Oxford
Idioms
Dictionary
for learners of English

D0920442

OXFORD
UNIVERSITY PRESS

OXFORD
UNIVERSITY PRESS
Great Clarendon Street, Oxford OX2 6DP

Oxford University Press is a department of the University of Oxford.
It furthers the University's objective of excellence in research, scholarship,
and education by publishing worldwide in

Oxford New York

Auckland Bangkok Buenos Aires Cape Town Chennai
Dar es Salaam Delhi Hong Kong Istanbul Karachi Kolkata
Kuala Lumpur Madrid Melbourne Mexico City Mumbai Nairobi
São Paulo Shanghai Taipei Tokyo Toronto

Oxford and Oxford English are registered trade marks of Oxford University Press
in the UK and in certain other countries

© Oxford University Press, 2001
Database right Oxford University Press (maker)
New edition. Previous edition published as
Oxford Learner's Dictionary of English Idioms (1994)

First published 2001
Third impression 2003

ISBN 0-19-431-545-2
10 9 8 7 6 5 4 3

Acknowledgements

Advisory Board: Dr Keith Brown; Prof. Guy Cook; Dr Alan Cruse; Ms Moira Runcie;
Prof. Gabriele Stein; Dr Norman Whitney; Prof. Henry Widdowson

Phonetics editor: Michael Ashby

A–Z pages designed by Peter Burgess
Non A–Z pages designed by Sarah Nicholson
Cover design by Richard Morris
Illustrations by: Lorna Barnard; Sophie Grillet; Karen Hiscock; Martin Shovel;
Technical Graphics Department, OUP; Harry Venning

Data capture and processing by Oxford University Press
Printed in Spain

CONTENTS

GUIDE to USING the DICTIONARY

Key to Dictionary Entries

Information about idioms in the dictionary is given in the form of entries under a keyword:

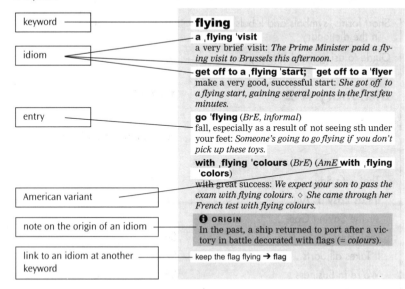

keyword

idiom

entry

American variant

note on the origin of an idiom

link to an idiom at another keyword

flying

a ˌflying 'visit
a very brief visit: *The Prime Minister paid a flying visit to Brussels this afternoon.*

get off to a ˌflying 'start; get off to a 'flyer
make a very good, successful start: *She got off to a flying start, gaining several points in the first few minutes.*

go 'flying (*BrE, informal*)
fall, especially as a result of not seeing sth under your feet: *Someone's going to go flying if you don't pick up these toys.*

with ˌflying 'colours (*BrE*) (*AmE* with ˌflying 'colors)
with great success: *We expect your son to pass the exam with flying colours.* ◇ *She came through her French test with flying colours.*

❶ ORIGIN
In the past, a ship returned to port after a victory in battle decorated with flags (= *colours*).

keep the flag flying → flag

Finding an idiom

Look up the idiom you want at the first important, or 'full', word in it. This will be a noun, an adjective, a verb or an adverb. Ignore any grammatical words such as articles, prepositions, etc. For example, if you want to find *a leap in the dark*, look at the keyword **leap**. 'A' does not count as a 'full' word:

If you want to find a plural noun, such as *by leaps and bounds*, it will be at the keyword **leaps**:

leap

a leap in the 'dark
an action or a risk that you take without knowing anything about the activity or what the result will be: *Government ministers are being accused of taking a leap in the dark as they prepare to radically change the education system.*

leaps

by/in ˌleaps and 'bounds
in large amounts or very quickly: *My knowledge of German increased by leaps and bounds when I lived in Germany for a year.* ◇ *Production is going up in leaps and bounds.*

Keywords are arranged in alphabetical order. If a noun and a verb are spelled the same, there will only be one keyword. For example the idioms *face to face* and *face the music* will be at the same keyword **face**. This is also the case with two words that have the same spelling even though they are pronounced differently, for example *a live wire* and *live and let live* are at the same keyword **live**.

If the first full word in an idiom is a verb, and the verb can be used with different subjects or in different tenses, you will find the idiom at the infinitive form of the verb. For example, the idiom *eat like a bird* is defined at **eat**, as you can say *She eats like a bird; I don't know how he stayed alive – he always ate like a bird.* etc.

However, the idiom *be barking up the wrong tree* is defined at the keyword **barking** as it is always used in progressive tenses.

Sometimes it is difficult to know where an idiom begins and ends. For example, if you meet the sentence *They decided to bury the hatchet and be friends again*, you might look up **hatchet**, if that is the only word you do not know. However, the idiom is *bury the hatchet*. To help you find it, a link to *bury the hatchet* is given at **hatchet**:

> ### hatchet
> **a 'hatchet job (on sb/sth)** (*informal*)
> strong criticism that is unfair or intended to harm sb/sth: *The press did a very effective hatchet job on her last movie.*
>
> bury the hatchet → bury

One 'full' word of an idiom can sometimes be replaced with another. For example, you can say *beam from ear to ear*, or you can use *smile* or *grin* instead of *beam*. In this case the idiom will be defined at the first full fixed word in it, **ear**, and is shown like this:

> ### ear
> **be out on your 'ear** (*informal*)
> be forced to leave a job, home, etc. suddenly: *You'll be out on your ear unless your work gets a lot better, my lad.*
>
> **beam/grin/smile from ear to 'ear**
> be smiling, etc. a lot because you are very pleased about sth: *I like your graduation photo, with you grinning from ear to ear and your parents looking so proud.*

You will also find links at each of the verbs *beam*, *grin* and *smile*.

In other idioms, many different words are possible. For example, in the phrase *in great measure*, **great** could be replaced by *large*, *full*, etc. This idiom is given in the dictionary as *in great*, *large*, *etc. measure* and you will find it at the first fixed word **measure**.

Some common verbs and adjectives such as **get**, **have**, **bad** and **good** have so many idioms that it is not possible to list them all at those words. Instead there is a note telling you to look at the next noun, adjective, etc:

> ### have
> Most idioms containing the verb **have** are at the entries for the nouns or adjectives in the idioms, for example **have (got) an eye for sth** is at **eye**.

Some idioms only contain grammar words, or grammar words and very common verbs, for example *in and out of something*, or *have it out with somebody*. You will find these at the first word in the idiom:

in

anything/nothing/something 'in it
any/no/some truth in what is being said: *'Is there anything in the story that he is leaving the company?' 'No, I'm sure there's nothing in it.'/'Yes, I think there's something in it.'*

,in and 'out of sth
(going) in and out of places all the time: *I've been in and out of the travel agency all this week, trying to arrange my holiday.* ◇ *After the accident, he was in and out of hospital for a couple of years.*

If you cannot find an idiom when you look it up, try looking for it at one of the other important words in the idiom.

Idioms and links are given in alphabetical order under each keyword. Grammatical words like **a/an** or **the**, **sb/sth** and the possessive forms **your**, **sb's**, **his**, **her**, etc. as well as words in brackets ( ) or after the symbol / are usually ignored.

Further Information and Practice

There is a 24-page section of study pages in the middle of this dictionary. You can use these on your own or in class with a teacher. They will help you to focus on certain idiomatic phrases and give you practice using them.

You will find answers to all the exercises in the 'Key to the Study Pages' section at the back of the dictionary.

Aa

A

from A to 'B
from one place to another: *I don't care what kind of car it is as long as it gets me from A to B.*

from A to 'Z
very thoroughly and in detail: *We need an expert who knows the subject from A to Z.*

(earn/get) straight A's ➔ straight

aah

um and aah (about sth) ➔ um

aback

be taken a'back (by sb/sth)
be shocked or surprised by sb/sth: *She was completely taken aback by his anger.*

abandon

with gay abandon ➔ gay

ABC

(as) easy as ABC/pie/falling off a log ➔ easy

about

be about to do sth
be going to do sth immediately: *I was about to phone him when he walked into the room.* ◇ *You'd better ask her now—I think she's about to leave.*

how/what about … ?
1 used when asking for information about sb/sth: *How about Ruth? Have you heard from her?* ◇ *I'm having fish. What about you?*
2 used to make a suggestion or offer: *How about going for a walk?* ◇ *You look cold. How about a nice hot drink?*
3 used for introducing sb/sth into a conversation or reminding sb of sb/sth: *I know she's very happy now, but what about him?* ◇ *'I've never been to Spain before.' 'What about the conference you went to in Madrid?'*

how/what about 'that (, then)! (*informal*)
used for expressing surprise, praise, great respect, etc: *'Have you heard Jane's been offered a film part in Hollywood?' 'Well, how about that, then!'*

not be about to do sth
not be willing to do sth; not intend to do sth: *I've never done any cooking and I'm not about to start now.*

that's about 'all/'it
used to say that you have finished telling sb about sth and there is nothing to add: *'Anything else?' 'No, that's about it for now.'*

above

above 'all ('else)
especially: *Don't spend too much money, don't forget to write, but above all, have a good time!* ◇ *He misses his family above all else.*

a,bove and be'yond sth (*formal*)
more than (your duty, etc.): *They showed commitment to the job above and beyond what was expected of them.*

be/get a'bove yourself (*disapproving*)
behave as if you are better or more important than you really are: *She's getting a bit above herself. She's only been working for me for two weeks and already she's telling me what to do!*

abreast

keep a'breast of sth
make sure that you know all the most recent facts about a subject: *It is almost impossible to keep abreast of all the latest developments in computing.*

absence

absence makes the heart grow fonder (*saying*)
used to say that when you are away from sb that you love, you love them even more

conspicuous by your absence ➔ conspicuous
leave of absence ➔ leave

accident

by 'accident
in a way that is not planned or organized: *We met by accident at the airport.* ◇ *Helen got into acting purely by accident.*

(whether) by ,accident or de'sign
if you say that sth happens **by accident or design**, you mean that you do not know if it has been planned or not: *Mary was wearing the same T-shirt as me—whether by accident or design, I never knew.*

an accident/a disaster waiting to happen ➔ waiting

accidentally

acci,dentally on 'purpose (*informal, ironic*)
intending to do sth, but wanting to appear to have done it by accident: *'We'd just finished our meal when John realized he'd accidentally left his chequebook at home.' 'Accidentally on purpose, you mean!'*

accidents

,accidents will 'happen (*saying*)
said when a small accident has happened, for example when sth has been broken, to show that you do not consider it to be serious, or to excuse

yourself for causing it: *'I'm so sorry, I've just broken a plate.' 'Oh, never mind, accidents will happen.'*

a chapter of accidents → **chapter**

accompli

a fait accompli → **fait**

accomplished

mission accomplished → **mission**

accord

of your own ac'cord
without being asked or forced: *I didn't need to tell her to apologize; she did it of her own accord.*

account

of little/no ac'count (*formal*)
not considered important: *His past achievements were of no account when it came to competing with the younger men.*

on account of sb/sth; on sb's account
because of sb/sth: *Flights were delayed on account of the bad weather.* ◇ *I can't go, but don't stay in on my account.*

on 'no account; not on 'any account
not for any reason: *On no account (should you) try to fix the heater yourself. All repairs should be done by a trained engineer.*

on your own ac'count
1 for yourself: *In 1992 Smith set up in business on his own account.*
2 because you want to and you have decided, not sb else: *No one sent me, I am here on my own account.*

put/turn sth to good ac'count (*formal*)
make good use of money, an ability, etc: *He put his experience as a teacher to good account as a writer of children's books.*

take sth into ac'count; take account of sth
consider sth when making a calculation or decision: *It's clear he didn't take his family's wishes into account when deciding to change jobs.* ◇ *We mustn't forget to take account of price increases when we do the budget for next year.*

call sb to account (for/over sth) → **call**
settle a score/an account (with sb) → **settle**
square your/an account (with sb) → **square**

accounted

all present and accounted for → **present**

accounting

there's no accounting for 'taste(s) (*saying*)
used to express surprise at another person's likes and dislikes which are different from your own: *'She's just painted her whole room purple.' 'Well, there's no accounting for taste!'*

accounts

by/from 'all accounts
used when the speaker does not have direct experience of the thing mentioned but is reporting the ideas, etc. of others: *I've never seen any of her films but she's a brilliant director, by all accounts.* ◇ *It was, from all accounts, a very interesting discussion.*

square accounts (with sb) → **square**

ace

within an ace of sth/of doing sth (*BrE*)
very close to sth: *We came within an ace of victory.*

have an ace in the hole = have (got) an ace/a trick up your sleeve → **sleeve**
play your ace → **play**

aces

have/hold (all) the 'aces (also **hold all the 'cards**)
be in a controlling position because you have certain advantages over another person: *The Labour candidate holds all the aces—he's local and well liked.*

❶ ORIGIN
This expression refers to card-playing. The *ace* usually has the highest value, and is associated with success.

Achilles

an/sb's Achilles 'heel
a hidden weakness or fault in sb which may be used to harm them: *The opposition realized they had found the Prime Minister's Achilles heel.*

❶ ORIGIN
This expression is named after the Greek hero *Achilles*. When he was a small child, his mother dipped him into the river Styx, which meant that he could not be injured. She held him by his heel, which therefore was not touched by the water. Achilles died after being wounded by an arrow in the heel.

acid

the ˌacid 'test (of sth)
a situation which finally proves whether sth is good or bad, true or false, etc: *They've always been good friends, but the acid test will come when they have to share a flat.*

acorns

great/tall oaks from little acorns grow → **oaks**

acquaintance

make sb's acquaintance; make the acquaintance of sb (*formal*)
meet sb for the first time: *I am delighted to make your acquaintance, Mrs Baker.* ◇ *I made the*

acquaintance of several musicians around that time.

have a nodding acquaintance with sb/sth → **nodding**
scrape (up) an acquaintance with sb → **scrape**

acquired

an acquired 'taste

a thing which you find unpleasant or do not appreciate at first but which you gradually learn to like: *Whisky is an acquired taste.*

Act

read (sb) the Riot Act → **read**

act

an ,act of 'God (*law*)

an event caused by natural forces which people cannot control or prevent, for example a hurricane, earthquake, etc: *The insurance policy covers your house against all types of damage, excluding those caused by acts of God.*

a 'balancing/'juggling act

a process in which sb tries to please two or more people or groups who want different things: *The UN must perform a delicate balancing act between the different sides involved in the conflict.*

Managing her home life and work was proving to be something of a juggling act.

be/get in on the 'act (*informal*)

be/become involved in a particular activity only after it has become successful: *Sales of 'green' products have increased dramatically and now a lot of manufacturers are trying to get in on the act.*

do/perform/stage a disap'pearing/'vanishing act (*informal*)

go away or be impossible to find when people need or want you: *Ian always does a disappearing act when it's time to wash the dishes.*

get your 'act together; get sth/it to'gether (*informal*)

manage to organize or control sth (better than you have done previously): *If Sally got her act together she'd be a great musician.* ◇ *He's been trying to get his life together.* ◇ *He seems to be getting it together at last.*

a hard/tough act to 'follow

a person or a group that is so good or successful at sth that it will be difficult for anyone else who comes after them to be as good or successful: *The last head teacher achieved a lot—she'll be a hard act to follow.*

act/be your age → **age**
act/play the fool → **fool**
act/play the goat → **goat**
behave/act as if you own the place = think you own the place → **think**
catch sb in the act (of doing sth) → **catch**
clean up your act → **clean**

action

'action stations (*spoken, especially BrE*)

used as an order to get ready for action: *Action stations! There's a bus full of tourists arriving in five minutes.*

in 'action

working, operating, etc.; doing a particular activity: *John's a great cook—you should see him in action.*

out of 'action

not working or operating as normal because of illness, injury, damage, etc: *Jane's broken leg will put her out of action for a while.* ◇ *He can't give you a lift today—his car's out of action.*

a piece/slice of the 'action (*informal*)

a share or role in an interesting or exciting activity, especially in order to make money: *Foreign firms will all want a piece of the action if the new airport goes ahead.*

where the 'action is

where the most exciting or important events are happening: *I'd hate to live out in the country—I like to be where the action is.*

a course of action → **course**
spring (in)to life/action → **spring**
swing into action → **swing**

actions

,actions speak ,louder than 'words (*saying*)

what you do is more important than what you say: *I know we don't speak the same language, but you know what they say: actions speak louder than words!*

ad

,ad 'hoc (*from Latin*)

arranged or happening when necessary and not

planned in advance: *The meetings will be held on an ad hoc basis.*

,ad infi'nitum *(from Latin)*

without ever coming to an end; again and again: *You cannot stay here ad infinitum without paying any rent.* ◇ *The problem would be repeated ad infinitum.*

> ❷ NOTE
> The meaning of the Latin phrase is 'to infinity'.

,ad 'nauseam *(from Latin)*

if a person says or does sth **ad nauseam**, they say or do it again and again so that it becomes boring or annoying: *Television sports commentators repeat the same phrases ad nauseam.*

> ❷ NOTE
> The meaning of the Latin phrase is 'to sickness'.

Adam

not know sb from Adam ➜ know

add

add ,fuel to the 'fire/'flames

do or say sth which makes a difficult situation worse, or makes sb even more angry, etc: *She was already furious and his apologies and excuses only added fuel to the flames.*

add ,insult to 'injury

hurt the feelings of, or harm, sb who has already been harmed in some other way: *She forgot to send me an invitation to her party and then added insult to injury by asking to borrow my jacket!*

addition

in addition (to sb/sth)

used when you want to mention another person or thing after sb/sth else: *In addition to these arrangements, extra ambulances will be on duty until midnight.* ◇ *There is, in addition, one further point to make.*

ado

without further/more a'do *(old-fashioned)*

without delaying; immediately: *So without further ado, let's get on with tonight's show.*

advance

in advance (of sth)

before the time that is expected; before sth happens: *a week/month/year in advance* ◇ *It's cheaper if you book the tickets in advance.* ◇ *People were evacuated from the coastal regions in advance of the hurricane.*

be ahead of/before/in advance of your time ➜ time

advantage

take ad'vantage of sth/sb

1 make good use of sth; to make use of an opportunity: *We made sure that we **took full advantage***

of the hotel facilities. ◇ *Take advantage of our special offer and get two books for the price of one!*
2 make use of sb/sth in a way that is unfair or dishonest: *He took advantage of my generosity* (= for example, by taking more than I had intended to give).

to sb's ad'vantage

so that sb benefits: *The rise in the value of the pound will work to the advantage of those planning a holiday abroad this summer.*

to (good, better, etc.) ad'vantage

in a way that produces a good result: *You would be spending your time to better advantage if you did what I suggested.* ◇ *That's a lovely picture but it's not seen to its best advantage on that wall. Why don't you hang it nearer the light?*

press home your advantage ➜ press
turn sth to your (own) advantage ➜ turn

advocate'

(a/the) devil's advocate ➜ devil

affairs

a state of affairs ➜ state

afield

far/farther/further a'field

far away from home; to or in places that are not near: *You can hire a car if you want to explore further afield.* ◇ *Journalists came from as far afield as China and Brazil.*

aforethought

with malice aforethought ➜ malice

afraid

I'm afraid (that) ... *(spoken)*

used as a polite way of telling sb sth that is unpleasant or disappointing, or sth that you are sorry about: *I'm afraid I can't come to your party.* ◇ *'Have you got change for ten pounds?' 'I'm afraid not.'* ◇ *I've got some bad news, I'm afraid.* ◇ *'Is this the best you can do?' 'I'm afraid so.'*

after

after 'all

1 used to show that sth is the opposite of what you first intend to do or expect to happen: *I think I will have something to eat after all.* ◇ *We could have left our coats at home—it didn't rain after all.*
2 used when you are explaining sth, or giving a reason: *Can't I stay up late tonight? After all, there's no school tomorrow!* ◇ *You got a fair price for your car. It's six years old, after all.*

again

a,gain and a'gain

many times; repeatedly: *I've told him again and again to shut the door but he always leaves it open.*

then/there a'gain (*informal*)
used for introducing an extra piece of information which explains sth or gives another explanation for sth: *I thought he liked me, but then again maybe he didn't.*

age

,**act/,be your 'age** (*informal*)
(often used as a command) stop behaving in a childish way: *Paul, act your age or I won't take you to the cinema again!*

,**come of 'age**
1 reach the age when you are considered by the law to be an adult: *He will inherit his father's money when he comes of age.*
2 (of an organization) become established: *With more and more people now aware of environmental issues, 'green' politics has really come of age.*

,**under 'age**
not yet an adult according to the law: *We don't serve alcohol to teenagers who are under age/to under-age teenagers.*

at/to a ripe old age → **ripe**
(be) at a tender age → **tender**
the awkward age → **awkward**
feel your age → **feel**
the golden age (of sth) → **golden**
a/the grand old age → **grand**
in this day and age → **day**
look your age → **look**
of a certain age → **certain**

aggregate

on 'aggregate (*BrE, sport*)
when the scores of a number of games are added together: *They won 4-2 on aggregate.*

agony

pile on the agony/gloom → **pile**
prolong the agony → **prolong**

agree

a,gree to 'differ
(of two or more people) allow each other to have different opinions about sth, especially in order to avoid more argument: *Our views on this matter are so different—I think we'll just have to agree to differ.*

I ,couldn't agree (with you) 'more
I completely agree (with you): *I couldn't agree with you more about the need to hire extra staff.*

agreement

a gentlemen's agreement = a gentleman's agreement → **gentleman**

aid

in aid of sb/sth (*BrE*)
in order to help sb/sth: *The children spent the day collecting money in aid of charity.*

what's (all) 'this, etc. in aid of? (*BrE, spoken*)
what is the purpose or cause of sth?: *What's all this crying in aid of?*

air

float/walk on 'air (*informal*)
be very happy about sth: *When I passed my driving test, I was walking on air for days.*

in the 'air
(of an idea, a feeling, a piece of information, etc.) felt by a number of people to exist or to be happening: *Spring is in the air.* ◇ *There was a strong feeling of excitement in the air.*

(up) in the 'air
(of plans, etc.) uncertain; not yet decided: *I'm hoping to take a holiday this month but my plans are still very much up in the air.* ◇ *At the end of the meeting, the matter was left in the air.*

,**on/,off the 'air**
(being) broadcast/not (being) broadcast on radio or television: *'Going Live' will go off the air for the summer, returning for a new series in the autumn.*

appear, etc. out of thin air → **thin**
a breath of fresh air → **breath**
(build) castles in the air → **castles**
clear the air → **clear**
disappear, etc. into thin air → **thin**
(as) free as (the) air/as a bird → **free**
hot air → **hot**
in the open air → **open**
(as) light as air/a feather → **light**
pluck sth out of the air → **pluck**
with your nose in the air → **nose**

airs

,**airs and 'graces** (*BrE, disapproving*)
behaviour which is elegant but unnatural and intended to impress others: *Her airs and graces didn't impress her fellow students at all.*

,**give yourself/,put ,on 'airs**
behave in a way which shows that you feel you are important: *The nice thing about her is that, in spite of being so rich, she doesn't put on any airs.*

aisle

go/walk down the 'aisle (*informal*)
get married: *I never thought you'd be the first one to walk down the aisle—you used to say you'd never marry!*

❷ NOTE
The *aisle* is the passage down the middle of a church between the two blocks of seats.

aisles

rolling in the aisles → **rolling**

aitches

drop your aitches → **drop**

Aladdin

an Aladdin's 'cave
a place full of valuable or interesting objects: *He kept for his private pleasure an Aladdin's cave of stolen masterpieces.*

> **❶ ORIGIN**
> This expression comes from a story in *The Arabian Nights*. Aladdin was trapped in a cave full of gold and jewels by a magician.

alarm
a false alarm → false

alec
a smart alec/aleck → smart

alert
on red alert → red

alike
share and share alike → share

alive

a͵live and 'kicking (*informal*)
still existing and strong or active: *The old prejudices were still very much alive and kicking.*

bring sth a'live
make sth interesting: *Maps and pictures bring the book alive.*

come a'live
1 (of a subject or an event) become interesting and exciting: *The game came alive in the second half.*
2 (of a place) become busy and full of activity: *The city starts to come alive after dark.*
3 (of a person) show interest in sth and become excited about it: *She came alive as she talked about her job.*

eat sb alive → eat
skin sb alive → skin

all

your 'all
everything you have: *They gave their all* (= fought and died) *in the war.*

all a'long
from the beginning: *I've said all along that this would happen.* ◇ *He knew who they were all along but he pretended he didn't.*

'all but
1 almost: *The snow all but covered the path, making it difficult to walk.* ◇ *The patient was all but dead when the doctor arrived.*
2 all (the people or things mentioned) except ...: *'Have you done your homework?' 'Yes, all but the last two questions.'*

͵all 'in
1 (of a price) with nothing extra to pay; inclusive:

The holiday cost £250 all in. ◇ *These are all-in prices—room, breakfast, service and tax.*
2 (*old-fashioned, informal*) very tired: *At the end of the race he was all in.*

all in 'all
when everything is considered: *All in all the film was a great success, despite the bad publicity.*

all of 'sth
(of size, weight, distance, etc.) at least: *'How old is she?' 'Oh, she must be all of fifty.'* ◇ (*ironic*) *He never visits his mother and she lives all of three miles away.*

all or 'nothing
a situation which will end either in complete success or complete failure

all 'over
1 everywhere: *We looked all over for the ring.* ◇ *The news was all over the office within minutes.*
2 what you would expect of the person mentioned: *That sounds like my sister all over.*

all 'round (*BrE*) (*AmE* all a'round)
1 in every way; in all respects: *a good performance all round*
2 for each person: *She bought drinks all round.*

͵all 'there (*informal*)
having a healthy mind; thinking clearly: *He behaves very oddly at times—I don't think he's quite all there.*

and 'all
1 also; included: *They're coming to stay for the weekend, dog and all.*
2 (*spoken*) too; as well: *And he stole £5 from me, and all.*
3 (*informal*) and other (connected) things: *She doesn't go out much in the evenings now, what with her work and all.*

and all 'that (rubbish, stuff, etc.) (*informal*)
and other similar things: *He was an intellectual—read Beckett and Barthes and all that.* ◇ *They're always kissing and all that romantic stuff.*

(not) at 'all
(used with a negative, in a question or in an *if*-clause) in any way; to any degree: *This isn't at all what I expected.* ◇ *Are you hungry at all?* ◇ *If you're at all unhappy about marrying him, then don't.*

be all about sb/sth (*informal*)
used to describe the subject or purpose of sth: *This book is all about Greece.* ◇ *Now then, what's this all about* (= what is the problem)? ◇ *It's all about money these days.*

be all sb can/could 'do (not) to do sth (*informal*)
be very difficult (not) to do sth: *His face looked so funny that it was all she could do not to laugh.*

(not) be/take all 'day, 'morning, etc. (to do sth); not have all 'day, etc. (*informal*)
(used as a request to hurry up) (not) take a long time (to do sth): *'Are you going to take all day shav-*

ing?' she shouted to him through the bathroom door.
◇ *Come on! We haven't got all day!*

be all for sth/for doing sth
believe strongly that sth should be done: *They're all for saving money where they can.*

be all 'go (*BrE, informal*)
be (a situation where people are) very active or busy: *It was all go in the office today.* ◇ *The election's on the eighteenth, so it's all go for the next three weeks.*

be all 'over sb (*informal*)
show a lot of affection for or enthusiasm about sb: *He was all over her at the party.*

be all the same to 'sb (also be all 'one to sb, *old-fashioned*)
not be important to sb: *If it's all the same to you, I'd prefer to go shopping on my own.*

in 'all
as a total quantity or number: *We've got six litres of milk in all.* ◇ *That's £10.29 in all, please.*

it's/they're ˌall 'yours
used when passing the responsibility for sb/sth or the use of sth to another person: *'There you are, Mr Brown,' she said, taking him into the classroom full of children, 'they're all yours.'*

not all that 'good, 'well, etc.
not particularly good, well, etc: *He doesn't sing all that well.*

not as bad(ly), tall, etc. as all 'that
not as much as has been suggested: *They're not as rich as all that.*

ˌnot at 'all
used to politely accept thanks or to agree to sth: *'Thanks a lot.' 'Not at all.'* ◇ *'Will it bother you if I smoke?' 'Not at all.'*

of ˌall the 'cheek, 'nerve, stupid things to 'do, etc.! (*informal*)
used to express annoyance, impatience, etc. at what another person has done or said: *Of all the idiots, leaving his car unlocked in the middle of town!*

> ❷ NOTE
> This expression is often used without a noun, especially to show that sb is annoyed: *She said I was fat? Well, of all the … !*

all-clear

give sb/get the all-'clear
give sb/get a sign that a particular situation is no longer dangerous: *She got the all-clear from the doctor and was sent home from the hospital.*

> ❶ ORIGIN
> This idiom refers to the signal that is sounded in wartime when a bombing raid is over.

alley

be (right) up your alley = be (right) up your street → **street**
a blind alley → **blind**

allow

allow 'me (*spoken*)
used to offer help politely: *'I'll just take these bags upstairs.' 'Allow me.'*

give/allow sb/sth free/full rein → **rein**

allowances

make al'lowances for sb
not judge sb too strictly because of certain problems or difficulties: *The court was asked to make allowances for the age of the accused.*

almighty

God almighty → **God**

alone

go it a'lone (*informal*)
do sth, especially sth difficult, without the help or support of others: *Andrew decided to go it alone and start his own business.*

leave/let sb/sth alone = leave/let sb/sth be → **leave**
let alone → **let**
let well enough alone = leave/let well alone → **well**

along

along with sth
in addition to sth: *Tobacco is taxed in most countries, along with alcohol.*

aloud

think aloud → **think**

always

as 'always
as usually happens or is expected: *As always, Polly was late for school.*

amends

make a'mends (to sb) (for sth/for doing sth)
do sth for sb in order to show that you are sorry for sth wrong or unfair that you have done: *I'm sorry I upset you—how can I make amends?* ◇ *He finished third in the 200 metres, but hopes to make amends in the 100 metres.*

American

as Aˌmerican as apple 'pie
used to say that sth is typical of America: *For me, baseball is as American as apple pie.*

amiss

not come/go a'miss (*BrE*)
be useful or pleasant in a particular situation: *A little luck wouldn't go amiss right now!*

take sth a'miss (*BrE*)
feel offended by sth, perhaps because you have understood it in the wrong way: *Would she take it amiss if I offered to help?*

amok

run amok → run

amount

any a'mount/'number of sth

a large quantity of sth: *There was any amount of food and drink at the party.* ◇ *You won't have any difficulty selling your car—there are any number of people who would buy it.*

no a'mount of sth

used for saying that sth will have no effect: *No amount of encouragement would make him jump into the pool.*

amount/come to the same thing → thing

amused

keep sb a'mused

give sb interesting things to do, or entertain them so that they do not become bored: *Playing with water can keep children amused for hours.*

analysis

in the ˌlast/ˌfinal a'nalysis

used to say what is most important after everything has been discussed, or considered: *In the final analysis, humour is a matter of individual interpretation.*

anchor

weigh anchor → weigh

angels

be on the side of the angels → side

anger

do sth more in sorrow than in anger → sorrow

answer

the answer to sb's prayers

a thing or a person that sb has waited for or wanted for a long time: *If you've been looking for a good quality fleece at a reasonable price, this one could be the answer to your prayers.*

not take no for an answer

refuse to accept that sb does not want sth, will not do sth, etc: *You're coming and I won't take no for an answer!*

a dusty answer → dusty

answers

have/know all the 'answers

be or seem to be more intelligent or know more than others: *He's an economist who thinks he knows all the answers.*

ante

raise/up the 'ante

increase the level of sth, especially demands or

sums of money: *His ex-wife has upped the ante in her alimony suit against him.*

> **❷ NOTE**
> The *ante* is the amount of money that players bet in a card game such as poker.

ants

have (got) ants in your pants (*informal*)

be unable to stay still because you are anxious or excited about sth: *Relax and enjoy yourself—you've really got ants in your pants about something tonight!*

anything

anything 'but

certainly not; just the opposite (of): *Ecologists are anything but optimistic about a change in the Government's attitude towards 'green' issues.* ◇ *'I suppose the weather in Scotland was terrible.' 'Oh no, anything but.'*

anything 'goes

there are no rules about how sb should behave; anything is acceptable: *John always has to wear a suit and tie to the office, but where I work anything goes.*

anything 'like

(used with a negative, in a question or in an *if* -clause) in any way similar to; nearly: *If the meal's anything like the one we had there, you'll really enjoy it.* ◇ *The car isn't anything like as fast as yours.*

(as) easy, clear, quick, etc. as anything (*informal*)

extremely easy, clear, quickly, etc: *It was only a small gift but Phil was as pleased as anything with it.*

like 'anything (*BrE, informal*)

very much or very enthusiastically: *My head hurt like anything.*

not for 'anything (*informal*)

definitely not: *I wouldn't give it up for anything.*

or anything (*spoken*)

or another thing of a similar type: *If you want to call a meeting or anything, just let me know.*

apart

be 'poles/'worlds apart

be widely separated; have no interests that you share: *Politically, the two leaders are poles apart.* ◇ *After hours of discussion and negotiation, they're still poles apart.*

come/fall apart at the 'seams (*informal*)

begin to fail or collapse: *The Government's economic policy is falling apart at the seams.* ◇ *After only six months, their marriage has come apart at the seams.*

be miles apart → miles
joking apart/aside → joking
rip sb/sth apart/to shreds, bits, etc. → rip

ape

go 'ape (also go'apeshit, ⚠) (*slang, especially AmE*)
become extremely angry or excited: *The manager
went ape when the team lost yet another game.*

apologies

make no apology/apologies for sth → **apology**

apology

an apology for sth
a very poor example of sth: *I'm sorry this is a bit of
an apology for lunch—we'll have a proper meal
tonight.*

make no a'pology/a'pologies for sth
if you say that you **make no apology/apologies** for
sth, you mean that you do not feel that you have said
or done sth wrong: *Having grown up in the north of
the country, I make no apologies for saying that people
there are more friendly than people in the south.*

appearances

keep up ap'pearances
hide the true situation and pretend that everything is still going well: *When she lost all her
money, she was determined to keep up appearances.*

to all ap'pearances
if sth/sb is judged only by what you can see: *The
house was, to all appearances, empty.* ◇ *Although
to all appearances they were the 'ideal couple', in
fact they were very unhappy.*

appetite

whet sb's appetite → **whet**

apple

the ˌapple of sb's 'eye
a person, usually a child, who sb loves very much;
a favourite child: *The second child, John, was the
apple of his mother's eye.*

as American as apple pie → **American**
a rotten apple → **rotten**
upset the/sb's apple cart → **upset**

approach

a/the softly-softly approach → **softly-softly**

approval

on ap'proval
(of goods) not paid for and to be returned, usually
within a few days, if the customer decides not to
buy them: *I've got it on seven days approval, so if
you don't like it I can take it back.*

a seal of approval → **seal**

apron

**(tied to) your mother's, wife's, etc. 'apron
  strings**
(too much under) the influence and control of your
mother, wife, etc: *The British prime minister is too
apt to cling to Washington's apron strings.*

area

a disaster area → **disaster**
a grey area → **grey**
a no-go area → **no-go**

argue

ˌargue the 'toss (*BrE, informal*)
continue to disagree about a decision, especially
when it is too late to change it or it is not very
important: *Look, just do it your way. I've got better
things to do than stand here all day arguing the toss
with you.*

argument

for the sake of argument → **sake**

ark

be out of the 'ark; went out with the 'ark
  (*BrE, spoken*)
(of an object or a custom) extremely old or old-
fashioned: *She was using a dictionary that was
straight out of the ark.*

> **❶ ORIGIN**
> This idiom refers to a story in the Bible. The *ark*
> was a large boat which Noah built to save his
> family and two of every type of animal from the
> flood.

arm

cost/pay an ˌarm and a 'leg (*informal*)
cost/pay a lot of money: *We want to redecorate the
living room, but I'm afraid it's going to cost us an
arm and a leg.*

keep sb at 'arm's length
avoid becoming too friendly with sb: *He's the kind of
man who's best kept at arm's length, in my opinion.*

put the 'arm/'bite on sb (*AmE, informal*)
ask sb for sth, especially money: *To pay for the tax
reductions, the government will put the bite on
smokers and motorists.*

(a list) as long as your arm → **long**
chance your arm → **chance**
the long arm of the law → **long**
a shot in the arm → **shot**
twist sb's arm → **twist**
would give your right arm for sth/to do sth → **right**

armchair

an armchair critic, traveller, etc.
a person who knows about a subject only from
what they have heard or read and not from personal experience: *He's what you might call an
'armchair traveller', having never actually been
outside Europe.*

armed

ˌarmed to the 'teeth (with sth) (*informal*)
carrying a lot of weapons or a lot of things needed
for a particular purpose: *The tourists got out of the
coach, armed to the teeth with cameras, binoculars,
and guidebooks.*

armour (*BrE*) (*AmE* armor)

a chink in sb's armour → **chink**
a knight in shining armour → **knight**

arms

up in 'arms (about/over sth) (*informal*)
very angry and protesting very strongly (about
sth): *Local residents are up in arms over plans to
build a new motorway.*

a babe in arms → **babe**
fold sb in your arms → **fold**
lay down your arms → **lay**
throw up your arms/hands in despair, horror, etc. → **throw**
with open arms → **open**

arrive

arrive/come on the scene → **scene**

arrow

(as) straight as an arrow → **straight**

arrows

the slings and arrows (of sth) → **slings**

arse

my arse! (*BrE*, ⚠, *slang*)
used by some people to show they do not believe
what sb has said: *An appointment at the dentist my
arse! She's gone shopping!*

kiss sb's arse → **kiss**
lick sb's arse → **lick**
not know your arse from your elbow → **know**
a pain in the arse/bum/backside → **pain**
think the sun shines out of sb's arse/backside → **think**
work your arse off → **work**

arsed

can't be 'arsed (to do sth) (*BrE*, ⚠, *slang*)
not want to do sth because it is too much trouble: *I
was supposed to do some work this weekend but I
couldn't be arsed.*

> ❷ NOTE
> A more polite way to express this is 'can't be
> bothered (to do sth)'.

art

have (got) sth down to a fine art → **fine**
state of the art → **state**

artistic

artistic/poetic licence → **licence**

as

as against sth
in contrast with sth: *They got 27% of the vote as
against 32% at the last election.*

ˌas and 'when
whenever; at the moment when: *We'll deal with
individual problems as and when they arise.*

as for sb/sth
turning to the subject of sb/sth: *I like Sue very
much, but as for her boyfriend—I wouldn't care if I
never saw him again!*

'as from (also **'as of** *especially AmE*)
used to indicate the time or date from which something starts: *As from next Monday she'll have a
new secretary.* ◇ *We shall be at our new address as
of mid-June.*

as 'if (*spoken*)
used to express anger at or disapproval of a suggestion, an explanation, etc., or to deny a possibility: *As if I really cared!* ◇ *'Don't tell Tom I said
that, will you?' 'Oh, as if (I would)!'*

as if/as though
in a way that suggests sth: *He behaved as if nothing had happened.* ◇ *It sounds as though you had a
good time.*

ˌas it 'is
as the situation is at the moment (often in contrast
to what was expected): *I wanted to have this report
ready by tomorrow but as it is, it may not be done
until Thursday.* ◇ *We won't be able to buy a new car
this year—we can only just afford a holiday as it is.*

as to sth
used when you are referring to sth: *As to tax, that
will be deducted from your salary.*

as you 'do (*BrE*)
used as a comment on sth that you have just said to
say that it is normal behaviour: *He smiled and I
smiled back, as you do.* ◇ (*ironic*) *She's just gone off
to the Bahamas for three weeks on holiday. As you
do!*

**it isn't as if/as though; it's not as if/as
though**
used to show that a particular explanation for sth
is not the correct one: *It isn't as if he didn't recognize me! He just walked straight past me as I stood
there.*

ashes

put on, wear, etc. sackcloth and ashes → **sackcloth**
rake over the ashes/the past → **rake**
rise from the ashes → **rise**

aside

joking apart/aside → **joking**

ask

'ask for trouble/it (*informal*)
(usually used in the progressive tenses) behave in

a way that is likely to result in problems: *They're asking for trouble, leaving young children alone in the house like that.* ◇ *She's really asking for it the way she comes in late every day.*

,don't 'ask (*spoken, informal*)
if you say **don't ask** to sb, you mean that you do not want to reply to their question, because it would be awkward, embarrassing, etc: *'How was your holiday?' 'Don't ask! It was a disaster!'*

,don't ask 'me (*spoken, informal*)
if you say **don't ask me**, you mean that you do not know the answer to a question and are annoyed you have been asked: *Don't ask me—nobody tells me anything around here.*

I 'ask you! (*spoken, informal*)
used to show strong surprise, disbelief, shock, etc: *So they just arrived without telling you they were coming? Well, I ask you!*

if you ask 'me (*spoken, informal*)
in my personal opinion: *If you ask me, Mark shouldn't have bought that car—it just wasn't worth the money.*

ask for/win sb's hand → **hand**
cry/ask for the moon → **moon**

asking

be sb's for the 'asking
be obtained simply by asking (for it); be very easily obtained: *If you want any of the furniture, it's yours for the asking.* ◇ *Fame and money were hers for the asking in those days.*

asleep

sound asleep → **sound**

ass

get your 'ass in gear (also **move your 'ass**) (⚠, *slang, especially AmE*)
a rude way of telling sb to hurry

get your ass over/in 'here, etc. (⚠, *slang, especially AmE*)
a rude way of telling sb to come here, etc.

cover your ass → **cover**
kick (some/sb's) ass → **kick**
kiss sb's ass → **kiss**
lick sb's ass → **lick**
not know your ass from your elbow → **know**
a pain in the ass/butt → **pain**
think the sun shines out of sb's ass → **think**
work your ass off → **work**

assured

rest assured (that   ) → **rest**

astray

go a'stray
1 become lost; be stolen: *Several letters went*

astray or were not delivered. ◇ *We locked up our valuables so they wouldn't go astray.*
2 go in the wrong direction or have the wrong result: *Fortunately the gunman's shots went astray.*

lead sb astray → **lead**

atmosphere

(you could) cut the atmosphere with a knife → **cut**
a heavy silence/atmosphere → **heavy**

attached

(with) no strings attached → **strings**

attempt

a last-ditch stand/attempt/effort → **last-ditch**

attendance

be in at'tendance (*formal*)
be present at a special event: *Several heads of state were in attendance at the funeral.*

take at'tendance (*AmE*)
check who is present and who is not present at a place and mark this information on a list of names: *The teacher took attendance at the beginning of every class.*

dance attendance on sb → **dance**

attention

get/have sb's undivided attention → **undivided**

attitude

strike a pose/an attitude → **strike**

attract

opposites attract → **opposites**

authority

have (got) sth on good au'thority
be able to believe sth because you trust the person who gave you the information: *I have it on good authority that the chairman is going to resign.*

automatic

be on ,automatic 'pilot
do sth without thinking because you have done the same thing many times before: *I got up and dressed on automatic pilot.*

> **❓ NOTE**
> The *automatic pilot* is the device in an aircraft that keeps it on a fixed course without the need for a person to control it. It is often shortened to 'autopilot': *I did the journey on autopilot.*

avail

of little/no a'vail (*formal*)
of little or no use: *Your ability to argue is of little avail if you get your facts wrong.*

to little/no a'vail (*formal*)
with little or no success: *The doctors tried everything to keep him alive but to no avail.*

averages

the law of averages → law

avoid

avoid sb/sth like the 'plague (*informal*)
avoid sb/sth completely: *It was the sort of restaurant that I would normally have avoided like the plague.*

> **❷ NOTE**
> A *plague* is an infectious disease that kills a lot of people.

fall into/avoid the trap of doing sth → trap

awakening

a rude awakening → rude

aware

be well aware of sth/that   → well

awe

be/stand in 'awe of sb/sth
admire sb/sth and be slightly afraid of them/it: *While Diana was in awe of her grandfather, she adored her grandmother.*

awkward

the 'awkward age
the period when some young people have difficulties as they approach adult life: *'Gary seems such a quiet boy.' 'Oh, he's just at that awkward age—he'll soon grow out of it.'*

AWOL

go 'AWOL
go missing without permission or explanation: *He's gone AWOL.* ◇ *The guitarist suddenly went AWOL in the middle of the tour.*

> **❷ NOTE**
> This expression is used in the armed forces when sb has left their group without permission. It stands for *Absent WithOut Leave* and is pronounced /'eɪwɒl/ in British English and /'eɪwɔːl/ in American English.

axe (*especially BrE*) (*AmE usually* **ax**)
have (got) an 'axe to grind
(usually used in negative sentences) have private, often selfish, reasons for being involved in sth: *Having no particular political axe to grind, he stood for election as an independent candidate.*

B b

B

from A to B → A

babe

a ‚babe in 'arms (*old-fashioned*)
1 a very young baby not able to walk or crawl
2 a helpless, inexperienced or innocent person: *He's a babe in arms in financial matters.*

a ‚babe in the 'woods (*AmE*)
somebody who lacks experience of life or knowledge and who is too willing to trust other people: *We're still babes in the woods when it comes to computer technology.*

babes

out of the mouths of babes (and sucklings) → mouths

baby

a 'baby boomer (*AmE also* **a 'boomer**)
a person born during a period when many more babies are born than usual (called a *baby boom*), especially after the Second World War: *The new President was a baby boomer, born in the 1950s.*

be sb's 'baby (*informal*)
be sth that sb has created, is dealing with, etc: *Mary's the lawyer, so the legal problem's her baby.*

be like taking candy from a baby → candy
leave sb holding the baby → leave
sleep like a baby → sleep
(as) smooth as a baby's bottom → smooth
throw the baby out with the bathwater → throw
wet the baby's head → wet

back

Most idioms containing **back** are at the entries for the nouns and verbs in the idioms, for example **on the back burner** is at **burner**.

(in) back of sth (*AmE, informal*)
behind sth: *There's a large garden in back of the house.*

the ‚back of be'yond (*informal*)
a lonely place that is a long way from any town: *That village they've moved to is really in the back of beyond!*

‚back to 'back
1 if two people stand **back to back**, they stand with their backs facing or touching each other
2 if two or more things happen **back to back**, they happen one after the other: *back-to-back victories / successes*

be on sb's 'back (*informal*)
annoy or criticize sb a lot: *My new boss is on my back all the time, saying I have to work harder.*

behind sb's 'back
without sb knowing, especially because they would not like it: *I feel guilty about going behind his back and complaining to the boss.* ◇ *People were often very rude about her behind her back.*

As she walked away, she could hear them whispering about her behind her back.

get/put sb's 'back up
make sb annoyed: *His silly remarks always get her back up.*

> **❶ ORIGIN**
> This idiom refers to the way cats arch their backs when they are angry.

get off sb's 'back; get sb off your 'back (*informal*)
stop annoying sb, for example by telling them what to do or trying to force them to do sth; make sb stop annoying you in this way: *I've done all that already, so why don't you just get off my back?* ◇ *If you let the newspaper take a photo of you, that'll get them off your back for a while.*

put your 'back into sth
work very hard at sth: *We'll get the job finished today if we put our backs into it.*

background

merge into the background → merge

backhanded

a ‚backhanded 'compliment (*AmE also* **a ‚left-handed 'compliment**)
a remark that seems to express admiration but could also be understood as an insult: *She told me that my essay was 'surprisingly good', which I thought was a backhanded compliment.*

back-room

the 'back-room boys (*BrE*)
scientists, researchers, etc. who do important work but do not have direct contact with the public: *It's thanks to the back-room boys more than to the sales people that the new product is such a success.*

backs

mind your backs! ➔ mind

back-seat

a ˌback-seat ˈdriver (disapproving)

1 a passenger in a vehicle who keeps giving advice to the driver about how he or she should drive

2 a person who wants to be in control of sth that is not really their responsibility: *There are too many back-seat drivers in this department. This is my project and I'm the one who's in charge!*

backside

a kick up the backside ➔ kick

a pain in the arse/bum/backside ➔ pain

think the sun shines out of sb's arse/backside ➔ think

backwards

bend/lean over ˈbackwards to do sth

try very hard to help or please sb: *We've bent over backwards to help the child, but she refuses to cooperate.*

backwards and forwards = back and forth ➔ forth

know sb/sth backwards ➔ know

backyard

in your (own) backˈyard

in or near the place where you live or work: *The residents didn't want a new factory in their backyard.* ◇ *The party leader is facing opposition in his own backyard* (= from his own members).

bacon

bring home the bacon ➔ home

save sb's bacon ➔ save

bad

Most idioms containing **bad** are at the entries for the nouns or verbs in the idioms, for example **bad blood** is at **blood**.

can't be bad (spoken)

used to try to persuade sb to agree that sth is good: *You'll save fifty dollars, which can't be bad, can it?*

have got it ˈbad (informal, humorous)

be very much in love: *You're not seeing him again tonight, are you? That's five times this week—you've got it bad!*

not (so/too) ˈbad (spoken)

quite good: *'How are you feeling today?' 'Not too bad, thanks.'* ◇ *Some of his recent books are really not bad.*

take the ˌbad with the ˈgood

accept the bad aspects of sth as well as the good ones: *You must learn to take the bad with the good in this job. Things don't always go as well as you hope think they should.*

(it's) too ˈbad (spoken)

1 used to show sympathy or disappointment: *It's too bad you can't come to the party.*

2 used to show that you are not sympathetic: *I know you don't want me to go. Well, too bad, I'm going!*

badly

badly ˈoff

1 not having much money; poor

2 not in a good situation: *I've got quite a big room so I'm not too badly off.*

be badly ˈoff for sth (BrE)

not have enough of sth: *My father also studied history at college, so I'm not badly off for books* (= I've got quite a lot).

bag

(not) your ˈbag (informal)

(not) sth that you are interested in or good at: *Poetry isn't really my bag.*

ˌbag and ˈbaggage

with all your belongings: *If you don't pay the rent, you'll be thrown out, bag and baggage.*

a ˈbag lady (informal)

a woman who has no home and who walks around carrying her possessions with her

a ˌbag of ˈbones (informal)

a very thin person or animal: *She refused to eat until eventually she was a bag of bones.*

in the ˈbag (informal)

(of a successful result) almost certain to be achieved: *With a three-goal lead and only ten minutes of the match left to play, victory seemed in the bag.*

a bag/bundle of nerves ➔ nerves

a bag/box of tricks ➔ tricks

be a mixed bag/bunch ➔ mixed

he, she, etc. couldn't punch his, her, etc. way out of a paper bag ➔ punch

let the cat out of the bag ➔ let

an old bag ➔ old

baggage

bag and baggage ➔ bag

bags

bags (I)/(I) bags (BrE) (AmE ˈdibs on …) (informal)

used especially by children for claiming the right to have or do sth before anyone else: *Bags I the front seat!* ◇ *I bags the biggest one!*

pack your bags ➔ pack

(yes sir, no sir) three bags full (sir) ➔ three

bait

fish or cut bait ➔ fish

rise to the bait ➔ rise

swallow the bait ➔ swallow

baker

a baker's 'dozen (old-fashioned)
thirteen

> **❶ ORIGIN**
> This phrase comes from bakers' old custom of adding one extra loaf to an order of a dozen (= twelve).

balance

(be/hang) in the 'balance
(be) at a point where sth could either develop well or badly; be uncertain: *With the election results due to be announced this afternoon, the future of the party still hangs very much in the balance.*

(catch/throw sb) off 'balance
1 make sb/sth unsteady and in danger of falling: *I was thrown off balance by the sudden gust of wind.*
2 make sb surprised and no longer calm: *The senator was clearly caught off balance by the unexpected question.*

on 'balance
when advantages and disadvantages, successes and failures, etc. have been compared: *It has been decided that, on balance, she is the best person for the job despite her lack of experience.*

redress the balance → **redress**
strike a balance (between A and B) → **strike**
swing the balance = tip the balance/scales → **tip**

balances

checks and balances → **checks**

balancing

a balancing/juggling act → **act**

bald

(as) bald as a 'coot
having no hair on your head at all: *Why did you buy him a hairbrush? He's as bald as a coot!*

> **❷ NOTE**
> A *coot* is a black bird with a white patch on its forehead that lives on or near water.

ball

a ˌball and 'chain (BrE)
1 a problem that prevents you from doing what you would like to do: *The business never made any money and was regarded more as a ball and chain than anything else.*
2 (humorous) sb's husband or wife: *I must get home to the ball and chain!*

> **❶ ORIGIN**
> In the past, prisoners had to wear a heavy metal ball on a chain around one leg so that they couldn't escape.

the ball is in your/sb's 'court
it is sb's turn to speak, act, etc. next: *I've given them a list of the changes that I think are necessary, so the ball's in their court now.*

be on the 'ball
be aware of what is happening and be able to react or deal with it quickly: *For the assistant manager's job we need someone who's really on the ball.*

a (whole) different/new 'ball game (informal)
a completely different kind of situation: *They used to go out every night, but now they've got a baby it's a whole new ball game.*

get/keep/set/start the 'ball rolling
begin/continue an activity, discussion etc: *I will start the ball rolling by introducing the first speaker.*

have (yourself) a 'ball (informal, especially AmE)
enjoy yourself very much: *When these exams are finally over, we're going to have a ball.*

play ball (with sb) → **play**

ballistic

go bal'listic (informal)
become very angry: *He went ballistic when I told him about the accident.*

balloon

when the bal'loon goes up (informal)
when the trouble or important event begins: *I don't want to be there when the balloon goes up.*

go down like a lead balloon → **lead**

ballpark

a 'ballpark figure
a number which is approximately correct: *I know we haven't really discussed costs yet, but can you give me a ballpark figure?*

be in the same/right 'ballpark (especially AmE)
be within the same/the right area or range of figures, etc: *The offers for the contract were all in the same ballpark.*

banana

slip on a banana skin → **slip**

bananas

go ba'nanas (slang)
become angry, crazy or silly: *If I'm late again my Dad'll go bananas.* ◇ *The clock's going bananas (= isn't working correctly).*

bandwagon

climb/jump on the 'bandwagon (informal, disapproving)
do sth that others are already doing because it is successful or fashionable: *As soon as their policies became popular all the other parties started to climb on the bandwagon.*

> **❶ ORIGIN**
> In the USA, political parades often included a band on a wagon. Political leaders would join them in the hope of winning popular support.

bane

the bane of sb's 'life/e'xistence
a person or thing that makes sb's life unpleasant or unhappy: *That car is always breaking down! It's the bane of my life.*

bang

bang for your 'buck (*AmE, slang*)
if you get more, better, etc. **bang for your buck**, you get better value for the money you spend or the effort you put in to sth: *Buyers get more bang for their buck with our cars.*

bang goes sth (*informal*)
sth is suddenly gone, finished, lost, etc: *I twisted my ankle and bang went my chances of playing in the match.*

bang/spot 'on (*informal*)
(of an estimate, a description, etc.) exactly right: *She was bang on when she called him an idiot: that's just what he is!* ◇ *Your sales estimate was spot on. Well done!*

bang to 'rights (*BrE*) (*AmE* dead to 'rights) (*informal*)
in the act of committing a crime, so that you cannot claim to be innocent: *We've got you bang to rights handling stolen property.*

go 'bang (*informal*)
burst or explode with a loud noise; make a sudden loud noise: *A balloon suddenly went bang.*

go (off) with a 'bang (*informal*)
(of an event, etc.) be very successful: *Last night's party really went off with a bang.*

bang/beat the drum (for sb/sth) → **drum**
bang/knock your/their heads together → **heads**
bang on time = (right) on time → **time**

bank

laugh all the way to the bank → **laugh**
not break the bank → **break**

baptism

a ˌbaptism of 'fire
an unpleasant or difficult first experience of sth: *Her first day in the job was a real baptism of fire because she had to deal with a very difficult case immediately.*

bar

bar 'none
without exception: *This is the best apple pie I've ever tasted, bar none.*

be all over ˌbar the 'shouting
(of a performance, contest, etc.) be finished or decided, with only the audience's reaction or the official announcement to follow: *Now that the first few election results have been declared, it's really all over bar the shouting.*

everything but/bar the kitchen sink → **kitchen**
prop up the bar → **prop**

bare

the bare 'bones (of sth)
the main or basic facts of a matter: *I had so little time that I could only tell him the bare bones of the story and had to supply the details later.*

bare your 'soul
tell sb your deepest feelings: *Finally she bared her soul to him, saying she had always loved him.*

bare your 'teeth
show your teeth in a fierce and threatening way: *The dog bared its teeth and growled.*

with your bare 'hands
with your hands only, without any tools or weapons: *He said he'd killed a crocodile with his bare hands!*

the cupboard is bare → **cupboard**
lay sth bare → **lay**

bargain

into the 'bargain (*AmE* in the 'bargain)
as well; in addition: *She gave us tea and some useful information into the bargain.*

drive a hard bargain → **drive**
strike a bargain/deal (with sb) → **strike**

bargaining

a 'bargaining counter (*BrE*) (also a 'bargaining chip *AmE, BrE*)
a special advantage in negotiations, disputes, etc. which can be offered in exchange for sth: *The proposed troop reductions were a useful bargaining counter in the disarmament talks.*

bargepole

not touch sb/sth with a bargepole → **touch**

bark

his, her, etc. bark is worse than his, her, etc. bite (*informal*)
sb is not really as angry or unkind as they seem: *Don't worry about my father being angry—his bark is worse than his bite.*

why keep a dog and bark yourself? → **dog**

barking

be barking 'mad; be 'barking (*BrE, informal*)
completely crazy: *You're playing tennis in this weather? You're barking mad!*

be barking up the wrong 'tree
be mistaken about sth: *The police are barking up the wrong tree if they think I had anything to do with the crime. I wasn't even in the country when it happened!*

barn

shut, etc. the barn door after the horse has escaped = shut/lock/close the stable door after the horse has bolted → **stable**

barred

(with) no holds barred → **holds**

barrel

(get/have sb) over a 'barrel (*informal*)
(put/have sb) in a position where they are forced to do what you want: *She has us over a barrel—if we don't pay her, we'll lose everything.*

a barrel/bundle of laughs → **laughs**
be like shooting fish in a barrel = be like taking candy from a baby → **candy**
lock, stock and barrel → **lock**
scrape (the bottom of) the barrel → **scrape**

barrelhead

cash on the barrelhead → **cash**

bars

behind 'bars (*informal*)
in prison: *Criminals like him ought to be put behind bars for life.*

base

off 'base (*AmE, informal*)
1 completely wrong about sth: *You're way off base with that guess.*
2 unprepared: *The question caught her off base.*

get to first base (with sb/sth) → **first**
reach/make first base (with sb/sth) → **first**
touch base (with sb) → **touch**

bash

have a bash at (doing) sth (*BrE, spoken*)
make an attempt at sth: *I'm going to have a bash at fixing the car myself.*

basics

get/go back to 'basics
think about the simple or most important ideas within a subject or an activity instead of new ideas or complicated details: *It's time for us all to get back to basics and concentrate on what really matters.*

bask

bathe/bask in reflected glory → **reflected**

basket

a 'basket case (*informal*)
1 a country or an organization whose economic situation is very bad: *A few years ago, the country was an economic basket case, but now things are different.*
2 a person who is slightly crazy and who has problems dealing with situations: *'How did the inter-*

view go?' 'Terrible! I'm sure they thought I was a complete basket case.'

put all your eggs into one basket → **eggs**

bat

bat your 'eyelashes/'eyes
open and close your eyes quickly, in a way that is supposed to be attractive: *There's no use batting your eyelashes at me, young lady!*

go to 'bat for sb (*AmE, informal*)
give sb help and support: *I'm going to go to bat for more police officers.*

like a bat out of 'hell (*informal*)
very fast: *If there were a fire, I wouldn't try to save any possessions. I'd be off like a bat out of hell!*

not bat an 'eyelid (*BrE*) (*AmE* **not bat an 'eye**) (*informal*)
not seem surprised, worried, afraid, etc: *She didn't bat an eyelid when they told her she'd lost her job. She just calmly walked out.*

(right) off the 'bat (*informal, especially AmE*)
immediately; without delay: *They liked each other very much, right off the bat.*

off your own 'bat (*BrE, informal*)
independently, without the encouragement or help of others: *Nobody had even tried to persuade Tim to give up smoking; he did it off his own bat.*

(as) blind as a bat → **blind**
an old bat → **old**
play a straight bat → **play**

bated

with bated 'breath
hardly able to breathe because you are very anxious about sth: *We watched with bated breath as the lion moved slowly towards him.*

bathe

bathe/bask in reflected glory → **reflected**

bathwater

throw the baby out with the bathwater → **throw**

bats

have (got) bats in the 'belfry (*old-fashioned, informal*)
be crazy or eccentric

batten

batten down the 'hatches
prepare yourself for a period of difficulty or trouble: *Hollywood is battening down the hatches in expectation of a strike by actors and writers this summer.*

> **❷ NOTE**
> A *batten* is a long piece of wood which was used to hold down strong material in order to cover a ship's *hatches* (= openings in the deck of a boat leading to the lower level) in a storm.

batteries

recharge your batteries → **recharge**

battle

the battle lines are 'drawn
used to say that people or groups have shown which side they intend to support in a dispute or contest that is going to begin: *The battle lines are being drawn between those who want to join the single currency, and those who don't.*

a battle of 'wills
a competition, argument or struggle where each side is very determined to win: *Annie and Phil were engaged in a silent battle of wills, each refusing to leave.*

a battle of 'wits
a competition, argument or struggle where each side uses their ability to think quickly to try to win: *It's a battle of wits between the hero and the villain.*

do/join 'battle (with sb)
fight, compete or argue (with sb): *Paul Wilkins will do battle with Ray Jobson tonight for the middleweight boxing championship.* ◇ *A group of local parents have decided to join battle with the council about their decision to close two of the town's schools.*

fight a losing battle → **fight**
half the battle → **half**
a pitched battle → **pitched**
a running battle → **running**
an uphill struggle/battle/task → **uphill**

battles

fight your own battles → **fight**

bay

at 'bay
when an animal that is being hunted is **at bay**, it must turn and face the dogs and hunters because it is impossible to escape from them

hold/keep sb/sth at 'bay
prevent sb/sth from coming too close or attacking: *Vitamin C helps to keep colds and flu at bay.*

> ❶ ORIGIN
> The Greeks and Romans believed the *bay tree* provided protection against thunderbolts because it was never struck by lightning, so they wore its leaves on their heads to protect themselves during thunderstorms.

be

Most idioms containing the verb **be** are at the entries for the nouns and adjectives in the idioms, for example **be the death of sb** is at **death**.

be 'at it (*informal*)
1 be talking or arguing too much: *It's time you two stopped arguing - you've been at it all morning!*
2 be having sex with sb

be your'self
act naturally: *Don't try to act sophisticated—just be yourself.*

so 'be it (*formal*)
used to show that you accept a situation but do not like it: *He never wants to speak to me again? So be it.*

beach

not the only pebble on the beach → **pebble**

beady

keep a beady 'eye on sb/sth; have (got) your beady 'eye on sb/sth
watch sb/sth very carefully because you do not really trust them/it: *He always kept a beady eye on his employees.*

be-all

the ˌbe-all and 'end-all (of sth) (*informal*)
the most important thing/person; the only thing/person that matters: *His girlfriend is the be-all and end-all of his existence.* ◇ *I'll never be rich, but money isn't the be-all and end-all, you know.*

beam

off 'beam (*informal*)
wrong; incorrect: *No, you're way off beam there.*

beam/grin/smile from ear to ear → **ear**
broad in the beam → **broad**

bean

not (have) a 'bean (*BrE, informal*)
(have) no money at all: *'How much have you saved?' 'Not a bean.'*

beans

full of beans → **full**
a hill of beans → **hill**
spill the beans → **spill**

bear

bear the 'brunt of sth
suffer most as the result of an attack, a loss, bad luck, etc: *We all lost money when the business collapsed, but I bore the brunt of it because I had invested the most.*

bear 'fruit
have the desired result; be successful: *The tireless efforts of campaigners have finally borne fruit and the prisoners are due to be released tomorrow.*

like a ˌbear with a sore 'head (*informal*)
very bad-tempered: *She's like a bear with a sore head in the mornings.*

bear/carry your cross → **cross**
bear/keep sb/sth in mind → **mind**
bear/keep in mind that … → **mind**
bear/give witness (to sth) → **witness**
bring pressure to bear (on sb) (to do sth) → **pressure**

grin and bear it ➔ **grin**

have (got) a (heavy) cross to bear ➔ **cross**

bearings

find/get your 'bearings
find out exactly where you are, or the details of the situation you are in, especially when this is new and unfamiliar: *We got off the bus right in the centre of town and it took us a moment or two to get our bearings.* ◇ *I've only been in the job for a week so I'm still finding my bearings.*

lose your bearings ➔ **lose**

beast

be no good/use to man or beast ➔ **man**

beat

,beat about the 'bush *(BrE)* *(AmE* ,beat around the 'bush)
take too long before saying what you want to say; avoid saying sth directly: *Don't beat about the bush. Tell me exactly what you think is wrong with my work.*

beat sb at their own 'game
be more successful than sb in their special activity, sport, etc.; defeat sb using their own methods: *If you thought someone was trying to cheat you, would you challenge him or try to beat him at his own game?*

beat your 'brains out *(informal, especially AmE)*
think very hard about sth for a long time: *I was beating my brains out all weekend trying to write the script.*

beat your 'breast *(often ironic)*
show that you know you have done sth wrong and are sorry for this: *If anything happens to the children while you're out enjoying yourself, don't come beating your breast to me about it afterwards.*

beat the 'clock
finish a task, race, etc. before a particular time

beat sb/sth 'hollow
beat sb easily in a contest, etc.; be much better than sb/sth: *As a cook he beats the professionals hollow.*

'beat it *(informal)*
(usually used as a command) go away: *You're not wanted here, so beat it.*

beat a path to sb's 'door
if a lot of people **beat a path to sb's door**, they are all interested in sth that person has to sell, or can do or tell them: *Top theatrical agents are beating a path to the teenager's door.*

beat the 'rap *(AmE, slang)*
escape without being punished: *This time he didn't beat the rap, and got three years in jail for robbery.*

beat a (hasty) re'treat
go away quickly from sb/sth: *I had a terrible head-ache from all the noise and smoke at the party, so my wife and I beat a hasty retreat.*

beat 'time
show the rhythm of a piece of music by striking sth, moving your hands, etc: *She beat time with her fingers.*

,can you 'beat it/'that? *(spoken)*
used to express disbelief, surprise, annoyance, etc: *Can you beat that? He's just broken another glass.*

if you can't 'beat them, 'join them *(saying)*
if you cannot defeat sb or be as successful as they are, then it is more sensible to join them in what they are doing and perhaps get some advantage for yourself by doing so: *Everybody else seems to be leaving early today, so I think I will too. After all, if you can't beat 'em, join 'em!*

a rod/stick to 'beat sb with
a fact, an argument, etc. that is used in order to blame or punish sb: *The results of the national exams this year are being used as another stick to beat teachers with.*

bang/beat the drum (for sb/sth) ➔ **drum**

beat/scare the (living) daylights out of sb ➔ **daylights**

beat/knock/kick the hell out of sb ➔ **hell**

your heart misses a beat ➔ **heart**

win (sth)/beat sb hands down ➔ **hands**

beaten

off the ,beaten 'track
far away from where people normally live or go: *Our house is a bit off the beaten track.*

beating

take a 'beating
1 be damaged or hurt: *The house took a terrible beating during the storms.* ◇ *Dad's good humour had taken a beating.*
2 lose a lot of money: *Share prices on the London Stock Exchange took a beating last week.*

take some 'beating *(BrE)*
be difficult to do or be better than: *As a place to live, Oxford takes some beating.*

beats

it ,beats 'me (why, how, etc.) *(informal)*
I cannot understand (why, how, etc.): *It beats me how he can afford a new car on his salary.* ◇ *What she does with her time beats me.*

beauty

,beauty is in the ,eye of the be'holder *(saying)*
what one person thinks is beautiful may not seem beautiful to somebody else: *Personally I don't think he's very attractive, but they say beauty's in the eye of the beholder, don't they?*

beauty is only skin-'deep *(saying)*
physical appearance is no guide to a person's char-acter: *My mother always used to say that beauty is*

only skin-deep. What's really important is the sort of person you are.

the beauty of (doing) sth
the advantage of (doing) sth: *The beauty of (having) a small car is that it makes it so much easier to find a parking space.*

get your 'beauty sleep *(humorous)*
go to bed early so that you wake up feeling healthy and looking attractive: *Look how late it is! I won't get my beauty sleep tonight.*

beaver
an eager beaver ➔ **eager**

beck
at sb's ,beck and 'call
always ready and required to do exactly what sb asks: *Working as a shop assistant means being at the customers' beck and call all day.*

> ❷ NOTE
> *Beck* is a shortened form of the word 'beckon' (= give sb a signal with your finger or hand, especially to tell them to come closer).

become
what will become/has become/became of sb/sth?
used to ask what will happen or what has happened to sb/sth: *What became of that student who used to live with you?* ◊ *I hate to think what will become of them if they lose their home.*

bed
get out of bed on the wrong side *(BrE)* *(AmE* get up on the wrong side of the bed*)*
be bad-tempered from the moment when you get up: *Why is Pete so irritable this morning? Did he get out of bed on the wrong side again?*

go to 'bed with sb *(informal)*
have sex with sb: *He asked her to go to bed with him.*

have ,made your bed and have to 'lie on it
have to accept a difficult or unpleasant situation that you have caused yourself: *Linda has borrowed more money than she can ever pay back, but I suppose she's made her bed and now she's got to lie on it.*

in 'bed
used to refer to sexual activity: *What's he like in bed?* ◊ *I caught them in bed together* (= having sex).

take to your 'bed
go to bed and stay there because of illness: *She has taken to her bed with a bad bout of flu.*

be a bed of roses = be all roses ➔ **roses**
die in your bed ➔ **die**
wet the/your bed ➔ **wet**

bedfellows
be/make strange bedfellows ➔ **strange**

bee
the ,bee's 'knees *(informal)*
a wonderful person or thing: *He thinks he's the bee's knees* (= has a high opinion of himself).

have (got) a 'bee in your bonnet *(informal)*
think or talk about sth all the time and believe that it is very important: *Harry's always going around opening windows. He's got a bee in his bonnet about fresh air.*

(as) busy as a bee ➔ **busy**
a busy bee ➔ **busy**

beeline
make a 'beeline for sb/sth *(informal)*
move directly towards sb/sth: *The children made a beeline for the food the moment they came in.*

> ❶ ORIGIN
> This idioms refers to the way bees fly in a straight line when they return to the hive.

been
,been 'there, ,done 'that *(informal)*
used to show that you think a place or an activity is not very interesting or impressive because you have already experienced it: *Not camping again! Been there, done that, got the T-shirt.*

have been a'round *(informal)*
1 have a wide experience of life: *She's been around a bit so she'll know how to deal with this type of problem.*
2 have had many sexual partners: *He'd had a lot of girlfriends before he met Sue. He'd certainly been around a bit.*

have been there be'fore *(informal)*
know all about a situation because you have experienced it: *I know how bad it is when your parents get divorced—I've been there before, remember?*

he, she, etc. has gone/been and done sth ➔ **done**

beer
small beer ➔ **small**

bees
the birds and the bees ➔ **birds**

beet
(as) red as a beet ➔ **red**

beetroot
(as) red as a beetroot ➔ **red**

beg
,beg, ,borrow or 'steal (also ,beg, ,steal or 'borrow)
obtain sth any way you can: *We'll have to beg, steal or borrow enough money to pay the fines.*

beg the 'question
1 make sb want to ask a question that has not yet been answered: *All of which begs the question as to who will fund the project.*
2 talk about sth as if it were definitely true, even though it might not be: *This proposal begs the question of whether a change is needed at all.*

I beg to 'differ
used to say politely that you do not agree with sth that has just been said: *I must beg to differ on this. I think you are quite mistaken.*

I beg your 'pardon (*formal, especially BrE*)
1 used as a polite way of saying sorry for sth you have just said or done: *Did I step on your toe? Oh, I beg your pardon!*
2 used to ask sb to repeat what they have just said because you did not hear: *'It's on Duke Street.' 'I beg your pardon?' 'Duke Street.'*
3 (*especially BrE*) used to show that you are angry or offended: *I beg your pardon! I'd rather you didn't refer to my father as 'that fat man'.*

beggar
beggar be'lief/de'scription
be too strange and unusual to be believed/described: *Tim left two windows wide open when he went on holiday. His stupidity beggars belief!* ◇ *The sight of him completely covered with mud and oil beggared description.*

beggars
beggars can't be 'choosers (*saying*)
when there is no choice, you have to be satisfied with whatever you can get: *I would have preferred a bed, but beggars can't be choosers so I slept on the sofa in the living room.*

if wishes were horses, beggars would/might ride ➔ wishes

begging
go 'begging (*BrE, spoken*)
(*go* is usually used in the progressive tenses) (of things) be unwanted: *I'll have that last potato if it's going begging.*

begin
to be'gin with
1 at first: *I found it tiring to begin with but I soon got used to it.* ◇ *We'll go slowly to begin with.*
2 used to introduce the first point you want to make: *'What was it you didn't like?' 'Well, to begin with, our room was far too small.'*

beginner
beginner's 'luck
good luck or success at the start of learning to do sth: *'You won the game! Well done!' 'It was probably just beginner's luck.'*

beginning
the beginning of the 'end
the first sign of sth ending: *The quarrel was the beginning of the end for our relationship.*

begins
charity begins at home ➔ charity

behalf
in behalf of sb; in sb's behalf (*AmE*)
in order to help sb: *We collected money in behalf of the homeless.*

on behalf of sb; on sb's behalf
1 as the representative of sb or instead of them: *On behalf of the department I would like to thank you all.* ◇ *Mr Knight cannot be here, so his wife will accept the prize on his behalf.*
2 because of sb; for sb: *Don't worry on my behalf.*
3 in order to help sb: *They campaigned on behalf of asylum seekers.*

take up the cudgels on behalf of sb/sth ➔ cudgels

behave
behave/act as if you own the place = think you own the place ➔ think

behold
lo and behold ➔ lo

beholder
beauty is in the eye of the beholder ➔ beauty

belfry
have (got) bats in the belfry ➔ bats

belief
beyond be'lief
(in a way that is) too great, difficult, etc. to be believed: *Dissatisfaction with the government has grown beyond belief.* ◇ *icy air that was cold beyond belief*

beggar belief/description ➔ beggar
contrary to popular belief/opinion ➔ contrary
to the best of your belief/knowledge ➔ best

believe
be,lieve it or 'not (*spoken*)
it is true, even though it does not sound likely: *Believe it or not, I've just won £1 000 in a competition!* ◇ *I am still, believe it or not, very nervous about speaking in public.*

be,lieve (you) 'me
used for emphasizing a statement, a promise or a threat: *I'll be seeing her tomorrow, and, believe you me, I'll tell her exactly what I think of her.*

don't you be'lieve it! (*spoken*)
used to tell sb that sth is definitely not true: *Some people say skiing is easy but don't you believe it!*

give sb to be'lieve/under'stand (that) …
(*formal*)
(often used in the passive) make sb believe/understand sth: *I was given to understand that she had resigned.*

I don't be'lieve it! (*spoken*)
used to say that you are surprised or annoyed about sth: *I don't believe it! What are you doing here?*

if you, they, etc. believe 'that, you'll, they'll, etc. believe 'anything (*informal*)
you, they, etc. would be very stupid to believe that: *He says he'll pay for your holiday? Well, if you believe that, you'll believe anything!*

I'll believe it/that when I see it (*informal*)
used for expressing doubt that sth will happen or be done: *'He says he's going to give up smoking.' 'I'll believe that when I see it.'*

make be'lieve (that …)
pretend (that …): *The journey seemed like an attempt to make believe that the modern world didn't exist.*

not be,lieve your 'eyes/'ears
(usually used with *can't* or *couldn't*) think that sth you see/hear is very surprising: *I couldn't believe my ears when I heard my name mentioned on the radio.* ◊ *I could hardly believe my eyes when I saw the professor arrive dressed as a clown.*

would you be'lieve (it)? (*spoken*)
used to show that you are surprised and annoyed about sth: *And, would you believe, he didn't even apologize!*

lead sb to believe (that …) ➔ **lead**
you/you'd better believe it! ➔ **better**

believer

be a great/firm believer in sth
believe strongly that sth is good, important or valuable: *My mother was a great believer in horoscopes all her life.* ◊ *The boss was a firm believer in developing strong teamwork.*

believing

seeing is believing ➔ **seeing**

bell

give sb a 'bell (*BrE, informal*)
call sb by telephone: *I'll give you a bell tomorrow.*

(as) clear as a bell ➔ **clear**
ring a bell ➔ **ring**
(be) saved by the bell ➔ **saved**
(as) sound as a bell ➔ **sound**

bells

bells and 'whistles
attractive extra features: *a software package with more new bells and whistles than ever*

belly

go belly 'up
if a business or a project **goes belly up**, it fails: *Everything started off well, but the business went belly up when one of the partners resigned.*

bellyful

have had a 'bellyful of sb/sth (*informal*)
have had too much of sb/sth: *I've had a bellyful of his complaining. If he doesn't stop, I'm leaving.*

belt

below the 'belt
(of a comment, attack, etc.) unfair and unkind: *Her remarks about his age were a bit below the belt.*

> **ⓘ ORIGIN**
> This expression comes from boxing, and refers to the rule that forbids boxers from hitting each other below the waist.

under your 'belt
already achieved and so making you feel more confident: *With ten years' experience under his belt, Mark was ready to start his own business.*

tighten your belt ➔ **tighten**

bend

bend sb's 'ear (about sth) (*informal*)
talk to sb a lot about sth, especially about a problem that you have: *Max has been bending my ear all night about his job.*

bend your 'mind/'efforts to sth (*formal*)
think very hard about or put a lot of effort into one particular thing

bend the 'truth
say sth that is not completely true: *In the end he admitted bending the truth. He had done some of his essay, but he hadn't finished it.*

(drive sb/be/go) round the 'bend/'twist (*informal, especially BrE*)
(make sb/be/become) crazy: *I'm going round the twist trying to repair this machine. Nothing I do seems to work.* ◊ *He practises the same tune all day; it drives me round the bend* (= annoys me very much).

bend/lean over backwards to do sth ➔ **backwards**
bend/stretch the rules ➔ **rules**

bended

on bended 'knee(s)
kneeling to ask for sth or to pray: *He went down on bended knee and asked her to marry him.*

benefit

for sb's 'benefit
especially in order to help or be useful to sb: *I have typed out some lecture notes for the benefit of those people who were absent last week.* ◊ *There's no need to repeat everything for my benefit.*

give sb the ˌbenefit of the ˈdoubt
accept that a person is right or innocent because you cannot prove that they are not: *The old man said that he had put the goods in his bag by mistake and the shopkeeper decided to give him the benefit of the doubt.*

bent

be ˈbent on sth/on doing sth (*informal*)
be determined to do or have sth: *I advised her against it, but she was bent on taking part in the marathon.*

berth

give sb/sth a wide berth ➔ **wide**

beside

beˈside yourself (with sth)
unable to control yourself because of the strength of emotion you are feeling: *He was beside himself with rage when he found out what she'd done.*

best

all the ˈbest
used when you are saying goodbye or ending a letter to give sb your best wishes: *All the best, then, Maria, and we'll see you in two weeks.* ◇ *Here's wishing you all the best for the coming year.*

as ˌbest you ˈcan
not perfectly but as well as you are able: *We'll manage as best we can.*

at ˈbest/ˈworst
taking the most/least hopeful or positive view: *Smoking is at best unpleasant and expensive, and at worst lethal.*

at the ˈbest of times
(even) when conditions are good: *This car does not go very fast at the best of times, and with four people in it it will go a lot slower.*

be (all) for the ˈbest
have a good result, though it does not seem good at first: *I was very disappointed when I didn't get the job but now I think it was for the best. I don't think I would have liked it.*

the/your best bet (*informal*)
the best thing for you to do in a particular situation: *Your best bet is to leave the car here and get a bus into town.*

your best bib and ˈtucker (*humorous*)
your best clothes that you only wear on special occasions: *Bill put on his best bib and tucker and booked a table at a top restaurant for a romantic dinner.*

> ❷ NOTE
> *Bib* and *tucker* are both items of clothing worn in the past.

the best ˈmedicine
the best way of improving a situation, especially of making you feel happier: *Laughter is the best medicine.*

the best of a bad ˈbunch/ˈlot (*BrE*)
a person or a thing that is a little better than the rest in a group, although none are very good

the best of ˈboth/ˈall (possible) worlds
the advantages of two/many very different situations: *We have the best of both worlds here—it's a peaceful village but we're only twenty minutes from the town centre.*

the best of (British) ˈluck (to sb) (also **the best of ˈBritish (to sb)**) (*old-fashioned, informal, often ironic*)
used to wish sb luck in an activity, especially one in which they are unlikely to be successful: *The four of you are going to live in that tiny flat? The best of British to you!*

the best of ˈthree, ˈfive, etc.
(especially in games and sports) up to three, five, etc. games played to decide who wins, the winner being the person who wins most of them

the best thing since sliced ˈbread (*informal, spoken*)
if you say that sth is **the best thing since sliced bread**, you think it is extremely good, interesting, etc: *My father doesn't like him very much, but my mother thinks he's the best thing since sliced bread!*

bring out the ˈbest in sb
make sb show their best qualities: *Sometimes it takes a crisis to bring out the best in people.*

do, mean, etc. sth for the ˈbest
do or say sth in order to achieve a good result or to help sb: *I just don't know what to do for the best.* ◇ *I'm sorry if my advice offended you—I meant it for the best.*

for a/some reason/reasons best known to himˈself, herˈself, etc. (*humorous*)
for a reason or reasons which other people find hard to understand: *For reasons best known to himself, he wears three pairs of socks.*

get/have the ˈbest of sth
gain more advantage from sth than sb else: *I thought you had the best of that discussion.*

give it your best ˈshot
try as hard as you can to do or achieve sth: *I probably won't win the game, but I'll give it my best shot.*

make the best of sth/things/a bad job
do as well as you can in a difficult situation: *It wasn't a very large room, but he made the best of it by using space carefully.* ◇ *I know the lighting isn't perfect but we'll have to make the best of a bad job and get the best photos we can.*

put your best foot ˈforward
go, work, etc. as fast as you can: *If we put our best foot forward, we should be there by noon.*

to the best of your beˈlief/ˈknowledge
as far as you know: *He never made a will, to the best of my knowledge.*

with the 'best of them

as well as anybody: *She may be seventy, but she can get up and dance with the best of them!*

with the ˌbest will in the 'world

even though you have tried very hard to be fair, generous etc: *He's quite competent, but with the best will in the world, I can't imagine him as head of a large company.*

be past your/its best → past

the better/best part of sth → part

do/try your level best (to do sth) → level

had better/best do sth → better

hope for the best → hope

know best → know

look your/its best → look

man's best friend → man

the next best thing → next

second best → second

your Sunday best → Sunday

bet

(you can) bet your bottom 'dollar/your 'life (on sth/that …) (*informal*)

(you can) be certain of sth: *You can bet your bottom dollar that he'll forget our anniversary.*

I('ll) 'bet (that …) (*informal*)

1 I am certain (that …): *I bet he'll get drunk at the party—he always does.*

2 used to show that you agree with sb or are not surprised to hear sth: *'I'm furious about what she said to me.' 'I bet (you are)!'*

I wouldn't 'bet on it; don't 'bet on it (*spoken*)

used to say that you do not think that sth is very likely: *'She'll soon get used to the idea.' 'I wouldn't bet on it.'*

ˌyou 'bet (*informal*)

certainly: *'Would you like an ice cream?' 'You bet!'* ◇ *'Are you hungry?' 'You bet I am!'*

the/your best bet → best

a safe bet → safe

bête

your, his, etc. bête 'noire (*from French*)

a person or thing that particularly annoys you and that you do not like: *Edward was furious when he discovered that he would be working with his old bête noire, Richard Watkins.*

> ❶ **NOTE**
> The meaning of the French phrase is 'black beast'.

betide

woe betide sb → woe

bets

hedge your bets → hedge

better

against your better 'judgement (*especially BrE*) (*AmE* usually **against your better 'judgment**)

although you know your action, decision, etc. is not sensible: *She was persuaded against her better judgement to lend him the money, and now she's regretting it.*

be better 'off

be richer, happier, more fortunate, etc: *'You'd be better off with a smaller house, now that your children have left home.'* ◇ *Under the new tax regulations I will be £17 a month better off.*

be better off (doing sth)

be more sensible (to do a particular thing): *You'd be better off resting at home with that cold.*

ˌbetter the ˌdevil you 'know (than the devil you don't) (*saying*)

it is better to deal with sb/sth bad, difficult, etc. that is familiar than to make a change and perhaps have to deal with sb/sth worse

(all) the better for sth

made better by (doing) sth; benefiting from sth: *You'll be all the better for (having had) a holiday by the sea.*

ˌbetter ˌlate than 'never (*saying*)

it is better to arrive, do sth, etc. late than not to arrive, do sth, etc. at all: *You were supposed to be here an hour ago, but better late than never, I suppose!*

ˌbetter luck 'next time (*spoken*)

used to encourage sb who has not been successful at sth

ˌbetter (to be) ˌsafe than 'sorry (*saying*)

it is better to be too careful than to do sth careless that you may later regret: *We'd better fill the car up with petrol now. It's better to be safe than sorry.*

the ˌbigger, ˌsmaller, ˌfaster, ˌslower, etc. the 'better

used to say that sth should be as big, small, etc. as possible: *As far as the hard disk is concerned, the bigger the better.*

do better to do sth

used to say that it would be more sensible to do sth: *You'd do better to buy a good-quality radio, even if it is more expensive.*

for ˌbetter or (for) 'worse

whether the result is good or bad: *I've decided, for better or for worse, to leave my job.*

get the 'better of sb/sth

defeat sb/sth: *She always manages to get the better of me at tennis.* ◇ *Eventually, his curiosity got the better of him and he had to take a look in the box.*

go one 'better (than sb/sth)

do sth better than sb else; improve on sth: *I bought a new tennis racket but my sister had to go one bet-*

ter (*than me*) *by buying the most expensive one in the shop.*

had better/best do sth
used to tell sb what you think they should do: *You'd better lock the door before you leave: there are lots of thieves about.* ◇ *Hadn't you better check to see if the baby is all right?* ◇ *'Shall I phone her now?' 'You'd best not. She might be asleep.'*

have seen/known better 'days
be in a worse condition than in the past: *That jacket of yours has seen better days—isn't it time you bought a new one?*

little/no 'better than
almost or just the same as; almost or just as bad as: *The path was no better than a sheep track.*

so much the 'better/'worse (for sb/sth)
it is better/worse for that reason: *'I seem to have made my curry hotter than usual.' 'So much the better. I love hot curries.'*

that's (much) 'better
1 used to give support to sb who has been upset and is trying to become calmer: *Dry your eyes now. That's better.*
2 used to praise sb who has made an effort to improve: *That's much better—you played the right notes this time.*

you/you'd better be'lieve it! (*spoken*)
used to tell sb that sth is definitely true: *'He's not a bad player, is he?' 'You'd better believe it!'*

your better/other half → half
the better/best part of sth → part
discretion is the better part of valour → discretion
half a loaf is better than none/no bread → half
kiss sth better → kiss
know better (than that/than to do sth) → know
the less/least said, the better → said
not know any better → know
an ounce of prevention is better than a pound of cure = prevention is better than cure → prevention
the sooner the better → sooner
take a turn for the better/worse → turn
think (the) better of sb → think
think better of it/of doing sth → think
two heads are better than one → two

betters
your elders and betters → elders

betting
what's the 'betting ... ?; the betting 'is that ... (*informal*)
it seems likely that ...: *What's the betting that he arrives late?* ◇ *The betting is that she'll get her own way.*

between
between our'selves/you and 'me
as a secret or private matter that nobody else

should know about: *Just between you and me, I've heard that the business made a big loss last year.*

in be'tween
neither one thing nor another, but having some qualities of both; between two states, kinds, sizes, etc: *'Would you call this dress green or blue?' 'I'd say it was in between.'*

betwixt
be,twixt and be'tween (*old-fashioned*)
in a middle position; neither one thing nor the other: *He found himself placed betwixt and between in the debate, agreeing with parts of each side's arguments.*

beyond
be be'yond sb (*informal*)
be impossible for sb to imagine, understand or do: *Why she decided to marry such a boring man is beyond me.* ◇ *Some of the questions in that exam were beyond me, I'm afraid.*

bib
your best bib and tucker → best

bide
bide your 'time
wait for a suitable opportunity to do sth: *She's just biding her time until the right job comes along.*

Big
Big 'Brother (is watching you)
a leader, a person in authority or a government that tries to control every aspect of people's lives: *We live in a society where all kinds of information about the individual may be stored on computer. Big Brother, if not actually watching you, can quickly check on you if he wants to.*

> ❶ ORIGIN
> This comes from the novel *Nineteen Eighty-Four* by George Orwell, in which the leader of the government, Big Brother, had total control over people. The slogan 'Big Brother is watching you' reminded people that he knew everything they did.

Mr Big → Mr

big
a ,big 'cheese/'wheel (*informal*)
an important person with a lot of influence in an organization, etc: *His father's a big wheel in the textile industry.*

> ❶ ORIGIN
> In this sense, 'cheese' comes from the Urdu word *chiz*, meaning 'thing'.

big 'deal (*informal, ironic*)
used for suggesting that sth is not as important or impressive as sb else thinks it is: *I've got tickets for*

next Saturday's football match.' 'Big deal! Who's interested in football anyway?'

the big enchi'lada *(AmE, informal, humorous)*
the most important person or thing: *New Hampshire is the big enchilada in American politics.*

a big fish (in a little pond)
an important person (but only in a small community, group, etc.): *I would rather stay here in the village and be a big fish in a little pond than go to the city where no one knows me.*

a big girl's 'blouse *(informal, humorous)*
used to say that you think the way a boy or a man is behaving is more typical of a woman than a man, especially when they appear weak or not brave: *Don't be a big girl's blouse and start crying!*

a big name/noise/shot *(informal)*
an important person: *'What does Ian's dad do?' 'Oh, he's a big shot in the City.'*

the big 'picture *(informal, especially AmE)*
the situation as a whole: *Right now forget the details and take a look at the big picture.*

'big time *(informal)*
1 (the big time) great success in a profession, especially the entertainment business: *a bit-part actor who finally made/hit the big time*
2 on a large scale; to a great extent: *This time they've messed up big time!*

give sb a big 'hand *(informal)*
clap your hands loudly and enthusiastically: *Let's have a big hand, ladies and gentlemen, for our next performer …*

make it 'big
be very successful: *He's hoping to make it big on television.*

me and my big 'mouth *(spoken)*
used when you realize that you have said sth that you should not have said

no big 'deal *(spoken)*
used to say that sth is not important or not a problem: *If I don't win it's no big deal.*

one big happy family *(informal)*
a group of people who live or work together happily and without disagreements: *We were always together. We were like one big happy family.* ◇ *(ironic) 'Is your office a happy place to work in?' 'Oh sure, we're just one big happy family. Everybody hates everybody else.'*

too ,big for your 'boots *(informal)*
thinking that you are more important than you really are: *His political rivals had decided that he was getting too big for his boots.*

dirty great/big ➔ **dirty**
do sth in a big/small way ➔ **way**
hit (it) big ➔ **hit**
talk big ➔ **talk**
think big ➔ **think**

bigger

your eyes are bigger than your stomach ➔ **eyes**
have (got) other/bigger fish to fry ➔ **fish**

bike

on your bike! *(BrE, informal)*
a rude or humorous way of telling sb to go away: *'Can I borrow some money, Dave?' 'On yer bike!'*

Bill

the Old Bill ➔ **Old**

bill

bill and 'coo *(old-fashioned, informal)*
(of lovers) kiss and speak quietly and lovingly together

head/top the 'bill
be (listed as) the most important item or performer in a show, play, etc: *Topping the bill tonight will be Robbie Williams.*

a clean bill of health ➔ **clean**
fit the bill ➔ **fit**
foot the bill (for sth) ➔ **foot**

billy-o

like 'billy-o *(BrE, informal)*
very much or very enthusiastically: *They worked like billy-o to get it finished on time.*

bind

in a 'bind *(AmE)*
in a difficult situation that you do not know how to get out of: *I'd be in a bind without a car. I drive everywhere these days.*

bind/tie sb hand and foot ➔ **hand**
in a double bind ➔ **double**

bird

the bird has 'flown
the person who was being chased or looked for has escaped or gone away: *The police raided the house at dawn, but the bird had flown.*

a bird in the ,hand is worth two in the 'bush *(saying)*
it is better to be satisfied with what you have got than to lose it trying to get sth more or better

a ,bird of 'passage
a person who does not stay in a place for very long

flip/give/shoot sb the 'bird *(AmE, slang)*
make a rude sign at sb with your middle finger

the early bird catches the worm ➔ **early**
eat like a bird ➔ **eat**
(as) free as (the) air/as a bird ➔ **free**
a home bird ➔ **home**
a little bird told me (that …) ➔ **little**
not say/hear a dicky bird ➔ **dicky**
a rare bird ➔ **rare**

birds

the birds and the 'bees (*old-fashioned* or *humorous*)
the basic facts about sex and reproduction, the 'facts of life', as told to children: *Now that Jamie is eleven, isn't it time you told him about the birds and the bees?*

birds of a 'feather (flock to'gether) (*saying*)
similar people (spend time together): *She spent most of her time abroad with other English speakers, which I suppose is only natural. Birds of a feather flock together, after all.*

(strictly) for the 'birds (*informal*)
not important or interesting: *Fishing? That's strictly for the birds, if you ask me.*

kill two birds with one stone → kill

bird's-eye

a ˌbird's-ˌeye 'view (of sth)
a good view of sth from high above: *From the church tower you get a bird's-eye view of the town.*

birth

give 'birth (to sb/sth)
produce a baby or young animal: *She died shortly after giving birth.* ◇ *Mary gave birth to a healthy baby girl.* ◇ *(figurative) It was the study of history that gave birth to the social sciences.*

birthday

in/wearing your 'birthday suit (*informal, humorous*)
wearing no clothes; naked: *The towel fell off, and there he was in his birthday suit!*

biscuit

take the 'biscuit (*BrE*) (also **take the 'cake** *AmE, BrE*) (*informal*)
be especially surprising, annoying, etc: *Well, that really takes the biscuit! She asks if she can borrow the car, then keeps it for a month!*

bit

be ˌchamping/ˌchomping at the 'bit (also **be ˌchafing at the bit**, *more formal*)
be impatient to do or to start doing sth: *The players were champing at the bit as the start of the match was delayed.* ◇ *I know you're chafing at the bit, so we'll start as soon as we can.*

> ❷ **NOTE**
> *Champ* and *chomp* mean to bite or eat something noisily. The *bit* is the piece of metal which goes in a horse's mouth and is used to control the horse.

the (whole) … bit (*informal, disapproving*)
behaviour or ideas that are typical of a particular group, type of person or activity: *She couldn't accept the whole drug-culture bit.*

bit by 'bit (also **little by 'little**)
a small amount at a time; gradually: *We managed to save the money bit by bit over a period of ten years.* ◇ *Little by little, she began to feel better after her illness.*

a bit 'much (*informal*)
too much to be acceptable; unreasonable: *Claiming £50 a day for expenses is a bit much, I think.* ◇ *Don't you think it's a bit much of him to give me most of the work and then take the afternoon off?*

a bit of a … (*informal, especially BrE*)
used when talking about unpleasant or negative things or ideas, to mean 'rather a … ': *We may have a bit of a problem on our hands.* ◇ *The rail strike is a bit of a pain.*

a bit of all 'right (*BrE, slang*)
a very attractive person: *He's a bit of all right, don't you think, Madge?*

a bit of 'rough (*BrE, slang*)
a person of a low social class who has a sexual relationship with sb of a higher class

a ˌbit on the 'side (*slang*)
a sexual relationship with sb who is not your regular partner: *He's always looking for a bit on the side.*

a bit 'thick/'strong (*old-fashioned, BrE, informal*)
not fair or acceptable: *It's a bit thick of him to expect me to pay every time we go out together.* ◇ *She said it was the worst book she'd ever read, which I think was a bit strong.*

do your 'bit (*informal*)
do your share of a task, help a cause, etc: *Everyone is expected to do their bit to make the business successful.* ◇ *In re-using this old paper I'm doing my bit for conservation of the rain forests.*

every bit as good, bad, etc. (as sb/sth)
just as good, bad, etc.; equally good, bad, etc: *Rome is every bit as beautiful as Paris.*

get/take the bit between your 'teeth (*informal*)
start doing sth in a determined and enthusiastic way: *Once he gets the bit between his teeth in an argument, no one can stop him.*

> ❶ **ORIGIN**
> The *bit* is the piece of metal which goes in a horse's mouth and is used to control the horse. If the horse learns to hold the bit between its teeth then it can no longer be controlled by the rider.

not a 'bit; not one (little) 'bit
not at all: *'Are you cold?' 'Not a bit.'* ◇ *I don't like that idea one bit.*

not a 'bit of it! (*BrE, informal*)
used for saying that sth that you had expected to happen did not happen: *You'd think he'd be tired after the journey but not a bit of it!* ◇ *I thought she would be glad to see him but not a bit of it—she made some excuse and left as soon as he got here.*

be a bit/rather steep → steep
the ˌbiter bit → biter

go a bit far = go too far ➔ **far**

not a blind bit of notice, difference, etc. ➔ **blind**

bitch

a/the son of a bitch ➔ **son**

bite

a bite at/of the 'cherry (also a second/ another bite at/of the 'cherry) (BrE)

an opportunity to do sth, or a second attempt at doing sth, especially sth you have failed to do earlier: *They all wanted a bite of the cherry.* ◇ *We've lost that contract with the German firm and we probably won't get another bite at the cherry.*

bite the 'bullet (informal)

realize that you cannot avoid sth unpleasant, and so accept it: *Getting your car repaired is often an expensive business, but all you can do is bite the bullet and pay up.*

> **❶ ORIGIN**
> This expression comes from the old custom of giving soldiers a bullet to bite on during medical operations, which had to be done without any drugs to stop the pain.

bite the 'dust (informal)

1 fail, or be defeated or destroyed: *Thousands of small businesses bite the dust every year.*
2 (*humorous*) die

bite the hand that 'feeds you

be unkind or disloyal to sb who has been kind or helpful to you, or who pays your wages: *When you say such nasty things about the organization, you're biting the hand that feeds you.*

bite your 'lip

force yourself not to express the negative emotions that you are feeling: *You could tell she thought the criticism was unfair but she bit her lip and said nothing.*

bite your '(finger)nails

(put or press your fingers to your mouth because you) feel very excited, nervous, or afraid ▶ '**nail-biting** *adj.* very exciting or tense: *What an exciting film that was—real nail-biting stuff!*

bite off ˌmore than you can 'chew (informal)

attempt to do sth that is too difficult for you or that you do not have enough time to do: *He's promised to get all this work finished by the weekend but I've got a feeling he's bitten off more than he can chew.*

bite your 'tongue

stop yourself from saying sth that might upset sb or cause an argument, although you want to speak: *I didn't believe her explanation but I bit my tongue.*

I, he, she, etc. won't 'bite (you) (humorous)

used to tell sb that they need not be afraid of sb: *You should tell your teacher that you don't understand—she won't bite you!*

bite/snap sb's head off ➔ **head**

his, her, etc. bark is worse than his, her, etc. bite ➔ **bark**

put the arm/bite on sb ➔ **arm**

biter

the biter 'bit

the person who wanted to do harm, cheat sb, etc., has harm done to them, is cheated, etc: *It was a case of the biter bit—she'd tried to make him look foolish and ended up being ridiculed herself.*

bits

ˌbits and 'bobs (BrE) (also ˌbits and 'pieces BrE, AmE) (informal)

small things of various kinds; belongings: *The box contained needles and thread and various bits and bobs for sewing.* ◇ *She let me store a few bits and pieces in her flat while I was abroad.*

pick, pull, etc. sb/sth to 'bits/'pieces

criticize sb/sth severely and find as many faults with them/it as you can: *The committee pulled his proposal to bits. They didn't have anything positive at all to say about it.* ◇ *As soon as she left the room, everyone started pulling her to pieces.*

to bits

1 into small pieces: *The book fell to bits in my hands.* ◇ *She took the engine to bits, then carefully put it together again.*
2 (*spoken, informal*) very much: *I love my kids to bits.* ◇ *She was thrilled to bits when I said I'd come.*

bitten

be bitten by/have (got) the bug ➔ **bug**

once bitten, twice shy ➔ **once**

bitter

a bitter 'pill (for sb) (to swallow)

a thing that is very difficult or unpleasant to accept: *He was a proud man, so having to ask for money must have been a bitter pill to swallow.*

to the bitter 'end

right to the end, no matter how long it takes; until everything possible has been done: *Now that we have begun this project, we must see it through to the bitter end.* ◇ *We are determined to fight to the bitter end.*

black

black and 'blue

covered with bruises (= blue, brown or purple marks on the body): *She was black and blue all over after falling down stairs.*

(in) black and 'white

(as) absolutely right or wrong, good or bad, with no grades between them: *My grandmother has very rigid ideas of character and behaviour; she sees everything in black and white.* ◇ *It's not a black-and-white issue.*

a black 'day (for sb)

a day when sth sad, unpleasant or disastrous happens (to sb): *It was a black day for this area when the local steel factory closed down.*

a black 'eye
an area of dark skin (= a bruise) around the eye caused by an accident, sb hitting you, etc: *How did you get that black eye?*

a black 'look
an angry or disapproving expression on sb's face: *She gave me a black look when I suggested she should do the washing-up.*

a black 'mark (against sb) (*BrE*)
sth that sb has done which makes other people dislike or disapprove of them: *It was another black mark against her that she had not gone to the last meeting.*

the black 'market
an illegal form of trade in which foreign money, or goods that are difficult to obtain, are bought and sold: *Tickets for the match are being sold on the black market for up to £200 each.*

a/the black 'sheep (of the family)
a person who is considered to have done sth bad, or to be a failure, by their family or the group to which they belong: *Debbie is the black sheep of the family, having left home at seventeen to live with her boyfriend.*

ⓘ ORIGIN
Shepherds used to dislike black sheep because their wool was not as valuable as white wool.

a 'black spot
a place where accidents often happen, especially on a road: *This junction is a well-known accident black spot.*

he, it, etc. is not as black as he, it, etc. is 'painted
he, it, etc. is not as bad as people say: *The boss is not as black as she's painted; in fact, I find her quite helpful and friendly.*

in black and 'white
in print or writing: *I want to see his statement down in black and white.*

look black → **look**
the pot calling the kettle black → **pot**

blame

be to 'blame (for sth)
be responsible for sth bad: *If anyone's to blame, it's me.* ◇ *Which driver was to blame for the accident?*

don't blame 'me (*spoken*)
used to advise sb not to do sth, when you think they will do it despite your advice: *Call her if you like, but don't blame me if she's angry.*

I don't 'blame you/her, etc. (for doing sth) (*spoken*)
used to say that you think what sb did was reasonable and the right thing to do: *'I just put the phone down when he said that.' 'I don't blame you!'*

blanche

carte blanche (to do sth) → **carte**

blank

a blank 'cheque (*BrE*) (*AmE* **a blank 'check**)
permission to act as you like (especially to spend money) in a particular task or situation: *Just because I asked you to speak on my behalf, that didn't mean you had a blank cheque to promise anything you liked.* ◇ *She was given a blank cheque and told to hire the best singers she could.*

ask, tell, etc. sb point blank → **point**
draw a blank → **draw**

blanket

a wet blanket → **wet**

blast

(at) full blast → **full**

blaze

blaze a/the 'trail
be the first to do sth important or interesting: *As the first female Member of Parliament, she blazed a trail for others to follow.*

blazes

like 'blazes (*old-fashioned, spoken*)
very hard; very fast: *By the time they reached the hotel it was raining like blazes.*

what / where / who the 'blazes … ? (*old-fashioned, spoken*)
used to emphasize that you are annoyed and surprised, to avoid using the word 'hell': *What the blazes have you done?*

ⓘ ORIGIN
This expression refers to the flames associated with hell.

bleed

bleed sb 'dry/'white (*disapproving*)
take away all sb's money: *He used to be quite wealthy, but his children have bled him dry.*

bleeds

your heart bleeds for sb → **heart**

blend

blend/fade into the woodwork → **woodwork**

bless

bless (*BrE, spoken, approving*)
used to express affection for sb when you hear about sth they have said or done: *'And then he offered to cook supper for us.' 'Oh, bless!'*

bless his, her, etc. (little) cotton 'socks (*BrE, humorous*)
used to express your affection for sb because of sth

they have said or done: *And the kids brought me breakfast in bed—bless their little cotton socks!*

'bless you (*spoken*)
said to sb after they have sneezed (= made a loud noise through the nose)

(God) 'bless you (*old-fashioned*)
used for expressing thanks or affection: *God bless you, my dear. It's most kind of you to help.*

'bless you, him, etc. (also **(God) ,bless your, his, etc. 'heart/'soul**, *less frequent*) (*spoken*)
used to express affection for sb who has just been mentioned: *Your mother, bless her heart, is the only friend I have.* ◇ *Sarah, bless her, had made a cup of tea.*

God bless → God

blessing

a blessing in dis'guise
a thing that seems bad, unpleasant, etc. at first but that has advantages in the end: *Not getting that job turned out to be a blessing in disguise, as the firm went out of business only a few months later.*

a mixed blessing → mixed

blessings

count your blessings → count

blind

a ,blind 'alley
a course of action which has no useful result in the end: *Our first experiment was a blind alley, but the second one gave us very promising results.*

(as) blind as a 'bat (*humorous*)
not able to see well: *I'm as blind as a bat without my glasses.*

a ,blind 'date
a social meeting between two people who have never met before, often arranged by friends, in the hope that it may lead to a love affair: *A friend of mine set up a blind date for me with his girlfriend's sister.*

blind 'drunk (*informal*)
extremely drunk: *I'm not surprised he can't remember what happened—he was blind drunk!*

the ,blind leading the 'blind (*saying*)
(an example of) a person with as little ability or knowledge as the person they are trying to help or teach: *I don't know why she asked me to show her how the computer works when I've hardly used it myself. It would be a case of the blind leading the blind!*

a/sb's 'blind spot
a small part of a subject that sb does not understand or know anything about: *I'm a real music lover but I have to say that modern jazz is a bit of a blind spot with me.*

,blind sb with 'science
deliberately confuse sb with your special know-

ledge, especially by using difficult or technical words which they do not understand: *Every time I ask her a simple question, she tries to blind me with science.*

not a 'blind bit of notice, difference, etc. (*BrE, spoken*)
no notice, difference, etc. at all: *She didn't take a blind bit of notice when I asked her to stop. She walked straight past me.*

love is blind → love
rob sb blind → rob
swear blind (that …) → swear
turn a blind eye (to sth) → turn

blinding

effing and blinding → effing

blink

in the blink of an 'eye
very quickly; in a short time: *He was gone in the blink of an eye.*

on the 'blink (*informal*)
(of a machine) not working properly: *Can I watch the film at your house? Our TV's on the blink again.*

bliss

ignorance is bliss → ignorance

block

put/lay your head/neck on the block
risk defeat, failure, etc.; put yourself in a situation where you might be blamed, criticized, etc: *The government laid its head on the block and said that if it loses this vote in Parliament tonight it will call an election.* ◇ *I'm prepared to put my neck on the block and promise that the new building will be ready by the end of the year.*

❶ ORIGIN
In the past when people were executed (= killed as a punishment), they had to lay their head on a block so that it could be chopped off.

a chip off the old block → chip
I'll knock your block/head off! → knock
a/the new kid on the block → new

Bloggs

Joe Bloggs → Joe

blood

bad 'blood (between A and B) (*old-fashioned*)
feelings of hatred or strong dislike between two or more people or groups: *There has always been bad blood between the two families.*

be after/out for sb's 'blood (*informal, often humorous*)
want to hurt or harm sb, especially as revenge: *They have been after my blood ever since I accidentally damaged their car.*

blood and 'guts (*informal*)
used to refer to extreme violence when it is shown in films/movies or on television: *Audiences seem to prefer movies with romance and humour rather than the blood and guts stuff.*

blood and 'thunder (*informal*)
sensational and very dramatic incidents in plays, films, stories, contests, etc: *I don't like blood-and-thunder novels.*

blood is thicker than 'water (*saying*)
your family is more important than other people: *Tony was angry with his brother for a while, but blood is thicker than water, and in the end he forgave him.*

your/sb's ,blood is 'up (*BrE*)
sb feels angry and aggressive: *Normally, he's a quiet man, but when his blood is up he can be very violent.*

,blood, sweat and 'tears
very hard work; a lot of effort: *The only way to succeed is through old-fashioned blood, sweat and tears.*

fresh/new/young 'blood
new members of a group or organization who have fresh ideas, skills, etc. and so make the group more efficient: *What this committee really needs is some new blood.*

have (got) (sb's) 'blood on your hands
be responsible for sb's death: *He's a tyrant with the blood of millions of innocent people on his hands.*

in the/sb's 'blood/'genes
part of sb's nature and shared by other members of their family: *Both his father and his mother were writers, so literature runs in his blood.*

like getting ,blood out of/from a 'stone
extremely difficult to obtain: *Getting an apology from him was like getting blood out of a stone.*

make sb's 'blood boil
make sb very angry: *Seeing him beating that little dog made my blood boil.*

make sb's ,blood run 'cold; make sb's blood 'freeze
make sb feel horror or extreme fear: *A terrifying scream in the blackness of the night made my blood run cold.*

burst a blood vessel → **burst**
flesh and blood → **flesh**
your (own) flesh and blood → **flesh**
have a rush of blood to the head → **rush**
in cold blood → **cold**
more than flesh and blood can stand, endure, etc. → **flesh**
spill (sb's) blood → **spill**
spit blood/venom → **spit**
stir sb's/the blood → **stir**
sweat blood → **sweat**

bloody

scream bloody murder → **scream**

bloom

in (full) bloom
(of trees, plants, gardens, etc.) with the flowers fully open: *Their garden was in full bloom.*

blot

blot your 'copybook (*old-fashioned*, *informal*)
spoil a previously good record: *He paid back the money he had stolen, but he had blotted his copybook and couldn't hope for promotion.*

a blot on the 'landscape
a thing, especially an ugly building, that spoils the appearance of a place: *That power station is rather a blot on the landscape.*

blouse

a big girl's blouse → **big**

Blow

Joe Blow → **Joe**

blow

at a (single) 'blow; at one 'blow
with a single action or effort; all at once: *By stopping all payments to her sons, she made all three of them poor at one blow.*

blow away the 'cobwebs (*informal*)
make you feel lively and refreshed, especially after you have been indoors for too long: *After sitting around for hours, we went out and had a long walk along the beach to blow the cobwebs away.*

blow your/sb's 'brains out (*informal*)
kill yourself/sb by shooting in the head: *He was so depressed about his debts that he wanted to blow his brains out.*

blow sb's 'cover (*informal*)
discover or reveal the real identity of sb, especially of a spy, etc: *She had been posing as a diplomat, but her cover was blown when she was found sending coded messages to agents.*

blow a 'fuse (*informal*)
get very angry: *It was only a suggestion, Rob. There's no need to blow a fuse.*

> ❷ NOTE
> A *fuse* is a device that makes a bomb explode.

blow the 'gaff (on sb/sth) (*BrE*, *informal*)
reveal a secret: *She didn't want anyone to know where she had been, but her husband blew the gaff.*

blow hot and 'cold (*informal*)
keep changing your opinions (about sb/sth): *She keeps blowing hot and cold about the job: one day she says it's marvellous, the next she hates it.*

blow it/your chances
waste an opportunity: *She blew her chances by arriving late for the interview.* ◇ *You had your chance and you blew it.*

blow 'me! (*old-fashioned, BrE, informal*)
used for expressing great surprise: *'Isn't that Alice over there?' 'Well, blow me! I thought she was in Japan!'*

blow your/sb's 'mind (*informal*)
make you/sb feel extreme pleasure, excitement, etc: *This new game will blow your mind!* ▶ **'mind-blowing** *adj.*: *We were stunned by the mind-blowing beauty of the landscape.*

blow sb/sth out of the 'water (*informal*)
1 destroy sb/sth completely
2 show that sb/sth is not good at all: *A DVD music system plays discs that look like CDs, but blows them out of the water.*

blow your own 'trumpet (*especially BrE*) (*AmE* usually **blow/toot your own 'horn**) (*informal*)
talk proudly about your own achievements, abilities, etc.; praise yourself: *I don't like to blow my own trumpet, but the office was much better run when I was in charge.*

❶ ORIGIN
This phrase refers to the custom of announcing important guests by blowing a horn.

blow sb/sth ˌsky-'high (*informal*)
destroy sb/sth completely in an explosion: *The explosives factory was blown sky-high when one of the workers lit a match.*

blow your 'top (*BrE*) (*AmE* **blow your 'stack**) (*informal*)
suddenly become very angry: *My mum blew her top when she found out that I'd damaged her car.*

blow up in sb's 'face
(of a situation, plan, project, etc.) end or fail suddenly, with bad results: *Starting up the business was difficult, and it all nearly blew up in his face when his partner fell sick at the last minute.*

blow the 'whistle (on sb/sth) (*informal*)
stop sb doing sth illegal or wrong by telling a person in authority about it: *One of the police officers blew the whistle on his colleagues when he found out they were taking bribes.*

cushion/soften the 'blow
make sth unpleasant seem less unpleasant and easier to accept: *When he lost his job he was offered a cash payment to soften the blow.*

blow/knock sb's socks off ➔ **socks**
blow/sod that for a lark ➔ **lark**
blow/sod this/that for a game of soldiers ➔ **game**
deal sb/sth a blow ➔ **deal**
deal a blow to sb/sth ➔ **deal**
puff and pant/blow ➔ **puff**
strike a blow for/against sth ➔ **strike**

blow-by-blow

a ˌblow-by-ˌblow ac'count, de'scription, etc.
an account, description, etc. in which all the details of an event are told in the order in which

they happened: *He gave us a blow-by-blow account of everything he had done that day.*

blowed

I'm/I'll be blowed if … = I'm/I'll be damned if … ➔ **damned**

blows

come to 'blows (over sth)
begin to hit each other: *They were shouting at each other so much that I thought they would come to blows.*

see which way the wind blows ➔ **see**

blue

out of the 'blue
suddenly and unexpectedly: *She had no idea that anything was wrong until he announced out of the blue that he wanted a divorce.*

(do sth) till you're ˌblue in the 'face (*informal*)
(do sth) with a lot of effort and for a very long time without success: *You can argue with John till you're blue in the face, he'll never agree with you.*

between the devil and the deep blue sea ➔ **devil**
black and blue ➔ **black**
a bolt from the blue ➔ **bolt**
the boys in blue ➔ **boys**
have a pink/blue fit ➔ **fit**
once in a blue moon ➔ **once**
scream blue murder ➔ **scream**

blue-eyed

your, his, sb's, etc. ˌblue-eyed 'boy (*informal, usually disapproving*)
the favourite, especially of a person in authority; a person who sb thinks is perfect: *Bob is certain to be promoted: he's the manager's blue-eyed boy.*

bluff

call sb's bluff ➔ **call**

blushes

save/spare sb's 'blushes (*informal*)
do not do sth which will make sb feel embarrassed: *Don't tell everybody about his excellent exam results. Spare his blushes.*

board

above 'board
honest and open; not secret: *All my dealings with the company have been completely above board.*

❶ ORIGIN
If card players keep their hands above the table (the *board*), other players can see what they are doing.

aˌcross the 'board
affecting everything or everyone in a society, organization, etc., equally: *The government claims that standards in education have fallen right*

across the board. ◇ *The union demanded an across-the-board salary increase.*

ˌboard and ˈlodging
accommodation and food: *I pay £70 a week for board and lodging.*

ˌgo by the ˈboard
(of a plan, idea, etc.) be abandoned or rejected: *Our research will certainly go by the board if the government doesn't agree to continue financing it.*

on ˈboard
on or in a ship, an aircraft or a train: *Have the passengers gone on board yet?* ◇ *(figurative) It's good to have you on board* (= working with us) *for this project.*

take sth on ˈboard (*informal*)
accept (an idea, suggestion, etc.); recognize (a problem, etc.): *I hope the committee takes our recommendations on board when coming to a decision.*

(it's) back to the drawing board → **drawing**
(as) stiff as a board → **stiff**
sweep the board → **sweep**

boards

tread the boards → **tread**

boat

be in the ˌsame ˈboat
be in the same difficult position or situation as sb else: *None of us could do the maths exam, so we're all in the same boat.*

miss the boat → **miss**
push the boat out → **push**
rock the boat → **rock**
when your ship/boat comes in → **ship**

boats

burn your boats = burn your bridges → **burn**

Bob

(and) Bob's your ˈuncle (*BrE, informal*)
often used after explaining how to do sth, solve a problem, etc. to emphasize how easy it is: *To make the alarm go off at the right time, you just press this button, set the clock, and Bob's your uncle!*

❶ ORIGIN
Bob is a short form of the name 'Robert'. This phrase might refer to the prime minister Robert Cecil. In 1887 he unexpectedly decided to give an important government position to his nephew, who was not considered a very important politician.

bobs

bits and bobs → **bits**

bode

bode ˈwell/ˈill (for sb/sth) (*written*)
be a good/bad sign for sb/sth: *These figures do not bode well for the company's future.*

body

body and ˈsoul
physically and mentally; completely: *She devoted herself body and soul to this political cause.* ◇ *The company doesn't own me body and soul just because it pays my salary.*

keep body and ˈsoul together (*often humorous*)
manage to stay alive: *I hardly earn enough to keep body and soul together.*

not have a cruel, malicious, vicious, etc. bone in your body → **bone**
over my dead body → **dead**

bog

bog ˈstandard (*BrE, informal*)
ordinary; with no special features: *All you need is a bog standard machine—nothing fancy.*

boggles

it boggles the mind = the mind boggles → **mind**

boil

off the ˈboil (*BrE*)
past the time of greatest activity, excitement, etc: *The team were playing brilliantly at the start of the season but seem to have gone off the boil now.*

on the ˈboil
in a lively or active condition: *Fresh discoveries kept their enthusiasm on the boil.*

make sb's blood boil → **blood**

boils

a watched pot never boils → **watched**

bold

be/make so ˈbold (as to do sth) (*formal*)
used especially when politely asking a question or making a suggestion which you hope will not offend anyone: *May I make so bold, sir, as to suggest that you try the grilled fish?*

(as) bold as ˈbrass (*BrE, informal*)
without seeming ashamed or embarrassed; very cheeky: *He came up to me, bold as brass, and asked me for five pounds.*

bolt

a ˌbolt from the ˈblue
an event or a piece of news which is sudden and unexpected; a complete surprise: *She had given us no warning she was going to leave; it came as a complete bolt from the blue.*

❶ ORIGIN
This idiom refers to a bolt of lightning·from a clear sky.

bolt ˈupright
with your back very straight in an upright position: *The noise woke her suddenly and she sat bolt upright in bed.*

make a 'bolt/'dash for it/sth (*informal*)
try to escape or get somewhere quickly: *The pris-oners made a bolt for it through an open window.* ◇ *We smelt smoke and made a dash for the door.*

shoot your bolt → **shoot**

bolted

shut/lock/close the stable door after the horse has bolted → **stable**

bolts

the nuts and bolts (of sth) → **nuts**

bomb

go down a 'bomb; go (like) a 'bomb (*BrE*)
be very successful: *Our performance went down a bomb.* ◇ *The party was really going (like) a bomb.*

go like a 'bomb (*BrE*)
(of a vehicle) go very fast: *Her new car goes like a bomb!*

bombshell

drop a, the, his, etc. bombshell → **drop**

bond

your, his, etc. word is (as good as) your, his, etc. bond → **word**

bone

,bone 'idle (*informal*)
(of a person) very lazy

a bone of con'tention
a matter about which there is a lot of disagree-ment: *The interpretation of this painting has long been a bone of contention among art historians.*

close to/near the 'bone (*informal*)
likely to offend or upset sb because, for example, a remark contains elements of truth: *Some of the things she said to him about his failure to find work were a bit close to the bone.*

cut, pare, etc. sth to the 'bone
reduce sth to the point where no further reduction is possible: *We have cut the costs of the business to the bone, but they are still too high for us to make any profit.*

have (got) a 'bone to pick with sb (*informal*)
have sth that you want to complain to sb about: *Here, I've got a bone to pick with you: why did you tell David I wasn't at home when he phoned?*

not have a cruel, malicious, vicious, etc. bone in your body
have none of the quality mentioned: *She was hon-est and hard-working, and didn't have an unkind bone in her body.*

be (nothing but/all/just) skin and bone(s) → **skin**
chill sb to the bone/marrow → **chill**

(as) dry as a bone → **dry**
work your fingers to the bone → **work**

bones

make no 'bones about (doing) sth
not hesitate to do sth; be honest and open about sth: *She made no bones about telling him she wanted a pay rise.* ◇ *He makes no bones about the fact that he's been in prison.*

a bag of bones → **bag**
the bare bones (of sth) → **bare**
feel (it) in your bones → **feel**

bonkers

(stark) raving mad/bonkers → **raving**

bonnet

have (got) a bee in your bonnet → **bee**

boo

he, she, etc. wouldn't say boo to a goose → **say**

book

bring sb to 'book (for sth) (*formal, especially BrE*)
make sb explain their actions, or punish them: *This is just another of the many crimes for which nobody was ever brought to book.*

by the 'book
strictly following the rules or the official way of doing sth: *He insists on doing everything by the book.*

in 'sb's book (*spoken*)
in sb's opinion; according to sb's judgement: *They took the car away without asking me, and in my book that's theft.*

close the book on sth → **close**
a closed book → **closed**
don't judge a book by its cover → **judge**
an open book → **open**
read sb like a book → **read**
suit your/sb's book → **suit**
take a leaf out of sb's book → **leaf**
throw the book at sb → **throw**
try, use, etc. every trick in the book → **trick**
a turn-up for the book(s) → **turn-up**

books

be in sb's 'good/'bad books (*informal*)
have/not have sb's favour or approval: *I'm in his bad books at the moment because I accidentally broke the window.* ◇ *'Why are you cleaning her shoes?' 'I'm trying to get into her good books.'*

cook the books → **cook**
the history books → **history**

boomer

a boomer = a baby boomer → **baby**

boot

the boot is on the other 'foot (*BrE*) (*AmE* **the shoe is on the other 'foot**) (*informal*)
a situation is now the opposite of what it was: *She used to be the one who had to obey orders, but the boot is on the other foot now she's been promoted.*

give sb/get the 'boot (*informal*)
dismiss sb/be dismissed from a job: *He got the boot for stealing money from the firm.*

put/stick the 'boot in (*BrE, informal*)
1 kick sb very hard, especially when they are on the ground
2 say or do sth cruel or unfair to sb, especially when they have already been harmed in some other way: *She was upset about losing her job and then her sister started putting the boot in, telling her she was lazy.*

to 'boot (*old-fashioned* or *humorous*)
in addition; as well: *She has a big house, an expensive car, and a holiday villa in Italy to boot.*

boots

fill sb's boots/shoes → **fill**
hang up your boots → **hang**
lick sb's boots → **lick**
(be) quaking/shaking in your boots/shoes → **quaking**
too big for your boots → **big**
(as) tough as old boots → **tough**

bootstraps

drag/pull yourself up by your (own) 'bootstraps (*informal*)
improve your situation yourself, without help from other people: *Nobody helped her get where she is today—she pulled herself up by her own bootstraps.*

bore

bore sb to 'tears; bore sb 'stiff; bore sb out of their 'mind (*informal*)
(often used in the passive) bore sb very much: *He bored me to tears with stories about his childhood.* ◇ *After listening to the speech for three hours I was bored stiff.* ◇ *You had to wait for five hours? You must have been bored out of your mind.*

bored

be scared/bored witless → **witless**

born

be born with a silver 'spoon in your mouth (*saying*)
be born into a very rich family: *They had both been born with silver spoons in their mouths, and never had to worry about money.*

‚born and 'bred
born and brought up (in a place): *He's Liverpool born and bred.* ◇ *Both my parents were born and bred in London.*

I wasn't born 'yesterday (*spoken*)
used to say that you are not stupid enough to believe what sb is telling you: *You don't expect me to believe that, do you? I wasn't born yesterday, you know.*

in all my born 'days (*old-fashioned, informal*)
never in my life (especially used when referring to sth unpleasant): *How dare you say that! I've never been spoken to like that in all my born days!*

there's one born every 'minute (*saying*)
used to say that sb is very stupid: *You really believed he would pay you that money back? There's one born every minute!*

be/be born/be made that way → **way**
not know you're born → **know**
(as if) to the manner born → **manner**

borrow

beg, borrow or steal → **beg**

borrowed

be/live on borrowed 'time
1 (of a person who is seriously ill) live longer than the doctors expected: *The doctors say he's living on borrowed time.*
2 be doing sth that other people are likely to soon stop you from doing: *The government is on borrowed time* (= they are not likely to be in power for long).

bosom

in the bosom of sth
surrounded or protected by: *He longed to be back safe in the bosom of his family.*

boss

show sb who's boss → **show**

bothered

can't be bothered (to do sth) (*BrE, informal*)
not willing to make the effort (to do sth): *I got home so late last night that I couldn't be bothered to cook dinner.* ◇ *He didn't have an excuse for not coming to the party—he just couldn't be bothered.*

I'm not 'bothered (*informal, especially BrE*)
I don't mind: *'What shall we have for supper tonight?' 'I'm not bothered.'*

(all) hot and bothered → **hot**

bottle

have, show, etc. (a lot of) bottle (*BrE, informal*)
have, show, etc. (a lot of) courage or confidence: *Carol went in and told the boss he wasn't doing his job properly. She's certainly got a lot of bottle!* ◇ *The match was very tough and United just didn't have the bottle for it.*

on the 'bottle (*informal*)
drinking a lot of alcoholic drinks regularly: *I see he's back on the bottle again.*

the genie is out of the bottle → genie
hit the bottle → hit
let the genie out of the bottle → let

bottom

at 'bottom
basically; in reality: *She seems rather unfriendly, but at bottom I think she's quite kind.*

at the bottom/top of the 'pile/'heap (*informal*)
in a low/high position in society: *You've no idea what life at the bottom of the pile is like, have you? When do you ever talk to ordinary people?*

be/lie at the 'bottom of sth
be the basic cause of sth: *Racist feelings almost certainly lie at the bottom of these recent attacks.*

the ˌbottom drops/falls out of the 'market
people no longer want to buy a particular product and so it has to be sold very cheaply: *She invested in coffee, but then the bottom dropped out of the market, and she lost a lot of money.*

the ˌbottom drops/falls out of sb's 'world
a person suddenly loses all their happiness, self-confidence, etc: *When his wife left him, the bottom dropped out of his world.*

the ˌbottom 'line (*informal*)
the important conclusion, judgement, or result: *We've had some success this year, but the bottom line is that the business is still losing money.*

from the ˌbottom of your 'heart
with deep feeling; very sincerely: *I thank you from the bottom of my heart for all your help.*

get to the 'bottom of sth
find the true cause of sth or the solution to sth: *We're determined to get to the bottom of this mystery.*

be at rock bottom → rock
(you can) bet your bottom dollar/your life (on sth/that …) → bet
from top to bottom → top
hit/reach rock bottom → rock
(as) smooth as a baby's bottom → smooth
touch bottom → touch

bottomless

a bottomless 'pit (of sth)
a thing or situation which seems to have no limits or seems never to end: *There isn't a bottomless pit of money for public spending.* ◇ *the bottomless pit of his sorrow*

bottoms

bottoms 'up! (*old-fashioned*, *spoken*)
used for telling people to finish their drinks, or to express good wishes when drinking alcohol: *Come on everybody, it's time to go home. Bottoms up!*

bound

be/feel duty/honour 'bound to do sth (*BrE*)
(*AmE* **be/feel duty/honor 'bound to do sth**)
(*formal*)
feel that you must do sth because of your sense of moral duty: *She felt honour bound to attend as she had promised to.* ◇ *Most people think that children are duty bound to look after their parents when they are old.*

bounds

out of 'bounds
1 (in some sports) outside the area of play which is allowed: *His shot went out of bounds.*
2 (*AmE*) not reasonable or acceptable: *His demands were out of bounds.*

out of 'bounds (to/for sb) (*especially BrE*)
(*AmE* usually ˌoff 'limits**)
outside the area sb is allowed to go: *The village is out of bounds to the soldiers in the camp.*

within 'bounds
within acceptable limits; under control: *Borrowing money from friends is all right as long as it's kept within bounds.*

by/in leaps and bounds → leaps
know no bounds → know

bow

ˌbow and 'scrape (*disapproving*)
be too polite to sb important in order to gain their approval: *I will not bow and scrape to him just to get a salary increase.*

have (got) another string/more strings to your bow (*BrE*)
something else that you can use or do if the thing you are using or doing fails: *If I don't succeed as an actor, I've got another string to my bow because I'm a trained music teacher.*

bows

(fire) a (warning) shot across sb's bows → shot

box

box 'clever (*BrE, informal*)
act in a clever way to get what you want, sometimes tricking and deceiving sb: *Suzie realized that she had to box clever. She had to let Adam think she trusted him.*

box sb's 'ears; give sb a box on the 'ears (*old-fashioned*)
hit sb with your hand on the side of their head as a punishment: *If you do that one more time I'll box your ears, boy!*

a bag/box of tricks → tricks
be out of your box = be out of your tree → tree

Pandora's box → Pandora
think out of/outside the box → think

boy

a 'mummy's/'mother's boy (*BrE*) (*AmE* **a
'mama's boy**) (*disapproving*)
a boy or man who is thought to be too weak
because he is influenced and controlled by his
mother: *He's a bit of a mummy's boy really. He
ought to leave home and become a bit more independent.* ◇ *She always makes sure he wears a
scarf—he's a real mother's boy.*

your, his, sb's, etc. blue-eyed boy → blue-eyed
a golden boy → golden
man and boy → man
old boy/girl → old
the old boy network → old
a whipping boy → whipping
a wide boy → wide

boys

the boys in 'blue (*old-fashioned, informal* or
humorous)
police officers: *If you're not careful, you'll get a
visit from the boys in blue!*

boys will be 'boys (*saying*)
you must not criticize boys or men too much for
behaving badly, being noisy, etc. as this is a natural
way for them to behave: *The children came home
covered in mud from head to foot, but I suppose boys
will be boys!*

the back-room boys → back-room
be one of the lads/boys/girls → lads
jobs for the boys → jobs
sort out/separate the men from the boys → men

brain

the 'brain drain
the loss of qualified scientists, doctors, engineers,
etc. to another country, especially one where they
are paid more for their work

have (got) sb/sth on the 'brain (*informal*)
think and/or talk a lot or too much about sb/sth:
*You do nothing but talk about your job; you've got
work on the brain!*

brains

brains and/versus brawn
intelligence and/compared with physical strength:
In this job you need both brains and brawn.

beat your brains out → beat
blow your/sb's brains out → blow
pick sb's brains → pick
wrack your brains = rack your brains → rack

brake

jam the brake(s) on = jam on the brake(s) → jam

branch

hold out/offer an olive branch (to sb) → olive
root and branch → root

brass

brass 'monkeys; brass 'monkey weather
(*BrE, slang*)
if you say that it is **brass monkeys** or **brass monkey weather**, you mean that it is very cold weather: *Wear a hat—it's brass monkeys out there!*

> **ⓘ ORIGIN**
> The full expression is 'cold enough to freeze the
> balls off a brass monkey', although this is not
> often used. It may refer to a brass rack called a
> *monkey* which was used to store cannonballs.
> When it was very cold, the brass contracted (=
> got smaller) and the balls fell off.

brass 'neck/'nerve (*BrE, informal*)
a combination of confidence and lack of respect: *I
didn't think she would have the brass neck to do
that.*

the brass 'ring (*AmE, informal*)
the opportunity to be successful; success that you
have worked hard to get: *The girls' outdoor track
team has grabbed the brass ring seven times.*

> **ⓘ ORIGIN**
> This comes from the custom of giving a free ride
> to any child who grabbed one of the rings hang-
> ing around the side of a merry-go-round at a fair-
> ground.

get down to brass 'tacks (*informal*)
begin to discuss and deal with the really important practical details: *Let's get down to brass tacks—
how much will it all cost?*

(as) bold as brass → bold
(the) top brass → top
where there's muck there's brass → muck

brassed

brassed off (with sb/sth) = browned off (with sb/sth) →
browned

brave

a brave new 'world (*often ironic*)
a situation or society that changes in a way that is
meant to improve people's lives but is often a
source of extra problems: *She promises us a brave
new world of high salaries and good working conditions after the reforms.*

> **ⓘ ORIGIN**
> This phrase comes from Shakespeare's play *The
> Tempest*. It was later used by Aldous Huxley as
> the title of his most famous book, which
> described a vision of the future.

put a brave 'face on sth; put on a brave 'face
try to appear brave or cheerful or to be managing
well in a difficult situation, when in fact you are
frightened or unhappy: *'How's Mrs O'Brien?'*

'She's trying to put a very brave face on things, but you can see that she's very unhappy.'

brawn

brains and/versus brawn → brains

breach

step into the breach → step

bread

your ,bread and 'butter
the work that sb does which provides them with enough money to live: *He's written one or two novels but journalism is his bread and butter.*

the best thing since sliced bread → best
your daily bread → daily
half a loaf is better than none/no bread → half
know which side your bread is buttered → know

breadline

on the 'breadline
very poor: *Most of the unemployed in this area are on the breadline.*

> **❶ ORIGIN**
> In North America, a *breadline* was a queue of poor people waiting to receive free food from the government.

breadth

a hair's breadth → hair
the length and breadth of sth → length

break

break your 'back doing sth/to do sth
work very hard (to achieve sth): *I've been breaking my back to sell as many books as I can.*

break the 'back of sth
finish the largest or most difficult part of a task: *I won't finish this essay tonight but I'd like to break the back of it before I go to bed.*

break 'even
make neither a profit nor a loss: *In the first year of the business we only just managed to break even.*

break fresh/new 'ground
make a discovery; use new methods, etc: *We're breaking fresh ground with our new freezing methods.* ▶ **'ground-breaking** *adj.: a ground-breaking discovery/report*

break sb's 'heart
make sb feel extremely unhappy: *That boy is breaking his mother's heart with his wild ways.* ◇ *It's a job I would like, but it won't break my heart if I don't get it.* ▶ **'heartbreak** *noun: He causes his mother nothing but heartbreak.* **'heartbreaking, 'heartbroken** *adjs.: a heartbreaking story* ◇ *We were heartbroken by the news.*

,break the 'ice
make a social situation more informal and

He broke her heart and then just walked away.

relaxed, especially at the beginning of a meeting, party, etc: *If you serve drinks as soon as they arrive it will help to break the ice.* ▶ **an 'ice-breaker** *noun: James told a very funny joke, which was a good ice-breaker.*

break a 'leg! (*spoken*)
used to wish sb good luck: *You'd better leave now if you want to arrive early for the exam. Break a leg!*

> **❶ ORIGIN**
> It is thought that wishing for something bad to happen will prevent it from happening. This expression is used especially in the theatre.

break the 'mould (of sth) (*BrE*) (*AmE* break the 'mold (of sth))
change what people expect from a situation, especially by acting in a dramatic and original way: *After a string of defeats, he finally broke the mould by getting through to the semi-finals of a major competition.*

(not) break your 'neck (doing/to do sth) (*informal*)
(not) make a great effort: *There's no need to break your neck trying to get here by five. We can always wait for you.*

break the 'news (to sb)
be the first to tell sb some bad news: *I'm sorry to be the one to break the news.*

break 'ranks
(of the members of a group) refuse to support a group or an organization of which they are members: *Large numbers of MPs felt compelled to break ranks over the issue.*

> **❶ ORIGIN**
> This idiom refers to soldiers, police etc. failing to remain in line.

break 'wind
let gas out from the bowels through the anus

give sb a 'break
give sb a chance; not judge sb too harshly: *Give the lad a break—it's only his second day on the job.*

give me a 'break! (*spoken*)
used when sb wants sb else to stop doing or saying

sth that is annoying, or to stop saying sth that is not true: *I didn't mean it like that, so give me a break!*

make a 'break for it (*informal*)
try to escape from prison, etc: *Six prisoners shot a guard and made a break for it in a stolen car.*

,make or 'break (*informal*)
the thing which decides whether sth succeeds or fails: *This film is make or break for the production company.* ◇ *This is a make-or-break year for us.*

not ,break the 'bank (*informal*)
not cost a lot of money, or more than you can afford: *Just lend me £10. That won't break the bank, will it?*

> ❷ NOTE
> If you *break the bank* in a game or competition, you win more money than the bank holds.

break/keep faith with sb → **faith**
break/cut/tear (sth) loose from sb/sth → **loose**
a clean break → **clean**
keep/break your word → **word**

breakfast

a dog's breakfast/dinner → **dog**
have/eat sb for breakfast = eat sb alive → **eat**

breaking

,breaking and 'entering
the act of getting into a building illegally by breaking a window etc: *Although they hadn't stolen anything, they were still found guilty of breaking and entering.*

without breaking 'stride (*especially AmE*)
without stopping what you are doing: *The police officers looked at him as they passed, but walked on without breaking stride.*

you can't make an omelette without breaking eggs → **omelette**

breaks

all hell breaks/is let loose → **hell**
be the straw that breaks the camel's back → **straw**

breast

beat your breast → **beat**
make a clean breast of sth → **clean**

breath

a breath of fresh 'air
a person or thing that is new and different and therefore interesting and exciting: *Having these young people living with us is like a breath of fresh air after years on our own.*

get your 'breath back
be able to breathe again properly after running,

etc: *She stopped at the top of the stairs to get her breath back.*

out of 'breath
not be able to breathe easily after physical effort: *I'm out of breath now after running for the bus.*

,say, etc. sth in the same 'breath (also ,say, etc. sth in one 'breath, and then in the next say ...)
say sth which appears to be the opposite of what you have just said: *He told me that my work had improved and then in the same breath said that I was lazy.*

take sb's 'breath away
surprise or amaze sb: *It quite took my breath away when they told me how much money I had won.*
▶ **'breathtaking** *adj.* very exciting; spectacular: *a breathtaking view*

under your 'breath
in a whisper (= a low voice), so that others cannot hear: *He muttered something under his breath.*

catch your breath → **catch**
don't waste your breath = save your breath → **save**
draw (a) breath → **draw**
hold your breath → **hold**
mention sb/sth in the same breath → **mention**
save your breath → **save**
waste your breath (on sb/sth) → **waste**
with bated breath → **bated**

breathe

breathe (easily/freely) again
no longer need to be afraid, worried, etc: *I was able to breathe easily again once I knew the children were safe.*

breathe down sb's 'neck (*informal*)
watch sb too closely, and so make them feel uncomfortable: *I can't work with people breathing down my neck the whole time.*

breathe your 'last (*formal*)
die: *Later that night, the King breathed his last.*

(not) breathe a 'word (about/of sth) (to sb)
(not) tell sb sth, especially sth secret: *Please don't breathe a word of this to anyone.*

live and breathe sth → **live**

breathing

a 'breathing space
a time for resting between two periods of effort; pause: *This holiday will give me a bit of breathing space before I start my new job.*

bred

born and bred → **born**

breeds

familiarity breeds contempt → **familiarity**

breeze

shoot the breeze/bull → **shoot**

brewing

there's trouble brewing → **trouble**

brick

be/come up against a brick 'wall (also **hit a brick 'wall**)
be unable to make any progress because there is a difficulty that stops you: *Since he had no more money to spend on the project, he was up against a brick wall.* ◇ *Plans to build a new road around the town hit a brick wall when local residents protested.*

a ˌbrick short of a 'load (also **two ˌsandwiches short of a 'picnic**) (*informal*)
(of a person) stupid; not very intelligent: *If you ask me, I think he must be one or two sandwiches short of a picnic!*

be banging, etc. your head against a brick wall → **head**
be built like a brick shithouse → **built**
drop a clanger/brick → **drop**
talk to a brick wall → **talk**

bricks

bricks and 'mortar
a building, especially when you are thinking of it in connection with how much it cost to build or how much it is worth: *A home isn't just bricks and mortar.* ◇ *We now need funding to turn the plans into bricks and mortar.*

> ❷ NOTE
> The modern way of doing business through the Internet as well as from buildings and shops can be referred to as *clicks and mortar*, where 'clicks' refers to the use of the mouse and the Internet.

make ˌbricks without 'straw (*BrE*)
try to do a piece of work without the necessary materials, equipment, or information: *I don't know how you expect me to cook dinner when there's hardly any food in the house. You can't make bricks without straw, you know.*

be/come down on sb like a ton of bricks → **ton**
like a cat on hot bricks → **cat**

bridge

bridge the 'gap (between A and B) (also **bridge the 'gulf (between A and B)**, *less frequent*)
make it easier to move from one thing to another or for two groups to communicate with each other: *The hostel helps to bridge the gap between prison and life on the outside.*

be like painting the Forth Bridge → **painting**
be (all) water under the bridge → **water**
cross a bridge when you come to it → **cross**

bridges

build bridges (between A and B/with sb) → **build**
burn your bridges → **burn**
cross your bridges when you come to them → **cross**

brief

in 'brief
in a few words: *I won't give a you a long history of the dispute; in brief, it led to the business closing.* ◇ *And now, the news in brief.*

hold no brief for sb/sth → **hold**

brigade

the heavy mob/brigade → **heavy**

bright

bright and 'early
early in the morning: *You're up bright and early this morning!*

(as) bright as a 'button (*BrE*)
clever and lively: *That child's as bright as a button!*

the bright 'lights (*informal*)
the big city seen as a centre of entertainment, enjoyment, etc: *Many people from other places are still tempted by the bright lights of London.*

(a) bright 'spark (*BrE, informal, often ironic*)
a lively and intelligent person: *What bright spark* (= stupid person) *left the front door open all night?*

a/the 'bright spot
a good or pleasant part of sth that is unpleasant or bad in all other ways: *The win last week was the only bright spot in their last ten games.*

look on the bright side → **look**

bright-eyed

ˌbright-eyed and ˌbushy-'tailed (*informal*)
lively and cheerful; pleased and proud: *She came in to see me, all bright-eyed and bushy-tailed, and announced she was leaving the next day.*

bring

Idioms containing the verb **bring** are at the entries for the nouns and adjectives in the idioms, for example **bring the house down** is at **house**.

brink

teeter on the brink/edge of sth → **teeter**

British

the best of British (to sb) → **best**

broad

a broad 'church (*BrE*)
an organization that accepts a wide range of opinions

broad in the 'beam (*informal*)
having wide hips: *Her waist is quite small, but she's rather broad in the beam.*

in broad 'daylight

in the clear light of day, when it is easy to see: *He was attacked right in the centre of town in broad daylight.*

it's as ˌbroad as it's 'long (*old-fashioned, BrE, spoken*)

there is no real difference between two possible alternatives: *'Shall we go today or tomorrow?' 'It's as broad as it's long, isn't it? You choose.'*

paint sth with a broad brush → **paint**

broke

go for 'broke (*informal*)

risk everything in one determined effort to do sth: *I decided to go for broke and start my own business.*

if it ain't 'broke, don't 'fix it

used to say that if sth is satisfactory and works well, it should not be changed: *Why do they have to keep suggesting 'improvements' when everything's working perfectly? If it ain't broke, don't fix it.*

be stony broke = be flat broke → **flat**

broom

a new broom (sweeps clean) → **new**

broth

too many cooks spoil the broth → **cooks**

Brother

Big Brother (is watching you) → **Big**

brothers

be (all) brothers/sisters under the skin → **skin**

brought

(look) like sth the cat brought/dragged in → **cat**

brow

by the sweat of your brow → **sweat**

browned

ˌbrowned 'off (with sb/sth) (also **ˌbrassed 'off (with sb/sth)**) (*BrE, informal*)

bored, unhappy and/or annoyed: *By now the passengers were getting browned off with the delay.*

brownie

'brownie points

if sb does sth to earn **brownie points**, they do it to make sb in authority have a good opinion of them: *She's only working late to win brownie points with the boss.*

❶ ORIGIN
The Brownies is a club for young girls who are not yet old enough to be Guides. They are awarded points for good behaviour and achievements.

brows

knit your brows → **knit**

brunt

bear the brunt of sth → **bear**

brush

(as) daft as a brush → **daft**
paint sth with a broad brush → **paint**
sweep/brush sth under the carpet → **carpet**
tar sb/sth with the same brush → **tar**

bubble

the bubble 'bursts

there is a sudden end to a good or lucky situation: *When the bubble finally burst, hundreds of people lost their jobs.*

burst sb's bubble → **burst**

buck

the buck stops 'here

used for telling sb that you are prepared to accept responsibility for sth: *We don't try to escape our responsibilities. The buck stops here.*

❶ ORIGIN
The *buck* is a small object in a poker game that is placed in front of the player whose turn it is to deal the cards.

buck up your i'deas (*informal*)

start to work harder or more efficiently; become more willing to do things: *He's been late every day for two weeks. He'll have to buck up his ideas if he wants to keep his job.*

make a fast/quick buck (*informal, often disapproving*)

earn money quickly and easily: *He didn't really care about the business—he just wanted to make a fast buck.*

bang for your buck → **bang**
buck naked = stark naked → **stark**
pass the buck → **pass**

bucket

a drop in the bucket → **drop**
kick the bucket → **kick**

buckets

rain buckets → **rain**

bucks

look/feel like a million dollars/bucks → **million**

bud

nip sth in the bud → **nip**

budge

not budge/give/move an inch → **inch**

buff

in the 'buff (*informal*)
wearing no clothes: *I'm sure I saw him swimming in the buff!*

buffers

hit the buffers ➔ hit

bug

be bitten by/have (got) the 'bug (*informal*)
have a sudden strong interest in or enthusiasm for sth: *My mum was never really interested in going abroad until she went to America last year. Now she's been bitten by **the travel bug** and hates staying at home!*

bug 'off! (*AmE, spoken*)
a rude way of telling sb to go away

(as) snug as a bug (in a rug) ➔ snug

buggers

play silly buggers (with sth) ➔ play

build

build 'bridges (between A and B/with sb)
if you **build bridges** between people who disagree on sth or who do not like each other, you try to find ways to improve the relationship between them: *The police are trying to build bridges with the local community.*

build up/raise sb's hopes ➔ hopes

built

be built like a ˌbrick 'shithouse (⚠, *slang*)
(of a person) be very big and strong: *He's a wrestler? Well, that doesn't surprise me—he's built like a brick shithouse!*

Rome wasn't built in a day ➔ Rome

bulging

be bursting/bulging at the seams (with sth) ➔ seams

bull

like a ˌbull in a 'china shop
very careless or clumsy, especially in a situation where you need to be careful: *He was like a bull in a china shop, treading on everyone's feet and apologizing constantly.* ◇ *The Prime Minister went into the negotiations like a bull in a china shop and only made the relations between the two countries worse.*

take the ˌbull by the 'horns (*informal*)
deal with a difficult or dangerous situation in a direct and brave way: *I decided to take the bull by the horns and ask the bank for a loan.*

a cock and bull story ➔ cock
(like) a red rag to a bull ➔ red
shoot the breeze/bull ➔ shoot

bullet

bite the bullet ➔ bite

bully

bully for 'sb! (*spoken*)
used to show that you do not think that what sb has said or done is very impressive: *'Janet's just won a free holiday in Spain.' 'Oh, bully for her! She's so rich anyway, she can afford to go away whenever she wants to.'*

bum

a bum 'steer (*AmE, informal*)
wrong or unhelpful information or advice: *Whoever recommended this software gave you a bum steer, I'm afraid.*

give sb/get the bum's 'rush (*slang, especially AmE*)
1 order or use force to make sb leave a place; be made to leave in this way: *The reporter was given the bum's rush out of the club.*
2 dismiss or get rid of sb that you do not want; be dismissed or got rid of: *I got the bum's rush from Smith & Co.*

a pain in the arse/bum/backside ➔ pain

bump

things that go bump in the night ➔ things

bumper

ˌbumper to 'bumper
if vehicles are **bumper to bumper**, there is so much traffic that they are very close together and can hardly move: *Being a Friday evening, it was bumper to bumper on the main road leading out of town.*

bumpkin

a country bumpkin/cousin ➔ country

bumpy

give sb/have a bumpy 'ride
make a situation difficult for sb; have a difficult time: *The business has had a bumpy ride over the last twelve months, but profits are growing again now.*

bums

bums on 'seats (*BrE, informal*)
used to refer to the number of people who attend a show, talk, etc., especially when emphasizing the need or desire to attract a large number: *They're not bothered about attracting the right audience—they just want bums on seats.*

bun

have (got) a 'bun in the oven (*informal, humorous*)
be pregnant

bunch

a bunch of 'fives (*old-fashioned* or *humorous*)
a punch (= a hard hit made with a closed hand)

be a mixed bag/bunch → mixed
the best of a bad bunch/lot → best
the pick of the bunch → pick

bundle

a bundle of 'joy (*informal*)
a baby

not go a 'bundle on sb/sth (*BrE, informal*)
not like sb/sth: *I don't go a bundle on that shirt he's
wearing.*

a bag/bundle of nerves → nerves
a barrel/bundle of laughs → laughs

bunk

do a 'bunk (*BrE, informal*)
leave a place quickly without telling anyone: *I
heard Jimmy did a bunk with all their money!*

buried

dead and buried/gone → dead

burn

burn your 'bridges (*BrE* also **burn your 'boats**)
do sth that makes it impossible for you to return to
a previous situation: *Once you sign this document,
you'll have burned your boats, and will have to go
ahead with the sale.*

burn the candle at both 'ends
make yourself very tired by doing too much, especially by going to bed late and getting up early: *You
look exhausted. Been burning the candle at both
ends, have you?*

burn the midnight 'oil
work or study until very late at night: *Before my
exams, I was burning the midnight oil every night.*

burn sth to a 'cinder/'crisp
cook sth for too long or with too much heat, so that
it becomes badly burnt: *Alan left the potatoes for so
long that they were burnt to a crisp.*

burn your fingers = get your fingers burnt → fingers
crash and burn → crash
do a slow burn → slow
have (got) money to burn → money

burner

on the back 'burner (*informal*)
(of an idea, a plan, etc.) left for the present time, to
be done or considered later: *The job was put on the
back burner when more important assignments
arrived.*

on the front burner → front

burning

his, her, etc. ears are burning → ears

burns

fiddle while Rome burns → fiddle
money burns a hole in sb's pocket → money

burnt

get your fingers burnt → fingers

burst

,burst a 'blood vessel (*informal*)
get very angry and excited: *When I told Dad I'd
damaged the car, he nearly burst a blood vessel.*

,burst sb's 'bubble
bring an end to sb's hopes, happiness, etc: *Things
are going really well for him. I just hope nothing
happens to burst his bubble.*

,burst 'open; ,burst (sth) 'open
open suddenly or violently; make sth open in this
way: *The door burst open.* ◇ *Firefighters burst the
door open and rescued them.*

bursting

(be) bursting to do sth (*informal*)
want to do sth so much that you can hardly stop
yourself: *She was just bursting to tell us the news.*

> ❷ NOTE
> *I'm bursting* when it is used on its own usually
> means 'I really need to go to the toilet'.

be full to bursting (with sth) = be bursting/bulging at the
seams (with sth) → seams

bursts

the bubble bursts → bubble

burton

gone for a burton → gone

bury

,bury the 'hatchet; ,bury your 'differences
(of two people or groups) agree to forget past disagreements and be friends again: *I've said I'm prepared to bury the hatchet, but John says he won't
forgive me for what happened.*

bury/hide your head in the sand → head

bush

,bush 'telegraph
the spreading of news quickly from one person to
another: *Everyone knew about it before it was officially announced: the bush telegraph had been at
work again.*

beat about/around the bush → beat
a bird in the hand is worth two in the bush → bird

bushel

hide your light under a bushel → hide

bushy-tailed
bright-eyed and bushy-tailed → bright-eyed

business
be (back) in 'business
be working or operating (again) as normal: *Once the switch has been fixed, we will be back in business and we can use the machine again.* ◇ *It looks as though we're in business: she's agreed to lend us the money.*

be none of sb's 'business; be no business of 'sb's (*informal*)
a person has no right to know sth: *'How much do you earn?' 'That's none of your business.'* ◇ *It's no business of yours who I go out with.*

the 'business end (of sth) (*informal*)
the part of a tool, weapon, etc. that performs its particular function: *Never pick up a knife by the business end.*

business is 'business
a way of saying that financial and commercial matters are the important things to consider and you should not be influenced by friendship, etc: *I'm afraid you will all have to stay late tonight. I'm sorry if you had other plans, but business is business.*

get down to 'business
start discussing or doing sth seriously, especially after a time of social talk: *Well, it's getting late—perhaps we'd better get down to business.*

go about your 'business
be busy with the things that you do every day: *He looked out onto the street and watched the people going about their daily business.*

have (got) no business doing sth; have (got) no business to do sth
have no right to do sth: *You have no business being here.*

it's business as 'usual
things continue normally, despite difficulties or disturbances: *It was business as usual at the theatre yesterday, in spite of all the building work going on.*

like 'nobody's business (*informal*)
very fast, very much, very hard, etc: *He's been spending money like nobody's business recently.*

not be in the business of doing sth
not intending to do sth (which it would be surprising for you to do): *I'm not in the business of getting other people to do my work for me.*

out of 'business
having stopped operating as a business because there is no more money or work available: *The new regulations will put many small firms out of business.* ◇ *Some travel companies will probably go out of business this summer.*

funny business → funny
mean business → mean
mind your own business → mind

monkey business → monkey
ply for hire/trade/business → ply

busman
a busman's 'holiday (*informal*)
a holiday spent doing the same kind of thing that you do at work: *The fire crew's annual outing turned into a busman's holiday when their bus caught fire. Fortunately, no one was hurt in the blaze.*

ⓘ ORIGIN
This phrase may refer to the drivers of horse-drawn vehicles in the 19th century. When they were not working, they often rode as passengers on their own buses to make sure that the replacement driver was treating their horses well.

bust
bust a 'gut (doing sth/to do sth) (*informal*)
make a very great effort: *I'm not going to bust a gut trying to be on time when I know she'll probably be late.*

go 'bust (*informal*)
(of a business) fail financially; become bankrupt: *The firm went bust and fifty workers lost their jobs.*

... or 'bust (*informal*)
used to say that you will try very hard to get somewhere or achieve sth: *For him it's the Olympics or bust.*

bustle
hustle and bustle → hustle

busy
(as) busy as a 'bee
very busy

a busy 'bee (*informal*)
a cheerful and busy person

keep yourself 'busy
find enough things to do: *Since she retired she's kept herself very busy.*

but
but for 'sb/'sth
except for sb/sth; without sb/sth: *But for a brief period after leaving university, he had never been unemployed.* ◇ *But for you, we would not have been able to start up the business.*

butcher
have/take a 'butcher's (*BrE, slang*)
have a look at sth: *Come over here and have a butcher's at this!*

ⓘ ORIGIN
This phrase comes from rhyming slang, in which *butcher's hook* stands for 'look'.

buts
ifs and/or buts → ifs

butt

be the butt of sth
be the person or thing that other people often joke about or criticize: *She was the butt of some very unkind jokes.*

a pain in the ass/butt ➔ **pain**

butter

,butter wouldn't ,melt in his, her, etc. 'mouth (*spoken*)
a person looks very innocent, but probably is not: *She looks as if butter wouldn't melt in her mouth, but don't be fooled by first impressions!*

your bread and butter ➔ **bread**
like a knife through butter ➔ **knife**

buttered

know which side your bread is buttered ➔ **know**

butterflies

get/have 'butterflies (in your stomach) (*informal*)
get/have a nervous feeling in your stomach before doing sth: *I always get butterflies (in my stomach) before an interview.*

button

'button it! (*BrE, spoken*)
used to tell sb rudely to be quiet

on the 'button (*informal, especially AmE*)
1 at exactly the right time or at the exact time mentioned: *We arrived at 4 o'clock on the button.*
2 exactly right: *You're on the button there!*

(as) bright as a button ➔ **bright**
(as) cute as a button ➔ **cute**
press/push the panic button ➔ **panic**

buy

buy the 'farm (*informal humorous, especially AmE*)
die: *I'd like to visit India one day, before I buy the farm.*

> **❶ ORIGIN**
> This comes from the military, perhaps referring to the dream of many soldiers and pilots of buying a farm when the war was over.

buy 'time
delay sth that seems about to happen: *This treatment can buy time for the patient, but I'm afraid it will not cure him.*

buy sth for a song = (go) for a song ➔ **song**
sell sb/buy a pup ➔ **pup**

buyer

a ,buyer's 'market
a situation in which there is a lot of a particular item for sale, so that prices are low and people buying have a choice: *We got a very good deal on our new car—it really is a buyer's market at the moment.*

buzz

give sb a 'buzz (*informal*)
1 telephone sb: *I'll give you a buzz before I leave.*
2 (also **get a buzz from sth/from doing sth**) if sth **gives** you **a buzz** or you **get a buzz from** it, it provides interest and enjoyment for you: *If the work gives you a buzz, then you do the job better.*

by

by and 'by (*old-fashioned*)
after a little time; soon: *Things will be better by and by.*

(all) by your'self, him'self, etc.
1 alone; without anyone else: *How long were you by yourself in the house?*
2 without help: *Are you sure he did this exercise by himself?*

bye

by the by/bye = by the way ➔ **way**

bygones

let bygones be bygones ➔ **let**

byways

highways and byways ➔ **highways**

Cc

caboodle

the ˌwhole caˈboodle; the ˌwhole kit and caˈboodle

everything: *I had new clothes, a new hairstyle—the whole caboodle.*

❶ ORIGIN
This idiom originally came from the Dutch word *boedel*, meaning 'possessions'.

cackle

cut the cackle ➔ cut

cage

rattle sb's cage ➔ rattle

cahoots

be in caˈhoots (with sb) (*informal*)

be planning or doing sth dishonest with sb else: *Some people believe that the company directors are in cahoots with the government.*

Cain

raise Cain/hell ➔ raise

cake

have your cake and ˈeat it (*BrE*) (also **have your cake and eat it too** *AmE, BrE*) (*informal*)

(often used with *can't*) enjoy the advantages of two things that cannot exist together: *'I'll have no money at all left after this holiday.' 'But you're having a great time, aren't you? You can't have your cake and eat it!'*

a ˌshare/slice of the ˈcake (*BrE*) (*AmE* **a ˌpiece/share/slice of the ˈpie**)

a share of the benefits or profits: *Third-world countries are discovering how their natural resources have been exploited by the rest of the world and now they want a bigger slice of the cake.*

the icing on the cake ➔ icing
a piece of cake ➔ piece
take the cake = take the biscuit ➔ biscuit

cakes

sell/go like hot cakes ➔ hot

calf

kill the fatted calf ➔ kill

call

(above and) beyond the call of ˈduty (*formal*)

used for describing a greater degree of courage or effort than is usual or expected in a job, etc: *The young policeman later received an award for bravery beyond the call of duty.*

call sb's ˈbluff

give sb the chance to do what they are threatening to do, because you believe they will not or cannot do it: *Next time she offers her resignation, they'll call her bluff and accept it.*

❷ NOTE
If you *call somebody's bluff* in the game of poker, you force them to show their cards.

call a ˈhalt (to sth)

stop (an activity): *We must call a halt to people leaving work early without permission.*

call it a ˈday (*informal*)

decide to stop doing sth, especially sth you have been doing for a long time: *We'd painted half the room and were feeling a bit tired so we decided to call it a day.*

call it ˈquits (*informal*)

decide to end an argument, a disagreement, etc. at a point where both sides are equal: *I know I upset you, but you said some nasty things to me too. Can't we just call it quits and try to forget it?*

call sb ˈnames

insult sb with rude or unpleasant names: *In the playground, the other children called him names.*

a call of ˈnature (*humorous*)

a need to go to the toilet: *He left the meeting to answer a call of nature.*

call sth your ˈown

claim sth as belonging to you: *At her age she needs a place she can call her own.*

call the ˈshots/the ˈtune (*informal*)

be in control: *Ask Jenny—she's the one who calls the shots around here.*

call a ˌspade a ˈspade

speak openly and directly about sth unpleasant: *I believe in calling a spade a spade. When a patient's going to die, I say so. Most people prefer to know the truth.*

call sb to acˈcount (for/over sth) (*formal*)

make sb explain (a mistake, loss, etc.): *His manager called him to account over the missing reports.*

call yourself a ˈteacher, ˈfriend, etc.? (*informal*)

used to say that you do not think sb is a very good teacher, friend, etc: *Call yourself a friend? Why did you forget my birthday then?* ◊ *How can he call himself a musician when he's never even heard of Schubert?*

don't call ˌus, we'll call ˈyou (*informal*)

used for indicating that the speaker has no interest in meeting sb, taking sth that sb is offering, etc:

I had hoped she might want me to work with her, but her attitude was one of 'don't call us, we'll call you.'

on 'call
(of a doctor, etc.) available for duty if needed: *Our qualified staff are on call 24 hours a day should you need any technical support.*

at sb's beck and call → **beck**
bring/call/put sth into play → **play**
bring/call/throw sth into question → **question**
bring/call sb/sth to mind → **mind**
a close shave/call → **close**
have (got) first call (on sb/sth) → **first**
a port of call → **port**
a wake-up call → **wake-up**
what-d'you-call-him/-her/-it/-them → **what**

calling
the pot calling the kettle black → **pot**

calls
duty calls → **duty**
he who pays the piper calls the tune → **pays**

calm
the calm/lull before the storm → **storm**

camel
be the straw that breaks the camel's back → **straw**

camera

on 'camera
being filmed or shown on television: *Are you prepared to tell your story on camera?*

camps
have (got) a foot in both camps → **foot**

can

a can of 'worms (*informal*)
if you open up **a can of worms**, you start doing sth that will cause a lot of problems and be very difficult: *I think if we start asking questions we'll open up a whole new can of worms. Perhaps we should just accept the situation.*

(be) in the 'can (*informal*)
(be) finished and ready for use; (be) already decided or arranged: *I don't need to worry about a grant—my application's been accepted so it's in the can.*

> **❷ NOTE**
> In American English slang, *in the can* can also mean 'in prison' or 'in the toilet'.

carry the can (for sb/sth) → **carry**

candle
burn the candle at both ends → **burn**
cannot hold a candle to sb/sth → **hold**
the game is not worth the candle → **game**

candy

be like taking ˌcandy from a 'baby (also be like shooting ˌfish in a 'barrel)
used to emphasize how easy it is to do sth: *I thought it was going to be difficult to get funding for the project, but in the end it was like taking candy from a baby.* ◇ *What do you mean you can't do it? It'll be like shooting fish in a barrel!*

cannon

'cannon fodder
large numbers of soldiers who are used in order to win a war, even though most of them are likely to be killed: *Their lives were not considered important—they were just the cannon fodder.* ◇ *(figurative) The team had no intention of being cannon fodder when they played the champions, and were determined to win.*

> **❷ NOTE**
> *Fodder* is food for horses and farm animals.

cap

go cap in 'hand (to sb) (*BrE*) (*AmE* go hat in 'hand)
beg sb for sth very respectfully: *I've run out of money, but I don't want to go cap in hand to my father.*

if the cap fits (, wear it) (*BrE*) (*AmE* if the shoe fits (, wear it)) (*saying*)
if a person feels that a critical remark applies to them, then it does: *'There are too many lazy people in this house.' 'Including me, I suppose?' 'If the cap fits, wear it.'*

a feather in your cap → **feather**
put your thinking cap on → **thinking**
to top/cap/crown it all → **top**

capital

make 'capital (out) of sth
use a situation or event in a way which benefits yourself; exploit sth: *The media made great capital out of his careless remarks in the interview.*

with a capital 'A, 'B, 'C, etc.
used to emphasize that a word has a stronger meaning in a particular situation; very: *When I say he's boring, I mean boring with a capital B!*

captain

a captain of 'industry
a person who manages a large industrial company: *He later moved to Seattle, where he became a well-known figure and captain of industry.*

carbon

a ˌcarbon 'copy
a person or thing that is exactly or extremely like another: *The recent robberies in Leeds are a carbon copy of those that have occurred in Halifax over the last few months.*

card

a/your trump card → trump

cards

keep/hold/play your cards ˌclose to your 'chest

not tell others what you are intending to do: *He keeps his cards pretty close to his chest. I don't know whether he plans to buy the house or not.*

on the 'cards (*BrE*) (*AmE* **in the** 'cards) (*informal*)

likely to happen: *With a rail strike on the cards for next week, airline bookings have been unusually high.*

put/lay your 'cards on the table (*informal*)

talk honestly and openly about your thoughts and intentions, especially when these have been secret until now: *I think it's time I put my cards on the table; I really can't afford the price you're asking.*

the cards/odds are stacked against sb/sth → stacked
the cards/odds are stacked in favour of sb/sth → stacked
hold all the cards = have/hold all the aces → aces
a house of cards → house
play your cards right → play

care

'care of sb (*AmE* also **in** 'care of sb)

used when writing to sb at another person's address: *Write to me care of my sister, because I'll be touring Africa for six months.*

> ❷ NOTE
> This expression is usually written as 'c/o' on envelopes.

I, he, etc. couldn't care 'less (*informal*)

I am, he is, etc. not at all interested in, or concerned about, sth: *I couldn't care less if I fail my exams—I don't want to go to university anyway.*

for all I, you, etc. 'care (*spoken*)

used to say that a person is not worried about or interested in what happens to sb/sth: *I could be dead for all he cares!*

in 'care (*BrE*)

(of children) living and looked after in an institution owned by the State: *She has been in care ever since her parents died.* ◊ *The social worker said that their baby would have to be taken into care.*

not have a ˌcare in the 'world; without a ˌcare in the 'world

not have any worry or anxiety at all: *Sam looked as if he didn't have a care in the world.* ◊ *She skipped along the road, without a care in the world.*

take 'care (that …/to do sth)

be careful: *Take care that you don't fall and hurt yourself.* ◊ *He took great care not to let his personal problems interfere with his work.*

take 'care of yourself/sb/sth

1 make sure that you are/sb is safe, well, healthy, etc.; look after yourself/sb: *I don't need your help! I can take care of myself quite well, thank you!* ◊

Don't worry about the children while you're away. They'll be taken good care of.

> ❷ NOTE
> '*Take care*' is often used alone when saying 'goodbye' to sb: *Bye then! Take care!*

2 be responsible for (dealing with) sb/sth: *Can you take care of the shopping if I do the cooking?* ◊ *There's no need for you to pay the bill. It's all taken care of* (= it is already done).

would you care for …; would you care to … (*formal*)

used to ask sb politely if they would like sth or would like to do sth, or if they would be willing to do sth: *Would you care for another drink?* ◊ *If you'd care to follow me, I'll show you where his office is.*

not care/give a damn (about/for sb/sth) → damn
not care/give a fig (about/for sb/sth) → fig
not care/give tuppence for/about sb/sth → tuppence
not care/give two hoots (about sb/sth) = not care/give a hoot (about sb/sth) → hoot

careful

you can't be too 'careful

used to warn sb that they should be careful to avoid danger or problems: *Don't stay out in the sun for too long—you can't be too careful.*

cares

who 'cares?; what do I, you, etc. care? (*informal*)

nobody cares; I, you, etc. do not care: *'Who do you think will win the next election?' 'Who cares?'*

caring

be beyond/past 'caring (about sth)

have reached a stage where you no longer care about or are no longer affected by sth: *She can't hurt him now because he's beyond caring about what she says.*

carpet

be on the 'carpet (*informal, especially AmE*)

be criticized, especially by an employer or sb in authority, because you have done sth wrong: *She's on the carpet for spending too much of the company's money on entertaining guests.*

sweep/brush sth under the 'carpet (*AmE* also **sweep sth under the** 'rug) (*informal*)

hide sth which might cause trouble, or which you do not want other people to know: *No matter how unwelcome the results of the enquiry may be, they must not be swept under the carpet.*

pull the carpet/rug out from under sb's feet → pull
the red carpet → red

carried

be/get carried a'way

be/get very excited or lose control of your feelings:

I got carried away and started shouting at the television.

carrot

the carrot and/or (the) stick
rewards offered to sb to persuade them to do sth or try harder, and/or punishment threatened if they do not: *She favoured a carrot-and-stick approach to teaching.*

carry

carry all be'fore you
be completely successful in a battle, competition, etc: *In three tournaments since June, this young tennis player has carried all before him, winning easy victories each time.*

carry the 'can (for sb/sth) *(BrE, informal)*
accept the responsibility or blame (for sth): *The teachers who were criticized said that they would not carry the can for the faults in the school system.*

> ❶ **ORIGIN**
> One theory about the origin of this expression is that it comes from military slang. One person would collect a can containing the whole group's beer ration and was then responsible for bringing it all back without spilling any.

carry a 'torch for sb
be in love with sb, especially sb who does not love you in return: *She's been carrying a torch for him for years.*

carry 'weight
be important or able to influence sb: *His opinions carry very little weight with his manager.*

as fast as your legs can carry you → **fast**
bear/carry your cross → **cross**
carry/win the day → **day**
carry/take sth to extremes → **extremes**
carry/take sth too, etc. far → **far**
fetch and carry (for sb) → **fetch**

cart

put the ,cart before the 'horse
put or do things in the wrong order: *Don't plan the menu before you've decided how many people to invite—it would be like putting the cart before the horse.*

upset the/sb's apple cart → **upset**

carte

,carte 'blanche (to do sth) *(from French)*
complete freedom or authority to do anything you like: *The detective was given carte blanche to read any files he liked in his search for the murderer.*

> ❷ **NOTE**
> The meaning of the French expression is 'blank paper'.

carved

be carved/set in stone → **stone**

case

as the ,case may 'be
used to say that one of two or more possibilities is true, but which one is true depends on the circumstances: *There may be an announcement about this tomorrow—or not, as the case may be.*

be on sb's 'case *(informal)*
criticize sb all the time: *She's always on my case about cleaning my room.*

be on the 'case
be dealing with a particular matter, especially a criminal investigation: *We have two of our best agents on the case.*

a case in 'point
a clear example of the problem, situation, etc. that is being discussed: *Many of the students are from Latin America. Carlos is a case in point—he's from Colombia.*

case the joint *(informal)*
look carefully around a building so that you can plan how to steal things from it at a later time: *I saw two men here earlier. Do you think they were casing the joint?*

get off sb's 'case *(informal)*
used to tell sb to stop criticizing you or another person: *I'm doing my best, so get off my case, will you?*

in 'any case
whatever may happen or has happened; anyway: *I don't know yet who'll bring it or what time, but in any case we'll make sure you get your car back tomorrow.* ◇ *My mother came to stay so I couldn't go to the party, but I didn't really want to go in any case.*

(just) in case
so as to be prepared for what may or may not happen: *Somebody should stay at home in case John phones.* ◇ *'Did Clara say she'd phone?' 'No, but somebody should stay here just in case.'*

in case of sth *(formal)*
if sth happens: *In case of fire, leave the building by the nearest exit.*

in 'that case
if that happens or has happened; if that is the situation: *'I've made up my mind.' 'In that case, there's no point discussing it.'*

make out a case (for sth)
argue in favour of sth: *In her report, she makes out a case for giving more funds to the health service.*

a basket case → **basket**
I rest my case → **rest**
an open-and-shut case → **open-and-shut**

cash

cash 'down *(BrE)* (also ,cash up 'front *AmE, BrE)*
with immediate payment of cash: *He paid for the car cash down.*

cash in your 'chips (especially AmE)

1 finish a gambling game

2 (slang) stop what you are doing and leave: The companies cashed in their chips and moved out of the valley.

3 (slang) die

,cash in 'hand (BrE, informal)

if you pay for goods and services **cash in hand**, you pay in cash, especially so that the person being paid can avoid paying tax on the amount: Most of his customers pay him cash in hand.

cash on the 'barrelhead (AmE)

if you pay for sth **cash on the barrelhead**, you pay in full at the time when you buy it: If I give you cash on the barrelhead, can I get a discount?

,cash on de'livery (abbr. **COD**)

a system of paying for goods when they are delivered: Do I need to pay now or will you take cash on delivery?

be strapped for cash → **strapped**

hard cash → **hard**

cast

cast/run an 'eye/your 'eyes over sth

look at or examine sth quickly: 'This looks great,' he said, casting an eye around the room. ◇ Could you just run your eyes over this report for me?

cast your 'mind back to sth

think about sth in the past: Cast your mind back to when you were a child.

cast ,pearls before 'swine (saying)

give or offer valuable things to people who do not understand their value: She decided not to buy the most expensive wine for dinner, thinking that would be casting pearls before swine.

❶ ORIGIN

This expression comes from the Bible. Swine are pigs.

cast/shed/throw (new) light on sth → **light**

cast/draw lots (for sth/to do sth) → **lots**

cast/spread your net wide → **net**

cast/draw/throw a veil over sth → **veil**

the die is cast → **die**

casting

the 'casting couch (informal, humorous)

used to refer to a situation in which sb, especially a woman, agrees to have sex with sb else in order to get work in a film/movie, television programme, etc: the Hollywood casting couch for starlets

castle

a man's home is his castle = an Englishman's home is his castle → **Englishman**

castles

(build) ,castles in the 'air

(have) plans, hopes, etc. which are unlikely to become reality: They talked about moving to Australia, but they knew they were really only building castles in the air.

cat

(play) cat and 'mouse (with sb) (informal)

(keep sb) in a state of uncertainty, being sometimes kind, sometimes cruel: He thought that the police were playing cat and mouse with him, just waiting for an opportunity to trap him. ◇ She plays **a cat-and-mouse game** with her boyfriend, telling him he's wonderful one day, and the next saying she doesn't want to see him any more.

❶ ORIGIN

This expression refers to the way a cat plays with a mouse before killing it.

(has the) cat got your, his, etc. tongue? (informal)

why don't you say anything?: What's the matter— cat got your tongue?

the cat's 'whiskers/py'jamas (informal, often ironic)

the best person, idea, thing, etc: She thinks she's the cat's whiskers.

(look) like sth the 'cat brought/dragged in (informal)

(look) dirty and untidy: Where have you been? You look like something the cat dragged in!

like a ,cat on hot 'bricks (BrE, informal)

very nervous: He'll be like a cat on hot bricks till he gets his exam results.

like the ,cat that got, stole, etc. the 'cream

very pleased or satisfied with yourself: Ever since she won that prize, she's been like the cat that ate the cream.

not have a cat in 'hell's chance (also **not have a 'dog's chance**) (informal)

have no chance at all: You haven't got a cat in hell's chance of buying a decent car for £500.

put/set the 'cat among the pigeons (BrE, informal)

do sth that is likely to cause trouble: She told all the staff they would have to cancel their holidays, and that really set the cat among the pigeons.

when the cat's a'way the mice will 'play (saying)

people enjoy themselves more and behave with greater freedom when the person in charge of them is not there

curiosity killed the cat → **curiosity**

a fat cat → **fat**

fight like cat and dog → **fight**

grin like a Cheshire cat → **grin**

let the cat out of the bag → **let**

no room to swing a cat → **room**

there's more than one way to skin a cat → **way**

catch

catch your 'breath
stop breathing for a moment (because of surprise, fear, shock, etc.): *The magnificent view made us catch our breath.*

catch your 'death (of cold) (*old-fashioned, informal*)
(usually said to emphasize how cold it is) get a very bad cold: *Don't go out without your coat— you'll catch your death.*

catch sb's 'eye
attract sb's attention: *I liked all the paintings, but the one that really caught my eye was a Matisse.* ◇ *Can you try to catch the waiter's eye?*

catch sb in the 'act (of doing sth)
find sb while they are doing sth they should not be doing: *She turned round to catch him in the act of trying to run upstairs.*

> **❷ NOTE**
> This expression is often used in the passive: *He was caught in the act of stealing a car.*

'catch it (*BrE*) (*AmE* **catch 'hell; 'get it**) (*spoken*)
be punished or spoken to angrily about sth: *If your dad finds out you'll really catch it!*

catch sb 'napping (*BrE, informal*)
find sb not prepared or not paying attention, and perhaps gain an advantage over them as a result: *Chelsea's defence was caught napping in the final moments of the game when Jones scored his second goal for Liverpool.*

> **❷ NOTE**
> *Nap* means 'sleep', usually for a short time and especially during the day.

catch sb off (their) 'guard
happen when sb is not prepared: *The question caught him off his guard and he couldn't answer.* ◇ *Businesses were caught off guard by the sudden rise in interest rates.*

catch sb on the 'hop (*BrE, informal*)
find sb in a situation where they are unprepared: *The early start of winter that year caught many farmers on the hop.*

catch sb red-'handed
find sb while they are doing sth wrong, committing a crime, etc: *The thief was caught red-handed as she was emptying the till.*

catch the 'sun
become red or brown because of spending time in the sun: *Look at the colour of you! You really caught the sun, didn't you?*

catch sb with their 'pants down (*BrE also* **catch sb with their 'trousers down**) (*informal*)
find or trap sb when they are unprepared or not paying attention: *After the devastating attack on its military bases, the country was determined not to be caught with its pants down a second time.*

catch/get sb's/the drift → **drift**
catch/take/tickle sb's fancy → **fancy**

catch/get/grab/take (a) hold of sb/sth → **hold**
catch/touch sb on the raw → **raw**
catch/get some Z's → **Z**
catch/take sb unawares → **unawares**
(be) a sprat to catch a mackerel → **sprat**

catch-22

(a) catch-22; a catch-22 situation (*informal*)
a difficult situation from which there is no escape because you need to do one thing before doing a second, and you cannot do the second thing before doing the first: *I can't get a job because I haven't got anywhere to live, but I can't afford a place to live until I get a job—it's a catch-22 situation.*

> **❶ ORIGIN**
> This phrase is the title of a novel by Joseph Heller, in which the main character pretends to be crazy in order to avoid dangerous situations in war. The authorities said that he could not be crazy if he was concerned about his own safety.

catch-as-catch-can

catch-as-catch-can (*AmE*)
using whatever is available: *The company took a catch-as-catch-can approach to IT training.* ◇ *The visit was arranged catch-as-catch-can.*

> **❶ ORIGIN**
> *Catch-as-catch-can* is a type of wrestling in which most things are allowed, including many that are not allowed in other forms of wrestling.

catches

the early bird catches the worm → **early**
if A catches a cold, B gets pneumonia = when A sneezes, B catches a cold → **sneezes**

cats

rain cats and dogs → **rain**

caught

be caught in the 'crossfire
become involved in a situation where two people or groups of people are arguing, and suffer as a result: *When two industrial giants clash, small companies can get caught in the crossfire.*

be caught/taken short → **short**
I, he, etc. wouldn't be seen/caught dead ... → **dead**

cause

be (all) for/in a good 'cause
worth doing, because it is helping other people: *Most motorists seem to accept that the speed cameras are all in a good cause (= they help to keep people safe on the roads by stopping people driving too fast).*

cause/create a stir → **stir**
a lost cause → **lost**
the root cause (of sth) → **root**
show good cause (for sth/doing sth) → **show**

caution

throw caution to the wind(s) → **throw**

cave

an Aladdin's cave → **Aladdin**

cease

wonders (will) never cease → **wonders**

ceiling

hit the roof/ceiling → **hit**

cent

a/one hundred per cent → **hundred**

not have a red cent → **red**

centre (*BrE*) (*AmE* center)

front and center → **front**

right, left and centre = left, right and centre → **left**

century

the turn of the year/century → **turn**

ceremony

without 'ceremony

in a very rough or informal way: *He found himself pushed without ceremony out of the house and into the street.*

stand on ceremony → **stand**

cert

a dead cert → **dead**

certain

for 'certain

without doubt: *No one can say for certain how the world's climate is likely to change.*

make 'certain (that …)

find out whether sth is definitely true: *I think there's a bus at 8 but you'd better call to make certain.*

make certain of sth/of doing sth

do sth in order to be sure that sth else will happen: *You'll have to leave soon to make certain of getting there on time.*

of a certain 'age

if you talk about a person being **of a certain age**, you mean that they are no longer young but not yet old: *The show is designed to appeal to an audience of a certain age.*

up to a (certain) point → **point**

chaff

sort out/separate the wheat from the chaff → **wheat**

chafing

be chafing at the bit = be champing/chomping at the bit → **bit**

chain

a ball and chain → **ball**

a link in the chain → **link**

yank sb's chain → **yank**

chair

on the edge of your seat/chair → **edge**

chalice

a poisoned chalice → **poisoned**

chalk

(like) ˌchalk and 'cheese (also **as different as ˌchalk and 'cheese**) (*BrE, informal*)

very different: *It's hard to imagine that Mark and John are brothers—they're like chalk and cheese.*

chalk it up to experience = put it down to experience → **experience**

not by a long chalk → **long**

challenge

rise to the occasion/challenge → **rise**

champing

be champing/chomping at the bit → **bit**

chance

as ˌchance/ˌluck would 'have it (also **as ˌchance 'has it**)

as it happens or happened, fortunately or unfortunately: *He asked whether we had a room to let and, as luck would have it, we did.* ◇ *I'm going to London myself tomorrow, as chance has it, so perhaps we can travel together.*

by 'any chance

used especially in questions, to ask whether sth is true, possible, etc: *Are you in love with him, by any chance?*

ˌchance your 'arm (*BrE, informal*)

take a risk (especially when you are unlikely to succeed): *He knew he wasn't likely to win the contest, but decided to chance his arm anyway.*

a ˌchance in a 'million (*informal*)

a very unlikely possibility: *If you lost your ring on the beach, it's a chance in a million that you'd find it again.*

'chance would be a fine thing (*BrE, spoken*)

used to say that you would like to do sth but will probably not have the opportunity: *'Are you going on holiday this year?' 'Chance would be a fine thing—I can't even afford a day trip to London!'*

'no chance (*spoken*)

there is no possibility of that: *'Lend us five pounds, will you?' 'No chance!'*

on the 'off chance (*informal*)

hoping that sth will happen, even if it is unlikely: *I called at their house on the off chance that they'd let me stay, but they weren't at home.*

take a 'chance (on sth)

do sth without being sure of success: *We took a chance on being able to get tickets on the day of the match, but they were sold out.*

(a) fat chance (of sth/doing sth) → **fat**

a fighting chance → **fighting**

give sb half a chance (to do sth) → **half**

have (got) an even chance (of doing sth) → **even**

have (got) an eye to/for the main chance → **eye**

not have a dog's chance = not have a cat in hell's chance → **cat**

not have a ghost of a chance (of doing sth) → **ghost**

not have a snowball's chance in hell (of doing sth) → **snowball**

a sporting chance → **sporting**

(not) stand a chance (of doing sth/with sb) → **stand**

chances

(the) chances 'are (that) (*informal*)

it is likely (that): *The chances are that he'll come if he can finish work on time.*

take 'chances

do risky things: *Take no chances: don't lend money to people you don't know.*

take your 'chances (*informal*)

make as much use as you can of your opportunities: *When the offer of a job in Singapore came, I accepted it. After all, you have to take your chances in life.*

blow it/your chances → **blow**

fancy your/sb's chances → **fancy**

change

change 'hands

pass to a different owner: *The house has changed hands several times.*

change your 'mind

change your decision or opinion: *He was intending to go to the party but now he's changed his mind and decided to stay in.*

a ,change of 'heart

a change in your attitude and feelings, especially becoming kinder, more friendly, etc: *The Government has had a change of heart over the proposed tax reforms and is now prepared to listen to public opinion.*

change the 'subject

start to talk about something different, especially because what was being discussed was embarrassing or difficult to talk about: *'You know I don't like talking about the war. Can't we change the subject?'*

change your 'tune (*informal*)

change your opinion about or your attitude to sb/sth: *Tom used to say that parents worry too much about their children, but he soon changed his tune when he became a parent himself!*

change your 'ways

start to live or behave in a different way from before: *I've learned my lesson and I'm going to try*

to change my ways. ◇ *It's unlikely your boss will change his ways.*

for a 'change

for variety; as an improvement on what usually happens: *We usually go to Cyprus on holiday but this year we've decided to stay at home for a change.* ◇ *Oh good! She's on time for a change.*

get no change out of sb; not get much/any change out of sb (*BrE, spoken*)

get no/little help or information from sb: *If you need any help, ask Manuel. You'll get more change out of him than the others.*

a wind/the winds of 'change

an event or a series of events that has started to happen and will cause important changes or results: *There's a wind of change in the attitude of voters.* ◇ *Winds of change were sweeping over the country.*

change/swap horses in midstream → **horses**

change/swap places (with sb) → **places**

chop and change → **chop**

a leopard cannot change its spots → **leopard**

plus ça change (, plus c'est la même chose) → **plus**

changes

ring the changes (on sth) → **ring**

chapter

,chapter and 'verse

the exact details of sth, especially the exact place where particular information may be found: *I can't give you chapter and verse, but I can tell you that the lines she quoted come from a Brecht play.*

a ,chapter of 'accidents

a series of unlucky events or mistakes in a short period of time: *The reorganization of the company has been a chapter of accidents!*

character

,in/,out of 'character

(of sb's behaviour, etc.) of the kind you would/would not expect from them; characteristic/uncharacteristic: *That unpleasant remark she made was quite out of character.* ◇ *'I'm sure it was Bill I saw from the bus. He was arguing with a police officer.' 'Well, that's in character, anyway!'*

charge

get a 'charge out of sth (*AmE*)

get a strong feeling of excitement or pleasure from sth: *If you like horror movies then you'll get a charge out of this film.*

in charge (of sb/sth)

having control or command (of sth): *The teacher in charge of the children has to accompany them on the coach.* ◇ *Who's in charge around here?*

take 'charge (of sth)

begin to have control or command: *The Chief*

Inspector took charge of the investigations into the murder.

cost/pay/charge the earth → **earth**

charity

,charity begins at 'home (*saying*)
people should look after their own family before they think about others

charm

third time is the charm → **third**
work like a charm → **work**

charmed

lead/have a ,charmed 'life
have a lot of good luck, avoiding accidents or harm: *Carol appeared to lead a charmed life, with her successful career in television, money and a happy home life.*

Charming

Prince Charming → **Prince**

chase

chase your (own) 'tail
be very busy but in fact achieve very little: *In my first month at college I was continually chasing my own tail and being late for everything.*

give 'chase
begin to run after sb/sth in order to catch them: *We gave chase along the footpath.*

cut to the chase → **cut**
a wild goose chase → **wild**

cheap

be going 'cheap (*informal*)
be sold at a low price: *These shirts were going cheap, so I bought two.*

cheap and 'cheerful (*informal*)
something that is **cheap and cheerful** does not cost a lot but is attractive and pleasant: *cheap and cheerful clothes / meals / rugs*

cheap and 'nasty (*informal*)
something that is **cheap and nasty** does not cost a lot and is of poor quality and not very attractive or pleasant: *The furniture was cheap and nasty.*

'cheap at the price (*BrE*) (*AmE* **cheap at 'twice the price**)
worth more than the price paid, even though it is expensive: *I know £6000 is a lot of money, but a great car like this is cheap at the price.*

not come 'cheap
be expensive: *Violins like this don't come cheap.* ◇ *Babies certainly don't come cheap* (= it is expensive to buy everything they need).

on the 'cheap (*informal*)
for less than the normal cost (and therefore of poor

quality): *He got it on the cheap so I wasn't surprised when it broke after a couple of months.*

life is cheap → **life**

check

keep/hold sb/sth in 'check
control sb/sth: *The disease is kept in check with drugs.* ◇ *It was difficult to hold their enthusiasm in check.*

a blank check → **blank**
take a rain check (on sth) → **rain**

checks

checks and balances
rules that are designed to control the amount of power, especially political power, that one person or group has: *These are the proposals for introducing a new system of checks and balances into the boardrooms of UK companies.*

cheek

,cheek by 'jowl (with sb/sth)
side by side (with sb/sth); very near: *If he'd known that he was to find himself seated cheek by jowl with his old enemy he wouldn't have attended the dinner.*

turn the other cheek → **turn**
with your tongue in your cheek = (with) tongue in cheek → **tongue**

cheeks

put the roses back in your cheeks → **roses**

cheerful

cheap and cheerful → **cheap**

cheers

(give) three cheers (for sb/sth) → **three**

cheese

a big cheese/wheel → **big**
as different as chalk and cheese = (like) chalk and cheese → **chalk**
hard cheese → **hard**
say cheese! → **say**

cheque (*BrE*) (*AmE* check)

a blank cheque → **blank**

cherry

a second/another bite at/of the cherry = a bite at/of the cherry → **bite**

Cheshire

grin like a Cheshire cat → **grin**

chest

,get sth off your 'chest (*informal*)
say sth that you have wanted to say for a long time
and feel better because you have done this: *If
something is worrying you, get it off your chest.*

His visit to a counsellor really helped him get things
off his chest.

keep/hold/play your cards close to your chest → **cards**
put hairs on your chest → **hairs**

chestnut

an/that old chestnut → **old**

chew

,chew the 'fat (*BrE*) (*AmE* **,chew the 'rag**)
(*informal*)
talk about unimportant things; chat: *They sit
around chewing the fat instead of working.*

bite off more than you can chew → **bite**

chicken

'chicken feed (*informal*)
a small and unimportant amount of money: *My
salary is chicken feed compared with hers.*

be no spring chicken → **spring**
run around like a headless chicken → **run**

chicken-and-egg

a chicken-and-'egg situation
a situation in which you do not know which of two
connected events is the cause of the other: *Is she
unhappy because she gets into debt, or does she get
into debt because she's unhappy? I suppose it's a
chicken-and-egg situation.*

chickens

(your/the) chickens come home to 'roost
after a long time you experience the unpleasant
effects of sth bad or stupid that you have done in
the past: *For years he avoided paying tax. But now
his chickens have come home to roost and he's got a
tax bill of £25 000.*

not count your chickens (before they're hatched) → **count**

chiefs

**there are too many ,chiefs and not enough
'Indians** (*BrE, informal*)
used to describe a situation in which there are too
many people telling other people what to do, and
not enough people to do the work

child

'child's play
a very easy job or task: *Mending the lamp was
child's play for an experienced electrician like him.*

spare the rod and spoil the child → **spare**

childhood

a/your second childhood → **second**

chill

chill sb to the 'bone/'marrow
frighten sb very much: *His threat chilled her to the
bone.*

> ❓ **NOTE**
> *Bone marrow* is a soft substance that fills the hol-
> low parts of bones.

a chill runs/goes down sb's spine = send a chill up/down
sb's spine → **send**

chimney

smoke like a chimney → **smoke**

chin

(keep your) 'chin up (*BrE* also **keep your
'pecker up**, *old-fashioned*) (*spoken*)
used to tell sb to stay cheerful in difficult circumstances: *Chin up! Things will get better soon.*

take sth on the 'chin (*informal*)
accept a difficult or unpleasant situation without
complaining, trying to make excuses, etc: *Losing
his job after so many years was a great shock, but he
took it on the chin.*

China

wouldn't do sth for all the tea in China → **tea**

china

like a bull in a china shop → **bull**

chink

a chink in sb's 'armour (*BrE*) (*AmE* **a chink in
sb's 'armor**)
a weakness in sb's argument, character, etc., that
can be used in an attack: *The one chink in her
armour is the lack of a sense of humour. She hates
people laughing at her.*

chip

a ,chip off the old 'block (*informal*)
a person who is very like one of his/her parents in

appearance or character: *Young Tom's a chip off the old block, isn't he? He looks exactly like his Dad!*

have (got) a 'chip on your shoulder (*informal*)
be sensitive about sth that happened in the past and easily offended if it is mentioned, because you think you were treated unfairly: *He's got a chip on his shoulder about not having been to university.*

❶ ORIGIN
This idiom comes from a nineteenth-century US custom. If a boy wanted to fight, he put a small piece of wood on his shoulder. He would begin a fight with whoever knocked the chip of wood off his shoulder.

a bargaining chip → **bargaining**

chips

have had your 'chips (*BrE, informal*)
be in a situation in which you are certain to be defeated or killed: *With the score at 3-0, it looked as if the Scottish team had had their chips.*

when the chips are 'down (*informal*)
when the situation is urgent and action must be taken: *Nobody wanted a war but when the chips were down and the enemy was ready to attack, everyone volunteered to defend their homeland.*

❷ NOTE
This idiom refers to the use of *chips* (= small flat pieces of plastic) to represent money when gambling.

cash in your chips → **cash**
let the chips fall where they may → **let**

choice

be spoilt/spoiled for 'choice
have so many opportunities or things to choose from that it is difficult to make a decision: *I've had so many job offers that I'm spoilt for choice.*

by 'choice
because you have chosen: *I wouldn't go there by choice.*

of 'choice (for sb/sth)
(used after a noun) that is chosen by a particular group of people or for a particular purpose: *It's the software of choice for business use.*

of your 'choice
that you choose yourself: *First prize will be a meal for two at the restaurant of your choice.*

Hobson's choice → **Hobson**
you pays your money and you takes your choice → **pays**

chomping

be champing/chomping at the bit → **bit**

choose

there's nothing, not much, etc. to choose between A and B
there is very little difference between A and B: *One*

of the computers has a larger monitor, but otherwise there's not much to choose between them.

pick and choose → **pick**
pick/choose your moment → **moment**

choosers

beggars can't be choosers → **beggars**

chop

be for the 'chop (*BrE, informal*)
1 (of a person) be likely to be dismissed from a job: *Who's next for the chop?*
2 (of a plan, project, etc.) be likely to be stopped or ended

chop and 'change (*BrE, informal*)
change your plans, opinions or methods too often: *I wish he'd make up his mind—I'm tired of all this chopping and changing.*

get/be given the 'chop (*BrE, informal*)
1 (of a person) be dismissed from a job: *The whole department has been given the chop.*
2 (of a plan, project, etc.) be stopped or ended: *Three more schemes have got the chop.*

chop-chop

chop-'chop! (*BrE, informal*)
hurry up!: *Come on then, chop-chop! If we don't leave now we'll miss the bus.*

❶ ORIGIN
This expression comes from pidgin English, based on a Chinese dialect word for 'quick'.

chord

strike/touch a 'chord (with sb)
say or do sth which speaks directly to sb's emotions or memories: *His war poetry struck a chord with people who remembered that period.*

Christmas

a white Christmas → **white**

chucking

it's 'chucking it down (*BrE, spoken*)
it is raining heavily: *They had to cancel the barbecue, as it started chucking it down.*

church

a broad church → **broad**
(as) poor as a church mouse → **poor**

cigar

close but no cigar → **close**

cinder

burn sth to a cinder/crisp → **burn**

circle

come/go full circle → **full**

square the circle ➜ **square**
a vicious circle ➜ **vicious**
the wheel has come/turned full circle ➜ **wheel**

circles

go round in 'circles
keep making the same points without making progress in a discussion, argument, etc: *This discussion is going round and round in circles. Let's make a decision.*

run around/round in circles ➜ **run**

circumstance

force of circumstance ➜ **force**
pomp and circumstance ➜ **pomp**

circumstances

in/under the 'circumstances
used before or after a statement to show that you have thought about the conditions that affect a situation before making a decision or a statement: *Under the circumstances, it seemed better not to tell him about the accident.*

in/under no circumstances
used to emphasize that sth should never happen or be allowed: *Under no circumstances should you lend Paul any money.*

reduced circumstances ➜ **reduced**

claim

‚claim to 'fame (*often humorous*)
one thing that makes a person or place important or interesting: *His main claim to fame is that he went to school with the Prime Minister.*

lay claim to sth ➜ **lay**
stake (out) a/your claim to sb/sth ➜ **stake**

clam

(as) happy as the day is long/as a clam/as Larry ➜ **happy**

clanger

drop a brick/clanger ➜ **drop**

clap

clap/lay/set eyes on sb/sth ➜ **eyes**

Clapham

the man (and/or woman) on the Clapham omnibus ➜ **man**

clappers

like the 'clappers (*BrE, informal*)
very fast: *We had to drive like the clappers to get there on time.*

class

be in a class of your, its, etc. own (also **be in a class by yourself, itself, etc.**)
be much better than any others of the same kind:
The winning competitor was in a class by herself. ◊ *For originality, Leo's designs are truly in a class of their own.*

have, etc. a touch of class ➜ **touch**
not be in the same league/class/street ➜ **league**

claw

claw your way back, into sth, out of sth, etc.
gradually achieve sth or move somewhere by using a lot of determination and effort: *She clawed her way to the top of her profession.* ◊ *Slowly, he clawed his way out from under the collapsed building.*

red in tooth and claw ➜ **red**

claws

get your 'claws into sb
1 (*disapproving*) if a woman **gets her claws** into a man, she tries hard to make him marry her or to have a relationship with her: *He was perfectly happy before she started trying to get her claws into him!*
2 criticize sb severely: *Wait until the media gets its claws into her.*

> **❷ NOTE**
> *Claws* are the sharp curved nails on the end of an animal's or a bird's foot.

clay

feet of clay ➜ **feet**

clean

(as) clean as a 'whistle (*informal*)
1 (also **(as) clean as a new 'pin**) very clean: *She scrubbed the kitchen floor until it was clean as a whistle.*
2 if sb is **as clean as a whistle**, they are not involved in anything illegal: *I don't know why the police want to talk to me. I'm as clean as a whistle!*

a clean bill of 'health
a statement that sb is well or sth is in a satisfactory condition: *The doctor's given her a clean bill of health.*

a clean 'break
a complete separation from a person, an organization, a way of life, etc: *She wanted to make a clean break with the past and start again.*

a clean 'sheet/'slate
a record of your work or actions that does not show any mistakes or bad things that you have done: *At the new school, you will start with a clean slate.* ◊ *They kept a clean sheet in the match* (= no goals were scored against them).

clean up your 'act (*informal*)
start behaving in a moral or responsible way: *He cleaned up his act and gave up the cigarettes and alcohol.*

come 'clean (with sb) (about sth) (*informal*)
tell the truth about sth, especially after lying or

keeping it secret: *I'll come clean with you—I've been reading your mail.* ◇ *He finally came clean and confessed.*

have (got) clean 'hands; your hands are 'clean
not be responsible for crime, dishonesty, etc: *After years of corrupt government, we want politicians with clean hands.*

make a clean 'breast of sth
admit fully sth that you have done wrong: *He decided to make a clean breast of it and tell the police.*

make a clean 'sweep (of sth) (*informal*)
1 remove unwanted things or people: *The Prime Minister is expected to make a clean sweep of the ministers who don't support the new policy.*
2 win all the prizes, etc. that are available: *Kenyan athletes made a clean sweep (of the medals) in yesterday's competition.*

keep your nose clean → nose
show (sb) a clean pair of heels → show
wipe the slate clean → wipe

cleaners

take sb to the 'cleaners (*informal*)
1 make sb lose a lot of money, often by cheating them: *He's heavily in debt—his ex-wife took him to the cleaners at the time of their divorce.*
2 defeat sb completely: *Our team got taken to the cleaners.*

clear

clear the 'air
remove the causes of disagreement, fear, doubts, etc. by talking about them honestly and openly: *Mary had been bad-tempered with me for days, so in an attempt to clear the air, I asked her what the matter was.*

(as) clear as a 'bell
easily and clearly heard: *'Can you hear me all right?' 'Clear as a bell!'*

(as) clear as 'day
easy to see or understand; obvious: *Although it's written on the door as clear as day, people still don't realize that this room is private.*

(as) clear as 'mud (*spoken*)
not clear at all; very difficult to understand: *The instructions in the manual are as clear as mud.*

clear the 'deck(s)
get ready for some activity by first dealing with anything not essential to it: *We had been doing some painting in the dining room, so we had to spend some time clearing the decks before our visitors came round in the evening.*

clear sb's 'name
prove that sb is innocent: *Throughout his years in prison, his family fought to clear his name.*

clear your 'throat
cough slightly, especially before speaking or to attract sb's attention: *The lawyer stood up, cleared his throat and began to address the jury.*

clear the 'way (for sth/for sth to happen)
remove things that are stopping the progress or movement of sth: *The ruling could clear the way for extradition proceedings.*

have/keep a clear 'head
be able to think clearly, especially because you have not had any alcohol, drugs, etc: *Don't give me any wine, I must keep a clear head for the meeting this afternoon.*

in the 'clear (*informal*)
no longer in danger or likely to be blamed, punished, etc: *She told the police that Jim was with her when the burglary happened, so that put him in the clear.*

steer/stay/keep clear (of sb/sth)
avoid sb/sth: *I'm trying to lose weight so I have to steer clear of fattening foods.* ◇ *It's best to stay clear of the bank at lunchtimes as it gets very busy.*

be clear sailing = be (all) plain sailing → plain
the coast is clear → coast
crystal clear → crystal
leave the field clear for sb → leave
loud and clear → loud

cleft

be (caught) in a cleft 'stick (*informal*)
be in a difficult situation when any action you take will have bad results: *I was in a cleft stick—my job was boring but I couldn't move to another firm without losing my company pension.*

clever

(a) 'clever Dick (also (a) 'clever clogs) (*BrE, informal, disapproving*)
a person who thinks that they are always right or that they know everything: *Come on then, clever clogs, tell us the answer!* ◇ *(ironic) Some clever Dick has parked his car so close to mine I can't get out!*

box clever → box

climb

climb/jump on the bandwagon → bandwagon

climbing

be climbing the walls (*informal*)
be extremely bored, worried, etc: *It's too cold and wet to play outside, and the kids are climbing the walls with frustration.*

clip

at a fast, good, steady, etc. 'clip (*especially AmE*)
quickly: *Land prices will rise at a healthy clip.*

clip sb's 'wings

limit sb's freedom or power: *The new law was seen as an attempt to clip the wings of the trade unions.*

clock

around/round the 'clock

for twenty-four hours without stopping: *The police watched the house round the clock but no one went in or came out.* ◇ *Her mother needs round-the-clock care and attention.*

put/turn the 'clock back

return to the past; return to old-fashioned ideas, customs, etc: *Sometimes I wish I could turn the clock back to my days as a student.* ◇ *These new restrictions on medical research will undoubtedly put the clock back (by) 20 years.*

against the clock = against time ➔ **time**
beat the clock ➔ **beat**
a race against time/the clock ➔ **race**
run out the clock ➔ **run**
watch the clock ➔ **watch**

clockwork

go/run like 'clockwork

(of arrangements, etc.) happen according to plan, without any difficulty or trouble: *The sports day went like clockwork, with every race starting and finishing on time.*

(as) regular as clockwork ➔ **regular**

clogs

(a) clever clogs ➔ **clever**
pop your clogs ➔ **pop**

close

at ‚close 'quarters

from/within a very short distance: *You have to examine the paint at close quarters in order to see the tiny scratches on it.*

close the 'book on sth

stop doing sth because you no longer believe you will be successful or will find a solution: *The police have closed the book on the case* (= they have stopped trying to solve it).

close but no cigar (*AmE, informal*)

used to say that the answer, result, etc. is not quite good enough

> ❶ ORIGIN
> This expression comes from the old US custom of giving a cigar as a prize in fairground games of skill, such as shooting games.

close 'by (sb/sth)

at a short distance (from sb/sth): *Our friends live close by.* ◇ *The route passes close by the town.*

close your 'mind (to sth)

be unwilling or unable to consider new ideas, proposals, etc: *His mind is closed to the possibility of reform.*

close on; close to

almost; nearly: *She is close on sixty.* ◇ *It's close on midnight.* ◇ *They made a profit close to £2000.*

close 'ranks

(of the members of a profession, group, etc.) co-operate closely to protect and defend each other: *Although the family quarrelled a good deal among themselves, they quickly closed ranks against any outsider who criticized one of them.*

a ‚close 'shave/'call (*informal*)

a situation where a disaster, accident, etc. almost happens: *We didn't actually hit the other car, but it was a close shave.* ◇ *Phew! That was a close call—she nearly saw us!*

close 'to; close 'up

in a position very near to sth: *The picture looks very different when you see it close to.*

close to 'home

if a remark or topic of discussion is **close to home**, it is accurate or connected with you in a way that makes you uncomfortable or embarrassed: *Her remarks about me were embarrassingly close to home.*

come 'close (to sth/to doing sth)

almost reach or do sth: *He'd come close to death.* ◇ *We didn't win but we came close.*

keep a close 'eye/'watch on sb/sth

watch sb/sth carefully: *Over the next few months we will keep a close eye on sales.*

too close for 'comfort

so near that you become afraid or anxious: *The exams are getting a bit too close for comfort.*

be close/dear/near to sb's heart ➔ **heart**
be close to/near the mark ➔ **mark**
a close/near thing ➔ **thing**
close to/near the bone ➔ **bone**
keep/hold/play your cards close to your chest ➔ **cards**
run sb/sth close ➔ **run**
sail close to the wind ➔ **sail**
shut/close the door on sth ➔ **door**
shut/close your ears to sb/sth ➔ **ears**
shut/close your eyes to sth ➔ **eyes**
shut/lock/close the stable door after the horse has bolted ➔ **stable**

closed

be‚hind closed 'doors

in private; without the public being allowed to attend: *Journalists protested that the trial was being held behind closed doors.*

a closed 'book (to sb)

a person or a subject that you know nothing about: *I'm afraid geophysics is rather a closed book to me.*

a closed 'shop

a factory, etc. where only people belonging to a certain union may work

(be able to do sth) with your eyes shut/closed ➔ **eyes**

close-run

a close-run thing = a near/close thing → **thing**

closet

come out of the 'closet
admit sth openly that you kept secret before, especially because of shame or embarrassment: *Homosexuals in public life are now coming out of the closet.*

a skeleton in the cupboard/closet → **skeleton**

cloth

cut your coat according to your cloth → **cut**
(to be) cut from the same cloth → **cut**
a man of God/the cloth → **man**

clothing

a wolf in sheep's clothing → **wolf**

cloud

a cloud hangs over sb/sth
if a **cloud hangs over sb/sth**, sth bad has happened that will affect them/it for a long time: *He didn't die, but there was a cloud hanging over his future.*

a (small) cloud on the ho'rizon
a sign of trouble or difficulty to come: *Although we are making good profits there is one cloud on the horizon—the government may increase taxes.*

every ˌcloud has a silver 'lining (*saying*)
there is always something hopeful about even the most difficult or unhappy situation

on cloud 'nine (*old-fashioned, informal*)
extremely happy: *She's been on cloud nine ever since she heard the news.*

under a 'cloud
suspected of having done sth wrong; in disgrace: *He'd been stealing, so he was asked to resign, and he left under a cloud.*

clouds

have (got) your head in the clouds → **head**

clover

in 'clover (*informal*)
in comfort or luxury: *Since winning the lottery, they've been living in clover.*

club

be in the 'club (*BrE, informal*)
be pregnant

join the club → **join**

clue

not have a 'clue (*informal*)
1 not know (anything about) sth: *'Who's that woman over there?' 'I'm afraid I don't have a clue.'*
◊ *I haven't a clue how to get there.*

2 (*disapproving*) be stupid; lack skill or ability: *It's a waste of time trying to teach him anything: he hasn't got a clue.*

clutch

clutch/grasp at straws → **straws**

coach

drive a coach and horses through sth → **drive**

coalface

at the 'coalface (*BrE*)
where the real work is done, not just where people talk about it: *Many of the best ideas come from doctors at the coalface.*

coals

(carry/take) coals to 'Newcastle (*BrE*)
(supply) sth that there is already a lot of: *Exporting wine to France would be like taking coals to Newcastle.*

ⓘ ORIGIN
Newcastle-upon-Tyne, in the north of England, was once an important coal-mining centre.

rake sb over the coals = haul sb over the coals → **haul**

coast

the ˌcoast is 'clear (*informal*)
there is no one around to see or stop what you are doing: *She looked left and right to make sure the coast was clear, then ran as fast as she could down the corridor.*

coat

cut your coat according to your cloth → **cut**

coat-tails

on sb's 'coat-tails
using the success and influence of another person to help yourself become successful: *She got where she is today on her brother's coat-tails.*

cobwebs

blow away the cobwebs → **blow**

cock

a ˌcock and 'bull story (*informal*)
a story, excuse or explanation that is so unlikely that no one believes it: *I asked him about his job and he gave me some cock and bull story about being so rich he didn't need to work.*

ⓘ ORIGIN
There is a story about the town of Stony Stratford in Britain, which was a famous stop for coaches and had two famous inns, *The Cock* and *The Bull*. Coach passengers would walk from one inn to another, their stories becoming more exaggerated as they drank more alcohol.

cock an 'ear/'eye at sth/sb
look at or listen to sb/sth carefully and with a lot of attention

cock a 'snook at sb/sth (*BrE, informal*)
1 make a rude gesture by putting your thumb to your nose
2 do or say sth that shows your lack of respect for sb/sth, especially when you cannot be punished for this: *She cocked a snook at her teachers by going to school with her hair dyed purple.*

cocked

knock sb/sth into a cocked hat → knock

cockles

warm the cockles (of sb's heart) → warm

coffee

wake up and smell the coffee → wake

coffin

a nail in sb's/sth's coffin → nail

cog

a cog in the ma'chine/'wheel (*informal*)
a person who plays a small part in a large organization or plan: *The firm tries hard to make its employees feel that they are more than simply cogs in the wheel.*

coil

shuffle off this mortal coil → shuffle

coin

'coin it (in); coin 'money (*informal*)
(normally used in progressive tenses) earn a lot of money: *They must be really coining it at that cafe on the corner. You can hardly get a seat at any time of day.*

to coin a 'phrase
used for introducing an expression that you have invented or to apologize for using a well-known idiom or phrase instead of an original one: *Oh well, no news is good news, to coin a phrase.*

the other side of the coin → side
toss a coin → toss
two sides of the same coin → two

cold

,cold 'comfort
a thing that is intended to make you feel better but which does not: *When you've just had your car stolen, it's cold comfort to be told it happens to somebody every day.*

a ,cold 'fish (*disapproving*)
a person who shows little or no emotion, or is unfriendly, reserved, etc: *When I first met him, he*

seemed rather a cold fish, but actually he's quite passionate.

cold 'turkey
the unpleasant state that drug addicts experience when they suddenly stop taking a drug, or a way of treating addicts that makes them experience this state: *The worst time was when he was going cold turkey.* ◇ *I quit smoking cold turkey* (= I stopped suddenly and completely).

come in from the 'cold
be included in a group, activity, etc. that you have had no part in before: *In that year, Finland came in from the cold and became a member of the EU.*

get/have cold 'feet (*informal*)
no longer want to continue what you intended or have started to do because you are nervous or afraid: *Do you still want to do this parachute jump or are you getting cold feet?*

Everything was fine until the last minute, when she suddenly got cold feet.

give sb/get the cold 'shoulder
treat sb/be treated in a deliberately unfriendly way: *I try to chat to my colleagues during the lunch hour, but for some reason they've been giving me the cold shoulder.*

> **ⓘ ORIGIN**
> One theory about the origin of this expression is that it refers to meat. Meat cut from the shoulder of an adult sheep was very cheap, so giving visitors this meat served cold was a sign that they were not welcome.

in cold 'blood
deliberately and calmly, without showing any pity: *The innocent victims were shot in cold blood.*
▶ **,cold-'blooded** *adj.*: *a cold-blooded murder*

in the ,cold light of 'day
when you have had time to think calmly about sth; in the morning when things are clearer: *In the cold light of day, the plans they'd made didn't seem such a good idea.*

pour/throw cold 'water on sth (*informal*)
discourage or try to prevent a plan, etc. from being
carried out; be unenthusiastic about sth: *I've had
lots of ideas about how to improve sales but my
manager pours cold water on all my suggestions.*

be in a cold sweat = be in a sweat → **sweat**

blow hot and cold → **blow**

go hot and cold (all over) → **hot**

if A catches a cold, B gets pneumonia = when A sneezes,
  B catches a cold → **sneezes**

leave sb cold → **leave**

left out in the cold → **left**

make sb's blood run cold → **blood**

when A sneezes, B catches a cold → **sneezes**

collar

hot under the collar → **hot**

collect

collect yourself/your thoughts
1 try to control your emotions and become calm:
I'm fine—I just need a minute to collect myself.
2 prepare yourself mentally for sth: *She paused to
collect her thoughts before entering the interview
room.*

collect/gather your wits → **wits**

collision

be on a col'lision course (with sb/sth)
1 be in a situation which is almost certain to
cause a disagreement or dispute: *I was on a collision course with my boss over the sales figures.*
2 be moving in a direction in which it is likely
that you will crash into sb/sth: *The ship was on a
collision course with a huge iceberg.*

colour (*BrE*) (*AmE* color)

off 'colour (*informal*)
1 (*BrE*) looking or feeling ill: *I'm feeling a bit off
colour this morning.*
2 (*especially AmE*) an **off-colour** joke is one that
people think is rude, usually because it is about
sex: *They describe their humor as suitable for the
family, with nothing off-color.*

lend colour to sth → **lend**

see the colour of sb's money → **see**

colours (*BrE*) (*AmE* colors)

in glowing terms/colours → **glowing**

nail your colours to the mast → **nail**

your, his, etc. true colours → **true**

with flying colours → **flying**

comb

go over/through sth with a fine-tooth comb → **fine-tooth**

combine

join/combine forces (with sb) → **forces**

come

Most idioms containing the verb **come** are at the
entries for the nouns or adjectives in the idioms,
for example **come a cropper** is at **cropper**.

as ,clever, ,stupid, etc. as they 'come
very clever, stupid, etc: *He's just about as mean as
they come. He wouldn't even lend me 50p!*

,come 'again? (*informal*)
used for asking sb to repeat sth because you have
not heard or understood: *'This is Peter—he's a
dermatologist.' 'Come again?' 'A dermatologist—
you know, a specialist in skin diseases.'*

,come and 'go
exist or be there for a short time and then stop or
leave: *Newspapers come and go, and unfortunately
the time has now come for this one to close.* ◇ *Feel
free to come and go as you please.*

,come, 'come; ,come, now
used for asking sb to act or speak in a sensible or
reasonable way: *Come, come! We all know that you
were in Manchester the day the crime was committed, so you may as well tell the whole story.*

come 'easily, 'naturally, etc. to sb
(of an activity, a skill, etc.) be easy, natural, etc. for
sb to do: *Acting comes naturally to her.*

,come it (with 'sb) (*informal*)
try to impress, persuade or deceive sb in the hope
of getting their attention, respect, sympathy, etc:
*Your leg hurts? Don't come it (with me)—get out
there and play with the rest of the team!*

come 'off it (*spoken*)
used to show that you do not believe sb/sth or that
you disagree with sb: *'I can't afford a holiday this
year.' 'Come off it, you've got plenty of money.'*

come to 'nothing; not 'come to anything/
  much
not have a successful result: *The latest attempt to
end the dispute came to nothing.* ◇ *They had a
scheme for making a lot of money quickly, but it
never came to anything.*

come to 'that; if it comes to 'that
used when you are going to add sth to what has just
been said: *It's been raining all day today. Come to
that, it's been raining non-stop since Friday.*

,come what 'may
whatever may happen: *My mother taught us to
always tell the truth, come what may.*

to 'come
(used after a noun) in the future: *They may well
regret the decision **in years to come**.* ◇ *This will be
a problem **for some time to come** (= for a period of
time in the future).*

comes

when it comes to sth/to doing sth
when it is a question of sth: *When it comes to getting things done, he's useless.*

comeuppance

get your come'uppance (*informal*)
receive a punishment for sth bad that you have done and that other people feel you really deserve: *I was glad to see that the bad guy got his comeuppance at the end of the movie.*

comfort

cold comfort ➔ cold
too close for comfort ➔ close

comfortably

,comfortably 'off
having enough money to buy what you want without worrying about the cost: *My brother is very comfortably off. He has a career in finance.*

sit comfortably/easily/well (with sth) ➔ sit

comforter

a Job's comforter ➔ Job

coming

have (got) it/that 'coming (to you) (*informal*)
be about to experience sth unpleasant, especially if you deserve it: *He's got a shock coming to him when he takes the exams and sees how difficult they are.* ◇ *He thinks he can break all the rules; but, believe me, he's got it coming to him one day.*

where sb is 'coming from (*informal, spoken*)
somebody's ideas, beliefs, personality, etc. that makes them say what they have said: *I see where you're coming from* (= I understand what you mean).

comings

,comings and 'goings
arrivals and departures; movement of people: *There were a lot of comings and goings at our neighbour's house all day.*

command

at your com'mand
if you have a skill or an amount of sth **at your command**, you are able to use it well and completely: *With four European languages at her command, she's thinking of working for the EU.*

be at sb's com'mand (*formal*)
be ready to obey sb: *I'm at your command—what would you like me to do?*

your wish is my command ➔ wish

commas

in inverted commas ➔ inverted

comment

,no 'comment
(said in reply to a question, usually from a journal-ist) I have nothing to say about that: *'Will you resign, sir?' 'No comment!'*

commission

in/out of com'mission
available/not available to be used: *Several of the airline's planes are temporarily out of commission and undergoing safety checks.*

common

,common or 'garden (*BrE*) (*AmE* **'garden-variety**) (*informal*)
ordinary; not unusual: *… a pet shop full of snakes and spiders, and not a common or garden rabbit or hamster in sight!*

the ,common 'touch
the ability of a powerful or famous person to talk to and understand ordinary people: *Despite being one of the richest and most famous women in the world, she never lost the common touch.*

have (got) sth in 'common (with sb/sth)
have the same interests, characteristics or experience as sb: *Come and meet my sister. I'm sure you two have got a lot in common.* ◇ *I have nothing in common with Mark, so I find it quite difficult to talk to him.*

in common with 'sb/'sth
together with sb/sth; similar to sb/sth: *The hospital buildings, in common with many others in this country, are sadly out of date.*

be common/public knowledge ➔ knowledge
the common/general run (of sth) ➔ run

company

the 'company sb keeps
the people with whom sb spends time: *People disapprove of the company he keeps.*

get into/keep bad 'company
be friends with people that others disapprove of: *I'm worried about Jo—I think he's getting into bad company.*

in company with sb/sth (*formal*)
together with or at the same time as sb/sth: *She arrived in company with the ship's captain.* ◇ *The US dollar went through a difficult time, in company with the oil market.*

in good 'company
if you say that sb is **in good company**, you mean that they should not worry about a mistake, etc. because sb else, especially sb more important, has done the same thing: *If you worry about your relationship with your teenage son or daughter, you're in good company. Many parents share the same worries.*

keep sb 'company
spend time with sb so that they are not alone: *I've promised to keep my sister company while her husband is away.*

excepting present company = present company excepted
→ **present**

part company (with/from sb/sth) → **part**

two's company (, three's a crowd) → **two**

compare

beyond/without com'pare (*literary*)

too good, beautiful, etc. to be compared with anyone or anything else: *The loveliness of the scene
was beyond compare.*

compare 'notes (with sb)

exchange ideas, opinions, with sb, especially about
shared experiences: *We met after the exam to compare notes on how well we had done.*

comparison

by com'parison (*written*)

used especially at the beginning of a sentence
when the next thing that is mentioned is compared
with sth in the previous sentence: *By comparison,
expenditure on education increased last year.*

by/in comparison (with sb/sth)

when compared with sb/sth: *The second half of
the game was dull by comparison with the first.* ◇
*The tallest buildings in London are small in com-
parison with New York's skyscrapers.*

there's no com'parison

used when comparing two people or things to
emphasize that one is much better, etc: *'Who is the
better player, Tom or Anna?' 'Anna is—there's no
comparison.'*

pale in/by comparison (with/to sth) → **pale**

complexion

put a new/different com'plexion on sth

change the way that a situation appears: *What the
police officer had just told me put quite a different
complexion on the mystery.*

compliment

a left-handed compliment = a backhanded compliment →
backhanded

return the compliment → **return**

compliments

fish for compliments → **fish**

compos

be ˌcompos 'mentis (*from Latin, formal* or
humorous)

having full control of your mind: *Are you sure she
was fully compos mentis when she said that?*

concentrate

ˌconcentrate the 'mind

make you think very clearly and seriously about
sth: *Being informed that you are likely to lose your
job unless you work harder concentrates the mind
wonderfully.*

concern

a ˌgoing con'cern

a business or an activity that is making a profit
and is expected to continue to do well: *He sold the
cafe as a going concern.*

conclusion

a foregone conclusion → **foregone**

conclusions

jump/leap to con'clusions

make a decision about sb/sth too quickly, before
you know or have thought about all the facts:
*There you go again—jumping to conclusions. Wait
till you hear my side of the story!*

condition

in mint condition → **mint**

confidence

be in sb's 'confidence

be trusted with sb's secrets: *He is said to be very
much in the President's confidence.*

take sb into your 'confidence

tell sb your secret plans, problems, etc: *She's the
only person I've taken into my confidence about it.*

conflict

conflict of 'interest(s)

a situation in which there are two jobs, aims, roles,
etc. and it is not possible for both of them to be
treated equally and fairly at the same time: *There
was a conflict of interest between his business dealings and his political activities.*

conjunction

in con'junction with (*formal*)

together with: *The police are working in conjunction with tax officers on the investigation.* ◇ *The
system is designed to be used in conjunction with a
word processing program.*

conjure

a name to conjure with → **name**

cons

(with) all mod cons → **mod**

the pros and cons (of sth) → **pros**

conscience

in all/good 'conscience

while being honest or just: *You cannot in all conscience think that is fair pay.*

on your 'conscience

making you feel guilty for doing or failing to do
sth: *I'll write and apologize. I've had it on my conscience for weeks.*

your conscience pricks you = prick your conscience →
 prick

search your heart/soul/conscience → **search**

consequence

in 'consequence (of sth) (*formal*)
as a result of sth: *The child was born deformed in
consequence of an injury to its mother.*

consideration

in conside'ration of sth (*formal*)
as payment for sth: *a small sum in consideration of
your services*

take sth into conside'ration
think about and include a particular thing or fact
when you are forming an opinion or making a decision: *The candidates' experience and qualifications
will be taken into consideration when the decision is
made.* ◇ *Taking everything into consideration, the
event was a great success.*

on mature reflection/consideration → **mature**

considered

your con,sidered o'pinion
your opinion that is the result of careful thought:
*In my considered opinion, 'Trainspotting' is one of
the best British movies ever made.*

all things considered → **things**

conspicuous

con,spicuous by your 'absence
not present in a situation or place, when it is obvious that you should be there: *When it came to cleaning up afterwards, Anne was conspicuous by her
absence.*

conspiracy

a con,spiracy of 'silence
an agreement not to talk publicly about sth which
should not remain secret: *As no one was ever
convicted of the murders, it is widely believed that
there may have been a conspiracy of silence maintained by the victims' friends and families.*

contact

lose touch/contact (with sb/sth) → **lose**
point of contact → **point**

contempt

beneath con'tempt
very shameful or disgusting: *Stealing the money
was bad enough. Trying to get someone else blamed
for it was beneath contempt.*

familiarity breeds contempt → **familiarity**

content

to your heart's content → **heart**

contention

in/out of con'tention (for sth)
with/without a chance of winning sth: *Only three
teams are now in contention for the title.* ◇ *With
that defeat, Marshall dropped out of contention.*

a bone of contention → **bone**

contradiction

a ,contradiction in 'terms
a statement or description containing two words
or phrases that contradict each other's meaning:
*They call their project 'a peace offensive', which
seems to me a contradiction in terms.*

contrary

contrary to popular be'lief/o'pinion
although it is not what most people consider to be
true: *Contrary to popular belief, many cats dislike
milk.*

on the 'contrary; ,quite the 'contrary
used to emphasize that the opposite of what has
been said is true: *It's not that I don't like him—on
the contrary, he seems very pleasant.* ◇ *I don't find
him funny at all. Quite the contrary.*

to the 'contrary
showing or proving the opposite: *Unless you hear
from me to the contrary, expect me on Friday at
about 6 o'clock.* ◇ *She was convinced that John was
not capable of murder, in spite of all the evidence to
the contrary.*

control

be in con'trol (of sth)
be able to organize your life well and keep calm: *In
spite of all her family problems, she's completely in
control.*

be, get, etc. out of con'trol
be or become impossible to manage or to control:
*The children are completely out of control since
their father left.* ◇ *A truck ran out of control on the
hill.*

be under con'trol
be being dealt with successfully: *Don't worry—
everything's under control!*

bring/get/keep sth under con'trol
succeed in dealing with sth so that it does not
cause any harm: *It took two hours to bring the fire
under control.* ◇ *Please will you keep your dog
under control!*

control/hold the purse strings → **purse**

convenience

at sb's con'venience (*formal*)
at a time or a place which is suitable for sb: *Can
you telephone me at your convenience to arrange a
meeting?*

at your earliest convenience → **earliest**

conventional

conventional/received wisdom → **wisdom**

converted

preach to the converted → **preach**

convictions

have/lack the courage of your convictions → **courage**

coo

bill and coo → **bill**

cook

,**cook the 'books** (*informal*)
change facts or figures in order to make the situation seem better than it is or to hide the fact that you have stolen money: *The two directors of the company had been cooking the books, a local court heard yesterday.*

,**cook sb's 'goose** (*informal*)
ruin sb's plans or chances of success: *He thought that the police would never find him but when he saw the officer coming towards him he realized that his goose was finally cooked.*

cookie

a/one smart cookie → **smart**
that's the way the cookie crumbles → **way**
a tough customer/cookie → **tough**

cooking

be cooking with 'gas (*AmE, informal*)
be doing sth very well and successfully: *Business may have been a little slow at first, but now we're cooking with gas!*

what's 'cooking? (*informal*)
what is being done or planned: *What's cooking in here? You all look very guilty!*

cooks

too many cooks spoil the 'broth (*saying*)
if too many people try to do sth it will not be done well or properly

cool

(as) ,cool as a 'cucumber (*informal*)
(of people) very calm, especially when the opposite might be expected, for example on a hot day or in a difficult situation: *Everyone was rushing round trying to get things ready, and he just sat there, cool as a cucumber.*

,**cool your 'heels** (*informal*)
be kept waiting: *The bank manager had asked to see her at four o'clock but she had to sit cooling her heels for almost 45 minutes.*

'**cool it** (*informal*)
behave in a less aggressive or excited way; calm down: *His friends were holding him back and tell-ing him to cool it, but he broke free and punched the barman on the nose.*

keep/lose your 'cool (*informal*)
stay calm/get angry, excited, etc: *He was very insulting. I really don't know how I managed to keep my cool.*

play it cool → **play**

coop

fly the coop → **fly**

coot

(as) bald as a coot → **bald**

cop

'**cop it** (*BrE, slang*)
be punished: *You'll cop it if your father finds out you broke the window!*

not much 'cop (*BrE, slang*)
not very good: *'What do you think of the book?' 'It's not much cop, really.'*

it's a fair cop → **fair**

copy

a carbon copy → **carbon**

copybook

blot your copybook → **blot**

core

to the 'core
very much; in every way: *He's a Welshman to the core.* ◊ *They believe that our society is rotten to the core* (= completely bad).

(the) hard core → **hard**

corner

back sb/yourself into a 'corner
(usually used in the passive) force sb/yourself into a very difficult position that they/you cannot escape from: *The President had backed himself into a corner by promising not to raise taxes.*

corner the 'market (in sth)
get control of the trade in a particular type of goods, so that you control its price and the conditions of sale: *By reducing prices so that the smaller shops can't compete and are forced to close, Bestsave has effectively cornered the market.*

just around/round the 'corner
very near; soon to happen: *We have been trying to develop the new drug for years, and now that success is just around the corner, the work must not be stopped.*

out of the corner of your 'eye
at the edge of your vision; indirectly: *I just caught sight of him out of the corner of my eye, so I couldn't say exactly what he looked like.*

in a tight corner/spot → **tight**
turn the corner → **turn**

corners

cut corners → **cut**
the four corners of the earth → **four**

correct

all present and correct → **present**
politically correct → **politically**

corridors

the corridors of 'power
the places where important decisions in government are made

cost

at 'any cost
under any circumstances: *He is determined to win at any cost.*

it will 'cost you (*spoken*)
used to say that sth will be expensive: *There is also a de luxe model available, but it'll cost you.*

to your 'cost
(know, discover, etc. sth) because of sth unpleasant that has happened to you: *Joanne's not a very reliable person, as I've recently discovered to my cost.*

cost/pay an arm and a leg → **arm**
cost/pay/charge the earth → **earth**
count the cost → **count**

costs

at 'all costs
whatever has to be done, suffered, etc: *He is determined to win at all costs.*

cotton

bless his, her, etc. (little) cotton socks → **bless**
wrap sb up in cotton wool → **wrap**

couch

a 'couch potato (*informal, disapproving*)
a person who spends a lot of time sitting and watching television

the casting couch → **casting**

counsel

keep your own 'counsel (*formal*)
keep your thoughts, plans, etc. secret: *Try to keep your own counsel when you're with him, or he'll tell everyone what you say.*

count

be able to count sb/sth on (the fingers of) one 'hand
used to say that the total number of sb/sth is very

His mother always warned him he'd turn into a couch potato if he watched too much TV.

small: *She could count on the fingers of one hand the people she actually enjoyed being with.*

count your 'blessings
realize how lucky you are and not complain: *Stop looking so miserable and count your blessings! At least you've still got a job and somewhere to live.*

count the 'cost
1 consider carefully what the risks or disadvantages may be before you do sth: *The job was attractive financially, but when I counted the cost in terms of separation from my family and friends, I decided not to take it.*
2 feel the bad effects of a mistake, an accident, etc: *We made a big mistake when we bought that old car, and we're still counting the cost—it breaks down almost every week!*

count 'sheep
imagine that sheep are jumping over a fence and count them, as a way of getting to sleep: *Doug closed his eyes and tried counting sheep, but he still couldn't get to sleep.*

keep/lose (a) 'count (of sth)
know/not know how many there are of sth: *He's had so many different jobs that I've lost count (of them all).* ◇ *Make sure you keep count of all the phone calls you make so you can claim the money back later.*

not count your 'chickens (before they're 'hatched)
not be too confident of success until it actually happens: *She said she was certain to be offered a part in the play, but I told her not to count her chickens, as a lot of other people wanted the same part.*

out for the 'count (*BrE*) (*AmE* ,down for the 'count)
unconscious or in a very deep sleep, either because you have been hit very hard or are very

tired: *After a whole day of walking around the city, I was out for the count!*

ℹ ORIGIN
This idiom refers to the rules in boxing. If a boxer is still down when the referee has finished counting to ten, he loses the game.

at the last count → last

counted

stand up and be counted → stand

counter

over the 'counter
goods, especially medicines, for sale **over the counter** can be bought without written permission from a doctor: *These tablets are available over the counter.*

under the 'counter
(of goods bought or sold in a shop) secretly or illegally: *Before the revolution, such luxuries were only sold under the counter.*

ℹ ORIGIN
This expression comes from World War II, when some shops held scarce or special goods for their best customers. They would hide them under the shop counter so that the other customers could not see or buy them.

a bargaining counter → bargaining

counting

who's 'counting? (*informal*)
used to say that you do not care how many times sth happens: *I've been late for school three times this week—but who's counting?*

country

a country 'bumpkin/'cousin (*informal, usually disapproving*)
a person from the countryside who is not used to towns or cities and seems unsophisticated: *He felt a real country bumpkin, sitting in that expensive restaurant, not knowing which cutlery to use.*

go to the 'country (*BrE*)
hold a general election: *The Prime Minister may decide to go to the country in the next few weeks.*

it's a free country → free
the mother country → mother

counts

it's the thought that counts → thought

couple

in a couple of shakes = in two shakes → two

courage

have/lack the courage of your con'victions
be/not be brave enough to do what you believe to be right: *You say that cruelty to animals is wrong, so why not have the courage of your convictions and join our campaign?*

pluck/screw/summon up (your/the) 'courage (to do sth)
force yourself to be brave enough to do sth: *I had liked her for a long time, and eventually I plucked up the courage to ask her out.* ◇ *I finally screwed up my courage and went to the dentist.*

take your ,courage in both 'hands
decide to do sth very brave: *I saw him screaming for help far out from the shore, so I took my courage in both hands and swam out to save him.*

Dutch courage → Dutch

course

a course of 'action
a way of doing, managing, or achieving sth: *What is the best course of action to take?* ◇ *Two alternative courses of action are open to us: either we deal with him directly or we get the help of a lawyer.*

in/over the course of …
(used with expressions for periods of time) during: *He's seen many changes in the course of his long life.* ◇ *The company faces some major challenges over the course of the next few years.*

in the ordinary, normal, etc. course of e'vents, 'things, etc.
as things usually happen: *In the normal course of events we would not treat her disappearance as suspicious.*

of 'course
1 (also **course**, *informal*) used to emphasize that what you are saying is true or correct: *'Don't you like my mother?' 'Of course I do!'* ◇ *'Will you be there?' 'Course I will.'*
2 (also **course**, *informal*) used as a polite way of giving sb permission to do sth: *'Can I come, too?' 'Course you can.'* ◇ *'Can I have one of those pens?' 'Of course—help yourself.'*
3 used as a polite way of agreeing with what sb has just said: *'I did all I could to help.' 'Of course,' he murmured gently.*
4 used to show that what you are saying is not surprising or is generally known or accepted: *Ben, of course, was the last to arrive.* ◇ *Of course, there are other ways of doing this.*

of 'course not (also **'course not**, *informal*)
used to emphasize the fact that you are saying 'no': *'Are you going?' 'Of course not.'* ◇ *'Do you mind?' 'No, of course not.'*

on 'course for sth/to do sth
likely to achieve or do sth because you have already started to do it: *The American economy is on course for higher inflation than Britain by the end of the year.*

run/take its 'course
(of a series of events, an illness, etc.) develop in the natural or usual way without being changed or

stopped: *The doctors agreed to let the illness run its course, rather than prescribe drugs which had little chance of success.* ◇ *We must allow justice to take its course.*

(do sth) as a matter of course → **matter**
be on a collision course (with sb/sth) → **collision**
be (about) par for the course → **par**
follow/steer/take a middle course → **middle**
in due course → **due**
pervert the course of justice → **pervert**
stay the course → **stay**

courses

horses for courses → **horses**

court

rule/throw sth out of 'court

make sth not worth considering; completely reject or exclude sth: *The committee ruled any further discussion on the matter out of court.* ◇ *My suggestion was ruled out of court because it was too expensive.*

the ball is in your/sb's court → **ball**
hold court → **hold**
laugh sb/sth out of court → **laugh**

courtesy

courtesy of sb/sth

1 (also **by courtesy of sb/sth**) with the official permission of sb/sth and as a favour: *The pictures have been reproduced by courtesy of the British Museum.*
2 given as a prize or provided free by a person or an organization: *Win a weekend in Rome, courtesy of Fiat.*
3 as the result of a particular thing or situation: *Viewers can see the stadium from the air, courtesy of a camera fastened to the plane.*

do sb the courtesy of doing sth

be polite by doing the thing that is mentioned: *Please do me the courtesy of listening to what I'm saying.*

have (got) the courtesy to do sth

know when you should do sth in order to be polite: *You think he'd at least have the courtesy to call to say he'd be late.*

cousin

a country bumpkin/cousin → **country**

Coventry

send sb to Coventry → **send**

cover

cover your 'back (*informal*) (*AmE* also **cover your 'ass** ⚠, *slang*)

realize that you may be attacked or criticized for sth later and make sure you avoid this: *Cover your back by getting everything in writing.*

cover your 'tracks

be careful not to leave any signs of sth secret or illegal that you have been doing: *He didn't want his wife to know he'd met an old girlfriend so he invented a story to cover his tracks.*

from ˌcover to 'cover

from the beginning to the end of a book, magazine, etc: *I've read the newspaper from cover to cover, but I can't find any mention of yesterday's accident.*

under 'cover

1 pretending to be sb else in order to do sth secretly: *a police officer working under cover*
2 under a structure that gives protection from the weather: *We'd better get under cover or we'll get very wet in this rain.*

under cover of sth

hidden or protected by sth: *They hoped to get into the enemy fortress under cover of darkness.*

blow sb's cover → **blow**
cover/hide a multitude of sins → **multitude**
don't judge a book by its cover → **judge**

cow

have a 'cow (*AmE, slang*)

suddenly become very excited or angry: *My dad spent $500 on a new coat and my mom had a cow.*

a sacred cow → **sacred**

cows

till/until the ˈcows come home (*informal*)

for a long time, or for ever: *You can talk till the cows come home, but you'll never persuade me to go with you!*

crack

crack a 'joke

tell a joke: *He's always cracking jokes in class.*

the crack of 'dawn (*informal*)

very early in the morning: *We'll have to get up at the crack of dawn to be there by 9 am.*

crack the 'whip

use your authority or power to make sb work very hard, usually by treating them in a strict way: *What you need to do is crack the whip and make sure that they do the job properly.*

have a ˈcrack at (doing) sth; get a ˈcrack at (doing) sth (*informal*)

make an attempt at doing sth: *Why not let me have a crack at fixing the kettle?* ◇ *When will we get a crack at the championship?*

a fair crack of the whip → **fair**
use a sledgehammer to crack a nut → **use**

cracked

not all, etc. he's, it's, etc. cracked 'up to be (*informal*)

not be as good, interesting, etc. as people claim: *The food in this restaurant is not all it's cracked up to be.* ◇ *She isn't the brilliant skier that she's been cracked up to be.*

cracking

get 'cracking (*informal*)
start doing sth quickly: *We'll have to get cracking with the painting if we want to be finished by Friday.* ◇ *There's an awful lot to do, so let's get cracking.*

cracks

paper over the cracks ➔ **paper**

cradle

from the ˌcradle to the 'grave
from birth to death; throughout your whole life: *The new ministry was formed to look after citizens' social welfare from the cradle to the grave.*

cramp

cramp sb's 'style
prevent sb from doing sth freely, or living as they want: *She thinks that having her parents to stay in her flat will cramp her style.* ◇ *Are you sure you don't mind me coming along? I'd hate to cramp your style!*

cranny

(in) every nook and cranny ➔ **nook**

crap

be full of shit/crap ➔ **full**
cut the crap ➔ **cut**

crash

crash and burn (*AmE, slang*)
1 fail completely: *She shot to fame, then crashed and burned.*
2 fall asleep or collapse because you are very tired

craw

stick in your throat/craw/gullet ➔ **stick**

crawl

come/crawl out of the woodwork ➔ **woodwork**
make your flesh creep/crawl ➔ **flesh**
make your skin crawl ➔ **skin**
a pub crawl ➔ **pub**

crazy

like 'crazy/'mad (*informal*)
very fast, hard, etc: *running/working like crazy*

cream

the ˌcream of the 'crop
the best people or things in a particular group: *Only the cream of the crop of the year's movies are nominated for an award.*

like the cat that got, stole, etc. the cream ➔ **cat**

create

cause/create a stir ➔ **stir**
create/make a scene ➔ **scene**
kick up/make/create/raise a stink (about sth) ➔ **stink**

creature

a creature of 'habit
a person who always does certain things at certain times: *My grandfather is a real creature of habit— he likes his meals at the same time every day.*

credit

do sb 'credit; do 'credit to sb; be to sb's 'credit
show sb's good qualities; make sb deserve praise: *The event was arranged with a speed and efficiency that does you credit.* ◇ *Their manager, to her credit, was always strongly opposed to the pay cuts.*

have sth to your 'credit
have achieved sth: *At the age of twenty-two he already has several tournament victories to his credit.*

on the 'credit side
used to introduce the good points about sb/sth, especially after the bad points have been mentioned: *If you work for yourself you may not make much money. On the credit side, you will be completely independent.*

creek

up the 'creek (*informal*) (also **up shit 'creek (without a 'paddle)** ⚠, *slang*)
in great difficulty: *Make sure you look after the money and passports—if they get stolen we'll be right up the creek.*

creep

make your flesh creep/crawl ➔ **flesh**

creeps

give sb the willies/heebie-jeebies/creeps ➔ **willies**

crème

the ˌcrème de la 'crème (*from French, formal* or *humorous*)
the best people or things of their kind: *This university takes only the crème de la crème of school leavers.* ◇ *Naturally, only the crème de la crème have been invited to the wedding.*

crest

(on) the crest of a 'wave
(at) the point of greatest success, wealth, happiness, etc: *He was fortunate to arrive in Hollywood when the film industry was on the crest of a wave.*

ride the crest of sth ➔ **ride**

crew

a skeleton crew/staff/service ➔ **skeleton**

cricket

it's (just) not 'cricket (*old-fashioned, BrE, informal*)
it is not a fair or honourable action or way of
behaving

crisp

burn sth to a cinder/crisp ➔ **burn**

crock

a ,crock of 'shit (⚠, *slang, especially AmE*)
something that is not true: *'He told me he was working yesterday.' 'What a crock of shit! I saw him
shopping in town!'*

crocodile

'crocodile tears
an insincere show of sadness: *They never visited
her when she was ill, but they came to her funeral
and wept a few crocodile tears.*

> ❶ ORIGIN
> When crocodiles produce tears, it is a physical
> response, not an emotional one.

Croesus

(as) rich as Croesus ➔ **rich**

crook

by hook or by crook ➔ **hook**

crop

the cream of the crop ➔ **cream**

cropper

come a 'cropper (*BrE, informal*)
1 fall (to the ground): *Pete came a cropper on his
motorbike and ended up in hospital.*
2 fail badly, usually when you are expected to do
well: *She's so confident she'll pass her exams without doing any work, but I've got a feeling she's going
to come a real cropper.*

cross

be/talk at cross 'purposes
(of two people or groups) misunderstand what the
other is referring to or trying to do: *Mary and I
spoke about Anne for a minute or two before I realized we were talking at cross purposes: I meant
Anne Smith and Mary meant Anne Harris.*

**cross a ,bridge when you 'come to it; cross
your ,bridges when you 'come to them**
deal with a problem only when it happens and not
worry about it before then: *'What will you do if you
can't afford to go on holiday next summer?' 'I'll
cross that bridge when I come to it.'*

cross sb's 'mind
(often used in negative sentences) (of a thought,
etc.) come into sb's mind for a short time: *He
intended to marry her and the thought never
crossed his mind that she might refuse.* ◇ *It had
crossed my mind that I hadn't seen her for a long
time so I decided to ring her.*

cross my 'heart (and hope to 'die)
used for emphasizing that you are sincere when
making a promise, or that what you say is true:
*'Don't tell anyone else about this, will you?' 'Cross
my heart, I won't.'*

cross sb's 'path; our/their paths 'cross
(we/they) meet by chance: *He never crossed my
path, the last person I
wanted to meet.* ◇ *Our paths crossed several times
during the war but after that I never saw him
again.*

cross the 'Rubicon (*formal*)
reach a point where an important decision is
taken which cannot be changed later: *Today we
cross the Rubicon. There is no going back.*

> ❶ ORIGIN
> This expression refers to the *Rubicon*, a stream
> which formed the border between Italy and
> Gaul. When Julius Caesar broke the law by
> crossing it with his army, it led inevitably to war.

cross 'swords (with sb)
have an argument (with sb): *At the committee meeting, I crossed swords with Professor Smith over her
department's overspending.*

**have (got) a (heavy) 'cross to bear; bear/
carry your 'cross**
suffer the trouble(s) that life brings to you: *We all
have our crosses to bear.*

cross your fingers = have/keep your fingers crossed ➔ **fingers**
dot the/your i's and cross the/your t's ➔ **dot**

crossed

**get your 'lines/'wires crossed; have (got)
crossed 'lines/'wires** (*informal*)
misunderstand each other: *I think we've got our
lines crossed somewhere. I said Venice, not Vienna.*
◇ *We must have got crossed wires. I thought you
were going to drive, not me.*

have/keep your fingers crossed ➔ **fingers**

crossfire

be caught in the crossfire ➔ **caught**

crossroads

at a 'crossroads
at a stage where a decision has to be made: *He's at
a crossroads in his career—either he stays in his
current job and waits for promotion, or he accepts
this new post in Brazil*

crow

as the 'crow flies (*informal*)
(of a distance) measured in a straight line: *From here to the village it's five miles as the crow flies, but it's a lot further by road.*

eat crow → eat

crowd

follow/go with the 'crowd (*often disapproving*)
do as everyone else does because you have no ideas of your own: *Dress in the way you like and try not to follow the crowd.*

crown

the jewel in the crown → jewel
to top/cap/crown it all → top

crows

stone the crows → stone

cruel

be ,cruel to be 'kind
use unpleasant methods because they are necessary to help sb: *I was worried about Katie getting too involved with Steve so I eventually told her about his drug addiction—you've got to be cruel to be kind sometimes.*

crumbles

that's the way the cookie crumbles → way

crunch

if/when it comes to the 'crunch (*informal*)
if/when the moment comes when sth must be decided or done, or a difficulty can no longer be avoided: *She was always threatening to leave him, but when it came to the crunch she didn't have the courage.*

crust

earn a/your crust → earn
the upper crust → upper

cry

cry your 'eyes out
cry a lot and for a long time: *My son cried his eyes out when we told him we couldn't afford a new bike.*

,cry 'foul (*informal*)
complain that sb else has done sth wrong or unfair: *When the Labour party candidate didn't win the election, he cried foul and demanded a recount.*

cry 'wolf
repeatedly say there is danger, etc. when there is none, or ask for help when there is no need (with the result that people do not think you are telling the truth when there is real danger or when you really need help): *Is the economic future really so bad? Or are the economists just crying wolf?*

❶ ORIGIN
This refers to the traditional story of the shepherd boy who shouted 'Wolf!' just to frighten people, so that when a wolf did come, nobody went to help him.

cry/ask for the moon → moon
a far cry from sth → far
a hue and cry → hue
in full cry → full
not know whether to laugh or cry → know
a shoulder to cry on → shoulder

crying

be a crying 'shame (*spoken*)
used to emphasize that you think sth is extremely bad or shocking: *It's a crying shame to waste all that food.*

a crying 'need (for sth)
a great and urgent need for sth: *There's a crying need for more roads, but at the same time the wildlife needs to be preserved.*

for ,crying out 'loud (*spoken, informal*)
used to express anger or frustration: *For crying out loud! How many times have I asked you not to do that?*

it's no good/use crying over spilt 'milk (*saying*)
it is a waste of time worrying, complaining or feeling sad about sth which is done and cannot be changed: *His decision to resign was disappointing, but it's no use crying over spilt milk. We need to concentrate on finding someone to replace him.*

crystal

,crystal 'clear
very easy to understand; completely obvious: *After Anne was late for the third time in a week, her boss made it crystal clear that it must not happen again.*

cucumber

(as) cool as a cucumber → cool

cudgels

take up the 'cudgels for sb/sth; take up the cudgels on behalf of sb/sth (*old-fashioned, written*)
start to defend or support sb/sth: *The local newspapers have taken up the cudgels on behalf of the woman who was unfairly dismissed from her job because she was pregnant.*

❷ NOTE
A *cudgel* is a short thick stick that is used as a weapon.

cue

(right) on 'cue
just at the appropriate moment: *The bell sounded for the beginning of the lesson, and, right on cue, the teacher walked in.*

take your 'cue from sb
be influenced in your actions by what sb else has done: *In designing the car, we took our cue from other designers who aimed to combine low cost with low petrol consumption.*

cuff

,off the 'cuff
without previous thought or preparation: *I don't know how you can stand up and give an after-dinner speech off the cuff like that.* ◇ *an off-the-cuff remark*

culpa

mea culpa ➔ **mea**

cup

not be sb's cup of 'tea (*informal, spoken*)
not be the (kind of) person, thing or activity that you like: *He invited me to the opera but it's not really my cup of tea.*

there's many a slip 'twixt cup and lip ➔ **slip**

cupboard

the ,cupboard is 'bare (*BrE*)
used to say that there is no money for sth: *They are seeking more funds but the cupboard is bare.*

> ❶ ORIGIN
> This expression refers to a children's nursery rhyme about Old Mother Hubbard, who had nothing in her cupboard to feed her dog.

'cupboard love (*BrE*)
affection that sb shows towards sb else in order to get sth: *The cat seems especially fond of her, but it's just cupboard love. She's the one who feeds him.*

a skeleton in the cupboard/closet ➔ **skeleton**

Cupid

play Cupid ➔ **play**

curate

(like) the curate's 'egg (, good in parts) (*BrE*)
sth that has some good things and some bad things about it: *'Is it an interesting book?' 'A bit like the curate's egg, good in parts. The dialogue's often quite amusing.'*

cure

kill or cure ➔ **kill**

an ounce of prevention is better than a pound of cure = prevention is better than cure ➔ **prevention**

curiosity

curiosity killed the 'cat (*saying*)
used to tell sb not to ask so many questions, especially in reply to a question that you do not want to answer: *'Are you two thinking of getting married by any chance?' 'Now, now. Curiosity killed the cat!'*

curl

make sb's hair curl ➔ **hair**
make sb's toes curl ➔ **toes**

curlies

get/have sb by the short and curlies ➔ **short**

curry

curry 'favour (with sb) (*BrE*) (*AmE* **curry 'favor (with sb)**) (*disapproving*)
try to get sb to like or support you by praising or helping them a lot: *He's always trying to curry favour with the director by telling her how talented she is.*

curtain

bring/ring down the 'curtain (on sth); bring/ring the 'curtain down (on sth)
bring an end to sth: *The BBC has finally decided to bring the curtain down on one of its oldest television programmes.*

the curtain comes down on sth
if the curtain comes down on sth, it ends: *On Saturday the curtain came down on another Olympic Games.*

curtains

be ,curtains for 'sb/'sth (*informal*)
cause the death of sb or the end of sth: *It'll be curtains for the business if the bank doesn't give us that loan.*

cushion

cushion/soften the blow ➔ **blow**

cushy

a cushy 'number (*BrE*)
an easy job; a pleasant situation that other people would like: *Sarah's new job sounds like a right cushy number—she only has to go to the office three days a week.*

customer

a tough customer/cookie ➔ **tough**

cut

be cut 'out for sb/sth; be cut 'out to be sth
be well suited in character or ability to sb, a job, or activity: *She wasn't a great journalist. She was more cut out for television reporting.* ◇ *Why did he join the army? He's really not cut out to be a soldier.*

a cut a'bove sb/sth

better than sb/sth: *This is a cut above the average weekly magazine—it publishes very good articles and short stories.*

cut and 'dried

(of matters, arrangements or opinions) completely decided and unlikely to be changed: *By the end of the evening their plans for carrying out the robbery were cut and dried, with nothing left to chance.* ◇ *The police thought they had a cut-and-dried case.*

cut and 'run (*BrE, informal*)

make a quick or sudden escape: *She can't rely on Jason—he's the type to cut and run as soon as things get difficult.*

the cut and 'thrust (of sth) (*BrE*)

the lively exchange of opinions or ideas; competitiveness: *He enjoys the cut and thrust of business.*

(you could) ,cut the ,atmosphere with a 'knife (*informal*)

used to say that the emotional tension, embarrassment, etc. shared by a group of people is very great: *When John came in with his new girlfriend, you could have cut the atmosphere with a knife.*

cut both/two 'ways

have an effect both for and against sb/sth: *Banning imports of cars could cut both ways: other countries may ban the import of cars produced here.*

cut the 'cackle (*informal*)

stop talking and start working, etc. properly; start talking about the important matters: *Let's cut the cackle and get down to business.*

cut your 'coat according to your 'cloth (*saying*)

do only what you have enough money to do and no more: *This has not been a good year for us financially, and we must be prepared to cut our coat according to our cloth.*

cut 'corners (*disapproving*)

do things in the easiest, quickest or cheapest way and not in the proper way: *Don't be tempted to cut corners when doing a home decorating job.*

cut the 'crap (⚠, *slang*)

used to tell sb in an impolite way to stop talking about unimportant things or talking nonsense and get to the main point: *Cut the crap and tell me what you really think, OK?*

cut a 'dash (*BrE*)

impress others by your elegant appearance or behaviour: *She cuts quite a dash with her designer clothes and expensive car.*

cut sb 'dead

pretend not to see sb or not greet sb in order to show your anger, dislike, etc: *Jim has just cut me dead in the street. I'm sure it must be because I criticized his work yesterday.*

cut sb down to 'size

show that sb is less important than they seem or

think: *Failing his exams has certainly cut him down to size.*

cut a fine, poor, sorry, etc. 'figure

have a fine, etc. appearance: *In his brand new uniform he cut a fine figure.*

(to be) cut from the same 'cloth

(be) very similar in character, quality, experience, etc: *Don't assume all the women in our family are cut from the same cloth.*

cut the ground from under sb/sb's 'feet

suddenly spoil sb's idea or plan by doing sth to stop them from continuing with it: *When he announced that all my figures were out of date, he really cut the ground from under my feet.*

cut it/things 'fine

allow only just enough time to do sth: *Your train leaves in twenty minutes and you're still here! You're cutting it a bit fine, aren't you?*

cut your 'losses

stop doing sth that is not successful before the situation becomes even worse: *When our rent went up we decided to cut our losses and shut the shop.*

(not) cut the 'mustard

(not) be as good as expected or required: *I didn't cut the mustard as a hockey player.*

❶ ORIGIN
This idiom probably comes from an old use of the word *mustard* meaning 'the best'.

cut no 'ice (with sb)

not impress or influence sb: *Her aggressive manner may be very useful at work, but it cuts no ice with me.* ◇ *Public protests don't cut much ice with this government.*

cut off your 'nose to spite your 'face (*informal*)

do sth, for example because you are angry or proud, that is intended to hurt sb else but in fact harms you: *Keeping your class in after school as a punishment is cutting off your nose to spite your face, because you have to stay in with them!*

cut your own 'throat

do sth that is likely to harm you, especially when you are angry and trying to harm sb else: *You cut your own throat when you told him to leave. How are you going to manage alone?*

cut sb 'short

stop sb speaking: *She was just about to say who had got the job, but I cut her short and asked her to keep it secret.*

cut sth 'short

make sth end before the natural time; interrupt sth: *We'll have to cut our stay short, I'm afraid. My husband's father is seriously ill.* ◇ *Our conversation was cut short by the arrival of the teacher.*

cut sb some 'slack (*informal, especially AmE*)

make things easier than usual for sb; allow sb more freedom to do things than they would normally have: *I know I made a mistake, but it's my first week on the job, so cut me some slack, OK?*

cut a 'swathe through sth
(of a person, fire, etc.) pass through a particular area destroying a large part of it: *The new road cut a swathe through the countryside.*

cut your 'teeth on sth
learn or gain experience from sth: *It was a small experimental theatre company and many of today's most successful actors cut their teeth there.*

cut to the 'chase (*informal, especially AmE*)
stop wasting time and do or say the important things that need to be done or said: *Let's cut to the chase. How much is it going to cost me?*

> ❶ ORIGIN
> This expression comes from the device used in films / movies of changing from a slower scene to a more exciting one, such as a car chase, to keep the audience interested.

cut sb to the 'quick
hurt sb's feelings; offend sb deeply: *It cut her to the quick to hear him criticizing her family like that.*

cut up 'rough/'nasty (*informal*)
behave or react in an angry, bad-tempered or violent way: *I didn't want to ask Jo for money, but Billy had cut up rough when I couldn't pay him back.*

to cut a long story 'short (*BrE*) (*AmE* to make a long story 'short) (*spoken*)
used when a speaker is not going to describe all the details of sth, only the final result: *'What happened at the meeting?' 'Well, to cut a long story short, ten people are going to lose their jobs.'*

break/cut/tear (sth) loose from sb/sth → **loose**
cut/untie the Gordian knot → **Gordian**
cut loose = let loose → **let**
fish or cut bait → **fish**
have (got) your work cut out (to do sth/doing sth) → **work**
a short cut (to sth) → **short**

cute

(as) cute as a 'button (*AmE*)
(usually used about a baby or a child, or sb/sth small) very attractive and charming: *Kate is four, and as cute as a button!*

cutting

(be at) the cutting 'edge (of sth)
(be at) the newest, most advanced stage in the development of sth: *working at the cutting edge of computer technology*

cylinders

firing/working on all 'cylinders (*informal*)
using all your energy to do sth; working as well as possible: *The 24-year-old player feels that he is not yet firing on all cylinders.*

D d

dab

be a dab 'hand at (doing) sth (*BrE, informal*)
be very good at doing sth: *Ask Neil to do it—he's a dab hand at carpentry.*

daddy

a sugar daddy → **sugar**

daft

(as) ˌdaft as a 'brush (*BrE, spoken*)
(of a person) very silly

daggers

be at daggers 'drawn (with sb)
(be ready to) fight or argue (with sb): *They've been at daggers drawn ever since he borrowed her car and smashed it up.*

> **❷ NOTE**
> If you *draw* a weapon (= a gun, a dagger, etc.), you take it out in order to attack sb.

look daggers at sb → **look**

daily

your daily 'bread
the food or money that you need to live: *Each one of us has to earn our daily bread somehow.*

daisies

be pushing up (the) daisies → **pushing**

daisy

(as) fresh as a daisy → **fresh**

dale

up hill and down dale → **hill**

damage

what's the 'damage? (*BrE, informal*)
how much do I need to pay you?: *Thanks for repairing the cooker. What's the damage?*

dammit

as near as dammit → **near**

damn

damn the consequences, expense, etc. (*spoken*)
used to say that you are going to do sth even though you know it may be expensive, have bad results, etc: *Let's celebrate and damn the expense!*

damn it (all) (*informal*)
used for expressing anger, annoyance, etc: *I've broken my pen again, damn it!*

damn sb/sth with faint 'praise
praise sb/sth so little that you seem to be criticizing them/it: *All he said was that I was 'capable'. Talk about damning someone with faint praise!*

not care/give a 'damn (about/for sb/sth) (*informal*)
not care at all about sb/sth: *Steve doesn't give a damn about anybody except himself.*

damned

I'll be 'damned (*old-fashioned, spoken*)
used for expressing surprise: *Well, I'll be damned! Isn't that Sarah Parker over there?*

I'm/I'll be 'damned if … (*BrE also* **I'm/I'll be 'blowed if …**) (*spoken*)
I certainly will not, do not, etc: *I'm damned if I will lend any money to that lazy son of mine.* ◇ *'Why is she so late?' 'I'll be blowed if I know.'*

damnedest

do/try your 'damnedest (*informal*)
try very hard; make a very great effort: *He was doing his damnedest to make me feel uncomfortable so that I would leave.*

Damocles

a/the sword of Damocles → **sword**

damp

a damp 'squib (*BrE, informal*)
an event, experience, etc. that is expected to be interesting or exciting, but is in fact boring or ordinary: *In the end, the party turned out to be rather a damp squib.*

> **❷ NOTE**
> A *squib* is a type of small firework. If it is damp, it will not burn properly.

damper

put a 'damper on sth (*also* **put a 'dampener on sth**) (*informal*)
make an event, etc. less enjoyable or cheerful: *The news of my father's illness put a bit of a damper on the birthday celebrations.*

> **❷ NOTE**
> A *damper* is a device in a piano that is used to reduce the level of the sound produced.

damsel

a ˌdamsel in diˈstress (*humorous*)
a woman who needs help from a man, often to solve
a practical problem: *When I got a flat tyre I had to
wait for my boyfriend to come and help me, like a
true damsel in distress!*

❷ **NOTE**
Damsel is an old word for a young woman who is
not married.

dance

ˌdance atˈtendance on sb (*BrE, formal*)
do a lot of small jobs in order to please sb: *She
always has an assistant dancing attendance on her.*

dance to sb's ˈtune (*BrE*)
do whatever sb tells you to: *They are richer and
more powerful than us so unfortunately we have to
dance to their tune.*

lead sb a (merry) dance → **lead**
make a song and dance about sth → **song**

dancing

all singing, all dancing → **singing**

danger

be on/off the ˈdanger list (*BrE*)
be so ill that you may die; no longer be very ill: *He's
been extremely sick, but thankfully he's off the danger list now.*

dangerous

dangerous ˈground
a situation or subject that is likely to make sb
angry, or that involves risk: *We'd be on dangerous
ground if we asked about race or religion.*

dare

don't you ˈdare (do sth)! (*spoken*)
used to tell sb strongly not to do sth: *'I'll tell her
about it.' 'Don't you dare!'* ◇ *Don't you dare say
anything to anybody.*

how ˈdare you, he, etc. (do sth)? (*spoken*)
used for expressing anger or shock about sth that
sb has done: *How dare you speak to me like that!* ◇
How dare he use my office without permission?

I dare ˈsay (*spoken*)
I suppose; it seems probable: *I dare say what you
say is true, but it's too late to change our plans now.*

dark

a dark ˈhorse (*BrE*)
a person who hides their feelings, plans, activities,
etc: *You're a dark horse! I had no idea you could
play the piano so well.*

❶ **ORIGIN**
This phrase comes from horse racing. Horses that
often won races were darkened to hide their identity
so that more money could be won from the betting.

in the ˈdark (about sth)
knowing nothing about sth: *Workers were kept in
the dark about the plans to sell the company.* ◇ *She
arrived at the meeting as much in the dark as everyone else.*

keep it/sth ˈdark (from sb) (*BrE, informal*)
keep sth secret: *I've got a new job, but keep it dark,
won't you?*

a shot/stab in the ˈdark
a guess; sth you do without knowing what the
result will be: *The figure he came up with was
really just a shot in the dark.*

a leap in the dark → **leap**
whistle in the dark → **whistle**

darken

not/never darken sb's ˌdoor aˈgain (*old-
fashioned or humorous*)
not/never come to sb's home again because you
are not welcome: *Go! And never darken my door
again!*

darn

ˈdarn it! (*spoken, especially AmE*)
used as a mild swear word to show that you are
angry or annoyed about sth, to avoid saying
'damn': *Darn it! I've lost my keys!*

darned

I'll be ˈdarned! (*spoken, especially AmE*)
used to show that you are surprised about sth:
Well, I'll be darned! Isn't that Lisa over there?

dash

cut a dash → **cut**
dash/shatter sb's hopes → **hopes**
make a bolt/dash for it/sth → **bolt**

date

ˌout of ˈdate
not modern; not including the latest information:
This atlas is out of date. ◇ *I'm afraid you must
have been using an out-of-date catalogue.*

to ˈdate
up to and including the present time: *To date,
we've received 40 bookings for the holiday, so we're
doing quite well.*

ˌup to ˈdate
1 possessing the most recent information, ideas,
etc. about sth/sb: *Are you keeping up to date with
the latest developments?* ◇ *I'm not really up to date
on John and Mary. Are they still together?*
2 the most recent, modern or fashionable: *His kitchen is **bang up to date**. He's got all the latest technology in it.*

be past its sell-by date → **past**
a blind date → **blind**

daughter

like father/mother, like son/daughter → **father**

daunted

nothing 'daunted (*BrE, formal*)
confident about sth difficult that you have to do:
*Nothing daunted, the people set about rebuilding
their homes after the fire.*

dawn

the crack of dawn → **crack**

dawns

(the) light dawns (on sb) → **light**

day

,all day and 'every day
without change for a long period of time: *I have to
be active. I couldn't just sit around all day and every
day now I've retired.*

all in a day's 'work
part of your normal working life and not unusual
(especially of events or activities that are considered difficult or unpleasant): *For a nurse, calm-
ing the fears of anxious relatives is all in a day's
work.*

any day (now) (*spoken*)
very soon: *The letter should arrive any day now.*

'any day (of the week)
used for showing that you prefer one thing or person to another: *I'd rather have him than his
brother any day of the week.*

carry/win the 'day (*formal*)
win a contest, argument, etc.; be successful: *It was
a difficult match, but the New Zealand team finally
carried the day.*

day after 'day
for many days, one after the other: *Day after day,
she came and waited in his office, until finally he
agreed to see her.*

day by 'day
all the time; as the days pass: *Day by day she grew
more confident about the job.*

day ,in, day 'out
every day for a long period of time: *I drive to work
day in, day out, and I'm getting tired of spending so
much time travelling.*

the day of 'reckoning (*formal*)
the time when good actions, successes, etc. or bad
actions, failures, etc. will be made known and punished or rewarded: *Tomorrow is the day of
reckoning; the accountant will tell me what my
profits were and how much tax I'll have to pay.*

don't give up the 'day job (*informal, humorous*)
used to tell sb that they should continue doing
what they are used to, rather than trying sth new
which they are likely to fail at: *So you want to be a
writer? Well my advice is, don't give up the day job.*

from day 'one (*spoken*)
from the beginning: *This arrangement has never
worked from day one.*

from day to 'day
1 with no thoughts or plans for the future: *They
both live from day to day, looking after their sick
daughter.*
2 if a situation changes **from day to day**, it
changes often: *A baby's need for food can vary from
day to day.*

from ,one day to the 'next
if a situation changes **from one day to the next**,
it is uncertain and not likely to stay the same each
day: *In this job, I never know what to expect from
one day to the next.*

have had your/its 'day
no longer be as successful, powerful, etc. as you
once were/it once was: *He used to be one of the
world's top soccer players but now, I'm afraid, he's
had his day.*

**he's, she's, etc. 60, 70, etc. ,if he's, she's,
etc. a 'day** (*informal*)
he's, she's, etc. at least 60, 70, etc. years old: *She
isn't forty! She's fifty-five if she's a day!*

in 'sb's day/time
1 when sb was most successful, famous, etc: *He
had, in his day, been one of the greatest opera singers in the world.*
2 at the time when sb was alive; when sb was
young: *In my grandmother's time, women were
expected to stay at home and look after the children.*
◇ *In my day, nobody would have spoken to the boss
like that.*

in 'this day and age
at the present time; nowadays: *It's surprising, in
this day and age, to discover that there are still
many homes which do not have telephones.*

make sb's 'day (*informal*)
make sb very happy: *Thanks for sending me those
flowers. It really made my day!*

make a 'day of it (*spoken*)
make a particular enjoyable activity last for a
whole day instead of only part of it: *Instead of
going home when we've done our shopping, why
don't we make a day of it and stay in town for
lunch?*

not be sb's 'day (*spoken*)
be a day when a lot of things go wrong for sb: *First
I tore my jacket, then my car broke down. This is definitely not my day!*

'one day
at some time in the future or in the past: *One day
I'd like to go to China.* ◇ *One day we decided to go to
the seaside.*

'some day
at a time in the future: *Some day you'll realize what
good parents you have.*

take it/things one ,day at a 'time (*spoken*)
not think about what will happen in the future: *I don't know if he'll get better. We're just taking things one day at a time.*

'that'll be the day (*spoken, ironic*)
used for saying that sth is unlikely: *'When I'm rich, I'll buy you a new car.' 'That'll be the day!'*

to the 'day
exactly: *It's ten years to the day since I first came to this town.*

to this 'day
up to now: *To this day I have not been able to find out anything about who my real parents were.*

at the end of the day → **end**
a bad hair day → **hair**
a black day (for sb) → **black**
call it a day → **call**
(as) clear as day → **clear**
day and night = night and day → **night**
every dog has his/its day → **dog**
the evil hour/day/moment → **evil**
from that day/time forth → **forth**
your good deed for the day → **deed**
(as) happy as the day is long/as a clam/as Larry → **happy**
have a field day → **field**
have a nice day! → **nice**
in the cold light of day → **cold**
late in the day → **late**
(see) the light of day → **light**
live to fight another day → **live**
name the day → **name**
night and day → **night**
not give sb the time of day → **time**
the order of the day → **order**
pass the time of day (with sb) → **pass**
(as) plain as day → **plain**
the present day → **present**
a red-letter day → **red-letter**
Rome wasn't built in a day → **Rome**
save the day/situation → **save**
save, keep, etc. it for a rainy day → **rainy**
till/to/until your dying day → **dying**

daylight

,daylight 'robbery (*informal*)
a price or fee that you think is far too high: *£3000 for a useless old car like this? That's daylight robbery!*

in broad daylight → **broad**
see daylight → **see**

daylights

beat/scare the (living) 'daylights out of sb (*informal*)
hit sb/sth very hard and repeatedly; frighten sb very much: *He said if I did it again he'd beat the living daylights out of me!* ◇ *I don't think I'll go to see that new horror film at the cinema. Jane said it scared the daylights out of her.*

days

your, its, etc. days are 'numbered
sb has not long left to live; sth will not last much longer: *Now that we're no longer getting any government support, the theatre's days are numbered.*

'one of these days
at some unspecified time in the future; before a long time has passed: *It's been nice talking to you. We must meet up again one of these days.* ◇ *One of these (fine) days you'll find that you have no friends left, and who'll help you then?*

(just) one of those 'days
a day on which unpleasant things happen: *It's been one of those days. I lost my keys and then I fell over running for the bus.*

'these days
at the present time, as compared with an earlier time; nowadays: *Divorce is getting more and more common these days.*

'those were the days
used for talking about a better or happier time in the past: *'They bought the house for £600 in 1930.' 'Ah, those were the days!'*

end your days/life (in sth) → **end**
the good/bad old days → **old**
have seen/known better days → **better**
high days and holidays → **high**
in all my born days → **born**
it's early days (yet) → **early**
a nine days' wonder → **nine**
your salad days → **salad**

dead

dead and 'buried/'gone
dead, especially for a long time; long past and forgotten: *Long after I'm dead and gone, you'll still be carrying on the same as you ever were.* ◇ *Why bring up old disagreements that have been dead and buried for years?*

(as) dead as a/the 'dodo (*informal*)
no longer in existence; very old-fashioned: *Old business practices are as dead as a dodo in the computer age.*

❷ NOTE
The dodo was a large bird that could not fly. It is now extinct (= it no longer exists).

(as) ,dead as a 'doornail (*informal*)
completely dead

a dead 'cert (*informal*)
a person or thing that is certain to win, succeed, etc: *'Would you ever bet money on a horse?' 'No, not unless it was a dead cert.'*

a dead 'duck (*informal*)
a plan, idea, etc. that has failed or is certain to fail and that is therefore not worth discussing: *They say that the new supermarket is going to be a dead duck because there's no demand for one in this area.*

a dead 'end (*informal*)
a point where no more progress can be made: *Lack of further clues meant that the murder investigation came to a dead end.* ◊ *He was in a dead-end job with no hope of promotion.*

the dead hand of sth (*written*)
an influence that controls or restricts sth: *We need to free business from the dead hand of bureaucracy.*

ˌdead in the 'water
a person or plan that is **dead in the water** has failed and has little hope of succeeding in the future: *Now the scandal is out, his leadership campaign is dead in the water.*

a dead 'letter
an idea, proposal, etc. that is no longer valid, useful, etc: *The plans for a new school are a dead letter, now that we know there will be no pupils for it.*

a dead 'loss
a person or thing that is useless or a complete failure: *This television is a dead loss; the picture fades completely after five minutes.*

dead 'meat (*informal*)
in serious trouble: *If anyone finds out, you're dead meat.*

(in) the ˌdead of (the) 'night; at ˌdead of 'night
in the quietest, darkest hours of the night: *She crept in at dead of night, while they were asleep.*

a dead 'ringer for sb (*informal*)
a person who looks extremely like sb else: *She's a dead ringer for her mother.*

> **❶ ORIGIN**
> This expression comes from horse racing. A *ringer* was a horse that was substituted for another in order to cheat in a race.

ˌdead to the 'world (*informal*)
deeply asleep: *Within two minutes of getting into bed, I was dead to the world.*

ˌdead 'wood (*informal*)
people or things that are no longer useful or necessary: *The management wants to cut costs by getting rid of all the dead wood in the factory. Fifty workers are to lose their jobs.*

I, he, etc. wouldn't be seen/caught 'dead … (*spoken*)
I, he, etc. would not do a certain thing because I, he, etc. would feel stupid or embarrassed: *I wouldn't be seen dead in a hat like that.* ◊ *She wouldn't be caught dead in a place like this.*

over ˌmy dead 'body (*spoken*)
used for saying that you will do everything possible to stop sth happening: *'Mum, can I get a tattoo?' 'Over my dead body!'*

cut sb dead → **cut**
dead to rights = bang to rights → **bang**
drop dead → **drop**
flog a dead horse → **flog**
kill sth stone dead → **kill**
knock sb dead → **knock**

stop dead → **stop**
wake the dead → **wake**

deaf

(as) deaf as a 'post (*informal*)
unable to hear anything: *You'll have to shout if you want her to hear you. She's as deaf as a post.*

fall on deaf ears → **fall**
turn a deaf ear (to sth) → **turn**

deal

deal sb/sth a 'blow; deal a blow to sb/sth
be a shock for sb; make sth fail, etc: *The death of her father dealt her a terrible blow.* ◊ *Losing his job dealt a blow to his hopes of buying his own house.*

a raw/rough 'deal
unfair treatment: *Many old people feel they are getting a raw deal from the state: they pay money towards a pension all their working life but discover it isn't worth much when they retire.*

big deal → **big**
a done deal → **done**
no big deal → **big**
strike a bargain/deal (with sb) → **strike**
wheel and deal → **wheel**

dear

dear me; (dear,) oh dear
used for expressing worry, sympathy, concern, etc: *Dear me! It's started to rain and I've just hung out the washing!*

for dear 'life; for your 'life
because you are in danger: *Run for your life! A tiger has escaped from the circus!* ◊ *They were clinging for dear life to the edge of the rock.*

be close/dear/near to sb's heart → **heart**
hold sb/sth dear → **hold**
an old dear → **old**

dearest

your nearest and dearest → **nearest**

death

at death's 'door (*often ironic*)
so ill that you might die: *Come on, get out of bed. You're not at death's door yet!*

be the 'death of sb (*often humorous*)
cause sb a lot of harm or worry: *You children are so badly behaved! You'll be the death of me one day!*

be ˌin at the 'death/'kill
be there when sth ends or fails: *I was in at the kill when the Professor finally won the debate against his opponents.*

ˌdo sth to 'death (*informal*)
talk or write about a subject, or perform a play, etc. so often that it is no longer interesting: *Some people think that the theme of romantic love has been done to death in poetry.*

like death warmed 'up (*BrE*) (*AmE* **like death warmed 'over**) (*informal*)
very ill or tired: *I feel like death warmed up this morning, but I'm going to go to work anyway.* ◇ *You should really go home to bed. You look like death warmed up.*

put sb to 'death
kill sb as a punishment; execute sb: *The prisoner will be put to death at dawn.*

to 'death
extremely; very much: *to be bored/frightened/scared/worried to death* ◇ *I'm sick to death of your endless criticism.*

to the 'death
until sb dies or is defeated: *There was a fight to the death between two men armed with knives.*

be tickled to death → **tickled**
catch your death (of cold) → **catch**
dice with death → **dice**
die a/the death → **die**
a fate worse than death → **fate**
flog sth to death → **flog**
hang on/hold on (to sth) like grim death → **grim**
the kiss of death → **kiss**
life after death → **life**
(a matter of) life and/or death → **life**
sign your own death warrant → **sign**
sound the death knell of sth → **sound**
sudden death → **sudden**
work yourself/sb to death → **work**

debt

be in sb's 'debt (*formal*)
be very grateful to sb because they have helped you: *After my divorce Ann was the only one prepared to listen to my problems, and I am forever in her debt.*

,get/,run into 'debt
begin to owe money: *After she lost her job, she began to run into debt.*

deck

all hands on deck → **hands**
clear the deck(s) → **clear**
hit the deck → **hit**

deckchairs

rearrange the deckchairs on the Titanic → **rearrange**

deed

your good deed for the 'day
a helpful, kind thing that you do: *Why don't you do your good deed for the day and help me cook dinner?*

deep

deep 'down (*informal*)
in your most private thoughts; in reality rather than in appearance: *She's very generous deep down, but this only comes out when you get to know her.* ◇ *He seems very confident but deep down I think he's quite shy.*

(in) deep 'water
(involved in) very difficult, complicated or dangerous affairs: *She was getting into deep water when she tried to argue that murder is sometimes justified for political reasons.*

go/run 'deep
(of emotions, beliefs, etc.) be felt in a strong way, especially for a long time: *Dignity and pride run deep in this community.*

go off the 'deep end (*informal*)
suddenly become very angry or emotional: *Don't tell your father that you lost the money—he'll just go off the deep end.*

jump in/be thrown in at the 'deep end (*informal*)
try to do sth difficult without help when you are not prepared or know very little about it: *On the first day of her new teaching job, she was thrown in at the deep end and was told to teach the most badly-behaved class.* ◇ *I didn't know anything about business when I started. I just had to jump in at the deep end.*

> **❶ ORIGIN**
> This phrase refers to the deep end of a swimming pool, where it is too deep to stand.

be in deep shit = be in the shit → **shit**
between the devil and the deep blue sea → **devil**
dig deep → **dig**
still waters run deep → **still**

default

by de'fault
1 a game or competition can be won **by default** if there are no other competitors: *The other team didn't even turn up, so we won by default.*
2 if sth happens **by default**, it happens because you have not made any other decision or choices which would make things happen differently: *It was never my ambition to get into teaching. I became a teacher more by default than by choice.*

in de'fault of sth (*formal*)
because of a lack of sth: *They accepted what he had said in default of any evidence to disprove it.*

defensive

on/onto the de'fensive
acting in a way that shows that you expect to be attacked or criticized; having to defend yourself: *Their questions about the money put her on the defensive.* ◇ *Warnings of an enemy attack forced the troops onto the defensive.*

degree

(give sb) the third degree → **third**
to the nth degree → **nth**

degrees

by de'grees
little by little; gradually: *The country's economy won't improve straight away, but will only get better by degrees.*

déjà

,déjà 'vu *(from French)*
the feeling that you have previously experienced sth which is happening to you now: *I had a strong sense of déjà vu as I walked into the room.*

> **❷ NOTE**
> The meaning of the French phrase is 'already seen'.

deliver

come up with/deliver/produce the goods → goods

delivered

signed, sealed and delivered → signed

delivery

cash on delivery → cash

delusions

delusions of 'grandeur *(often humorous)*
a belief that you are more important than you really are: *He's been suffering from delusions of grandeur ever since he became manager.*

demand

in de'mand
wanted by many people; popular: *Beautiful old houses like this one are always in great demand.* ◊ *Well-qualified young people with experience in marketing are very much in demand at the moment.*

on de'mand
done or happening whenever sb asks: *Feed the baby on demand.*

by popular demand → popular

demon

the demon 'drink *(BrE, humorous)*
alcoholic drink: *It was the demon drink that made me act in that way.*

demur

without de'mur *(formal)*
without objecting or hesitating: *They accepted without demur.*

den

a den of i'niquity/'vice *(disapproving)*
a place where people do bad things: *She thinks that just because we sit around smoking and drinking beer the club must be a real den of iniquity.*

the lion's den → lion

dent

make a 'dent/'hole in sth *(informal)*
reduce sth: *Having to pay out unexpectedly for car repairs made a big hole in my savings.* ◊ *The embarrassing stories about his past made quite a dent in his reputation.*

department

be sb's department *(spoken)*
be sth that sb is responsible for or knows a lot about: *Don't ask me about it—that's Helen's department, not mine.*

departure

a point of departure → point

depends

it/that (all) de'pends *(informal)*
perhaps; possibly: *'Would you marry him if he asked you to?' 'I might. It all depends.'* ◊ *'But is it right to send people to prison?' 'It depends what you mean by right!'*

depth

,in 'depth
thoroughly: *The report treats the subject of homelessness in some depth.* ◊ *an in-depth analysis, discussion, etc.*

out of your 'depth *(informal)*
in a situation that is too difficult for you to deal with or understand: *When they start talking about economics, I'm out of my depth.*

depths

in the depths of sth
at the worst or most unpleasant stage of sth: *in the depths of despair, poverty, depression, etc.* ◊ *in the depths of winter*

plumb the depths of sth → plumb

description

beggar belief/description → beggar

deserting

(like rats) deserting/leaving a sinking ship → sinking

deserts

your/sb's (just) de'serts
what you/sb deserves, especially when it is sth bad: *The family of the victim said that the killer had got his just deserts when he was jailed for life.*

> **❶ ORIGIN**
> This phrase originates from the old French word *deservir*, meaning 'to deserve'.

deserve

,get what you de'serve; de,serve all/everything
 you 'get (informal)
used to say that you think sb has earned the bad
things that happen to them: I'm not sorry he's in
prison. In my opinion he got what he deserved.

deserves

he, she, etc. de,serves a 'medal (spoken)
used to say that you admire sb because they have
done sth difficult or unpleasant: You deserve a
medal for what you've done for him over the years.

one good turn deserves another → turn

design

(whether) by accident or design → accident

designs

have (got) de'signs on sb/sth
intend to take sb/sth for yourself, for example a
job or a person who you find sexually attractive:
Several people have got designs on the office
manager's post. ◇ I think she's got designs on you,
Peter.

desired

leave a lot, much, etc. to be desired → leave

detail

go into 'detail(s)
explain sth fully: I can't go into details now; it
would take too long.

devices

leave sb to their own devices → leave

devil

be a 'devil (BrE)
said to encourage sb to do sth that they are not
sure about doing: Go on, be a devil, Catherine! Buy
yourself some new clothes for once!

between the ,devil and the deep blue 'sea
in a situation where you have to choose between
two things that are equally bad: In this situation,
the government finds itself caught between the devil
and the deep blue sea.

the 'devil (old-fashioned)
very difficult or unpleasant: These berries are the
devil to pick because they're so small.

the ,devil looks after his 'own (saying)
bad people often seem to have good luck

the devil makes work for idle 'hands (saying)
people who do not have enough to do often start to
do wrong: She blamed the crimes on the local jobless
teenagers. 'The devil makes work for idle hands,'
she would say.

a/the 'devil of a job, nuisance, fellow, etc.
 (old-fashioned)
a difficult or unpleasant example of sth: We're
going to have a devil of a job getting the roots of
that tree out of the ground.

(the) devil take the 'hindmost (saying)
everyone should look after themselves and not
care about others: I like the way people here always
queue up. Back home we just push and shove, and
the devil take the hindmost!

(a/the) devil's 'advocate
a person who argues against sth, even though they
really agree with it, just to test the arguments for
it: Helen doesn't really think that women shouldn't
go out to work. She just likes to play (the) devil's
advocate.

go to the 'devil! (old-fashioned, spoken)
used, in an unfriendly way, to tell sb to go away

like the 'devil (old-fashioned, informal)
very fast, hard, etc: We had to work like the devil to
be finished on time. ◇ I ran like the devil, but I still
missed the bus.

speak/talk of the 'devil (informal, saying)
said when sb who has just been mentioned
appears unexpectedly: 'I haven't seen Leo for a
while.' 'Well, speak of the devil, here he is!'

who, what, where, etc. the 'devil … (old-
 fashioned, informal)
used in questions for showing that you are
annoyed or surprised: Who the devil are you? ◇
Where the devil have I put my glasses?

better the devil you know (than the devil you don't) →
 better
hell/the devil to pay → pay
the luck of the devil → luck

devoured

be de'voured by sth
be filled with a strong emotion that seems to control you: She was devoured by envy and hatred.

diamond

a diamond in the rough = a rough diamond → rough

dibs

dibs on … = bags (I)/(I) bags → bags

dice

the 'dice are loaded against sb
a person has little chance of succeeding in sth, perhaps for unfair reasons: If you apply for a job when
you're over 40, the dice are loaded against you.

> **❶ ORIGIN**
> This phrase refers to putting a piece of lead (= a
> heavy metal) inside a dice so that it always falls
> in a particular way.

,**dice with 'death** (*informal*)
risk your life by doing sth very dangerous: *Racing drivers dice with death every time they race.*

no 'dice (*spoken, especially AmE*)
used to show that you refuse to do sth or that sth cannot be done: *'Did you get that job?' 'No dice.'*

❶ ORIGIN
When you throw dice in a game, if they do not fall flat or they land on top of each other, the throw is invalid and considered *no dice*.

Dick

(a) clever Dick → **clever**
every/any Tom, Dick and/or Harry → **Tom**

dicky

not say/hear a 'dicky bird (*BrE, informal*)
say/hear nothing: *Don't look at me! I didn't say a dicky bird. ◇ We haven't heard a dicky bird from her for weeks.*

❶ ORIGIN
This idiom is from rhyming slang, in which *dicky bird* stands for 'word'.

diddly

diddly; diddly-squat (*AmE, informal*)
(often used in negative sentences) not anything; nothing: *I don't know what's wrong with him—he tells me diddly-squat. ◇ She doesn't know diddly about it* (= she doesn't know anything).

die

die a/the 'death (*BrE, informal*)
end suddenly and completely; fail: *Our fund-raising appeal died a death when the government failed to support it. ◇ He died the death as Othello, and never got another role after that.*

die 'hard
not be easily changed or removed: *Old habits die hard, and I'm finding it difficult to give up smoking.*
▶ **'diehard** *noun, adj.*: *A few diehards are trying to stop the reforms. ◇ diehard supporters of the exiled king*

die in your 'bed
die of old age or illness

die in 'harness
die while you are still working

the die is 'cast (*saying*)
a decision has been made, or a risk has been taken, and the situation cannot now be changed: *Once he'd signed the papers, he knew the die had been cast and there was no turning back.*

❶ NOTE
Die here means 'dice'. *Cast* means 'thrown.'

die 'laughing (*informal*)
find sth extremely funny: *I nearly died laughing when he said that.*

to 'die for (*informal*)
if you think sth is **to die for**, you really want it, and would do anything to get it: *She was wearing a dress to die for.*

die/drop/fall like flies → **flies**
never say die → **say**
(as) straight as a die → **straight**

differ

agree to differ → **agree**
I beg to differ → **beg**

difference

make a, no, some, etc. 'difference (to/in sb/sth)
have an effect/no effect on sb/sth: *The rain didn't make much difference to the game. ◇ Your age shouldn't make any difference to whether you get the job or not. ◇ Changing schools made a big difference to my life.*

make all the 'difference (to sb/sth)
have an important effect on sb/sth; make sb feel better: *A few kind words at the right time make all the difference if you're upset.*

same 'difference (*spoken*)
used to say that you think the differences between two things are not important: *'She's divorced from her husband.' 'No she's not, she's only separated.' 'Same difference.'*

with a 'difference (*informal*)
(used after nouns) of an unusual kind: *This is a house with a difference: it has a swimming pool in the living room.*

as near as makes no difference → **near**
split the difference → **split**
a/the world of difference (between A and B) → **world**

differences

bury your differences → **bury**
sink your differences → **sink**

different

a different kettle of 'fish (*informal*)
a person or thing that is completely different from sb/sth else previously mentioned: *You may be able to read French well, but speaking it fluently is a different kettle of fish entirely.*

as different as chalk and cheese = (like) chalk and cheese → **chalk**
be another/a different matter → **matter**
be on the same wavelength/on different wavelengths → **wavelength**
a (whole) different/new ball game → **ball**
a (quite) different story = (quite) another story → **story**
know different/otherwise → **know**
put a new/different complexion on sth → **complexion**
sing a different song/tune → **sing**
speak/talk the same/a different language → **language**

difficult

make life difficult (for sb) → life

dig

dig 'deep

1 search thoroughly for information: *You'll need to dig deep into the records to find the figures you want.*

2 try hard to provide the money, equipment, etc. that is needed: *We're asking you to dig deep for the earthquake victims.*

dig your 'heels in (*informal*)

refuse to do sth or to change your views: *A number of councils have dug their heels in over the government's request to reduce spending.*

dig your own 'grave; dig a 'grave for yourself

do sth that will bring harm to yourself: *If you give up your job now, you'll be digging your own grave, because you won't find it easy to get another one.*

dig yourself (into) a 'hole

get yourself into a bad situation that it will be very difficult to get out of: *When I started lying to him, I realized that I was digging myself into a hole which would be very difficult to get out of.*

dignity

be,neath sb's 'dignity (*often ironic*)

seeming so unimportant or unpleasant that sb thinks they are too important to do it: *She considers it beneath her dignity to help with the housework now and again.*

stand on your dignity → stand

dilemma

(on) the horns of a dilemma → horns

dim

take a dim/poor view of sb/sth → view

dime

a dime a dozen = two/ten a penny → penny

dine

wine and dine (sb) → wine

dinner

a dog's breakfast/dinner → dog

dinners

more sth/more often than sb has had hot dinners → hot

dint

by dint of sth/doing sth (*formal*)

as a result of (doing) sth; through: *By dint of sheer hard work, she managed to pass all her exams.*

dirt

dish the dirt (on sb) → dish

hit/strike pay dirt → pay

treat sb like dirt → treat

dirty

dirty great/big (*BrE, informal*)

used to emphasize how large sth is: *When I turned round he was pointing a dirty great gun at me.*

(give sb/get) a dirty 'look (*informal*)

look at sb/be looked at in an angry, or a disapproving way: *She gave me a dirty look when I suggested that she should go and wash the dishes.*

a ,dirty old 'man (*informal, disapproving*)

an older man who thinks too much about sex: *Lots of dirty old men stood around looking at pornographic magazines.*

a ,dirty week'end (*BrE, humorous*)

a weekend spent away from home in order to have sex, usually with sb who is not your usual partner: *They went away for a dirty weekend in Brighton.*

a dirty word

a thing or idea that sb finds unpleasant or offensive: *Work is a dirty word to these lazy kids.*

(do sb's) 'dirty work

(do) the unpleasant or dishonest jobs that sb else does not want to do: *Tell him yourself! I don't see why I should have to do your dirty work for you!*

do the 'dirty on sb (*BrE, informal*)

cheat sb or treat them unfairly: *Mike felt that his fellow students had done the dirty on him by telling the lecturer he'd cheated in the exam.*

get your hands dirty → hands

talk dirty → talk

wash your dirty linen in public → wash

disadvantage

put sb/be at a disad'vantage

make it/be difficult for sb to succeed: *My lack of experience put me at a disadvantage in comparison with the other candidates for the job.*

disappear

disappear/vanish off the face of the earth → face

disappearing

do/perform/stage a disappearing/vanishing act → act

disaster

a di'saster area

1 (*informal*) a place or situation that has a lot of problems, is a failure, or is badly-organized: *The room was a disaster area* (= very untidy), *with stuff piled everywhere and nowhere to sit.* ◇ *The current system of taxation is a disaster area.*

2 a place where a disaster has happened and which needs special help: *After the floods, the whole region was declared a disaster area.*

an accident/a disaster waiting to happen → waiting

discretion

at sb's di'scretion
according to what sb decides or wishes to do: *Bail is granted at the discretion of the court.* ◇ *There is no service charge and tipping is at your discretion.*

di,scretion is the better part of 'valour (*BrE*) (*AmE* **di,scretion is the better part of 'valor**) (*saying*)
you should avoid danger and not take unnecessary risks

❶ ORIGIN
This comes from Shakespeare's play *Henry IV*.

disguise

a blessing in disguise → **blessing**

dish

,dish the 'dirt (on sb) (*informal*)
tell people unkind or unpleasant things about sb, especially about their private life: *When the newspaper offered her £10000, she was only too happy to dish the dirt on her friends.*

dishwater

(as) dull as dishwater → **dull**

disposal

at your/sb's dis'posal
available for use as you prefer/sb prefers: *He will have a car at his disposal for the whole month.* ◇ *Well, I'm at your disposal* (= I am ready to help you in any way I can).

disservice

do sb a dis'service
do sth that harms sb and the opinion that other people have of them: *The minister's comments do teachers a great disservice.*

distance

at/from a 'distance
from a place or time that is not near; from far away: *She had loved him at a distance for years.*

go the (full) 'distance
continue playing in a competition or sports contest until the end: *Nobody thought he would last 15 rounds but he went the full distance.*

in/into the 'distance
far away but still able to be seen or heard: *We saw lights in the distance.* ◇ *Alice stood staring into the distance.*

keep your 'distance (from sb/sth); keep sb/ sth at a 'distance
not be too friendly or familiar with sb/sth: *She tends to keep her distance from her neighbours, so none of them know her very well.*

within shouting distance = within spitting distance (of sth) → **spitting**
within striking distance (of sth) → **striking**

distant

the (,dim and) ,distant 'past
a long time ago: *stories from the distant past*

in the not too ,distant 'future
not a long time in the future; fairly soon: *We're thinking of having a baby in the not too distant future.*

distraction

to di'straction
so that you become upset, excited, or angry and not able to think clearly: *The children are **driving me to distraction** today.*

distress

a damsel in distress → **damsel**

district

the red-light district → **red-light**

ditchwater

(as) dull as ditchwater → **dull**

dive

make a 'dive (for sth)
suddenly move or jump forward to do sth or reach sb/sth: *The goalkeeper made a dive for the ball.*

take a 'dive (*informal*)
suddenly get worse: *Profits really took a dive at the end of last year.*

divide

di,vide and 'rule
keep control over people by making them disagree with and fight each other, therefore not giving them the chance to unite and oppose you together: *a policy of divide and rule*

dividend

a/the peace dividend → **peace**

dividends

pay dividends → **pay**

do

Most idioms containing the verb **do** are at the entries for the nouns or adjectives in the idioms, for example **do a runner** is at **runner**.

be/have to ,do with 'sb/'sth
be connected or concerned with sb/sth: *'What do you want to see me about?' 'It's to do with the letter you sent.'* ◇ *I'm not sure what he does for a living but I know it's something to do with computers.*

could 'do with sth (*spoken*)
want or need sth: *I could really do with a coffee.* ◇ *Her hair could have done with a wash.* ◇ *You look as if you could do with a good night's sleep.*

could/can do with'out sth (*spoken*)
not want sth, for example criticism, advice or complaints: *I could do without him telling me what to say all the time.* ◇ *I could have done without her ringing me up just as I was about to go out.*

do a 'sb (*informal*)
do or behave as sb did or would do: *Now don't go and do a Mr. Carpenter on us. He told us he was leaving only three weeks before he went, and it took us months to find a replacement.*

'do something for sb/sth (*informal*)
make sb/sth look better: *You know, that hat really does something for you!*

do's and 'don'ts (*informal*)
what to do and what not to do; rules: *This book is a useful guide to the do's and don'ts of choosing and buying your first car.*

it/that (just) won't 'do; it/that will never 'do (*especially BrE*)
used to say that a situation is not satisfactory and should be changed or improved: *He's spending every afternoon in the park with his friends instead of going to school, and that just won't do!* ◇ *I feel very upset but it would never do to show it.*

not do anything/a lot/much for sb (*informal*)
used to say that sth does not make sb look attractive: *That hairstyle doesn't do anything for her.*

that will 'do (*informal*)
used to order sb to stop doing or saying sth: *That'll do! I've heard enough of your complaints.*

what did you, etc. do with sth?
(usually in perfect and simple past tenses) where did you, etc. put, lose or hide sth?: *What have you done with my scissors? They were on the kitchen table the last time I saw them.*

what do you do for sth?
used to ask how sb manages to obtain the thing mentioned: *It's very quiet, isn't it? What do you do for entertainment out here?*

dock

put sb in the 'dock
accuse sb of doing sth wrong: *The government is being put in the dock for failing to warn the public about the flu epidemic.*

> **❷ NOTE**
> The *dock* in a court of law is the place where the person who has been accused of a crime stands or sits during a trial.

doctor

just what the doctor 'ordered (*humorous, saying*)
exactly what sb wants or needs: *Ah, a long, cool, refreshing drink! Just what the doctor ordered!*

doddle

(it's) a 'doddle (*BrE, informal*)
used to refer to a task or an activity that is very easy: *The first year of the course was an absolute doddle.*

dodo

(as) dead as a/the dodo → **dead**

does

that 'does it (*informal*)
used to show that you will not tolerate sth any longer: *That does it! You've called me a liar once too often. I'm leaving!*

dog

be like a dog with two 'tails
be extremely happy: *'Is he pleased about his new job?' 'He's like a dog with two tails!'*

,dog eat 'dog (*informal*)
fierce competition, with no concern for the harm done or other people's feelings: *In the modern business world, it's dog eat dog in the search for success.*

dog sb's 'footsteps
(of a problem or bad luck) seem to follow sb everywhere: *Bad luck seems to have dogged our footsteps from the beginning.*

a ,dog in the 'manger
a person who selfishly stops other people from using or enjoying sth which he/she cannot use or enjoy himself/herself ▶ ,dog-in-the-'manger *adj.*: *a dog-in-the-manger attitude*

> **❶ ORIGIN**
> This expression comes from Aesop's fable about a dog which lay in a manger (= a long open box) filled with hay. In this way he stopped the other animals eating the hay, even though he could not eat it himself.

a dog's 'breakfast/'dinner (*BrE, informal*)
a very untidy piece of work; a mess: *Don't ask Julie to help you with the decorating—she made a complete dog's breakfast of painting the kitchen!*

a 'dog's life (*informal*)
a life in which there is not much pleasure or freedom: *It's a dog's life having to do two jobs in order to survive.*

every dog has his/its 'day (*saying*)
(often used to encourage sb) everyone will, at some time in their life, be successful or lucky: *They say every dog has its day, and mine is on Wednesday, when I will be interviewed for a television programme!*

give a dog a bad 'name (and 'hang him) (*saying*)
when a person already has a bad reputation, it is difficult to change it because others will continue to blame or suspect him/her

why keep a dog and bark yourself? (*informal, saying*)

if sb can do a task for you, there is no point in doing it yourself: *My mother always cleans the house before the cleaning lady comes, but why keep a dog and bark yourself?*

fight like cat and dog → **fight**

the hair of the dog (that bit you) → **hair**

let the tail wag the dog = the tail (is) wagging the dog → **tail**

not have a dog's chance = not have a cat in hell's chance → **cat**

(as) sick as a dog → **sick**

the tail (is) wagging the dog → **tail**

(you can't) teach an old dog new tricks → **teach**

there's life in the old dog yet → **life**

top dog → **top**

work like a dog/slave/Trojan → **work**

doggo

lie doggo → **lie**

doghouse

in the 'doghouse (*informal*)

in a situation where sb is angry with you because you have done sth wrong: *I'm in the doghouse with my wife at the moment: I forgot it was her birthday yesterday!*

Mr Brown was in the doghouse again.

dogs

go to the 'dogs (*AmE* also **go to hell in a 'handbasket**) (*informal*)

(often used of a company, organization, country, etc.) become less powerful, efficient, etc. than before: *Many people think this country's going to the dogs.*

let sleeping dogs lie → **let**

rain cats and dogs → **rain**

doing

can't be 'doing with sth (*informal*)

used to say that you do not like sth and are unwilling to accept it: *I can't be doing with people who complain all the time.*

take some 'doing; take a lot of 'doing

be hard work; be difficult: *Getting it finished by tomorrow will take some doing.* ◇ *It's going to take some doing to do the report on time, but we should manage it.*

what is sb/sth doing ... ?

used to ask why sb/sth is in the place mentioned: *What are these shoes doing on my desk?*

doldrums

in the 'doldrums

quiet or depressed: *Property sales have been in the doldrums for some time.* ◇ *He was in the doldrums for the whole winter.*

> **❶ ORIGIN**
> The *doldrums* is a place in the ocean near the equator where there are sudden periods of calm. A sailing ship caught in this area can be stranded due to a lack of wind.

dollar

(you can) bet your bottom dollar/your life (on sth/that ...) → **bet**

the million dollar question = the sixty-four thousand dollar question → **sixty-four**

pay, earn, charge, etc. top dollar → **top**

dollars

look/feel like a million dollars/bucks → **million**

done

be 'done for (*informal*)

be in serious trouble: *The supplies are so low that we will be done for in a few days if help doesn't come soon.* ◇ *I think the project is done for—the money's almost gone and we've got no results after three years' hard work.*

be/get 'done for sth/for doing sth (*BrE, informal*)

be caught and punished for doing sth illegal but not too serious: *I got done for speeding on my way back home.*

be/have 'done with sb/sth (*especially BrE*)

no longer be involved with sb/sth or do sth, especially sth unpleasant: *I'm fed up with you lot! I'm done with you for ever!* ◇ *Let's have done with this silly argument.*

be ,over and 'done with

(often used of sth unpleasant, upsetting, etc.) be completely finished: *Well I'm glad that's over and done with. I was so nervous.*

done and 'dusted (*informal*)

if a project, activity, etc. is **done and dusted**, it is

completely finished or ready: *Everybody else seems to think the deal will be done and dusted by lunchtime, but I'm not so sure.*

a done 'deal (*especially AmE*)
used to describe a decision, arrangement, project, etc. that is completed and cannot be changed: *The managing director denied that the merger was a done deal, and said they were still in negotiations.*

done 'in (*informal*)
extremely tired: *I feel absolutely done in!*

the done 'thing (*BrE*)
the socially correct way to behave: *Smoking while somebody else is eating is not the done thing.* ◇ *It's the done thing to dress for dinner in this hotel.*

done to a 'turn (*BrE*)
cooked for exactly the right amount of time: *We had a wonderful dinner, with chicken done to a turn and home-grown vegetables.*

he, she, etc. has gone/been and done sth (*informal*)
used to express surprise, annoyance, etc. at sb's actions: *Someone's gone and locked the door and I haven't got a key!* ◇ *What's he been and done now?*

be/feel hard done by → **hard**
been there, done that → **been**
easier said than done → **easier**
no harm done → **harm**
no sooner said than done → **sooner**
when all is said and done → **said**

donkey

the 'donkey work (*informal*)
the hard, boring parts of a job: *Why is it always me who has to do the donkey work?*

'donkey's years (*BrE, informal*)
a very long time: *She's lived in that house for donkey's years.*

talk the hind leg(s) off a donkey → **talk**

donna

(a) prima donna → **prima**

don'ts

do's and don'ts → **do**

doom

,doom and 'gloom; ,gloom and 'doom
a general feeling of having lost all hope and of pessimism (= expecting things to go badly): *Despite the obvious setbacks, it's not all doom and gloom for the England team.*

a doom merchant = a prophet of doom → **prophet**

doomsday

till 'doomsday (*informal*)
a very long time; for ever: *This job's going to take me till doomsday.*

door

be on the 'door
work at the entrance to a theatre, club, etc., for example collecting tickets from people as they enter: *We should be able to get in free because I know the guy on the door.*

by/through the back 'door
in an indirect or unofficial way: *She has powerful friends, so she got into the diplomatic service by the back door.*

(from) ,door to 'door
1 from the place of departure to the place you are going to; from building to building: *The whole journey took me four hours from door to door.*
2 from one house, flat, etc. to the next: *The church distributes leaflets from door to door.* ◇ *a door-to-door salesman*

shut/close the 'door on sth
make it unlikely that sth will happen; refuse to consider an idea, a plan, etc: *I think this company should remain open to ideas and not shut the door on change.* ◇ *She was careful not to close the door on the possibility of further talks.*

at death's door → **death**
beat a path to sb's door → **beat**
get/have a/your foot in the door → **foot**
keep the wolf from the door → **wolf**
lay sth at sb's door → **lay**
leave the door open (for/on sth) → **leave**
lie at sb's door → **lie**
not/never darken sb's door again → **darken**
open the door to/for sb/sth → **open**
show sb the door → **show**
shut, etc. the barn door after the horse has escaped = shut/lock/close the stable door after the horse has bolted → **stable**

doornail

(as) dead as a doornail → **dead**

doors

out of ,doors
in the open air; outdoors: *You should spend more time out of doors in the fresh air.*

behind closed doors → **closed**

doorstep

on the/your 'doorstep
very near your/sb's home: *It's easy to be concerned with problems across the other side of the world and not see the poverty and unhappiness on your own doorstep.*

dos

fair dos/do's → **fair**

dose

like a dose of 'salts (old-fashioned, BrE, informal)
very fast and easily: *We'll go through this house like a
dose of salts, cleaning everything from top to bottom.*

give sb a taste/dose of their own medicine → medicine

dot

dot the/your ,i's and cross the/your 't's
pay great attention to small details in order to
complete sth; be very thorough and careful in
what you do or say: *We reached a broad agreement,
and decided to dot the i's and cross the t's later.*

on the 'dot (informal)
at exactly the right time or at the exact time mentioned: *He always finishes work at 4.30 on the dot.* ◇
She arrived on the dot of 6.00.

from, since, etc. the year dot → year

dotage

be in your 'dotage (often humorous)
be old and not always able to think clearly: *Sarah
moved back in with her father so that she could look
after him in his dotage.* ◇ *Sometimes the kids talk to
me as if I'm in my dotage!*

dotted

sign on the dotted line → sign

double

at the 'double (BrE) (AmE **on the 'double**)
(informal)
very quickly; immediately: *Go and get my boots, on
the double!* ◇ *The boss wants you to go and see her
at the double.*

do a ,double 'take
react to sth surprising or unusual only after a
short delay: *I had to do a double take when she
walked in—she looked exactly like her mother!*

,double 'Dutch (BrE, informal)
language that is impossible to understand: *I wish
someone would explain this contract in simple language—it's all double Dutch to me!*

,double or 'quits (BrE) (AmE **,double or
'nothing**)
(in gambling) a risk in which you could win twice
the amount you pay, or you could lose all your
money

,double 'quick (BrE, informal)
very quick(ly): *If the machine starts making a hiss-
ing noise, then turn it off double quick.*

a double 'whammy (informal)
two unpleasant situations or events that happen at
the same time and cause problems for sb/sth: *With
this government we've had a double whammy of
tax increases and benefit cuts.*

ⓘ ORIGIN
This phrase comes from the 1950s American car-
toon L'il Abner, in which one of the characters

could shoot a whammy (= put a curse on sb) by
pointing a finger with one eye open, or a double
whammy with both eyes open.

in a ,double 'bind
in a situation in which it is difficult to choose what
to do because whatever you choose will have negative results: *The company is **caught in a double
bind**. If it doesn't modernize it won't make money,
but if it does modernize they'll have to make people
redundant because they won't need them any more.*

double-edged

be a double-edged 'sword/'weapon
be sth that has both advantages and disadvantages: *This new 'miracle diet' is a double-edged
sword—it'll make you lose weight fast but you may
have some unpleasant side effects.*

doubt

in 'doubt
not certain: *The future of the company is still in
doubt.* ◇ *If in doubt, call for an ambulance.*

,no 'doubt
probably, almost certainly: *No doubt you know why
I have asked you to come and see me.* ◇ *You will no
doubt have already heard that the chairman has
resigned.*

without/beyond (a) 'doubt
certainly: *This is without a doubt the finest wine I
have ever drunk.*

beyond/without a shadow of (a) doubt → shadow
give sb the benefit of the doubt → benefit
there isn't a shadow of a doubt (that …) → shadow

doubting

a ,doubting 'Thomas
a person who will not believe sth without proof:
*Now, for all you doubting Thomases who thought I
couldn't win an important race, here's my medal to
prove it!*

ⓘ ORIGIN
This expression comes from the Bible. Thomas
refused to believe that Jesus had been brought
back to life until he saw Jesus for himself and
touched his wounds.

doubts

have (got) your 'doubts (about sth)
have reasons why you are not certain about
whether sth is good or whether sth good will happen: *I've had my doubts about his work since he
joined the company.* ◇ *It may be all right. Personally, I have my doubts.*

down

be down to 'sb/'sth (informal)
1 be caused by a particular person or thing: *She
claimed her problems were down to the media.* ◇

Our defeat in last week's game is down to the goal-keeper, who played very badly.
2 be the responsibility of sb: *It's down to you to check the doors and windows before we leave.*

be down to 'sth
have nothing except one or a few items of the kind mentioned: *I'm down to my last penny.*

down and 'out
having no home or job and living on the streets of a city; very poor: *It must be terrible to be down and out in this cold weather.* ▶ ,**down-and-'out** *noun* person who is down and out: *Life is hard for the city's down-and-outs.*

down through sth (*written*)
during a long period of time: *Down through the years this town has seen many changes.*

down to 'sb/'sth
even including the last item of a whole list of people or things: *Everybody was affected by the economic crisis, from the president down to the poorest citizen.* ◇ *She's thought of everything down to the tiniest details!*

down 'under (*informal*)
in or to Australia and/or New Zealand: *TV stars from down under*

down with 'sb/'sth!
shouted as a protest against sb/sth: *Down with the dictator!*

downhill

(all) down'hill; ,**downhill all the 'way** (*informal*)
1 very easy compared with the difficulties that came before: *It's all downhill from here. We'll soon be finished.* ◇ *I've done three out of the four parts of the course, so it should be downhill all the way from now on.*
2 getting worse very quickly: *I took on far too much work and after that it was downhill all the way for my health.*

go down'hill
get worse: *My work has been going downhill ever since my divorce.* ◇ *This restaurant has definitely gone downhill since I last came here.*

downs

ups and downs ➔ **ups**

dozen

by the 'dozen
many at the same time: *On her birthday, she always receives cards by the dozen.*

a baker's dozen ➔ **baker**
a dime a dozen = two/ten a penny ➔ **penny**
it's six of one and half a dozen of the other ➔ **six**
talk, etc. nineteen to the dozen ➔ **nineteen**

drabs

in dribs and drabs ➔ **dribs**

drag

drag your 'feet/'heels
do sth very slowly or delay doing sth because you do not want to do it: *How much longer will the government go on dragging its feet about whether to invest more money in the railways?*

drag/pull yourself up by your (own) bootstraps ➔ **boot-straps**

dragged

(look) like sth the cat brought/dragged in ➔ **cat**

drain

(go) down the 'drain (*BrE* also **(go) down the 'plughole**) (*informal*)
(be) wasted or lost; (get) much worse: *He watched his business, which had taken so long to build up, go slowly down the drain.*

the brain drain ➔ **brain**
laugh like a drain ➔ **laugh**
money down the drain ➔ **money**

drama

make a 'drama out of sth
make a small problem or event seem more important or serious than it really is: *Oh come on, it's only a tiny scratch—you always make such a drama out of everything!*

draught

on 'draught (*BrE*)
(of beer) taken from a barrel (= a large container): *This beer is not available on draught* (= it is available only in bottles or cans).

feel the draught ➔ **feel**

draw

be fast/quick on the 'draw
1 (*informal*) be quick to understand or react in a new situation: *You can't fool him, he's always quick on the draw.*
2 be quick at pulling out a gun in order to shoot it

draw a 'blank
not find sth that you are looking for: *There was no sign of the murder weapon. The police searched every inch of the forest but drew a blank.*

draw 'breath (*BrE*) (*AmE* **draw a 'breath**)
1 stop doing sth and rest: *She talks all the time and hardly stops to draw breath.*
2 (*literary*) live; be alive: *He was as kind a man as ever drew breath.*

draw the 'line (at sth)
refuse to do or accept sth: *I don't mind cooking dinner for you occasionally, but I draw the line at iron-*

ing your shirts! ◇ He refused to tolerate her lies any longer. The line had to be drawn somewhere.

,**draw the short 'straw** (*BrE*) (*AmE* **get the** ,**short end of the 'stick**)
be the person in a group who is chosen or forced to do sth unpleasant that nobody wants to do: *You've drawn the short straw, I'm afraid. You're going to have to work on Christmas Day.*

,**draw 'straws (for sth)**
decide on sb to do or have sth, by choosing pieces of paper, etc: *We drew straws for who went first.*

cast/draw lots (for sth/to do sth) → **lots**
cast/draw/throw a veil over sth → **veil**
draw/pull in your horns → **horns**
draw yourself up/rise to your full height → **full**
the luck of the draw → **luck**
take/draw sb to one side → **side**

drawer

not the sharpest knife in the drawer → **sharpest**

drawing

(**it's**) **back to the 'drawing board**
a new plan must be prepared because an earlier one has failed: *She's refused to consider our offer, so it's back to the drawing board, I'm afraid.*

drawn

the battle lines are drawn → **battle**
be at daggers drawn (with sb) → **daggers**

dread

I shudder/dread to think (how, what, etc. ...) → **think**

dreaded

the ,**dreaded 'lurgy** (*informal, humorous*)
an illness that is easy to catch but not serious, for example a cold: *Ann's not coming out tonight—she's got the dreaded lurgy so she's at home in bed.*

dream

dream 'on (*spoken, informal*)
used to tell sb that an idea is not practical or likely to happen: *'Do you think if I ask my boss for a pay rise, I'll get one?' 'Dream on!'*

like a bad 'dream
(of a situation) so unpleasant that you cannot believe it is true: *In broad daylight the events of the night before seemed like a bad dream.*

not 'dream of (doing) sth
(often used with *would*) not even consider (doing) sth under any circumstances: *'Don't tell Gary what I've bought him for his birthday.' 'I wouldn't dream of it.' ◇ Only a couple of years ago he would never have dreamt of going abroad on his own, and now he's travelling around India!*

work/go like a 'dream (*informal*)
work/go very well: *The plan worked like a dream, and everybody got what they wanted.*

a pipe dream → **pipe**

dreams

in your 'dreams (*spoken*)
used to tell sb that sth they are hoping for is not likely to happen: *'I'll be a manager before I'm 30.' 'In your dreams.'*

beyond your wildest dreams → **wildest**

dress

look/dress the part → **part**

dressed

dressed to 'kill (*informal*)
(especially of a woman) wearing your best clothes, especially clothes that attract attention: *She went to the party dressed to kill.*

dressed (up) to the 'nines (*informal*)
wearing very elegant or formal clothes, especially to attract attention: *She was dressed up to the nines in her furs and jewellery.*

> **❶ ORIGIN**
> One theory about the origin of this expression is that it refers to suit-making. A well-made, good quality suit needs nine yards (= approximately 8.2 metres) of fabric.

be mutton dressed (up) as lamb → **mutton**

dribs

in ,**dribs and 'drabs** (*informal*)
in small amounts or numbers: *People started arriving in dribs and drabs from nine o'clock onwards. ◇ He paid back the money in dribs and drabs.*

dried

cut and dried → **cut**

drift

catch/get sb's/the drift (*informal*)
understand the general meaning of what sb says or writes: *Do you catch my drift? ◇ My German isn't very good, but I got the drift of what he said. ◇ He wasn't the sort of boy you'd introduce to your mother, **if you get my drift** (= I have not told you all the details, but I am sure you can understand what I mean).*

lose the drift/thread of sth → **lose**

drink

drink sb's 'health
wish sb good health as you lift your glass, and then drink from it

drink like a 'fish (*informal*)
regularly drink too much alcohol: *Her husband drinks like a fish.*

drink sb under the 'table (*informal*)
drink more alcohol than sb without becoming as drunk as they do: *Believe me, she can drink anyone under the table!*

be meat and drink (to sb) → **meat**

the demon drink → **demon**

drive sb to drink → **drive**

eat, drink and be merry → **eat**

spike sb's drink → **spike**

a stiff drink → **stiff**

(be) the worse for drink → **worse**

you can take/lead a horse to water, but you can't make it drink → **horse**

drive

drive a coach and 'horses through sth
succeed in avoiding certain rules, conditions, etc. in an obvious and important way, without being punished: *The wage increase we've been given is three times the government's limit. We've driven a coach and horses right through their pay policy.*

drive a hard 'bargain
make sure that you always gain an advantage in business deals, etc: *I wouldn't try to do business with Jack; he's got the reputation of driving a hard bargain.*

drive sb in'sane
make sb more and more angry or irritated, especially over a long period of time: *This job is driving me insane.*

drive sb out of their 'mind/'wits (*informal*)
make sb crazy, or very nervous or worried: *That noise is driving me out of my mind!*

drive sb to 'drink (*often humorous*)
make sb so annoyed, worried, etc. that they begin to drink too much alcohol: *A week with those noisy kids is enough to drive anyone to drink!*

drive a wedge between A and B
make two people become less friendly or loving towards each other: *The disagreements over money finally drove a wedge between them, and they ended up getting divorced.*

drive/hammer sth home (to sb) → **home**

drive/send sb up the wall → **wall**

drive/run/work yourself into the ground → **ground**

driven

(as) pure as the driven snow → **pure**

driver

a back-seat driver → **back-seat**

in the driver's seat = in the driving seat → **driving**

driving

the driving 'force (behind sth)
the person or thing that makes sth happen: *She is the driving force behind this new road safety campaign.*

in the 'driving seat (*BrE*) (*AmE* in the 'driver's seat)
managing or controlling sth, for example a business: *With a younger person in the driving seat, we can expect some big changes in the company.*

what sb is 'driving at
the thing sb is trying to say: *What are you driving at? Try to explain what you mean more clearly.* ◇ *I wish I knew what they were really driving at.*

drop

at the ˌdrop of a 'hat (*informal*)
immediately and without hesitating: *He's the sort of person who can sing any song at all at the drop of a hat.*

ˌdrop your 'aitches
not pronounce the 'h' sound, especially at the beginning of a word, where it is pronounced in standard English

> **❷ NOTE**
> This is a feature of certain English accents, for example the London one.

drop a, the, his, etc. 'bombshell
announce sth which is unexpected and usually unpleasant: *It was then that he dropped the bombshell—he wasn't planning to come with us.*

drop a 'brick/'clanger (*BrE, informal*)
say or do sth that offends or embarrasses sb, although you did not intend to: *I dropped a real clanger when I mentioned the party. He hadn't been invited.*

drop 'dead
1 (*informal*) die very suddenly
2 (*spoken*) used as a rude way of telling sb to go away: *Drop dead, will you!*

drop a 'hint (to sb); drop sb a 'hint
suggest sth in an indirect way: *He tried to drop a hint about it being time to leave, but they didn't seem to take any notice.* ◇ *She's dropped me a few hints about what she'd like for her birthday.*

drop sb 'in it (*BrE, informal*)
put sb in an embarrassing situation, especially by telling a secret that you should not have told: *Don't mention Paul to my parents or you'll really drop me in it—I haven't told them about him yet.*

a ˌdrop in the 'ocean (*BrE*) (*AmE* a ˌdrop in the 'bucket)
a very small amount in comparison to the much larger amount that is needed: *£10 million is only a drop in the ocean compared to what is needed to help these people effectively.*

drop sb a 'line/'note (*informal*)
write a short letter, message, etc. to sb: *I dropped her a line inviting her to my birthday party.*

drop 'names
mention famous people you know or have met in order to impress others ▶ 'name-dropping *noun*: *I can't stand all this name-dropping! Does he really know Liam Gallagher?*

fit/ready to 'drop (*informal*)
very tired; exhausted: *I feel fit to drop.* ◇ *We danced until we were ready to drop.*

die/drop/fall like flies → **flies**

drop/dump sth in sb's lap → **lap**

drop/fall into sb's lap → **lap**
let sth drop → **let**
you could have heard a pin drop → **heard**

drops

the bottom drops/falls out of the market → **bottom**
the bottom drops/falls out of sb's world → **bottom**
your jaw drops → **jaw**
the penny drops → **penny**

drown

drown your 'sorrows (*informal, often humorous*)
try to forget your problems or a disappointment by
drinking alcohol: *Whenever his team lost a match
he could be found in the pub afterwards drowning
his sorrows.*

drowned

like a drowned 'rat (*informal*)
very wet: *She came in from the storm looking like a
drowned rat.*

drugged

drugged up to the 'eyeballs
have taken or been given a lot of drugs: *She was
drugged up to the eyeballs, but still in a lot of pain.*

drum

bang/beat the 'drum (for sb/sth) (*especially
BrE*)
speak with enthusiasm in support of sb/sth: *She's
really banging the drum for the new system.*

drunk

(as) drunk as a 'lord (*BrE*) (*AmE* **(as) drunk as
a 'skunk**) (*informal*)
very drunk: *I eventually found them in a bar, both
as drunk as skunks.*

blind drunk → **blind**
roaring drunk → **roaring**

dry

(as) dry as a 'bone
very dry

(as) dry as 'dust
extremely boring: *Her lectures are very useful, but
they're dry as dust.*

milk/suck sb/sth 'dry
get from sb/sth all the money, help, information,
etc. they have, usually giving nothing in return: *It
was only later that we found out he'd milked his
grandmother dry of all her money before she died.*

not a dry eye in the 'house (*humorous*)
used to say that everyone was very emotional
about sth: *There wasn't a dry eye in the house when
they announced their engagement.*

bleed sb dry/white → **bleed**

high and dry → **high**
home and dry → **home**
keep your powder dry → **powder**
run dry → **run**
squeeze sb dry → **squeeze**

duck

(take to sth) like a ˌduck to 'water
(be able to do sth) naturally and without any difficulty: *'Do the children like living in the country?'
'They've taken to it like ducks to water. They've
never been happier!'*

be (like) water off a duck's back → **water**
a dead duck → **dead**
a lame duck → **lame**
a sitting duck/target → **sitting**

duckling

an ugly duckling → **ugly**

dudgeon

in high dudgeon → **high**

due

give sb their 'due
give sb the praise that they deserve: *Helen may not
be bright, but to give her her due, her work is always
very accurate.*

in ˌdue 'course
at the right time in the future; eventually: *Thank
you for your letter applying for the post of manager.
We will be in contact with you again in due course.*

dull

(as) dull as 'ditchwater (*BrE*) (*AmE* **(as) dull
as 'dishwater**)
very boring: *Best-seller or not, the book sounds as
dull as ditchwater to me.*

dumb

be struck dumb (with sth) → **struck**

dump

drop/dump sth in sb's lap → **lap**

dumps

down in the 'dumps (*informal*)
depressed; miserable: *I've been feeling a bit down
in the dumps since I lost my job.*

duration

for the du'ration (*informal*)
until the end of a particular situation: *Kate has the
flu so badly that she's confined to her room for the
duration.*

dust

after/when the 'dust settles

when all the exciting events, changes, etc. are over: *When the dust finally began to settle, certain facts about the Prime Minister's resignation started to emerge.*

bite the dust → **bite**

(as) dry as dust → **dry**

gather dust → **gather**

leave sb/sth in the dust → **leave**

let the dust settle → **let**

like gold dust → **gold**

not see sb for dust → **see**

wait for the dust to settle = let the dust settle → **let**

dusted

done and dusted → **done**

dusty

a dusty 'answer (*old-fashioned, BrE*)

an unhelpful or sharp response to a request or question: *When I asked the company what their policy was on this matter, I received a very dusty answer.*

Dutch

Dutch 'courage (*BrE, informal*)

courage or confidence that you get by drinking alcohol: *I was afraid of having to tell my wife about what had happened, so I went to the pub to get some Dutch courage.*

go 'Dutch (with sb) (*informal*)

share the cost of a meal, cinema trip, etc. equally with sb else: *She always insists on going Dutch when they go out together.*

double Dutch → **double**

duty

duty 'calls

used to say that you must do sth that cannot be avoided, especially when you have to stop doing sth pleasant: *Ah, duty calls, I'm afraid—I really must go and finish off those letters.*

on/off 'duty

(of nurses, police officers, etc.) working/not working at a particular time: *Who's on duty today?* ◇ *What time do you go off duty?*

be/feel duty/honour bound to do sth → **bound**

(above and) beyond the call of duty → **call**

in the line of duty → **line**

dying

be 'dying for sth/to do sth (*informal*)

want to have or do sth very much: *I'm dying for a drink.* ◇ *She's heard so much about you. She's dying to meet you.*

be 'dying of sth (*informal*)

have a very strong feeling of sth, for example hunger or boredom: *We're all dying of curiosity—come on, tell us what happened!* ◇ *I'm dying of thirst.*

till/to/until your ,dying 'day

for as long as you live: *I swear I won't forgive her to my dying day!*

Ee

eager

an eager 'beaver (*informal*)
a person who is enthusiastic about work, etc: *She always starts work early and leaves late. She's a real eager beaver.*

eagle

an/sb's ,eagle 'eye (*informal*)
if sb has an **eagle eye**, they watch things carefully and are good at noticing things: *Nothing the staff did escaped the eagle eye of the manager* (= he saw everything they did). ▶ **,eagle-'eyed** *adj.*: *An eagle-eyed student spotted the mistake.*

ear

be out on your 'ear (*informal*)
be forced to leave a job, home, etc. suddenly: *You'll be out on your ear unless your work gets a lot better, my lad.*

beam/grin/smile from ear to 'ear
be smiling, etc. a lot because you are very pleased about sth: *I like your graduation photo, with you grinning from ear to ear and your parents looking so proud.*

go in 'one ear and out the 'other (*informal*)
(of information, advice, an order, etc.) be immediately forgotten or ignored: *He never remembers anything I tell him. It just goes in one ear and out the other.*

have, get, win, etc. sb's 'ear; have, get, etc. the ear of sb (*formal*)
gain the attention of sb important in order to influence them or get their help: *We'll have to gain the ear of the Senator to win support for our cause.* ◇ *He had the ear of the monarch.*

have (got) an 'ear for sth
be able to recognize and copy sounds well: *He has an ear for the rhythm of Irish speech.* ◇ *The child certainly has an ear for music.*

keep/have an/your ear (close) to the 'ground
(try to) be well-informed about what is or will be happening: *Jane keeps her ear pretty close to the ground and can usually tell you what the mood of the staff is.*

bend sb's ear (about sth) → **bend**
cock an ear/eye at sth/sb → **cock**
give sb/get a thick ear → **thick**
have (got) a tin ear (for sth) → **tin**
have a word in sb's ear → **word**
lend an ear (to sb/sth) → **lend**
listen with half an ear → **listen**
make a pig's ear (out) of sth → **pig**
make a silk purse out of a sow's ear → **silk**

play (sth/it) by ear → **play**
turn a deaf ear (to sth) → **turn**
(send sb away/off) with a flea in their ear → **flea**

earliest

at your earliest con'venience (*written*)
as soon as possible: *Please telephone at your earliest convenience.*

early

the ,early bird catches the 'worm (*saying*)
you have to get up early or do sth before others in order to be successful ▶ **an 'early bird** *noun* (*humorous*) a person who gets up, arrives, etc. very early

early 'on
at an early stage of a situation, relationship, period of time, etc: *I knew quite early on that I wanted to marry her.*

it's early 'days (yet) (*BrE*)
it is too soon to be certain about (the results of) sth: *We look forward to the time when Europe will operate as a single economic unit, though of course it's early days yet.*

bright and early → **bright**
have an early/a late night → **night**
the small/early hours → **hours**

earn

,earn a/your 'crust (*BrE, informal*)
earn enough money to live on: *He's a musician now, but he used to earn a crust by cleaning windows.*

❶ NOTE
The *crust* is the hard, outer surface of bread.

,earn your 'keep
be useful, helpful, successful, etc. enough to balance any costs that you cause: *Jill more than earns her keep with the help she gives me around the house.* ◇ *Though it's expensive to buy and maintain, the new computer is earning its keep as we've been able to reduce the number of staff.*

win/earn your spurs → **spurs**

earnest

in 'earnest
1 more seriously and with more force or effort than before: *The work on the house will begin in earnest on Monday.*
2 very serious and sincere about what you are saying and about your intentions; in a way that shows that you are serious: *You may laugh but I'm in **deadly earnest**.* ◇ *I could tell she was speaking in earnest.*

ears

be all 'ears (*informal*)
listen very carefully and with great interest: *Go on, tell me what happened—I'm all ears.*

be up to your 'ears in sth
have a lot of sth to deal with: *I'm afraid I'm up to my ears in work at the moment. Can we talk later in the week?*

come to/reach sb's 'ears
hear about sth, especially when other people already know about it: *News of the affair eventually reached her ears.*

his, her, etc. 'ears are burning
a person thinks or knows that other people have been talking about them: *Jenny's ears must have been burning last night: we talked about her for hours.*

his, her, etc. 'ears are flapping (*BrE, informal*)
a person is trying to listen to sb else's conversation: *I think you'd better tell me later when we're alone—ears are flapping here.*

shut/close your 'ears to sb/sth
refuse to listen to sb/sth; ignore sb/sth: *The government has shut its ears to our protests.*

be (like) music to your ears → **music**
box sb's ears → **box**
your ears prick up = prick up your ears → **prick**
fall on deaf ears → **fall**
give sb a box on the ears → **box**
not believe your eyes/ears → **believe**
prick up your ears → **prick**
ring in your ears/head → **ring**
walls have ears → **walls**
(still) wet behind the ears → **wet**

earshot

out of 'earshot (of sb/sth)
too far away to hear sb/sth or to be heard: *We waited until Ted was safely out of earshot before discussing it.*

within 'earshot (of sb/sth)
near enough to hear sb/sth or to be heard: *As she came within earshot of the group, she heard her name mentioned.*

earth

bring sb/come (back) down to 'earth (with a 'bang, 'bump, etc.)
(make sb) have to deal with sth unpleasant, especially after a time when things seemed to be going well or life was enjoyable: *After such a wonderful holiday, losing all her money certainly brought her back down to earth with a bump.* ▶ ,**down-to-'earth** *adj.* (*approving*) sensible and practical: *Even though she's a movie star, she's still friendly and down-to-earth.*

cost/pay/charge the 'earth (*BrE, informal*)
cost/pay/charge a lot of money: *Redecorating your home needn't cost the earth if you use a little*

imagination. ◊ *They paid the earth to see the Rolling Stones play live.*

go to 'earth/'ground (*BrE*)
hide, especially to escape from sb who is chasing you: *His family never saw him again. He went to ground and they heard nothing else of him until he died last year.*

> ❶ ORIGIN
> This expression refers to a fox hiding underground when it is hunted.

how, what, why, etc. on 'earth/in the 'world … (*informal*)
used with questions to express the speaker's surprise, anger, etc: *How on earth did you know I was coming today when I didn't know myself until the last minute?* ◊ *Why on earth would anyone give up such a good job?*

like ,nothing on 'earth
very ill or unattractive: *After two hours in that tiny boat I felt like nothing on earth.* ◊ *I hadn't slept for 48 hours. I must have looked like nothing on earth.*

nothing on 'earth (*informal*)
absolutely nothing: *Nothing on earth would make me tell anyone our secret.*

disappear/vanish off the face of the earth → **face**
the four corners of the earth → **four**
a heaven on earth → **heaven**
a hell on earth → **hell**
move heaven and earth (to do sth) → **move**
promise (sb) the moon/earth/world → **promise**
run sb/sth to earth/ground → **run**
the salt of the earth → **salt**
the scum of the earth → **scum**
to the ends of the earth → **ends**
wipe sth off the face of the earth → **wipe**

earthly

no earthly 'use, 'reason, etc. (*informal*)
used to emphasize that there is no use, reason, etc. at all: *There's no earthly reason why she shouldn't come with us.*

not (have) an 'earthly (chance) (*BrE, informal*)
(have) no chance at all: *You haven't an earthly chance of beating her at tennis—she is one of the best players in the country.* ◊ *'Any chance of getting a ticket for the concert?' 'Not an earthly, I'm afraid.'*

ease

(stand) at 'ease
(in the military) (an order to soldiers to) stand in a relaxed position, with the feet apart: *The platoon stood at ease while the officer explained the battle plan.*

at (your) 'ease
relaxed and confident and not nervous or embarrassed: *I never feel completely at ease with him.* ◊ *No matter what situation she was in, somehow she always managed to look completely at her ease.*

put/set sb at (their) 'ease
make sb feel relaxed, not shy, etc: *Try to put the
candidate at ease by being friendly and informal.*

ill at ease ➜ **ill**
put/set sb's mind at ease/rest ➜ **mind**

easier

,easier ,said than 'done (*saying*)
it is easier to suggest doing sth than actually to do
it: *'All you have to do is climb a ladder and mend the
roof.' 'Easier said than done—I'm terrified of
heights!'*

easily

sit comfortably/easily/well (with sth) ➜ **sit**

easy

(as) ,easy as AB'C/'pie/falling off a 'log
(*informal*)
very easy: *Try using the new photocopier. It's as
easy as pie.*

,easy 'come, ,easy 'go (*saying*)
something that has been obtained very easily and
quickly may be lost or wasted in the same way: *Her
parents have given her all the money she wants, but
she's always in debt. With her, it's a case of easy
come, easy go.*

,easy/,gently/,slowly 'does it (*informal*)
used for telling sb to be careful, calm, etc: *Easy
does it! Just lift it a little bit and I think it'll go
through the door.*

,easy 'game
a person or thing that is easy to attack, criticize, or
make a victim: *Customers who know nothing about
cars are easy game for dishonest dealers.*

,easy 'money
money earned for very little work or effort, often
by doing sth dishonest: *There's a lot of easy money
to be made in this business.*

,easy on the 'eye, 'ear, etc.
pleasant to look at, listen to, etc: *When decorating
your bedroom, it's best to choose colours that are
easy on the eye.*

go 'easy on sb (*informal*)
not be too strict with sb, especially when they have
done sth wrong: *Go easy on the child, she didn't
mean to break the window.*

go 'easy on sth
do not use too much of sth, speak too much about
sth, etc: *Go easy on the spices. I don't like very hot
curry.* ◇ *When you're talking to Jim, go easy on the
subject of marriage—his wife's just left him.*

have an easy 'time of it (*BrE, informal*)
be in a very favourable situation: *She has a very
easy time of it in her job—she only works about 20
hours a week.*

I'm 'easy (*BrE, informal*)
used to say that you do not have a strong opinion

when sb has offered you a choice: *'Tea or coffee?'
'Oh, I'm easy—I'll have whatever you're having.'*

on 'easy street (*AmE*)
enjoying a comfortable way of life with plenty of
money and no worries: *The box office success of his
first movie put him and his family on easy street.*

take the easy way 'out
end a difficult situation by choosing the simplest
solution, even if it is not the best one: *Rather than
trying to save his business, he took the easy way out
and declared himself bankrupt.*

take it/things 'easy (*informal*)
relax and avoid working too hard or doing too
much; not get angry, excited, etc: *Bob's still running the business on his own. He really ought to be
taking things easy at his age.* ◇ *Take it easy, Jenny!
There's no need to get so annoyed.*

free and easy ➜ **free**
(give sb, have, etc.) a rough/an easy ride ➜ **ride**
the soft/easy option ➜ **option**
a soft/an easy touch ➜ **touch**

eat

eat sb a'live (*informal*)
1 (also **have/eat sb for 'breakfast**) criticize or
punish sb severely because you are extremely
angry with them
2 (also **have/eat sb for 'breakfast**) defeat sb
completely in an argument, a competition, etc:
*The defence lawyers are going to eat you alive
tomorrow.* ◇ *The union leader eats managers for
breakfast!*
3 (usually used in the passive) (of insects, etc.)
bite sb many times: *I was being eaten alive by mos-
quitoes.*

,eat, drink and be 'merry (*saying*)
said to encourage sb to enjoy life now, while they
can, and not to think of the future

eat your 'heart out (for sb/sth) (*especially BrE*)
be very unhappy because you want sb/sth that you
cannot have: *He's eating his heart out for that
woman.*

,eat humble 'pie (*BrE*) (*AmE* **eat 'crow**)
say and show that you are sorry for a mistake that
you made: *I had to eat humble pie when Harry, who
I said would never have any success, won first prize.*

❶ ORIGIN
This comes from a pun on the old word *umbles*,
meaning 'offal' (= the inside parts of an animal),
which was considered inferior food.

eat like a 'bird
eat very little: *She's so afraid of putting on weight
that she eats like a bird.*

eat like a 'horse
eat very large quantities of food: *My brother eats
like a horse but never puts on any weight.*

eat sb out of ˌhouse and ˈhome (*informal, often humorous*)

eat all the food that sb has: *She eats us out of house and home every time she comes to stay.*

eat your ˈwords

be forced to admit that what you have said before was wrong: *Nick told everyone that he'd be picked for the team, but when he wasn't chosen he had to eat his words.*

eat your ˈheart out (*spoken*)

used to compare two things and say that one of them is better: *Look at him dance! Eat your heart out, John Travolta* (= he dances even better than John Travolta).

I could eat a ˈhorse (*spoken*)

I am very hungry: *What's for dinner? I could eat a horse!*

I'll eat my ˈhat! (*spoken*)

used to say that you think sth is very unlikely to happen: *They're always late—if they get here before eight o'clock, I'll eat my hat.*

he, she, etc. won't ˈeat you (*informal*)

said to encourage sb to speak to or approach sb who seems frightening: *Come on, Emma, Santa Claus won't eat you! If you go closer, he'll give you a present!*

dog eat dog ➔ **dog**
have your cake and eat it (too) ➔ **cake**

eating

have (got) sb eating out of your ˈhand

have sb completely in your control so that they will do whatever you want: *Once they knew that they would never be able to escape without his help, he had them eating out of his hand.*

what's eating ˈsb? (*spoken*)

used to ask why sb is worried, unhappy, etc: *You seem a bit quiet today. What's eating you?*

ebb

the ˌebb and ˈflow (of sb/sth)

the repeated, often regular, movement from one state to another; the repeated change in level, numbers or amount: *the ebb and flow of money/ seasons* ◇ *She sat quietly, enjoying the ebb and flow of conversation.*

❶ ORIGIN
This expression refers to the movement of the sea away from and towards the land.

(at) a low ebb ➔ **low**

economical

economical with the ˈtruth

a way of saying that sb has left out some important facts, when you do not want to say that they are lying: *It was only after the trial that he admitted that he had occasionally been economical with the truth.*

edge

have, etc. an/the edge on/over sb/sth

be slightly better, faster, etc. than sb/sth; have an advantage over sb/sth: *Max's design is very good, but I think Paul's has the edge on it.* ◇ *Extra training will give our team an edge over the opposition.*

on ˈedge

nervous, worried or anxious: *Most people feel on edge before exams.*

on the ˌedge of your ˈseat/ˈchair

very excited and giving your full attention to sth: *The film was so exciting it had me on the edge of my seat right until the last moment.*

take the ˈedge off sth

make sth less strong, unpleasant, etc: *He tried to take the edge off the bad news by promising to help them in their difficulties.* ◇ *I had an apple before lunch, which took the edge off my appetite.*

(be at) the cutting edge (of sth) ➔ **cutting**
on a razor's edge = on a knife-edge ➔ **knife-edge**
set sb's teeth on edge ➔ **set**
teeter on the brink/edge of sth ➔ **teeter**

edges

fray at/around the edges/seams ➔ **fray**
rough edges ➔ **rough**

edgeways

(not) get a word in edgeways ➔ **word**

edgewise

(not) get a word in edgewise ➔ **word**

educated

an ˌeducated ˈguess

a guess made on the basis of facts, good information, etc., and so probably fairly accurate: *I can't tell you exactly how much the building work will cost, but I can make an educated guess.*

eel

(as) slippery as an eel ➔ **slippery**

effect

bring/put sth into efˈfect

make sth, for example an idea, plan, etc. happen: *The government wants to put its new housing policy into immediate effect.*

come/go into efˈfect

(of laws, rules, etc.) begin to be used, applied, etc: *The winter timetable comes into effect in November.*

in efˈfect

in actual practice; in fact: *They may seem different, but in effect, the two systems are almost identical.*

of/to no efˈfect

not having the result hoped for: *Their warnings were of no effect.* ◇ *They tried to persuade him to change his mind, but to no effect.*

take ef'fect
1 have the intended result: *It will be some time before the painkillers take effect.*
2 (*formal*) start to be valid: *Your promotion takes effect from the end of the month.*

to the ef'fect that ...; to this/that ef'fect
used when giving the basic meaning of what sb has said or written, without using their exact words: *A letter was sent to the employees to the effect that the store would have to close down.* ◇ *She told me not to interfere, or words to that effect.*

to good, little, etc. ef'fect
with a good, etc. result: *Her talent as a dancer is shown to considerable effect in this new production.*

with effect from ... (*formal*)
starting from ...: *The Minister has announced a 10p increase in the price of petrol, with effect from 6th April.*

a ripple effect → ripple

effing

effing and 'blinding (*BrE, informal*)
using swear words (= rude and offensive words): *There was a lot of effing and blinding going on.*

effort

a last-ditch stand/attempt/effort → last-ditch

efforts

bend your mind/efforts to sth → bend

egg

(have) 'egg on your face (*informal*)
be made to look stupid: *Let's think this out carefully. I don't want to end up with egg on my face.*

(like) the curate's egg (, good in parts) → curate
kill the goose that lays the golden egg/eggs → kill
a nest egg → nest

eggs

put all your eggs into one 'basket
risk all your money, effort, etc. on one thing, so that if it is not successful, you have no other chance: *It may be better to invest a small amount of money in several businesses rather than putting all your eggs into one basket.*

kill the goose that lays the golden egg/eggs → kill
(as) sure as eggs is eggs → sure
teach your grandmother to suck eggs → teach
you can't make an omelette without breaking eggs → omelette

eggshells

walk on eggshells → walk

eight

be/have one over the 'eight (*informal*)
be slightly drunk: *From the way he was walking it was obvious he'd had one over the eight.*

❶ ORIGIN
This idiom probably comes from the time when officials at the Royal Court were allowed eight pints of beer to drink per day. If people drank more, they were assumed to have had too much.

elbow

at your 'elbow
very near; within arm's reach: *I always like to have a dictionary at my elbow to check spellings.*

'elbow grease (*informal*)
the effort used in physical work, especially in cleaning: *The bath was so old and stained that we couldn't get it clean no matter how much elbow grease we used.*

'elbow room (*informal*)
1 enough space to move in: *October is a good time to visit as there are fewer tourists and more elbow room in the restaurants.*
2 the freedom to do sth: *Teachers often feel they have little elbow room to try new methods.*

give sb the 'elbow (*BrE, informal*)
tell sb that you no longer want to have a relationship with them: *I hear she's finally given her boyfriend the elbow.*

more power to sb's elbow → power
not know your arse/ass from your elbow → know

elbows

rub elbows with sb → rub

elder

an ,elder 'statesman
1 a person who has had an important job in government, business, etc. and who, though he may have retired (= stopped work), is still likely to be asked for his opinion and advice
2 any experienced and respected person whose advice or work is valued: *He is regarded as TV's elder statesman, having worked for the giant CBS network for nearly twenty years.*

elders

your ,elders and 'betters
people who are older and wiser than you and whom you should respect: *You may not want to go, but your elders and betters think you should.*

element

in your 'element
doing sth that you enjoy and do well, especially

with other similar people: *Julie is in her element with anything mechanical. She just loves fixing things.*

out of your 'element
in a situation that you are not used to and that makes you feel uncomfortable: *I feel out of my element talking about politics.*

elephant

a white elephant → white

elephants

see pink elephants → see

eleventh

the e,leventh 'hour
the moment when it is almost, but not quite, too late to do sth, avoid sth, etc: *Our pianist had fallen ill, and then, at the eleventh hour, when we thought we'd have to cancel the performance, Jill offered to replace him.* ▶ **e,leventh-'hour** *adj.*: *an eleventh-hour decision*

else

if all else 'fails (*spoken*)
used to introduce an idea or a suggestion that you could try if nothing else works: *Let's try phoning her at this number and then emailing her. If all else fails, we can always contact her parents.*

or else
1 used to introduce the second of two possibilities: *I can't get through to Sally. She's out, or else she's decided not to answer the telephone.*
2 (*informal*) used to threaten or warn sb: *You'd better clean up this mess, or else!*

something 'else
1 a different thing; another thing: *He said something else that I thought was interesting.*
2 (*informal*) a person, a thing or an event that is much better than others of a similar type: *I've seen some fine players, but she's something else.*

embarrassment

an em,barrassment of 'riches
so many good things that it is difficult to choose just one: *Stratford has an embarrassment of riches, what with three theatres and lovely country-side too.*

embryo

in 'embryo
still in a very early stage of development: *We have just one editor and a reporter, so you could say that the newspaper exists in embryo.*

empty

the ,empty 'nest
the situation that parents are in when their children have left home: *the empty nest syndrome*

on an empty 'stomach
without having eaten anything: *If I travel on an empty stomach, I always feel sick.*

enchilada

the whole enchi'lada (*AmE, informal*)
the whole situation; everything: *We had a great time on vacation, and it only cost us $500 for the whole enchilada.*

❷ NOTE
An *enchilada* is a Mexican dish consisting of a tortilla filled with meat or cheese and covered with a spicy sauce.

the big enchilada → big

end

at the ,end of the 'day (*BrE, spoken*)
when everything has been considered: *At the end of the day, it's your decision and nobody else's.*

be at an 'end (*formal*)
be finished: *Our negotiations are at an end, and we have reached an agreement.*

be at the ,end of your 'tether (*BrE*) (*AmE* **be at the ,end of your 'rope**)
having no more patience or strength left: *After two hours of hearing the children shout and argue, I really was at the end of my tether.*

be the 'end (*BrE, spoken*)
be very annoying; be impossible to tolerate: *Your children really are the end!* ◇ *I'd seen dirty houses before, but theirs was the absolute end!*

come to a bad/sticky 'end (*informal*)
finish in an unpleasant way; finish by having sth unpleasant happen to you, usually because of your own actions: *The neighbours used to shake their heads at his behaviour and say that he'd come to a bad end.*

days, weeks, etc. on 'end
several days, weeks, etc., one after another: *She stays away from home for days on end.* ◇ *He sits watching TV for hours on end.*

,end your 'days/'life (in sth)
spend the last part of your life in a particular state or place: *He ended his days in poverty.*

an ,end in it'self
a thing that is itself important and not just a part of sth more important: *Speech is not an end in itself, but a means to communicate something.*

,end in 'tears (*spoken*)
if you say that sth will **end in tears**, you are warning sb that what they are doing will have an unhappy or unpleasant result: *You'd better keep your promise or it'll end in tears.*

,end it 'all
kill yourself; commit suicide: *After years of suffering, she had decided to end it all.*

the end justifies the 'means (*saying*)
bad or unfair methods of doing sth are acceptable
if the result of that action is good or positive

the ‚end of the 'road/'line
the point where sb/sth cannot continue: *The workers see the closure of the pit as the end of the line for
mining in this area.* ◇ *It's the end of the road for
our relationship. We just can't agree about anything any more.*

end of 'story (*spoken*)
used when you are stating that there is nothing
more that can be said or done about sth: *Look, I
told you I can't give you a job here. End of story.*

‚end to 'end
in a line, with the ends touching: *They arranged
the tables end to end.*

get/have your 'end away (*BrE, slang*)
have sex

in the 'end
after or in spite of everything that has gone before;
finally: *I looked for my keys for hours, and in the
end I found them in the car.* ◇ *They tried to get him
to confess, and in the end he did.*

keep your 'end up (*BrE, informal*)
stay cheerful or perform well in a difficult situation: *She managed to keep her end up even though
she was suffering from flu.* ◇ *I had trouble keeping
my end up in the conversation, because I didn't
know anything about the subject.*

no 'end (*spoken*)
very much: *Your visit pleased her no end.*

no 'end of (*spoken*)
a lot of: *Making new friends has done him no end of
good.* ◇ *We've had no end of offers of help.*

not be the ‚end of the 'world (*spoken*)
not be a disaster: *It wouldn't be the end of the world
if you couldn't get into college. I'm sure you'd be
able to find a good job anyway.* ◇ *Why are you so
upset? It's not the end of the world.*

**not know/not be able to tell one end of sth
from the other** (*informal*)
know absolutely nothing about sth, for example a
machine: *Don't ask me to fix the car. I don't know
one end of an engine from the other.*

put an 'end to yourself; put an 'end to it all
kill yourself: *She told me that sometimes she felt so
bad that she just felt like putting an end to it all.*

the sth to end all sths
used to emphasize how large, important, exciting,
etc. you think sth is: *The movie has a car chase to
end all car chases.* ◇ *Many people said that World
War I would be the war to end all wars.*

at a loose end → **loose**
be at your wits' end → **wits**
be on/at the receiving end (of sth) → **receiving**
be (at) the sharp end (of sth) → **sharp**
the beginning of the end → **beginning**
the business end (of sth) → **business**

a dead end → **dead**
get the short end of the stick = draw the short straw
→ **draw**
get (hold of) the wrong end of the stick → **wrong**
go off the deep end → **deep**
your hair stands on end → **hair**
hear/see the end/the last of sb/sth → **hear**
jump in/be thrown in at the deep end → **deep**
(see the) light at the end of the tunnel → **light**
(be) a means to an end → **means**
not see beyond/past the end of your nose → **see**
(at) the tail end (of sth) → **tail**
the thin end of the wedge → **thin**
to the bitter end → **bitter**

end-all

the be-all and end-all (of sth) → **be-all**

ends

make (both) ends 'meet
earn enough to pay your living expenses: *Since I
lost my job, I'm finding it harder to make ends meet.*

to the ‚ends of the 'earth
a very great distance: *He would go to the ends of the
earth to be with her.*

all's well that ends well → **well**
at loose ends → **loose**
burn the candle at both ends → **burn**
the loose ends/threads → **loose**
odds and ends → **odds**

enemy

be your own worst enemy → **worst**
public enemy number one → **public**
wouldn't wish sth on my, etc. worst enemy → **wish**

English

the ‚King's/‚Queen's 'English (*old-fashioned*
or *humorous*)
(in Britain) correct standard English: *I can't
understand a word you're saying. Can't you speak
the Queen's English?*

in plain English → **plain**

Englishman

an ‚Englishman's ‚home is his 'castle (*BrE*)
(*AmE* **a ‚man's ‚home is his 'castle**) (*saying*)
a person's home is a place where they can be private and safe and do as they like

engraved

**be engraved/etched on/in your 'heart/
'memory/'mind**
be sth that you will never forget because it affected
you so strongly: *Although he was very young at the
time, the date of his father's funeral was engraved
on his heart.* ◇ *The image of their son holding up
the championship trophy would be etched on their
memories forever.*

enough

,curiously, ,funnily, ,oddly, ,strangely, etc. e'nough
used to show that sth is surprising: *Funnily enough, I was born on exactly the same day as my wife.*

e,nough is e'nough (*saying*)
used when you think that sth should not continue any longer: *Enough is enough! I don't mind a joke, but now you've gone too far!*

have had e'nough (of sb/sth)
used when sb/sth is annoying you and you no longer want to do, have or see them/it: *I've had enough of driving the kids around.*

enter

enter sb's 'head
be thought of by sb; occur to sb: *It never even entered my head that we might not win.*

enter sb's/your 'name (for sth); put sb's/ your 'name down (for sth)
apply for a place at a school, in a competition, etc. for sb or yourself: *Have you entered your name for the quiz yet?*

get/enter into the spirit of sth → spirit

entering

breaking and entering → breaking

entirety

in its/their en'tirety
as a whole, rather than in parts: *The poem is too long to quote in its entirety.*

envelope

push the envelope → push

envy

be the envy of sb/sth
be a person or thing that other people admire and that causes feelings of envy: *Our new games console was the envy of all the kids in the street.*

green with envy → green

equal

be without 'equal; have no 'equal (*formal*)
be better than anything else or anyone else of the same type: *He was a violinist without equal.*

on equal 'terms (with sb/sth); on the same 'terms (as sb/sth)
with no difference or advantage over another person; as equals: *We're not competing on equal terms; the other team has one more player.* ◇ *A good teacher should treat all her students on the same terms.*

,some (people, members, etc.) are more equal than 'others (*saying*)
although the members of a society, group, etc. appear to be equal, some get better treatment than others

> ❶ ORIGIN
> This phrase is used by one of the pigs in the book *Animal Farm* by George Orwell: 'All animals are equal but some animals are more equal than others.'

other/all things being equal → things

equals

first among equals → first

err

err on the side of 'sth
show slightly too much rather than too little of a (usually good) quality: *When I am marking exam papers, I always try to err on the side of generosity* (= I give slightly higher marks than the students may deserve).

errand

a fool's errand → fool

error

the ,error of your 'ways (*formal* or *humorous*)
what is wrong and should be changed about the kind of life you are leading: *While he was in prison, a social worker and a priest both visited him in an attempt to make him see the error of his ways.*

by trial and error → trial

escape

escape sb's 'notice
not be noticed by sb: *It may have escaped your notice but I'm very busy right now. Can we talk later?*

make ,good your e'scape (*written*)
manage to escape completely: *In the confusion at the border, the woman made good her escape.* ◇ *He made good his escape from a crowd of journalists by jumping over a fence.*

a narrow escape/squeak → narrow

escaped

shut, etc. the barn door after the horse has escaped = shut/lock/close the stable door after the horse has bolted → stable

essence

of the 'essence
absolutely necessary: *Time is of the essence* (= we must do things as quickly as possible).

etched

be engraved/etched on/in your heart/memory/mind → engraved

eternal

hope springs eternal → hope

even

be 'even (*informal*)
no longer owe sb money or a favour: *If I pay for the meals then we're even.*

be/get 'even with sb (*informal*)
cause sb the same amount of trouble or harm as they have caused you: *I'll get even with him some day for making those nasty comments about me.*

even as (*formal*)
just at the same time as sb does sth or as sth else happens: *Even as he shouted the warning the car skidded.*

even if/though
in spite of the fact or belief that; no matter whether: *I'll get there, even if I have to walk.* ◇ *I like her, even though she can be annoying at times.*

even 'now/'then
1 in spite of what has/had happened: *I've shown him the photographs but even now he won't believe me.* ◇ *Even then she would not admit her mistake.*
2 (*formal*) at this or that exact moment: *The troops are even now preparing to march into the city.*

,even the 'score
harm or punish sb who has harmed or cheated you in the past: *When he discovered how Martha had tricked him, Jack was determined to even the score.*

,even 'so
in spite of that: *There are a lot of spelling mistakes; even so, it's quite a good essay.*

have (got) an even 'chance (of doing sth)
be equally likely to do or not do sth: *She has more than an even chance of winning tomorrow.*

on an even 'keel
living, working or happening in a calm way, with no sudden changes, especially after a difficult time: *After all the troubles of the past weeks, life seems to be getting back on an even keel again.*

> ❷ NOTE
> The *keel* is the long piece of wood or steel along the bottom of a ship which helps it to keep upright in the water.

break even → break
even/much/still less → less
honours are even → honours

event

in the e'vent
as it actually happened, contrasted with what was expected: *We all thought he was rather lazy, but in the event he worked very hard and passed all his exams.*

in the event of sth; in the event that sth happens
if sth happens: *The money will be paid to your fam-* ily *in the event of your death.* ◇ *In the event of an emergency please call the following number …*

be wise after the event → wise
a/the happy event → happy

events

at 'all events; in 'any event
whatever happens; anyway: *James may arrive this evening or tomorrow morning. In any event, I would like you to meet him at the airport.* ◇ *At all events, there will be a change of government.*

a/the turn of events → turn

ever

did you 'ever (…)! (*old-fashioned, informal*)
used to show that you are surprised or shocked: *Did you ever hear anything like it?*

ever more (*formal*)
more and more: *She grew ever more impatient as time passed.*

ever since (…)
continuously since the time mentioned: *He's had a car ever since he was 18.* ◇ *I was bitten by a dog once and I've been afraid of them ever since.*

'ever so/'ever such (a) … (*spoken, especially BrE*)
very: *Thanks ever so much for all your help.* ◇ *She plays the piano ever so well.* ◇ *He's ever such a nice man.*

if ,ever there 'was (one) (*spoken*)
used to emphasize that sth is certainly true: *That meal was a disaster if ever there was one!*

yours 'ever/ever 'yours
sometimes used at the end of an informal letter, before you write your name

everything

and everything (*spoken*)
and so on; and other similar things: *Have you got his name and address and everything?* ◇ *She told me about the baby and everything.*

money, winning, etc. isn't 'everything
money, etc. is not the most important thing: *Work isn't everything. You must learn to relax a bit more.*

evidence

in 'evidence
present and clearly seen: *There were very few local people in evidence at the meeting.* ◇ *What's the matter with John? His sense of humour hasn't been much in evidence recently.*

turn King's/Queen's evidence → turn
turn State's evidence → turn

evil

the evil 'hour/'day/'moment
the time when you have to do sth difficult or unpleasant: *I'd better go and see the dentist—I can't put off the evil hour any longer.* ◇ *I worried for*

weeks about how I would tell him the bad news but eventually I couldn't put off the evil day any longer.

give sb the evil 'eye
look at sb in a very angry, unfriendly or unpleasant way, as if you are trying to harm them by magic power: *I don't know why you're giving me the evil eye—I haven't done anything wrong!*

the lesser evil → **lesser**
a necessary evil → **necessary**

evils

the lesser of two evils → **lesser**

exactly

not e'xactly (*spoken*)
1 used when you are saying the opposite of what you really mean: *He wasn't exactly pleased to see us—in fact he refused to open the door.* ◊ *It's not exactly beautiful, is it?* (= it's ugly)
2 used when you are correcting sth that sb has said: *'So he told you you'd got the job?' 'Not exactly, but he said they were impressed with me.'*

examined

need, want, etc. your head examined → **head**

example

make an e'xample of sb
punish sb severely for a mistake, crime, etc. so that others will be less likely to do wrong: *The judge decided to make an example of the leaders of the riot in order to prevent other disturbances.*

be a shining example (of sb/sth) → **shining**
set (sb) a (good, bad, etc.) example → **set**

excellence

par excellence → **par**

excepted

present company excepted → **present**

excepting

excepting present company = present company excepted
  → **present**

exception

the ex,ception (that) proves the 'rule (*saying*)
if sth is different from or the opposite of a belief or theory, this shows that the belief or theory is true in general: *English people are supposed to be very reserved, but Pete is the exception that proves the rule—he'll chat to anyone!*

make an ex'ception
allow sb not to follow the usual rule on one occasion: *Children are not usually allowed in, but I'm prepared to make an exception in this case.*

take ex'ception to sth
be very offended by a remark, suggestion, etc: *I*

take great exception to your suggestion that I only did this for the money.*

with the ex'ception of
except; not including: *All his novels are set in Italy with the exception of his last.*

without ex'ception
used to emphasize that the statement you are making is always true and everyone or everything is included: *All students without exception must take the English examination.*

exchange

have/exchange words (with sb) (about sth) → **words**

excuse

ex'cuse me
1 used before you do or say sth that might annoy sb, or to get sb's attention: *Excuse me, is anybody sitting here?* ◊ *Excuse me, could you tell me the time, please?*
2 used for saying sorry or disagreeing with sb, or for showing that you are annoyed: *Excuse me, but I think you're mistaken.* ◊ *Excuse me, sir, but you can't park there!*
3 used when you are leaving the room for a short time: *Excuse me a minute, I'll be right back.*
4 (*especially AmE*) used for saying sorry for something you have done: *Excuse me, did I step on your toe?*
5 (*especially AmE*) used when you did not hear what sb said and you want them to repeat it

excuse/pardon my French → **French**

exhibition

make an exhi'bition of yourself (*disapproving*)
behave in a stupid or embarrassing way that makes people notice you: *She got angry and made a real exhibition of herself at the party.*

existence

the bane of sb's life/existence → **bane**

expect

what (else) do you ex'pect? (*spoken*)
used to tell sb not to be surprised by sth: *She shouted at you? What do you expect when you treat her like that?*

expected

be (only) to be ex'pected
be likely to happen; be quite normal: *A little tiredness after taking these drugs is to be expected.* ◊ *'I'm afraid I'm very nervous.' 'Don't worry, that's only to be expected.'*

expecting

be ex'pecting (*informal*)
be pregnant: *I hear Sue's expecting.*

expense

at sb's expense
1 paid for by sb: *When Joe is travelling at the firm's expense, he goes first class.*
2 (of jokes, etc.) making sb seem foolish: *They all had a good laugh at Pete's expense.*

at the expense of sb/sth
causing damage or loss to sb/sth else: *We could lower the price, but only at the expense of quality.*

go to the expense of sth/of doing sth; go to a lot of, etc. expense
spend money on sth: *They went to all the expense of redecorating the house and then they moved.*

put sb to the expense of sth/of doing sth; put sb to a lot of, etc. expense
make sb spend money on sth: *Their visit put us to a lot of expense.*

spare no expense/pains/trouble (to do sth/(in) doing sth)
→ spare

experience

put sth down to ex'perience (also chalk it up to ex'perience *especially AmE*)
accept a failure, loss, etc. as being sth that you can learn from: *When her second novel was rejected by the publisher, she put it down to experience and began another one.*

explain

ex'plain yourself
1 give sb reasons for your behaviour, especially when they are angry or upset because of it: *I really don't see why I should have to explain myself to you.*
2 say what you mean in a clear way: *Could you explain yourself a little more—I didn't understand.*

extent

to ... extent
used to show how far sth is true or how great an effect it has: *To a certain extent, we are all responsible for this tragic situation.* ◇ *He had changed to such an extent (= so much) that I no longer recognized him.* ◇ *The pollution of the forest has seriously affected plant life and, to a lesser extent, wildlife.* ◇ *To what extent is this true of all schools?*

extra

go the extra mile (for sb/sth) → extra

extreme

boring, silly, etc. in the ex'treme
extremely boring, silly, etc: *I must admit, it's puzzling in the extreme just how these books found their way here.*

extremes

go to ex'tremes; carry/take sth to ex'tremes
behave in a way that is not moderate or normal: *She really goes to extremes, spending such huge sums of money on entertaining her friends.* ◇ *You never go out after dark? That's taking being careful to extremes, isn't it?*

eye

an ,eye for an 'eye (and a ,tooth for a 'tooth) (*saying*)
a person who treats sb else badly should be treated in the same way

> ❶ ORIGIN
> This expression comes from the Bible.

get your 'eye in (*BrE*)
(in ball games) get to the point where you start to judge distances, the speed of the ball, etc., accurately and so start to play well: *The batsman began slowly but once he got his eye in he started to play some very good shots.*

have (got) an 'eye for sth
be good at judging sth: *He's always had an eye for a bargain.*

have (got) your 'eye on sb/sth
watch sb/sth closely; want to have sth: *A house that I'd had my eye on for some time suddenly came up for sale.*

have (got) an eye to/for the main 'chance (*BrE, usually disapproving*)
be good at using opportunities for your own benefit: *She's certainly got an eye for the main chance. Her business has become highly successful.*

have (got) one eye/half an eye on sth
look at or watch sth while doing sth else, especially in a secret way so that other people do not notice: *During his talk, most of the delegates had one eye on the clock.*

keep an/your 'eye on sb/sth
take responsibility for sb/sth; make sure that sb/sth is safe: *It's my job to keep an eye on how the money is spent.* ◇ *Keep an eye on my bag while I go and make a phone call, will you?*

She found it difficult to relax when she had to keep an eye on young Lucy.

keep an 'eye out (for sb/sth) (*informal*)
watch or look carefully (for sb/sth): *Can you keep an eye out for the taxi and let me know when it arrives?*

my 'eye! (*BrE, spoken*)
used to show that you do not believe sb/sth: *'It's an antique.' 'An antique, my eye!'*

one in the eye for sb/sth (*informal*)
a result, action, etc. that represents a defeat or disappointment for sb/sth: *The appointment of a woman was one in the eye for male domination.*

under the (watchful) eye of sb
being watched carefully by sb: *The children played under the watchful eye of their father.*

what the eye doesn't 'see (the heart doesn't 'grieve over) (*saying*)
if a person does not know about sth that they would normally disapprove of, then it cannot hurt them: *What does it matter if I do use his flat while he's away? What the eye doesn't see ... !*

with an eye to (doing) sth
intending to do sth: *She's doing an interpreters' course with an eye to getting a job abroad.*

would give your eye 'teeth for sth/to do sth (*informal*)
would give anything for sth; want sth very much: *I'd give my eye teeth to own a car like that.* ◇ *He'd give his eye teeth for a job in television.*

the apple of sb's eye → **apple**
as far as the eye can/could see → **far**
beauty is in the eye of the beholder → **beauty**
a black eye → **black**
cast/run an eye/your eyes over sth → **cast**
catch sb's eye → **catch**
cock an ear/eye at sth/sb → **cock**
an/sb's eagle eye → **eagle**
give sb the evil eye → **evil**
have (got) your beady eye on sb/sth → **beady**
have (got) a roving eye → **roving**
hit sb in the eye → **hit**
in the blink of an eye → **blink**
in your mind's eye → **mind**
in a pig's eye → **pig**
in the public eye → **public**
(do sth) in the twinkling of an eye → **twinkling**
keep a beady eye on sb/sth → **beady**
keep a close eye/watch on sb/sth → **close**
keep a weather eye on sth/open for sth → **weather**
(be unable to) look sb in the eye(s)/face → **look**
meet the/your eye(s) → **meet**
the naked eye → **naked**
not bat an eye → **bat**
not a dry eye in the house → **dry**
out of the corner of your eye → **corner**
please the eye → **please**
a private eye → **private**
(not) see eye to eye (with sb) (about/on/over sth) → **see**
there's more to sb/sth than meets the eye → **meets**
turn a blind eye (to sth) → **turn**

eyeball

,eyeball to 'eyeball (with sb) (*informal*)
standing very close, facing one another, for example in a fight: *The two men stood eyeball to eyeball, shouting insults at each other.*

eyeballs

be up to your eyes/eyeballs in sth → **eyes**
drugged up to the eyeballs → **drugged**

eyebrows

raise your eyebrows (at sth) → **raise**

eyeful

have/get an 'eyeful (of sth) (*BrE, spoken*)
look carefully at sth that is interesting or unusual: *Quick! Come and get an eyeful of this!*

eyelashes

bat your eyelashes/eyes → **bat**

eyelid

not bat an eyelid → **bat**

eyes

all eyes are on sb/sth
if **all eyes are on sb/sth**, everyone is looking at sb/sth in an interested way: *All eyes were on him as he walked onto the stage.*

be all 'eyes
watch with close attention and usually with great interest: *The children were all eyes as, one by one, I took the toys out of the bag.*

be up to your 'eyes/'eyeballs in sth
have a lot of sth to deal with: *He was up to his eyes in debt.*

'Lunch? No way – I'm up to my eyes in it here!'

before your (very) 'eyes
right in front of you, where you can see sth very clearly: *There, before my very eyes, he took the plane ticket and ripped it into tiny pieces.*

clap/lay/set 'eyes on sb/sth (*informal*)
see sb/sth: *I've no idea who she is. I've never clapped eyes on her before.* ◇ *From the moment I set eyes on the house, I knew I could be happy living there.*

your ,eyes are bigger than your 'stomach (*informal, humorous*)
used to say that sb has been greedy by taking more

food than they can eat: *Can't you finish your food? Your eyes are bigger than your stomach!*

your eyes nearly pop out of your 'head (*informal*)

sb has an expression of great surprise on their face: *Our eyes nearly popped out of our heads when we saw a giraffe walking down the High Street.*

for sb's eyes 'only

to be seen only by sb: *This letter is for your eyes only, so keep it locked in your desk.*

have (got) eyes in the back of your 'head (*informal*)

seem to be able to see everything and know what is going on: *You have to have eyes in the back of your head to keep control of six lively children.*

have (got) eyes like a 'hawk

be able to notice or see everything: *Mrs Fielding's bound to notice that chipped glass. The woman has eyes like a hawk!*

in the eyes of 'sb/'sth; in 'sb's eyes

according to sb/sth; in sb's opinion: *You may believe that what you are doing is right, but in the eyes of the law it's a crime.*

keep your 'eyes open/peeled/skinned (for sb/sth)

watch carefully (for sb/sth): *Keep your eyes peeled, and if you see anything suspicious, call the police immediately.*

make 'eyes at sb (*informal*)

look at sb in a way that tries to attract them sexually: *He did nothing all holiday but make eyes at the girls!*

not take your 'eyes off sb/sth

(often used with *can* or *could*) not stop looking at sb/sth: *She couldn't take her eyes off the beautiful picture.*

only have eyes for sb; have eyes only for sb

be interested in, or in love with a particular person and nobody else: *John has been trying to get Helen to go out with him, but she only has eyes for Chris.*

shut/close your 'eyes to sth

pretend that you have not noticed sth so that you do not have to deal with it: *My son has his faults—and I've never closed my eyes to them—but dishonesty isn't one of them.* ◇ *Politicians seemed to be shutting their eyes to corruption in the police force.*

through the eyes of 'sb; through 'sb's eyes

from the point of view of sb: *You must try to see it through the eyes of the parents, not just from the teacher's point of view.* ◇ *Can't you look at the situation through my eyes?*

with your 'eyes open

knowing what you are doing, what to expect, and what the results may be: *If a marriage is to work, both partners must go into it with their eyes open.*

(be able to do sth) with your 'eyes shut/ closed

(be able to do sth) very easily, especially because you have done it many times before: *She's driven up to Scotland so often that she can do it with her eyes shut.*

bat your eyelashes/eyes → **bat**
be a sight for sore eyes → **sight**
cast/run an eye/your eyes over sth → **cast**
cry your eyes out → **cry**
feast your eyes (on sb/sth) → **feast**
have (got) stars in your eyes → **stars**
meet sb's eyes → **meet**
not believe your eyes/ears → **believe**
open your/sb's eyes (to sth) → **open**
pull the wool over sb's eyes → **pull**
the scales fall from sb's eyes → **scales**

Ff

FA
sweet FA → sweet

face

be in your 'face (*informal*)
if an attitude, performance, etc. is **in your face** it is aggressive in style and designed to make people react strongly to it: *This band's famous for their live performances, which are always loud and in your face.* ▶ **'in-your-face** *adj.*: *I don't really like in-your-face action thrillers.*

disappear/vanish off the face of the 'earth
disappear completely: *Keep looking—they can't just have vanished off the face of the earth.*

your/sb's face doesn't fit
used to say that sb will not get a particular job or position because they do not have the appearance, personality, etc. that the employer wants, even when this should not be important: *It doesn't matter how qualified you are, if your face doesn't fit, you don't stand a chance.*

your face falls
you suddenly look disappointed or upset: *He was quite cheerful until we told him the price. Then his face fell.*

his, her, etc. face is like 'thunder; he, she, etc. has (got) a face like 'thunder
sb looks very angry: *'What's wrong with Julia?' 'I don't know, but she's had a face like thunder all morning.'*

face the 'music (*informal*)
accept the difficulties, criticism and unpleasant results that your words or actions may cause: *He's been cheating us out of our money for years and now it's time for him to face the music.*

> **ℹ️ ORIGIN**
> This idiom might come from the days when, if a soldier was dismissed from his regiment, he was *drummed out*, which meant that the reason(s) for his dismissal were read out in front of the whole group while someone beat the drums.

,face to 'face (with sb/sth)
1 in the presence of sb and close enough to meet, talk, see, etc. them: *The two leaders came face to face for the first time in Moscow this morning.* ◇ *The programme brought Anna face to face with her father for the first time in her life.* ◇ *face-to-face discussions, negotiations, etc.*
2 in a situation where you have to accept that sth is true and deal with it: *The crisis brought her face to face with a lot of problems she had been trying not to think about.*

,face 'up/'down
1 (of a person) with your face and stomach facing upwards/downwards: *She lay face down on the bed.*
2 (of a playing card) with the number or picture facing upwards/downwards: *Place the card face up on the pile.*

in the face of 'sth
even though sth, usually a danger, problem or unpleasant situation, etc. exists: *In the face of all the evidence against you, how can you say that you're innocent?* ◇ *She married him in the face of opposition from both her parents.* ◇ *In the face of very dangerous conditions, they managed to rescue all the men from the ship.*

let's 'face it (*informal*)
we must accept the unpleasant facts; let's be honest: *Let's face it—we just don't have enough money to buy a new car.* ◇ *Let's face it. He married her for her money, not for love.*

look/stare you in the 'face
(usually used in progressive tenses) (of a fact, an answer, a situation, etc.) be obvious but not noticed: *The answer to the problem had been staring her in the face for years but she hadn't seen it.* ◇ *'Where's that book?' 'There in front of you, looking you in the face.'*

on the 'face of it (*informal*)
as sth appears to you when you first look at or consider it, especially when your first impression may be or was wrong: *On the face of it the pay offer looked wonderful, but in fact it wasn't nearly as good as we thought.* ◇ *'Well, what do you think of the new plans?' 'On the face of it, they look good but I think we need to look at them more closely.'*

take sb/sth at (his, its, etc.) face value
accept that sb/sth is exactly as they/it first appears: *You can't take everything she says at face value.* ◇ *A diplomat learns not to take everything at face value.*

to sb's 'face
(say sth) openly, when speaking to sb: *Would you really call her a liar to her face?* ◇ *I think he's guilty but I'd never dare say it to his face.*

'what's his/her face (*spoken*)
used to refer to a person whose name you cannot remember: *Are you still working for what's her face?*

be written all over sb's face → written
blow up in sb's face → blow
cut off your nose to spite your face → cut
(have) egg on your face → egg
fall flat on your face → fall
fly in the face of sth → fly

have (got) the face to do sth = have (got) the nerve to do sth ➔ **nerve**

laugh in sb's face ➔ **laugh**

laugh on the other side of your face ➔ **laugh**

(pull, wear, etc.) a long face ➔ **long**

(be unable to) look sb in the eye(s)/face ➔ **look**

lose face ➔ **lose**

not just a pretty face ➔ **pretty**

(as) plain as the nose on your face ➔ **plain**

pull/make faces/a face (at sb/sth) ➔ **pull**

put a brave face on sth ➔ **brave**

put on a brave face ➔ **brave**

a red face ➔ **red**

save (sb's) face ➔ **save**

set your face against sth ➔ **set**

show your face ➔ **show**

shut your mouth/trap/face/gob! ➔ **shut**

a slap in the face ➔ **slap**

smash sb's face/head in ➔ **smash**

stare sth in the face ➔ **stare**

(keep) a straight face ➔ **straight**

(do sth) till you're blue in the face ➔ **blue**

wipe sth off the face of the earth ➔ **wipe**

wipe the/that smile, grin, etc. off your/sb's face ➔ **wipe**

facelift

give sth a 'facelift

improve the appearance of sth, for example a building, room, etc: *We've given our offices a facelift—new furniture, new lighting and a new carpet.* ◇ *The whole street needs a facelift.*

> ❷ NOTE
> A *facelift* is an operation to lift and tighten the skin on your face in order to make you look younger.

faces

pull/make faces/a face (at sb/sth) ➔ **pull**

fact

ˌafter the 'fact

after sth has happened or been done when it is too late to prevent it or change it: *On some vital decisions employees were only informed after the fact.*

a ˌfact of 'life

something difficult or unpleasant that cannot be changed and has to be accepted or dealt with: *Taxes are a fact of life. You just have to pay them.* ◇ *It is a fact of life that some people are born more intelligent than others.*

in (actual) 'fact

1 used to emphasize a statement, especially one that is the opposite of what has just been mentioned: *This £10 note looks genuine but it is, in actual fact, a fake.* ◇ *I thought the lecture would be boring but in fact it was very interesting.*
2 used to give extra details about sth that has just been mentioned: *It was cold. In fact, it was freezing.*

is that a 'fact? (*spoken*)

used in reply to a statement that you find interesting or surprising, or that you do not believe: *'She says I'm one of the best students she's ever taught.' 'Is that a fact?'*

as a matter of fact ➔ **matter**

the fact/truth of the matter ➔ **matter**

in point of fact ➔ **point**

facts

the ˌfacts of 'life

the facts about sex, how babies are born, etc., especially when told to children: *When do you think you should tell your children the facts of life?*

the facts speak for them'selves

it is not necessary to give any further explanation about sth because the information that is available already proves that it is true: *The film producers say they were careful not to present their own opinions, simply letting the facts speak for themselves.*

hard facts ➔ **hard**

fade

blend/fade into the woodwork ➔ **woodwork**

fail

without 'fail

used for emphasizing that sth always happens or must happen: *She sends me a Christmas card every year without fail.* ◇ *You must be here by 8.30 without fail.*

words fail me ➔ **words**

fails

if all else fails ➔ **else**

faint

damn sb/sth with faint praise ➔ **damn**

faintest

not have the 'faintest/'foggiest (idea) (*BrE, informal*)

have no idea at all about sth; not know anything at all: *I haven't got the faintest idea what to buy Roger for his birthday.* ◇ *'Where are we?' 'I'm afraid I haven't the foggiest.'*

fair

all's fair in love and 'war (*saying*)

normal rules of behaviour do not apply in situations like war and love: *'I told Sarah that John had another girlfriend.' 'But that's not true; he hasn't.' 'I know, but all's fair in love and war.'*

ˌbe 'fair! (*spoken*)

used to tell sb to be reasonable in their judgement of sb/sth: *Be fair! She didn't even know you were coming today.*

by ˌfair means or ˈfoul
even if unfair methods are used: *He's determined to buy that company by fair means or foul.*

fair and ˈsquare (also fairly and ˈsquarely)
1 completely and fully: *They were the better team and they beat us fair and square.*
2 directly and with force: *I hit him fair and square on the chin.*

a fair crack of the ˈwhip (BrE, informal)
a fair or reasonable opportunity to do sth or to show that you can do sth: *I don't think he was really given a fair crack of the whip. He only had five minutes to present his suggestions.* ◇ *We all got a fair crack of the whip. We can't complain.*

fair eˈnough (informal)
1 used for accepting a suggestion, etc: *'I think £200 is a reasonable price.' 'Fair enough. Can I pay you at the end of the week?'*
2 used for showing that you think that sth is reasonable: *Letting the students work the machines on their own is fair enough, but they do need some training first.*

fair ˈgame
if a person or thing is said to be **fair game**, it is considered acceptable to play jokes on them, criticize them, etc: *The younger teachers were considered fair game by most of the kids.*

> ❷ NOTE
> In this idiom, *game* refers to birds and animals that people hunt for sport or food.

a fair ˈhearing
the opportunity for sb to give their point of view about sth before deciding if they have done sth wrong, often in a court of law: *I'll see that you get a fair hearing.*

fair ˈplay
not breaking the rules or cheating; honest or correct behaviour: *We want to see fair play in this competition.* ◇ *It may be legal, but it's not fair play.*

a fair ˈshake (AmE, informal)
a fair chance or fair treatment: *This new pay deal means a fair shake for all the workers.*

(more than) your fair ˈshare of sth
(more than) the usual, expected or desired amount of sth: *I've had more than my fair share of problems recently, but now things seem to be getting better again.* ◇ *We've all paid our fair share except Delia, who's never got any money.*

fair's ˈfair (BrE also fair ˈdos/ˈdo's) (spoken)
used, especially as an exclamation, to say that you think that an action, decision, etc. is acceptable and appropriate because it means that everyone will be treated fairly: *You may not like her, but fair's fair; she's a good teacher.* ◇ *Look, Mike, fair's fair. I've helped you lots of times. Now you can help me.*

it's a fair ˈcop (BrE, spoken, humorous)
used by sb who is caught doing sth wrong, to say that they admit that they are wrong: *He just said, 'it's a fair cop' and handed the bag to one of the policemen there.*

make, etc. sth by/with your own fair ˈhand (humorous)
make, etc. sth yourself: *I made this birthday card for you with my own fair hand.*

be set fair → **set**
play fair/straight (with sb) → **play**

faire
savoir faire → **savoir**

fairer
you can't say fairer (than that) → **say**

fairly
fairly and squarely = fair and square → **fair**

fairness

in (all) ˈfairness (to sb)
used to introduce a statement that defends sb who has just been criticized, or that explains another statement that may seem unreasonable: *In all fairness to him, he did try to stop her leaving.*

fair-weather

a ˌfair-weather ˈfriend (disapproving)
somebody who is only a friend when it is pleasant for them, and stops being a friend when you are in trouble: *I really thought she'd be here to help me, but it seems that she's just a fair-weather friend.*

fairy

a/your ˌfairy ˈgodmother
a person who helps you unexpectedly when you most need help: *You'll need a fairy godmother to get you out of your present difficulties.*

> ❷ NOTE
> The fairy godmother is the magical character in the story of *Cinderella* who helps Cinderella go to the ball.

fait

a ˌfait accomˈpli (from French)
something that has already happened or been done and that you cannot change: *We got married secretly and then presented our parents with a fait accompli.*

faith

bad ˈfaith
1 lack of trust between two people: *The dispute was the cause of a lot of bad faith and bitterness.*
2 dishonest behaviour: *There were many accusations of bad faith on the part of the government.*

break/keep ˈfaith with sb
break/keep a promise that you have made to sb;

stop/continue being loyal to sb: *The government claims they have kept faith with the people by reducing the crime rate.*

good 'faith
the intention to do sth right: *They handed over their weapons as a gesture of good faith.*

in bad 'faith
knowing that what you are doing is wrong: *She insists that she did not act in bad faith, and that the mistakes were due to a computer error.*

in good 'faith
believing that sth is correct; believing that what you are doing is right, especially when it has bad consequences: *When I recommended Simon for the job, I did it in good faith. I didn't realize that he had been in trouble with the police.*

pin your faith/hopes on sb/sth ➔ pin

faithfully

Yours faithfully (*BrE, formal, written*)
used at the end of a formal letter before you sign your name, when you have addressed sb as 'Dear Sir/Dear Madam,' etc. and not by their name

fall

fall about (laughing/with laughter) (*BrE, informal*)
laugh a lot: *When he watches Charlie Chaplin films, he falls about laughing. I don't find them funny at all!*

fall between two 'stools (*BrE*)
not be successful, acceptable, etc. because it is neither one thing nor another: *The book falls between two stools. It's neither a love story nor a crime story.*

fall by the 'wayside
not be able to continue sth that needs effort, discipline, etc.; begin to be dishonest, immoral, etc: *Some 150 people used to go to the church service regularly, but many have fallen by the wayside, and now we have only 95.*

> **ⓘ ORIGIN**
> This idiom comes from a story in the Bible, in which the seeds that fell on the *wayside* (= the path) did not grow.

fall 'flat
if a joke, a story, or an event **falls flat**, it completely fails to amuse people or to have the effect that was intended: *I didn't think the comedian was funny at all—most of his jokes fell completely flat.*

fall ,flat on your 'face (*informal*)
fail completely in an attempt to do sth, especially in a noticeable way: *I thought I would pass my driving test easily but I fell flat on my face.*

fall foul of 'sb/'sth
do sth which gets you into trouble with sb/sth: *They fell foul of the law by not paying their taxes.* ◊ *Try not to fall foul of Mr. Jones. He can be very unpleasant.*

fall from 'grace
lose people's approval, for example through a mistake or immoral behaviour: *The government minister fell from grace as a result of the financial scandal.*

fall into sb's 'hands/the hands of 'sb
be taken, captured or obtained by sb: *The city has fallen into enemy hands.* ◊ *These documents must not fall into the hands of the wrong people.*

fall into 'step (beside/with sb) (*written*)
change the way you are walking so that you start walking in the same rhythm as the person you are walking with: *He caught her up and fell into step beside her.*

fall on deaf 'ears
(of a question, request, etc.) be ignored or not noticed: *Our request for money fell on deaf ears.*

fall on hard 'times
become poor: *She has fallen on hard times and hardly has enough money to live on.*

fall on stony 'ground
fail to produce the result or the effect that you hope for; have little success: *She tried to warn him, but her words fell on stony ground.*

fall 'over yourself to do sth (*informal*)
do everything you can for sb because you want to please and impress them: *After he became manager, people were suddenly falling over themselves to help him.*

fall 'short of sth
fail to reach the standard that you expected or need: *Your performance at work has fallen short of what is required in this company.*

fall to 'pieces
1 (usually used in the progressive tenses) (of things) become very old and in bad condition because of long use: *Our car is falling to pieces, we've had it so long.*
2 (of a person, an organization, a plan, etc.) stop working; be destroyed: *He's worried that the business will fall to pieces without him.*

fall 'victim (to sth) (*written*)
be injured, damaged or killed by sth: *Many plants have fallen victim to the sudden frost.*

be in/go into free fall ➔ free
be/fall prey to sth ➔ prey
be riding for a fall ➔ riding
be/fall wide of the mark ➔ wide
come/fall apart at the seams ➔ apart
die/drop/fall like flies ➔ flies
drop/fall into sb's lap ➔ lap
fall into/avoid the trap of doing sth ➔ trap
fall/land on your feet ➔ feet
let the chips fall where they may ➔ let
let fall sth ➔ let
pride comes before a fall ➔ pride
the scales fall from sb's eyes ➔ scales
stand or fall by sth ➔ stand

falling

(as) easy as ABC/pie/falling off a log → **easy**

falls

the bottom drops/falls out of the market → **bottom**
the bottom drops/falls out of sb's world → **bottom**
your face falls → **face**

false

by/on/under false pre'tences (*BrE*) (*AmE* **by/ on/under false 'pretenses**)
by lying about your identity, qualifications, financial or social position, etc: *She was sent to prison for six months for obtaining money under false pretences.* ◇ *He got me there under false pretences. He told me he wanted to discuss a business deal, but when I got there, it was a surprise birthday party.*

a false a'larm
a warning of sth, especially sth unpleasant or dangerous, which does not in fact happen: *They thought the packet contained a bomb but it was a false alarm.*

(make) a/one false 'move (*informal*)
in an already dangerous or risky situation, (do) sth which makes your position even more dangerous: *She's in a difficult financial situation, and if she makes a false move now she could lose everything.* ◇ *'One false move and you're dead,' he shouted at the bank clerk.*

(make) a false 'start
make an attempt to begin sth that is not successful: *After a few false starts, I finally managed to work the fax machine.* ◇ *He made a few false starts early on in his acting career, but then found success with the Royal Shakespeare Company.*

> ❷ NOTE
> In sport, a *false start* is a situation when a competitor in a race starts before the official signal has been given.

sound/strike a false 'note
seem wrong, not appropriate, etc. in a certain situation: *I really thought his speech at the conference struck a false note. Instead of saying how serious the housing situation was, he was telling jokes about it.*

ring true/false/hollow → **ring**

fame

claim to fame → **claim**

familiar

have (got) a familiar 'ring (about/to it)
sound familiar: *His complaints have a familiar ring. Others have said exactly the same thing about our designs.* ◇ *The music in the film had a familiar ring to it. I think it was Schumann.*

familiarity

familiarity breeds con'tempt (*saying*)
you have little respect, liking, etc. for sb/sth that you know too well: *George's father is regarded by everyone as a great artist, but George doesn't think he is. Familiarity breeds contempt!*

family

in the 'family way (*old-fashioned, informal*)
pregnant

one big happy family → **big**
run in the family → **run**

famous

famous last words (*informal, humorous*)
used when you think sb has been too optimistic about sth: *'The journey won't take more than three hours on the high-speed train.' 'Famous last words! That train is always late!'*

> ❶ ORIGIN
> This phrase refers to a collection of quotations of the dying words of famous people.

famously

get on/along 'famously (*old-fashioned, informal*)
have a very good relationship: *My mother and my mother-in-law are getting on famously.*

fan

fan the 'flames (of sth)
make a feeling such as anger, hatred, etc. worse: *His writings fanned the flames of racism.*

(when) the shit hits the fan → **shit**

fancy

as, whenever, etc. the fancy 'takes you
as, whenever, etc. you feel like doing sth: *We bought a camper van so we could go away whenever the fancy took us.*

catch/take/tickle sb's 'fancy (*informal*)
please or attract sb: *Mary seems afraid some other girl will catch Alan's fancy.* ◇ *She saw that the picture had taken my fancy and insisted on giving it to me as a present.*

fancy your/sb's 'chances (*informal*)
think (often wrongly) that you will be successful; be (too) confident about what you/sb can do: *He fancies his chances as a racing driver, even though he has hardly ever driven a racing car.* ◇ *'Do you think he'll win?' 'No, I don't fancy his chances at all.'*

(just) fancy 'that (*old-fashioned, BrE, spoken*)
used as an expression of surprise: *'He passed all his exams with grade A.' 'Well, fancy that.'*

take a 'fancy to sb/sth (*especially BrE*)
begin to like sb/sth; be attracted by sb/sth: *He's taken quite a fancy to Chinese cooking.* ◇ *She's taken a fancy to one of the team.*

a flight of fancy → **flight**

fancy-free

footloose and fancy-free → **footloose**

far

as/so 'far as ...
as much as; to the extent that: *I will help you as far as I am able.* ◇ *As far as I'm concerned, the whole matter is no longer my responsibility and is now with the police.*

as far as the eye can/could 'see
to the horizon: *There was only sand as far as the eye could see.*

as/so far as it 'goes
to a limited degree, usually less than is satisfactory: *It's a good plan as far as it goes, but there are a lot of things they haven't thought of.*

by 'far
by a very great amount; much: *This is by far the best painting / This is the best painting by far.* ◇ *Our holiday this year was better by far than last year's.*

carry/take sth too, etc. 'far
continue doing sth beyond reasonable limits: *Of course we should show him respect, but I think expecting us to stand up whenever he walks into the room is taking things a bit far.*

(by) far and a'way
(used with superlative adjectives) very much; by a very great amount: *The company has by far and away the biggest share of the car market in this country.* ◇ *Her essay is far and away the best.*

far and 'wide
everywhere and many places; over a large area: *People come from far and wide to visit the monument.* ◇ *The police were searching far and wide for the missing child.*

far be it from me to do sth, but ... (*informal*)
used when you are just about to disagree with sb or criticize them and you would like them to think that you do not really want to do this: *Far be it from me to interfere, but don't you think you've been arguing for long enough?*

a far cry from sth
very different from sth: *This house is a far cry from our little flat.* ◇ *Her designs are a far cry from the eccentric clothes she used to make.*

far from sth/doing sth
almost the opposite of sth or of what is expected: *It is far from clear* (= it is not clear) *what he intends to do.* ◇ *Far from being grateful for our help, she said we had ruined the evening.*

far 'from it (*informal*)
not at all; certainly not: *'Isn't he generous with money?' 'Far from it! He spends it all on himself.'* ◇ *'Are you ready, Alex?' 'Far from it, I'm afraid.'*

far 'gone (*informal*)
very drunk, ill, tired, etc: *When we arrived, she was already too far gone to recognize us, and she only lived for a few more hours.* ◇ *She seemed quite far gone, even though she'd only had two glasses of sparkling wine.*

go as/so far as to do sth
be willing to go to extreme or surprising limits in dealing with sth: *She's a brilliant painter, but I wouldn't go so far as to say she is the best in the country.* ◇ *I don't like people smoking but I wouldn't go so far as to forbid it.*

go 'far
(of people) be successful in the future: *Linda is an excellent manager. She should go far.*

go too 'far; go a bit 'far
say or do sth which is considered too extreme or socially unacceptable: *Getting a bit drunk at a party is OK, but arriving completely drunk—that's really going too far.* ◇ *You've gone too far this time, Joanna.*

in so 'far as (also **inso'far as**)
to the extent that: *In so far as I am a judge of these things, the repairs to the car have been done very well.* ◇ *It was a good report in so far as it showed what needs to be done.*

not far 'off/'out/'wrong (*informal*)
almost correct: *She said she thought it would be sold for £90, and she wasn't far wrong: someone paid £100 for it.* ◇ *The original sales' estimate was not far off.*

not go 'far
1 (of money) not be enough to buy a lot of things: *Five pounds doesn't go very far these days.*
2 (of a supply of sth) not be enough for what is needed: *Four bottles of wine won't go far among twenty people.*

'so far
up to this point; up to now: *There haven't been any accidents in this factory so far, and let's hope that none happen in future.*

,so far, so 'good (*saying*)
used to say that things have been successful until now and you hope they will continue like this, but you know the task, etc. is not finished yet: *'How's the operation going?' 'So far, so good.'*

be far/further/furthest removed from sth → **removed**
far/farther/further afield → **afield**
few and far between → **few**
so near and yet so far → **near**

farm

buy the farm → **buy**

farther

far/farther/further afield → **afield**

fashion

after a 'fashion
(do sth) but not very well: *'Can you skate?' 'Yes, after a fashion.'* ◇ *'Have you mended the radio?' 'Yes, after a fashion.'*

after the fashion of sb/sth (*formal*)
in the style of sb/sth: *The new library is very much after the fashion of Nash.*

in (a) ... 'fashion (*formal*)
in a particular way: *How could they behave in such a fashion?* ◇ *She was proved right, in dramatic fashion, when the whole department resigned.*

like it's going out of 'fashion (*spoken*)
used to emphasize that sb is doing sth or using sth a lot: *She's been spending money like it's going out of fashion.*

fast

as fast as your legs can carry you
as quickly as you can: *When he heard the police sirens, he ran off as fast as his legs could carry him.*

fast and 'furious
(of games, amusements, etc.) noisy and very active: *Ten minutes before the race, the betting was fast and furious.*

a fast 'talker
a person who can talk very quickly and easily, but who cannot always be trusted: *The salesman was a real fast talker, and somehow managed to convince me to buy the most expensive model!*

a fast 'worker (*informal*)
a person who wastes no time in gaining an advantage, especially a person who can quickly gain sb's affection: *She's a fast worker! She's only known him for two days, and they've already arranged to go on holiday together!*

in the 'fast lane (*informal*)
the exciting and sometimes risky way of life typical of very successful people: *I hear you've just been made chief of the Berlin office, Joan. How's life in the fast lane?*

> ❷ **NOTE**
> The *fast lane* is the part of a main road such as a motorway, where vehicles drive fastest.

not so 'fast (*informal*)
often used for telling sb who may have done sth wrong, etc. to stop or wait: *Not so fast, young man! Let me see your ticket!* ◇ *'I'm going out to play now, Dad.' 'Not so fast, David. You've got to tidy your room first.'*

be fast/quick on the draw → **draw**
hard and fast → **hard**
hold fast to sth → **hold**
make a fast/quick buck → **buck**
play fast and loose (with sb/sth) → **play**

pull a fast one (on sb) → **pull**
stand fast/firm → **stand**
stick fast → **stick**
thick and fast → **thick**

fat

a ,fat 'cat (*informal, disapproving*)
a person who earns, or has, a lot of money (especially when compared to people who do not earn much): *The company director is described as a fat cat, who enjoys his luxury lifestyle but doesn't care about his employees.*

(a) 'fat chance (of sth/doing sth) (*spoken*)
used when you think that there is no possibility of sth happening: *He said he'd give me a job if I passed my exam with a grade A. A fat chance I have of that!* ◇ *'Do you think she'll lend me the money?' 'Fat chance.'*

the fat is in the 'fire (*informal*)
something has been said or done that is certain to cause anger, fighting, offended feelings, or other trouble: *The fat's in the fire now. Jim has just told his wife that he has taken a job in another town without mentioning it to her first.*

a 'fat lot of good/help/use (*spoken*)
not at all good/helpful/useful: *A fat lot of use that would be! What a stupid idea.* ◇ *He was a fat lot of help, I must say!*

it ain't/it's not over till the fat lady sings (*saying*)
used near the end of a competition, race, etc. to say that it is not finished yet, especially when you think that the person/team who is losing still have a chance to win: *Some people think he's already lost the election, but it ain't over till the fat lady sings, you know!*

chew the fat → **chew**
live off/on the fat of the land → **live**
run to fat → **run**

fatale

(be) a femme fatale → **femme**

fate

a ,fate worse than 'death (*often humorous*)
a terrible experience: *Go on holiday with the Trumans? You're joking. It would be a fate worse than death.*

tempt fate/providence → **tempt**

father

like ,father/,mother, like 'son/'daughter (*saying*)
a child is similar to its father/mother in a particular way: *Young Jim is turning out to be as hardworking as his dad—like father, like son.*

the founding father(s) of sth → **founding**
the wish is father to the thought → **wish**

fatted

kill the fatted calf → kill

fault

at fault

responsible for doing wrong, making a mistake, etc.; to be blamed: *The inquiry will decide who was at fault over the loss of the funds.* ◇ *I don't feel that I am at fault. After all, I didn't know I was breaking a rule.*

to a 'fault *(written)*

used to say that sb has a lot, or even too much of a particular good quality: *He was generous to a fault.*

find fault (with sb/sth) → find

faux

(make/commit) a ˌfaux ˈpas *(from French)*

an action or a remark that causes embarrassment because it is not socially correct: *I immediately made a faux pas when I forgot to take my shoes off before I went into the house.* ◇ *They were kind enough to overlook my faux pas and continued as if nothing had happened.*

> **❷ NOTE**
> The meaning of the French expression is 'wrong step'.

favour *(BrE)* *(AmE* **favor***)*

be (all) in favour of (doing) sth

support or approve an idea, course of action, etc: *As far as Joe's suggestion about saving money is concerned, I'm all in favour of it. Some people are in favour of restoring the death penalty for major crimes.* ◇ *All those in favour, raise their hands.*

do me a 'favour

1 *(informal)* used when asking sb to help you: *Do me a favour and answer the door, will you?*
2 *(spoken)* you can't expect me to believe that: *'It's worth £2 000. The man in the antique shop told me.'* · *'Do me a favour. It's not even worth £200.'*

in sb's/sth's 'favour

to sb's advantage: *The court decided in the employee's favour.* ◇ *The fact that the dollar is falling is in your favour.*

in/out of 'favour (with sb)

supported/not supported or liked/not liked by sb: *I seem to be out of favour with the head of department after my remarks at the meeting.* ◇ *He stays late every afternoon because he wants to stay in favour with the boss.*

the cards/odds are stacked in favour of sb/sth → stacked
curry favour (with sb) → curry
without fear or favour → fear

favourite *(BrE)* *(AmE* **favorite***)*

sb's favourite 'son

a performer, politician, sports player, etc., who is popular where they were born: *Everyone in the* town was proud and excited to see their favourite son nominated for an Oscar.

favours *(BrE)* *(AmE* **favors***)*

do sb no 'favours; not do sb any 'favours

do sth that is not helpful to sb or that gives a bad impression of them: *You're not doing yourself any favours, working for nothing.* ◇ *The orchestra did Beethoven no favours.*

fear

be/go in fear of your 'life

be afraid all the time that you may be killed, attacked, etc: *After she got involved with the drug dealers, she went in fear of her life.*

for fear of (doing) sth; for fear (that) …

because you do not want sth bad to happen: *I'm not going to put it in the washing machine for fear of spoiling it.* ◇ *I had to leave for fear (that) he might one day kill me.*

in fear and 'trembling (of sb/sth) *(written)*

feeling very frightened or anxious: *They lived in fear and trembling of being discovered by the police.*

ˌno ˈfear! *(BrE, spoken)*

used to say that you definitely do not want to do sth: *'Who's coming for a midnight swim?' 'No fear! It's much too cold.'*

put the fear of 'God into sb *(informal)*

frighten sb very much, especially in order to force them to do what you want: *The first thing that happens when you go into the army is that they put the fear of God into you.*

there's no fear of sth

there's no possibility or danger of sth happening: *I've got a new alarm clock so there's no fear of me oversleeping again.*

without ˌfear or ˈfavour *(BrE)* *(AmE* **without ˌfear or ˈfavor***)* *(formal)*

(judge, decide sth, etc.) in a completely fair way without being influenced by anybody: *The newspaper reprinted the facts, without fear or favour.*

feast

feast your 'eyes (on sb/sth)

look at sb/sth and get great pleasure: *Wow! Come and feast your eyes on this birthday cake!*

feather

a 'feather in your cap

an achievement, success or honour which you can be proud of: *It's a real feather in his cap to represent his country in the Olympics.*

> **❶ ORIGIN**
> This idiom comes from the American Indian custom of giving a feather to somebody who had been very brave in battle.

feather your (own) 'nest
make yourself richer, especially by spending money on yourself that should be spent on sth else: *He's been feathering his own nest at the expense of the people he was supposed to be helping.*

birds of a feather (flock together) ➔ **birds**

(as) light as air/a feather ➔ **light**

you could have knocked me, etc. down with a feather ➔ **knocked**

feathered

our feathered 'friends (*informal, humorous*)
birds: *We mustn't forget to put out food for our feathered friends during the cold winter months.*

feathers

the feathers/fur/sparks will fly ➔ **fly**

ruffle sb's/a few feathers ➔ **ruffle**

smooth (sb's) ruffled feathers ➔ **smooth**

feature

a redeeming feature ➔ **redeeming**

fed

fed up to the back teeth with sb/sth (also **sick to the back teeth of sb/sth**) (*informal*)
depressed, annoyed or bored by sb/sth: *I'm fed up to the back teeth with listening to you complaining.* ◇ *She's always playing the same CD, and I'm sick to the back teeth of it!*

feed

chicken feed ➔ **chicken**

feeding

a 'feeding frenzy (*especially AmE*)
a period of time during which sb/sth eats, spends, etc. a lot in a way that does not seem to be controlled: *The news about their marriage started a media feeding frenzy, with all the newspapers trying to get photos and interviews.*

feeds

bite the hand that feeds you ➔ **bite**

feel

be/feel 'out of it/things
not be/feel part of a group, conversation, activity, etc: *I didn't know anybody at the party so I felt a bit out of it really.*

feel your 'age
realize from your physical condition, opinion, views, etc. that you are getting old: *He's not as energetic as he used to be—beginning to feel his age, I suppose.* ◇ *Listening to this rap music really makes me feel my age.*

feel the 'draught (*informal*)
suffer financially as a result of economic, social or political changes around you: *Because of the world*

trade recession, a lot of third world countries are feeling the draught.

> **❷ NOTE**
> A *draught* is a flow of cold air in a room or other enclosed space.

feel 'free (to do sth) (*informal*)
(used to give sb permission to do sth) you may do as you want; nobody will object if you do sth: *'May I borrow your bike?' 'Feel free!'* ◇ *Feel free to come and go as you like.*

feel (it) in your 'bones (*informal*)
sense or suspect sth without really knowing why: *That's funny—I felt in my bones that there was something wrong—and now you tell me there's been an accident.* ◇ *'How can you be so sure she's going to win?' 'I can feel it in my bones.'*

feel like (doing) sth
want sth/to do sth or think that you would enjoy (doing) sth: *Do you know what I feel like? A nice cup of tea!* ◇ *I'm so tired that I feel like going straight to bed.*

feel the 'pinch (*informal*)
be under pressure because you do not have as much money as you had before: *Schools all over the country are beginning to feel the pinch after the government cut back its spending on education.*

feel 'strange
not feel comfortable in a situation; have an unpleasant physical feeling: *She felt strange sitting at her father's desk.* ◇ *It was terribly hot and I started to feel strange.*

feel your 'way
1 move along carefully, for example when it is dark, by touching walls, objects, etc.
2 be careful about how you do sth because you are just learning how to do it or you don't yet have enough information: *I don't know how they will react to the proposal, so at the moment I'm still feeling my way.* ◇ *He's only been in the job for three months, so he's still feeling his way.*

get the 'feel of sth (*informal*)
become familiar with or get used to sth: *When you're learning to drive a car, you'll probably find changing gear difficult, but you'll soon get the feel of it.* ◇ *Once you get the feel of a Ferrari, you'll never want any other car.*

have (got) a 'feel for sth (*informal*)
have an understanding of sth or be naturally good at doing it: *A good politician has to have a feel for what people want.*

not feel your'self
not feel as healthy, happy, etc. as you usually feel: *I don't feel myself this morning; I think I'll stay at home.*

be/feel duty/honour bound to do sth ➔ **bound**

be/feel hard done by ➔ **hard**

be/feel honoured (to do sth) ➔ **honoured**

be/feel like jelly ➔ **jelly**

be/feel lost without sb/sth ➔ lost
be/feel sick at heart ➔ sick
be/feel sorry for sb ➔ sorry
be/feel sorry for yourself ➔ sorry
feel a chill running/going down your spine = send a chill up/down sb's spine ➔ send
feel that high = look/feel small ➔ small
look/feel like a million dollars/bucks ➔ million
look/feel small ➔ small

feelers

put out/have 'feelers
try to find out what people think about a particular course of action before you do it: *They're putting out feelers about the possibility of building a new sports complex in Leeds.*

> ❷ NOTE
> An insect has *feelers* (= antennae) on its head, which it uses to feel or sense things.

feeling

bad/ill 'feeling(s)
anger between people, especially after an argument or disagreement: *There was a lot of bad feeling between the two groups of students.*

get/have the 'feeling (that …)
feel that sth is true although you have no direct knowledge or facts: *I get the feeling that he's got another girlfriend somewhere.* ◇ *Have you ever had the feeling that you were being watched?*

(get/have) a/that sinking feeling ➔ sinking
that Monday morning feeling ➔ Monday

feelings

have (got) mixed feelings (about sb/sth) ➔ mixed
no hard feelings ➔ hard
spare sb's feelings ➔ spare

feet

at sb's 'feet
respecting and admiring sb, and so being influenced by them: *As a young man, he had the whole of Paris at his feet.*

be/get ˌrun/ˌrushed off your 'feet
be very busy: *In the last few days before Christmas, the sales assistants were rushed off their feet.*

fall/land on your 'feet (*informal*)
be lucky in finding a good position, job, place to live, etc., especially when your previous situation was difficult: *Well, you really fell on your feet this time, didn't you? A job in Rome, a large flat, a company car …*

> ❶ ORIGIN
> This expression refers to the way a cat always lands safely.

ˌfeet 'first (*informal*)
dead or unconscious: *If you want me to leave this*

house, you'll have to carry me out feet first (= you'll have to kill me first).

feet of 'clay
a surprising fault or weakness in the character of sb who is admired and respected: *Why are people always surprised when they discover that their heroes have feet of clay.*

> ❶ ORIGIN
> This idiom comes from a story in the Bible, where the king of Babylon saw an image with a head of gold and feet of clay.

have/keep both/your feet on the 'ground
have a sensible and realistic attitude to life: *He is always talking about his big plans to be a great actor. You should tell him to keep his feet on the ground.*

on your 'feet
1 standing up: *Being a shop assistant means that you're on your feet all day long.*
2 (of a business etc.) in a strong position again after a period of difficulty, uncertainty, etc: *Only our party's policies will really get the country on its feet again.* ◇ *The company seems to be back on its feet now.*

put your 'feet up
relax by sitting, or lying down; enjoy a period of rest from work, etc: *After work, I like to have a cup of tea and put my feet up.* ◇ *You've worked for this company for 35 years, Jack. Now it's time for you to put your feet up and relax.*

under sb's 'feet
annoying sb because you are getting in their way and/or stopping them from working, etc: *It's difficult to do housework with the children under my feet all the time.*

cut the ground from under sb/sb's feet ➔ cut
drag your feet/heels ➔ drag
find your feet ➔ find
get/have cold feet ➔ cold
get/have itchy feet ➔ itchy
have (got) two left feet ➔ two
have (got) the world at your feet ➔ world
in your stocking(ed) feet ➔ stocking
not let the grass grow under your feet ➔ let
the patter of tiny feet ➔ patter
pull the carpet/rug out from under sb's feet ➔ pull
six feet under ➔ six
stand on your own two feet ➔ stand
sweep sb off their feet ➔ sweep
take the weight off your feet ➔ weight
think on your feet ➔ think
throw yourself at sb's feet ➔ throw
vote with your feet ➔ vote
walk sb off their feet ➔ walk

fell

at/in one fell 'swoop
with a single action or movement; all at the same

time: *Only a foolish politician would promise to lower the rate of inflation and reduce unemployment at one fell swoop.*

felt

make your presence felt → **presence**

femme

(be) a ‚femme fa'tale (*from French*)
(be) a beautiful woman that men find sexually attractive but who brings them trouble or unhappiness: *The film follows the relationship between sexy femme fatale Suzy and young lawyer Jim, which eventually leads to a murderous crime of passion.*

> **❷ NOTE**
> The meaning of the French expression is 'disastrous woman'.

fence

my, her, the other, the same, etc. side of the fence → **side**
sit on the fence → **sit**

fences

mend (your) fences (with sb) → **mend**

fetch

fetch and 'carry (for sb)
be always doing small jobs for sb; act as if you were sb's servant: *I hate having to fetch and carry for my husband all day. Why can't he do more for himself?*

fettle

in fine/good 'fettle (*old-fashioned, informal*)
healthy and cheerful: *After ten hours' sleep and a good long run, I was in fine fettle.*

fever

at 'fever pitch
in a state of great excitement or great activity: *The audience was at fever pitch. I've never seen such excitement at a concert.* ◇ *We're working at fever pitch to get the hall ready for the concert at eight.*

few

few and far be'tween
not frequent; not happening often: *Since her illness, the former Minister's public appearances have been few and far between.* ◇ *Houses for sale are few and far between in this part of town.*

have had a few (too many) (*informal*)
have drunk a lot of alcohol: *Look, he's had a few and he really shouldn't drive home.* ◇ *You've had a few too many, Paul. You don't know what you're saying.*

a man/woman of few 'words
a person who does not talk much: *Mr Robins was a*

man of few words, but his opinions were always respected.

a good few = quite a few → **quite**
precious few/little → **precious**
ruffle sb's/a few feathers → **ruffle**

fiction

truth is stranger than fiction → **truth**

fiddle

fiddle while Rome burns
do nothing or waste your time when you should be dealing with a dangerous or serious situation: *With the world's population growing fast and millions getting hungrier every day, the leaders of the rich nations just seem to be fiddling while Rome burns.*

> **❶ ORIGIN**
> This phrase refers to the Roman emperor Nero, who fiddled (= played the violin) during the burning of Rome in AD 64.

on the 'fiddle (*BrE, informal*)
getting money by doing dishonest things, usually at work, for example stealing from your employer, making false claims for expenses, etc: *He was on the fiddle for years and his boss never suspected a thing.*

(as) fit as a fiddle → **fit**
play second fiddle → **play**

field

have a 'field day
enjoy a time of great excitement or activity: *Whenever this novelist brings out a new book, the critics have a field day, and she is attacked from all sides.* ◇ *When the royal family go skiing, press photographers have a field day.*

be (way out/over) in left field → **left**
leave the field clear for sb → **leave**
leave sb in possession of the field → **leave**
a level playing field → **level**
level the playing field → **level**
play the field → **play**

fierce

something 'fierce (*AmE, spoken*)
very much; more than usual: *I sure do miss you something fierce!*

fifth

a fifth/third wheel → **wheel**

fifty-fifty

‚fifty-'fifty (*informal*)
divided equally between two people, groups or possibilities: *Let's split the bill fifty-fifty.* ◇ *She has a fifty-fifty chance of winning.*

fig 120

fig

not care/give a 'fig (about/for sb/sth) (old-fashioned, BrE, informal)
not care at all about sth; think that sth is not important: *I don't give a fig about him!*

fight

fight ˌfire with 'fire
use similar methods in a fight or an argument to those your opponent is using: *The only way we can win this match is to fight fire with fire.*

ˌfight for (your) 'life
make a great effort to stay alive, especially when you are badly injured or seriously ill: *A young cyclist is fighting for his life after the accident.*

ˌfight it 'out
continue fighting or arguing until one person wins: *I'm not going to interfere. They can just fight it out between themselves.*

fight like cat and 'dog (informal)
argue fiercely very often: *They fight like cat and dog, but they are really very fond of each other.*

fight a ˌlosing 'battle
try without success to achieve or prevent sth: *I'm fighting a losing battle with my weight. I can't lose any.* ◇ *The police are fighting a losing battle against car theft.*

fight your 'own battles
be able to win an argument or get what you want without anyone's help: *I wouldn't get involved—he's old enough to fight his own battles.*

fight 'shy of sb/of (doing) sth
avoid sb/(doing) sth; not want to meet sb/do sth: *I tend to fight shy of getting involved in protests, but in this case I feel very strongly that we should complain.* ◇ *He fights shy of any real contact with people.*

fight (sb/sth) ˌtooth and 'nail; fight ˌtooth and 'nail for sb/sth
fight in a very determined way: *We fought the government tooth and nail to prevent the new road being built.* ◇ *She's prepared to fight tooth and nail to get the job.*

put up a (good) 'fight
fight or compete bravely against sb/sth stronger than you: *The team put up a good fight but in the end they were beaten.* ◇ *She won't accept the decision—she'll put up a fight.*

live to fight another day → **live**
pick a fight/quarrel (with sb) → **pick**

fighting

a ˌfighting 'chance
a slight but real chance of succeeding, avoiding sth, etc: *With five minutes of the game left, our team still has a fighting chance of winning.* ◇ *Things*

don't look very hopeful for John Brown in the presidential elections, but he's still in with a fighting chance.

fighting 'spirit
a feeling that you are ready to fight very hard for sth or to try sth difficult: *Come on, don't give up now! Where's your fighting spirit?*

'fighting talk
comments or remarks that show that you are ready to fight very hard for sth: *What we want from the management is fighting talk.*

fighting fit = (as) fit as a fiddle → **fit**

figment

a figment of sb's imagi'nation
something which sb only imagines: *Doctor, are you suggesting the pain is a figment of my imagination?*

figure

a figure of 'fun
somebody who is often laughed at by other people: *As a young man he was admired, but as an old man he became a figure of fun.*

put a 'figure on sth
give the exact amount or exact value of sth: *It's difficult to put a figure on a table like this, but it's probably worth about £5000.* ◇ *'We're going to invest a great deal of money in our new business.' 'Excuse me, Sir, could you put a figure on that?'*

a ballpark figure → **ballpark**
cut a fine, poor, sorry, etc. figure → **cut**

figures

in round 'figures/'numbers
approximately, to the nearest 10, 100 or 1 000: *In round figures, how much do you think the work will cost?*

it/that figures (informal)
used to say that sth was expected or seems logical: *'We're going to need new offices when the company expands next year.' 'That figures.'* ◇ *'I think he killed her to get the insurance money.' 'That certainly figures.'*

have (got) a (good) head for figures → **head**

file

(in) single/Indian 'file
in a line, one person after another: *The whole class walked along behind the teacher in single file.*

> **❶ ORIGIN**
> When American Indians walked in a group, each person walked in the footsteps of the person in front so that they could not be counted by the enemy.

(the) rank and file → **rank**

fill

fill sb's 'boots/'shoes
do sb's job in a satisfactory way when they are not there: *Mr Carter is retiring and we need a new director to fill his shoes.*

have had your 'fill of sb/sth
have had enough of sb/sth: *I've had my fill of Agatha Christie films. I never want to see another one as long as I live.* ◇ *She's had her fill of him and his awful temper and she's left him.*

final

be the last/final straw → straw
in the last/final analysis → analysis
your/the last/final word (on/about sth) → word

find

find 'fault (with sb/sth)
look for faults or mistakes in sb/sth, often so that you can criticize them/it: *He's always finding fault with the children, even when they are doing nothing wrong.* ◇ *I can find no fault with this essay; it's the best I've ever read.*

find your 'feet (*informal*)
become used to a new job, place, etc. and start functioning well: *After moving from teaching to industry, it took her a long time to find her feet in a very different job.*

(not) find it in your heart to 'do sth (also (not) find it 'in yourself to do sth) (*literary*)
(not) be able to persuade yourself to do sth: *I wish you could find it in your heart to forgive her.* ◇ *I can't find it in myself to criticize her work after she's tried so hard.*

find your 'voice/'tongue (*informal*)
finally be able to speak after being too nervous or shy to do so: *He sat silent through the first half of the meeting before he found his tongue.*

find your/its 'way (to/into ...)
come to a place or a situation by chance or without intending to: *After several other jobs, he eventually found his way into acting.*

take sb as you 'find them
accept sb as they are without expecting them to behave in a special way or have special qualities: *The house is in chaos, so when you come you must take us as you find us.*

find/get your bearings → bearings
find/meet your match (in sb) → match
like looking for/trying to find a needle in a haystack → needle
scratch A and you'll find B → scratch

finders

ˌfinders 'keepers (*saying*)
(often used by children) anyone who finds sth has a right to keep it: *I just found a ten-pound note on the ground. Finders keepers, so it's mine!*

fine

have (got) sth down to a fine 'art (*informal, often humorous*)
learn through experience how to do sth perfectly: *I found it difficult to organize the timetables at first, but now I've got it down to a fine art.* ◇ *She has complaining in restaurants down to a fine art! Head waiters are terrified of her.*

not to put too fine a 'point on it
used when you are about to speak very directly or honestly: *Not to put too fine a point on it, I think you've been a complete idiot.*

all very well/fine (for sb) (to do sth) but ... → well
chance would be a fine thing → chance
cut it/things fine → cut
the fine print = the small print → small
in fine/good fettle → fettle
the small print → small
tread/walk a fine/thin line → line
you're a fine one to talk = you can/can't talk → talk

fine-tooth

go over/through sth with a ˌfine-tooth 'comb (*informal*)
search or look at sth very closely or carefully: *I went through the accounts with a fine-tooth comb to see if there was any mention of this money.* ◇ *The police went through his room with a fine-tooth comb.*

finger

the ˌfinger of su'spicion
if **the finger of suspicion** points or is pointed at sb, they are suspected of having committed a crime, being responsible for sth, etc: *The woman's still missing, and the finger of suspicion is now being pointed at her husband.*

get/pull your 'finger out (*BrE, informal*)
used to tell sb to start doing some work or making an effort: *I wish the police would get their finger out and solve the crime!* ◇ *If you pull your finger out, we might finish on time.*

give sb the 'finger (*AmE, informal*)
raise your middle finger in the air with the back part of your hand facing sb, done to be rude to sb or to show them that you are angry: *Did you see what he just did? He gave me the finger!*

have (got) a finger in every 'pie (*informal*)
be involved in everything that happens: *Jane likes to have a finger in every pie.*

have/keep your finger on the 'pulse (of sth)
know all that is happening; be aware of new developments in a particular situation: *Successful politicians need to keep their finger on the pulse of the voters.*

❷ NOTE
A doctor takes your *pulse* by putting his fingers on your wrist and counting the number of times the blood beats in a minute.

not put your finger on sth (*informal*)
not be able to say exactly what is wrong or different about a particular situation: *I knew something she had said wasn't true, but I couldn't quite put my finger on it.* ◇ *There's something wrong with these statistics but I just can't put my finger on what it is.*

lay a finger on sb → lay
(not) lift a finger (to do sth) → lift
point a/the finger (at sb) → point
twist/wind/wrap sb around/round your little finger → little

fingers

get your 'fingers burnt; burn your 'fingers
suffer as a result of doing sth without realizing the possible bad results, especially in business: *She got her fingers burnt when she set up a business and had all her money stolen by her partner.*

have/keep your 'fingers crossed; cross your 'fingers (*informal*)
hope that sth will be successful; wish sb good luck: *I'm going to give my first lecture tomorrow, so keep your fingers crossed for me, won't you?* ◇ *Good luck, Ingrid. **Fingers crossed!***

> ❶ NOTE
> People often cross the first two fingers of one hand when they use this expression.

be all fingers and thumbs = be all thumbs → thumbs
green fingers → green
have (got) your fingers/hand in the till → till
have (got) sticky fingers → sticky
put/stick two fingers up at sb → two
slip through sb's fingers → slip
snap your fingers → snap
tick sth off on your fingers → tick
work your fingers to the bone → work

fingertips

have (got) sth at your 'fingertips
be so familiar with a subject that you can produce any facts about it easily and quickly: *The Minister was well prepared for the interview. She had all the facts at her fingertips.*

to your 'fingertips (*BrE*)
(of a particular type of person) completely; in every way: *He is an artist to his fingertips.* ◇ *She's a professional to her fingertips.*

finish

be in at the 'finish
be present when sth ends: *I was one of the first people on this project and I certainly want to be in at the finish.*

finishing

the finishing 'touch(es)
the final detail(s) that complete(s) or decorate(s) sth: *We've been putting the finishing touches to the Christmas decorations.*

fire

be/come under 'fire
1 be shot at: *While defending the town we came under fire again last night.*
2 be criticized, insulted, etc: *The government is already under fire over its housing policy.*

fire 'questions, 'insults, etc. at sb
ask sb a lot of questions one after another or make a lot of comments very quickly: *The room was full of journalists, all firing questions at them.*

on 'fire
giving you a painful burning feeling: *He couldn't breathe. His chest was on fire.*

add fuel to the fire/flames → add
a baptism of fire → baptism
the fat is in the fire → fat
fight fire with fire → fight
get along/on like a house on fire → house
hang fire → hang
have (got) many, etc. irons in the fire → irons
hold your fire → hold
not/never set the Thames on fire → set
not/never set the world on fire → set
open fire (on sb/sth) → open
out of the frying pan (and) into the fire → frying
play with fire → play
set sth on fire/set fire to sth → set
there's no smoke without fire → smoke
where there's smoke, there's fire → smoke

firing

be in the 'firing line (*BrE*) (*AmE* **be on the 'firing line**)
be in a position where you are likely to be affected, attacked, criticized, etc: *The newspapers are criticizing the government's policy again, and the Prime Minister is in the firing line.* ◇ *In the latest round of spending cuts, teachers' jobs are again in the firing line.*

firing/working on all cylinders → cylinders

firm

be on firm 'ground
be sure about one's beliefs, knowledge, etc.; be confident: *I don't know a lot about physics, I'm afraid. I'm on firmer ground with mathematics, which I studied at university.*

a firm 'hand
strong discipline and control: *What his son needs, if you ask me, is a firm hand!*

take a firm 'line/'stand (on/against sth)
make your beliefs known and try to make others follow them: *We need to take a firm line on tobacco advertising.* ◇ *They took a firm stand against drugs in the school.*

be a great/firm believer in sth → believer
hold firm (to sth) → hold
stand fast/firm → stand

first

at first 'glance/'sight
as things seem at first; judging by first appearances: *At first glance, the exam paper looked fairly difficult, but once I got started I found it quite easy.*

come 'first
be treated as the most important person or thing in sb's life: *His work always came first with Joe, which upset his wife a lot.*

first among 'equals
the person or thing with the highest status in a group: *Our history classes were usually open discussion-groups between us and our teacher, with the teacher as first among equals.*

first and 'foremost
before everything else; most importantly: *First and foremost, we must ensure that the children are safe.* ◇ *Don't forget, he is first and foremost an actor, not a singer.*

first and 'last
mainly; only: *The book is, first and last, an account of a poet's development.* ◇ *I saw him for the first and last time at his father's funeral.*

first 'come, ˌfirst 'served (*saying*)
people will be dealt with, seen, etc. strictly in the order in which they arrive, apply, etc: *We have 100 tickets for the performance, and they will be distributed on a first come, first served basis.*

(in) the first flush of 'youth, en'thusiasm, etc.
when sth is new or sb is young: *In the first flush of enthusiasm, we were able to get everyone interested in helping.* ◇ *By then, he was no longer in the first flush of youth.*

(at) first 'hand
from your own experience or knowledge, rather than from sb else; directly: *I know at first hand what it is like to be poor; we always had very little money at home.* ◇ *We have a first-hand account of the raid from a witness.*

first of 'all
1 before doing anything else; at the beginning: *First of all, let me ask you something.*
2 as the most important thing: *The content of any article needs, first of all, to be relevant to the reader.*

first 'off/'up (*informal*)
before anything else; to begin with: *First off, we will choose the teams, then we can start the game.*

(give sb, have, etc.) (the) first re'fusal
(give sb, etc.) the opportunity to buy sth before it is offered for sale to others: *She promised to give me first refusal if she ever decides to sell the flat.*

first 'thing (tomorrow, in the morning, etc.)
at the beginning of the period of time mentioned, before doing anything else: *I always like a cup of tea first thing in the morning.* ◇ *Can you lend me some money? I'll pay you back first thing tomorrow.*

ˌfirst things 'first (*often humorous*)
the most important or necessary duties, matters, etc. must be dealt with before others: *First things first. We must make sure the electricity is turned off before we start repairing the cooker.* ◇ *We have a lot to discuss, but, first things first, let's have a cup of coffee!*

(be) the 'first/'last (person) to do sth
be very willing or likely/unwilling or unlikely to do sth: *I'd be the first person to admit that I'm not perfect.* ◇ *Mary is the last person you'd see in a pub—she hates pubs.*

from the (very) 'first
from the beginning: *They were attracted to each other from the first.*

from ˌfirst to 'last
from beginning to end; during the whole time: *It's a fine performance that commands attention from first to last.*

get to first 'base (with sb/sth) (also reach/ make first 'base (with sb/sth)) (*informal, especially AmE*)
successfully complete the first stage of sth: '*How are you getting on with that new girlfriend of yours?*' '*I haven't even got to first base yet*' (= possibly 'I haven't even held her hand or kissed her yet'). ◇ *The project hasn't even reached first base yet. Why all this delay?*

have (got) first 'call (on sb/sth)
be the most important person or thing competing for sb's time, money, etc. and be dealt with or paid for before other people or things: *The children always have first call on her time.*

in the 'first instance (*formal*)
as the first part of a series of actions: *In the first instance, notify the police and then contact your insurance company.*

make the first 'move
do sth before sb else, for example in order to end an argument or to begin sth: *If he wants to see me, he should make the first move.*

put sb/sth 'first
treat sb/sth as the most important person or thing: *A politician should always put the needs of the country first and not his personal ambitions.* ◇ *He never put his family first.*

there's a first time for everything (*saying, humorous*)
the fact that something has not happened before does not mean that it will never happen: '*The flood water has never reached the house before.*' '*Well, there's a first time for everything.*'

feet first → **feet**
head first → **head**
in the first/top flight → **flight**
in the first place → **first**
last in, first out → **last**
love at first sight → **love**

not know the first thing about sb/sth → **know**
of the highest/first order → **order**
see sb in hell first → **see**

fish

fish for compliments
encourage sb indirectly to say nice things about you: *Stop asking me if you look OK. You're just fishing for compliments.*

fish or cut 'bait (*AmE, informal*)
used to tell sb to make a decision and take the necessary action: *There's been enough discussion. It's time for the government to fish or cut bait.*

> **❶ NOTE**
> *Bait* is the food you put on a hook to catch fish. If you *cut bait*, you stop fishing.

a ,fish out of 'water (*informal*)
a person who feels uncomfortable or embarrassed in unfamiliar surroundings: *Everybody else knew each other really well, so I felt a bit like a fish out of water.*

have (got) 'other/'bigger fish to fry (*informal*)
have more important, interesting or useful things to do: *He's not interested in reviewing small provincial exhibitions like this one; he's got much bigger fish to fry.* ◇ *So you aren't coming out with us tonight? I suppose you've got other fish to fry.*

neither ,fish nor 'fowl
neither one thing nor another: *Graduate teaching assistants are neither fish nor fowl, neither completely students nor teachers.*

an ,odd/a ,queer 'fish (*old-fashioned, BrE*)
a strange person: *He's an odd fish. He's got a lot of very strange ideas.*

there are plenty/lots more fish in the 'sea; there are (plenty of) other fish in the 'sea (*informal*)
there are many other people or things that are as good as the one sb has failed to get: *'I'll never love anyone as much again.' 'Look, Julie, there are lots more fish in the sea, you know.'*

be like shooting fish in a barrel = be like taking candy from a baby → **candy**
a big fish (in a little pond) → **big**
a cold fish → **cold**
a different kettle of fish → **different**
drink like a fish → **drink**

fist

make a better, good, poor, etc. 'fist of sth (*BrE, informal*)
make a good, bad, etc. attempt to do sth: *The Irish rugby team are hoping to make a better fist of it than the English did yesterday.*

an iron fist/hand in a velvet glove → **iron**
make/lose money hand over fist → **money**
shake your fist (at sb) → **shake**

fit

(as) ,fit as a 'fiddle (also ,fighting 'fit)
very healthy and active: *After our walking holiday I came back feeling fit as a fiddle.*

fit the 'bill (*informal*)
be suitable for a purpose: *We need a new sofa for the living room, and I think this one will fit the bill quite nicely.*

fit (sb) like a 'glove
(of a coat, dress, etc.) be the perfect size or shape for sb: *You look wonderful in that dress. It fits you like a glove.*

have/throw a 'fit (*informal*)
become very excited or angry: *Your father will throw a fit when he sees you've broken yet another window!*

have a pink/blue 'fit (*BrE, informal*)
be very angry: *If your mother catches you smoking she'll have a pink fit.*

see/think 'fit (to do sth) (*formal, often disapproving*)
think it is right or acceptable to do sth: *You obviously didn't see fit to inform us of what you were going to do.* ◇ *You should warn her about his behaviour if you see fit.*

your/sb's face doesn't fit → **face**
fit/ready to drop → **drop**

fits

in ,fits and 'starts
not steadily; often starting and stopping:: *'How's the book?' 'Oh, I'm working on it in fits and starts. I sometimes wonder if I'll ever finish it.'* ◇ *He made progress in fits and starts at first but now he's improving rapidly.*

if the shoe fits (, wear it) = if the cap fits (, wear it) → **cap**

fittest

(the) survival of the fittest → **survival**

five

,give sb 'five (*informal*)
hit the inside of sb's hand with the inside of your hand as a greeting or to celebrate a victory: *Give me five!*

nine to five → **nine**

fives

a bunch of fives → **bunch**

fix

be/get in a 'fix (*informal*)
be/get in a difficult situation: *I'm in a bit of a fix. Can you help me?*

fix sb with a 'look, 'stare, 'gaze, etc.
look directly at sb for a long time: *He fixed her with an angry stare.*

if it ain't broke, don't fix it → **broke**

fixed

how are you, etc. 'fixed (for sth)? (*spoken*)
used to ask how much of sth a person has, or to ask about arrangements: *How are you fixed for cash?* ◇ *How are we fixed for Saturday* (= have we arranged to do anything)?

flag

fly/show/wave the 'flag
show your support for your country, an organization or an idea in order to encourage or persuade others to do the same: *This exhibition of Scottish painting is our way of flying the flag.*

keep the 'flag flying
continue to support an idea, principle, activity, etc. which is in danger of disappearing: *They try to keep the flag flying in the British film industry.* ◇ *There are only two of us left now to keep the flag flying.*

flagrante

in fla'grante (delicto) (*from Latin, literary or humorous*)
if sb is found or caught **in flagrante**, they are discovered doing sth that they should not be doing, especially having sex: *One of the gentlemen was caught in flagrante with the wife of the club's President, which of course caused a huge scandal.*

> ❷ **NOTE**
> The meaning of the Latin phrase is 'in the heat (of the crime)'.

flak

get/take (the) 'flak (for sth) (*informal*)
receive severe criticism: *He's taken a lot of flak for his unpopular decisions.* ◇ *Why do I always get the flak when something goes wrong around here?*

flame

an old flame → old

flames

add fuel to the fire/flames → add
fan the flames (of sth) → fan

flap

be in/get into a flap (*informal*)
be in/get into a state of worry or excitement: *Julia's getting into a real flap about her exams.*

flapping

his, her, etc. ears are flapping → ears

flash

a ˌflash in the 'pan (*informal*)
a success which lasts for a short time and is not likely to be repeated: *He scored a lot of goals early in the season, but hasn't scored any since, so it may have been just a flash in the pan.*

> ❶ **ORIGIN**
> This expression refers to an old type of gun; sometimes the gunpowder exploded with a flash in the *pan* of the gun instead of firing the shot.

flash sb a 'smile, 'look, etc.
smile, look, etc. at sb suddenly and quickly: *She flashed him a quick smile, then was gone before he could say anything.*

in/like a 'flash (*informal*)
very quickly; suddenly: *'Sixty-six!' she answered in a flash.* ◇ *This new liquid will clean your floor in a flash.*

(as) quick as a flash → quick

flat

and ˌthat's 'flat! (*BrE, spoken*)
that is my final decision and I will not change my mind: *I'm not lending you any more money, and that's flat!*

be flat 'broke (*BrE also* **be stony 'broke**) (*informal*)
have no money at all: *I'm afraid I can't come away with you this weekend—I'm flat broke!*

(as) flat as a 'pancake (*informal*)
completely flat: *There are one or two hills in Norfolk, but otherwise the landscape is as flat as a pancake.*

flat 'out (*informal*)
1 as fast as possible; with all the energy, strength, etc. you have: *If I worked flat out, I could get all the repairs done today.*
2 lying down, especially because you are ill or extremely tired: *He was flat out on the bed.*
3 (*especially AmE*) in a definite and direct way; completely: *I told him flat out 'No'.* ◇ *It's a 30-year mortgage, which we just flat out can't handle.*

in two minutes, ten seconds, etc. 'flat (*informal*)
used to say that sth happened or was done very quickly, in no more than the time stated: *He tidied his room in ten minutes flat.* ◇ *She spent nine months writing the first half of the book and then finished it in three months flat.*

fall flat → fall
fall flat on your face → fall

flattery

flattery will get you 'everywhere/'nowhere (*spoken, humorous*)
praise that is not sincere will/will not get you what you want: *Just remember—flattery will get you nowhere. There's no use trying to be nice to me so I'll give you what you want.*

flaunt

if you've ˌgot it, 'flaunt it (*humorous, saying*)
used to tell sb that they should not be afraid of
allowing other people to see their qualities and
abilities: *Don't worry about what other people
think! As my grandmother always used to say, 'if
you've got it, flaunt it'!*

flavour (*BrE*) (*AmE* flavor)

flavour of the ˈmonth (*especially BrE*)
a person who is especially popular at the moment:
*If I were you, I'd keep quiet at the staff meeting.
You're not exactly flavour of the month with the
boss at the moment.*

flea

(send sb away/off) with a ˈflea in their ear
(refuse sb's request) very angrily: *When he came to
ask for his job back, we sent him away with a flea in
his ear.*

flesh

ˌflesh and ˈblood
the human body; the weaknesses, desires, fears,
etc. that human beings have: *'Why did he do it?'
'Look, he'd been away from home for six months
and he was lonely. He's only flesh and blood, you
know.'*

your (own) ˌflesh and ˈblood
(members of) your own family: *How can I possibly
not help him? He's my own flesh and blood, isn't he?*

in the ˈflesh
in sb's actual presence; in person: *It's very strange
seeing somebody in the flesh after seeing them on
television for years.*

make your ˈflesh creep/crawl
make you feel afraid or full of disgust: *This is a film
to make your flesh creep.* ◊ *The way he looked at me
made my flesh crawl.*

**more than flesh and blood can stand,
endure, etc.**
too painful or unpleasant to tolerate: *Sometimes
the pain is so bad that it is more than flesh and
blood can stand.*

put flesh on (the bones of) sth
develop a basic idea, etc. by giving more details to
make it more complete: *The strength of the book is
that it puts flesh on the bare bones of his argument.*

be a thorn in your flesh/side → **thorn**

go the way of all flesh → **way**

(take, demand, etc.) your pound of flesh → **pound**

press (the) flesh → **press**

the spirit is willing but the flesh (it) is weak → **spirit**

flex

flex your ˈmuscles
show that you are ready and prepared to use your
power, abilities, etc: *He's flexing his muscles, waiting for the day he becomes president.*

❷ NOTE
Athletes *flex* (= stretch and tighten) their muscles
before a race, a fight, a game, etc.

flies

die/drop/fall like ˈflies
die, become ill, etc. in large numbers: *During the
epidemic people were dropping like flies.*

(there are) no flies on ˈsb (*informal*)
1 sb is not stupid and therefore cannot be tricked
or deceived easily: *You can't just tell her that you've
lost the money; she'll never believe you. There are no
flies on Jane, you know.*
2 sb is skilful or clever at doing sth: *There are no
flies on Jim. He can persuade anybody to buy a car
from him.*

as the crow flies → **crow**

time flies → **time**

flight

a ˌflight of ˈfancy
an idea or a statement that is very imaginative but
not practical or sensible: *The idea is not just a
flight of fancy. It has been done before.*

in the first/top ˈflight
among the best of a particular group: *Everybody
hopes that the new manager will be able to keep the
team in the top flight next year.*

take ˈflight
run away: *The gang took flight when they heard the
police car.*

fling

have a ˈfling (*informal*)
1 enjoy yourself without worrying or thinking
seriously about anything, especially when it is the
last opportunity you will have: *Before I started
training, I had one last fling and went to Paris with
a group of friends for the weekend.*
2 have a short sexual relationship with sb: *'Do
you know Sally Taylor?' 'Yes, I know her quite well
in fact. We had a bit of a fling a few years ago.'*

fling/sling/throw mud (at sb) → **mud**

flip

flip your ˈlid (*informal*)
1 become very angry: *When he saw the damage to
his car, he flipped his lid.*
2 go mad; become mentally ill: *After the divorce,
she just flipped her lid. She was in hospital for
months.*

flip/give/shoot sb the bird → **bird**

flit

do a moonlight flit → **moonlight**

float

float/walk on air ➔ **air**

flog

,flog a dead 'horse (BrE, informal)
waste your effort by trying to do sth that is no longer possible: *Pam's flogging a dead horse trying to organize the theatre trip. It's quite obvious that nobody's interested.*

> **❷ NOTE**
> If an animal or a person is *flogged*, it is/they are hit many times with a whip or a stick, usually as a punishment.

,flog sth to 'death (BrE, informal)
talk/write about or deal with a subject so often that there is no longer any interest in it: *The word 'new' has really been flogged to death in advertisements, and nobody believes it any more.*

flood

,flood the 'market
offer for sale large quantities of a product, often at a low price: *Importers flooded the market with cheap toys just before Christmas.*

floodgates

open the floodgates (to sth) ➔ **open**

floods

be in floods (of tears) (informal)
be crying a lot: *She was in floods of tears after a row with her family.*

floor

,take the 'floor
1 stand up to talk in a debate, etc: *Next, the chairman asked the treasurer, Ms. Jones, to take the floor.*
2 begin dancing: *A few couples took the floor.*

be, come, get, etc. in on the ground floor ➔ **ground**
hold the floor ➔ **hold**
wipe the floor with sb ➔ **wipe**

flotsam

,flotsam and 'jetsam
1 parts of boats, pieces of wood or rubbish, etc. that are found floating on the sea or along the shore; any kind of rubbish: *The beaches are wide and filled with interesting flotsam and jetsam.*
2 people who have no home or job and who move from place to place, often rejected by society: *Under the bridge, you see the human flotsam and jetsam of a big city.*

flow

go with the 'flow (informal)
be relaxed and not worry about what you should do: *He's very stubborn so there's really no point in trying to change his mind. It's best to just go with the flow.*

the ebb and flow (of sb/sth) ➔ **ebb**

flower

the flower of sth (literary)
the finest or best part of sth: *The people of the village will never forget the war and their young men, killed in the flower of youth.*

flown

the bird has flown ➔ **bird**

flush

(in) the first flush of youth, enthusiasm, etc. ➔ **first**

fly

the ,feathers/,fur/,sparks will 'fly (informal)
there will be anger, annoyance, etc: *The fur will really fly when she tells him he can't go out tonight.*

fly the 'coop (informal, especially AmE)
escape from a place: *He was never happy living at home with his parents, so as soon as possible he flew the coop and got his own place.*

> **❷ NOTE**
> A *coop* is a cage for chickens, hens, etc.

fly 'high
be successful: *The business is flying high at the moment, making large profits and attracting a lot of investors.*

fly in the face of 'sth (written)
oppose or be the opposite of sth that is usual or expected: *Such a proposal is flying in the face of common sense.*

a/the fly in the 'ointment (informal)
a person or thing that stops a situation, activity, plan, etc. from being as good or successful as it could be: *We lead a very happy life here. The only fly in the ointment is that there's too much traffic on our road.*

fly into a 'rage, 'temper, etc.
suddenly become very angry: *She flies into a rage every time anybody suggests that she should stop working so hard.*

fly a 'kite (BrE, informal)
release a bit of information, etc. in order to test public reaction to sth that you plan to do at a later date: *Let's fly a kite. Tell the papers that the government is thinking of raising the school leaving age to 18, and we'll see what the reaction is.*

> **❷ NOTE**
> A *kite* is a kind of toy that you fly in the air at the end of a one or more long strings. It will tell you which way the wind is blowing.

(go) fly a/your 'kite (AmE, informal)
used to tell sb to go away and stop annoying you or interfering

ˌfly the ˈnest
1 (of a young bird) become able to fly and leave its nest
2 (*informal*) (of sb's child) leave home and live somewhere else: *Their children have all flown the nest now.*

fly off the ˈhandle (*informal*)
suddenly become very angry: *There's no need to fly off the handle!*

a fly on the ˈwall
a person who watches others without being noticed: *I'd love to be a fly on the wall when the committee is discussing the report I wrote!* ◇ *fly-on-the-wall documentaries* (= in which people are filmed going about their normal lives as if the camera were not there)

he, she, etc. wouldn't harm/hurt a ˈfly
he, she, etc. is kind and gentle, and would not hurt anyone: *The dog may look very fierce, but he wouldn't hurt a fly.*

on the ˈfly (*informal*)
1 if you do sth **on the fly**, you do it quickly while sth else is happening, and without thinking about it very much: *I usually eat my breakfast on the fly.*
2 (in computing) if sth is produced **on the fly**, it is created immediately while the computer program is running: *This is a new program that creates GIF images on the fly.*

fly/show/wave the flag → **flag**
go/fly off at a tangent → **tangent**
let fly (at sb/sth) (with sth) → **let**
pigs might fly → **pigs**
when pigs fly → **pigs**

flyer
get off to a flyer = get off to a flying start → **flying**

flying
a ˌflying ˈvisit
a very brief visit: *The Prime Minister paid a flying visit to Brussels this afternoon.*

get off to a ˌflying ˈstart; get off to a ˈflyer
make a very good, successful start: *She got off to a flying start, gaining several points in the first few minutes.*

go ˈflying (*BrE, informal*)
fall, especially as a result of not seeing sth under your feet: *Someone's going to go flying if you don't pick up these toys.*

with ˌflying ˈcolours (*BrE*) (*AmE* **with ˌflying ˈcolors**)
with great success: *We expect your son to pass the exam with flying colours.* ◇ *She came through her French test with flying colours.*

❶ ORIGIN
In the past, a ship returned to port after a victory in battle decorated with flags (= *colours*).

keep the flag flying → **flag**

foam
foam at the ˈmouth (*informal*)
be extremely angry: *He stood there foaming at the mouth. I've never seen anybody so angry.*

❷ NOTE
If an animal *foams at the mouth*, it has a mass of small bubbles in an around its mouth, especially because it is very ill or angry.

fodder
cannon fodder → **cannon**

fog
in a ˈfog (*informal*)
uncertain and confused: *Thank you for your explanation, but I'm afraid I'm still in a fog over what happened.*

fogey (also fogy)
an old fogey/fogy → **old**

foggiest
not have the faintest/foggiest (idea) → **faintest**

fold
fold sb in your ˈarms (*literary*)
put your arms around sb and hold them against your body: *When he saw how upset she was, he folded her in his arms.*

return to the fold → **return**

follow
follow in sb's ˈfootsteps
do the same job as sb else, especially a parent, has done before; lead a similar life to sb else: *He followed in his dad's footsteps and became a lawyer.*

follow your ˈnose
1 be guided by your sense of smell: *He followed his nose to the kitchen, and found Marina making tomato soup.*
2 go straight forward: *The garage is a mile ahead up the hill—just follow your nose.*
3 act according to what seems right or reasonable, rather than following any particular rules: *In situations like this, I think all we can do is follow our noses.*

follow ˈsuit
act or behave in the way that sb else has just done: *One of the oil companies put up the price of petrol today, and the others are expected to follow suit.*

❷ NOTE
If you *follow suit* in card games, you play a card of the same suit (= either hearts, clubs, diamonds or spades) that has just been played.

follow/steer/take a middle course → **middle**
follow/go with the crowd → **crowd**
a hard/tough act to follow → **act**

fonder

absence makes the heart grow fonder → absence

food

be off your 'food

have no appetite, probably because you are ill or depressed: *She's off her food, she's sleeping very badly and she can't concentrate.*

food for 'thought

an event, remark, fact, etc. which should be considered very carefully because it is interesting, important, etc: *The lectures were very interesting and gave much food for thought.*

fool

act/play the 'fool

behave in a stupid way to make people laugh, especially in a way that may also annoy them: *It's impossible to have a decent game of tennis with Frank—he acts the fool the whole time.* ◇ *If you played the fool in class a little less and worked a bit harder, you could do quite well.*

any fool can/could … (*spoken*)

used to say that sth is very easy to do: *Any fool could tell she was lying.*

be ˌno/ˌnobody's 'fool

be a clever person who cannot easily be tricked or cheated by anyone: *You won't be able to cheat her— she's nobody's fool.* ◇ *Don't underestimate him. He's no fool.*

a ˌfool and his ˌmoney are soon 'parted (*saying*)

a foolish person usually spends money too quickly or carelessly, or is cheated by others

a 'fool's errand

a journey, task, etc. that is a waste of time because it was not necessary: *Are you sending me on a fool's errand again? The last time you sent me to get tickets, the play wasn't even on.*

a fool's 'paradise

a state of happiness which cannot last because sth which you have not thought of is threatening to destroy it: *You've been living in a fool's paradise. How long do you think we can go on spending our money without earning more?*

make a 'fool of sb/yourself

make sb/yourself appear stupid or ridiculous: *Last time you drank champagne, you made a complete fool of yourself.* ◇ *The interviewer made a real fool of me; I just couldn't answer her question.*

ˌmore fool 'you,ˈthem, etc. (*spoken*)

(used as an exclamation) you, etc., were very foolish to do sth: *'He's not going to accept that job in Vienna.' 'More fool him. He'll never get another chance like that again.'*

(there's) ˌno fool like an 'old fool (*saying*)

an older person who behaves foolishly appears more foolish than a younger person who does the same thing, because experience should have taught him not to do it: *Fred is going to marry a woman thirty years younger than him. There's no fool like an old fool.*

fooled

you could have ˌfooled 'me! (*informal*)

used for expressing your surprise about a statement, claim, etc: *'He's quite intelligent, you know.' 'You could have fooled me! I've never heard him say anything intelligent at all.'*

fools

fools rush in (where angels fear to tread) (*saying*)

people with little experience attempt to do the difficult or dangerous things which more experienced people would not consider doing

not suffer fools gladly → suffer

foot

foot the 'bill (for sth)

(used of a large amount of money) be responsible for paying for sth: *The local council will have to foot the bill for damage done to the roads in last year's floods.*

get/have a/your ˌfoot in the 'door

start/have started to be accepted in an organization, group, profession, etc. that could bring you success: *It's difficult to get your foot in the door as a young actor without any experience.* ▶ **foot-in-the-door** *adj.*: *aggressive, foot-in-the-door sales techniques*

get/start off on the right/wrong 'foot (with sb) (*informal*)

start a relationship well/badly: *I seem to have got off on the wrong foot with the new boss.*

have (got) a foot in both 'camps (*informal*)

be involved with two separate groups, etc. that have different ideas: *She works in industry and at a university, so she's got a foot in both camps.*

have (got) ˌone foot in the 'grave (*informal, humorous*)

be so old or ill that you probably will not live much longer: *I may be retired, but that doesn't mean I've got one foot in the grave, you know.*

… my 'foot! (*informal, humorous*)

a strong way of saying that you disagree completely with what has just been said: *'Ian can't come because he's tired.' 'Tired my foot! Lazy more like!'*

not/never put/set a foot 'wrong (*informal*)

never make a mistake: *According to her colleagues, she never put a foot wrong.*

on foot

walking, in contrast to other ways of travelling: *It'll take you half an hour on foot, or five minutes in the car.*

put your 'foot down (*informal*)

1 drive faster in a car: *If you put your foot down, we might be home by seven o'clock.*

2 use your authority to stop sb doing sth: *When she asked if she could stay out until midnight, I put my foot down and insisted that she come home by eleven at the latest.*

put your 'foot in it (*BrE*) (also put your foot in your 'mouth *AmE, BrE*) (*informal*)

say or do sth that upsets, offends or embarrasses sb without intending to: *He really put his foot in it when he mentioned the party to her. She hadn't been invited.*

bind/tie sb hand and foot → **hand**
from head to foot/toe → **head**
put your best foot forward → **best**
set foot in/on sth → **set**
the shoe is on the other foot = the boot is on the other foot → **boot**
shoot yourself in the foot → **shoot**
wait on sb hand and foot → **wait**

football

a political football → **political**

footloose

footloose and fancy-'free

free to go where you like or do what you want because you have no responsibilities: *Here she was, at forty, footloose and fancy-free in New York.*

footsie

play footsie (with sb) → **play**

footsteps

dog sb's footsteps → **dog**
follow in sb's footsteps → **follow**

for

A for B

comparing A with B: *The packets of washing powder are all different sizes, but, weight for weight, this one is the cheapest.* ◇ *Man for man, our soldiers are better trained and better equipped than theirs.*

for 'all

1 in spite of: *For all his qualifications, he isn't really very good at the job.* ◇ *For all her claims to be efficient, she is a very slow worker.*

2 used for saying that the thing you mention does not matter or make any difference: *He can do what he wants, for all I care* (= I don't care what he does). ◇ *'Where's Peter?' 'For all I know, he may be dead.'*

there's/that's ... for you

used to say that sth is a typical example of its kind: *She calls him at least four times a day, but that's love for you I suppose.* ◇ (*ironic*) *He might at least have called to explain. There's gratitude for you!*

forbid

God/Heaven for'bid (that ...) (*spoken*)

used to say that you hope that sth will not happen: *'Maybe you'll end up as a lawyer, like me.' 'Heaven forbid!'*

(Some people find this use offensive.)

forbidden

for,bidden 'fruit

something that you are not allowed to have, do, etc. and for this reason is more attractive: *He felt very attracted to his best friend's wife, but admitted that it was partly because she was forbidden fruit.*

> **❶ ORIGIN**
> This expression refers to the story of Adam and Eve in the Bible, in which Eve ate an apple when she wasn't allowed to.

force

bring sth/come into 'force

(cause a law, rule, etc. to) start being used: *After the new housing law comes into force, we will find it easier to buy our own home.* ◇ *The government says it will bring the new rules into force on July the first.*

force sb's 'hand

force sb to do sth differently or sooner than planned: *By applying pressure to get the law changed, the opposition party wants to force the government's hand.*

> **❶ NOTE**
> In card games if you *force sb's hand*, you force sb to show the cards that they are holding.

'force the issue

do sth to make people take action quickly: *The management certainly seemed sympathetic to our concerns, but I think it would be best to wait a while and not try to force the issue just yet.*

force of 'circumstance

a situation in which you are forced to do sth by factors beyond your control: *He claimed he turned to crime through force of circumstance. He hadn't been able to find a job and his family was starving.*

force of 'habit

a tendency always to do things in a certain way because you have always done them in that way: *I don't know why I check all the locks every time I leave the house. It's force of habit, I suppose.*

force the 'pace (*especially BrE*)

make sb do sth more quickly or make sth happen more quickly: *The government is forcing the pace on economic reforms and the public don't like it.*

> **❶ NOTE**
> If you *force the pace* in a race, you force the other runners to run as fast as you because you want them to get tired.

a force to be 'reckoned with
a person or thing that has a lot of power and influence and should therefore be treated seriously: *The increased size of the country's army means that it is now a force to be reckoned with.* ◊ *Be very careful how you deal with her because she's a force to be reckoned with.*

in 'force/'strength
(of people) present in large numbers: *The police were out in force to deal with any trouble at the demonstration.* ◊ *Party members appeared in strength to welcome the Prime Minister.*

the driving force (behind sth) → **driving**
a show of force → **show**
a spent force → **spent**
a tour de force → **tour**

forces

the forces of 'nature
the power of the wind, rain, etc., especially when it causes damage or harm: *This is one of the few areas of the country where the forces of nature are in control, which is why people don't live here.*

join/combine 'forces (with sb)
work together in order to achieve a shared aim: *The two firms joined forces to win the contract.*

fore

be/come to the 'fore (*BrE*) (*AmE* **be at the 'fore**)
be or become important and noticed by people; play an important part: *She came very much to the fore in the area during the local campaign against the new bypass.*

bring sth to the 'fore
make sth become noticed by people: *His political opinions have been brought to the fore recently, particularly after his television appearance last week.*

forearmed

forewarned is forearmed → **forewarned**

forefront

at/in/to the 'forefront (of sth)
in or into an important or leading position in a particular group or activity: *The new product took the company to the forefront of the computer software market.* ◊ *The court case was constantly in the forefront of my mind* (= I thought about it all the time).

foregone

a ,foregone con'clusion
a result that is certain to happen: *It's a foregone conclusion that Spain will win tonight's match.*

forelock

touch/tug your 'forelock (*disapproving*)

show (too much) respect for a person of a higher rank or status: *This is a democratic country and we don't want people tugging their forelocks.*

> **ℹ ORIGIN**
> In the past people of the lower classes either took off their hats or pulled on their *forelocks* (= the hair above the forehead) to show respect.

foremost

first and foremost → **first**

foreseeable

for/in the foreseeable 'future
for/in the period of time when you can predict what is going to happen, based on the present circumstances: *The statue will remain in the museum for the foreseeable future.* ◊ *It's unlikely that the hospital will be closed in the foreseeable future* (= soon).

forest

not see the forest for the trees → **see**

forewarned

fore,warned is fore'armed (*saying*)
if you know about problems, dangers, etc. before they happen, you can be better prepared for them: *Jim says that Betty is very angry with me still. Well, forewarned is forearmed, and I'll have to think up an excuse before I see her.*

forget

for'get it (*spoken*)
1 used to tell sb that sth is not important and that they should not worry about it: *'I still owe you for lunch yesterday.' 'Forget it—it was my treat!'*
2 used to tell sb that you are not going to repeat what you said: *'Now, what were you saying about John?' 'Forget it, it doesn't matter.'*
3 used to emphasize that you are saying 'no' to sth: *'Any chance of you helping out here?' 'Forget it, I've got too much to do.'*
4 used to tell sb to stop talking about sth because they are annoying you: *Just forget it, will you?*

forgive and forget → **forgive**

forgetting

not forgetting … (*BrE*)
used to include sth in the list of things that you have just mentioned: *I share the house with Jim, Ian and Sam, not forgetting Spike, the dog.*

forgive

for,give and for'get
decide to forget an argument, an insult, etc: *Come on, it's time to forgive and forget.* ◊ *Many of his victims find it impossible to forgive and forget.*

forgiven

he, she, etc. could/might be for'given for doing sth

used to say that it is easy to understand why sb does or thinks sth, although they are wrong: *Looking at the crowds out shopping, you could be forgiven for thinking that everyone has plenty of money to spend.*

form

good/bad 'form (*old-fashioned, BrE*)

a way of doing things that is socially acceptable/ not socially acceptable: *I think it was very bad form for Joe to arrive late for the funeral.* ◇ *Apparently, good form requires you to wear a hat on these occasions.*

on/off 'form (also in (good)/out of 'form)

in a good/poor mental or physical state; doing as well/worse than normal: *She had been ill and was off form, so she didn't do so well in the exam.* ◇ *He's really on form tonight and is answering all the questions correctly and very quickly.* ◇ *The team are in good form this season.*

take 'form (*formal*)

gradually form into a particular shape; gradually develop: *In her body a new life was taking form.*

(do sth) as a matter of form → **matter**
in any (way,) shape or form → **shape**
in the shape/form of sb/sth → **shape**
on present form → **present**
(happen, go, etc.) true to form → **true**

former

be a shadow/ghost of your/its former 'self

not have the strength, influence, etc. that you/sth used to have: *He'd been ill for some time, and he looked a shadow of his former self.* ◇ *The old house, which had once been so full of life, was now just a ghost of its former self.*

fort

hold down the fort = hold the fort → **hold**

Forth

be like painting the Forth Bridge → **painting**

forth

and 'so forth (also and ˌso on (and 'so forth))

used to show that a story, list, etc. continues in an expected way: *I'm in a bit of a hurry. I've got to pack my bags, find my passport and so on, all before tomorrow morning.*

ˌback and 'forth (also ˌbackwards and 'forwards)

in one direction and then in the opposite one, repeatedly: *The rope swung back and forth from the branch.* ◇ *She travels backwards and forwards between the factory and head office.*

from that day/time 'forth (*literary*)

beginning on that day; from that time: *He never saw his mother again from that day forth.*

hold forth (about/on sth) → **hold**

fortune

fortune 'smiles on sb

a person is lucky and successful: *At first, fortune smiled on him and the business was successful.*

make a 'fortune

make a lot of money: *He made a fortune buying and selling nineteenth-century paintings.*

a hostage to fortune → **hostage**
seek your fortune → **seek**
a small fortune → **small**

forty

forty 'winks (*informal*)

a short sleep, especially during the day: *I managed to get forty winks after lunch.*

forward

one step forward, two steps back → **step**
put your best foot forward → **best**

forwards

backwards and forwards = back and forth → **forth**

foul

by fair means or foul → **fair**
cry foul → **cry**
fall foul of sb/sth → **fall**

found

all 'found (*old-fashioned*)

with free food and accommodation in addition to your wages: *My grandmother told me how she used to work as a maid, and was paid £3 a week all found.*

nowhere to be 'found/'seen (also nowhere in 'sight)

impossible to find: *They searched the house but the necklace was nowhere to be found.* ◇ *By the time I arrived at the station, the others were nowhere in sight.*

foundations

shake/rock the 'foundations of sth; shake/rock sth to its 'foundations

cause people to question their basic beliefs about sth: *This issue has shaken the very foundations of French politics.*

founding

the ˌfounding 'father(s) of sth (*formal*)

the people who found or start a country, an organization, a branch of science, etc: *Charles Babbage, the founding father of computer science.*

four

the four ˌcorners of the ˈearth
the parts of the world furthest away: *People come from the four corners of the earth to attend the annual festival.*

these four ˈwalls
used when you are talking about keeping sth secret: *Don't let this go further than these four walls* (= don't tell anyone else who is not in the room now).

four-letter

a ˌfour-letter ˈword
a short word that is considered rude or offensive, especially because it refers to sex or other functions of the body: *Four-letter words used to be banned on radio and television.*

fours

on all ˈfours
with your knees, toes and hands on the floor: *The ceiling of the tunnel was so low that we had to crawl along on all fours.*

fowl

neither fish nor fowl ➔ fish

frame

be in/out of the ˈframe
be taking part/not taking part in sth: *We won our match last week, so we're still in the frame for the championship.*

a frame of ˈmind
a particular way of thinking, mood, etc: *You should ask her for permission when she's in a better frame of mind.* ◊ *I wonder what frame of mind he was in when he wrote the letter.*

franca

a lingua franca ➔ lingua

fray

ˌfray at/around the ˈedges/ˈseams
start to come apart or to fail: *Support for the leader was fraying at the edges.*

frazzle

be burnt, worn, etc. to a ˈfrazzle *(informal)*
be completely burnt/extremely tired: *After working all weekend at the hospital, Deborah was worn to a frazzle.*

free

be in/go into free fall
be falling/start to fall rapidly: *Share prices are in free fall in Tokyo this morning.* ◊ *The value of the euro against the dollar went into free fall as soon as the news was announced.*

> **❷ NOTE**
> From the moment you jump out of a plane until the moment your parachute opens, you are in *free fall*.

(get, do, etc. sth) for ˈfree
1 without having to pay: *Some children got into the cinema for free by using old tickets.*
2 used for emphasizing how strongly you feel about sth: *The whole plan is a disaster. I can tell you that for free.*

free and ˈeasy
informal and relaxed: *They had to settle down. Life wasn't free and easy any more.*

(as) free as (the) ˈair/as a ˈbird
completely free: *You can't imagine what it's like to feel as free as the air. Nobody who hasn't been in prison can imagine it.*

get, have, etc. a free ˈhand
be given permission or an opportunity to do what you want in your work, plans, etc: *My boss gives me a free hand in deciding which outside contractor to use.* ◊ *She has a free hand in choosing her staff.*

get, take, etc. a free ˈride
have an advantage or benefit from a situation without doing anything to deserve it: *You can come with us, but don't expect to get a free ride. You'll have to help us with the work.*

it's a free ˈcountry *(spoken)*
used as a reply when sb suggests that you should not do sth: *It's a free country and I'll say what I like!*

make free with ˈsth *(disapproving)*
use sth a lot, even though it does not belong to you: *Don't you think he'll have something to say about you making free with all his things while he's away?*

of your own free ˈwill
because you want to do sth rather than because sb has told or forced you to do it: *She left of her own free will.*

feel free (to do sth) ➔ feel
give/allow sb/sth free/full rein ➔ rein
home free ➔ home
there's no such thing as a free lunch ➔ thing
walk free ➔ walk

freedom

freedom of/room for manoeuvre ➔ manoeuvre

freeze

make sb's blood freeze ➔ blood
stop/halt/freeze in your tracks ➔ tracks

freezes

when hell freezes over ➔ hell

French

ex,cuse/,pardon my 'French (*informal, humorous*)
used for saying you are sorry when you have used
or are going to use rude or offensive language:
Ouch, bloody hell! Oops, excuse my French! ◇ *If
you'll pardon my French, he's a complete bloody
fool.*

take French 'leave (*BrE, old-fashioned* or
humorous)
leave your work, duty, etc. without permission; go
away without telling anyone: *I think I might take
French leave this afternoon and go to the cinema.*

> **ⓘ ORIGIN**
> This idiom is said to refer to the eighteenth-cen-
> tury French custom of leaving a dinner or party
> without saying goodbye to the host or hostess.

frenzy

a feeding frenzy → **feeding**

fresh

(as) fresh as a 'daisy
lively or clean and neat: *Even when it's so hot, she
looks as fresh as a daisy. How does she do it?*

fresh out of sth (*informal, especially AmE*)
having recently finished a supply of sth: *Sorry,
we're fresh out of milk.*

get 'fresh (with sb) (*informal*)
rude and too confident in a way that shows a lack
of respect for sb or a sexual interest in sb: *Don't get
fresh with me!*

break fresh/new ground → **break**
a breath of fresh air → **breath**
fresh/new/young blood → **blood**

Freudian

a ,Freudian 'slip
a mistake in speaking or writing which shows
what you really think or feel about sb/sth: *'I've
never loved, I mean I've never stopped loving, my
mother.' 'Was that a Freudian slip?'*

> **ⓘ ORIGIN**
> This expression is named after Sigmund Freud
> and his theories of subconscious thought.

friend

a ,friend in 'need (is a ,friend in'deed) (*saying*)
a friend who helps you when you are in trouble (is
a real friend): *I'll always be grateful to Christine
for lending me the money; a friend in need is a friend
indeed!*

a fair-weather friend → **fair-weather**
man's best friend → **man**

friends

be (just) good 'friends
used to say that two friends are not having a
romantic relationship with each other: *People*

*often think Ian and I are a couple, but we're just
good friends.*

have (got) ,friends in high 'places
know important people with power and influence
who can help you: *Ask Geoff to help with the campaign. He's got friends in high places.*

He never did anything special in his life, but he had
friends in high places.

make 'friends (with sb)
become sb's friend: *Roger was new to the district
but he soon made friends with other boys of his age.*
◇ *She's a very open sort of person and tends to
make friends easily.*

what's sth between friends? (*spoken*)
used for refusing an offer by a friend to pay you for
sth because the amount is small: *'I owe you 50p for
that coffee.' 'Don't be silly, Steve, what's 50p between
friends?'*

our feathered friends → **feathered**

fright

the ,fright of your 'life
an experience that makes you feel great fear: *I got
the fright of my life when I saw the gun pointing at
me.* ◇ *He gave me the fright of my life when I saw
him hanging out of the window.*

take 'fright (at sth) (*written*)
be frightened by sth: *The horse took fright and galloped off as the car passed.*

look a fright → **look**

frighten

frighten/scare the life out of sb → **life**
frighten/scare sb out of their wits → **wits**

frightened

be frightened/nervous/scared of your own shadow →
shadow

frighteners

put the 'frighteners on (sb) (*BrE, slang*)
threaten sb so that they will do what you want:
*They started putting the frighteners on the witness,
sending him threatening letters.*

fringe

the lunatic fringe → lunatic

fritz

on the 'fritz (*AmE, informal*)
not working: *The TV is on the fritz again.*

fro

to and fro → to

frog

have (got) a 'frog in your throat (*informal*)
not be able to speak clearly because your throat is
sore, you want to cough, etc: *She had a frog in her
throat, so she had a drink of water before she went
on speaking.*

froing

toing and froing → toing

front

back to 'front
with the front part where the back should be:
You've got your jumper on back to front.

front and 'center (*AmE*)
in or into the most important position: *On Thursday night the new presidential candidate will be
front and center, talking about his policies.*

in the front line (of sth)
doing work that will have an important effect on
sth: *a life spent in the front line of research*

on the 'front burner (*informal, especially AmE*)
(of an issue, a plan, etc.) being given a lot of attention because it is considered important: *Anything
that keeps education on the front burner is good.*

up 'front (*informal*)
(of money) as payment in advance: *We finally
agreed to pay him half the fee up front and the
other half when he'd finished.* ▶ **,up'front** *adj.*
1 not trying to hide what you think or do: *If that's
what they're doing, they ought to be more upfront
about it.*
2 (of money) paid in advance: *There will be an
upfront fee of 4%.*

cash up front → cash
lead from the front → lead
on the home front → home

fruit

the fruit(s) of sth
the good results of an activity or a situation: *Enjoy
the fruits of your labours* (= the rewards for your

hard work). ◇ *The book is the fruit of years of
research.*

bear fruit → **bear**
forbidden fruit → **forbidden**

fruitcake

(as) nutty as a fruitcake → nutty

fry

have (got) other/bigger fish to fry → **fish**
small fry → **small**

frying

out of the 'frying pan (and) into the 'fire (*saying*)
out of one situation of danger or difficulty into
another (usually worse) one: *It was a case of out of
the frying pan into the fire: she divorced her husband, who was an alcoholic, and then married
another man with the same problem.*

fuel

add fuel to the fire/flames → **add**

full

at full 'stretch
to the full extent of your powers, abilities, etc:
*We've been working at full stretch for weeks to get
the hall ready for the conference.*

be at/below full 'strength
have/not have the necessary number of people to
do sth: *We're working below strength at the
moment; it's not easy to deliver all the orders on
time.* ◇ *When we're working at full strength, we
employ 600 people.*

be full of 'shit/'crap (⚠, *slang*)
say, write, etc. stupid or wrong things: *She's so full
of shit.* ◇ *You're all full of crap and I'm not listening any more!*

come/go full 'circle
after a long period of changes, return to the position or situation in which sth/you started: *The
wheel of fashion has come full circle. I was wearing
shoes like that thirty years ago.*

come to a full 'stop (*BrE*)
stop unexpectedly before sth is or seems to be finished: *It's a very strange book—you're in the middle
of the story and it suddenly comes to a full stop.* ◇
*She came to a full stop and seemed unable to go on
with her speech.*

draw yourself up/rise to your full 'height
stand straight and tall in order to show your determination or high status: *When the sales assistant
said he couldn't help her, she drew herself up to her
full height and demanded to see the manager.*

(at) full 'blast
with great noise, power, speed, etc: *Tom had his
radio on at full blast—it was deafening.* ◇ *The heating was on full blast all day.*

full 'marks (to sb for doing sth) (BrE)

used for praising sb for being or doing sth: *Full marks to Hannah for being so helpful this morning.* ◇ *Full marks, Dominic. You sang that very well.*

the ˌfull ˈmonty

the full amount that people expect or want: *They'll do the full monty* (= take off all their clothes) *if you pay them enough.*

❶ ORIGIN
This expression may refer to Field Marshal Montgomery ('*Monty*'), who insisted on a full cooked English breakfast wherever he went; or it might refer to a full three-piece suit from the tailors *Montague Burton.*

full of ˈbeans

very lively, active and healthy: *Ray is certainly full of beans again after his illness.*

❶ ORIGIN
This phrase was originally used to talk about horses that were fed on beans.

full of the joys of ˈspring

very happy, cheerful and lively: *You look full of the joys of spring this morning.*

ˈfull of yourself (disapproving)

feeling successful and very proud of yourself because of it: *He came to see us last week, very full of himself because he had just been promoted.*

(at) full ˈpelt/ˈspeed/ˈtilt

with great speed, force, etc: *The police were chasing him so he ran full pelt down the road.* ◇ *We drove down the road at full tilt.*

full steam/speed aˈhead

with as much speed or energy as possible: *We were working full steam ahead to finish the project by the end of April.*

❶ ORIGIN
This expression refers to the order given on a ship by the captain to the engine room.

full ˈstop (BrE) (also **period** AmE, BrE) (spoken)

used to emphasize that there is nothing more to say about a subject: *I don't have to give you any reasons. You can't have a motorbike, full stop.* ◇ *I don't like him, period.*

(at) full ˈthrottle

if you do sth **at full throttle**, you do it with as much speed and energy as you can: *He's determined to live his whole life at full throttle.*

❷ NOTE
The *throttle* is a device that controls the amount of fuel going into the engine of a vehicle.

in ˈfull

completely; with nothing missing: *I paid the debt in full.* ◇ *The programme reported on the latest developments in full.*

in full ˈcry

chasing or attacking sth with a lot of noise and enthusiasm: *The newspapers are in full cry over this new banking scandal.* ◇ *The government is having difficulties, and its critics are in full cry again.*

❶ ORIGIN
This idiom refers to hounds (= hunting dogs) and the noise they make when they are chasing a fox.

in full ˈswing

at the height (of an event, party, election, etc.); at its busiest or liveliest time: *When we arrived at 10 o'clock, the party was already in full swing.* ◇ *The tourist season in London is in full swing at the moment.*

in full ˈview (of sb/sth)

where you can easily be seen (by sb/sth): *The player committed the foul in full view of the referee, and was sent off the field.*

to the ˈfull

as completely or as much as possible: *You'll be able to enjoy life to the full again after your operation.*

be full to bursting (with sth) = be bursting/bulging at the
   seams (with sth) ➔ **seams**
full/short measure ➔ **measure**
give/allow sb/sth free/full rein ➔ **rein**
have (got) your hands full ➔ **hands**
know sth full/perfectly/very well ➔ **know**
pump sb full of sth ➔ **pump**
(yes sir, no sir) three bags full (sir) ➔ **three**
the wheel has come/turned full circle ➔ **wheel**

fullness

in the fullness of ˈtime (formal)

when (enough) time has passed; eventually: *I knew that, in the fullness of time, somebody with your abilities would emerge and become leader.*

fun

for ˈfun; for the ˈfun of it

for the pleasure or enjoyment of sth, not because it's important or serious: *I entered the competition just for fun—I never thought I'd win.* ◇ *'Why did you say it if you didn't mean it?' 'For the fun of it. I just wanted to see his reaction.'*

fun and ˈgames (informal)

1 activities that are not serious and that other people may disapprove of: *It's not all fun and games at this school—we make our children work hard as well.*
2 (humorous) trouble: *We had some fun and games putting up those new shelves yesterday.*

in ˈfun

in order to amuse sb, not to upset them: *I didn't mean to upset you. It was only said in fun.*

make ˈfun of sb/sth (also **poke ˈfun at sb/sth**)

make unkind remarks or jokes about sb: *People enjoy making fun of the clothes I wear, though they seem all right to me.* ◇ *It's a programme that likes to poke fun at the royal family.*

a figure of fun ➔ **figure**

funeral

it's 'your funeral (*informal*)
used to tell sb that they, and nobody else, will have
to deal with the unpleasant results of their own
actions: *I think you're making a big mistake, but if
you don't want to listen to me that's fine—it's your
funeral.*

funny

'funny business (*informal*)
something that is suspicious and probably illegal
or dishonest: *Now, behave yourself! I don't want
any of your funny business.* ◇ *If there's any funny
business going on, we'll soon find out.*

fur

the feathers/fur/sparks will fly → **fly**

furious

fast and furious → **fast**

furniture

part of the furniture → **part**

furrow

plough a lonely, your own, etc. furrow → **plough**

further

further along/down the 'road
at some time in the future: *There are certain to be
more job losses further down the road.*

go 'further
1 say more about sth, or make a more extreme
point about it: *I would go even further and suggest
that the entire government is corrupt.*
2 last longer; serve more people: *They watered
down the soup to make it go further.*

go no 'further; not go any 'further
if you tell sb that a secret will **go no further**, you
promise not to tell it to anyone else: *Can I have
your assurance that this will go no further?*

**,nothing could be ,further from my 'mind,
the 'truth, etc.**
used to emphasize that what sb has said you are
thinking is definitely not true: *'You must be thinking how terrible I look.' 'Nothing could be further
from my mind. You're as beautiful as always.'* ◇
*People expect the richest people to be the most gener-
ous, but in fact nothing could be further from the
truth.*

take sth 'further
take more serious action about sth or speak to sb
at a higher level about it: *I am not satisfied with
your explanation and I warn you that I intend to
take the matter further.*

be far/further/furthest removed from sth → **removed**
far/farther/further afield → **afield**
without further/more ado → **ado**

furthest

be far/further/furthest removed from sth → **removed**

fury

like 'fury (*informal*)
with great energy, speed, etc: *I worked like fury to
get everything done by five o'clock.*

hell hath no fury (like a woman scorned) → **hell**

fuse

be on/have a short fuse → **short**
blow a fuse → **blow**

fuss

a ,fuss about 'nothing
a lot of anger or worry about sth that is not important: *She complained about her food twice in the restaurant. She was making a lot of fuss about
nothing—I thought everything was fine.*

make a 'fuss of/over sb/sth
pay a lot of attention to sb/sth; show concern,
affection, etc. for sb/sth: *It's sometimes quite pleasant being ill, with people making a fuss of you all
the time.*

fussed

not be 'fussed (about sb/sth) (*BrE, informal*)
not mind about sth; not have feelings about sth:
It'd be good to be there, but I'm not that fussed.

future

in 'future (*BrE*) (*AmE* **in the 'future**)
from now on: *Please be more careful in future.* ◇ *In
future, make sure the door is never left unlocked.*

for/in the foreseeable future → **foreseeable**
in the not too distant future → **distant**

Gg

gab
a gift for/of gab ➔ gift
the gift of the gab ➔ gift

gaff
blow the gaff (on sb/sth) ➔ blow

gain
gain 'ground
1 (of soldiers) move forward in a battle: *Our men began to gain ground, forcing the enemy back towards the river.*
2 (of an idea, development, etc.) become more popular or successful: *Diesel cars seem to be gaining ground because they are cheaper to run.*

gain 'time
delay sth so that you can have more time to make a decision, deal with a problem, etc: *Instead of answering the question, he asked for a glass of water to gain time.*

gained
nothing ventured, nothing gained ➔ ventured

gallery
play to the gallery ➔ play
a rogues' gallery ➔ rogues

game
blow/sod ⚠ 'this/'that for a game of soldiers (*BrE, slang*)
used by sb who does not want to do sth because it is annoying or involves too much effort: *After waiting for twenty minutes more, he thought 'sod this for a game of soldiers', and left.*

your/sb's (little) 'game (*informal*)
your/sb's trick, plan or intention: *So that's your little game—getting me moved to a different office and then doing my job for me.*

the ˌgame is not worth the 'candle (*old-fashioned, saying*)
sth is not worth the effort needed: *After trying to get permission to build the office for a whole year, we gave up, because the game was just not worth the candle.*

> **❶ ORIGIN**
> In the past, people used to play cards by candle-light. If the money being gambled was less than the cost of the candle, it was not worth playing the game.

the game is 'up (*BrE, informal*)
said to sb who has done sth wrong, when they are caught and the crime or trick has been discovered: *The game's up, Malone. We're arresting you for the murder of Joe Capella.* ◇ *The game is up for the Democrats. They'll never win the next election after this scandal.*

give the 'game away (*informal*)
(accidentally) reveal your own or another person's secret plan, trick, etc. and so spoil it: *Don't laugh when he comes in or you'll give the game away. The birthday present's got to be a surprise.* ◇ *He can't keep a secret, so never tell him anything important in case he gives the game away.*

(be/go) on the 'game (*BrE, slang*)
be/become a prostitute

what's sb's/your 'game? (*BrE, spoken*)
used to ask why sb is behaving as they are: *Dan's looking very nervous. Why? What's his game?*

be a mug's game ➔ mug
beat sb at their own game ➔ beat
a (whole) different/new ball game ➔ ball
easy game ➔ easy
fair game ➔ fair
a game that two can play = two can play at that game ➔ two
the name of the game ➔ name
a/the numbers game ➔ numbers
play sb at their own game ➔ play
play the game ➔ play
play the same game (as sb) = play sb's game ➔ play
the rules of the game ➔ rules
two can play at that game ➔ two
(play) a waiting game ➔ waiting

gamekeeper
poacher turned gamekeeper ➔ poacher

games
fun and games ➔ fun
play (silly) games (with sb) ➔ play

gamut
run the gamut of sth ➔ run

gander
have/take a 'gander (at sth) (*informal*)
look at sth: *Come over here and have a gander at what I've got!*

what's sauce for the goose is sauce for the gander ➔ sauce

gangbusters
like 'gangbusters (*AmE, informal*)
with a lot of energy and enthusiasm: *At the time, we were spending money like gangbusters.*

gap

bridge the gap (between A and B) → **bridge**

garden

everything in the garden is 'lovely/'rosy (*BrE, saying, often ironic*)

everything is satisfactory, is going well, or could not be better: *She pretends that everything in the garden is rosy, but I've heard that she's heavily in debt.*

common or garden → **common**

lead sb up the garden path → **lead**

garden-variety

garden-variety = common or garden → **common**

garters

have sb's guts for garters → **guts**

gas

be cooking with gas → **cooking**

step on the gas → **step**

gasp

your/the last gasp → **last**

gatepost

between you, me and the 'gatepost (*BrE, informal*)

used to show that what you are going to say next is a secret: *Well, between you, me and the gatepost, I heard that she's pregnant.*

Gates

the Pearly Gates → **Pearly**

gather

gather 'dust

(of plans, recommendations, etc.) be forgotten or ignored: *As usual the report was left to gather dust and not dealt with by the authorities for years.*

collect/gather your wits → **wits**

gauntlet

take up the 'gauntlet

accept sb's invitation to fight or compete: *The country needs enormous help to rebuild its economy, and it's time to take up the gauntlet and do what we can.*

ⓘ ORIGIN

A *gauntlet* is a kind of glove. In medieval times a knight threw his gauntlet at the feet of another knight as a challenge to fight. If he accepted the challenge, the other knight would pick up the glove.

run the gauntlet → **run**

throw down the gauntlet → **throw**

gay

with gay a'bandon (*old-fashioned*)

without thinking about the results or effects of a particular action: *Although she was nervous at first, she was soon singing and dancing with gay abandon.*

gaze

look/stare/gaze into space → **space**

gear

get into 'gear; get sth into 'gear

start working, or start sth working, in an efficient way: *Sorry, I can't seem to get my brain into gear this morning.*

(slip/be thrown) out of 'gear

(of emotions or situations) (become) out of control: *She said nothing when he arrived in case her temper slipped out of gear.*

get your ass in gear → **ass**

general

in 'general

in most cases; usually: *The money is due to come on the first of every month; in general it arrives punctually, but at holiday times it's sometimes late.*

the common/general run (of sth) → **run**

genes

in the/sb's blood/genes → **blood**

genie

the genie is out of the bottle

used to say that an action has been taken that will cause a big and permanent change in people's lives, especially one which might make a situation worse: *Now that genetically modified foods are on our supermarket shelves, the genie is out of the bottle and cannot be put back in.*

ⓘ ORIGIN

In Arabian stories, a *genie* is a spirit with magical powers, especially one that lives in a bottle or lamp.

let the genie out of the bottle → **let**

gentleman

a ,gentleman's a'greement (also a ,gentlemen's a'greement)

an agreement, contract, etc. in which nothing is written down because both people trust each other not to break it: *'Why don't you tell him you don't want to sell it now?' 'I can't possibly. It was a gentleman's agreement and I must keep to it.'*

gently

easy/gently/slowly does it → **easy**

get

Most idioms containing the verb **get** are at the entries for the nouns or adjectives in the idioms, for example **get on sb's nerves** is at **nerves**.

can't get 'over sth (*spoken*)

used to say that you are shocked, surprised, amused, etc. by sth: *I can't get over how rude she was to me.*

get a'long/a'way/'on (with you)! (*old-fashioned, BrE, informal*)

used for expressing surprise, disbelief, annoyance, etc: *Get away with you! You don't expect me to believe that story, do you?*

get a'way from it all (*informal*)

go away somewhere on holiday, etc. in order to escape from pressures at work, home, city life, etc: *We went walking to get away from it all for a while.* ◇ *Why don't you get away from it all and have a weekend in the country?*

get it (in the neck) (*informal*)

be criticized, blamed or punished: *You'll get it when your mother sees all this mess.* ◇ *We'll get it in the neck if we arrive late.*

get it 'on (with sb) (*slang, especially AmE*)

have sex with sb

get sb 'nowhere/not get sb 'anywhere

not help sb make progress: *His job is getting him nowhere. He ought to try and find another one.* ◇ *All these questions aren't getting us anywhere. We need to make a decision.*

(not) get somewhere/nowhere/anywhere

(not) make progress: *Now at last we're getting somewhere!* ◇ *You'll get nowhere in life if you don't work harder.* ◇ *Are you getting anywhere with that new manager?*

'get there (*informal*)

finally achieve your aim or complete a task: *Peter is a slow learner, but he gets there in the end.*

how selfish, stupid, ungrateful, etc. can you 'get? (*spoken*)

used to express surprise or disapproval that sb has been so selfish, stupid, etc: *I can't believe he didn't even say thank you. How ungrateful can you get?*

getting

be getting 'on (*informal*)

1 (of people) be becoming old: *I'm getting on a bit now and I can't walk as well as I used to.*

2 (of the time) be becoming late: *It's getting on, so I'd better be off home.*

getting on for ... (*especially BrE*)

near to or approaching a certain time, number, age, etc: *I've lived here getting on for five years now.* ◇ *She's getting on for ninety.*

there's no getting a'way from it (*informal*)

we cannot ignore an important and possibly unpleasant fact: *There's no getting away from it. He's simply a better player than me.*

what are you, was he, etc. 'getting at? (*spoken*)

used to ask, especially in an angry way, what sb is/was suggesting: *I'm partly to blame. What exactly are you getting at?*

ghost

give up the 'ghost

1 (*old-fashioned*) die

2 (*humorous*) (of a machine, etc.) stop working because it is so old: *My old computer has finally given up the ghost, so I'm getting a new one.*

3 (of a person) stop making an effort; stop working: *She persuaded me to carry on when I was tempted to give up the ghost.*

not have a 'ghost of a chance (of doing sth) (*informal*)

have no chance at all (of doing sth): *He doesn't have a ghost of a chance of passing the exam this year.*

be a shadow/ghost of your/its former self → **former**

(as) white as a sheet/ghost → **white**

gift

the gift of the 'gab (*BrE*) (*AmE* **a gift of/for 'gab**) (*informal, sometimes disapproving*)

the ability to speak easily and to persuade other people with your words: *To be a successful sales executive you need the gift of the gab.*

❶ ORIGIN

Gab is possibly from the Irish word for *mouth*. The Irish have a reputation as good talkers.

God's gift (to sb/sth) → **God**

(not) look a gift horse in the mouth → **look**

gild

gild the 'lily

try to improve sth which is already perfect, and so spoil it: *The dress is perfect. Don't add anything to it at all. It would just be gilding the lily.*

❶ ORIGIN

This idiom is a misquotation from Shakespeare's *King John*: 'to gild refined gold, to paint the lily ... is wasteful and ridiculous excess'.

gills

to the 'gills (*informal*)

completely full: *I was stuffed to the gills with chocolate cake.*

green about the gills → **green**

gilt

take the gilt off the 'gingerbread

spoil sth so that you find it less attractive than before: *He's offered us his villa by the sea for two weeks. The only problem is that we can only have it in February, which rather takes the gilt off the gingerbread.*

gingerbread

take the gilt off the gingerbread → gilt

gird

gird (up) your 'loins (*literary* or *humorous*)
prepare yourself for action, hard work, etc:
*There's a lot of hard work to be done before the
weekend, so let's gird up our loins and start.*

> ❶ ORIGIN
> In the Bible, to *gird your loins* meant to pick up
> your robe and tie it about your waist so that you
> could run or move much more quickly.

girl

a big girl's blouse → big
old boy/girl → old

girls

be one of the lads/boys/girls → lads

give

Most idioms containing the verb **give** are at the
entries for the nouns or adjectives in the idioms,
for example **give sb a break** is at **break**.

don't give me 'that (*spoken*, *informal*)
used to tell sb that you do not accept what they say:
'I didn't have time to do it.' 'Oh, don't give me that!'

give and 'take
be willing to listen to other people's wishes and
points of view and to change your demands, if this
is necessary: *If we want this marriage to be successful, we both have to learn to give and take.*
▶ **give and 'take** *noun*: *We can't all expect to have
exactly what we want. There has to be some give
and take.*

give as good as you 'get
defend yourself very well when you fight or argue
with sb: *Don't worry about her. She can give as good
as she gets.*

give me sth/sb ('any day/time) (*spoken*)
used for saying you like sth much more than the
thing just mentioned: *I hate going to clubs. Give me
a nice meal at a restaurant any day.* ◇ *I don't like
cricket very much. Give me football any time.*

give or 'take (sth)
if sth is correct **give or take** a particular amount,
it is approximately correct: *It took us three hours,
give or take a few minutes.* ◇ *It'll cost about £1 000,
give or take.*

give sb what 'for; 'give it to sb (*BrE*, *spoken*)
punish sb severely: *If you take my car again without asking me, I'll give you what for.* ◇ *The manager will really give it to you when he finds out what
you've done.*

I/I'll give you 'that (*spoken*)
used when you are admitting that sth is true. *I said
an hour ago that I thought we were going the wrong
way, didn't I?' 'Yes, you did, I'll give you that.'*

given

be given to sth/to doing sth (*formal*)
do sth often or regularly: *She's much given to out-
bursts of temper.* ◇ *He's given to going for long
walks on his own.*

gives

what 'gives? (*spoken*, *informal*)
what is happening?; what is the news?: *I haven't
seen you for a few weeks! What gives?*

glad

'glad rags (*old-fashioned*, *informal*)
smart clothes worn for a party, etc: *We put our glad
rags on and went to the theatre.*

gladly

not suffer fools gladly → suffer

glance

at a (single) 'glance
immediately; with only a quick look: *He could tell
at a glance what was wrong.*

at first glance/sight → first
steal a glance/look (at sb/sth) → steal

glass

people (who live) in glass houses shouldn't throw stones
→ people
raise your glass (to sb) → raise

glistens

all that glitters/glistens/glisters is not gold → gold

glisters

all that glitters/glistens/glisters is not gold → gold

glitters

all that glitters/glistens/glisters is not gold → gold

gloom

gloom and doom = doom and gloom → doom
pile on the agony/gloom → pile

glory

bathe/bask in reflected glory → reflected

glove

fit (sb) like a glove → fit
hand in glove (with sb) → hand
an iron fist/hand in a velvet glove → iron

gloves

the gloves are 'off (*informal*)
in an argument, dispute, etc., stop being gentle
with sb and start fighting them with force and
determination: *Up to now both sides in the dispute*

have been cautious, but now the gloves are off and a serious confrontation is expected.

> **❶ ORIGIN**
> This idiom refers to boxers taking off their gloves.

'Right, that's it! The gloves are off now!'

handle, treat, etc. sb with kid gloves → **kid**

glowing

in glowing 'terms/'colours (*BrE*) (*AmE* **in glowing 'terms/'colors**)
(describe sb/sth) in a very positive way: *He describes Manchester in glowing terms. I never realized it was such an interesting place.* ◇ *He spoke of her performance in the film in glowing terms.*

glued

be 'glued to sth (*informal*)
give all your attention to sth; stay very close to sth: *He spends every evening glued to the TV.* ◇ *Her eyes were glued to the screen* (= she did not stop watching it).

glued/rooted to the spot → **spot**

glutton

a glutton for punishment, work, etc. (*informal*)
a person who seems to like doing unpleasant or difficult things: *You're going to drive all the way to London and back in a day? You're a glutton for punishment, aren't you?* ◇ *She's a glutton for work. She stays late every evening.*

gnash

gnash your 'teeth
feel very angry and upset about sth, especially because you cannot get what you want: *He'll be gnashing his teeth when he hears that we lost the contract.*

go

Most idioms containing the verb **go** are at the entries for the nouns or adjectives in the idioms, for example **go for broke** is at **broke**.

as things, people, etc. 'go
compared to the average thing of that type: *As government statements go, this one was fairly honest.* ◇ *As titles for abstract paintings go, 'Field with Figures' is better than most.*

at/in one 'go (*BrE*)
in one single action; all at the same time: *I don't think I'll be able to solve all the problems at one go.* ◇ *He ate the whole cake in one go.*

be on the 'go (*informal*)
be busy and active: *I've been on the go all day and I'm exhausted.* ◇ *She's always on the go. I wish she would just sit down and relax sometimes.*

don't go doing sth (*spoken*)
used to tell or warn sb not to do sth: *Don't go getting yourself into trouble.*

first, second, etc. 'go (*BrE*)
at the first, second, etc. attempt: *I passed my driving test first go.*

go all 'out for sth; go all out to 'do sth (*informal*)
make a very great effort to get or do sth: *We knew that only one of the firms would get the order for computers and so we went all out to get the contract.* ◇ *We must go all out to increase our membership.*

go and do sth (*informal*)
used for expressing anger that sb has done sth: *Why did you have to go and tell him? It was a secret.* ◇ *Look what you've gone and done now! That was my favourite vase.*

go down 'well, 'badly, etc. (with sb) (also **go off 'well**)
used to talk about whether people like sth such as a speech, performance, etc: *Her speech went down well with the audience.*

'go for it (*spoken*)
used for encouraging sb to try and achieve sth that is difficult or considered difficult: *Don't listen to him, Jeannie, go for it! How will you ever know unless you try?*

go 'on (with you) (*old-fashioned*)
used to express the fact that you do not believe sth, or that you disapprove of sth: *Go on with you—you're never forty. You don't look a day over thirty.*

have a 'go (at sb) (*informal*)
attack, criticize (sb): *She had a go at me last night about crashing the car.* ◇ *He's always having a go at me about my spelling.*

have a 'go (at sth/at doing sth) (*informal*)
attempt to do, win or achieve sth: *I'm sure I could do better than that. Let me have a go!* ◇ *I've got the time, so I'll have a go at the decorating myself.*

have (got) sth on the 'go (*informal*)
be dealing with, working on, etc. sth: *She's a very*

busy architect and always has some project on the go. ◇ 'Have you got anything interesting on the go at the moment?' 'Yes, I'm working on a programme about the origins of sport.'

no 'go (*informal*)
impossible; unsuccessful: *I asked him if I could have an extra week's holiday, but it was no go.* ◇ *'Could you lend me your car this weekend, Mike?' 'No go, I'm afraid. I need it myself.'*

... to 'go
1 still remaining before sth happens, finishes or is completed: *There's only a few seconds to go before the rocket takes off.* ◇ *With only two kilometres to go, Max is still first.*
2 (*especially AmE, informal*) (of food bought in a restaurant, shop, etc.) to be taken away and eaten somewhere else: *Two coffees to go, please.*

goalposts
move the goalposts → **move**

goat
act/play the 'goat (*informal*)
deliberately behave in a silly or foolish way: *Stop acting the goat or I'll send you out. I'm warning you.*

get sb's 'goat (*informal*)
annoy sb very much: *That woman really gets my goat. She does nothing but complain.* ◇ *It really gets my goat when people smoke in non-smoking areas.*

goats
sort out/separate the sheep from the goats → **sheep**

gob
shut your mouth/trap/face/gob! → **shut**

God
by 'God! (*old-fashioned, spoken*)
used to emphasize a feeling of determination or surprise: *By God, I never thought I'd say this, but I'm proud of you!*
(Some people find this use offensive.)

(good) 'God; God al'mighty; God in 'heaven; my/oh 'God (*spoken*)
used for expressing anger, surprise, etc: *Good God! What on earth have you done to my car?* ◇ *Oh my God! I've broken my watch again!* ◇ *God almighty! You're not going to wear that terrible old suit to the wedding, are you?*
(Some people find these expressions offensive.)

God 'bless
used when you are leaving sb, to say that you hope they will be safe, etc: *Good night, God bless.*

God 'rest his, her, etc. soul; God 'rest him, her, etc. (*old-fashioned, spoken*)
used to show respect when you are talking about sb who is dead: *My grandfather, God rest his soul,*

would never think of leaving the house without a suit and tie on.

God 'willing (*spoken*)
used for expressing your hope that sth will happen: *We've had a lovely holiday and we'll be back again next year, God willing.*

God's gift (to sb/sth) (*ironic*)
a person who thinks that they are particularly good at sth or who thinks that sb will find them particularly attractive: *He seems to think he's God's gift to women.*

to 'God/'goodness/'Heaven
used after a verb to emphasize a particular hope, wish, etc: *I wish to God you'd learn to pay attention!* (Some people find the use of **God** here offensive.)

an act of God → **act**
for the love of God → **love**
God/Heaven forbid (that ...) → **forbid**
God/Heaven help sb → **help**
God/goodness/Heaven knows → **knows**
honest to God/goodness → **honest**
in God's/Heaven's name → **name**
in the name of God/Heaven → **name**
a man of God/the cloth → **man**
play God → **play**
please God → **please**
put the fear of God into sb → **fear**
thank God! → **thank**
there but for the grace of God (go I) → **grace**
work all the hours God sends → **work**

godmother
a/your fairy godmother → **fairy**

gods
in the lap of the gods → **lap**

going
be going on (for) sth (*BrE*)
be nearly a particular age, time or number: *It was going on for midnight by the time we left.*

be good 'going; be not bad 'going (*informal*)
be good progress: *'It only took me two hours to get to Birmingham.' 'That's good going.'* ◇ *'I've written 20 pages today.' 'That's not bad going.'*

enough/something to be going 'on with (*BrE*)
something that is enough for a short time: *£50 should be enough to be going on with.*

have (got) a lot, something, nothing, etc. 'going for you
have (got) many, some, no, etc. achievements, skills, advantages, etc: *As the very intelligent daughter of rich parents, she's got a lot going for her.* ◇ *No job, no qualifications, nowhere to live. He doesn't have much going for him, does he?*

while the ‚going is 'good (*BrE*) (*AmE* **while the ‚getting is 'good**)
before a situation changes and it is no longer pos-

sible to do sth: *He thinks the company is going to go bankrupt soon, so he's getting out while the going is good.* ◇ *Don't you think we should quit while the going is good?*

goings

comings and goings → **comings**

gold

,**all that** ,**glitters/**,**glistens/**,**glisters is not** '**gold** (*saying*)
not everything that seems good, attractive, etc. is actually good, etc: *Don't imagine that because they are rich, they are happy. All that glitters is not gold.*

a 'gold mine
a business or an activity that makes a large profit: *That Internet cafe of his is a real gold mine.*

(as) good as 'gold
(of children) very well-behaved: *The children were good as gold. They sat quietly and read all afternoon.*

like 'gold dust
very difficult to obtain because everyone wants it/ them: *You can't get those new trainers anywhere. They're like gold dust.*

be worth your/its weight in gold → **worth**
have (got) a heart of gold → **heart**
the streets are paved with gold → **streets**
strike gold → **strike**

golden

the 'golden age (of sth)
the period during which sth is very successful, especially in the past: *This book looks back on the golden age of steam engines, and all railway fans will enjoy it immensely.*

a 'golden boy
a young man who is very successful and popular: *He had been the golden boy of Welsh rugby.*

a golden 'handshake
a large sum of money given to sb when they leave their job, or to persuade them to leave their job: *The directors will each get a large golden handshake and a pension.*

the golden 'rule
the most important rule, principle, etc. to remember when you are doing sth: *When you're playing a stroke in golf, the golden rule is to keep your eye on the ball.*

the happy/golden mean → **mean**
kill the goose that lays the golden egg/eggs → **kill**
silence is golden → **silence**

gone

gone for a '**burton** (*old-fashioned, BrE, informal*)
lost, destroyed or broken: *The custom of couples saving up for a long time before they get married*

has long gone for a burton. ◇ *Sorry I didn't reply to your email. My computer's gone for a burton!*

> **❶ ORIGIN**
> This expression was used during World War II to refer to pilots missing and perhaps killed in action. It may refer to a popular type of beer at the time called *Burton ale.*

dead and buried/gone → **dead**
far gone → **far**
he, she, etc. has gone/been and done sth → **done**
here today, gone tomorrow → **today**

good

Most idioms containing **good** are at the entries for the nouns or verbs in the idioms, for example **a good Samaritan** is at **Samaritan**.

,all to the 'good
used to say that if sth happens, it will be good, even if it is not exactly what you were expecting: *'I'm afraid we've arrived a bit early.' 'Don't worry. It's all to the good. It means we can start the meeting earlier.'*

as 'good as …
so close to sth happening that you consider that it has happened: *I thought the car was as good as sold and then the man suddenly decided not to buy it.* ◇ *She as good as told me she didn't want to come.*

as ,good as it 'gets
used when you are saying that a situation is not going to get any better: *The past year has been very special—as good as it gets as far as I'm concerned.*

be 'good for sth
1 be likely to be able to give or provide sth: *I'll ask my aunt if she can help us. She'll be good for a few pounds, I'm sure.*
2 be likely to live, last, etc. for a period of time: *This car's probably good for another 20 000 miles.*

be no 'good; not be any/much 'good
1 not be useful; have no useful effect: *This gadget isn't much good.* ◇ *It's no good trying to talk me out of leaving.* ◇ *Was his advice ever any good?*
2 not be interesting or enjoyable: *His latest film isn't much good.*

do 'good
be kind and generous to people who need help, for example by working for a charity: *She tries to do good by visiting prisoners' families when she can.*
▶ ,do-'gooder *noun* (*informal, disapproving*) a person who tries to help others but does it in a way that is annoying

do sb 'good
help sb; have a good effect on sb: *A holiday at the seaside would do you a lot of good.*

for 'good (*BrE also* for ,good and 'all)
permanently; for ever: *I'm going away for good.* ◇ *Today I gave up smoking for good.*

for your (own) good
(of sth unpleasant) so that you will benefit: *I don't*

like criticizing you but it's for your own good. ◇ I know he doesn't want to do all this extra homework, but it's for his own good.

good and ... (*informal*)
completely: I won't go until I'm good and ready.

good for 'you, 'him, etc. (also **good 'on you, him, etc.**) (*informal*)
used to praise sb for doing sth well: 'I've decided to give up smoking as from tomorrow.' 'Good for you, Philip.' ◇ 'He's saving up his pocket money to buy a football.' 'Good for him.'

to the 'good
in profit: She bought the painting for £250 and then sold it for £550, so she's £300 to the good, lucky woman.

up to no 'good (*informal*)
doing or planning sth wrong or dishonest: He doesn't work but he seems to have lots of money. I'm sure he's up to no good. ◇ Where have those children gone? They're probably up to no good.

very good (*old-fashioned, formal*)
used for saying 'yes' when a person in authority gives you an order: 'Brown, bring me a bottle of champagne and two glasses, please.' 'Very good, Sir.'

goodbye

kiss/say goodbye to sth; kiss sth goodbye (*informal*)
give up hope of getting sth that you want very much: You'll have to say goodbye to your chances of becoming a doctor if you don't pass the exams. ◇ After this letter from the bank, we can kiss goodbye to our holiday in Australia.

goodness

out of the ˌgoodness of your 'heart
from feelings of kindness, without thinking about what advantage there will be for you: You're not telling me he offered to lend you the money out of the goodness of his heart?

God/goodness/Heaven knows → knows
honest to God/goodness → honest
thank goodness/Heaven(s)! → thank
to God/goodness/Heaven → God

goods

come up with/deliver/produce the 'goods (*informal*)
do what you are expected or have promised to do: You can depend on him to come up with the goods. If he says he'll do something, he always does it.

goody-goody

a ˌgoody-goody; a goody ˌtwo-shoes (*informal, disapproving*)
a person who behaves very well to please people in authority such as parents or teachers: Don't be such a goody-goody! ◇ He's a real goody two-shoes.

He'd never do anything that might get him into trouble.

goose

cook sb's goose → **cook**
he, she, etc. wouldn't say boo to a goose → **say**
kill the goose that lays the golden egg/eggs → **kill**
what's sauce for the goose is sauce for the gander → **sauce**
a wild goose chase → **wild**

gooseberry

play gooseberry → **play**

Gordian

cut/untie the ˌGordian 'knot
solve a very difficult or complicated problem with forceful action: Will the negotiators be able to untie the Gordian knot?

> **❶ ORIGIN**
> This expression comes from the legend in which King Gordius tied a very complicated knot and said that whoever untied it would become the ruler of Asia. Alexander the Great cut through the knot with his sword.

gospel

take sth as/for gospel (truth) (*informal*)
believe sth without questioning it or without any real proof: You can't always take what she says as gospel—she's not the most honest person in the world. ◇ It would be foolish to take everything in the newspapers for gospel.

grab

how does ... grab you? (*spoken*)
used to ask sb whether they are interested in sth or in doing sth: How does the idea of a trip to Rome grab you?

catch/get/grab/take (a) hold of sb/sth → **hold**
grab/hit/make the headlines → **headlines**

grabs

be up for 'grabs (*informal*)
be available to anyone who is interested in getting it, buying it, etc: The contract for repairing the damaged buildings will soon be up for grabs. ◇ There are £25000 worth of prizes up for grabs in our competition!

grace

have (got) the (good) grace to do sth
be polite enough to do sth: Fortunately, she had the grace to apologize as soon as she realized she had offended them. ◇ He didn't even have the grace to say thank you.

there but for the grace of 'God (go 'I) (*saying*)
used to say that you could easily have been in the same difficult or unpleasant situation that sb else

is in: *Whenever I think of poor Fran and her problems, I think there but for the Grace of God go I.*

with (a) good/bad 'grace

(do or accept sth unpleasant, unfair, boring, etc.) in a willing and pleasant/unwilling and rude way: *It is very important in sport to accept defeat with good grace.* ◊ *I've never seen anybody do anything with such bad grace.*

fall from grace → **fall**

in a state of grace → **state**

a saving grace → **saving**

graces

be in sb's good 'graces (*formal*)

have sb's approval and be liked by them: *Having bought them all dinner, he is now firmly in their good graces.*

airs and graces → **airs**

grade

make the 'grade (*informal*)

reach a high enough standard in an exam, a job, etc: *You'll never make the grade if you don't work hard before the exams.* ◊ *Do you think she'll ever make the grade as a journalist?*

grain

be/go against the 'grain

be or do sth different from what is normal or natural: *Voting for the Liberal Party goes against the grain with him. He's voted Conservative all his life.* ◊ *It goes against the grain for her to spend a lot of money on clothes.*

❷ NOTE
The *grain* is the natural direction of lines in a piece of wood.

grand

a/the ˌgrand old 'age

a great age: *She finally learned to drive at the grand old age of 70.*

a/the ˌgrand old 'man (of sth)

an old man who is very experienced and respected in a particular profession, etc: *At eighty, he is the grand old man of the British film industry.*

grandeur

delusions of grandeur → **delusions**

grandmother

teach your grandmother to suck eggs → **teach**

granted

take sb/sth for 'granted

not value sb/sth just because they are/it is always there: *Your problem is that you take your wife for granted. When was the last time you told her how much you appreciated her?* ◊ *We take so many*

things for granted these days: electricity, running water, cars …

take sth for 'granted (that …)

believe that sth is/will be true, will happen, etc. without checking to make sure: *We took it for granted that there would be some rooms available at the hotel but we were wrong.* ◊ *He took it for granted that he would get the job, and so he was very surprised when he didn't.*

grapes

sour grapes → **sour**

grapevine

on/through the 'grapevine

by talking in an informal way to other people: *I heard on the grapevine that you're leaving.*

grasp

grasp the 'nettle (*BrE*)

deal with a difficult matter, firmly and with courage: *The government will have to grasp the nettle. If they don't, the traffic congestion is going to get out of control.*

❷ NOTE
A *nettle* is a plant with leaves that sting if you touch them lightly, but not if you grasp them firmly.

clutch/grasp at straws → **straws**

grass

the grass is (always) greener on the other side (of the fence) (*saying*)

things always seem better in another place, job, etc: *She says she would be able to do business better in France, but the grass is always greener on the other side!*

the ˌgrass 'roots

the ordinary people in an organization, for example a political party or trade union, and not the officials: *The leaders of this union are losing contact with their members. They need to get back in touch with the grass roots.* ▶ ˌgrass-'roots *adj.*: *a grass-roots movement*

put/turn/send sb out to 'grass (*informal, humorous*)

force sb to stop doing their job, especially because they are old: *Old Harry doesn't seem able to remember anything nowadays. Isn't it time he was put out to grass?*

❶ ORIGIN
This expression refers to old farm horses or other animals, which no longer work and stay in the fields all day.

not let the grass grow under your feet → **let**

a snake in the grass → **snake**

grasshopper

knee-high to a grasshopper → **knee-high**

grata

persona non grata → **persona**

grateful

be grateful/thankful for small mercies → **small**

grave

dig your own grave → **dig**

from the cradle to the grave → **cradle**

have (got) one foot in the grave → **foot**

roll in his, her, etc. grave = turn in his, her, etc. grave → **turn**

(as) silent as the grave → **silent**

turn in his, her, etc. grave → **turn**

gravy

the 'gravy train (*informal, especially AmE*)
(of a particular job or situation) an easy way of getting a lot of money and other benefits: *Banking and financial services produce very high earnings, and a lot of people are trying to get onto the gravy train.*

gray (*especially AmE*) = **grey**

grease

grease sb's 'palm (*old-fashioned, informal*)
give sb money in order to persuade them to do sth dishonest: *Luckily, Mick was able to grease a few palms, thus helping his brother to escape.*

elbow grease → **elbow**

grease the wheels = oil the wheels → **oil**

greased

like greased 'lightning (*informal*)
very fast: *After the phone call, he was out of the door like greased lightning.*

great

be a 'great one for (doing) sth
do sth a lot; enjoy sth: *I've never been a great one for writing letters.* ◇ *You're a great one for quizzes, aren't you?*

be no great 'shakes (*informal*)
be not very good, efficient, suitable, etc: *He's no great shakes as a teacher.* ◇ *'What did you think of the film?' 'It was no great shakes.'*

go great 'guns (*informal*)
(usually in the progressive tenses) do sth quickly and successfully: *She's halfway through the race, and is going great guns.* ◇ *He's going great guns on his new book at the moment.*

be a great/firm believer in sth → **believer**

dirty great/big → **dirty**

a good/great many → **many**

great/tall oaks from little acorns grow → **oaks**

greater

be greater/more than the sum of its parts → **sum**

Greek

it's all 'Greek to me (*informal, saying*)
it is too difficult for me to understand: *This contract is written in such complicated language that it's all Greek to me.*

green

give sb/get the ˌgreen 'light (*informal*)
allow sb/be allowed to begin sth: *The council has given the green light for work to begin on the new shopping centre.* ◇ *As soon as we get the green light, we'll start advertising for new staff.*

❶ ORIGIN
This expression refers to the green light on traffic lights, which means 'go'.

ˌgreen about the 'gills (*informal*)
looking or feeling as if you are going to be sick, especially at sea; seasick: *You look a bit green about the gills. Go up on deck and get some fresh air.*

ˌgreen 'fingers (*BrE*) (*AmE* a ˌgreen 'thumb)
if you have **green fingers**, you are good at making plants grow: *I do envy you your green fingers. Your garden always looks so beautiful.*

ˌgreen with 'envy
very jealous (= wanting sth that sb else has): *He was green with envy when he saw their expensive new car.*

greener

the grass is (always) greener on the other side (of the fence) → **grass**

green-eyed

the ˌgreen-eyed 'monster (*humorous*)
a feeling of anger or unhappiness because sb you like or love is showing interest in sb else; jealousy: *In next week's programme we'll be looking at the green-eyed monster, jealousy.*

❶ ORIGIN
This comes from Shakespeare's play *Othello*.

greetings

(the) season's greetings → **season**

grey (*especially BrE*) (*AmE* usually **gray**)

a 'grey area
an area of a subject or situation that is not clear or does not fit into a particular group and is therefore difficult to define or deal with: *The question of police evidence in cases like this is a grey area. We will need to consult our lawyers about it.*

'grey matter (*informal*)
intelligence or mental powers: *Mark hasn't got much grey matter, but he tries hard.*

(men in) grey 'suits
people working in politics, law, etc. who have power but are not known to the public: *It will be the men in grey suits who decide whether the Prime Minister stays or goes.*

grief

come to 'grief (*informal*)
be destroyed or ruined; have an accident and hurt yourself: *All our plans have come to grief.* ◇ *I was riding my bike very fast round that corner when I hit a stone and came to grief over there.*

give sb 'grief (about/over sth) (*informal*)
be annoyed with sb and criticize their behaviour: *Stop giving me grief and let me finish this!*

good 'grief! (*informal*)
used for expressing surprise or disbelief: *Good grief! You're not going out dressed like that, are you?*

grim

hang on/hold on (to sth) like grim 'death
hold sb/sth very tightly, usually because you are afraid or determined not to let go: *As the horse galloped off, you could see poor Sarah hanging on like grim death.* ◇ *The robbers tried to steal my bag, but I held on to it like grim death.*

grin

grin and 'bear it (*informal*)
(only used as an infinitive and in orders) accept sth unpleasant without complaining: *If the holiday is a disaster, you'll just have to grin and bear it.*

grin like a Cheshire 'cat
smile widely in a foolish or self-satisfied way: *She sat there grinning like a Cheshire cat while we tried to put the tent up.*

❶ ORIGIN
The Cheshire Cat is a character in Lewis Carroll's story, *Alice in Wonderland.*

beam/grin/smile from ear to ear → **ear**

grind

grind to a 'halt/'standstill; come to a grinding 'halt
stop slowly: *All work on the building has ground to a halt because of a shortage of materials.* ◇ *Every Friday night traffic comes to a grinding halt in Hammersmith.*

❶ ORIGIN
This idiom refers to the way a very large machine slowly stops working.

have (got) an axe to grind → **axe**

grindstone

keep your nose to the grindstone → **nose**

grip

get/take a 'grip/'hold on yourself (*informal*)
make an effort to control your feelings, especially in a difficult situation: *I know you're nervous, but you must get a grip on yourself. You're due to go on stage in five minutes.* ◇ *Look, Ben, get a grip, will you? If we panic now, we'll be finished.*

in the 'grip of sth
experiencing sth unpleasant that cannot be stopped: *The whole country is in the grip of a serious recession.*

lose your grip (on sth) → **lose**

grips

come/get to 'grips with sb/sth
begin to understand or to deal properly with a person, problem, subject, etc: *The government has yet to get to grips with the problem of homelessness.* ◇ *I'm trying to come to grips with Russian grammar.*

grist

grist for/to sb's 'mill
(of an experience, a piece of information, etc.) useful to sb: *As a novelist, I feel that any experience, good or bad, is grist to my mill.*

❷ NOTE
Grist is corn that is ground to make flour in a mill.

grit

grit your 'teeth
be determined to continue to do sth in a difficult or an unpleasant situation: *When I was a boy, I was forced to have a cold shower every morning. I hated it but I just had to grit my teeth and do it.* ◇ *She shouted at me but I just gritted my teeth and said nothing.*

groan

groan under the weight of sth (*written*)
used to say that there is a lot or too much of sth: *The dining table was groaning under the weight of all the food.*

groove

be (stuck) in a 'groove (*BrE*)
be unable to change sth that you have been doing the same way for a long time and that has become boring: *While other businesses are attracting new customers, this one seems to be stuck in a groove, and has been losing money for the last two years.*

ground

be, come, get, etc. in on the ground 'floor (*informal*)
become involved at the beginning of a plan, company, organization, etc. and possibly profit from this later: *Reg came in on the ground floor and saw the value of his investment double in two years.*

drive/run/work yourself into the 'ground
work so hard that you become extremely tired: *You need to be careful, or you'll run yourself into the ground before long.* ◇ *With only two or three hours' sleep a night, he was driving himself into the ground.*

get (sth) off the 'ground
(of a plan, project, etc.) get sth started successfully/start successfully: *By this time next year the new company should be just getting off the ground.* ◇ *We're looking for a new manager to help get this project off the ground.*

give/lose 'ground (to sb/sth)
allow sb/sth to obtain more power, influence, etc. than yourself: *The government has lost ground to the opposition, according to the opinion polls.*

hold/stand your 'ground
face a situation and refuse to run away: *In spite of the enemy's fierce attack, we stood our ground and eventually they had to retreat.* ◇ *After arguing about future policy for three hours, he was still standing his ground.*

on the 'ground
among ordinary people or people closely involved in sth: *On the ground, there are hopes that the fighting will soon stop.* ◇ *There's a lot of support for the policy on the ground.*

thick/thin on the 'ground (BrE)
if people or things are **thick/thin on the ground**, there are a lot/not many of them in a place: *Customers are thin on the ground at this time of year.* ◇ *Good science teachers are thin on the ground.*

be on firm ground → **firm**
be riveted to the spot/ground → **riveted**
break fresh/new ground → **break**
cut the ground from under sb/sb's feet → **cut**
dangerous ground → **dangerous**
fall on stony ground → **fall**
gain ground → **gain**
go to earth/ground → **earth**
a happy hunting ground → **happy**
have/keep both/your feet on the ground → **feet**
hit the ground running → **hit**
keep/have an/your ear (close) to the ground → **ear**
on neutral ground/territory → **neutral**
prepare the ground (for sth) → **prepare**
run sb/sth into the ground → **run**
run sb/sth to earth/ground → **run**
shift your ground → **shift**
suit sb (right) down to the ground → **suit**
take, claim, seize, etc. the moral high ground → **moral**

grow

grow like 'Topsy
grow very fast: *After many contributions, our website has grown like Topsy, and is now being completely revised.* ◇ *The number of gardening and cooking magazines has grown like Topsy in recent years.*

> **ⓘ ORIGIN**
> Topsy was a female character in Harriet Beecher Stowe's novel *Uncle Tom's Cabin*.

absence makes the heart grow fonder → **absence**
great/tall oaks from little acorns grow → **oaks**
money doesn't grow on trees → **money**
not let the grass grow under your feet → **let**

growing

growing pains
the problems, difficulties, etc. which happen in the early stages of sth: *The troubles that are affecting the company are more than just growing pains.*

guard

be on/off your 'guard
be prepared/not be prepared for sth, for example an attack, a danger, a surprise, etc. to happen: *We must all be on our guard against bomb attacks.* ◇ *He hit me while I was off my guard.*

> **❷ NOTE**
> Your *guard* is a position you take when you want to defend yourself, especially in a sport such as boxing or fencing.

mount/stand/keep 'guard (over sb/sth)
act as a guard: *Two soldiers stood guard over the captured weapons.*

catch sb off (their) guard → **catch**
the old guard → **old**

guess

'anybody's/'anyone's guess (informal)
nobody knows: *Who will win the next game is anybody's guess.*

at a 'guess
as a rough estimate: *At a guess, I would say there were about thirty people in the room.*

,guess 'what (informal)
used to introduce sth surprising or exciting that you want to tell sb: *Guess what, Angela's getting married next month!*

your ,guess is as good as 'mine (informal)
neither of us knows the answer: *'If the government knows how to run the country, why aren't things getting any better?' 'Your guess is as good as mine!'*

an educated guess → **educated**

guessing

keep sb 'guessing (informal)
not tell sb about your plans or what is going to happen next: *It's the kind of book that keeps you guessing right to the end.*

(there are) no prizes for guessing what … , who … , etc. → **prizes**

guest

be my 'guest (*informal*)
used to give sb permission to do sth that they have asked to do: *'May I look at this book?' 'Be my guest.'*

guilt

a 'guilt trip (*informal*)
things you say to sb in order to make them feel guilty about sth: *Don't lay a guilt trip on your child about schoolwork.*

guinea

a 'guinea pig
a person used in medical or other experiments: *Students in fifty schools are to act as guinea pigs for these new teaching methods.*

> ❷ NOTE
> A *guinea pig* is a small animal with short ears and no tail, often kept as a pet or used for laboratory research.

gulf

bridge the gulf (between A and B) → **bridge**

gullet

stick in your throat/craw/gullet → **stick**

gum

,by 'gum! (*old-fashioned, BrE, informal*)
used as an expression of surprise: *By gum! You've grown. You'll be as tall as your father soon.*

gum up the 'works (*informal*)
make progress or an activity impossible: *The building was going well, but the delay in delivering more bricks has really gummed up the works.*

> ❷ NOTE
> The *works* are the moving parts of an engine.

up a 'gum tree (*BrE, informal*)
in a very difficult or awkward situation: *I've got bills to pay and the bank is refusing to lend me any more money. I'm really up a gum tree.*

> ❶ ORIGIN
> This idiom refers to the animal opossum which hides up a eucalyptus (= *gum*) tree when it is being hunted.

gun

have (got) a 'gun to your head (*informal*)
be forced to do sth that you do not want to do: *'Why did he go back to his wife?' 'Because he had a gun to his head. She said she would never let him see the children again.'*

hold/put a 'gun to sb's head
force sb to do sth that they do not want to do by making threats: *He had to sack a hundred workers last week. He didn't want to, but the bank was holding a gun to his head.*

jump the gun → **jump**
a/the son of a gun → **son**

guns

go great guns → **great**
spike sb's guns → **spike**
stick to your guns → **stick**

gut

bust a gut (doing sth/to do sth) → **bust**

guts

have (got) the 'guts (to do sth) (*informal*)
have the courage (to do sth): *She didn't have the guts to tell him she was going to move out.* ◇ *He'll never agree to sail across the Atlantic with you. He hasn't got the guts.*

have sb's ,guts for 'garters (*BrE, informal*)
be very angry with sb and punish them severely for sth they have done: *She'd have my guts for garters if she knew I'd lent you her car.*

slog/sweat/work your 'guts out (*informal*)
work very hard: *I've slogged my guts out digging this ditch, and I'm completely exhausted.* ◇ *You sweat your guts out all your life and what do you get when you retire? Next to nothing.*

blood and guts → **blood**
hate sb's guts → **hate**
(a) misery guts → **misery**
spill your guts (to sb) → **spill**

gutter

the ,gutter 'press (*disapproving*)
popular newspapers which print a lot of shocking stories about people's private lives rather than serious news: *Somebody must control the gutter press in this country.*

Guy

Mr Nice Guy → **Mr**

guy

a tough guy → **tough**
a wise guy → **wise**

gyp

give sb 'gyp (*BrE, informal*)
cause sb a lot of pain: *My back's been giving me gyp again lately.*

H h

habit

make a 'habit/'practice of sth
do sth regularly: *I don't usually make a practice of staying up so late, but there was a film on TV I wanted to watch.*

a creature of habit → **creature**
force of habit → **force**

hackles

your, his, etc. 'hackles rise
become angry: *Ben felt his hackles rise as the speaker continued.*

make sb's 'hackles rise; raise 'hackles
make sb angry: *He really makes my hackles rise, that man. He's so rude to everybody.* ◇ *Her remarks certainly raised hackles.*

> ❷ NOTE
> A dog's *hackles* are the hairs on the back of its neck. These hairs often rise when the dog is angry or irritated.

hair

a bad 'hair day (*spoken, humorous*)
a day when everything seems to go wrong: *Today is definitely a bad hair day—you know, one of those days when nothing gets done no matter how hard you try.* ◇ *What's wrong—are you having a bad hair day?*

> ❷ NOTE
> This expression refers to the fact that if you think your hair looks bad, then you feel that you look unattractive and nothing in the day will go right for you.

get in sb's 'hair
annoy sb by preventing them from doing sth: *I can do the housework much more quickly when the children aren't getting in my hair all the time.*

the hair of the 'dog (that bit you) (*informal*)
an alcoholic drink taken in the morning in order to help cure the unpleasant effects of drinking too much alcohol the night before: *'Why are you drinking whisky at 8 o'clock in the morning?' 'Hair of the dog. I've got the most terrible hangover.'*

> ❶ ORIGIN
> In the past, if a person was bitten by a dog, burnt hair from the same dog was used as a protection against infection.

a ˌhair's 'breadth
a very small distance or amount: *He escaped death by a hair's breadth. If the other car had been going any faster, he would certainly have been killed.* ◇ *She was within a hair's breadth of winning.*

your 'hair stands on end (*informal*)
you feel very frightened, nervous or angry: *This is a film which will make your hair stand on end.* ◇ *When I first read the report my hair stood on end.*

keep your 'hair on (also **keep your 'shirt on**, *less frequent*) (*BrE, informal*)
used for telling sb who is angry or very excited about sth to keep calm: *Keep your hair on, Mum. You can hardly see the damage.* ◇ *Keep your shirt on! We've got plenty of time to get to the airport.*

make sb's 'hair curl (*informal, humorous*)
shock or disturb sb: *The film contains some sex scenes that are enough to make your hair curl.*

not a 'hair out of place
looking very smart, well-dressed, etc.: *How does she manage to look so good at the end of a long journey? There's never a hair out of place.*

not harm/touch a hair of sb's 'head
not hurt sb physically in any way at all: *If he harms a hair of my daughter's head, I'll kill him.*

hang by a hair/a thread → **hang**
let your hair down → **let**
not see hide nor hair of sb/sth → **see**
not turn a hair → **turn**
tear your hair (out) → **tear**

hairs

put 'hairs on your chest (*informal, humorous*)
(especially of alcoholic drinks) make you feel strong, etc.: *This Polish vodka will put hairs on your chest.*

get/have sb by the short hairs → **short**
split hairs → **split**

hale

hale and 'hearty
(especially of old people) strong and healthy: *She was still hale and hearty in her nineties.*

half

and a 'half (*informal*)
bigger, better, more important, etc. than usual: *That was a meal and a half. I haven't eaten so well for months.*

your better/other 'half (*informal, humorous*)
your wife or husband: *I'll have to ask my better half about that.*

give sb half a 'chance (to do sth) (*informal*)
give sb even a small opportunity (to do sth): *Given half a chance, I'd go and work in the USA, but it's so difficult to get a visa.* ◇ *If you give him half a chance, he'll show how well he can do the job.*

half the 'battle
(complete, achieve, etc.) the most difficult part of sth: *If you manage to keep calm when you're taking your driving test, that's half the battle.*

half the 'fun, 'trouble, etc. of sth (*informal*)
much or a great deal of the enjoyment, etc. of sth: *Half the pleasure of coming home is finding out what's been happening while you were away.* ◇ *'The team should play better with a new manager.' 'That's half the trouble—everybody expects too much of him.'*

half a loaf is better than none/no bread (*saying*)
you should be grateful for sth, even if it is not as good, much, etc. as you really wanted; something is better than nothing: *They're only going to agree to some of this, but half a loaf is better than none, I suppose.*

half a 'minute, 'tick, 'second, etc. (*informal*)
(wait) a very short time: *I'll be with you in half a moment! I've just got to put my coat on.* ◇ *Just give me half a tick, will you? I've left the keys upstairs.*

the 'half of it
only some of the facts of a particular situation, not all of them: *The public knows that he's had an affair with his secretary, but that's only the half of it.* ◇ *'I hear you've been having trouble with the new managers.' 'You don't know the half of it, Ray. It's been an absolute nightmare.'*

'half the time (*informal*)
most of the time: *Do tell me whether you are coming home for lunch or not. I don't know where you are half the time.*

how the other half 'lives
the life of people in circumstances very different from your own, especially those much richer or poorer: *You should go and see the homeless in our big cities, then you'd know how the other half lives.* ◇ *Look at these photos of houses in Hollywood! How the other half lives, eh?*

in 'half the time
in a much shorter time than expected: *I don't think much of his work. I could have done the same job in half the time, and much better too.*

no half 'measures (*BrE*)
used for emphasizing that you want sth done as well, fully, etc. as possible: *He entertained the visitors very well indeed. There were no half measures: the best food, the best wine, the best silver …*

ˌnot 'half (*BrE, informal*)
used to emphasize a statement or an opinion: *It wasn't half good* (= it was very good). ◇ *'Is it hot outside?' 'Not half. It's much too hot for me.'*

not half as good, nice, etc. as sb/sth
not nearly as good, nice, etc. as sb/sth: *She's not half as nice as her sister.* ◇ *His new book isn't half as interesting as his last one.*

not half 'bad (*informal*)
(used to show surprise) not bad at all; good: *The food really isn't half bad, is it?*

too clever, quick, etc. by 'half (*BrE, informal, disapproving*)
much too clever, quick, etc: *That boy is too charming by half—he can get you to do anything he wants.* ◇ *I don't like her at all—she's too clever by half.*

go half and half = go halves (with sb) → **halves**
have (got) one eye/half an eye on sth → **eye**
it's six of one and half a dozen of the other → **six**
listen with half an ear → **listen**

half-cock

go off at ˌhalf-'cock (*informal*)
start without enough preparation, so that the effect or result is not satisfactory: *Let's not go off at half-cock. We must get enough people together before we start the meeting.*

half-hour

on the hour/half-hour → **hour**

halfway

a ˌhalfway 'house
1 a place where prisoners, mental patients, etc. can stay for a short time after leaving a prison or hospital, before they start to live on their own again: *We're opening several halfway houses for people who've been in this hospital.*
2 a compromise between two plans, wishes, etc: *We really wanted to build a completely new hospital, but we didn't have the money, so this extension is a kind of halfway house.*

meet sb halfway → **meet**

hallmarks

have (got) all the 'hallmarks of sb/sth
have all the characteristics or typical features of sb/sth: *The burglary had all the hallmarks of a professional job.*

> ❷ NOTE
> *Hallmarks* are marks put on gold and silver objects that show the quality of the metal and give information about when and where they were made.

halt

call a halt (to sth) → **call**
come to a grinding halt = grind to a halt/standstill → **grind**
stop/halt sb in their tracks → **tracks**
stop/halt/freeze in your tracks → **tracks**

halved

a trouble shared is a trouble halved → **trouble**

halves

do nothing/not do anything by 'halves
do whatever you do completely and thoroughly: *She does nothing by halves. When she decided to write a book, it was 1 000 pages long.*

go 'halves (with sb); go ,half and 'half (with sb) (*informal*)

share the total cost of sth equally with sb else: *If you drive me up to Edinburgh, we'll go halves on the petrol.*

ham

,ham it 'up (*informal*)

(especially of actors) when people **ham it up**, they deliberately exaggerate their emotions or movements: *When we realised we were being filmed, we all started behaving differently, hamming it up for the cameras.*

hammer

be/go at sb/sth ,hammer and 'tongs (*informal*)

do sth, especially argue or fight, with a lot of energy and noise: *The boss went at me hammer and tongs. I've never seen him so angry.* ◇ *The couple in the flat upstairs are always at it hammer and tongs.*

ⓘ ORIGIN
This idiom refers to the loud noise made by a blacksmith at work when he is making horseshoes. He uses a pair of *tongs* to hold the hot iron and a *hammer* to beat the iron into the shape of the shoe.

come/go under the 'hammer

be offered for sale at an auction (= a sale at which things are sold to the person who offers the most money): *The house and all its contents are to come under the hammer next Thursday.*

❷ NOTE
The person in charge of an auction hits the table with a *hammer* to show that he/she has accepted the highest offer.

drive/hammer sth home (to sb) → home

hammering

give sb/get a 'hammering (*BrE, informal*)

beat sb/be beaten severely or easily; punish sb/be punished hard: *Real Madrid gave the other team a hammering.* ◇ *When I was young, I once stole some money from my mother. I got a real hammering when she found out.*

hand

ask for/win sb's hand (*old-fashioned*)

ask for/get permission to marry sb: *'Did John ask your father for your hand?' 'No. Nobody does that any more, do they?'*

(close/near) at 'hand

near in distance or time: *Some people think that the end of the world is at hand.* ◇ *It's a very convenient place to live. We've got everything close at hand—shops, schools, and a library.*

bind/tie sb hand and 'foot

remove or restrict sb's freedom of action or movement: *Staying at home to look after a sick parent often means that a person is tied hand and foot.* ◇ *I can do nothing to help you because I'm bound hand and foot by my present contract.*

by 'hand

1 (of a letter, etc.) if a letter is delivered **by hand**, it is delivered by the person who wrote it, or by messenger rather than by post: *There's a postal strike on at the moment, so we'll have to deliver these invitations by hand.*
2 made/done without using machinery: *Several local farmers still milk their cows by hand.* ◇ *These wine glasses were made by hand.*

get out of 'hand

become difficult or impossible to control: *How can we stop price increases getting out of hand?* ◇ *The student teacher saw that the class was getting completely out of hand, so he asked for help.*

give sb a 'hand (with sth)

help sb (to do sth): *I can't lift this piano on my own. Can you give me a hand, Carlos?* ◇ *Let me give you a hand with these suitcases.*

go hand in 'hand (with sth)

be closely connected (with sth): *Poverty tends to go hand in hand with disease, and raising people's incomes usually helps to improve their health.* ◇ *A bad economic situation and rising crime usually go hand in hand.*

,hand in 'glove (with sb)

very closely associated with sb, usually in sth dishonest: *The terrorists are working hand in glove with the drug traffickers.* ◇ *They are hand in glove with the secret police.*

,hand in 'hand

(of people) holding each other's hand, usually as a sign of affection: *The lovers walked along the river bank, hand in hand.*

hand sth to sb on a plate; hand sb sth on a plate (*informal*)

give sth to sb without the person concerned having to make any effort to get it: *She was handed the job on a plate. Somebody just telephoned her one afternoon and asked her if she'd like to work for the BBC.* ◇ *A contract's not just going to be handed to you on a plate, you know. You have to earn it.*

have/take a hand in (doing) sth

be involved in (doing) sth, especially sth bad, wrong, etc: *We think all three of you had a hand in planning the robbery. So, come on, confess.* ◇ *I'm sure he had a hand in creating this problem.*

have (got) to 'hand it to sb (*informal*)

admit, perhaps unwillingly, that you admire sb for their skill, achievements, determination, etc: *You have to hand it to him; he certainly knows how to play tennis.* ◇ *To be honest, I didn't think she could cook, but I have to hand it to her. Tonight's meal was fantastic.*

in 'hand
1 (of a task, matter, etc.) now being dealt with, thought about, discussed, etc: *Let's stop talking about other subjects and get back to the matter in hand.*
2 still to be used, played, spent, etc.; remaining: *The two teams have an equal number of points, but Liverpool still have a game in hand.* ◇ *The club still has money in hand for the improvements.*

keep your 'hand in
practise a skill occasionally, so that you do not lose it: *The director likes to teach a class occasionally, just to keep her hand in.*

lift/raise a 'hand against sb
threaten to hit sb: *She never raised a hand against her daughter because she didn't believe in hitting children.*

not do a hand's 'turn (*old-fashioned*)
do no work: *She hasn't done a hand's turn all week.*

on either/every 'hand (*literary*)
on both/all sides; in every direction: *We were surrounded on every hand by dancing couples.*

on 'hand
near and available; present: *We have a doctor on hand in case of emergency.*

on (the) 'one hand ... on the 'other (hand) ...
used to show two different aspects of the same situation: *On the one hand, it's very cheap living here. On the other, it costs a lot to get home!*

out of 'hand
immediately and without thinking about sth fully or listening to other people's arguments: *They rejected my suggestion out of hand.*

put your ˌhand in(to) your 'pocket (*BrE*)
spend or give money: *One of our colleagues is retiring, so I expect they'll want us to put our hands into our pockets for a present.* ◇ *He's one of the meanest men I know. He never puts his hand in his pocket for anything.*

(at) second, third, etc. 'hand
by being told about sth by sb else who has seen it or heard about it, not by experiencing, seeing, etc. it yourself: *I'm fed up of hearing about these decisions third hand!*

show/reveal your 'hand (*BrE*) (*AmE* tip your 'hand)
do sth which reveals your intentions, plans, etc: *The problem is that we can't say anything to the management without showing our hand, and we wanted to be able to take them by surprise.* ◇ *In court a good lawyer never reveals his hand too soon.*

ˌtake sb/sth in 'hand
begin to control or look after sb/sth, especially in order to make improvements in their behaviour, their performance, etc: *That child is very badly behaved; someone should take her in hand.* ◇ *The new manager hopes to take the organization in hand, because in recent months it has been in chaos.*

(ready) to 'hand
(have sth) with or near you; easy to reach or get: *I don't seem to have my diary to hand at the moment—can I ring you back and make an appointment?* ◇ *Surgeons need their instruments ready to hand during an operation.*

with your ˌhand on your 'heart; ˌhand on 'heart
speaking very honestly and telling the truth: *I can tell you, hand on heart, that I never took any money out of your purse.* ◇ *How can you stand there with your hand on your heart and tell me that?*

with one hand tied behind your 'back (*informal*)
1 unable to use your full powers: *The government has one hand tied behind its back in these negotiations.*
2 very easily; with little effort: *She could run the restaurant with one hand tied behind her back.*

be able to count sb/sth on (the fingers of) one hand → **count**
be a dab hand at (doing) sth → **dab**
a bird in the hand is worth two in the bush → **bird**
bite the hand that feeds you → **bite**
cash in hand → **cash**
the dead hand of sth → **dead**
a firm hand → **firm**
(at) first hand → **first**
force sb's hand → **force**
get, have, etc. a free hand → **free**
get, have, gain, etc. the upper hand (over sb) → **upper**
get, have, hold, etc. the whip hand (over sb) → **whip**
give sb a big hand → **big**
go hat in hand = go cap in hand → **cap**
have (got) sb eating out of your hand → **eating**
have (got) your fingers/hand in the till → **till**
have (got) sb in the palm of your hand → **palm**
heavy hand → **heavy**
a helping hand → **helping**
hold sb's hand → **hold**
an iron fist/hand in a velvet glove → **iron**
know sth like the back of your hand → **know**
the left hand doesn't know what the right hand's doing → **left**
lend (sb) a hand (with sth) → **lend**
live (from) hand to mouth → **live**
make, etc. sth by/with your own fair hand → **fair**
make/lose money hand over fist → **money**
an old hand at (doing) sth → **old**
overplay your hand → **overplay**
rule (sb/sth) with a rod of iron/with an iron hand → **rule**
shake sb by the hand → **shake**
sleight of hand → **sleight**
stay your hand → **stay**

strengthen your hand → **strengthen**
throw your hand in → **throw**
try your hand (at sth/doing sth) → **try**
turn your hand to sth → **turn**
wait on sb hand and foot → **wait**

handbasket

go to hell in a handbasket = go to the dogs → **dogs**

handle

get/have a handle on sb/sth (*informal*)
become/be familiar with and so understand sb/
sth: *I can't really get a handle on the situation here.
What's happening?*

fly off the handle → **fly**
too hot to handle → **hot**

hands

all ,hands on 'deck (also **all ,hands to the
'pump**) (*saying, humorous*)
everyone helps or must help, especially in an
emergency: *There are 30 people coming to dinner
tonight, so it's all hands on deck.* ◇ *When the kitchen staff became ill, it was all hands to the pump
and even the manager did some cooking.*

> ❷ **NOTE**
> On a ship, a *hand* is a sailor.

at the hands of sb; at sb's hands (*written*)
if you experience sth **at the hands of sb**, they are
the cause of it: *So far hundreds of innocent civil-
ians have died at the hands of the terrorists.*

be good with your 'hands
be skilful at making or doing things with your
hands: *I'm not surprised he's become an artist—he
always was good with his hands.*

get your 'hands dirty
do physical work: *He's not frightened of getting his
hands dirty.*

get/lay your 'hands on sb
(used mostly in threats) catch sb who has done sth
wrong: *Just wait until I get my hands on the person
who stole my bike!*

get/lay your hands on 'sth
obtain sth that you want or need very much: *Do
you know where I can get my hands on a Russian
dictionary? I need to check a translation.* ◇ *I'd buy
a new car if only I could lay my hands on the money.*

get/keep/take your) ,hands 'off (sb/sth)
(*spoken*)
used to tell sb not to touch sb/sth: *Those cakes are
for tea, so hands off!* ◇ *Keep your hands off my
tools, please.*

hands 'up! (*spoken*)
1 used to tell a group of people to raise one hand
in the air if they know the answer to a question,
etc: *Hands up all those who want to go swimming.*
2 used by sb who is threatening people with a gun
to tell them to raise both hands in the air

have (got) your 'hands full
be very busy: *I've got my hands full looking after
four children.* ◇ *You look as if you've got your
hands full today. Would you like me to help you?*

in the hands of 'sb; in sb's 'hands
in the control of sb or sb's responsibility: *I'll leave
the matter entirely in your hands.* ◇ *The future of
the industry now lies in the hands of the government.*

in safe/good 'hands
being taken care of by a responsible person or
organization, and unlikely to be harmed or damaged: *When the child is with my mother, I know she's
in good hands.* ◇ *It's a good hospital. I'm sure he's
in safe hands.*

many hands make light 'work (*saying*)
a task is done easily if a lot of people share the
work

off sb's 'hands
no longer the responsibility of sb: *Now that the
children are off my hands, I've got more time for
other things.*

on sb's 'hands
1 (of work, etc.) to do: *I've got a lot of work on my
hands at the moment.*
2 for which/whom sb is responsible: *I've got the
neighbour's children on my hands this afternoon.*

on your ,hands and 'knees
with your knees, toes and hands on the ground:
*The tunnel was so low in places that we had to crawl
along on our hands and knees.* ◇ *She was down on
her hands and knees looking for her earring.*

,out of sb's 'hands
no longer in the control of or the responsibility of
sb: *I'm afraid the matter is now out of my hands.
You'll have to write to the Area Manager.*

take sth/sb off sb's 'hands
take sth away from sb who no longer wants it or
take a responsibility from sb who needs a rest: *I
wish somebody would take this old table off my
hands. I haven't got room for it.* ◇ *Look, you and
Tony relax at the weekend, and I'll take the children
off your hands for a couple of days.*

win (sth)/beat sb ,hands 'down
win (sth)/beat sb very easily: *Holland won the
match hands down. The score was five nil.*

change hands → **change**
the devil makes work for idle hands → **devil**
fall into sb's hands/the hands of sb → **fall**
your hands are clean = have (got) clean hands → **clean**
have (got) (sb's) blood on your hands → **blood**
have (got) clean hands → **clean**
have (got) time on your hands → **time**
I've only got one pair of hands → **pair**
join hands (with sb) → **join**
a pair of hands → **pair**
play (right) into sb's hands → **play**
(like) putty in sb's hands → **putty**
shake hands (with sb) → **shake**

a show of hands → show
take your courage in both hands → courage
take the law into your own hands → law
take your life in your hands → life
take matters into your own hands → matters
throw up your arms/hands in despair, horror, etc. → throw
tie sb's hands → tie
wash your hands of sb/sth → wash
with your bare hands → bare
wring your hands → wring

handshake

a golden handshake → golden

handwriting

the handwriting (is) on the wall = the writing (is) on the wall
→ writing

handy

,come in 'handy/'useful (*informal*)
be useful when needed: *The money my aunt gave me will come in handy to pay for my music lessons.*

hang

can go hang (*old-fashioned, informal*)
used for saying that you do not care about sb/sth or about what happens to sb/sth: *I don't care what the critics say about my film. As far as I'm concerned, they can all just go hang.*

get the 'hang of sth (*informal*)
learn or begin to understand how to do, use, etc. sth: *I haven't got the hang of how to use the coffee-making machine yet.* ◇ *It took him a long time to get the hang of all the irregular verbs.*

'hang sth (*BrE, spoken*)
used to say that you are not going to worry about sth: *Oh, let's get two boxes and hang the expense!*

hang by a 'hair/a 'thread
be in a very uncertain situation: *After the operation, his life hung by a thread for several hours.* ◇ *The future of this company hangs by a thread. Unless we get two or three big orders by the end of the month, we're finished.*

hang 'fire
delay or be delayed: *We'll have to hang fire on that decision, I'm afraid.*

ⓘ ORIGIN
This phrase refers to a gun which does not fire immediately.

hang your head (in/for shame)
look or feel embarrassed or ashamed: *When I think of how I behaved, I have to hang my head in shame.* ◇ *The thief hung his head as he was led away through the crowd.*

hang (on) 'in there (*informal*)
used for encouraging sb to continue trying to

achieve sth: *'I'll never find a job.' 'Look, just hang on in there. I'm sure you'll get something soon.'*

hang a 'left/'right (*AmE*)
take a left/right turn

hang on sb's 'words/every 'word
listen to what sb says with great attention: *The professor was talking to a group of students, who hung on her every word.*

hang over sb's 'head; hang 'over sb
(of a possible problem, etc.) worry sb: *With the threat of job losses hanging over their heads, the staff are all very worried.* ◇ *She can't enjoy herself with all these financial problems hanging over her.*

hang 'tough (*AmE*)
be determined and refuse to change your attitude or ideas: *Employees are being urged to hang tough and continue negotiations with management.*

hang up your 'boots
stop playing football, etc. because you are too old or ill to continue: *At the age of 38 he decided it was time to hang up his boots.*

hang/lie heavy (on sb/sth) → heavy
hang/stay loose → loose
hang on/hold on (to sth) like grim death → grim
let it all hang out → let
a peg to hang sth on → peg
a peg on which to hang sth → peg

hanged

(you, etc.) may/might as well be hanged/hung for a sheep as (for) a lamb → well

hangs

a cloud hangs over sb/sth → cloud
a question mark hangs over sb/sth → question
time hangs/lies heavy (on your hands) → time

ha'porth

spoil the ship for a ha'porth/ha'penny-worth of tar → spoil

happen

anything can/might 'happen
used to say that it is not possible to know what the result of sth will be: *'There's no way we're going to win this match!' 'How can you be so sure—anything can happen!'*

an accident/a disaster waiting to happen → waiting
accidents will happen → accidents
these things happen → things

happens

as it 'happens
used when you say sth that is surprising, or still connected with what sb else has just said: *I agree with you, as it happens.* ◇ *As it happened, I had a spare set of keys in my bag.*

it (just) so 'happens that …
by chance: *It just so happened they'd been invited to the party too.*

in the event that sth happens → event

happy

(as) happy as the day is 'long/as a 'clam/as 'Larry (*informal*)
very happy: *Grandpa's as happy as a clam helping the children to fly their kites.*

a/the ˌhappy 'event (*humorous*)
the birth of a baby: *'When's the happy event, then?' 'At the end of July.'*

a happy 'hunting ground (*humorous*)
a very good place to find what you want: *The Sunday antique market is a happy hunting ground for collectors.*

a/the happy 'medium
a sensible balance between two extremes: *I like to know my colleagues well, but not too well. The sort of friendship I have with them now is a happy medium.* ◇ *In life generally we should try to find the happy medium. Extreme solutions to problems always lead to difficulties.*

many happy re'turns (of the 'day)
used to wish sb a happy and pleasant birthday: *Here's your present. Many happy returns!*

the happy/golden mean → mean
one big happy family → big

hard

be hard 'at it
be working hard: *She's been hard at it all day.* ◇ *When I left at six, he was still hard at it.*

be/feel hard 'done by (*informal*)
be/feel unfairly treated: *I think you've been hard done by—you worked twice as long as anyone else.*

be 'hard on sb
1 treat, criticize or punish sb too severely: *Don't be too hard on little Emma. She didn't intend to break the cup.*
2 be unfair to sb; be unfortunate for sb: *It's hard on the people who have to work on Christmas Day.*

be hard 'up (*informal*)
have very little money: *In those days we were so hard up that meat was a real luxury.*

be hard 'up for sth
have too few or too little of sth: *We're hard up for ideas at the moment.*

do/learn sth the 'hard way
learn sth from experience, especially when this is unpleasant: *I learned the hard way not to trust door-to-door salesmen.* ◇ *Why do you always do everything the hard way?*

hard and 'fast
(of rules, etc.) that cannot be changed: *These regulations are not hard and fast. They can be changed by general consent.* ◇ *There are no hard and fast rules about this.*

(as) hard as 'nails
(of a person) not sensitive or sympathetic: *She doesn't care what happens to anybody. She's as hard as nails.*

hard 'cash
real money, not shares, cheques, etc: *How much is it worth in hard cash?*

hard 'cheese (*BrE, informal*)
used as a way of saying that you are sorry about sth, usually in an ironic way (= you really mean the opposite): *I've made my decision—I'm going to the sell the car, and if he doesn't agree with that then it's hard cheese.*

(the) hard 'core (*BrE*)
the small central group in an organization, or in a particular group of people, who are the most active or who will not change their beliefs or behaviour: *It's only really the hard core that bother(s) to go to meetings regularly.* ▶ **'hard-core** *adj.*
1 having a belief or a way of behaving that will not change: *a hard-core political activist*
2 relating to pornography (= books, videos, etc. that describe or show naked people and sexual acts) of an extreme kind: *hard-core sex magazines*

hard 'facts
the real or true facts of a situation, etc: *I'm not interested in your opinion. I want hard facts.* ◇ *This is a newspaper which deals in hard facts, not rumours.*

ˌhard 'going
difficult to understand or needing a lot of effort: *I'm finding his latest novel very hard going.*

ˌhard 'luck/'lines (*BrE*)
used to tell sb that you feel sorry for them: *'Failed again, I'm afraid.' 'Oh, hard luck.'*

hard of 'hearing
unable to hear well: *He's become rather hard of hearing.* ◇ *The television programme has subtitles for the hard of hearing.*

hard 'put (to it) to do sth; hard 'pressed/ 'pushed to do sth
able to do sth only with great difficulty: *I'd be hard put to name all the countries in the world.*

the 'hard stuff (*informal*)
strong alcoholic drinks like whisky, brandy, etc: *a drop of the hard stuff*

make hard 'work of sth
make sth more difficult or complicated than it should be: *I don't know why he's making such hard work of his maths homework. It's really quite easy.*

no hard 'feelings
used for saying that you would still like to be friendly with sb you have just beaten in a fight, competition, argument, etc: *When he heard that he had won the contract, he turned to his competitor and said, 'No hard feelings, I hope.'*

take sth 'hard
be very upset by sth: *He took his wife's death very hard.*

too much like hard 'work
so difficult, tiring, etc. that you do not want to do it: *This job is a bit too much like hard work for me. I'm going to look for something easier.*

(caught/stuck) between a rock and a hard place ➔ **rock**
die hard ➔ **die**
drive a hard bargain ➔ **drive**
fall on hard times ➔ **fall**
a hard/tough act to follow ➔ **act**
a hard/tough nut (to crack) ➔ **nut**
hard/hot on sb's heels ➔ **heels**
hit sb/sth hard ➔ **hit**
play hard to get ➔ **play**

harden

ˌharden your 'heart against sb/sth
no longer be emotionally affected by sb/sth because you feel angry, bitter, etc., towards them/ it: *Doctors have to harden their hearts against the suffering they see every day.*

hard-luck

a ˌhard-'luck story
a story about yourself that you tell sb in order to get their sympathy or help: *He stopped me in the street and told me a long hard-luck story about his wife leaving him. All he really wanted was some money.* ◇ *Don't give me any of your hard-luck stories, John. I don't believe them.*

hardly

I, he, etc. can hardly wait = I, he, etc. can't wait ➔ **wait**

hare

(as) mad as a March hare ➔ **mad**
run with the hare and hunt with the hounds ➔ **run**

harm

ˌno 'harm done (*spoken*)
used to tell sb not to worry because they have caused no serious damage or injury: *Forget it, Dave, no harm done.*

not come to (any) 'harm; come to no 'harm
not be injured, badly treated or damaged, etc: *The child will come to no harm if she stays there.*

out of harm's 'way
in a place where sb/sth cannot cause or suffer injury, accident, loss, etc: *Most people think that dangerous criminals should be locked up out of harm's way.* ◇ *You should put these glasses out of harm's way. They're too valuable to use every day.*

there's no harm in (sb's) doing sth; it does no harm (for sb) to do sth
used to tell sb that sth is a good idea and will not cause any problems: *He may say no, but there's no harm in asking.* ◇ *It does no harm to ask.*

he, she, etc. wouldn't harm/hurt a fly ➔ **fly**
mean (sb) no harm ➔ **mean**
not harm/touch a hair of sb's head ➔ **hair**
not mean (sb) any harm ➔ **mean**

harness

in 'harness (*BrE*)
doing your normal work, especially after a rest or a holiday: *After so many weeks away, it felt good to be back in harness again.*

in 'harness (with sb) (*BrE*)
working closely with sb in order to achieve sth: *The manager told us to remember that we're a team and that we can achieve much greater results if we're working in harness.*

die in harness ➔ **die**

Harry

every/any Tom, Dick and/or Harry ➔ **Tom**

harvest

reap a/the harvest ➔ **reap**

hash

make a mess/hash of sth/doing sth ➔ **mess**

haste

ˌmore 'haste, ˌless 'speed (*BrE, saying*)
if you try to do sth quickly, you are more likely to make mistakes and so take a longer time than necessary: *I had to send the email twice because I forgot to add the attachment. More haste, less speed.*

marry in haste (, repent at leisure) ➔ **marry**

hat

ˌkeep sth under your 'hat (*informal*)
keep sth secret: *I'm going to apply for another job but keep it under your hat for a while, will you?*

pick, etc. sth out of a hat (*informal*)
choose sb/sth completely by chance: *We couldn't decide where to go on holiday so we just picked a place out of a hat.*

take your 'hat off to sb; hats 'off to sb (both *especially BrE*) (*AmE* usually **tip your 'hat to sb**) (*informal*)
used for expressing admiration for what sb has done: *I take my hat off to the doctors and nurses of the hospital. They were magnificent.* ◇ *Hats off to you. That's the best fish soup I've ever tasted.*

at the drop of a hat ➔ **drop**
go hat in hand = go cap in hand ➔ **cap**
I'll eat my hat! ➔ **eat**
knock sb/sth into a cocked hat ➔ **knock**
old hat ➔ **old**
pass round the hat = pass the hat round/around ➔ **pass**
pull sth/a rabbit out of the hat ➔ **pull**
talk through your hat ➔ **talk**
throw your hat into the ring ➔ **throw**

hatch

down the 'hatch (*informal*)
said before you drink alcohol: *He raised his glass, said 'Down the hatch', and then drank it all at once!*

hatches

batten down the hatches ➔ **batten**

hatchet

a 'hatchet job (on sb/sth) (*informal*)
strong criticism that is unfair or intended to harm sb/sth: *The press did a very effective hatchet job on her last movie.*

bury the hatchet ➔ **bury**

hate

hate sb's 'guts (*informal*)
dislike sb very much: *Don't invite that man to the party. I hate his guts.*

your, his, etc. pet hate ➔ **pet**

hath

hell hath no fury (like a woman scorned) ➔ **hell**

hats

hats off to sb = take your hat off to sb ➔ **hat**

hatter

(as) mad as a hatter ➔ **mad**

haul

haul sb over the 'coals (*BrE*) (*AmE* rake sb over the 'coals) (*informal*)
criticize sb very strongly for sth they have done: *I was hauled over the coals for being late.*

a long haul ➔ **long**

have

Most idioms containing the verb **have** are at the entries for the nouns or adjectives in the idioms, for example **have (got) an eye for sth** is at **eye**.

and what 'have you (*spoken*)
other things, people, etc. of the same kind: *He does all sorts of things—building, gardening, fencing and what have you.* ◇ *If you add up the cost of petrol, insurance, repairs and what have you, running a car certainly isn't cheap.*

have 'had it (*informal*)
1 be in a very bad condition; be unable to be repaired: *This television's had it; we'll have to get a new one.* ◇ *The car had had it.*
2 be extremely tired: *I've had it! I'm going to bed.*
3 have lost all chance of surviving sth: *When the truck smashed into me, I thought I'd had it.*
4 be going to experience sth unpleasant: *Dad saw you scratch the car—you've had it now!*
5 (also **have had it up to here (with sb/sth)**) be

unable to accept a situation any longer: *I've had it with him—he's let me down once too often.* ◇ *I've had it up to here with these tax forms.*

'have it (that ...)
say that ... ; claim that ...: *Rumour has it that you're going to retire. Is that true?* ◇ *She will have it that her brother is a better athlete than you, but I don't believe her.*

have (got) it 'in you (to do sth)
have the unexpected ability, determination, courage, etc. to do sth: *She managed to finish the crossword all on her own! I didn't know she had it in her!* ◇ *He stood up and gave a brilliant speech to 1 000 people. I didn't know he had it in him.*

have (got) it 'in for sb (*informal*)
want to harm or cause trouble for sb because you have had a bad experience with them: *She's had it in for those boys ever since they damaged her roses.* ◇ *The government has had it in for the trade unions for years.*

have it 'off/a'way with sb (*BrE, slang*)
have sex with sb

have it 'out with sb
have a serious discussion with sb in order to end a disagreement, quarrel, etc: *You must stop ignoring Fred because of what he said, and have it out with him once and for all.*

(not) have a lot, anything, etc. on
be busy/not busy: *I'm sorry I can't come with you, but I've got a lot on at the moment.* ◇ *I haven't got much on next week, so I might be able to spend some time with the kids.*

have-nots

the haves and the have-nots ➔ **haves**

haves

the haves and the have-nots
the rich people and the poor people: *You can see the haves and the have-nots in this city—the millionaires in their huge houses and the homeless sleeping on the streets.*

having

he, she, etc. isn't having any (of it) (*informal*)
he, she, etc. is not willing to listen to or believe sth: *I suggested sharing the cost, but he wasn't having any of it.* ◇ *I tried to persuade her to wait but she wasn't having any.*

havoc

play/wreak 'havoc with sth
cause damage, destruction or disorder to sth: *The terrible storms wreaked havoc with electricity supplies, because so many power lines were down.*

haw

hum/hem and haw = um and aah (about sth) ➔ **um**

hawk

have (got) eyes like a hawk → eyes
watch sb/sth like a hawk → watch

hay

make hay while the 'sun shines (*saying*)
make the best use of opportunities and favourable conditions while they last: *Opportunities for starting your own business will never be better, so make hay while the sun shines and go and see your bank manager today.*

hit the sack/hay → hit

haystack

like looking for/trying to find a needle in a haystack → needle

haywire

go 'haywire (*informal*)
go out of control; start functioning or behaving in a very strange way: *My printer's gone haywire. It keeps stopping and starting.*

head

above/over sb's 'head
too difficult for sb to understand: *It was clear from the expression on his face that the lecture went completely over his head.*

be banging, etc. your head against a brick 'wall (*informal*)
try for a long time to achieve sth, persuade sb to do sth, etc. without success: *I realized they weren't even listening to my protests. I was just banging my head against a brick wall.*

bite/snap sb's 'head off (*informal*)
speak to sb angrily without good reason: *He was only making a suggestion—there's no need to snap his head off!*

The teacher must be having a bad day. I only asked her a question and she bit my head off!

bring sth/come to a 'head
(cause sth to) reach a point when you are forced to deal with sth quickly because it suddenly becomes very bad: *Matters came to a head yesterday when an emergency meeting was called to demand the directors' resignation.* ◇ *Her recent public remarks about company policy have finally brought matters to a head.*

bury/hide your ˌhead in the 'sand
refuse to deal with unpleasant realities, possible dangers, etc. by pretending they do not exist: *Stop burying your head in the sand, Tim. Don't pretend that everything's all right.*

ℹ️ ORIGIN
This phrase refers to the common belief that the ostrich buries its head in the sand when it is in danger.

can't make head (n)or 'tail of sth (*informal*)
not be able to understand sth at all: *I can't make head or tail of this picture—is it upside down?*

do sb's 'head in (*BrE, informal*)
make sb feel confused, upset and/or annoyed: *Shut up! You're doing my head in.*

do sth/go ˌover sb's 'head
do sth without telling the people who have a right to know: *He gets angry when you go over his head and talk to his boss.*

from ˌhead to 'foot/'toe
all over your body; completely: *She was dressed from head to foot in white.* ◇ *He was covered from head to foot in mud.*

get your 'head down (*informal*)
1 work or study hard: *If you want to pass that French exam, you'll have to get your head down.*
2 go to bed and sleep: *It's time to get our heads down; we have to be up early tomorrow morning.*

get your 'head round sth (*BrE, informal*)
understand sth difficult, often with a lot of effort: *The plan is so complicated—I'm still trying to get my head round it.*

get sth into your/sb's (thick) 'head (*informal*)
succeed in understanding or in making sb understand sth fully: *When are you going to get it into your thick head that you don't need to worry about money? You're rich now.* ◇ *I'm still trying to get it into my head that I'm free to do what I want now.*

get/take it into your 'head that ... (*informal*)
understand or believe sth, often wrongly: *Somehow she's taken it into her head that her husband is trying to poison her.*

give sb their 'head
give sb the freedom to do what they want: *We must give the new art teacher her head, so that she has the freedom to do things differently.*

ℹ️ ORIGIN
This idiom refers to allowing a horse to go as fast as it likes when you are riding it.

go to your 'head
1 (of alcohol) make you feel a bit drunk: *I can't drink more than two pints of beer—it goes straight to my head.*
2 (of success, fame, praise, etc.) make you feel too proud of yourself in a way that other people find

annoying: *Just because you've become a film actor, don't let it go to your head!*

have (got) a good 'head on your shoulders
be a sensible person: *Don't worry about the children—Laura's with them and she's got a good head on her shoulders.*

have (got) a (good) head for 'figures
be good at doing sums, etc: *If you want to be successful in business, you must have a good head for figures.*

have (got) a (good) head for 'heights
be able to stand on a high place without feeling ill or afraid: *I won't go up the church tower with you. I've no head for heights.*

have (got) your head in the 'clouds *(informal)*
not be realistic because you are always thinking of your own hopes, ideas, dreams, etc: *He wants us to start a business together but it would never work. He's got his head in the clouds half the time.*

have (got) your 'head screwed on (the right way) *(informal)*
be sensible: *You can certainly trust Ann with your money. She's got her head screwed on the right way.*

a/per 'head
for each person: *The meal shouldn't cost more than $20 a head.*

head and 'shoulders above sb/sth
very much better, greater, etc. than sb/sth: *He's head and shoulders above the other candidates.*

,head 'first
1 moving forwards or downwards with your head in front of the rest of your body: *He fell head first down the stairs.*
2 without thinking carefully about sth before acting: *She got divorced and rushed head first into another marriage.*

(the) head 'honcho *(informal, especially AmE)*
the person who is in charge; the boss: *Claude is the studio's head honcho, so talk to him if you have a problem.*

❶ ORIGIN
This phrase comes from the Japanese word *hanchō*, meaning 'group leader'.

head over 'heels (in 'love)
completely in love: *He's head over heels in love with his new girlfriend.*

a ,head 'start (on/over sb)
an advantage that sb already has before they start doing sth: *Being able to speak French gave her a head start over the other candidates.*

in over your 'head
involved in sth that is too difficult for you to deal with: *After a week in the new job, I soon realized that I was in over my head.*

keep your 'head
think clearly and remain calm: *If there is a robbery, you should try to keep your head and do as you are told.*

keep your 'head above water
succeed in staying out of debt; manage to deal with tasks, responsibilities, etc: *The company had great difficulty keeping its head above water during the economic crisis.* ◇ *I don't know how she manages to keep her head above water. She has so much to do.*

keep your 'head down *(informal)*
1 avoid being noticed or being seen in public: *She's so unpopular with the voters that the Prime Minister has told her to keep her head down until after the election.* ◇ *In the army you soon learn to keep your head down and stay out of trouble.*
2 work very hard: *He kept his head down for weeks before the entrance exam.*

need, want, etc. your 'head examined *(informal)*
used for saying that sb is behaving in a crazy or stupid way: *She spent £300 on a pair of shoes? She needs her head examined.*

on sb's (own) head 'be it
(often used for warning sb) somebody is alone responsible for the results of their action or decision: *You refuse to go to your own daughter's wedding? On your head be it!* ◇ *On his own head be it if he decides to leave university early.*

out of/off your 'head *(BrE, informal)*
1 crazy: *Are you off your head?*
2 not knowing what you are saying or doing because of the effects of alcohol or drugs: *Don't even try to have a proper conversation with him—he's off his head.*

put your ,head in the lion's 'mouth
deliberately put yourself in a dangerous or risky situation: *So I put my head in the lion's mouth and asked my boss for a pay rise.*

put sth out of your 'head
stop thinking about or wanting sth: *I am not going to let you go to the party, so you can put that idea out of your head.*

rear/raise its (ugly) 'head
(used of sth considered unpleasant) appear again after being hidden or forgotten: *Political corruption has reared its ugly head again.* ◇ *Famine has raised its head again in many parts of the world.*

scream, shout, etc. your 'head off *(informal)*
scream, shout, etc. a lot and very loudly: *She screamed her head off when I jumped out at her.*

stand/turn sth on its 'head
1 turn sth upside down
2 make people think about sth in a completely different way: *He stood the argument on its head, saying that the plan wouldn't save money and would, in fact, cost more.*

take it into your head to do sth
suddenly decide to do sth: *She's taken it into her head to give all her books away.*

be/go soft in the head → **soft**
do sth standing on your head → **standing**
enter sb's head → **enter**

your eyes nearly pop out of your head → **eyes**

hang your head (in/for shame) → **hang**

hang over sb's head → **hang**

have/keep a clear head → **clear**

have (got) eyes in the back of your head → **eyes**

have (got) a gun to your head → **gun**

have a rush of blood to the head → **rush**

head/top the bill → **bill**

hit the nail on the head → **hit**

hold/put a gun to sb's head → **gun**

hold your head up (high) → **hold**

I'll knock your block/head off! → **knock**

keep a level head → **level**

knock sth on the head → **knock**

laugh your head off → **laugh**

let your heart rule your head → **let**

like a bear with a sore head → **bear**

lose your head → **lose**

need/want sth like (you need/want) a hole in the head → **hole**

not harm/touch a hair of sb's head → **hair**

off the top of your head → **top**

(have) an old head on young shoulders → **old**

a price on sb's head → **price**

put/lay your head/neck on the block → **block**

put ideas in(to) sb's head → **ideas**

ring in your ears/head → **ring**

a roof over your head → **roof**

scratch your head (over sth) → **scratch**

shake your head → **shake**

smash sb's face/head in → **smash**

talk your head off → **talk**

talk through the back of your head → **talk**

a thick head → **thick**

turn sb's head → **turn**

use your head → **use**

wet the baby's head → **wet**

win, lose, etc. by a short head → **short**

headless

run around like a headless chicken → **run**

headlines

grab/hit/make the 'headlines (*informal*)
be an important item of news in newspapers or on the radio or television: *His reputation has suffered a lot since the scandal over his love affair hit the headlines.*

heads

bang/knock your/their 'heads together (*informal*)
force people to stop arguing and behave in a sensible way: *I'd like to bang those stupid politicians' heads together.*

heads or 'tails? (*spoken*)
used to ask sb which side of a coin they think will be facing upwards after it has been thrown in the air in order to decide sth by chance: *'Let's toss for it. Heads or tails?' 'Heads.' 'Heads it is. You win.'*

heads will 'roll (for sth) (*spoken, usually humorous*)
used to say that some people will be punished because of sth that has happened: *Have you seen this article about police corruption? Heads will roll, I'm sure.* ◇ *When the spy scandal was exposed, many said that heads should roll in the government.*

put your, their, etc. 'heads together (*informal*)
think about or discuss sth as a group: *If we all put our heads together, we might find a way to solve the problem.*

two heads are better than one → **two**

head-to-head

(go) head-to-'head (with sb)
(deal with sb) in a very direct and determined way, especially in a competition between two people, organizations, etc: *They are set to meet head-to-head in next week's final.*

headway

make 'headway
make progress, especially when this is slow or difficult: *We are making little headway with the negotiations.* ◇ *The boat was unable to make much headway against the tide.*

health

a clean bill of health → **clean**

drink sb's health → **drink**

heap

collapse, fall, etc. in(to) a 'heap
fall down heavily and not move: *He collapsed in a heap on the floor.*

at the bottom/top of the pile/heap → **bottom**

heap/pour scorn on sb/sth → **scorn**

on the scrap heap → **scrap**

heaps

heaps 'better, 'more, 'older, etc. (*BrE, informal*)
a lot better, etc: *Help yourself—there's heaps more.* ◇ *He looks heaps better than when I last saw him.*

hear

can't hear yourself think (*informal*)
there is so much noise around you that you cannot think clearly: *Can you turn the volume down? I can't hear myself think in here.*

hear, 'hear!
called out, usually at a public meeting, etc. to express agreement and approval: *'It is the wish of this government that both unemployment and inflation be reduced to acceptable levels.' 'Hear, hear!'*

hear/see the 'end/the 'last of sb/sth
(often used with not, never, etc.) hear/see sb/sth for the last time: *We'll never hear the end of her visit to Buckingham Palace.* ◇ *He says he's not*

going to come back to England, but I'm sure we haven't seen the last of him.

hear 'tell (of sth) (*old-fashioned* or *formal*)
hear people talking about sth: *I've often heard tell of such things.*

not 'hear of sth
not allow sth to happen: *'May I pay for the phone call?' 'Don't be silly! I wouldn't hear of it!'* ◇ *He won't hear of his daughter becoming a police officer. He thinks it's much too dangerous.*

(do) you 'hear me? (*spoken*)
used to tell sb in an angry way to pay attention and obey you: *You can't go—do you hear me?*

not say/hear a dicky bird → **dicky**
see/hear things → **things**

heard

you could have heard a 'pin drop
it was extremely quiet: *As the Minister told Parliament of the crisis you could have heard a pin drop.*

the last I heard → **last**
make your voice heard → **voice**

hearing

in/within (sb's) 'hearing
near enough to sb so that they can hear what is said: *She shouldn't have said such things in your hearing.*

a fair hearing → **fair**
hard of hearing → **hard**

heart

at 'heart
used to say what sb is really like even though they may seem to be different: *He seems strict but he's a very kind man at heart.*

be close/dear/near to sb's 'heart
be a person or thing that sb is very fond of, concerned about, interested in, etc: *The campaign to keep our local hospital open is something that is very close to my heart.*

(off) by 'heart
(learn sth) so that you can remember it perfectly: *There was a time when I knew the whole poem off by heart.*

do sb's heart 'good
make sb feel happy, more cheerful, hopeful, etc: *It did my heart good to see him looking so well.*

(come) (straight) from the 'heart
(be) genuine and sincere: *The letter comes straight from the heart. He means every word of it.*

have a 'heart (*spoken*)
used for asking sb to be sympathetic or kind: *'We'll work until midnight.' 'Have a heart, Joe. Can't we stop earlier than that?'*

have (got) a heart of 'gold
have a very kind and helpful nature, even though

it is not always obvious: *I know he's often bad-tempered but really, you know, he's got a heart of gold.*

have (got) a heart of 'stone
be a person who does not show others sympathy or pity: *Don't ask her to give any money to the fund—she's got a heart of stone.*

(your) heart and 'soul
(with) a lot of energy and enthusiasm: *She puts her heart and soul into the job.* ◇ *A dancer must throw herself heart and soul into every performance.*

your heart 'bleeds for sb (*ironic*)
used to say that you do not feel sympathy or pity for sb: *'I have to get up at 6 o'clock tomorrow!' 'Oh, my heart bleeds for you—I have to do that every single day!'*

your heart goes 'out to sb
you feel great pity or sympathy for sb: *My heart goes out to all those who lost relatives in the disaster.*

your heart is in your 'mouth (*informal*)
you feel very anxious or afraid: *My heart was in my mouth as I waited to hear whether the jury would find me guilty or not guilty.*

your, his, etc. heart is in the right 'place
used to say that sb's intentions are kind and sincere even though they sometimes do the wrong thing: *I know she gets angry sometimes, but basically her heart is in the right place.*

your/sb's 'heart is not in it
sb does not give all their enthusiasm, interest and energy to sth: *He agreed to write the book for a large sum of money, but his heart wasn't in it, and it was never finished.*

your heart 'leaps
used to say that you have a sudden feeling of happiness or excitement: *Her heart leapt when she heard a knock on the door, thinking it might be him.*

your ˌheart misses a 'beat
used to say that you have a sudden feeling of fear, excitement, etc: *For a moment she thought she saw the dead man's face looking in through the window and her heart missed a beat.*

the 'heart of the matter
the most central and important part of a situation, problem, etc: *And now we come to the heart of the matter. Who is going to pay for all this?*

your heart 'sinks
used to say that you suddenly feel sad or depressed about sth: *My heart sank when I realized I would have to walk home in the rain.*

in good 'heart (*BrE*)
happy and cheerful: *Despite their bad living conditions and lack of money, the families were still in good heart.*

in your ˌheart of 'hearts
in your deepest feelings or thoughts: *I know in my heart of hearts that you're right, but I still find it difficult to accept.*

a man, woman, etc. after your own 'heart
a person you particularly like because they have
the same interests, opinions, etc. as you: *You love
football too? Then you're a man after my own heart!*

not have the 'heart (to do sth)
not be able or willing to do sth which could hurt sb
else: *I didn't have the heart to take the money from
him—it was all he had.*

rip/tear the 'heart out of sth
destroy the most important part or aspect of sth:
*Protestors say that closing the factory will tear the
heart out of the local economy.*

take 'heart (from sth)
feel more positive about sth, especially when you
thought that you had no chance of achieving sth:
*The government can take heart from the results of
the latest opinion polls.*

take sth to 'heart
1 be very upset or offended by sb's criticism: *Her
review of your book is stupid. Don't take it so much
to heart.*
2 pay great attention (to sb's suggestions, etc.):
*I'm pleased to see that they have taken my sugges-
tions to heart and followed my advice.*

to your heart's con'tent
as much or as long as you want: *On holiday I'll be
able to read to my heart's content.*

with all your 'heart/your whole 'heart
used for emphasizing how strongly you feel about
sth: *She hoped with all her heart that she would
never have to see him again.* ◇ *I love you with all
my heart.*

with a ,heavy/,sinking 'heart
with a feeling of sadness or fear: *It was with a
heavy heart that he left the school for the last time.*

absence makes the heart grow fonder → **absence**
be engraved/etched on/in your heart/memory/mind →
  engraved
be/feel sick at heart → **sick**
be, stay, etc. young at heart → **young**
(God) bless your, his, etc. heart/soul → **bless**
break sb's heart → **break**
a change of heart → **change**
cross my heart (and hope to die) → **cross**
eat your heart out (for sb/sth) → **eat**
(not) find it in your heart to do sth → **find**
from the bottom of your heart → **bottom**
hand on heart → **hand**
harden your heart against sb/sth → **harden**
have (got) your heart/mind set on sth/doing sth → **set**
have (got) sb's (best) interests at heart → **interests**
home is where the heart is → **home**
let your heart rule your head → **let**
lose heart → **lose**
lose your heart (to sb/sth) → **lose**
open your heart (to sb) → **open**
out of the goodness of your heart → **goodness**
pour your heart out (to sb) → **pour**
search your heart/soul/conscience → **search**

set your heart/mind on sth/doing sth → **set**
sob your heart out → **sob**
steal sb's heart → **steal**
strike fear, terror, etc. into sb/sb's heart → **strike**
the way to sb's heart → **way**
wear your heart on your sleeve → **wear**
win sb's heart → **win**
with your hand on your heart → **hand**
with a light heart → **light**

hearts
in your heart of hearts → **heart**

heartstrings
tug at sb's heartstrings → **tug**

hearty
hale and hearty → **hale**

heat
in the ,heat of the 'moment
while in a state of strong emotion or excitement: *I
must apologize for the rude things I said yesterday
in the heat of the moment.*

take the 'heat out of sth
make a situation less tense, emotional, dangerous,
etc: *The police tried to take the heat out of the situation by withdrawing for a while.*

if you can't stand the heat (get out of the kitchen) → **stand**
turn on the heat → **turn**

heave-ho
give sb the (old) heave-'ho (*informal*)
dismiss sb from their job; end a relationship with
sb: *'Are Julie and Mike still together?' 'Oh no, she
gave him the old heave-ho a couple of months ago.'*

heaven
a heaven on 'earth
a place or situation where everything is perfect:
The island is a real heaven on earth.

a ,marriage/,match made in 'heaven
a combination of two people or things which
seems perfect: *When she married Dave, everyone
thought that theirs was a match made in heaven.* ◇
*A merger between the two leading mobile phone net-
works would appear to be a marriage made in
heaven, but will consumers lose out?*

be in (your) seventh heaven → **seventh**
God/Heaven forbid (that …) → **forbid**
God/Heaven help sb → **help**
God in heaven → **God**
God/goodness/Heaven knows → **knows**
in God's/Heaven's name → **name**
in the name of God/Heaven → **name**
manna from heaven → **manna**
move heaven and earth (to do sth) → **move**
smell/stink to high heaven → **high**
to God/goodness/Heaven → **God**

heavens

(Good) 'Heavens!; Heavens a'bove! (*spoken*)
used to show that you are surprised or annoyed:
Good Heavens! What have you done to your hair?

the heavens 'open
it suddenly begins to rain very heavily: *We were
walking back from the bus stop when suddenly the
heavens opened.*

heavy

get 'heavy (*informal*)
become very serious, because strong feelings are
involved: *They started shouting at me and it soon
got very heavy.*

hang/lie 'heavy (on sb/sth)
1 (of a feeling or sth in the air) be very noticeable
in a particular place in a way that is unpleasant:
Smoke lay heavy on the far side of the water. ◇ *Despair hangs heavy on the air.*
2 cause sb/sth to feel uncomfortable or anxious:
The crime lay heavy on her conscience.

heavy 'going
boring, tiring, difficult, etc: *I do find her novels
very heavy going.* ◇ *The last part of the journey
was rather heavy going because of the muddy
paths.*

> ❷ NOTE
> The *going* is the condition of the ground, espe-
> cially in horse racing.

heavy 'hand
a way of doing sth or of treating people that is
much stronger and less sensitive than it needs to
be: *the heavy hand of management* ▶ **heavy-
'handed** *adj.: a heavy-handed approach / manner*

the 'heavy mob/brigade (*BrE, informal*)
a group of strong, often violent people employed to
do sth such as protect sb: *I had to laugh when he
turned up at the meeting with his heavy mob, as if
he was a mafia boss or something.*

a heavy 'silence/'atmosphere
a situation when people do not say anything, but
feel embarrassed or uncomfortable: *There was a
heavy silence for a few minutes before anybody
finally spoke.*

make heavy 'weather of (doing) sth
make sth seem more difficult than it really is:
*You're making very heavy weather of repairing
that bike. What's the problem?*

time hangs/lies heavy (on your hands) ➔ time
with a heavy/sinking heart ➔ heart

heck

for the 'heck of it (*informal*)
just for pleasure rather than for a reason: *'Why are
you doing that?' 'Just for the heck of it.'*

what the 'heck! (*informal*)
used to say that you are going to do sth that you

know you should not do: *It means I'll be late for
work but what the heck!*

hedge

hedge your 'bets (*informal*)
try to reduce the risk of losing your money, being
wrong about sth, etc. by choosing two or more
courses of action at the same time: *She's invested
her money in two quite different businesses, so she's
hedging her bets.*

> ❶ ORIGIN
> This idiom refers to putting money on more
> than one horse in a race to increase your
> chances of winning money.

heebie-jeebies

give sb the willies/heebie-jeebies/creeps ➔ willies

heed

**give/pay 'heed (to sb/sth); take 'heed (of sb/
sth)** (*formal*)
pay careful attention to sb/sth: *They gave little
heed to the rumours.* ◇ *I paid no heed at the time but
later I had cause to remember what he'd said.*

heel

bring sb to 'heel/come to 'heel
(make sb) obey the rules: *He'll soon come to heel if I
start to get nasty with him.* ◇ *Tell him you'll leave
him if he does it again. That'll bring him to heel,
I'm sure.*

> ❷ NOTE
> If you tell a dog to *come to heel*, you make it come
> close to you.

down at 'heel
(of sb's appearance) looking poor: *Since he lost his
job, he has begun to look rather down at heel.*

> ❶ ORIGIN
> This idiom refers to the worn heels of old shoes.

turn/ spin on your 'heel
suddenly turn around and leave, often because
you are angry or annoyed: *Quite unexpectedly he
turned on his heel and walked out of the door.*

under the 'heel of sb (*literary*)
completely in sb's control; dominated by sb: *For
years, the country was under the heel of a dictator.*

an/sb's Achilles' heel ➔ Achilles

heels

at/on sb's 'heels
following closely behind sb: *Every day she walks
past my house, with her little black dog at her heels.*

hard/hot on sb's 'heels
following sb closely because you want to catch
them: *Jane has the most points at the moment, but
the other competitors are hot on her heels.* ◇ *The
police are hard on his heels.*

take to your 'heels
run away very quickly: *The burglars took to their heels when they heard the police arrive.*

cool your heels → **cool**
dig your heels in → **dig**
drag your feet/heels → **drag**
head over heels (in love) → **head**
kick your heels → **kick**
kick up your heels → **kick**
show (sb) a clean pair of heels → **show**
tread on sb's heels → **tread**

height

draw yourself up/rise to your full height → **full**

heights

have (got) a (good) head for heights → **head**

hell

all 'hell breaks/is let loose (*informal*)
there is suddenly an angry, noisy reaction to sth; suddenly everything becomes confused, noisy, etc: *When soldiers fired shots into the crowd, all hell broke loose.* ◇ *All hell broke loose when they heard that their pay had been cut.*

beat/knock/kick the 'hell out of sb/sth (*informal*) (also **beat, etc. the 'shit out of sb/sth** ⚠, *slang*)
beat, etc. sb/sth very hard: *If the crowd had managed to get hold of the robber, they would have beaten the hell out of him.* ◇ *The gang knocked the hell out of him for no reason at all.*

(just) for the 'hell of it (*informal*)
just for fun, with no particular reason: *The youths had nothing to do so they went round breaking windows just for the hell of it.*

from 'hell (*informal*)
used to describe a very unpleasant person or thing; the worst that you can imagine: *They are the neighbours from hell.*

get the hell 'out (of ...) (*spoken*)
get out of or leave a place very quickly: *Here come the police. Let's get the hell out of here.* ◇ *Get the hell out of my house and don't come back!*
(Some people find the use of this idiom offensive.)

give sb 'hell (*informal*)
1 make life unpleasant for sb: *Her back is giving her hell at the moment; she's in constant pain.*
2 shout at or speak angrily to sb because they have done sth wrong: *His mother gave him hell for coming home so late.*

go to hell (*spoken, offensive*)
used to tell sb to go away or to stop saying/doing sth because it is annoying: *He wanted to come back but she told him to go to hell.* ◇ *'Why don't you answer my question, Jim?' 'Oh, go to hell, will you? I'm tired of your stupid questions.'*

hell for 'leather (*old-fashioned, BrE, informal*)
with the greatest possible speed, energy, etc: *I saw*

a man going hell for leather down the street, with two policemen running after him.

hell hath no 'fury (like a woman 'scorned) (*BrE*)
used to refer to sb, usually a woman, who has reacted very angrily to sth, especially the fact that her husband or lover has been unfaithful (= has had a sexual relationship with another woman): *He should have known better than to leave her for that young girl. Hell hath no fury like a woman scorned.*

a/one hell of a ... (*spoken, slang*)
sb/sth that is very bad, good, unusual, impressive, etc: *We had a hell of a good time at the night club.* ◇ *I had one hell of a hangover the next morning.*

> ❶ NOTE
> This is sometimes written as 'a/one helluva'.

a hell on 'earth
a place or situation that is extremely bad or unpleasant: *Life for the ordinary soldiers was hell on earth.*

(come) hell or high 'water
whatever the difficulties or opposition may be: *Come hell or high water, we've got to reach the injured men tonight.*

Hell's 'teeth (*old-fashioned, BrE, spoken*)
used to express anger or surprise: *Hell's teeth, look at the time! I'm going to be late for work!*

like 'hell
1 (*informal*) very hard, very much, very fast, etc. in an effort to achieve, etc. sth: *I had to run like hell to catch the bus.*
2 (*spoken*) used to give emphasis when saying no to a suggestion, idea, etc: *'He thinks you're going to lend him your car this weekend.' 'Like hell I am.'* (Some people find this use offensive.)

scare, annoy, etc. the 'hell out of sb (*informal*)
scare, annoy, etc. sb very much: *The sight of a man with a gun scared the hell out of her.* ◇ *Louise suddenly surprised the hell out of us by announcing that she was pregnant!*

to 'hell and back (*informal*)
used to say that sb has been through a difficult situation: *We'd been to hell and back together and we were still good friends.*

to 'hell with sb/sth (*spoken*)
used to express anger or dislike and to say that you no longer care about sb/sth and will take no notice of it/them: *To hell with this stupid car. I'm going to buy a new one.*
(Some people find this use offensive.)

what the 'hell! (*spoken*)
it doesn't matter; I don't care: *'Do you want a cigarette?' 'No, thanks, I've given up. Oh, what the hell! Yes, I will have one, after all.'*
(Some people find this use offensive.)

when 'hell freezes over (*informal*)
if you say something will happen **when hell**

freezes over, you mean that you think it will never happen: *'They might give you a pay rise soon.' 'Yeah, right. When hell freezes over!'*

catch hell → **catch**

go to hell in a handbasket = go to the dogs → **dogs**

hell/the devil to pay → **pay**

like a bat out of hell → **bat**

not have a cat in hell's chance → **cat**

not have a hope in hell → **hope**

not have a snowball's chance in hell (of doing sth) → **snowball**

play (merry) hell with sb/sth → **play**

raise Cain/hell → **raise**

the road to hell is paved with good intentions → **road**

see sb in hell first → **see**

(as) sure as hell → **sure**

hell-bent

be ,hell-'bent on (doing) sth

be absolutely determined to do sth stupid, dangerous, etc: *Have you seen how fast he drives that car? I'd say he was hell-bent on killing himself.*

helm

at the 'helm/'tiller

in control of an organization, etc: *The company began to make profits again with the new managing director at the helm.*

> **❷ NOTE**
> A *helm* or a *tiller* is used for controlling the direction of a ship or a boat.

take (over) the 'helm

take control of an organization, etc. from another person: *When Mr Davies retired, his daughter took the helm.*

help

can't help (doing) sth; can't help but do sth

not be able to avoid or resist doing sth: *A kleptomaniac is a person who can't stop stealing things.* ◇ *'I'm sorry, I can't help it,' she said, bursting into tears.* ◇ *He's a bit of a fool, but you can't help but like him.*

God/Heaven 'help sb (*spoken*)

used to say that you are afraid sb will be in danger or that sth bad will happen to them: *God help us if this doesn't work.*

(Some people find this use offensive.)

not if 'I can help it

used for saying you do not want sth to happen: *'Your daughter told me that she wants to leave school when she's 16.' 'Not if I can help it.'*

so 'help me ('God)

used when making a serious promise, threat, etc: *I'll catch the man who did this to my son, so help me God.* ◇ *I'll kill him, so help me.*

> **❷ NOTE**
> In a court of law a witness swears to 'tell the truth, the whole truth and nothing but the truth, so help me God'.

there's no 'help for it (*especially BrE*)

it is not possible to avoid doing sth that may harm sb in some way: *There's no help for it. We shall have to call the police.*

a fat lot of good/help/use → **fat**

helping

a ,helping 'hand

help: *The new charity tries to offer a helping hand to young people who have become addicted to drugs.* ◇ *A helping hand would be very welcome at the moment.*

hem

hum/hem and haw = um and aah (about sth) → **um**

hen

(as) rare/scarce as hen's teeth (*old-fashioned*)

extremely rare: *Critics always complain that good movies that the whole family can see together are as scarce as hen's teeth.*

hence

six, a few, etc. days, weeks, etc. 'hence (*formal*)

six, etc. days, etc. from now: *The true consequences will only be known several years hence.*

herd

ride herd on sb/sth → **ride**

here

,here and 'now

1 at this moment; immediately: *I'm afraid I can't tell you the answer here and now. I'll try and find out for you later.*

2 the present situation: *Don't worry so much about the future. You need to concentrate more on the here and now.*

,here and 'there

to or in various places: *Here and there in the crowd I saw people I recognized.*

,here 'goes; ,here we 'go

said before you begin to do sth dangerous, exciting, difficult, etc: *Is everybody ready? OK, here goes. Turn on the electricity and let's see what happens.*

,here goes 'nothing (*AmE*)

said before you begin to do something that you do not think will be successful: *'Well, here goes nothing!' she said, getting ready to jump.*

,here, there, and 'everywhere

in, to or from many different places: *The letters came from here, there, and everywhere.* ◇ *We searched here, there, and everywhere, but couldn't find the document they wanted.*

,here we go a'gain

often used for showing you are angry or annoyed that sth is starting to happen again: *Here we go again! They're digging up the road—it's the third* time this year. ◇ *Here we go again—another train cancelled. This is getting ridiculous.*

‚here you 'are; ‚here you 'go (*spoken*)
used when you are giving sth to sb: *Here you are. This is what you were asking for.* ◇ *Here you go. Four copies, is that right?*

here's to 'sb/'sth!
used for wishing sb/sth health, success, happiness, etc., especially when lifting your glass and drinking a toast to sb/sth: *Here's to the happy couple! May they have a long and happy marriage!* ◇ *What a wonderful meal. Here's to the cook!* ◇ *Here's to success!*

neither ‚here nor 'there
not important because it is not connected with the subject being discussed; irrelevant: *The fact that she's the director's daughter is neither here nor there. She's the most suitable person for the job.* ◇ *What might have happened is neither here nor there.*

herring

a red herring → **red**

hesitates

he who 'hesitates (is 'lost) (*saying*)
if you delay in doing sth you may lose a good opportunity: *You should have applied for that job. I'm sure you would have got it. Remember, he who hesitates …*

hey

hey 'presto (*BrE*) (*AmE* **'presto**)
people sometimes say **hey presto** when they have just done sth so quickly and easily that it seems to have been done by magic: *You just press the button and, hey presto, a perfect cup of coffee!*

❶ NOTE
Presto is an Italian word meaning 'quick' or 'quickly'.

what the 'hey! (*AmE*, *spoken*)
it doesn't matter; I don't care: *This is probably a bad idea, but what the hey!*

hide

hide your ‚light under a 'bushel (*BrE*)
not let people know that you are good at sth: *We didn't know you could play the guitar! You've been hiding your light under a bushel all this time!*

❶ ORIGIN
This phrase comes from the Bible.

bury/hide your head in the sand → **head**
cover/hide a multitude of sins → **multitude**
have (got) a hide/skin like a rhinoceros → **rhinoceros**
not see hide nor hair of sb/sth → **see**
save sb's/your (own) neck/skin/hide → **save**

hiding

be on a ‚hiding to 'nothing (*BrE*, *informal*)
have no hope of succeeding, whatever happens: *The Government is on a hiding to nothing in these elections.*

high

be for the 'high jump (*BrE*, *informal*)
be about to be punished, criticized, dismissed, etc: *When your father sees your school report, you'll be for the high jump.*

be/get on your ‚high 'horse
be annoyed because you think that sb has not treated you with enough respect: *When they suggested that she might have made a mistake, she got on her high horse and asked them how they dared question her ability.*

have a 'high old time (*old-fashioned*, *informal*)
enjoy yourself very much: *When I left them they were having a high old time singing and dancing on the tables!*

‚high and 'dry
in a difficult situation without help or money: *When the travel company went bankrupt, many holidaymakers were left high and dry abroad or waiting at the airport.*

❶ ORIGIN
This expression refers to boats left on the beach after the tide has gone out.

‚high and 'low
(search, etc. for sth) in every possible place; everywhere: *I've been hunting high and low for that pen, where did you find it?*

‚high and 'mighty (*informal*)
behaving as though you think you are more important than other people: *He's too high and mighty to mix with ordinary people like us!*

(as) high as a 'kite (*informal*)
in an excited state, especially because of drugs, alcohol, etc: *He was as high as a kite when they came to arrest him.*

‚high days and 'holidays
festivals and special occasions: *This 19th-century dish was traditionally made on high days and holidays, and is still often eaten at Christmas.*

‚high 'jinks (*old-fashioned*, *informal*)
a lot of fun and amusement: *They got up to all sorts of high jinks on the trip.*

the 'high point/spot of sth
the best, most interesting, entertaining, etc. part of sth: *The high spot of our holiday was the visit to Rome.* ◇ *It was the high point of the evening.*

in ‚high 'dudgeon (*old-fashioned*, *written*)
in an angry or offended mood, and showing other people that you are angry: *After being refused entry to the club, he went off in high dudgeon.*

on 'high

1 (*formal*) in a high place: *We gazed down into the valley from on high.*

2 (*humorous*) the people in senior positions in an organization: *An order came down from on high that from now on lunchbreaks were to be half an hour and no longer.*

3 in heaven: *The disaster was seen as a judgement from on high.*

on the ,high 'seas

in international waters; on a part of the sea which does not belong to any country: *What happens if a crime is committed on the high seas?*

smell/stink to high 'heaven (*informal*)

1 have a very strong and unpleasant smell: *When was the last time you cleaned the dog kennel? It stinks to high heaven.*

2 seem to be very dishonest or morally unacceptable: *This whole deal stinks to high heaven. I'm sure somebody was bribed.*

take the 'high road (in sth) (*AmE*)

take the most positive course of action: *He took the high road in his campaign.*

adopt, keep, etc. a high/low profile → **profile**
be in high/low spirits → **spirits**
feel that high = look/feel small → **small**
fly high → **fly**
have (got) friends in high places → **friends**
(come) hell or high water → **hell**
hold your head up (high) → **hold**
it is high/about time (that) … → **time**
of a high order = of the highest/first order → **order**
riding high → **riding**
run high → **run**
set your sights high/low → **set**
take, claim, seize, etc. the moral high ground → **moral**

highest

of the highest/first order → **order**

highly

speak highly of sb → **speak**
think highly of sb/sth → **think**

hightail

'hightail it (*informal, especially AmE*)

leave somewhere very quickly: *As soon as the bell went for the end of lessons, Jack ran out of the school gates and hightailed it for home.*

high-water

high-'water mark

the highest stage of achievement: *This was the high-water mark of the ancient Greek civilization.*

highways

,highways and 'byways

(on/along) all the roads, large and small, of a country, area, etc: *She travelled the highways and byways of Scotland collecting folk songs and local traditions.*

hike

take a 'hike (*AmE, informal*)

a rude way of telling sb to go away: *Take a hike, will you?*

hill

a ,hill of 'beans (*old-fashioned, AmE, informal*)

something that is not worth much: *He's so rich that as far as he's concerned, the money he lost doesn't amount to a hill of beans.*

over the 'hill (*informal*)

no longer young; past your best: *Some people think if you're 30, you're over the hill!*

up ,hill and down 'dale

to or from many places; everywhere: *They cycled up hill and down dale, glad to be away from the city.*

hills

(as) old as the hills → **old**

hilt

(up) to the 'hilt

(support, etc. sb) completely: *I will support you to the hilt on this.*

❶ ORIGIN
This expression refers to the full length of a sword, up to its handle (= the *hilt*).

hind

talk the hind leg(s) off a donkey → **talk**

hindmost

(the) devil take the hindmost → **devil**

hint

take a/the 'hint

understand what sb wants you to do, even though they tell you in an indirect way: *She yawned and said, 'Goodness, it's late.' 'OK,' said Pete, 'I can take a hint. I'll go now.'* ◇ *Sarah hoped he'd take the hint and leave her alone.*

drop a hint (to sb) → **drop**

hip

shoot from the hip → **shoot**

hire

ply for hire/trade/business → **ply**

history

go down in/make 'history

be or do sth so important that it will be recorded in history: *Roger Bannister made history as the first man to run a mile in less than four minutes.* ◇ *This battle will go down in history as one of our most important victories.*

the 'history books
the record of great achievements in history: *She has earned her place in the history books.*

the rest is history → rest

hit

be/make a (big, etc.) 'hit with sb
be liked very much by sb when they first meet you: *You've made quite a hit with my mother. She really likes you.* ◊ *The new teacher is a big hit with all the students as well as the other members of staff.*

hit (it) 'big (*informal*)
be very successful: *The band has hit big in the US.*

hit the 'bottle (*informal*)
regularly drink too much: *She managed to resist alcohol for a year, then hit the bottle again when her husband died.* ◊ *He's really hitting the bottle at the moment.*

hit the 'buffers (*informal*)
if a plan, sb's career, etc. **hits the buffers**, it suddenly stops being successful: *His big ideas for expanding the business hit the buffers yesterday when the board of directors rejected his proposals.*

hit the 'deck (*informal*)
1 fall to the ground suddenly: *When we heard the shooting we hit the deck.* ◊ *The champion landed another heavy punch and the challenger hit the deck for the third time.*
2 (*AmE*) get out of bed: *Come on! It's time to hit the deck.*

hit the ground 'running (*informal*)
start doing sth and continue very quickly and successfully: *What we need for this project is someone who will hit the ground running.*

> **❶ ORIGIN**
> This idiom possibly refers to soldiers who are expected to land from parachutes or from helicopters and get straight into action.

hit sb/sth 'hard
affect sb/sth very badly: *The death of her daughter hit her very hard.*

> **❷ NOTE**
> In the passive, we usually say 'hard hit by' instead of 'hit hard by': *Pensioners have been particularly hard hit by the rise in heating costs.*

hit sb in the 'eye (*informal*)
be very obvious or striking: *The strange combination of colours hits you in the eye as soon as you enter the room.*

'hit it (*spoken*)
used to tell sb to start doing sth, such as playing music: *Hit it, Louis!*

hit it 'off (with sb) (*informal*)
quickly form or have a good relationship with sb: *I*

met a girl at the party, and we hit it off straight away.

hit the 'jackpot
suddenly win, earn, etc. a lot of money; suddenly be very successful: *She's hit the jackpot with her latest book—it's sold millions.*

a 'hit list (*informal*)
a list of people, organizations, etc. against whom some unpleasant action is being planned: *The gang have drawn up a hit list of about 50 politicians.* ◊ *Be careful how you speak to her because I think you're on her hit list.*

hit the nail on the 'head (*informal*)
say sth that is exactly right: *'So you want to move to another department.' 'You've hit the nail on the head. That's exactly what I want.'*

hit the 'road (also hit the 'trail *especially AmE*) (*informal*)
begin a journey: *Well, we'd better hit the road, we've a long way to go.*

hit the 'roof/'ceiling (*informal*)
suddenly become very angry: *Every time I mention Patricia, Sam hits the roof.*

When Dad found out I'd crashed the car, he hit the roof.

hit the 'sack/'hay (*informal*)
go to bed: *I think it's time to hit the sack.*

hit the 'spot (*informal*)
if sth **hits the spot** it does exactly what it should do: *I decided I wasn't really hungry, but the coffee really hit the spot and I drank a whole pot.*

hit the 'streets; hit the 'shops/'stores (*informal*)
become widely available for sale: *The new games console hits the streets tomorrow.*

hit sb when they're 'down
continue to hurt sb when they are already defeated: *You wouldn't hit a man when he's down, would you?*

hit sb where it 'hurts
affect sb where they will feel it most: *After four years of marriage, she really knows how to hit him where it hurts, and isn't afraid to do it either.*

grab/hit/make the headlines → **headlines**
hit a brick wall = be/come up against a brick wall → **brick**
hit/knock sb/sth for six → **six**
hit/strike home → **home**
hit/miss the mark → **mark**
hit/touch a (raw) nerve → **nerve**
hit/strike pay dirt → **pay**
hit/strike the right/wrong note → **note**
hit/reach rock bottom → **rock**
hit (your) stride = get into your stride → **stride**
not know what hit you → **know**
a smash hit → **smash**

hit-and-miss

‚hit-and-'miss (also ‚hit-or-'miss, *less frequent*)
not done in a careful or planned way and therefore not likely to be successful: *The advertisements were rather hit-and-miss and not based on proper market research.* ◇ *They use rather hit-and-miss techniques for selecting new staff.*

hit-and-run

‚hit-and-'run
a road accident in which a driver leaves the place where the accident happened without stopping to give help, leave his name, etc: *a hit-and-run accident/driver*

hitch

hitch your wagon to a star; hitch your wagon to sb/sth
try to succeed by forming a relationship with sb/sth that is already successful: *She quit the group and hitched her wagon to the dance band 'Beats'.* ◇ *We must be careful. We don't want to hitch our wagon to the wrong star.*

thumb/hitch a lift → **lift**

hitched

get 'hitched (*informal*)
get married: *They got hitched last year without telling anybody about it.*

hither

‚hither and 'thither (*especially literary*)
in many different directions: *When you look down at the square, you see all the people hurrying hither and thither.*

hits

(when) the shit hits the fan → **shit**

Hobson

‚Hobson's 'choice
the choice of taking what is offered or nothing at all, in reality no choice at all: *It's Hobson's choice really, as this is the only room they have empty at the moment.*

❶ ORIGIN
This expression refers to a 17th-century Cambridge man, Tobias Hobson, who hired out horses; he would give his customers the 'choice' of the horse nearest the stable door or none at all.

hoc

ad hoc → **ad**

hock

be in 'hock (to sb) (*informal*)
owe money: *I'm in hock for about £5000.*

hog

go the ‚whole 'hog (*informal*)
do sth thoroughly or completely: *They painted the kitchen and then decided to go the whole hog and do the other rooms as well.*

a road hog → **road**

hoist

be hoist/hoisted by/with your own petard → **petard**

hold

cannot hold a candle to sb/sth (*informal*)
is not as good as sb or sth else: *She is a good player, but she can't hold a candle to a champion like Jane.*

❶ ORIGIN
Before electricity, a helper would hold a candle for somebody to do something in the dark. Somebody who cannot even hold the candle for somebody else is no good at all.

catch/get/grab/take (a) 'hold of sb/sth
have or take sb/sth in your hands: *He caught hold of her wrists so she couldn't get away.* ◇ *Quick, grab a hold of that rope.*

get 'hold of sb/sth
obtain sth; reach or contact sb: *Do you know where I can get hold of a telephone directory for Paris?* ◇ *I spent all morning on the phone trying to get hold of the manager.*

hold your 'breath
1 stop breathing for a short time, for example because you are afraid of or very anxious about sth: *I held my breath as the car skidded towards me.*
2 be anxious while you are waiting for sth that you are worried about: *'When will you hear about your university application?' 'Not till next week. I'm holding my breath until then.'*
3 (*informal*) **don't hold your breath** used for telling sb that it's not worth waiting for sth: *We'll let you know if there's any work for you, but don't hold your breath.*

hold 'court (*often ironic*)
be the centre of attention in a group of people who

find what you say interesting and amusing: *There was Professor Johnson, holding court as usual in the students' coffee bar.*

hold sb/sth 'dear (*formal*)

feel that sb/sth is of great value: *He laughed at the ideas they held dear.*

hold 'fast to sth

refuse to stop believing in (a theory, principle, religion, etc.): *She knew that whatever happened in her life, she would hold fast to her religious beliefs.*

hold your 'fire

1 delay or stop shooting for a while: *Hold your fire! I think they're going to surrender.*
2 stop attacking sb: *She told the journalists to hold their fire. If they didn't listen to her, how would they know what she thought?*

hold 'firm (to sth) (*formal*)

believe sth strongly and not change your mind: *She held firm to her principles.*

,hold the 'floor

speak at a public meeting, etc. for a long time, often stopping others from speaking: *The American delegation held the floor for three quarters of an hour, putting forward their proposals.*

hold the 'fort (*BrE*) (*AmE* hold down the 'fort) (*informal*)

be in charge or taking care of sth while the person usually responsible is not there: *I'm going abroad for a few weeks, and Kathy will hold the fort while I'm away.*

hold 'forth (about/on sth) (*disapproving*)

speak for a long time about sth in a way that other people might find boring: *The politician held forth on the importance of living in a society free from social injustice.* ◇ *He's a real bore. He's always holding forth about something or other.*

hold 'good/'true

be or remain true, valid, correct, etc: *This principle holds true in every case.* ◇ *Will your promise hold good even if you don't get the money?*

hold sb's 'hand

give sb help, comfort, support, etc. in a difficult situation: *Industry cannot expect the government to hold its hand every time it has problems.* ◇ *This is Jane's first day in the office, so I've asked Mary to hold her hand a bit.*

hold your 'head up (high)

not feel ashamed, guilty or embarrassed about sth: *After this scandal, he will never be able to hold his head up high again.*

'hold it (*informal*)

wait a moment: *Hold it a second! I just have to make sure the doors are locked.*

hold no 'brief for sb/sth (*formal*)

not be in favour of or not support sb/sth, for example a cause, an idea, etc: *I hold no brief for long prison sentences but this terrible crime really deserves one.*

hold out little, etc. 'hope (of sth/that ...); not hold out any, much, etc. 'hope

offer little, etc. reason for believing that sth will happen: *The doctors did not hold out much hope for her recovery.*

hold your 'own

remain in a strong position when sb is attacking you, competing with you, etc: *There was a lot of competition but she managed to hold her own.* ◇ *'How's your father?' 'He's holding his own, but only just. We'll just have to hope that he'll start getting better soon.'*

,hold your 'peace/'tongue (*old-fashioned*)

say nothing; remain silent although you would like to give your opinion: *We don't want anyone to know what's happened, so you'd better hold your tongue—do you understand?* ◇ *I didn't want to start another argument, so I held my peace.*

hold 'sway (over sb/sth) (*literary*)

(of a person, movement, idea, etc.) have power, control or great influence over sb/sth: *Rebel forces hold sway over much of the island.* ◇ *These ideas held sway for most of the century.*

hold sb to 'ransom

1 hold sb as a prisoner until money has been paid for their release: *The kidnappers held the little girl to ransom for more than eight hours.*
2 try to force sb to do what you want by using threats: *The government said that the workers were holding the country to ransom by demanding a ten per cent pay rise.*

hold 'water (*informal*)

(of a theory, etc.) remain true even when examined closely: *Your argument just doesn't hold water.*

hold your 'horses (*informal*)

used for asking sb to stop for a moment, speak more slowly, etc: *Hold your horses! We haven't finished the last question yet.*

on 'hold

delayed until a later time or date: *We can't find the money, so all our plans are on hold at the moment.* ◇ *We'll have to put the decision on hold until we get more details.*

take (a) 'hold

begin to have complete control over sb/sth; become very strong: *Panic took hold of him and he couldn't move.* ◇ *They managed to get out of the house just before the flames took hold.* ◇ *It is best to treat the disease early before it takes a hold.*

control/hold the purse strings ➜ **purse**
get/take a grip/hold on yourself ➜ **grip**
hang on/hold on (to sth) like grim death ➜ **grim**
hold all the cards = have/hold (all) the aces ➜ **aces**
hold/keep sb/sth at bay ➜ **bay**
hold/stand your ground ➜ **ground**
hold/put a gun to sb's head ➜ **gun**
hold out/offer an olive branch (to sb) ➜ **olive**
keep/hold/play your cards close to your chest ➜ **cards**
keep/hold sb/sth in check ➜ **check**

holding

there's no 'holding/'stopping sb
a person cannot be prevented from doing sth
because of their enthusiasm, energy, determination, etc: *There was no holding him once he started
talking about his life in India.* ◇ *You know
Hannah—once she's decided to do something there's
no stopping her.*

leave sb holding the baby → **leave**

holds

(with) ,no ,holds 'barred
(of fighting, competition, etc.) with no or very few
rules or restrictions: *This started off as a very
clean election campaign, but now it's no holds
barred.* ◇ *a no-holds-barred row over the latest political scandal*

> ❷ NOTE
> In wrestling, *no holds barred* means that there
> are no strict rules about which holds are allowed
> and which are not.

hole

in a 'hole (*informal*)
in a difficult situation: *Somehow he had got himself
into a hole and it was going to be difficult to get out
of it.*

in the 'hole (*AmE, informal*)
in debt; owing money: *We started the current fiscal
year $3 million in the hole.*

**need/want sb/sth like (you need/want) a
hole in the head** (*informal*)
definitely not need/want sb/sth at all: *I had to get
home before midnight, and just then I needed a flat
tyre like a hole in the head.*

dig yourself (into) a hole → **dig**
have an ace in the hole = have (got) an ace/a trick up your
  sleeve → **sleeve**
make a dent/hole in sth → **dent**
money burns a hole in sb's pocket → **money**

holes

pick holes (in sth) → **pick**

holiday

a busman's holiday → **busman**

holidays

high days and holidays → **high**

holies

holy of holies → **holy**

hollow

beat sb/sth hollow → **beat**
ring true/false/hollow → **ring**

holy

,holy of 'holies (*humorous*)
a special place which only certain people can
enter: *This room is the holy of holies. It contains the
most valuable books in the world.* ◇ *The boss
invited me into his holy of holies this morning.
What a fantastic office he's got!*

> ❷ NOTE
> In a Jewish temple, the *holy of holies* is the inner
> part, which only the chief priest can enter.

home

at 'home
1 (feeling) comfortable or relaxed, as if you are in
your own home: *I like the city. I feel at home here.* ◇
*Come in and make yourself at home while I finish
cooking the dinner.*
2 (of a sports event) at your own ground, club, etc:
*We're at home to Oxford United on Saturday, and
the week after we're away to Luton.*
3 (of a subject, topic of conversation, etc.) know
about and feel confident discussing sth: *I'm not
really at home with seventeenth-century literature. I
specialize in the nineteenth century.*

bring home the 'bacon (*informal*)
be successful in sth; be the person who earns
money for a family, organization, etc: *The firm
wants very much to get this contract, and we're
expecting you to bring home the bacon.* ◇ *He's the
one who brings home the bacon, not his wife.*

bring sth 'home to sb
make sb realize how important, difficult or serious sth is: *This documentary brought home the
tragedy of the poor to many people.* ◇ *Visiting that
hospital for the mentally ill really brought home to
me how sad some people's lives are.*

come 'home (to sb)
become fully clear or understood: *The danger of
the situation we were in suddenly came home to me.*

drive/hammer sth 'home (to sb)
make sure that sb understands sth completely, for
example by repeating it often: *The instructor tried
to drive home to us the need for safety precautions
before diving.* ◇ *Police used statistics to hammer
home their warning about car theft.*

hit/strike 'home
1 (of an insult, a remark, criticism, etc.) affect or
hurt sb in the intended way; make sb really understand sth: *His criticism of my work struck home. I
knew he was right.* ◇ *My remarks last week obviously hit home because he has not been late for work
since.*
2 (of a punch, a blow, an arrow, a bullet, etc.) hit
sb/sth where you intended; hit the target: *The
punch hit home and Ferguson fell to the floor.*

home and 'dry (*BrE*) (*AmE* **home 'free**)
in a safe or good position because you have successfully completed or won sth: *When we've won
four out of six games, we'll know that we're home*

and dry. ◇ *All they have to do is sign the contract and then we'll be home free.*

a 'home bird

a person who spends most of the time at home because they are happiest there: *Sheila's a home bird really. She likes to spend her free time around the house or in the garden.*

a ˌhome from 'home (*BrE*) (*AmE* a ˌhome away from 'home)

a place where you feel as comfortable, happy, etc. as in your own home: *They used to stay in their father's flat in Brighton every holiday. It was a real home from home.*

ˌhome is where the 'heart is (*saying*)

a home is where the people you love are: *When I ask him if he's happy travelling around the world all the time, he just says, 'Home is where the heart is. If my wife and children are with me, then I'm happy.'*

home sweet 'home (*often ironic*)

used to say how pleasant your home is (especially when you really mean that it is not pleasant at all)

a ˌhome 'truth

an honest criticism of a person said directly to them: *It's time someone told you a few home truths, my boy!*

on the 'home front

happening at home, or in your own country, rather than in a foreign country: *There will be heavy snow across most of France, while on the home front we can expect to see similar conditions at least until the weekend.*

on the ˌhome 'straight/'stretch

approaching the end of a task, project, course, etc: *Ten exams done and two more to do—you're on the home straight now.* ◇ *I never thought the prison sentence would end, but I feel I'm on the home straight now.*

> ❶ ORIGIN
> This expression refers to the last part of a horse race when the horses are approaching the finishing line.

who's 'sb when he's, they're, etc. at home? (*informal, humorous*)

used for asking who the person that has just been mentioned is: *'Shirley Hughes wants to meet you.' 'Who's she when she's at home?'*

be nothing, not much, etc. to write home about → **write**
be sb's spiritual home → **spiritual**
charity begins at home → **charity**
(your/the) chickens come home to roost → **chickens**
close to home → **close**
eat sb out of house and home → **eat**
an Englishman's home is his castle → **Englishman**
the lights are on but nobody's home → **lights**
a man's home is his castle = an Englishman's home is his castle → **Englishman**
press sth home → **press**

press home your advantage → **press**
ram sth home → **ram**
romp home/to victory → **romp**
set up house/home (with sb/together) → **set**
till/until the cows come home → **cows**

homework

do your 'homework (on sth)

find out the facts, details, etc. of a subject in preparation for a meeting, speech, article, etc: *He had just not done his homework for the interview. He couldn't answer our questions.*

honcho

(the) head honcho → **head**

honest

honest! (*spoken*)

used to emphasize that you are not lying: *I didn't mean it, honest!*

honest to 'God/'goodness

used for emphasizing the truth of what you are saying: *I didn't tell anybody—honest to God!*
▶ ˌhonest-to-'goodness *adj.* (*approving*) simple and good: *This book is an honest-to-goodness attempt to describe life as a political leader.*

make an honest 'woman of sb (*old-fashioned or humorous*)

marry a woman who you have been having a sexual relationship with: *When are you going to make an honest woman of her, Peter?*

honesty

in all 'honesty

speaking honestly: *I can't in all honesty say that I've had much experience of this kind of work, but I'm willing to try it.*

honey

a/the land of milk and honey → **land**

honeymoon

a/the 'honeymoon period

a period of time at the beginning of sth, for example a relationship, a job, a period in government, etc., when everybody is pleased with you and there appear to be no problems: *The honeymoon period is over now for the new President.*

honour (*BrE*) (*AmE* honor)

do sb an 'honour; do sb the 'honour (of doing sth) (*formal*)

do sth to make sb feel very proud and pleased: *Would you do me the honour of dining with me?*

have the 'honour of sth/of doing sth (*formal*)

be given the opportunity to do sth that makes you feel proud and happy: *May I have the honour of the next dance?*

(there is) honour among 'thieves (*saying*)
used to say that even criminals have standards of
behaviour that they respect

in 'honour of sb/sth; in sb's/sth's 'honour
in order to show respect and admiration for sb/
sth: *a ceremony in honour of those killed in the
explosion* ◇ *A banquet was held in her honour.*

on your 'honour (*old-fashioned*)
1 used to promise very seriously that you will do
sth or that sth is true: *I swear on my honour that I
knew nothing about this.*
2 be trusted to do sth: *You're on your honour not to
go into my room.*

be/feel duty/honour bound to do sth → **bound**
a point of honour → **point**
your, his, etc. word of honour → **word**

honoured (*BrE*) (*AmE* honored)

be/feel honoured (to do sth)
feel proud and happy: *I was honoured to have been
mentioned in his speech.*

honours (*BrE*) (*AmE* honors)

do the 'honours (*often humorous*)
perform a social duty or ceremony, such as pouring drinks, making a speech, etc: *Harry, could you
do the honours? Tom and Angela both want gin and
tonic.* ◇ *His father was ill, so Charles did the honours with the welcome speech.*

honours are 'even (*BrE*)
no particular person, team, etc. is doing better
than the others in a competition, an argument, etc:
*After a competitive first day of the series, I'd say
honours are even.*

hoof

'hoof it (*informal*)
go somewhere on foot; walk somewhere: *We hoofed
it all the way to 42nd Street.*

on the 'hoof (*BrE, informal*)
if you do sth **on the hoof**, you do it quickly and
without giving it your full attention because you
are doing sth else at the same time: *We made the
decision on the hoof, late at night and without really
thinking about the consequences.*

> **❷ NOTE**
> Meat that is sold, transported, etc. *on the hoof* is
> sold, etc. while the cow or sheep is still alive.

hook

by ‚hook or by 'crook
(of sth difficult) by any method, whether it is honest or not: *Don't worry—we'll have the money ready
by 4 o'clock, by hook or by crook.*

> **❶ ORIGIN**
> In medieval times workers were allowed to use
> the tools of their trade (*billhooks* for farm work-
> ers, *crooks* for shepherds) to get down twigs and
> branches from their employers' trees to use for
> firewood.

get sb off the 'hook (*informal*)
help sb to avoid punishment, etc: *You're going to
need a very clever lawyer to get you off the hook.*

hook, line and 'sinker
(accept or believe sth) completely, either because
you have been deceived or because you believe
things too easily: *Are you telling me that you swallowed his absurd lies hook, line and sinker?*

> **❷ NOTE**
> All three words in this expression are items
> used for catching a fish.

off the 'hook
if you leave or take the telephone **off the hook**,
you take the receiver (= the part that you pick up)
off the place where it usually rests, so that nobody
can call you: *So many people were calling me that in
the end I got tired of it and left the phone off the
hook.*

let sb off the hook → **let**
ring off the hook → **ring**
sling your hook → **sling**

hookey (also hooky)

play hookey/hooky → **play**

hooks

get your 'hooks into sb
gain influence or control over sb: *He was perfectly
happy living alone until that woman got her hooks
into him.*

hoops

jump through hoops → **jump**

hoot

not care/give a 'hoot (about sb/sth) (also **not
care/give two 'hoots (about sb/sth)**) (*informal*)
not care at all: *I don't care two hoots about having
money, as long as I'm happy.*

hop

'hop it (*old-fashioned, BrE, informal*)
usually used in orders to tell sb to go away: *Go on,
hop it!*

catch sb on the hop → **catch**
hop to it = jump to it → **jump**

hope

be beyond 'hope (of sth)
be in a situation where no improvement is possible: *After so many months, the captives were
beyond hope of escape and of ever seeing their families again.*

‚hope against 'hope (that …)
continue to hope for sth, even if this seems useless
or foolish: *It was a couple of days since the earthquake, but the family were still hoping against hope
that their son was safe.*

,hope for the 'best

hope that everything will go well, even if there are doubts that it will: *There is nothing more the doctors can do. All we can do now is hope for the best.*

,hope springs e'ternal (*saying*)

human beings never stop hoping: *She's sure that he'll come back to her one day. I'm not so sure, but hope springs eternal.*

> **❶ ORIGIN**
> This comes from *An Essay on Man* by Alexander Pope: 'Hope springs eternal in the human breast'.

I should hope so/not; so I should hope (*spoken*)

used to say that you feel very strongly that sth should/should not happen: *'Nobody blames you.' 'I should hope not!'* ◇ *'She did apologize.' 'So I should hope!'*

in the hope of sth; in the hope that ...

because you want sth to happen: *I called early in the hope of catching her before she went to work.* ◇ *He asked her again in the vain hope that he could persuade her to come* (= it was impossible).

not have a ,hope in 'hell (*informal*)

not have any chance at all: *You haven't got a hope in hell of winning the race—you're far too slow!*

not a 'hope; some 'hope(s)! (*BrE, spoken*)

there is no or little chance of sth happening: *Some hope of your becoming manager—you're far too lazy!* ◇ *'Your dad will lend you the money, won't he?' 'Not a hope.'*

live in hope → **live**
not hold out any, much, etc. hope = hold out little, etc. hope (of sth/that ...) → **hold**
the one/a ray of hope → **ray**

hopes

build up/raise sb's 'hopes

make sb feel hopeful about sth or persuade them that sth good is going to happen: *Don't raise her hopes too much. She may not win.*

dash/shatter sb's 'hopes

destroy sb's hopes of doing or getting sth: *Any hopes that the museum would be built this year were dashed yesterday when the council announced its plans to spend less money on the arts.* ◇ *His poor performance in the exam shattered his hopes of becoming a lawyer.*

pin your faith/hopes on sb/sth → **pin**

hopping

,hopping 'mad (about/over sth) (*informal*)

extremely angry about sth: *Anne was hopping mad about the sales figures.*

horizon

on the ho'rizon

soon to happen: *The change of government means*

that there are new developments on the horizon.

a (small) cloud on the horizon → **cloud**

horn

blow/toot your own horn = blow your own trumpet → **blow**

hornet

a 'hornet's nest

a lot of trouble: *When Charles got the manager's job, it stirred up a real hornet's nest, because everyone was angry about his fast promotion.*

> **❶ NOTE**
> A *hornet* is a large wasp that has a very powerful sting.

horns

draw/pull in your 'horns

start being more careful in your behaviour, especially by spending less money than before: *After making huge losses, the company had to draw in its horns by cancelling some major projects.*

(on) the horns of a di'lemma

(in) a situation in which you must make a choice between things which are equally unpleasant: *I'm really on the horns of a dilemma. I need the car but I can't afford it.*

lock horns (with sb) (over sth) → **lock**
take the bull by the horns → **bull**

horror

,horror of 'horrors (*BrE, humorous* or *ironic*)

used to emphasize how bad a situation is: *I stood up to speak and—horror of horrors—realized I had left my notes behind.*

shock horror → **shock**

horse

(straight) from the horse's 'mouth (*informal*)

(of information, etc.) directly from the person who really knows because they are closely connected with its source: *'How do you know he's leaving?' 'I got it straight from the horse's mouth. He told me himself.'*

you can ,take/,lead a horse to ,water, but you ,can't make it 'drink (*saying*)

you can give sb the opportunity to do sth, but you cannot force them to do it if they do not want to

back the wrong horse → **wrong**
be/get on your high horse → **high**
a dark horse → **dark**
eat like a horse → **eat**
flog a dead horse → **flog**
I could eat a horse → **eat**
(not) look a gift horse in the mouth → **look**
put the cart before the horse → **cart**
shut, etc. the barn door after the horse has escaped = shut/lock/close the stable door after the horse has bolted → **stable**

horses

change/swap horses in mid'stream
change to a different or new activity while you are in the middle of sth else; change from supporting one person or thing to another: *'I don't believe in changing horses in midstream,' he said. 'Give this policy a chance before you think of changing it.'*

,horses for 'courses (*BrE*)
people or things should only be used for the purpose which they are most suitable for: *I think Johnson would be much better for this job. It's a question of horses for courses.*

❶ ORIGIN
This expression refers to the fact that horses race better on a track that suits them.

drive a coach and horses through sth **→ drive**
hold your horses **→ hold**
if wishes were horses, beggars would/might ride **→ wishes**
wild horses couldn't/wouldn't drag sb there, prevent sb doing sth, etc. **→ wild**

hostage

a ,hostage to 'fortune
an action which may cause you great trouble in the future: *Are you really sure you want to know who your real mother is? It may be taking a hostage to fortune, you know.*

hot

go ,hot and 'cold (all 'over) (*informal*)
suddenly feel very worried, upset or frightened when you remember sth very unpleasant: *I go hot and cold all over when I think of that train accident. It was so terrible.*

hot 'air (*informal*)
impressive but worthless or empty promises: *Don't believe anything she says. It's all hot air.*

(all) hot and 'bothered (*informal*)
worried and upset: *Ministers are getting all hot and bothered about official secrets getting out.* ◊ *You're looking a bit hot and bothered. Is everything OK?*

(too) 'hot for sb (also too hot to 'handle) (*informal*)
(too) difficult, dangerous, etc. for sb: *When the scandal became public, things got too hot for the Minister and she resigned.* ◊ *The newspapers won't print the story—it's just too hot to handle.*

a 'hot line (to sb)
a special telephone line to an important person, such as a president, etc. which is used in emergencies: *The President of the United States spoke on the hot line with the Prime Minister about the crisis.*

,hot off the 'press
news that is **hot off the press** has just appeared in the newspapers and is fresh and usually exciting: *Listen to this story—it's hot off the press!*

hot on sb's/sth's 'tracks/'trail (*informal*)
close to catching or finding the person or thing that you have been chasing or searching for: *The burglar ran away, with the police hot on his trail.*

a hot po'tato (*informal*)
a very sensitive matter that is difficult or embarrassing to deal with: *The minister's resignation is a political hot potato.*

a 'hot spot (*informal*)
1 a place where fighting is common, especially for political reasons: *As a journalist, I get sent to one hot spot after another.*
2 a place where there is a lot of activity or entertainment: *We went clubbing in some of Ibiza's most famous hot spots.*

hot 'stuff (*informal, especially BrE*)
1 sb/sth of very high quality: *He's really hot stuff as a tennis player.*
2 a sexually attractive person; (of a film, book, etc.) exciting in a sexual way: *She seems to think he's really hot stuff.* ◊ *His new book is really hot stuff.*

hot under the 'collar (*informal*)
annoyed, embarrassed or excited: *He gets very hot under the collar if people disagree with him.*

in hot pur'suit (of sb/sth)
chasing sb; trying to catch sb: *He grabbed the jewels and ran, with the shopkeeper in hot pursuit.*

in the 'hot seat (*informal*)
a position of responsibility in which you must deal with difficult questions, criticism or attacks: *Our radio phone-in today is on transport, and the Minister of Transport will be in the hot seat, ready to answer your questions.*

in hot 'water (*informal*)
in trouble: *She got into hot water for being late.* ◊ *The new clerk was in hot water because she forgot to ask for a receipt for the money.* ◊ *This sort of behaviour will land him in hot water.*

make it 'hot for sb (*informal*)
make a situation very difficult or uncomfortable for sb: *If you insist on staying here, I can make it very hot for you.*

more sth/more often than sb has had hot dinners (*informal, often humorous*)
used for emphasizing how much/many or how often sb has done sth: *He's won more medals than you've had hot dinners.* ◊ *She's been to France more often than you've had hot dinners.*

not so/too 'hot (*informal*)
not very well, healthy, etc.; not very good: *'How do you feel today?' 'Not so hot.'* ◊ *Her work's not too hot, is it? I thought she'd be better than this!*

sell/go like 'hot cakes (*informal*)
be sold quickly in great quantities: *The band's latest record is selling like hot cakes.*

blow hot and cold **→ blow**
hard/hot on sb's heels **→ heels**

like a cat on hot bricks ➔ **cat**
strike while the iron is hot ➔ **strike**

hotfoot

'hotfoot it (*informal*)
walk or run somewhere quickly: *Once the police arrived, we hotfooted it out of there.*

hots

get/have the 'hots for sb (*informal*)
be sexually attracted to sb: *I reckon Jim's really got the hots for you!*

hounds

run with the hare and hunt with the hounds ➔ **run**

hour

at an un,earthly/un,godly 'hour (*informal*)
very early or very late, especially when this is annoying: *The job involved getting up at some unearthly hour to catch the first train.* ◇ *I heard him come home at some ungodly hour again last night.*

in your hour of need (*often humorous*)
when you really need help: *Where were you in my hour of need? Sitting in the pub with your friends!*

on the 'hour/half-'hour
at exactly 5 o'clock, 6 o'clock, etc./ 5.30, 6.30, etc: *Buses leave here for Oxford on the hour.*

the eleventh hour ➔ **eleventh**
the evil hour/day/moment ➔ **evil**

hours

,after 'hours
after the period during which a shop, pub, etc. is open: *Pubs are not allowed to sell drinks after hours.*

at 'all hours
at any time during the night or day; all the time: *He comes here at all hours, sometimes in the middle of the night.*

keep ... 'hours
if you **keep** regular, strange, etc. **hours**, the times at which you do things (especially getting up or going to bed) are regular, strange, etc: *Keeping irregular hours is hard on children, so try to set a regular bedime and regular morning time.*

the 'small/'early hours (also **the wee (small) 'hours**)
the period of time very early in the morning, soon after midnight: *He died in the early hours of Saturday morning.* ◇ *We stayed up talking into the small hours.*

till/until 'all hours
until very late at night or early next morning: *She sat up till all hours trying to finish her essay.*

work all the hours God sends ➔ **work**

house

bring the 'house down (*informal*)
make everyone laugh a lot or clap their hands loudly, especially at a performance in the theatre: *Their act brought the house down when they played in London.* ◇ *'Did he sing well?' 'He brought the house down!'*

get on like a 'house on fire (*BrE*) (*AmE* **get along like a 'house on fire**) (*informal*)
quickly develop a very friendly relationship with sb: *I was worried about introducing my boyfriend to my parents, but they got on like a house on fire.*

a ,house of 'cards
a plan, an organization, etc., that is so badly arranged that it could easily fail: *His plans collapsed like a house of cards when he was told he hadn't won the scholarship.*

keep 'house
cook, clean and do all the other jobs around the house: *She had given up her career to devote herself to the task of keeping house and raising a family.*

on the 'house
(especially of alcoholic drinks) given to a customer free by the hotel, restaurant, bar, etc: *Drinks are on the house tonight!*

put/set your (own) 'house in order
organize your own business or improve your own behaviour before you try to criticize sb else: *A government minister warned the newspaper industry to put its own house in order before it started to tell other industries how they should be run.*

eat sb out of house and home ➔ **eat**
a halfway house ➔ **halfway**
in the doghouse ➔ **doghouse**
not a dry eye in the house ➔ **dry**
(keep) open house ➔ **open**
pack the house ➔ **pack**
set up house/home (with sb/together) ➔ **set**

household

a ,household 'name/'word
a name/word that is extremely well known: *The business she founded made her into a household name.* ◇ *Microsoft is a household name.*

houseroom

not give sb/sth 'houseroom (*BrE*)
not want sb/sth in your house because you dislike or do not approve of it/them; completely reject sb/sth: *I wouldn't give that ugly old furniture houseroom.* ◇ *She won't give any of these theories houseroom.*

houses

go all round the 'houses (*BrE, informal*)
do sth or ask a question in a very complicated way instead of in a simple, direct way: *If you want to ask her something, just ask her directly—there's no need to go all round the houses!*

people (who live) in glass houses shouldn't throw stones → **people**

(as) safe as houses → **safe**

housetops

shout, etc. sth from the 'housetops/ 'rooftops (*informal*)

tell sth to everyone: *Don't shout it from the housetops, will you? I want to keep it a secret just between us for a while.* ◊ *If you tell her it's a secret, she'll announce it from the rooftops.*

how

how 'can/'could you! (*spoken*)

used to show that you strongly disapprove of sb's behaviour or are very surprised by it: *Ben! How could you? After all they've done for us!* ◊ *Ugh! How can you eat that stuff?*

how 'come (…)? (*spoken*)

used to say you do not understand how sth can happen and would like an explanation: *'They've decided not to buy the house.' 'How come? I thought they definitely wanted it.'* ◊ *If she spent five years in Paris, how come her French is so bad?*

how do you 'do (*becoming old-fashioned*)

used as a formal greeting when you meet sb for the first time. The usual reply is also *How do you do?*

how's 'this/'that for a … ? (*informal*)

used for asking for sb's reaction to sth: *'How's that for a surprise present?' 'It looks wonderful. Thank you!'* ◊ *'Well, how's that for bad hotel service?' 'Unbelievable.'*

huddle

get/go into a 'huddle (with sb)

move close to sb so that you can talk about sth without other people hearing: *Every time she asked a question, the group went into a huddle before giving her an answer.*

hue

a ˌhue and 'cry

loud opposition, protest, etc: *There was a great hue and cry among the parents when it was announced that the school was to close.* ◊ *If the government raises taxes too much, there'll be a real hue and cry.*

> **ⓘ ORIGIN**
> This phrase refers to the medieval law 'hu e cri', which stated that the public had to chase and try to catch a criminal.

huff

ˌhuff and 'puff

1 breathe heavily while making a great physical effort: *They huffed and puffed as they carried the sofa upstairs.*
2 make it obvious that you are annoyed about sth

without doing anything to change the situation: *After much huffing and puffing, he agreed to help.*

in a 'huff (*informal*)

in a bad mood, especially because sb has annoyed or upset you: *She went off in a huff.*

hum

hum/hem and haw = um and aah (about sth) → **um**

human

the milk of human kindness → **milk**

humble

eat humble pie → **eat**

hump

give sb/get the 'hump (*BrE, informal*)

annoy sb/become annoyed, angry, etc: *She gets the hump when people don't listen to her.* ◊ *'What's wrong with Jake?' 'Oh, I don't know. He's got the hump about something.'*

over the 'hump (*informal*)

past the largest, worst or most difficult part of a job, illness, etc: *I'll be over the hump when I've done this exam—then there'll be just two left.*

hundred

a hundred/thousand/million and one (things, etc. to do, etc.) (*informal*)

very many or too many (things to do, people to see, etc.): *I'm so busy—I've got lectures to prepare and a hundred and one letters to write—I just don't know where to start.* ◊ *She's always got a thousand and one excuses for everything.*

a/one hundred per 'cent

completely: *I agree with you one hundred per cent.*

ninety-nine times out of a hundred = nine times out of ten → **nine**

not a hundred/thousand/million miles away/from here → **miles**

hung

(you, etc.) may/might as well be hanged/hung for a sheep as (for) a lamb → **well**

hunkers

on your 'hunkers

sitting on your heels with your knees bent up in front of you: *The little boy took out his favourite red sports car, and was delighted when Tom went down on his hunkers and admired the toy.*

hunt

run with the hare and hunt with the hounds → **run**

hunting

a happy hunting ground → **happy**

hurry

in a 'hurry

1 very quickly or more quickly than usual: *He had to leave in a hurry.*

2 not having enough time to do sth: *Sorry, I haven't got time to do it now—I'm in a hurry.*

in a 'hurry to do sth

impatient to do sth: *My daughter is in such a hurry to grow up.* ◇ *Why are you in such a hurry to sell?*

in no 'hurry (to do sth); not in a/any 'hurry (to do sth)

1 having plenty of time: *I don't mind waiting—I'm not in any particular hurry.* ◇ *Serve this lady first—I'm in no hurry.*

2 not wanting or not willing to do sth: *We were in no hurry to get back to work after the holiday.*

I, he, etc. won't do sth again in a 'hurry (*spoken*)

used to say that sb does not want to do sth again because it was not enjoyable: *I won't be going there again in a hurry—the food was terrible.*

(be in) a tearing hurry/rush → **tearing**

hurt

it won't/wouldn't 'hurt sb to do sth

it will/would be better for sb to do sth; it would be a good idea for sb to do sth: *It wouldn't hurt her to walk instead of going in the car all the time.*

he, she, etc. wouldn't harm/hurt a fly → **fly**

hurts

hit sb where it hurts → **hit**

hustle

,hustle and 'bustle

busy and excited activity: *I can't concentrate on my work with all this hustle and bustle going on around me.* ◇ *I've always loved the hustle and bustle of big cities.*

Hyde

a Jekyll and Hyde → **Jekyll**

hymn

sing from the same song/hymn sheet → **sing**

hysterics

have hy'sterics (*spoken*)

be extremely upset and angry: *My mum'll have hysterics when she sees the colour of my hair.*

I i

i

dot the/your i's and cross the/your t's → dot

ice

put sth on 'ice

decide to take no action on sth for a period of time; postpone sth: *They have put the plans for the new hospital on ice because of the economic situation.* ◇ *My plans for going to the USA are on ice for now.*

be skating/walking on thin ice → thin
break the ice → break
cut no ice (with sb) → cut

iceberg

be the tip of the iceberg → tip

icing

the icing on the 'cake

something attractive, but not necessary, which is added to sth already very good: *The meal was perfect, the wonderful view from the restaurant the icing on the cake.*

idea

get the i'dea (*informal*)

understand sth when it has been explained to you: *'Do you understand how it works now?' 'Yes, I think I've got the idea. Thanks for showing me.'*

have (got) no i'dea; not have the first, slightest, etc. i'dea

not know sth at all; not know how to do sth at all: *I've no idea what time it is.* ◇ *Don't ask him to mend it; he hasn't got the first idea about cars.*

the (very) i'dea! (*old-fashioned*, *spoken*)

used to express surprise or disapproval at the way sb behaves: *She expected me to pay for everything. The idea!*

'that's an idea! (*spoken*)

used to reply in a positive way to a suggestion that sb has made: *Hey, that's an idea! And we could get a band, as well.*

'that's the idea! (*spoken*)

used to encourage people and to tell them that they are doing sth right: *That's the idea! You're doing just fine.*

you have (got) no i'dea ... (*spoken*)

used to show that sth is hard for sb else to imagine: *You've no idea how much traffic there was tonight.*

have (got) the right idea → right
run away with the idea/notion → run

ideal

in an ideal/a perfect world → world

ideas

give sb i'deas (also put i'deas in(to) sb's head)

give sb hopes about sth that may not be possible or likely; make sb act or think in an unreasonable way: *Don't keep telling him about your adventures in Africa. You're giving him ideas.* ◇ *Who's been putting ideas into his head?*

buck up your ideas → buck

idle

bone idle → bone
the devil makes work for idle hands → devil

if

ˌif and 'when

used to say sth about an event that may or may not happen: *If and when we ever meet again I hope he remembers what I did for him.*

if 'anything

used to express an opinion about sth, or after a negative statement to suggest that the opposite is true: *I'd say he was more like his father, if anything.* ◇ *She's not thin—if anything she's a little plump.*

if ˌI were 'you

used to introduce a suggestion or a piece of advice: *If I were you, I wouldn't buy that car. You can see it's been in an accident.*

if it wasn't/weren't for ...

used to say that sb/sth stopped sb/sth from happening: *If it weren't for you, I wouldn't even be here today.*

if 'not

1 used to introduce a different suggestion, after a sentence with *if*: *I'll go if you're going. If not* (= if you are not) *I'd rather stay at home.*

2 used after a yes/no question to say what will or should happen if the answer is 'no': *Are you ready? If not, I'm going without you.* ◇ *Do you want that cake? If not, I'll have it.*

3 used to suggest that sth may be even larger, more important, etc. than was first stated: *They cost thousands if not millions of pounds to build.*

if 'only

used to express a wish that something had happened or would happen: *If only she'd done what I told her, she wouldn't be in this trouble.* ◇ *If only you'd let me explain.*

ifs

ˌifs and/or 'buts

(often used in negative sentences) used to stop sb arguing, protesting or making excuses when you tell them to do sth: *I want this work finished by Fri-day and no ifs and buts.*

ignorance

‚ignorance is 'bliss (*saying*)
if you do not know about sth, you cannot worry about it: *Some doctors believe ignorance is bliss and don't give their patients all the facts.*

ill

for ‚good or 'ill (*formal*)
whether the effect of an action, fact, etc. is good or bad: *Look, for good or ill, you chose this profession. You can't just leave it now.*

‚ill at 'ease
nervous, especially in a social situation: *He always feels ill at ease at parties.* ◇ *She looked very ill at ease during her speech.*

it's an ‚ill 'wind (that blows nobody any good) (*saying*)
no problem is so bad that it does not bring some advantage to sb: *The fire destroyed half the village. For the builders business has never been better. It's an ill wind …*

speak/think 'ill of sb (*formal*)
say or think bad things about sb: *You shouldn't speak ill of the dead.*

bad/ill feeling(s) → **feeling**
bode well/ill (for sb/sth) → **bode**
wish sb/sth well/ill → **wish**

image

be the image of sb/sth; be the living/spitting/very image of sb/sth
be very similar to, or look exactly like sb/sth else: *She's the spitting image of her mother.*

imagination

by no stretch of the imagination → **stretch**
a figment of sb's imagination → **figment**
not by any stretch of the imagination → **stretch**

immemorial

from/since time immemorial → **time**

impression

be under the im'pression (that) …
believe, usually wrongly, that …: *I was under the impression you were coming tomorrow, not today.*

in

anything/nothing/something 'in it
any/no/some truth in what is being said: *'Is there anything in the story that he is leaving the com-pany?' 'No, I'm sure there's nothing in it.' / 'Yes, I think there's something in it.'*

anything/nothing/something in it for sb (*informal*)
any/no/some advantage, especially financial, to sb: *He wanted to know more about the business but I told him there was nothing in it for him.*

be in at sth
present when sth happens: *They were in at the start of the economic boom.*

be 'in for sth
1 be about to get or experience sth unpleasant, for example a shock, a surprise, trouble, bad weather, etc: *He'll be in for a big surprise when he opens that letter.* ◇ *I think we're in for trouble with the new boss.*
2 be taking part in sth, for example, a competition; be trying to get sth, for example, a job: *I'm in for both the 100 metres race and the long jump.* ◇ *I hope Jan gets that professorship she's in for.*

be 'in for it (*BrE* also **be 'for it**) (*informal*)
be going to get into trouble or be punished: *We'd better hurry or we'll be in for it.*

be/get 'in on sth (*informal*)
knowing about sth; included in sth: *I'd like to be in on this project if you'll have me.* ◇ *She wants to get in on what the others are doing.* ◇ *Shall we let him in on the secret?*

be/keep (well) 'in with sb (*informal*)
be friendly with sb, not because you like them, but because they may be useful to you: *If you want to do well in this company, keep well in with the boss.*

‚in and 'out of sth
(going) in and out of places all the time: *I've been in and out of the travel agency all this week, trying to arrange my holiday.* ◇ *After the accident, he was in and out of hospital for a couple of years.*

in that (*written*)
for the reason that; because: *She was fortunate in that she had friends to help her.*

inch

every inch a/the leader, film star, etc.
a leader, star, etc. in every way; completely a leader, star, etc: *She was every inch a leader.* ◇ *He looked every inch the romantic hero.* ◇ *That horse looks every inch a winner.*

give sb an 'inch (and they'll ‚take a 'yard/'mile) (*saying*)
if you say yes to sb for a small request, they will want much more: *I said Joe could borrow my car occasionally, and then he started to borrow it every night! Give him an inch!*

‚inch by 'inch
very slowly and with great care or difficulty: *She crawled forward inch by inch.*

not budge/give/move an 'inch
refuse to change your position, decision, etc. even
a little: *We tried to negotiate a lower price but they
wouldn't budge an inch.*

within an 'inch of (doing) sth
very near/close to (doing) sth: *I came within an
inch of death in that car accident.* ◇ *They came
within an inch of winning the match.* ◇ *They beat
him within an inch of his life* (= very severely).

not trust sb an inch ➔ **trust**

inconsiderable

not incon'siderable (*formal*)
large; large enough to be considered important:
*We have spent a not inconsiderable amount of
money on the project already.*

Indian

an ‚Indian 'summer
1 a period of unusually dry, warm weather in the
autumn: *We had a splendid Indian summer last
October.*
2 a period of success or happiness near the end of
sb's life: *He made his best films in his seventies; it
was for him a real Indian summer.*

(in) single/Indian file ➔ **file**

Indians

there are too many chiefs and not enough Indians ➔
  chiefs

industry

a captain of industry ➔ **captain**

infinitum

ad infinitum ➔ **ad**

influence

under the 'influence
(used of sb driving a car) having had too much
alcohol to drink: *She was fined £500 for driving
under the influence.*

information

for your infor'mation
1 (*abbr.* **FYI**) written on documents that are sent
to sb who needs to know the information in them
but does not need to deal with them
2 (*informal*) used to tell sb that they are wrong
about sth: *For your information, I don't even have a
car.*

a mine of information (about/on sb/sth) ➔ **mine**

iniquity

a den of iniquity/vice ➔ **den**

initiative

(do sth) on your own i'nitiative
do sth which is your own idea, not a suggestion or
order from another person: *Did you ask him to
organize a meeting, or was it on his own initiative?*

take the i'nitiative
lead people by being the first to act in a situation:
France took the initiative in the peace talks. ◇
*California took the initiative in banning smoking
in public places.*

injury

do sb/yourself an 'injury (*often humorous*)
hurt sb/yourself physically: *I nearly did myself an
injury carrying those heavy suitcases.*

add insult to injury ➔ **add**

injustice

do yourself/sb an in'justice
judge yourself/sb unfairly: *We may have been
doing him an injustice. This work is good.*

inner

the ‚inner 'man/'woman
1 your mind or soul: *Prayer and meditation are
good for the inner man.*
2 (*humorous*) your appetite: *It's time to do something for the inner man; let's look for a restaurant.*

innings

a good 'innings (*BrE, informal*)
(of a person who has died or who is at the end of
their life or career) a long (and successful) life
and/or career: *He's had a good innings but now it's
time for him to retire and let someone younger take
over as director.*

inroads

make inroads in/into sth
1 reduce the amount of sth: *Repairs to the house
had made deep inroads into their savings.*
2 advance successfully into a new area: *Doctors
are making great inroads in the fight against cancer.* ◇ *Their products are already making inroads
in these new markets.*

ins

the ‚ins and 'outs (of sth)
all the details of sth, which are often difficult to
understand: *It would take me too long to explain all
the ins and outs of the problem.* ◇ *I don't know all
the ins and outs of the case.*

insane

drive sb insane ➔ **drive**

inside

,inside 'out
with the part that is usually inside facing out:
You've got your sweater on inside out. ◇ *Turn the
bag inside out and let it dry.*

on the in'side
working in an organization and possessing secret
information about it: *Someone on the inside must
have passed on the information to the bank robbers.*

know sb/sth inside out → **know**
turn sth inside out/upside down → **turn**

insignificance

pale into insignificance → **pale**

insofar

insofar as = in so far as → **far**

instance

for 'instance
as an example: *Some of my books have sold well.
My most recent one, for instance, sold 100 000 copies.*

in the first instance → **first**

instant

not for a/one minute/moment/second/instant → **minute**

insult

add insult to injury → **add**

intentions

the road to hell is paved with good intentions → **road**

intents

to all intents and 'purposes (*BrE*) (*AmE* for all intents and 'purposes)
in almost every important way: *The fighting has
stopped, so to all intents and purposes, the war is
over.*

interest

in the interest(s) of sth
in order to help or achieve sth: *In the interests of
safety, smoking is forbidden.*

pay sth back/return sth with 'interest
react to the harm sb has done to you by doing sth
even worse to them: *Peter pushed his sister, so she
paid him back with interest by kicking him hard.*

> ❷ NOTE
> *Interest* is the extra money you receive or pay
> when you lend or borrow money.

conflict of interest(s) → **conflict**
have (got) a vested interest (in sth) → **vested**

interests

have (got) sb's (best) interests at 'heart
want sb to be happy and successful even though

your actions may not show this: *As a father, he
always had the little girl's best interests at heart.*

interim

in the 'interim
during the period of time between two events;
until a particular event happens: *Despite everything that happened in the interim, they remained
good friends.* ◇ *Her new job does not start until May
and she will continue in the old job in the interim.*

intervals

at (...) intervals
1 with time between: *Buses to the city leave **at
regular intervals**.* ◇ *The runners started at 5-
minute intervals.*
2 with spaces between: *Flaming torches were pos-
itioned at intervals along the terrace.*

into

be 'into sth (*informal*)
be interested in sth in an active way: *He's into
snowboarding in a big way.*

invention

necessity is the mother of invention → **necessity**

inverted

in inverted 'commas (*spoken*)
used to show that you think a particular word,
description, etc. is not true or appropriate: *The
manager showed us to our 'luxury apartment', in
inverted commas.*

> ❷ NOTE
> *Inverted commas* are another name for quota-
> tion marks (' ') or (" ").

invitation

an open invitation (to sb) → **open**

Irish

the luck of the Irish → **luck**

iron

an ,iron ,fist/,hand in a ,velvet 'glove
harsh treatment of sb that is hidden behind a gentle manner: *The president ruled his country by
using an iron fist in a velvet glove.*

pump iron → **pump**
rule (sb/sth) with a rod of iron/with an iron hand → **rule**
strike while the iron is hot → **strike**

irons

have (got) many, etc. irons in the 'fire
have (got) many, etc. different plans, projects, etc.
at the same time, often with the hope that at least
one will be successful: *She's still got several irons*

in the fire: her television work, her film work and her writing.

> **❶ ORIGIN**
> This idiom refers to blacksmiths (= people whose job it is to make and repair things made of iron), who have several pieces of iron in the fire at a time, so that there is always one piece that is hot enough to work with.

issue

(the point, etc.) at 'issue
the most important part of the subject that is being discussed: *The point at issue here is his honesty, not the quality of his work.*

make an 'issue (out) of sth
behave as if sth is more serious or important than it really is: *Look, it's not important who did it. Let's not make an issue out of it.*

take 'issue with sb (about/on/over sth) (*formal*)
disagree and argue with sb about sth: *I'd like to take issue with you about what you just said.*

force the issue → force

itch

the seven year itch → seven

itchy

get/have itchy 'feet (*informal*)
a desire to travel, move house, change your job, etc: *He never stays in a job long. He gets itchy feet after two or three years.*

item

be an 'item (*informal*)
be involved in a romantic or sexual relationship: *Are they an item?*

itself

be ˌpatience, ˌhonesty, sim'plicity, etc. it'self
be an example of complete patience, etc: *The manager of the hotel was courtesy itself.* ◇ *Programming the video is simplicity itself.*

in it'self
considered separately from other things; in its true nature: *In itself, it's not a difficult problem to solve.*

ivory

an ˌivory 'tower (*disapproving*)
a way of life in which people avoid the unpleasant realities of life: *Just because I'm a writer, it doesn't mean I live in an ivory tower. I have to earn a living like anyone else.* ◇ *What do professors and academics sitting in their ivory towers know about the real world?*

J j

Jack

a ,Jack the 'Lad (BrE, slang)

a young man who is very confident in a noisy way, and enjoys going out with male friends, drinking alcohol and trying to attract women: *He used to be a bit of a Jack the Lad—I never thought he'd settle down and get married.*

> **❶ ORIGIN**
> This was originally the nickname of an 18th-century thief called Jack Sheppard.

before you can say Jack Robinson ➔ **say**
I'm all right, Jack ➔ **right**

jack

a jack of 'all trades

a person who can do many different kinds of work, but perhaps does not do them very well: *He repairs cars, he paints houses, he makes furniture. He's a real jack of all trades.*

> **❷ NOTE**
> The full expression is 'jack of all trades and master of none'.

jackpot

hit the jackpot ➔ **hit**

jam

be in a 'jam (informal)

be in a difficult situation: *I'm in a bit of a jam. Could you give me a lift to the train station?*

jam on the 'brake(s); jam the 'brake(s) on

make a vehicle stop very suddenly by operating the brakes with force: *The car skidded as he jammed on the brakes.*

jam to'morrow (BrE, informal)

good things that are promised for the future but never happen: *They refused to settle for a promise of jam tomorrow.*

money for jam ➔ **money**

Jane

a plain Jane ➔ **plain**

jaw

your 'jaw drops

your mouth opens because you are very surprised: *When they told her that she had won a million pounds, her jaw dropped in amazement.*

jaws

the jaws of 'death, de'feat, etc. (literary)

used to describe an unpleasant situation that

almost happens: *The team snatched victory from the jaws of defeat.*

jazz

and all that 'jazz (spoken, informal)

and things like that: *I was no good at history at school—dates and battles and all that jazz.*

Jekyll

a ,Jekyll and 'Hyde

a person with two separate personalities or ways of behaving, one good, pleasant, etc. and one evil, unpleasant, etc: *He's a real Jekyll and Hyde. At home he shouts at his wife and children all the time; at work he's always charming and friendly.*

> **❶ ORIGIN**
> This expression comes from a story by Robert Louis Stevenson, *Dr Jekyll and Mr Hyde*, in which Dr Jekyll takes a drug which separates the good and bad sides of his personality into two characters. All the negative aspects go into the character of Mr Hyde.

jelly

be/feel like 'jelly (also turn to 'jelly)

(of legs or knees) feel weak because you are nervous or frightened.: *She couldn't move—her head was swimming, her mouth was dry and her legs felt like jelly.*

shake like a jelly/leaf ➔ **shake**

jest

in 'jest

as a joke: *The remark was made half in jest.* ◇ *'Many a true word is spoken in jest,' thought Rosie* (= people often say things as a joke that are actually true).

jet

the 'jet set

the group of very rich and fashionable people who travel a lot, either on business or for pleasure: *She's really joined the jet set now, skiing in St. Moritz, winter holidays in Barbados, shopping in Paris ...* ▶ **'jet-setter** *noun* a person who belongs to the jet set: *His job takes him to New York, Tokyo, Rome and Madrid. He's a real jet-setter.*

jetsam

flotsam and jetsam ➔ **flotsam**

jewel

the jewel in the 'crown

the most attractive or valuable part of sth: *Most*

critics agree that this artist's latest work is the jewel in the crown of an exceptional body of work.

jinks

high jinks → high

jitters

get/have the 'jitters (*informal*)
feel anxious and nervous, especially before an important event or before having to do sth difficult: *I always get the jitters before exams.* ◊ *Louise had the pre-wedding jitters so badly she nearly didn't make it to the church.*

Job

a ,Job's 'comforter (*old-fashioned*)
a person who is sympathetic but says things which make you feel even more unhappy than you are already: *Ann came to see me when I was in hospital. She was a real Job's comforter! She told me about somebody who had the same operation as me, and then died a month later.*

❶ ORIGIN

Job is a character in the Bible. His friends pretended to comfort him but were actually criticizing him.

the patience of a saint/of Job → patience

job

do a good, bad, etc. 'job (on sth); make a good, bad, etc. job of sth
do sth well, badly, etc: *They did a very professional job.* ◊ *You've certainly made an excellent job of the kitchen* (= for example, painting it).

do the 'job/'trick (*informal*)
do what is needed or wanted: *These pills should do the job. You'll feel better in no time.* ◊ *I tried many different ways to stop smoking. Acupuncture finally did the trick.*

give sb/sth up as a bad 'job (*informal*)
decide that it is impossible to do sth or to change sb and then stop trying to do it: *'Are you still studying Japanese?' 'No, I gave it up as a bad job. It was far too difficult for me!'*

good 'job! (*AmE, spoken*)
used to tell sb that they have done well at sth: *You finished already? Good job!*

(it's) a good 'job/'thing (that) … (*spoken*)
(it's) lucky: *It's a good job he was here. We couldn't have moved the piano without him.* ◊ *It's a good job my luggage was insured.*

(and) a ,good job/thing 'too (*spoken*)
used to show that you are pleased to hear some news, especially if you have been waiting for it for a long time: *'They've cut the price of petrol.' 'And a good thing too.'* ◊ *He's given up smoking, and a good job too in my opinion.*

have a (hard/difficult) job doing/to do sth
find it difficult to do sth: *I had a job getting to work on time this morning. The traffic was terrible.* ◊ *He had a hard job to make himself heard.*

a job of 'work (*BrE, old-fashioned* or *formal*)
work that you are paid to do or that must be done: *There was a job of work waiting for him that he was not looking forward to.*

just the 'job/'ticket (*informal*)
exactly what was wanted or needed: *That cup of tea was just the job.*

more than your 'job's worth (to do sth) (*BrE, spoken*)
not worth doing because it is against the rules or because it might cause you to lose your job: *I'm afraid I can't do that. It would be more than my job's worth.*

on the 'job
1 (while) actually working, and not drinking coffee, talking, wasting time, etc: *I've been on the job all day, and I feel exhausted.* ◊ *At work we can smoke in the canteen, but not on the job.*
2 (*BrE, slang*) having sex

don't give up the day job → day
a hatchet job (on sb/sth) → hatchet
lie down on the job → lie
make the best of sth/things/a bad job → best
a put-up job → put-up
a snow job → snow
walk off the job → walk

jobs

jobs for the 'boys (*BrE, informal, disapproving*)
(giving) good jobs, positions or contracts to people only or mainly because they are friends, relatives or supporters: *The city officials here are completely corrupt. It's jobs for the boys.*

odd jobs → odd

Joe

,Joe 'Bloggs (*BrE*) (*AmE* **,Joe 'Blow**) (*informal*)
a way of referring to a typical ordinary person: *What will this promised cut in taxes really mean to Joe Bloggs and his family?* ◊ *As the son of a senator, of course he has advantages that the average Joe Blow doesn't have.*

,Joe 'Public (*BrE*) (*AmE* **,John ,Q. 'Public**) (*informal*)
people in general; the public: *Once again, it seems that Joe Public is paying the price for inefficient management.*

jog

jog sb's 'memory
help sb to remember sth: *So you don't remember Mary Woodson? Well, here's a photograph of you with her which might jog your memory.*

John

John Q. Public = Joe Public → **Joe**

joie

ˌjoie de ˈvivre (*from French, written*)
a feeling of great happiness and enjoyment of life: *After the depressing events of the last few months, Mina felt that it was time to put a little joie de vivre back into their lives.*

> ❷ NOTE
> The meaning of the French phrase is 'joy of living'.

join

join the ˈclub
said as a reply to sb who tells you their bad news when you are or have been in the same situation yourself; an expression of sympathy: *'I failed the exam again!' 'Join the club! Pete, Sarah and I have as well, so don't worry!'*

join ˈhands (with sb)
1 if two people **join hands**, they hold each other's hands
2 work together in doing sth: *Education has been reluctant to join hands with business.*

do/join battle (with sb) → **battle**
if you can't beat them, join them → **beat**
join/combine forces (with sb) → **forces**

joint

out of ˈjoint
1 (of a bone) pushed out of its correct position
2 not working or behaving in the normal way: *Time is thrown completely out of joint in the opening chapters.*

case the joint → **case**
put sb's nose out of joint → **nose**

joke

be/get/go beyond a ˈjoke
be no longer funny; be serious: *This has got beyond a joke! Open this door and let me out at once!* ◇ *The state of the roads in this country is beyond a joke.*

be no ˈjoke
be serious or difficult: *Trying to find a job nowadays is no joke.* ◇ *It's no joke living on such a small income.*

the joke's on ˈsb (*informal*)
used to say that sb who tried to make another person look ridiculous now looks ridiculous instead

make a ˈjoke of sth
laugh about sth that is serious or should be taken seriously: *Don't make a joke of it! I could lose my job because of this!*

take a ˈjoke
find a joke or trick which is played on you amusing and accept it: *He didn't think it was funny at all when we put that pin on his chair. He really can't take a joke, can he?*

crack a joke → **crack**
(play) a practical joke (on sb) → **practical**

joker

the ˌjoker in the ˈpack
a person or thing who could change the way that things will happen in a way that cannot be predicted: *Everyone knew each other well, except for the new guy Jason, who was the joker in the pack.*

> ❷ NOTE
> The *pack* here is a set of playing cards. In every pack there are two extra cards, which are called *jokers*.

joking

ˌjoking aˈpart/aˈside (*BrE*)
used to show that you are now being serious after you have said sth funny: *No, but joking apart, do you think we should go and see if she's OK?*

you must be ˈjoking!; you're ˈjoking! (*informal*)
used to show that you do not believe sth, or that you find sth ridiculous: *'It's the best film I've ever seen.' 'You must be joking!'* ◇ *'The boss wants us to work late again.' 'What? You're joking!'*

jolly

jolly ˈgood! (*old-fashioned, BrE, spoken*)
used to show that you approve of sth that sb has just said: *So you and Alan are going away for the weekend, are you? Jolly good.*

ˈjolly well (*old-fashioned, BrE*)
used to emphasize a statement when you are annoyed about sth: *If you don't come now, you can jolly well walk home!*

Joneses

keep up with the ˈJoneses (*informal, disapproving*)
try to have all the possessions and social achievements that your neighbours or other people around you have, especially by buying what they buy: *First the Smiths got a swimming pool, and now their neighbours, the Sinclairs, are building one. It's silly the way people always have to keep up with the Joneses.*

> ❷ NOTE
> *Jones* is a very common surname, and is used to refer to neighbours in general.

jot

not one/a jot (or tittle) (*informal*)
not even the smallest amount: *There's not a jot of truth in the story.* ◇ *It seems that his divorce has not affected him one jot.* ◇ *She doesn't seem to care a jot what I do.*

Jove

by 'Jove (*old-fashioned, spoken, especially BrE*)
used to express surprise or to emphasize a statement: *By Jove, I think you might be right!*

❶ ORIGIN
Jove is another name for *Jupiter*. In Roman mythology, he was the king of the gods.

jowl

cheek by jowl (with sb/sth) → cheek

joy

(get/have) no 'joy (from sb) (*informal*)
(get/have) no success or luck in getting sth you want: *I tried to find that record but no joy.* ◇ *'I've just been fishing.' 'Any joy?' 'Yes, I caught a big one.'* ◇ *You won't get any joy from her. She doesn't give money to any kind of charity.*

a bundle of joy → bundle
your pride and joy → pride

joys

full of the joys of spring → full

judge

don't judge a ˌbook by its 'cover (*saying*)
used to say that you should not form an opinion about sb/sth from their appearance only: *When we arrived we found that the hotel we'd booked looked awful, but as they say, you should never judge a book by its cover.*

(as) sober as a judge → sober

judgement (*especially BrE*) (*AmE usually* judgment)

against your better judgement → better
pass judgement (on/about sb/sth) → pass
sit in judgement (on/over sb) → sit
a value judgement → value

juggling

a balancing/juggling act → act

jugular

go for the 'jugular (*informal*)
attack sb's weakest point during a discussion in an aggressive way: *Harry decided that there was no point trying to be nice to these people—he would have to go straight for the jugular.*

❷ NOTE
The *jugular vein* is a large vein in the neck that carries blood from the head to the heart.

jump

be/stay one jump a'head (of sb/sth)
have/keep your advantage over sb by taking action before they do or by making sure you know more than they do: *For years he has managed to* stay one jump ahead of the police. ◇ *People who are successful in business are always one jump ahead of the competition.*

go (and) jump in a/the 'lake (*spoken*)
used to tell sb in a rude way to go away or to stop doing something: *I'm sick of you and your stupid questions. Go and jump in the lake!* ◇ *She made me so angry that I told her to go jump in a lake.*

jump down sb's 'throat (*informal*)
react to sth that sb has said or done by suddenly speaking to them angrily: *He asked her a very simple question and she jumped down his throat. He couldn't believe it.* ◇ *It's not my fault. Don't jump down my throat.*

jump the 'gun (*informal*)
do sth before the right time: *They jumped the gun by building the garage before they got permission from the town council.*

❶ ORIGIN
This idiom refers to an athlete in a race who starts running before the starter has fired the gun.

jump the 'lights (*informal*)
drive on when the traffic lights are red: *A policeman stopped us for jumping the lights.*

jump out of your 'skin (*informal*)
make a quick, sudden movement because sth has suddenly frightened you: *When I heard the explosion, I nearly jumped out of my skin.* ◇ *She nearly jumped out of her skin when somebody banged on the door in the middle of the night.*

The sight of a spider made her jump out of her skin.

jump the 'queue (*BrE*) (*AmE* **jump the 'line**)
go to the front of a line of people without waiting for your turn: *I get very angry with people who jump the queue.*

jump 'ship
1 (of a sailor) leave the ship on which you are

serving, without permission: *Two of the sailors jumped ship in New York.*
2 leave an organization that you belong to, suddenly and unexpectedly: *When they realized that the company was in serious financial trouble, quite a few of the staff jumped ship.*

jump through 'hoops
do sth difficult or complicated in order to achieve sth: *How did you manage to get permission for this? Did you have to jump through hoops?*

jump 'to it (*AmE* also **hop 'to it**) (*informal*)
used to tell sb to hurry and do sth quickly: *You have got ten minutes to clean this room. Now jump to it.* ◇ *Hop to it, will you? We don't have much time.*

be for the high jump → **high**
climb/jump on the bandwagon → **bandwagon**
jump in/be thrown in at the deep end → **deep**
jump/leap to conclusions → **conclusions**
a quantum jump → **quantum**
take a running jump → **running**

jungle
the law of the jungle → **law**

jury
the jury is/are (still) 'out (on sth)
people have not yet decided if sth is good or bad: *No one knows whether the government's housing policy is popular or not. The jury is still out on that until the next election.* ◇ *Was he a good leader? The jury is still out on that question.*

❷ NOTE
The *jury* is a group of members of the public who listen to the facts of a case in a court of law and decide whether or not sb is guilty of a crime. They leave the courtroom to discuss the case and make their decision in secret.

just
could/might just as well …
used to say that you/sb would have been in the same position if you had done sth else, because you got little benefit or enjoyment from what you did do: *The weather was so bad we might just as well have stayed at home.*

just about (*informal*)
1 almost; nearly: *I've just about finished my essay.* ◇ *'Do you feel all right?' 'I suppose so, just about.'*
2 approximately; about: *The company has lost just about a million pounds this year.* ◇ *It was just about midnight when they arrived.*

just like 'that
suddenly and unexpectedly: *She announced that she was leaving her job at the end of this week, just like that.*

just a 'minute/'moment/'second (*informal*)
used to ask sb to wait for a short time: *'Is Mr Burns available?' 'Just a second, please, I'll check.'*

just 'now
1 at this moment: *Come and see me later—I'm busy just now.*
2 during this present period: *Business is good just now.*
3 only a short time ago: *I saw her just now.*

just 'so
1 as it should be; with everything in its proper place or with everything done properly: *He likes his office to be just so, with everything in its place.*
2 (*old-fashioned, formal*) yes, I agree: *'This must never happen again.' 'Just so.'*

just 'then
at that moment: *Just then, someone knocked at the front door.*

not just 'yet
not now but probably quite soon: *I can't give you the money just yet.*

that's just 'it (also **that's just the 'trouble**) (*informal*)
that is exactly the problem: *'You only need to spend £5 more and you can get a really good dictionary.' 'That's just it, I'm afraid—I haven't got another £5.'*

justice
bring sb to 'justice
arrest sb for a crime and put them on trial in a court of law: *It is his job to bring the murderer to justice.*

do justice to 'sb/'sth; ,do sb/sth 'justice
say or do sth which shows that you know or recognize the true value of sb/sth; show the true value of sth: *They were not hungry and couldn't do justice to her excellent cooking.* ◇ *This picture doesn't do him justice; he's much better-looking in real life.*

,do yourself 'justice
do sth as well as you can in order to show other people how good you are: *She's a very good painter, but in her recent work she hasn't done herself justice.* ◇ *He didn't do himself justice in the match. He hadn't trained hard enough.*

pervert the course of justice → **pervert**
poetic justice → **poetic**
rough justice → **rough**

justifies
the end justifies the means → **end**

K k

keel

on an even keel → even

keen

(as) ˌkeen as ˈmustard (*BrE*, *informal*)
wanting very much to do well at sth; enthusiastic: *She's as keen as mustard. She always gets here first in the morning and she's the last to leave work in the evening.*

be mad keen (on sb/sth) → mad

keep

Most idioms containing the verb **keep** are at the entries for the nouns or adjectives in the idioms, for example **keep your nose clean** is at **nose**.

ˌkeep ˈgoing
1 make an effort to live normally when you are in a difficult situation or when you have experienced great suffering: *You just have to keep yourself busy and keep going.*
2 (*spoken*) used to encourage sb to continue doing sth: *Keep going, Sarah, you're nearly there.*

ˌkeep sb ˈgoing (*informal*)
be enough for sb until they get what they are waiting for: *Why don't you have an apple to keep you going till dinner time?*

ˌkeep it ˈup
used to tell sb to continue doing sth as well as they are already doing it: *They've done well so far. I just wonder how long they can keep it up.*

ˌkeep sth to yourˈself
not tell other people about sth: *I don't want John to know about this, so keep it to yourself.*

keep yourˌself to yourˈself
avoid meeting people socially or becoming involved in their affairs: *My neighbour keeps himself to himself. We smile and say 'good morning,' but that's all.*

keepers

finders keepers → finders

keeping

in sb's ˈkeeping
being taken care of by sb: *The documents were all in the safe keeping of the family solicitor, and would remain so until her death.*

in ˈkeeping (with sth)
appropriate or expected in a particular situation; in agreement with sth: *The furniture should be in keeping with the style of the house.*

out of ˈkeeping (with sth)
not appropriate or expected in a particular situation; not in agreement with sth: *Her remarks were quite out of keeping with the formality of the occasion.*

keeps

for ˈkeeps (*informal*)
permanently; for ever: *'Are you really giving me this beautiful ring?' 'Yes, it's yours. For keeps.'*

ken

beyond/outside your ˈken (*old-fashioned*)
not within your knowledge or understanding: *Such things are beyond my ken.*

> **❷ NOTE**
> *Ken* is another word for 'knowledge'.

kettle

a different kettle of fish → different
the pot calling the kettle black → pot

key

under lock and key → lock

kibosh

put the ˈkibosh on sth (*old-fashioned*, *informal*)
stop sth from happening: *Melissa's parents put the kibosh on her plans for a big party at her house on her birthday.*

> **❶ ORIGIN**
> The word *kibosh* possibly comes from a Yiddish word meaning 'suppress'.

kick

get a ˈkick from/out of sth (*informal*)
get a feeling of excitement, enjoyment, etc. out of sth: *She got a real kick from seeing her photo in the newspaper.*

ˌkick against the ˈpricks
harm yourself by protesting when it is useless to do so: *People in prison learn very quickly not to kick against the pricks. If they complain, the prison officers make their lives very difficult.*

kick (some/sb's) ˈass (⚠, *slang*, *especially AmE*)
punish or defeat sb

ˌkick the ˈbucket (*BrE*, *informal* or *humorous*)
die: *He got married for the first time when he was 85 and a week later he kicked the bucket.*

> **❶ ORIGIN**
> This idiom refers to the killing of animals for food. They were hung from a wooden frame (the *bucket*), which they would kick as they were dying.

kick the 'habit, 'drug, 'booze, etc.

stop doing sth harmful that you have done for a long time: *According to research, only one smoker in a hundred is able to kick the habit without some kind of help.*

kick your 'heels (*BrE, informal*)

have nothing to do while you are waiting for sth: *I've been kicking my heels here for an hour, waiting for the passport office to open.*

kick sb in the 'teeth (*informal*)

treat sb badly or fail to give them help when they need it: *The workers feel they've been kicked in the teeth by their employers. They have met all their orders this year but are still being made redundant.*
▶ **a kick in the 'teeth** *noun*: *I expected to get that job. It was a real kick in the teeth when I didn't.*

kick over the 'traces (*old-fashioned, BrE*)

start to behave badly and refuse to accept any discipline or control: *She smokes and she drinks. She's really kicking over the traces, and her parents don't know what to do with her.*

> **❶ ORIGIN**
> This expression refers to a horse trying to break free from the straps that attach it to a carriage or wagon (= the *traces*).

a kick up the 'backside (also a kick in the 'pants) (*informal*)

a shock, strong criticism, etc. which encourages sb to do sth or to behave better: *What he needs is a good kick up the backside. Then he'd do some work.*

kick up a 'fuss, 'row, etc. (*informal*)

complain very noisily and loudly about sth: *He kicked up a real fuss about the slow service in the restaurant.* ◇ *Every time her newspaper arrives late, she kicks up a fuss.*

kick up your 'heels (*informal, especially AmE*)

be relaxed and enjoy yourself: *Now that he's more confident in his job, perhaps he can kick up his heels and stop looking so worried all the time.*

kick sb up'stairs (*informal*)

move sb to a job that seems to be more important but which actually has less power or influence: *They couldn't sack him, so they kicked him upstairs onto the board of directors, where he could do less damage.*

kick sb when they're 'down

continue to hurt sb when they are already defeated, etc: *George generally believed that you should never kick a man when he's down, but thought that this time he might make an exception.*

'kick yourself (*informal*)

be angry with yourself for sth you have done or not done: *Buy it. It's a real bargain. You'll kick yourself if you don't.* ◇ *I told John that Susan was really lazy. Then somebody told me that she was a good friend of his. I could have kicked myself for being so stupid.*

beat/knock/kick the hell out of sb ➔ **hell**
kick up/make/create/raise a stink (about sth) ➔ **stink**

kicking

alive and kicking ➔ **alive**

kicks

for 'kicks (*informal*)

(especially of crime or violence) done for excitement and pleasure: *They destroyed the telephone boxes just for kicks.* ◇ *'Why did he steal the car?' 'Just for kicks. He was bored.'*

kid

handle, treat, etc. sb with kid 'gloves

treat sb very carefully and gently because you do not want to upset them or make them angry: *She is so easily upset that I feel I have to treat her with kid gloves all the time.*

kid stuff = kids' stuff ➔ **kids**
a/the new kid on the block ➔ **new**

kidding

no 'kidding (*spoken*)

1 (*sometimes ironic*) used to emphasize that sth is true or that you agree with sth that sb has just said: *'It's cold!' 'No kidding!'*
2 used to show that you mean what you are saying: *I want the money back tomorrow. No kidding.*

you're 'kidding; you must be 'kidding (*spoken*)

used to show that you are very surprised at sth that sb has just said: *'Did you hear about Christine? She won some money on the lottery.' 'You're kidding! How much?'*

kids

'kids' stuff (*BrE*) (*AmE* 'kid stuff)

something that is very easy to do or understand: *'What did you think of the maths exam?' 'Kids' stuff. I'm sure I've passed.'*

kill

kill the fatted 'calf

welcome home sb who has been away for a long time by having a big celebration: *My brother's coming home tomorrow, so I expect my parents will be killing the fatted calf for him.*

> **❶ ORIGIN**
> This comes from a story in the Bible, in which a father arranged a banquet when his son returned to the family.

kill the goose that lays the golden 'egg/'eggs (*saying*)

destroy sth that would make you rich, successful, etc: *By trying to stop people smoking, the govern-*

ment may be killing the goose that lays the golden eggs, because it makes millions of pounds from the tax on cigarettes.

❶ ORIGIN
This saying comes from a Greek legend about a farmer who had a goose that laid golden eggs. The farmer thought that he would make himself rich by killing the goose, expecting to get all the eggs inside. However, by killing the goose, the farmer ended up with nothing.

kill or 'cure (*BrE*)
extreme action which will either be a complete success or a complete failure: *This new chemical will either clean the painting perfectly or it will damage it badly. It's kill or cure.*

kill sth stone 'dead (*informal*)
completely destroy sth; end sth: *This has killed my chances of promotion in this company stone dead.*

kill 'time, a couple of 'hours, etc.; have (got) 'time, a couple of 'hours, etc. to kill
do sth to help pass the time while you are waiting for sth: *'What did you do at the airport when your plane was late?' 'We killed time by playing cards and doing crosswords.'* ◇ *I had two hours to kill before the train left, so I went to see a film.*

kill two birds with one 'stone
manage to achieve two aims by doing one thing: *If we have to go to Manchester for the meeting, then let's visit Joan on the way there. We can kill two birds with one stone.*

kill sb with 'kindness
harm sb by being too kind to them, usually without realizing what you are doing: *The patient needs lots of exercise. Don't let him stay in bed—you'll kill him with kindness.*

kill yourself (laughing) (*BrE, informal*)
laugh a lot: *It was a very funny film. We killed ourselves laughing from beginning to end.* ◇ *He just stood there, killing himself laughing.*

kill yourself doing sth (*informal*)
make a very great effort to do sth: *It would be good to leave at 7 o'clock, but don't kill yourself getting here by then. We can leave a bit later if we need to.* ◇ *I nearly killed myself finishing the report in time for this meeting.*

be in at the death/kill → **death**
dressed to kill → **dressed**
if looks could kill … → **looks**

killed

curiosity killed the cat → **curiosity**

killing

make a 'killing (*informal*)
make a lot of money quickly: *He was clever. He invested a lot of money in property. When prices went up, he made a killing.*

kilter

out of 'kilter
out of harmony or balance; not working properly: *Long-haul flights tend to throw your body clock out of kilter for a couple of days.*

kin

kith and kin → **kith**
your next of kin → **next**

kind

in 'kind
1 (of payment) in the form of goods or services, not money: *People in the country used to pay the doctor in kind with meat, vegetables, eggs and things like that.*
2 do the same thing to sb as they have done to you, usually something unpleasant: *If they attack our troops, we will retaliate in kind.*

'kind of/'sort of (*informal*)
used with adjectives, adverbs and verbs when something is difficult to describe or when the word you use is not exactly what you mean: *My new dress is sort of green.* ◇ *He said it sort of nervously.* ◇ *She kind of smiled at me.*

❷ NOTE
These phrases are sometimes written or spoken as *kinda* or *sorta*.

nothing of the 'kind/'sort (*informal*)
not at all as sb said or as you expected: *The brochure said it would be a beginners' course but it's nothing of the sort.* ◇ *I said nothing of the kind. She completely misunderstood me.*

(two) of a 'kind/'sort
(two) people or things with similar characteristics: *Uncle Fred and your father are two of a kind; football and beer, that's all they seem to be interested in.* ◇ *He always uses the same style of photography and similar music so all his films are very much of a kind.*

of a 'kind/'sort (*disapproving*)
(used after a noun) of poor quality; not what sb/sth should be: *He is a poet of a kind.* ◇ *They gave us meat of a sort; we could hardly eat it.*

one of a 'kind
the only one like this: *My father was one of a kind—I'll never be like him.*

something of the/that 'kind/'sort
something like what has been said: *'He's resigning.' 'I'd suspected something of the kind.'*

be cruel to be kind → **cruel**

kindly

not take 'kindly to sb/sth
find it difficult to accept sb/sth: *I don't take kindly to criticism from him.* ◇ *She didn't take kindly to my suggestion.*

look kindly on/upon sth/sb → **look**

kindness

kill sb with kindness → **kill**
the milk of human kindness → **milk**

King

the King's/Queen's English → **English**
turn King's/Queen's evidence → **turn**

king

a ˌking's 'ransom (*literary*)

a very large amount of money: *We don't exactly get paid a king's ransom in this job.*

> **🛈 ORIGIN**
> In the past, if a king was captured in a war, his country would pay a ransom for his release.

live like a king → **live**
(be) the uncrowned king/queen (of sth) → **uncrowned**

kingdom

blow, send, etc. sb to kingdom 'come (*informal*)

kill sb, especially with a gun, a bomb or other very violent methods: *'If you try to call the police, I'll blow you to kingdom come.'*

till/until kingdom 'come (*old-fashioned*)

for a long time, for ever: *You can dig here until kingdom come, but you will never find water.*

kiss

ˌkiss and 'tell

a way of referring to sb talking publicly, usually for money, about a past sexual relationship with sb famous: *Despite all the money the tabloids were offering for her story, she was determined not to kiss and tell.*

kiss sb's 'arse (*BrE*) (*AmE* kiss sb's 'ass) (⚠, slang)

be very nice to sb in order to persuade them to help you or to give you sth

> **❓ NOTE**
> A more polite way to express this is 'lick sb's boots.'

ˌkiss sth 'better (*spoken*)

take away the pain of an injury by kissing it: *Come here and let me kiss it better.*

the kiss of 'death (*informal, often humorous*)

an action or event that seems good, but is certain to make sth else fail: *When the chairman said he had every confidence in me, I knew it was the kiss of death. A week later I was looking for another job.*

> **🛈 ORIGIN**
> This expression comes from a mafia custom, where a kiss from the mafia boss meant that the person receiving it would soon die.

the kiss of 'life (*BrE*)

1 a method of helping sb who has stopped breathing to breathe again by placing your mouth on theirs and forcing air into their lungs: *He gave the child the kiss of life, but unfortunately it was too late to save her.*
2 any thing or action that saves an organization, business, etc: *This loan is the kiss of life that our company needs.*

kiss sth goodbye = kiss/say goodbye to sth → **goodbye**
steal a kiss (from sb) → **steal**

kit

get your 'kit off (*BrE, slang*)

take your clothes off

the whole kit and caboodle = the whole caboodle → **caboodle**

kitchen

everything but/bar the kitchen 'sink (*informal, humorous*)

many more things than are necessary: *She was only staying for a few days, but she brought everything with her bar the kitchen sink!*

They always take everything but the kitchen sink when they go on holiday.

kite

fly a kite → **fly**
(go) fly a/your kite → **fly**
(as) high as a kite → **high**

kith

kith and 'kin (*old-fashioned*)

friends and relatives: *He has returned to live in Italy, where he'll be surrounded by his kith and kin.*

kittens

have 'kittens (*BrE, informal*)

be nervous and anxious, especially when you are waiting for news of sth: *Your poor mother's having kittens. She hasn't heard anything from Simon for three weeks.*

knee

at your mother's knee ➔ **mother**
on bended knee(s) ➔ **bended**

knee-high

knee-high to a 'grasshopper (*informal, humorous*)
(of a child) very young and small: *I haven't seen you since you were knee-high to a grasshopper!*

knees

bring sb to their 'knees
show sb that they are weak; defeat sb, especially in a war

bring sth to its 'knees
badly affect an organization, etc. so that it can no longer function: *The strikes brought the industry to its knees.*

your/sb's knees are knocking (*informal*)
if your/sb's **knees are knocking**, they are shaking because you are nervous or afraid: *It was the first time I'd ever spoken in public, and my knees were knocking!*

on your 'knees
1 kneeling down: *He was on his knees praying.* ◇ *She was on her knees looking for the coin.*
2 in a very weak state: *The country's economy is on its knees.*

the bee's knees ➔ **bee**
be/go weak at the knees ➔ **weak**
on your hands and knees ➔ **hands**

knell

sound the death knell of sth ➔ **sound**

knickers

get/have your 'knickers in a twist (*BrE, informal*)
react too strongly to a difficult situation by getting angry, upset, confused, etc: *Don't get your knickers in a twist! It's not the end of the world.* ◇ *The boss is getting his knickers in a twist about these sales figures.*

wet your pants/knickers ➔ **wet**

knife

get your knife into sb; have (got) your knife in sb (*informal*)
harm and continue to harm sb (usually not physically) whom you consider your enemy: *He's had his knife into me for months, and every time I make a mistake, he tells my boss.*

go under the 'knife (*informal*)
have a medical operation: *Peter hates his nose so much that he's seriously considering going under the knife to have it made smaller.*

like a knife through 'butter
(cut/go) through sth hard easily: *It went through the metal door like a knife through butter.*

turn/twist the 'knife (in the wound)
deliberately remind sb of sth they are already upset about, and so upset them even more: *After the divorce, her friend turned the knife in the wound by saying she had always thought that the marriage wouldn't last.* ◇ *All right. I know I was stupid. You don't have to twist the knife.*

(you could) cut the atmosphere with a knife ➔ **cut**
not the sharpest knife in the drawer ➔ **sharpest**

knife-edge

on a 'knife-edge (also **on a 'razor's edge**)
in a very dangerous or difficult situation where there is a risk of sth terrible happening: *The future of this company is on a razor's edge.* ◇ *He was balanced on a knife-edge between life and death.*

knifepoint

at 'knifepoint
while being threatened, or threatening sb, with a knife: *She was attacked at knifepoint.*

knight

a knight in shining 'armour (*BrE*) (*AmE* **a knight in shining 'armor**) (*usually humorous*)
a person (usually a man) who arrives to help you when you are in trouble or danger: *My car broke down at the roundabout. Luckily, a knight in shining armour stopped to help me.*

knit

knit your 'brows
frown (= move your eyebrows together), to show that you are thinking hard, feeling angry, etc: *She knitted her brows, trying to think how she could have spent so much money in one week.*

knives

the knives are 'out (for sb)
the situation has become so bad that people are preparing to make one person take the blame, for example by taking away their job: *The knives are out for the chancellor. People are demanding his resignation.*

knobs

with 'knobs on (*BrE, slang*)
used to say that sth is a more complicated version of what you mention: *It isn't art—it's just a horror movie with knobs on!*

knock

I'll knock your 'block/'head off! (*BrE, spoken*)
used to threaten sb that you will hit them

knock sb 'dead (*spoken*)
impress sb very much: *You look fabulous—you'll knock 'em dead tonight.*

knock sb/sth into a cocked 'hat (*BrE*)
be very much better than sb/sth: *This new soft-*

ware is going to knock everything else on the market into a cocked hat.

knock it 'off! (*spoken*)
used to tell sb to stop making a noise, annoying you, etc: *Knock it off, will you? I'm trying to work.*

knock sb off their 'perch/'pedestal
show that sb does not deserve to be admired so much: *These revelations will really knock him off his pedestal.*

knock sth on the 'head (*BrE, informal*)
stop doing sth; stop sth from happening: *By lunchtime we were all exhausted so we knocked it on the head.* ◇ *The increase in prices has knocked our plan to buy a house on the head.*

knock sb 'sideways (*informal*)
surprise or shock sb so much that they are unable to react immediately: *Losing his job has really knocked him sideways.*

knock 'spots off sb/sth (*BrE, informal*)
be very much better than sb/sth else: *This book knocks spots off all the other books on Napoleon.* ◇ *You'll knock spots off her. You're a much better player.*

knock the 'stuffing out of sb (*informal*)
make sb feel weak, mentally and/or physically: *When his wife left him, it seemed to knock the stuffing out of him.* ◇ *This flu has really knocked the stuffing out of me.*

take a (hard, nasty, etc.) 'knock
have an experience that makes sb/sth less confident or successful; be damaged: *His reputation has taken a bit of a knock since the newspapers printed stories about his private life.*

bang/knock your/their heads together ➜ **heads**
beat/knock/kick the hell out of sb ➜ **hell**
blow/knock sb's socks off ➜ **socks**
get/knock/lick sb/sth into shape ➜ **shape**
hit/knock sb/sth for six ➜ **six**
knock/throw sb for a loop ➜ **loop**
knock on wood = touch wood ➜ **touch**
knock/talk some sense into sb ➜ **sense**

knocked

you could have knocked me, etc. down with a 'feather (*informal*)
used to tell sb about a very surprising experience: *When they said how much the painting was worth, you could have knocked me down with a feather!*

knocking

your/sb's knees are knocking ➜ **knees**

knot

cut/untie the Gordian knot ➜ **Gordian**
tie the knot ➜ **tie**

knots

at a rate of knots ➜ **rate**
tie sb/yourself up in knots ➜ **tie**

knotted

get knotted = get stuffed ➜ **stuffed**

know

be not to 'know
have no way of realizing or being aware that you have done sth wrong: *'I'm sorry I called when you were asleep.' 'Don't worry—you weren't to know.'*

before you know where you 'are
before you have time to realize that sth has happened: *We were whisked off in a taxi before we knew where we were.* ◇ *Before she knew where she was, her bag had been snatched and the thief was running away with it.*

for all 'I, 'you, etc. know (*spoken*)
used to emphasize that sb does not know sth: *She could be dead for all I know.*

in the 'know (*informal*)
having information or knowledge that most other people do not have: *Only a few of us were in the know about the date of the wedding. We didn't want the press to find out.* ◇ *People in the know say that this is the best Spanish wine you can buy.*

it ˌtakes one to 'know one (*informal, disapproving*)
you are the same kind of person as the person you are criticizing: *'Your brother is a real idiot.' 'Well, it takes one to know one.'*

know sb/sth 'backwards (*informal, especially BrE*)
know sb/sth extremely well: *He must know the play backwards by now—he's seen it six times!*

know 'best
know what should be done in a situation because you have knowledge and/or experience: *'I want to get up.' 'But the doctor said you were to stay in bed, and he knows best.'* ◇ *Everyone said that I shouldn't go there alone but I thought I knew best.*

know 'better (than that/than to do sth)
be sensible enough not to do sth: *You left the car unlocked? I thought you'd know better.* ◇ *He knows better than to judge by appearances.*

know sb by 'sight
recognize sb and know who they are, without having spoken to them: *I haven't actually met Dr. Galston, but I know him by sight of course.*

know 'different/'otherwise (*informal*)
have more information about sth: *She thought he was upset about the divorce, but I knew different.*

know sth ˌfull/ˌperfectly/ˌvery 'well
used when you wish to indicate that the person you are speaking to already knows sth you have just said or are about to say: *You know full well that smoking is forbidden in this room.* ◇ *You know perfectly well what I am referring to.*

know sb/sth inside 'out (*informal*)
know sb/sth very well: *You've read that book so*

often that you must know it inside out by now. ◇ She knows me inside out. I can't hide anything from her.

know sth like the back of your 'hand (*informal*)
know a place very well: *As a taxi-driver, you have to know the city like the back of your hand.*

know no 'bounds
(usually with abstract nouns) be without limits; be very great: *His generosity knows no bounds.*

know your 'onions (*old-fashioned, BrE, informal*)
know a lot about a particular subject: *He's spent years studying Roman archaeology, so he really knows his onions.*

know your own 'mind
know what you want or like: *At 25 you're old enough to know your own mind and make these decisions for yourself.*

know your 'place
behave in a way that shows that you know what your social position is and which people are more important than you: *My grandfather believed that life was simpler when he was young, when everybody knew their place.*

know the 'score (*informal*)
know the true situation, especially if this is bad: *Look, you know the score, we can't afford a holiday right now.*

know your 'stuff (*informal*)
know everything that you should know about a job, a subject, etc: *I was very impressed by your lawyer. He really knows his stuff.*

know a thing or two (about sb/sth) (*informal*)
know a lot about sb/sth from your own experience: *After ten years as a teacher, I know a thing or two about how children learn.* ◇ *'How much do you know about computers?' 'Oh, I know a thing or two.'*

know your way a'bout/a'round (sth)
be familiar with a place, with how things are done etc.; be experienced: *I'd used the library before, so I knew my way around and found the book quite quickly.*

know what you're 'doing/a'bout (*informal*)
have experience of doing sth and therefore understand it fully: *'I'm worried about David using that machine.' 'Don't worry. He knows what he's doing.'*

know what you're 'talking about (*informal*)
have good knowledge of sth; be an expert on sth: *I really enjoyed that lecture. She certainly knows what she's talking about.* ◇ *That history teacher doesn't know what he's talking about. He makes a lot of mistakes.*

know what's 'good for you
know what is necessary for you to do to be successful, etc.; know how to avoid trouble: *If you know what's good for you, young man, you'll talk to nobody about what you've seen here tonight.*

know what it 'is to be/do sth
have personal experience of being/doing sth: *I*

know what it is to be a mother, so believe me when I say it is very hard work.

know what's 'what (*informal*)
know all that needs to be known in a particular situation or in general: *Ask Ann. She knows what's what. She's been here for years.*

know where you 'are/'stand
know what your position is; know what sb expects of you: *I don't know where I stand with him. I don't know what he feels about me.* ◇ *Has she talked to you about your chances of promotion? Do you know where you stand?*

know where you're going
know clearly what you want to achieve (in life, in your job, etc.): *He knows exactly where he's going. He wants to be an actor.*

know which side your 'bread is buttered (*informal*)
know what to do in order to gain advantages, stay in a favourable situation, etc: *I'm sure Ray will make a special effort to please the new supervisor—after all, he knows which side his bread is buttered!*

not know any 'better
not behave well, politely, etc. because you have never learned how to: *You can't blame him for his bad table manners; he doesn't know any better.*

not know you're 'born (*BrE, spoken*)
not realize how easy your life or situation is compared to other people's: *Young people today don't know they're born. Life was much harder when I was a child.*

not know your ˌarse from your 'elbow (*BrE*) (*AmE* **not know your ˌass from your 'elbow**) (⚠, *slang*)
be very stupid or completely lacking in skill: *Don't ask him to organize things! He doesn't know his arse from his elbow!*

not know the first 'thing about sb/sth
know nothing at all about sb/sth: *I don't know the first thing about Chinese history.*

not know sb from 'Adam (*informal*)
not know who sb is: *This man came into the office and he said that he knew me. I didn't know him from Adam, which was a bit embarrassing.*

not know the 'meaning of the word (*disapproving*)
not have enough experience of sth to understand what it really is; not be capable of really understanding sth: *Love? He doesn't know the meaning of the word.* ◇ *They talk about justice, but they don't know the meaning of the word.*

not know what you're 'missing
not realize how good, amusing, interesting, etc. sth is because you have never tried it: *'I'm not really interested in snowboarding.' 'Oh, you should give it a try. You don't know what you're missing.'*

not know what 'hit you (*informal*)
be so surprised by sth that you do not know how to

react: *You should have seen his reaction! He didn't know what had hit him!*

not know what to 'do with yourself
not know how to spend your time: *I hardly know what to do with myself when the children go back to school. I have so much free time.*

not know whether you're 'coming or 'going (*informal*)
be confused about what you are doing, because you are doing too many things at the same time: *I've got so much work to do that I don't know whether I'm coming or going.*

not know whether to 'laugh or 'cry (*informal*)
be unable to decide how to react to a bad or unfortunate situation: *Can you believe she said that to me? I didn't know whether to laugh or cry!*

not know which way/where to 'look (*informal*)
not know how to react or behave in an embarrassing situation: *When a half-naked woman walked into the room, nobody knew where to look.*

not know which way/where to 'turn
not know what to do, where to get help, etc. in a difficult situation: *She didn't know where to turn for help when her daughter started taking drugs.*

(well) what do you 'know (about 'that)? (*informal*)
used to express surprise: *Well, what do you know? Look who's here!*

‚you 'know (*informal*)
1 used when you are thinking of what to say next: *He's, you know, strange. It's hard to explain.*
2 used to show that what you are referring to is known or understood by the person you are speaking to: *You know I bought a new bag? Well, someone stole it last night.*
3 used to emphasize sth that you are saying: *I'm not stupid, you know.*

‚you know as well as 'I do
used when you are trying to convince sb that sth is true: *You know as well as I do that if she finds out, she'll stop us going.*

you know 'who/'what (*spoken*)
used to refer to sb/sth without mentioning a name: *I saw you know who this morning. She didn't even say hello to me.*

you never 'know (with sb/sth)
you cannot be sure (about the behaviour of sb/sth or the quality of sth): *Don't throw away those old stamps. You never know, they might be valuable one day.* ◇ *You never know with him; one day he's smiling and laughing, the next day he won't speak to anybody.*

better the devil you know (than the devil you don't) → **better**
have/know all the answers → **answers**
have/know/get sth off pat → **pat**
have/know sth down pat → **pat**
I don't know what the world's coming to = what is the world coming to? → **world**

I know what = I/I'll tell you what → **tell**
the left hand doesn't know what the right hand's doing → **left**
let sb know → **let**
not know/not be able to tell one end of sth from the other → **end**
not want to know (about sth) → **want**
show sb/learn/know the ropes → **ropes**

knowing
there's no 'knowing/'saying/'telling ...
it is impossible to know/say/tell: *There is no telling what he may do when he gets angry.* ◇ *There's no saying what will happen.*

knowledge
be common/public 'knowledge
be sth that everyone knows, especially in a particular community or group: *What do you mean you're surprised he's leaving? I thought it was common knowledge that he was looking for another job!*

come to sb's 'knowledge (*formal*)
become known by sb: *It has come to our knowledge that you have been taking time off without permission.*

to your 'knowledge
from the information you have, although you may not know everything: *'Are they divorced?' 'Not to my knowledge.'*

have (got) a working knowledge of sth → **working**
safe in the knowledge that ... → **safe**
to the best of your belief/knowledge → **best**

known
make yourself 'known to sb
introduce yourself to sb: *I made myself known to the hotel manager.*

for a/some reason/reasons best known to himself, herself, etc. → **best**
have seen/known better days → **better**
if (the) truth be known/told → **truth**
let it be known; make it known that ... → **let**

knows
God/goodness/Heaven knows (*spoken*)
1 I do not know; no one knows: *'What's going to happen next?' 'God knows.'*
2 used for adding emphasis to a statement, opinion, etc: *God knows how he manages to survive on such a small salary.* ◇ *I'm no gardening expert, goodness knows!*
(Some people may find the use of **God knows** offensive.)

Lord (only) knows (what, where, why, etc.) ... → **Lord**

knuckles
give sb, get, etc. a rap over the knuckles → **rap**
rap sb over the knuckles → **rap**

LI

labour (BrE) (AmE labor)

a ˌlabour of ˈlove
work that you do for your own pleasure and satisfaction, not for money or profit: *This tablecloth is a real labour of love. It took her years to make it.*

labour the ˈpoint
continue to repeat or explain sth that is already clear: *I think you've said enough—there's no need to labour the point.*

lack

have/lack the courage of your convictions → **courage**
not for lack/want of trying → **trying**

Lad

a Jack the Lad → **Jack**

ladder

(at) the top of the tree/ladder → **top**

ladies

a ˈladies' man
a man who likes the company of women and is successful with them: *Jim had always been a bit of a ladies' man, and he didn't marry until he was 45.*

lads

be one of the ˈlads/ˈboys/ˈgirls (*informal*)
be a member of a group of friends of the same sex and a similar age, who meet regularly to enjoy themselves: *His wife doesn't understand that he likes being one of the lads from time to time.* ◇ *She's never really been one of the girls. She much prefers the company of men.*

lady

a bag lady → **bag**
it ain't/it's not over till the fat lady sings → **fat**

lager

a ˈlager lout (*BrE*)
a young man who drinks too much alcohol and then behaves in a noisy and unpleasant way: *The police will be cracking down on lager louts this summer.*

lake

go (and) jump in a/the lake → **jump**

lam

on the ˈlam (*AmE, informal*)
escaping from sb, especially from the police: *The man disappeared just before he was due to go to jail and has been on the lam ever since.*

lamb

be mutton dressed (up) as lamb → **mutton**
in two shakes of a lamb's tail → **two**
(like) a lamb/lambs to the slaughter → **slaughter**
(you, etc.) may/might as well be hanged/hung for a sheep as (for) a lamb → **well**

lame

a ˌlame ˈduck (*informal*)
a person or an organization that is in serious difficulties and needs help in order to survive: *My uncle is a bit of a lame duck. The family has to help him all the time.* ◇ *The shipping industry had become a lame duck.*

land

in the ˌland of the ˈliving (*humorous*)
alive: *Nice to see you. I'm glad to see that you're still in the land of the living.*

in the ˌland of ˈNod (*old-fashioned, humorous*)
asleep: *Pete and Jo were still in the land of Nod, so I went out for a walk in the morning sunshine.*

land a ˈblow, ˈpunch, etc.
succeed in hitting sb/sth: *She landed a punch on his chin.*

a/the land of ˌmilk and ˈhoney
a place where life is pleasant and easy and people are very happy: *She had always longed to travel to the United States and to see what she imagined as the land of milk and honey.*

> ❶ ORIGIN
> This phrase comes from the Bible, referring to the Promised Land.

see, etc. how the ˈland lies (*BrE*)
find out about a situation: *Let's wait and see how the land lies before we do anything.*

fall/land on your feet → **feet**
land yourself/sb in the soup = be in the soup → **soup**
the lay of the land = the lie of the land → **lie**
live off/on the fat of the land → **live**
live off the land → **live**
the promised land → **promised**
spy out the land → **spy**

landscape

a blot on the landscape → **blot**

lane

in the fast lane → **fast**
in the slow lane → **slow**
take a trip down memory lane = take sb/go down memory lane → **memory**

language

mind/watch your 'language
be careful about what you say in order not to upset or offend sb: *Watch your language, young man!*

speak/talk the same/a different 'language
share/not share ideas, experiences, opinions, etc., that make real communication or understanding possible: *Unions and managers are at last beginning to speak the same language.* ◇ *Artists and scientists simply talk a different language.*

lap

drop/dump sth in sb's 'lap (*informal*)
make sth the responsibility of another person: *They dropped the problem firmly back in my lap.*

drop/fall into sb's 'lap (*informal*)
be obtained without any effort: *A job's not going to just fall in your lap, you know. You'll have to go out and find one!*

in the lap of the 'gods
(the success of something is) uncertain because it depends on luck or on things beyond your control: *I don't know what's going to happen—it's in the lap of the gods now. All we can do is wait.*

in the lap of 'luxury
in easy, comfortable conditions, and enjoying the advantages of being rich: *I really enjoyed living in the lap of luxury for a couple of weeks. It was a wonderful hotel.*

the last lap → last

large

at 'large
1 (after a noun) as a whole, in general: *The public at large does not know enough about this problem.*
2 (of a dangerous person or animal) free; not captured: *Her killer is still at large.*

by and 'large (*informal*)
used when you are saying something that is generally, but not completely, true: *By and large, I enjoyed my time at university.*

in 'large part; in no small part (*formal*)
to a large extent: *The speech was in large part an attack on the Prime Minister.* ◇ *She was in no small part responsible for the success of this company and we mustn't forget that.*

(as) large as 'life (*humorous*)
used of sb who is seen in person, often unexpectedly: *I thought she'd left the country, but there she was, large as life, in the supermarket!*

loom large → loom
writ large → writ

larger

larger than 'life
looking or behaving in a way that is more interesting or exciting than other people, and so is likely to attract attention: *He's one of those larger than life characters.*

lark

be ,up/,rise with the 'lark
get up early in the morning: *She was up with the lark this morning.*

blow/sod⚠ that for a lark (*BrE, slang*)
used by sb who does not want to do sth because it involves too much effort: *Sod that for a lark! I'm not doing any more tonight.*

Larry

(as) happy as the day is long/as a clam/as Larry → happy

last

at (long) 'last
at the end of a period of waiting, trying etc.; finally: *At long last she's got a job in a theatre in Stratford.*

at the last 'count
according to the latest information about the numbers of sth: *She'd applied for 30 jobs at the last count.*

at the last 'minute/'moment
as late as possible; almost too late: *Why do you always have to arrive at the last moment?* ▶ **last-minute** *adj.*: *last-minute changes of plan, decisions, preparations, etc.*

the day, week, month, etc. before 'last
the day, week, etc. just before the most recent one; two days, weeks, etc. ago: *I haven't seen him since the summer before last.*

every last ...
every person or thing in a group: *We spent every last penny we had on the house.*

have the last 'laugh (*informal*)
be successful at sth in the end, even though other people thought that this was not possible: *When he invented this machine, everybody laughed at it, but he's sold 10000 of them. He certainly had the last laugh.*

have the last 'word
make the final point in a discussion or argument: *She always likes to have the last word in any argument.*

,last but not 'least; ,last but by no means 'least
used to say that the last person or thing on a list, etc. is as important as the others: *He thanked everyone for their help: Mr Watkins, Ms Smith, Ms Jackson, and last, but by no means least, Mr Jones.*

your/the last 'gasp
the point at which you/sth can no longer continue living, fighting, existing, etc: *People are saying that the group's latest actions are simply the last gasp of a dying campaign.*

the last I 'heard (*spoken*)

used to give the most recent news you have about sb/sth: *The last I heard he was still working at the garage.*

‚last ˈin, ‚first ˈout

used, for example in a situation when people are losing their jobs, to say that the last people to be employed will be the first to go

the last 'lap

the final part of sth which has taken a long time: *Her medical studies finish next year, so she's on the last lap now.* ◊ *They are on the last lap of their journey round the world.*

> ❷ NOTE
> A *lap* is a single circuit of a running track.

(as) a last re'sort

a thing you decide to do when everything else has failed: *Nobody wanted to lend me the money. As a last resort I asked my brother-in-law, and luckily he was able to help me.*

last 'thing (at night)

immediately before going to bed or to sleep: *They always had a cup of cocoa last thing at night.*

the ‚last 'word (in sth)

the most recent, most fashionable, etc. of its type: *They say that this new car is the last word in luxury.* ◊ *This is the last word in computer technology.*

on your/its ‚last 'legs

about to die or stop functioning very soon; be very weak or in bad condition: *He was on his last legs and would never paint another picture.* ◊ *This photocopier is on its last legs.*

to/till the 'last

until the last possible moment, especially until death: *He died protesting his innocence to the last.* ◊ *They loved each other till the last.*

be the last/final straw → **straw**
breathe your last → **breathe**
famous last words → **famous**
first and last → **first**
(be) the first/last (person) to do sth → **first**
from first to last → **first**
he who laughs last laughs longest → **laughs**
hear/see the end/the last of sb/sth → **hear**
in the last/final analysis → **analysis**
your/the last/final word (on/about sth) → **word**
a week yesterday, last Monday, etc. → **week**

last-ditch

a last-‚ditch 'stand/at'tempt/'effort

a final attempt to avoid defeat: *They are making a last-ditch stand to save the company.* ◊ *This is a last-ditch attempt to stop the strike.*

latch

on the 'latch (*BrE*)

closed but not locked: *Can you leave the door on the latch so I can get in?*

late

‚late in the 'day (*disapproving*)

(do sth) later than you should: *It's a bit late in the day to tell me you can't come. I've already bought the tickets.*

late of ... (*formal*)

until recently working or living in the place mentioned: *Professor Jones, late of York University*

of 'late (*formal*)

recently: *He has been feeling rather unwell of late. He ought to see the doctor.*

better late than never → **better**
have an early/a late night → **night**

later

later 'on (*informal*)

at a time in the future; after the time you are talking about: *I'm going out later on.* ◊ *Much later on, she realized what he had meant.*

see you later → **see**
sooner or later → **sooner**
sooner rather than later → **sooner**

lather

get into a 'lather; work yourself into a 'lather (*BrE, informal*)

get anxious or angry about sth, especially when it is not necessary: *Look, don't worry! There's no point getting yourself into a lather over this!*

in a 'lather (*BrE, informal*)

in a nervous, angry or excited state: *What's going on? Chris has just come rushing into my office all in a lather, saying something about a lost report.*

laugh

don't make me 'laugh (*spoken*)

used to show that you think what sb has just said is impossible or stupid: *'Will your dad lend you the money?' 'Don't make me laugh!'*

for a laugh; for laughs

for fun and amusement: *'Why did you hide her glasses?' 'Oh, just for a laugh.'* ◊ *We all went swimming at 2am for a laugh.*

have a (good) 'laugh (about sth)

find sth amusing: *I was angry at the time but we had a good laugh about it afterwards.*

laugh all the way to the 'bank (*informal*)

make a lot of money easily and feel very pleased about it: *With profits continuing to rise, both investors and company bosses are laughing all the way to the bank.*

laugh your 'head off

laugh very loudly and for a long time: *If old Mr Bradley could see you now he'd laugh his head off.*

laugh in sb's 'face (*informal*)

show in a very obvious way that you have no respect for sb: *When I made my suggestion at the meeting, everybody just laughed in my face.*

laugh like a 'drain (*BrE*)
laugh very loudly: *When I told him what had happened he laughed like a drain, as if it was the funniest thing he'd ever heard.*

laugh on the other side of your 'face (*BrE, informal*)
be forced to change from feeling pleased or satisfied to feeling disappointed or annoyed: *If you think you've tricked me, then you're wrong! You'll soon be laughing on the other side of your face!*

laugh sb/sth out of 'court (*BrE, informal*)
refuse, in an unpleasant way, to consider seriously sb's suggestion, opinion, etc. because you think it's stupid: *When she suggested trying the new treatment, they laughed her out of court.*

laugh up your 'sleeve (at sb/sth) (*informal*)
be secretly amused by sth: *Only he knew the whole story about the money. He must have been laughing up his sleeve all along.*

you have (got) to 'laugh (*spoken*)
used to say that you think there is a funny side to a situation: *Well, I'm sorry you've lost your shoes, but you've got to laugh, haven't you?*

have the last laugh → **last**
not know whether to laugh or cry → **know**
raise a laugh/smile → **raise**

laughing

be 'laughing (*spoken, informal*)
be in a fortunate position; have no worries: *If you can play like that in tomorrow's game you'll be laughing!*

a 'laughing stock
a person that everyone laughs at because they have done sth stupid: *I can't wear this to the party! I'll be a laughing stock!*

no laughing 'matter
something which is too serious to joke about: *Trying to find a place to live is no laughing matter.*

die laughing → **die**

laughs

a barrel/bundle of 'laughs (*informal, often ironic*)
very amusing; a lot of fun: *Life hasn't exactly been a barrel of laughs lately.*

he who laughs last laughs 'longest (*saying*)
do not be too proud of your present success; in the end another person may be more successful than you: *You think just because you've won this game, that means you're the best player. Well, wait until the championship. Remember, he who laughs last laughs longest.*

for laughs = for a laugh → **laugh**

laurels

look to your laurels → **look**
rest on your laurels → **rest**

Law

Murphy's Law → **Murphy**
Sod's Law → **Sod**

law

go to 'law (*BrE*)
ask a court of law to settle a problem or disagreement: *They went to law to get their property back.*

have the 'law on sb (*BrE, informal*)
(often used as a threat) report sb to the police: *If you have just one more noisy party, I'll have the law on you.*

law and 'order
a situation in which most people in a country respect and obey the law; public order: *There has been a breakdown in law and order in some parts of the country.* ◇ *The President praised the forces of law and order* (= the police and the army).

the ˌlaw of 'averages
the principle that one thing will happen as often as another if you try enough times: *Keep applying for jobs and by the law of averages you'll get one sooner or later.*

the ˌlaw of the 'jungle
a situation in which people are prepared to harm other people in order to succeed: *The police daren't go into certain parts of the city. It's the law of the jungle in there.* ◇ *In this business it's the law of the jungle.*

a law unto him'self, her'self, etc.
a person who does what they want, even when this is against the rules and customs of a group or society in general: *That man is a law unto himself. He comes to work when he likes, and when he's here he doesn't do what he's supposed to do.*

take the law into your own 'hands
take action personally against sb who has broken the law or done sth wrong, instead of calling the police: *I knew who had stolen my car, so I took the law into my own hands. I went to his house and beat him up. The police arrested both of us!*

there's no 'law against sth (*spoken*)
used to tell sb who is criticizing you that you are not doing anything wrong: *I'll sing if I want to—there's no law against it.*

lay down the law → **lay**
the letter of the law → **letter**
the long arm of the law → **long**
on the wrong side of the law → **wrong**
Parkinson's law → **Parkinson**
possession is nine points/tenths/parts of the law → **possession**
your, his, etc. word is law → **word**

lay

lay sth at sb's door (*formal*)
blame sb for sth: *The failure of the talks cannot be laid at the government's door.*

lay sth 'bare
reveal sth which has never been seen before: *She laid bare her feelings for him.* ◇ *The report lays bare the shocking housing conditions in this city.*

lay 'claim to sth
state that you have a right to sth: *'The Lamb and Flag' lays claim to being the oldest pub in London.*

lay down your 'arms
stop fighting in a war etc: *Tell your men to lay down their arms—the war's over.*

lay down the 'law (*informal, disapproving*)
give sb orders and express your opinions in an unpleasant, aggressive way, often when you have no right to do so: *He came in here this morning and started laying down the law about all kinds of things. Who does he think he is?*

lay down your 'life (for sb/sth) (*formal*)
die for (your country, a cause etc.): *Thousands of young men laid down their lives in the war so that we could live in freedom.*

lay a 'finger on sb (*informal*)
(often in negative sentences) touch sb with the intention of hurting them physically: *If you lay a finger on her, I'll call the police.*

lay/pile it 'on (thick/with a trowel)
say that sth is much better or much worse than it really is because you want to impress sb: *He told her that she was his favourite author and that she deserved the Nobel Prize for literature. He really laid it on with a trowel.* ◇ *My father really piled it on, shouting at me for ages about my exam results.*

lay it on the 'line (*informal*)
tell sb sth in an honest, direct and forceful way: *She laid it on the line, telling us that we would fail the exam unless we worked harder.*

lay sb 'low (*informal*)
(of an illness) cause sb to go to bed or be unable to work normally: *That flu laid her low for a couple of weeks.*

lay 'siege to sth
surround a building, especially in order to speak to or question the person or people living or working there: *The press and paparazzi laid siege to the star's London flat in the hope of getting a photograph of her.*

> ❷ NOTE
> A *siege* is a military operation in which an army tries to capture a town by surrounding it and stopping the supply of food, etc. to the people inside.

lay sb to 'rest (*formal*)
bury sb: *He was laid to rest beside his parents.*

lay sth to 'rest
stop sth by showing that it is not true: *The media speculation about their relationship has finally been laid to rest.*

lay sth 'waste; lay 'waste to sth (*formal*)
destroy everything, especially in a war: *As the army retreated, it laid waste to thousands of acres of farmland.*

clap/lay/set eyes on sb/sth → **eyes**
get/lay your hands on sb → **hands**
get/lay your hands on sth → **hands**
the lay of the land = the lie of the land → **lie**
put/lay your cards on the table → **cards**
put/lay your head/neck on the block → **block**

lays
kill the goose that lays the golden egg/eggs → **kill**

lead

give a 'lead (on sth)
give people encouragement to do sth by doing it yourself first: *The government should give a lead on protection of the environment.*

go ,down like a lead bal'loon (*informal*)
be very unsuccessful; not be accepted by people: *As you can imagine, the new proposals went down like a lead balloon, so we'll have to think again.*

> ❷ NOTE
> In this idiom, *lead* is pronounced /led/, meaning a heavy soft grey metal (Symbol Pb).

lead sb a'stray
encourage sb to behave in a silly or criminal way: *Small children are easily led astray by older children.* ◇ *He's a weak character, who's easily led astray.*

lead sb by the 'nose
make sb do everything you want; control sb completely: *Unfortunately, she's allowed herself to be led by the nose for years, so it doesn't surprise me that she isn't happy.*

lead sb a (merry) 'dance
cause sb a lot of trouble or worry: *Where have you been? You've led us a merry dance—we've been looking all over for you!*

lead from the 'front
take an active part in what you are telling or persuading others to do: *If you want to succeed in this business, you need to lead from the front. We need people who can motivate their team to get the best possible results.*

lead (sb) 'nowhere
have no successful result for sb: *This discussion is leading us nowhere.*

lead sb to be'lieve (that ...)
make sb think sth is true, usually wrongly: *I was led to believe that I didn't need a visa to enter the country, and now it appears that I do.* ◇ *She led me to believe that she was a student, but she wasn't.*

lead sb up the garden 'path (*informal*)
cause sb to believe sth that is not true; deceive sb: *I think you're just leading us up the garden path—now, come on, tell us the truth!* ◇ *He had led her up the garden path, telling her he wasn't married.*

lead the 'way
1 go in front of sb in order to show them the way: *She led the way to the conference hall.*
2 be the first to do or develop sth: *The United States was leading the way in space research.*

lead/have a charmed life → **charmed**
lead/live the life of Reilly/Riley → **life**
swing the lead → **swing**
you can take/lead a horse to water, but you can't make it drink → **horse**

leading
a ,leading 'light (in/of sth)
an important and respected member of a group, an organization, a profession, etc: *Mr Harris is a leading light in the local business community.*

a ,leading 'question
a question that you ask in a particular way in order to get the answer you want: *That's a leading question.* ◇ *Lawyers are experts on leading questions. You have to be very careful when you answer them.*

the blind leading the blind → **blind**

leads
one thing leads to another → **thing**

leaf
take a leaf out of sb's 'book
follow sb's example because you admire them and their way of doing sth: *If you're having difficulty with the children, take a leaf out of Sandra's book. She knows how to control them.*

shake like a jelly/leaf → **shake**
turn over a new leaf → **turn**

league
in 'league (with sb)
making secret plans with sb: *They accused him of being in league with the terrorists, which of course he denied.*

not be in the same league/class/street
(*informal*)
be of a much lower standard than sb/sth: *He was a good painter, but not in the same league as Picasso.* ◇ *We're not in the same class as the Swiss ski team. They're the best in the world.*

leak
take a 'leak (*slang*)
pass urine (= waste liquid) from the body: *I'm just going to take a leak before we leave.*

spring a leak → **spring**

lean
bend/lean over backwards to do sth → **backwards**

leap
a leap in the 'dark
an action or a risk that you take without knowing anything about the activity or what the result will be: *Government ministers are being accused of taking a leap in the dark as they prepare to radically change the education system.*

jump/leap to conclusions → **conclusions**
look before you leap → **look**
a quantum leap → **quantum**

leaps
by/in ,leaps and 'bounds
in large amounts or very quickly: *My knowledge of German increased by leaps and bounds when I lived in Germany for a year.* ◇ *Production is going up in leaps and bounds.*

your heart leaps → **heart**

learn
learn your 'lesson
learn what (not) to do in the future because you have had a bad experience in the past: *I used to carry a lot of money on me, until one day my bag was stolen. Since then, I've learned my lesson.*

do/learn sth the hard way → **hard**
live and learn → **live**
show sb/learn/know the ropes → **ropes**

lease
a (,new) lease of 'life (*BrE*) (*AmE* a (,new) lease on 'life)
a chance for sb/sth to live/last longer; a chance to get more enjoyment and satisfaction out of life: *The successful heart operation gave him a new lease of life.* ◇ *The outside of the town hall has just been thoroughly cleaned and it's given the old place a new lease of life.*

leash
keep sb/sth on a tight leash → **tight**
strain at the leash → **strain**

least
at 'least
1 (of a number) not less than: *There were at least 70 000 people at the concert.*
2 the minimum sb should do: *I know it's difficult for him to telephone me, but he could at least write.*
3 used for talking about the only advantage or good point of sb/sth: *This car is slow, it uses a lot of petrol, but at least it doesn't break down.*
4 used to show you are not completely sure of sth: *It's true. At least, I think so.*

at the (very) 'least
used after amounts to show that the amount is the lowest possible: *It'll take a year, at the very least.*

(₁not) in the ˈleast
(used in negative sentences, questions and *if* -
clauses) (not) at all: *She wasn't in the least afraid.*
◇ *If you are in the least worried about it, then ask
somebody for help.*

the (very) ˈleast you can/could do
the minimum you should do: *The least you can do
is apologize.* ◇ *'Thank you so much for helping me.'
'Well, it was the least I could do.'*

ˌleast ˈsaid ˌsoonest ˈmended (*BrE, saying*)
a bad situation will pass or be forgotten most
quickly if nothing more is said about it: *She's still
very angry, of course, but if you ask me it's a case of
least said soonest mended.*

not ˈleast (*written*)
especially: *There are a lot of complaints about the
new road, not least because of the noise.*

last but by no means least ➔ **last**
last but not least ➔ **last**
the less/least said, the better ➔ **said**
(choose, follow, take, etc.) the line of least resistance ➔
  line
to say the (very) least ➔ **say**

leather

hell for leather ➔ **hell**

leave

leave/let sb aˈlone; leave/let sb ˈbe
stop annoying sb or trying to get their attention:
*She's asked to be left alone but the press photog-
raphers follow her everywhere.* ◇ *Leave him be—he
obviously doesn't want to talk about it.*

leave/let sth aˈlone; leave/let sth ˈbe
stop touching, changing or moving sth: *I've told
you before—leave my things alone!*

leave a bad/nasty ˈtaste in the/your mouth
(of an experience) make you feel angry, bitter, or
disgusted: *The idea that the money had been stolen
from her sick mother left a nasty taste in the mouth.*
◇ *When you see someone being treated so unkindly,
it leaves a bad taste in your mouth.*

leave sb ˈcold
fail to affect or interest sb: *Classical music leaves
me absolutely cold, but I love rock.* ◇ *His kind of
humour just leaves me cold.*

leave the ˈdoor open (for/on sth)
make sure that there is still the possibility of
doing sth: *The management were intelligent
enough to leave the door open for further negotiations with the union.*

**leave the field ˈclear for sb; leave sb in pos-
  session of the ˈfield**
enable sb to be successful in a particular area of
activity because other people or groups are not
competing with them any longer: *Many of our
more experienced players are injured or resting,
which leaves the field clear for new talent.*

ˌleave ˈgo (of sth) (*BrE, informal*)
stop holding on to sth: *Leave go of my arm—you're
hurting me!*

leave sb holding the ˈbaby (*informal*)
leave sb to take the responsibility or blame for sth:
*It's always the same. We all agree to do something,
then you all say you're too busy to arrange it, and
I'm left holding the baby.*

leave sb/sth in the ˈdust (*AmE*)
leave sb/sth far behind: *The four-minute mile barrier has been left in the dust by a generation of
faster runners.* ◇ *In the local elections, Jackson
won easily, leaving all other candidates in the dust.*

leave sb in the ˈlurch (*informal*)
leave sb who is in a difficult situation and needs
your help: *You can't resign now and leave us all in
the lurch. It wouldn't be fair.*

leave it at ˈthat (*informal*)
say or do no more about sth: *We talked about it for a
few minutes, I made a few suggestions, and we left it
at that.* ◇ *We've done enough for today. Let's leave it
at that, shall we?*

ˌleave it ˈout (*BrE, spoken*)
used to tell sb to stop doing sth: *Leave it out, will
you? I'm trying to study!*

leave a lot, much, etc. to be deˈsired
not be good enough: *Your standard of work has
gone down. In fact it leaves a great deal to be
desired.* ◇ *The acting in some of those early films
left much to be desired.*

leave no stone unˈturned
try everything possible to find or obtain sth: *The
police left no stone unturned in their efforts to find
the little girl.*

leave of ˈabsence (*formal*)
permission to be away from work for a certain
period of time: *Several of my colleagues have had
leave of absence to go on training courses.*

leave sb/sth ˈstanding (*informal*)
be much better than sb/sth: *In maths and science
she leaves the others standing.*

leave sb ˈto it (*informal*)
allow sb to continue doing sth on their own, without your help: *Oh well, we'll leave you to it, Derek—
you seem to be managing very well by yourself.*

leave sb/sth to the mercy/mercies of sb/sth
leave sb/sth in a situation that may cause them to
suffer or to be treated badly: *The soldiers had no
choice but to run across open fields, which left them
to the mercy of enemy gunners.*

leave sb to their own deˈvices
leave sb to do sth without your help, or to spend
their time as they like: *I've explained everything to
him. Now I'm leaving him to his own devices, and
we'll see how he manages.* ◇ *The children were usually left to their own devices in the summer holidays.*

leave 'word (with sb)

leave a message with sb: *He left word with his secretary about where to contact him if necessary.*

not leave sb's 'side

stay with sb, especially in order to take care of them: *While he was in hospital she didn't leave his side for more than a couple of hours at a time.*

take it or 'leave it

1 used to say that you do not care if sb accepts or rejects your offer: *£200 is my final offer, take it or leave it.* **2** (*informal*) (with *can*, not used in the negative) not feel strongly about sth, not mind sth: *'Do you like Indian food?' 'I can take it or leave it.'*

take (your) 'leave (of sb) (*formal*)

say goodbye: *With a nod and a smile, she took leave of her colleagues.*

take ,leave of your 'senses (*informal, humorous*)

behave as if you are mad: *You want £25000 for it? Have you taken leave of your senses?* ◇ *I think my aunt has taken leave of her senses. She wants to make a will leaving all her money to a dogs' home.*

without (so much as) a ,by your 'leave (*old-fashioned*)

without asking permission; rudely: *What do you think you're doing, coming in here without so much as a by your leave?*

keep/leave (all) your options open → **options**
leave/make your/its mark (on sth/sb) → **mark**
leave/put sth on/to one side → **side**
leave/let well alone → **well**
love you and leave you → **love**
take French leave → **French**

leaving

(like rats) deserting/leaving a sinking ship → **sinking**

leeway

make up 'leeway (*BrE*)

get out of a bad position that you are in, especially because you have lost a lot of time: *By now, James was so far behind in the race that he knew he had little chance of making up the leeway.*

left

be (way out/over) in left 'field (*AmE, informal*)

completely wrong; strange or unusual: *He's way out in left field if he thinks we're going to support him on this.*

> ❶ ORIGIN
> This idiom refers to the left part of the field in baseball.

the left hand doesn't know what the right hand's doing (*informal*)

one part of an organization, group, etc. does not know what another part is doing: *First I got a letter from them saying they couldn't return my money, and then the next day they sent me a cheque. Obviously the left hand doesn't know what the right hand's doing.*

left ,out in the 'cold

excluded from a group or an activity; ignored: *Everyone had something to do or somewhere to go. I felt left out in the cold.*

,left, right and 'centre; ,right, left and 'centre (*BrE*) (*AmE* ,left, right and 'center; ,right, left and 'center) (*informal*)

in or from all directions: *He was shouting orders left, right and centre.* ◇ *She was criticized right, left and centre for her views on education.*

hang a left/right → **hang**
have (got) two left feet → **two**
left and right = right and left → **right**

left-handed

a left-handed compliment = a backhanded compliment → **backhanded**

leg

get your 'leg over (*BrE, informal*)

have sex

'leg it (*informal, especially BrE*)

run, especially in order to escape from sb: *We saw the police coming and legged it down the road.*

not have a ,leg to 'stand on (*informal*)

not be able to prove what you say: *He claims he wasn't there, but four people saw him, so he doesn't have a leg to stand on.*

break a leg! → **break**
cost/pay an arm and a leg → **arm**
pull sb's leg → **pull**
shake a leg → **shake**
talk the hind leg(s) off a donkey → **talk**

legend

a legend in your own lifetime = a living legend → **living**

legs

as fast as your legs can carry you → **fast**
on your/its last legs → **last**
stretch your legs → **stretch**
with your tail between your legs → **tail**

leg-up

give sb a 'leg-up

1 (*BrE, informal*) help sb climb up or onto sth, for example, a horse or a wall: *I gave him a leg-up.* **2** (*informal*) help sb, usually by giving them money: *His father gave him a leg-up when he was starting his business.*

leisure

at (your) 'leisure

without needing to hurry, at a convenient time for you: *I'm not going to read this report now; I'll read it later at my leisure.*

lend

lend 'colour to sth (*BrE*) (*AmE* lend 'color to sth)
make sth seem probable: *The tracks outside the house lend colour to her claim that somebody tried to break in last night.*

lend an 'ear (to sb/sth)
listen to what sb is telling you: *He's a good friend. He's always ready to lend a sympathetic ear.*

lend (sb) a 'hand (with sth)
help (to do sth): *I saw two men pushing a broken-down car along the road so I stopped to lend them a hand.* ◇ *She stayed with us for three weeks and didn't once lend a hand with the housework!*

lend your 'name to sth (*formal*)
let it be known in public that you support or agree with sth: *Famous actors sometimes lend their names to political causes.*

lend sup'port, 'weight, 'credence, etc. to sth
make sth seem more likely to be true or genuine: *This latest evidence lends support to her theory.*

length

at 'length
1 (*literary*) after a long time: *'I'm not sure,' he said at length.*
2 in great detail and taking a long time: *She talked at length about her work in hospitals.*

the length and 'breadth of sth
everywhere in an area: *I've travelled the length and breadth of Europe, but I've never seen such beautiful scenery as here.*

keep sb at arm's length → arm

lengths

go to any, great, etc. 'lengths (to do sth)
try very hard (to do sth); do whatever is necessary: *She went to great lengths to find this book.* ◇ *They were prepared to go to any lengths to find their son.*

leopard

a leopard cannot change its 'spots (*saying*)
a person's character does not change: *A dictator is unlikely to become a good leader in a democracy. A leopard cannot change its spots.*

less

even/much/still 'less
and certainly not: *I don't want even to see her, much less speak to her.* ◇ *I don't like beer, even less do I like warm, weak English beer.*

no 'less (*often ironic*)
used to suggest that sth is surprising or impressive: *She's having lunch with the Director, no less.*

no less than ...
used to emphasize a large amount: *The guide contains details of no less than 115 hiking routes.*

lesser

the ˌlesser of two 'evils; the ˌlesser 'evil
the less unpleasant of two unpleasant choices: *Neither candidate seemed capable of governing the country. People voted for him as the lesser of two evils.*

lesson

learn your lesson → learn
an object lesson → object
teach sb a lesson → teach

let

let a'lone
used after a statement to emphasize that because the first thing is not true or possible, the next thing cannot be true or possible either: *I wouldn't speak to him, let alone trust him or lend him money.* ◇ *She didn't even apologize, let alone offer to pay for the damage.*

let ˌbygones be 'bygones
decide to forget about disagreements that happened in the past: *This is a ridiculous situation, avoiding each other like this. Why can't we let bygones be bygones?*

let the 'cat out of the bag (*informal*)
make known a secret, usually without realizing what you are doing: *'Who let the cat out of the bag?' 'I'm afraid I did. I thought everybody already knew.'* ◇ *Nobody knew she had been offered the job until her husband let the cat out of the bag.*

let the chips fall where they 'may (*AmE, informal*)
used to say that you are not worried about anything that may happen, particularly as a result of sth you do: *Don't argue with him. Just tell the truth and let the chips fall where they may.*

let sth 'drop
no longer speak, write, etc. about sth: *I've heard enough about this subject. Can we let it drop now?*

let the 'dust settle (also wait for the 'dust to settle)
wait for a situation to become clear or certain: *Let's not make any decisions now—we'll wait for the dust to settle and then decide what to do.*

ˌlet 'fall
mention sth in a conversation, by accident or as if by accident: *She let fall a further heavy hint.*

let 'fly (at sb/sth) (with sth) (*informal*)
1 throw, shoot, etc. sth with great force: *He aimed his gun and let fly.*
2 attack sb/sth: *When I told him that I couldn't find the letter, he let fly at me.* ◇ *She let fly at her neighbour with a stream of insults.*

let the ˌgenie out of the 'bottle
do sth that causes a big and permanent change in people's lives, especially one which might make a

situation worse: *Once you make carrying guns legal, you let the genie out of the bottle.*

> **ⓘ ORIGIN**
> In Arabian stories, a *genie* is a spirit with magical powers, especially one that lives in a bottle or lamp.

¡let sb 'go
1 allow sb to be free: *Will they let the hostages go?* **2** make sb have to leave their job: *They're having to let 100 employees go because of falling profits.*

¡let sb/sth 'go; ¡let 'go (of sb/sth)
1 stop holding sb/sth: *Let go of me! You're hurting!* ◇ *Don't let go of my hand, or you'll get lost.* **2** give up an idea or an attitude, or control of sth: *It's time to let the past go.* ◇ *Some people find it hard to let go of their inhibitions.*

¡let yourself 'go
1 behave in a relaxed way without worrying about what people think of your behaviour: *Come on, enjoy yourself, let yourself go!* **2** stop being careful about how you look and dress, etc: *He has let himself go since he lost his job.*

let your 'hair down (*informal*)
relax completely and enjoy yourself, especially after a period when you have not been able to do so: *Why don't you let your hair down a bit? Come out with us for the evening.*

> **ⓘ ORIGIN**
> In the past, young girls put their long hair up to show that they were grown up, mature adults. When they were playing in private, they would let their hair down again.

The office party was a good opportunity for everyone to let their hair down.

let sb 'have it (*spoken, informal*)
punish sb or speak to them very angrily: *She annoyed me so much that I let her have it.* ◇ *Dad will let you have it when he sees that mess.*

let your ¡heart rule your 'head
act according to what you feel rather than what

you think is sensible: *Don't let your heart rule your head. I know you like him but are you sure you can really trust him?*

let it all hang 'out (*informal*)
express your feelings freely: *Sometimes you just have to let it all hang out and say what you really think.*

let it be 'known; make it 'known that ... (*formal*)
make sure that people are informed about sth, especially by getting sb else to tell them: *The President has let it be known that he does not intend to run for election again.*

let it 'go (at that)
say or do nothing more about sth: *I could have disagreed with him, but I let it go. I don't like arguments.* ◇ *The police spoke firmly to the boy about the damage and then let it go at that.*

let sb 'know
tell sb about sth: *I don't know if I can come, but I'll let you know soon.* ◇ *Let me know how I can help.*

let 'loose (*BrE*) (*AmE* cut 'loose) (*informal*)
do sth or happen in a way that is not controlled: *Teenagers need a place to let loose.*

let 'loose sth
make a noise or remark, especially in a loud or sudden way: *She let loose a stream of abuse.*

let sb/sth 'loose
1 free sb/sth from whatever holds them/it in place: *She let her hair loose and it fell around her shoulders.* ◇ *Who let the dogs loose?* **2** give sb complete freedom to do what they want in a place or situation: *He was at last let loose in the kitchen.* ◇ *A team of professionals were let loose on the project.*

¡let me 'see/'think
used when you are thinking or trying to remember sth: *Now let me see—where did he say he lived?*

let sb off the 'hook (*informal*)
allow sb to escape from a difficult situation or punishment: *We'll let you off the hook this time, but if you make any more mistakes like that, you'll lose your job.* ◇ *There won't be time for me to read my report to the committee, so that's let me off the hook.*

> **ⓘ ORIGIN**
> This expression refers to a fish escaping after it has been caught.

¡let off 'steam (*informal*)
release energy, strong feelings, nervous tension, etc. by intense physical activity or noisy behaviour: *He lets off steam by going to the gym after work.* ◇ *All children need to let off steam from time to time.*

let sth 'pass
pay no attention to sth that sb says or does because you think it is better not to argue about it or criticize it: *He started saying terrible things about my mother again but I let it pass. It only makes things worse if I say something.*

let sth 'ride (*informal*)
decide to do nothing about a problem that you know you may have to deal with later: *The manager knows who is leaving work early, but he's decided to let it ride for the moment.*

let sth 'rip (*informal*)
allow a car, boat, etc. to go as fast as possible: *There's a straight road ahead. Let it rip!*

let 'rip (at sb) (with sth) (*informal*)
speak or do sth with great force, enthusiasm, etc. and without control: *He was furious. He let rip at me with a stream of abuse.* ◇ *In the last song, the singer really let rip.*

let the 'side down (*especially BrE*)
fail to give your friends, family, etc. the help and support they expect, or behave in a way that makes them disappointed: *Everyone in the sales team has increased their sales except you. You're letting the side down badly.*

let ˌsleeping dogs 'lie (*saying*)
do not disturb a situation which could cause trouble: *I was very careful about what I said. It's best to let sleeping dogs lie, I think.*

let 'slip sth
give sb information that is supposed to be secret: *She tried not to let slip what she knew.* ◇ *I happened to let it slip that he had given me £1 000 for the car.*

let sb 'stew (in their own 'juice) (*informal*)
leave sb to worry and suffer the unpleasant effects of their own actions: *We told her not to trust him but she wouldn't listen—so let her stew in her own juice!*

let us 'say
used when making a suggestion or giving an example: *I can let you have it for, well let's say £100.*

not let the ˌgrass grow under your 'feet
be very active and do the things that need to be done very quickly: *The new owner didn't let the grass grow under her feet, and immediately started to change the whole layout of the shop.*

all hell breaks/is let loose → **hell**
get off/be let off lightly → **lightly**
leave/let sb be = leave/let sb alone → **leave**
leave/let sth be = leave/let sth alone → **leave**
leave/let well alone → **well**
let the tail wag the dog = the tail (is) wagging the dog → **tail**
let well enough alone = leave/let well alone → **well**
live and let live → **live**

letter

the ˌletter of the 'law (*often disapproving*)
the exact words of a law or rule rather than its general meaning: *They insist on sticking to the letter of the law.*

to the 'letter
with attention to every detail; exactly: *I followed your instructions to the letter.*

a dead letter → **dead**

an open letter → **open**
a poison pen letter → **poison**

level

do/try your level 'best (to do sth)
try as hard as you can: *I'll do my level best to be there by ten o'clock, but I can't promise anything.*

keep a level 'head
remain calm and sensible, even in difficult situations: *She managed to keep a level head when all the others panicked.* ▶ **ˌlevel-'headed** *adj.*: *Nurses need to be level-headed.*

ˌlevel 'pegging (*BrE*)
making progress at the same rate as another person or group: *There's ten minutes left, and the teams are still level pegging.*

a ˌlevel 'playing field
a situation in which everyone has the same opportunities: *Many small businesses complain that they are not competing on a level playing field and that they are the ones who lose out.*

ˌlevel the 'playing field
create a situation where everyone has the same opportunities: *There is a high demand for new laws and restrictions to be introduced in order to level the playing field.*

on the 'level (*AmE* also **on the ˌup and 'up**) (*informal*)
honest; legal: *I promise you that he's on the level. He's never been involved in anything criminal.*

sink to sb's level → **sink**

liberties

take 'liberties (with sb/sth)
be more free with sb/sth than you should be: *The translator has taken too many liberties with this. The original meaning is lost.* ◇ *He uses our phone without asking, which I think is taking liberties.*

liberty

at 'liberty (to do sth) (*formal*)
having permission to do sth: *You are at liberty to leave, if you wish.*

take the liberty of doing sth (*formal*)
do sth without permission: *I have taken the liberty of giving your address to a friend who is visiting London. I hope you don't mind.*

licence (*BrE*) (*AmE* **license**)

artistic/poetic 'licence (*often ironic*)
the freedom of artists or writers to change facts in order to make a story, painting, etc. more interesting or beautiful: *He was using poetic licence when he described this room as 'large, modern and comfortable'.* ◇ *The only photo we had of her as a young woman was very out of focus, so a bit of artistic licence was needed to show what she probably looked like.*

a licence to print 'money (*disapproving*)
used to describe a business which makes a lot of
money with little effort: *Many people think that the
national lottery is nothing more than a licence to
print money.*

lick

at a (fair) 'lick (*informal*)
fast; at a high speed: *You must have been driving at
a fair lick to get here so quickly!*

lick sb's 'boots (*informal*) (*BrE* also **lick sb's
'arse** ⚠, *slang*) (*AmE* **lick sb's 'ass** ⚠, *slang*)
show too much respect for sb in authority because
you want to please them: *It makes me very angry
when I see Andrew licking Mr Smith's boots all the
time.*

a lick of 'paint (*informal*)
a coat of fresh paint: *All this house needs is a good
clean and a lick of paint.*

lick your 'wounds
spend time trying to get your strength and confidence back after a defeat or disappointment: *'He
heard this morning that he hasn't got the job.'
'Where is he?' 'Licking his wounds somewhere,
probably.'*

get/knock/lick sb/sth into shape → **shape**
lick/smack your lips → **lips**

lid

keep/put a/the 'lid on sth
try to make sure that people do not do sth or find
out about sth: *The government wants to keep the lid
on discussion of tax reforms at the moment.*

lift, blow, etc. the 'lid off sth (*informal*)
tell people unpleasant or shocking facts about sth:
*The story in today's paper really lifts the lid off the
use of drugs in horse racing.*

put the (tin) 'lid on sth (*BrE*, *informal*)
bring to an end an activity, your hopes or plans:
*I've got a place at an American university but I
can't afford to go, so that's put the lid on that.* ◇ *It
rained and rained, which put the tin lid on our
plans for a picnic in the park.*

flip your lid → **flip**

lie

give the 'lie to sth (*formal*)
show that sth is not true: *These statistics give the lie
to the government's claim that inflation is under
control.*

lie at sb's 'door (*formal*)
(of the responsibility for a mistake, etc.) belong to
sb: *The main problem is the design of the building
and the responsibility for that lies clearly at the
architect's door.*

lie 'doggo (*old-fashioned, informal*)
be very still or hide somewhere so that you will not

be found: *I lay doggo in the shed while the police
searched the house for me.*

lie down on the 'job (*informal*)
not do a job properly: *I'm not going to employ anybody here who lies down on the job. I only want
people who work hard.*

lie in 'state
(of the body of an important person) be placed for
people to see before it is buried: *Before the funeral,
Churchill's body lay in state in Westminster Abbey.*

lie in 'store (for sb)
(of events, etc.) be waiting to happen (to sb): *I wonder what lies in store for us in our new life in
California.*

lie in 'wait
hide and wait for sb so that you can attack them:
*The police think the murderer must have been lying
in wait for his victim.*

lie 'low (*informal*)
hide or keep quiet for a short time: *The thieves lay
low for a few days in a farmhouse, then tried to leave
the country with the money.*

the ˌlie of the 'land (*BrE*) (*AmE* **the ˌlay of the
'land**)
1 the way the land in an area is formed and what
physical characteristics it has
2 the way a situation is now and how it is likely to
develop: *Check out the lie of the land before you
make a decision.*

lie through your 'teeth (*informal*)
tell very obvious lies without being embarrassed:
The witness was clearly lying through his teeth.

lie your way into/out of sth
get yourself into/out of a situation by telling lies: *I
lied my way into the concert by claiming to be a journalist.* ◇ *You can't lie your way out of it this time,
I'm afraid.*

be/lie at the bottom of sth → **bottom**
hang/lie heavy (on sb/sth) → **heavy**
have made your bed and have to lie on it → **bed**
I tell a lie → **tell**
let sleeping dogs lie → **let**
live a lie → **live**
a white lie → **white**

lies

a pack of lies → **pack**
see, etc. how the land lies → **land**
there is/lies the rub → **rub**
therein lies … → **therein**
time hangs/lies heavy (on your hands) → **time**
a tissue of lies → **tissue**

lieu

in lieu (of sth) (*formal*)
instead of: *They took cash in lieu of the prize they
had won.* ◇ *We work on Saturdays and have a day
off in lieu during the week.*

life

be sb's 'life
be the most important person or thing to sb: *My children are my life.* ◇ *Writing is his life.*

bring sb/sth to 'life
make sb/sth more lively, interesting or attractive: *It was only her performance that brought the film to life.* ◇ *If you put a couple of pictures on the wall it might bring the room to life a bit.*

come to 'life
1 become more interesting, exciting or full of activity: *The match finally came to life in the final minutes of the second half.*
2 start to act or move as if alive: *In my dream all my toys came to life.*

frighten/scare the 'life out of sb
frighten sb very much: *Don't do that! You scared the life out of me creeping up on me like that!*

get a 'life (*spoken*)
used to tell sb to stop being boring and to do sth more interesting: *Simon, all you do is sit at home all day playing video games! Get a life!*

lead/live the life of 'Riley (*informal*)
have a comfortable and enjoyable life without any worries: *He inherited a lot of money and since then he's been living the life of Riley.*

life after 'death
the possibility or belief that people continue to exist in some form after they die: *Do you believe in life after death?*

(a matter of) ,life and/or 'death (*informal*)
used to describe a situation that is very important or serious: *We need that business deal, it's a matter of life or death to the company.* ◇ *It's hardly a life-and-death decision whether we go by bus or take the train, is it?*

the life and 'soul of the party (*BrE*)
very cheerful or enthusiastic: *People always expect Jane to be the life and soul of the party.*

life is 'cheap (*disapproving*)
used to say that there is a situation in which it is not thought to be important if people die or are treated badly: *In areas like this, drugs are hard currency and life is cheap.*

(have) a life of its 'own
(of an object) seeming to move or function by itself without a person touching or working it: *When he was painting, he said, the brush used to take on a life of its own and take him in directions he never intended to go.*

make life 'difficult (for sb)
cause problems for sb: *She does everything she can to make life difficult for him.*

make sb's life a 'misery
make sb's life very unpleasant or difficult: *Ever since he joined the company he's made my life a misery.* ◇ *Her arthritis makes her life a misery; she's in constant pain.*

the 'man/'woman in your life (*informal*)
the man or woman that you are having a sexual or romantic relationship with

not for the 'life of me, etc.
used for saying that you cannot do sth, however hard you try: *I can't for the life of me remember his first name.* ◇ *He couldn't for the life of him understand why she was so annoyed with him.*

not on your 'life (*spoken*)
used to refuse very firmly to do sth: *Go out and miss the football match on TV? Not on your life!* ◇ *Lend him £50? Not on your life.*

such is 'life (*informal*)
used when you are disappointed about sth but know that you must accept it: *He didn't get the prize he was hoping for. But such is life, I suppose.*

take sb's 'life (*formal*)
kill sb: *In my opinion, the state does not have the right to take a person's life.*

take your ,life in your 'hands
risk being killed, injured, attacked, etc: *You take your life in your hands if you let him drive.* ◇ *The reason that his photos are so good is because he takes his life in his hands to get them.*

take your own 'life (*formal*)
kill yourself; commit suicide: *His children died in a house fire and shortly afterwards he took his own life.*

,that's 'life (also ,c'est la 'vie *from French*) (*spoken*)
used when you are disappointed about sth but know that you must accept it: *Some people are born intelligent and some people are not. That's life.* ◇ *I didn't get that job I wanted. They said I didn't have enough experience. Oh well, c'est la vie.*

there's ,life in the old dog 'yet (*humorous*)
a person is old but is still active and enjoys life: *At 70 he's decided to go round the world. There's life in the old dog yet!* ◇ *I'm not too old to enjoy myself! There's life in the old dog yet, you know.*

this is the 'life!
used to show that you are very happy with the situation you are in: *Sunshine, a swimming pool and champagne. This is the life!*

to the 'life
(of a painting, sculpture, description, etc.) exactly like the person/thing painted, etc: *This new portrait really is Prince Charles to the life.* ◇ *When I read her description of him, I could see him again so clearly. It was him to the life.*

what a 'life!
used to show that you think your life is very difficult or unpleasant: *Three hours travelling to work in a crowded train every day. What a life!* ◇ *Cooking, cleaning and ironing seven days a week. What a life!*

where there's 'life (, there's 'hope) (*saying*)
in a terrible situation you must not give up hope because there is always a chance that it will

improve: *The doctors are doing all they can to save her. Where there's life, there's hope.*

at my, your, etc. time of life → **time**

the bane of sb's life/existence → **bane**

be/go in fear of your life → **fear**

(you can) bet your bottom dollar/your life (on sth/that …) → **bet**

can't do sth to save your life → **save**

a dog's life → **dog**

end your days/life (in sth) → **end**

a fact of life → **fact**

the facts of life → **facts**

fight for (your) life → **fight**

for your life = for dear life → **dear**

the fright of your life → **fright**

have the time of your life → **time**

in the prime of (your) life → **prime**

in real life → **real**

the kiss of life → **kiss**

(as) large as life → **large**

larger than life → **larger**

lay down your life (for sb/sth) → **lay**

lead/have a charmed life → **charmed**

a (new) lease of/on life → **lease**

the light of sb's life → **light**

lose your life → **lose**

risk life and limb → **risk**

see life → **see**

a slice of life → **slice**

spring (in)to life/action → **spring**

the staff of life → **staff**

that's the story of my life → **story**

true to life → **true**

variety is the spice of life → **variety**

a walk of life → **walk**

a/the/sb's way of life → **way**

lifetime

the chance, etc. of a 'lifetime

a wonderful opportunity, etc. that you are not likely to get again: *This is your chance to win the holiday of a lifetime!*

a legend in your own lifetime = a living legend → **living**

lift

(not) lift a 'finger (to do sth) (*informal*)

(not) make any effort at all to do sth, especially to help sb: *He didn't lift a finger to help me when I was in trouble.* ◇ *She does all the work in the house. Nobody else lifts a finger.*

thumb/hitch a 'lift

stand by the side of the road with your thumb out because you want a driver to stop and take you somewhere: *We tried to hitch a lift, but nobody stopped to pick us up.*

lift/raise a hand against sb → **hand**

lift/raise the roof → **roof**

light

be in sb's 'light

be between sb and a source of light: *Could you move, please? You're in my light.*

be light on sth

not have enough of sth: *We seem to be light on fuel.*

be/go out like a 'light (*informal*)

fall asleep very quickly or suddenly lose consciousness: *She went out like a light after an exhausting day at work.* ◇ *One minute she was talking and laughing and the next minute she was out like a light. It was very frightening.*

bring sth to 'light

show information, evidence, etc: *The police investigation brought to light evidence of more than one crime.* ◇ *These documents have brought new information to light about Shakespeare's early life.*

cast/shed/throw (new) 'light on sth

make a problem, etc. easier to understand: *This book sheds new light on the role of the CIA.* ◇ *'Can you throw any light on the matter?'*

come to 'light

become known; be revealed: *It recently came to light that he'd been in trouble with the police before.*

in a ˌgood, ˌbad, ˌfavourable, etc. 'light

if you see sth or put sth **in a good, bad, etc. light**, it seems good, bad, etc: *You must not view what happened in a negative light.* ◇ *They want to present their policies in the best possible light.*

in the 'light of sth (*BrE*) (*AmE* in 'light of sth)

after considering sth: *In the light of what you have just told me, I am prepared to increase your loan to £5000.*

(as) light as 'air/a 'feather

weighing very little; very light: *I love this jacket— it's really warm but it's as light as a feather.* ◇ *Her sponge cakes are as light as air.*

(see the) ˌlight at the end of the 'tunnel

(see) the possibility of success, happiness, etc. in the future, especially after a long period of difficulty: *Business has been bad recently, but I think we're beginning to see some light at the end of the tunnel.*

(the) light 'dawns (on sb)

somebody suddenly understood or began to understand sth: *I puzzled over the problem for ages before the light suddenly dawned on me.*

(see) the light of 'day

be thought of or discovered by sb, or become known to a lot of people at a particular time: *It was then that the idea of a European parliament first saw the light of day.*

the light of sb's 'life

the person sb loves more than any other: *Elizabeth was his only child, the light of his life.*

a light 'touch

the ability to deal with sth in a delicate and relaxed

way: *She handles this difficult subject with a light touch.*

make 'light of sth
treat sth or behave as if sth is less serious, important etc. than it really is: *She was in great pain but she always made light of it.* ◇ *They made light of their difficulties but it was obvious that things were going badly.*

make light 'work of sth (*informal*)
do sth very easily; defeat sb very easily: *She made light work of that translation.* ◇ *They made light work of their match against Lazio and won the championship.*

with a light 'heart
with a feeling of happiness or relief: *She left the doctor's with a light heart. There was nothing wrong with her after all.* ▶ ˌlight-'hearted *adj.*
1 (of a person) cheerful and happy
2 (of a situation, etc.) amusing, not serious: *The programme takes a light-hearted look at the tourist industry.*

be all sweetness and light → **sweetness**
be a shining light → **shining**
give sb/get the green light → **green**
hide your light under a bushel → **hide**
in the cold light of day → **cold**
a leading light (in/of sth) → **leading**
many hands make light work → **hands**
see the light → **see**
set light to sth → **set**
travel light → **travel**

lightly

get off/be let off 'lightly (*informal*)
be lucky and escape serious injury, punishment or trouble: *Only two years in prison for stealing all that money? I think he got off very lightly.*

lightning

at/with ˌlightning 'speed
very fast: *The lecturer talked at lightning speed.* ◇ *They're a very efficient company. They reply to your letters with lightning speed.*

lightning never strikes twice (in the same place) (*saying*)
an unusual or unpleasant event is not likely to happen in the same place or to the same person twice

like greased lightning → **greased**

lights

the lights are 'on but nobody's 'home (*saying, humorous*)
used to describe sb who is stupid, not thinking clearly or not paying attention: *Don't try discussing anything intelligent with Alice. The lights are on but nobody's home, I'm afraid.*

the bright lights → **bright**
jump the lights → **jump**
shoot the lights → **shoot**

like

Most idioms containing **like** are at the entries for the nouns and verbs in the idioms, for example **like gold dust** is at **gold**.

and the 'like (*informal*)
and similar people or things: *Professional people include lawyers, doctors, architects and the like.*

anything/nothing/something like that
anything, etc. of that kind: *Do you do aerobics or play tennis, or anything like that?* ◇ *She's an expert in the preservation of paper or something like that.* ◇ *No, there's nothing like that available yet.*

how would 'you like it?
used to emphasize that sth bad has happened to you and you want some sympathy: *How would you like it if someone called you a liar?*

I like your 'nerve, 'cheek, etc.; I like 'that! (*informal, ironic*)
used for saying that you think sb's behaviour is very unreasonable or unfair: *She crashed into my car and now she wants me to pay for hers to be repaired. Well I like her nerve!* ◇ *He wants me to do his work for him while he goes to a football game! Well, I like that!*

if you 'like (*spoken*)
1 used to politely agree to sth or to suggest sth: *'Shall we stop now?' 'If you like.'* ◇ *If you like, we could go out this evening.*
2 used when you express sth in a new way or when you are not confident about sth: *It was, if you like, the dawn of a new era.*

(as) like as 'not; like e'nough; most/very 'like (*informal*)
quite/very probably: *As like as not, he'll be late. He usually is.*

(just) like 'that
without hesitating: *I asked him for £100 and he gave it to me just like that.*

likely

as ˌlikely as 'not; most/very 'likely
very probably: *As likely as not she's forgotten all about it.*

a 'likely story (*spoken, ironic*)
used for showing that you do not believe what sb has said: *They said they'd found the wallet on the ground outside the pub—a likely story!*

not (bloody⚠, etc.) 'likely! (*spoken, especially BrE*)
used to disagree strongly with a statement or a suggestion: *Sign a blank cheque for you? Not bloody likely!*

likes

the likes of sb (*informal*)
people like sb: *Champagne isn't for the likes of you and me. Beer's more our style.*

liking

for 'your liking
if you say, for example, that sth is too hot **for your liking**, you mean that you would prefer it to be less hot: *The town was too crowded for my liking.*

to sb's 'liking (*formal*)
suitable, and how sb likes sth: *The coffee was just to his liking.*

lily

gild the lily → **gild**

limb

out on a 'limb (*informal*)
in a risky or difficult position because you are saying or doing sth which does not have the support of other people: *When he started that company, he really went out on a limb. It might have been a disaster.* ◇ *I seem to be out on a limb here. Does nobody agree with my idea?*

risk life and limb → **risk**
tear sb limb from limb → **tear**

limbo

in 'limbo
in a state of uncertainty or between two states: *We're in limbo at the moment because we've finished our work in this country and now we're waiting for our next contract.* ◇ *Our plans for buying a flat in Spain are in limbo at the moment.*

limelight

out of/in the 'limelight
receiving no/a lot of public attention: *If you are married to a Prime Minister, you are always in the limelight.*

> **❶ ORIGIN**
> In theatres, *lime* used to be burnt in front of the stage to give a bright light.

limit

be the (absolute) 'limit (*old-fashioned, spoken*)
be a very annoying person or thing: *You're the limit, Michael. I've been waiting for you for over two hours. Where on earth have you been?* ◇ *The trains on this line are the absolute limit. They are never on time.*

the sky's the limit → **sky**

limits

within 'limits
1 to a certain extent; not completely: *'Do you support what he says?' 'Yes, within limits!'*

2 as long as it is reasonable; to a reasonable degree: *I will do anything I can to help you, within limits, of course.*

off limits = out of bounds → **bounds**

line

all along/down the 'line; right down the 'line (*informal*)
completely; at every stage: *We've had problems with this software all along the line. It was a complete waste of money.* ◇ *He supported their campaign right down the line.*

bring sb/sth into 'line (with sb/sth)
(make sb/sth) behave, function, etc. in the same way as other people, organizations, etc: *He's a very clever child but he's naughty. I feel that he needs bringing into line a bit.* ◇ *We're trying to bring our production methods more into line with our Japanese competitors.*

in 'line for sth
likely to get sth: *She's in line for promotion.*

in the ˌline of 'duty
while doing a job: *A police officer was injured in the line of duty yesterday.*

(be) in/out of 'line with sb/sth
be in agreement/disagreement with sth: *Her views on education are quite out of line with the official view.* ◇ *The changes being made are in line with the new policy.*

(choose, follow, take, etc.) the line of least re'sistance
when you have a choice between two or more courses of action, choose the one which causes you the least trouble: *You'll never get anywhere in life if you always take the line of least resistance.*

line your (own)/sb's 'pocket(s) (*informal*)
make a lot of money dishonestly, especially by stealing it from your employer: *He'd been lining his pockets for years before it was discovered.* ◇ *We thought he was giving our money to the Church Building Fund and in fact he was busy lining his own pockets.*

on the 'line
(of a job, your career, reputation, etc.) at risk: *If I don't get enough contracts this month, my job will be on the line.* ◇ *By making such an unusual film, he has really put his reputation on the line.*

somewhere, etc. along/down the 'line
at some particular moment or stage during sth: *With an idiot like him to advise you, it was certain that you would get into trouble somewhere along the line.* ◇ *'How did it happen?' 'I don't know. I just know that somewhere along the line we stopped loving each other.'*

tread/walk a fine/thin 'line
be in a difficult or dangerous situation where you could easily make a mistake: *He was walking a fine line between being funny and being rude.*

be in/on the firing line → firing
be/get out of line = step out of line → step
the bottom line → bottom
draw the line (at sth) → draw
drop sb a line/note → drop
the end of the road/line → end
hook, line and sinker → hook
a hot line (to sb) → hot
in the front line (of sth) → front
jump the line → jump
lay it on the line → lay
out of line = out of order → order
overstep the mark/line → overstep
the party line → party
pitch a line/story/yarn (to sb) → pitch
sign on the dotted line → sign
step out of line → step
take a firm line/stand (on/against sth) → firm
toe the line → toe

linen

wash your dirty linen in public → wash

lines

on/along the 'lines of sth; on/along the same 'lines as sth (spoken)

1 similar to sth; in a similar way, style, etc. to sth: *I'm looking for a silver teapot, something along the lines of this one here.*
2 used for giving a summary of sth you have read or heard: *'What did he say in his defence?' 'Something along the lines of his being so drunk that he didn't realize what he was doing.'*

the battle lines are drawn → battle
get your lines/wires crossed → crossed
hard luck/lines → hard
have (got) crossed lines/wires → crossed
read between the lines → read

lingua

a ˌlingua 'franca (from Italian)

a shared language that is used for communication by people whose main languages are different: *In the middle of the 20th century, English suddenly became the lingua franca of the world.* ◇ *The majority of our group being South American, we used Spanish as a lingua franca.*

lining

every cloud has a silver lining → cloud

link

a link in the 'chain

one of the stages in a process or a line of argument: *Many people believe that coming from a broken home may be one of the first links in the chain that eventually leads to a life of crime.*

the weak link (in the chain) → weak

lion

the ˌlion's 'den

a difficult situation in which you have to face a person or people who are unfriendly or aggressive towards you: *Before each one of her press conferences, she felt as if she were going into the lion's den.*

the 'lion's 'share (of sth) (BrE)

the largest part of sth that is being shared: *The lion's share of the awards have gone to American films again.*

> **ⓘ ORIGIN**
> This idiom comes from one of Aesop's fables. The lion is helped by other animals to kill a stag, but then refuses to share it with them.

put your head in the lion's mouth → head

lions

throw sb to the wolves/lions → throw

lip

bite your lip → bite
(keep) a stiff upper lip → stiff
there's many a slip 'twixt cup and lip → slip

lips

lick/smack your 'lips

1 move your tongue over your lips, especially before eating sth good
2 (informal) show that you are excited about sth and want it to happen soon: *They were licking their lips at the thought of clinching the deal.*

my lips are 'sealed (informal, humorous)

I promise not to tell your secret: *Don't worry, I won't tell anybody. My lips are sealed.*

on everyone's 'lips

if sth is **on everyone's lips**, they are all talking about it: *The question on everyone's lips at the moment is: will they get married or not?*

not pass your lips → pass
read my lips → read

lip-service

pay lip-service to sth → pay

list

be on/off the danger list → danger
a hit list → hit

listen

listen with half an 'ear

not listen with your full attention: *I was watching television and listening with half an ear to what he was telling me.*

little

a little 'bird told me (that …) (spoken)

I have heard about sth but I do not want to say who told me: *A little bird told me you might be applying for another job. Is that true?* ◇ *'How did you know I was getting married?' 'Oh, a little bird told me.'*

ˌlittle by 'little
slowly; gradually: *Her English is improving little by little.* ◇ *Little by little she began to feel better.*

make 'little of sth
1 treat sth as unimportant or less important than expected: *She made little of all the problems in the department and said everything was all right.*
2 hardly understand sth: *I read the article on the relationship between physics and art, but I'm afraid I could make little of it.*

more than a little ex'cited, 'shocked, etc.
quite or very excited, shocked, etc: *Peter was more than a little disappointed not to be chosen for the team.* ◇ *I was more than a little surprised to see it still there two days later.*

twist/wind/wrap sb around/round your little 'finger (*informal*)
be able to persuade or influence sb very easily, usually because they like you: *I can twist my parents round my little finger.*

great/tall oaks from little acorns grow → **oaks**
little/no better than → **better**
little by little = bit by bit → **bit**
little/nothing short of sth → **short**
(it's) no/small/little wonder (that) … → **wonder**
of little/no account → **account**
precious few/little → **precious**
to little/no avail → **avail**
to little/good/some/no purpose → **purpose**

live

go 'live
(of a computer system) become operational (= ready to be used): *Good news! Our website is going live tomorrow!*

ˌlive and 'breathe sth
be very enthusiastic about sth: *He just lives and breathes football.*

live and 'learn
1 learn through your mistakes or experience: *I left my bike unlocked for five minutes and it was stolen. You live and learn I suppose.*
2 used for expressing surprise at sth new which you have just heard, read, etc: *It says in this book that the Romans were the first to have a state postal service. Well, you live and learn, don't you?*

live and 'let live (*saying*)
used to say that you should accept other people's opinions and behaviour even though they are different from your own: *If we could all learn to live and let live a little more, the world would be a much happier place.*

live beyond/within your 'means
live on more/less money than you have or earn: *They seemed wealthy but they were living well beyond their means.* ◇ *I find it very hard to live within my means.*

live by/on your 'wits
earn money by clever or sometimes dishonest means: *Patrick did not go to university, as expected, but learned to live very successfully on his wits.*

live (from) ˌhand to 'mouth
spend all the money you earn on basic needs such as food, without being able to save any money: *There's no way we can even think about going on holiday this year, as we are literally living from hand to mouth.* ▶ **hand-to-mouth** *adj.: a hand-to-mouth existence*

live in 'hope
believe there is a chance that what you want to happen will happen one day: *The situation doesn't look too good, but we live in hope.* ◇ *The Johnsons live in hope that one day their son will come home.*

live in 'sin (*old-fashioned or humorous*)
live together and have a sexual relationship with sb, without being married: *Are you two married yet or are you still living in sin?*

live it 'up (*informal*)
have a very enjoyable time, often spending a lot of money: *Since his retirement he has been living it up in the south of Spain.* ◇ *We are very careful with our money, but for two weeks a year while we're on holiday, we really live it up.*

live a 'lie
keep sth important about yourself a secret from other people, so that they do not know what you really think, what you are really like, etc: *In the end she found that she couldn't go on living a lie, and told him the truth.*

live like a 'king
live in very comfortable surroundings, enjoying all the advantages of being rich: *In this luxury resort, you can live like a king.* ◇ *One day we'll be rich, and you and I will live like kings.*

live off/on the ˌfat of the 'land (*informal*)
have plenty of money to spend on the best food, drink, entertainment, etc: *Money was no problem then. We were living off the fat of the land in those days.* ◇ *It's always the same: the rich live off the fat of the land and complain that the poor are lazy.*

live off the 'land
eat whatever food you can grow, kill or find yourself: *Having grown up on a farm, Jack was more used to living off the land than the rest of the group.*

ˌlive to fight another 'day (*saying*)
used to say that although you have failed or had a bad experience, you will continue: *She only just lost the election, so she lives to fight another day.*

live to tell the 'tale (*informal, often humorous*)
survive a terrible experience: *Only one man out of fifteen lived to tell the tale.* ◇ *It will be a difficult experience, but I expect you'll live to tell the tale!*

live up to your/its repu'tation
be as good, bad, etc. as people say: *The restaurant lived up to its reputation. We had a wonderful meal.* ◇ *I'm afraid that he lived up to his reputation. He*

got more and more drunk all evening and finally
went to sleep under the table.

a live 'wire (*informal*)
a lively and enthusiastic person: *You must invite
her to your party—she's a real live wire.* ◇ *We need
a live wire like him in this department. Let's give
him the job.*

be/live in each other's pockets → **pockets**
be/live on borrowed time → **borrowed**
lead/live the life of Reilly/Riley → **life**
live/sleep rough → **rough**

lived

you haven't 'lived
used to tell sb that if they have not had a particular
experience their life is not complete: *You've never
been to New York? You haven't lived!*

lively

look lively/sharp → **look**

lives

have (got) nine lives → **nine**
how the other half lives → **half**

living

be ,living 'proof of sth
show sth is true simply by being alive or existing:
*He plays tennis and golf. He's living proof that a
heart attack doesn't mean the end of an active life.*

in/within ,living 'memory
that can be remembered by people who are alive
now: *These are the worst floods in Britain within
living memory.*

a living 'legend (also **a ,legend in your own
'lifetime**)
a person who has become famous while still alive:
*Her 30-year study of chimpanzees made her a living
legend.*

be the living/spitting/very image of sb/sth → **image**
in the land of the living → **land**
(think) the world owes you a living → **world**

lo

,lo and be'hold (*humorous*)
used when telling a story to introduce sb's unexpected appearance: *I walked into the pub and, lo
and behold, there was my boss with his wife.*

load

get a load of 'this (*spoken*)
used to tell sb to look at or listen to sb/sth: *Get a
load of this. They want to build a new road right
across here.*

a load of (old) 'rubbish, 'nonsense, etc.
(*informal*)
nonsense; worthless: *Don't bother to watch that
film. It's a load of old rubbish.*

a brick short of a load → **brick**
(take) a load/weight off sb's mind → **mind**

loaded

the dice are loaded against sb → **dice**

loaf

half a loaf is better than none/no bread → **half**
use your loaf → **use**

lock

,lock 'horns (with sb) (over sth)
argue or fight with sb: *The lawyers did not want to
lock horns with the judge.*

> ❶ ORIGIN
> This idiom refers to fighting with horns or ant-
> lers between animals such as bulls, stags, etc.

Smith and Jenkins have locked horns over the deal.

,lock, stock and 'barrel
including everything; completely: *They were all
emigrating so they were selling everything they
had, lock, stock and barrel.*

> ❷ NOTE
> The *lock*, *stock* and *barrel* are the three main
> parts of a rifle.

under ,lock and 'key
locked up in prison, in a safe, etc: *The escaped prisoners are now safely under lock and key.* ◇ *The
exam papers must be kept under lock and key until
half an hour before the exam.*

pick a lock → **pick**
shut/lock/close the stable door after the horse has bolted
→ **stable**

loco

in ,loco pa'rentis (*from Latin, formal*)
having the same responsibility for a child as a par-

ent has: *Teachers at a boarding school are acting much more in loco parentis than at a day school.*

lodging

board and lodging → **board**

log

(as) easy as ABC/pie/falling off a log → **easy**
sleep like a log/top → **sleep**

loggerheads

at ˈloggerheads (with sb) (over sth)
disagreeing or arguing very strongly (with sb): *The students are at loggerheads with the college over the price of food in the canteen.* ◇ *Management and staff are at loggerheads over the plan.*

> ❶ ORIGIN
> In the past, a *loggerhead* was a long iron instrument which may have been used as a weapon.

loins

gird (up) your loins → **gird**

lone

a ˌlone ˈwolf
a person who chooses to work, live, be, etc. alone: *In the police force he had the reputation of being something of a lone wolf.*

long

as/so ˈlong as
on condition that: *As long as you tidy your room first, you can go out to play.* ◇ *I'll lend you my car so long as you promise to take great care of it.*

(a list) as long as your ˈarm (*informal*)
(of a list) with many things to do, buy, etc. on it: *I've got a list as long as your arm of things I need to buy for the party.*

for (so) ˈlong
for (such) a long time: *Will you be away for long?* ◇ *I'm sorry I haven't written to you for so long.*

go back a long ˈway
(of two or more people) have known each other for a long time: *We go back a long way, he and I.*

have come a long ˈway
have made good progress and achieved a lot: *The manager has come a long way since she joined the company as a messenger.*

have (got) a long way to ˈgo
need to make a lot of progress before you can achieve sth: *She still has a long way to go before she's fully fit.*

how long is a piece of ˈstring? (*BrE, spoken*)
used to say that there is no definite answer to a question: *'How long will it take?' 'How long's a piece of string?'*

in the ˈlong run
over or after a long period of time; in the end: *Buy-*

ing your own house is a big expense at first but in the long run it's cheaper than paying rent.

it's a ˌlong ˈstory (*informal*)
used to say that the reasons for sth are complicated and you would prefer not to give all the details: *'So why did you leave?' 'Oh, it's a long story—I'll tell you some other time.'*

the long and (the) ˈshort of it
the basic fact of a situation, etc. is: *The examiners discussed your paper for at least an hour, but I'm afraid the long and the short of it is that you have failed.*

the long arm of the law
the ability of the police and the legal system to find criminals and punish them: *You have to be a very clever criminal to escape the long arm of the law.*

(pull, wear, etc.) a long ˈface
(have) a sad or disappointed expression: *I asked him if he wanted to come out but he pulled a long face and said no.* ◇ *Why the long face?*

a long ˈhaul (*informal*)
a long and difficult task or journey: *It was a long haul doing the degree part-time, but it was worth it.* ◇ *They started on the long haul back to the camp.*

(be) ˌlong in the ˈtooth (*humorous, especially BrE*)
old: *I'm a bit long in the tooth for all-night parties.*

> ❶ ORIGIN
> This idiom refers to the fact that some animals' teeth keep growing as they grow older.

a ˈlong shot (*informal*)
an attempt or a guess which you do not expect to be successful but which is worth trying: *Try ringing him at home. It's a long shot, I know, but he might just be there.* ◇ *'Are you going to apply for the manager's job?' 'I don't know. It's a bit of a long shot, isn't it?'*

long time no ˈsee (*spoken*)
used when you greet sb you have not seen for a long time: *Well, hello! Long time no see.*

not by a ˈlong chalk (*BrE*) (also not by a ˈlong shot *AmE, BrE*) (*informal*)
not nearly; not at all: *'Do you think she's ready to take the First Certificate exam?' 'No, not by a long chalk.'* ◇ *This election isn't over yet, not by a long chalk. We need to take our decision.*

not long for this world (*old-fashioned*)
likely to die soon: *She looked extremely ill and I fear she's not long for this world.*

so ˈlong (for now) (*informal*)
goodbye until we next meet: *So long for now. I'll see you soon.*

take a long (cool/hard) ˈlook at sth
think about a problem or possibility very carefully: *After taking a long hard look at the cost of employing an extra person, we decided against it.* ◇ *We need to take a long look at the plan before we make a decision.*

take the 'long view (of sth)
think about the possible future effects of sth rather than its immediate effects: *You always have to take the long view when you are thinking about spending money on education.* ◇ *If we really want to save the planet, we must take the long view in our energy policy.*

go a long/some way towards doing sth → **way**
(as) happy as the day is long/as a clam/as Larry → **happy**
(do sth) in the long/medium/short term → **term**
it's as broad as it's long → **broad**
to make a long story short = to cut a long story short → **cut**

longer

no/any 'longer
used to say that sth which was possible or true before is not now: *I can't wait any longer.* ◇ *He no longer lives here.*

longest

he who laughs last laughs longest → **laughs**

look

by/from the 'look(s) of it/things (*informal*)
judging from the way things seem to be: *From the look of it, there's going to be another war.* ◇ *By the looks of things, we're going to be late.*

look your 'age
seem as old as you really are and not younger or older: *I was surprised when I last saw her—she's really starting to look her age now.*

look 'bad; not look 'good
1 (of behaviour) give a bad impression: *It will look bad if you don't go to the funeral.* ◇ *It doesn't look good if you forget people's names.*
2 suggest probable failure, problems, etc: *Things don't look good for the economy at the moment.*

look before you 'leap (*saying*)
think carefully about the possible risks and effects before you decide to do sth: *I know you don't like this job but don't just accept the first job offered to you. Remember to look before you leap.*

look your/its 'best
look as attractive, neat, etc. as possible: *The garden looks its best when all the flowers are out.*

look 'black
show no signs of hope or improvement: *I know things look black at the moment but I'm sure you'll get a job soon.*

look 'daggers at sb
look at sb very angrily but not say anything: *He looked daggers at her across the room when she mentioned his divorce.*

look down your 'nose (at sb/sth) (*informal, especially BrE*)
behave in a way that suggests that you think that you are better than sb, or that sth is not good enough for you: *Why do you always look down your nose at people who have less money than you?*

look for 'trouble
behave in a way that is likely to cause an argument, violence, etc: *Bored youths hang around outside looking for trouble.*

look a 'fright (*old-fashioned, BrE*)
look ugly or ridiculous: *Oh no, just look at what the hairdresser's done to my hair! I look a fright!*

(not) look a ˌgift horse in the 'mouth (*informal*)
(not) find sth wrong with sth given to you free: *He didn't want to accept the offer of a free holiday but I told him not to look a gift horse in the mouth.*

> ❶ ORIGIN
> The usual way to judge the age of a horse is to look at its teeth.

look 'good
show success or that sth good might happen: *This year's sales figures are looking good.*

ˌlook 'here! (*old-fashioned*)
used when you are going to say sth important to sb and you are annoyed or angry: *Look here, I've been waiting to be served for half an hour. The service here is terrible.* ◇ *Look here, I paid a lot of money for this car. I certainly didn't expect it to break down after a month.*

(be unable to) look sb in the 'eye(s)/'face
(be unable to) look at sb directly (because you feel embarrassed, ashamed, etc.): *I knew he was lying because he wouldn't look me in the eye when he spoke.*

look 'kindly on/upon sb/sth (*formal*)
approve of sb/sth: *He hoped they would look kindly on his request.*

look 'lively/'sharp (*BrE, informal*)
do sth quickly; hurry up: *Come on, look lively or we won't get to the station in time.*

look on the 'bright side
be cheerful or hopeful about a bad situation, for example by thinking only of the advantages and not the disadvantages: *I know it's inconvenient to be without a car, but look on the bright side—at least you'll save money on petrol.*

look the other 'way
ignore sb/sth deliberately: *We only had three tickets but the woman at the door looked the other way and let all four of us in.*

look a 'sight (*old-fashioned, BrE*)
be ugly or untidy: *She looked a real sight. A yellow hat, pink dress, black stockings, blue shoes.* ◇ *Your bedroom looks a sight. Go and tidy it.*

look to your 'laurels
do sth to protect your good position or reputation from competition by others: *He thinks he's the best in the class but there's a new girl who is very good. He's going to have to look to his laurels.*

look sb ˌup and 'down (*informal*)
openly look at sb from head to foot in a way that makes them feel embarrassed: *When I started working there, I could feel people looking me up and down and wondering what I was like.*

(not) look your'self (*informal*)
(not) look as healthy as you normally do: *She wasn't looking herself at all yesterday.* ◇ *He looks more himself this morning. His temperature's come right down.*

never/not look 'back (*informal*)
(after a change of career, etc.) become very successful: *She hasn't looked back since she started her own business five years ago.* ◇ *He moved to New York and never looked back.*

not be much to 'look at (*informal*)
not be very attractive: *The boat is not much to look at but it's easy to sail.* ◇ *He's not much to look at, but he's got a great sense of humour.*

to 'look at sb/sth; by the 'look of sb/sth (*informal*)
judging from the way sb/sth appears: *To look at him, you wouldn't think he was the richest person in the country.* ◇ *To look at them, you'd never imagine that they tasted so delicious.*

be/look past it → **past**
be/look a picture → **picture**
a black look → **black**
(give sb/get) a dirty look → **dirty**
look/stare you in the face → **face**
look/stare/gaze into space → **space**
look/feel like a million dollars/bucks → **million**
look/dress the part → **part**
look/feel small → **small**
look/sound suspiciously like sth → **suspiciously**
look who's talking = you can/can't talk → **talk**
not know which way/where to look → **know**
steal a glance/look (at sb/sth) → **steal**
take a long (cool/hard) look at sth → **long**

look-in

not get/have a 'look-in (*BrE, informal*)
not get the chance to do sth you want because of other people who are better or more determined than you: *There are too many good players, so I never get a look-in when they're choosing the team.*

looking

be just 'looking
used in a shop/store to say that you are not ready to buy sth: *'Can I help you?' 'I'm just looking, thank you.'*

be looking over your 'shoulder
be anxious and have the feeling that sb is going to do sth unpleasant or harmful to you: *Many employees are looking over their shoulders, because jobs are at risk and nobody knows who'll be next.*

be looking to do sth
try to find ways of doing sth: *The government is looking to reduce inflation.*

like looking for/trying to find a needle in a haystack → **needle**

lookout

be 'sb's (own) lookout (*BrE, informal*)
be sb's problem because they are responsible for causing it: *If he wants to invest all his money in one company, that's his lookout.* ◇ *It's my own lookout if I fail this exam.*

be on the 'lookout (for sb/sth); keep a 'lookout (for sb/sth)
be searching (for sb/sth): *We're always on the lookout for good computer programmers.* ◇ *I'm on the lookout for a good book on German history.*

looks

if looks could 'kill ...
used to describe the very angry or unpleasant way sb is/was looking at you: *If looks could kill, she thought, seeing the expression that came over his face when he saw her, she'd be dead on the pavement.* ◇ *I don't know what I've done to upset him, but if looks could kill ...*

the devil looks after his own → **devil**

loom

loom 'large
(of an important problem, event, etc.) approach and seem worrying or frightening: *With the local elections looming large, the Conservative party is beginning to look nervous.* ◇ *In your last year of school, public exams loom very large in your mind.*

loop

be in the 'loop; be out of the 'loop (*informal, especially AmE*)
be part of a group of people that is dealing with sth important; not be part of this group: *A lot of people want to be in the loop on this operation.* ◇ *Lawton had gradually been cut out of the information loop.*

knock/throw sb for a 'loop (*AmE, informal*)
shock or surprise sb: *The result of the election knocked most people for a loop.*

loop the 'loop
fly or make a plane fly in a circle going up and down: *The plane looped the loop then disappeared into the distance.*

loose

at a loose 'end (*BrE*) (*AmE at loose 'ends*)
having nothing to do; not knowing what to do: *I'm at a bit of a loose end this afternoon. Do you fancy a game of tennis?*

break/cut/tear (sth) 'loose from sb/sth
separate yourself or sb/sth from a group of people or their influence, etc: *The organization broke loose from its sponsors.* ◇ *He cut himself loose from his family.*

hang/stay 'loose (*informal, especially AmE*)
remain calm; not worry: *It's OK—hang loose and stay cool.*

have (got) a loose 'tongue
talk too much, especially about things that are private: *Be careful what you tell Sam—she's got a very loose tongue, you know.*

the loose 'ends/'threads
the minor details of sth which have still not been dealt with or explained: *We've almost finished the report. There are just a few loose ends to tie up and then it'll be ready.* ◇ *It's a very unsatisfactory detective story. You know who committed the murder, but there are far too many loose ends.*

(be) on the 'loose
1 (of an escaped prisoner, animal, etc.) be free: *There are ten prisoners on the loose.*
2 be enjoying a period of freedom from your normal life or usual rules and restrictions: *Her boyfriend's on the loose in Paris this weekend, but she doesn't seem to mind.*

all hell breaks/is let loose → **hell**
cut loose = let loose → **let**
have (got) a screw loose → **screw**
let loose → **let**
let loose sth → **let**
let sb/sth loose → **let**
play fast and loose (with sb/sth) → **play**
tear (yourself/sth) loose (from sb/sth) → **tear**

loosen

loosen sb's 'tongue
make sb talk more freely than usual: *A bottle of wine had loosened Harry's tongue.*

Lord

(good) 'Lord!; oh 'Lord!
used to show that you are surprised, annoyed or worried about sth: *Good Lord, what have you done to your hair!*
(Some people may find these expressions offensive.)

'Lord ('only) knows (what, where, why, etc.) ... (*spoken*)
used to say that you do not know the answer to sth: *She comes and goes as she pleases. Lord knows when we'll see her again.* ◇ *'Why did she say that?' 'Lord knows!'*
(Some people may find this use offensive.)

lord

'lord it over sb (*disapproving*)
act as if you are better or more important than sb: *A good manager does not lord it over his or her team.*

(as) drunk as a lord → **drunk**

lorry

off the ˌback of a 'lorry (*BrE, informal, humorous*)
goods that **fell off the back of a lorry** were probably stolen. People say or accept that they came 'off the back of a lorry' to avoid saying or asking where they really came from: *Where did you get a new DVD player at a price like that? Off the back of a lorry?*

lose

lose your 'bearings
become lost or suddenly confused: *The old man seemed to have lost his bearings for a moment.*

lose the 'drift/'thread of sth
be unable to follow a story, discussion, etc. because you cannot understand the relationship between events, facts, etc: *I had to go out in the middle of the film and when I came back I found I'd lost the thread entirely.* ◇ *When they started talking about artificial intelligence, I completely lost the drift of the argument.*

lose 'face
lose the respect of other people because you have been defeated: *The government can't agree to the changes without losing face.* ▶ **a loss of 'face** *noun*: *This gives him an opportunity to change his mind without loss of face.*

lose your 'grip (on sth) (*informal*)
be unable to control or do sth as well as you did before: *She's definitely made some bad decisions recently. I think she's losing her grip.*

lose your 'head (*informal*)
become unable to act in a calm or sensible way: *It's a very frightening situation, but we mustn't lose our heads.*

lose 'heart
become discouraged: *The revolutionaries lost heart after their leader was killed.*

lose your 'heart (to sb/sth) (*written*)
fall in love (with sb/sth): *I've quite lost my heart to those little kittens of yours. Can we take one home?*

'lose it (*spoken*)
be unable to stop yourself from crying, laughing, etc.; become crazy: *Then she just lost it completely and started screaming.*

lose your 'life
be killed: *Sixty people lost their lives in the air crash.* ▶ **loss of 'life** *noun*: *Fortunately there was no loss of life in the fire.*

lose your 'marbles (*informal*)
become crazy or mentally confused: *They say the old man has lost his marbles because of the strange things he's been saying, but I'm not so sure.*

lose your 'mind
become mentally ill

lose the 'plot (*BrE, informal*)
lose your ability to understand or deal with what is happening: *You should have seen Jimmy yesterday. I really thought he'd lost the plot!*

lose your 'rag (*BrE, informal*)
become very angry and behave in an uncontrolled way: *He really lost his rag when the children broke another window with their ball.*

lose your 'shirt (*informal*)
lose all or a lot of your money and possessions: *'How did you two get on at the races?' 'I won £80 and Paul lost his shirt.'*

lose 'sight of sth
(of a purpose, aim, etc.) stop considering sth; forget sth: *The government seem to have lost sight of their aims and are now just trying to survive.*

lose your 'touch
lose the skill or ability to do sth which you used to do very well: *I don't know what's happened to her playing. She seems to have lost her touch.* ◇ *He's not as good a salesman as he used to be. He's losing his touch.*

lose 'touch/'contact (with sb/sth)
not write/speak to sb or not hear/read about sb/sth as you did in the past: *She lost touch with most of her old friends when she moved to London.*

lose your 'way
1 become lost: *We lost our way in the dark.*
2 forget or move away from the purpose or reason for sth: *I feel that the project has lost its way.*

not lose any sleep over sb/sth; lose no sleep over sb/sth (*informal*)
not worry a lot about sb/sth: *The business does have problems at present but it's nothing I'm going to lose any sleep over.*

give/lose ground (to sb/sth) → ground
keep/lose your cool → cool
keep/lose (a) count (of sth) → count
keep/lose your temper (with sb) → temper
keep/lose track (of sb/sth) → track
lose/waste no time (in doing sth) → time
make/lose money hand over fist → money
there's no time to lose → time
win or lose → win
you win some, you lose some → win

losing
fight a losing battle → fight

loss

at a 'loss (*informal*)
uncertain about what to do or how to do sth: *We're at a loss to know what to do with all this food from the party yesterday.* ◇ *I was completely at a loss. I couldn't understand the instructions.*

at a ˌloss for 'words
unable to say anything: *He's never at a loss for words, in fact it's difficult sometimes to stop him talking.* ◇ *I was completely at a loss for words. I had never been spoken to like that in my whole life.*

a dead loss → dead

losses
cut your losses → cut

lost

ˌall is not 'lost (*saying*)
there is still a chance that you may succeed, survive, etc: *I know things look bad, but all is not lost.*

be lost for 'words
be so surprised, confused, etc. that you do not know what to say: *When he told me what she'd done to him I was lost for words.*

be 'lost in sth
be giving all your attention to sth so that you do not notice what is happening around you: *to be lost in thought/admiration*

be 'lost on sb
not be understood or noticed by sb: *I'm afraid that joke was lost on me.* ◇ *Good writing is lost on him. He's just not interested in literature.*

be lost to the 'world
be giving all your attention to sth so that you do not notice what is happening around you: *When I went into his office he was staring out of the window, apparently lost to the world.*

be/feel 'lost without sb/sth
feel unable to work or live without sb/sth: *I left my watch at home and I feel lost without it.* ◇ *I'm completely lost without my diary.*

get 'lost! (*informal*)
an impolite way of telling sb to go away, or of refusing sth: *I told him to get lost, but it makes no difference, he just keeps following me around.*

give sb/sth up for 'lost (*formal*)
stop looking for sb/sth because you no longer expect to find them/it: *The fishermen had been given up for lost in the storm but they have now arrived safely back.*

a lost 'cause
an ambition, project or aim which seems certain to end in failure: *For many years he supported the development of the electric car, but he now thinks it's a lost cause.* ◇ *Trying to help him to improve his pronunciation is a lost cause.*

make up for lost 'time
do sth quickly or very often because you wish you had started doing it sooner: *The building work is now behind schedule, but contractors are confident that they can make up for lost time.*

there's no love lost between A and B → love
there's no time to be lost → time

lot

a bad 'lot (*old-fashioned, BrE*)
a person who is dishonest: *I'm not surprised. I always said he was a bad lot, didn't I?*

by 'lot
using a method of choosing sb to do sth in which each person takes a piece of paper, etc. from a container and the one whose paper has a special mark is chosen: *The committee is chosen by lot and its members change annually.*

lots

cast/draw 'lots (for sth/to do sth)
decide who is going to do sth by giving each person

a piece of paper or a stick so that the person who has the paper with a mark on or the shortest stick is chosen: *They drew lots to see who should speak to the parents.*

loud

‚loud and 'clear (*informal*)
said in a very clear voice or expressed very clearly: *The message of the book is loud and clear: smoking kills.* ◇ *He let us know loud and clear that he would not accept students arriving late for his lectures.*

‚out 'loud
in a voice that can be heard by other people: *I almost laughed out loud.* ◇ *Please read the letter out loud.*

for crying out loud → **crying**
think out loud → **think**

louder

actions speak louder than words → **actions**

lout

a lager lout → **lager**

love

(do sth) (just) for 'love/for the 'love of sth
without payment or other reward, because you like the work or the person you are working for: *She works in the museum during the summer but she doesn't get paid. She helps for the love of it.*

for the love of 'God (*old-fashioned, spoken*)
used when you are expressing anger and the fact that you are impatient: *For the love of God, be quiet! I'm trying to concentrate.*

give/send my love to sb (*informal*)
used to send friendly greetings to sb: *Give my love to Mary when you see her.* ◇ *Bob sends his love.*

love at first 'sight
falling in love with sb the first time you meet them: *I never really believed in love at first sight until I met my husband.*

'love from; lots of 'love (from) (*written, informal*)
used at the end of a letter to a friend or to sb you love, followed by your name: *Lots of love, Jenny*

love is 'blind (*saying*)
when you are in love with sb, you cannot see their faults: *I don't like him at all, but she's crazy about him. Well, they say love is blind, don't they?*

‚love you and 'leave you (*spoken, humorous*)
used to say that you must go, although you would like to stay longer: *Well, time to love you and leave you, I'm afraid.*

make 'love (to sb)
have sex (with sb): *They made love all night long.*

not for love (n)or 'money (*informal*)
used to say that it is impossible to do sth: *The show is sold out. You can't get a ticket for love nor money.*

there's no 'love lost between A and B (*informal*)
two people dislike each other: *They may have been the best of friends when they were younger but there's no love lost between them now.*

all's fair in love and war → **fair**
cupboard love → **cupboard**
a labour of love → **labour**
tough love → **tough**

lovely

lovely and 'warm, 'cold, 'quiet, etc. (*BrE, spoken*)
used when you are emphasizing that sth is good because of the quality mentioned: *It's lovely and warm in here.*

everything in the garden is lovely/rosy → **garden**

low

be/run 'low (on sth)
not have much of sth left: *We're running low on petrol. Do you think we'll have enough to get home?*

(at) a low 'ebb
not as good, strong, successful, etc. as usual: *Business confidence is at a low ebb at the moment.* ◇ *Our family fortunes are at a bit of a low ebb.*

> **❶ ORIGIN**
> This idiom refers to a very low tide, when the sea is a long way from the land.

adopt, keep, etc. a high/low profile → **profile**
be in high/low spirits → **spirits**
high and low → **high**
lay sb low → **lay**
lie low → **lie**
set your sights high/low → **set**
sink so low → **sink**
stoop so low (as to do sth) → **stoop**

low-down

give sb/get the 'low-down (on sb/sth) (*informal*)
give sb/get the important and true facts about sb/sth: *Can you give me the low-down on this deal with the Bank of China?*

lower

lower the 'tone (of sth)
make the general character and attitude of sth, such as a piece of writing or the atmosphere of an event, less polite or respectable: *Residents were afraid that a fast-food restaurant would lower the tone of the street.*

'lower yourself (by doing sth)
(usually used in negative sentences) behave in a way that makes other people respect you less: *I wouldn't lower myself by working for him.*

raise/lower your sights → **sights**
raise/lower the temperature → **temperature**

luck

any 'luck? (*spoken*)

used to ask sb if they have been successful with sth: *'Any luck?' 'No, they're all too busy to help.'*

be down on your 'luck (*informal*)

have no money because of a period of bad luck: *He employed a retired soldier who was down on his luck to tidy up the garden.*

do sth for 'luck

1 do sth because you believe it will bring you good luck, or because this is a traditional belief: *Take something blue. It's for luck.*

2 do sth for no particular reason: *I hit him once more for luck.*

good 'luck (with sth) (*spoken*)

used to wish sb success with sth: *Good luck with your exams.* ◇ *Good luck! I hope it goes well.*

good 'luck to sb (*spoken*)

used to say that you do not mind what sb does as it does not affect you, but you hope they will be successful: *It's not something I would care to try myself but if she wants to, good luck to her.*

you're in 'luck; your 'luck is in

you are lucky at the moment: *I knew my luck was in today when all the traffic lights were green on my way to work. And now I've found that money I lost.*

just my, his, etc. 'luck (*informal*)

my, his, etc. typical bad luck: *I wanted the steak but there wasn't any left. Just my luck!* ◇ *They sold the last tickets to the people in front of us. Just our luck.*

the luck of the 'devil; the luck of the 'Irish

very good luck: *You need the luck of the devil to get a seat on the train in the rush hour.* ◇ *It was the luck of the Irish that saved him.*

the ˌluck of the 'draw

the result of chance only: *Some teachers get a job near home, others are sent hundreds of miles away. It's the luck of the draw.*

no such 'luck (*informal*)

unfortunately not: *I thought I might finish early today, but no such luck.*

tough/bad 'luck (*informal*)

1 (*BrE*) used to show sympathy for sth unfortunate that has happened to sb: *'I failed by one point.' 'That's tough luck.'*

2 (also **tough**) (also **tough 'shit** ⚠, *slang*) (*ironic*) used to show that you do not feel sorry for sb who has a problem: *'If you take the car, I won't be able to go out.' 'Tough luck!'* ◇ *If you don't like the idea, tough. You should have said something earlier.*

as chance/luck would have it → **chance**
beginner's luck → **beginner**
the best of (British) luck (to sb) → **best**
better luck next time → **better**
hard luck/lines → **hard**
push your luck → **push**
take pot luck → **pot**

try your luck (at sth) → **try**
worse luck → **worse**

lucky

lucky 'you, 'me, etc. (*spoken*)

used to show that you think sb is lucky to have sth, be able to do sth, etc: *'I'm off to Paris.' 'Lucky you!'*

'you'll, 'he'll, etc. be lucky (also **'you, 'he, etc. should be so lucky**) (*spoken*)

what you expect or hope for is unlikely to happen: *You were hoping I'd come and collect you from the airport after midnight? You'll be lucky! Try a taxi!* ◇ *'Come and see us if you are ever in Australia.' 'I should be so lucky.'*

strike (it) lucky → **strike**
thank your lucky stars (that …) → **thank**
third time lucky → **third**

lull

the calm/lull before the storm → **storm**

lump

have, etc. a 'lump in your throat

feel a tight feeling in your throat caused by a strong emotion: *I didn't cry but I did have a lump in my throat.*

(like it or) 'lump it (*informal*)

accept sth unpleasant because there is no other choice: *I'm sorry you're not happy about it but you'll just have to lump it.* ◇ *That's the situation— like it or lump it!*

lumps

take your 'lumps (*AmE, informal*)

accept bad things that happen to you without complaining: *If we make mistakes, we'll take our lumps.*

lunatic

the ˌlunatic 'fringe (*disapproving*)

members of an organization or group who are more extreme than the others; extreme groups: *It's the lunatic fringe of the Animal Liberation Front which smashes the windows of butchers' shops, not ordinary members like us.*

> **❶ ORIGIN**
> The word *lunatic* means crazy. It comes from the Latin word *luna*, meaning 'moon', because people believed that the changes in the moon caused temporary madness.

lunch

there's no such thing as a free lunch → **thing**

lurch

leave sb in the lurch → **leave**

lurgy

the dreaded lurgy → **dreaded**

luxury

in the lap of luxury → **lap**

lying

take sth lying 'down (*informal*)

accept an insult or offensive act without protesting or reacting: *I'm not going to take this stupid decision lying down. If necessary, I'll take the company to court.* ◇ *She's the kind of person who won't take defeat lying down.*

lyrical

wax lyrical (about sth) → **wax**

M m

machine
a cog in the machine/wheel → cog

mackerel
(be) a sprat to catch a mackerel → sprat

mad
be mad 'keen (on sb/sth) (*informal*)
be very interested in or enthusiastic about sb/sth:
*She's been mad keen on African music ever since she
came back from Zimbabwe last year.* ◇ *He's mad
keen on getting into the army.*

(as) mad as a 'hatter (*informal*)
(of a person) crazy

❶ ORIGIN
The Mad Hatter was a character in Lewis
Carroll's *Alice's Adventures in Wonderland.*
Because of the chemicals used in hat-making,
workers often suffered from mercury poisoning,
which can cause loss of memory and damage to
the nervous system.

(as) mad as a March 'hare (*informal*)
(of a person) crazy

❶ ORIGIN
In the spring hares do a strange leaping dance in
the fields.

be barking mad → barking
hopping mad (about/over sth) → hopping
like crazy/mad → crazy
(stark) raving mad/bonkers → raving

made
have (got) it 'made (*informal*)
be sure of success; have everything that you want:
With his brains and energy, he's got it made. ◇ *A
good job, a beautiful house, lovely children: she's
really got it made.*

(be) 'made for sb/each other
be completely suited to sb/each other: *Jen and
Alan seem made for each other, don't they?*

madness
there's method in sb's madness → method

magic
(have) a/the magic 'touch
(have) a special ability that means you do sth very
well: *She seems to have a magic touch with the children and they do everything she asks.*

weave your magic → weave

maid
an old maid → old

mail
snail mail → snail

main
in the 'main
mostly; on the whole: *In the main, the students did
well in the exam.*

have (got) an eye to/for the main chance → eye

majority
the silent majority → silent

make
Most idioms containing the verb **make** are at the
entries for the nouns or adjectives in the idioms,
for example **make no bones about (doing) sth** is
at **bones**.

make as if to do sth (*written*)
make a movement that makes it seem as if you are
just going to do sth: *He made as if to speak.*

make 'do (with sth); make (sth) 'do
manage with sth that is not really satisfactory: *I
really need a large frying pan but if you haven't got
one I'll have to make do with that small one.* ◇ *I
didn't have time to go shopping today so we'll just
have to make do.*

make a 'go of sth (*informal*)
be successful in sth: *We've had quite a few problems in our marriage, but we're both determined to
make a go of it.*

make 'good (*informal*)
become rich and successful, especially when you
have started your life poor and unknown: *He's a
local boy **made good**.*

make good sth
1 pay for, replace or repair sth that has been damaged or lost: *The suitcase went missing at the airport so the airline have agreed to make good the
loss.* ◇ *The mechanic explained that they would
have to make good the damage to the body of the car
before they resprayed it.*
2 do what you promised, threatened, intended,
etc. to do: *When she became President she made
good her promise to ensure equal pay for both men
and women.*

'make it
1 be successful in your job: *She's a very good dancer but I'm not sure she'll make it as a professional.*
◇ *He wants to be a professor by the time he's 30. Do
you think he'll make it?*

2 succeed in reaching a place: *The train leaves in ten minutes. Hurry up or we won't make it.* ◇ *I don't think we'll make it before dark.*
3 survive after an illness, accident, etc: *'Do you think she's going to make it, doctor?' 'It's really too soon to say.'*

'**make it with sb** (*AmE, slang*)
have sex with sb

make like … (*AmE, informal*)
pretend to be, know or have sth in order to impress people: *He makes like he's the greatest actor of all time.*

make the 'most of sth
get as much good as you can out of sth: *The meeting finished early so I decided to make the most of being in London and do some shopping.* ◇ *The opportunity won't come again so make the most of it now.*

make the 'most of yourself, himself, etc.
look as attractive as possible: *She's a pretty girl but she doesn't make the most of herself.*

make 'much of sb/sth (*written*)
treat sb/sth as important: *The media made much of the fact that she was the first woman pilot to fly a jumbo jet.*

make nothing 'of sth
treat sth as easy or unimportant: *I know that she lost a lot of money on that property deal, but when I asked her about it, she made nothing of it at all.* ◇ *He made nothing of it—pretended he didn't mind.*

'**make something of yourself**
be successful in your life: *I really wanted to make something of myself, so I decided to stay on at school and then maybe go to university.*

on the 'make (*informal, disapproving*)
1 trying openly to become successful, rich, etc: *Bill Johnson? Now, there's a young man on the make. Success at any price—that's what he wants.*
2 trying to find a sexual partner: *It was one of those terrible parties where half the men were on the make and the other half were really boring.*

Maker
meet your Maker → meet

making
be the 'making of sb/sth
be the reason that sb/sth succeeds or develops well: *It was only a small part on a TV show, but it was the making of her.* ◇ *Those two years of hard work were the making of him.*

in the 'making
developing into sth or being made: *He's very good at public speaking—I think he's a politician in the making.*

of your own 'making
(used about a problem or difficulty) caused by you rather than by sb/sth else: *The problem is of your own making, so don't try to blame anyone else.*

makings
have (got) the 'makings of sth
(of a person) have the necessary qualities or character to become sth: *She's got the makings of a good tennis player, but she needs to practise much harder.*

malice
with ˌmalice aˈforethought (*law*)
with the deliberate intention of committing a crime or harming sb: *Suddenly Guy, more by way of a nervous twitch than with malice aforethought, pulled the trigger.*

mama
a mama's boy = a mummy's/mother's boy → **boy**

man
be sb's 'man/'woman
be the best person to do a particular job, etc: *If you need a driver, then I'm your man.* ◇ *If you need a good music teacher, she's your woman.*

be 'man enough (to do sth/for sth)
be brave enough (to do sth): *He won't fight—he's not man enough!*

be no good/use to ˌman or 'beast (*informal*)
be completely useless: *Since the Chernobyl disaster the land round here has been no use to man or beast.*

be your own 'man/'woman
act or think independently, not following others or being ordered: *Working for himself meant that he could be his own man.*

every man has his 'price; everyone has their 'price (*saying*)
everyone can be persuaded to do sth against their moral principles if you offer them enough money

it's every ˌman for him'self (*saying*)
you must think about your own interests, safety, etc. first, before the interests, etc. of other people: *In business, it's every man for himself.*

make a 'man (out) of sb
make a young man develop and become more adult: *My father was very old-fashioned. He was always trying to 'make a man of me' by taking me fishing or camping with him.*

a/the ˌman about 'town
a man who frequently goes to fashionable parties, clubs, theatres, etc.

ˌman and 'boy
from when sb was young to when they were old or older: *He's been doing the same job for 50 years—man and boy.*

the ˌman (and/or ˌwoman) in the 'street (*BrE* also **the man (and/or woman) on the ˌClapham 'omnibus**, *old-fashioned*)
an average or ordinary person, either male or female: *You have to explain it in terms that the man in the street would understand.*

a ˌman of 'God/the 'cloth (old-fashioned, formal)
a religious man, especially a priest or a clergyman

the ˌman of the 'match (BrE, sport)
the man who plays the best in a game of football,
cricket, etc.

a ˌman of the 'people
(especially of a politician) a man who understands
and is sympathetic to ordinary people: The main
reason he was so popular was that despite being one
of the most powerful men in the country, he was also
a man of the people.

a ˌman of 'straw
a weak or cowardly person: You don't need to be
frightened of him—he's a man of straw.

ˌman to 'man
between two men who are treating each other honestly and equally: I'm telling you all this man to
man. ◇ a man-to-man talk

man's best 'friend
a way of describing a dog

a 'man's man
a man who is more popular with men than with
women

one man's ˌmeat is another man's 'poison
(saying)
used to say that different people like different
things; what one person likes very much, another
person does not like at all: I'm amazed that Tim
enjoys cricket so much. Still, one man's meat is
another man's poison, as they say.

to a 'man (written)
used to emphasize that sth is true of all the people
being described: To a man, they all agreed.

you can't keep a good man 'down (saying)
a person who is determined or wants sth very
much will succeed: He failed his driving test twice,
but passed on the third try—you can't keep a good
man down!

as one man = as one → **one**
be a man/woman of his/her word → **word**
be a/the poor man's sth/sth → **poor**
be twice the man/woman (that sb is) → **twice**
a dirty old man → **dirty**
a/the grand old man (of sth) → **grand**
the inner man/woman → **inner**
a ladies' man → **ladies**
like a man/woman possessed → **possessed**
a man's home is his castle = an Englishman's home is his
castle → **Englishman**
the man/woman in your life → **life**
a man/woman of few words → **few**
a man/woman of (many) parts → **parts**
a man/woman of the world → **world**
a marked man → **marked**
a new man → **new**
the odd man/one out → **odd**
old man → **old**
your right-hand man → **right-hand**
white-van man → **white-van**

maneuver (AmE) = manoeuvre

manger
a dog in the manger → **dog**

manna
manna from 'heaven
something unexpected, for example a gift of
money, which comes to help you when you are in
difficulties: That cheque for £1000 from my aunt
came like manna from heaven as I had three or four
big bills to pay.

> ❶ ORIGIN
> This phrase comes from the Bible. Manna was
> the food the Israelites found in the desert.

manner
all 'manner of sb/sth
many different types of people or things: The problem can be solved in all manner of ways.

in the manner of sb/sth (formal)
in a style that is typical of sb/sth: a painting in the
manner of Raphael

in a ˌmanner of 'speaking
if you think about it in a certain way: 'Are they
married?' 'In a manner of speaking—they've lived
together for 15 years.'

(as if) to the ˌmanner 'born (formal)
as if a job, a social position, etc. were completely
natural to you: He rides round in a Rolls Royce as if
to the manner born.

what manner of ... (formal or literary)
what kind of ...: What manner of man could do
such a terrible thing?

manoeuvre (BrE) (AmE **maneuver**)
freedom of/room for ma'noeuvre
the chance to change the way that sth happens and
influence decisions that are made: Small businesses have limited room for manoeuvre.

many
as many as ...
used to show surprise that the number of people or
things involved is so large: There were as many as
200 people at the lecture.

a good/great many
very many; a lot: A good many people think she's
right. ◇ There are a great many places in the world
I'd like to visit.

map
(be) off the 'map
(be) far away from other places; (be) remote: It's a
little house in the country, a bit off the map.

put sb/sth on the 'map
make sb/sth famous or important: Her perform-

ance in her first film really put her on the map. ◇ *The newspaper story put the village on the map.*

wipe sth off the map ➜ **wipe**

marbles

lose your marbles ➜ **lose**

March

(as) mad as a March hare ➜ **mad**

march

quick march ➜ **quick**

steal a march on sb ➜ **steal**

marching

get your 'marching orders (*BrE, informal*)
be ordered to leave a place, a job, etc: *When he kept arriving late he got his marching orders.*

give sb their 'marching orders (*BrE, informal*)
tell sb to leave a job, a relationship, etc: *When she found out he was seeing another woman, she gave him his marching orders.*

mare

a 'mare's nest
1 a discovery that seems interesting but is found to have no value
2 a very complicated situation: *This area of the law is a veritable mare's nest.*

marines

(go) tell it/that to the marines ➜ **tell**

mark

be close to/near the 'mark
almost correct or accurate: *The estimate of the total cost had been pretty close to the mark, in fact.* ◇ *She thinks it will take six months to complete the job, but I think eight would be nearer the mark.*

be ,quick/,slow off the 'mark
be quick/slow to do sth or understand sth: *You have to be quick off the mark when you answer a newspaper advertisement for a flat.* ◇ *Jenny was rather slow off the mark, and they had to explain the joke to her.*

get off the 'mark
start scoring, especially in cricket: *Stewart got off the mark with a four.*

,hit/,miss the 'mark
succeed/fail in achieving or guessing sth: *He blushed furiously and Robyn knew she had hit the mark.*

,leave/,make your/its 'mark (on sth/sb)
do sth important, that has a lasting effect or makes a lasting impression (on sth/sb): *As Minister for Education, he left his mark on British politics.* ◇ *Her two unhappy marriages have left their mark (= have made her an unhappy person).*

,make your 'mark
become famous because you are very good at sth: *He's an actor who has made his mark in comedy films.*

,mark my 'words (*old-fashioned, spoken*)
(often used for introducing a warning) listen carefully to what I am saying: *He'll be back, mark my words! He never stays away for long.*

mark 'time
stay in one situation, job, etc., not making any progress, but waiting for an opportunity to do so: *'What are you doing at the moment?' 'I'm just marking time until somebody offers me a better job.'*

> **❶ NOTE**
> If soldiers *mark time*, they march on one spot without moving forward.

,mark 'you (*old-fashioned, spoken, especially BrE*)
used to remind sb of sth they should consider in a particular case: *She hasn't had much success yet. Mark you, she tries hard.*

,up to the 'mark
as good as it/they should be: *His English and History are very good, but his maths is not really up to the mark.* ◇ *I don't think we should promote her. She's just not up to the mark.*

be (a long) way off the mark = be/fall wide of the mark ➜ **wide**

a black mark (against sb) ➜ **black**

high-water mark ➜ **high-water**

overshoot the mark ➜ **overshoot**

overstep the mark/line ➜ **overstep**

a question mark hangs over sb/sth ➜ **question**

there's a question mark (hanging) over sb/sth ➜ **question**

toe the mark ➜ **toe**

marked

a marked 'man
a man who is in danger of being killed by his enemies: *When they discovered he was a spy, he became a marked man.*

market

(be) in the 'market for sth (*informal*)
(be) interested in buying sth: *I'm not in the market for a car as expensive as that.* ◇ *Do you know anyone in the market for some stereo equipment?*

on the 'market
available for sale: *This computer isn't on the market yet. You should be able to buy one early next year.* ◇ *This house only came on the market yesterday.* ◇ *We're putting a new range of cosmetics on the market next month.*

the black market ➜ **black**

the bottom drops/falls out of the market ➜ **bottom**

a buyer's market ➜ **buyer**

corner the market (in sth) ➜ **corner**

flood the market ➜ **flood**

on the open market ➜ **open**

play the market ➜ **play**

price yourself/sth out of the market → **price**
a seller's market → **seller**

marks

on your ˌmarks, get ˌset, ˈgo!

used to tell runners in a race to get ready and then to start: *He raised the starting gun. 'On your marks, get set, go!' he shouted, and fired into the air.*

full marks (to sb for doing sth) → **full**

marriage

a marriage/match made in heaven → **heaven**

marrow

chill sb to the bone/marrow → **chill**

marry

marry in ˈhaste (, repent at ˈleisure) *(saying)*

people who marry quickly, without really getting to know each other, will discover later that they have made a mistake

marry ˈmoney

marry a rich person: *His sister married money— she lives in Bermuda now.*

mass

be a ˈmass of sth

be full of or covered with sth: *The garden was a mass of flowers.*

mast

nail your colours to the mast → **nail**

master

be your own ˈmaster/ˈmistress

be free to make your own decisions rather than being told what to do by sb else: *There's no point trying to tell him what to do. He's his own master, as you know.*

a past master (in/of/at sth) → **past**

mat

lay, put, roll, etc. out the welcome mat (for sb) → **welcome**

match

be no ˈmatch for sb/sth

not be as good, etc. as sb/sth; not be able to compete successfully against sb/sth: *He's no match for Woods. Woods is much the better player.* ◇ *We are no match for the Japanese when it comes to making cameras.*

find/meet your ˈmatch (in sb)

meet sb who is as good at doing sth as you are, and perhaps better: *He thought he could beat anyone, but he's finally found his match.* ◇ *As a saleswoman, she's met her match in Lorna.*

the man of the match → **man**
a marriage/match made in heaven → **heaven**

mix and match → **mix**
a slanging match → **slanging**
the whole shooting match → **shooting**

matter

(do sth) as a matter of ˈcourse

(do sth) as a regular habit, or as a normal way of behaving: *Before making any important decision, I discuss it with my wife as a matter of course.* ◇ *As a matter of course, you should go to the dentist at least once a year.*

as a matter of ˈfact *(spoken)*

used when you are telling sb sth interesting, new or important: *I'm going home early today. As a matter of fact, it's my birthday.* ◇ *I don't agree, as a matter of fact.*

(do sth) as a matter of ˈform

(do sth) because it is polite, or because it is the usual way of doing sth: *We knew everyone agreed, but we had a vote as a matter of form.* ◇ *I need your signature, just as a matter of form.*

be another/a different ˈmatter

be very different: *I know which area they live in, but whether I can find their house is a different matter altogether.*

be the ˈmatter (with sb/sth)

be the reason for unhappiness, pain, problems, etc: *What's the matter, Gail? You look ill.* ◇ *John's been very quiet recently. I wonder if there's anything the matter with him.* ◇ *Don't worry, there's nothing the matter.* ◇ *There's something the matter with this radio. It's stopped working.*

be (all) a matter of sth/doing sth

depend on sth/doing sth: *Success in business is all a matter of experience.* ◇ *Doing anything well is a matter of practice.*

be a matter of oˈpinion

be sth which people disagree about: *'She's a great singer.' 'That's a matter of opinion'* (= I do not agree).

the ˈfact/ˈtruth of the matter

used when you want to show you are being honest, or when you are telling sb sth unusual or surprising: *I didn't take anything, and that's the truth of the matter.* ◇ *The fact of the matter is that they only got married so she could stay in the country.*

for ˈthat matter *(spoken)*

used to say that the second thing mentioned is just as important or true as the first thing: *Don't shout at your mother like that—or at anyone else, for that matter.* ◇ *She thought that TV—and cinema too, for that matter—was bad for children.*

a matter of ˈdays, ˈmiles, ˈpounds, etc.

a certain number of days, miles, etc., especially when this number is small: *Don't worry, it'll only be a matter of hours before he gets back.* ◇ *It will only cost us a matter of a few pounds.* ◇ *Travelling by boat could take us a matter of weeks.*

no matter who, what, where, when, etc.

used to say that sth is always true, whatever the situation is, or that sb should certainly do sth: *Don't open the door, no matter who comes.* ◇ *No matter what he says, don't trust him.* ◇ *I'll find her, no matter where she's hiding.*

grey matter → **grey**
the heart of the matter → **heart**
it's only, just, etc. a matter/question of time (before …) → **time**
mind over matter → **mind**
no laughing matter → **laughing**

matters

take matters into your own 'hands
do sth yourself, because you are tired of waiting for sb else to do it: *The police were doing nothing about finding my car, so I decided to take matters into my own hands and look for it myself.*

not mince matters → **mince**

mature

on mature re'flection/conside'ration (*formal*)
after thinking about sth carefully and for a long time: *He wanted to ban his staff from using the Internet at work, but on mature reflection he decided that this would not be good for morale.*

may

be that as it 'may; that's as 'may be (*formal*)
in spite of that: *I know he's tried hard; be that as it may, his work is just not good enough.* ◇ *'That dress cost £800.' 'That's as may be, I still don't like it.'*

McCoy

the real McCoy → **real**

mea

mea 'culpa (*from Latin, often humorous*)
used when you are admitting that sth is your fault: *'Who broke this glass?' 'Mea culpa,' Frank said.*

❷ NOTE
The meaning of the Latin phrase is 'my fault'.

meal

make a 'meal (out) of sth (*informal*)
do sth with more effort and care than it really needs; treat sth as more serious than it really is: *Just write her a short note—don't make a meal of it.* ◇ *It's only a small mistake. There's no need to make such a meal out of it, is there?*

a 'meal ticket (*informal*)
a person or thing that you see only as a source of money and food: *He suspected that he was just a meal ticket for her.* ◇ *His violin had become little more than a meal ticket.*

a square meal → **square**

mean

be no mean 'sth (*approving*)
be a thing of a very high quality; be a very good example of sth: *This is no mean whisky, Bob. Where did you get it?* ◇ *Cycling around France at the age of 75 is no mean feat.*

be/mean 'nothing to sb (*informal*)
not be important for sb; not be a person that sb loves: *Why should he go to the funeral? The dead man was nothing to him.* ◇ *The danger meant nothing to them.*

the happy/golden 'mean (*approving*)
a course of action that is not extreme: *To be honest, I don't like either of the proposals. What we really need is a golden mean between the two.*

I mean (*spoken*)
used to explain or correct what you have just said: *I blame the parents. I mean, would you allow a 13-year-old to stay out until 2 o'clock in the morning?*

mean 'business (*informal*)
be serious about what you plan to do; be determined: *He means business. If we try to escape, he'll shoot us.* ◇ *I'm not joking. This time I really mean business.*

mean (sb) no 'harm; not mean (sb) any 'harm
not have any intention of hurting sb: *Try not to worry about what he said. I know you thought he was rude, but he didn't mean any harm by it.*

mean to 'say
used to emphasize what you are saying or to ask sb if they really mean what they say: *I mean to say, you should have known how he would react!* ◇ *Do you mean to say you've lost it?*

'mean well (*usually disapproving*)
have good intentions, although their effect may not be good: *Your father means well, I know, but I wish he'd stop telling us what to do.* ◇ *She's always suggesting ways I could improve my cooking. I know she means well but it really annoys me.*
▶ **,well-'meaning** *adj.*: *She's very well-meaning, but she only makes the situation worse.*

be/mean (all) the world to sb → **world**
what's that supposed to mean? → **supposed**

meaning

get sb's 'meaning (*informal*)
understand what sb is really saying: *I get your meaning. You don't need to say any more.*

not know the meaning of the word → **know**

means

by 'all means (*spoken*)
used to say that you are very willing for sb to have sth or do sth: *'Can I smoke?' 'By all means.'* ◇ *'Do you think I could borrow this dictionary?' 'Yes, by all means.'*

by means of sth (*formal*)

with the help of sth: *The load was lifted by means of a crane.*

by 'no (manner of) means; not by 'any (manner of) means

in no way at all; definitely not: *She is by no means poor, believe me. She only pretends to be.* ◇ *He hasn't won yet, not by any manner of means.*

(be) a ˌmeans to an 'end

a thing you do only in order to achieve or obtain sth else: *He saw his marriage simply as a means to an end—he was only interested in his wife's money.*

by fair means or foul → **fair**
the end justifies the means → **end**
last but by no means least → **last**
live beyond/within your means → **live**
ways and means → **ways**

meant

be meant to be sth

be generally considered to be sth: *This restaurant is meant to be excellent.*

meantime

in the 'meantime/'meanwhile

in the time between two things happening: *In five minutes, there's the news. In the meantime, here's some music.* ◇ *The bus doesn't leave until six o'clock. In the meantime we can go and have a coffee.* ◇ *I hope to go to medical school eventually. In the meanwhile, I'm going to study chemistry.*

measure

beyond 'measure (*formal*)

very much: *His relief was beyond measure.* ◇ *It has improved beyond measure.*

(do sth) for good 'measure

(do sth) extra in order to make certain that everything is all right, safe, etc: *Put a couple more spoonfuls of tea in the pot for good measure. There's nothing worse than weak tea.* ◇ *I've put new locks on all the doors, and just for good measure, I've put locks on all the downstairs windows too.*

full/short 'measure

the whole of sth or less of sth than you expect or should have: *We experienced the full measure of their hospitality.* ◇ *The concert only lasted an hour, so we felt we were getting short measure.*

get/have/take the 'measure of sb; get/have/take sb's 'measure (*formal*)

form an opinion about sb's character or abilities so that you can deal with them: *After only one game, the champion had the measure of his young opponent.*

in great, large, etc. 'measure (*formal*)

to a great extent or degree: *His success is in great measure the result of good luck.* ◇ *You are in large measure responsible for all our problems.* ◇ *My expectations had been met in full measure.*

in some, equal, etc. 'measure (*formal*)

to some, etc. extent or degree: *The introduction of a new tax accounted in some measure for the downfall of the government.* ◇ *Our thanks are due in equal measure to every member of the team.*

make sth to 'measure (*BrE*)

make a piece of clothing especially for sb, by taking personal measurements: *All his shirts are made to measure.* ▶ ˌmade-to-'measure *adj.*: *a made-to-measure suit*

measures

no half measures → **half**

meat

be meat and 'drink (to sb)

be sth that a person enjoys very much or is very interested in: *Stories about the royal family are meat and drink to journalists.*

dead meat → **dead**
one man's meat is another man's poison → **man**

meat-and-potatoes

ˌmeat-and-po'tatoes (*AmE*)

dealing with or interested in the most basic and important aspects of sth: *a meat-and-potatoes argument* ◇ *My father always was a meat-and-potatoes man* (= a person who likes simple things).

medal

he, she, etc. deserves a medal → **deserves**

medicine

give sb a taste/dose of their own 'medicine

treat sb in the same unpleasant, unkind, rude, etc. way that they have treated you: *Give her a dose of her own medicine and make her wait for you. Then maybe she won't be so slow next time.*

take your 'medicine (like a 'man) (*usually humorous*)

accept sth unpleasant, for example, punishment, without protesting or complaining: *He really hates shopping, but he goes anyway and takes his medicine like a man.*

the best medicine → **best**

medium

a/the happy medium → **happy**
(do sth) in the long/medium/short term → **term**

meet

meet the/your 'eye(s)

be seen: *A strange sight met our eyes.*

meet sb's 'eyes (also **meet sb's 'gaze, 'look, etc.**)

look straight at sb because you realize that they are looking at you: *She was afraid to meet my eyes because she knew what I was thinking.* ◇ *She met his gaze without flinching.*

meet sb half'way
reach an agreement with sb by giving them part of what they want: *I can't agree to all your sugges-tions, but I am prepared to meet you halfway.*

meet your 'Maker (*especially humorous*)
die: *The car was out of control. There was nothing I could do except prepare to meet my maker!*

,meet your Water'loo
be finally defeated: *She can usually beat anyone at chess, but I think with Kathy she's met her Waterloo.*

> **ⓘ ORIGIN**
> This idiom refers to the Battle of Waterloo in 1815, in which Napoleon was finally defeated and taken prisoner.

find/meet your match (in sb) → **match**
I'm (very) pleased to meet you → **pleased**
make (both) ends meet → **ends**
never the twain shall meet → **twain**

meeting

a meeting of 'minds
people thinking in the same way about sth; a spe-cial understanding between people: *I think there will be a meeting of minds on this subject.* ◇ *The discussions were a failure. There was no meeting of minds between the two parties.*

meets

there's more to sb/sth than meets the 'eye
a thing or a person is more complicated, difficult, interesting, etc., than it appears: *Sailing isn't easy—there's a lot more to it than meets the eye.* ◇ *Colleagues felt that there was more to his resigna-tion than met the eye.*

melt

,melt in your 'mouth
(of food) be soft and very good to eat: *They serve steaks that just melt in your mouth.*

butter wouldn't melt in his, her, etc. mouth → **butter**

melting

in the 'melting pot (*especially BrE*)
likely to change; in the process of changing: *The project is in the melting pot at the moment, so we'd better wait for a while before we make any decisions.*

memory

if my ,memory serves me 'well, cor'rectly, etc.; if ,memory 'serves
if I remember correctly: *I first went to Canada in June 1982, if my memory serves me right.* ◇ *It was 1997, if memory serves.*

(do sth) in memory of sb
(do sth) to remember sb who is dead, especially to show love and respect: *He goes to France every year in memory of his late wife, who was French.* ◇ *Monuments were built in memory of those who died in the war.*

take sb/go down ,memory 'lane; take a trip down ,memory 'lane
(make sb) remember pleasant things that hap-pened a long time ago: *Reading those letters took me down memory lane.* ◇ *We'll be taking a trip down memory lane this evening when Mary Smithson talks about her 50 years in film-making.*

be engraved/etched on/in your heart/memory/mind → **engraved**
have (got) a mind/memory like a sieve → **sieve**
in/within living memory → **living**
jog sb's memory → **jog**
refresh sb's/your memory → **refresh**
slip sb's memory/mind → **slip**

men

sort out/separate the ,men from the 'boys
show or prove who is brave, skilful, etc. and who is not: *OK everybody, today we're going to do a phys-ical fitness test, which will soon sort out the men from the boys!*

be all things to all men/people → **things**

mend

be on the 'mend (*informal, especially BrE*)
be getting better after an illness or injury: *Jan's been very ill, but she's on the mend now.*

make do and 'mend (*especially BrE*)
mend, repair or make things yourself instead of buying new things: *Anybody who has lived through a war knows how to make do and mend.*

mend (your) 'fences (with sb) (*BrE*)
find a solution to a disagreement with sb: *Is it too late to mend fences with your ex-wife?*

mend your 'ways (*BrE*)
improve your behaviour, way of living, etc: *If Richard doesn't mend his ways, they'll throw him out of college.*

mended

least said soonest mended → **least**

mental

go 'mental (*BrE, slang*)
become very angry: *My dad'll go mental when he sees what we've done!*

make a mental 'note of sth/to do sth
make an effort to remember sth (without writing it down): *I must make a mental note to order more wood.* ◇ *She made a mental note of the car's regis-tration number.*

mention

don't 'mention it (*spoken*)
used as a polite reply when a person thanks you: *'Thanks—that's very kind!' 'Don't mention it.'*

mention sb/sth in the same 'breath
compare a person or thing with another much better person or thing: *How can you mention the Beatles and the Spice Girls in the same breath?*

not to mention sth
used to introduce extra information and emphasize what you are saying: *He's got a house in London and a cottage in the country, not to mention the villa in Spain.*

mentis

be compos mentis → compos

merchant

a doom merchant = a prophet of doom → prophet

mercies

be grateful/thankful for small mercies → small
leave sb/sth to the mercy/mercies of sb/sth → leave

mercy

(be) at the mercy of sb/sth
not be able to stop sb/sth harming you because they have power or control over you: *Small businesses are completely at the mercy of the banks these days.* ◇ *The little ship was at the mercy of the storm.*

have (got) sb at your 'mercy
have (got) sb completely in your power or under your control: *I've got you at my mercy now. What shall I do with you?*

leave sb/sth to the mercy/mercies of sb/sth → leave
throw yourself on sb's mercy → throw

merge

merge into the 'background
(of a person) behave quietly when you are with a group of people so that they do not notice you: *Nick didn't say anything during the meeting, and it was obvious that he was desperately trying to merge into the background.*

merrier

the ˌmore the 'merrier (*saying*)
the more people or things there are, the better the situation will be or the more fun people will have: *Bring as many friends as you like to the party. The more the merrier.*

merry

make 'merry (*old-fashioned*)
enjoy yourself by singing, laughing, drinking, etc: *There was a group of rugby players making*

merry in the bar last night until gone 2 o'clock.
▶ 'merrymaking *noun*: *There was a lot of merrymaking in this town when Leeds won the cup final.*

eat, drink and be merry → eat

mess

make a 'mess/'hash of sth/doing sth (*informal*)
do sth very badly: *We tried making some wine, but we made a mess of it* (= it did not taste good). ◇ *I made a complete hash of the whole exam.*

message

get the 'message (*BrE, informal*)
understand what sb means, even if they do not say it directly: *She said she was too busy to see me—I got the message, and didn't ask her again.*

on/off 'message
(of a politician) stating/not stating the official point of view of their political party: *Despite their internal problems, the party maintains a public front of staying on message.*

messing

ˌno 'messing (*informal*)
used to show that you are telling the truth, or to ask sb if they are telling the truth: *That's the honest truth! No messing!* ◇ *Are you sure? No messing?*

method

there's ˌmethod in sb's 'madness
there is a reason for your behaviour and it is not as strange or as stupid as it seems: *'Why do you always read your newspaper backwards?' 'Ah, there's method in my madness—the back pages are where the sport is.'*

> **❶ ORIGIN**
> This comes from Shakespeare's play *Hamlet*: 'Though this be madness, yet there is method in't (= in it).'

mettle

be on, show, prove, etc. your 'mettle
(be prepared to) do the best work you can or perform as well as you can in a particular situation: *When the boss comes round, I want you all to show your mettle.* ◇ *He'll have to be on his mettle if he wants to win the next race.*

> **❶ NOTE**
> *Mettle* is the ability and determination to do sth successfully in spite of difficult conditions.

put sb on their 'mettle
make sb do the best work they can, or perform as well as they can: *The school inspection is going to put the teachers on their mettle.*

mice

when the cat's away the mice will play → cat

mickey

take the 'mickey/'mick (out of sb/sth) (*BrE, informal*)
make fun of sb/sth: *Are you taking the mickey?* ◇ *People are always trying to take the mickey out of him because of his funny accent.*

microcosm

in 'microcosm
on a small scale: *The developments in this town represent in microcosm what is happening in the country as a whole.*

Midas

(have) the 'Midas touch
be very successful in making money: *Stephanie has the Midas touch—she makes lots of money whatever she does.*

> **ⓘ ORIGIN**
> In Greek legend, whatever King Midas touched turned to gold.

middle

be in the middle of sth/of doing sth
be busy doing sth: *They were in the middle of dinner when I called.* ◇ *I'm in the middle of writing a difficult letter.*

be sb's middle 'name (*informal*)
used to say that sb has a lot of a particular quality: *'Patience' is my middle name!*

They say 'clumsy' is her middle name.

follow/steer/take a middle 'course; find, etc. a/the middle 'way
follow, find, etc. a plan that is halfway between two opposing plans; compromise: *Kate wanted to stay for the rest of the week, and I wanted to leave straight away, so in the end we followed a middle course and stayed a couple of days.* ◇ *In politics you often have to steer a middle course.*

(be/live) in the middle of 'nowhere (*informal*)
(be/live) somewhere that is a long way from other buildings, towns, etc: *They own a small farm in the middle of nowhere.* ◇ *The house isn't easy to find—it's in the middle of nowhere.*

(be) pig/piggy in the 'middle (*informal*)
(be) a person who is caught between two people or groups who are fighting or arguing: *Her parents quarrelled a lot, and unfortunately she was always piggy in the middle.*

> **❷ NOTE**
> This is the name of a children's game where two children throw a ball to each other, and a third child in the middle tries to catch it.

split sth down the middle → split

midnight

burn the midnight oil → burn

midst

in our, their, its, etc. 'midst (*formal*)
among or with us, them, etc: *There is a traitor in our midst.*

in the 'midst of sth/of doing sth
while sth is happening or being done; while you are doing sth: *a country in the midst of a recession* ◇ *She discovered it in the midst of sorting out her father's things.*

midstream

stop, pause, etc. in mid'stream
stop, pause, etc. in the middle of doing sth or while sth is still happening: *The speaker stopped in midstream, coughed, then started up again.* ◇ *She interrupted him in midstream.*

change/swap horses in midstream → horses

might

might is 'right (*saying*)
having the power to do sth gives you the right to do it: *Their foreign policy is based on the principle that 'might is right'.*

mightier

the pen is mightier than the sword → pen

mighty

high and mighty → high

mildly

put it 'mildly
used for showing that you could have said sth much stronger or more critical, etc: *He was annoyed, to put it mildly* (= he was very angry). ◇ *'She said you didn't like it.' 'That's putting it mildly—it's hideous!'*

mile

go the ,extra 'mile (for sb/sth)
make a special effort to achieve sth, help sb, etc:
Both sides involved in the fighting say they are willing to go the extra mile for peace.

see, spot, smell, etc. sth a 'mile off (*informal*)
see or know (sth) very easily because it is so obvious: *He's wearing a wig—you can see it a mile off.* ◇
You could tell they were tourists a mile off.

stand/stick out a 'mile (*informal*)
be easy to see or notice; be obvious: *He's not telling
the truth—it stands out a mile.* ◇ *It sticks out a mile
that they're having problems.*

a miss is as good as a mile → **miss**
run a mile (from sb/sth) → **run**

miles

be 'miles apart
(of two sides in an argument, dispute, etc.) not at
all close to reaching agreement: *The Government
and the trade unions are still miles apart in this dispute.* ◇ *We're miles apart on our understanding of
the problem.*

be 'miles away (*informal*)
be thinking deeply about sth and not aware of
what is happening around you: *When I ask him a
question in class, he just looks at me. He's always
miles away.* ◇ *'What do you think of Anne's idea,
Dan?' 'Sorry, I was miles away. What idea is that?'*

(be/live) miles from 'anywhere/'nowhere
(be/live) far away from a town, village, other
houses, etc: *The car broke down when they were
miles from anywhere.* ◇ *They live in the country,
miles from nowhere.*

**not a hundred/thousand/million miles away/
from here** (*humorous*)
used to identify sb/sth indirectly: *The person I'm
talking about is not a hundred miles from here, but
I'm not in a position to say who he is.* ◇ *We're talking about a factory not a million miles away.*

milk

the milk of human 'kindness
kind feelings: *There's not much of the milk of
human kindness in him. I've never known such a
hard man.*

❶ ORIGIN
This expression comes from Shakespeare's play
Macbeth.

it's no good/use crying over spilt milk → **crying**
a/the land of milk and honey → **land**
milk/suck sb/sth dry → **dry**

mill

put sb/go through the 'mill
(make sb) experience sth difficult or painful: *It
was a very difficult interview. They really put me
through the mill.* ◇ *She's been through the mill this*

*year. First she lost her job and then her house was
burgled.*

❷ NOTE
A *mill* is a machine for crushing or grinding a
solid substance into powder.

grist for/to sb's mill → **grist**

million

look/feel like a million 'dollars/'bucks (*informal*)
look/feel extremely good: *With her new haircut
and new clothes, she felt like a million dollars, and
looked it too.*

one, etc. in a 'million
a person or thing that is very unusual or special:
My assistant's one in a million. ◇ *It's an opportunity in a million, and we shouldn't waste it.* ◇ *If you
lost your ring on the beach, it's a chance in a million
that you'll find it again.* ◇ *I think there's about a
one-in-a-million chance of winning.*

a hundred/thousand/million and one (things, etc. to do,
etc.) → **hundred**
the million dollar question = the sixty-four thousand dollar
question → **sixty-four**
not a hundred/thousand/million miles away/from here
→ **miles**

millstone

be a millstone around/round sb's 'neck
sth which limits your freedom or makes you
worry: *My debts are a millstone round my neck.*

mince

not mince your 'words (also **not 'mince matters**)
speak openly or directly; say what you think, even
though you may offend sb: *Sir John, never a man to
mince his words, said in a TV interview that the
government had lied.* ◇ *I won't mince matters: I
think it's a stupid idea.*

mincemeat

make 'mincemeat of sb/sth (*informal*)
defeat sb completely in a fight, argument, etc.;
completely destroy sb's argument, theory, etc:
*France made mincemeat of Portugal, beating them
5 goals to nil.* ◇ *The professor made mincemeat of
the speaker at the conference.*

mind

at/in the ,back of your 'mind
in your thoughts, but not your main interest or
concern: *I think your father knew at the back of his
mind that he was being deceived.*

be all in sb's/the 'mind
not be true or real; be imagined: *She's not really
ill—it's all in the mind.*

be of one/the same 'mind (about/on sb/sth)
have the same opinion about sb/sth: *Doctors are of*

one mind about the dangers of smoking. ◇ *I am afraid that he and I are not of the same mind.*

be/go ˌout of your 'mind
1 be/go crazy: *You want to go on a parachuting holiday? Are you out of your mind?*
2 confused and upset because of worry, illness, etc: *She's out of her mind with worry.*

bear/keep sb/sth in 'mind; bear/keep in 'mind that ...
not forget about sb/sth: *We'll bear you in mind if a job becomes available.* ◇ *I'll keep your advice in mind.* ◇ *Do bear in mind that the tickets are usually sold very quickly.*

bring/call sb/sth to 'mind
remind you of sb/sth: *Her paintings bring to mind hot summer days in Provence.*

come/spring to 'mind
if sth **comes** or **springs to mind**, you suddenly remember or think of it: *'Have you any suggestions?' 'Nothing springs to mind, I'm afraid.'* ◇ *Just say whatever comes to mind—it doesn't matter.*

do you 'mind (if ...)?
1 used to ask permission or make a polite suggestion to do sth: *Do you mind if I smoke?* ◇ *Do you mind if we discuss this later?*
2 (*ironic*) used to show that you are annoyed about sth that sb has just said or done: *This man pushed into me without apologizing so I turned round and said, 'Do you mind?' and he looked very embarrassed.*

don't mind 'me
1 used when you ask people to ignore you because you do not want to disturb a meeting, lesson, meal, etc: *Don't mind me. Carry on with your supper.*
2 (*ironic*) used for showing your anger at not being included in sth or being asked about sth: *What's the matter with Joanna this morning? I opened the window in the office and she said, 'Don't mind me, will you,' in a really unpleasant voice.*

give your 'mind to sth
think hard about sth: *He hadn't really been giving his mind to the problem.* ◇ *I'm sure you'll learn it if you give your mind to it.*

go over sth in your 'mind
think very carefully about sth that happened to you: *I go over that terrible moment in my mind every day.*

have (got) a good mind to 'do sth; have (got) half a mind to 'do sth
1 used to say that you think you will do sth, although you are not sure: *I've got half a mind to sell my car and buy a new one.* ◇ *I've a good mind to give up this stupid job.*
2 used to say that you disapprove of what sb has done and should do sth about it, although you probably will not: *I've got a good mind to write and tell your parents about it.*

have (got) sth in 'mind; have (got) it in 'mind to do sth
plan or intend to do sth: *What do you have in mind for dinner tonight?* ◇ *How long have you had this in mind?*

have (got) sb/sth in 'mind (for sth)
be planning to ask sb to do a job, or use sth to do a job: *I need a secretary, but I haven't got anyone in mind.* ◇ *I've got a picture by Hockney in mind for the front cover of the book.*

have (got) a mind of your 'own
1 (of people) have your own opinion and make your own decisions without being influenced by other people: *She certainly doesn't need your advice; she's got a mind of her own, that girl.*
2 (*humorous*) (of machines, etc.) behave in a way that you do not expect: *This photocopier has a mind of its own. If I ask for ten copies it does one; if I ask for five, it does fifteen.*

have (got) your ˌmind on other 'things; your ˌmind is on other 'things
not give sb/sth your full attention because you are thinking about sth else: *'He's made a few mistakes today. What's the matter with him?' 'He's got his mind on other things. Family problems mainly.'*

have (got) a mind to do sth
want to do or achieve sth: *He could pass the exam easily, if he really had a mind to.* ◇ *I have a mind to find out the truth behind all this.*

have (got) sth on your 'mind; sth is on your 'mind
be worried about sth; be thinking a lot about a problem, etc: *His daughter's very ill, so he's got a lot on his mind just now.* ◇ *She asked me if there was anything on my mind.*

I don't mind ad'mitting, 'telling you ... , etc.
used to emphasize what you are saying, especially when you are talking about sth that may be embarrassing for you: *I was scared, I don't mind telling you!*

I don't mind if I 'do (*spoken, informal*)
used to say politely that you would like sth you have been offered: *'Another glass of wine, Gary?' 'I don't mind if I do.'*

I wouldn't mind (*spoken*)
used to say that you would like sth or would like to do sth: *I wouldn't mind a coffee.* ◇ *I wouldn't mind living abroad for a few years. What about you?*

if you ˌdon't 'mind; if you ˌwouldn't 'mind (*spoken*)
1 used to check that sb does not object to sth you want to do, or to ask sb politely to do sth: *I'd like to ask you a few questions, if you don't mind.* ◇ *Can you read that form carefully, if you wouldn't mind, and then sign it.*
2 (*often ironic*) used to show that you object to sth that sb has said or done: *I give the orders around here, if you don't mind.*
3 used to refuse an offer politely: *'Will you come*

with us tonight?' 'I won't, if you don't mind—I've got a lot of work to do.'

if you ˌdon't mind me/my ˈsaying so ... (*spoken*)
used when you are going to criticize sb or say sth that might upset them: *That colour doesn't really suit you, if you don't mind my saying so.*

in your ˌmind's ˈeye
as a picture in your mind or in your imagination: *I can see his face quite clearly in my mind's eye.* ◇ *Try to picture in your mind's eye the scene that day.*

keep your mind on sth; your mind is on sth
think about sth; concentrate on sth: *I'll write her a letter later. I can't keep my mind on anything today.* ◇ *Your mind's not on your work today, is it?*

(take) a load/weight off sb's mind
(cause sb to feel) great relief, because a problem has been solved: *Selling the house was an enormous weight off my mind.* ◇ *'I've finished all my essays.' 'I bet that's a load off your mind.'* ◇ *It took a load off my mind when the doctor said there was nothing wrong with me.*

make up your ˈmind
decide sth: *I've made up my mind to be a doctor.* ◇ *She's finally made her mind up.* ◇ *My mind is made up and nothing will change it.*

Shopping with Tom was a nightmare—he could never make up his mind.

the mind ˈboggles (at sth); it boggles the ˈmind (*informal*)
you find it difficult to imagine sth because it is so surprising, strange or complicated: *The mind boggles at the thought of a boxer dressed up as a fairy.* ◇ *The vastness of space really boggles the mind.*
▶ ˈmind-boggling *adj.*: *Distances in space are mind-boggling.*

ˌmind how you ˈgo (*informal*)
1 used to tell sb to be careful: *Mind how you go with that knife—it's very sharp!*
2 used when saying goodbye to sb: *Goodbye then! Mind how you go!*

ˌmind over ˈmatter
the influence of the mind on the body; the power to change things by thinking: *'How does he manage to work when he's so ill?' 'Mind over matter.'*

ˌmind your own ˈbusiness (*spoken, informal*)
think about your own affairs and not ask ques-

tions about or try to get involved in other people's lives: *'Who was the girl I saw you with last night?' 'Mind your own business!'* ◇ *I was sitting in a café minding my own business when a man came up to me and hit me in the face.*

mind your ˌP's and ˈQ's (*informal*)
be careful how you behave; remember to be polite: *Sally's got very strict ideas about how her children should behave, so mind your P's and Q's.*

> **❷ NOTE**
> This expression probably refers to the *P* in 'please' and the pronunciation of 'thank you' which sounds like *Q*.

mind the ˈshop (*BrE*) (*AmE* mind the ˈstore)
be in charge of sth for a short time while sb is away: *Who's minding the shop while the boss is abroad?*

ˌmind ˈyou (*spoken*)
1 used to add to what you have just said, especially sth that makes it less strong: *It's a fantastic restaurant. Expensive, mind you.* ◇ *She's a very unpleasant woman, in my opinion. But a very good doctor, mind you.* ◇ *I've heard they're getting divorced. Mind you, I'm not surprised—they were always arguing.*
2 used after a word you want to emphasize: *When we were children, we used to walk, walk mind you, five miles to and from school every day.*

ˌmind your ˈbacks! (*informal*)
used to tell people to move out of your way, for example when you are carrying something: *Mind your backs! I'm coming through!*

never ˈmind
1 (*especially BrE*) used to tell sb not to worry or be upset: *You failed your driving test, did you? Never mind, they say the best drivers always fail the first time.*
2 used to suggest that sth is not important: *This isn't the place I wanted to take you to—but never mind, it's just as good.*
3 used to emphasize that what is true about the first thing you have said is even more true about the second: *I never thought she'd win once, never mind twice!*

never mind (about) (doing) sth
used to tell sb that they should not think about sth or do sth because it is not as important as sth else, or because you will do it: *Never mind the washing-up—we haven't got time.* ◇ *Never mind saying how sorry you are, who's going to pay for the damage you've done?*

ˌnever you ˈmind (*informal*)
used to tell sb not to ask about sth because you are not going to tell them: *'How much did you pay for it?' 'Never you mind.'* ◇ *Never you mind why I want it, just give it to me.*

put you in mind of sb/sth (*old-fashioned*)
remind you of sb/sth: *Her way of speaking puts me*

in mind of my mother. ◇ *That music always puts me in mind of holidays in Turkey.*

put/set sb's 'mind at ease/rest
do or say sth to sb which stops them worrying about sth: *If you'd phoned me it would have put my mind at ease.* ◇ *He was nervous about meeting my parents, so I tried to set his mind at rest.*

put/set/turn your 'mind to sth
give all your effort and attention to (achieving) sth: *You could be a very good writer if you put your mind to it.* ◇ *He can turn his mind to the detail if he has to.*

put/get sth out of your 'mind
stop thinking about sth; try to forget sth: *Let's put the problems with the bank out of our minds and try to enjoy ourselves a bit. There's no point worrying all the time.*

take sb's 'mind off sth
make sb forget about sth unpleasant for a short time: *I went out to see a film to try to take my mind off my problems.* ◇ *We're trying to take his mind off things a bit.*

to 'my mind (*spoken*)
in my opinion: *To my mind, his earlier works are better.*

with sth in 'mind
for a particular reason: *He wrote the book with his son in mind* (= for his son). ◇ *I went out for a drive, with no particular destination in mind.*

be engraved/etched on/in your heart/memory/mind → **engraved**
bend your mind/efforts to sth → **bend**
blow your/sb's mind → **blow**
bore sb out of their mind → **bore**
cast your mind back to sth → **cast**
change your mind → **change**
close your mind (to sth) → **close**
concentrate the mind → **concentrate**
cross sb's mind → **cross**
drive sb out of their mind/wits → **drive**
a frame of mind → **frame**
give sb a piece of your mind → **piece**
have (got) your heart/mind set on sth/doing sth → **set**
have (got) a mind/memory like a sieve → **sieve**
have (got) a one-track mind → **one-track**
have/keep an open mind (on/about sth) → **open**
(not) in your right mind → **right**
know your own mind → **know**
lose your mind → **lose**
mind/watch your language → **language**
mind/watch your step → **step**
of unsound mind → **unsound**
out of sight, out of mind → **sight**
peace of mind → **peace**
play on sb's mind = prey on sb's mind → **prey**
a practical, scientific, etc. turn of mind → **turn**
presence of mind → **presence**
prey on sb's mind → **prey**
push sth to the back of your mind → **push**
read sb's mind/thoughts → **read**

set your heart/mind on sth/doing sth → **set**
slip sb's memory/mind → **slip**
speak your mind → **speak**
stick in your mind → **stick**
stoned out of your mind → **stoned**
turn sth over in your mind → **turn**
weigh on your mind → **weigh**

minds
be in/of two minds about sth/doing sth → **two**
a meeting of minds → **meeting**

mine
a mine of infor'mation (about/on sb/sth)
a person, book, etc. that can give you a lot of information on a particular subject: *My grandmother was a mine of information on the family's history.* ◇ *People criticize television, but for children it's a mine of information.*

a gold mine → **gold**
your guess is as good as mine → **guess**

minority
be in a/the mi'nority
form much less than half of a large group: *Men are in the minority in this profession.*

be in a minority of 'one (*often humorous*)
be the only person to have a particular opinion or to vote a particular way: *Hannah didn't like the music, but she realized that she'd be in a minority of one if she said anything negative about it.*

mint
in mint con'dition
new or as good as new; in perfect condition: *The books were 30 years old but they were in mint condition.* ◇ *My bicycle isn't exactly in mint condition so I really can't ask much for it.*

make, etc. a 'mint (of money) (*informal*)
make a lot of money: *They've made a mint of money with their new range of travel books.* ◇ *You can earn a mint selling ice cream on the beach in July and August.*

> ❷ NOTE
> A *mint* is a place where money is made.

minus
plus or minus → **plus**

minute
(at) any 'minute/'moment ('now)
very soon: *Hurry up! He'll be back any minute now.*

the minute/moment (that) …
as soon as …: *I want to see him the minute he arrives.*

not for a/one 'minute/'moment/'second/ 'instant (*informal*)
not at all; definitely not: *I didn't think for a minute*

that he was married. ◇ *Not for one instant would I ever consider going there on holiday again.*

this 'minute
immediately; now: *Come down from there this minute!* ◇ *I don't know what I'm going to do yet—I've only just this minute found out.*

to the 'minute
exactly: *The train arrived at 9.05 to the minute.*

‚up to the 'minute (*informal*)
1 fashionable and modern: *She's a tremendous follower of fashion. Everything she wears is up to the minute.*
2 having the most recent information: *Our reporters will keep you up to the minute with the latest developments in Florida.*

at the last minute/moment → last
just a minute/moment/second → just
there's one born every minute → born
wait a minute/moment/second → wait

miracles
work/do wonders/miracles (for/on/with sb/sth) → work

mischief

‚do sb/yourself a 'mischief (*BrE, informal or humorous*)
hurt sb/yourself: *You could do yourself a mischief wearing such tight trousers!*

make 'mischief
deliberately do or say sth that annoys or upsets sb; make trouble for sb: *She told those lies because she was jealous and wanted to make mischief.*

miserable
(as) miserable/ugly as sin → sin

misery

(a) 'misery guts (*informal*)
a way to describe sb who is never happy or who complains a lot: *What's the matter with you, misery guts?* ◇ *He used to be good fun, but he seems to be turning into an old misery guts.*

put sb/sth out of their/its 'misery
1 (*informal*) stop sb worrying by telling them sth that they are anxious to know: *You can't keep telling him to wait for your answer. Put him out of his misery and tell him now.*
2 kill an animal which is badly injured or very ill in order to end its suffering: *You can't let a horse go on suffering such terrible pain. Put it out of its misery, please.*

make sb's life a misery → life

miss

give sth a 'miss (*informal, especially BrE*)
decide not to do sth: *I usually go to a yoga class on Mondays, but I think I'll give it a miss this week.*

‚miss the 'boat (*informal*)
lose the opportunity to do or get sth because you do not act quickly enough: *I'm afraid we've missed the boat—all the tickets for Saturday's performance have been sold.*

a ‚miss is as ‚good as a 'mile (*saying*)
there is no real difference between only just failing in sth and failing in it badly because the result is still the same: *What's the difference between failing an exam with 35% or 10%? Absolutely nothing; a miss is as good as a mile.*

he, she, etc. doesn't miss a 'trick (also **he, she, etc. doesn't 'miss much**) (*spoken*)
used to say that sb notices every opportunity to gain an advantage: *I'm sure Julie knows your secret—she never misses a trick!* ◇ *How did he know it was the right time to sell all his shares in the company? He doesn't miss much, does he?*

hit/miss the mark → mark
a near miss → near

misses
your heart misses a beat → heart

missing
not know what you're missing → know

mission

‚mission ac'complished
used when you have successfully completed what you have had to do: *Mission accomplished. Let's go and have a drink.*

mistake

and 'no mistake! (*old-fashioned, especially BrE*)
used to show that that you are sure about the truth of what you have just said: *The dinner party was a disaster, and no mistake!*

by mi'stake
accidentally; without intending to: *I took your bag instead of mine by mistake.*

in mi'stake for sth
thinking that sth is sth else: *Children may eat pills in mistake for sweets.*

‚make no mi'stake (about sth) (*spoken*)
used to emphasize what you are saying, especially when you want to warn sb about sth: *Make no mistake (about it), this is one crisis that won't just go away.*

mistaking

there's no mi'staking sb/sth
sb/sth is easy to recognize; sth is obvious: *There's no mistaking her voice—she's got a very strong Scottish accent.* ◇ *There's no mistaking the new mood of optimism in the country.*

mistress

be your own master/mistress → master

mix

,mix and 'match
combine things in different ways for different purposes: *You can mix and match courses to suit your requirements.*

'mix it (with sb) *(BrE)* *(AmE* **,mix it 'up (with sb))** *(informal)*
argue with sb or cause trouble: *Don't take any notice of what he says. You know what he's like—always trying to mix it.*

mixed

be a ,mixed 'bag/'bunch *(informal)*
a group of people or things of different types or of different abilities: *The entries to the competition were a real mixed bag—some excellent, some awful.* ◇ *This year's students are rather a mixed bunch.*

be/get mixed 'up in sth
be/become involved in sth, especially sth illegal or dishonest: *What have you got yourself mixed up in now?*

be/get mixed 'up with sb
be/become friendly with or involved with sb that other people do not approve of: *I told her I didn't think she should get mixed up with that group, but as usual she ignored my advice.*

have (got) ,mixed 'feelings (about sb/sth)
have both positive and negative feelings (about sb/sth): *I've got mixed feelings about leaving college—it's great to finish my studies, but I'm rather worried about finding a job.* ◇ *They had mixed feelings about their new boss. She seemed very pleasant but not very organized.*

a ,mixed 'blessing
sth good, pleasant, fortunate, etc. which also has disadvantages: *Living in such a beautiful old castle is something of a mixed blessing. Just think of the heating bills, for example.*

mixer

a good/bad 'mixer
a person who finds it easy/difficult to talk to people they do not know, for example at a party: *Whoever we appoint for this position will be dealing directly with our clients. We are looking for someone who is friendly, a good mixer, reliable and practical.*

mob

the heavy mob/brigade → heavy

mockers

put the 'mockers on sth *(BrE, informal)*
stop sth from happening or spoil its chances for success: *According to the weather forecast, it's going to rain, which will really put the mockers on our plans for a barbecue.*

mockery

make a 'mockery of sth
make sth seem worthless or foolish: *This decision makes a mockery of the government's economic policy.*

> **❷ NOTE**
> If you *mock* somebody or something, you laugh at them or it in an unkind way.

mod

(with) all mod 'cons *(BrE, informal)*
(of a house, caravan, etc.) (having) all the things that make living there easier and more comfortable, for example a washing machine, a shower, etc: *We want a campsite with all mod cons.* ◇ *From the outside it looks really primitive but inside it's got all mod cons—even a microwave oven.*

> **❷ NOTE**
> This phrase is a short form of 'modern conveniences'.

Mohammed

if the mountain will not come to Mohammed, Mohammed must go to the mountain → mountain

mold *(AmE)* = mould

molehill

make a mountain out of a molehill → mountain

moment

at the 'moment
now; at the present time: *'The number is engaged at the moment.' 'OK, I'll phone again later.'* ◇ *I'm unemployed at the moment.*

the man, woman, etc. of the 'moment
the person most admired and talked about at a particular time: *This is the woman of the moment: the first Olympic gold medalist in gymnastics in this country.*

the ,moment of 'truth
a time when sb/sth is tested, or when important decisions are made: *He asked her if she still loved him. It was a moment of truth.* ◇ *Right, now for the moment of truth. Switch it on and see if it works!*

of 'moment
(after nouns) very important: *matters of great moment*

pick/choose your 'moment
carefully choose the right time to do sth: *I wanted to make sure she agreed, so I picked my moment, when she was in a good mood.* ◇ *(ironic) You told her you wanted a divorce two days after her operation! You really picked your moment, didn't you?*

(at) any minute/moment (now) → minute
at the last minute/moment → last
at a moment's notice = at (very) short notice → short
the evil hour/day/moment → evil

for the moment / present = for the time being → **time**

in the heat of the moment → **heat**

just a minute / moment / second → **just**

the minute / moment (that) … → **minute**

a moment of weakness = a weak moment → **weak**

not for a / one minute / moment / second / instant → **minute**

(do sth) on the spur of the moment → **spur**

the psychological moment → **psychological**

wait a minute / moment / second → **wait**

a weak moment → **weak**

moments

have your/its 'moments

have short times that are better, more interesting, etc. than others: *My job's rather boring most of the time but it does have its moments.* ◇ *'What did you think of the film?' 'Well, it had its moments, but on the whole it wasn't very good.'*

Monday

that Monday 'morning feeling

a feeling of being depressed because you have to start a new week back at work: *Now I've got a new job, I never have that awful Monday morning feeling.*

money

be in the 'money (*informal*)

have a lot of money to spend: *I'll be in the money if I get this job.*

be 'made of money (*informal*)

be rich; have a lot of money: *I can't afford that! I'm not made of money, you know!* ◇ *Why do people always think that lawyers are made of money?*

for 'my money (*informal*)

in my opinion: *For my money, he's one of the greatest pianists of all time.*

get/have your 'money's worth

get good value for the money you have spent: *What an exciting final it was! The crowd certainly had its money's worth.* ◇ *The film was only an hour long, so we felt that that we didn't really get our money's worth.*

good 'money

a lot of money; money that you earn with hard work: *Thousands of people paid good money to watch the band perform.* ◇ *Don't waste good money on that!*

have (got) ‚money to 'burn

have so much money that you can spend as much as you like: *I was staying at the Ritz—I had money to burn in those days!* ◇ *He's got money to burn. He's just spent £4 000 on a picture of Mickey Mouse.*

have (got) more ‚money than 'sense

have a lot of money, and waste it by spending it in a foolish way: *Collectors with more money than sense pay thousands of pounds for these spoons.*

make/lose money ‚hand over 'fist (*informal*)

make/lose money very fast and in large quan-

tities: *Some of these tennis players are making money hand over fist.*

money burns a hole in sb's pocket (*informal*)

sb spends or wants to spend money very quickly and carelessly: *She can't wait to spend her prize money—it's burning a hole in her pocket.* ◇ *He gets paid on Friday and by Monday he's spent it all. Money just burns a hole in his pocket.*

money doesn't grow on 'trees (*saying*)

used to say that you should be careful about how much money you spend because the amount you have is limited: *'Dad, I've seen a really nice tennis racket in town. It's only £60.' 'I haven't got £60 for a tennis racket, Alice. Money doesn't grow on trees, you know.'*

‚money down the 'drain (*informal*)

a waste of money: *Her father feels that all her expensive education will just be money down the drain if she gets a job in a cafe.*

money for old 'rope (also money for 'jam) (both *BrE, informal*)

money that is earned very easily and with very little effort: *All I have to do in my job is answer the phone occasionally—it's money for old rope.*

money 'talks (*saying*)

if you have a lot of money you can persuade people to do things, get special treatment, have more power, etc: *Of course he'll get what he wants. Money talks, doesn't it?*

on the 'money (*AmE*)

correct; accurate: *His prediction was right on the money.*

put 'money into sth

invest money in sth: *She put the money into stocks and shares.* ◇ *The Government should put more money into the film industry.*

put (your) 'money on sb/sth

1 bet that a horse, dog, etc. will win a race: *He put his money on Second Wind for the 3.30.*

2 (*informal*) be certain that sb will do sth, or that sth will happen: *I'd put money on him passing that exam.* ◇ *I wouldn't put any money on that car lasting much longer.*

put your money where your 'mouth is (*informal*)

show that you really mean what you say, by actually doing sth, giving money, etc. rather than just talking about it: *The government talks about helping disabled people, but doesn't put its money where its mouth is.* ◇ *You think she'll win? Come on, then, put your money where your mouth is* (= have a bet with me).

coin money → **coin**

easy money → **easy**

a fool and his money are soon parted → **fool**

a licence to print money → **licence**

marry money → **marry**

not for love (n)or money → **love**

pin money → **pin**

(be) rolling in it/money → **rolling**
a (good) run for your money → **run**
see the colour of sb's money → **see**
the smart money is on sb/sth → **smart**
throw good money after bad → **throw**
throw your money about/around → **throw**
throw money at sth → **throw**
time is money → **time**
you pays your money and you takes your choice → **pays**

monkey

I don't/couldn't give a 'monkey's (*BrE, slang*)
used to say, in a way that is not very polite, that you
do not care about sth, or are not at all interested in
it: *To be honest, I couldn't give a monkey's whether
you go or not.*

make a 'monkey out of sb
make sb seem stupid or foolish: *No one makes a
monkey out of me.* ◇ *Are you trying to make a monkey out of me? Don't tell me it costs £20 when I know
it only costs £15.*

'monkey business (*informal*)
dishonest or silly behaviour: *There's money missing from the office and it's not the first time it's happened. I think there's some monkey business going
on.* ◇ *That's enough monkey business. Let's get
down to more serious matters. This is a meeting, not
a party.*

brass monkey weather → **brass**

monkeys

brass monkeys → **brass**

monster

the green-eyed monster → **green-eyed**

month

month after 'month
over a period of several months: *Prices continue to
rise month after month.*

month by 'month
as the months pass; each month: *Her pain
increased month by month.*

(not for/in) a ,month of 'Sundays (*spoken*)
used to emphasize that sth will never happen: *'Do
you think she'll be able to sell the house at that
price?' 'Not in a month of Sundays. It's far too
much.'*

flavour of the month → **flavour**

monty

the full monty → **full**

mood

**be in the mood for sth/doing sth; be in the
mood to do sth**
have a strong desire to do sth; feel like doing sth:
*I'm in the mood for going out and having a good
time.* ◇ *She said she wasn't in the mood to dance.*

**be in no mood for sth/doing sth; be in no
mood to do sth**
not want to do sth; not feel like doing sth: *I'm in no
mood for jokes—just tell me the truth.*

moon

be over the 'moon (*informal, especially BrE*)
be very happy and excited: *'How does it feel to have
won the championship?' 'I'm over the moon.'*

❶ **ORIGIN**
This comes from a children's nursery rhyme, in
which *the cow jumped over the moon.*

cry/ask for the 'moon (also **want the 'moon**)
(*BrE, informal*)
want or ask for sth you cannot get, or sth that will
not be given to you: *Is it asking for the moon to hope
for peace in this country?* ◇ *I don't want the moon; I
just want him to listen to me for once.*

once in a blue moon → **once**
promise (sb) the moon/earth/world → **promise**

moonlight

do a moonlight 'flit (*BrE, informal*)
leave the place where you have been living quickly
and secretly, usually to avoid paying your debts,
rent, etc: *When I called to get the money she owed
me, I found she'd done a moonlight flit.*

moons

many 'moons ago (*literary*)
a very long time ago: *Many moons ago, when I was
young …*

moot

be a moot 'point/'question
be a subject that people disagree on or are uncertain about: *It's a moot point whether women or men
make better drivers.*

moral

(give sb) ,moral sup'port
(give sb) your friendship, encouragement,
approval, etc. rather than financial or practical
help: *Will you stay and give me some moral support
while I explain to him why I'm late?* ◇ *Your moral
support alone isn't enough. We need money to fund
this cause.*

**take, claim, seize, etc. the moral 'high
ground**
claim that your side of an argument is morally better than your opponents' side; argue in a way that
makes your side seem morally better: *Don't you try
to take the moral high ground with me! You're just
as bad as I am!*

more

be more than glad, ready, etc. (to do sth)
be very glad, etc. (to do sth): *If you ever want to borrow the car, I'll be more than happy to lend it to you.*

◇ *The project's made very good progress—I'm more than satisfied.*

more 'like (it) (*informal*)

1 better; more satisfactory: *This is more like it! Fresh vegetables—not that canned rubbish.* ◇ *Turn the music up louder! That's more like it!*

2 used to give what you think is a better description of sth: *'How many people were there—about 40?' 'No, more like 20.'* ◇ *Just talking? Arguing more like it.*

,more or 'less

1 almost: *I've more or less finished reading the book.* ◇ *She's finished, more or less.*

2 approximately: *It cost £200, more or less.*

morning

the morning 'after (the night be'fore) (*informal*)
the morning after an occasion when sb has drunk too much alcohol and is feeling tired, ill, etc: *She was suffering from the effects of the morning after.* ◇ *a morning-after headache*

morning, noon and 'night
at all times of the day and night (used to emphasize that sth happens very often or that it happens continuously): *When Sally was a baby she used to cry morning, noon and night.*

that Monday morning feeling → **Monday**

mortal

shuffle off this mortal coil → **shuffle**

mortar

bricks and mortar → **bricks**

most

at (the) 'most
not more than this amount; as a maximum: *I'll be away for a week, or perhaps ten days at the most.* ◇ *There were 50 people there at the very most.*

mother

at your ,mother's 'knee
when you were very young: *I learnt these songs at my mother's knee.*

be 'mother (*old-fashioned, informal or humorous*)
pour the tea: *The tea's ready. Shall I be mother?*

the 'mother country
the country where you or your family were born and which you feel a strong emotional connection with: *The cafe was a meeting place for the immigrants, a welcome reminder of the tastes of the mother country.*

the 'mother (and 'father) of (all) sth (*informal*)
used to emphasize that sth is very large, important, etc: *There was the mother of all storms that night. It lasted for hours.* ◇ *Sorry we're so late. We got stuck in the mother of all traffic jams on the way.*

your ,mother 'tongue
the language you first learned to speak as a child; your native language: *She was born in Singapore, but her mother tongue is French.*

like father/mother, like son/daughter → **father**
a mummy's/mother's boy → **boy**
necessity is the mother of invention → **necessity**

motion

put/set sth in 'motion (also **set the wheels in 'motion**)
do what is necessary to make a start on a (large) project, plan, meeting, etc: *The Government wants to put the new reforms in motion before the election.* ◇ *It will be many years before we see any results, but at least we know that the wheels are in motion.*

ⓘ ORIGIN
This expression refers to starting a large and complicated piece of machinery.

motions

go through the 'motions (of doing sth)
do sth or say sth because you have to, not because you really want to: *He went through the motions of welcoming his friends, but then quickly left the room.* ◇ *She's not really interested in the subject—she's just going through the motions.*

mould (*BrE*) (*AmE* mold)

break the mould (of sth) → **break**

mount

mount/stand/keep guard (over sb/sth) → **guard**

mountain

if the mountain will not come to Mohammed, Mohammed must go to the mountain (*saying*)
if a person cannot or refuses to come and see you, you must go and see them: *He's refused to fly to the USA to see the Defence Secretary, so it's a case of if the mountain won't come to Mohammed …*

ⓘ ORIGIN
This phrase comes from a story about the prophet Mohammed.

make a ,mountain out of a 'molehill (*disapproving*)
make a small or unimportant problem seem much more serious than it really is: *It's not such a big problem! You're making a mountain out of a molehill!*

mountains

move mountains (to do sth) → **move**

mouse

(play) cat and mouse (with sb) → **cat**

(as) poor as a church mouse → **poor**
(as) quiet as a mouse → **quiet**

mouth

be all 'mouth (*BrE* also **be all mouth and (no) 'trousers**) (*informal*)
if you say sb is **all mouth**, you mean that they talk a lot about doing sth, but are, in fact, not brave enough to do it: *Don't be scared of her. She won't hurt you—she's all mouth.*

down in the 'mouth (*informal*)
unhappy and depressed: *Why is she looking so down in the mouth?*

make sb's 'mouth water
make sb feel hungry; make sb want to do or have sth very much: *The smell of your cooking is making my mouth water.* ◇ *The sight of all that money made his mouth water.* ▶ **'mouth-watering** *adj.*: *a mouth-watering smell*

be born with a silver spoon in your mouth → **born**
butter wouldn't melt in his, her, etc. mouth → **butter**
by word of mouth → **word**
foam at the mouth → **foam**
(straight) from the horse's mouth → **horse**
have (got) a plum in your mouth → **plum**
your heart is in your mouth → **heart**
keep your mouth/trap shut → **shut**
leave a bad/nasty taste in the/your mouth → **leave**
live (from) hand to mouth → **live**
(not) look a gift horse in the mouth → **look**
me and my big mouth → **big**
melt in your mouth → **melt**
open your (big) mouth → **open**
put your foot in your mouth → **foot**
put your head in the lion's mouth → **head**
put your money where your mouth is → **money**
put words in(to) sb's mouth → **words**
shoot your mouth off (about sth) → **shoot**
shut sb's mouth → **shut**
shut your mouth/trap/face/gob! → **shut**
take the words (right) out of sb's mouth → **words**
watch your mouth/tongue → **watch**

mouths

out of the ˌmouths of 'babes (and 'sucklings) (*saying*)
used when a small child has just said sth that seems very wise or clever: *It was my daughter who told me I should enjoy life more. She's only four years old, but out of the mouths of babes …*

move

get a 'move on (*spoken*)
hurry; do sth faster: *You'd better get a move on or you'll be late.*

make a 'move
1 (*BrE, informal*) leave one place in order to go to another: *It's getting late. I think it's time we made a*

move. ◇ *I've been in this job far too long already, it's time I made a move.*
2 (also **make your 'move**) do the action that you intend to do or need to do in order to achieve sth: *We're waiting to see what our competitors will do before we make a move.* ◇ *The rebels waited until nightfall before making their move.*

> **ℹ ORIGIN**
> This phrase refers to moving your pieces in a game such as chess.

move the 'goalposts (*BrE, informal, disapproving*)
change the rules for sth, or the conditions under which it is done, so that the situation becomes more difficult for sb: *I've cleaned all the windows, and now you say I've got to clean the car as well. That's what I call moving the goalposts, Dad.*

move heaven and 'earth (to do sth) (also **move 'mountains (to do sth)**)
do everything you can in order to help sb, achieve sth, etc: *His friends moved heaven and earth to free him from prison.* ◇ *Faith can move mountains (= achieve the impossible).*

not move a 'muscle
(of a person) stay very still, without moving: *The patient didn't move a muscle for weeks.*

on the 'move
1 moving or travelling from one place to another: *The army is on the move at last.*
2 very active or busy: *It is important for patients to keep on the move while they are recovering.* ◇ *I can't wait to sit down and relax—I've been on the move all day.*

(do sth) as/if/when the spirit moves you → **spirit**
(make) a/one false move → **false**
make the first move → **first**
move your ass = get your ass in gear → **ass**
not budge/give/move an inch → **inch**

mover

a prime mover → **prime**

movers

ˌmovers and 'shakers
people with power in important organizations: *He is one of the principle movers and shakers in the political arena.*

moves

(do sth) as/if/when the spirit moves you → **spirit**

moving

get 'moving (*informal*)
begin, leave, etc. quickly: *It's late: we ought to get moving.* ◇ *The tourist trade doesn't really get moving until June.*

get sth 'moving (*informal*)

cause sth to make progress: *The new management really got the business moving.*

the moving spirit

the person who begins and leads a group, for example a political party, a group of artists, etc: *He was one of the moving spirits in the establishment of the United Nations.*

Mr

Mr 'Big (*informal, disapproving*)

the most important person in a group, area, etc: *Harry Turner, considered the local Mr Big of the criminal underworld, was found dead today at his home in Wandsworth.*

,Mr 'Nice Guy (*informal*)

a way of describing a man who is very honest and thinks about the wishes and feelings of other people: *He is famous for being football's Mr Nice Guy.* ◇ *I've given them plenty of chances, but now I've had enough. It's no more Mr Nice Guy!*

Mr 'Right (*informal*)

the man who would be the ideal husband for a particular woman: *I'm not going to get married in a hurry—I'm waiting for Mr Right to come along.*

much

as 'much (as)

the same (as): *Please help me—you know I'd do as much for you.* ◇ *I thought as much* (= that's what I expected).

as much as sb can/could 'do (not) to do sth

used to say that sth is/was difficult to do: *No dessert for me, thanks. It was as much as I could do to finish the main course.*

be not so much sth as sth

be one thing but also something else which is more important: *He's not so much unintelligent as uninterested in schoolwork.*

be too 'much (for sb)

1 be stronger or better than sb; beat sb: *Cambridge were too much for Oxford in the boat race this year.*

2 be more than sb is able to do: *A cycling holiday would be too much for an unfit person like me.*

3 used for showing that sb/sth annoys you: *His rudeness towards her is just too much.*

'much as/though

although: *Much as I'd like to stay, I really must leave now.* ◇ *He agreed, much though he disliked the idea of selling the business.*

not be 'much of a sth

not be a good sth: *You're not much of a help, standing there with your hands in your pockets.* ◇ *I'm not much of a cook.* ◇ *It wasn't much of a speech really.*

not much 'in it

used to say that there is little difference between two things: *I won, but there wasn't much in it* (= our scores were nearly the same).

not 'up to much (*BrE*)

not very good: *His French isn't up to much but his German is excellent.* ◇ *The weather wasn't up to much, unfortunately.*

,so much for 'sb/'sth

1 used to show that you have finished talking about sth: *So much for the situation in the Far East. Now let's turn our attention to South America.*

2 used to suggest that sth has not been useful or successful: *She gave the job to the other manager. So much for all her promises to me.*

,so much 'so that

to such an extent that: *His nose wouldn't stop bleeding—so much so that we had to take him to hospital.*

'this much

used to introduce sth positive or definite: *I'll say this much for him—he never leaves a piece of work unfinished.*

very 'much so

used for emphasizing 'yes': *'I understand you are interested in German politics.' 'Yes, very much so.'*

without so much as sth/doing sth; not so much as sth/doing sth

used for emphasizing that sb does not do sth that you expected them to do: *He didn't so much as look at her when she came in.* ◇ *She took the money without so much as a thank you.*

muchness

be ,much of a 'muchness

be very similar (especially of people or things which are not very good): *It's hard to choose between them—they're all much of a muchness.* ◇ *All the restaurants round here are much of a muchness.*

muck

where there's ,muck there's 'brass (*BrE, saying*)

used to say that sb has made a lot of money from an unpleasant or dirty business activity: *When they saw his enormous house and flash car they looked at each other, both thinking 'Where there's muck there's brass.'*

❷ NOTE

Brass is an old-fashioned informal word for 'money'.

mud

fling/sling/throw 'mud (at sb) (*informal*)

try to damage sb's reputation by telling other people bad things about them: *Just before an election, politicians really start to sling mud at each other.* ▶ **'mud-slinging** *noun*: *There's too much mud-slinging by irresponsible journalists.*

,mud 'sticks (also **if you throw enough mud, some of it will stick**) (*saying*)

people remember and believe the bad things they hear about other people, even if they are shown to be false: *Although he was proved innocent, mud sticks, and he found it very difficult to get a job afterwards.*

(as) clear as mud → **clear**

your, his, etc. name is mud → **name**

muddy

muddy the 'waters (*disapproving*)
make sth which seemed clear and easy to understand before seem much less clear now: *Recent research findings have muddied the waters considerably—scientists are having to re-examine all their existing theories.* ◇ *They're just muddying the waters with all this new information.*

mug

be a 'mug's game (*disapproving, especially BrE*)
an activity which brings little or no benefit to you: *Don't start smoking—it's a mug's game.* ◇ *The money's terrible in this job—it's a real mug's game.*

> **❷ NOTE**
> *Mug* here means 'fool'.

mule

(as) stubborn as a mule → **stubborn**

multitude

cover/hide a multitude of sins (*often humorous*)
used to say that sth is not as good as it looks, sounds, etc: *The term 'abstract art' covers a multitude of sins.* ◇ *A coat of paint can hide a multitude of sins.*

mum

keep 'mum (*informal*)
say nothing about a secret; stay silent: *I just kept mum when she asked me where Ben was. She'd be furious if she knew.* ◇ *Please will everyone keep mum about Saturday. We want to give them a real surprise.*

mum's the 'word! (*informal*)
used for telling sb to keep a secret or for telling sb that you will keep a secret: *'Nobody must mention this project outside the office. I hope that's clear.' 'We understand, John. Mum's the word!'*

> **❶ ORIGIN**
> These two idioms refer to the sound you make when your mouth is closed.

mummy

a mummy's/mother's boy → **boy**

munchies

have (got) the 'munchies (*informal*)
suddenly feel hungry: *Can I borrow £2? I've got the munchies and I haven't got any money to buy anything.*

murder

get away with 'murder (*informal, often humorous*)
do sth wrong without being punished, criticized, etc: *His latest book is rubbish! He seems to think that because he's a famous author he can get away with murder!* ◇ *She lets the students get away with murder.*

I could 'murder a ... (*spoken*)
used to say that you very much want to eat or drink sth: *I could murder a beer.*

he, she, etc. will 'murder you (*spoken*)
used to warn sb that another person will be very angry with them: *Your Dad will murder you when he finds out what you've done to his car!*

scream bloody murder → **scream**

scream blue murder → **scream**

murky

(be in/get into) murky/uncharted waters → **waters**

murmur

(do sth) with,out a 'murmur
(do sth) without complaining: *She paid the extra money for the holiday without a murmur.*

Murphy

Murphy's 'Law (*humorous*)
a statement of the fact that, if anything can possibly go wrong, it will go wrong: *Of course it had to be the day of my job interview that the car broke down—it's Murphy's Law.*

> **❶ ORIGIN**
> This expression was named after Edward A. Murphy, Jr., an engineer in the US Air Force.

muscle

not move a muscle → **move**

muscles

flex your muscles → **flex**

music

be (like) ,music to your 'ears
(of information, etc.) be sth that is pleasant to hear: *The news that she'd finally left was like music to my ears.* ◇ *The bell at the end of the lesson is always music to my ears.*

face the music → **face**

must

if you 'must (do sth)
used to say that sb may do sth but you do not really want them to: *'Can I smoke?' 'If you must.'* ◇ *It's from my boyfriend, if you must know.*

mustard

(not) cut the mustard → **cut**

(as) keen as mustard → **keen**

muster

pass muster → **pass**

mutton

be mutton dressed (up) as 'lamb (*BrE, informal, disapproving*)
used to describe a woman who is trying to look younger than she really is, especially by wearing clothes that are designed for young people: *Have you seen her? Mutton dressed as lamb. Somebody should remind her that she's 55, not 25.*

> **NOTE**
> *Mutton* is the meat from an adult sheep, while *lamb* is the meat from a young sheep.

STUDY PAGES

When you are having a conversation, fixed expressions and idioms will link your ideas and show the listener(s) that you are making a new point, disagreeing, etc. Using these phrases gives you time to think about what you are going to say next, and helps your listeners to know what they can expect and so understand your argument better.

A Read the following dialogue and notice the use of the expressions in italics.

> *I say*, have you heard? Richard Smith's leaving. You could apply for his job at the London office.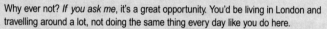
>
> *Funnily enough*, you're the third person who's said that today. Actually, I did know about it, but I wasn't planning to apply.
>
> Why ever not? *If you ask me*, it's a great opportunity. You'd be living in London and travelling around a lot, not doing the same thing every day like you do here.
>
> Yes, but I don't want to live in London. *For one thing*, it would mean leaving all my friends, and for another, I'd be further away from my parents, and they're not getting any younger. And *on top of that*, I'd have to find somewhere to live in London.
>
> *There is that*. Accommodation would be more difficult to find and it would be more expensive. *On the other hand*, you could afford to pay more money because you'd have a better salary.
>
> *Believe me*, I have thought about it, but I really don't think I want to take on more responsibility.
>
> Well, *at the end of the day* it's your decision. You have to do what you think is best.
>
> Yes, and I've made my decision. I'm happy here, so *can we leave it at that*?

B Match each expression in italics with its use.

Which expression is used…

1   to give your opinion? _____
2   to emphasize what you are about to say? _____
3   to introduce a different, often contrasting point of view? _____
4   to give the first reason for something? _____
5   to give another, perhaps more important reason? _____
6   to introduce a topic of conversation? _____
7   to say something that will surprise the other person? _____
8   to agree with what somebody has just said? _____
9   to put an end to an argument? _____
10 to show that you have considered all the various aspects of the question? _____

C Match these other expressions to the uses in B above. There are two for each use.

what's more	by the way	to my mind
I'm telling you	for my money	to be sure
believe it or not	(and/so) that's that	when all is said and done
to begin with	as it happens	for a start
guess what	all in all	goodness knows
into the bargain	end of story	the other side of the coin (is that…)
mind you	you've got a point there	

D Look at the following and check the main part of the dictionary for more information on each expression.

Idioms you can use when…

1 …you don't know the answer to something

> I haven't a clue.
> Search me.
> Your guess is as good as mine.
> Goodness knows.
> I haven't got the foggiest.
> I have no idea.

4 …you understand what somebody is telling you

> I get the message.
> I get the picture.
> I take your point.
> Enough said.
> Tell me about it.
> Say no more.

2 …you are surprised

> Well I never!
> You don't say!
> Is that a fact?
> Get away with you!
> Good grief!
> My word!

5 …you want somebody to hurry up

> Get your skates on!
> Get a move on!
> Jump to it!
> Hop to it!
> Make it snappy!
> Shake a leg!

3 …you want to tell somebody to keep calm

> Keep you hair on!
> Keep your shirt on!
> It's not the end of the world.
> Don't get your knickers in a twist.
> Don't make a mountain out of a molehill.
> Take it easy.

6 …you do not believe what somebody has told you

> Pull the other one!
> As if!
> My eye!
> Tell me another!
> You're joking!
> A likely story!

E Choose an idiom that could be used in reply to the following.

1 Where's Mark?
2 My interview starts in ten minutes.
3 Rachel's getting married!
4 My life's a complete disaster!
5 Paul says he's met George W. Bush.
6 I'd better not get home late again tonight. It would be the third time this week.

It's as easy as *ABC*! If something is as easy as learning the alphabet, something that we all do as children, it must be very easy indeed.

There are lots of expressions like this in English, using **as x as y** to mean 'very x'. Sometimes we can easily see where the idea has come from, but in other idioms, it is no longer quite as obvious.

A Look at the phrases below and try to decide which adjective is the correct one to make the idiom.

1 as _____ as mustard
   hot   yellow   keen

2 as _____ as two peas in a pod
   round   like   green

3 as _____ as falling off a log
   painful   crazy   easy

4 as _____ as a mule
   stubborn   miffed   mule

5 as _____ as a fiddle
   fit   jolly   French

6 as _____ as a cucumber
   crisp   cool   green

7 as _____ as a bee
   annoying   noisy   busy

8 as _____ as a pancake
   flat   sweet   pale

B Here the nouns in the idioms have been mixed up. Find the right combination.

1 After an hour of aerobics, my face was as red as a picture.   _a beet_

2 Without his glasses he's as blind as a brush.   _____

3 Don't expect a sensible answer from him – he's as daft as toast.   _____

4 In her new dress, she looked as pretty as a bat.   _____

5 He answered the question as quick as ~~a beet.~~   _____

6 It was cold outside but we were as warm as a flash.   _____

C In these phrases, two of the nouns are commonly used in idioms. Can you identify the one that is not?

a hatter   a March hare   potatoes   day   air   a feather

as mad as…   as plain as…   as light as…

monkeys   the nose on your face   a bubble

D Comparisons with 'like'

We can say that a good swimmer 'swims like a fish'. Choose the correct noun from the box to complete these sentences.

1 No wonder she's so thin. She eats like _____ .

2 We need to order some more of those umbrellas. They're selling like _____ .

3 I was so tired, I went out like _____ .

4 The rumour spread like _____ .

5 She was running around like _____ trying to get everything done.

6 He doesn't care what people say about him. He's got a hide like _____ .

7 Before I had to sing my solo I was shaking like _____ .

8 What's he so pleased about? He's been grinning like _____ all morning.

wildfire
hot cakes
a bird
a rhinoceros
a leaf
a Cheshire cat
a headless chicken
a light

In this dictionary you will find many phrases labelled as 'saying', such as **look before you leap**. It seems that there is a saying to fit almost every situation in human life.

A What can you say?

In the box there is a keyword to help you find a saying that could be used in each of these situations.

1 Ah, you've finally arrived! I've been waiting an hour! *Better late than never*.
2 My aunt sent me the most awful knitted sweater for my birthday. I really don't like it!
3 She's always complaining about her boyfriend when he's at home, but she says she really misses him now that he's working abroad.
4 I really wish I hadn't resigned from my job. I should have stayed there for longer.
5 I don't know where Joe has got to…oh look, there he is now!
6 Look, all you need to do is find a cheaper place to live and get a better-paid job.
7 I was trying to get the letter done so quickly that I accidentally deleted it and had to start all over again.
8 She had to spend some time in hospital after the operation, but while she was there she met the man who would become her husband.

absence

devil

crying

thought

cloud

haste

easier

~~better~~

B The beginning of the end

Some sayings are so well known that it is not even necessary to finish the whole expression. The first half of the idiom is enough for everyone to know what you mean.

For each of the beginnings of the idioms in box A, find the (optional) ending in box B.

A		B	
1	When the going gets tough…	a	makes Jack a dull boy.
2	Two's company…	b	and he'll take a yard/mile.
3	A rolling stone…	c	the tough get going.
4	The proof of the pudding…	d	is lost.
5	He who hesitates…	e	three's a crowd.
6	Give him an inch…	f	gathers no moss.
7	All work and no play…	g	is in the eating.
8	What the eye doesn't see…	h	the heart doesn't grieve over.

Now match the sayings above to their meanings below.

i If you do not take action quickly, you could miss out on a good opportunity.
ii If you offer him something, he will take more than you intended.
iii When two people are together, they don't want anyone else with them.
iv A person who keeps moving on never makes much money or many friends, but is free from responsibilities.
v If you don't know about something, it can't hurt you.
vi When things get difficult, strong people start working even harder to succeed.
vii You can't judge whether something is successful until it has been tried out or used.
viii It isn't healthy to work all the time.

A Look at the following idioms, all of which are connected with the way people look, and fit them into the categories below. There are two idioms per category.

You look rather off colour.	He cut quite a dash in his suit.	He looks a bit past it.
He's no oil painting.	She looks the picture of health.	He gave her a dirty look.
We were all in our Sunday best.	She had a face like thunder.	She's not much to look at.
She's starting to look her age.	He doesn't look so hot.	He was all smiles.

Well/Happy
1 _____
2 _____

Old
1 _____
2 _____

Angry/Unhappy
1 _____
2 _____

Well-dressed
1 _____
2 _____

Unwell/Ill
1 _____
2 _____

Unattractive
1 _____
2 _____

B Write an idiomatic phrase that could be used to describe each of the following situations. You will find one of the words in each idiom in the box on the right.

1 When her boss told her she was getting a pay rise, she looked very pleased with herself.
   She _looked like the cat that got the cream._

2 She walked all the way home in the rain without an umbrella. By the time she got here she was completely wet.
   She _____

3 He definitely takes after his father. They look the same, and have similar personalities too.
   He's _____

4 Nobody had to tell me she was Joan's sister. It's amazing how similar they are.
   She's _____

5 She certainly wanted everyone to notice her at the party in her silky black mini-dress.
   She _____

6 You don't have to tell me you're upset. I can see it clearly in your face.
   It's _____

7 Life hasn't been good for her lately and she's feeling a bit depressed.
   She's _____

8 He makes such stupid mistakes sometimes; it's difficult not to laugh.
   It's difficult _____

9 It was really wonderful to see her after such a long time.
   She _____

10 I really don't think she should be wearing those clothes at her age. She's trying to look like a young woman.
   She's _____

image
chip
written
sight
mouth
cream
straight
kill
mutton
drowned

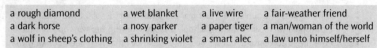

A Types of People

Match the person with the description.

a rough diamond	a wet blanket	a live wire	a fair-weather friend
a dark horse	a nosy parker	a paper tiger	a man/woman of the world
a wolf in sheep's clothing	a shrinking violet	a smart alec	a law unto himself/herself

What type of person...

1   has a lot of experience of life and is not easily shocked?
2   seems friendly and nice but is actually quite dangerous and threatening?
3   seems to be dangerous but in fact is not?
4   is too interested in other people's private affairs?
5   is not enthusiastic about things and stops other people from enjoying themselves?
6   does not follow the rules or customs that others in a group or society follow?
7   hides their feelings and experiences?
8   stops being your friend when you are in trouble?
9   has a good nature, although they may not always seem polite, educated, etc?
10 is lively and enthusiastic?
11 is very shy and easily frightened?
12 tries to show that they are cleverer than other people?

B The answer to each crossword clue is one word from the idiom.

Across (→)

1   She gets angry rather easily. She's got a quick ____. (6)
4   He can always speak easily and persuade other people. He has the gift of the ____. (3)
6   He talks a lot about what he's going to do, but never does anything. He's all talk and no ____. (6)
8   Once she starts talking she won't stop. She could talk the hind leg off a ____. (6)
9   He would never hurt anyone. He wouldn't harm a ____. (3)
10 She's not realistic or practical. She has her head in the ____. (6)
12 He doesn't like new ideas, he prefers old and traditional ways. He's an old ____. (5)
13 She's never done anything wrong in her life. She's as pure as the driven ____. (4)
14 He never shows any emotion and seems unfriendly. He's a cold ____. (4)
15 He will always try to help people who need it. He's a good ____. (9)

Down (↓)

2   She has good intentions even though she sometimes does the wrong thing. Her heart is in the right ____. (5)
3   She's always sensible and reasonable. She's got a good head on her ____. (9)
5   She seems to be frightened of everyone. She wouldn't say ____ to a goose. (3)
7   He can never do anything right. He's a waste of ____. (5)
8   He always expects things to go badly. He's a prophet of ____. (4)
11 She thinks she's better than other people and always has to get what she wants. She's a prima ____. (5)

 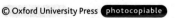

S8 We're in Business

A Read the following story and then match the idiomatic
expressions with the definitions below.

> Joe Fisher was in trouble. He'd just **got the sack** from his job at the local factory.
> He'd worked there since leaving school, steadily **working his way up** from tea boy
> to the firm's accountant, but his boss had found out that he'd been **cooking the
> books**. He'd started doing it because he was fed up with seeing the **fat cats** at the
> top of the company **making money hand over fist** while he **slogged his guts
> out** just to **make ends meet**. So he started stealing from the company. For a few
> months it **went like a dream** and nobody suspected anything. Then he started
> **living beyond his means**, buying a new house and an expensive car. People got
> suspicious and began to wonder how he could **throw** so much **money around** on
> his salary. That's when the boss found out and everything **went pear-shaped**. He
> wondered what would happen now. Perhaps he could **throw in the towel** and
> leave **the rat race** altogether. After all, he could sell that big new house and buy
> himself a nice little cottage in the country...

1 work extremely hard: _slog your guts out_
2 be dismissed from your job: _____
3 be paid enough money to live on: _____
4 give up (a project): _____
5 spend more than you earn: _____
6 make money very easily: _____
7 change facts or figures in a dishonest or an illegal way: _____
8 go badly wrong: _____
9 work very successfully: _____
10 spend money in a careless way: _____
11 get yourself more responsible jobs within a company: _____
12 a competitive struggle for success in jobs and business: _____
13 a wealthy and powerful person: _____

B Now look at the following idiomatic expressions and match them into pairs
that have a similar meaning. One has been done for you.

a a fat cat
b come a cropper
c get off to a flying start
d sell like hot cakes
e do a roaring trade
f sink or swim
g fall flat on your face
h hit the ground running
i make or break
j a big shot

_a & j_   _____   _____   _____   _____

C Now complete the following sentences with an appropriate expression from
exercise B, changing the form as necessary.

1 He was a very skilled businessman and his new company … .
2 The new computer games were both original and exciting, and … .
3 This year is our last chance to succeed. It's … .
4 He was far too ambitious and when he tried to set up yet another company, … .

A Is it a sign of good health ☺ or bad health ☹ if you…

	☺	☹		☺	☹
▶ are green about the gills?		✓	▶ are in shape?		
▶ are in the pink?	✓		▶ have been in the wars?		
▶ feel like a million dollars?			▶ feel the worse for wear?		
▶ have the dreaded lurgy?			▶ are off your food?		
▶ are on form?			▶ are as right as rain?		

B Look up the words in the boxes to help you complete these sentences with an idiom:

1 I got food poisoning on holiday and for three days I was _s i c k_ _a s_ _a_
2 I went for a check-up and the doctor gave me a _ _ _ _ _ _ _ _ _ _ _
3 I've got a headache and a sore throat, and I feel generally a bit _ _ _ _ _ _ _ _
4 He was about to come out of hospital but then he took a _ _ _ _ _ _ _ _ _ _

worse.
weather.
health.
dog.

5 It's such a dangerous operation that only 10% of patients _ _ _ _
6 She's given up smoking and started jogging, and she looks _ _ _ _ _ _ _
7 The meat I had tasted strange, and the next morning I felt a bit _ _ _
8 She's been very poorly for months, but now she's _ _ _ _ _ _

mend.
shape.
colour.
through.

9 I'm exhausted. I need a holiday to _ _ _ _ _ _ _ _ _ _
10 I'm back at work now, but I still don't feel _ _ _ _ _ _ _ _ _ _ _
11 He made a full recovery from his operation and now he's _ _ _ _ _ _ _ _
12 They came back from their holiday looking _ _ _ _ _ _ _ _ _ _ _ _

cent.
health.
batteries.
fit.

13 He's getting better now, but after the crash he was _ _ _ _ _ _ _
14 My dog is very old and the vet says he's _ _ _ _ _ _ _ _ _
15 I went to sleep on my arm and now I've got _ _ _ _ _ _ _
16 There's a virus going round. My students are _ _ _ _ _ _ _ _ _ _ _ _ _

needles.
flies.
way.
legs.

17 The two passengers died, but the driver is still _ _ _ _ _ _ _ _ _ _ _ _ _ _ _ _
18 My grandmother is 97 and she's _ _ _ _ _ _ _ _ _ _ _ _
19 When the sea got rough I had to rush to the toilet to _ _
20 The dog was so badly injured that they had to have it _ _ _ _ _

strong.
sick.
sleep.
life.

21 Once my granddad got ill, he quickly _ _ _ _
22 For a man his age, he's still _ _ _ _ _ _
23 He got the flu, and for the last week he's been _ _ _ _ _ _ _ _ _
24 Her condition was critical for a week but now she's _ _ _ _ _ _ _ _ _ _ _ _

nick.
downhill.
list.
back.

© Oxford University Press *photocopiable*

A Read the following story and answer the questions below. Sometimes there is more than one answer:

> Belinda was an attractive young woman, but she ***wasn't just a pretty face***. She had a great job and she was ***as clever as they come***. She also had a handsome boyfriend. His name was Ben and he was ***a whizz-kid*** in the City. He had a stressful job but he could ***think on his feet*** and ***keep his head*** under pressure. Belinda and Ben seemed like the perfect couple, and she couldn't wait to see him after her business trip.
>
> They'd arranged to meet at a restaurant and when she saw him, she immediately started telling him about her great trip. Ben was such ***a bright spark*** and was usually very interested in her career, but today it seemed he ***wasn't all there***. He smiled at her a lot but he hardly spoke. By the end of the meal she was ***racking her brains*** for things to talk about. Finally, the bill arrived and Ben began to check it carefully. He ***had a good head for figures*** but today it took him ages. In the end, Belinda, who ***didn't suffer fools gladly***, shouted, 'Come on, Ben! ***You don't have to be a rocket scientist*** to work it out!' She walked off and left him sitting there on his own.
>
> As she sat in the taxi on her way home, she just couldn't ***get her head round*** it: Why had Ben acted so strangely? When she got home, there was a message on her answerphone. It said, 'Hi, it's Ben. Sorry I couldn't tell you to your face, but I've found a new girlfriend. Her name's Bella and she's a millionairess. I hope you enjoyed meeting my twin brother, Bill. He can be a bit ***slow on the uptake***, but I'm sure you'll get on really well.'

1 Who was very rich?	5 Who went to the restaurant?	**a** Belinda
2 Who was good-looking?	6 Who got angry?	**b** Ben
3 Who was good at maths?	7 Who couldn't think of anything to say?	**c** Bill
4 Who was very intelligent?	8 Who paid the bill?	**d** Bella

B Now find an idiom from the story to fit each of these definitions:

1 stay calm: _keep your head_
2 be good at maths: _____
3 think quickly: _____
4 not understand things quickly and easily: _____
5 a highly successful young person: _____
6 it isn't necessary to be very intelligent: _____
7 be impatient with stupid people: _____
8 not just good-looking but also intelligent: _____
9 very intelligent: _____
10 think very hard about something: _____
11 not be mentally aware: _____
12 understand something difficult: _____
13 a clever, lively person: _____

C Read the following sentences and decide whether the speaker thinks 'he' is intelligent 👍 or not 👎:

	👍	👎
❯ He's not the sharpest knife in the drawer.		✓
❯ He really uses his loaf.	✓	
❯ He's as thick as two short planks.		
❯ He's two sandwiches short of a picnic.		
❯ There are no flies on him.		
❯ He's nobody's fool.		
❯ The lights are on but nobody's home.		
❯ He's one smart cookie.		

There are many idioms in English that are connected with animals. For example, if you think something is 'the bee's knees', you think it is excellent. Try the following exercises to help you be 'top dog' at animal idioms!

A Fill in the gaps with the name of one of the animals shown.

1 The traffic was moving at a _____'s pace.

2 Don't forget it was him who did all the _____ work.

3 Criticism doesn't affect him – it's like water off a _____'s back.

4 The US athletes won the _____'s share of the medals at last year's games.

5 I've known him since he was knee-high to a _____ .

B Match the two halves of the sentence and fill in the missing word.

1 I felt like a fish out of	_____ about something or other.
2 I decided to take the bull by the	_water_ when I started in this company.
3 The tourist office sent us on a wild goose	_____ before I have to give a speech.
4 I always get butterflies in my	_____ to a hotel which had closed down.
5 I made a real pig's	_____ of the letter so I had to do it again.
6 The boss has always got a bee in his	_____ and tell the boss what I thought.

7 I nearly let the cat out of the	_____ , but there's no direct road.
8 I could talk about football till the cows	_____ about how he'd been in a famous band.
9 He told us some cock and bull	_____ and told Jim about his surprise party.
10 My house is quite near as the crow	_____ _____ , but I don't want to bore you.

C The nouns in italics have got mixed up. Can you move the last word in each sentence to its correct idiom?

Hold your *chickens*.	Hair of the *horse*.	He's no spring *wolf*.
She had ~~tears~~. kittens	He's a dark *dog*.	Don't count your *dogs*.
They're crocodile *horses*.	It's gone to the ~~kittens~~.	He's a lone *chicken*.

D Which of the idioms in C above could be used as a response to the following? Use each one once only.

1 What did Sandra say when she saw her phone bill?   _She had kittens._

2 Come on, come on! I'm ready, so let's hurry up and go!   _____

3 Why is she crying if she doesn't care?   _____

4 Can you believe Dave's going out with a supermodel?   _____

5 I'm amazed you're drinking beer today after last night's party!   _____

6 I think I've got the job. I'm going to go out to celebrate.   _____

7 Ali doesn't seem to have any friends.   _____

8 This used to be a nice neighbourhood, didn't it?   _____

9 Dad can't run as fast as he used to.   _____

A There are many idioms which have come from sport, but which are used to talk about other situations. Which sport do you think the following expressions came from? If you need help, check the NOTE/ORIGIN boxes in the main part of the dictionary.

football   swimming   golf   horse-racing   cricket   baseball   boxing

▶ hit/knock sb for six
▶ below par
▶ pull no punches
▶ be way out in left field

▶ move the goalposts
▶ par for the course
▶ out of your depth
▶ be on a sticky wicket

▶ be thrown in at the deep end
▶ on the ropes
▶ win/lose by a short head
▶ out for the count

B Match the heads and tails of the sporting idioms, then fit each one into an appropriate gap in the article, changing the form as necessary.

pull no	ball
thrown in at the deep	depth
on the	end
out of your	game
a whole new ball	punches

Almost 20 million viewers tuned in to Channel 2 last night to see the long-awaited live debate between Prime Minister Turner and Leader of the Opposition Simon Stand.

Mr Stand must have felt he'd been (1) *thrown in at the deep end* , appearing in his first TV debate so soon after becoming leader. He has had a highly successful career as an MP, but this is (2)_____.
Mr Turner knew he had the advantage, and he (3)_____. Mr Stand, who is usually (4)_____ and very skilled at handling questions, appeared flustered and (5)_____.

ballpark	figure
move the	goalposts
set the ball	mark
throw in the	rolling
way off the	towel

Mr Turner (6)_____ by asking Mr Stand how much money he intended to spend on the health service. Mr Stand mentioned a (7)_____ that was (8)_____, as Mr Turner was quick to point out. Mr Stand looked as if he wanted to (9)_____ at this stage, but recovered enough to accuse the government of (10)_____ by changing the tax limits in order to suit their policies. Mr Turner appeared to hesitate before giving an unconvincing reply.

back to square	course
know the	one
a one-horse	race
par for the	score

Simon Stand has long complained that people are more interested in how politicians come across on TV than in their policies. As leader, he must now accept that this is (11)_____. Mr Turner (12)_____, and receives regular 'media training'.

The debate will no doubt prove a disaster for Mr Stand, who is already a long way behind in the opinion polls. So it's (13)_____ for him and his party. If they don't come up with some solid and convincing policies very soon, the election looks like being (14)_____.

A The words in the puzzle below are all connected with the sea and sailing. If you have completed it correctly, the shaded column will spell out the name of a sea.

1   the action of moving your body through water (8)
2   a big area of salt water (5)
3   the top outside floor of a ship or boat (4)
4   a person who works on a ship (6)
5   a large flat shellfish that can be eaten or that produces shiny white jewels called pearls (6)
6   the piece of wood or metal along the bottom of a boat that keeps it upright in the water (4)
7   a structure that is built over a river so that people or vehicles can cross it (6)
8   a heavy metal object that is dropped over the side of a boat to keep it in one place (6)
9   a line of water that moves across the surface of the sea (4)
10 the sport or activity of travelling in a boat or ship (7)
11 the regular rise and fall in the level of the sea (4)
12 the person who is in command of a ship (7)
13 go down below the surface or towards the bottom of the sea (4)

1 | S | W | I | M | M | I | N | G |
2 | O |
3 | D |
4 | S |
5 | O |
6 | K |
7 | B |
8 | A |
9 | W |
10 | S |
11 | T |
12 | C |
13 | S |

B When Commander Bill Seaman left the Navy, he couldn't help using idioms connected with the sea whenever he talked. When he was interviewed for a magazine, the journalist took them all out and put another phrase in.

Replace the phrases (a) – (m) to find out what he really said about his change of career. Remember to change the form of the idiom where necessary.

When I left the Navy, I was still young and fit and I felt that (a) *I could do whatever I wanted,* so I decided to set up in business on my own. I have to admit that it wasn't all (b) *without difficulties,* but I (c) *run things very efficiently* and business soon picked up. My assistant manager was a bit of (d) *a strange character,* but he worked hard and didn't (e) *upset the balance,* which suited me. Orders were flooding in and it was (f) *necessary for everyone to work very hard* to keep up!

Then something happened that (g) *made me feel less confident.* My assistant suddenly decided to (h) *leave,* taking the month's profits with him! At first I thought I was sunk, but in fact the sum involved was really just (i) *a small amount* and, as to finding a new assistant, there were (j) *lots more potential candidates.* I soon got the business (k) *happening in a calm way again* and our problems are all (l) *in the past* now. In fact, things are going so well that my wife and I have decided to really (m) *be very extravagant* on our next holiday: we're thinking of going on a round-the-world cruise!

the world was my oyster (above phrase a)

run a tight ship	all hands on deck	water under the bridge
the world is your oyster	jump ship	rock the boat
push the boat out	an odd fish	plain sailing
back on an even keel	plenty more fish in the sea	
a drop in the ocean	take the wind out of sb's sails	

A First, label the diagram on the right with the correct word and check your answers in the key.

B Using the words you have added to the diagram, find an appropriate idiom to complete these sentences. The numbers correspond to the numbers on the diagram, but remember that some of the nouns may be plural.

1 The smell of onions frying really _made my mouth water._

2 When the teacher said she had some exciting news to tell us, we were _ _ _ _ _ _ _.

3 I don't care if he leaves or stays – it's no _ _ _ _ _ _ _ my _ _ _ _.

4 He says he broke his arm falling out of bed, but I think there's _ _ _ _ _ _ it _ _ _ _ _ _ _ _ _ the _ _ _.

5 I'm sure we can think of a present for Mark if we _ _ _ our _ _ _ _ _ _ _ _ _ _ _ _.

6 I was very surprised to see him here. We don't get many visitors _ _ this _ _ _ _ _ _ the _ _ _ _ _.

7 If you're feeling worried or upset you should talk to someone and _ _ _ it _ _ _ your _ _ _ _ _.

8 Why are you giving me the _ _ _ _ _ _ _ _ _ _ _ _? Have I done something to upset you?

9 I'd give my _ _ _ _ _ _ _ _ for the opportunity to study abroad for a year.

10 Can't you finish all your food, Billy? Your _ _ _ _ were _ _ _ _ _ _ _ _ _ _ your _ _ _ _ _ _ _.

11 His parents want him to become more independent and learn to _ _ _ _ _ _ _ _ his _ _ _ _ _ _ _.

12 He ran as fast as he could, with the angry shopkeeper _ _ _ _ _ his _ _ _ _ _ _.

13 He didn't really mean what he said. I think he was just _ _ _ _ _ _ _ _ your _ _ _.

14 The teacher does tests without warning, just to _ _ _ _ the class _ _ their _ _ _ _.

15 The thought of having to giving a speech made him go _ _ _ _ _ _ the _ _ _ _ _.

C Each of the following sentences contains an idiom with a mistake in it. Can you find it and correct it?

1 I nearly jumped out /my skin when the fire alarm went off.

2 If she loses any more weight she'll be just bones and skin.

3 I had to bite my tongue off and keep quiet about what really happened.

4 He seems the ideal candidate, but does he have any skeletons in the cellar?

5 He was lucky – he passed the exam by the skin of his tooth.

6 She may be over sixty, but she's still young at her heart.

7 Keep your hairs on! It's not time to leave yet.

8 I asked him to lend me the money, but it was like trying to get blood out of a bone.

A This cookery writer has got carried away with her love of food and has used too many idioms connected with food in her article. Can you work out the meaning of the underlined idioms? Look them up in the main part of the dictionary if you are not sure.

Wine and dine your guests – without breaking the bank!

<u>Too much on your plate?</u> No time and no money to entertain? Coping with the pressures of work and family life is <u>no picnic</u>, even without the extra burden of shopping and cooking for guests. But don't worry: with a little forward planning, a dinner party needn't be <u>a recipe for disaster</u>. Here's our simple guide to give you <u>food for thought</u>.

For the main course, let's <u>talk turkey</u>. It's low-fat, reasonably priced and versatile, and it's <u>saved my bacon</u> on many occasions. Of course, if your guests are not the <u>meat-and-potatoes</u> types, you may need to find vegetarian alternatives.

<u>Can't</u> bake <u>for toffee</u>? There's no need to <u>go bananas</u> over desserts. If your puddings always <u>go pear-shaped</u>, go for a simple alternative such as fresh fruit salad. There's no point in <u>over-egging the pudding</u>, and you can prepare this light and refreshing dish in advance.

And when you're really <u>in a pickle</u>, remember that when it comes to entertaining friends, the food is just <u>the icing on the cake</u>. They've really come to see you, so try to relax and enjoy yourself!

B Replace a part of each of the following sentences with one of the idioms from the text above.

    She's got a lot on her plate
1 ~~She's got a lot to deal with~~, what with the new job and moving house.
2 Letting the kids decorate their own rooms sounds to me like *an idea that can only have bad results*.
3 What's wrong with her? I was only five minutes late and she *got really angry*.
4 The dinner party *all went wrong* when Henry arrived with his new girlfriend.
5 *I'm a terrible cook*, I'm afraid.
6 Let's *discuss the practical details*. How much money can we afford to spend?
7 We're both working 7 days a week, so life is *not much fun* at the moment.
8 My parents *rescued me from a very difficult position* by lending me the money.

C Complete the following sentences with an item of food or drink.

1 I'd rather not go clubbing with you. It's not really my cup of <u>tea</u> .
2 You can't have your c_____ and eat it. If you want a higher salary you have to accept more responsibility.
3 He doesn't usually speak to me, but he was as nice as p_____ to me today. I wonder why?
4 I'm sure Dave will be a successful businessman. He's one smart c_____ .
5 Don't invest all your money in one company. It's never a good idea to put all your e_____ in one basket.
6 Well, we've missed our chance to enter the competition this year. I wonder if we'll get another bite of the c_____?
7 My salary is just small p_____ compared to what some people earn.
8 According to them, the new software is the best thing since sliced b_____ .

A Fill in the colour to make common idioms or expressions:

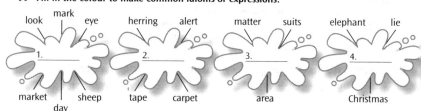

look
mark   eye   herring   alert   matter   suits   elephant   lie

1. _____   2. _____   3. _____   4. _____

market   sheep   tape   carpet   area   Christmas
day

B Match the beginnings and endings to make full sentences. The first one has been done for you.

1 The public scandal was a *black*	**a** *spectacles* — she's always so positive about things.
2 She really *put out the red*	**b** *fingers*. In fact, all my plants seem to die.
3 I kept telling him *till I was blue in the*	**c** *moon* because we're both so busy.
4 Sue really does see the world through *rose-coloured*	**d** *tape* drives me crazy. There are so many forms to fill in before you can do anything.
5 I wouldn't say I've got *green*	**e** *carpet* when her in-laws came round. What a welcome!
6 I hardly ever see him now; we only get to meet *once in a blue*	**f** *light* so we can start the project straight away.
7 Well, what harm will a little *white*	**g** *mark* against him.
8 They've finally *given us the green*	**h** *lie* do? I could hardly tell her what I really thought.
9 They really *painted the town*	**i** *face* but he wouldn't listen.
10 All this *red*	**j** *red*. Well, there was a lot to celebrate.

C Read the following dialogue. Both speakers use a number of colour idioms, but do they use them correctly? Check in the main part of the dictionary and change any colours that are wrong.

At the police station

PC Green	Can I help you, sir?
Mr Blue	I'm here to report an accident
PC Green	Yes, I see you're hurt. Where exactly did this occur?
Mr Blue	Down by the roundabout on Main Street.
PC Green	Mm, that is a bit of a red spot.
Mr Blue	Anyway, this car suddenly came out in front of me. It was a real bolt from the black, and I couldn't stop in time.
PC Green	How serious was the accident, sir? Is the other driver OK?
Mr Blue	Oh, she was healthy enough to scream red murder and attract a crowd. There wasn't even any damage and neither of us was hurt.
PC Green	How did you get that yellow eye then?
Mr Blue	We were exchanging details when she hit me. She said I was giving her a black look. Talk about the pot calling the kettle brown! Anyway, I came down here to see you boys in white because I want to report her.
PC Green	We'd better get all this down in pink and green. Here's a pen…

S17 Naming Names

A Places

Complete the sentences with the name of a place or a nationality. The words are in the box below, but be careful: there are a few extra words that you will not need!

1 The other children said they'd send him to __Coventry__ if he told the teacher.
2 I wouldn't do her job for all the tea in _____ .
3 I've read this chapter twice but I'm afraid it's all _____ to me.
4 You're taking wine with you to France? Isn't that a bit like taking coals to _____ ?
5 I can't believe he won the game! He has the luck of the _____ , that boy.
6 I don't want you to pay for my meal as well as your own. Let's go _____ .
7 Don't try to rush things. _____ wasn't built in a day, you know.
8 I've had a bloody awful day! Oops, pardon my _____ !

> China   Greek   Irish   Rome   American   Coventry
> French   Newcastle   Indian   Dutch   Cheshire

B People

All the answers in this crossword are people's names. If you need help, one word in each clue will lead you to the correct part of the dictionary.

Across (→)

1 By his Law, everything that can go wrong, will go wrong. (6)
5 It's easy when he's your uncle. (3)
7 He's got the most patience. (3)
8 He has a law that says that work will take as much time as you have. (9)
9 He's the American Uncle. (3)
12 He has the golden touch. (5)
14 He likes to have a good time, this Lad. (4)
15 This man is always so happy. (5)
16 This Old man is in the police force. (4)
17 His heel is the only weak point. (8)

Down (↓)

2 His choice is no choice at all. (6)
3 With Tom and Harry, he could be anyone. (4)
4 His pony is really your feet. (6)
6 You don't know who he is at all. (4)
7 Mr Blow or Mr Public, just ordinary guys. (3)
8 Open her box and the results could be disastrous. (7)
10 This is the Prince that every girl would like to meet. (8)
11 He's Mr Hyde's other side. (6)
12 He's the real thing, the best example. (5)
13 We would all like to live this man's life. (5)
14 She's a plain girl. (4)

A Choose the idiom which would be appropriate in the following situations:

1 You're so proud of your child.
   a He's the apple of my eye.
   b He's for my eyes only.
   c He looks a sight.

2 You're pleased/relieved to see someone.
   a She's robbed me blind.
   b I take a dim view of her.
   c She's a sight for sore eyes.

3 You can see a little hope for the future in difficult times.
   a I can see stars.
   b Feast your eyes on that.
   c There's light at the end of the tunnel.

4 She's good at noticing things around her.
   a She can see things in her mind's eye.
   b She has eyes in the back of her head.
   c She can see her way clear to doing that.

5 There's too much information for you to see clearly.
   a I can't see the wood for the trees.
   b I just watch the world go by.
   c I need to keep my eyes open.

6 You don't want anyone else to see something.
   a This is for your eyes only.
   b Keep your eyes peeled.
   c Feast your eyes on this.

7 He looks terrible.
   a I take a dim view of him.
   b He looks a sight.
   c I know him by sight.

8 Somebody seems to be daydreaming.
   a Has he got second sight?
   b He's all eyes.
   c He's just staring into space.

B Julie's talking about her friend Clare. Use the idioms in the box to replace the phrases 1–10, changing the form as necessary.

cry your eyes out	love is blind	not see sb for dust	have (got) a roving eye
look daggers at sb	beauty is in the eye of the beholder		swear blind
not take your eyes off sb	see the light	turn a blind eye	

couldn't take her eyes off
   It all started in a club on holiday. She just (1) **couldn't stop looking at** this guy, and of course eventually he came over. Personally I didn't think he was very attractive, but (2) **we all have a different opinion of what's good looking**, after all. I could tell he (3) **was always looking for the chance to start a new sexual relationship** but she just wouldn't listen.
   Well, (4) **when people are in love they just don't see things clearly**, as they say. She was already talking about marriage, after just two days! But one night, she caught him kissing someone else. Well, you know Clare. She would never (5) **pretend not to notice something**, so she marched over and threw her drink over him. He (6) **looked at her in a terrible way**, and then left. I'm not surprised — if that had happened to me you (7) **wouldn't see me because I'd leave so quickly**. She spent the rest of the holiday (8) **crying all the time**, but I'm glad she (9) **understood what the real situation was**. She (10) **says definitely** that she'll never look at another man again, but I'm sure she'll get over it...

A Decide which noun completes the expression on the left. The first has been done for you.

		ear	sound	noise	music	ring
1	have (got) an _____ for sth	✓				
2	face the _____					
3	be out on your _____					
4	make a lot of _____ (about sth)					
5	play it by _____					
6	a big _____					
7	love the _____ of your own voice					
8	go in one _____ and out the other					
9	have (got) a familiar _____ to it					
10	be like _____ to your ears					

B Using the expressions from above, how can you say the following more idiomatically?

1 I recognize it.   *It...* _____
2 He enjoys speaking a lot.   _____
3 It's really good to hear that.   _____
4 I won't plan things—I'll just see how things go.   _____
5 I'll have to accept the criticism for what I've done.   _____
6 She's good at imitating the sounds of other languages.   *She has an ear for languages.*
7 He never pays attention to what I say.   *It...* _____
8 He's an important person.   _____

C In the dialogue below, one word in each idiom is incorrect. Can you find the errors and correct them?

Jo	I just *can't ~~understand~~* ^{believe} *my ears*, it seems so incredible! So, what happened next? I'm *total ears*.
Jen	Well, later that evening, we went to Pete's. You should have heard what he was saying about Cathy! I told him to calm down but it just *fell on closed ears*.
Jo	And?
Jen	In walked Cathy. The front door was open, only Tom didn't notice.
Jo	What happened?
Jen	Tom eventually realized, and of course we were all really embarrassed. *You could've heard a feather drop*. Nobody said a word.
Jo	What about Cathy?
Jen	Finally, she turned to Tom and said, "*My ears were steaming*. I thought I'd come round here and find out exactly what you thought of me."
Jo	Oh dear.
Jen	She stormed out, packed a suitcase and left. Tom can't believe it but *for shouting out loud*, what does he expect? He said some terrible things.
Jo	What's the situation now?
Jen	Your guess is as good as mine. *Keep your ear to the floor* and let me know if you hear anything.

A Look at the words in the box below and sort them into two categories /areas.

taste	smell

~~taste~~	~~smell~~	mouth	sweet	odour
bitter	nose	flavour	sour	tongue
lips	stink	scent	sniff	

B Choose a word from the box to complete the following.

1 If you can't quite remember something, it is on the tip of your _____ .
2 If you have a low opinion of somebody, you look down your _____ at them.
3 If information spreads by people talking, it spreads by word of _____ .
4 If you like to eat sugary things such as cakes, you have a _____ tooth.
5 If a lot of people are talking about something, it is on everyone's _____ .
6 If an experience, relationship, etc. becomes less pleasant or enjoyable, it turns _____ .

C Put the domino cards in the right order so that the two halves make an idiom, for example:

in it.	Don't look a gift horse	**+**	in the mouth.	Put your money	**+**	where your mouth is.	Straight from

1	in the mouth.	Give her a taste	11	and smell the coffee.	Kick up
2	of the tongue.	Throw somebody	12	to spite your face.	Follow
3	got your tongue?	Wake up	13	the horse's mouth.	Flavour
4	your nose.	Straight from	14	the nose on your face.	Keep
5	for taste.	Get your tongue	15	off the scent.	An acquired
6	taste.	To the	16	of her own medicine.	Has the cat
7	of the month.	Butter wouldn't melt	17	bitter end.	It was no skin
8	your mouth water.	A slip	18	a stiff upper lip.	Make
9	a stink.	There's no accounting	19	around something.	Cut off your nose
10	in his mouth.	As plain as	20	off my nose.	Never look a gift horse

1																			20

D Put the correct idioms from the dominoes game into the spaces in the following story. The information in italics gives the meaning of the idiom you need in each case.

...Well, it was like this. I was just sitting in the park, relaxing and enjoying the sunshine. Then a woman with a little kid came along, sat down and started chatting. She offered me some of the picnic she had for her and her boy. Well, I believe that you should (1) _____. *(Don't complain when someone wants to give you something for free.)*

So we sat together, having lunch. After ten minutes or so, she asked me to look after her kid while she went to the shop, and I said yes of course. After all, (2) _____. *(It didn't annoy me or affect me in a bad way.)*

Off she went and I started asking the boy about his toys, what games he liked and things like that. Oh, it was impossible—the kid just wouldn't talk to me. So I said, "(3) _____?" *(Why aren't you saying anything?)*

I gave up trying to talk, and eventually his Mum came back and said thanks and goodbye. An hour later, I was in the shops myself and when I went to pay, I realized that my purse was gone. I was so angry and upset. That little boy! You'd think to look at him that (4) _____. *(He looked so sweet and innocent.)* How wrong can you be?

How could a boy of six be stealing already? I suppose the mother had told him to do it. I wish someone would (5) _____ *(treat her in the same unpleasant way as she treated me).* If I ever see her again...

E Which definition is correct? Choose a, b or c.

1	If you whisper *sweet nothings,* you are	a	talking a load of rubbish.
		b	saying romantic things to someone.
		c	saying nothing of interest.
2	If you have *a good sniff round,* you	a	examine a place carefully.
		b	have a cold.
		c	show your disapproval of something.
3	If you are *down in the mouth,* you are	a	unhappy and depressed.
		b	unsure of what to say.
		c	not able to find the right words.
4	If something *gets up your nose,* it	a	makes you feel uncomfortable.
		b	makes you laugh.
		c	irritates you.
5	If *your lips are sealed,* you will	a	keep a secret.
		b	find it impossible to say anything.
		c	refuse to speak because you are angry.

A There are ten words connected with hands in the box below, reading across (→), down (↓) or diagonally (↘). One has been found for you, can you find the others?

K	O	C	A	F	I	S	T
N	N	L	W	U	H	K	E
G	Q	U	T	O	U	C	H
L	P	T	C	L	P	R	A
O	A	C	H	K	A	B	N
V	Z	H	F	U	L	O	D
E	M	I	S	S	M	E	U
F	I	N	G	E	R	B	S
A	N	G	R	A	S	P	S

1 *hand* _____
2 _____
3 _____
4 _____
5 _____
6 _____
7 _____
8 _____
9 _____
10 _____

B Now use one of the words from the grid above to complete the idiom in each of the following sentences.

1 He's quite ill, but he'll be OK on the day of the exam, _____ wood!
2 She won't lift a _____ round the house, Jo does everything.
3 John's a dab _____ at that kind of thing – ask him to do it.
4 That dress looks great on you – it fits like a _____.
5 He'll do anything she tells him to do – he's really under her _____.
6 We got a rap over the _____ for being late.
7 He says he'll do anything to save the marriage, but in my opinion he's just _____ at straws.
8 They're making money hand over _____ now they're doing business over the Internet.

C Jean and Sheila are talking about a bad experience, but the lines of the dialogue have been mixed up. Can you put the correct order in the box on the right? The first line has been done for you.

1	Sheila	You dropped them?	3
2	Jean	Well, I *took my courage in both hands* and went over to these two men to ask for help.	
3	Sheila	How well do you know the city?	
4	Sheila	I bet they wouldn't have been able to take it off you. You're stronger than you look.	
5	Jean	*Like the back of my hand*. I've lived here for years. But when I first arrived I got lost one night and my car broke down.	
6	Sheila	So how did you manage to *slip through their fingers* then?	
7	Jean	I really thought *it was touch-and-go* whether I'd get out alive.	
8	Sheila	Ooh, that was brave of you!	
9	Jean	What else could I do? Anyway, one of them told me to give him my keys. Well, I was *all fingers and thumbs*…	
10	Sheila	What did you do?	
11	Jean	Well, it was all rather embarrassing. They turned out to be plain-clothes police officers. I was *in* perfectly *safe hands* after all!	
12	Jean	Yes, but I held on to my bag *for dear life*! They were both stepping towards me…	

The following two pages give you an opportunity to test yourself on the idioms that have been focused on in the study pages. Do this after you have completed the previous pages as they are not in order.

1 If somebody is criticizing you for a fault that they have themselves, you can say, 'Talk about *the pot calling the kettle* ...'
   a silver **b** grey **c** black

2 If you make a lot of money very quickly, you *make money hand over* ...
   a hand **b** foot **c** fist

3 If you have the freedom to do what you want and go where you want, *the world is your* ...
   a oyster **b** ocean **c** business

4 For their daughter's wedding, they really *pushed the* ... *out* and hired a whole orchestra.
   a ship **b** boat **c** tide

5 If you have a very angry expression on your face, you have *a face like* ...
   a a storm **b** fire **c** thunder

6 If you have a lot of things to do and a lot of responsibilities, you have *a lot on your* ...
   a dish **b** plate **c** table

7 She's so thin that she's really nothing more than *skin and* ...
   a flesh **b** skeleton **c** bones

8 Your Mum's going to *have* ... when she sees what you've done to your hair!
   a bananas **b** monkeys **c** kittens

9 This machine is so easy to use, all you have to do is push this button, and ... *'s your uncle!*
   a Bill **b** Bob **c** Sam

10 If you deal with a difficult or dangerous situation in a direct and brave way, you *take the bull by the* ...
   a leg **b** tail **c** horns

11 If you stop doing something because you know that you cannot succeed, you *throw in the* ...
   a towel **b** ghost **c** hand

12 If you make a small problem seem much more serious than it really is, you *make a mountain out of* ...
   a an anthill **b** a molehill **c** a hill

13 If you understand what somebody means, even if they do not say it directly, you *get the* ...
   a picture **b** painting **c** scene

14 If you make a mess of something, you make *a pig's* ... *of it.*
   a nose **b** ear **c** face

15 If you wouldn't like to do something at all, you wouldn't do it *for all the* ... *in China.*
   a rice **b** tea **c** people

16 After Jake's announcement, it was so quiet in the room that *you could have heard* ... *drop.*
   a a feather **b** a pin **c** aitches

17 If you look very angrily at somebody without speaking, you *look* ... *at them.*
   a murder **b** knives **c** daggers

18 If something is very easy to see or understand, it's *as plain as* ...
   a Jane **b** day **c** pie

19 If you give an important visitor a very special welcome, you put out *the red* ...
   a tape **b** herring **c** carpet

20 Somebody you are very pleased or relieved to see is *a sight for* ... *eyes.*
   a sore **b** bad **c** blind

21 A person who moves around a lot and so does not have many possessions or responsibilities is *a rolling* ...
    a stone b wave c cloud

22 If you say *'It's no use crying over spilt* ...', you think that it is a waste of time to worry or complain about something that is done and cannot be changed.
    a toffee b cream c milk

23 If you change the rules for something so that it becomes more difficult for somebody, *you move the* ...
    a mountain b target c goalposts

24 Somebody who is very shy and doesn't like meeting new people is *a shrinking* ...
    a rose b violet c daisy

25 Do you want to talk about it? It might make you feel better if you *get things off your* ...
    a back b chest c shoulders

26 If a piece of clothing fits you perfectly, it *fits like a* ...
    a skin b dream c glove

27 Trying to keep two jobs and look after the family too is *no* ...., believe me.
    a picnic b barbecue c feast

28 If an emotion can clearly be seen in somebody's expression, it is *written all over his/her* ...
    a face b look c eyes

29 I've lived here all my life, so I know the city *like the back of my* ...
    a head b hand c eyes

30 If news, information, etc. spreads in spoken, not written, words, it spreads by *word of* ...
    a tongue b mouth c speech

31 Pleasant, romantic words that lovers say to each other are called '*sweet* ...'
    a nothings b whisperings c wordings

32 If a person is intelligent and has good ideas, he/she is *a smart* ...
    a biscuit b cookie c cake

33 If somebody is very good at doing something, he/she is *a dab* ... *at* it.
    a touch b finger c hand

34 If you are completely wrong, you are *way out in left* ...
    a field b pitch c court

35 If somebody has good intentions even though they sometimes do the wrong thing, *their* ... *is in the right place.*
    a mind b soul c heart

36 If you try very hard to think of something or remember something, you *rack your* ...
    a head b mind c brains

37 My grandfather's nearly seventy, but he's still ... *fit.*
    a fighting b boxing c kicking

38 If you cannot quite remember a name, word, etc., but feel that you will soon, it is *on the* ... *of your tongue.*
    a end b tip c edge

39 If you are not as well or cheerful as usual, you are *under the* ...
    a rain b clouds c weather

40 If you think something is extremely good, interesting, useful, etc., you think it is *the best thing since* ... *bread.*
    a toasted b crusty c sliced

N n

nail

nail your colours to the 'mast (*especially BrE*)
show clearly which side you support: *It's time to
nail our colours to the mast and condemn this
dreadful policy.*

ℹ ORIGIN
In this expression, *colours* are flags. In a battle at
sea, a ship would *nail its colours to the mast* to
show its intention to continue fighting and not
surrender.

a nail in sb's/sth's 'coffin
something, especially one of a series of things,
which makes the failure or destruction of sth
more likely: *If we don't succeed with this campaign, it'll be the final nail in our coffin.* ◇ *The
increase in petrol prices drove another nail into the
company's coffin.* ◇ *The new tax is another nail in
the coffin of the British film industry.*

nail sb to the 'wall (*informal*)
punish sb and/or make them suffer because you
are very angry with them: *I'm going to nail him to
the wall for what he's done!*

on the 'nail (*informal*)
(of payment) without delay: *They're good customers who always pay on the nail.*

fight (sb/sth) tooth and nail → **fight**
fight tooth and nail for sb/sth → **fight**
hit the nail on the head → **hit**

nails

bite your (finger)nails → **bite**
(as) hard as nails → **hard**
(as) tough as nails → **tough**

naked

the naked 'eye
the normal power of your eyes without the help of
an instrument: *Bacteria are invisible to the naked
eye.*

the naked 'truth
the truth, which may be unpleasant: *If you want
the naked truth about it, he'll certainly give it to you!*

buck naked = stark naked → **stark**

name

by 'name
using the name of sb/sth: *She asked for you by
name.* ◇ *The principal knows all the students by
name.* ◇ *I only know her by name* (= I have heard
about her but I have not met her).

by the name of … (*written*)
who is called: *The play stars a young actor by the
name of Tom Rees.*

go by the name of …
use a name that may not be your real one:
*Although she was born Mary Jones, she now goes
by the name of Natasha, which she feels is more
appropriate to her glamorous image.*

**have (got) sb's 'name on it; with your 'name
on it** (*informal*)
if sth **has your name on it**, or there is sth **with
your name on it**, it is intended for you: *He took my
place and got killed. It should have been me—that
bullet had my name on it.* ◇ *Are you coming round
for dinner this evening? I've got a steak here with
your name on it!*

(not) have sth to your 'name (*informal*)
(not) possess sth: *I've only got two dresses to my
name.* ◇ *She didn't have a penny to her name when
she arrived here.*

in ˌall but 'name
used to describe a situation which exists in reality
but that is not officially recognized: *He runs the
company in all but name.*

**in 'God's/'Heaven's name; in the name of
'God/'Heaven**
used especially in questions to show that you are
angry, surprised or shocked: *What in God's name
was that noise?* ◇ *Where in the name of Heaven
have you been?*

in the name of 'sb/'sth; in sb's/sth's 'name
1 using the authority of sb/sth; as a representative of sb/sth: *I arrest you in the name of the law.*
2 used to give a reason or an excuse for doing sth,
often when what you are doing is wrong: *crimes
committed in the name of religion* ◇ *I'm asking
you, in the name of love, to stop meeting that
woman.*
3 for sb; showing that sth officially belongs to sb:
The reservation was made in the name of Brown. ◇
The car is registered in my name.

in 'name only
officially recognized but not existing in reality:
He's party leader in name only.

make a 'name for yourself; make your 'name
become successful and well known because of
your skill in doing sth very well: *She quickly made
a name for herself as one of the best brain surgeons
in the country.* ◇ *He made his name in the theatre
and then moved into films.*

name the 'day
choose the date for a wedding: *They are engaged
but they haven't named the day yet.*

your, his, etc. name is 'mud (*informal, usually
humorous*)
used to say that sb is not liked or popular because
of sth they have done: *Your name will be mud at*

home if you don't write to your family soon. ◇ *My name is mud at the moment. It's all because I forgot to book our holidays in time.*

ⓘ ORIGIN
Some people say that this expression refers to Dr Mudd, the doctor who treated the broken leg of the man who shot and killed Abraham Lincoln. Mudd claimed he didn't know that the man had just killed the President, but he was still sent to prison.

name 'names
give the names of people who are involved in sth, especially sth wrong or illegal: *If the newspapers really know the people responsible for these terrible crimes, then they should name names.* ◇ *I won't name names, but there are some people in this room who have broken several of the club's rules.*

the name of the 'game (informal)
the thing that is considered central or really important in a particular situation: *Survival is the name of the game when you're in the jungle.* ◇ *In the art world good publicity is the name of the game, not talent.*

a name to 'conjure with
1 the name of a well-known, very respected and admired person, group or thing in a particular field: *My great grandfather went to school with Charlie Chaplin—now there's a name to conjure with!*
2 (*humorous*) used when you mention a name that is difficult to remember or pronounce: *The soup was called chlodnik—now there's a name to conjure with!*

put a 'name to sb/sth
know or remember what sb/sth is called: *I recognize his face but I can't put a name to it.*

take sb's name in 'vain
show a lack of respect when using sb's name: *Don't worry about what he says about me—he's always taking my name in vain.* ◇ *I get very upset when people take God's name in vain.* ◇ (*humorous*) *Have you been taking my name in vain again?*

you ˌname it, sb's 'got it (informal)
sb has everything you can think of: *He's got an amazing collection of jazz records—you name it, he's got it.*

be sb's middle name → **middle**
a big name/noise/shot → **big**
clear sb's name → **clear**
enter sb's/your name (for sth) → **enter**
give a dog a bad name (and hang him) → **dog**
a household name/word → **household**
lend your name to sth → **lend**
put sb's/your name down (for sth) = enter sb's/your name (for sth) → **enter**
a rose by any other name (would smell as sweet) → **rose**
what's-his-/-her-/-its-/-their-name → **what**
worth the name = worthy of the name → **worthy**

nameless

somebody, who will/shall remain/be nameless (*humorous*)
used to say that you will not mention sb's name, either because the people listening to you already know who you are talking about, or because you do not want to embarrass sb: *Somebody, who will remain nameless, actually managed to drink two bottles of champagne!*

names

call sb names → **call**
drop names → **drop**
name names → **name**

nanny

the 'nanny state (*BrE*)
a disapproving way of talking about the fact that government seems to get too much involved in people's lives and to protect them too much, in a way that limits their freedom: *We're living in a nanny state; the government watches over you for everything and nobody's responsible for their own actions any more.*

napping

catch sb napping → **catch**

narrow

a narrow e'scape/'squeak
a situation where sb only just avoids injury, danger or failure: *We had a narrow escape on the way here. The wind blew a tree down just in front of us. We could have been killed.*

keep to, stay on, etc. the straight and narrow → **straight**

nasty

get/turn 'nasty
1 become threatening and violent: *You'd better do what he says or he'll turn nasty.*
2 become bad or unpleasant: *It looks as though the weather is going to turn nasty again.*

a nasty piece of 'work (*BrE, informal*)
a very unpleasant and dangerous person: *Keep away from Bill Smith—he's a very nasty piece of work.* ◇ *The factory manager was a nasty piece of work. We were all terrified of him.*

cheap and nasty → **cheap**
cut up rough/nasty → **cut**
leave a bad/nasty taste in the/your mouth → **leave**

native

go 'native (*often humorous*)
(of a person staying in another country) try to live and behave like the local people: *She was one of a number of artists who had emigrated before the war and gone native.*

naturally

come 'naturally (to sb/sth)
if sth **comes naturally** to you, you are able to do it
very easily and very well: *Making money came naturally to him.*

nature

against 'nature
not natural; not moral: *Murder is a crime against
nature.*

(get, go, etc.) back to 'nature
return to a simple kind of life in the country, away
from cities and technology: *'Did you enjoy your
camping trip?' 'Well, not really. Getting back to
nature isn't really my thing. I'd have preferred to
stay in a luxury hotel!'*

in the nature of 'sth
similar to sth; a type of sth; in the style of sth: *His
speech was in the nature of an apology.*

in the 'nature of things
used for saying that sth that happens is normal in
a particular situation: *Don't worry about it. It's in the nature of things for
children to argue with their parents when they're
teenagers.* ◇ *In the nature of things, people who
have power don't like losing it.*

be second nature (to sb) → **second**
a call of nature → **call**
the forces of nature → **forces**

nauseam

ad nauseam → **ad**

near

as ,near as 'dammit (also **as ,near as makes
no 'difference**) (*BrE, spoken*)
very nearly; so nearly sth or so like sth that you
can consider it the same: *The bill for the meal was
£100, as near as dammit.* ◇ *Here's some paint to
cover that scratch on the car. It's not an exact match
but it's as near as makes no difference.*

near e'nough (*BrE, spoken*)
used to say that sth is so nearly true that the difference does not matter: *We've been here twenty years,
near enough.*

a near 'miss
a situation in which an accident, usually involving two moving objects, is only just avoided: *There
was another near miss this afternoon just over
Heathrow Airport when a jet nearly hit a small private plane.* ◇ *He drove like a maniac. We had one
near miss after another.*

nowhere/not anywhere 'near
not nearly: *The bus was nowhere near full.* ◇ *The
test wasn't anywhere near as difficult as I expected.*

so ,near and ,yet so 'far
used to describe a situation in which sb is very
near to success, but finally fails: *He came second in
the piano competition, only one point behind the
winner. So near and yet so far.*

be close/dear/near to sb's heart → **heart**
be close to/near the mark → **mark**
a close/near thing → **thing**
close to/near the bone → **bone**
pretty near → **pretty**

nearest

your ,nearest and 'dearest (*informal, often
humorous*)
your close family and friends: *It must be difficult
for him here, so far away from his nearest and dearest.* ◇ *She usually spends Christmas with her nearest and dearest and then leaves as soon as she can.*

nearly

not 'nearly
much less than; not at all: *It's not nearly as hot as
last year.* ◇ *There isn't nearly enough time to get
there now.*

your eyes nearly pop out of your head → **eyes**
pretty nearly → **pretty**

necessarily

,not neces'sarily
used to say that sth is possibly true but not definitely or always true: *The more expensive articles
are not necessarily better.* ◇ *Biggest doesn't necessarily mean best.* ◇ (*spoken*) *'We're going to lose.'
'Not necessarily.'*

necessary

a ,necessary 'evil
a thing that is unpleasant or even harmful, but
which must be accepted because it brings some
benefit: *Injections against tropical illnesses are a
necessary evil when you are planning to travel to
that part of the world.* ◇ *I suppose all these security
measures are a necessary evil.*

necessity

ne,cessity is the ,mother of in'vention (*saying*)
a very difficult new problem forces people to think
of, design, produce, etc. a solution to it: *'So how did
you manage to open the bottle?' 'I used a bit of wire
and a stick. Necessity is the mother of invention, as
the saying goes.'*

make a virtue of necessity → **virtue**

neck

**be up to your 'neck in sth; be in sth up to
your 'neck**
1 have a lot of sth to deal with: *I've been up to my
neck in job applications for weeks.*
2 be deeply involved in sth, especially sth dangerous or criminal: *He says he knows nothing about
the drug smuggling, but the police are sure he's in it
(= trouble) up to his neck.*

need

by a 'neck
if a person or an animal wins a race **by a neck**, they win it by a short distance: *The final was very close, with Molina finally winning by a neck.*

ˌget it in the 'neck (*BrE, informal*)
be shouted at or punished because of sth that you have done: *Look at the time! I really should get back to work, or I'll get it in the neck.*

in your, this, etc. ˌneck of the 'woods (*informal*)
in a particular area or part of the country: *Hi, Jim! What are you doing in this neck of the woods?* ◇ *Not much happens in our neck of the woods. It's very quiet.*

ˌneck and 'neck (with sb/sth) (also ˌnip and 'tuck (with sb) *especially AmE*)
(in a race, competition, etc.) level with each other: *With another 100 metres to go, Jones and Saville are neck and neck.*

be a millstone around/round sb's neck → **millstone**
brass neck/nerve → **brass**
(not) break your neck (doing/to do sth) → **break**
breathe down sb's neck → **breathe**
by the scruff of sb's/the neck → **scruff**
a pain in the neck → **pain**
put/lay your head/neck on the block → **block**
risk your neck → **risk**
save sb's/your (own) neck/skin/hide → **save**
stick your neck out → **stick**
wring sb's neck → **wring**

need

if need(s) 'be
if it is necessary: *We should have enough money, but if need be, we can cash one of our traveller's cheques.* ◇ *Give him a tablet now to relieve the pain; you can give him another one later if needs be.*

that's 'all I need (*informal*)
used when sth bad happens in a situation which is already bad: *The car's broken down? That's all I need!*

a crying need (for sth) → **crying**
a friend in need (is a friend indeed) → **friend**
in your hour of need → **hour**
need/want sth like (you need/want) a hole in the head → **hole**

needle

like looking for/trying to find a ˌneedle in a 'haystack
very difficult to find: *How can we ever find the quotation if you don't even know what part of the book it comes from? It'll be like looking for a needle in a haystack.*

needles

be on pins and needles = (be) on tenterhooks → **tenterhooks**
have (got) pins and needles → **pins**

needless

ˌneedless to 'say
as you would expect: *Needless to say, the student who had studied mathematics before did better in the statistics exam.* ◇ *He got home from the party the next morning. Needless to say, his parents were furious.*

needs

needs 'must (when the devil drives) (*saying*)
in certain situations it is necessary for you to do sth you do not like or enjoy: *Of course I'd rather go to the beach than sit here studying for my exams but needs must I suppose.*

neighbourhood (*BrE*) (*AmE* neighborhood)

in the 'neighbourhood of
(of a number or an amount) approximately; not exactly: *It cost in the neighbourhood of £500.*

nelly

not on your 'nelly (*old-fashioned, BrE, informal*)
definitely not: *You want to borrow my new car? Not on your nelly!*

nerve

have (got) a 'nerve (*informal*)
behave in a way that other people think is rude or not appropriate: *She had a nerve, arriving half an hour late for the meeting.* ◇ *She borrowed my new bicycle without asking.* **What a nerve!**

have (got) the nerve to do sth (*BrE also* have (got) the face to do sth) (*informal*)
do sth that other people think is rude or not appropriate without feeling embarrassed or ashamed: *He had the nerve to ask me for a pay rise after only three weeks in the job.* ◇ *I don't know how she's got the face to criticize my designs. She doesn't know anything at all about architecture.*

hit/touch a (raw) 'nerve
say sth which upsets sb because they are very sensitive about that subject: *You touched a raw nerve when you talked to the manager about the need for better communications within the company.*

brass neck/nerve → **brass**
strain every nerve/sinew (to do sth) → **strain**

nerves

a bag/bundle of 'nerves (*informal*)
a person who is very frightened, worried or nervous about sth: *She was a bundle of nerves at the start of the interview but she became more confident later.* ◇ *He's a bag of nerves. He needs a holiday.*

get on sb's 'nerves (*informal*)
annoy sb a lot: *It really gets on my nerves the way he only ever talks about his job and his car.* ◇ *By the end of the week, they were all getting on each other's nerves.*

have (got) nerves of 'steel
not be easily frightened in a difficult or dangerous situation: *She won't be nervous about doing it. She's got nerves of steel.*

a war of nerves → war

nervous

be frightened/nervous/scared of your own shadow → shadow

nest

a 'nest egg (*informal*)
a sum of money saved for the future: *She has a nice little nest egg which she intends to use for travelling round the world one day.*

the empty nest → empty
feather your (own) nest → feather
fly the nest → fly
a hornet's nest → hornet
a mare's nest → mare

net

cast/spread your net 'wide
consider a wide range of possibilities or cover a large area, especially to try to find sb/sth: *Unless we spread our net a bit wider, this company will never get enough business.*

slip through the net → slip

nettle

grasp the nettle → grasp

network

the old boy network → old

neutral

on neutral 'ground/'territory
in a place that has no connection with either of the people or sides who are meeting and so does not give an advantage to either of them: *We decided to meet on neutral ground.*

never-never

on the ˌnever-'never (*BrE, informal*)
on hire purchase (= by making payments over a long period of time): *He bought a new car on the never-never.*

new

(as) ˌgood as 'new; like 'new
in very good condition, as it was when it was new: *I've had your coat cleaned—it's as good as new now.*

a new 'broom (sweeps clean) (*BrE, saying*)
a person who has just started to work for an organization, department, etc., especially in a senior job, and who is likely to make a lot of changes: *The new managing director is clearly a new broom. He's*
already got rid of ten members of staff and now he's looking at our working methods.

a/the new kid on the block (*informal*)
sb who is new to a place, organization, etc: *Despite his six years in politics, he was still regarded by many as the new kid on the block.*

a ˌnew 'man (*BrE*)
a man who shares the work in the home that is traditionally done by women, such as cleaning, cooking and taking care of children. New men are considered sensitive and not aggressive: *He is comfortable with his 'new man' image, and has been known to leave the office early to go home and cook dinner for his family.*

a ˌnew one on 'me
a story, joke or piece of information that you have not heard before and which you may find difficult to believe: *Butter that always stays soft—that's a new one on me.* ◇ *No, I've never heard that story before. It's a new one on me.*

what's 'new? (*spoken, informal*)
used as a friendly greeting: *Hi! What's new?*

a brave new world → brave
break fresh/new ground → break
(as) clean as a new pin → clean
a (whole) different/new ball game → ball
fresh/new/young blood → blood
pastures new → pastures
put a new/different complexion on sth → complexion
ring out the old (year) and ring in the new → ring
(you can't) teach an old dog new tricks → teach
turn over a new leaf → turn

Newcastle

(carry/take) coals to Newcastle → coals

news

be bad 'news (for sb/sth)
be likely to cause problems for sb/sth: *Central heating is bad news for indoor plants.*

be good news (for sb/sth)
be likely to be helpful or give an advantage for sb/sth: *The cut in interest rates is good news for homeowners.*

it's/that's ˌnews to 'me
used to express surprise at some information that you have just heard: *'Max is thinking of leaving his job.' 'Really? That's news to me. I thought he was happy there.'*

ˌno news is 'good news (*saying*)
if there were bad news you would hear it, so if you have not heard anything that means everything must be all right: *He's been in the mountains for a week without contacting us. I just hope no news is good news.*

break the news (to sb) → break

newt

(as) pissed as a newt → pissed

next

as good, well, etc. as the 'next person
as good/well etc. as most other people: *I can swim as well as the next person, but I can't compete with her—she's an Olympic champion.*

the next best 'thing
the best alternative for a thing that you cannot have: *I couldn't find any more of that Italian ice cream but this is the next best thing in my opinion.*

your ,next of 'kin (*formal*)
your closest living relative or relatives: *The hospital need to contact her next of kin—she is very ill indeed.* ◇ *This form must be signed by your next of kin.*

the 'next thing (I knew) (*informal*)
used when sb tells a story and wants to say that sth happened suddenly or unexpectedly: *I was just walking down the road and the next thing I knew someone was pointing a gun at my face.*

next to 'nothing
a very small amount; almost nothing: *He knows a great deal about flowers but next to nothing about trees and shrubs.* ◇ *He was able to buy the neighbouring farm for next to nothing.*

the 'next world
(according to some religious beliefs) the place you go to when you die: *She had had a difficult life but she was convinced her reward would come in the next world.*

better luck next time → better

from one day to the next → day

say, etc. sth in one breath, and then in the next say ... → breath

nibs

his 'nibs (*old-fashioned, BrE, informal*)
used to refer to a man who is, or thinks he is, more important than other people: *And how is his nibs this morning?*

Nice

Mr Nice Guy → Mr

nice

have a nice 'day! (*spoken, especially AmE*)
a friendly way of saying goodbye, especially to customers

,nice and 'peaceful, 'comfortable, 'warm, etc.
pleasantly peaceful, etc: *Sit by the fire. It's nice and warm there.* ◇ *Drink your coffee while it's nice and hot.*

(as) ,nice as 'pie (*informal*)
very kind and friendly, especially when you are not expecting it: *He'd been very nervous about meeting everyone, but they were all as nice as pie.*

'nice one! (*BrE, spoken*)
used to show you are pleased when sth good has happened or sb has said sth amusing: *You got the job? Nice one!*

nice 'work! (*spoken, especially BrE*)
used to show you are pleased when sb has done sth well: *You did a good job today. Nice work, James!*

nice 'work if you can get it (*informal, humorous*)
used for saying how lucky a person is to have such a pleasant and well-paid job: *She has to see all the latest films as part of her job. Nice work if you can get it.*

nicely

do 'nicely
1 (usually used in progressive tenses) be making good progress: *Her new business is doing very nicely.*
2 be satisfactory: *Tomorrow at ten will do nicely* (= will be a good time).

nick

in good, bad, etc. 'nick (*BrE, informal*)
in good/bad condition or health: *When I last saw him he looked in pretty good nick.* ◇ *She wants to sell the bike, but she won't get very much for it because it's in terrible nick.*

in the ,nick of 'time (*informal*)
at the last possible moment; just in time: *He got to the railway station in the nick of time.* ◇ *He remembered in the nick of time that his passport was in his coat pocket.*

night

have an early/a late 'night
go to bed earlier or later than usual: *I'd better have an early night if I want to get up at 6 o'clock.* ◇ *I've had a lot of late nights recently.*

have a good/bad 'night
sleep well/badly during the night: *He was very tired after his bad night, and wanted very much to take the day off work.*

make a 'night of it (*informal*)
decide to spend the whole evening doing sth enjoyable: *They met some old friends in the pub after work and decided to make a night of it by going to a restaurant and then on to a nightclub.*

,night and 'day; ,day and 'night
all the time; without stopping: *She worked night and day on the computer program until it was finished.*

night 'night
used by children or to children, to mean 'Good night': *'Night night, sleep tight!'*

a night 'out
an evening that you spend enjoying yourself away from home: *They enjoy a night out occasionally.*

a 'night owl (*informal*)

somebody who feels more lively at night and usually goes to bed very late: *She's a night owl and has always done her best work after midnight.*

be (like) ships that pass in the night → **ships**

(in/at) the dead of (the) night → **dead**

it'll be all right on the night → **right**

like a thief in the night → **thief**

morning, noon and night → **morning**

a night (out) on the town/on the tiles = (out) on the town → **town**

spend the night with sb/together → **spend**

stay the night → **stay**

the still of the night → **still**

things that go bump in the night → **things**

nine

have (got) nine 'lives

be very lucky in dangerous situations: *We were called to the hospital twice, but the old man seemed to have nine lives, and before long made a complete recovery.*

> ❶ ORIGIN
> This idiom refers to the traditional saying that cats have nine lives.

a ,nine days' 'wonder

a person or thing that attracts a lot of attention, but only for a short time: *The satellite that landed in their garden made the family a bit of a nine days' wonder, but no one remembers their name now.*

,nine times out of 'ten (also ,ninety-nine ,times out of a 'hundred)

almost always: *Nine times out of ten our opponents will beat us. We just hope this is the one in ten.* ◇ *Ninety-nine times out of a hundred she's right about people but this time she was wrong.*

,nine to 'five

normal office working hours: *After years working nine to five in a boring job, he set off to sail round the world.* ◇ *She'd had a typical nine-to-five job in the civil service before she worked in the theatre.*

the ,whole ,nine 'yards (*informal, especially AmE*)

everything, or a situation which includes everything: *When Des cooks dinner he always goes the whole nine yards, with three courses and and a choice of dessert.*

> ❷ NOTE
> A *yard* is a unit for measuring length, equal to 0.9144 of a metre.

on cloud nine → **cloud**

possession is nine points/tenths/parts of the law → **possession**

ninepins

,go down, ,drop, etc. like 'ninepins (*informal*)

1 (of large numbers of people) become ill, be killed or die at the same time: *In last year's flu epidemic both children and teachers at this school were going down like ninepins.* ◇ *As the enemy advanced, men and horses went down like ninepins.*

2 (of businesses, etc.) fail, go out of business, etc: *Small businesses are going down like ninepins at the moment.*

> ❷ NOTE
> In the game of *ninepins*, you roll a ball towards a group of nine wooden objects (= *skittles*) in order to knock down as many of them as possible.

nines

dressed (up) to the nines → **dressed**

nineteen

talk, etc. nineteen to the 'dozen (*BrE, informal*)

talk a lot and very fast, usually in an informal conversation: *An hour later they were still sitting there talking nineteen to the dozen.*

ninety-nine

ninety-nine times out of a hundred = nine times out of ten → **nine**

nip

nip sth in the 'bud

stop sth in its early stages because you think it is dangerous to let it develop: *I do not want drugs in this school. It's essential that we nip the problem in the bud so I want a meeting with all the parents next week.* ◇ *The scheme to allow all pensioners a free travel pass was nipped in the bud by the government, who said it would cost too much.*

nip and tuck (with sb/sth) = neck and neck (with sb/sth) → **neck**

nitty-gritty

get down to the nitty-'gritty (*informal*)

start discussing the basic, especially the practical aspects of a matter/decision: *Let's get down to the nitty-gritty. Who's going to pay for the renovations?* ◇ *We talked for an hour without really getting down to the nitty-gritty of the problem.*

Nod

in the land of Nod → **land**

nod

get the 'nod (*informal*)

be chosen for sth; be given permission or approval to do sth: *He got the nod from the team manager (= he was chosen for the team).* ◇ *The proposal should get the nod.*

give sb the 'nod (*informal*)

give sb permission to do sth; tell sb that you are willing or ready for sth to happen: *Just give me the nod when you've decided, and I'll make all the necessary arrangements.*

a ˌnod is as good as a ˈwink (to a blind man)
(*saying*)
used for telling the speaker that it is unnecessary
to explain sth further because you have already
understood: *'I've invited Marie to dinner. What
time will you be coming home?' 'Don't worry, a nod
is as good as a wink. I'll be back very late.'*

on the ˈnod (*BrE, informal*)
(of a matter being discussed by a committee, etc.)
agreed to by all the members of the group, so that a
vote or further discussion is unnecessary: *The
decision to increase bus fares went through on the
nod.*

nodding

be on ˈnodding terms with sb
know sb not very well, but well enough to say
'hello' when you meet them: *We're on nodding
terms with our neighbours but we don't know anyone else at all.*

have a nodding acˈquaintance with sb/sth
know sb slightly/know a little about sth: *I have a
nodding acquaintance with some members of the
committee.* ◇ *You need at least a nodding acquaintance with the rules of chess to understand the book.*

no-go

a no-ˈgo area (*especially BrE*)
an area, especially in a city, which is dangerous for
people to enter, or that the police or army do not
enter, often because it is controlled by a violent
group: *Several parts of the city have become no-go
areas for the police.* ◇ *(figurative) This subject is
definitely a no-go area* (= we must not discuss it).

noire

your, his, etc. bête noire → **bête**

noise

make a (lot of) ˈnoise (about sth) (*informal*)
talk or complain about sth a lot: *People are making
more noise these days about pollution.* ◇ *The
unions are making a lot of noise about the new
legislation.*

a big name/noise/shot → **big**

noises

make ˈnoises (about sth) (*informal*)
show that you are interested in (doing) sth, but not
in a direct way: *The government has been making
noises about listening to the public but it still hasn't
changed any of its policies.* ◇ *She hasn't exactly
said that she wants to change her job but she has
been making noises in that direction.*

make (all) the right noises → **right**

none

have/want ˈnone of it/that (*informal*)
refuse to do, become involved in, accept or agree to
sth: *She wants me to work late again this week but
I'm having none of it. I've told her I won't do it.* ◇
*The management has offered a 3% pay rise but the
workers want none of it. They're demanding a 10%
increase.*

ˈnone but (*literary*)
only: *None but he knew the truth.*

none ˈother than sb
used to emphasize who or what sb/sth is, when
this is surprising: *And who do you think was
responsible for the mistake? None other than the
director himself!*

none too ˈclever, ˈhappy, ˈquickly, etc.
not at all clever, quickly, etc: *The driver was none
too pleased about having to leave so early.* ◇ *Her
chances of winning are none too good, I'm afraid.*

no-no

a ˈno-no (*informal*)
a thing or a way of behaving that is not acceptable
in a particular situation: *Women wearing trousers
used to be a bit of a no-no, but now it's completely
normal.*

nonsense

make (a) ˈnonsense of sth
reduce the value of sth by a lot; make sth seem
ridiculous: *If people can bribe police officers, it
makes a complete nonsense of the legal system.*

stuff and nonsense → **stuff**

nook

(in) every ˌnook and ˈcranny (*informal*)
everywhere; (in) all parts of a place: *I've looked in
every nook and cranny but I can't find it.* ◇ *She
knows every nook and cranny of the city, so she's the
perfect guide.*

noon

morning, noon and night → **morning**

normal

as per usual/normal → **per**

north

up ˈnorth
to or in the north of a country, especially England:
They've gone to live up north.

nose

get up sb's ˈnose (*BrE, informal*)
annoy sb: *It gets right up my nose, the way they keep
telling you how successful they are.*

have (got) a ˈnose for sth (*informal*)
have a natural ability in finding or recognizing
sth: *Don't worry about your money, he'll invest it
wisely. He's got a nose for that sort of thing.* ◇ *She
seems to have a nose for good restaurants.*

have (got) your nose in a 'book, maga'zine, etc. (*informal*)
be reading sth and giving it all your attention: *She's always got her nose in a book.*

have a nose 'round (*BrE, informal*)
look around a place; look for sth in a place: *Let's have a quick nose round before we leave.*

keep your 'nose clean (*informal*)
do nothing that will get you into trouble with the police or other authorities: *After he came out of prison, he was determined to keep his nose clean.*

keep your nose out of sth (*informal*)
not interfere in sth that does not concern you: *Keep your nose out of my business affairs, will you? It's nothing to do with you.*

keep your ˌnose to the 'grindstone (*informal*)
continue to work very hard: *Keep your nose to the grindstone and you should pass the exam easily.*

> ❷ **NOTE**
> A *grindstone* is a machine used for grinding, sharpening and polishing knives and tools.

ˌnose to 'tail (*BrE*)
if cars, etc. are **nose to tail**, they are moving slowly in a long line with little space between them: *I'm sorry I'm late—the traffic was nose to tail going through the town centre.*

on the 'nose (*informal, especially AmE*)
exactly: *The budget should hit the $136 billion target on the nose.*

poke/stick your nose in/into 'sth (*informal*)
interfere in the affairs or business of other people: *She's always sticking her nose into other people's affairs. It's really annoying.* ◇ *What happens in this department does not concern him. Why does he have to poke his nose into everything all the time?*

We were managing fine until Brian started sticking his nose in.

put sb's 'nose out of joint (*informal*)
upset or annoy sb, especially by not giving them enough attention: *The new teacher speaks much better German than he does. That's going to put his nose out of joint.*

(right) under sb's 'nose (*informal*)
1 very close to sb, even though they cannot see it: *'Where are the car keys?' 'There, right under your nose.'*

2 used to talk about sth bad that happens over a period of time, but which nobody has noticed: *Stealing from the kitchen has been going on right under their noses for years.*

with your 'nose in the air (*informal, disapproving*)
in a way that is unfriendly and suggests that you think that you are better than other people: *I hate the way she walks round with her nose in the air. She thinks she's better than us just because her family is rich.* ◇ *He sat with his nose in the air and never bothered to speak to anybody.*

cut off your nose to spite your face → **cut**
follow your nose → **follow**
it's no skin off my, your, his, etc. nose → **skin**
lead sb by the nose → **lead**
look down your nose (at sb/sth) → **look**
not see beyond/past the end of your nose → **see**
pay through the nose (for sth) → **pay**
(as) plain as the nose on your face → **plain**
(go to) powder your nose → **powder**
rub sb's nose in it → **rub**
thumb your nose at sb/sth → **thumb**
turn your nose up at sth → **turn**

nosy

a ˌnosy 'parker (*BrE, informal, becoming old-fashioned*)
a person who is too interested in other people's private lives: *Our next door neighbour is a real nosy parker. He always has to know everything about everybody on our street.*

note

hit/strike the right/wrong 'note (*especially BrE*)
do, say or write sth that is suitable/not suitable for a particular occasion: *Somehow, her clothes and manner struck just the right note of gracious elegance.*

of 'note
(used after a noun) important or famous: *The old theatre is one of the town's few buildings of note.*

sound/strike a 'note (of 'sth)
express feelings or opinions of a particular kind: *She sounded a note of warning in her speech.*

take 'note of sth
notice and think about or remember sth: *Well, Ms Brown, I've taken note of everything you've told me, and I'll give you my answer next week.* ◇ *I'd like everyone to take note of the changes I've made to the timetable.*

drop sb a line/note → **drop**
make a mental note of sth/to do sth → **mental**
sound/strike a false note → **false**

notes

compare notes (with sb) → **compare**

nothing

be/have nothing to 'do with sb/sth
1 have no connection with sb/sth: *I'm absolutely sure that the stars have nothing to do with our personalities.* ◇ *Wynne-Williams plc is nothing to do with Owen Wynne-Williams. It's a completely different company.* ◇ *Go away! It's got nothing to do with you* (= you have no right to know about it).
2 avoid or refuse contact with sb/sth: *She wants to have nothing to do with drugs, thank God.* ◇ *She will have absolutely nothing to do with that organization. She doesn't approve of it.*

for 'nothing
1 without paying; free: *We got into the concert for nothing because my uncle works there.* ◇ *They were giving packets of sweets away for nothing at the supermarket this morning.*
2 (do sth and) not achieve what you wanted; (do sth) for no reason or purpose: *All that hard work for nothing!* ◇ *When I got to Berlin, he'd already left. I'd made the journey for nothing.*

have (got) nothing on sb (*informal*)
1 have much less of a particular quality than sth/sb: *I'm quite a fast worker, but I've got nothing on her!* ◇ *Although all four children could play the piano well, the three boys had nothing on Joan, who played like an angel.*
2 (of the police, etc.) have no information that could show sb to be guilty of sth: *Look, they've got nothing on you, so stop worrying!*

not for 'nothing do, will, etc. I, they, etc. do sth
used to emphasize that there is a good reason for sth: *Not for nothing do people call this beer the best in the world. It's absolutely wonderful.*

'nothing but
only: *Nothing but the freshest vegetables are used in our restaurant.*

ˌnothing 'doing (*informal*)
used to refuse a request: *'Can you lend me ten dollars?' 'Nothing doing!'*

'nothing if not sth (*informal*)
(used for emphasis) very; very much a particular type of person: *She's nothing if not fair.* ◇ *Her work is nothing if not original.*

(there's) nothing 'in it
1 (*informal*) used to talk about a contest where the competitors are level and it is hard to say who will win: *Right up to the end of the game, there was nothing in it. Either team could have won.*
2 (of a rumour, report, story, etc.) there's no truth in it: *There was a rumour that he was about to resign, but apparently there's nothing in it.*

nothing 'less than
(used for emphasis) very; completely: *Their defeat was nothing less than amazing.* ◇ *Her survival was nothing less than a miracle.*

nothing 'like (*informal*)
not; not at all like sth: *It's nothing like as bad as he said.* ◇ *We've sold nothing like enough books to make a profit.*

nothing 'more than
(used for emphasis) only: *The injury isn't serious—it's nothing more than a sprained ankle.*

ˌnothing 'much
not a great amount of sth; nothing of great value or importance: *There's nothing much in the fridge.* ◇ *I got up late and did nothing much all day.*

there's nothing (else) 'for it (but to do sth)
there is only one possible action in a particular situation: *When the river flooded, there was nothing for it but to move everything upstairs.* ◇ *There was nothing for it but to try to swim to the shore.*

there's nothing like sth
used to say that you enjoy sth very much: *There's nothing like a brisk walk on a cold day!*

there's nothing 'to it (*informal*)
it is easy to do: *It's not difficult to use. All you have to do is pull these two switches and it starts. You see, there's nothing to it!* ◇ *I finished the work very quickly. There was nothing to it really.*

nothings

sweet nothings → sweet

notice

at a moment's notice = at (very) short notice → short
escape sb's notice → escape

notion

run away with the idea/notion → run

nouveau

the ˌnouveau 'riche (*from French, disapproving*)
people who have recently become rich and like to show how rich they are in a very obvious way: *As a member of the nouveau riche, Tom can often be seen at New York's most fashionable and sophisticated venues.*

> ❷ NOTE
> The meaning of the French phrase is 'new rich'.

now

ˌany minute, day, time, etc. 'now
in the next few minutes, days, etc: *The taxi will be here any minute now.*

as of 'now
from now on; from this moment on: *As of now, smoking is forbidden in this house.*

it's ˌnow or 'never
you must do sth now because you will not get another opportunity to do it: *If we don't climb it now, we never will. It's now or never.*

(every) now and a'gain/'then
occasionally: *We see each other every now and again.* ◇ *She sat by the window, looking out now*

and then to see if they were coming. ◊ *'How often do you go to the cinema?' 'Now and then. Not often.'*

now for 'sb/'sth
used when turning to a fresh activity or subject: *And now for some travel news.*

,now, 'now (*informal*)
1 used for comforting sb who is upset: *Now, now, darling. What's the matter? Stop crying and tell me what's happened.*

2 used for introducing a friendly warning or criticism: *Now, now, that's no way to speak to your father!*

now ... now ...
at one time ... at another time ...: *Her moods kept changing—now happy, now sad.*

'now then
1 used for getting sb's attention before you start to tell them or ask sth: *Now then, let's begin the next exercise.* ◊ *Now then, lads, what's going on here?*

2 used when you are trying to remember sth: *The capital of Cuba? Now then, let me think ...*

'now what? (*spoken*)
1 (also **what is it 'now?**) used when you are annoyed because sb is always asking questions or interrupting you: *'Yes, but Dad ... ' 'Now what?'*

2 used to say that you do not know what to do next in a particular situation: *Well, that idea didn't work. Now what?*

nth

for the nth 'time (*informal*)
used when you are stating that sth is the last in a long series and emphasizing how often sth has happened, especially when you are annoyed: *I told him, for the nth time, to tidy his room but he's done nothing to it at all.*

to the nth de'gree (*informal*)
to the greatest possible amount, level, etc.; very much: *This book is boring to the nth degree.* ◊ *Not only was he an excellent musician, he was also a gentleman to the nth degree.*

> **❷ NOTE**
> *Nth* in these two idioms is pronounced /enθ/.

nude

in the 'nude
wearing no clothes; naked: *It's a painting of the Duchess of Alba in the nude.* ◊ *People sunbathe in the nude on the rocks above the creek.*

nudge

,nudge 'nudge, ,wink 'wink; a ,nudge and a 'wink
used to suggest sth to do with sex without actually saying it: *They've been spending a lot of time together, nudge nudge, wink wink.*

null

,null and 'void (*formal*)
(of a legal agreement) no longer effective or valid: *The contract was declared null and void.*

number

have (got) 'sb's number (*informal*)
really understand what type of person sb is and what they plan to do: *Don't worry, I've got his number. I shall be very careful in any business I do with him.* ◊ *You can't fool me, you know. I've got your number.*

your/sb's (lucky) 'number comes up (*informal*)
sb is very lucky in a competition, etc: *If my lucky number comes up, we'll have a holiday in Venice.*

your/sb's number is 'up (*informal*)
sb is about to die or experience sth very unpleasant: *There's no point worrying about getting killed in a plane crash. When your number's up, your number's up.* ◊ *The police have the evidence they need to arrest him, so it looks as if his number's up.*

,number 'one (*informal*)
1 the most important or best person or thing: *We're number one in the used car business.* ◊ *He's the world's number one athlete.*

2 (*often disapproving*) yourself: *She doesn't care about other people and their problems. She just looks after number one.* ◊ *Take care of number one and forget everybody else. That's his philosophy.*

your/sb's number 'two (*informal*)
the second most important person in a company, organization, etc: *Brian Jones is the new number two at the ministry.*

any amount/number of sth → **amount**
a cushy number → **cushy**
your opposite number → **opposite**
public enemy number one → **public**

numbered

your, its, etc. days are numbered → **days**

numbers

by 'numbers
sth done easily but without imagination; following instructions: *I'm not a great cook, I just do it by numbers.* ◊ *I once got a painting by numbers set for my birthday.*

a/the 'numbers game
a way of considering an activity, etc. that is concerned only with the number of people doing sth, things achieved, etc., not with who or what they are: *Candidates were playing the numbers game as the crucial vote drew closer.*

in round figures/numbers → **figures**
there's safety in numbers → **safety**
(do sth by) weight of numbers → **weight**

nut

do your 'nut (*BrE, informal, spoken*)
be very angry or worried: *He'll do his nut when he sees all that mess.* ◇ *She's doing her nut because she hasn't heard from her son for weeks. She's sure that something terrible must have happened.*

a hard/tough 'nut (to crack) (*informal*)
a very difficult problem to solve; a very difficult person to deal with: *Persuading drivers to leave their cars at home and use public transport will be a very tough nut to crack.* ◇ *You'll find it difficult to make him change his mind. He's a tough nut.*

,off your 'nut (*BrE, informal, spoken*)
crazy: *Is he completely off his nut?*

use a sledgehammer to crack a nut → use

nuts

the nuts and 'bolts (of sth) (*informal*)
the most important and practical details of sth: *If we look at the nuts and bolts of the plan, what problems are there?* ◇ *He worked there for two years, long enough to learn the nuts and bolts of the business.*

nutshell

(put sth) in a 'nutshell (*informal*)
(say or express sth) in a very clear way, using few words: *Unemployment is rising, prices are increasing; in a nutshell, the economy is in trouble.* ◇ *'Do you like his new girlfriend?' 'To put it in a nutshell, no.'*

nutty

(as) nutty as a 'fruitcake (*informal, humorous*)
(of a person) completely crazy: *He's as nutty as a fruitcake. Do you know what he did yesterday? He had lunch out in the garden in the pouring rain.*

O o

oaks

great/tall oaks from little acorns grow (*saying*)
large and successful organizations, businesses,
etc. sometimes begin in a very small or modest
way: *Welcome to my new website! It may not look
much at the moment, but great oaks from little
acorns grow!*

> **❷ NOTE**
> An *oak* is a large tree and the *acorn* is its fruit.

oar

put/stick your 'oar in (*BrE, informal*)
interfere in the affairs of other people: *This project
is nothing to do with Dave. Why does he keep trying
to stick his oar in all the time?*

oath

on/under 'oath (*law*)
having made a formal promise to tell the truth in a
court of law: *Is she prepared to give evidence on
oath?* ◇ *The judge reminded the witness that he was
still under oath.*

oats

get your 'oats (*BrE, informal*)
have sex regularly: *What's the matter with you,
John? Not getting your oats?*

sow your wild oats → sow

object

money, expense, etc. is no 'object
there is no need to worry about the amount of
money, etc., because there is enough or because it
has no importance: *Choose whatever you like from
the menu. It's your birthday so money is no object.*
◇ *He was ready to travel anywhere. Distance was
no object.*

an 'object lesson
a practical example of what you should or should
not do in a particular situation: *It was an object lesson in how not to make a speech. He did absolutely
everything wrong.*

occasion

have occasion to do sth (*formal*)
have a reason or need to do sth: *If you ever have
occasion to visit Zurich, you will always be welcome
to stay with us.*

on oc'casion(s)
sometimes; not very often: *I don't smoke cigarettes
but I like to smoke a cigar on occasion.*

rise to the occasion/challenge → rise
a sense of occasion → sense

ocean

an ocean of sth (*BrE also* **oceans of sth**)
(*informal*)
a large amount of sth: *oceans of food*

a drop in the ocean → drop

odd

,odd 'jobs
various small, practical tasks, repairs, etc. in the
home, often done for other people: *I've got some
odd jobs to do around the house; the bedroom door
needs to be painted and the wall light fixed.* ▶ **,odd-
'job man** *noun* (*especially BrE*) a person who is
employed to do odd jobs

the odd man/one 'out
a person or thing that is different from others or
does not fit easily into a group or set: *That's the
problem with 13 people in a group. If you need to
work in pairs, there's always an odd one out.* ◇ *Tom
is nearly always the odd man out. He never wants to
do what we want to do, or go where we want to go.*

an odd/a queer fish → fish

odds

against all (the) 'odds
in spite of great difficulties or problems; although
it seemed impossible: *Against all the odds this
little-known man succeeded in becoming President.*
◇ *It's a romantic story of love surviving against all
odds.*

be at 'odds (with sb/sth) (about/over sth)
1 not be in agreement with sb about sth: *I'm at
odds with her on the question of nuclear energy.*
2 (of two things) not match or correspond to each
other: *His colourful and confident way of dressing
is strangely at odds with his shy personality.*

it makes no 'odds (to sb/sth) (*spoken, especially BrE*)
used to say that sth is not important: *It makes no
odds to me what you decide to do.*

odds and 'ends (*BrE also* **odds and 'sods**)
(*informal*)
small items that are not valuable or are not part of
a larger set: *She's got all kinds of interesting odds
and ends on her desk.* ◇ *I've got a few odds and ends
(= small jobs) to do before leaving.*

the odds 'are (that ...) (*also* (**it's) odds-'on
(that ...)**)
it is very likely that: *I don't think we can come. The
odds are that we won't be able to get a babysitter—
not on Christmas Eve.* ◇ *It was odds-on that they
would decide to get married, so no one was surprised.*

the odds are a'gainst sth/sb doing sth
sth is very unlikely: *The odds are against them*

winning, I'm afraid. ◇ *The odds are against her because she's less experienced than the other applicants.*

over the 'odds (*informal*)
more than the usual price: *He paid over the odds for that bike and now he's regretting it.*

what's the 'odds? (*BrE, informal*)
what difference does it make?; what does it matter?: *Work this weekend or next weekend? What's the odds? You get the same money.*

the cards/odds are stacked against sb/sth → **stacked**
the cards/odds are stacked in favour of sb/sth → **stacked**

odds-on
(it's) odds-on (that ...) = the odds are (that ...) → **odds**

odour (*BrE*) (*AmE* odor)

be in good/bad 'odour (with sb) (*formal*)
have/not have sb's approval and support: *He's in rather bad odour with his boss at the moment.*

off

be ,off for 'sth (*informal*)
have a particular amount of sth: *How are we off for coffee* (= how much have we got)*?*

,off and 'on; ,on and 'off
not regularly; not continuously: *It rained on and off all week.*

offence (*BrE*) (*AmE* offense)

no of'fence (*spoken*)
used to say that you do not mean to upset or insult sb by sth you say or do: *No offence, but I'd really like to be on my own.*

offensive

be on the of'fensive
be attacking sb/sth rather than waiting for them to attack you: *The Scots were on the offensive for most of the game.* ◇ *The government is very much on the offensive in the fight against drugs.*

go on(to) the of'fensive; take the of'fensive
start attacking sb/sth before they start attacking you: *The president decided to take the offensive by developing a new strategy to discourage competition.*

offer

have (got) sth to 'offer
have sth available that sb wants: *Barcelona has a lot to offer its visitors in the way of entertainment.* ◇ *He's a young man with a great deal to offer* (= who is intelligent, has many skills, etc.).

on 'offer
1 that can be bought, used, etc: *The following is a list of courses currently on offer.* ◇ *Prizes worth more than £20 000 are on offer to the winner.*

2 (*especially BrE*) on sale at a lower price than normal for a short period of time: *Italian wines are on* (*special*) *offer this week.*

under 'offer (*BrE*)
if a house or other building is **under offer**, sb has agreed to buy it at a particular price: *They've already sold two of their properties, and the third is currently under offer.*

hold out/offer an olive branch (to sb) → **olive**

offering

a peace offering → **peace**

offices

through sb's good 'offices (*formal*)
with sb's help: *He eventually managed to find employment, through the good offices of a former colleague.*

offing

in the 'offing (*informal*)
likely or about to happen soon: *There's a pay rise in the offing, I hear.*

> **ℹ ORIGIN**
> The *offing* is the furthest part of the sea that you can see from land. Ships that are *in the offing* will soon arrive at the land.

often

,every so 'often
occasionally: *She pays someone to do the gardening every so often.*

(as) ,often as 'not; more ,often than 'not
frequently; usually: *As often as not I watch TV after dinner.*

oil

be no 'oil painting (*BrE, humorous*)
used to say that a person is not attractive to look at: *He's no oil painting but he's a marvellous actor.*

oil the 'wheels (*BrE*) (*AmE* grease the 'wheels)
help sth to happen easily and without problems, especially in business or politics: *He doesn't worry about bureaucratic procedures because he knows just where to oil the wheels.*

burn the midnight oil → **burn**
pour oil on troubled waters → **pour**

ointment

a/the fly in the ointment → **fly**

OK (also okay)

be doing OK/okay (*informal*)
be successful; be making a lot of money: *'How's business?' 'We're doing OK, thanks.'* ◇ *They're doing more than okay with those new restaurants. They're making a fortune.*

give sb/get the OK/okay (*informal*)
give sb/receive approval or permission: *We're waiting for the Ministry to give us the OK, and then we can go ahead with production.* ◇ *They can't start until they've got the OK.*

Old

the Old 'Bill (*BrE, informal*)
the police: *Put it down or I'll call the Old Bill!*

old

'any old how (*spoken*)
in a careless or untidy way: *You can't just dress any old how for such an important occasion.*

'any old thing, time, place, etc. (*spoken*)
it does not matter which thing, when, where, etc: *Come on, let's go out now—you can do the housework any old time.* ◇ *We can't have any old person looking after the kids—it has to be someone reliable.*

for old 'times' sake
because of pleasant memories of things you did together in the past: *I saw John Smith today. I hadn't seen him for years. We had a drink together for old times' sake.* ◇ *I lent him the money for old times' sake.*

the 'good/'bad old days
an earlier period of time in your life or in history that is seen as better/worse than the present: *That was in the bad old days of very high inflation.*

it's the (same) old 'story
something unpleasant or bad which happens again and again: *He says we haven't got enough money to go on holiday. It's the same old story every year.*

of 'old (*formal* or *literary*)
in or since past times: *in days of old* ◇ *We know him of old* (= we have known him for a long time).

of the 'old school
following old methods, standards, etc: *He's one of the old school, a teacher who believes in discipline and politeness.*

(as) old as the 'hills
very old; ancient: *That joke's as old as the hills!*

an old 'bag (*disapproving, offensive*)
an annoying and unpleasant woman: *Some old bag came in here complaining that we'd charged her too much.*

an ,old 'bat (*BrE, informal, disapproving*)
a silly or annoying old person: *She never hears what I'm saying to her—the silly old bat.*

old 'boy, 'chap, 'man, etc. (*old-fashioned, BrE, informal*)
used by older men of the middle and upper classes as a friendly way of addressing another man: *Terribly sorry, old chap!*

old 'boy/'girl (*informal*)
1 an older man/woman: *There's a nice old boy living next door.*
2 a former pupil of a school: *He's one of our most famous old boys.* ◇ *We have an old girls' reunion every five years.*

the ,old 'boy network (*BrE, informal*)
the practice of men who went to the same school using their influence to help each other at work or socially

an/that old 'chestnut (*informal*)
a joke or story that has often been repeated and as a result is no longer amusing: *'He told us all about the police arresting him for climbing into his own house.' 'Oh, no, not that old chestnut again.'*

an old 'dear (*informal*)
an old woman: *And then this old dear came in looking very ill, so I asked the doctor to see her before the other patients.*

an old 'flame (*informal*)
a person you were once in love with; a former boyfriend or girlfriend: *My mother has an old flame who sends her a bottle of perfume once a year.*

an old 'fogey/'fogy (*usually disapproving*)
(usually of an older person) a person with very old-fashioned or traditional views, opinions, etc: *I'm not such an old fogey that I can't remember what it was like to be a student.*

> ❷ **NOTE**
> A young person with old-fashioned views, style of dress, etc. is sometimes called a 'young fogey': *He's one of the young fogies who write for the 'Spectator'.*

the old 'guard
the original or older members of a group or an organization, who are often against change but whose ideas and ways of working are being replaced: *The old guard in European politics is being challenged by fresh new ideas.*

an old 'hand at (doing) sth
a person who is very experienced at (doing) sth: *Pete's an old hand at negotiating our contracts—he's been at the firm nearly twenty years, so he knows all the procedures.*

,old 'hat
something that is old-fashioned and no longer interesting: *This is supposed to be a new method of learning English, but frankly, it's a bit old hat.*

(have) an old head on young 'shoulders
used to describe a young person who acts in a more sensible way than you would expect for a person of their age: *He's only seventeen, but he has an old head on young shoulders and remains calm under pressure.*

an old 'maid (*old-fashioned, disapproving*)
a woman who has never married and is now no longer young

old 'man (*informal*)
a person's husband or father: *I go to see my old man every month. He's 77 now, you know.* ◇ *Ask your old man if he can mend it.*

the ,old school 'tie (*BrE*)
an informal system in which upper class men educated at the same private school help each other with jobs, contracts, etc. in their adult lives: *People say that the bank is run on the old school tie system.*

an old 'wives' tale (*disapproving*)
an old idea or belief that has proved not to be scientific: *When you're expecting a baby, people tell you all sorts of old wives' tales.* ◇ *The belief that make-up ruins your skin is just an old wives' tale.*

old 'woman (*informal, especially BrE*)
1 a person's wife or mother: *Give your old woman a surprise and take her out for a nice meal.*
2 (*disapproving*) a man who worries about things that are not important: *My boss is a real old woman. He gets so annoyed if I make even the smallest mistake.*

at/to a ripe old age → **ripe**
a chip off the old block → **chip**
a dirty old man → **dirty**
a/the grand old age → **grand**
a/the grand old man (of sth) → **grand**
have a high old time → **high**
money for old rope → **money**
(there's) no fool like an old fool → **fool**
poor old sb/sth → **poor**
reopen old wounds → **reopen**
ring out the old (year) and ring in the new → **ring**
settle an old score → **settle**
(you can't) teach an old dog new tricks → **teach**
there's life in the old dog yet → **life**
(as) tough as old boots → **tough**

olive

hold out/offer an 'olive branch (to sb)
show that you want to make peace with sb: *After their argument, he was the first one to hold out an olive branch.*

❶ ORIGIN
The olive branch is an ancient symbol of peace.

omelette (*AmE* also **omelet**)

you can't make an ,omelette without breaking 'eggs (*saying*)
you cannot make an important change in sth without causing problems for sb: *I know that all these changes in the car industry are painful to many people, but you can't make an omelette without breaking eggs.*

omnibus

the man (and/or woman) on the Clapham omnibus → **man**

on

be 'on about sth (*informal*)
talk about sth; mean sth: *I didn't know what he was on about. It didn't make sense.*

be/go/keep 'on about sth (*informal, disapproving*)
keep talking about the same thing so that people become bored or annoyed: *What's she on about now?* ◇ *Don't keep on about your terrible holiday. It's so boring.*

be/go/keep 'on at sb (to do sth) (*informal, disapproving*)
keep criticizing sb or telling them what to do, etc: *He keeps on at her all the time about her smoking.*

(just) not 'on (*informal*)
not a good or an acceptable way to behave: *He told her that using his bike without asking just wasn't on.* ◇ *It's not on—you should know better.*

,on and 'on
without stopping; continuously: *The road seemed to go on and on.* ◇ *The band played on and on, repeating the same tunes.*

you're 'on! (*informal*)
1 used for showing that you agree to sb's good, interesting, etc. suggestion: *'You pay for the wine and I'll pay for the food.' 'You're on!'*
2 used for accepting a bet from sb: *'I bet you £5 that New Zealand beat Australia.' 'You're on!'*

once

,all at 'once
suddenly: *All at once it began to rain.*

at 'once
1 immediately: *I'm afraid there's a problem. I must ask you to leave the building at once.*
2 at the same time: *Don't all speak at once!* ◇ *I'm not superwoman, you know. I can't do a hundred things at once.*

(just) for 'once; just this 'once (*spoken*)
on this occasion (which is in contrast to what happens usually): *For once he was early.* ◇ *Try and get here on time for once, will you?* ◇ *Can't you two be nice to each other just this once?*

once a'gain/once 'more
one more time; another time: *Once again the train was late.* ◇ *Let me hear it just once more.*

once a … , always a …
in certain respects people do not change, although circumstances change: *He can't resist explaining things in detail. Once a teacher, always a teacher.*

,once and for 'all
finally and definitely: *I've decided once and for all that this city is not the place for me.*

,once 'bitten, ,twice 'shy (*saying*)
if something has gone wrong once, you are very careful not to let sth similar happen again: *'Will she marry again, do you think?' 'I doubt it—once bitten, twice shy.'*

,once in a blue 'moon (*informal*)
very rarely: *Sue's daughter only visits her once in a blue moon.*

> **ⓘ ORIGIN**
> Very occasionally two full moons occur in the same month. The second one is sometimes referred to as a *blue moon*.

(every) ,once in a 'while
occasionally: *We go to the theatre once in a while, but there's not much worth seeing.*

,once or 'twice
a few times: *I don't know her well, I've only met her once or twice.*

,once too 'often
used to say that sb has done sth wrong or stupid again, and this time they will suffer because of it: *You've tried that trick once too often.*

,once upon a 'time
used, especially at the beginning of children's stories, to mean 'a long time in the past': *Once upon a time in a faraway land there lived a princess in a big castle.*

you're only young once → **young**

once-over

give sb/sth a/the 'once-over (*informal*)
1 look at sb/sth quickly to see what they are/it is like: *The landlord gave the house the once-over to check if anything was broken or missing.*
2 clean sth quickly: *She gave the room a quick once-over before the guests arrived.*

one

Most idioms containing **one** are at the entries for the nouns and verbs in the idioms, for example **one for the road** is at **road**.

you, etc. are a 'one! (*old-fashioned, especially BrE*)
used for showing that you find sb's behaviour surprising or amusing: *'She's just about to marry for the fifth time.' 'Ooh, she is a one, isn't she?'*

as 'one (also **as one 'man**) (*formal*)
in agreement; all together: *We spoke as one on this matter.* ◇ *As Keith approached the finishing line, the crowd rose to their feet as one man, cheering him on.*

(be) at 'one (with sb/sth) (*formal*)
feel that you completely agree with sb/sth, or that you are part of sth: *Both political parties are at one on the question of foreign imports.* ◇ *This is the kind of place where you can feel at one with nature.*

be (a) one for (doing) sth (*informal*)
be a person who enjoys sth, or does sth often or well: *They live in the country and they're great ones for long walks.* ◇ *She's not one for staying up late— she likes to be in bed by eleven.* ◇ *I've never been a great one for fish and chips.*

be/get/have one 'up on sb (*informal*)
be in a better position than sb; have an advantage over sb: *Why do you always have to be one up on everybody else?* ▶ **one-'upmanship** *noun* (*disapproving*) the skill of getting an advantage over other people

No matter what Sam did, her sister always managed to get one up on her.

I, you, etc. for 'one
used to emphasize that a particular person does sth and that you believe other people do too: *'Who is definitely coming to the meeting?' 'Well, Mr Davies is, for one, and I'm almost sure Jill is too.'*

get/put one 'over on sb/sth (*informal*)
get an advantage over sb/sth: *I'm not going to let them get one over on me!* ◇ *Don't believe a word he says. He's just trying to put one over on you.*

(you've, he's, etc.) got it in 'one (*informal*)
used when sb understands or gets the right answer immediately: *'I don't think this job really suits me.' 'So you're thinking of leaving.' 'Yes, Dick, you've got it in one.'*

have had ,one too 'many (*informal*)
have drunk too much alcohol: *I think David's had one too many. He can hardly stand up.*

in 'one
used to say that sb/sth has different roles, contains different things or is used for different purposes: *She's a mother and company director in one.* ◇ *It's a public relations office, a press office and a private office all in one.*

it's a hundred, etc. to one that sb/sth will (not) do sth
it is almost certain that sb/sth will (not) do sth: *It's a hundred to one that the train will be late.* ◇ *It's a million to one that she'll finish before us. She always does.*

,one after a'nother/the 'other
first one person or thing, and then another, and then another, up to any number or amount: *The bills kept coming in, one after another.*

,**one and** '**all** (*old-fashioned*, *informal*)
everyone in a particular group: *Happy New Year to one and all!*

the ,one and '**only**
used to emphasize that sb is famous or that sth is the only one of its kind: *That was the one and only James Brown, with 'Try me'.* ◇ *My trip to France is the one and only time I've been out of the country.*

,**one and the** '**same**
used for emphasis to mean 'the same': *In some countries, the police and the army are one and the same thing.*

,**one by** '**one**
one after another: *She read all of Agatha Christie's novels one by one.* ◇ *One by one the guests left.*

when you've seen, heard, etc. '**one, you've seen, heard, etc. them** '**all** (*saying*)
used to say that all types of the things mentioned are very similar: *I don't like science fiction novels much. When you've read one, you've read them all.*

one-horse

a one-horse '**race**
a competition, etc. in which there is only one team or candidate with a chance of winning: *It seems that the presidential elections are going to be a one-horse race this time.*

a one-horse '**town** (*informal*)
a small, boring town where nothing happens: *The President likes to remind people that he grew up in a small one-horse town in the Midwest.*

one-night

a ,one-night '**stand**
1 (*informal*) a sexual relationship that lasts for a single night; a person that sb has this relationship with: *I wanted it to be more than a one-night stand.* ◇ *For him I was just a one-night stand.*
2 one performance, concert, etc. in a town, given by an orchestra, theatre company, etc. which is travelling round from town to town: *He left the band because he got tired of one-night stands. It's not much fun moving from place to place all the time.*

one-off

a ,one-'**off** (*BrE*)
1 a thing that is made or that happens only once and not regularly: *This plate is a one-off produced by Minton in 1898.* ◇ *'Are they going to do another concert in the church this year?' 'I don't think so. It was just a one-off.'*
2 (*informal*, *humorous*) a person who is quite unlike other people: *There'll never be another Charlie Chaplin. He was a one-off.*

one-track

have (got) a ,one-track '**mind**
think only about one subject: *James will always*
bring sex into a conversation if he can. He's got a one-track mind.

onions

know your onions → **know**

only

not only ... but (also) ...
both ... and ...: *He not only read the book, but also remembered what he had read.*

'**only if**
used to state the only situation in which sth can happen: *Only if a teacher has given permission is a student allowed to leave the room.* ◇ *Only if the red light comes on is there any danger to employees.*

only '**just**
1 not long ago/before: *We've only just arrived.*
2 almost not: *He only just caught the train.* ◇ *I can afford it, but only just.*

only to do sth (*written*)
used to show that sth happened immediately after sth else, especially when this is disappointing, surprising, etc: *I arrived at the museum only to find that it was closed for the day.* ◇ *She tried to be friendly to him, only to be shouted at again.*

only too '**glad,** '**ready, etc. (to do sth)**
very glad, ready, etc: *If you want any advice, I'd be only too willing to give it.* ◇ *She was only too pleased to help.*

onside

get/keep sb on'**side**
get/keep sb's support: *The government needs to keep the major national newspapers onside to help win votes in the election.*

onto

be '**onto sb**
1 (*informal*) know about what sb has done wrong: *She knew the police would be onto them.*
2 (also **get** '**onto sb**) be talking to sb, usually in order to ask or tell them sth: *They've been onto me for ages to get a job.* ◇ *I must get onto the local council about all the rubbish in the street.*

be '**onto sth**
know about sth or be in a situation that could lead to a good result for you: *Researchers believe that they are onto something big.* ◇ *She's onto a good thing with that new job.*

open

be '**open to sth**
be willing to consider sth: *We are open to any suggestions you care to make.*

have/keep an ,open '**mind (on/about sth)**
be willing to change your opinion (on/about sth): *I've still got an open mind on the question of nuclear defence.* ▶ ,**open-**'**minded** *adj.*: *You can*

talk to her about anything—she's very open-minded.

(out) in(to) the 'open
no longer/not hidden or secret: *The whole banking scandal came into the open after somebody found some confidential documents on a train.*

in the open 'air
outside; not indoors: *In summer I think it's nice to eat in the open air.* ▶ **,open-'air** *adj.*: *an open-air swimming pool*

on the open 'market
available to buy without any restrictions: *Firearms are not freely available on the open market.*

an ,open 'book
a person whose behaviour, attitudes, thoughts, etc. are very easy to understand, either because you know them very well or because they are very open and honest: *After living with her for 20 years, she's an open book to me.* ◇ *His life is an open book. He has no secrets.*

open the 'door to/for sb/sth
provide sb with the chance or opportunity to do sth new, interesting, etc: *Going to university opened the door to a whole new world for her.*

open your/sb's 'eyes (to sth)
realize or make sb realize the truth about sth: *The trip to China really opened the Minister's eyes.* ◇ *He opened my eyes to the beauty of poetry.* ▶ **an 'eye-opener** *noun: The film on police methods was a real eye-opener for me.*

open 'fire (on sb/sth)
start shooting (at sb/sth): *The officer gave the order to open fire on the enemy.*

open the 'floodgates (to sth)
1 remove the restrictions or controls which for a long time have prevented a lot of people from doing sth they want to do: *Political changes in eastern Europe opened the floodgates to thousands of people who wished to emigrate.*
2 do sth which allows sb to express feelings which have been kept under control for a long time: *The discussion sessions allow people to open the floodgates to their deepest fears.*

open your 'heart (to sb)
tell sb about your feelings, problems or worries: *She longed to be able to open her heart to someone who would understand.*

(keep) open 'house
be willing to receive guests in your home at any time, and give them food, drink, etc: *It was always open house at their place.*

an ,open invi'tation (to sb)
1 an invitation to sb to visit you at any time
2 if sth is **an open invitation** to criminals, etc., it encourages them to commit a crime by making it easier: *Leaving your camera on the seat in the car is an open invitation to thieves.*

an ,open 'letter
a letter containing a protest, piece of advice, etc. to a well-known person, which is published in a newspaper: *In an open letter to the Prime Minister, six well-known authors attacked the government's policy on the arts.*

open your (big) 'mouth (*informal*)
say sth when you should not: *Why do you always have to open your big mouth? Can't you just keep quiet sometimes?*

an ,open 'question (also **open to 'question**)
a matter that cannot be decided easily or that people hold several different views on: *Whether private schools give children a better education is open to question.* ◇ *It's an open question whether meat is bad for you.*

an ,open 'secret
a fact that is supposed to be a secret but that everyone knows: *It's an open secret that they're getting married.*

open 'sesame (*humorous*)
an easy way to gain or achieve sth that is usually very difficult to get: *Academic success is not always an open sesame to a well-paid job.* ◇ *The bank had just closed but I banged on the door and—open sesame—they let me in!*

> ❶ ORIGIN
> This expression comes from the story *Ali Baba and the Forty Thieves*. The words *open sesame* opened the door of the thieves' cave where they kept their treasure.

open the way for sb/sth (to do sth)
make it possible for sb to do sth or for sth to happen: *A group of diplomats was sent first, in order to open the way for a personal visit by the President himself.*

with ,open 'arms
if you welcome sb **with open arms,** you are extremely happy and pleased to see them: *Don't expect her to welcome you with open arms. She's still very angry with you.*

be wide open → **wide**
burst (sth) open → **burst**
the heavens open → **heavens**
keep your eyes open/peeled/skinned (for sb/sth) → **eyes**
keep/leave (all) your options open → **options**
keep a weather eye on sth/open for sth → **weather**
leave the door open (for/on sth) → **leave**
(lay/leave yourself) wide open (to sth) → **wide**
with your eyes open → **eyes**

open-and-shut

an ,open-and-shut 'case
(of a legal case, crime, etc.) so clear or simple that it can be dealt with or solved very easily and quickly: *It's an open-and-shut case. His fingerprints were on the gun and he can't prove where he was that night.*

openers

for 'openers (*informal, especially AmE*)
to begin with; for a start: *For openers, I don't think
his work is very original.*

operation

come into ope'ration
start working; start having an effect: *The new rules
come into operation from next week.*

in ope'ration
working, being used or having an effect: *The system needs to be in operation for six months before it
can be assessed.* ◇ *Temporary traffic controls are in
operation on New Road.*

put sth into ope'ration
make sth start working; start using sth: *It's time to
put our plan into operation.*

operative

the ,operative 'word
used to emphasize that a particular word or
phrase is the most important one in a sentence: *I
was in love with her—'was' being the operative
word.*

opinion

be of the o'pinion that ... (*formal*)
think or believe that ...: *I'm firmly of the opinion
that smoking should be banned in all public places.*

have (got) a good, bad, high, low, etc.
o'pinion of sb/sth
think that sb/sth is good, bad, etc: *The boss has a
very high opinion of her.*

be a matter of opinion → **matter**

your considered opinion → **considered**

contrary to popular belief/opinion → **contrary**

opportunity

a window of opportunity → **window**

opposed

as op'posed to (*written*)
used to make a contrast between two things: *200
people attended, as opposed to 300 the previous year.*
◇ *This exercise develops suppleness as opposed to*
(= rather than) *strength.*

opposite

your ,opposite 'number
a person who holds the same position as you in
another country, organization, company, etc: *The
American Secretary of State will meet his Russian
opposite number tomorrow.* ◇ *She's my opposite
number in IBM.*

the ,opposite 'sex
the other sex: *He found it difficult to talk to members of the opposite sex.*

opposites

,opposites at'tract
used to say that people who are very different are
often attracted to each other: *'Aren't you surprised
that Peter and Sally are together?' 'A little. But they
say opposites attract, don't they?'*

opposition

in oppo'sition to sb/sth
1 disagreeing strongly with sb/sth, especially
with the aim of preventing sth from happening:
*Protest marches were held in opposition to the pro-
posed law.*
2 contrasting two people or things that are very
different: *Leisure is usually defined in opposition to
work.*

option

the ,soft/,easy 'option (*often disapproving*)
an easier way of doing sth; an easier course of
action because it involves less effort, difficulty, etc:
*If you want to go for the soft option, you can get the
qualification in three years rather than two.* ◇ *He
decided to take the easy option and give them what
they wanted.*

options

keep/leave (all) your 'options open
avoid making a decision now so that you still have
a choice in the future: *Doing business with him is
sometimes quite stressful. He likes to keep all his
options open until the very last minute.*

order

in 'order
1 (of an official document) that can be used
because it is all correct and legal: *If the documents
are not in order, the house cannot be sold.*
2 (*formal*) as it should be: *Is everything in order
for you, sir?*
3 if sth is **in order**, it is a suitable thing to do or
say on a particular occasion: *I think a drink would
be in order.*

in/of the 'order of (*BrE*) (*AmE* on the 'order
of) (*formal*)
(of an amount) about; approximately: *They own a
business worth in the order of fifteen million
pounds.* ◇ *We employ in the order of 4 000 people in
this factory.*

in order that (*formal*)
so that sth can happen: *All those concerned must
work together in order that agreement can be
reached on this issue.*

in order to do sth
with the purpose or intention of doing or achieving sth: *She arrived early in order to get a good seat.*
◇ *In order to get a complete picture, further information is needed.*

of the highest/first 'order; of a high 'order
of the best, worst, most extreme, etc. type: *It was a scandal of the first order.*

on 'order
requested from a shop, factory, etc. but not yet received: *We've got 1000 copies of the book on order. They should be here later this week.*

the ,order of the 'day
what is normally done, etc. or should be done in a particular situation; the usual attitudes, beliefs, etc. of a particular group of people: *Dinner jackets and evening dresses are the order of the day at these parties.*

,out of 'order
1 (of a machine, etc.) broken or not working properly: *The phone is out of order again.* ◇ *There was a notice on the toilet door saying 'out of order'.*
2 (*BrE*) (*AmE* ,out of 'line) (*informal*) (of behaviour, remarks, etc.) not acceptable in a particular situation: *Your remarks were completely out of order at a meeting like that.*

in running order = in (full/good) working order → **working**
in short order → **short**
law and order → **law**
a/the pecking order → **pecking**
put/set your (own) house in order → **house**
a tall order → **tall**

ordered
just what the doctor ordered → **doctor**

orders
be in/take (holy) 'orders
be/become a priest: *He wanted to take holy orders, but his father had other plans for him.*

be under 'orders (to do sth)
have been ordered or commanded (to do sth): *Prisoners of war were under orders to reveal only their name, rank and number.*

get your marching orders → **marching**
give sb their marching orders → **marching**
under starters orders → **starters**

ordinary
in the ordinary 'way (*BrE*)
used to say what normally happens in a particular situation: *In the ordinary way, she's not a nervous person.*

out of the 'ordinary
unusual; strange: *His new book is certainly out of the ordinary. I've never read anything like it before.*

other
Most idioms containing **other** are at the entries for the nouns and verbs in the idioms, for example **in other words** is at **words**.

every other (person/thing)
every second (person/thing): *We go abroad for our holidays every other year.* ◇ *I buy milk every other day.*

the ,other 'day, 'morning, etc.
only a few days ago: *The other evening we went for a drive in the country.* ◇ *I saw Jake the other day while I was out shopping.*

other than
1 except: *I don't know any French people other than you.* ◇ *We're going away in June but other than that I'll be here all summer.*
2 (*written*) different or differently from; not: *I have never known him to behave any other than selfishly.*

'somebody/'something/'somewhere or other
used when you do not think it is necessary to be more exact about sb/sth, or to show that the person/thing/place mentioned does not have much importance or value in your opinion: *'What did you have for pudding?' 'Oh, something or other covered with cream.'* ◇ *'Where's your pen?' 'Oh, I lent it to someone or other at work and he forgot to give it back.'*

otherwise
or 'otherwise
used to refer to sth that is different from or the opposite of what has just been mentioned: *It was necessary to discover the truth or otherwise of these statements.* ◇ *We insure against all damage, accidental or otherwise.*

know different/otherwise → **know**

ounce
an ounce of prevention is better than a pound of cure = prevention is better than cure → **prevention**

out
be (all) out to do sth; be (all) out for sth
want or plan to do or get sth: *I think he's out to kill me.* ◇ *I'm not interested in a few thousand pounds. I'm out for a million!*

,out and a'bout (*BrE*)
able to go outside again after an illness: *I saw Mrs Neve in town this morning. I was pleased to see her out and about again.*

'out of it (*informal*)
not aware of what is happening, usually because of drinking too much alcohol, or taking drugs: *He looks completely out of it.*

'out with it!
used to make sb tell you sth they are hiding, or hesitating to tell you: *Come on, out with it! I want to know the truth!*

outs
the ins and outs (of sth) → **ins**

outset

at/from the 'outset (of sth)
at/from the beginning of sth: *I made it clear right from the outset that I disapproved.*

outside

at the 'outside
(of an amount, number, etc.) at the most; as a maximum: *I doubt if this factory makes more than 500 cars a year at the very outside.*

on the 'outside
1 used to describe how sb appears or seems: *On the outside she seems calm, but I know she's quite worried.*
2 not in prison: *Life on the outside took some getting used to again.*

the outside 'world; the world out'side
the rest of the world; somewhere where you are in contact with or have the normal way of life of most people: *After 15 years in a monastery, he got a job in the outside world. It was quite a shock for him.*

beyond/outside your ken → **ken**

outstay

outstay/overstay your welcome → **welcome**

oven

have (got) a bun in the oven → **bun**

over

(all) over a'gain
once more; for a second time: *I'm not sure if I could stand seeing the film over again.* ◇ *He told me the work was so bad that I would have to do it all over again.*

,over and a'bove
in addition to sth: *Higher safety standards are needed over and above the ones already in place.* ◇ *He gets a big annual bonus over and above his basic salary.*

,over and 'over (a'gain)
many times; repeatedly: *Her doctor warned her over and over about the dangers of smoking.*

overboard

go 'overboard (about/for sb/sth) (*informal*)
be too excited or enthusiastic about sth or about doing sth: *I told her just to cook a simple meal but she went completely overboard.* ◇ *He doesn't just like her. He's gone completely overboard about her.*

throw sth overboard → **throw**

overdo

over'do it/things
do too much: *He rather overdid it last Saturday playing football, and now he's aching all over.* ◇ *I've been overdoing things a bit recently. I really need a holiday.*

overdrive

go, etc. into 'overdrive
begin to work much harder, increase production, etc: *Production at the factory has shifted into overdrive in an attempt to meet the new orders on time.*

over-egg

,over-egg the 'pudding
used to say that you think sb has done more than is necessary, or has added unnecessary details to make sth seem better or worse than it really is: *If you're telling lies, keep it simple—never over-egg the pudding.*

overplay

overplay your 'hand
spoil your chance of success by judging your position to be stronger than it really is: *Some say that the actors overplayed their hand, asking for too much money for each appearance.*

overshoot

overshoot the 'mark
make a mistake when you are judging the amount, etc. of sth: *He overshot the mark by about £3 million.*

overstay

outstay/overstay your welcome → **welcome**

overstep

overstep the 'mark/'line
go beyond the limit of what is polite or acceptable: *I don't mind him being friendly, but when he tried to kiss me he was really overstepping the mark.*

overtime

be working overtime → **working**

overtures

make 'overtures (to sb)
try to make friends, start a business relationship, have discussions, etc. with sb: *On my first day at work everyone made friendly overtures.* ◇ *If we want to stay in business I think we ought to start making overtures to the bank manager!*

owes

(think) the world owes you a living → **world**

owl

a night owl → **night**

own

Most idioms containing **own** are at the entries for the nouns and verbs in the idioms, for example **off your own bat** is at **bat**.

come ,into your/its 'own
have the opportunity to show how good or useful you are or sth is: *When the traffic's as bad as this, a*

bicycle really comes into its own. ◇ *It was only when she became Health Secretary that she came into her own.*

get your 'own back (on sb) (*informal*)
do sth to sb in return for harm they have done to you; get revenge: *I got my own back by writing a very rude article about him in the newspaper.*

(all) on your 'own
1 alone; without anyone else: *Why are you sitting here on your own?*
2 without help: *She made it all on her own.*

oyster

the world is your oyster → **world**

Pp

pace

do sth at your own 'pace
do sth at the speed you prefer: *When you are learning a language at home, you can work at your own pace.*

keep 'pace (with sb/sth)
1 move, progress or develop at the same speed or rate as sb/sth: *In this business we have to keep pace with our foreign competitors.* ◇ *He isn't really keeping pace with the other children in his class.*
2 keep informed about sth which is changing very fast: *I find it difficult to keep pace with all the political changes that are taking place.*

at a snail's pace → snail
force the pace → force
set the pace → set
(not) stand the pace → stand

paces

go through your 'paces; show your 'paces
perform a particular activity in order to show other people what you are capable of doing: *We watched the trainee waiters going through their paces.*

put sb/sth through his, their, its, etc. 'paces
test sb's/sth's ability to do sth by making them/it show how well they/it can actually perform certain actions, tasks, etc: *We watched the trainer putting the police dog through its paces.* ◇ *They're putting the new machinery through its paces.*

❶ ORIGIN
These expressions refer to judging the performance of a horse before deciding to buy it.

pack

ˌpack your 'bags (*informal*)
prepare to leave a place permanently, especially after a disagreement: *He hadn't paid any rent for three months so she told him to pack his bags.*

ˌpack it 'in (*informal, especially BrE*)
stop doing sth: *Your guitar playing is getting on my nerves. Pack it in, will you?* ◇ *I didn't like my last job so I packed it in.*

a ˌpack of 'lies (*informal*)
a lot of lies told at the same time: *The police discovered that her story was a pack of lies.* ◇ *He told me a pack of lies when I asked him about previous jobs.*

ˌpack a (hard, etc.) 'punch (*informal*)
1 be able to hit very hard: *He's a boxer who packs a nasty punch!*

2 have a powerful effect on sb: *Don't drink too much of his home-made beer—it packs quite a punch!* ◇ *Their latest advertising campaign packs a hard punch.*

pack them in; pack the house
attract a large audience; fill a theatre, hall, etc: *This group's been playing for twenty years but they're still packing them in.* ◇ *The city orchestra always plays to a packed house.*

the joker in the pack → joker

packed

packed (together) like sar'dines (*informal*)
(of people) pressed tightly together in a way that is uncomfortable or unpleasant: *On the tube in the rush hour the passengers are packed like sardines.*

❷ NOTE
Sardines are a type of fish that are sold packed tightly together in small tins.

packet

make, lose, spend, etc. a 'packet (*informal*)
make, etc. a large amount of money: *He went to the USA and made a packet in office property.* ◇ *We spent a packet on our weekend away—everything was so expensive.*

packing

send sb packing → send

page

the printed word/page → printed

paid

put 'paid to sth (*informal*)
make it impossible for sth to happen or continue: *Her poor exam results have put paid to any chance she had of getting into medical school.*

paid-up

a (fully) ˌpaid-up 'member, etc.
1 a person who has paid the money necessary to become a member of a group, etc: *The society has got over 10 000 paid-up members.*
2 (*informal*) a strong and enthusiastic supporter of a group, etc: *He is a fully paid-up supporter of the Green Party.*

pain

on/under pain of sth (*formal*)
with the threat of having sth done to you as a punishment if you do not obey a command: *They were forbidden on pain of death to talk to any of the*

other prisoners. ◇ *We were told to pay within three days, on pain of a £1 000 fine if we didn't.*

a pain in the 'neck (*BrE* also **a pain in the 'arse**⚠/**'bum**/**'backside**) (*AmE* also **a pain in the 'ass**⚠/**'butt**) (*informal*)

a person or thing that you find annoying: *Her new boyfriend is a real pain in the neck—he never stops talking.*

pains

be at (great) pains to do sth

put a lot of effort into doing sth correctly: *The manager was at great pains to point out that no one would lose their job after reorganization.* ◇ *She was at pains to make us feel welcome in her home.*

for your 'pains (*especially BrE, often ironic*)

as payment, reward or thanks for sth you have done: *I helped them in the shop for a week, and all I got for my pains was a box of chocolates.*

take (great) 'pains with sth/to do sth; go to great 'pains to do sth

make a great effort to do sth well, carefully, properly, etc: *It looks easy but in fact he went to great pains to achieve that particular effect in his paintings.* ◇ *She takes great pains with the flower arrangements.*

growing pains → **growing**

spare no expense/pains/trouble (to do sth/(in) doing sth) → **spare**

paint

paint a terrible, depressing, rosy, etc. 'picture (of sb/sth)

describe sth in a particular way; give a particular impression of sb/sth, often a negative one: *You paint a depressing picture of your childhood!* ◇ *People who don't like students paint the worst possible picture of their behaviour.* ◇ *The book paints a vivid picture of life in the city.*

paint the town 'red (*informal*)

go to a lot of different bars, clubs, etc. and enjoy yourself: *It was the end of term and students decided to go out and paint the town red.*

paint sth with a ˌbroad 'brush

describe sth in a general way, ignoring the details: *His description of national politics is painted with a very broad brush, although some areas are described in a little more detail than others.*

a lick of paint → **lick**

painted

he, it, etc. is not as black as he, it, etc. is painted → **black**

painting

be like painting the Forth 'Bridge (*BrE*)

if a job is **like painting the Forth Bridge**, it is so big that by the time you get to the end you have to start at the beginning again: *Cleaning a house this size is a bit like painting the Forth Bridge. As soon as I've finished it's time to start again!*

❶ ORIGIN

The *Forth Bridge* is a very big bridge over the river Forth in Edinburgh.

be no oil painting → **oil**

pair

I've only got one pair of 'hands (*spoken*)

used to say that you are too busy to do anything else: *Give me a chance! I've only got one pair of hands you know!*

a pair of 'hands (*informal*)

a person who can do, or is doing, a job: *We need an extra pair of hands if we're going to finish on time.* ◇ *Colleagues regarded him as a **safe pair of hands** (= sb who can be relied on to do a job well).*

show (sb) a clean pair of heels → **show**

pairs

in 'pairs

in groups of two objects or people: *Students worked in pairs on the project.*

pajamas (*AmE*) = pyjamas

pale

beˌyond the 'pale

considered socially unacceptable: *Her behaviour towards her employees is completely beyond the pale. She treats them like servants.*

❶ ORIGIN

In the fourteenth century, the part of Ireland that was under English rule was called the *pale*. The area outside this was *beyond the pale*.

'pale beside/next to sth; 'pale in/by comparison (with/to sth); 'pale into insignificance

seem less important when compared with sth else: *Last year's riots pale in comparison with this latest outburst of violence.*

palm

have (got) sb in the ˌpalm of your 'hand

have sb completely under your control or influence: *Her boyfriend will do anything for her; she's got him in the palm of her hand.*

grease sb's palm → **grease**

pan

go down the 'pan (*BrE, slang*)

be wasted or spoiled: *That's another brilliant idea down the pan.*

a flash in the pan → **flash**

out of the frying pan (and) into the fire → **frying**

pancake

(as) flat as a pancake → flat

Pandora

Pandora's 'box

a source of great trouble and suffering, although this may not be obvious at the beginning: *The publication of the diaries opened up a real Pandora's box.*

❶ ORIGIN
In Greek mythology, Pandora was the first woman on earth. Zeus gave her a box that she was forbidden to open, and when she opened it, all the evils flew out of it into the world.

panic

'panic stations (*BrE, informal*)

a situation in which people feel anxious and there is a lot of confused activity, especially because there is a lot to do in a short period of time: *At the moment it's panic stations in the office because we're preparing for the president's visit next week.*

press/push the 'panic button (*BrE*)

react in a sudden or extreme way to sth unexpected that has frightened you: *Although the team lost yet another match on Saturday, their manager is refusing to press the panic button.*

pant

puff and pant/blow → puff

pants

scare, bore, etc. the 'pants off sb (*informal*)

scare, bore, etc. sb very much: *He would creep up behind people and scare the pants off them.* ◇ *He was clearly boring the pants off his audience.*

(fly) by the seat of your pants → seat
catch sb with their pants down → catch
have (got) ants in your pants → ants
a kick in the pants → kick
wear the pants → wear
wet your pants/knickers → wet

paper

on 'paper

considering sth from what is written down about it, rather than what is actually true in practice; in theory: *This idea looks very good on paper, but I'm not sure that it's very practical.*

,paper over the 'cracks

try to hide a problem or disagreement in a way that is temporary and not likely to be successful: *These new prison reforms are just papering over the cracks. What we need is a fundamental change in the prison system.*

❶ ORIGIN
This expression refers to putting wallpaper on a wall in order to hide the cracks in the plaster.

a ,paper 'tiger

a person or thing that is less strong, powerful, dangerous, etc. than they/it appears: *He claimed that the enemies of his party were paper tigers and not to be feared.*

he, she, etc. couldn't punch his, her, etc. way out of a paper bag → punch
not worth the paper it's printed/written on → worth
put pen to paper → pen

papers

get your walking papers → walking
give sb their walking papers → walking

par

be below/under 'par

less well, good, etc. than is usual or expected: *I've been feeling rather below par recently—I think it's time I took a holiday.* ◇ *His performance at the concert was well under par.*

be on a 'par with sb/sth

be equal to sb/sth; be at the same level as sb/sth (in importance, rank, value, etc.): *He doesn't think his salary is on a par with his position in the company.* ◇ *As actors, I would say they were on a par.*

be (about) ,par for the 'course (*disapproving*)

be normal; be what you would expect to happen: *'The food on this plane is terrible.' 'Well, that's about par for the course.'*

be up to/above 'par

of an acceptable standard, quality, etc.; better than the usual standard, quality, etc: *You don't need to worry. Your work is well above par.* ◇ *His driving wasn't quite up to par and he lost the race.*

par excellence (*from French*)

(only used after the noun it describes) better than all the others of the same kind; a very good example of sth: *She turned out to be an organizer par excellence.*

parade

rain on sb's parade → rain

paradise

a fool's paradise → fool

paragon

a paragon of 'virtue

a person who is without faults; a completely perfect person: *Unfortunately we can't expect all policemen to be paragons of virtue.*

parallel

in 'parallel (with sb/sth)

with and at the same time as sb/sth else: *The new degree and the existing certificate courses would run in parallel.* ◇ *Ann wanted to pursue her own career in parallel with her husband's.*

parcel

be part and parcel of sth → part

pardon

,pardon 'me (*spoken*)

1 (*especially AmE*) used to ask sb to repeat sth because you did not hear it or do not understand it: *'You look miles away.' 'Pardon me?'*

2 used by some people to say 'sorry' when they have accidentally made a rude noise or done sth wrong

,pardon ,me for 'doing sth (*informal*)

used to show that you are upset or offended by the way that sb has spoken to you: *'This is a meeting for women only, so get out and mind your own business.' 'Oh, pardon me for existing!'* ◇ *'Oh, just shut up.' 'Well, pardon me for breathing!'*

excuse/pardon my French → French

I beg your pardon → beg

parentis

in loco parentis → loco

parker

a nosy parker → nosy

Parkinson

'Parkinson's law (*humorous*)

the idea that work will always take as long as the time you have to do it: *I don't know why this essay is taking me so long. Parkinson's law, I suppose.*

❶ ORIGIN
This is the title of a book by C. Northcote Parkinson about inefficient administration.

parrot-fashion

(learn, repeat, etc. sth) 'parrot-fashion (*BrE, disapproving*)

(learn, repeat, etc. sth) without understanding the meaning: *When we were at school we used to learn history parrot-fashion; all I can remember now is the dates.*

❶ ORIGIN
This idiom refers to the fact that parrots can learn certain phrases and repeat them after you.

(as) sick as a parrot → sick

part

be part and ,parcel of 'sth

be an essential part of sth: *Long hours spent planning lessons are part and parcel of a teacher's job.*

the better/best part of sth

most of sth: *I worked at the camp for the better part of the summer.* ◇ *He had lived there for the best part of fifty years.*

for the 'most part

mainly; on the whole; generally: *I agree with you for the most part but there are a few details I'd like to discuss further.*

for 'my, 'his, etc. (own) part

as far as I am, he is, etc. concerned: *For my part I don't care whether they win or not.*

have/play/take/want no 'part in/of sth

not be involved or refuse to be involved in sth, especially because you disapprove of it: *He had no part in the decision.* ◇ *I want no part of this sordid business.*

have (got) a part to 'play (in sth)

be able to help sb: *We all have a part to play in the fight against crime.*

in 'part

partly; to some extent: *Her success was due in part to luck.*

look/dress the 'part

have an appearance or wear clothes that are suitable for a particular job, position, etc: *I think Tim Evans should play Robin Hood. He really looks the part.* ◇ *He's a funny kind of bank manager; he doesn't dress the part at all.*

on 'sb's part; on the part of 'sb

(of an action) done, made or performed by sb: *The argument started because of an angry remark on his part.* ◇ *If you want to go camping, son, there'd be no objection on our part.*

part 'company (with/from sb/sth)

1 leave sb; separate and go in different directions: *We walked down into town together and then parted company at the station.* ◇ *They've finally parted company after a long, unhappy marriage.*

2 disagree with sb: *I'm afraid I have to part company with you on the question of nuclear energy.*

3 (*humorous*) come apart; separate: *In the high winds the sail and the boat parted company.*

part of the 'furniture (*informal*)

sb who has worked or been in a particular place for such a long time that people hardly notice them: *The librarian had been there so long he seemed like part of the furniture.*

take sth in good 'part (*BrE*)

accept sth slightly unpleasant without complaining or being offended: *They played a trick on her by putting a plastic spider in her bed, but she took it in good part.* ◇ *He took my criticism in good part.*

take 'part (in sth)

be one of a group of people doing sth together; participate in sth: *He's taking part in a golf competition this weekend.* ◇ *She never takes part in any community activities.*

take sb's 'part (*BrE*)

defend or support what sb has said or done, especially in an argument: *Personally I take Emma's part on this matter.* ◇ *He never takes my part in an argument.*

discretion is the better part of valour → discretion

in no small part = in large part → **large**

play a/your part (in sth) → **play**

parted

a fool and his money are soon parted → **fool**

Parthian

a Parthian shot = a parting shot → **parting**

particular

in par'ticular

1 especially or particularly: *He loves reading, science fiction in particular.*

2 special or specific: *Peter was lying on the sofa doing nothing in particular* ◇ *Is there anything in particular you'd like for dinner?* ◇ *She directed the question at no one in particular.*

parting

a/the ˌparting of the 'ways

1 the place where two or more people who have been travelling together separate and take different routes: *We travelled to India together, and in Delhi it was the parting of the ways. Ray went on to China and I went on to Australia.*

2 the time when two or more people who have been working, living, etc. together separate and begin a new period in their lives: *After college it was the parting of the ways. We all went to live in different parts of the country and gradually we lost touch.*

a ˌparting 'shot (also a ˌParthian 'shot)

a remark or action, often an unkind one, that somebody makes just as they are leaving: *As Jim walked out of the door, his parting shot was, 'I never want to see any of you again.'*

> **ⓘ ORIGIN**
> Parthia was a kingdom in ancient times. The Parthians used to fire arrows at the enemy as they were retreating from battle.

parts

a ˌman/woman of (many) 'parts

a person who can do many different things well: *My grandfather was a man of many parts: a talented musician, a skilled gardener and not a bad painter.*

round/in these parts (*old-fashioned*)

in this area: *We don't see many tourists round these parts.* ◇ *What are the food specialities in these parts?*

be greater/more than the sum of its parts → **sum**

possession is nine points/tenths/parts of the law → **possession**

private parts → **private**

party

be (a) 'party to sth (*formal*)

take part in a (secret) plan, agreement, etc., and therefore be partly responsible for it: *'Were you a party to this, Anna?' 'No, Mrs Jones, I was away on holiday at the time.'* ◇ *How many people were party to the plan?*

the ˌparty 'line

the beliefs or policies of a political party: *Ministers in the government are expected to follow the party line.* ◇ *She has gone against the party line again.* ◇ *No one seems to know exactly what the party line is on this issue.*

your 'party piece (*BrE, informal*)

the same song, poem, trick, etc. that you often do in order to entertain people at parties: *His party piece is to stand on his head and drink a glass of water.*

the party's 'over

a period of freedom, enjoyment, very good luck, etc. has now come to an end and life is about to return to normal: *We've had a good time while the manager's been away, but now the party's over.*

the life and soul of the party → **life**

pas

(make/commit) a faux pas → **faux**

pass

ˌcome to 'pass (*old use*)

happen: *And so it came to pass that the old king died and his son was named king of all the land.*

(things) come to a (pretty) 'pass (*old-fashioned or humorous*)

reach a sad or difficult state: *Things have come to a pretty pass when children are begging in the streets.*

make a 'pass at sb (*informal*)

make a direct approach to sb you are interested in sexually: *He can't resist making a pass at every woman he meets.*

not pass your 'lips

1 if words do **not pass your lips**, you say nothing

2 if food or drink does **not pass your lips**, you eat or drink nothing: *He promised her that nothing would pass his lips before dinner.*

ˌpass the 'buck (*informal*)

refuse to accept responsibility for a mistake, accident, important decision, etc. and try to get another person, organization, etc. to accept responsibility for it instead: *The same thing happens after every disaster. All the officials and ministries involved just try to pass the buck.*

▶ **'buck-passing** *noun: The public is tired of all this political buck-passing. They just want to know who was responsible for the decision.*

> **ⓘ ORIGIN**
> The *buck* is a small object in a poker game that is placed in front of the player whose turn it is to deal.

pass the 'hat round/around; pass round the 'hat (*informal*)

collect money from a number of people, for example to buy a present for sb: *Anthony had his car radio stolen, so his friends passed the hat round and bought him a new one.*

pass 'judgement (on/about sb/sth) (*especially BrE*) (*AmE usually* **pass 'judgment (on/about sb/sth)**)

give your opinion about sb/sth, especially if this is critical: *Don't be too quick to pass judgement, you're not perfect yourself, you know.*

pass 'muster

be good enough; be acceptable: *I didn't think Charlie's parents would like me, but evidently I pass muster.*

pass the/your time (doing sth)

spend your time (doing sth), often while you are waiting for sth else: *They told each other jokes to pass the time while they waited for the next train.* ◇ *We passed our time making holiday plans.*

pass the time of 'day (with sb)

greet sb and have a short conversation with them about things that are not very important: *I don't know any of the neighbours very well, only just enough to pass the the time of day.*

pass 'water (*formal*)

pass urine (= waste liquid) out of your body; urinate: *The patient was having difficulty in passing water.*

be (like) ships that pass in the night → **ships**
let sth pass → **let**

passage

a bird of passage → **bird**

passing

in 'passing

done or said while you are giving your attention to sth else: *'What did the minister say about educational reform?' 'Not very much. He just mentioned it in passing.'* ◇ *Could I just say in passing that … ?*

past

be/look 'past it (*BrE, informal*)

1 (of a person) be too old to do sth as well as you used to in the past: *He might look past it, but I bet he can run faster than you.*
2 (of a thing) be no longer in good condition or functioning well because of its age: *Those shoes are a bit past it, aren't they? You need a new pair.*

be past your/its 'best

be no longer as strong, fresh, young, beautiful, etc. as before: *What do you mean, somebody over 35 is past their best? That's nonsense.*

be past its 'sell-by date (*informal*)

be no longer useful or valued: *His ideas on economics are well past their sell-by date, in my opinion.*

> ❷ **NOTE**
> The *sell-by date* is the date written on food packaging after which the food must not be sold.

I wouldn't put it 'past sb (to do sth)

used to say that you think sb is quite capable of doing sth surprising, unusual, etc: *'Do you think he'd ever steal from his friends?' 'I wouldn't put it past him.'*

a ˌpast 'master (in/of/at sth)

a person who is very good at doing sth: *He's a past master at making other people feel guilty.*

be beyond/past caring (about sth) → **caring**
the (dim and) distant past → **distant**
not see beyond/past the end of your nose → **see**
rake over the ashes/the past → **rake**
a thing of the past → **thing**

pasting

give sb/get a 'pasting (*informal, especially BrE*)

1 beat sb/be beaten very easily: *Our team was given a real pasting on Saturday. We lost 6-0.* ◇ *The Democrats got a real pasting at the local elections.*
2 criticize sb/be criticized very severely: *His new film got a pasting in the newspaper yesterday.* ◇ *She gave me a real pasting for handing in my essay a week late.*

pasture

put sb out to 'pasture (*informal, humorous*)

ask sb to leave a job because they are getting old; make sb retire: *Isn't it time some of these politicians were put out to pasture?*

> ❶ **ORIGIN**
> This expression refers to old farm horses or other animals, which no longer work and stay in the fields (= *pastures*) all day.

pastures

ˌpastures 'new

a new job, place to live, way of life, etc: *After 10 years as a teacher, Jen felt it was time to move on to pastures new.* ◇ *Without warning, she left him for pastures new.*

pat

give sb/yourself a ˌpat on the 'back; pat sb/ yourself on the 'back (for doing sth)

praise sb/yourself for sth they/you have done well: *I think we should give James a pat on the back for working so hard.* ◇ *I feel I'm entitled to pat myself on the back for having everything ready on time.*

have/know/get sth off 'pat (*BrE*) (*AmE* **have/ know sth down 'pat**)

know or have learned sth so well that you can repeat it at any time: *I'm afraid I haven't got the answer off pat.* ◇ *She has all our names and telephone numbers down pat.*

stand pat → **stand**

patch

go through, hit, etc. a 'bad/'sticky patch
come to a difficult time in your business, marriage, etc: *We've struck a bad patch in our marriage.* ◇ *High inflation meant that her business went through a sticky patch.*

not be a 'patch on sb/sth (*informal, especially BrE*)
not be nearly as good as sb/sth: *The film isn't a patch on the book.*

path

beat a path to sb's door → **beat**
lead sb up the garden path → **lead**
the primrose path (to ruin, destruction, etc.) → **primrose**
smooth the path/way → **smooth**
tread a difficult, solitary, etc. path → **tread**

paths

our/their paths cross = cross sb's path → **cross**

patience

the patience of a 'saint/of 'Job
very great patience: *I don't know how she does it— she's got the patience of a saint, that woman!* ◇ *You need the patience of Job to deal with customers like that.*

❶ ORIGIN
Job was a character in the Bible who lost his family, his home and his possessions, but still did not reject God.

try sb's patience → **try**

patter

the patter of tiny 'feet (*informal or humorous*)
(the sound of) young children around you in your home; a baby: *She's not particularly interested in having children, but her husband longs for the patter of tiny feet.*

Paul

rob Peter to pay Paul → **rob**

pause

give (sb) pause for 'thought; give (sb) 'pause (*formal*)
make sb think seriously about sth or hesitate before doing sth: *His remarks on the conditions in our prisons gave me pause for thought. Until that moment I'd never realized things were so bad.*

a pregnant pause/silence → **pregnant**

pave

pave the 'way (for sb/sth)
make the arrival of sb/sth easier; prepare for sb/sth: *Babbage's early work on calculating machines in the nineteenth century paved the way for the development of computers.*

paved

the road to hell is paved with good intentions → **road**
the streets are paved with gold → **streets**

pay

be in sb's/sth's pay; be in the pay of sb/sth (*usually disapproving*)
be working for sb or for an organization, often secretly: *He's been in the pay of our rivals for the last ten years.*

'hell/the 'devil to pay (*informal*)
a lot of trouble: *There'll be hell to pay when your father sees that broken window.*

hit/strike 'pay dirt (*informal, especially AmE*)
suddenly be in a successful situation, especially one that makes you rich: *The band hit pay dirt two years ago with their first album, but have since been less successful.*

pay 'dividends
produce great advantages or profits: *Learning a foreign language will always pay dividends.* ◇ *Hard work while you're young pays dividends later.*

❶ NOTE
If you invest in a company, the money you receive as your share of the profit is called a *dividend*.

pay for it'self
(of a new system, sth you have bought, etc.) save as much money as it cost: *The rail pass will pay for itself after only about two trips.*

pay 'lip-service to sth
if a person **pays lip-service to sth**, they pretend to support or agree with sth, without proving their support by what they actually do: *He doesn't really believe in equal opportunities. He just pays lip-service to it because he doesn't want to appear old-fashioned.*

pay the 'price/'penalty (for sth/for doing sth)
suffer as a result of bad luck, a mistake or sth you have done: *She insisted on marrying him against everybody's advice, and now she's paid the penalty. She's terribly unhappy.* ◇ *I'm really paying the price for that whisky I drank last night. I've never had such a headache.*

pay your re'spects (to sb) (*formal*)
show respect for sb by visiting them, attending their funeral, etc: *At the funeral the whole neighbourhood came out to pay their respects (to him).*

pay through the 'nose (for sth) (*informal*)
pay a very high price for sth: *Why pay through the nose for a used car? Come to Smith's for prices you can afford!*

pay 'tribute to sb/sth
show that you respect or admire sb/sth: *Members of the musical profession paid tribute to the late Leonard Bernstein.*

pay sb/sth a visit; pay a visit to sb/sth

visit sb/sth: *I think it's time we paid Jo a visit, don't you?*

pay your/its (own) 'way

(of a person, group, etc.) have or make enough money to support yourself/itself: *While she was a student she had to work as a waitress in order to pay her way.* ◇ *The local theatre doesn't get a grant from the Arts Council so it has to pay its own way.*

cost/pay an arm and a leg → **arm**
cost/pay/charge the earth → **earth**
give/pay heed (to sb/sth) → **heed**
pay sth back/return sth with interest → **interest**
rob Peter to pay Paul → **rob**

pays

he who pays the ˌpiper calls the 'tune (*saying*)

the person who provides the money for sth has the right to say how it should be spent; the person with power makes the decisions: *The Rockefeller Foundation helps the project financially, and they have the right to say 'no' to any part of it. He who pays the piper …*

it always/never pays to do sth

it is always/never wise to do sth: *It always pays to get good professional advice.* ◇ *It never pays to cheat in exams because you will always be discovered eventually.*

you ˌpays your ˌmoney and you ˌtakes your 'choice (*saying*)

used to say that there is not much difference between two or more alternatives, so you should choose whichever you prefer: *'I can't decide whether to buy this book—it is well written but it's rather short.' 'Well, you pays your money and you takes your choice.'* ◇ *It's hard to say which explanation is more likely; it's more a matter of you pays your money and you takes your choice.*

peace

be at 'peace

1 not be fighting: *In 1945 the western world was once again at peace.*

2 be calm or quiet: *He's much more at peace with himself now than he used to be.*

3 (of sb who has recently died) no longer suffering: *We have to comfort ourselves with the knowledge that she's at peace now.*

ˌkeep the 'peace

1 prevent people from fighting, arguing, etc: *The United Nations is sending in troops to keep the peace.* ◇ *If I'm at home I can keep the peace; if I'm not, they fight all day long.*

2 (*formal*) not create a disturbance in a public place: *The court ordered him to keep the peace.*

make (your) 'peace with sb

end an argument, quarrel, etc. with sb, for example by saying sorry to them: *He made his peace with his mother just before she died.*

peace and 'quiet

a period of calm, silence, etc., especially after noise, stress, etc: *Why don't you all go out and play in the garden? Your mother needs a bit of peace and quiet.*

a/the 'peace dividend

money that governments save by not buying weapons: *The Health Service should benefit from the peace dividend.*

peace of 'mind

freedom from worry, anxiety, guilt, etc: *He seemed to find peace of mind in the last few weeks of his life.*

a 'peace offering

a present that you give to sb to show that you are sorry for sth or want to make peace after an argument: *He left a box of chocolates as a peace offering, hoping that she would forgive him.*

hold your peace/tongue → **hold**
there's no peace/rest for the wicked → **wicked**

pearls

pearls of 'wisdom (*usually ironic*)

good advice; wise remarks: *They all gathered round her, hoping for some of her pearls of wisdom.*

cast pearls before swine → **cast**

Pearly

the ˌPearly 'Gates (*humorous*)

the gates of heaven: *What's going to happen when I get to those Pearly Gates? Have I lead a good life?*

pear-shaped

go 'pear-shaped (*BrE, informal*)

if things **go pear-shaped**, they go wrong: *Everything was going really well for Dave until the last week of the course, when it all went a bit pear-shaped and he failed an assignment.*

After a promising start, it all seemed to go a bit pear-shaped.

peas

as like as (two) 'peas in a pod (*informal*)
very similar in appearance: *I had never met his brother before but I recognized him immediately because they're as like as two peas in a pod.*

pebble

not the 'only pebble on the beach (*informal, disapproving*)
not the only person who is important or who should be considered: *'She thinks she should be chosen to go to the meeting in Paris.' 'She's not the only pebble on the beach, you know.'*

pecker

keep your pecker up = keep your chin up → chin

pecking

a/the 'pecking order (*informal, often humorous*)
the way a group is organized, with some members being more important or powerful than others: *You don't get a company car unless you're pretty high up in the pecking order.*

> ❶ ORIGIN
> This expression was first used by a scientist in the 1920s after studying groups of birds; he noticed there was a hierarchy when birds were feeding.

pedestal

put/set/place sb on a 'pedestal
admire sb so much that you are unable to see their faults: *Don't try to put her on a pedestal, she's as guilty as the rest of them!*

knock sb off their perch/pedestal → knock

peeled

keep your eyes open/peeled/skinned (for sb/sth) → eyes

Peeping

a ,Peeping 'Tom (*disapproving*)
a person who likes to watch people secretly, especially when they are taking off their clothes

> ❶ ORIGIN
> In 1040 in the English town of Coventry, Lady Godiva rode through the streets completely naked in an attempt to make her husband change his mind about forcing people to pay high taxes. In the legend, only one man, Tom, watched her and he suddenly became blind.

peeve

your, his, etc. pet peeve → pet

peg

,bring/,take sb 'down a peg (or two) (*informal*)
make sb realize that they are not as good, important, etc. as they think they are: *He didn't win first*

prize after all. That'll bring him down a peg or two. ◇ *It's time that somebody took that woman down a peg or two. She behaves as if she were the queen.*

,off the 'peg (*BrE*) (*AmE* ,off the 'rack)
(of a suit, etc.) ready to wear; not made specially to fit one person: *He couldn't afford a made-to-measure suit, so he bought one off the peg.*

a peg to 'hang sth on; a peg on which to 'hang sth
an event, occasion, subject of discussion, etc. which is used by sb to express opinions or ideas about sth else: *The professor makes any subject a peg on which to hang his political views.*

be a square peg (in a round hole) → square

pegging

level pegging → level

pelt

(at) full pelt/speed/tilt → full

pen

the ,pen is ,mightier than the 'sword (*saying*)
people who write books, poems, etc. have a greater effect on history and human affairs than soldiers and wars

put ,pen to 'paper (*formal*)
write or start to write sth: *He spent hours thinking about what he should write, and it was midnight before he finally put pen to paper.*

a poison pen letter → poison
a slip of the tongue/pen → slip

penalty

pay the price/penalty (for sth/for doing sth) → pay

pennies

pinch pennies → pinch

penny

,in for a 'penny, ,in for a 'pound (*saying*)
once you have decided to start doing sth, you may as well do it as well as you can, even if this means spending a lot of time, energy, money, etc: *The new carpet made everything else look old, so we thought 'in for a penny, in for a pound', and we painted the room and bought a new sofa too!*

the ,penny 'drops (*informal, especially BrE*)
suddenly understand the meaning or significance of sth: *She never understands jokes. It usually takes about half an hour for the penny to drop.* ◇ *There was a long silence on the stage, and then the penny finally dropped—it was my turn to speak.*

a ,penny for your 'thoughts (also **a 'penny for them**) (*saying*)
used to ask sb what they are thinking about: *A penny for your thoughts, Hugh! You haven't said anything all evening!*

two/ten a 'penny (*BrE*) (*AmE* **a ˌdime a 'dozen**)
very cheap or very common, and therefore not valuable: *In the small towns on the coast, lobsters are two a penny.* ◇ *Finding a job will be difficult. History teachers are ten a penny at the moment.*

a pretty penny → pretty
spend a penny → spend
turn up like a bad penny → turn

people

of 'all people/places/things
used to emphasize that the person/place/thing is the most or least likely in the circumstances: *You of all people should be sympathetic, having just had a similar accident yourself.* ◇ *If it's a rest they need, then why go to New York of all places?*

people (who live) in glass ˌhouses shouldn't throw 'stones (*saying*)
you should not criticize other people for faults that you have yourself: *'He said you weren't entirely honest in business.' 'Oh, did he? Well tell him from me that people who live in glasshouses shouldn't throw stones. He'll know what I mean.'*

be all things to all men/people → things
a man of the people → man

pep

a 'pep talk (*informal*)
a talk by sb to give people confidence or encouragement: *Just before the exams, our teacher gave us all a pep talk.*

per

as per sth
following sth that has been decided: *The work was carried out as per instructions.*

as per 'usual/'normal (*spoken*)
in the usual or normal manner: *'What time is the lesson?' 'Thursday at 3 o'clock, as per usual.'* ◇ *'Is he in a bad mood this morning?' 'Yes, as per normal.'*

a/per head → head
a/one hundred per cent → hundred

perch

knock sb off their perch/pedestal → knock

perfect

in an ideal/a perfect world → world
practice makes perfect → practice

perfectly

know sth full/perfectly/very well → know

perform

do/perform/stage a disappearing/vanishing act → act

peril

(do sth) at your (own) 'peril
(often used as a warning) at the risk of serious danger: *People who go climbing in winter do so at their own peril.* ◇ *You go in Mike's car at your peril. He's a terrible driver.*

period

a/the honeymoon period → honeymoon
period = full stop → full

perish

ˌperish the 'thought! (*spoken, often humorous*)
I hope it will not happen; may it never happen: *'A picnic is a good idea but what if it rains?' 'Perish the thought!'*

perpetuity

in perpe'tuity (*formal*)
for all time in the future; forever: *They do not own the land in perpetuity.*

person

about/on your 'person (*formal*)
carried with you, for example in a pocket or bag: *The defendant had 100 grams of cocaine on his person.*

in 'person
personally; physically present: *I'm sorry, I won't be able to come in person, but I'll send my assistant.*

in the person of sb (*formal*)
in the form or shape of sb: *Help arrived in the person of his mother.*

as good, well, etc. as the next person → next

persona

perˌsona non 'grata (*from Latin*)
a person who is not welcome in a particular place because of sth they have said or done: *Persona non grata in Hollywood, Jake moved to New York to try and make a living on the stage.*

❷ NOTE
The meaning of *non grata* is 'not pleasing'.

personally

take sth 'personally
feel personally offended by sb's general remark, etc: *I was talking about people having smelly socks, and I'm afraid Mike took it personally.* ◇ *Look, don't take this personally, Sue, but there are several people in this office who are not working hard enough.*

persons

be no respecter of persons → respecter

perspective

get, put, etc. sth in/out of per'spective
be able/not be able to see or understand the rela-

tive importance of certain events, facts, etc: *When you're depressed, it's very easy to get things out of perspective. Everything worries you.* ◇ *Let's try and put your present problems in perspective, then you'll see that things aren't as bad as you think.*

persuasion

of a/the … persuasion (*formal* or *humorous*)
of the type mentioned: *As a young man, Max had always been of an artistic persuasion.* ◇ *peers of the Liberal persuasion*

pervert

per‚vert the course of 'justice (*law*)
tell a lie or do sth in order to prevent the police, etc. from finding out the truth about a crime: *He was arrested and charged with attempting to pervert the course of justice.*

pet

your, his, etc. pet 'hate (*BrE*) (*AmE* **your, his, etc. pet 'peeve**)
something that you particularly dislike: *She didn't mind people smoking, but her pet hate was people blowing smoke in her face.*

petard

be hoist/hoisted by/with your own pe'tard (*BrE*)
be caught in the trap that you were preparing for another person

❶ ORIGIN
This comes from Shakespeare's play *Hamlet*. A *petard* is a kind of firework.

Pete

for Pete's 'sake (*BrE*)
used to emphasize that it is important to do sth, or when you are annoyed or impatient about sth: *For Pete's sake, what are you doing in that bathroom? You've been in there for nearly an hour.*

Peter

rob Peter to pay Paul ➔ **rob**

pew

‚take a 'pew (*BrE, spoken, humorous*)
used to tell sb to sit down: *Good to see you! Take a pew and I'll get us a drink.*

❷ NOTE
A *pew* is a long wooden seat in a church.

phase

in 'phase/out of 'phase (with sth) (*BrE*)
working/not working together in the right way: *The traffic lights were out of phase.*

phone

be on the telephone/phone ➔ **telephone**

phrase

to coin a phrase ➔ **coin**
a turn of phrase ➔ **turn**

pick

‚pick and 'choose
take time and care to choose sth you really want: *There are so few jobs in banking at the moment that you're not really in a position to pick and choose.*

pick sb's 'brains (*informal*)
ask sb who knows a lot about a particular subject for information or ideas: *I need some help with my homework. Can I pick your brains?*

pick a 'fight/'quarrel (with sb)
deliberately start a fight or argument (with sb): *Why do you always pick fights with boys smaller than you?* ◇ *At work he's always picking quarrels.*

pick 'holes (in sth) (*informal*)
criticize sth or find fault with sth, for example a plan, reason, argument, etc: *It's easy for you to pick holes in my explanation, but have you got a better one?*

pick a 'lock
open a lock without a key, using sth such as a piece of wire: *I can't find my front door key. I don't suppose you know how to pick a lock, do you?*

the pick of the 'bunch (*informal*)
the best example of a group of people or things: *This Australian wine is the pick of the bunch.*

pick sb's 'pocket
steal money or other things from sb's pocket without them realizing: *I can't find my wallet. I think somebody's picked my pocket!* ◇ *If she's not careful she'll get her pocket picked.* ▶ **'pickpocket** noun a person who picks pockets: *Be careful of pickpockets when you're on the underground in London.*

pick up the 'pieces
do what you can to get your life, a situation, etc. back to normal after a disaster, shock, etc: *After his son was killed in a car accident, it took him a long time to pick up the pieces.* ◇ *It's always the same with her husband. He upsets everyone and then leaves her to pick up the pieces.*

pick up 'speed
go faster: *The train began to pick up speed.*

pick up the 'tab (for sth) (*informal*)
pay the bill, especially for a group of people in a restaurant, etc: *Her father picked up the tab for all the champagne at the wedding.*

pick up the 'threads
start sth, for example an activity, relationship, career, again after a break: *It's not easy for women returning to work to pick up the threads of their earlier careers.*

pick your 'way (across, over, etc. sth)
walk carefully, choosing the safest, driest, etc. place to put your feet: *She picked her way delicately over the rough ground.*

pick a 'winner

1 choose a horse, etc. that you think is most likely to win a race

2 (*informal*) make a very good choice: *Good choice, George. I think you've picked a winner there!*

take/have your 'pick (of sth)

choose whatever you like: *With that much money you can have your pick of any car in the showroom.* ◇ *There's ham, cheese or egg sandwiches. Take your pick!*

get up/pick up steam → **steam**

have (got) a bone to pick with sb → **bone**

pick/choose your moment → **moment**

pickle

in a (real, right, etc.) 'pickle (*informal*)

in a difficult situation; in a mess: *Things are in a real pickle at the moment, I'm afraid. My assistant's left and I'm completely lost without him!* ◇ *Can you help me? I'm in a bit of a pickle.*

picnic

be no 'picnic (*informal*)

be difficult or unpleasant: *Living with someone like her is no picnic, believe me.*

two sandwiches short of a picnic = a brick short of a load → **brick**

picture

be/look a 'picture

look very beautiful or special: *The garden looks a picture in the summer.*

be the ˌpicture of 'health, 'happiness, etc.

be completely or extremely healthy, etc: *She's the picture of happiness in this photo.* ◇ *He's the picture of misery, isn't he? Look at him standing there in the rain.*

get the 'picture (*spoken*)

understand sth: *I get the picture—you want me to keep it a secret.*

in/out of the 'picture (*informal*)

involved/not involved in a situation: *Morris is likely to win, with Jones out of the picture now.*

put/keep sb in the 'picture (*informal*)

give sb the information they need in order to understand a particular situation, etc: *Before you start work, let me put you in the picture about the way the office is run.*

the big picture → **big**

paint a terrible, depressing, etc. picture (of sb/sth) → **paint**

(as) pretty as a picture → **pretty**

a/one side of the story/picture → **side**

pie

ˌpie in the 'sky (*informal*)

ideas that are not practical; false hopes or promises: *Most voters know that the big promises which politicians make before an election are just pie in the sky.* ◇ *He says he's going to make a film in Hollywood, but I think it's all pie in the sky.*

as American as apple pie → **American**

(as) easy as ABC/pie/falling off a log → **easy**

eat humble pie → **eat**

have (got) a finger in every pie → **finger**

(as) nice as pie → **nice**

a piece/share/slice of the pie = a share/slice of the cake → **cake**

piece

give sb a piece of your 'mind (*informal*)

angrily tell sb your true opinion of them; criticize sb angrily: *If he doesn't turn that music down soon, I'm going to give him a piece of my mind.*

(all) in one 'piece (*informal*)

not hurt or harmed, especially after being in danger or in an accident: *'Are you all right, Richard?' 'Yes, thanks. I'm still in one piece, I think. I've torn my jacket, that's all.'*

(all) of a 'piece (with sth) (*formal*)

possessing the same character or qualities; consistent (with sth): *When you see a lot of his paintings together, you feel that his work is all of a piece.* ◇ *The pews, the pulpit and the altar are of a piece with the simple elegance of the church itself.*

ˌpiece by 'piece

one part at a time: *He took his motorcycle apart piece by piece, cleaned it, and put it back together.*

a piece of 'cake (*informal*) (*BrE* also **a piece of 'piss** ⚠, *slang*)

(of a task, etc.) very easy to do: *After climbing mountains in the Swiss Alps, going up English hills is a piece of cake.* ◇ *Taking the photo should be a piece of cake with the new lens I've got.*

how long is a piece of string? → **long**

a nasty piece of work → **nasty**

a piece/slice of the action → **action**

a piece/share/slice of the pie = a share/slice of the cake → **cake**

your party piece → **party**

say your piece → **say**

the villain of the piece → **villain**

pièce

your/the ˌpièce de ré'sistance (*from French*)

the most important or impressive part of a group or series of things: *I hope you all enjoyed your main course. And now for my pièce de résistance: chocolate gateau!*

pieces

go (all) to 'pieces (*informal*)

after a terrible shock, etc., become so upset or nervous that you can no longer lead your life normally: *After he lost his job he just seemed to go to pieces.*

bits and pieces → **bits**

fall to pieces → **fall**

pick, pull, etc. sb/sth to bits/pieces ➔ **bits**
pick up the pieces ➔ **pick**
tear sb/sth to pieces/shreds ➔ **tear**

pig

in a pig's 'eye (*AmE, informal*)
used to say that you think that sth is not at all true
or that sth will definitely not happen: *He told you
his father owns the company? In a pig's eye!* ◊
*'Apparently this is the best hotel in town.' 'In a pig's
eye it is!'*

make a 'pig of yourself (*informal*)
eat and drink too much; be greedy: *She always
makes such a pig of herself.*

make a pig's 'ear (out) of sth (*BrE, informal*)
do sth very badly: *He made a real pig's ear of his
geography exam.*

(buy) a pig in a 'poke
buy or pay for sth without seeing it or examining it
carefully first ◊ *Make sure you take the car for a
proper test drive—you don't want to buy a pig in a
poke, do you?*

❶ ORIGIN
This expression refers to an old market trick of
putting a rat in a bag (= a *poke*) and selling it as a
young pig.

'pig it (*informal*)
live or behave in a dirty way: *'Where does he live?'
'He pigs it in a tiny old flat in Camden.'*

a pig of a sth (*BrE, informal*)
a difficult or unpleasant thing or task: *I've had a
pig of a day.*

a guinea pig ➔ **guinea**
(be) pig/piggy in the middle ➔ **middle**
sweat like a pig ➔ **sweat**

pigeon

be sb's pigeon (*old-fashioned, BrE*)
be sb's responsibility or business: *Somebody needs
to write a report on training for the manager, but it's
not my pigeon.* ◊ *Gustav will have to tell them first,
it's his pigeon.*

pigeons

put/set the cat among the pigeons ➔ **cat**

piggy

(be) pig/piggy in the middle ➔ **middle**

pigs

pigs might 'fly (*BrE*) (*AmE* **when pigs 'fly**)
(*ironic, saying*)
used when you do not believe sth will ever happen:
*'You might get into the football team if you practise
hard.' 'Yes, and pigs might fly!'*

pike

come down the 'pike (*AmE, informal*)
happen; become noticeable: *We're hearing a lot
about new inventions coming down the pike.*

❷ NOTE
Pike here is short for 'turnpike', which is a type
of large road in the US.

pikestaff

(as) plain as a pikestaff ➔ **plain**

pile

make a/your 'pile (*informal*)
make a lot of money: *If you want to make a pile,
don't go into the restaurant business.*

pile on the 'agony/'gloom (*informal, especially
BrE*)
1 make sth unpleasant sound much worse than it
really is in order to gain sympathy from other
people: *He always piles on the agony when he has a
cold; you'd think he was dying.*
2 make sb feel even worse about an unpleasant
situation: *The latest fare increase just piles on the
gloom for rail passengers, who already feel they are
paying too much.*

at the bottom/top of the pile/heap ➔ **bottom**
lay/pile it on (thick/with a trowel) ➔ **lay**

pill

be on the 'pill
(of women) be regularly taking a medicine that
will stop you getting pregnant (= the contraceptive
pill): *When I went to see the doctor, he asked me if I
was on the pill.*

sugar/sweeten the 'pill
make sth unpleasant seem less unpleasant: *He
tried to sweeten the pill by telling her she'd only be
in hospital a few days.*

a bitter pill (for sb) (to swallow) ➔ **bitter**

pillar

be driven, pushed, etc. from ,pillar to 'post
be forced to go from one person or situation to
another without achieving anything: *Vast numbers of refugees have been pushed from pillar to
post in that area.*

a pillar of so'ciety, etc.
a person who is respected in society, etc.; a person
of importance: *I couldn't believe that a pillar of the
community like him had been caught stealing from
his employer.*

a pillar/tower of strength ➔ **strength**

pillow

'pillow talk (*informal*)
a conversation in bed between lovers when promises are made which should not be taken too ser-

iously, or secrets are revealed: *'He said he'd never been so deeply in love in the whole of his life.' 'That was just pillow talk.'* ◇ *'How did he find out about that?' 'Pillow talk, probably.'*

pilot

be on automatic pilot → **automatic**

pin

pin your 'faith/'hopes on sb/sth

put your trust in sb/sth; hope for sb/sth: *He's pinning his faith on the revival of the economy.* ◇ *The idea that he'll be out of prison in five years is all she's got to pin her hopes on.*

'pin money (*informal*)

a small amount of money that you earn, especially when this is used to buy things that you want rather than things that you need: *She teaches a little French now and then, just for pin money.*

(as) clean as a new pin → **clean**
you could have heard a pin drop → **heard**

pinch

at a 'pinch/'push (*BrE*) (*AmE* **in a 'pinch**) (*informal*)

possible if you try very hard or if it is absolutely necessary: *We usually only accept 55 guests but at a pinch, we could take 60.*

pinch 'pennies (*informal*)

try to spend as little money as possible: *We've been pinching pennies all year so that we can visit my relatives in Australia in December.*

take sth with a pinch of 'salt (*informal*)

not believe everything sb says: *She told me she knew people in the film industry, but I took that with a pinch of salt.* ◇ *I take everything he says with a large pinch of salt.*

feel the pinch → **feel**

pink

(be) in the 'pink (of condition/health) (*old-fashioned, informal*)

(be) in very good health or excellent physical condition: *The dog that won the competition was in the pink of condition.*

be tickled pink → **tickled**
have a pink/blue fit → **fit**
see pink elephants → **see**

pins

have (got) pins and 'needles

have an uncomfortable feeling in your arm or leg when it has been in the same position for a long time: *The best thing to do when you have pins and needles in your leg is to stamp your foot on the floor several times.*

on your 'pins (*old-fashioned, informal*)

on your legs; when standing up or walking: *He's not as steady on his pins as he used to be. I worry about him going out.*

be on pins and needles = (be) on tenterhooks → **tenterhooks**
for two pins → **two**

pint

get/pour/put a quart into a pint pot → **quart**

pip

pip sb at/to the 'post (*BrE, informal*)

beat sb in a race, competition, etc. by only a small amount or at the last moment: *We thought we'd won the contract, but we were pipped at the post by a rival company.* ◇ *I was winning the race until Tina came up behind me and pipped me to the post.*

pipe

a 'pipe dream

a hope, belief, plan, etc. that will probably never come true: *She's got this pipe dream about being a pop star.*

❶ ORIGIN
This expression refers to smoking the drug opium, which makes you sleep and gives you powerful dreams.

put 'that in your pipe and smoke it (*informal*)

used after telling sb an unpleasant fact or truth, to say that they should accept it: *I'm not giving you any more money to spend on that car. So put that in your pipe and smoke it!*

pipeline

in the 'pipeline

already being considered, planned, prepared or developed, but not yet ready: *We have an interesting new database program in the pipeline. It should be on sale early next year.*

piper

he who pays the piper calls the tune → **pays**

pique

pique sb's 'interest, curi'osity, etc. (*especially AmE*)

make sb very interested in sth: *The film has certainly piqued public interest in this rare bird.*

piss

be on the 'piss (*BrE, ⚠, slang*)

be out at a pub, club, etc. and drinking a large amount of alcohol: *I'm not sure if Jerry will be at work today—he was out on the piss with his mates last night.*

'piss yourself (laughing) (*BrE, ⚠, slang*)

laugh very hard: *Poor Kath—she was lying on the floor and we were all pissing ourselves laughing!*

take the 'piss (out of sb/sth) (*BrE*, ⚠, *slang*)
make fun of sb/sth: *He told me he thought I had a fantastic singing voice, but I think he was taking the piss* (= he was only joking). ◇ *Are you taking the piss out of me?*

a piece of piss → **piece**

pissed

(as) pissed as a 'newt (*BrE*, ⚠, *slang*)
very drunk: *You should have seen Tom when he got home last night—he was pissed as a newt!*

pit

make a 'pit stop (*informal, especially AmE*)
stop for a short time during a long journey by road for a rest, meal, etc: *I'm getting a bit hungry. Shall we make a pit stop at the next service station?*

❶ NOTE
In motor racing, a *pit stop* is an occasion when a car stops during a race for more fuel, etc.

the pit of your/the 'stomach
the bottom of the stomach where people say they feel strong feelings, especially fear: *He had a sudden sinking feeling in the pit of his stomach.*

,pit your 'wits (against sb/sth)
compete with sb/sth in a test of intelligence or knowledge: *He's pitting his wits against the computer chess game.*

a bottomless pit (of sth) → **bottomless**

pitch

make a 'pitch for sb/sth; make a 'pitch to sb
(*especially AmE*)
make a determined effort to get sth or to persuade sb of sth: *Both presidential candidates have promised to make a pitch for better roads and schools.*

,pitch a 'line/'story/'yarn (to sb) (*informal*)
tell sb a story or make an excuse that is not true: *He assured me that it really happened, but I reckon he was just pitching me a line.*

at fever pitch → **fever**
queer sb's pitch → **queer**

pitched

a ,pitched 'battle
1 a fight that involves a large number of people: *There was a pitched battle earlier today between police and demonstrators. Two hundred people were injured, ten seriously.*
2 a military battle fought with soldiers arranged in prepared positions

pits

be the 'pits (*informal*)
be very bad; be the worst kind of sth: *The teaching at this school is the pits.* ◇ *This newspaper really is the pits.*

pity

,more's the 'pity (*BrE, informal*)
unfortunately: *He can't read and he doesn't want to learn, more's the pity.*

place

all 'over the place (*informal*)
1 everywhere: *In my job I have to travel all over the place.*
2 not neat or tidy; not well organized: *There were books and papers all over the place.* ◇ *Your calculations are all over the place* (= completely wrong).

(not) be sb's place to do sth
not have the right to do sth, for example to criticize sb, suggest sth, etc: *'Why didn't you tell him?' 'It wasn't my place to.'* ◇ *He told his secretary that it wasn't her place to question what he said.*

fall, drop, slide, etc. into 'place
1 because of a new piece of information, the relationship between several events, facts, etc. suddenly becomes clear: *When I found out that he was Lucy's uncle, everything fell into place.* ◇ *When we got the final result of our experiment, everything slotted into place.*
2 (of a complex situation) finally reach a satisfactory conclusion: *Last year everything was so difficult; then John changed his job, I started work, the children moved school and everything finally fell into place.*

give 'place to sb/sth (*formal*)
be replaced by sb/sth: *Houses and factories gave place to open fields as the train gathered speed.*

if ,I was/were in 'your place
used to introduce a piece of advice you are giving to sb: *If I were in your place, I'd resign immediately.*

in the 'first place
1 used at the beginning of a sentence to introduce the different points you are making in an argument: *In the first place it's not your car, and in the second you're not old enough to drive it. Is that clear?*
2 used at the end of a sentence to talk about why sth was done or whether it should have been done or not: *I should never have taken that job in the first place.*

in 'my, 'your, etc. place
in my, your, etc. situation: *I wouldn't like to be in your place.*

in 'place
prepared and ready: *Everything seems to be in place for a successful peace conference.*

in place of sb/sth; in sb's/sth's 'place
instead of sb/sth: *You can use milk in place of cream in this recipe.* ◇ *He was unable to go to the ceremony, but he sent his son in his place.*

out of 'place
1 not in the correct place: *Some of these files seem to be out place.*

2 not suitable for a particular situation: *Your silly remarks were completely out of place at such an important meeting.* ◇ *I feel quite out of place at a smart party like this.*

a place in the 'sun

(of a person) a very favourable position, especially in your professional life: *When he was offered a professorship at Caltech, he felt that he had finally found his place in the sun.*

put sb in their 'place

remind sb forcefully of their real position in society or at work: *That young man needs putting in his place. He behaves as if he were the manager here.*

take 'place

happen: *The meeting will take place at eight o'clock.* ◇ *Some strange things had taken place in that old castle.*

take sb's 'place; take the place of 'sb

do sth which another person was doing before; replace sb: *Miss Jones has left the school and this term her place has been taken by Mr Carter.* ◇ *I was ill, so Bill took my place at the meeting.*

take your 'place

1 go to the physical position that is necessary for an activity: *Take your places for dinner.*
2 take or accept the status in society that is correct or that you deserve: *He is ready now to take his place as one of the fastest swimmers in history.*

behave/act as if you own the place = think you own the place → **think**

(caught/stuck) between a rock and a hard place → **rock**

your, his, etc. heart is in the right place → **heart**

know your place → **know**

not a hair out of place → **hair**

(give sth) pride of place → **pride**

put/set/place sb on a pedestal → **pedestal**

put/place a premium on sth → **premium**

put yourself in sb's shoes/place → **shoes**

think you own the place → **think**

placed

be well, ideally, better, etc. placed for sth/to do sth

1 be in a good, ideal, etc. position or have a good, ideal, etc. opportunity to do sth: *Engineering graduates are well placed for a wide range of jobs.* ◇ *The company is now better placed to take advantage of the new legislation.*
2 be situated in a pleasant or convenient place: *The hotel is ideally placed for restaurants, bars and clubs.*

places

change/swap 'places (with sb)

(of two people, groups, etc.) exchange seats, positions, situations, etc: *The Smiths can afford to go away a lot because they haven't got a family to bring up. But I wouldn't want to change places with*

them. ◇ *Can you see the whiteboard where you are, or would you like to swap places?*

'go places (*informal*)

be successful or likely to be successful in your life or job: *If you're young, energetic and want to go places, write to this address and we'll send you a job application form.* ◇ *He's a young architect who's really going places.*

have (got) friends in high places → **friends**

of all people/places/things → **people**

plague

avoid sb/sth like the plague → **avoid**

plain

be (all) plain 'sailing (*AmE* also **be clear 'sailing**)

be simple and free from trouble: *Life with him isn't all plain sailing, you know.* ◇ *She answered the first question well and from then on it was all plain sailing.*

in plain 'English

simply and clearly expressed, without using technical language: *I don't understand these documents at all. Why can't they write them in plain English?*

(as) plain as a 'pikestaff; (as) plain as 'day; (as) plain as the nose on your 'face (*informal*)

easy to see or understand; obvious: *It's as plain as a pikestaff; this government is ruining the economy.* ◇ *You can't miss the sign, it's right there, as plain as the nose on your face.*

a plain 'Jane (*disapproving*)

a girl or woman who is not very pretty or attractive: *She was a shy girl, who always thought of herself as a plain Jane.*

'That thing? What planet are you on?'

planet

be on another 'planet; what 'planet is sb on? (*spoken, humorous*)

used to suggest that sb's ideas are not realistic or

practical: *He can't really think we're going to finish the job today, can he? What planet is he on?*

plank

walk the plank → **walk**

planks

(as) thick as two short planks → **thick**

plant

plant/sow the seeds of sth → **seeds**

plate

have (got) enough, a lot, etc. on your 'plate (*informal*)

have enough, a lot of things, etc. to do or be responsible for: *I can't help you next week, I've got too much on my plate.* ◇ *She has a lot on her plate at the moment; that's why she looks so worried all the time.*

hand sth to sb on a plate → **hand**

platter

(hand sth to sb) on a silver platter → **silver**

play

bring/call/put sth into 'play

make sth begin to work or operate; involve sth in sth: *The exercise brings many skills into play.* ◇ *This latest decision calls many new factors into play.*

come into 'play

(begin to) operate or be active; have an effect or influence: *It's time for the first part of our plan to come into play.* ◇ *A lot of different factors came into play in making this decision.*

have (got) money, time, etc. to 'play with (*informal*)

have plenty of money, time, etc. for doing sth: *We need to make a decision now, as we haven't got much time to play with.*

in/out of 'play

(of the ball) in/out of a position where it can be played according to the rules of the game: *The defender kicked the ball out of play.* ◇ *The ball's in play, so play on.*

make great, much, etc. 'play of/with sth

put a lot of emphasis on sth; behave as if sth is very important: *The English love of gardening is something he makes great play of in his latest book.* ◇ *He always makes great play of the fact that he went to a famous school.*

make a 'play for sb/sth (*especially AmE*)

make a well-planned attempt to get sth you want: *He was making a play for a top government position.* ◇ *If you want to make a play for her, send her flowers.*

play your 'ace

use your best argument, etc. in order to get an advantage in a situation: *I think it's time we played our ace, which is the fact that without us they wouldn't be able to run this place.*

> **❷ NOTE**
> In most card games the ace has the highest value, and is associated with success.

play 'ball (with sb) (*informal*)

be willing to work with other people in a helpful way, especially so that sb can get what they want: *We need their help, but will they play ball?* ◇ *So he won't play ball, eh? He'll soon realize he can't manage without us.*

play (sth) by 'ear

1 play (music) which you have heard or remembered but which you have not seen written down: *She can't read music very well, so she plays all the tunes by ear.*

2 (also **play it by 'ear**) (*informal*) decide how to act in a situation as it happens or develops, rather than by planning in advance: *You can't really prepare for the questions the interviewer will ask—you'll just have to play it by ear, I'm afraid.*

play by sb's (own) 'rules

if sb **plays by their own rules** or makes other people **play by their rules**, they set the conditions for doing business or having a relationship: *If we want to win this contract, we're going to have to play by their rules for a while.*

play by the 'rules

deal fairly and honestly with people: *You know how we conduct business here, and I expect you all to play by the rules in future.*

play your 'cards right (*informal*)

deal successfully with a particular situation so that you achieve some advantage or sth that you want: *If you play your cards right you could get promotion in a year or two.*

play 'Cupid

try to start a romantic relationship between two people: *Martha was busy playing Cupid as usual, trying to get me to go out with her cousin Terry.*

play 'fair/'straight (with sb)

act honestly and fairly: *I don't think it's playing fair to blame her for other people's mistakes.*

play fast and 'loose (with sb/sth) (*old-fashioned*)

treat sb/sth in a way that shows that you feel no responsibility or respect for them: *If he plays fast and loose with my daughter's feelings, I'll make sure he regrets it.*

play the 'field (*informal*)

have romantic or sexual relationships with a lot of different people: *He told me he didn't want to get married yet because he was having too much fun playing the field.*

play 'footsie (with sb)
touch sb's feet lightly with your own feet, especially under a table, as an expression of affection or sexual interest: *They were very embarrassed when her mother caught them playing footsie under the dinner table.*

play for 'time
try to delay sth or prevent sth from happening now because you think there will be an advantage to you if you act later: *If I can play for time a bit longer, they might lower their price.*

play the 'game
behave in a fair and honest way: *That's the third time this week you've left me to finish all your work. You're not playing the game, Luke.*

play sb's 'game; play the same 'game (as sb)
(also **play sb at their own 'game**)
use the same methods as a competitor, opponent, enemy, etc: *Safeway started cutting their food prices, so Asda decided to play them at their own game by cutting prices even more.*

play (silly) 'games (with sb)
not treat a situation seriously, especially in order to cheat or deceive sb: *Don't play silly games with me; I know you did it.*

play 'God
behave as if you control events or other people's lives: *It is unfair to ask doctors to play God and end someone's life.*

play 'gooseberry (BrE)
be a third person with two people who have a romantic relationship and want to be alone together: *Dave and Michelle invited me to go out with them but I don't want to play gooseberry all evening.*

play hard to 'get (informal)
pretend not to be interested in sb/sth in order to increase sb's interest in or desire for you: *She's playing hard to get, but I'm sure she really wants to go out with me.* ◇ *My advice is, play hard to get for a while and they might offer you more money.*

play (merry) 'hell with sb/sth (BrE, informal)
disturb, upset or trouble sb/sth very much: *These storms play merry hell with our TV reception.*

play (right) into sb's 'hands
do exactly what an enemy, opponent, etc. wants so that they gain the advantage in a particular situation: *The thieves played right into the hands of the law by trying to sell stolen property to a police informer.*

play it 'cool (informal)
not appear excited, worried, angry, etc: *If you play it cool and don't seem too interested, he might lower the price.* ◇ *He was shouting at me, but I played it cool—I didn't want him to see how angry I was.*

play it 'straight (also play a straight 'bat)
be honest and not try to deceive sb: *'Do you think we should try and hide this from the newspapers?'*

'No, play it straight; I'm sure the public will see our point of view.'

> **❶ ORIGIN**
> These idioms refer to one way of holding the bat in the game of cricket.

play the 'market
buy and sell stocks and shares in order to make a profit: *He's been playing the market for 30 years, but is quick to warn people of the risks involved.*

a play on 'words
a clever or amusing use of a word that has more than one meaning, or of words that have different meanings but sound similar/the same; a pun: *When Elvis Presley had his hair cut off in the army he said, 'Hair today and gone tomorrow'. It was a play on words—the usual expression is 'here today and gone tomorrow.'*

play a/your part (in sth)
be involved in sth; be a reason for sth happening: *You too can play a part in helping your community.* ◇ *Arguments within the party played a part in the downfall of the government.*

play 'possum (informal)
pretend to be asleep or not aware of sth, in order to deceive sb: *Jake decided that his best course of action would be to play possum and wait for her to give up.*

> **❶ ORIGIN**
> A *possum* is a small Australian and American animal that pretends to be dead if it is in danger.

play (it) 'safe
avoid danger; act safely, even if another course of action would be quicker, more successful, etc: *I know all these locks seem unnecessary but I believe it's always better to play safe.*

play second 'fiddle
have a lower or less important position than another person: *She wants to be the boss, not play second fiddle to somebody else.*

> **❷ NOTE**
> *Fiddle* is an informal word for 'violin'.

play 'silly buggers (with sth) (BrE, informal)
behave in a stupid and annoying way: *Stop playing silly buggers and answer the question.*

play to the 'gallery
behave in an exaggerated way to attract ordinary people's attention: *The most popular and successful politicians in our history have always known how to play to the gallery.*

> **❷ NOTE**
> In a theatre, the *gallery* is the highest level where the cheapest seats are.

play 'truant (BrE) (AmE play 'hookey/'hooky informal) (old-fashioned)
stay away from school without permission: *Is she off school because she's ill, or is she playing truant?*

play with 'fire

take unnecessary and dangerous risks: *Be very careful, Mike. You're playing with fire.* ◇ *If you ask me she's playing with fire, getting involved with a married man.*

act/play the fool → **fool**
act/play the goat → **goat**
all work and no play (makes Jack a dull boy) → **work**
child's play → **child**
fair play → **fair**
have/play/take/want no part in/of sth → **part**
have (got) a part to play (in sth) → **part**
keep/hold/play your cards close to your chest → **cards**
play/wreak havoc with sth → **havoc**
play on sb's mind = prey on sb's mind → **prey**
the state of play → **state**
two can play at that game → **two**
when the cat's away the mice will play → **cat**

playing

what's sb 'playing at?

used to ask in an angry way about what sb is doing: *What do you think you're playing at?*

a level playing field → **level**
level the playing field → **level**

please

if you 'please

1 (*old-fashioned, formal*) used when politely asking sb to do sth: *Take a seat, if you please.*
2 (*old-fashioned, especially BrE*) used to say that you are annoyed or surprised at sb's actions: *And now, if you please, he wants me to rewrite the whole thing!*

,please the 'eye

be very attractive to look at: *We are proud to present our new lunchtime buffet, where we're sure you will find dishes to please the eye as well as the palate.*

,please 'God

used to say that you very much hope or wish that sth will happen: *Please God, don't let him be dead.*

,please your'self (*spoken*)

used to tell sb that you are annoyed with them and do not care what they do: *'I don't think I'll bother finishing this.' 'Please yourself.'*

,please your'self; ,do as you 'please

be able to do whatever you like: *There were no children to cook for, so we could just please ourselves.*

pleased

I'm (very) pleased to 'meet you (*formal*)

said when you are meeting sb for the first time, often as you shake hands: *'John, this is Dr Savary.' 'I'm pleased to meet you.'*

none too 'pleased

not pleased; angry: *She was none too pleased at having to do it all again.*

only too 'pleased (to do sth)

very happy or willing to do sth: *We're only too pleased to help.*

(as) ,pleased as 'Punch (*BrE*)

very pleased; delighted: *My brother was as pleased as Punch when he passed his driving test.*

> **ⓘ ORIGIN**
> This idiom refers to the character Mr Punch in the traditional puppet play *Punch and Judy*.

'pleased with yourself (*often disapproving*)

too proud of sth you have done: *He was looking very pleased with himself.*

pleasure

at your/sb's 'pleasure (*formal*)

as you want; as sb else wants: *The land can be sold at the owner's pleasure.*

have had the 'pleasure (*formal*)

have been introduced to sb before: *'Tony, have you met Angela Evans?' 'No, I don't think I've had the pleasure.'*

it's a 'pleasure

used after sb thanks you for doing sth to help them: *'Thanks for coming to help us.' 'It's a pleasure.'*

with 'pleasure (*formal*)

used for accepting an offer, invitation, etc. or for saying that you are willing to do what sb has requested: *'Would you like to come and have lunch on Sunday?' 'With pleasure. I'd love to come.'*

pledge

sign/take the 'pledge (*old-fashioned*)

promise never to drink alcohol: *He hasn't been much fun since he took the pledge.*

> **ⓘ ORIGIN**
> In the nineteenth century there were anti-drinking campaigns, when people were encouraged to sign a promise (= a *pledge*) never to drink alcohol.

plot

the plot 'thickens (*often humorous*)

used to say that a situation is becoming more complicated and difficult to understand: *Aha, so both Karen and Steve had the day off work yesterday? The plot thickens!*

lose the plot → **lose**

plough (*BrE*) (*AmE* plow)

,plough a lonely, your own, etc. 'furrow (*literary*)

do things that other people do not do, or be interested in things that other people are not interested in: *There are several English teachers at the school, but Jeanne continues to plough a lonely furrow, teaching French and German.*

ploughshares (*BrE*) (*AmE* plowshares)

turn swords into ploughshares → **turn**

pluck

pluck sth out of the 'air

say a name, number, etc. without thinking about it, especially in answer to a question: *I just plucked a figure out of the air and said: 'Would £1 000 seem reasonable to you?'*

pluck/screw/summon up (your/the) courage (to do sth) → **courage**

plug

pull the plug on sth → **pull**

plughole

(go) down the plughole = (go) down the drain → **drain**

plum

have (got) a 'plum in your mouth (*BrE, disapproving*)

speak in a way that is thought to be typical of the English upper classes: *She speaks as if she's got a plum in her mouth.*

plumb

plumb the 'depths of sth

reach the lowest or most extreme point of sth: *When his friend was killed, he plumbed the depths of despair.*

plunge

take the 'plunge (*informal*)

decide to do sth new, difficult or risky, especially after working at it for some time: *After working for twenty years he's decided to take the plunge and go back to college.*

> ❷ NOTE
> A *plunge* is an act of jumping or diving into water.

plus

plus ça 'change (, plus c'est la même 'chose) (*from French, saying*)

some things never really change, even though details such as time and people involved may be different: *Despite assurances that this year's competition would welcome new talent and new ideas, none of the newcomers have reached the final round. Plus ça change …*

> ❷ NOTE
> The meaning of the full expression in French is 'the more it changes, the more it stays the same'.

plus or 'minus

used when the number mentioned may actually be more or less by a particular amount: *The margin of error was plus or minus three percentage points.*

ply

ply for 'hire/'trade/'business (*BrE*)

look for customers, passengers, etc. in order to do business: *There are plenty of taxis plying for hire outside the theatre.*

ply your 'trade (*written*)

do your work or business: *This is the restaurant where he plied his trade as a cook.*

pneumonia

if A catches a cold, B gets pneumonia = when A sneezes, B catches a cold → **sneezes**

poacher

poacher turned 'gamekeeper (*BrE*)

a person who has changed from one situation or attitude to the opposite one, especially sb who used to oppose people in authority but is now in a position of authority: *Since his days as a militant student, he has cut his hair, put on a suit and is now the classic example of the poacher turned gamekeeper.*

pocket

be ˌin/ˌout of 'pocket (*especially BrE*)

have gained/lost money as a result of sth: *That one mistake left him thousands of pounds out of pocket.* ◇ *Even after paying the extra fee, we were still £100 in pocket.*

in sb's 'pocket (*informal*)

in sb's control, under sb's influence, etc: *She makes all the decisions, not him. He's completely in her pocket.* ◇ *The gang had hundreds of police officers in their pockets.*

out of your own 'pocket

with your own money: *He paid for the trip out of his own pocket.*

line your (own)/sb's pocket(s) → **line**
money burns a hole in sb's pocket → **money**
pick sb's pocket → **pick**
put your hand in(to) your pocket → **hand**

pockets

be/live in each other's 'pockets (*BrE*)

if two people are **in each other's pockets**, they are too close to each other or spend too much time with each other: *They live together, work together and socialize together. If you ask me, it can't be healthy to live in each other's pockets like that.*

pod

as like as (two) peas in a pod → **peas**

poetic

poetic 'justice

a punishment or reward that is deserved: *If you ask me it's poetic justice. He tried to get you fired, and now he's lost his job himself.*

artistic/poetic licence → **licence**

point

ask, tell, etc. sb point 'blank
ask, tell, etc. sb very directly, and perhaps rudely: *I told him point blank that we no longer wanted him to work for us.* ◇ *She asked me point blank why I didn't like her.*

be on the 'point of doing sth
be about to do sth: *I was on the point of posting the letter when I saw it didn't have a stamp on it.*

beside the 'point
of no importance to the matter being discussed; irrelevant: *His political interests are beside the point. All I want to know about him is whether he can do the job properly.*

come/get (straight) to the 'point
talk about the most important problem, matter, etc. immediately rather than have a general conversation first: *Stop avoiding the issue and come to the point!* ◇ *Let me get straight to the point. I don't think you'll pass this exam unless you work harder.*

get the 'point (of sth)
understand sb's explanation: *You haven't got the point of what I'm trying to say.* ◇ *Oh, I see. I get the point.*

have (got) a 'point (there)
have made a good suggestion; have a good idea: *He's got a point there; if you sell the house now you'll lose money, so why not wait till next year?* ◇ *Animal rights campaigners have a point when they say that a lot of animal testing is unnecessary.*

if/when it ,comes to the 'point
if/when the time comes when you have to do or decide sth: *I'm not frightened of flying, but when it comes to the point I'd rather travel by train.*

in point of 'fact
used to say what is true in a situation: *'Picasso painted this picture in 1935.' 'In point of fact, Joanna, he painted it in 1934.'* ◇ *I'll visit you next time I'm in Berlin. In point of fact, I'm supposed to be going there next month, so why don't I come and see you then?*

make your 'point
explain your opinion fully; tell sb exactly what you mean: *They were all talking so loudly I didn't get a chance to make my point.* ◇ *Look, I think you've made your point, Mr Davies. Perhaps we should hear somebody else's opinion.*

make a 'point of doing sth
make sure you do sth; make an effort to do sth because you think it's the correct way to do things: *I always make a point of locking up at night.* ◇ *She made a point of thanking all the staff before she left the office.*

,more to the 'point
more important to the subject being discussed than what has already been mentioned: *Drink driving is against the law and, more to the point, extremely dangerous.*

point a/the 'finger (at sb)
say you think sb is responsible for sth; accuse sb of doing sth: *It was his wife who pointed the finger at him in the end.*

,point of 'contact
a place where you go or a person that you speak to when you are dealing with an organization: *The receptionist is the first point of contact most people have with the clinic.*

a ,point of de'parture
1 a place where a journey starts
2 (*formal*) an idea, a theory or an event that is used to start a discussion, an activity, etc: *Professor Brown's recent essay will certainly be the point of departure for future research on the subject.*

a ,point of 'honour (*BrE*) (*AmE* a ,point of 'honor)
a thing that sb considers to be very important for their honour or reputation: *His refusal to talk to the press about his private life had always been a point of honour for him.*

the ,point of ,no re'turn
the time when you must continue with what you have decided to do, because it is not possible to get back to an earlier situation: *We've invested so much in the project that we simply must finish it. We've reached the point of no return.*

a ,point of 'view
1 sb's opinion about sb/sth: *I don't agree with her, but she has a right to her point of view.*
2 one way of looking at or judging sth: *From the businessman's point of view these new hourly flights to Paris are just what is needed.*

point the 'way (to/towards sth)
show how things will develop in future: *New high-speed trains are pointing the way to a new age of European travel.*

take sb's 'point
understand and accept the truth of what sb has said, especially during an argument, discussion, etc: *I take your point, Simon, but I don't think it's as simple as you think.* ◇ *'Look, Jane. I know a lot more about physics than you, so why do you keep disagreeing with what I say?' 'OK, point taken.'*

to the 'point
expressed in a simple, clear way without any extra information or feelings: *The speech was short and to the point.*

to the 'point of (doing) 'sth
to such an extent that a stronger description could be used: *The restaurant staff were unhelpful to the point of rudeness.* ◇ *His remarks were unkind to the point of being cruel.*

up to a (certain) 'point
to some extent; not completely: *I'm willing to help you up to a point, but after that you'll have to look after yourself.* ◇ *I agree with you up to a point, but not completely.*

be a moot point/question → **moot**
be your strong point/suit → **strong**
a case in point → **case**
the high point/spot of sth → **high**
labour the point → **labour**
not to put too fine a point on it → **fine**
(get to, reach, etc.) saturation point → **saturation**
score a point/points off/over/against sb → **score**
a sore point (with sb) → **sore**
stretch a point → **stretch**

points

have (got) your 'good, 'plus, etc. points

have (got) some good qualities or aspects: *Europe has its good points, but I prefer the Eastern way of life.* ◊ *She often seems rather unfriendly, but I suppose she's got her plus points.*

brownie points → **brownie**
possession is nine points/tenths/parts of the law → **possession**
score a point/points off/over/against sb → **score**

poison

a ,poison 'pen letter

an unpleasant letter which is not signed and is intended to upset the person who receives it: *Most politicians get poison pen letters, sometimes threatening their lives.*

what's your 'poison? (*spoken, humorous*)

used to ask sb what alcoholic drink they would like: *Right, would anyone like a drink? Bill, what's your poison?*

one man's meat is another man's poison → **man**

poisoned

a poisoned 'chalice (*especially BrE*)

a thing which seems attractive when it is given to sb but which soon becomes unpleasant: *He inherited a poisoned chalice when he took over the job as union leader.*

poke

have a ,poke a'round (*informal*)

look carefully around a place to see what you can find; try to find out information about sb/sth: *I thought I'd go and have a poke around the new shopping centre later. Do you want to come with me?*

take a 'poke at sb/sth (*old-fashioned, AmE, informal*)

make an unkind remark about sb/sth; laugh at sb/sth: *Then he took a poke at my hair, telling me I looked like a scarecrow!*

(buy) a pig in a poke → **pig**
poke fun at sb/sth = make fun of sb/sth → **fun**
poke/stick your nose in/into sth → **nose**

poker

(as) stiff as a poker → **stiff**

pole

be up the 'pole (*old-fashioned, BrE, informal*)

1 be mad, crazy, etc: *My neighbour's really up the pole. I can hear him singing and shouting night after night.*
2 be in trouble or difficulties: *The whole industry is up the pole at the moment. Nobody knows what its future will be.*

not touch sb/sth with a ten-foot pole → **touch**

poles

be poles/worlds apart → **apart**

polish

spit and polish → **spit**

political

a po,litical 'football

an issue or problem that causes argument and disagreement and that different political groups use to gain votes: *It is sad that education is still being used as a political football, instead of action being taken to improve it.*

politically

po,litically cor'rect (*abbr.* **PC**)

used to describe language or behaviour that deliberately tries to avoid offending particular groups of people: *These days everybody has to be politically correct. I even heard someone the other day calling a short person 'vertically challenged'!*

pomp

pomp and 'circumstance

formal and impressive ceremony: *The Prince was welcomed with warmth, but not with all the pomp and circumstance he was used to.*

pond

across the 'pond (*informal*)

on the other side of the Atlantic Ocean from Britain/the US: *And now let's hear some news and gossip from across the pond, with our reporter in New York.*

pony

(on) Shanks's pony → **Shanks**

poor

be a/the ,poor man's 'sb/'sth

be a person or thing that is similar to but of a lower quality than a particular famous person or thing: *Try some of this sparkling white wine—the poor man's champagne.*

be/come a poor second, third, etc. (*especially BrE*)

finish a long way behind the winner in a race, competition, etc: *The Socialists won the election easily* with 40% of the vote, with the Democrats coming a poor second with only 26%.

(as) poor as a church 'mouse
very poor: *She was as poor as a church mouse, living on a tiny pension.*

,poor old 'sb/'sth (*informal*)
used to express sympathy: *Poor old Mrs Kirk's just gone into hospital again.* ◇ *She sat down to rest her poor old legs.*

a poor re'lation
sb/sth with less importance, respect or power than others: *At the peace conference, our country was treated very much as the poor relation.*

in good/poor spirits → spirits
take a dim/poor view of sb/sth → view

pop

pop your 'clogs (*BrE, humorous*)
die

pop the 'question (*informal*)
ask sb to marry you: *Where were you when he popped the question?*

your eyes nearly pop out of your head → eyes

popular

by popular de'mand
because a lot of people have asked for sth: *By popular demand, the play will run for another week.*

contrary to popular belief/opinion → contrary

porkies

tell porkies → tell

porridge

do 'porridge (*BrE, informal*)
be in prison serving a sentence: *He's doing porridge again, this time for armed robbery.*

port

any port in a 'storm (*saying*)
when you are in trouble you will accept help, etc. that would be unacceptable otherwise: *When he went to work there he had been unemployed for a year. It was a case of any port in a storm.*

a ,port of 'call (*informal*)
a place where you go or stop for a short time, especially when you are going to several places: *Our first port of call this morning is the bank.*

❶ ORIGIN
These two idioms refer to ports where ships stop for a short time during a voyage.

pose

strike a pose/an attitude → strike

positive

proof positive → proof
think positive → think

possessed

like a man/woman pos'sessed; like one pos'sessed
with a lot of force or energy: *He flew out of the room like a man possessed.*

what(ever) pos'sessed sb to do sth?
used to ask why sb did sth bad, stupid, unexpected, etc: *'She drove straight to the airport and got on the first plane.' 'What possessed her to do that?'*

❶ ORIGIN
This phrase refers to the belief that people can be possessed by an evil spirit.

possession

possession is nine points/tenths/parts of the 'law (*saying*)
if you already have or control sth, it is difficult for sb else to take it away from you, even if they have the legal right to it

take pos'session (of sth) (*formal*)
become the owner of sth: *He couldn't pay his taxes, so the government took possession of his property.*

leave the field clear for sb → leave
leave sb in possession of the field → leave

possibility

beyond/within the realms of possibility → realms

possible

as quickly, much, soon, etc. as 'possible
as quickly, much, soon, etc. as you can: *We will get your order to you as soon as possible.*

possum

play possum → play

post

be driven, pushed, etc. from pillar to post → pillar
(as) deaf as a post → deaf
pip sb at/to the post → pip

postal

go 'postal (*AmE, informal*)
become extremely angry or start behaving in a violent and angry way: *According to one eye witness, the man 'went postal, and started hitting his computer'.*

❶ ORIGIN
This expression originated in the USA in the 1990s, where there were several incidents of postal workers losing control and shooting members of the public in post offices.

posted

keep sb 'posted (on/of/about sth) (*informal*)
keep sb informed: *There's no news at the moment,*

but I'll keep you posted. ◇ *He said he'd keep me posted of his movements.*

post-haste

,post-'haste *(literary)*
with great speed: *I shall send the invitations off post-haste.*

pot

go (all) to 'pot *(informal)*
be spoiled because people are not working hard or taking care of things: *This whole country's going to pot.* ◇ *She used to write very nicely, but her handwriting's really gone to pot recently.*

the ,pot calling the kettle 'black *(saying, informal)*
used to say that you should not criticize sb for a fault that you have yourself: *'You haven't done any work all morning.' 'Neither have you! Talk about the pot calling the kettle black!'*

> ❶ ORIGIN
> When cooking was done over a fire, the smoke made cooking pots turn black.

take ,pot 'luck *(informal)*
choose sth or go somewhere without knowing very much about it, but hope that it will be good, pleasant, etc: *'Did somebody recommend the hotel to you?' 'No, we just took pot luck. It was the first hotel in the brochure.'* ◇ *You're welcome to stay for supper, but you'll have to take pot luck* (= eat whatever is available).

get/pour/put a quart into a pint pot → **quart**
in the melting pot → **melting**
a watched pot never boils → **watched**

potato

a couch potato → **couch**
a hot potato → **hot**

potatoes

small potatoes → **small**

potshot

take a 'potshot/'potshots (at sb/sth) *(informal)*
1 fire at sb without aiming carefully: *Somebody took a potshot at him as he drove past.*
2 criticize sb suddenly and without thinking: *The newspapers took potshots at his attempts to get into the movie business.*

pound

(take, demand, etc.) your pound of 'flesh
(take, demand, etc.) the full amount that sb owes you, even if this will cause them trouble or suffering: *They want their pound of flesh; they want every penny we owe them by next Monday.* ◇ *I didn't realize working here was going to be such hard*

work. *They really demand their pound of flesh, don't they?*

> ❶ ORIGIN
> This phrase comes from Shakespeare's *Merchant of Venice*, in which the moneylender Shylock demanded a pound of flesh from Antonio's body if he could not pay back the money he borrowed.

in for a penny, in for a pound → **penny**
an ounce of prevention is better than a pound of cure = prevention is better than cure → **prevention**

pour

pour your 'heart out (to sb)
tell sb all about your troubles, feelings, etc: *When I asked her what was the matter, she burst into tears and poured out her heart to me.*

pour oil on troubled 'water(s)
try to settle a disagreement or dispute; take action which will calm a tense or dangerous situation: *There's going to be big trouble unless somebody pours oil on troubled waters fast.* ◇ *He was always having rows with his son and his wife's attempts to pour oil on troubled water usually made things worse.*

> ❶ ORIGIN
> Sailors used to pour oil on a rough sea to calm the water in order to make a sea rescue easier.

get/pour/put a quart into a pint pot → **quart**
heap/pour scorn on sb/sth → **scorn**
pour/throw cold water on sth → **cold**

pours

it never rains but it pours → **rains**
when it rains, it pours → **rains**

powder

keep your 'powder dry *(old-fashioned)*
remain ready for a possible emergency: *The minister refused to be specific about the government's plans, but it appears that they are keeping their powder dry.*

(go to) powder your 'nose *(old-fashioned or humorous)*
a polite way of referring to the fact that a woman is going to the toilet: *I'm just going to powder my nose and I'll be with you in a minute.*

take a 'powder *(AmE, informal)*
leave suddenly; run away: *She hung about all morning getting in my way, so in the end I told her to take a powder.*

power

be the (real) power behind the 'throne
be the person who really controls a family, business, country, etc., even though people think sb else controls it: *It's not the president who makes the*

important decisions; his wife is the real power behind the throne.

do sb/sth a 'power/'world of good (old-fashioned)
do sb/sth a lot of good; benefit sb/sth: *She's under a lot of stress at work, and a few days at the seaside would do her a power of good.*

more power to sb's 'elbow (old-fashioned, BrE, informal)
used to express support or encouragement for sb to do sth: *'He's so angry at his train being late every morning that he's made an official complaint.' 'Good for him. More power to his elbow.'*

the corridors of power → corridors

powers

the ˌpowers that 'be (often ironic)
the people who control a country, organization, etc: *It's the powers that be who decide things. We just have to live with their decisions.*

practical

for (all) 'practical purposes
in actual fact; in reality: *Your daughter does so little work at school, Mrs Brown, that for all practical purposes she might as well not be here at all.*

(play) a ˌpractical 'joke (on sb)
play a trick on sb which involves using an object, physical action, etc: *They put a frog in his bed as a practical joke.* ▶ a ˌpractical 'joker *noun* a person who plays practical jokes

practice

in 'practice
in reality; in fact; in a real or normal situation: *The pilot is there to fly the plane, but in practice it flies itself most of the time.* ◇ *In theory it should work very well, but in practice it doesn't.*

ˌin/ˌout of 'practice
having practised/having not practised a skill regularly for a period of time: *I've got to keep in practice if I'm going to win this race.* ◇ *I haven't played the piano for a while so I'm a bit out of practice.*

ˌpractice makes 'perfect (saying)
a way of encouraging people by telling them that if you do an activity regularly you will become very good at it: *If you want to learn a language, speak it as much as you can. Practice makes perfect!*

put sth into 'practice
actually do or carry out sth which was only planned or talked about before: *It's not always easy to put your ideas into practice.*

make a habit/practice of sth → habit
sharp practice → sharp

practise (BrE) (AmE practice)

ˌpractise what you 'preach (saying)
live or act the way you advise others to live or act:

He's always telling me to go on a diet, but he doesn't practise what he preaches. He needs to lose weight too!

praise

praise sb/sth to the 'skies
praise sb/sth very much; say sb/sth is very good, beautiful, etc: *She's always praising you to the skies: she says she's never had such a good assistant before.*

damn sb/sth with faint praise → damn

praises

sing sb's/sth's praises → sing

prayer

not have a 'prayer (of doing sth)
have no chance of succeeding: *She's done no work at all this term, so she doesn't have a prayer of passing her exams.*

on a wing and a prayer → wing

prayers

the answer to sb's prayers → answer

preach

preach to the con'verted
tell people to support a view or idea when they already support it: *Why do they keep telling us about the importance of women in industry? They're preaching to the converted here.*

practise what you preach → practise

precious

precious 'few/'little (informal)
very few/little: *There are precious few places around here where you can get really good Indian food.* ◇ *Look, darling, don't ask me for any more pocket money this month. We've got precious little money for anything at the moment.*

precise

to be (more) pre'cise (also **more pre'cisely**)
used to show that you are giving more detailed and accurate information about sth you have just mentioned: *The shelf is about a metre long—well, 98 cm, to be precise.* ◇ *The problem is due to discipline, or, more precisely, the lack of discipline, in schools.*

preference

give (a) preference to sb/sth
treat sb/sth in a way that gives them an advantage over other people or things: *Preference will be given to graduates of this university.*

in preference to sb/sth
rather than sb/sth: *She was chosen in preference to her sister.*

pregnant

a pregnant 'pause/'silence
a pause/silence in which everyone is waiting or listening for sth, or a moment of silence which is full of meaning: *There was a pregnant pause while everyone waited to hear what she had to say.*

prejudice

without 'prejudice (to sth) (*law*)
without affecting any other legal matter: *They agreed to pay compensation without prejudice (= without admitting guilt).*

premium

at a 'premium
having great value or importance; difficult or expensive to buy, find, obtain, etc: *During a war, ordinary foods like bread or meat are often at a premium.* ◇ *Good mathematics teachers are always at a premium in this country.*

put/place a 'premium on sth
consider sth very important or valuable: *This company puts a high premium on the loyalty of its employees.*

prepare

prepare the 'ground (for sth)
do something which makes it possible or easier for sth to happen: *By making her his deputy, the chairman was preparing the ground for her to replace him after he retired.* ◇ *The meeting was to prepare the ground for next week's peace talks.*

presence

in the presence of 'sb; in sb's 'presence
with sb in the same place: *The document was signed in the presence of two witnesses.* ◇ *She asked them not to discuss the matter in her presence.*

make your presence 'felt
do sth which makes people notice your importance, strength, abilities, etc: *In the first half of the game the Turkish team really made their presence felt.* ◇ *The demonstrators made their presence felt by shouting and waving banners.*

,presence of 'mind
the ability to react quickly and stay calm in a difficult or dangerous situation: *A little girl from Leeds showed remarkable presence of mind yesterday when she saved her brothers from a fire in their home.* ◇ *The boy had the presence of mind to switch off the gas.*

present

all ,present and cor'rect (*BrE*) (*AmE* all ,present and ac'counted for) (*spoken*)
used to say that all the things or people who should be there are now there: *'Now, is everybody here?' 'All present and correct, Sir!'*

at 'present
now; at the moment: *How many people are living in this house at present?*

make a 'present of sth (to sb)
make it easy for sb to take or steal sth from you, or to gain an advantage over you, because you have been careless: *Before you go out, lock all the doors and windows. Don't make a present of your property (to thieves).*

on 'present form
judging by sb/sth's present performance or behaviour; as things are at the moment: *On present form I'd say he should win easily.* ◇ *A watercolour by Durant could sell for well over a million on present form.*

present company ex'cepted (also excepting present 'company)
used as a polite remark to show that the criticisms you are making are not directed at the people you are talking to: *My feeling is that the people around here, present company excepted of course, are rather unfriendly.*

the ,present 'day
modern times; now: *These customs have continued right up to the present day.* ◇ *Present-day attitudes to women are very different.*

for the moment/present = for the time being ➔ time
(there's) no time like the present ➔ time

press

get/have a good, bad, etc. 'press
get/have good, bad, etc. things said about you in the newspapers, on television, etc: *The royal family's been getting a good press recently, for a change.* ◇ *Zoos have been getting a bad press over the last few years.*

,press (the) 'flesh
(of a famous person or a politician) shake hands with members of the public in order to persuade them to vote for you: *The presidential candidates were out on the streets again today, smiling for the cameras and pressing the flesh.*

,press sth 'home
make a point in an argument or discussion with force: *She kept pressing home the point that more money should be spent on education.*

press ,home your ad'vantage
make good use of the fact that you are in a stronger position than your opponent, enemy, etc: *Once they realized that the management was so weak, the union leaders pressed home their advantage and asked for another three days' holiday.*

,press sb/sth into 'service
use sb/sth for a purpose that they were not trained or intended for because there is nobody or nothing

else available: *Every type of boat was pressed into service to rescue passengers from the sinking ferry.*

❶ ORIGIN
This expression comes from the eighteenth century, when groups called *press gangs* forced young men to join the military.

the gutter press ➔ **gutter**
hot off the press ➔ **hot**
press/push the panic button ➔ **panic**

pressed

be pressed/pushed for money, space, time, etc.
have very little money, time, etc: *I'll have to do those letters tomorrow—I'm a bit pushed for time this afternoon.* ◇ *I'm afraid we're a bit pushed for space in this office.*

hard pressed/pushed to do sth ➔ **hard**

pressure

put 'pressure on sb (to do sth); bring pressure to 'bear (on sb) (to do sth)
force or try to persuade sb to do sth: *The landlord is putting pressure on us to move out.* ◇ *If the ministry won't listen, we'll have to bring some more pressure to bear.*

under 'pressure
1 if a liquid or a gas is kept **under pressure**, it is forced into a container so that when the container is opened, the liquid or gas escapes quickly
2 being forced to do sth: *The director is under increasing pressure to resign.*
3 made to feel anxious about sth you have to do: *The team performs well under pressure.*

presto

hey presto ➔ **hey**

pretences *(BrE)* *(AmE* **pretenses)**

by/on/under false pretences ➔ **false**

pretty

not just a pretty 'face *(humorous)*
used to emphasize that you have particular skills or qualities: *'I hear you passed all your exams.' 'Yes, I'm not just a pretty face, you know!'*

not a pretty 'sight *(humorous)*
a very unpleasant or shocking sight: *When he stepped out of that boxing ring, he wasn't a pretty sight, I can tell you.*

(as) ,pretty as a 'picture
very pretty: *This charming cottage dates back to the 15th century and is as pretty as a picture, with its thatched roof and secluded garden.*

pretty 'much/'well *(BrE* also **pretty 'nearly)** *(AmE* also **pretty 'near)** *(spoken)*
almost; just about: *This nightclub is pretty much the best this town can offer.* ◇ *I'm pretty well dis-*

gusted by your behaviour.* ◇ *It's worth pretty near a thousand dollars.*

a pretty 'penny *(old-fashioned)*
a lot of money: *Have you seen the neighbour's new car? That must have cost a pretty penny.*

be sitting pretty ➔ **sitting**

prevention

pre,vention is better than 'cure *(BrE)* *(AmE* **an ounce of pre,vention is better than a pound of 'cure)** *(saying)*
it is better to stop sth bad from happening rather than try to deal with the problems after it has happened: *Remember that prevention is better than cure, so brush your teeth at least twice a day and visit your dentist for regular check-ups.*

preview

a sneak preview ➔ **sneak**

prey

be/fall 'prey to sth *(formal)*
be harmed or affected by sth bad: *He was often prey to doubt and despair.* ◇ *Thousands of small businesses are falling prey to high interest rates.*

❷ NOTE
Prey is an animal, a bird, etc. that is hunted, killed and eaten by another animal.

,prey on sb's 'mind *(also* **,play on sb's 'mind)**
worry or trouble sb very much: *The death of his father is really preying on his mind at the moment. He thinks it was his fault.* ◇ *The question of whether to accept the new job and move to Scotland had been playing on his mind for days.*

price

at 'any price
without considering how much it might cost or how many unpleasant things you might have to do (to achieve sth): *They wanted victory at any price.* ◇ *Be elected president at any price; that's his aim.*

at a 'price
(get sth) only by paying a high price, by spending a lot of time, effort, etc: *Accommodation is only available in the city centre at a price.* ◇ *He knew he could be a successful businessman, but at a price— he'd hardly ever see his family.*

beyond/without 'price *(formal or literary)*
so valuable that it cannot be bought; priceless: *These paintings are almost beyond price.*

not at 'any price
used to say that no amount of money would persuade you to do or sell sth: *'What about joining the army?' 'Not at any price. That's the last thing I want to do.'*

a 'price on sb's head
a reward for finding or killing a criminal: *In the*

Wild West there were cowboys who used to hunt down any man with a price on his head.

price yourself/sth out of the 'market
demand such a high price for sth that no one wants to buy it: *If you charge too much, you'll price yourself out of the market.*

put a 'price on sth
give the value of sth in money: *Any businessman will tell you it's hard to put a price on public confidence.* ◇ *I've never seen a gun like this before, so I'm afraid I can't put a price on it.*

what price 'sth ... ? (*BrE, spoken*)
1 used to say that you think that sth you have achieved may not be worth all the problems and difficulties it causes: *What price fame and fortune?*
2 used to say that sth seems unlikely: *What price England winning the World Cup?*

cheap at twice the price = cheap at the price → **cheap**
everyone has their price = every man has his price → **man**
pay the price/penalty (for sth/for doing sth) → **pay**

prick

prick your 'conscience; your 'conscience pricks you
make you feel guilty about sth; feel guilty about sth: *Her conscience pricked her as she lied to her sister.*

,prick up your 'ears; your 'ears prick up
start to listen carefully: '*And the winner is ... ' He pricked up his ears. ' ... Michael Poole.*'

❶ ORIGIN
This expression refers to the way dogs, horses and other animals raise their ears when they listen with attention.

pricks

kick against the pricks → **kick**
your conscience pricks you = prick your conscience → **prick**

pride

your ,pride and 'joy
sb/sth that you are very proud and pleased to have: *That car's his pride and joy.* ◇ *His granddaughter is his real pride and joy.*

pride comes before a 'fall (*saying*)
if you are too proud or confident, sth may happen which will make you look foolish: *Remember, John, pride comes before a fall. Don't go round talking about your success in business all the time.*

(give sth) pride of 'place
(give sth) the best or most important position: *All the entries in the flower show are good, but pride of place must go to Cynthia Jones's roses.* ◇ *Sally gave her award pride of place on the mantelpiece.*

take 'pride in sb/sth
be proud of sb/sth; consider sth to be worth doing

well: *She takes a lot of pride in running such a successful business.*

swallow your pride → **swallow**

prim

prim and 'proper
(of a person) very correctly behaved and easily shocked by anything that is rude: *Don't invite her to the party. She's so prim and proper.*

prima

(a) ,prima 'donna (*from Italian, disapproving*)
a person who thinks they are very important because they are good at sth, and who behaves badly when they do not get what they want: *Stop behaving like a prima donna—you're not the only person around here.* ◇ *In her new film, Victoria plays a prima donna television presenter.*

❷ NOTE
The *prima donna* is the main woman singer in an opera performance or an opera company. The phrase means 'first lady'.

prime

in the prime of (your) 'life
at the time in your life when you are strongest or most successful: *He was struck down in the prime of his life by a heart attack.* ◇ *What do you mean, I'm old? I'm still in the prime of life!*

a prime 'mover
a person or a thing that starts sth and has an important influence on its development: *The prime mover in setting up the group was ex-lawyer James Stanley.* ◇ *Economic factors are the prime mover of change.*

prime the 'pump
give sb, an organization, etc. financial help in order to support a project, business, etc. when it is beginning: *The government should really prime the pump in new high technology projects. That's the only way they'll be able to survive in the current economic climate.* ▶ **'pump-priming** *noun*: *The nation is relying on pump-priming to get the economy started.*

primrose

the primrose 'path (to ruin, destruction, etc.) (*literary*)
an easy life that is full of pleasure but that causes you harm in the end: *If we followed your advice we'd all be walking down the primrose path to ruin.*

❶ ORIGIN
This phrase comes from Shakespeare's play *Hamlet*.

Prince

,Prince 'Charming (*usually humorous*)
a man who seems to be a perfect boyfriend or hus-

band because he is attractive, kind, etc: *I'm still waiting for my Prince Charming!*

ⓘ ORIGIN
This expression refers to a character in fairy tales such as *Cinderella*.

principle

in 'principle
1 according to the general principles or theory: *In principle it should work in all different types of climate, but we haven't actually tried it out abroad yet.*
2 in general but not necessarily in detail: *In principle I agree with you, but I'm not sure that it's the most effective solution to the problem.*

on 'principle
because of your beliefs or ideas about what is right or how people should behave: *I quite like meat, but I don't eat it on principle.*

print

get into 'print
have your work printed and published (for the first time): *If you want to get into print, you have to know the right people.*

in 'print
1 (of a book) still available from the company that publishes it: *Is this edition still in print?*
2 (of a person's work) printed in a book, newspaper, etc: *It was the first time he had seen his name in print.*

out of 'print
(of a book) no longer available from the company that publishes it: *Her first novel is now out of print.*

the fine print = the small print → **small**
a licence to print money → **licence**

printed

the printed 'word/'page
stories, articles, etc. printed in a book, magazine, newspaper, etc.

not worth the paper it's printed/written on → **worth**

priorities

get your pri'orities right/straight
do or get things in the right order of importance: *If you think enjoying yourself is more important, then you need to get your priorities straight.* ◇ *The country has got its priorities right—it has invested in industry to achieve economic success.*

private

a ˌprivate 'eye (*informal*)
a detective who is not in the police, but who can be employed to find out information, find a missing person, follow sb, etc: *They hired a private eye to look for more evidence.*

private 'parts
a polite way of referring to the sexual organs without saying their names

prizes

(there are) no prizes for guessing what … , who … , etc. (*informal*)
(it is) not difficult to guess or find the answer to sth: *No prizes for guessing who does all the work round here.*

pro

quid pro quo → **quid**

probability

in ˌall proba'bility (*written*)
very probably: *The changes were, in all probability, made before 1600.*

problem

do you have a 'problem with that? (*spoken*)
used to show that you are impatient with sb who disagrees with you

ˌit's/ˌthat's not 'my problem (*spoken, informal*)
used to show that you do not care about sb else's difficulties: *Well, I'm sorry you feel that way, but I'm afraid it's not my problem.*

no 'problem (*spoken, informal*)
1 (also **not a 'problem**) used for saying that you can do sth or are happy to do sth for sb: *'Can you be here at 7.30 tomorrow morning?' 'No problem.'*
2 used after sb has thanked you or said they are sorry for sth: *'Thanks for the ride.' 'No problem.'*

that's 'your, 'his, etc. problem (*spoken, informal*)
used to show that you think sb should deal with their own difficulties: *If she doesn't like it, that's her problem, not mine!*

what's your problem? (*spoken, informal*)
used to show that you think sb is being unreasonable: *What's your problem? I only asked if you could help me for ten minutes.*

problems

have, etc. teething problems/troubles → **teething**

probs

no 'probs (*spoken*)
used to mean 'there is no problem': *I can let you have it by next week, no probs.*

process

in the 'process (of doing sth)
1 while doing sth: *In the process of cleaning the furniture, I found six pound coins.* ◇ *He was supposed to be cutting my hair, but he nearly cut off my ear in the process.*
2 in the middle of doing sth: *We're still in the process of trying to find somewhere to live.*

prodigal

a/the prodigal 'son (*formal, disapproving* or *humorous*)

a person who leaves home as a young man and wastes his money and time on a life of pleasure, but who is later sorry about this and returns to his family: *All the family went to the airport to welcome home the prodigal son.*

ℹ️ **ORIGIN**
This expression comes from a story in the Bible.

produce

come up with/deliver/produce the goods → **goods**

production

on pro'duction of sth (*formal*)

when you show sth: *Discounts will only be given on production of your student ID card.*

profile

in 'profile

(of a face) seen from the side: *In profile he's got a nose like an eagle!*

adopt, keep, etc. a ˌhigh/ˌlow 'profile

try to/try not to attract other people's interest, attention, etc: *If I were you, I'd try and keep a low profile until she's forgotten about the whole thing.* ◇ *In the run-up to the elections all three candidates maintained a high profile.*

prolong

proˌlong the 'agony

make an unpleasant situation last longer than is necessary: *Don't prolong the agony. Just say yes or no, and then I'll know where I stand.*

promise

I (can) 'promise you (*informal*)

used as a way of encouraging or warning sb about sth: *I can promise you, you'll have a wonderful time.* ◇ *If you don't take my advice, you'll regret it, I promise you.*

promise (sb) the 'moon/'earth/'world (*informal*)

make very big or impossible promises that you are unlikely to keep: *He promised her the moon, but after ten years of marriage they hardly had enough to live on.*

promised

the promised 'land

a place or situation in which people expect to find happiness, wealth, freedom etc: *For millions of people in Europe, the USA was seen as the promised land.* ◇ *The Prime Minister's speech seemed to suggest that we had already reached the promised land.*

ℹ️ **ORIGIN**
This expression comes from the Bible and refers to the land that God promised the Israelites.

promises

he, it, etc. promises 'well

sb/sth seems likely to do well in future: *The new trainee promises well.* ◇ *The harvest promises well this year.*

proof

the proof of the 'pudding (is in the 'eating) (*saying*)

you can only say sth is a success after it has actually been tried out or used: *I know you didn't think it was a very good product, but just look at the fantastic sales figures. That's the proof of the pudding.*

proof 'positive

definite or convincing proof: *It's proof positive of her belief in the company that she's investing her own money in it.*

be living proof of sth → **living**

prop

ˌprop up the 'bar (*informal, disapproving*)

spend a lot of time drinking in a pub or a bar: *'Where's Paul?' 'Propping up the bar in the King's Head, as usual.'*

proper

ˌgood and 'proper (*BrE, spoken*)

completely; thoroughly: *That's messed things up good and proper.*

prim and proper → **prim**

property

be public property → **public**

prophet

a ˌprophet of 'doom; a 'doom merchant

a person who always expects that things will go very badly: *Various prophets of doom have suggested that standards in education are worse than ever.*

proportion

ˌkeep sth in pro'portion

react to sth in a sensible way and not think it is worse or more serious than it really is: *Listen, I know you're all upset but let's try to keep things in proportion, shall we?*

out of (all) pro'portion (to sth)

greater or more important, serious, etc. than it really is or should be: *When you're depressed, it's very easy to get things out of proportion.* ◇ *The punishment is out of all proportion to the crime.*

propose

propose a 'toast (to sb)

ask people to wish sb health, happiness and success by raising their glasses and drinking: *I'd like to propose a toast to the bride and groom.*

❶ ORIGIN
In the past, people liked to dip a piece of toast into their wine or beer, either to improve the flavour, or to collect the material that settled at the bottom.

pros

the pros and 'cons (of sth)
the arguments for and against sth; the advantages and disadvantages (of sth): *Your idea is interesting, but let's look carefully at its pros and cons before we take any decisions.*

❶ ORIGIN
This expression comes from the Latin words *pro*, meaning 'for', and *contra*, meaning 'against'.

protest

under 'protest
unwillingly and after expressing disagreement: *The new contract was finally accepted, but only under protest.*

proud

do sb 'proud (*old-fashioned, BrE*)
look after a guest very well, especially by giving them good food, entertainment, etc: *We spent the holidays with them and they really did us proud.*

do yourself/sb 'proud
do sth that makes you proud of yourself or that makes other people proud of you: *The team did us proud by winning 3-0 on Saturday.*

proves

the exception (that) proves the rule → exception

providence

tempt fate/providence → tempt

prowl

be/go on the 'prowl
1 (of animals) move around quietly while hunting for food: *Our cats go on the prowl at night, and then they sleep here all day.*
2 (of people) be moving around quietly because you are trying to catch sb or intending to commit a crime: *Look out for burglars on the prowl. If you see anything suspicious, call the police immediately.*

psychological

the ,psychological 'moment
the best time to do sth in order for it to be successful: *The publication of her first novel came at the psychological moment, and she became well known very quickly.*

pub

a 'pub crawl (*BrE, informal*)
a visit to several pubs, going straight from one to the next and drinking in each one: *We went on a pub crawl last night.*

Public

John Q. Public = Joe Public → Joe

public

be ,public 'property
be known or talked about by everyone: *When you're famous, you and your life suddenly become public property.*

go 'public
1 (of a company) sell shares to the public: *We're hoping to go public early next year.*
2 make a public statement about a private matter because you think this is the right thing to do: *He decided to go public about his drug problem in order to warn other athletes of the dangers.*

in the public 'eye
well known because you are often seen on television or in newspapers: *The royal family are always in the public eye.*

public enemy number one
a person or a thing that is thought to be the greatest threat to a group or community: *Genetically modified foods have replaced nuclear power as public enemy number one.* ◇ *The gangster Kline became America's public enemy number one during the Depression.*

be common/public knowledge → knowledge
wash your dirty linen in public → wash

pudding

over-egg the pudding → over-egg
the proof of the pudding (is in the eating) → proof

puff

,puff and 'pant/'blow (*informal*)
breathe quickly and loudly through your mouth after physical effort: *Eventually, puffing and panting, he arrived at the gate.*

huff and puff → huff

puffed

be puffed up with 'pride, etc.
be too full of pride, etc: *He felt grown-up, puffed up with self-importance.*

pull

on the 'pull (*BrE, slang*)
(of a person) trying to find a sexual partner: *What are you all dressed up for? Are you going out on the pull again tonight?*

pull the ˌcarpet/ˌrug out from under sb's 'feet (informal)

take the help, support or confidence away from sb suddenly: *I was just about to ask her out when she pulled the rug out from under my feet by telling me she's getting married next month.* ◊ *The bank's pulled the carpet out from under his feet, unfortunately. It looks as if he'll have to sell the business.*

pull/make 'faces/a 'face (at sb/sth)

produce an expression on your face to show that you do not like sb/sth or in order to make sb laugh: *What are you pulling a face at now?* ◊ *Every time I give him fish for lunch, he makes a face.* ◊ *The little girl stood outside the restaurant window making faces at everybody.*

pull a 'fast one (on sb) (slang)

tell lies or cheat sb to get their money, possessions, etc.; deceive sb: *Don't try to pull a fast one on me. I'm not stupid, you know.*

pull sb's 'leg (informal)

tell sb sth which is not true, as a joke: *'You came first! You've won the prize!' 'Really? Or are you just pulling my leg?'*

pull the 'other one (—it's got bells on!) (BrE, spoken)

used to show that you do not believe what sb has just said: *'I've been offered a job in New York.' 'Pull the other one!' 'No, really!'*

pull out all the 'stops (informal)

do everything you can to make sth successful: *We'll have to pull out all the stops to get this order ready by the end of the week.*

❶ ORIGIN
You pull out the *stops* on an organ when you want to make the music very loud.

pull the 'plug on sth (informal)

destroy or bring an end to sth, for example sb's plans, a project, etc: *The banks are threatening to pull the plug on the project.* ◊ *They've pulled the plug on that new comedy programme on Channel Four.*

pull your 'punches (informal)

(usually used in negative sentences) express sth less strongly than you are able to, for example to avoid upsetting or shocking sb: *Her articles certainly don't pull any punches.* ◊ *I don't believe in pulling punches. If they're wrong, let's say so.*

pull sth/a ˌrabbit out of the 'hat (informal)

suddenly produce sth as a solution to a problem: *We had almost given up hope when Mick pulled a rabbit out of the hat by coming up with a great new idea.*

pull 'rank (on sb)

make unfair use of your senior position, authority, etc. in an organization, etc: *I was really looking forward to going to Rome on business, but then my manager pulled rank on me and said she was going instead.*

❶ NOTE
The position, especially a high one, that sb has in the army, etc. is called a *rank*.

pull your 'socks up (BrE, informal)

work harder, be more determined, etc: *You really must pull your socks up if you want to beat Jackie in the competition.*

pull 'strings (for sb) (AmE also pull 'wires) (informal)

use your influence in order to get an advantage for sb: *She doesn't want me to pull any strings for her; she says she prefers to be offered a place on her own merit.* ◊ *I'm sure his uncle in the BBC must have pulled strings for him.*

pull the 'strings

(secretly) control the actions of other people: *I don't understand this situation at all. I want to know exactly who is pulling the strings.*

❶ ORIGIN
These two expressions refer to the strings which are attached to puppets, marionettes, etc.

pull up 'stakes (AmE)

leave your home and go to live in a different place: *When the factories and businesses closed, most of the community were forced to pull up stakes and move south.*

pull your 'weight

do your fair share of the work: *If everyone pulls their weight we're going to win this prize with no trouble at all.* ◊ *She's annoyed because she feels that certain people are not pulling their weight.*

pull the 'wool over sb's eyes (informal)

deceive sb; hide the truth from sb: *It's no use you trying to pull the wool over my eyes; you didn't go to school again today, did you?*

❶ ORIGIN
This idiom comes from the time when people wore wigs made out of wool. If someone pulled the wig down over these people's eyes, they would not be able to see.

pull yourself to'gether

bring your feelings under control and start acting normally; stop feeling sorry for yourself: *I know she's upset but it's time for her to pull herself together and stop crying.*

bring/pull sb up short → short
drag/pull yourself up by your (own) bootstraps → bootstraps
draw/pull in your horns → horns
get/pull your finger out → finger

pulse

have/keep your finger on the pulse (of sth) → finger

pump

pump sb full of sth
fill sb with sth, especially drugs: *They pumped her full of painkillers.*

pump 'iron (*informal*)
do exercises in which you lift heavy weights in order to strengthen your muscles: *I should take more exercise, but I'm not interested in pumping iron at the local gym three evenings a week.*

pump sb's 'stomach
remove the contents of sb's stomach using a pump, because they have swallowed sth harmful: *She had to go to the hospital and* **have her stomach pumped**.

all hands to the pump → **hands**
prime the pump → **prime**

Punch

(as) pleased as Punch → **pleased**

punch

he, she, etc. couldn't punch his, her, etc. way out of a paper bag (*informal, humorous*)
a person is so weak, shy, etc. that they would never dare react forcefully to sth: *You don't need to worry about what Jim would do; he couldn't punch his way out of a paper bag.*

pack a (hard, etc.) punch → **pack**

punches

pull your punches → **pull**
roll with the punches → **roll**

pup

sell sb/buy a 'pup (*old-fashioned, BrE, informal*)
sell sb or be sold sth that has no value or is worth much less than the price paid for it: *I'm wondering whether this really is a genuine Rolex. Do you think I've been sold a pup?*

ℹ️ ORIGIN
This expression refers to an old market trick of putting a puppy in a bag and selling it as a young pig.

pure

,pure and 'simple
and nothing else: *They are terrorists, pure and simple, and must be punished.* ▶ **,purely and 'simply** *adv.*: *I am basing my opinion purely and simply on the facts of the case.*

(as) pure as the driven 'snow (*often humorous*)
innocent or morally good: *I don't think you're really in a position to criticize her. You're hardly as pure as the driven snow yourself!*

purpose

(do sth) on 'purpose
(do sth) deliberately: *He took the worst jobs he*

could find on purpose, and then wrote a book about his experiences.* ◇ *Don't shout at me like that. I didn't break it on purpose.*

to little/good/some/no 'purpose (*formal*)
with little, good, etc. result or effect: *Another meeting was held, to little purpose.* ◇ *She had used the profits to good purpose and upgraded their software.*

accidentally on purpose → **accidentally**
serve the purpose (of doing sth) = serve a, his, its, etc. purpose → **serve**

purposes

be/talk at cross purposes → **cross**
for/to all intents and purposes → **intents**
for (all) practical purposes → **practical**

purse

control/hold the 'purse strings (*informal*)
be the person who controls the amount of money spent and the way in which it is spent: *I'm the one who controls the purse strings in this office, and you must come to me if you want any more money.*

make a silk purse out of a sow's ear → **silk**

pursuit

in hot pursuit (of sb/sth) → **hot**

push

give sb/get the 'push (*BrE, informal*)
1 tell sb/be told to leave your job: *He was stealing from the firm so the manager gave him the push.* ◇ *The company is in trouble. Who will be the next to get the push?*
2 end a relationship with sb/be rejected by sb you have had a relationship with: *His girlfriend gave him the push and he's a bit upset.* ◇ *Why is it always me that gets the push? What's wrong with me?*

if/when push comes to 'shove (*informal*)
if/when there is no other choice; if/when everything else has failed: *I don't want to sell the house, but if push comes to shove, I might have to.*

push the 'boat out (*BrE, informal*)
spend a lot of money on food, drinks, etc. when celebrating a special occasion: *They really pushed the boat out for their daughter's wedding.*

push the 'envelope
do sth in an extreme way in order to find out to what degree sth is possible: *Advertisements seem to be pushing the envelope of taste every day.* ◇ *People these days like to push the envelope with extreme sports.*

ℹ️ ORIGIN
This expression comes from the aeroplane industry. A plane's *envelope* was the limit of its performance. Test pilots would need to *push (the edge of) the envelope* to see what the plane could and could not do.

push your 'luck; 'push it/things (*informal*)
(often used as a warning) take a risk because you
have successfully avoided problems in the past:
*You've already got a good pay rise. Now don't push
your luck by asking for more holidays.* ◇ *Look, boys,
I told you ten minutes ago to leave, so don't push it.
Get out of here now or I'll call the police.*

push sth to the ˌback of your 'mind
try to forget about sth unpleasant: *I tried to push
the thought to the back of my mind.*

at a pinch/push → pinch
press/push the panic button → panic

pushed

be pressed/pushed for money, space, time, etc. →
ˌpressed
hard pressed/pushed to do sth → hard

pushing

be ˌpushing '40, '50, etc. (*informal*)
be nearly 40, 50, etc. years old: *My grandmother's
pushing eighty but she's as fit as ever.*

be ˌpushing up (the) 'daisies (*old-fashioned,
humorous*)
be dead and in a grave: *I'll be pushing up daisies by
the time that happens.*

> ❷ NOTE
> A *daisy* is a small white flower that often grows
> in grass.

put

Most idioms containing the verb **put** are at the
entries for the nouns or adjectives in the idioms,
for example **put your foot in it** is at **foot**.

put it a'bout (*BrE, informal*)
have many sexual partners: *He was a man who had
always put it about.*

put it 'on (*informal*)
pretend that you are hurt, angry, etc: *She's not
really scared. She's only putting it on.*

put it 'there!
used when you are offering to shake hands with sb
because you agree with them or want to praise
them

put it to sb that … (*formal*)
suggest sth to sb to see if they can argue against it:
*I put it to you that you are the only person who had a
motive for the crime.*

put sb 'through it (*especially BrE, informal*)
force sb to do sth difficult or unpleasant: *During
the training they really put you through it; I was
exhausted!*

put to'gether
used when comparing or contrasting sb/sth with a
group of other people or things to mean
'combined' or 'in total': *Your department spent
more last year than all the others put together.*

putty

(like) putty in sb's 'hands (*informal*)
willing to do anything sb wants or tells you to do:
As soon as she starts crying, I'm putty in her hands.

> ❷ NOTE
> *Putty* is a soft flexible substance used for fixing
> glass in windows.

put-up

a 'put-up ˌjob (*BrE, informal*)
something that is planned to trick or deceive sb:
*The whole thing was a put-up job. He set fire to the
shop himself so that he could claim the insurance
money.*

pyjamas (*BrE*) (*AmE* pajamas)

the cat's whiskers/pyjamas → cat

Pyrrhic

a ˌPyrrhic 'victory
a victory which is achieved at too high a price and
therefore not worth having: *It was a Pyrrhic victory. They won the strike but then most of them lost
their jobs.*

> ❶ ORIGIN
> This idiom refers to Pyrrhus, King of Epirus,
> who in 279BC defeated the Romans but lost all
> his best officers and men.

Q q

Q

,QE'D

that is what I wanted to prove and I have proved it: *He can't have done it. Someone broke into the bank around 6.30 and he was with me at the time. QED.*

John Q. Public = Joe Public → **Joe**

mind your P's and Q's → **mind**

q

on the q.t. = on the quiet → **quiet**

qua

a sine qua non (of/for sth) → **sine**

quaking

(be) ,quaking/,shaking in your 'boots/'shoes
be very worried or frightened: *The prospect of facing the team again in the semi-final had everyone quaking in their boots.*

quandary

in a 'quandary
uncertain about what to do in a particular situation: *She's in a bit of a quandary about which of the jobs to accept.*

quantity

an unknown quantity → **unknown**

quantum

a quantum 'leap (also **a quantum 'jump**, *less frequent*)
a sudden very large increase, advance or improvement in sth: *This latest research represents a quantum leap in our understanding of the universe.* ◇ *The quantum leap in writing technology came with the introduction of personal computers.*

❶ ORIGIN
Quantum comes from the Latin word meaning 'how much'.

quarrel

pick a fight/quarrel (with sb) → **pick**

quart

get/pour/put a ,quart into a pint 'pot (*BrE*)
try to do sth impossible, especially to try to put sth into a space which is too small for it: *30 people in this small room! You can't put a quart into a pint pot, you know.*

❷ NOTE
A *pint* is 0.568 litres and a *quart* is 1.136 litres.

quarters

at close quarters → **close**

Queen

the King's/Queen's English → **English**

turn King's/Queen's evidence → **turn**

queen

'queen it over sb
(of women) behave in an unpleasant way to sb because you think you are better or more important than they are: *She sits in her office queening it over all the junior staff.*

(be) the uncrowned king/queen (of sth) → **uncrowned**

queer

queer sb's 'pitch; queer the 'pitch (for sb) (*BrE, informal*)
spoil sb's plans or their chances of getting sth: *Somebody must have told her boss about her plans to leave. Who was trying to queer her pitch?*

an odd/a queer fish → **fish**

question

beyond/without 'question
without any doubt: *She is without question the best student in the class.* ◇ *The view is, beyond question, the most spectacular in the whole area.*

bring/call/throw sth into 'question
cause sth to become a matter for doubt and discussion: *Scandals like this call into question the honesty of the police.* ◇ *The high number of accidents has brought government policy on industrial safety into question.*

,good 'question! (*spoken*)
used to show that you do not know the answer to an important question: *'How much is all this going to cost?' 'Good question!'*

in 'question (*formal*)
1 that is being discussed: *On the day in question we were in Cardiff.* ◇ *The money in question doesn't belong to you; it belongs to your sister.*
2 in doubt; uncertain: *The future of public transport is not in question.*

it's (just, etc.) a 'question of sth
it concerns sth; it is really about sth: *It's not a question of money; it's much more a question of principle.* ◇ *If it's a question of paying you a bit more, then I think we can consider that.*

out of the 'question
impossible and so not worth considering: *An expensive holiday is out of the question this year.*

a 'question mark hangs over sb/sth; there's a 'question mark (hanging) over sb/sth

there is some doubt about sb/sth: *A question mark hangs over the future of this club.* ◇ *There's a question mark over his loyalty to the company.*

there's some/no question of sth/doing sth

there is some/no possibility of sth/doing sth: *I'm afraid there is no question of you leaving work early this afternoon.* ◇ *Apparently there is some question of our getting three days' extra holiday this year. I hope we do.*

(do sth) without 'question

do sth without arguing or complaining about it: *I expect officers to obey my orders without question.* ◇ *Her version of events was accepted without question.*

be a moot point/question → **moot**

beg the question → **beg**

it's only, just, etc. a matter/a question of time (before …) → **time**

a leading question → **leading**

the million dollar question = the sixty-four thousand dollar question → **sixty-four**

open to question = an open question → **open**

pop the question → **pop**

the sixty-four thousand dollar question → **sixty-four**

a vexed question → **vexed**

queue

jump the queue → **jump**

quick

have (got) a quick 'temper

become angry easily: *Just be careful how you tell him—he's got a very quick temper and he's quite scary when he's angry!* ▶ ,**quick-'tempered** *adj.*: *She's quite a quick-tempered woman.*

(as) quick as a 'flash

very fast or suddenly: *Quick as a flash he replied that he had never seen it before.* ◇ *When the cat appeared, the bird flew away, as quick as a flash.*

,quick 'march

used for telling sb to walk faster: *Come on! Quick march or we'll miss the bus.*

> ❷ NOTE
> '*Quick march*' is also a command given to soldiers.

a 'quick one (*BrE, informal*)

a drink, usually alcoholic, which you have a short time for before doing sth else: *Have you got time for a quick one before your train goes?*

be fast/quick on the draw → **draw**

be quick/slow off the mark → **mark**

be quick/slow on the uptake → **uptake**

cut sb to the quick → **cut**

double quick → **double**

make a fast/quick buck → **buck**

quid

,quid pro 'quo (*from Latin*)

a thing that is given in return for sth else: *The management have agreed to begin pay talks as a quid pro quo for suspension of strike action.*

> ❷ NOTE
> The meaning of the Latin phrase is 'something for something'.

quids

quids 'in (*BrE, informal*)

in a position of having made a profit, especially a good profit: *I've just received three cheques so we're quids in at the moment.*

> ❷ NOTE
> A *quid* is an informal word for one pound in money.

quiet

keep quiet about sth; keep sth quiet

say nothing about sth; keep sth secret: *I've decided to resign but I'd rather you kept quiet about it.*

on the 'quiet (also **on the q.t.**, *old-fashioned*) (*informal*)

without telling anyone; secretly: *Well, just on the quiet, she's actually leaving her job next month. Don't tell anyone, will you?* ◇ *Just remember that whatever I tell you is on the q.t.*

> ❷ NOTE
> *Q.t.* is an abbreviation of 'quiet'.

(as) quiet as a 'mouse

(of a person) saying very little or making very little noise: *He's quiet as a mouse in class.* ◇ *Be as quiet as a mouse when you go upstairs—the baby's asleep in our bedroom.*

peace and quiet → **peace**

quite

not ,quite the 'thing

1 not considered socially acceptable: *It wouldn't be quite the thing to turn up in jeans and trainers.*
2 (*old-fashioned*) not healthy or normal

'quite a/some sb/sth (*informal*)

used to show that you think sb/sth is impressive, unusual, remarkable, etc: *That's quite some swimming pool you've got there. I've never seen one so large in a private garden.* ◇ *We found it quite a change when we moved abroad.*

quite the best, the worst, etc. sth (*informal*)

absolutely the best, worst, etc: *It was quite the worst film I've ever seen.*

quite a 'few (*BrE also* **a good 'few**)

a fairly large number: *I've been there quite a few times.* ◇ *They've been here a good few years now.*

quite 'so (*BrE, formal*)

used to agree with sb or to show that you understand them: '*It's a very interesting book.*' '*Quite so. That's why I wanted you to read it.*'

quite some 'time

quite a long time: *Quite some time has passed since
I last saw my brother.*

be not all / quite there → **there**

quite the contrary = on the contrary → **contrary**

quits

be 'quits (with sb) (*informal*)

1 be in a position in which neither of two people
owe each other money any more: *If I give you this
£10, then we're quits, aren't we?*

2 have done sth unpleasant to sb who did sth
unpleasant to you: *He crashed my motorbike last
year and now I've crashed his car, so we're quits.*

call it quits → **call**

double or quits → **double**

quo

quid pro quo → **quid**

the status quo → **status**

quoi

je ne sais quoi → **sais**

quote

'quote (... 'unquote) (*spoken*)

used by a speaker to show the beginning (and end)
of a word, phrase, etc. that has been said or written
by sb else: *This, quote, 'novel of the century',
unquote, is probably the most boring book I've ever
read.*

R r

R
the three R's → three

rabbit
pull sth/a rabbit out of the hat → pull

race

a ,race against 'time/the 'clock
a situation in which you have to do sth or finish sth very fast before it is too late: *It was a race against time to reach the shore before the boat sank.*

a one-horse race → one-horse
the rat race → rat

rack

go to ,rack and 'ruin
get into bad condition because of lack of care: *The house has gone to rack and ruin over the last few years.* ◇ *The country is going to rack and ruin under this government.*

(be) on the 'rack
(be) in a state of anxiety, stress, pain, etc: *After three weeks had passed and she had still not heard from her daughter, Joan was on the rack.*

> **❶ ORIGIN**
> The *rack* was an instrument of torture, used in the past for punishing and hurting people. Their arms and legs were tied to a wooden frame and then pulled in opposite directions, stretching the body.

rack your 'brains (also wrack your 'brains, *less frequent*) (*informal*)
try very hard to think of sth or remember sth: *I've been racking my brains all day trying to remember his name.*

off the rack = off the peg → peg

rag

the 'rag trade (*old-fashioned, informal*)
the business of designing, making and selling clothes: *He's worked in the rag trade all his life.*

chew the rag → chew
lose your rag → lose
(like) a red rag to a bull → red

rage

all the 'rage (*informal*)
very popular or fashionable: *Short hair is all the rage at the moment.*

ragged
run sb ragged → run

rags

from ,rags to 'riches (*informal*)
from being very poor to being very rich, especially in a short period of time: *She went from rags to riches in less than five years.* ▶ ,rags-to-'riches *adj.*: *It was a real rags-to-riches story.*

glad rags → glad

rails

get back on the 'rails (*informal*)
become successful again after a period of failure, or begin functioning normally again: *Even after losing all three of their last matches, the club assures fans that they will get back on the rails in time for their next game.*

go off the 'rails (*BrE, informal*)
start behaving in a way which shocks or upsets other people: *Away from the routine of army life some ex-soldiers go completely off the rails.*

> **❶ ORIGIN**
> These idioms refer to a train leaving the track that it runs on.

rain

come ,rain, come 'shine; (come) ,rain or 'shine (*informal*)
whatever the weather is like; whatever happens: *They met in the park, come rain or shine, every Saturday morning for twenty years.*

rain cats and 'dogs (also rain 'buckets) (*informal*)
(usually used in progressive tenses) rain very heavily: *We can't possibly play golf today. It's raining cats and dogs out there.* ◇ *It's been raining buckets all morning.*

> **❶ ORIGIN**
> The expression 'raining cats and dogs' may come from Norse mythology. Cats were supposed to have an influence over the weather, while dogs were the signal of storms.

,rain on sb's 'parade (*AmE*)
spoil sth for sb: *Drugs again rained on the Olympics' parade as another athlete tested positive for an illegal substance.*

take a 'rain check (on sth) (*informal, especially AmE*)
used to refuse an offer or invitation but to say that you will accept it later: *'Would you like to try that new restaurant tonight?' 'I'm afraid I'm busy tonight, but can I take a rain check?'*

> **❶ ORIGIN**
> A *rain check* was originally a ticket that was given to spectators at an outdoor event if it was

cancelled or interrupted by rain. They could then use this ticket at a future event.

(as) right as rain → **right**

rains

it ˌnever ˌrains but it 'pours (*BrE*) (*AmE* **when it rains, it 'pours**) (*saying*)

when one thing goes wrong, so do others: *It never rains but it pours! First I found that the car had been stolen and then I lost the keys to my flat.*

rainy

save, keep, etc. it for a ˌrainy 'day (*informal*)

save money or things for a time in the future when you might need them: *'Don't spend it all at once,' his aunt said to him. 'Save some of it for a rainy day.'*

raise

raise 'Cain/'hell (*informal*)

complain or protest noisily and angrily, often as a way of getting sth you want: *He'll raise hell if we don't finish on time.* ▶ **'hell-raiser** *noun* a violent and destructive person

> **❶ ORIGIN**
> *Cain* was the first murderer in the Bible.

raise your 'eyebrows (at sth)

show, by the expression on your face, that you disapprove or are surprised by sth: *Eyebrows were raised when he arrived at the wedding in jeans.* ◇ *When he said he was leaving, there were a lot of raised eyebrows.*

raise your 'glass (to sb)

hold up your glass and wish sb happiness, good luck, etc. before you drink: *Now, would everybody please raise their glasses and drink a toast to the bride and groom.*

raise a 'laugh/'smile

do or say sth that makes other people laugh/smile: *If the speeches are not going well, ask Paula to speak; she can always raise a laugh.* ◇ *His jokes didn't even raise a smile, which was embarrassing.*

raise the 'spectre of sth (*BrE*) (*AmE* **raise the 'specter of sth**)

make people afraid that sth unpleasant might happen: *The news of more cuts has raised the spectre of redundancies once again.* ◇ *The arrival of warm weather raises the specter of disease and increased rat infestations caused by rotting garbage.*

raise sb's 'spirits

make sb happier: *Good weather always raises her spirits.*

raise your 'voice

speak in a louder voice, often because you are angry: *Don't raise your voice at me. It wasn't my fault.*

raise a/your voice a'gainst sb/sth

say publicly that you do not agree with sb's actions, plans, etc: *He was the only person to raise his voice against the plan.*

build up/raise sb's hopes → **hopes**
kick up/make/create/raise a stink (about sth) → **stink**
lift/raise a hand against sb → **hand**
lift/raise the roof → **roof**
raise/up the ante → **ante**
raise hackles = make sb's hackles rise → **hackles**
raise/lower your sights → **sights**
raise/lower the temperature → **temperature**
rear/raise its (ugly) head → **head**

raison

his, your, etc. ˌraison 'd'être (*from French*)

the most important reason for sb's/sth's existence: *Work seems to be her sole raison d'être.*

> **❷ NOTE**
> The meaning of the French phrase is 'reason for being'.

rake

rake over the 'ashes/the 'past (*informal, disapproving*)

discuss with sb unpleasant things that happened between you in the past: *When they met each other again, ten years after the divorce, they both tried hard not to rake over the past.*

rake sb over the coals = haul sb over the coals → **haul**
(as) thin as a rake → **thin**

ram

ram sth 'home (*especially BrE*)

force sb to understand sth important: *The terrible injuries I saw in that accident really rammed home for me the importance of wearing seat belts.*

rampage

be/go on the 'rampage

run round the streets causing damage to shops, cars, etc: *After their team lost, some of the crowd went on the rampage through the town.*

ramrod

ˌramrod 'straight; (as) straight as a 'ramrod

(of a person) with a very straight back and looking serious and formal: *As she walked in she could feel the tension in the room, with her mother sitting ramrod straight in her chair.*

range

in/within 'range (of sth)

near enough to be reached, seen or heard: *He shouted angrily at anyone within range.*

out of 'range (of sth)

too far away to be reached, seen or heard: *The cat stayed well out of range of the children.* ◇ *Harry stayed up against the wall, out of range of the security guards.*

rank

(the) ‚rank and 'file
(the) ordinary members of a group or organization: *I can see that you are happy with the plan but what will the rank and file think?* ◇ *The rank-and-file members don't elect the leader.*

> **❶ ORIGIN**
> In the military, the *rank and file* are ordinary soldiers who are not officers.

pull rank (on sb) ➔ pull

ranks

come up/rise through the 'ranks
after starting your career at the bottom or low down in an organization, finally reach a high position in it: *The new managing director has come up through the ranks, which is quite unusual these days.*

> **❶ ORIGIN**
> In the military, the *ranks* refers to the position of ordinary soldiers rather than officers. Some may become officers if they have the right qualities.

break ranks ➔ break
close ranks ➔ close

ransom

hold sb to ransom ➔ hold
a king's ransom ➔ king

rant

‚rant and 'rave (*disapproving*)
show that you are angry by shouting or complaining loudly for a long time: *He stood there for about twenty minutes ranting and raving about the colour of the new paint.*

rap

‚rap sb over the 'knuckles; give sb, get, etc. a ‚rap over the 'knuckles (*informal*)
criticize sb/be criticized for doing sth wrong: *He got a rap over the knuckles for spending too much money on his business lunches.*

take the 'rap (for sb/sth) (*informal*)
be blamed or punished, especially for sth you did not do: *She was prepared to take the rap for the broken window, even though it was her brother who had kicked the ball.*

beat the rap ➔ beat

raptures

be in/go into 'raptures (about/over sb/sth)
be extremely enthusiastic about sb/sth you like: *Each time I mention your name, he goes into raptures about you.*

rare

a rare 'bird
a person or thing that is unusual, often because they have/it has two very different interests or qualities: *Jill is a very rare bird, a good politician and an excellent listener.*

> **❶ ORIGIN**
> This expression is a translation of the Latin idiom 'rara avis'.

(as) rare/scarce as hen's teeth ➔ hen

raring

raring to go (*informal*)
very enthusiastic about starting sth: *At the start of the project we were raring to go but unfortunately we've lost a lot of our early enthusiasm.*

rat

the 'rat race (*disapproving*)
intense competition for success in jobs, business, etc., typical of a big city: *Paul got caught up in the rat race and was never at home.* ◇ *They longed to escape from the rat race and move to the countryside.*

like a drowned rat ➔ drowned
smell a rat ➔ smell

rate

at 'any rate (*spoken*)
1 used to say that a particular fact is true in spite of what has happened in the past or what may happen in the future: *Well, that's one good piece of news at any rate.*
2 used to show that you are being more accurate about sth that you have just said: *He said he'd be here on the 5th. At any rate, I think that's what he said.*
3 used to show that what you have just said is not as important as what you are going to say: *There were maybe 80 or 90 people there. At any rate, the room was packed.*

at a rate of 'knots (*BrE, informal*)
very fast: *You must have been going at a rate of knots to have finished so soon.*

> **❷ NOTE**
> The speed of a boat or ship is measured in *knots*.

at 'this/'that rate (*spoken*)
if the situation continues as it is: *This traffic's terrible. At this rate we'll never get to the airport on time.*

the ‚going 'rate (for sth)
the usual amount of money paid for goods or services at a particular time: *They pay slightly more than the going rate for freelance work.*

rather

rather than
instead of sb/sth: *I think I'll have a cold drink rather than coffee.* ◇ *Why didn't you ask for help, rather than trying to do it on your own?*

rather you, etc. than 'me (also **sooner you, etc. than 'me**) (*especially BrE*)
used for saying that you are pleased that you do not have to do a difficult or unpleasant thing: *'She works every weekend.' 'Rather her than me.'*

would rather … (than)
would prefer to: *She'd rather die than give a speech.* ◇ *'Do you want to come with us?' 'No, I'd rather not.'* ◇ *Would you rather walk or take the bus?* ◇ *'Do you mind if I smoke?' 'Well, I'd rather you didn't.'*

be a bit/rather steep ➔ steep

rattle

,rattle sb's 'cage (*informal*)
annoy sb: *Who's rattled his cage?*

rave

rant and rave ➔ rant

raving

(stark) raving 'mad/'bonkers (*informal*)
completely crazy; suddenly very angry with sb: *Are you stark raving mad, jumping off a moving train?* ◇ *When I told her I'd crashed her car, she went stark raving bonkers.*

raw

catch/touch sb on the 'raw (*BrE*)
upset sb by reminding them of sth they are particularly sensitive about: *She touched him on the raw by criticizing his driving.*

in the 'raw
in a way that does not hide the unpleasant aspects of sth: *If you want to see life in the raw, get a job as a police officer.*

a raw/rough deal ➔ deal

ray

the one/a ray of 'hope
the one small sign of improvement in a difficult situation: *They've actually stopped fighting, so perhaps there's a ray of hope after all.* ◇ *Our one ray of hope is my father. He might be able to lend us the money.*

a ray of 'sunshine (*informal*)
a person or thing that makes sb's life happier: *She calls her granddaughter her 'little ray of sunshine'.*

razor

on a razor's edge = on a knife-edge ➔ knife-edge

razzle

be/go out on the 'razzle (*BrE, informal*)
go out drinking, dancing and enjoying yourself: *It's a long time since I went out on the razzle, but your birthday will be a wonderful excuse.*

reach

reach for the 'stars
try to be successful at sth that is difficult: *She decided very early that she was going to reach for the stars and get to the top of her profession.*

within (easy) 'reach (of sth)
close to sth: *The house is within easy reach of schools and sports facilities.*

hit/reach rock bottom ➔ rock
come to/reach sb's ears ➔ ears
reach/make first base (with sb/sth) ➔ first

read

,read between the 'lines
find or look for a hidden or extra meaning in sth a person says or writes, usually their real feelings about sth: *Reading between the lines, it was obvious that he was feeling lonely.*

,read sb like a 'book (*informal*)
understand sb so well that you can guess what they will say or do before they say or do it: *She found that after living with him for a year or more, she could read him like a book.*

,read sb's 'mind/'thoughts (*informal*)
understand what sb is thinking, feeling, planning, etc: *I can't read your mind! If you don't tell me what's worrying you, I can't help you.*

,read my 'lips (*spoken*)
used to tell sb to listen carefully to what you are saying: *Read my lips: no new taxes* (= I promise there will be no new taxes).

read (sb) the 'Riot Act (*BrE*)
tell sb forcefully and angrily that you will punish them if they do not stop behaving badly; be angry with sb who has behaved badly: *The headmaster came in and read the Riot Act. He said he would keep us in after school if there was one more complaint about us.* ◇ *My dad read us the Riot Act when we broke the kitchen window. He was furious.*

ⓘ ORIGIN
In 1715 the Riot Act was passed in Parliament. Groups of more than twelve people were not allowed to meet in public. If they did, an official came to read them the Riot Act, which ordered them to stop the meeting.

,take sth/it as 'read (*BrE*)
consider that sth does not need discussing because everyone already knows, understands, or agrees about it: *Can I take it as read that we all agree on this matter?*

ⓘ ORIGIN
This comes from an expression used in committees. At the start of each meeting the committee must agree that the minutes (= notes) of the last meeting are a correct record. To save time the members are asked if the minutes can be *taken as read*.

ready

at the 'ready
prepared for immediate action or use: *Cameras and microphones at the ready, they waited for the new President to appear.*

make 'ready (for sth) (*formal*)
prepare (for sth): *Everyone is very busy here making ready for the royal visit.*

ready, steady, 'go! (*BrE*) (also (get) ready, (get) set, 'go! *AmE, BrE*)
what you say to tell people to start a race

,ready to 'roll (*informal*)
ready to start: *The show is just about ready to roll.*

ready when 'you are
used for telling sb that you are ready and are waiting for them to do sth: *'When would you like me to begin?' 'Ready when you are.'*

fit/ready to drop → **drop**
rough and ready → **rough**

real

for 'real
1 (do sth) which is real rather than imagined, practised or talked about, etc: *You might think that jumping out of a plane is easy, but when you do it for real, it's terrifying.* ◇ *He's joked about emigrating to Canada in the past, but this time I think it's for real.*
2 genuine: *Do you think this offer of a free holiday is for real?*

get 'real (*informal*)
used to tell sb that they are behaving in a stupid or unreasonable way: *You really think people are going to listen to your crazy ideas? Get real!*

in real 'life
not the life people have in books, films, plays, etc.: *She plays the role of an alcoholic in this play, but in real life she doesn't drink at all.*

the ,real Mc'Coy (*informal*)
the original and therefore the best type of sth; the best example of sth: *It's an American flying jacket, the real McCoy.* ◇ *This apple pie is the real McCoy. I haven't eaten one like this for years.*

> **ⓘ ORIGIN**
> This idiom possibly refers to the American boxing champion Kid McCoy. So many people pretended to be him that he started calling himself Kid 'The Real' McCoy.

the real 'thing (*informal*)
the genuine thing: *Are you sure it's the real thing (= love), not just infatuation?* ◇ *'What kind of whisky is this?' 'This is the real thing. You can't buy better whisky than this.'*

reality

in re'ality
used to say that a situation is different from what has just been said or from what people believe: *Outwardly she looked confident but in reality she felt extremely nervous.*

realms

beyond/within the realms of possi'bility
not possible/possible: *A successful outcome is not beyond the realms of possibility.*

reap

reap a/the 'harvest (*BrE*)
benefit or suffer as a direct result of sth that you have done: *His attacking policies have reaped a particularly good harvest overseas, where he is well known as a shrewd businessman.*

you ,reap what you 'sow (*saying*)
you have to deal with the bad effects or results of sth that you originally started: *He's so mean! When I went to him for some sympathy and understanding, all he said was 'you reap what you sow'!*

> **ⓘ ORIGIN**
> These two phrases refer to farmers cutting and collecting crops from a field.

rear

,bring up the 'rear
1 be the last person or group to appear in a line or procession: *The President led the way out of the courtyard, followed by senior ministers of government. Junior ministers brought up the rear.*
2 finish last in a race or competition: *Smith finished in 2nd place, Warren in 3rd, with poor Davis bringing up the rear in 12th place.*

rear/raise its (ugly) head → **head**

rearrange

rearrange the deckchairs on the Titanic
if sth is like **rearranging the deckchairs on the Titanic**, it is an activity that is not worth doing because it cannot improve the situation: *None of the staff believe that the new system will improve anything. It's simply a case of rearranging the deckchairs on the Titanic.*

> **ⓘ ORIGIN**
> This expression refers to the famous ship that sank after hitting an iceberg on its first voyage.

reason

within 'reason
on the condition that it is sensible or reasonable: *She wanted it repaired immediately and said she would pay whatever we asked, within reason.*

for a/some reason/reasons best known to himself, herself, etc. → **best**
it stands to reason (that …) → **stands**
neither/no/without rhyme (n)or reason → **rhyme**
(make sb) see sense/reason → **see**

rebound

on the 'rebound

while you are sad and confused, especially after a relationship has ended: *She married John on the rebound from Geoff. I knew it wouldn't last.*

> ❷ NOTE
> If a ball *rebounds*, it bounces back after it has hit a hard surface.

recall

beyond re'call

impossible to bring back to the original state; impossible to remember: *When the plans to build the new highway were announced, we knew that the beautiful landscape around our house would soon be damaged beyond recall.*

received

conventional/received wisdom → **wisdom**

receiving

be on/at the re'ceiving end (of sth) (*informal*)

be the person that an action, etc. is directed at, especially an unpleasant one: *He's been on the receiving end of a lot of criticism recently.*

recharge

recharge your 'batteries (*informal*)

rest for a while to get more energy (for the next period of activity): *You've been working too much. What you need is a good holiday to recharge your batteries.*

recipe

a recipe for di'saster, suc'cess, etc.

a method or an idea that seems likely to have a particular result: *If you ask me, that idea sounds like a recipe for disaster.* ◇ *What's her recipe for success?*

reckoned

a force to be reckoned with → **force**

reckoning

in/into/out of the 'reckoning (*especially BrE*)

(especially in sport) among/not among those who are likely to win or be successful: *Phelan is fit again and could come into the reckoning.*

the day of reckoning → **day**

recognition

change, alter, etc. beyond/out of (all) recog'nition

change, etc. such a lot that people do not recognize you, it, etc: *I went back to Birmingham after 20 years and it had changed beyond all recognition.* ◇ *She had changed beyond all recognition since I last saw her.*

record

be/go on 'record; put sth on 'record

say sth publicly (perhaps in a newspaper) so that what you say is written down: *He is on record as saying that he never wanted to become President, but now he's fighting for the job.*

(just) for the 'record

so that the facts should be recorded or remembered correctly: *I'd like to make it clear, just for the record, that I disagree with the committee's decision.*

off the 'record

if you tell sb sth **off the record**, it is not yet official and you do not want them to repeat it publicly: *If you speak to me off the record, I won't quote you by name.* ◇ *It was an off-the-record remark and you shouldn't have attached my name to it.*

on 'record

officially noted or written down: *It was the warmest day on record.*

put/set the 'record straight (*informal*)

give a correct version, explanation of events, facts, etc. because you think sb has made a mistake: *Let's put the record straight—we do not owe you £5000.*

a track record → **track**

red

(as) red as a 'beetroot (*BrE*) (*AmE* **(as) red as a 'beet**) (*informal*)

with red cheeks, because you feel angry, embarrassed or hot: *I could feel myself going as red as a beetroot when she said that my work had been chosen for the prize.* ◇ *My face is always as red as a beet when I come out of the sauna.*

in the 'red (*informal*)

in debt: *At this time of year we are usually in the red.*

> ❶ ORIGIN
> In bank accounts, an amount that was owed used to be written in red figures, not black.

not have a red 'cent (*AmE, informal*)

have no money at all: *I wish I could come skiing with you, but I don't have a red cent at the moment.*

on ‚red a'lert

prepared for an emergency or for sth dangerous to happen: *Following the bomb blast, local hospitals have been put on red alert.*

the red 'carpet

a very special welcome given to an important visitor: *When I went to my girlfriend's house for the first time, her family really put out the red carpet for me.* ◇ *It was an unofficial visit so the guests didn't get the usual red carpet treatment.*

> ❶ ORIGIN
> A strip of red carpet is usually laid on the ground for an important visitor to walk on when he or she arrives.

a red 'face (*informal*)
embarrassment: *There are going to be a lot of red faces at the bank when they discover their mistake.*

a red 'herring
a fact, etc. which sb introduces into a discussion because they want to take people's attention away from the main point: *Look, the situation in French agriculture is just a red herring. We're here to discuss the situation in this country.*

❶ ORIGIN
This idiom comes from the custom of using the scent of a smoked, dried herring (which was red) to train dogs to hunt.

red in ˌtooth and 'claw
involving opposition or competition that is violent and without pity: *nature, red in tooth and claw*

(like) a red rag to a 'bull
certain to make a particular person very angry or even violent: *Don't mention anything about religion to your uncle. It's like a red rag to a bull.*

❶ ORIGIN
This expression refers to the belief that bulls do not like the colour red.

red 'tape (*disapproving*)
official rules that seem more complicated than necessary and prevent things from being done quickly: *Do you know how much red tape you have to go through if you want to import a car?*

❶ ORIGIN
This phrase comes from the custom of tying up official documents with red ribbon or tape.

paint the town red → paint
see red → see

redeeming

a redeeming 'feature
sth good or positive about sb/sth that is otherwise bad: *Her one redeeming feature is her generosity.* ◇ *The only redeeming feature of the hotel was the swimming pool. Apart from that, it was the worst hotel I've ever stayed in.*

red-handed

catch sb red-handed → catch

red-letter

a red-'letter day
a very special day which is remembered because sth important or good happened: *Today was a red-letter day. We heard we had won a free holiday in Japan.* ◇ *The arrival of a new camcorder is a red-letter day in the life of any household.*

❶ ORIGIN
Religious holidays and other important dates used to be printed in red on calendars.

red-light

the red-'light district
the part of a city where prostitutes work and sex shops are found: *I got lost and found myself in the red-light district all alone!*

redress

redress the 'balance
make a situation equal or fair again: *Nowadays, it appears that too many films are being produced, and a tax on films will help to redress the balance.*

reduced

reˌduced 'circumstances
the state of being poorer than you were before. People use 'living in reduced circumstances' to avoid saying 'poor': *As time passed, his reduced circumstances became more and more obvious to his friends and colleagues.*

reference

in/with 'reference to (*formal* or *written*)
used to say what you are talking or writing about: *With reference to your letter of July 22 …*

reflect

reflect well, badly, etc. on sb/sth
make sb/sth appear to be good, bad, etc. to other people: *This incident reflects badly on everyone involved.*

reflected

bathe/bask in reflected glory
get attention and fame not because of sth you have done but through the success of sb else connected to you: *She wasn't happy to bathe in the reflected glory of her daughter's success, as she wanted to succeed on her own.*

reflection

a sad, poor, etc. reflection on sth
a thing which damages sb's/sth's reputation: *The increase in crime is a sad reflection on our society today.*

on mature reflection/consideration → mature

refresh

reˌfresh sb's/your 'memory
remind sb/yourself of sth that you have forgotten: *Refresh my memory, will you? How many children has he got?* ◇ *Before I interviewed Ms Waters, I read her book again just to refresh my memory.*

refusal

(give sb, have, etc.) (the) first refusal → first

regard

have re'gard to sth (*law*)
remember and think carefully about sth: *It is*

always necessary to have regard to the terms of the contract.

in/with re'gard to sb/sth (*formal*)
concerning sb/sth: *a country's laws in regard to human rights* ◇ *The company's position with regard to overtime is made clear in the contracts.*

in this/that re'gard (*formal*)
concerning what has just been mentioned: *I have nothing further to say in this regard.*

regards

as regards sb/sth (*formal*)
about or concerning sb/sth: *As regards the method of payment, a decision will be made after the contract has been signed.*

region

in the 'region of
approximately: *The house should sell for something in the region of £100000.*

regular

(as) regular as 'clockwork
very regularly; happening at the same time in the same way; reliable: *She arrives at work on her bicycle at 8.45 every day, as regular as clockwork.*

rein

give/allow sb/sth free/full 'rein; give/allow free/full 'rein to sb/sth
not restrict, limit or control sth: *In a novel the author need not keep to the facts, but a textbook is not the place to give free rein to your imagination.*

> ❷ NOTE
> A *rein* is a long leather band that is fastened around a horse's neck and used by the rider to control the speed of the horse.

keep a tight rein on sb/sth ➔ tight

reinvent

reinvent the 'wheel
waste time creating sth that already exists and works well: *There's no point in us reinventing the wheel. Why can't we just leave things as they are?*

relation

a poor relation ➔ poor

relatively

relatively 'speaking
used when you are comparing sth with all similar things: *Relatively speaking, these jobs provide good salaries.*

religion

get re'ligion (*informal, often disapproving*)
suddenly become interested in religion: *He got religion while he was touring in Australia.*

remain

somebody, who will/shall remain/be nameless ➔ nameless

remember

something to re'member sb by (*informal*)
a punishment, especially a physical one: *If I ever catch you stealing my apples again, I'll give you something to remember me by.*

remembered

be re'membered as/for sth
be famous or known for a particular thing that you have done in the past: *He is best remembered as the man who brought jazz to Britain.* ◇ *A natural journalist, he will be remembered for his words rather than his actions.*

removed

be far/further/furthest re'moved from sth
be very different from sth; not be connected with sth: *Many of these books are far removed from the reality of the children's lives.*

reopen

reopen old 'wounds
remind sb of sth unpleasant that happened or existed in the past: *Look, let's try not to reopen any old wounds this time, OK?*

repair

beyond re'pair
impossible to repair: *The engine was damaged beyond repair.*

in good, bad, etc. re'pair (also **in a good, bad, etc. state of re'pair**) (*formal*)
in good, bad, etc. condition: *The house is in a terrible state of repair.* ◇ *If it were in a better state of repair, this old table would be worth a lot of money.*

reputation

live up to your/its reputation ➔ live

reserve

in re'serve
available to be used in the future or when needed: *The money was being kept in reserve for their retirement.* ◇ *200 police officers were held in reserve.*

residence

in 'residence
having an official position in a particular place such as a college or university: *a writer/an artist/a musician in residence*

resistance

(choose, follow, take, etc.) the line of least resistance ➔ line

résistance

your/the pièce de résistance → pièce

resort

(as) a last resort → last

respect

in re'spect of (*formal*)
1 concerning: *Large increases can now be expected in respect of fuel prices.*
2 in payment for sth: *Please state the money you have received in respect of overtime worked.*

with (all due) re'spect (*formal*)
used before disagreeing with sb in order to seem polite: *With respect, sir, I cannot agree.*

with respect to 'sth (*formal*)
(often used in business) concerning sth; with reference to sth: *With respect to your enquiry about the new pension scheme, I have pleasure in enclosing our leaflet.*

respecter

be no respecter of 'persons
treat everyone in the same way, without being influenced by their importance, wealth, etc: *Though still young, she was a very confident girl. She was no respecter of persons and never thought before she spoke.*

respects

pay your respects (to sb) → pay

rest

and the 'rest (*spoken*)
used to say that the actual amount or number of sth is much higher than sb has stated: *'We've run up a cost of £250 ... ' 'Yeah, and the rest!'*

and (all) the 'rest (of it) (*spoken*)
used at the end of a list to mean everything else that you might expect to be on the list: *She believes in God and heaven and hell and all the rest.*

at 'rest
1 (*technical*) not moving: *At rest the insect looks like a dead leaf.*
2 dead and therefore free from trouble or anxiety. People say 'at rest' to avoid saying 'dead': *She now lies at rest in the family grave.*

come to 'rest
stop moving: *The car crashed through the barrier and came to rest in a field.* ◇ *His eyes came to rest on Clara's face.*

for the 'rest (*BrE, formal*)
as far as other less important matters are concerned: *The most important thing in life is to do your duty. For the rest I care nothing.*

(why don't you) give it a 'rest! (*BrE, spoken*)
used to tell sb to stop doing sth or talking about sth because they are annoying you: *Give it a rest will you! That's the third time you've criticized my driving this morning.*

give sth a 'rest (*informal*)
stop doing sth for a while: *He first started his university degree some ten years ago, but gave it a rest for a few years before starting again in 1995.*

I ˌrest my 'case (*spoken, law* or *humorous*)
have no more to say about sth, especially because you think you have proved your point: *You see what I mean about him always arriving late? It's nearly ten o'clock and he's not here yet. I rest my case!*

rest as'sured (that ...) (*formal*)
be completely certain or confident that ...: *You can rest assured that we will do everything we can to get your money back.*

the rest is 'history
used when you are telling a story to say that you do not need to tell the end of it, because everyone knows it already: *She moved here two years ago, met Steve last summer, and the rest is history.*

ˌrest on your 'laurels (*usually disapproving*)
be satisfied with the success(es) you have already gained and so no longer try to improve your position, etc: *I know you got a very good degree from Oxford but what are you going to do with your life now? You can't rest on your laurels for ever, you know.*

> ❶ ORIGIN
> Laurel leaves were used in Roman times to make a crown for the winner of a race or competition.

God rest him/her → God
God rest his/her soul → God
lay sb to rest → lay
lay sth to rest → lay
put/set sb's mind at ease/rest → mind
there's no peace/rest for the wicked → wicked

retreat

beat a (hasty) retreat → beat

retrospect

in 'retrospect
thinking about a past event or situation, often with a different opinion of it from the one you had at the time: *In retrospect, I think that I was wrong.* ◇ *The decision seems extremely odd, in retrospect.*

return

by re'turn (of 'post) (*BrE*)
using the next available post; as soon as possible: *Please reply by return of post.*

in re'turn (for sth)
1 as a way of thanking sb or paying them for sth they have done: *What will you give me in return for this information?*
2 as a response or reaction to sth: *I asked her opinion, but she just asked me a question in return.*

re,turn the 'compliment

do or say the same pleasant thing that sb else has done or said to you: *Thanks for a lovely meal. We'll try and return the compliment very soon.*

re,turn to the 'fold (*literary*)

come back to a group or community (especially a religious or political society): *She left the party 10 years ago but has recently returned to the fold.*

❶ ORIGIN
This idiom refers to the comparison in the Bible between the lost sheep which returns to the fold (= the place where sheep are kept) and the sinner who is sorry for what he or she has done.

pay sth back/return sth with interest → interest
(get to, reach, etc.) the point of no return → point

returns

many happy returns (of the day) → happy

reveal

show/reveal your hand → hand

revelation

come as/be a reve'lation (to sb)

be a completely new or surprising experience; be different from what was expected: *His performance in the race today was a revelation to everyone. ◇ My trip to Texas was a revelation.*

reverse

go/put sth into re'verse

start to happen or make sth happen in the opposite way: *In the 1980s economic growth went into reverse.*

in re'verse

in the opposite order or way; backwards: *The secret number is my phone number in reverse. ◇ We did a similar trip to you, but in reverse.*

revert

revert to 'type (*formal*)

return to the way you would expect sb to behave when you remember their family, sex, work, history, etc: *She was a student revolutionary for a while but now she's reverted to type. I saw her in a Mercedes the other day.*

reward

virtue is its own reward → virtue

rhinoceros

have (got) a hide/skin like a rhi'noceros (*informal*)

be tough and not easily offended; have no fear of criticism from others: *Say what you like about him, he won't care; he's got a skin like a rhinoceros.*

rhyme

neither/no/without ,rhyme (n)or 'reason

no sense or logical explanation: *There is neither rhyme nor reason in his actions. ◇ Changes were being made without rhyme or reason.*

❶ ORIGIN
This phrase comes from Shakespeare's play *As You Like It*: 'But are you so much in love as your rhymes speak?' 'Neither rhyme nor reason can express how much'.

ribbons

cut, tear, etc. sth to 'ribbons

cut, tear, etc. sth very badly: *She was so furious when she discovered her husband with another woman that she cut all his clothes to ribbons.*

rich

(as) rich as Croesus (*informal*)

extremely rich

❶ ORIGIN
Croesus was a very rich king in Lydia, Asia Minor, in the sixth century BC.

that's 'rich (*spoken, especially BrE*)

used to show surprise and amusement at sb's words or actions: *Me? Lazy? That's rich, coming from you!*

be stinking rich → stinking
strike it rich → strike

riche

the nouveau riche → nouveau

riches

an embarrassment of riches → embarrassment
from rags to riches → rags

rid

be 'rid of sb/sth (*formal*)

be free of sb/sth that has been annoying you or that you do not want: *I was glad to be rid of the car when I finally sold it. ◇ (BrE) He was a nuisance and we're all **well rid of** him* (= we'll be much better without him).

get 'rid of sb/sth

make yourself free of sb/sth that is annoying you or that you do not want; throw sth away: *Try and get rid of your visitors before I get there. ◇ I can't get rid of this headache. ◇ We got rid of all the old furniture.*

want rid of sb/sth → want

riddance

good 'riddance (to sb/sth)

an unkind way of saying that you are pleased that sb/sth has gone: *'Goodbye and good riddance!' she said to him angrily as he left.*

riddled

be 'riddled with sth
be full of sth, especially sth bad or unpleasant: *His body was riddled with cancer.* ◇ *Her typing was slow and riddled with mistakes.*

ride

be/go along for the 'ride (*informal*)
join a group of people because you are interested in what they are doing, although you do not want to take an active part in it: *Some of the group are not really interested in politics—they're just along for the ride.*

ride the 'crest of sth
enjoy great success or support because of a particular situation or event: *The band is riding the crest of its last tour.*

ride 'herd on sb/sth (*AmE, informal*)
keep watch or control over sb/sth: *Police are riding herd on crowds of youths on the streets.*

ride 'roughshod over sb/sth (*especially BrE*) (*AmE* usually **run 'roughshod over sb/sth**)
treat sb/sb's feelings, ideas, protests, etc. with no respect at all because you do not consider them important: *The local authority rode roughshod over the protests of parents and closed down the school.*

ride 'shotgun (*AmE, informal*)
ride in the front passenger seat of a car or truck: *My turn to ride shotgun today!*

ride a/the 'wave of sth
enjoy or be supported by the particular situation or quality mentioned: *Schools are riding a wave of renewed public interest.*

(give sb, have, etc.) a rough/an easy 'ride (*informal*)
(give sb/get) unpleasant/gentle treatment or questioning: *The government has had a rough ride from the popular press recently.* ◇ *The minister won't be given an easy ride in parliament over government cuts in education.*

take sb for a 'ride (*informal*)
cheat or deceive sb: *If you've paid £6 000 for that car you've been taken for a ride!*

get, take, etc. a free ride → **free**

give sb/have a bumpy ride → **bumpy**

if wishes were horses, beggars would/might ride → **wishes**

let sth ride → **let**

ride out/weather the storm (of sth) → **storm**

ridiculous

from the sublime to the ridiculous → **sublime**

riding

be riding for a 'fall
behave in a way which will cause problems for you later: *He's riding for a fall if he keeps talking to the boss so rudely.*

riding 'high
very successful or confident: *The company has been riding high for the last two years, but will their success continue?*

Right

Mr Right → **Mr**

right

as of 'right (also **by 'right**) (*formal*)
according to the law: *The house is hers as of right but it is not clear who owns the furniture and paintings.*

be all right (by/with sb)
be convenient (for sb); be allowed: *'Yes, thank you, I will stay the night if it's all right with you.'* ◇ *Is it all right to park here?*

do 'right by sb (*old-fashioned*)
treat sb fairly: *The factory will close but the company have promised to do right by the workforce and find jobs for those who want them.*

get sth 'right/'straight
understand sth clearly and correctly: *Have I got this right? You want me to jump off the bridge and onto a moving train? Never!* ◇ *Let's get one thing straight. I'm the boss and I tell you what to do.*

have (got) the right i'dea
have found a very good or successful way of living, doing sth, etc: *He's certainly got the right idea, retiring at 55.*

I'm all 'right, Jack (*BrE, informal*)
used by or about sb who is happy with their own life and does not care about other people's problems: *He has a typical 'I'm all right, Jack' attitude—as long as he's doing well he doesn't care about anyone else.*

in your own 'right
because of your own skills, qualifications, work, etc. and not because of other people: *She is the daughter of a world-famous actor but this prize will make her famous in her own right.*

(be) in the 'right
(be) in a legally or morally correct position in a particular situation: *The problem with Kate is that she always thinks she's in the right. She will never accept that sometimes she gets things wrong.*

(not) in your right 'mind
(not) mentally normal: *Nobody in their right mind would buy a used car without driving it first.*

it'll be all ˌright on the 'night (*saying*)
used to say that a performance, an event, etc. will be successful even if the preparations for it have not gone well

it's/that's all 'right
used as a response to sb thanking you or saying sorry for sth: *'Thank you so much for the flowers.' 'Oh, that's all right.'* ◇ *'I'm sorry I didn't call*

you yesterday.' 'Oh, it's all right—I'd forgotten all about it.'

it's ‚all right for 'some

used to show that you are jealous of another person's good luck: *Jane's going to Paris next week—it's all right for some, isn't it?*

make (all) the right 'noises (*informal*)

behave as if you support or agree with sth, usually because it is fashionable or to your advantage to do so: *The doctors are making the right noises about the reforms to the health service, but I'm not sure that they actually agree with them.*

put sth 'right

correct sth; repair sth: *There seems to be a mistake in my hotel bill. I wonder if you could put it right, please?* ◇ *There's nothing seriously wrong with your television. I can put it right in ten minutes.*

put/set sb 'right

1 tell sb the truth about sth because they have not understood or they have the wrong information: *She was telling everybody that I'd written the report so I soon put her right.*
2 make sb feel better: *These tablets should put you right.*

right you 'are! (*BrE, informal*)

used to show that you accept a statement or an order: *'Two teas, please.' 'Right you are!'*

‚right and 'left; ‚left and 'right

everywhere: *She owes money right and left.*

(as) right as 'rain (*informal*)

in good health or condition: *Get lots of fresh air and rest and you'll soon be feeling as right as rain again.*

right a'way/'off

immediately; without any delay: *They asked him to start right away.* ◇ *I told him right off what I thought of him.*

right e'nough (*spoken*)

certainly; in a way that cannot be denied: *You heard me right enough* (= so don't pretend that you did not).

right 'now

1 at this moment: *He's not in the office right now.*
2 immediately: *Do it right now!*

right 'on (*spoken*)

used to express strong approval or encouragement
▶ ‚right-'on *adj.* (*informal, sometimes disapproving*) having political opinions or being aware of social issues that are fashionable and left-wing: *They pretend to be so right-on, but are they really?*

‚right side 'up (*AmE*)

with the top part turned to the top; in the correct, normal position: *I dropped my toast, but luckily it fell right side up.*

right a 'wrong

do sth to correct an unfair situation or sth bad that you have done: *The families have now been given back their land, in an attempt to right a wrong that*

was committed generations ago.

too 'right/'true (*informal*)

used for showing that you completely agree with sb/sth: *Too right! This is the worst team we've had for years.*

would ‚give your right 'arm for sth/to do sth (*informal*)

want sth very much: *I'd give my right arm to own a horse like that.*

be in the same/right ballpark **→ ballpark**

be on the right/wrong side of 40, 50, etc. **→ side**

be on the right/wrong track **→ track**

a bit of all right **→ bit**

do sb right = see sb (all) right **→ see**

get/start off on the right/wrong foot (with sb) **→ foot**

get/keep on the right/wrong side of sb **→ side**

get your priorities right/straight **→ priorities**

hang a left/right **→ hang**

your, his, etc. heart is in the right place **→ heart**

hit/strike the right/wrong note **→ note**

the left hand doesn't know what the right hand's doing **→ left**

left, right and centre **→ left**

might is right **→ might**

play your cards right **→ play**

put things right **→ things**

right down the line = all along/down the line **→ line**

right, left and centre = left, right and centre **→ left**

see sb (all) right **→ see**

serve sb right (for doing sth) **→ serve**

two wrongs don't make a right **→ two**

right-hand

your ‚right-hand 'man (*informal*)

an assistant who you trust with everything: *'I'd like to introduce you to Peter Davies, my right-hand man. He'll help you when I am away.'*

rights

by 'rights

according to what should happen or what you would expect: *By rights I should feel sorry for shouting at her, but I don't.*

put/set sth to 'rights

correct a situation, especially one which is unfair; put things in their right places or right order: *As a young politician, she wanted to set the world to rights.* ◇ *It took me ages to put things to rights after the workmen had left.*

(be) within your 'rights

have the moral or legal right to do sth: *They were acting perfectly within their rights when they refused to let you into their house.*

dead to rights = bang to rights **→ bang**

riled

be/get (all) ‚riled 'up (*informal, especially AmE*)

be/get very annoyed about sth: *Instead of getting*

all riled up about this, we should try to figure out what to do.

Riley

lead/live the life of Riley → life

ring

give sb a 'ring (*BrE, informal*)
make a telephone call to sb: *I'll give you a ring tomorrow.*

ring a 'bell (*informal*)
sound familiar; help you remember sth, but not completely: *That name rings a bell but I can't remember exactly where I've heard it before.*

ring the 'changes (on sth) (*BrE*)
make changes to sth in order to have greater variety: *I'm pleased to see that they're ringing the changes in the staff canteen. The new menus are much more interesting.*

> ❶ ORIGIN
> This expression refers to bell-ringing, where the bells can be rung in different orders.

ring in your 'ears/'head
make you feel you can still hear sth: *Months later, the applause at the Berlin concert was still ringing in her ears.*

ˌring off the 'hook (*AmE*)
(of a telephone) ring many times: *The phone has been ringing off the hook with offers of help.*

ˌring out the ˌold (year) and ˌring in the 'new
celebrate the end of one year and the start of the next one

ring 'true/'false/'hollow
seem true/false/insincere: *What you've said about Jim just doesn't ring true. Are we talking about the same person?* ◇ *His apology rings a little hollow.*

the brass ring → brass
bring/ring down the curtain (on sth) → curtain
have (got) a familiar ring (about/to it) → familiar
throw your hat into the ring → throw

ringer

a dead ringer for sb → dead

rings

run rings around/round sb/sth → run

ringside

have (got) a ringside 'seat/'view (*informal*)
be in a very good position to see sth happen: *My flat overlooks the central square, so I had a ringside view of the demonstration.*

> ❷ NOTE
> At a boxing match or a circus, a *ringside seat* is one which is closest to the ring.

Riot

read (sb) the Riot Act → read

riot

run riot → run

rip

rip sb/sth aˈpart/to 'shreds, 'bits, etc.
destroy sth; criticize sb/sth very strongly: *Can you believe it? I spent all that time preparing my report, only to have it ripped to shreds!*

let sth rip → let
let rip (at sb) (with sth) → let
rip/tear the heart out of sth → heart

ripe

at/to a 'ripe old age; at/to the ripe old age of …
at/to a very old age: *My grandmother lived to a ripe old age.* ◇ *My uncle was still driving a car at the ripe old age of 89.*

the time is ripe (for sb) (to do sth) → time

ripple

a 'ripple effect
a situation in which an event or action has an effect on sth, which then has an effect on sth else: *His resignation will have a ripple effect on the whole department.*

> ❷ NOTE
> A *ripple* is a small wave on the surface of a liquid, especially water in a lake, etc.

rise

get a 'rise out of sb
make sb react in an angry way by saying sth that you know will annoy them, especially as a joke: *Don't take any notice of him—he's just trying to get a rise out of you.* ◇ *She always got a rise out of him by copying his accent.*

give 'rise to sth (*formal*)
cause sth to happen or exist: *The novel's success gave rise to a number of sequels.*

ˌrise and 'shine (*old-fashioned*)
used for telling sb to get out of bed in the morning: *Rise and shine, everyone, we've got a lot to do today.*

ˌrise from the 'ashes
become successful or powerful again after defeat or destruction: *Can a new party rise from the ashes of the old one?*

> ❶ ORIGIN
> This idiom refers to the story of the phoenix, a mythological bird which burns to death and then *rises from the ashes* to be born again.

rise to the 'bait
act or react to sth in exactly the way another per-

son wants you to: *I knew he was trying to get me angry, but I didn't rise to the bait.*

❷ NOTE
A fisherman uses *bait* to attract fish to his hook.

rise to the oc'casion/'challenge
do sth successfully in a difficult situation, emergency, etc: *When the lead singer became ill, Cathy had to take her place. Everyone thought she rose to the occasion magnificently.* ◇ *This company must be prepared to rise to the challenge of a rapidly changing market.*

be up/rise with the lark ➔ **lark**
come/up rise through the ranks ➔ **ranks**
draw yourself up/rise to your full height ➔ **full**
your, his, etc. hackles rise ➔ **hackles**
make sb's hackles rise ➔ **hackles**

risk
at 'risk (from/of sth)
in danger of sth unpleasant or harmful happening: *As with all diseases, certain groups will be more at risk than others.* ◇ *If we go to war, innocent lives will be put at risk.*

at the 'risk of doing sth
used to introduce sth that may sound stupid or may offend sb: *At the risk of showing my ignorance, how exactly does the Internet work?*

at risk to yourself/sb/sth
with the possibility of harming yourself/sb/sth: *He dived in to save the dog at considerable risk to his own life.*

do sth at your ,own 'risk
do sth even though you have been warned about the possible dangers and will have to take responsibility for anything bad that happens: *Persons swimming beyond this point do so at their own risk* (= on a notice). ◇ *Valuables are left at their owner's risk* (= on a notice).

risk ,life and 'limb
risk being killed or injured in order to do sth: *She risked life and limb to save her son from the fire.*

risk your 'neck (*informal*)
take a big risk by doing sth dangerous, stupid, etc: *I'm not going to risk my neck complaining about the boss.*

take a 'risk; take 'risks
do sth even though you know that sth bad could happen as a result: *That's a risk I'm not prepared to take.* ◇ *You have no right to take risks with other people's money.*

run the risk (of doing sth) ➔ **run**

risks
run risks ➔ **run**
take risks = take a risk ➔ **risk**

river
sell sb down the river ➔ **sell**

riveted
be ,riveted to the 'spot/'ground
be so shocked or frightened that you cannot move: *As he walked away towards his car she wanted to run after him, but she felt frozen, riveted to the spot.*

road
off the 'road
(of a car) need to be repaired and therefore impossible to use: *We'll have to go by bus. My car's off the road at the moment.*

on the 'road
1 travelling, especially for long distances or periods of time: *The band has been on the road for six months.*
2 (of a car) in good condition so that it can be legally driven: *It will cost about £500 to get the car back on the road.*
3 moving from place to place, and having no permanent home: *Life on the road can be very hard.*

on the ,road to re'covery, 'stardom, etc.
on the way to achieving sth desirable: *The operation was a success and the patient is now well on the road to recovery.* ◇ *After many years struggling to get their company started, they are now firmly on the road to success.*

on the ,road to 'ruin, di'saster, etc.
following a course of action that will lead to ruin, disaster, etc: *I don't know whether it was losing his job or alcohol that set him on the road to ruin.*

one for the 'road (*spoken*)
a last alcoholic drink before you leave a party, etc: *How about one for the road, Jim?*

❶ ORIGIN
This expression is is thought to come from the custom of offering criminals a final drink at a pub on the way to their public execution.

a 'road hog (*informal, disapproving*)
a person who drives in a dangerous way without thinking about the safety of other road users: *Keep left, you road hog!*

❷ NOTE
If you *hog the road*, you drive so that other vehicles cannot pass.

the road to hell is paved with good intentions (*saying*)
it is not enough to intend to do good things, behave better, etc.; you must actually do them, be better, etc.

the end of the road/line ➔ **end**
further along/down the road ➔ **further**
get the show on the road ➔ **show**
hit the road ➔ **hit**
take the high road (in sth) ➔ **high**

roaring

do a roaring 'trade (in sth) (*informal*)
sell sth very quickly or do a lot of business: *Toy shops do a roaring trade just before Christmas.*

,roaring 'drunk
extremely drunk and noisy: *They came home roaring drunk again last night.*

a ,roaring suc'cess (*informal*)
a very great success: *The musicians were such a roaring success that they have been asked to stay for an extra week.* ◇ *His films haven't exactly been a roaring success, have they?*

roasting

give sb/get a 'roasting (*informal*)
criticize sb or be criticized in an angry way: *I'd better go. I'll get a roasting if I'm late again!*

rob

,rob sb 'blind (*informal*)
get a lot of money from sb by deceiving them or charging them too much for sth: *He robbed his clients blind, taking about 25% of their profits.*

rob ,Peter to pay 'Paul (*saying*)
take money from one area and spend it in another: *Government spending on education has not increased. Some areas have improved, but only as a result of robbing Peter to pay Paul.*

robbery

daylight robbery → **daylight**

robin

a ,round 'robin
a letter of protest, etc. that has been signed by many people in such a way that no single person can be blamed or punished for sending it: *Did you sign that round robin that was sent to the manager this week?*

Robinson

before you can say Jack Robinson → **say**

rock

(caught/stuck) between a ,rock and a 'hard place
in a situation where you have to choose between two things, both of which are unpleasant: *The workers now feel that they are caught between a rock and a hard place. They don't agree with the new terms and conditions, but if they go on strike they may lose their jobs altogether.*

hit/reach ,rock 'bottom; be at ,rock 'bottom
reach or be at the lowest point or level that is possible: *Demand for new cars is at rock bottom. This month's sales figures are the lowest in ten years.* ◇ *I really hit rock bottom after my marriage broke up.*

▶ ,rock-'bottom *adj.*: *For rock-bottom prices, come to McArthur's Furniture Store.*

rock the 'boat (*informal*)
do sth that might upset sb/sth, cause problems or change the balance of a situation in some way: *Politicians who are prepared to rock the boat are popular with newspapers but not with their parties.*

shake/rock the foundations of sth → **foundations**
shake/rock sth to its foundations → **foundations**
(as) solid as a rock → **solid**
(as) steady as a rock → **steady**

rocker

,off your 'rocker (*informal, spoken*)
(of a person) crazy: *Spend a thousand pounds on a dress! Are you off your rocker?*

rocket

give sb a 'rocket (*BrE, informal*)
criticize sb very strongly for doing sth wrong: *His boss gave him a rocket for losing the contract.*

it's not 'rocket science
used in order to emphasize that sth is not complicated or difficult to do or understand: *Oh, I'm sure I'll manage. It's not exactly rocket science, is it?*

you don't have to be a 'rocket scientist (to do sth); it doesn't take a 'rocket scientist (to do sth)
used to emphasize that sth is easy to understand: *Of course this model sells more than the others—it's the cheapest! It doesn't take a rocket scientist to work that one out.*

rocks

on the 'rocks
1 in danger of failing or being destroyed: *Their marriage is on the rocks.* ◇ *The economy of this country is on the rocks. Something must be done before it's too late.*
2 (of drinks) served with ice but no water: *'How would you like your whisky?' 'On the rocks, please.'*

rod

make a rod for your own 'back
do sth which is likely to cause problems for yourself, especially in the future: *I think she's making a rod for her own back by not telling him she's leaving. When he finds out, there'll be trouble.*

a rod/stick to beat sb with → **beat**
rule (sb/sth) with a rod of iron/with an iron hand → **rule**
spare the rod and spoil the child → **spare**

rogues

a ,rogues' 'gallery (*informal, humorous*)
a collection of photographs of criminals: *Have you seen these photos of the new government ministers? What a rogues' gallery!*

roll

be on a 'roll (*informal*)
be experiencing a period of success at what you are doing: *Don't stop me now—I'm on a roll!*

'roll on...! (*BrE, spoken*)
used to say that you want sth to happen or arrive soon: *Roll on the spring! I hate winter.* ◇ *Roll on Friday!*

roll up your 'sleeves (*informal*)
get ready for hard work: *We've just moved into a bigger house and there's a lot to do. I guess we'll just have to roll up our sleeves and get on with it.*

roll with the 'punches
adapt yourself to a difficult situation: *Well, there's nothing we can do to change things. We'll just have to learn to roll with the punches.*

> **❶ ORIGIN**
> This idiom comes from a technique used in boxing, where the boxer moves away from the punch to avoid a direct hit.

heads will roll (for sth) → heads
ready to roll → ready
roll in his, her, etc. grave = turn in his, her, etc. grave → turn
roll/slip/trip off the tongue → tongue

rolled

(all) rolled into 'one
several qualities/things combined in one place, person, object, etc: *It's a penknife, scissors, corkscrew all rolled into one.* ◇ *He's a writer, scientist and journalist rolled into one.*

rolling

'rolling in the 'aisles (*informal*)
laughing a lot: *The comedian was very good indeed. He had the audience rolling in the aisles.*

(be) 'rolling in it/money (*informal*)
(be) very rich: *She's been the managing director of the company for 10 years, so she must be rolling in it by now.*

a rolling 'stone (gathers no 'moss) (*saying*)
a person who moves from place to place, job to job, etc. and so does not have a lot of money, possessions or friends but is free from responsibilities

get/keep/set/start the ball rolling → ball

Rome

Rome wasn't built in a 'day (*saying*)
it takes time, patience, and hard work to do a difficult or important job: *She asked me why the film wasn't finished yet so I reminded her that Rome wasn't built in a day.*

when in 'Rome (do as the 'Romans do) (*saying*)
follow the example of other people and act as they do, especially if you are a stranger or new to a place or situation: *I don't take taxis usually but it seemed to be what everyone did in the city; so I thought 'when in Rome...'*

fiddle while Rome burns → fiddle

romp

'romp home/to victory (*informal*)
win easily, especially in a race, election, etc: *The Queen's horse romped home in the first race.* ◇ *The Democratic Party romped to victory in the recent elections.*

roof

go through the 'roof (*informal*)
1 become very angry: *He went through the roof when I told him I'd lost the money.*
2 (of prices, numbers) rise or increase very quickly: *Prices have gone through the roof since the oil crisis began.*

lift/raise the 'roof (also **bring the 'roof down**) (*informal*)
(of a large group of people) make a very loud noise, for example by shouting or singing: *The audience raised the roof when the band played their favourite song.* ◇ *The crowd brought the roof down when the home team scored. I had never ever heard such cheering.*

a 'roof over your head (*informal*)
a place to live; a house: *Everyone needs a roof over their heads but thousands remain homeless.*

under one/the same 'roof (*informal*)
in the same house, etc: *There were three generations of the family living under one roof.*

under your 'roof
in your home: *I don't want that woman under my roof ever again!*

hit the roof/ceiling → hit

rooftops

shout, etc. sth from the housetops/rooftops → housetops

room

no room to swing a 'cat (*informal*)
(of a room) very small; not big enough: *In most modern student accommodation there's not enough room to swing a cat.* ◇ *I'd love a bigger kitchen. There isn't room to swing a cat in this one.*

> **❶ ORIGIN**
> This expression refers to a special kind of whip, the 'cat-o'-nine-tails', which was used to punish sailors.

elbow room → elbow
freedom of/room for manoeuvre → manoeuvre

roost

(your/the) chickens come home to roost → chickens
rule the roost → rule

root

get to the 'root of sth
be able to see or do sth about the main cause (of a problem, etc.): *We must get to the root of the drugs problem.*

,root and 'branch
completely; thoroughly: *The independence movement has been destroyed root and branch.*

the ,root 'cause (of sth)
the main cause of sth, such as a problem or difficult situation: *Poverty is the root cause of most of the crime in the city.*

take 'root
become firmly established: *His ideas on education never really took root; they were just too extreme.*

rooted

glued/rooted to the spot → **spot**

roots

put down (new) 'roots
go to live in a place and gradually become part of a local community: *We've moved around a lot because of my job and it seems to get more difficult to put down new roots each time.*

the grass roots → **grass**

rope

give sb enough 'rope (and he'll/she'll hang himself/herself) (*saying*)
deliberately give sb enough freedom for them to make a mistake and get into trouble: *I'm going to give John enough rope to hang himself. Then the police will be forced to take some action.*

be at the end of your rope → **end**
money for old rope → **money**

ropes

on the 'ropes (*informal*)
very near to failure or defeat: *The company is on the ropes; unless the bank extends their loan, they're finished.*

> **❶ ORIGIN**
> This idiom refers to a boxer that is against the ropes of a boxing ring.

show sb/learn/know the 'ropes (*informal*)
explain to sb/learn/know how to do a particular job, task, etc. correctly: *It will take me a couple of weeks to learn the ropes but after that I should be fine.* ◇ *Mrs Brian will show you the ropes.*

> **❶ ORIGIN**
> This expression refers to a sailor learning the different ropes for the sails of a ship.

rose

a 'rose by any other name (would smell as 'sweet) (*saying*)
what is important is what people or things are, not what they are called

> **❶ ORIGIN**
> This phrase comes from Shakespeare's play *Romeo and Juliet.*

rose-coloured (*BrE*) (*AmE* rose-coloured)

look at, see, etc. sth through rose-tinted/rose-coloured spectacles → **spectacles**

roses

be all 'roses; be a bed of 'roses (also **be ,roses, ,roses all the 'way**) (*informal*)
be easy, comfortable or pleasant: *Being a film star isn't all roses, you know.* ◇ *Don't expect married life to be a bed of roses, because it's not.*

everything's coming up 'roses (*informal*)
everything is happening as well as or better than you hoped: *She's had an unhappy time recently but everything seems to be coming up roses for her now.*

put the 'roses back in your cheeks (*BrE*, *informal*)
make you look healthier because you are not so pale: *A week in the countryside will put the roses back in your cheeks.*

come up/out of sth smelling of roses → **smelling**

rose-tinted

look at, see, etc. sth through rose-tinted/rose-coloured spectacles → **spectacles**

rosy

everything in the garden is lovely/rosy → **garden**

rot

the rot sets 'in
a situation starts to get worse: *The rot really set in when the team's best player left the club last year.*

stop the rot → **stop**

rotten

a rotten 'apple
one bad person who has a bad effect on others in a group: *In response to the allegations of mass corruption within the team, a former player said today, 'There may be the odd rotten apple in the pack, but the majority are clean and honest.'*

spoil sb rotten → **spoil**

rough

in 'rough (*especially BrE*)
if you write or draw sth **in rough**, you make a first version of it, not worrying too much about mistakes or details: *I've already written the essay in rough, but I need to write it out again this evening.*

live/sleep 'rough
live or sleep outside in the streets because you have no home or money: *Hundreds of people are sleeping rough on the streets of the city.*

,rough and 'ready
1 simple and prepared quickly but good enough for a particular situation: *I can give you a rough-*

and-ready estimate of the cost of the work now and a more detailed estimate later.
2 (of a person) not very polite, educated or fashionable: *His approach was rather rough and ready, but he was very popular with his customers.*

rough and 'tumble
1 a situation in which people compete with each other and are aggressive in order to get what they want: *In the rough and tumble of politics you can't trust anyone.*
2 a noisy but not serious fight: *The toddlers often join in the rough and tumble of the older children's games.*

a ,rough 'diamond (*BrE*) (*AmE* a ,diamond in the 'rough)
a person who has many good qualities even though they do not seem to be very polite, educated, etc: *Don't be put off by your first impressions—he's something of a rough diamond.*

rough 'edges
small parts of sth or of a person's character that are not yet as good as they should be: *The ballet still had some rough edges.* ◇ *He had the rough edges knocked off him at school.*

'rough it (*informal*)
live in a way that is not very comfortable for a short time: *We can sleep on the beach. I don't mind roughing it for a night or two.*

rough 'justice
punishment or rewards given without enough care so that people feel they have been unfairly treated: *The pensioners complained that they had received rough justice when their claim for an increase in benefits was rejected without discussion.*

take the ,rough with the 'smooth
accept the unpleasant part of sth as well as the pleasant: *It certainly isn't all fun and games when you're a student, but you have to learn to take the rough with the smooth.*

a bit of rough → **bit**
cut up rough/nasty → **cut**
a raw/rough deal → **deal**
(give sb, have, etc.) a rough/an easy ride → **ride**

roughshod
run roughshod over sb/sth = ride roughshod over sb/sth → **ride**

round

,round a'bout (*especially BrE*) (*AmE* usually a,round a'bout)
1 in the area near a place: *in Oxford and the villages round about*
2 approximately: *We're leaving around about ten.* ◇ *A new roof will cost round about £3000.*

,round 'here (*especially BrE*) (*AmE* usually a,round 'here)
near where you are now or where you live: *There are no decent schools round here.*

roundabouts
swings and roundabouts → **swings**

rounds

do the 'rounds (of sth) (*BrE*) (also **make the 'rounds** *AmE, BrE*)
1 go from place to place or from person to person: *We did the rounds of the local pubs but he wasn't in any of them.*
2 be passed from person to person: *News of her resignation soon made the rounds and it wasn't long before another company offered her work.* ◇ *This cold seems to be doing the rounds at the moment.*

route

en 'route (*from French*)
on the way; while travelling from/to a particular place: *We stopped for a picnic en route.* ◇ *The bus broke down en route from Boston to New York.*

roving

have (got) a roving 'eye (*old-fashioned*)
be always looking for a chance to start a new love affair or get sth that you want: *Be careful of Brian—he's got a roving eye.*

row

in a 'row
(of a number of events, etc.) happening one after another; consecutively: *We've won five games in a row.*

(on) skid row → **skid**

rub

rub sb's 'nose in it (also **rub it 'in**) (*informal*)
continue reminding sb about a mistake they have made or an unpleasant truth: *She's always rubbing my nose in it. She's never forgiven me for not taking that job.* ◇ *I know I made the wrong decision, but there's no need to rub it in, is there?*

rub 'salt into the wound/into sb's wounds
make sb who is already feeling upset, angry, etc. about sth feel even worse: *She was already upset about not getting the job, but when they gave it to one of her own trainees it really rubbed salt into the wound.*

rub 'shoulders (with sb) (*AmE* also **rub 'elbows with sb**) (*informal*)
meet and talk (to rich, famous, etc. people): *I used to rub shoulders with some very wealthy people when I worked in banking.*

rub sb up the wrong 'way (*BrE*) (*AmE* **rub sb the wrong 'way**) (*informal*)
make sb annoyed or angry, often without intending to, by doing or saying sth that offends them: *She's a very good lawyer but she does sometimes rub clients up the wrong way.*

there is/lies the 'rub

that is the main difficulty: *To get a job you need somewhere to live, and there's the rub—I have nowhere to live and so I can't get a job.*

❶ ORIGIN
This expression comes from Shakespeare's play *Hamlet*.

not have two brain cells, pennies, etc. to rub together → **two**

Rubicon

cross the Rubicon → **cross**

rude

a rude a'wakening (*written*)

a sudden, unexpected discovery of an unpleasant fact, truth, etc: *If he thinks that the exam's going to be easy, he's going to get a rude awakening.*

ruffle

ruffle sb's/a few 'feathers (*informal*)

annoy sb by doing sth that upsets and disturbs them: *All this talk of a strike has clearly ruffled the management's feathers.*

ruffled

smooth (sb's) ruffled feathers → **smooth**

rug

pull the carpet/rug out from under sb's feet → **pull**
sweep sth under the rug = sweep/brush sth under the carpet → **carpet**

ruin

go to rack and ruin → **rack**

ruins

in 'ruins

badly damaged or destroyed: *The city was in ruins at the end of the war.* ◇ *Their life was in ruins after the death of their only child.*

rule

as a (general) 'rule

usually: *It's lucky for you that I'm still awake. As a rule I'm in bed by eleven.*

make it a 'rule to do sth

always do sth because you think it is a good idea or the right thing to do: *I make it a rule to invite all my students to a party at my house once a year.*

a rule of 'thumb

a quick, practical, but not exact, way of measuring or calculating sth: *As a rule of thumb you need a litre of paint to every 12 square metres of wall.*

❶ ORIGIN
This idiom comes from the old practice of using your thumb to measure things.

rule the 'roost (*informal*)

be the person who controls a group, family, community, etc: *It is a family firm, where the owner's mother rules the roost.*

❷ NOTE
A *roost* is a place where birds sleep.

rule (sb/sth) with a rod of 'iron/with an iron 'hand (*informal*)

control sb/sth in a very strong or strict way: *They ruled the country with an iron hand and anybody who protested was arrested.*

divide and rule → **divide**
the exception (that) proves the rule → **exception**
the golden rule → **golden**
let your heart rule your head → **let**
rule/throw sth out of court → **court**

rules

bend/stretch the 'rules

allow sb to break the rules to some extent because you think there is a good reason: *We don't normally employ people over 50, but in your case we're prepared to bend the rules a little.*

the rules of the 'game

the standards of behaviour that most people accept or that actually operate in a particular area of life or business: *It was a very competitive and aggressive business, so I had to learn the rules of the game very quickly.*

play by sb's (own) rules → **play**
play by the rules → **play**

run

the common/general 'run (of sth)

the average or usual type (of sth): *This programme is better than the general run of television comedies.*

give sb/get/have the 'run of sth (*informal*)

allow sb/be allowed to use freely a house, etc. that belongs to another person: *He was very kind and let us have the run of his house while he was at work.*

on the 'run

1 (of an escaped prisoner, criminal, etc.) be running away or hiding from the police: *Four prisoners escaped this morning. Three of them were caught but one of them is still on the run.*
2 be very busy or active: *She's been on the run all day. It's not surprising she's tired.*
3 (of an enemy, opponent, etc.) in the process of being defeated: *Liverpool have got Manchester United on the run.* ◇ *The rebels are on the run now. Victory is ours.*

run a'mok

behave in a wild or uncontrolled way: *The crowd*

*ran amok through the city streets when they heard
their leaders had been killed.*

❶ ORIGIN
*Amok comes from the Malay word for 'attack
fiercely'.*

run around in 'circles (*BrE* also **run round in
'circles**) (*informal*)
be busy doing sth without achieving anything
important or making progress: *He has a tendency
to run around in circles getting more and more
worked up.*

run around like a ˌheadless 'chicken
be very busy and active trying to do sth, but not
very organized, with the result that you do not succeed: *What a day! I've been running around like a
headless chicken all day!*

run a'way with the idea/notion (*spoken*)
believe sth that is not true: *Don't run away with the
idea that you're going to be famous just because
you've appeared on television once.*

(try to) run before you can 'walk (*informal*)
try to do sth that is difficult before you have succeeded in doing sth easy: *The important thing
about cooking is not to try and run before you can
walk. Get the basics right and the rest will follow.*

run sb/sth 'close (*BrE*)
be nearly as good, fast, successful, etc. as sb/sth
else: *Germany ran Argentina very close in the final.*

run 'dry
stop supplying water; be all used so that none is
left: *The wells in most villages in the region have
run dry. ◇ Vaccine supplies started to run dry as the
flu outbreak reached epidemic proportions.*

'run for it (*informal*)
run away from danger very quickly: *Run for it.
There's a bomb in here!*

a (good) run for your 'money (*informal*)
1 a lot of satisfaction or pleasure from sth; good
value for sth: *I've had a good run for my money as
director of this company, but now I think it's time
someone younger took over.*
2 strong and satisfying competition, opposition,
etc: *They may not beat your team but they'll certainly give you a good run for your money.*

run the 'gamut of sth
experience or describe a range of sth: *This poem
runs the gamut of emotions from despair to joy.*

run the 'gauntlet
be attacked or criticized by many people at the
same time: *The Prime Minister's car had to run the
gauntlet of a large group of protesters outside the
conference hall.*

❶ ORIGIN
This phrase refers to a an old army punishment
where a man was forced to run between two
lines of soldiers hitting him.

run 'high
(especially of feelings) be strong and angry or

excited: *As usual, emotions ran high at the awards
ceremony last night.*

run in the 'family
(of a physical characteristic or moral quality) be
sth that many members of a family have: *He was
never going to live long because heart disease runs
in both families. ◇ Good looks run in the family.*

run sb/sth into the 'ground
use sth so much that it breaks; make sb work so
hard that they are no longer able to work: *In just
one year, she managed to run her new car into the
ground. ◇ These children are running me into the
ground.*

run a 'mile (from sb/sth) (*informal*)
show that you are very frightened of sb/sth: *She
likes him but she'd run a mile if he proposed to her.*

I knew if she tried to kiss him he'd run a mile.

run out the 'clock (*AmE*)
if a sports team tries to **run out the clock** at the
end of a game, it stops trying to score and just tries
to keep hold of the ball to stop the other team from
scoring

run out of 'steam (*informal*)
lose the energy, enthusiasm, etc. that you had
before: *His presidential campaign began well but
ran out of steam after a couple of months.*

ˌrun sb 'ragged (*informal*)
make sb do a lot of work or make a big effort so that
they become tired: *You look really exhausted. Have
the children been running you ragged?*

run 'rings around/round sb/sth (*informal*)
do sth very well and so make your opponent look
foolish: *I don't want to compete against her in the
debate, she'll run rings around me.*

run 'riot
get out of control: *They allow their children to run
riot—it's not surprising that the house is always in
such a mess. ◇ His imagination ran riot as he
thought what he would do if he won the money.*

run the 'risk (of doing sth); run 'risks
be or put yourself in a situation in which sth bad could happen to you: *We'd better give them what they want. We don't want to run the risk of losing their business.* ◊ *Investment is all about running risks.*

run the show (*sometimes disapproving*)
be in control of a plan, project, organization, etc: *Why does Sheila always have to run the show? There are plenty of other people who could organize the event just as well as her.*

run a ˌtight 'ship
run an organization in a strict and efficient way: *The boss runs a very tight ship and everybody is expected to work very hard.*

run sb/sth to 'earth/'ground (*informal*)
find sb/sth after a long, difficult search: *I spent years looking for the stolen picture but eventually ran it to ground in London.* ◊ *The escaped prisoner was run to ground within a couple of days.*

run to 'fat
(of people) begin to get fat: *After he stopped playing football he quickly ran to fat.*

run 'wild (*informal*)
grow or behave in an uncontrolled way: *Their parents believed in letting the children run wild when they were young and it doesn't seem to have done them any harm.* ◊ *I just let the roses run wild in this part of the garden.*

run with the hare and hunt with the hounds
try to remain friendly with both sides in a quarrel: *I know you want to keep everyone happy, but I'm afraid you can't run with the hare and hunt with the hounds on this issue.*

be/run low (on sth) → **low**
be/get run/rushed off your feet → **feet**
be/run short of sth → **short**
cast/run an eye/your eyes over sth → **cast**
cut and run → **cut**
drive/run/work yourself into the ground → **ground**
get/run into debt → **debt**
go/run deep → **deep**
go/run like clockwork → **clockwork**
go/run to seed → **seed**
go/run to waste → **waste**
have/run a temperature → **temperature**
in the long run → **long**
in the short run → **short**
make sb's blood run cold → **blood**
run/take its course → **course**
run roughshod over sb/sth = ride roughshod over sb/sth
→ **ride**
still waters run deep → **still**
a trial run → **trial**

runaround

give sb the 'runaround (*informal*)
treat sb badly by not telling them the truth, or by not giving them the help or the information they need, and sending them somewhere else: *Residents claim they were given the runaround by the local council, from whom they had no help at all.*

run-in

have a 'run-in with sb (*informal*)
have an argument or disagreement with sb: *She had a run-in with her son's teacher this morning. She doesn't think he gives the children enough homework.*

runner

do a 'runner (*BrE, informal*)
leave or escape from sb/a place, often after doing sth wrong: *He stole all the money in the office and did a runner.* ◊ *'What happened to his wife?' 'She did a runner. Nobody's seen her for months.'*

running

come 'running
be pleased to do what sb wants: *He expects his wife to come running every time he wants something.*

in/out of the 'running (for sth) (*informal*)
having some/no chance of succeeding or achieving sth: *She's definitely in the running for a prize.* ◊ *He's out of the running for the Paris job now.*

make the 'running (*BrE, informal*)
lead or be very active in sth, which other people must then follow or join: *In the field of electronics, it's the Japanese who are making the running.*

> **❶ ORIGIN**
> This idiom refers to the person in a race who determines the speed of the race by running faster than the others.

a running 'battle
an argument, dispute, etc. which continues over a long period of time: *There's been a running battle between John and his neighbour for years about the garden fence.*

take a running 'jump (*old-fashioned, spoken*)
used to tell sb in an angry or impolite way to go away: *He asked me if I'd sell him the painting for £5, so I told him to take a running jump.*

ˌup and 'running
working fully and correctly: *It will be a lot easier when we have the database up and running.*

feel a chill running/going down your spine = send a chill up/down sb's spine → **send**
hit the ground running → **hit**
in running order = in (full/good) working order → **working**

runs

a chill runs/goes down sb's spine = send a chill up/down sb's spine → **send**
a shiver runs/goes down sb's spine = send a shiver up/down sb's spine → **send**

rush

have a rush of blood to the 'head (*humorous*)
because of a strong emotion, suddenly (decide to)
do sth foolish or dangerous: *I don't really know
why I bought that vase. I just had a rush of blood to
the head and wrote a cheque.*

fools rush in (where angels fear to tread) → **fools**
give sb/get the bum's rush → **bum**
(be in) a tearing hurry/rush → **tearing**

rushed

be/get run/rushed off your feet → **feet**

rut

in a 'rut
in a fixed, rather boring way of doing things: *I suddenly realized one day that I'd been in a rut for
years: same job, same flat, same friends, same holiday every year ...*

> ❷ NOTE
> A *rut* is a deep track that a wheel makes in soft
> ground and which causes wheels to get stuck.

Ss

sack

give sb/get the 'sack (*informal*)
tell sb/be told to leave a job, usually because of sth
that you have done wrong: *If you don't work
harder you'll get the sack.* ◇ *She gave him the sack
because he was always late.*

> **ℹ ORIGIN**
> This expression probably comes from the days
> when boys who were training for employment
> used to carry the equipment necessary for their
> job in a sack. When they left the job they used to
> take the sack of equipment with them.

hit the sack/hay → **hit**

sackcloth

put on, wear, etc. ,sackcloth and 'ashes
behave in a way that shows that you are sorry for
sth that you have done: *Look, I've said I'm sorry!
What do you want me to do—put on sackcloth and
ashes?*

sacred

nothing is 'sacred
often used by sb to complain that people do not
respect traditions, ideas, values, etc. as much as
they should: *For journalists these days nothing is
sacred* (= they will write about anything).

a sacred 'cow (*disapproving*)
a person, belief or institution that a group of
people greatly respect and never criticize: *The
National Health Service is a political sacred cow.
No one likes to criticize it.*

> **❶ ORIGIN**
> In the Hindu religion, cows are respected and
> never harmed.

saddle

be in the 'saddle
be in a position of responsibility and control in an
organization: *It's too early to say if she is a good
manager. She hasn't been in the saddle for very
long.*

> **❷ NOTE**
> In horse riding the *saddle* is the leather seat for
> the rider.

safe

,safe and 'sound
safe; not hurt or harmed: *Fortunately, the police
found the missing children safe and sound.*

(as) safe as 'houses (*BrE*)
very safe; not dangerous: *Investing your money
with us is as safe as houses.*

a safe 'bet (*informal*)
something that is likely to be right or successful: *If
you want a cheap holiday with lots of sunshine,
then Spain is a safe bet.*

safe in the knowledge that …
confident because you know that sth is true or will
happen: *She went out safe in the knowledge that she
looked fabulous.*

to be on the 'safe side
to be careful or prepared; just in case sth unpleasant or unexpected happens: *I'll go and check
whether the gas is off, just to be on the safe side.* ◇
You'd better take an umbrella, to be on the safe side.

better (to be) safe than sorry → **better**
in safe/good hands → **hands**
play (it) safe → **play**

safety

there's ,safety in 'numbers (*saying*)
it is safer for a group of people to do something
which could be dangerous for one person alone:
*We decided there was safety in numbers, so we asked
everyone in the office to sign our letter of complaint.*

said

e,nough 'said
used to say that you understand a situation and
there is no need to say any more: *'He's a politician,
remember.' 'Enough said.'*

the less/least said, the 'better (*saying*)
it is better in a difficult situation to say nothing or
very little (because you might make it worse): *He's
very angry and she's very upset, so don't say anything about cars or accidents. Remember, the less
said, the better.*

**there's something, not much, etc. to be
'said for (doing) sth; sth has (got) something, not much, etc. to be 'said for it**
sth has a lot of advantages or good qualities:
There's a lot to be said for eating sensibly. ◇ *There's
not much to be said for this book; in fact, it's the
worst book I've ever read.*

when ,all is said and 'done
when all the facts are considered: *She doesn't have
a lot of experience but, when all is said and done,
she's the best person for the job.*

you 'said it! (*informal*)
I agree completely; that is very true: *'That was the
most boring lecture I've ever heard.' 'You said it!'*

easier said than done → **easier**
least said soonest mended → **least**
no sooner said than done → **sooner**
well said! → **well**

sail

sail close to the 'wind
behave in a way that is almost illegal or socially unacceptable: *Isn't he sailing a bit close to the wind, driving without a licence?* ◇ *She's been late for work three times this week, which is sailing very close to the wind, I think.*

sailing
be clear sailing = be (all) plain sailing ➔ **plain**

sails
take the wind out of sb's sails ➔ **wind**
trim your sails ➔ **trim**

saint
the patience of a saint/of Job ➔ **patience**

sais

,je ne sais 'quoi *(from French, often humorous)*
a good quality that is difficult to describe: *He has that je ne sais quoi that distinguishes a professional from an amateur.* ◇ *It has a certain je ne sais quoi that really appeals to me.*

> **❶ NOTE**
> The meaning of the French phrase is 'I do not know what'.

sake

for God's, heaven's, pity's, etc. 'sake
used to emphasize that it is important to do sth or when you are annoyed about sth: *For God's sake try and control yourself!* ◇ *Do be careful, for goodness' sake.* ◇ *Oh, for heaven's sake!*
(Some people find the use of **God** here offensive.)

(do sth) for its 'own sake
(do sth) because you are interested in it, and not because you could gain from doing it: *I'm not learning Arabic for any special reason; I'm doing it for its own sake, because I enjoy it.*

for the sake of sb/sth; for sb's/sth's sake
in order to help sb/sth or because you like sb/sth: *They stayed together for the sake of the children.* ◇ *You can do it. Please, for my sake.* ◇ *I hope you're right, for all our sakes* (= because this is important for all of us).

for the sake of 'argument
as a starting point for a discussion; to discuss things in theory only: *For the sake of argument, let's say that prices continue to rise by 20 per cent a year.*

for old times' sake ➔ **old**
for Pete's sake ➔ **Pete**

salad

your 'salad days *(old-fashioned)*
the time when you are young and do not have much experience of life: *Back in my salad days my friends and I used to go dancing every Saturday night.*

> **❶ ORIGIN**
> This comes from Shakespeare's play *Antony and Cleopatra*.

sale

for 'sale
available to be bought, especially from the owner: *I'm sorry, it's not for sale.* ◇ *They've put their house up for sale.*

on 'sale
1 available to be bought, especially in a shop/store: *Tickets are on sale from the booking office.* ◇ *The new model goes on sale next month.*
2 *(especially AmE)* being offered at a reduced price: *All video equipment is on sale today and tomorrow.*

salt

the salt of the 'earth
a very good and honest person that you can always depend on: *Tim's the salt of the earth—he'd do anything he can for you.*

> **❶ ORIGIN**
> This expression comes from the Bible.

rub salt into the wound/into sb's wounds ➔ **rub**
take sth with a pinch of salt ➔ **pinch**
worth your/its salt ➔ **worth**

salts
like a dose of salts ➔ **dose**

Sam
Uncle Sam ➔ **Uncle**

Samaritan

a ,good Sa'maritan
a person who gives help and sympathy to people who need it: *He stole money from an old woman while pretending to be a good Samaritan and help carry her shopping.*

same
Idioms containing **same** are at the entries for the nouns and verbs in the idioms, for example **be in the same boat** is at **boat**.

,all/,just the 'same
in spite of this; nevertheless: *I don't want a lift, but thanks all the same.* ◇ *'You don't need a raincoat! The weather's fine!' 'All the same, I think I'll take one; you never know.'*

(the) ,same a'gain *(spoken)*
used to ask sb to serve you the same drink as before: *Same again, please!*

same 'here (*spoken*)
used to say that the same is also true of you: '*I thought it was a terrible film.' 'Same here.'*

(the) ,same to 'you
used to reply to a greeting, an insult, etc: '*Have a good weekend.' 'And the same to you.'* ◇ '*Get lost!'* '*Same to you!'*

sand

bury/hide your head in the sand → **head**

sands

(the) shifting sands (of sth) → **shifting**

sandwiches

two sandwiches short of a picnic = a brick short of a load → **brick**

sardines

packed (together) like sardines → **packed**

satisfaction

to sb's satis'faction
1 if you do sth **to sb's satisfaction**, they are pleased with it: *The affair was settled to the complete satisfaction of the client.*
2 if you prove sth **to sb's satisfaction**, they believe or accept it: *Can you demonstrate to our satisfaction that your story is true?*

saturation

(get to, reach, etc.) satu'ration point
so full that you cannot add any more: *The refugee camps have reached saturation point.*

sauce

what's ,sauce for the ,goose is ,sauce for the 'gander (*old-fashioned, saying*)
if one partner (in a marriage or relationship) can behave in a certain way, then the other partner should also be allowed to behave in this way: *If she can go out with her friends, why can't I? What's sauce for the goose is sauce for the gander.*

> ❷ NOTE
> A *gander* is a male goose.

sausage

not a 'sausage (*old-fashioned, informal*)
nothing at all: *There's nothing in here at all. Not a sausage!*

save

can't do sth to ,save your 'life (*informal*)
cannot do sth at all or can only do sth very badly: *He can't cook to save his life.*

save sb's 'bacon (*informal*)
rescue sb from a difficult or dangerous situation:

Thank you for helping me with my exam preparation. You really saved my bacon.

save your 'breath (*spoken*)
do not waste your time speaking to sb because they will not listen to your comments, advice, suggestions, etc: *Save your breath. He never listens to anybody.*

> ❶ ORIGIN
> This phrase comes from a longer saying: 'save your breath to cool your porridge'.

save the 'day/situ'ation
do sth that changes probable failure into success: *Jones saved the day for England with a last-minute goal.*

save (sb's) 'face
do sth in order to keep the respect of other people: *The announcement was an attempt by the government to save face.* ▶ **'face-saving** adj.: *face-saving measures*

save sb's/your (own) 'neck/'skin/'hide (*informal*)
save sb or yourself from a dangerous or unpleasant situation: *Don't rely on him for help, he's only interested in saving his own skin.*

save/spare sb's blushes → **blushes**

saved

(be) ,saved by the 'bell
(be) saved from a difficult, embarrassing, etc. situation at the last moment: *Saved by the bell! He was just asking me why my essay was two weeks late when you came in.*

> ❶ ORIGIN
> This expression refers to the bell that marks the end of a round in a boxing match.

saving

a ,saving 'grace
a quality which prevents sb/sth from being completely bad: *She can be difficult at times. Her saving grace is her sense of humour.*

savoir

savoir 'faire (*from French, approving*)
the ability to behave in the appropriate way in certain situations: *He was renowned throughout the diplomatic world for his savoir faire.*

> ❷ NOTE
> The meaning of the French phrase is 'know how to do'.

say

as they 'say (also **as the saying 'goes**)
often used before or after a saying or idiom: *We can kill two birds with one stone, as they say.* ◇ *He was, as the saying goes, as mad as a hatter.*

before you can say Jack 'Robinson (*old-fashioned*)
very quickly or suddenly: *I'll do that for you. I'll have it finished before you can say Jack Robinson.*

have your 'say (*informal*)
give your opinion about sth: *You've had your say, now let me have mine.*

have (got) something, nothing, etc. to 'say for yourself
1 be able/unable to explain your actions: *I've asked him what he was doing here in the middle of the night, but he's got nothing to say for himself.*
2 be able/unable to hold a conversation or express your opinions: *She seems very nice but she doesn't have much to say for herself.*

he, she, etc. wouldn't say ,boo to a 'goose (*informal*)
sb is very shy and afraid of upsetting or annoying people: *How could he ever succeed in politics? He wouldn't say boo to a goose.*

I 'must say (*spoken*)
used to emphasize an opinion: *Well, I must say, that's the funniest thing I've heard all week.*

,I 'say (*old-fashioned, BrE, spoken*)
used to attract sb's attention when you want to tell them something: *I say, our train leaves in twenty minutes. We'd better hurry.*

I ,wouldn't say 'no (to sth) (*spoken*)
used to say that you would like sth or to accept sth that is offered: *I wouldn't say no to a pizza.* ◇ *'Tea, Brian?' 'I wouldn't say no.'*

'I'll say! (*old-fashioned, spoken*)
used to say 'yes' in a very forceful way: *'Is his dog dangerous?' 'I'll say! It nearly bit my hand off!'*

,never say 'die (*saying*)
do not stop trying or hoping for sth

'not to say
used to suggest that you could, with good reason, use a stronger word to describe sb/sth: *He is very difficult, not to say impossible, to understand.*

say 'cheese!
used to ask sb to smile before you take their photograph: *Is everybody ready? Right, say cheese!*

,say no 'more (*spoken*)
it is not necessary for sb to continue speaking because you already understand the situation: *'He's only 21, and he's marrying a rich old lady of 65.' 'Say no more!'*

say your 'piece (*informal*)
say exactly what you feel or think: *I went to see the boss this morning and I said my piece about our working conditions. He wasn't very happy about it.*

say 'what? (*AmE, spoken*)
used to express surprise at what sb has just said: *'He's getting married.' 'Say what?'*

say 'when
used to ask sb to tell you when you should stop pouring a drink or serving food for them because they have enough

(just) say the 'word
used to show that you are willing and ready to do something as soon as sb asks: *If you need any help, just say the word.*

that is to 'say
in other words: *We'll meet again three days from now, that is to say on Friday.*

to ,say the (very) 'least
used to say that you are using the least strong way of saying sth: *I'm not very happy with his work, to say the least.*

to say 'nothing of sth
and also; not forgetting: *She is an expert in Chinese, to say nothing of speaking several European languages.*

,what would/do you 'say (to sth/doing sth)? (*spoken*)
would you like sth/to do sth?: *What would you say to a weekend in Paris?* ◇ *What do you say to eating out tonight?*

whatever you 'say (*spoken*)
used to agree to sb's suggestion because you do not want to argue: *'Just do it now!' 'Whatever you say.'*

who can 'say (...)? (*spoken*)
used to say that nobody knows the answer to a question: *Who can say what will happen next year?*

who's to 'say (...)? (*spoken*)
used to say that sth might happen or might have happened in a particular way, because nobody really knows: *Who's to say we wouldn't have succeeded if we'd had more time?*

you can say 'that again! (*spoken*)
I agree completely; I know that already: *'She's the most boring person I've ever met.' 'You can say that again!'*

you can't say 'fairer (than 'that) (*BrE, spoken*)
used to say that you think the offer you are making is reasonable or generous: *Look, I'll give you £100 for it. I can't say fairer than that.*

you don't 'say! (*spoken, often ironic*)
used to express surprise: *'My brother's an astronaut, you know.' 'You don't say!'* ◇ *'I was in the Scouts for six years.' 'You don't say.'* (= I'm not interested/surprised.)

I dare say → **dare**
I'm sorry to say → **sorry**
kiss/say goodbye to sth → **goodbye**
let us say → **let**
mean to say → **mean**
needless to say → **needless**
not/never have a good word to say for/about sb/sth → **word**
not say/hear a dicky bird → **dicky**
suffice (it) to say (that) ... → **suffice**

saying

it ,goes without 'saying (that ...); that ,goes without 'saying
it is obvious, already known or natural (that ...):

Of course I'll visit you in hospital. It goes without saying! ◊ *'You realize that this is a very responsible job, don't you?' 'Yes, that goes without saying.'*

it's/that's not 'saying much, etc.

used to show that what you have just said is not particularly remarkable or impressive: *She's a better player than me, but that's not saying much* (= because I'm a very bad player).

as the saying goes = as they say → say
if you don't mind me/my saying so … → mind
there's no knowing/saying/telling … → knowing

says

it, etc. says a 'lot, 'much, etc. about/for sb/sth (that …)

something reveals a lot, etc. about sb's/sth's qualities, personality, etc: *It says much about the high quality of these instruments that many of them are still in use today.* ◊ *The kind of car you drive says a great deal about you.*

what/whatever sb says, 'goes (*informal, often humorous*)

when a certain person in authority gives an order, this order must be obeyed: *Sarah wanted the kitchen painted green, and whatever she says, goes.* ◊ *Don't argue with me. I'm the boss here and what I say goes.*

who 'says (…)? (*spoken*)

used to disagree with a statement or an opinion: *Who says I can't do it?*

say-so

on sb's 'say-so

based on a statement that sb makes without giving any proof: *He hired and fired people on his partner's say-so.*

scales

the scales fall from sb's eyes (*literary*)

sb finally understands the truth about sth: *It wasn't until much later that the scales fell from his eyes and he realized that she'd been lying to him.*

tip the balance/scales → tip
tip the scales at sth → tip

scarce

,make yourself 'scarce (*informal*)

leave the place you are in in order to avoid an embarrassing or difficult situation: *I could see they wanted to be alone, so I made myself scarce.*

(as) rare/scarce as hen's teeth → hen

scare

scare the 'shit out of sb; scare sb 'shitless (⚠, *slang*)

frighten sb very much: *You scared the shit out of me, creeping around in the dark like that!*

beat/scare the (living) daylights out of sb → daylights

frighten/scare the life out of sb → life
frighten/scare sb out of their wits → wits

scared

be frightened/nervous/scared of your own shadow → shadow
be scared/bored witless → witless

scene

arrive/come on the 'scene

arrive in/at a place, probably to change the existing situation: *John and I were really happy together until she came on the scene.* ◊ *By the time the police arrived on the scene, it was too late.*

create/make a 'scene

complain noisily, behave badly, etc. especially in a public place: *She refused to pay for the shopping, so Roger made a scene in the supermarket.* ◊ *Please don't create a scene in public.*

(not) sb's 'scene (*informal*)

(not) the kind of place, activity, etc. that sb likes or feels comfortable with: *The holiday wasn't really our scene. Most of the people were much older than us and there wasn't any nightlife.* ◊ *I don't like going to clubs. A quiet evening with friends is much more my scene.*

set the scene/stage (for sth) → set

scenes

behind the 'scenes

(of discussions, arrangements, etc.) not seen by the public: *The general public knows very little about what happens behind the scenes in politics.* ◊ *There was a lot of behind-the-scenes activity at the peace conference.*

❶ ORIGIN
This expression refers to the parts of the stage in a theatre which the audience cannot see.

scent

be on the 'scent (of sb/sth)

have information that will lead you to sb/sth: *The police are on the scent of the criminals.*

❷ NOTE
Animals such as dogs follow the *scent* (= smell) of other animals, especially when hunting.

put/throw sb off the 'scent

give sb false information to prevent them from finding out or knowing sth: *I threw the police off the scent by pretending I was in Mexico City on the day of the crime.*

scheme

the/sb's 'scheme of things

the way the world and other things are or seem to be organized: *Low-paid workers like us don't have a very important place in the scheme of things.* ◊ *Don't worry too much about your exam results;*

they're not really important in the great scheme of things.

school

a school of 'thought
theories or opinions held by certain groups of people: *There are two schools of thought on this matter.*

of the old school → old
the old school tie → old
tell tales out of school → tell

schtum (also shtum)

keep 'schtum/'shtum (*BrE, informal*)
say nothing: *I think we'd better keep schtum about this money, don't you?*

> **❶ ORIGIN**
> This originally comes from the German word *stumm*, meaning 'silent'.

science

blind sb with science → blind
it's not rocket science → rocket

scientist

you don't have to be a rocket scientist (to do sth) → rocket
it doesn't take a rocket scientist (to do sth) → rocket

score

on 'that/'this score
as far as that/this is concerned: *The accommodation is excellent so I don't think we need to worry on that score.*

'score a ,point/'points off/over/against sb
(*especially BrE*)
defeat sb in an argument; deliberately say sth that makes sb appear stupid: *Why don't you try to solve the problem instead of scoring points over each other?* ◇ *I don't like David. He's always trying to score points off everybody.*

even the score → even
know the score → know
settle an old score → settle
settle a score/an account (with sb) → settle

scorn

heap/pour 'scorn on sb/sth
speak about sb/sth in a way that shows that you do not respect them or have a good opinion of them: *She poured scorn on his plans to get rich quickly.*

scot-free

get off/go ,scot-'free (*informal*)
escape from a situation without receiving the pun-

ishment you deserve: *It seemed so unfair that sh was punished while the others got off scot-free!*

> **❶ ORIGIN**
> This idiom comes from the old English word *sceot*, meaning a 'tax'. People were *scot-free* if they didn't have to pay the tax.

scrap

on the 'scrap heap (*informal*)
no longer wanted or considered useful: *With the closure of the factory, thousands of workers have been thrown on the scrap heap.*

scrape

scrape (up) an ac'quaintance with sb (*informal*)
try to become friends with sb because they migh be useful to you

scrape (the bottom of) the 'barrel (*disapproving*)
use things or people of a low quality because al the good ones have already been used: *Television is terrible at the moment, it's nothing but old films They're really scraping the barrel, aren't they?*

bow and scrape → bow

scratch

do sth from 'scratch
do sth from the beginning, not using any work done earlier: *The fire destroyed all the plans. Now we'll have to start again from scratch.*

scratch A and you'll find B
(used to speak about certain types of people in general) carefully consider or examine sb/sth and you will find that they are different from their outside appearance: *Scratch a senator from Texas and you'll find a cowboy.*

scratch your 'head (over sth)
think hard in order to find an answer to sth: *We're all scratching our heads for an answer to the problem.*

(only) scratch (at) the 'surface (of sth)
deal with, understand, or find out about only a small part of a subject or problem: *This report only scratches the surface of the problem.*

up to 'scratch
at the good standard that is expected or needed: *The level of safety in our power stations must be brought up to scratch.* ◇ *If he doesn't come up to scratch, get rid of him.*

> **❶ ORIGIN**
> This expression comes from boxing: the line in the ring which the boxers have to come to when they start to fight is called the *scratch*.

,you scratch 'my back and ,I'll scratch 'yours
(*saying*)
used to say that if sb helps you, you will help them, even if this is unfair to others ▶ 'back-scratching

noun: There is too much back-scratching in local politics in this town.

scream

scream blue 'murder (*BrE*) (*AmE* **scream bloody 'murder**) (*informal*)
shout, scream, etc. very loudly and for a long time; make a lot of noise or fuss because you disagree very strongly with sth: *Jill will scream blue murder if Ann gets promoted and she doesn't.*

screen

the silver screen → silver
the small screen → small

screw

have (got) a 'screw loose
be slightly crazy: *He dresses his cats up in little coats for the winter. Sometimes I think he must have a screw loose.*

screw 'him, 'you, 'that, etc. (⚠, *slang*)
an offensive way of showing that you are annoyed or do not care about sb/sth

pluck/screw/summon up (your/the) courage (to do sth) → courage
a turn of the screw → turn

screwed

have (got) your head screwed on (the right way) → head

screws

put the 'screws on (sb) (*informal*)
force sb to do sth, especially by frightening and threatening them: *The electricity company is really putting the screws on. We've got a week to pay before our supply is cut off!*

🛈 **ORIGIN**
This idiom refers to *thumbscrews*, which were used in the past for torturing people by crushing their thumbs.

scrounge

be/go on the 'scrounge (for sth) (*BrE, informal, disapproving*)
ask sb for money, food, etc. without doing any work for it or paying for it: *She's always on the scrounge for cigarettes. Why doesn't she buy her own?*

scruff

by the scruff of sb's/the 'neck
(hold sb or an animal) by the back of the neck: *The barman took her by the scruff of the neck and threw her out.*

scum

the scum of the earth (*informal*)
a person or a group of people thought to be worth-

less, evil or completely without good qualities: *Drug dealers are the scum of the earth.*

❓ **NOTE**
Scum is a layer of dirt on the surface of water.

sea

all, completely, etc. at 'sea
confused; not organized: *We're still completely at sea trying to understand the new regulations.*

between the devil and the deep blue sea → devil
there are plenty/lots more fish in the sea → fish

seal

a ,seal of ap'proval
the formal support or approval of a person or organization: *Our project has the director's seal of approval.*

set the seal on sth → set

sealed

my lips are sealed → lips
signed, sealed and delivered → signed

seams

be bursting/bulging at the 'seams (with sth)
(also **be full to 'bursting (with sth)**) (*informal*)
be very or too full (of sth): *All of our hospitals are bursting at the seams; we have to build new ones urgently.*

come/fall apart at the seams → apart
fray at/around the edges/seams → fray

seamy

the 'seamy side (of life, etc.)
the unpleasant, dishonest or immoral aspects (of life, etc.): *It's well known that the world of entertainment has its seamy side: drug abuse, corruption, alcoholism ...*

search

search your 'heart/'soul/'conscience (*formal*)
think carefully about your feelings or your reasons for doing sth: *If I searched my heart I'd probably find that I don't always tell the truth.*
▶ **'heart-searching, 'soul-searching** *nouns*: *His divorce forced him to do a lot of soul-searching.*

,search 'me (*spoken*)
I don't know; I've no idea: *'What's the capital of Queensland?' 'Search me!'*

seas

on the high seas → high

season

,in/,out of 'season
1 (of fruit, vegetables, fish, etc.) available/not available in shops because it is the right/wrong

time of year for them: *Peaches are in season at the moment.*

2 during the most/least popular time of year for holidays: *Hotels are much cheaper out of season.*

3 during the time of year when you can/cannot hunt animals: *You can't shoot ducks out of season.*

(the) season's 'greetings (*written*)
used as a greeting at Christmas, especially on Christmas cards

the silly season → silly

seat

(fly) by the seat of your 'pants
act without careful thought and without making a plan in advance, hoping that you will be lucky and successful: *He made careful plans and then found that everything had changed at the last minute, so in the end he had to fly by the seat of his pants.*

take a back 'seat
change to a less important role or function: *After forty years in the business, it's time for me to take a back seat and let someone younger take over.*

have (got) a ringside seat/view → ringside
in the driver's seat = in the driving seat → driving
in the hot seat → hot
on the edge of your seat/chair → edge

seats

bums on seats → bums

second

be second 'nature (to sb)
be sth that you do automatically, without thinking about it, because you have done it for so long or so often: *It took a while to learn to drive, but now it's second nature (to me).*

be ,second ,only to 'sb/'sth
be in a position where only one person or thing is better, more important, etc: *As a pianist, he was second only to Rubinstein.*

get your second 'wind (*informal*)
find energy, strength or enthusiasm after feeling tired or after a period when you produce little: *After midnight the dancers seemed to get their second wind and went on till dawn.*

❶ ORIGIN
This expression comes from running; after feeling out of breath at the beginning of a race, you later find it easier to breathe.

have second 'thoughts
change your opinion about sth; have doubts about sth: *We were going to go to Italy, but we had second thoughts and came here instead.*

on 'second thoughts (*BrE*) (*AmE* **on 'second thought**)
used when you want to change what you have said or decided: *On second thoughts, I won't have a beer, I'll have a whisky.*

second 'best
not as good as the best; not exactly what you want: *The two teams seemed evenly matched, but Arsenal came off second best* (= did not win). ◇ *Sometimes you have to settle for* (= be content with) *second best.*

a/your second 'childhood
a period in life, especially in old age, when you sometimes act like a child, forget things, etc: *I had to feed her and dress her. She's really in her second childhood.*

,second 'sight
the special ability to know what will happen in the future or what is happening somewhere else: *Sometimes I think I've got second sight because my dreams seem to come true.*

second to 'none
very good; as good as the best: *This airline's safety record is second to none.*

without a second 'thought
immediately; without stopping to think about sth further: *He dived in after her without a second thought.*

just a minute/moment/second → just
not for a/one minute/moment/second/instant → minute
play second fiddle → play
a second/another bite at/of the cherry → bite
a split second → split
wait a minute/moment/second → wait

secrecy

swear sb to secrecy → swear

secret

an open secret → open
(be) top secret → top
a trade secret → trade

see

be glad, etc. to see the 'back of sb/sth (*informal, especially BrE*)
be happy that you will not have to deal with or see sb/sth again because you do not like them/it: *Was I pleased to see the back of her!* ◇ *This year's been awful, I'll be glad to see the back of it.*

for all (the world) to 'see
clearly visible; in a way that is clearly visible: *The relief that the audience felt when the performance finished was clear for all to see.*

not see beyond/past the ,end of your 'nose
not notice anything apart from what you are doing at present: *I'm so busy running the office day to day that I can't see beyond the end of my nose.*

not see sb for 'dust (*informal*)
not see sb because they have left a place very quickly: *If I ever win a lot of money, you won't see me for dust. I'll be on the next plane for New York.*

not see ˌhide nor ˈhair of sb/sth (*spoken*)
not see sb/sth for some time: *I haven't seen hide nor hair of her for a month.*

not see the ˌwood for the ˈtrees (*BrE*) (*AmE* **not see the ˌforest for the ˈtrees**) (*informal*)
not have a clear understanding of a situation because you are only looking at small aspects of it and not considering the situation as a whole: *The situation is so complex that many people are unable to see the wood for the trees.*

see both ˈsides (of the question, problem, etc.)
understand why one person or group has an opinion, and why a different person or group disagrees with it: *When people are in politics, it's difficult for them to see both sides of a question.*

see the ˌcolour of sb's ˈmoney (*BrE*) (*AmE* **see the ˌcolor of sb's ˈmoney**) (*informal*)
make sure that sb has enough money to pay you, especially if you think they might not have it: *I want to see the colour of his money before I start doing such a dangerous job for him.*

see sb ˈcoming (*informal*)
know that sb is innocent or stupid and decide to lie to them or cheat them: *'I paid £500 for it, and it doesn't work!' 'They must have seen you coming.'*

see sth ˈcoming
realize that there is going to be a problem before it happens: *We should have seen it coming. There was no way he could keep going under all that pressure.*

see ˈdaylight
begin to understand sth that you didn't understand before: *It was a long time before he finally saw daylight and realized what was going on.*

(not) see eye to ˈeye (with sb) (about/on/ over sth)
(not) have the same opinion or attitude as sb else (about a particular issue, problem, etc.): *My boss and I don't see eye to eye over the question of finance.*

see sb/sth for what they ˈare/it ˈis
realize that sb/sth is not as good, pleasant, etc. as they/it seems: *I used to really like him, but now I can see him for what he really is—selfish and arrogant!*

ˌsee for yourˈself
see or experience sth yourself so that you will believe it is true: *Don't you believe she's here? Well, come in and see for yourself.*

see sb in ˈhell first (*informal*)
used to emphasize that you have no intention of agreeing to or doing what sb has suggested: *You want me to invite that woman to this house? I'll see her in hell first.*

see ˈlife
see and experience different ways of living, for example by travelling, working with many different kinds of people, etc: *She's seen life, that's for sure.* ◇ *He's certainly seen a bit of life.*

see the ˈlight
1 understand or accept sth after you have spent a lot of time thinking about it: *I think he's finally seen the light and is going to retire while he's still able to enjoy himself.*
2 change what you believe as a result of a religious experience: *She was an atheist but now she says she's seen the light.*

see a lot, nothing, etc. of sb
often, never, etc. see sb socially: *'Do you see much of Jennifer these days?' 'No, but I see a great deal of her sister.'*

see pink ˈelephants (*informal*)
see things that are not really there, because you are drunk: *I think I ought to stop drinking that whisky. If I have any more tonight I'll be seeing pink elephants.*

see ˈred (*informal*)
suddenly become very angry: *Cruelty to animals makes him see red.*

see sb (all) right (*AmE* also **do sb ˈright**) (*informal*)
make sure that sb is treated correctly, paid properly for sth they have done, etc: *If I die, then the company will see my wife right.*

(make sb) see ˈsense/ˈreason
(cause sb to) begin to act and think more reasonably than before: *Ah, you've given up smoking! I'm glad you've seen sense at last.* ◇ *It's time somebody made him see reason.*

see ˈservice
1 be in the army, navy or air force: *He saw service in Korea and later in Vietnam.*
2 be used: *This new type of engine won't see service until next year.*

see the ˈsights
visit the famous places in a city, country, etc: *We spent our first day in Rome seeing the sights.*
▶ **ˈsightseeing, ˈsightseer** *nouns*: *We spent the afternoon sightseeing.* ◇ *There are always sightseers outside Buckingham Palace.*

see ˈstars (*informal*)
see small bright lights for a few moments, for example after being hit on the head: *There was a bang. I saw stars, and the next thing I knew, I was lying on the kitchen floor.*

ˈsee to it (that …)
make certain (that): *I want you to see to it that she never comes in here again.* ◇ *This report must be sent to Head Office immediately. Would you see to it for me?*

see your ˈway (ˈclear) to doing sth
find that it is possible or convenient to do sth: *Could you see your way clear to lending me £10 until next week?*

see which way the ˈwind blows
see what most people think, or what is likely to happen before you decide how to act yourself: *Most politicians are careful to see which way the wind's blowing before they make up their minds.*

see the 'world
travel, live or work in many different parts of the world: *A lot of students take a year off after university to travel and see the world.*

'see you (a'round); ,see you 'later (also (I'll) be 'seeing you) (*spoken*)
used to say goodbye to sb who you expect to see again soon

so I 'see!
used to say that sb does not need to tell you about the present situation because it is obvious, especially when you are not happy about it: *'I'm afraid I'm a bit late this morning.' 'So I see.'*

you 'see (*spoken*)
used when you are explaining sth: *You see, the thing is, we won't be finished before Friday.*

as far as the eye can/could see → **far**
hear/see the end/the last of sb/sth → **hear**
I'll believe it/that when I see it → **believe**
let me see/think → **let**
long time no see → **long**
see/think fit (to do sth) → **fit**
see/hear things → **things**
suck it and see → **suck**
wait and see → **wait**
what the eye doesn't see (the heart doesn't grieve over) → **eye**

seed

go/run to 'seed (*informal*)
(of a person) become untidy or dirty because you no longer care about your appearance, etc: *I was very surprised when I saw her. She has really run to seed in the last few months.*

> **ⓘ ORIGIN**
> This idiom refers to the fact that when the flower in a plant dies, seeds are produced.

seeds

plant/sow the 'seeds of sth
start a process which will develop into sth large, important, etc: *What first planted the seeds of doubt in your mind?* ◇ *The seeds of conflict were sown when oil was discovered on the border between the two countries.*

seeing

seeing as/that
because; considering that; since: *Seeing as we're both going the same way, can I give you a lift?*

,seeing is be'lieving (*saying*)
if you see sth, you can be sure that it is true or that it really exists: *He might be telling the truth, but seeing is believing, I always say.*

(I'll) be seeing you = see you (around) → **see**

seek

seek your 'fortune (*literary*)
try to find a way to become rich, especially by

going to another place: *At the age of twenty, he decided to emigrate and seek his fortune in Canada.*

seen

have seen/known better days → **better**
I, he, etc. wouldn't be seen/caught dead ... → **dead**
nowhere to be found/seen → **found**

self

be a shadow/ghost of your/its former self → **former**

sell

sell sb down the 'river (*informal*)
act very unfairly to sb who trusts you; betray sb you have promised to help: *The workers thought that their own leaders had sold them down the river.*

> **ⓘ ORIGIN**
> This idiom comes from the days of slavery in the US. A slave who was sold to a plantation owner further down the Mississippi would experience harsher conditions than before.

sell sb 'short
cheat sb by giving them less than they have paid for: *He sold us short! We paid for five kilos of mushrooms and only got four!*

sell your 'soul (*informal, often humorous*)
do something morally or legally wrong in order to get sth that you want very much: *He'd sell his soul to get that job.*

> **ⓘ ORIGIN**
> This expression refers to selling your soul to the devil in exchange for power, money, etc.

sell yourself/sb/sth 'short
describe yourself/sb/sth as being less good, valuable, etc. than you, sb, etc. really are: *Don't sell yourself short when you go for an interview.* ◇ *It was a great idea, but you sold it short.*

sell/go like hot cakes → **hot**
sell sb/buy a pup → **pup**

sell-by

be past its sell-by date → **past**

seller

a ,seller's 'market
a situation in which people selling sth have an advantage, because there is not a lot of a particular item for sale, and prices can be kept high: *We just can't afford to buy a house at the moment. It's a seller's market, and there's nothing we can do about it.*

send

send a 'chill up/down sb's spine; a 'chill runs/goes down sb's spine
cause sb to feel horror and fear: *The picture sent a chill up my spine.* ◇ *When I read the details of the murder, a chill ran down my spine.* ▶ 'spine-chilling *adj.*: *a spine-chilling horror novel*

send sb 'packing (*informal*)

tell sb firmly or rudely to go away because they are annoying or disturbing you; dismiss sb from a job: *He wanted to borrow money off me, but I sent him packing.* ◇ *They caught him stealing company property and he was sent packing.*

send a 'shiver up/down sb's spine; a 'shiver runs/goes down sb's spine

cause sb to feel excitement or anxiety: *This piece of music sends shivers down my spine.* ◇ *When I heard all those people shouting and cheering, a shiver ran down my spine.*

send sb to 'Coventry (*BrE*)

refuse to speak to sb, as a way of punishing them for sth they have done: *Joe worked all through the strike, so when it was over, the other workers sent him to Coventry.*

❶ ORIGIN
Coventry is a town in the centre of England. It is said that in the past, people there did not like soldiers and refused to talk to any who were sent to the town.

drive/send sb up the wall → **wall**
give/send my love to sb → **love**
put/turn/send sb out to grass → **grass**

sends

work all the hours God sends → **work**

sense

in 'no sense

not in any way: *In no sense do I agree with this suggestion.*

in a 'sense; in 'one sense

considered in one way, rather than in other ways: *In a sense we are all responsible for the problem of starvation in the world.*

knock/talk some 'sense into sb (*informal*)

try to persuade sb to stop behaving in a stupid way, sometimes using rough or violent methods: *I wish somebody would knock some sense into our politicians.* ◇ *Try and talk some sense into her before she makes the wrong decision.*

make 'sense

1 have a meaning that you can easily understand: *This sentence doesn't make sense—there's no verb in it.*

2 be a sensible or practical thing to do: *It makes sense to buy a house now because prices will certainly go up soon.*

3 be easy to understand or explain: *John wasn't making much sense on the phone.*

make 'sense of sth

understand sth that is difficult or not very clear: *I don't understand these instructions. Can you make any sense of them?*

a sense of oc'casion

a feeling or understanding that an event is important or special: *Candles on the table gave the evening a sense of occasion.*

have (got) more money than sense → **money**
(make sb) see sense/reason → **see**
a sixth sense → **sixth**

senses

come to your 'senses

1 (also **bring sb to their 'senses**) stop behaving in an unreasonable or stupid way; do sth to stop sb behaving in this way: *At last he has come to his senses. He now understands that a restaurant in this part of town will never succeed.*

2 wake up from being unconscious: *When I came to my senses I found myself in a hospital bed.*

take leave of your senses → **leave**

sent

these things are sent to try us → **things**

separate

go your separate 'ways

(of two or more people) stop seeing each other socially, because you are living in different places, doing different jobs, etc: *After school we went our separate ways.*

sort out/separate the men from the boys → **men**
sort out/separate the sheep from the goats → **sheep**
sort out/separate the wheat from the chaff → **wheat**

sequitur

a ˌnon 'sequitur (*from Latin, formal*)

a statement that does not seem to follow what has just been said in any natural or logical way: *In the middle of a discussion about the weather, Liz started talking about fish. Everyone ignored the non sequitur completely.*

❷ NOTE
The meaning of the Latin phrase is 'it does not follow'.

seriously

take sb/sth 'seriously

consider or treat sth as important or serious: *We told him he was in danger but he didn't take us seriously.*

seriousness

in all 'seriousness

seriously; not jokingly: *Surely you're not telling me, in all seriousness, that you want to work in a factory for the rest of your life!*

serve

serve a, his, its, etc. 'purpose; serve the 'purpose (of doing sth) (*BrE* also **serve his, its, etc. 'turn**)

be useful for a particular purpose or period of time; be good or useful enough for sb: *It's not a very good radio, but it serves its purpose.* ◇ *He used his friends and then abandoned them when they had served their turn.*

serve sb 'right (for doing sth) (*informal*)
used to say that sth that has happened to sb is their own fault and they deserve it: *After the way you've treated her, it will serve you right if she never speaks to you again!* ◇ *I told you the dog would bite if you teased it. It serves you right.*

do/serve time → time

served

first come, first served → first

serves

if memory serves → memory
if my memory serves me well, correctly, etc. → memory

service

be at sb's 'service (*formal*)
be ready to help sb: *If you need to know anything else, I'm at your service.*

be of 'service (to sb) (*formal*)
be helpful (to sb): *If I can be of service, please let me know.*

do sb a/no 'service (*formal*)
do sth that is helpful/not helpful to sb: *She was doing herself no service by remaining silent.*

press sb/sth into service → press
see service → see
a skeleton crew/staff/service → skeleton

sesame

open sesame → open

set

be, look, etc. (all) 'set (for sth/to do sth)
be ready or prepared to do sth: *They were all set to go out when the phone rang.* ◇ *The team looks set for another easy win.*

be (,dead) 'set against sth/doing sth
be strongly opposed to sth: *I've tried to persuade him to move house, but he's dead set against it.* ◇ *She's not very well, but she's set against going to the doctor.*

be set 'fair (*BrE*)
1 (of weather) good and with no sign of change: *Apparently the weather is set fair for the rest of the week.*
2 likely to be successful: *They are set fair to win the championship.*

be ,set in your 'ways
be unable or unwilling to change your behaviour, habits or ideas, usually because you are old: *He's too set in his ways to agree to a holiday on a boat.*

be (,dead) 'set on sth/doing sth
want to do or have sth very much; be determined

to do or have sth: *She's dead set on leaving her job and emigrating to Canada.*

not/never set the 'world on fire (*BrE* also not/never set the 'Thames on fire) (*informal*)
never do anything exciting, unusual or wonderful: *He's good, but he'll never set the world on fire. He's not dynamic enough.*

> ❷ NOTE
> The Thames is the large river that runs through London.

set (sb) a (good, bad, etc.) e'xample
show a (good, etc.) standard of work or behaviour for others to follow or copy: *You shouldn't use bad language in front of your children—it sets a bad example.* ◇ *She sets us all an example* (= a good example).

set your face against sth (*written, especially BrE*)
be strongly opposed to sth and refuse to change your opinion: *Her father had set his face against the marriage.*

set 'foot in/on sth
enter or visit a place: *Neil Armstrong was the first man to set foot on the moon, in July 1969.* ◇ *She's been complaining from the moment she set foot in this hotel.*

set your 'heart/'mind on sth/doing sth; have (got) your heart/mind 'set on sth/doing sth
want sth very much; want to do or achieve sth very much: *When she was a small girl, her heart was set on a horse of her own.* ◇ *He set his mind on becoming a doctor.* ◇ *I have my heart set on a new guitar.*

set 'light to sth (*especially BrE*)
make sth start burning: *A spark from the fire had set light to a rug.*

set sth on 'fire/set 'fire to sth
1 cause sth to start burning because you want to destroy or damage it: *Three youths were accused of setting the house on fire.*
2 make sb/sth very interested or excited: *Her new book has really set the literary critics on fire.*

set the 'pace
do sth at a speed which other people must follow if they want to be successful; lead by being better, cleverer, more original, etc. than other people: *Jones set the pace in the 5000 metres.* ◇ *This new style of bicycle has really set the pace for the rest of the industry.* ▶ 'pacesetter *noun*: *Richard Rogers is a pacesetter in modern architecture.*

> ❷ NOTE
> In athletics, one person in a race *sets the pace* for the other competitors by running faster than them.

set the 'seal on sth (*formal*)
be the highest or best thing to happen in a successful career, project, etc: *His Nobel prize set the seal on a brilliant academic career in physics.*

set the 'scene/'stage (for sth)

1 give sb the information they need in order to understand what comes next: *The first few chapters of the book just set the scene.*
2 create the conditions in which sth can easily happen: *His arrival set the scene for another argument.* ◇ *With so many economic and political problems, the stage was set for another war.*

set your sights 'high/'low

be ambitious/not ambitious; expect a lot/little from your life: *If you set your sights high, you could do anything.*

set your 'sights on sth/doing sth; have (got) your sights 'set on sth/doing sth

try to achieve or get sth: *She's set her sights on an Olympic gold.* ◇ *He has his sights on owning the biggest property company in the USA.*

> ❷ **NOTE**
> You look through the *sights* of a gun to aim at the target.

set sb's 'teeth on edge

1 (of a sound) make sb feel physically uncomfortable: *That noise is really setting my teeth on edge! Can you stop?*
2 annoy sb; make sb feel tense: *It sets my teeth on edge when I hear him talking to his mother so rudely.*

set the 'tone (of/for sth)

create or establish a general feeling or atmosphere among a group of people (about a particular subject): *His very clever and very funny speech set the tone for the rest of the evening.*

set 'tongues wagging (*informal*)

cause people to start talking about sb's private affairs: *A careless remark about his family really set tongues wagging.*

set up 'house/'home (with sb/together)

start to live with sb (rather than with your parents): *They didn't have much money, so they set up house in an old caravan.* ◇ *They got married and set up home together in Hull.*

set up 'shop

start a business (in a particular place): *He worked as a writer for several years, then set up shop as a small publisher.* ◇ *The young lawyer set up shop in a new office in the centre of town.*

be carved/set in stone → **stone**
clap/lay/set eyes on sb/sth → **eyes**
get/keep/set/start the ball rolling → **ball**
go/set about your work → **work**
go/set to work (on sth) → **work**
the jet set → **jet**
not/never put/set a foot wrong → **foot**
on your marks, get set, go! → **marks**
put/set sb at (their) ease → **ease**
put/set the cat among the pigeons → **cat**
put/set your (own) house in order → **house**

put/set sth in motion → **motion**
put/set sb's mind at ease/rest → **mind**
put/set/turn your mind to sth → **mind**
put/set/place sb on a pedestal → **pedestal**
put/set the record straight → **record**
put/set sb right → **right**
put/set (no, great, little, etc.) store by sth → **store**
put/set sb straight (about/on sth) → **straight**
put/set sth to rights → **rights**
put/set sb to work (on sth) → **work**
(get) ready, (get) set, go! → **ready**
set the wheels in motion = put/set sth in motion → **motion**

sets

the rot sets in → **rot**

settle

settle a 'score/an ac'count (with sb); settle an old 'score

hurt or punish sb who has harmed or cheated you in the past; get revenge: *I've got a score to settle with him after the terrible things he said about my girlfriend.* ◇ *Before he left the school, he wanted to settle an old score with one of his classmates.*

wait for the dust to settle = let the dust settle → **let**

settles

after/when the dust settles → **dust**

seven

the seven year 'itch (*informal*)

the wish for a new sexual partner because you are bored with your husband or wife: *He's started looking at all the women in the office. It must be the seven year itch.*

sevens

be at sixes and sevens → **sixes**

seventh

be in (your) seventh 'heaven

be extremely happy: *When she has all her grandchildren around her, she's in seventh heaven.*

> ❶ **ORIGIN**
> This expression comes from the belief that God and the highest class of angels live in the seventh heaven.

sex

the opposite sex → **opposite**

shade

put sb/sth in the 'shade (*informal*)

be much better or more successful than sb/sth: *The new player really puts the rest of the team in the shade.*

shadow

be frightened/nervous/scared of your own 'shadow
be very easily frightened; be very nervous: *Since the attack he's been a changed man. He's nervous of his own shadow and doesn't like to go out alone at night.*

beyond/without a ˌshadow of (a) 'doubt; there isn't a ˌshadow of a 'doubt (that …)
there is no doubt at all (that …); absolutely certainly: *He's innocent beyond a shadow of a doubt.* ◇ *There isn't a shadow of doubt in my mind about the safety of the system.*

in/under the 'shadow of
1 very close to: *The new market is in the shadow of the City Hall.*
2 when you say that sb is **in/under the shadow of** another person, you mean that they do not receive as much attention as that person: *Most of her childhood had been spent in the shadow of her elder sister.*

be a shadow/ghost of your/its former self → former

shaft

give sb the 'shaft (*AmE, informal*)
treat sb unfairly: *It seems to me that the big corporations are keeping all the money for themselves and giving the shaft to ordinary consumers, as usual.*

shaggy-dog

a ˌshaggy-'dog story (*informal*)
a long, complicated story or joke, which has no proper ending and is not very funny: *He told us this joke, which turned out to be a shaggy-dog story, and I hate those!*

shake

more sth than you can shake a 'stick at (*informal*)
used to emphasize the large number of sth: *This music magazine has more reviews than you can shake a stick at.*

shake your 'fist (at sb)
hold up your fist (= your closed hand) at sb because you are angry or because you want to threaten them: *He got out of the car, shaking his fist in anger at the driver in the car behind.*

shake 'hands (with sb); shake sb's 'hand; shake sb by the 'hand
take hold of sb's hand and move it up and down as a greeting or to show that you agree about sth: *The television pictures of the two presidents shaking hands were shown all over the world.*

shake your 'head
move your head from side to side as a way of saying 'no', or to show sadness, disagreement, disapproval, etc: *She didn't say anything—she just shook her head and sighed.*

shake a 'leg (*old-fashioned, informal*)
used to tell sb to start to do sth or to hurry: *Come on, shake a leg or we'll be late!*

shake like a 'jelly/'leaf (*informal*)
shake with fear; be very afraid or nervous: *Before I went into the exam room I was shaking like a leaf.*

shake (hands) on it/sth
shake hands with sb to show that you have made an agreement, a deal, etc: *'OK, I'll let the car go for £5000.' 'Do you want to shake on it?'* ◇ *Let's shake on it.*

a fair shake → fair

shake/rock the foundations of sth → foundations
shake/rock sth to its foundations → foundations

shakers

movers and shakers → movers

shakes

be no great shakes → great
in a couple of shakes = in two shakes → two
in two shakes of a lamb's tail → two

shaking

(be) quaking/shaking in your boots/shoes → quaking

shame

put sb/sth to 'shame
be much better than sb/sth: *This new stereo puts our old one to shame.*

'shame on you, him, etc. (*spoken*)
an exclamation said to sb who has behaved badly or done sth they should be ashamed of: *Shame on you for forgetting your mother's birthday!*

be a crying shame → crying

Shanks

(on) Shanks's 'pony (*BrE, informal*)
walking, rather than travelling by car, bus, etc.; on foot: *'How are we going to get there?' 'I suppose it'll have to be Shanks's pony.'* ◇ *You young people go everywhere by car these days. When I was young all we had was Shanks's pony.*

shape

be in (good, bad, etc.) 'shape
1 (of a person) be in good, bad, etc. health or physical condition: *He's in good shape for a man of his age.* ◇ *She goes to the gym three times a week to stay in shape.*
2 (of a thing) be well, badly, etc. organized or in good, bad, etc. condition: *The economy's in very bad shape and is likely to get worse.*

be out of 'shape
1 not having the normal shape: *The wheel had been twisted out of shape.*
2 (of a person) not be in good physical condition: *I*

hadn't been training for months and was really out of shape.

be the ,shape of ,things to 'come (also be a ,taste of ,things to 'come)

be a sign or example of how things are likely to be in the future: *These new computers are the shape of things to come.* ◇ *Telephones with television screens: could this be a taste of things to come?*

get (yourself) (back) into 'shape

take exercise, etc. to become fit and healthy (again): *After she had the baby, she started swimming every day, to get back into shape.*

get/knock/lick sb/sth into 'shape

make sb/sth more acceptable or organized; improve sb/sth: *Do you think you can lick this company into shape?*

give 'shape to sth (formal)

express or explain a particular idea, plan, etc.

in any (way,) shape or 'form (informal)

of any kind: *I don't approve of violence in any shape or form.*

in the shape/form of sb/sth

follows a general word and introduces a particular example of it: *There was entertainment on the ship, in the form of a disco and a cinema.* ◇ *Help arrived in the shape of a policeman.*

'shape up or ship 'out (AmE, informal)

used to tell sb that if they do not improve, work harder, etc. they will have to leave their job, position, etc: *He finally faced up to his drug problem when his band told him to shape up or ship out.*

take 'shape

develop to a point where you can see what sth will finally be like: *After months of discussion, a peace agreement is gradually taking shape.* ◇ *An idea for a new book started to take shape in his mind.*

shapes

come in all shapes and sizes

be of many different forms or types: *Pasta comes in all shapes and sizes.* ◇ *The containers come in all shapes and sizes.*

share

share and share a'like (saying)

share things equally: *Children must learn to share and share alike.*

(more than) your fair share of sth → **fair**
the lion's share (of sth) → **lion**
a piece/share/slice of the pie = a share/slice of the cake → **cake**

shared

a trouble shared is a trouble halved → **trouble**

sharp

be (at) the 'sharp end (of sth) (BrE, informal)

be (doing) the job or activity of greatest difficulty

or responsibility: *He started work at the sharp end of business, as a salesman.* ◇ *As head of the school, I'm at the sharp end if there are complaints.*

have (got) a sharp 'tongue (informal)

(of a person) often speak in an unkind or unpleasant way: *You've got to be careful of her, she's got a sharp tongue.* ▶ **sharp-'tongued** *adj.*: *a sharp-tongued old man*

sharp 'practice

clever but dishonest methods of business, etc: *There's a lot of sharp practice in the second-hand car business.*

look lively/sharp → **look**

sharpest

not the sharpest knife in the 'drawer (humorous)

not intelligent: *I know he's good-looking, but he's not exactly the sharpest knife in the drawer, is he?*

shatter

dash/shatter sb's hopes → **hopes**

shave

a close shave/call → **close**

shebang

the ,whole she'bang (informal)

the whole thing; everything: *It's not just a computer we need. We're going to have to get a printer, a scanner, a CD-writer, the whole shebang.*

> **❷ NOTE**
> The original meaning of the word *shebang* was a hut or shelter.

shed

cast/shed/throw (new) light on sth → **light**

sheep

like 'sheep (disapproving)

(do sth) because other people are doing it rather than thinking or deciding for yourself: *If John says that something must be done, they do it. They just follow his orders like sheep.*

sort out/separate the ,sheep from the 'goats

separate the good people from the bad people: *The exams at the end of the first year usually separate the sheep from the goats.*

a/the black sheep (of the family) → **black**
count sheep → **count**
(you, etc.) may/might as well be hanged/hung for a sheep as (for) a lamb → **well**
a wolf in sheep's clothing → **wolf**

sheet

a clean sheet/slate → **clean**
sing from the same song/hymn sheet → **sing**
(as) white as a sheet/ghost → **white**

sheets

(be) three sheets to the wind → **three**

shelf

buy, get, etc. sth off the 'shelf
buy, etc. sth which is not made especially for sb, and is found in an ordinary shop: *Did they buy the computer system off the shelf or was it designed specially for them?*

on the 'shelf (*informal*)
1 (especially of women) not married and unlikely to marry because you are no longer young: *Some women used to think they were on the shelf if they weren't married at 30.*
2 not wanted by anyone; not used: *Unemployed people often feel they've been left on the shelf.*

Angie's biggest fear was ending up on the shelf.

shell

come out of your 'shell; bring sb out of their 'shell (*informal*)
become less shy and more confident when talking to other people: *When Anna first joined the club, it took her a long time to come out of her shell.*

go, retreat, withdraw, etc. into your 'shell
become more shy and avoid talking to other people: *If you ask him about his family, he goes into his shell.*

Sherlock

no shit, Sherlock! → **shit**

shift

shift your 'ground (*usually disapproving*)
change your opinion or position during an argument: *He's shifted his ground a bit; he still believes in the death penalty, but now only for murderers.*

shifting

(the) ,shifting 'sands (of sth)
used to describe a situation that changes so often that it is difficult to understand or deal with it: *the shifting sands of the digital age*

shine

take the 'shine off sth (*informal*)
make sth seem much less good than it did at first: *Allegations of cheating have taken the shine off the successful exam results.*

take a 'shine to sb/sth (*informal*)
begin to like sb/sth as soon as you see/meet them/it: *I think you'll get the job—they seemed to take quite a shine to you.*

come rain, come shine → **rain**
(come) rain or shine → **rain**
rise and shine → **rise**

shines

make hay while the sun shines → **hay**
think the sun shines out of sb's arse/backside → **think**
think the sun shines out of sb's ass → **think**

shining

be a shining e'xample (of sb/sth) (also **be a shining 'light**)
be a very good example of sb/sth, which other people can follow or copy: *Their friends think Phillip and Joan are a shining example of a happily married couple.* ◊ *His books on grammar are a shining light in a very difficult and confused field.*

a knight in shining armour → **knight**

ship

when your 'ship/'boat comes in (*informal*)
when you are suddenly successful or have a lot of money: *Perhaps, when our ship comes in, we'll be able to buy that flat in Paris.*

(like rats) deserting/leaving a sinking ship → **sinking**
jump ship → **jump**
run a tight ship → **run**
shape up or ship out → **shape**
spoil the ship for a ha'porth/ha'penny-worth of tar → **spoil**

ships

be (like) ,ships that ,pass in the 'night (*informal*)
(of people) meet for a short time, by chance, and perhaps for the only time in your lives: *We met on holiday in Spain and had a wonderful time together. But we both knew that we were just ships that pass in the night.*

shirt

put your 'shirt on sth (*BrE, informal*)
bet a lot or all of your money in a horse race, etc.; invest all your money in sth: *I've put my shirt on*

Diamond Lady in the 10.15. ◇ *He put his shirt on the future of the company.*

the ˌshirt off sb's 'back
anything that sb has, including the things they really need themselves, that sb else takes from them or they are willing to give: *He's the type of person who would give the shirt off his back if he thought it would help.*

keep your shirt on = keep your hair on → **hair**

lose your shirt → **lose**

a stuffed shirt → **stuffed**

shirtsleeves

in (your) 'shirtsleeves
wearing a shirt without a jacket, etc. on top of it: *Even though it was the middle of winter, it was so hot in the office that we were all in our shirtsleeves.*

shit

be in the 'shit; be in ˌdeep 'shit (⚠, *slang*)
be in a lot of trouble: *I'll be in the shit if I don't get this work finished today.* ◇ *You're in deep shit now.*

like 'shit (⚠, *slang*)
very bad; ill/sick etc.; really badly: *I woke up feeling like shit.* ◇ *We get treated like shit in this job.*

no 'shit! (⚠, *slang*)
1 used to show that you are surprised, impressed, etc. or to show that what you are saying is true: *'That guy's my brother.' 'No shit! Really?'*
2 (also **no shit, Sherlock!**) used when you think sb has said sth that is obvious or that you already know: *'If it rains we'll all get wet.' 'No shit, Sherlock!'*

> **❶ ORIGIN**
> *Sherlock* in this expression refers to Sherlock Holmes, the fictional detective.

not give a 'shit (about sb/sth) (⚠, *slang*)
not care at all about sb/sth: *I don't give a shit what Marie thinks. I'll do what I want!*

(when) the ˌshit hits the 'fan (⚠, *slang*)
(when) sb in authority finds out about sth bad or wrong that sb has done: *When the committee finds out what actually happened, the shit will really hit the fan.*

be full of shit/crap → **full**

beat, etc. the shit out of sb = beat/knock/kick the hell out of sb → **hell**

a crock of shit → **crock**

scare the shit out of sb → **scare**

(as) thick as shit → **thick**

tough shit = tough/bad luck → **luck**

up shit creek (without a paddle) = up the creek → **creek**

shithouse

be built like a brick shithouse → **built**

shitless

scare sb shitless → **scare**

shiver

a shiver runs / goes down sb's spine = send a shiver up/ down sb's spine → **send**

shivers

give sb/get the 'shivers (*informal*)
make sb feel fear and horror: *That old portrait gives me the shivers.* ◇ *I get the shivers every time I hear his name.*

shock

ˌshock 'horror (*BrE, informal, often humorous*)
used when you pretend to be shocked by sth that is not really very serious or surprising: *Shock horror! You're actually on time for once!*

shoe

if the shoe fits (ˌwear it) = if the cap fits (ˌwear it) → **cap**

the shoe is on the other foot = the boot is on the other foot → **boot**

shoes

be in sb's 'shoes (*informal*)
be in sb's position: *I'd leave that job immediately if I were in his shoes.*

put yourself in sb's 'shoes/'place
consider what you would do or feel if you were in the position of sb else: *Put yourself in his shoes! If your mother had just died, how would you feel?*

fill sb's boots/shoes → **fill**

(be) quaking/shaking in your boots/shoes → **quaking**

step into sb's shoes → **step**

shoestring

(do sth) on a 'shoestring (*informal*)
(do sth) with very little money: *In the early years, the business was run on a shoestring.*

shoot

shoot your 'bolt (*informal*)
make a final attempt to do something, especially if this attempt comes too early to be successful: *In an argument it's important not to shoot your bolt too soon. Keep one or two good points for the end.*

> **❶ ORIGIN**
> In this idiom, *bolt* refers to an arrow that was shot from a crossbow.

shoot the 'breeze/'bull (*informal, especially AmE*)
talk in a friendly, informal way; chat: *We sat around in the bar, shooting the breeze.*

shoot sb/sth down (in flames) (*informal*)
be very critical of sb's ideas, opinions, suggestions, etc: *I thought it was a brilliant idea, but she shot it down in flames.*

ˌshoot from the 'hip
react quickly without thinking carefully first: *As a manager, he was sometimes accused of shooting*

from the hip, but he was always popular with his colleagues.

ˌshoot it 'out (with sb) (informal)
fight against sb with guns, especially until one side is killed or defeated: *The gang decided to shoot it out with the police.* ▶ **'shoot-out** noun: *The film ended with a shoot-out, which of course the hero won.*

shoot the 'lights (informal)
go through red traffic lights: *In this city people shoot the lights all the time.*

shoot your 'mouth off (about sth)
1 talk publicly or carelessly about things which should be secret: *This is a secret. Please don't shoot your mouth off to everyone about it.*
2 talk loudly and with too much pride about sth: *Mark is always shooting his mouth off about all the money he earns.*

shoot yourself in the 'foot (informal)
do or say sth stupid which is against your own interests: *You'd better prepare your argument carefully—you don't want to shoot yourself in the foot.*

flip/give/shoot sb the bird → **bird**

shooting

the ˌwhole 'shooting match (BrE, informal)
everything, or a situation which includes everything: *The whole shooting match is being computerized, which should significantly reduce delays.*

be like shooting fish in a barrel = be like taking candy from a baby → **candy**

shop

all 'over the shop (AmE also all 'over the lot) (informal)
everywhere: *I've been looking for you all over the shop. Where have you been?* ◇ *Since you explained idioms to me, I keep seeing them all over the shop.*

a closed shop → **closed**
like a bull in a china shop → **bull**
mind the shop → **mind**
set up shop → **set**
shut up shop → **shut**
talk shop → **talk**

shops

hit the shops/stores → **hit**

short

at (very) short 'notice (also at a moment's 'notice)
with very little warning; without much time to prepare: *In this job you have to be able to work weekends at short notice.*

be caught/taken 'short (BrE, informal)
suddenly need to go to the toilet in a place where it is difficult to find one

be in ˌshort sup'ply
not be enough of sth; be scarce: *During the war, many things were in short supply.*

be on/have a short 'fuse (informal)
be likely to get angry easily, because you are tired, stressed, etc: *Your father's having trouble at work, so his temper's on a short fuse today.* ◇ *Be careful what you say to the director. She has a very short fuse.*

❶ NOTE
A *fuse* is a piece of string or paper which is lit to make a bomb explode.

be ˌshort and 'sweet (informal)
last for a short time, but still be good or pleasant; be good because it is short: *The patient is very tired, so make your visit short and sweet.* ◇ *The chairman promised to make the introduction short and sweet.*

be/run short of sth
not have enough of sth; only have a small amount of sth left: *We're running short of butter. Can you get some more today?* ◇ *I'm a bit short of money at the moment.*

bring/pull sb up 'short
make sb stop what they are doing because sth attracts their attention or because they suddenly realize sth: *His criticism of my work pulled me up short, because I thought he was pleased with it.*

for 'short
as a shorter way of saying sth: *Her name's Joanna, but her friends call her 'Jo' for short.*

get/have sb by the short 'hairs (also get/have sb by the short and 'curlies) (informal)
get/have sb in a position where they must agree to what you want: *We can't go on strike because the boss will simply hire new staff. He's got us by the short and curlies.*

give sb/sth short 'shrift; get short 'shrift
give sb/sth/get little attention or sympathy: *Mrs Jones gave my suggestion very short shrift. I was quite surprised.* ◇ *When Ann complained about the toilets, she got very short shrift.*

go 'short (of sth)
not have as much of sth as you need: *Give the boy some pocket money. I don't want him to go short.*

in 'short
in a few words; briefly: *This picture has been badly damaged, and besides, it's not signed: in short, it's worthless.*

in ˌshort 'order
quickly and without trouble: *A decision will have to be made in short order if the new system is to be in place by September.*

in the 'short run
concerning the immediate future: *In the short run, unemployment may fall.*

little/nothing short of 'sth
used when you are saying that sth is almost true, or is equal to sth: *Last year's figures were little short of disastrous.* ◇ *The transformation has been nothing short of a miracle.*

make short 'work of sth/sb
do or finish sth very quickly; defeat sb very easily: *The children certainly made short work of the chocolate biscuits!* ◇ *The champion made very short work of the challenger in the title fight.*

a short back and 'sides
a conventional haircut for men where the hair is cut very short around the ears and above the neck

a 'short cut (to sth)
1 a shorter way to go to a place: *I usually take a short cut behind the post office to get to college.*
2 a way of doing sth more quickly or easily: *Producing a quality wine takes years—there are really no short cuts.*

short of (doing) sth
without (doing) sth; unless sth happens: *Short of a miracle, we're certain to lose.* ◇ *Short of asking her to leave (= and we don't want to do that), there's not a lot we can do about the situation.*

win, lose, etc. by a short 'head
win, lose, etc. but by only a little

❶ ORIGIN
This expression refers to a close finish in horse racing.

cut sb short → **cut**
cut sth short → **cut**
draw the short straw → **draw**
fall short of sth → **fall**
full/short measure → **measure**
get the short end of the stick = draw the short straw → **draw**
(do sth) in the long/medium/short term → **term**
the long and (the) short of it → **long**
sell sb short → **sell**
sell yourself/sb/sth short → **sell**
stop short → **stop**
(as) thick as two short planks → **thick**
to make a long story short = to cut a long story short → **cut**
two sandwiches short of a picnic = a brick short of a load → **brick**

shot

be (all) shot (to pieces) (*informal*)
be destroyed or in very bad condition: *All my dreams were shot to pieces when I heard the news.* ◇ *This engine's totally shot. I'll have to get a new one.*

be/get 'shot of sb/sth (*BrE, informal*)
get rid of sb/sth that you do not want/like or which has given you trouble: *It's time we got shot of this car—it's falling apart.*

have/take a 'shot (at sth/at doing sth) (also **give sth a 'shot**) (*informal*)
try to do sth: *We all had a shot at solving the riddle.* ◇ *I don't know if I'll be any good at editing the newsletter, but I'll give it a shot.*

(do sth) like a 'shot (*informal*)
(do sth) immediately or quickly, without hesitating: *I'd be off like a shot if he offered me a job abroad.* ◇ *If she wanted him, he'd go back to her like a shot.*

(fire) a (warning) shot across sb's 'bows
do sth to warn an enemy, competitor, etc. that you will take further action against them if necessary: *The minister's speech on Friday was a shot across the bows of the banks. If they don't change their policies, he will change the law.*

❶ ORIGIN
This expression refers to encounters between ships of hostile nations. One ship might fire a shot at another, not in order to hit it, but to warn it to move.

a shot in the 'arm (*informal*)
a thing or an action that gives sb/sth new energy, help or encouragement or provides a quick solution to a problem: *The discovery of gas reserves was a much-needed shot in the arm for the economy.*

❶ ORIGIN
This phrase refers to an injection of a drug.

shot through with sth
containing a lot of a particular colour, quality or feature: *He spoke in a voice shot through with emotion.*

a big name/noise/shot → **big**
give it your best shot → **best**
a long shot → **long**
not by a long shot → **long**
a Parthian shot = a parting shot → **parting**
a shot/stab in the dark → **dark**

shotgun

a shotgun 'wedding (*old-fashioned, informal*)
a marriage which takes place because the woman is pregnant

❶ ORIGIN
This expression probably refers to the father of a woman, who threatens to shoot the man unless he marries her.

ride shotgun → **ride**

shots

call the shots/the tune → **call**

shoulder

be, stand, act, etc. ,shoulder to 'shoulder (with sb)
be supporting sb or in agreement with sb: *We fought shoulder to shoulder to defend our country.*

◇ *I stand shoulder to shoulder with Julia on this important issue.*

put your shoulder to the 'wheel
start working very hard at a particular task: *We're really going to have to put our shoulders to the wheel if we want to get this ready on time.*

a shoulder to 'cry on
a person who listens to your troubles and offers sympathy and kindness: *When you're depressed, you need a shoulder to cry on.*

be looking over your shoulder ➔ looking
give sb/get the cold shoulder ➔ cold
have (got) a chip on your shoulder ➔ chip
tell, etc. sb straight from the shoulder (that …) ➔ straight

shoulders

on sb's 'shoulders
if blame, guilt, etc. is **on sb's shoulders**, they must take responsibility for it: *I feel like all the responsibility is on my shoulders, which is quite stressful.*

be a weight off your shoulders ➔ weight
have (got) a good head on your shoulders ➔ head
head and shoulders above sb/sth ➔ head
(have) an old head on young shoulders ➔ old
rub shoulders (with sb) ➔ rub

shout

be ˌin with a 'shout (of sth/of doing sth) (*informal*)
have a good chance of winning sth or of achieving sth: *The interview seemed to go well, so I think I'm in with a shout of getting the job.*

give sb a 'shout (*spoken*)
tell sb sth: *Give me a shout when you're ready.*

be nothing, not much, etc. to shout about = be nothing, not much, etc. to write home about ➔ write

shouting

be all over bar the shouting ➔ bar
within shouting distance = within spitting distance (of sth) ➔ spitting

shove

'shove it (*informal, especially AmE*)
used to say rudely that you will not accept or do sth: *'The boss wants that report now.' 'Yeah? Tell him he can shove it.'*

if/when push comes to shove ➔ push

show

be on 'show
be shown or displayed, often for sale: *A couple of the new models are on show at the BMW garage.* ◇ *At weddings the gifts given by the guests are often on show.*

do sth/be for 'show
do sth/be done to attract attention or admiration,

and for no other purpose: *That expensive computer is just for show; he doesn't really know how to use it.* ◇ *She doesn't really like whisky; she just drinks it for show.*

get the ˌshow on the 'road (*spoken*)
start an activity or journey, especially one that needs a lot of organization: *Right, everyone! Let's get this show on the road!*

(jolly) good 'show! (*old-fashioned, BrE, informal*)
used to show that you like sth or to say that sb has done sth well

have (got) something, nothing, little, etc. to 'show for sth
have or produce sth, etc. as a result of your efforts, work, etc: *Students who fail the final exam have nothing to show for years of hard work.*

it (just/only) goes to 'show (that …)
used to say that sth is an example of a general truth or principle: *He had all his money stolen? It just goes to show you should always lock your doors.*

put on a good, poor, wonderful, etc. show
make a good, poor, etc. attempt at doing sth, especially in spite of difficulties: *Considering that the children had no help, they put on a marvellous show.*

show (sb) a clean pair of 'heels (*informal*)
run away; get ahead of sb in a competition: *They ran after her, but she showed them a clean pair of heels.* ◇ *As makers of quality software, they've shown the rest of the industry a clean pair of heels.*

show sb the 'door (*informal*)
tell sb to leave because of an argument or bad behaviour: *If she spoke to me like that, I'd show her the door!*

show your 'face
be in or go to a place, especially when you are not welcome: *After what happened yesterday, I don't know how you dare show your face here.* ◇ *If he ever shows his face in here again, there'll be trouble.*

show good 'cause (for sth/doing sth) (*law*)
give a good reason for sth: *Can you show good cause for your accusation?* ◇ *She could show no good cause for being in the office at midnight.*

a show of 'force
an act which clearly shows your power or gives a warning to people not to act against you: *The government sent in tanks as a show of force, and the rebels left the town.*

a show of 'hands
a method of voting in which each person shows their opinion by raising their hand: *If you like, we can settle this debate with a show of hands.*

show your 'teeth (*BrE*)
do sth that shows that you are able to act aggressively and use your power in a situation if it is necessary: *Up until now the police have been very patient with the strikers, but today they really showed their teeth.*

show the 'way

do sth first so that other people can follow: *The future lies in changing the way we do business, and this Internet company is showing the way.*

show sb who's 'boss

make it clear to sb that you have more power and authority than they have: *I think it's time we showed these people who's boss, don't you?*

show 'willing (*BrE*)

show that you are ready to help, work hard, etc. if necessary: *The meeting wasn't due to start for another half an hour, but she thought she'd better go early to show willing.*

fly/show/wave the flag → **flag**
run the show → **run**
show/reveal your hand → **hand**
show your paces = go through your paces → **paces**
show sb/learn/know the ropes → **ropes**
steal the show → **steal**

shreds

in 'shreds

1 very badly damaged: *After a stressful week, her nerves were in shreds.* ◇ *The country's economy is in shreds.*
2 torn in many places: *The document was in shreds on the floor.*

tear sb/sth to pieces/shreds → **tear**

shrift

get short shrift → **short**
give sb/sth short shrift → **short**

shrinking

a ˌshrinking 'violet (*humorous*)

a very shy person who is easily frightened: *I can't imagine why a dynamic young woman like her is marrying a shrinking violet like him.*

shtum

keep schtum/shtum → **schtum**

shudder

I shudder/dread to think (how, what, etc. ...) → **think**

shuffle

shuffle off this mortal 'coil (*old-fashioned* or *humorous*)

die: *They believe that when they shuffle off this mortal coil their souls will become stars.*

❶ ORIGIN
This expression comes from Shakespeare's play *Hamlet*.

shufti

have/take a 'shufti (at sb/sth) (*BrE*, *informal*)

have a (quick) look (at sb/sth): *I don't mind having a shufti at the bike, but I can't afford to buy it.*

❶ ORIGIN
This comes from military slang, from an Arabic word meaning *try to see*.

shut

shut sb's 'mouth

stop sb from saying sth, especially from revealing a secret: *His employers tried to shut his mouth by offering him money, but he told the story to the newspapers anyway.*

shut your 'mouth/'trap/'face/'gob! (also keep your 'mouth/'trap shut) (*slang*)

a rude way of telling sb to be quiet or stop talking: *'Shut your face', Roger said, 'or I'll kick you out.'* ◇ *Why can't you learn to keep your big mouth shut?*

❷ NOTE
Trap and *gob* are slang words for 'mouth'.

shut up 'shop (*BrE*, *informal*)

close a business permanently or stop working for the day: *The family ran a small grocer's for years, but when the old man died they shut up shop.* ◇ *It's 6 o'clock—time to shut up shop and go home.*

shut/close the door on sth → **door**
shut/close your ears to sb/sth → **ears**
shut/close your eyes to sth → **eyes**
shut/lock/close the stable door after the horse has bolted → **stable**
(be able to do sth) with your eyes shut/closed → **eyes**

shutters

ˌbring/ˌput down the 'shutters

stop letting sb know what your thoughts or feelings are; stop letting yourself think about sth: *He brought down the shutters on the terrible image of the car accident.*

shy

fight shy of sb/of (doing) sth → **fight**
once bitten, twice shy → **once**

sick

be 'sick (*BrE*)

bring food from your stomach back out through your mouth; vomit: *I was sick three times in the night.* ◇ *The dog had been violently sick on the floor.*

be off 'sick

not be at work or school because you are not well: *He broke his arm and was off sick for a fortnight.*

be/feel sick at 'heart (*formal*)

be very unhappy or disappointed: *When I realized the accident was my fault, I felt sick at heart.*

make sb 'sick (*informal*)
make sb angry or disgusted: *You make me sick, lying around in front of the TV all day!* ◇ *Look how much these people are earning! It makes you sick.*

(as) sick as a 'dog (*informal*)
feeling very ill; vomiting a lot: *I was sick as a dog last night.*

(as) sick as a 'parrot (*BrE, humorous*)
very disappointed: *She was as sick as a parrot when she found out that her sister had been nominated for a prize and she hadn't.*

sick (and tired) of sb/sth (*informal*)
bored with or annoyed by sb, or by sth that has been happening for a long time which you want to stop: *I'm sick and tired of hearing you complaining all day long.*

sick to your 'stomach
disgusted or angry: *I feel sick to my stomach every time I think about the way that child was punished.*

be sick with worry = be worried sick ➔ **worried**
sick to the back teeth of sb/sth = fed up to the back teeth with sb/sth ➔ **fed**

side

be (a bit, a little, etc.) on the 'cold, 'small, etc. side (*informal*)
be slightly too cold, small, etc: *These boots are a bit on the big side, but they're quite comfortable.* ◇ *It's a little on the cold side this morning.*

be on the ˌright/ˌwrong side of '40, '50, etc. (*informal, often humorous*)
be younger/older than 40, 50, etc: *'How old is she?' 'On the wrong side of forty, I'd say.'*

be on sb's 'side
support and agree with sb: *I'm definitely on your side in this.* ◇ *Whose side are you on anyway?*

be on the side of the 'angels
having correct moral principles and behaving correctly: *The policemen in Scobie's crime novels are not always on the side of the angels.*

come down/out on the side of sb/sth
decide, especially after considering sth carefully, to choose or support sb/sth: *After much discussion, they finally came down on the side of nuclear energy.* ◇ *In the argument that followed, my father came down firmly on my side.*

from ˌside to 'side
moving to the left and then to the right: *He shook his head slowly from side to side.* ◇ *The ship rolled from side to side.*

get/keep on the right/wrong 'side of sb
try to please sb and not annoy them/annoy sb and make them dislike you: *She got on the wrong side of her boss after criticizing him in a meeting.*

have (got) sth on your 'side
have sth as an advantage that will make it more likely that you will achieve sth: *She may not win this year, but she does have youth on her side.*

leave/put sth on/to one 'side
put sth in a separate place so that you can deal with it later: *After you've taken the bread out of the oven, leave it on one side to cool.* ◇ *Leaving that to one side for now, are there any other questions?*

my, the other, the same, etc. side of the 'fence
my, the opposite, the same, etc. point of view or position in an argument: *The former allies are now on opposite sides of the fence.* ◇ *Make up your mind—which side of the fence are you on?*

(do sth) on the 'side
1 (do sth) in addition to your main job: *He's a teacher but he does some journalism on the side.*
2 (*informal*) (do sth) secretly: *Her husband doesn't know it, but she's got a boyfriend on the side.*

the other side of the 'coin
the other aspect of the situation; a different or opposite way of looking at a situation: *Third World countries receive a lot of money from developed countries, but the other side of the coin is that they have to spend this money on expensive imports.*

ˌside by 'side (with sb/sth)
1 close together and facing in the same direction: *The two dogs lay side by side on the floor.* ◇ *There were two children ahead, walking side by side.*
2 together, without any difficulties: *Party members fought side by side with trade unionists for a change in the law.* ◇ *We have been using both systems, side by side, for two years.*

a/one side of the 'story/'picture
only one way of looking at a situation: *There are two sides to this story, and you've only heard Jim's.* ◇ *This programme on the dispute only shows one side of the picture.*

take/draw sb to one 'side
take sb away from a group of people in order to speak to them in private: *She took me to one side to explain why she hadn't given me the job.*

this side of …
before a particular time, event, age, etc: *They aren't likely to arrive this side of midnight.*

be a thorn in your flesh/side ➔ **thorn**
a bit on the side ➔ **bit**
err on the side of sth ➔ **err**
from/on every side = from/on all sides ➔ **sides**
from/on the wrong side of the tracks ➔ **wrong**
get up on the wrong side of the bed = get out of bed on the wrong side ➔ **bed**
the grass is (always) greener on the other side (of the fence) ➔ **grass**
have (got) time on your side ➔ **time**
know which side your bread is buttered ➔ **know**
laugh on the other side of your face ➔ **laugh**
let the side down ➔ **let**
look on the bright side ➔ **look**
not leave sb's side ➔ **leave**
on the credit side ➔ **credit**
on the wrong side of the law ➔ **wrong**

right side up → **right**

the seamy side (of life, etc.) → **seamy**

take sb's side = take sides → **sides**

time is on sb's side → **time**

to be on the safe side → **safe**

sidelines

on the 'sidelines

(watching what is happening while) not taking an active part; waiting to take an active part in sth: *The Prime Minister's husband talked about what it was like on the sidelines of political life.* ◇ *He's waiting on the sidelines for a chance to re-enter politics.*

sides

from/on all 'sides; from/on every 'side

from every direction: *People are criticizing him from all sides.*

take 'sides; take sb's 'side

support one person or group in an argument or disagreement: *I refuse to take sides in this argument. It's nothing to do with me.* ◇ *Whenever we quarrel, you always take Carole's side.*

see both sides (of the question, problem, etc.) → **see**

a short back and sides → **short**

split your sides (laughing/with laughter) → **split**

two sides of the same coin → **two**

sideways

knock sb sideways → **knock**

siege

under 'siege

1 surrounded by an army or the police: *The city has now been under siege for more than three weeks.* **2** being criticized all the time or put under pressure by problems, questions, etc: *The latest revelations put more pressure on the minister, who is already under siege for his economic policies.*

lay siege to sth → **lay**

sieve

have (got) a mind/memory like a 'sieve (*informal*)

forget things easily or quickly: *I'm terribly sorry I didn't remember your birthday—I've got a memory like a sieve.*

> ❶ NOTE
>
> A *sieve* is a kitchen tool with small holes in it, used for separating solids from liquids or very small pieces of food from larger pieces.

sight

be in/within 'sight

1 be close enough to be seen: *In fine weather the mountains are just within sight.* **2** likely to happen, almost a reality: *Prison reform is now within sight.* ◇ *The end of our problems is in sight at last.*

be a ˌsight for sore 'eyes (*spoken*)

be a person or thing that you are happy to see; be welcome or much needed: *Ah! You're a sight for sore eyes!*

do sth on 'sight

do or feel sth as soon as you see sb/sth: *She complained constantly about the hotel, which she hated on sight.* ◇ *The soldiers were ordered to shoot on sight.*

hate, be sick of, etc. the 'sight of sb/sth (*informal*)

hate, etc. sb/sth very much: *I'm sick of the sight of him!*

in the sight of sb; in sb's sight (*formal*)

in sb's opinion: *We are all equal in the sight of God.*

keep sight of sb/sth; keep sb/sth in sight

1 stay in a position where you can see sb/sth: *If you keep the tower in sight, you won't get lost.* **2** remain aware of sth; not forget sth: *It's important to keep sight of the fact that you have a small chance of winning.*

ˌout of 'sight, ˌout of 'mind (*saying*)

used to say that sb will quickly be forgotten when they are no longer with you

a (damn, etc.) sight 'better, 'worse, 'bigger, etc. (than sb/sth) (*informal*)

a lot better, etc. (than sb/sth): *Life would be a sight easier if we had a little more money!* ◇ *A car that big would use a darn sight more petrol than ours.*

a (damn, etc.) sight too 'good, too 'much, too 'small, etc. (*informal*)

much too good, etc: *There's a damn sight too much rubbish on TV.*

sight un'seen

if you buy sth **sight unseen**, you do not have an opportunity to see it before you buy it: *We bought the table sight unseen and were pleased to find it was perfect for our kitchen.*

at first glance/sight → **first**

know sb by sight → **know**

look a sight → **look**

lose sight of sth → **lose**

love at first sight → **love**

not a pretty sight → **pretty**

nowhere in sight = nowhere to be found/seen → **found**

second sight → **second**

sights

raise/lower your 'sights

increase/reduce your hopes and ambitions: *You should raise your sights and apply for the director's job.* ◇ *Some women feel that staying at home and having a family means lowering their sights.*

have (got) your sights set on sth/doing sth = set your sights on sth/doing sth → **set**

see the sights → **see**

set your sights high/low → **set**

set your sights on sth/doing sth → **set**

sign

(be) a ˌsign of the ˈtimes
something that shows the way the world is changing: *Seventy per cent of last year's graduates are still unemployed—a sign of the times, I'm afraid.*

sign on the dotted ˈline (*informal*)
sign your name at the bottom of a contract and so agree to a deal, etc: *The house isn't mine until I've signed on the dotted line.*

sign your own ˈdeath warrant
do sth that results in your own death, defeat or failure: *By refusing to play pop music this new radio station is signing its own death warrant.*

sign/take the pledge → **pledge**

signed

ˌsigned, ˌsealed and deˈlivered; ˌsigned and ˈsealed
definite, because all the legal documents have been signed: *At the conference they hope to have a treaty signed, sealed and delivered by Tuesday.*

silence

ˌsilence is ˈgolden (*saying*)
it is sometimes best not to say anything in a difficult or dangerous situation

> **❷ NOTE**
> The complete saying is 'speech is silver, silence is golden'.

a conspiracy of silence → **conspiracy**
a heavy silence/atmosphere → **heavy**
a pregnant pause/silence → **pregnant**

silent

give sb/get the ˈsilent treatment
refuse to talk to sb, usually because you are angry with them; be treated in this way: *Are you going to talk to me now, or are you still giving me the silent treatment?*

(as) ˌsilent as the ˈgrave
without any noise at all: *The playground, which had been filled with the noises of children at play, suddenly became silent as the grave.*

the ˌsilent maˈjority
the large number of people in a country who think the same as each other, but do not express their views publicly: *The government is appealing to the silent majority to support its foreign policy.*

> **❶ ORIGIN**
> The US President, Richard Nixon, used this phrase during the Vietnam War.

silk

make a silk ˌpurse out of a sow's ˈear
succeed in making sth good out of material that does not seem very good at all: *If you're serious about taking up painting, invest in good quality brushes and canvas. After all, it's no good trying to make a silk purse out of a sow's ear.*

(as) smooth as silk → **smooth**

silly

ˌdrink, ˌlaugh, ˌshout, etc. yourself ˈsilly (*informal*)
drink, laugh, shout, etc. so much that you cannot behave in a sensible way: *Everyone was too busy laughing themselves silly to notice her quietly leave the room.*

the ˈsilly season (*BrE*)
the time, usually in the summer, when newpapers are full of unimportant stories because there is little serious news

play silly buggers (with sth) → **play**

silver

(hand sth to sb) on a silver ˈplatter
give sth to sb without expecting them to do or give anything in return: *I don't like her at all—she expects to be handed everything on a silver platter as if she's better than other people.*

the silver ˈscreen (*old-fashioned*)
the film industry: *the heroes and heroines of the silver screen*

be born with a silver spoon in your mouth → **born**
every cloud has a silver lining → **cloud**
a silver/smooth tongue → **tongue**

simple

pure and simple → **pure**

sin

(as) miserable/ugly as ˈsin (*spoken*)
used to emphasize that sb is very unhappy or ugly: *He arrived at the party looking as miserable as sin.* ◇ *Some babies are as ugly as sin at that age.*

live in sin → **live**

sincerely

Yours sincerely (*BrE*) (*AmE* Sincerely (yours)) (*formal, written*)
used at the end of a formal letter before you sign your name, when you have addressed sb by their name

sine

a sine qua ˈnon (of/for sth) (*from Latin, formal*)
something that is essential before you can achieve sth else: *Many people believe that grammar is the sine qua non of language learning.*

sinew

strain every nerve/sinew (to do sth) → **strain**

sing

sing a different 'song/'tune
(be forced to) change your opinion: *Anne says she wants a large family but I'm sure she'll be singing a different tune when she's had one or two children.*

sing for your 'supper (*old-fashioned*)
do sth for sb in order to get what you want or need: *Susan has to clean her room before she's allowed to go out with her friends—she really has to sing for her supper!*

sing from the same 'song/'hymn sheet (*informal*)
say the same things and agree about a subject, especially in public: *We really need to make sure we are all singing from the same hymn sheet before the press conference.*

sing sb's/sth's 'praises (*informal*)
praise sb/sth very much or with great enthusiasm; say that sb/sth is very good: *Both her grandsons are doctors, and she never stops singing their praises.* ◇ *One day he's singing your praises; the next day he's telling you you're stupid.*

singing

,all 'singing, ,all 'dancing (*BrE, informal*)
(of a machine or system) having a lot of advanced technical features and therefore able to perform many different functions: *With these extras your PC will become the all singing, all dancing box the salesman claimed it would be.*

single

(in) single/Indian file → **file**

sings

it ain't/it's not over till the fat lady sings → **fat**

sink

sink your 'differences
agree to forget or ignore your past arguments or disagreements: *The two groups sank their political differences and joined together to beat the ruling party.*

,sink or 'swim (*saying*)
either succeed without help from other people, or fail: *The government refused to give the company any help, and just left it to sink or swim.*

,sink so 'low; sink to sth
have such low moral standards that you do sth very bad: *Stealing from your friends? How could you sink so low?* ◇ *I can't believe that anyone would sink to such depths.*

sink to sb's 'level
stop behaving well and begin to behave badly, especially in an argument or a fight, because other people are behaving in this way: *Use words, not violence, or you'll just be sinking to their level.*

everything but/bar the kitchen sink → **kitchen**
sink, vanish, etc. without (a) trace → **trace**

sinker

hook, line and sinker → **hook**

sinking

(like rats) deserting/leaving a sinking 'ship (*humorous, disapproving*)
used to talk about people who leave an organization, a company, etc. that is having difficulties, without caring about the people who are left: *One by one, employees began looking for other jobs, like rats deserting a sinking ship.* ◇ *I might have known he'd be the first rat to desert this sinking ship!*

(get/have) a/that 'sinking feeling (*informal*)
(get/have) a feeling that sth bad has happened/is going to happen: *Most people know that sinking feeling you get when a bill arrives in the post.*

with a heavy/sinking heart → **heart**

sinks

your heart sinks → **heart**

sins

(do/be sth) for your sins (*spoken humorous, especially BrE*)
be/do sth as a punishment: *'I hear you're going to be the new manager.' 'Yes, for my sins.'*

cover/hide a multitude of sins → **multitude**

sir

,no 'sir!; ,no sir'ree! (*spoken, especially AmE*)
certainly not: *We will never allow that to happen! No sir!*

,yes 'sir!; ,yes sir'ree! (*spoken, especially AmE*)
used to emphasize that sth is true: *That's a fine car you have. Yes sirree!*

sirree

no sirree! = no sir! → **sir**
yes sirree! = yes sir! → **sir**

sisters

be (all) brothers/sisters under the skin → **skin**

sit

sit comfortably/easily/well (with sth) (*written*)
seem right, natural, suitable, etc. in a particular place or situation: *His views did not sit comfortably with the management line.*

sit in 'judgement (on/over sb) (*especially BrE*)
(*AmE usually* **sit in 'judgment (on/over sb)**))
judge or decide if sb is wrong or right, even if you have no right to do so: *What gives you the right to sit in judgement over us?*

sit on the 'fence
avoid deciding between two sides of an argument, discussion, quarrel, etc: *You must say if you support me or not. You can't sit on the fence all your life.*

◇ *Politicians cannot sit on the fence. People expect them to have clear views.* ▶ **'fence-sitter** *noun* a person who cannot or does not want to decide which side of an argument, etc. to support

sit 'tight

not move; not change your position, in the hope that your present difficulties will be solved or go away: *If your car breaks down on the motorway, sit tight and wait for the police.* ◇ *In a period of recession businessmen have to sit tight and hope for better times in the future.*

sitting

be ˌsitting 'pretty (*informal*)

be rich, successful or in a pleasant situation: *If you make £50000 profit when you sell this house, you'll be sitting pretty.*

do sth in/at one 'sitting

do sth in one continuous period of activity, without getting up from your chair: *I read the book in one sitting.*

a ˌsitting 'duck/'target

a person or thing that is very easy to attack or criticize: *It's always easy to criticize teachers; they're just sitting ducks.*

(as) sure as I'm standing/sitting here → sure

situ

in 'situ (*from Latin*)

in the original or correct place: *Much of the original furniture has been left in situ so that we can view the room almost as it looked a hundred years ago.*

❷ **NOTE**
Situ literally means 'position'.

situation

a catch-22 situation → catch-22
a chicken-and-egg situation → chicken-and-egg
save the day/situation → save

six

hit/knock sb/sth for 'six (*BrE*)

1 (often of sth unpleasant) surprise sb a lot: *It really hit me for six to find that my father had written about me in his book.*
2 completely destroy a plan, an idea, a suggestion, etc.; knock sb/sth over/down: *The stock market crash has hit the economy for six.* ◇ *Toby took a step backwards and knocked the video camera for six.*

❶ **ORIGIN**
This phrase refers to a score of six runs in the game of cricket.

it's six of ˌone and half a dozen of the 'other (*saying*)

used to say that there is no real difference between two possible choices: *Patrick said John started the fight, but I think it was probably six of one and half a dozen of the other.* ◇ *I've tried both ways of getting to Oxford and as far as I can see it's six of one and half a dozen of the other* (= they both take the same time).

❷ **NOTE**
A *dozen* means 'twelve'.

six feet 'under (*informal, humorous*)

dead (and buried in the ground): *By then, all the witnesses were six feet under.*

sixes

be at ˌsixes and 'sevens (*informal*)

be in a state of confusion; not be well organized: *I'm completely at sixes and sevens this week. My secretary's ill, I've got a report to write, and we're moving offices.*

sixth

a sixth 'sense

a special ability to know sth without using any of the five senses that include sight, touch, etc: *A kind of sixth sense told her that there was someone else in the room, and she turned round quickly.*

sixty-four

the sixty-four thousand dollar 'question (also **the million dollar 'question**)

a very important question which is difficult or impossible to answer: *The sixty-four thousand dollar question for modern astronomy is 'Is there life elsewhere in the universe?'*

❶ **ORIGIN**
This phrase originated in the 1940s as 'the sixty-four-dollar question'. It came from a popular US radio quiz programme at the time on which the top prize was $64.

size

that's about the 'size of it (*spoken*)

that is a good or fair description of the situation: *'So you're leaving university just to go travelling?' 'Yes, that's about the size of it.'*

cut sb down to size → cut

sizes

come in all shapes and sizes → shapes

skates

get/put your 'skates on (*BrE, informal*)

hurry up: *If you don't put your skates on, you'll be late for work.*

skating

be skating/walking on thin ice → thin

skeleton

a skeleton 'crew/'staff/'service
the minimum number of staff necessary to run an organization or service: *Over Christmas we have a skeleton staff to deal with emergencies.*

a skeleton in the 'cupboard/'closet
something shocking, embarrassing, etc. that has happened to you or your family in the past that you want to keep secret: *The new presidential candidate is certainly popular, but does he have any skeletons in the closet?*

> **ⓘ ORIGIN**
> This phrase comes from the fairy tale of Blue Beard (a rich man). He gave all the keys of the house to his wife when he left on business, saying that the only place where she could not go was a closet at the end of a long corridor. She opened it, and there she found the dead bodies of his previous wives.

skid

(on) skid 'row (*informal, especially AmE*)
people who are **on skid row** live in a very poor part of town where there are many social problems: *When he went bankrupt he lost everything, and ended up living on skid row for a few years.*

skids

on the 'skids (*informal*)
moving towards disaster; declining: *It was clear months ago that the firm was on the skids.*

put the 'skids under sb/sth (*informal*)
make sb/sth fail; stop sb/sth doing sth: *Unfortunately the government has put the skids under the hospital building programme.*

skies

praise sb/sth to the skies → **praise**

skin

be (all) brothers/sisters under the 'skin
be men/women with similar feelings, in spite of outside appearances, such as skin colour, beauty, dress, etc: *Actors and politicians are brothers under the skin. They both need public approval.*

be (nothing but/all/just) skin and 'bone(s) (*informal*)
be very or too thin: *After two years in prison, he was nothing but skin and bone.*

do sth by the ˌskin of your 'teeth (*informal*)
only just do sth; nearly fail to do sth: *We thought we'd miss the plane, but in the end we caught it by the skin of our teeth.*

get under sb's 'skin (*informal*)
attract or disturb sb: *I've tried to forget her, but I know that I've got her under my skin.* ◇ *He gets under his opponents' skins and they make stupid mistakes.*

it's no skin off 'my, 'your, 'his, etc. nose (*informal*)
used to say that sb is not upset or annoyed about sth because it does not affect them in a bad way: *It's no skin off my nose if the price of cigarettes goes up. I don't smoke.*

make your 'skin crawl
make you feel afraid or full of disgust: *It makes my skin crawl when I think of what he might have done to me. Thank God you were there!*

skin sb a'live
(used as a threat or warning) punish sb very severely: *Your mother would skin you alive if she knew you'd started smoking!*

(have) a thick/thin 'skin (*informal*)
(be) not affected/affected by criticism or unkind remarks: *A traffic warden needs a thick skin to take so much abuse from motorists.* ◇ *He's got rather a thin skin for a politician. He'll have to learn to take the odd unkind remark.* ▶ ˌthick-'skinned, ˌthin-'skinned *adjs.*

be/get soaked to the skin → **soaked**
have (got) a hide/skin like a rhinoceros → **rhinoceros**
jump out of your skin → **jump**
save sb's/your (own) neck/skin/hide → **save**
slip on a banana skin → **slip**
there's more than one way to skin a cat → **way**

skin-deep

beauty is only skin-deep → **beauty**

skinned

keep your eyes open/peeled/skinned (for sb/sth) → **eyes**

skip

'skip it (*spoken, informal*)
used to tell sb impolitely that you do not want to talk about sth or repeat what you have said: *'What were you saying?' 'Oh, skip it!'*

skunk

(as) drunk as a skunk → **drunk**

sky

the sky's the 'limit (*spoken, informal*)
there is no limit or end to sth, especially sb's success or progress: *For an ambitious young woman in this business, the sky's the limit.*

pie in the sky → **pie**

sky-high

blow sb/sth sky-high → **blow**

slack

take up the 'slack
improve the way money or people are used in an organization: *The export market has failed to take*

up the slack in recent years, which has led to financial losses.

> ❷ NOTE
> The *slack* is the part of a rope that is hanging loosely. If there is no slack, the rope is tight.

cut sb some slack → cut

slanging

a 'slanging match (*BrE, informal*)
a noisy, angry argument: *It started as a peaceful discussion, but it ended in a real slanging match.*

slap

(a bit of) slap and 'tickle (*old-fashioned, BrE, informal*)
kissing and cuddling between lovers: *We used to do anything to get a bit of slap and tickle when we were young lads.*

a slap in the 'face
an action that seems to be intended as a deliberate insult to sb: *The bank refused to lend her any more money, which was a real slap in the face for her.*

a slap on the 'wrist (*informal*)
a small punishment or warning: *I got a slap on the wrist from my secretary today for leaving the office so untidy.*

slate

(put sth) on the 'slate (*informal*)
(put sth) on your account in a shop, a bar, etc. to be paid for later: *Can I put this on the slate?*

a clean sheet/slate → clean
wipe the slate clean → wipe

slaughter

(like) a lamb/lambs to the 'slaughter
(do sth or go somewhere) without protesting, probably because you do not realize that you are in danger: *When the war started, thousands of young men went off to France, like lambs to the slaughter.*

slave

be a slave to/of sth
be a person whose life is completely controlled by sth, for example a habit, a job, an interest, etc: *She's a slave to fashion; she's always buying new clothes.*

work like a dog/slave/Trojan → work

sledgehammer

use a sledgehammer to crack a nut → use

sleep

be able to do sth in your 'sleep (*informal*)
be able to do sth very easily because you have done it many times before: *He'd done the journey so many times that he almost felt as if he could do it in his sleep.*

,go to 'sleep (*informal*)
(of your leg, arm, hand, etc.) be unable to feel anything in your leg, etc. because it has been in a particular position for a long time

not sleep a 'wink; not get a 'wink of sleep
not sleep at all: *I didn't sleep a wink last night because I was worrying about my driving test.*

put sb/sth to 'sleep
1 give sb drugs (= an anaesthetic) before an operation to make them unconscious: *Before the operation we'll put you to sleep, so don't worry, you won't feel a thing.*
2 kill a sick or injured animal by giving it drugs so that it dies without pain: *She took her old dog to the vet and he put it to sleep.*

sleep like a 'log/'top (also **sleep like a 'baby**) (*informal*)
sleep very well; sleep without waking: *After our long walk yesterday, I slept like a log.*

'sleep on it
not make a decision until the following day so that you can have more time to think about it: *If you aren't sure what to do, sleep on it and give us your decision tomorrow.*

sleep 'tight! (*informal, spoken*)
used especially to children before they go to bed to say that you hope they sleep well: *Good night, Pat, sleep tight!*

get your beauty sleep → beauty
live/sleep rough → rough
lose no sleep over sb/sth = not lose any sleep over sb/sth → lose

sleeping

let sleeping dogs lie → let

sleeve

have (got) an ,ace/a ,trick up your 'sleeve (*BrE*) (*AmE* **have an ,ace in the 'hole**) (*informal*)
have an idea or plan which you keep secret and can use if you need to (especially in order to gain an advantage over sb): *They think they've won the contract but we've still got a couple of aces up our sleeve.*

have/keep sth up your 'sleeve (*informal*)
have a good idea, plan or piece of information which you are not telling anyone about now, but which you intend to use later: *John was smiling to himself all through the meeting; I'm sure he's got something up his sleeve.*

laugh up your sleeve (at sb/sth) → laugh
wear your heart on your sleeve → wear

sleeves

roll up your sleeves → roll

sleight

sleight of 'hand
1 something done with very quick and skilful movements of the hand(s) so that other people cannot see what really happened: *The trick is done simply by sleight of hand.*
2 skilful use of facts or figures to give people the wrong impression of sth or to make them believe sth which is not true: *We now realize that much of Burt's research was presented with a statistical sleight of hand.*

slice

a slice of 'life
a story, play or film that shows aspects of ordinary life: *In this book Dickens shows us a slice of nineteenth-century London life.*

any way you slice it → **way**
a piece/slice of the action → **action**
a piece/share/slice of the pie = a share/slice of the cake → **cake**

sliced

the best thing since sliced bread → **best**

slightest

not in the 'slightest
not at all; not in the least: *Flying doesn't worry me in the slightest.*

sling

sling your 'hook (*BrE, informal*)
(often used in orders) go away: *That boy's a real nuisance. I tried telling him to sling his hook but he simply ignored me.*

fling/sling/throw mud (at sb) → **mud**

slings

the slings and 'arrows (of sth)
the problems and difficulties (of sth): *As a politician you have to deal with the slings and arrows of criticism from the newspapers.*

ⓘ ORIGIN
This comes from Shakespeare's play *Hamlet*: 'the slings and arrows of outrageous fortune'.

slip

give sb the 'slip (*informal*)
get away from sb who is following you: *The police were chasing us but we managed to give them the slip.*

slip sb's 'memory/'mind
forget about sth or forget to do sth: *I was supposed to go to the dentist today, but it completely slipped my mind.*

a 'slip of a boy, girl, etc. (*old-fashioned*)
a small or thin, usually young, person: *They were*
amazed that such a slip of a girl could cause so much trouble.

a slip of the 'tongue/'pen
a small mistake when speaking or writing: *Did I say North Street? Sorry, that was a slip of the tongue—I meant South Street.*

slip on a ba'nana skin (*informal*)
(usually of a public figure) make a stupid mistake: *The new minister slipped on a banana skin before he had been in the job a week.*

slip through sb's 'fingers
(of an opportunity, money, etc.) escape or be missed: *I wouldn't let a wonderful opportunity like this slip through your fingers if I were you.*

slip through the 'net
when sb/sth **slips through the net**, an organization or a system fails to find them/it and deal with them/it: *We tried to contact all former students, but one or two slipped through the net.*

there's many a 'slip 'twixt cup and 'lip (*saying*)
(of plans, hopes, etc.) nothing is completely certain until it happens because things can easily go wrong: *We should get to London before 7 o'clock, but there's many a slip 'twixt cup and lip.*

❷ NOTE
The word *'twixt* is a short form of the old word *betwixt*, meaning 'between'.

a Freudian slip → **Freudian**
let slip sth → **let**
roll/slip/trip off the tongue → **tongue**

slippery

(as) slippery as an 'eel (*informal*)
dishonest and good at not answering questions, etc: *The man the police want to talk to is slippery as an eel, and has so far escaped arrest.*

the slippery 'slope
a situation or way of behaving that could quickly lead to danger, disaster, failure, etc: *My mother seems to think that even a small drink is the start of the slippery slope towards alcoholism.*

slipping

be 'slipping (*informal*)
(of sb's behaviour or performance) not be as good, tidy, efficient, etc. as usual; not be up to sb's usual high standard: *You're slipping, Edwina: this essay is full of spelling mistakes.* ◇ *That's three times he's beaten me—I must be slipping!*

slog

slog/slug it 'out (*BrE, informal*)
(of people, organizations, competitors, etc.) fight very hard until one person or group finally wins: *The boxers slugged it out to the finish.* ◇ *The two teams will slog it out for second place.*

slog/sweat/work your guts out → **guts**

slope

the slippery slope ➔ slippery

slouch

be no 'slouch (at sth/doing sth) (*informal*)
be good at sth/doing sth: *He's no slouch in the kitchen—you should try his spaghetti bolognese.*

slow

do a slow 'burn (*AmE, informal*)
slowly get angry: *It makes me do a slow burn when it takes longer to check out at the grocery store than it took to shop.*

go 'slow (on sth)
show less enthusiasm for achieving sth: *The government is going slow on tax reforms.*

in the 'slow lane
not making progress as fast as other people, countries, companies, etc: *According to the latest survey, the country is expected to remain in the slow lane of economic recovery.*

be quick/slow off the mark ➔ mark
be quick/slow on the uptake ➔ uptake

slowly

slowly but 'surely
used for describing definite but slow progress in sth: *Attitudes to women at work are changing slowly but surely.*

easy/gently/slowly does it ➔ easy

slug

slog/slug it out ➔ slog

slum

'slum it (*informal, often humorous*)
live in worse conditions than you do usually: *We're slumming it tonight. No champagne, just ordinary table wine.*

sly

do sth on the 'sly
do sth secretly: *She didn't seem to have much appetite for dinner. I wonder if she's been eating chocolates on the sly?*

smack

lick/smack your lips ➔ lips

small

be grateful/thankful for small 'mercies
be happy that a bad situation is not even worse: *The thieves took the TV and stereo but didn't take any jewellery, so let's be thankful for small mercies.*

it's a ,small 'world (*saying*)
used when you meet or hear about sb you know, in an unexpected place: *It turns out that he's a friend of my brother's! It's a small world, isn't it?*

look/feel 'small (also **feel 'that high**)
feel stupid, embarrassed or ridiculous in front of other people: *Why did you tell everyone that I'd failed all my school exams? I felt so small.* ◇ *Mrs Jones made him feel that high when she criticized his work in front of everybody.*

> **❶ NOTE**
> When using the expression *feel that high*, you often use your thumb and finger to indicate something small.

small 'beer (*BrE*) (*AmE* **small po'tatoes**)
something that has little importance or value: *Jacob earns about £25 000, but that's small beer compared with his brother's salary.*

a ,small 'fortune (*informal*)
a lot of money: *This house cost hardly anything when we bought it, but now it's worth a small fortune.*

'small fry (*informal*)
people, groups or businesses that are not considered to be important or powerful: *These local companies are only small fry compared to the huge multinationals.*

the 'small print (*BrE*) (*AmE* **the 'fine print**)
the parts of a written agreement or legal contract that are printed in very small letters, but which may contain important information: *Make sure you read the small print before you sign the contract.*

the small 'screen
(the) television (when contrasted with cinema): *Cinema films reach the small screen very quickly these days.*

(make) 'small talk
(take part in) polite conversation about unimportant things: *Maria introduced me to her parents, and we sat there making small talk for a while.*

do sth in a big/small way ➔ way
don't sweat the small stuff ➔ sweat
in no small part = in large part ➔ large
(it's) no/small/little wonder (that) … ➔ wonder
the small/early hours ➔ hours
the still small voice ➔ still

smart

a 'smart alec/aleck (*informal, disapproving*)
a person who tries to show that they are cleverer than everyone else: *Some smart alec wrote in to say that the last edition of the newspaper contained 37 printing errors.*

a/one smart 'cookie (*AmE, informal*)
a clever person with good ideas: *Jed is one smart cookie. I'm sure he'll do the right thing.*

the 'smart money is on sb/sth
if **the smart money is on** sb or sth, people with intelligence or knowledge think sb will succeed or sth will happen: *This year, the smart money is on Roe to win the tournament.*

smash

smash sb's 'face/'head in (*BrE, informal*)
hit sb very hard in the face/head: *Give me the money or I'll smash your head in.*

a ˌsmash 'hit (*informal*)
(of a record, play or film) very popular and a great success: *Still at number one, it's The Rubber Band, with their smash hit, 'Love me'.* ◇ *Up to now, actress Donna May has been in 15 Broadway smash hits.*

smell

ˌsmell a 'rat (*informal*)
think or suspect that sth is wrong or that sb is trying to deceive you: *She says that the business is making a lot of money, but I smell a rat somewhere. The figures are too good to be true.*

smell/stink to high heaven → **high**
the sweet smell of success → **sweet**
wake up and smell the coffee → **wake**

smelling

come up/out of sth smelling of 'roses (*informal*)
still have a good reputation, even though you have been involved in sth that might have given people a bad opinion of you: *Nobody ever knew the details and he came out of the deal smelling of roses.*

smile

beam/grin/smile from ear to ear → **ear**
raise a laugh/smile → **raise**

smiles

be all 'smiles
be very happy and smiling, especially after feeling sad or worried about sth: *He was really depressed about the business last week, but he's all smiles now. A very big order has just come in.*

fortune smiles on sb → **fortune**

smithereens

blow, smash, etc. sth to smithe'reens (*informal*)
destroy sth completely by breaking it into small pieces: *The bomb blew the car to smithereens.*

smoke

go up in 'smoke
1 be destroyed by fire: *Their home went up in smoke before their eyes.*
2 (of plans, etc.) be destroyed or ruined: *Her plans to become a member of parliament went up in smoke when the newspapers printed a story about her drink problem.*

ˌsmoke like a 'chimney (*informal*)
smoke a lot of cigarettes: *You think I smoke a lot? You should meet Joe—he smokes like a chimney.*

there's no ˌsmoke without 'fire (*BrE*) (*AmE* **where there's smoke, there's 'fire**) (*saying*)
if a lot of people are saying that sth bad is happening, it must be partly true: *Although he had been found not guilty in court, people are saying that there's no smoke without fire.*

put that in your pipe and smoke it → **pipe**

smokescreen

(put up) a 'smokescreen
(do) sth that hides your real intentions, feelings, or activities: *She couldn't answer the question, so she tried to put up a smokescreen by talking angrily about the interviewer's rudeness.*

smooth

(as) smooth as 'silk (also **(as) smooth as a baby's 'bottom**, *humorous*)
very smooth: *He had just shaved and his face was as smooth as a baby's bottom.*

smooth the 'path/'way
make it easier for sth to happen: *The President's speech smoothed the way for talks with the rebel leaders.*

smooth (sb's) ruffled 'feathers
make sb feel less angry or offended: *According to his teachers, Nick was a sweet and loving child who always tried to smooth ruffled feathers and always supported his classmates and friends.*

a silver/smooth tongue → **tongue**
take the rough with the smooth → **rough**

snail

at a 'snail's pace (*informal*)
very slowly: *My grandmother drove the car at a snail's pace.*

'snail mail (*informal, humorous*)
used especially by people who use email on computers to describe the system of sending letters by ordinary mail: *I'd love to hear from you, either by email or snail mail.*

snake

a ˌsnake in the 'grass (*disapproving*)
a person who pretends to be your friend but who cannot be trusted: *We used to be friends, but who knew he'd turn out to be such a snake in the grass?*

snap

be a 'snap (*AmE, informal*)
be very easy to do: *This job's a snap.*

snap your 'fingers
1 attract sb's attention by making a sound with your thumb and middle finger: *Waiters don't like customers in restaurants who snap their fingers and shout 'waiter!'*
2 show you do not care about sb/sth: *He snapped his fingers at the committee and walked angrily out of the room.*

ˌsnap 'out of it; ˌsnap sb 'out of it (*informal*)
try to stop feeling unhappy or depressed; help sb

stop feeling this way: *For heaven's sake, Ann, snap out of it! Things aren't that bad!* ◇ *She wouldn't talk to anyone for days, but her friends helped snap her out of it.*

‚snap 'to it (*informal*)
used, especially in orders, to tell sb to start working harder or more quickly: *Come on! Snap to it!*

bite/snap sb's head off ➜ **head**

snappy

‚make it 'snappy (*informal*)
used to tell sb to do sth quickly or to hurry: *If you don't make it snappy, we'll miss the train.* ◇ *Come on, make it snappy! There's not much time left!*

snatches

in 'snatches
for short periods rather than continuously: *Sleep came to him in brief snatches.*

sneak

a ‚sneak 'preview
an opportunity to look at or watch sth, for example a book or a film, before it is shown to the public: *She gave me a sneak preview of her latest painting.*

sneezed

not to be 'sneezed/'sniffed at (*informal*)
important or worth having: *If I were you, I'd take the job. A salary like that's not to be sneezed at.*

sneezes

when A 'sneezes, B catches a 'cold (also **if A catches a 'cold, B gets pneu'monia**, *less frequent*)
if one person, organization, country, etc. has a problem, the effects of this on another person, organization or country are much more serious: *When Wall Street sneezes, the world catches a cold.*

sniff

have a (good) ‚sniff a'round
examine a place carefully: *Come and visit our website and have a sniff around!*

not get a 'sniff of sth (*informal*)
not succeed in obtaining sth: *I worked in Hollywood for years, but I never got a sniff of the big money.*

sniffed

not to be sneezed/sniffed at ➜ **sneezed**

sniffles

get, have, etc. the 'sniffles (*informal*)
get, have, etc. a slight cold: *'Are you ill?' 'No, I've just got the sniffles.'*

snook

cock a snook at sb/sth ➜ **cock**

snow

a 'snow job (*AmE, informal*)
an attempt to deceive sb or to persuade them to support sth by telling them things that are not true, or by praising them too much: *That guy gave me a real snow job. If I'd known the truth I never would have given him the money.*

(as) pure as the driven snow ➜ **pure**

snowball

not have a ‚snowball's chance in 'hell (of doing sth) (*informal*)
have no chance at all of doing sth: *Look at this traffic! I'm afraid we haven't got a snowball's chance in hell of getting to the airport in time.*

❶ ORIGIN
This idiom refers to the belief that hell is a place of fire.

snowed

be snowed 'under (with sth)
have more things, especially work, than you feel able to deal with: *I'd love to come but I'm completely snowed under at the moment.*

snuff

'snuff it (*BrE, slang, humorous*)
die: *Old Jack was over 90 when he snuffed it.*

(be) up to 'snuff (*informal*)
(be) of the required standard or quality: *Many people believe that the new senator is not up to snuff politically.*

❶ ORIGIN
This idiom possibly refers to the ability to identify the type and quality of *snuff*, which is tobacco in the form of powder that people used to take by breathing it into their noses.

snuffles

get, have, etc. the 'snuffles (*informal*)
get, have, etc. a cold: *According to research, non-drinkers are more likely to develop the winter snuffles than moderate drinkers.*

snug

(as) snug as a bug (in a rug) (*informal, humorous*)
very warm and comfortable: *In his sleeping bag he'll be as snug as a bug in a rug.*

so

be ‚so much/many 'sth
be completely sth; be just or only sth: *All his fine speeches are so much rubbish if he doesn't keep his promises.* ◇ *All these politicians are just so many names to me. I don't know any of them.*

... or so

used after a number, an amount, etc. to show that it is not exact: *He stayed for a week or so.* ◇ *Take a kilo or so of sugar ...*

so as to do sth

with the intention of doing sth: *We went early so as to get good seats.*

'so much/many (sth)

a certain amount/number (of sth): *At the end of every working week I have to write in my notebook that I drove so many miles at so much per litre.*

soaked

be/get ˌsoaked to the 'skin

(of a person) be/get very wet: *Don't go out in this rain—you'll get soaked to the skin.*

soapbox

be/get on your 'soapbox (*informal*)

express the strong opinions that you have about a particular subject: *Don't mention the Internet in front of him, or he'll get on his soapbox and we'll be here all night listening to his opinions about the evils of modern technology.*

sob

sob your 'heart out

cry noisily for a long time because you are very sad: *After the argument she spent an hour sobbing her heart out in the bedroom.*

a 'sob story (*informal, disapproving*)

a story that sb tells you so that you will feel sorry for them, especially one that does not have that effect or is not true: *Then she gave me another of her sob stories, this time about an argument with her boyfriend.*

sober

(as) sober as a 'judge

not at all affected by alcohol: *I was driving, so of course I was sober as a judge.*

stone-cold sober → stone-cold

sock

put a 'sock in it (*old-fashioned, BrE, informal*)

be quiet; stop talking or making a noise: *Put a sock in it, will you? I'm on the phone.*

> **ⓘ ORIGIN**
> This expression probably refers to early gramophones, which had no volume controls. To play records more quietly, people used to put a sock into the trumpet.

'sock it to sb (*informal or humorous*)

do sth or tell sb sth in a strong and effective way: *Go in there and sock it to 'em!*

socks

blow/knock sb's 'socks off (*informal*)

surprise or impress sb very much: *With that dress and your new haircut you'll really knock their socks off!*

bless his, her, etc. (little) cotton socks → bless

pull your socks up → pull

Sod

Sod's 'Law (*BrE, humorous*)

the tendency for things to happen in just the way that you do not want, and in a way that is not useful: *The band always plays better when they're not being recorded—but that's Sod's Law, isn't it?*

sod

blow/sod that for a lark → lark

blow/sod this/that for a game of soldiers → game

sods

odds and sods → odds

soft

be/go soft in the 'head (*informal, disapproving*)

be/become crazy or stupid: *Sometimes I talk to myself in the street; people must think I'm soft in the head.*

have (got) a soft 'spot for sb/sth (*informal*)

particularly like sb/sth: *I've always had a soft spot for my little cousin Clare.*

a soft/an easy touch → touch

the soft/easy option → option

soften

cushion/soften the blow → blow

softly-softly

a/the softly-'softly approach (*BrE, informal*)

a/the gentle, patient and careful way of doing sth, especially when dealing with people: *The police are now trying a more softly-softly approach with football hooligans.*

sold

be 'sold on sth (*informal*)

be very enthusiastic about sth: *We were really sold on the idea.*

soldiers

blow/sod this/that for a game of soldiers → game

solid

(as) solid as a 'rock

extremely solid and reliable: *The Irish team were solid as a rock in defence.*

some

'some such

used to say that sth is similar to another thing or things: *I think this music's by Bartok or some such composer.*

something

have (got) something 'on sb (*informal*)

have information about sb which is proof of their criminal activities or which would make them embarrassed if you told other people: *The press have got something on him, but for the moment they're keeping quiet.*

or something (*informal*)

or another similar thing: *Would you like some coffee or something?* ◇ *Why won't you tell her? Are you frightened of her or something?* ◇ *Let's go for a walk or something.*

something 'else

1 a different thing; another thing: *He said something else that I thought was interesting.*
2 (*informal*) a person, a thing or an event that is much better than others of a similar type: *I've seen some fine players, but she's something else!*

,something like 'sb/'sth

similar or partly the same as sb/sth; approximately (a number): *'Is he a travel agent?' 'Yes, something like that.'* ◇ *Something like twenty people came to the meeting.*

(be/have) something of a sth

(be/have) quite or rather a sth; (be/have) sth to an extent: *He has something of a reputation as a sportsman.* ◇ *Our walk home turned out to be something of an adventure.*

there's something about sb/sth

sb/sth has a strange, attractive or unusual quality that influences you, but which is difficult to explain: *There's something about her I don't like, but I can't put it into words.*

son

a/the ,son of a 'bitch (⚠, *slang*)

an offensive way to refer to a person that you think is bad or very unpleasant: *That's the son of a bitch who stole my car!*

a/the ,son of a 'gun (*AmE, informal, spoken*)

a person or thing that you are annoyed with: *My car's at the shop—the son of a gun broke down again.*

sb's favourite son → **favourite**
like father/mother, like son/daughter → **father**
a/the prodigal son → **prodigal**

song

(buy sth, go, etc.) for a 'song (*informal*)

(buy sth, be sold, etc.) for much less money than its real value: *I bought this car for a song.*

make a song and 'dance about sth (*informal, disapproving*)

worry or be excited about sth which is not very important: *My aunt makes a real song and dance about people arriving late, so hurry up.*

on 'song (*informal*)

working or performing well: *The whole team was on song.*

sing a different song/tune → **sing**
sing from the same song/hymn sheet → **sing**

soon

,anytime 'soon (*AmE*)

used in negative sentences and questions to refer to the near future: *Do you think she'll be back anytime soon?*

he, she, etc. would (just) as soon do A (as B)

sb wants to do one thing as much as another thing; it does not matter to sb what they do: *Susan can have my ticket for the show. I'd just as soon stay at home (as go out) anyway.* ◇ *He'd just as soon have pizza as a hamburger.*

none too 'soon

1 almost too late: *They were rescued none too soon; they'd already finished all the food and only had water for a couple more days.*
2 used for saying that sb should have done sth a long time ago: *'I've mended the lamp in the children's room.' 'None too soon. It's been broken for weeks.'*

a fool and his money are soon parted → **fool**
speak too soon → **speak**

sooner

no ,sooner ,said than 'done

(of a request) done immediately: *When he said he wanted to go to the zoo on his birthday it was no sooner said than done.*

no sooner ... than ... (*written*)

used to show that one thing, which is unexpected, happens immediately after another thing: *No sooner had she got in the bath than the front door bell rang.*

the ,sooner the 'better

very soon; as soon as possible: *'When shall I tell him?' 'The sooner the better.'*

,sooner or 'later

at some time in the future, even if you are not sure exactly when: *The police will find him sooner or later.*

,sooner rather than 'later

after a short time rather than after a long time: *We urged them to sort out the problem sooner rather than later.*

I, etc. would sooner do sth (than sth else)

I, etc. would prefer to do sth (than do sth else): *She'd sooner share a house with other students than live at home with her parents.*

sooner you, etc. than me = rather you, etc. than me → **rather**

soonest

least said soonest mended → **least**

sore

a ˌsore ˈpoint (with sb)
a subject or matter that makes sb feel angry or hurt: *The tax increases are a sore point with Jake, as he's going to lose a lot of money.*

stand/stick out like a sore ˈthumb (*informal*)
be very obvious or noticeable in an unpleasant way: *He's going to stick out like a sore thumb if he doesn't wear a suit to the wedding.*

be a sight for sore eyes → **sight**
like a bear with a sore head → **bear**

sorrow

do sth more in ˌsorrow than in ˈanger
do sth because you feel sad or sorry rather than angry: *One of the interrogators pretended to be acting more in sorrow than in anger.*

sorrows

drown your sorrows → **drown**

sorry

be/feel ˈsorry for sb
feel sympathy or pity for sb: *I feel sorry for all the people who are alone at Christmas.*

be/feel ˈsorry for yourself (*informal, disapproving*)
be/feel unhappy because you think other people have treated you badly, etc: *You can't sit there feeling sorry for yourself all day.*

I'm ˈsorry to say
used for saying that sth is disappointing: *He didn't accept the job, I'm sorry to say.*

better (to be) safe than sorry → **better**

sort

kind of/sort of → **kind**
nothing of the kind/sort → **kind**
something of the/that kind/sort → **kind**
of a kind/sort → **kind**
sort out/separate the men from the boys → **men**
sort out/separate the sheep from the goats → **sheep**
sort out/separate the wheat from the chaff → **wheat**

sorts

be, feel, etc. out of ˈsorts (*especially BrE*)
be, feel, etc. ill or bad-tempered: *I was out of sorts for a couple of weeks after I came out of hospital.* ◇ *What's the matter with Jane? She looks rather out of sorts today.*

it takes ˈall sorts (to make a world) (*saying*)
different people like different things; different people have different characters and abilities: *'I don't understand Bill. He spends nearly all weekend cleaning and polishing his car.' 'Well, it takes all sorts.'*

of ˈsorts (*informal*)
used when you are saying that sth is not a good example of a particular type of thing: *He offered us an apology of sorts and we accepted it.*

soul

be the soul of sth
be a perfect example of a good quality: *She's the soul of discretion.*

good for the ˈsoul (*humorous*)
good for you, even if it seems unpleasant: *'Want a ride?' 'No thanks. Walking is good for the soul.'*

bare your soul → **bare**
(God) bless your, his, etc. heart/soul → **bless**
body and soul → **body**
God rest his/her soul → **God**
(your) heart and soul → **heart**
keep body and soul together → **body**
the life and soul of the party → **life**
search your heart/soul/conscience → **search**
sell your soul → **sell**

sound

like, love, etc. the ˌsound of your own ˈvoice (*disapproving*)
talk too much, usually without listening to others: *That man does like the sound of his own voice. We couldn't stop him talking.*

(as) sound as a ˈbell (*informal*)
in perfect condition: *There's nothing wrong with her. She's been examined and she's sound as a bell.*

sound aˈsleep
deeply and peacefully asleep: *He had fallen sound asleep in the chair by the fire.* ◇ *The children are sound asleep upstairs.*

sound the ˈdeath knell of sth
be the reason why sth ends, goes out of fashion, or is replaced: *The arrival of large supermarkets sounded the death knell of many small local shops.*

look/sound suspiciously like sth → **suspiciously**
safe and sound → **safe**
sound/strike a false note → **false**
sound/strike a note (of sth) → **note**

soup

be in the ˈsoup; land yourself/sb in the ˈsoup (*informal*)
be in/get (sb) into trouble or difficulties: *If we don't get paid soon, we'll be in the soup.* ◇ *I've really landed myself in the soup this time; I've crashed my father's car.*

sour

go/turn ˈsour
become less enjoyable, pleasant or good: *Relations between the two nations have recently gone sour.*

sour 'grapes (*saying*)

used to describe the behaviour of sb who pretends that sth they cannot have is of little value or interest: *When she failed the entrance exam, she started saying that she never wanted to go to university anyway, but I think that's just sour grapes.*

❶ ORIGIN

This idiom comes from one of Aesop's fables. A fox cannot reach some grapes so he decides that they are not ready to eat.

sow

sow your wild 'oats (*informal*)

(usually used of young men) enjoy yourself before you get married and settle down: *The problem is that he never sowed his wild oats before he got married, and he wants to sow them now.*

make a silk purse out of a sow's ear → **silk**

plant/sow the seeds of sth → **seeds**

you reap what you sow → **reap**

space

in the space of a 'minute, an 'hour, a 'morning, etc.

during the period of a minute, an hour, etc: *I went from Glasgow to Edinburgh twelve times in the space of a few days.*

look/stare/gaze into 'space

look straight in front of you without looking at a particular thing, usually because you are thinking about sth: *I asked her twice if she was ready to leave but she just sat there staring into space.*

a breathing space → **breathing**

a waste of space → **waste**

watch this space → **watch**

spade

call a spade a spade → **call**

spades

in 'spades (*informal*)

in large amounts or to a great degree: *He'd got his revenge now, and in spades.*

span

spic and span = spick and span → **spick**

spanner

put/throw a 'spanner in the works (*BrE*) (*AmE* **throw a ('monkey) 'wrench in the works**) (*informal*)

spoil or prevent the success of sb's plan, idea, etc: *Let's get this finished before the boss comes along and throws a spanner in the works.*

spare

go 'spare (*BrE, informal*)

be very angry: *When she found the children drawing on the walls, she went spare.*

spare sb's 'feelings

be careful to avoid offending or upsetting sb: *Eric got no votes at all, but we didn't tell him because we wanted to spare his feelings.* ◇ *She didn't spare my feelings at all—she told me exactly why she didn't like me.*

spare no expense/pains/trouble (to do sth, (in) doing sth)

spend as much time, money or effort as is necessary: *His twenty-first birthday party was amazing—his parents had spared no expense.* ◇ *The ship's crew will spare no pains to make your Mediterranean cruise unforgettable.* ◇ *It will be a wonderful holiday, **no expense spared**.*

spare the 'rod and spoil the 'child (*saying*)

if you do not punish a child for behaving badly, he/she will behave badly in future

a spare 'tyre (*BrE*) (*AmE* **a spare 'tire**)

a roll of flesh around the waist: *He went on a diet to try and lose his spare tyre.*

to 'spare

if you have time, money, etc. **to spare**, you have more than you need: *I've got absolutely no money to spare this month.* ◇ *We arrived at the airport with five minutes to spare.*

save/spare sb's blushes → **blushes**

spark

(a) bright spark → **bright**

sparks

the feathers/fur/sparks will fly → **fly**

spate

in (full) 'spate (*especially BrE*)

1 (of a river) containing more water and flowing more strongly than usual: *After heavy rain, the river was in spate.*

2 (of a person) completely involved in talking and not likely to stop or not able to be interrupted: *Celia was in full spate as usual, so I just sat there waiting for her to finish.*

speak

no sth/nothing/not anything to 'speak of

nothing very important or worth mentioning: *We looked through his private papers, but we didn't find anything to speak of.* ◇ *He's got no money to speak of.*

so to 'speak (also **as it 'were**)

used to emphasize that you are expressing sth in an unusual or amusing way: *They were all very similar. All cut from the same cloth, so to speak.* ◇ *Night fell and the city became, as it were, a different place entirely.*

speak for it'self/them'selves

be so clear or obvious that no explanation or comment is needed: *The expressions on their faces spoke for themselves—they hated the film.*

speak for my'self, him'self, etc.
express what you think or want yourself, rather than sb else doing it for you: *I'm quite capable of speaking for myself, thank you!*

speak for your'self (*spoken, informal*)
used to tell sb that a general statement they have just made is not true of you: *'We didn't play very well.' 'Speak for yourself!'* (= I think that I played well.)

speak 'highly of sb
praise sb because you admire or respect their personal qualities or abilities: *His teacher speaks very highly of him.* ◇ *Professor Heynman was very highly spoken of by his students.*

speak your 'mind
say exactly what you think, in a very direct way: *I like a man who speaks his mind.*

speak too 'soon
say sth, and find afterwards that what you said is not true: *'I'm glad Simon didn't come.' 'You spoke too soon. Here he comes now.'*

speak 'volumes (about/for sb/sth)
show or express a lot about the nature or quality of sb/sth: *Her face spoke volumes. You could see how much she had suffered.* ◇ *The progress he's made since the operation speaks volumes for his courage.*

actions speak louder than words → **actions**
the facts speak for themselves → **facts**
speak/think ill of sb → **ill**
speak/talk of the devil → **devil**
speak/talk the same/a different language → **language**

speaking

be on 'speaking terms (with sb)
1 know sb well enough to speak to them, perhaps sb famous or important: *He's on speaking terms with a number of senior politicians.*
2 (also **be 'speaking (to sb)**) be talking to each other again after an argument: *Tony and Craig had a big row and are not on speaking terms.* ◇ *You're lucky I'm still speaking to you after what you did!*

in a manner of speaking → **manner**
relatively speaking → **relatively**
strictly speaking → **strictly**

spec

do sth on 'spec (*BrE, informal*)
go somewhere without a ticket, appointment, etc. in the hope that you will be able to get sth you want: *That restaurant's very popular. You'll never get a table if you just turn up on spec.*

spectacle

make a 'spectacle of yourself
draw attention to yourself by behaving or dressing in a ridiculous way in public: *He made a spectacle of himself by shouting at the barman.*

spectacles

look at, see, etc. sth through ,rose-tinted/ ,rose-coloured 'spectacles
notice only the pleasant things in life and think things are better than they really are; be too optimistic: *She is convinced the company will make a big profit, but then she does tend to see things through rose-tinted spectacles.*

spectre (*BrE*) (*AmE* specter)
raise the spectre of sth → **raise**

speed

up to 'speed (on sth)
1 (of a person, company, etc.) performing at an expected rate or level: *the cost of bringing the chosen schools up to speed*
2 (of a person) having the most recent and accurate information or knowledge: *I'll bring you up to speed on the latest developments.*

at/with lightning speed → **lightning**
full steam/speed ahead → **full**
(at) full pelt/speed/tilt → **full**
more haste, less speed → **haste**
pick up speed → **pick**
a turn of speed → **turn**

spell

(be) under sb's 'spell
(be) so attracted to or interested in sb that you are in their power and will do what they say: *When he tells a story, the children are completely under his spell.*

weave a spell (over sb) → **weave**

spend

spend the 'night with sb/together
stay with sb for a night and have sex with them: *James told me Kim and Robin spent the night together.*

spend a 'penny (*old-fashioned, BrE, informal*)
go to the toilet; urinate: *Do you want to spend a penny before we leave?*

❶ ORIGIN
In the past, public toilets in England had coin operated locks, which cost one penny to open.

spent

a ,spent 'force
a person or group that no longer has any power or influence: *The new album is proof that this band is not a spent force just yet.*

spice
variety is the spice of life → **variety**

spick (also spic)

,spick and 'span (also ,spic and 'span)
clean, tidy and fresh: *The boss likes everything spick and span in the office.*

spike

spike sb's 'drink
add (more) alcohol or drugs to sb's drink, without their knowledge: *It wasn't until later that I discovered they'd spiked my drink. That's why I was so ill!*

spike sb's 'guns (BrE)
spoil sb's plans because you do not want them to succeed: *She was jealous of David's progress in the company, so she spiked his guns by telling the boss that David had a drinking problem.*

spill

spill the 'beans (informal)
tell sb sth that should be kept secret or private: *We were trying to keep it a secret from Pete, but Marcia spilled the beans.* ◇ *Come on, spill the beans! What did your father say?*

spill (sb's) 'blood (formal or literary)
kill or wound people: *Nothing can justify spilling innocent blood.*

spill your 'guts (to sb) (AmE, informal)
tell sb everything you know or feel about sth, because you are upset: *I know you're upset about what I did, but did you have to spill your guts to my parents?*

spills

(the) thrills and spills (of sth) → thrills

spilt

it's no good/use crying over spilt milk → crying

spin

in a (flat) 'spin
very confused, worried or excited: *Her resignation put her colleagues in a spin.*

spin (sb) a 'yarn/'tale
tell (sb) a (usually long) story, which is often not true: *She came an hour late and spun him a yarn about her car breaking down.*

turn/spin on your heel → heel

spine

a chill runs/goes down sb's spine = send a chill up/down sb's spine → send

a shiver runs/goes down sb's spine = send a shiver up/down sb's spine → send

spirit

(do sth) as/if/when the spirit 'moves you
(do sth) when you want to, rather than when you have to or are forced to: *She works in the garden occasionally, when the spirit moves her.*

be with sb in 'spirit
be thinking of sb who is in another place because you would like to be with them but cannot be: *I'm afraid I can't come to the wedding, but I'll be with you in spirit.*

get/enter into the 'spirit of sth
take part in an activity or event with enthusiasm: *Every year he gets into the spirit of Christmas by decorating his whole house with coloured lights.* ◇ *The party went well because everyone entered into the spirit of things.*

the ,spirit is 'willing but the ,flesh (it) is 'weak (saying, humorous)
you intend to do good things but are too tired, lazy etc. to actually do them

,that's the 'spirit!
used to encourage sb or to tell them that they are doing sth well: *'I'm rather tired, but I think I can run another mile.' 'That's the spirit!'*

fighting spirit → fighting
the moving spirit → moving

spirits

be in high/low 'spirits (also in good/poor 'spirits)
be happy and cheerful/sad and miserable: *John was in rather low spirits all evening.* ▶ ,high-'spirited, ,low-'spirited adjs.: *high-spirited children*

raise sb's spirits → raise

spiritual

be sb's ,spiritual 'home
be a place where sb could be happy, because they like the people, customs, culture, etc. there: *I've always thought that Australia was his spiritual home.*

spit

spit and 'polish (informal)
cleaning and polishing: *This table will look as good as new with a bit of spit and polish.*

spit 'blood/'venom
show that you are very angry; speak in an angry way: *That man made me so angry that by the end of the meeting I was spitting blood!*

,spit it 'out! (spoken)
usually used in orders to tell sb to say sth when they seem frightened or unwilling to speak: *What did you tell her about me? Come on, spit it out!*

spite

in 'spite of sth
if you say that sb does/did sth in spite of a fact, you mean it is surprising that that fact does/did not prevent them from doing it; despite: *In spite of his age, he still leads an active life.* ◇ *They went swimming in spite of all the danger signs.* ◇ *English became the official language for business in*

spite of the fact that the population was largely Chinese.

(do sth) in 'spite of yourself
(do sth) even though you do not want or expect to: *He was a bit depressed so I tried to cheer him up with a joke. He smiled in spite of himself.*

cut off your nose to spite your face → **cut**

spitting

within 'spitting distance (of sth) (*BrE*) (also **within 'shouting distance** *AmE, BrE*) (*informal*)
very near a place: *We live within spitting distance of the sea.*

be the living/spitting/very image of sb/sth → **image**

splash

make, cause, etc. a 'splash (*informal*)
attract a lot of attention, for example in the newspapers, because you are famous: *Their wedding created quite a splash in the newspapers.*

spleen

vent your spleen → **vent**

spliced

get 'spliced (*old-fashioned, BrE, informal*)
get married

split

split the 'difference
agree on an amount (of money) which is halfway between two others: *John offered £60, but Peter wanted £100. Finally they split the difference and agreed on £80.*

split sth down the 'middle
divide people into two groups, who disagree: *The local Conservative party is split down the middle on the matter of taxation.*

split 'hairs (*disapproving*)
pay too much attention in an argument to differences that are very small and not important: *You might think I'm just splitting hairs, but what exactly do you mean by 'a significant improvement'?* ▶ **'hair-splitting** *noun*

a ˌsplit 'second
a very short time: *I heard a loud explosion and a split second later I was on the floor.* ▶ **'split-second** *adj.: split-second timing/reactions*

split your 'sides (laughing/with laughter)
laugh a lot; laugh loudly: *When she started singing in that funny voice, we nearly split our sides.*

split the 'ticket (*AmE, politics*)
vote for candidates from more than one party: *Election officials are reminding voters that they may 'split their ticket' in the November election, unlike a state primary election.*

spoil

spoil sb 'rotten
give sb everything they want or ask for: *She spoils the children rotten.*

spoil the ship for a ha'porth/ha'penny-worth of tar (*saying*)
spoil sth good because you did not spend any or enough money on a small but essential part of it: *Always buy good quality floppy disks. Don't spoil the ship for a ha'porth of tar.*

spare the rod and spoil the child → **spare**
too many cooks spoil the broth → **cooks**

spoiled

be spoilt/spoiled for choice → **choice**

spoiling

be ˌspoiling for a 'fight, argument, etc.
want to fight, argue, etc. with sb very much: *Are you spoiling for a fight?* ◇ *The teachers' union is spoiling for a fight with the Government.*

spoilt

be spoilt/spoiled for choice → **choice**

spoke

put a 'spoke in sb's wheel (*BrE*)
make it difficult for sb to do sth or to carry out their plans: *If the management try to cut our pay, we can put a spoke in their wheel by going on strike.*

spoken

the spoken/written word → **word**

sponge

throw in the towel/sponge → **throw**

spoon

be born with a silver spoon in your mouth → **born**
get, win, take, etc. the wooden spoon → **wooden**

sport

be a (good) 'sport (*informal*)
be generous, cheerful and pleasant, especially in a difficult situation: *She's a good sport.* ◇ *Go on, be a sport* (= used when asking sb to do sth for you).

sporting

a ˌsporting 'chance
a reasonable chance of success: *I know it's going to be tough, but I think I'm in with a sporting chance of winning.*

spot

ˌglued/ˌrooted to the 'spot
not able to move, for example because you are frightened or surprised: *He shouted at her to run,*

but she just stood there, glued to the spot. ◇ *She stood there rooted to the spot when she saw the body.*

on the 'spot

1 at the place where sth is happening: *Our man on the spot is Geoff Davies. He's going to tell us exactly what's happening in Cairo.*

2 immediately; without any delay: *The police officer asked me for my driving licence and I gave it to him on the spot.*

put sb on the 'spot

put sb in a difficult position, perhaps by asking them a difficult or embarrassing question: *Her question about my future plans really put me on the spot.*

bang/spot on → bang
be riveted to the spot/ground → riveted
a black spot → black
a/sb's blind spot → blind
a/the bright spot → bright
have (got) a soft spot for sb/sth → soft
the high point/spot of sth → high
hit the spot → hit
a hot spot → hot
in a tight corner/spot → tight

spotlight

in/under the 'spotlight

getting attention from newspapers, television and the public: *Unemployment has once again come under the spotlight.* ◇ *He's a shy man, who really doesn't enjoy being in the spotlight.*

spots

knock spots off sb/sth → knock
a leopard cannot change its spots → leopard

spout

be/go up the 'spout (*BrE, slang*)

be/go wrong; be spoilt or not working: *It looks like our holiday plans are up the spout.* ◇ *This information the bank sent me is totally up the spout.*

sprat

(be) a ‚sprat to catch a 'mackerel (*informal*)

(be) a fairly small or unimportant thing which is offered or risked in the hope of getting sth bigger or better: *The competition and prize of a free car is a sprat to catch a mackerel. The publicity will mean good business for months to come.*

spread

spread like 'wildfire

(especially of news or disease) travel or spread very quickly: *Rumours about a fall in the price of oil spread like wildfire in the city.* ◇ *Cholera spread like wildfire through the camps.*

spread your 'wings

become more independent and confident enough to try new activities, etc: *Studying at university*

should help you to spread your wings and become independent.

spread the 'word

tell people about sth: *Because of her contacts in the business world, he asked Kate to spread the word about his latest venture.*

spread yourself too 'thin

try to do so many different things at the same time that you do not do any of them properly: *Are you sure you can manage an evening job as well? Don't you think you're spreading yourself a bit too thin?*

cast/spread your net wide → net

spring

be ‚no spring 'chicken (*humorous*)

be no longer young: *I'm no spring chicken, but still like going on long walks.* ◇ *Are you sure he should be playing squash at his age? He's no spring chicken, you know!*

spring a 'leak

(of a boat, roof, container, etc.) start to let water in: *The boat sprang a leak halfway across the Atlantic.*

spring (in)to 'life/'action

(of a person or thing) suddenly become active or start to work: *As soon as he heard the alarm bell, he sprang into action.* ◇ *This machine will spring into life at the touch of a button.*

spring a 'trap

1 make a trap for catching animals close suddenly **2** try to trick sb into doing or saying sth; succeed in this: *The burglars were arrested after the police sprung a trap on them last night.*

come/spring to mind → mind
full of the joys of spring → full

springs

hope springs eternal → hope

spur

(do sth) on the ‚spur of the 'moment

(do sth) as soon as you think of it, without planning or preparation: *When they telephoned me with the offer of a job abroad, I decided on the spur of the moment to accept.* ◇ *It was a spur-of-the-moment decision.*

spurs

win/earn your 'spurs (*formal*)

become successful or famous: *You'll win your spurs as a teacher if you can control class 5.*

spy

‚spy out the 'land

find out about a situation, place, organization, etc. before you make a decision: *The manager is sending Mark to Iceland to spy out the land. He wants to know whether we can do business there.*

square

be/go back to square 'one (also **start again from square 'one**) (*informal*)
start sth again from the beginning because your first idea, plan, action, etc. has failed or has been stopped: *The experiment didn't work, so it's back to square one, I'm afraid.*

> **❶ ORIGIN**
> This idiom might have come from the early days of broadcasting, when people listened to football matches on the radio. A numbered grid diagram of the pitch was published, with *Square One* at the centre where teams returned to each time a goal was scored.

be (all) 'square (with sb) (*informal*)
1 have the same score in a competition: *Liverpool were all square with Chelsea at half-time.*
2 (of two people) not owe money (or anything else) to each other: *Here's a pound—now we're square.*

be a square 'peg (in a round 'hole) (*BrE, informal*)
not fit in well or easily into an organization, job, etc. because you are different: *I don't have the right personality for the job. I feel like a square peg in a round hole.*

square your/an ac'count (with sb); square ac'counts (with sb)
1 pay sb the money you owe them: *You can square your account at the end of the week.*
2 hurt sb, usually because they have done sth bad to you: *I'm here to square accounts with Murphy for what he did to my sister.*

square the 'circle
(try to) do sth that is or seems impossible: *The Government is trying to square the circle when it says it will spend more on the health service without raising taxes.*

a square 'meal
a large and satisfying meal: *The children get three square meals a day.*

fair and square → **fair**

squarely

fairly and squarely = fair and square → **fair**

squeak

a narrow escape/squeak → **narrow**

squeeze

put the 'squeeze on sb (to do sth) (*informal*)
put pressure on sb to act in a particular way; make a situation difficult for sb: *Rising fuel prices are putting the squeeze on farmers and transport businesses.*

₁squeeze sb 'dry
get as much money, information, etc. out of sb as you can: *The war, as well as the economic sanctions*

imposed by foreign powers, have squeezed the economy dry.

a tight squeeze → **tight**

squib

a damp squib → **damp**

stab

have a stab at sth/doing sth (*informal*)
try sth/doing sth, especially if you have never done it before: *I had a stab at fishing once but I found it boring.*

stab sb in the 'back; get, etc. a stab in the 'back (*informal*)
do or say sth that harms sb who trusts you; be treated this way: *Jane promised to support me at the meeting, but then she stabbed me in the back by supporting David instead.* ▶ **a 'back-stabber, 'back-stabbing** *nouns*: *This party is full of back-stabbers.* ◇ *There is always a lot of back-stabbing in academic life.*

a shot/stab in the dark → **dark**

stable

shut/lock/close the stable door after the horse has 'bolted (*BrE*) (*AmE* **shut, etc. the barn door after the horse has e'scaped**)
take action to prevent sth bad from happening after it has already happened: *Last week all their silver was stolen; this week they're putting in a burglar alarm! That's really shutting the stable door after the horse has bolted.*

stack

blow your stack → **blow**

stacked

the cards/odds are stacked a'gainst sb/sth
it is not likely that sb/sth will succeed, because they/it will have many problems or difficulties: *The cards are stacked against this plan. The public are against it.*

the cards/odds are stacked in 'favour of sb/sth (*BrE*) (*AmE* **the cards/odds are stacked in 'favor of sb/sth**)
it is likely that sb/sth will succeed because the conditions are good or because the conditions are good or because sb/sth has an advantage: *The odds are heavily stacked in favour of Manchester United, who are having a very successful season and who will be playing in front of the home crowd.*

staff

the ₁staff of 'life (*literary*)
a basic food, especially bread

a skeleton crew/staff/service → **skeleton**

stage

be/go on the 'stage
be/become an actor: *Maria has always wanted to go on the stage.*

do/perform/stage a disappearing/vanishing act → **act**

set the scene/stage (for sth) → **set**

stake

(be/have a lot, etc.) at 'stake
that can be won or lost, depending on the success of a particular action: *The team must win the game on Saturday to stay in the competition. With so much at stake, everyone has to play their very best.* ◇ *This decision has put our lives at stake.*

stake (out) a/your 'claim to sb/sth
say that you have a special interest in sb/sth, or have a right to own sth, especially to warn other people not to take it: *Both countries have staked out a claim to the land.*

stakes

in the … stakes
used to say how much of a particular quality a person has, as if they were in a competition in which some people are more successful than others: *John doesn't do too well in the personality stakes.*

pull up stakes → **pull**

stand

you, he, etc. can't 'stand (the sight/sound of) sb/sth (*informal*)
you, he, etc. dislikes or hates (seeing/hearing) sb/sth: *If you can't stand the sight of blood, you won't make a very good nurse!* ◇ *I can't stand the sight of her.*

if you can't stand the 'heat (get out of the 'kitchen) (*informal*)
used to tell sb to stop trying to do sth if they find it too difficult, especially in order to suggest that they are less able than other people: *'It seems a bit risky to me. Are you sure we should do this?' 'Well, if you can't stand the heat … '*

make a 'stand (against/for/over/about/on sth); take a 'stand (on/over sth)
argue, protest or fight because of sth you believe in: *This must never happen again; it's time to make a stand.*

not stand in sb's 'way
not try to stop sb from doing sth: *If you want to become a singer, we won't stand in your way.*

(not) stand a chance (of doing sth)
(not) have a chance (of doing sth): *You stand a very good chance of winning the prize.* ◇ *He doesn't stand a chance with her* (= she won't want to have a relationship with him).

stand 'fast/'firm
refuse to move back; refuse to change your opin-

ions or behaviour: *When he was arrested, his friends and colleagues all stood firm in his support.*

stand sb in good 'stead
be useful to sb: *Learning German will stand her in good stead when she goes to work in the export department.*

stand on 'ceremony (*BrE*)
behave in a very formal way: *Come on—don't stand on ceremony! Start eating or the food will get cold!*

,stand on your 'dignity (*formal*)
say firmly that you wish to be treated with the respect that you deserve: *The teacher stood on his dignity and insisted that the pupils be punished for being rude to him.*

stand on your own two 'feet
not need the help of other people; be independent: *I left home to show my parents that I can stand on my own two feet.* ◇ *Isn't it about time you learned to stand on your own two feet?*

stand or 'fall by sth
succeed or fail, or be judged good or bad, because of one thing: *A salesman stands or falls by the number of sales he makes—if he doesn't make enough, he loses his job.*

(not) stand the 'pace
not be able to work, live or compete under pressure: *You want to be a journalist? Are you sure you could stand the pace?*

stand 'pat (*especially AmE*)
refuse to change your mind about a decision you have made or an opinion you have: *There has been a lot of controversy over the new proposals, but the government is standing pat.*

stand a 'round (of drinks)
buy a drink at the same time for each of your friends in a pub, bar, etc: *It's my turn to stand a round, so what are you all having?*

stand 'tall (*especially AmE*)
show that you are proud and able to deal with anything: *Speaking on television, she said that her former manager's advice to stand tall and be proud of herself was what helped her to succeed.*

stand the test of 'time
be considered valuable or useful by people for many years: *Dickens' books have stood the test of time—they are as popular now as they were a century ago.*

stand up and be 'counted
say publicly that you support sb or you agree with sth: *I think that people who disagree with the policy should stand up and be counted.*

as things stand → **things**

be/stand in awe of sb/sth → **awe**

hold/stand your ground → **ground**

know where you are/stand → **know**

a last-ditch stand/attempt/effort → **last-ditch**

mount/stand/keep guard (over sb/sth) → **guard**

not have a leg to stand on → **leg**

a one-night stand → one-night

stand/turn sth on its head → head

stand/stick out like a sore thumb → sore

stand/stick out a mile → mile

take a firm line/stand (on/against sth) → firm

standard

bog standard → bog

standby

on 'standby

1 ready to do sth immediately if needed or asked: *The emergency services were put on standby after a bomb warning.*

2 ready to travel or go somewhere if a ticket or sth that is needed suddenly becomes available: *He was on standby for the flight to New York.*

standing

do sth standing on your 'head (*informal*)

do sth very easily, without any effort: *This exam's no problem. I could do it standing on my head.*

leave sb/sth standing → leave

(as) sure as I'm standing/sitting here → sure

stands

it ˌstands to 'reason (that …) (*informal*)

it is quite clear, obvious or easy to understand: *It stands to reason that the less you eat, the thinner you get.*

your hair stands on end → hair

standstill

grind to a halt/standstill → grind

star

hitch your wagon to a star → hitch

stare

stare sth in the 'face

be unable to avoid sth: *They were staring defeat in the face.*

look/stare you in the face → face

look/stare/gaze into space → space

stark

stark 'naked (*BrE*) (*AmE* **buck 'naked**)

completely naked: *He always walks around his apartment buck naked.*

stars

have (got) 'stars in your eyes

if you **have stars in your eyes**, you are happy and excited about the future, because you believe that you will be successful and famous: *Hundreds of young actors, all with stars in their eyes, are here for the auditions.* ▶ ˌstarry-'eyed *adj.*: *I was just a*

starry-eyed teenager, dreaming of singing at Wembley stadium.

reach for the stars → reach

see stars → see

thank your lucky stars (that …) → thank

start

ˌdon't 'start (also **ˌdon't 'you start**) (*spoken, informal*)

used to tell sb not to complain or be critical: *Don't start! I told you I'd be late.*

for a 'start; to 'start with (also **for 'starters**, *informal*)

used for giving the first of several things or reasons: *You're not going to marry him. For a start, you're much too young. For another thing, he hasn't got a job.* ◊ *She wasn't keen on the idea to start with.*

'start something/anything (*informal*)

begin a fight or an argument: *Don't try to start anything with him, he has a knife.* ◊ *Are you trying to start something?*

(make) a false start → false

get/keep/set/start the ball rolling → ball

get/start off on the right/wrong foot (with sb) → foot

get off to a flying start → flying

a head start (on/over sb) → head

start again from square one = be/go back to square one → square

start the wheels turning = put/set sth in motion → motion

started

you, he, she, etc. 'started it (*spoken, informal*)

you, he, she, etc. began a fight or an argument: *'Stop fighting, you two!' 'He started it!'*

starters

under ˌstarters 'orders

(of a runner, rider, etc.) waiting for a signal to start the race

for starters = for a start → start

starts

in fits and starts → fits

starving

be 'starving (for sth) (also **be 'starved** *especially AmE*) (*informal*)

feel very hungry: *When's dinner? I'm starving!*

State

turn State's evidence → turn

state

be in a 'state; get into a 'state (*informal*)

1 be/get worried, nervous or upset: *Her husband was injured in a car crash yesterday, so she's in a* terrible state. ◇ *He got into a state over his driving test.*

2 be/get dirty or untidy: *This house is in a real state!*

in a state of 'grace
(in the Roman Catholic Church) having been forgiven by God for the wrong or evil things you have done: *He died in a state of grace.*

a state of af'fairs
general situation or circumstances: *We don't know very much about the present state of affairs in China.*

‚state of the 'art
using the most modern or advanced techniques or methods; as good as it can be at the present time: *The security system we're using is state of the art.* ◇ *This new computer uses state-of-the-art technology.*

the state of 'play
what is happening now in a situation which is developing or changing: *We go to our correspondent for the latest state of play in the peace talks.*

in a good, bad, etc. state of repair = in good, bad, etc. repair → **repair**
lie in state → **lie**
the nanny state → **nanny**

statesman

an elder statesman → **elder**

stations

action stations → **action**
panic stations → **panic**

status

the status 'quo (*from Latin*)
the situation as it is now, or as it was before a recent change: *The conservatives are keen to maintain the status quo.*

a 'status symbol
an expensive possession which shows people that you are rich: *These cars are status symbols in Britain.*

stay

be here to 'stay; have come to 'stay
be accepted or used by most people and therefore a permanent part of our lives: *It looks as if televised trials are here to stay.*

stay! (*spoken*)
used to tell a dog not to move

stay the 'course
continue doing sth until it has finished or been completed, even though it is difficult: *Very few of the trainees have stayed the course.*

stay your 'hand (*old-fashioned or literary*)
stop yourself from doing sth; prevent you from doing sth: *She was about to leave when the sight of two women coming down the stairs stayed her hand.*

stay the 'night (*especially BrE*)
sleep at sb's house for one night: *You can always stay the night at our house.*

stay 'put (*informal*)
stay where you are; not travel, escape, look for another job, etc: *I'd like to move house, but my wife wants to stay put.*

be/stay one jump ahead (of sb/sth) → **jump**
hang/stay loose → **loose**
keep/stay out of sb's way → **way**
steer/stay/keep clear (of sb/sth) → **clear**

stead

in sb's/sth's 'stead (*formal*)
instead of sb/sth: *Foxton was dismissed and John Smith was appointed in his stead.*

stand sb in good stead → **stand**

steady

go 'steady (with sb) (*old-fashioned, informal*)
have sb as a regular boyfriend or girlfriend: *Martin and Ingrid have been going steady for nearly a year.*

(as) steady as a 'rock
extremely steady and calm; that you can rely on: *Even though she must have been frightened, her voice was as steady as a rock and she looked him straight in the eyes when she spoke.*

steady 'on! (*informal*)
be more careful about what you do or say; slow down: *Steady on, you two, don't get angry!* ◇ *Steady on, you'll break it!*

ready, steady, go! → **ready**

steal

be a 'steal (*especially AmE*)
be for sale at an unexpectedly low price: *This suit is a steal at $80.*

steal a 'glance/'look (at sb/sth) (*written*)
look quickly at sb/sth, so that nobody notices you looking: *He stole a glance at her out of the corner of his eye.*

steal sb's 'heart (*literary*)
make sb fall in love with you: *As he became more well known, his good looks and charm stole young girls' hearts all across the country.*

steal a 'kiss (from sb) (*literary*)
kiss sb suddenly or secretly: *This is the place where he first stole a kiss from me when I was only twelve.*

steal a 'march on sb (*written*)
do sth before sb else, and so gain an advantage: *The 'Daily News' stole a march on our paper by printing the story first.*

❶ ORIGIN
This expression probably comes from the military, referring to armies secretly marching to higher ground in order to be in a better position than the enemy.

steal the 'show
attract more attention and praise than other people in a particular situation: *Actors don't like working with animals because they often steal the show.*

steal sb's 'thunder
spoil sb's attempt to surprise or impress, by doing sth first: *He had planned to tell everyone about his discovery at the September meeting, but his assistant stole his thunder by talking about it beforehand.*

❶ ORIGIN
In the eighteenth century, John Dennis invented a machine that made the sound of thunder, and used it in his own play. The play was not a success, and was replaced by another play by a different company. When Dennis went to the opening night, he was angry to hear his thunder machine being used.

beg, borrow or steal → **beg**

steam

,get up/,pick up 'steam
1 gradually increase speed: *As the train came out of the tunnel, it picked up steam.*
2 (*informal*) gradually get bigger, more active or popular: *The election campaign is getting up steam now; it is only two weeks to election day.* ◇ *I'm trying to get up enough steam to finish writing this book, but it's not easy.*

(get/go somewhere) under your own 'steam
(*BrE, informal*)
(get/go somewhere) without help from others: *Don't worry about arranging transport for us. We can get there under our own steam.*

full steam/speed ahead → **full**
let off steam → **let**
run out of steam → **run**

steamed

be/get (all) steamed 'up (about/over sth)
(*BrE*) (*AmE* be '**steamed (about sth)**) (*informal*)
be/become very angry or excited (about sth): *There's no need to get so steamed up over such a small problem.*

steel

of 'steel
having a quality like steel, especially a strong, cold or hard quality: *She felt a hand of steel* (= a strong, firm hand) *on her arm.* ◇ *There was a hint of steel in his voice* (= he sounded cold and firm).

have (got) nerves of steel → **nerves**

steep

be a bit/rather 'steep (*informal*)
(of a price or a request) be too much; be unreasonable: *£2.50? That seems a bit steep for a small piece*

of cheese. ◇ *It's a bit steep to expect us to work longer hours for no extra money.*

steeped

be 'steeped in sth (*written*)
have a lot of a particular quality: *This is a city steeped in history.*

steer

a bum steer → **bum**
follow/steer/take a middle course → **middle**
steer/stay/keep clear (of sb/sth) → **clear**

stem

from ,stem to 'stern
all the way from the front of a ship to the back: *It was a small boat, less than thirty feet from stem to stern.*

,stem the 'tide (of sth)
stop the large increase of sth bad: *The police are unable to stem the rising tide of crime.*

step

be in/out of 'step (with sb/sth)
1 putting your feet on the ground in the right/wrong way, according to the rhythm of the music or the people you are moving with: *I found myself marching in step with the music.*
2 having ideas that are the same as or different from other people's: *He's completely out of step with other cancer specialists; his ideas about treatment are quite different.* ◇ *The government no longer seems to be in step with the attitudes of the people.*

mind/watch your 'step
1 walk carefully: *Mind your step, it's wet there.*
2 behave or act carefully: *You've got to watch your step with Simon. He gets angry very quickly.*

one step ,forward, two steps 'back (*saying*)
used to say that every time you make progress, something bad happens that means that the situation is worse than before: *Trying to get the law changed has been a frustrating business. It's a case of one step forward, two steps back.*

a/one step a'head (of sb/sth)
when you are **one step ahead** of sb/sth, you manage to avoid them or to achieve sth more quickly than they do: *One of the reasons why they're so successful as a business is because they always seem to be one step ahead of the competition.*

(do sth) ,step by 'step
(do sth) slowly, one thing after another; (do sth) gradually: *If you take it step by step, learning a language is easy.* ◇ *There are step-by-step instructions on how to build your bookcase.*

step into the 'breach
do sb's job or work when they are suddenly or unexpectedly unable to do it: *The cook at the hotel*

fell ill, so the manager's wife stepped into the breach.

step into sb's 'shoes
take over a job from another person: *Mike stepped into his father's shoes when his father retired as company director.*

'step on it; step on the 'gas *(informal)*
drive a car faster; accelerate: *You'll be late if you don't step on it.*

step out of 'line; be/get out of 'line
behave badly or break the rules: *The teacher warned them that she'd punish anyone who stepped out of line.*

fall into step (beside/with sb) → fall

step/tread on sb's toes → toes

steps

take steps to do sth
take the necessary action to achieve or get sth: *The government is taking steps to control the rising crime rate.*

one step forward, two steps back → step

stern

from stem to stern → stem

sterner

be made of sterner 'stuff
(of a person) have a stronger character and be more able to deal with difficulties and problems than other people: *Did she cry? I thought she was made of sterner stuff.*

stew

be in a 'stew (about/over sth); get (yourself) into a 'stew (about/over sth) *(informal)*
be/become very worried or nervous (about sth): *She's in a stew over what she's going to wear to the party tonight.*

let sb stew (in their own juice) → let

stick

get/take 'stick from sb *(BrE, informal)*
be angrily told you are wrong or at fault; be blamed or criticized: *The new member of the team took a lot of stick from the crowd. He played terribly.* ◇ *The government has been getting a lot of stick from the press recently.*

give sb 'stick *(BrE, informal)*
criticize sb: *The crowd gave the players a lot of stick for their terrible performance.*

,stick 'em 'up! *(spoken)*
used to tell sb to put their hands above their head when you are pointing a gun at them: *This is a robbery! Stick 'em up!*

stick 'fast
be firmly fixed in a place and unable to move or be moved: *The boat was stuck fast in the mud.*

stick in your 'mind
(of a memory, idea, picture, etc.) be remembered for a long time because it made a strong impression on you: *The image of the dead child's face stuck in my mind for years.* ◇ *That poem has always stuck in my mind.*

stick in your 'throat/'craw/'gullet *(informal)*
(sth is) difficult or impossible to agree with or accept: *It really sticks in my throat that I get paid less than the others for doing the same job.*

stick your 'neck out *(informal)*
do or say sth which other people are afraid to do, and as a result attract attention or trouble: *Joe stuck his neck out at the meeting; he told the boss that the new sales policy wasn't working.*

stick to your 'guns *(informal)*
refuse to change your actions, opinions, etc. in spite of criticism: *If the government sticks to its guns we'll get through this economic crisis.*

be (caught) in a cleft stick → cleft

the carrot and/or (the) stick → carrot

get the short end of the stick = draw the short straw → draw

get (hold of) the wrong end of the stick → wrong

if you throw enough mud, some of it will stick = mud sticks → mud

more sth than you can shake a stick at → shake

poke/stick your nose in/into sth → nose

put/stick the boot in → boot

put/stick your oar in → oar

put/stick two fingers up at sb → two

a rod/stick to beat sb with → beat

stand/stick out like a sore thumb → sore

stand/stick out a mile → mile

tell sb where to put/stick sth → tell

sticks

(out) in the 'sticks *(informal)*
in the country, far from towns and cities: *I like living out in the sticks, but it can be a bit boring.*

,up 'sticks (and go, etc.) *(BrE, informal)*
leave your home in order to move to another one: *Things weren't working out for them there, so they upped sticks and went to Chicago.*

mud sticks → mud

sticky

have (got) sticky 'fingers *(informal)*
be likely to steal sth: *Be careful about leaving your things lying around. Some people here have got very sticky fingers!*

(be on) a ,sticky 'wicket *(BrE, informal)*
(be in) a situation in which it is difficult to defend yourself against criticism or attack: *Don't be too*

confident about getting the contract. After our problems with the last one we're on a sticky wicket there.

❶ ORIGIN
This idiom comes from the game of cricket. A *sticky wicket* is difficult for the batsman to play on.

come to a bad/sticky end ➔ **end**
go through, hit, etc. a bad/sticky patch ➔ **patch**

stiff

(as) stiff as a 'board
(of things) very firm and difficult to bend or move: *He left his gloves outside in the snow, and when he found them again they were as stiff as a board.*

(as) stiff as a 'poker (*informal*)
(usually of people) very straight or upright in the way you sit or stand: *The old lady was sitting upright in her chair, stiff as a poker.*

a ˌstiff 'drink
a strong alcoholic drink: *That was a shock—I need a stiff drink!*

(keep) a stiff upper 'lip
keep calm and hide your feelings when you are in pain or in a difficult situation: *The English gentleman is famous for his stiff upper lip.*

bore sb stiff ➔ **bore**

still

be still going 'strong (*informal*)
1 be still active, successful or working: *After nine hours of chess, both players are still going strong.* ◇ *My car was made in the fifties, but it's still going strong.*
2 be still strong and healthy, in spite of being old: *She's 91 years old and still going strong.*

the still of the 'night (*literary*)
the time during the night when it is silent and calm

the still small 'voice
the voice of your conscience, especially when you are thinking of doing sth wrong or bad

still waters run 'deep (*saying*)
a person who seems to be quiet or shy may surprise you by knowing a lot or having deep feelings: *I know he seems very quiet and content with his life, but still waters run deep, you know.*

even/much/still less ➔ **less**

sting

a ˌsting in the 'tail (*informal*)
an unpleasant feature that comes at the end of a story, an event, etc: *Roald Dahl's stories often have a sting in the tail; that's why I like them.*

take the 'sting out of sth
(of a situation) take away the part that is unpleasant or dangerous: *We pay our phone bill in instalments, which takes the sting out of it.*

stink (*written*)

kick up/make/create/raise a 'stink (about sth) (*informal*)
show that you are angry about a situation, often by protesting in public: *He kicked up a stink about the noise from the new nightclub, writing to all the papers and complaining to the council.*

smell/stink to high heaven ➔ **high**

stinking

be 'stinking rich (*informal, usually disapproving*)
be extremely rich: *He doesn't need to work for a living—he's stinking rich.*

stint

do sth without 'stint (*written*)
do sth generously and in large amounts: *She praises her pupils without stint.*

stir

cause/create a 'stir
make a number of people feel interest, excitement or shock: *His sudden resignation caused quite a stir.*

stir sb's/the 'blood
make sb excited or enthusiastic: *His political speeches are designed to stir the blood.*

stir your 'stumps (*old-fashioned, BrE, informal*)
begin to move; hurry: *You stir your stumps and get ready for school, my girl!*

stitch

not have a stitch 'on; be without a stitch 'on (*informal*)
have no clothes on; be naked: *He was in the garden without a stitch on.*

a ˌstitch in 'time (saves 'nine) (*saying*)
if you act immediately when sth goes wrong, it will save you a lot more work later, because the problem will get worse if you leave it: *We'd better fix that leak before it does any permanent damage. A stitch in time …*

stitches

in 'stitches (*informal*)
laughing a lot: *The film had the audience in stitches.*

stock

(be) in/out of stock
(be) available/not available for sale in a shop: *Have you got any mozzarella cheese in stock?* ◇ *The book you want is out of stock at the moment.*

take 'stock (of sb/sth)
think again carefully (about sb/sth); think about what sth really means: *After a year in the job, she decided it was time to take stock* (= think again

whether it was the job she wanted). ◇ *He stopped to take stock of what he had read.*

a laughing stock → **laughing**
lock, stock and barrel → **lock**

stocking

in your stocking(ed) 'feet (*old-fashioned*)
wearing socks or stockings but not shoes: *Our feet were too sore to put into shoes, so we walked home in our stockinged feet.*

stocks

on the 'stocks
in the process of being made, built or prepared: *Our new model is already on the stocks and will be available in the spring.*

stock-still

be, stay, stand, etc. ˌstock-'still
be, stay, etc. still, without moving at all: *When I heard footsteps on the stairs, I stood stock-still and held my breath.*

stomach

have (got) no 'stomach for sth
have no desire or appetite for sth because you find it unpleasant: *He has no stomach for this kind of job. He should never have become a salesman.*

your eyes are bigger than your stomach → **eyes**
have (got) a strong stomach → **strong**
make sb's stomach turn = turn sb's stomach → **turn**
on an empty stomach → **empty**
the pit of your/the stomach → **pit**
pump sb's stomach → **pump**
sick to your stomach → **sick**
turn sb's stomach → **turn**

stone

be carved/set in 'stone
(of a decision, plan, etc.) unable to be changed: *People should remember that our proposals aren't carved in stone.*

ˌstone the 'crows; ˌstone 'me (*old-fashioned, BrE*)
used to express surprise, shock, anger, etc: *Stone the crows! You're not going out dressed like that, are you?*

a 'stone's throw
a very short distance: *We're just a stone's throw from the shops.*

have (got) a heart of stone → **heart**
kill sth stone dead → **kill**
kill two birds with one stone → **kill**
leave no stone unturned → **leave**
like getting blood out of/from a stone → **blood**
a rolling stone (gathers no moss) → **rolling**

When the brochure said the hotel was just a stone's throw from the beach…

stone-cold

ˌstone-cold 'sober
having drunk no alcohol at all: *By the time I arrived at the party, everyone else had had quite a few drinks, whereas I was stone-cold sober.*

stoned

ˌstoned out of your 'mind (*slang*)
not behaving or thinking normally because of the effects of a drug such as marijuana or alcohol: *Last night I got stoned out of my mind.*

stones

people (who live) in glass houses shouldn't throw stones → **people**

stony

be stony broke = be flat broke → **flat**
fall on stony ground → **fall**

stools

fall between two stools → **fall**

stoop

stoop so 'low (as to do sth) (*written*)
lower your moral standards far enough to do sth bad or unpleasant: *I hope none of my friends would stoop so low as to steal.* ◇ *She suggested advertising in a magazine for a boyfriend, but I'd never stoop so low.*

stop

stop at 'nothing
do anything, even sth immoral or criminal in order to get sth: *He'd stop at nothing to make a success out of his business.*

stop the 'rot

stop sth getting worse, especially in politics or business: *Our company's profits were falling, so a new director was appointed to stop the rot.*

stop 'short

1 stop (sb) short suddenly stop (sb) doing sth because sth has surprised you or you have just thought of sth important: *When I read how many people had died, I stopped short and stared in disbelief at the newspaper.*
2 stop short (of sth/of doing sth) nearly but not actually do sth, for example because you are afraid or you think it is a bad idea: *The manager told her that he was unhappy with her work, but he stopped short of dismissing her from her job.*

come to a full stop → full

full stop → full

make a pit stop → pit

stop/halt sb in their tracks → tracks

stop/halt/freeze in your tracks → tracks

stopping

there's no holding/stopping sb → holding

stops

the buck stops here → buck

pull out all the stops → pull

store

be in 'store (for sb)

be coming in the future; be about to happen: *I can see trouble in store.* ◇ *There's a surprise in store for you.*

put/set (no, great, little, etc.) 'store by sth

think that sth has (no, great, little, etc.) importance or value: *She sets little store by what her husband says.* ◇ *Why do some people put such great store by their horoscopes?*

store up 'trouble, etc. for yourself

have problems in the future because of things that you are doing or not doing now: *If you don't deal with the problem now, you'll be storing up trouble for yourself later.*

lie in store (for sb) → lie

mind the store → mind

stores

hit the shops/stores → hit

storm

the ˌcalm/ˌlull before the 'storm (*saying*)

a period of unnatural calm before an attack, violent activity, etc: *What the country was experiencing was not peace, but just the calm before another storm.*

ⓘ ORIGIN
This phrase refers to the period just before a thunderstorm when the wind drops completely.

dance, talk, etc. up a 'storm (*informal, especially AmE*)

dance, talk, etc. with enthusiasm and energy: *They spent the evening celebrating the end of the exams, dancing up a storm at the college party.* ◇ *Campbell won an award for his first novel, and has been writing up a storm ever since.*

ride out/weather the 'storm (of sth)

manage to survive a difficult period or situation: *The government has managed to ride out the recent storm.* ◇ *Many companies are having difficulty weathering the present economic storm.*

a storm in a 'teacup (*BrE*) (*AmE* a tempest in a 'teapot) (*informal*)

a small or unimportant problem which is treated as much more serious than it really is: *Don't worry. It's a storm in a teacup. Everyone will have forgotten about it by tomorrow.*

take sb/sth by 'storm

1 take or seize a town, castle, building, etc. with a sudden and fierce attack: *The police took the building by storm; two people were injured during the operation.*
2 be extremely successful very quickly in a particular place or among particular people: *ET took the whole world by storm; it was one of the most successful films ever made.*

any port in a storm → port

story

(quite) another 'story; a (quite) different 'story

1 very different from what has just been said: *Her English is excellent, but her French is another story.*
2 used when you are talking about one thing and then mention another thing, which you are not going to talk about on that occasion: *I once met Paul McCartney, but that's another story. I'll tell you about that one day.*

so the story 'goes ...; the story 'goes (that) ...

used to describe sth that people are saying, although it may not be correct: *He used to be a doctor, or so the story goes.*

that's the ˌstory of my 'life (*informal*)

used for saying that sth that happens to you or to another person is typical of the bad luck you always have: *'I meet somebody I really like and she tells me she's married. That's the story of my life!'*

a cock and bull story → cock

end of story → end

a hard-luck story → hard-luck

it's a long story → long

it's the (same) old story → old

a likely story → likely

pitch a line/story/yarn (to sb) → pitch

a shaggy-dog story → shaggy-dog

a/one side of the story/picture → side

a sob story → sob

a tall story → tall

tell its own tale/story ➜ **tell**

tell the same, a different, another, etc. tale/story (of sth) ➜ **tell**

to make a long story short = to cut a long story short ➜ **cut**

straight

give it to me 'straight (*spoken, informal*)
used when you want sb to tell you sth in an honest and direct way, especially if you think it will be unpleasant: *So, now you've met him, give it to me straight—what do you think of him?*

go 'straight (*informal*)
(of a former criminal) live according to the law: *After his years in prison, he was determined to go straight this time.*

keep to, stay on, etc. the ˌstraight and 'narrow (*informal*)
live your life according to strict moral principles: *She's stopped drinking and now she's trying to stay on the straight and narrow.*

❶ ORIGIN
This phrase comes from the Bible, describing the path to Heaven.

put/set sb 'straight (about/on sth)
make sure that sb is not mistaken about the real facts in a situation: *He thought I was a doctor of medicine, so I put him straight and told him I was a doctor of philosophy.*

put sth 'straight
make sth neat and tidy; organize or settle sth properly: *Please put all your papers straight before you leave the office.* ◇ *When he discovered that he was dying, he started to put all his affairs straight.*

(earn/get) straight 'A's (*especially AmE*)
(get) the best marks/grades in all your classes: *She got straight A's in all her exams.* ◇ *He's always been a straight A student.*

(as) straight as an 'arrow
in a straight line or direction: *You can't get lost if you follow this track. It runs as straight as an arrow through the middle of the wood.*

(as) straight as a 'die
1 in a straight line or direction: *The road runs northwards, as straight as a die.*
2 honest: *Carol would never steal anything—she's as straight as a die.*

ˌstraight a'way
immediately; without delay: *I'll do it straight away.*

(keep) a straight 'face
manage not to laugh: *When she told me about her accident with the pig, I couldn't keep a straight face.*

ˌstraight 'off/'out (*informal*)
without hesitating: *She asked him straight off what he thought about it all.* ◇ *I told her straight out that she was wrong.*

ˌstraight 'up (*BrE, spoken, informal*)
used for telling sb that what you are saying is completely true: *'I got the best marks in the class.' 'Straight up?' 'Straight up.'*

tell, etc. sb ˌstraight from the 'shoulder (that …)
tell sb honestly and directly (that …): *He's an outspoken politician who speaks straight from the shoulder.*

get your priorities right/straight ➜ **priorities**

get sth right/straight ➜ **right**

on the home straight/stretch ➜ **home**

play fair/straight (with sb) ➜ **play**

play it straight ➜ **play**

play a straight bat ➜ **play**

put/set the record straight ➜ **record**

(as) straight as a ramrod = ramrod straight ➜ **ramrod**

think straight ➜ **think**

strain

strain at the 'leash (*informal*)
want to be free from control; want to do sth very much: *Why don't you let her leave home? Can't you see she's straining at the leash?* ◇ *He's straining at the leash to leave Britain for somewhere sunnier.*

❷ NOTE
A *leash* is a long piece of leather, chain or rope used for holding and controlling a dog.

strain every 'nerve/'sinew (to do sth) (*written*)
try as hard as you can (to do sth): *He strained every sinew to help us, but didn't succeed.*

strange

be/make strange 'bedfellows
be two very different people or things that you would not expect to find together: *Art and rugby may seem strange bedfellows, but the local rugby club donated £2 000 to help fund an art exhibition.*

feel strange ➜ **feel**

stranger

be no/a 'stranger to sth (*formal*)
be familiar/not familiar with sth because you have/have not experienced it many times before: *He is no stranger to controversy.*

truth is stranger than fiction ➜ **truth**

strapped

be ˌstrapped for 'cash (*informal*)
have very little money: *I can't come to the cinema tonight—I'm a bit strapped for cash.*

straw

be the last/final 'straw (also be the ˌstraw that breaks the camel's 'back)
be the last in a series of bad events, etc. that makes it impossible for you to accept a situation any longer: *I've had a terrible day, and this traffic is the last straw, I can't take any more.*

a straw in the 'wind (*BrE*)
an unimportant incident or piece of information which shows you what might happen in the future: *Journalists are always looking for straws in the wind.*

draw the short straw → **draw**
make bricks without straw → **bricks**
a man of straw → **man**

straws

clutch/grasp at 'straws
try all possible means to find a solution or some hope in a difficult or unpleasant situation, even though this seems very unlikely: *The doctors have told him that he has only 6 months to live, but he won't accept it. He's going to a new clinic in Switzerland next week, but he's just clutching at straws.*

draw straws (for sth) → **draw**

strays

waifs and strays → **waifs**

streak

a yellow streak → **yellow**

stream

be/come on 'stream
(of a factory, machine etc.) be/start working or operating: *The new printing machines come on stream in March.* ◇ *We're waiting for the new software to come on stream; it will make our jobs much easier.*

go, swim, etc. with/against the 'stream/ 'tide
behave/not behave in the same way as most other people: *He's a fashion designer who's always swum against the stream; his work is very original.* ◇ *Why do you always have to go against the tide?*

street

be (right) up your 'street (*especially BrE*) (*AmE* usually **be (right) up your 'alley**) (*informal*)
be suitable for you: *Why don't you apply for this job? It looks right up your street.*

the man (and/or woman) in the street → **man**
not be in the same league/class/street → **league**
on easy street → **easy**

streets

be 'streets ahead (of sb/sth) (*BrE, informal*)
be very much better (than sb/sth): *Japan is streets ahead of us in computer technology.*

on the 'streets (*informal*)
1 without a home: *He was weak and ill and he knew he wouldn't survive on the streets.*
2 working as a prostitute: *She's been on the streets since she was fifteen.*

the streets are ,paved with 'gold (*saying*)
used to say that it seems easy to make money in a place: *More and more people are moving to the big cities, where they believe the streets are paved with gold.*

hit the streets → **hit**
walk the streets → **walk**

strength

go from ,strength to 'strength
have more and more success: *Since she became the boss, the company's gone from strength to strength.*

on the strength of sth
mainly because of sth: *I got the job on the strength of my experience in sales.* ◇ *They were sent to prison on the strength of a tiny piece of evidence.*

a ,pillar/,tower of 'strength
a person who gives you the courage and determination to continue when you are in a bad situation: *My wife has been a tower of strength during my illness.* ◇ *During your five years in prison, Terry was a pillar of strength.*

be at/below full strength → **full**
in force/strength → **force**

strengthen

,strengthen your 'hand
give you more power to do sth or act against sb/sth: *The new anti-drug laws will strengthen the hand of the police.*

stretch

at a 'stretch
(of periods of time) without stopping; continuously: *She practises the piano for hours at a stretch.*

by 'no stretch of the imagination; not by 'any stretch of the imagination
it is completely impossible to say; by no means: *By no stretch of the imagination could you call him clever.* ◇ *You couldn't say that factory was beautiful, not by any stretch of the imagination!*

stretch your 'legs
walk about after sitting or lying for a long time: *I'd been working at my desk all morning, so I went outside to stretch my legs for ten minutes.*

stretch a 'point
allow sb to break the rules for a good reason: *You are usually only allowed one hour for lunch, but I'm prepared to stretch a point if there's an emergency.*

at full stretch → **full**
bend/stretch the rules → **rules**
on the home straight/stretch → **home**

strictly

strictly 'speaking
if you are using words or rules in their exact or correct sense: *Strictly speaking, nobody under 18 can join this club, but as you are nearly 18 ...* ◇

Strictly speaking, a tomato is a fruit, not a vegetable.

stride

get into your 'stride (*BrE*) (*AmE* **hit (your) 'stride**)
begin to do sth with confidence and at a good speed after a slow, uncertain start: *She found the job difficult at first, but now she's got into her stride and she loves it.*

put sb off their 'stride/'stroke
make sb take their attention off what they are doing and stop doing it so well: *All sorts of things can put a player off his stroke.*

(match sb) ,stride for 'stride
keep doing sth as well as sb else, even though they keep making it harder for you: *We've managed to match our closest competitors stride for stride as regards prices.*

take sth in your 'stride (*BrE*) (*AmE* **take sth in 'stride**)
accept and deal with sth difficult without worrying about it too much: *Joey was upset when we moved house, but Ben seems to have taken it all in his stride.*

without breaking stride ➔ breaking

strides

make great, rapid, etc. strides (in sth/doing sth)
improve quickly or make fast progress (in sth/doing sth): *Ann's made huge strides in her piano-playing. ◇ Tom has made enormous strides at school this year.*

strike

strike a 'balance (between A and B)
find a sensible middle point between two demands, extremes, courses of action, etc: *We need to strike a balance between protecting him and letting him become more independent. ◇ Children need to strike a balance between work and play at school.*

strike a 'bargain/'deal (with sb)
come to an agreement (with sb), especially after a lot of discussion or argument: *They struck a bargain with the landlord to pay less rent in return for painting the house.*

strike a blow for/against sth
act forcefully in support of/against sth (for example a belief, principle or group of people): *The protest was a chance to strike a blow for freedom. ◇ The new law would strike a blow against racism.*

strike ,fear, ,terror, etc. into sb/sb's 'heart (*formal*)
make sb feel fear, terror, etc: *His crimes struck horror into the nation's heart.*

strike 'gold
find happiness, wealth, etc.; find exactly what you

need: *She hasn't always been lucky with her boyfriends, but I think she's struck gold this time. ◇ We've struck gold here. This book has everything we need.*

strike it 'rich (*informal*)
become rich suddenly: *He struck it rich when a relative died and left him two million.*

strike (it) 'lucky (*informal*)
have good luck: *We certainly struck it lucky with the weather—it's beautiful today. ◇ He bets on the horses, and sometimes he strikes lucky.*

strike a 'pose/an 'attitude
sit, stand or lie in a position in order to attract attention: *He was striking a pose, leaning against the ship's rail.*

,strike while the ,iron is 'hot (*saying*)
do sth immediately because now is a particularly good time to do it: *He seems in a good mood. Why don't you strike while the iron is hot and ask him now?*

ⓘ ORIGIN
This expression refers to a blacksmith making a shoe for a horse. He has to strike/hammer the iron while it is hot enough to bend into the shape of the shoe.

hit/strike home ➔ home
hit/strike pay dirt ➔ pay
hit/strike the right/wrong note ➔ note
sound/strike a false note ➔ false
sound/strike a note (of sth) ➔ note
strike/touch a chord (with sb) ➔ chord

strikes

lightning never strikes twice (in the same place) ➔ lightning

striking

within 'striking distance (of sth)
near enough to be reached or attacked; near: *In one minute the aircraft can be within striking distance of the target. ◇ There are lakes, mountains and forests all within striking distance.*

string

have/keep sb on a 'string
make sb do what you want because you have control over them: *Of course, he's rich and powerful enough to keep several people on a string.*

ⓘ ORIGIN
This idiom refers to a puppet (= a model of a person or an animal) that is controlled with strings attached to parts of its body.

have (got) another string/more strings to your bow ➔ bow
how long is a piece of string? ➔ long

strings

(with) no 'strings attached (also **without 'strings**)
with no special rules, conditions or limits: *I got a*

loan of £3000 with no strings attached. ◇ *It was a relationship without strings* (= without too much responsibility or commitment) *which suited them both.*

control/hold the purse strings → **purse**
have (got) another string/more strings to your bow → **bow**
(tied to) your mother's, wife's, etc. apron strings → **apron**
pull strings (for sb) → **pull**
pull the strings → **pull**

strip

tear a strip off sb = tear sb off a strip → **tear**

stroke

at a/one (single) 'stroke
(something happens) as a result of one sudden action or event: *All my problems were solved at a stroke when an aunt left me some money.*

not do a stroke (of work)
not do any work at all: *He's useless—he hasn't done a stroke of work today.* ◇ *'Does your husband help in the house?' 'No, he doesn't do a stroke.'*

on/at the stroke of eight, midnight, etc.
at exactly eight o'clock, midnight, etc: *She gets to work at the stroke of nine every day.*

put sb off their stride/stroke → **stride**

strong

be 'strong on sth
1 be good at sth: *I'm not very strong on dates* (= I can't remember the dates of important events).
2 have a lot of sth: *The report was strong on criticism, but short on practical suggestions.*

be your 'strong point/suit
be a thing that you do well: *Writing letters has never been my strong point.* ◇ *Logic is definitely not his strong suit.*

come on 'strong (with sb) (*informal*)
make your feelings clear in an aggressive way: *Do you think I came on too strong at that meeting?*

have (got) a strong 'stomach
not feel sick or upset when you see or do unpleasant things: *You've got to have a strong stomach to watch animals being killed.*

be still going strong → **still**
a bit thick/strong → **bit**

struck

be 'struck by/on/with sb/sth (*informal*)
be impressed or interested by sb/sth; like sb/sth very much: *I was struck by her youth and enthusiasm.* ◇ *We're not very struck on that new restaurant.*

be struck 'dumb (with sth)
be suddenly unable to speak (because of shock, fear, etc.): *We were struck dumb at the sight of three armed soldiers in the kitchen.* ◇ *The witnesses were struck dumb with terror.* ▶ **'dumbstruck** *adj.*:

When I found out that I had won first prize, I was dumbstruck.

struggle

an uphill struggle/battle/task → **uphill**

strut

,strut your 'stuff (*informal*)
proudly show your ability, especially at dancing or performing: *I saw you at the club last night, strutting your stuff on the dance floor!*

stubborn

(as) ,stubborn as a 'mule (*often disapproving*)
very determined not to change your opinion or attitude; obstinate: *If you tell her what to do, she won't do it because she's as stubborn as a mule. Why not just suggest it to her?*

stuck

,get stuck 'in(to sth) (*BrE, informal*)
start doing sth in an enthusiastic way: *Here's your food. Now get stuck in* (= start eating). ◇ *We got stuck into the job immediately.*

stuff

do your 'stuff (*informal*)
do sth you are good or skilled at (often while other people watch): *Joy got her guitar and went on stage to do her stuff.*

not give a 'stuff (*BrE, slang*)
not care at all about sth: *I don't give a stuff what you think!*

stuff and 'nonsense (*spoken, old-fashioned*)
used to say that you think sth is not true or stupid: *A hotel for the night? Stuff and nonsense! You're staying here with us.*

stuff him, that, etc. (*spoken, informal*)
used to show strong dislike of sb or a refusal to do what they want: *'Switch that radio off, I'm trying to work!' 'Stuff you, I'll do what I like!'* ◇ *He wants me to do extra work this week. Well, he can stuff it!*

that's the 'stuff (*informal*)
used for telling sb that they are doing sth correctly or well, or doing sth good: *'I'd like my hair cut shorter at the front.' 'Like this?' 'Yeah, that's the stuff.'*

be made of sterner stuff → **sterner**
don't sweat the small stuff → **sweat**
the hard stuff → **hard**
hot stuff → **hot**
kid stuff = kids' stuff → **kids**
know your stuff → **know**
strut your stuff → **strut**

stuffed

get 'stuffed (also get 'knotted, *less frequent*) (*BrE, spoken*)
used to tell sb in a rude and angry way to go away,

or that you do not want sth: *If they don't offer you more money, tell them to get stuffed.* ◇ *Get stuffed, you idiot!*

a stuffed 'shirt (*informal, disapproving*)
a person who is very serious, formal or old-fashioned: *This office is full of stuffed shirts; there's no one fun that I can have a laugh with.*

stuffing

knock the stuffing out of sb → knock

stumps

stir your stumps → stir

style

be (not) sb's 'style
be (not) the type of thing that sb enjoys; be (not) the way sb usually behaves: *Classical music's not my style; I prefer rock.* ◇ *I don't like living in town much. The country is more my style.* ◇ *I'm sure he didn't say that; it's not his style at all. He's always so polite.*

in (great, grand, etc.) style
in an impressive way: *She always celebrates her birthday in style.* ◇ *He won the championship in fine/great style.*

cramp sb's style → cramp

subject

change the subject → change

sublime

from the sub,lime to the ri'diculous
used to describe a situation in which sth serious, important or of high quality is followed by sth silly, unimportant or of poor quality: *His works as an artist range from the sublime to the ridiculous, with very little in between.*

substance

a woman, man, person, etc. of 'substance (*formal*)
a person who is important, powerful or rich: *In those days, a station master was a man of substance in the community.*

succeeds

nothing suc,ceeds like suc'cess (*saying*)
success encourages you and often leads to more success: *The first task the students do should be one they are likely to do well. This is because nothing succeeds like success.*

success

nothing succeeds like success → succeeds
a roaring success → roaring
the sweet smell of success → sweet

such

… and such
and similar things or people: *The centre offers activities like canoeing and sailing and such.*

as 'such
1 in the usual sense or meaning of the word: *There is no theatre as such in the town, but plays are sometimes performed in the town hall.*
2 considering sth only in theory, not in practice or in relation to a particular person or thing: *I am not interested in money as such, but I do like the freedom it can buy.*
3 because sb/sth is what it is: *The government is the main contributor and, as such, controls the project.*

such as
1 for example: *Wild flowers such as orchids and primroses are becoming rare.* ◇ *'I met a lot of important people in Canada.' 'Such as?'* (= give me an example).
2 of a kind that; like: *Opportunities such as this don't come along every day.*

,such as it 'is
used to say that there is not much of sth or that it is of poor quality: *You're welcome to join us for lunch, such as it is—we're only having soup and bread.* ◇ *Later we went to the local nightclub, such as it was, but there was hardly anyone there.*

suck

,suck it and 'see (*BrE, informal*)
used to say that the only way to know if sth is suitable is to try it: *With so many different models of mobile phone available, the best way to find out if one is right for you is to suck it and see.*

,suck it 'up (*AmE, informal*)
accept sth bad and deal with it well, controlling your emotions: *I admired the way he never stopped trying. Even when the audience started shouting abuse at him, he sucked it up and continued singing.*

milk/suck sb/sth dry → dry
teach your grandmother to suck eggs → teach

sudden

,all of a ,sudden
suddenly and unexpectedly: *I was sitting reading my book when all of a sudden the lights went out.*

,sudden 'death
a way of deciding the winner of a game when scores are equal at the end. The players or teams continue playing and the game ends as soon as one of them gains the lead: *If no one scores in the next five minutes the game will go to sudden death.* ◇ *They won the match after a sudden-death play-off.*

suffer

not suffer fools 'gladly
not be patient or polite with people who are less intelligent than you: *He says what he thinks and*

doesn't suffer fools gladly. Some people consider him a bit arrogant.

sufferance

on 'sufferance
if you do sth **on sufferance**, sb allows you to do it although they do not really want you to: *He's only staying here on sufferance.*

suffice

suffice (it) to say (that) … (*formal*)
used for saying that you could say much more about sb/sth but you do not want or need to: *I won't tell you all that was said at the meeting. Suffice it to say that they approved our plan.* ◇ *Suffice it to say that the figures were not included in the official report.*

sugar

a 'sugar daddy (*informal*)
an older man who has a much younger woman as a girlfriend and gives her presents, money, etc: *When you tell him that he's a sugar daddy, he gets very angry. He says she isn't interested in his money, only in him.*

sugar/sweeten the pill → **pill**

suggestion

at/on sb's sug'gestion
because sb suggested it: *At his suggestion, I bought the more expensive printer.*

suit

,suit your/sb's 'book (*BrE, informal*)
be convenient or useful for you/sb: *Well, if you're honest and hard-working, that suits our book.*

suit sb (right) ,down to the 'ground (*BrE, informal*)
suit sb completely: *I've found a job that suits me down to the ground: the pay's great and I can work from home.* ◇ *'We've only got beer, I'm afraid.' 'That suits me right down to the ground—that's just what I wanted.'*

,suit your'self (*informal*)
1 do exactly what you like: *I choose my assignments to suit myself.*
2 usually used in orders to tell sb to do what they want, even though it might annoy you: *'I don't want anything to eat, I'm on a diet.' 'All right, suit yourself!'*

be your strong point/suit → **strong**
follow suit → **follow**
in/wearing your birthday suit → **birthday**

suits

(men in) grey suits → **grey**

sum

be greater/more than the ,sum of its 'parts
be better or more effective as a group than you would think just by looking at the individual members of the group: *After their victory, the captain was full of praise for his team, saying that it was a classic case of the whole being greater than the sum of its parts.*

in 'sum (*formal*)
used to introduce a short statement of the main points of a discussion, speech, etc: *In sum, there are significant gaps in technological development across countries.*

summer

an Indian summer → **Indian**
one swallow doesn't make a summer → **swallow**

summon

pluck/screw/summon up (your/the) courage (to do sth) → **courage**

sun

under the 'sun
of any kind; in the world: *He's tried every medicine under the sun, but nothing works.* ◇ *I've got stamps from every country under the sun.*

catch the sun → **catch**
make hay while the sun shines → **hay**
a place in the sun → **place**
think the sun shines out of sb's arse/backside → **think**
think the sun shines out of sb's ass → **think**

Sunday

your Sunday 'best (*informal, humorous*)
your best clothes: *She got all dressed up in her Sunday best to meet her boyfriend's parents.*

Sundays

(not for/in) a month of Sundays → **month**

sundry

,all and 'sundry (*informal*)
everyone; people of all kinds: *I don't like you talking about my personal problems to all and sundry.*

sunk

be 'sunk in sth
be in a state of unhappiness or deep thought: *She just sat there, sunk in thought.*

sunshine

a ray of sunshine → **ray**

supper

sing for your supper → **sing**

supply

be in short supply → **short**

support

(give sb) moral support → **moral**

suppose

I don't suppose you could ...
used as a very polite way of asking sb to do sth for you: *I don't suppose you could carry this bag for me, could you?* ◇ *I don't suppose you could lend me £10, could you?*

I sup'pose so
used for showing that you agree but you are not happy about it: *'Can I borrow the car?' 'Yes, I suppose so, but be careful.'* ◇ *'Can I invite him to the party?' 'I suppose so.'*

supposed

(not) be sup'posed to (do sth)
1 (not) be expected or required to do sth by rules, the law, an agreement, etc: *She's supposed to do an hour's homework every evening.* ◇ *We're not supposed to be at the party for an hour yet.*
2 (used only in negative sentences) be not allowed to do sth: *You're not supposed to walk on the grass.*

what's 'that supposed to mean? (*informal*)
used when you are angry at what sb has said, or do not fully understand it: *'You aren't the most popular person at school, you know.' 'What's that supposed to mean?'* ◇ *'He says you're not suitable for the job.' 'What's that supposed to mean?'*

sure

be sure to do sth (also **be sure and do sth**, *spoken*)
used to tell sb to do sth: *Be sure to give your family my regards.* ◇ *Be sure and call me tomorrow.*

for 'sure (*informal*)
definitely: *'What time will you be here?' 'I don't know for sure yet.'* ◇ *I'll be there for sure; don't worry.*

make 'sure (of sth/that ...)
1 check that sth is true or has been done: *I think the door's locked, but I'd better go and make sure.* ◇ *Have you made sure that we've got enough money?* ◇ *I phoned to make sure the train had arrived.*
2 do sth in order to be certain that sth else happens: *I want to make sure that the party is a success.* ◇ *Make sure there's enough to eat tonight.*

(as) sure as eggs is 'eggs (also **(as) sure as I'm standing/sitting 'here**) (*old-fashioned, BrE, informal*)
absolutely certain; without any doubt: *If he goes on driving at that speed, he'll end up in hospital, as sure as eggs is eggs.* ◇ *That's exactly what she said, as sure as I'm standing here.*

(as) sure as 'hell (*AmE, informal*)
certainly; without doubt: *Joe sure as hell won't want to dress up in a suit and tie.*

sure e'nough
exactly as expected or as sb said: *She said she was going to give up her job and, sure enough, she did.* ◇ *They said it would rain, and, sure enough, it did.*

'sure of yourself (*sometimes disapproving*)
very confident: *She seems very sure of herself.*

,sure 'thing (*spoken, especially AmE*)
yes; of course: *'Will you come tonight?' 'Sure thing!'* ◇ *'Can you help me with this table?' 'Sure thing.'*

to be 'sure (*formal*)
used to admit that sth is true: *He is intelligent, to be sure, but he's also very lazy.*

surely

slowly but surely → **slowly**

surface

below/beneath the 'surface
what you cannot see but can only guess at or feel: *She seems very calm but beneath the surface I'm sure that she's very upset.* ◇ *Beneath the surface of this beautiful city there is terrible poverty and suffering, which tourists never see.*

on the 'surface
when you consider the obvious things, and not the deeper, hidden things: *On the surface she can be very pleasant and helpful, but underneath she's got problems.* ◇ *The plan seems all right on the surface.*

(only) scratch (at) the surface (of sth) → **scratch**

surprise

sur,prise, sur'prise (*spoken, ironic*)
used when you are not surprised about sth: *'There's nothing worth watching on TV tonight.' 'Surprise, surprise'* (= there is usually nothing worth watching).

take sb by sur'prise
happen to sb unexpectedly; surprise sb: *The announcement of his promotion took us all by surprise.* ◇ *They didn't know she was coming, so her arrival took them by surprise.*

survival

(the) sur,vival of the 'fittest
the principle that only the people or things that are best adapted to their surroundings will continue to exist: *In this climate of economic recession, many businesses are at risk, and it really is a case of survival of the fittest.*

suspicion

be a,bove/be,yond su'spicion
be so good or honest that nobody thinks you would do sth bad: *He is absolutely beyond suspicion.*

be under su'spicion (of sth)
be the person that the police think has committed a crime (although they cannot prove it yet): *He was still under suspicion and he knew the police were watching him.*

the finger of suspicion → finger

suspiciously

look/sound suspiciously like sth (*often humorous*)
be very similar to sth: *Their latest single sounds suspiciously like the last one.*

swallow

one ˌswallow doesn't make a 'summer (*saying*)
you must not take too seriously a small sign that sth is happening or will happen in the future: *'We got a big order from Sweden this morning. Things are getting better.' 'One swallow doesn't make a summer, you know. Don't be too optimistic.'*

swallow the 'bait (*informal*)
accept an offer, etc. which has been made or prepared specially by sb in order to get you to do sth: *When people read the words 'Free Gift' on a magazine they usually swallow the bait and buy it.*

 NOTE
A fisherman uses *bait* to attract fish to his hook.

swallow your 'pride
decide to act in a way you are ashamed of or embarrassed by because you want or need sth very much: *I didn't know what to do, so I swallowed my pride and asked my father for the money to pay the bill.* ◇ *She is very independent and it was hard for her to swallow her pride and ask for help.*

swap

change/swap horses in midstream → horses
change/swap places (with sb) → places

swathe

cut a swathe through sth → cut

sway

hold sway (over sb/sth) → hold

swear

swear 'blind (that) … (*informal*)
say that sth is definitely true: *She swore blind that she had not taken the money, and I believe her.*

swear like a 'trooper (*old-fashioned, BrE*)
use many swear words; use bad language: *She's only fourteen, but she swears like a trooper.*

 NOTE
A *trooper* is a soldier.

swear sb to 'secrecy
make sb promise not to tell a secret: *Before telling her what happened, I had sworn her to secrecy.* ◇

Everyone was sworn to secrecy about what had happened.

sweat

be in a 'sweat
1 (also **be all of a 'sweat**) (*informal*) be wet with sweat because it is hot or you have been running, etc: *I had to run to work this morning because I got up late. I was in a real sweat when I arrived.*
2 (also **be in a cold 'sweat**) be very frightened or worried about sth: *I woke up during the night in a cold sweat worrying about the exam.*

by the sweat of your 'brow (*literary*)
by your own hard work or physical effort: *They had to live by the sweat of their brow.*

don't 'sweat it (*AmE, spoken*)
used to tell sb to stop worrying about sth: *If we're a few minutes late he'll wait for us, so don't sweat it.*

don't sweat the 'small stuff (*AmE, spoken*)
used to tell sb not to worry about small details or unimportant things

no 'sweat (*spoken*)
used as a way of saying that sth is not difficult or any trouble: *'Thanks for driving me to the station.' 'No sweat* (= it is no trouble).*' ◇ 'How was the exam?' 'I passed that one, no sweat.'*

sweat 'blood (*informal*)
1 work very hard; make a very great effort: *I sweated blood to get that essay finished on time.*
2 be very worried or afraid: *He sweats blood every time the telephone rings, in case it's the police.*

sweat it 'out (*informal*)
suffer an unpleasant situation; wait for sth unpleasant to end: *I hate this job, but I'm going to sweat it out and hope something better comes along.* ◇ *After the competition we just had to sit there and sweat it out until the result was announced.*

sweat like a 'pig (*informal*)
sweat very much: *It's 35 degrees inside the factory, and the workers are sweating like pigs.*

blood, sweat and tears → blood
slog/sweat/work your guts out → guts

sweep

sweep the 'board
win all or most of the prizes, games, money, etc: *At the awards ceremony last night France swept the board, with six major prizes.*

sweep sb off their 'feet
attract sb very strongly because you are exciting, charming, etc: *She's waiting for a nice young man to come and sweep her off her feet.* ◇ *I was swept off my feet by her wit and charm.*

make a clean sweep (of sth) → clean
sweep sth under the rug = sweep/brush sth under the carpet → carpet

sweet

be 'sweet on sb (*old-fashioned, informal*)
like sb very much in a romantic way: *I think he's sweet on her—he always waits for her to finish work so he can walk her home.*

do sth in your ˌown sweet 'time/'way (*informal*)
do sth how and when you want to, even though this might annoy other people: *I tried to give her some advice but she just went on in her own sweet way.* ◇ *It's no use trying to hurry him. He'll do it in his own sweet time.*

have (got) a sweet 'tooth
like to eat sweet things: *I've got a sweet tooth, so I'd find it difficult to give up sugar in my tea.*

keep sb 'sweet (*informal*)
be pleasant and nice to sb, so that they will treat you well: *I have to keep my mother sweet because I want to borrow the car.*

sweet F'A (*BrE, informal*)
nothing; nothing important: *'What happened while I was away?' 'Sweet FA.'*

❷ NOTE
FA stands for 'fuck all' (⚠, *slang*) or the more polite 'Fanny Adams'.

sweet 'nothings (*informal, usually humorous*)
pleasant but unimportant words said by lovers: *He was whispering sweet nothings in her ear.*

the sweet smell of suc'cess (*informal*)
the pleasant feeling of being successful

be short and sweet → **short**
home sweet home → **home**

sweeten

sugar/sweeten the pill → **pill**

sweetness

be all ˌsweetness and 'light
1 (of a person) be pleasant, friendly and polite: *She's all sweetness and light as long as you're doing what she wants.*
2 (of a situation) be enjoyable and easy to deal with: *Their quarrel seems to be over. Everything's all sweetness and light at the moment.*

swim

in(to) the 'swim (of things) (*informal*)
involved in things that are happening in society or in a particular situation: *After being away for two years, it took her a while to get back into the swim of things.*

sink or swim → **sink**

swine

cast pearls before swine → **cast**

swing

get in/into the 'swing (of sth) (*informal*)
become involved in sth and start to do it well and enjoy it: *I've only been at university a week, so I haven't got into the swing of things yet.* ◇ *He was just getting in the swing of his performance when all the lights went out.*

go with a 'swing (*BrE*)
(of a party or entertainment) be lively, enjoyable and successful: *Their house-warming party really went with a swing.*

swing both 'ways (*informal*)
be bisexual (= sexually attracted to both men and women)

ˌswing into 'action
start to act efficiently and quickly: *When the police heard about the the bomb, they swung into action, searching the area with dogs and moving the public to safety.*

ˌswing the 'lead (*old-fashioned, BrE, informal*)
(usually used in the progressive tenses) pretend to be ill when you are not, especially to avoid work: *I don't think there's anything wrong with her—she's just swinging the lead.*

❶ ORIGIN
The *lead* (pronounced /led/) was a weight at the bottom of a line that sailors used to measure how deep the water was when the ship was near land. *Swinging the lead* was considered an easy job, and came to mean avoiding hard work.

in full swing → **full**
no room to swing a cat → **room**
swing the balance = tip the balance/scales → **tip**

swings

ˌswings and 'roundabouts (*BrE, informal*)
used when you want to say that gaining one thing usually means losing another thing: *Higher earnings mean more tax, so it's all swings and roundabouts.* ◇ *What you gain on the swings you'll probably lose on the roundabouts.*

swoop

at/in one fell swoop → **fell**

sword

a/the sword of 'Damocles (*literary*)
a bad or unpleasant thing that might happen to you at any time and that makes you feel worried or frightened: *Now the news of my divorce is public, I'm relieved in a way. It had been hanging over my head like the sword of Damocles.*

❶ ORIGIN
This expression comes from the Greek legend in which *Damocles* had to sit at a meal with a sword hanging by a single hair above his head. He had

praised King Dionysius' happiness, and Dionysius wanted him to understand how quickly happiness can be lost.

be a double-edged sword/weapon ➔ **double-edged**
the pen is mightier than the sword ➔ **pen**

swords

cross swords (with sb) ➔ **cross**
turn swords into ploughshares ➔ **turn**

syllable

in words of one syllable ➔ **words**

symbol

a status symbol ➔ **status**

sympathy

in 'sympathy with sth (*written*)

happening because sth else has happened: *Share prices slipped again today, in sympathy with the German market.*

out of 'sympathy with sb/sth (*written*)

not wanting to support or not wanting to support sb/ sth: *It is generally believed that he is out of sympathy with government policies.*

sync

in/out of 'sync (*informal*)

moving or working/not moving or working at exactly the same time and speed as sb/sth else: *The soundtrack is not in sync with the picture.* ◇ *Can we try that part of the dance again? I think we were out of sync.*

system

get sth out of your 'system (*informal*)

do sth so that you no longer feel a very strong emotion or have a strong desire: *Tell him how angry you really feel. That'll get it out of your system.* ◇ *When I was young I was obsessed with ballet, but by the time I left school I had got it out of my system.*

systems

all systems 'go! (*informal, humorous*)

let's go; let's begin: *Have we got everything we need? Right, it's all systems go!*

T t

T

to a 'T/'tee (*BrE, informal*)
exactly; perfectly: *This new job suits me to a T* (= it is perfect for me). ◇ *This portrait is excellent—it's Rosemary to a T.*

> **ℹ ORIGIN**
> This expression probably refers to a *T-square*, which is an instrument in the shape of a 'T' and is used to accurately draw or measure right angles.

t

dot the/your i's and cross the/your t's → dot
on the q.t. = on the quiet → quiet

tab

pick up the tab (for sth) → pick

table

on the 'table (*BrE*)
used in business, to talk about a suggestion, plan or amount of money which is being discussed or offered: *In today's meeting there were several new proposals on the table.* ◇ *The company can put an extra one per cent on the table, in return for an agreement on overtime.*

drink sb under the table → drink
put/lay your cards on the table → cards

tables

turn the tables (on sb) → turn

tabs

keep (close) 'tabs on sb/sth (*informal*)
watch sb/sth very carefully; keep informed about sb/sth: *I'm not sure about Johnson—we'd better keep tabs on him until we know we can trust him.* ◇ *I'm keeping tabs on the number of private phone calls you all make from the office.*

tacks

get down to brass tacks → brass

tail

on sb's 'tail (*informal*)
(of the police, a spy, etc.) following behind sb very closely: *I had the feeling there was someone on my tail.*

(at) the tail 'end (of sth)
(at) the final or last part (of sth): *I didn't hear most of the conversation—I only came in at the tail end.*

the tail (is) wagging the 'dog (also **let the tail wag the 'dog**)
used to describe a situation where a small, unim-

portant thing controls a larger, more important thing: *In this company the workers tell the manager what he can and cannot do. It's a real case of the tail wagging the dog.*

with your tail between your 'legs (*informal*)
feeling ashamed, embarrassed or unhappy because you have been defeated or punished: *They thought they would win easily, but they've gone home with their tails between their legs.*

> **ℹ ORIGIN**
> This idiom refers to the way a dog behaves when it is punished.

can't make head (n)or tail of sth → head
chase your (own) tail → chase
in two shakes of a lamb's tail → two
nose to tail → nose
a sting in the tail → sting
top and tail sth → top
turn tail (and run, flee, etc.) → turn

tails

be like a dog with two tails → dog
heads or tails? → heads

take

Most idioms containing the verb **take** are at the entries for the nouns or adjectives in the idioms, for example **take sth with a pinch of salt** is at **pinch**.

be on the 'take (*informal*)
accept money from sb for helping them in a dishonest or illegal way: *It now seems that some of the officials were on the take, accepting bribes and then issuing fake passports.*

I, you, etc. can't take sb 'anywhere (*informal, often humorous*)
used to say that you cannot trust sb to behave well in public: *You've got soup all over your shirt—I can't take you anywhere, can I?*

take sth as it 'comes
deal with difficulties as they happen, without worrying too much: *I don't plan for the future. I like to take life as it comes.*

'take it (*informal*)
(often used with can/could) be able to bear or tolerate sth difficult or unpleasant such as stress, criticism or pain: *They argued so much that finally he couldn't take it any more and he left her.* ◇ *People are rude to her in her job, and she feels she's taken it for long enough.*

'take it (that …)
think or suppose (that sth is true, will happen, etc.): *'I take it that you won't be back for lunch,' she said as they left.* ◇ *You speak French, I take it?*

take it from 'here/'there
start doing sth on your own that another person
has been doing before you, or has been explaining
to you: *I explained how to start the machine, and let
him take it from there.*

take it from 'me (that …) (*informal*)
you should believe me, because I have personal
experience of …: *Take it from me that it's not easy
to become a professional writer.*

take it on/upon yourself to do sth
decide to do sth without asking anyone for permission: *He took it upon himself to dismiss my secretary, which he had no right to do.*

take it 'out of sb; take a lot 'out of sb
make sb very tired or weak: *Driving all day really
takes it out of you.* ◇ *That flu bug has really taken
it out of her.*

take it out on 'sb (*informal*)
behave in an unpleasant way towards sb because
you feel angry, disappointed, etc., although it is not
their fault: *I know you've had a bad day at work,
but don't take it out on me.*

take sb 'out of himself, herself, etc.
amuse or entertain sb and so make them feel less
worried about their problems or less unhappy: *She
was very depressed when they split up. We took her
on holiday to try to take her out of herself.*

takes

have (got) what it 'takes (to do sth) (*informal*)
have the qualities, ability, etc. needed to be successful: *He's certainly ambitious, but if you ask me
he hasn't really got what it takes to be the best.*

taking

**be sb's for the 'taking; be there for the
'taking**
if sth is **yours for the taking** or **there for the
taking**, it is easy to get: *She was surprised to find
the money on the kitchen table, just there for the taking.* ◇ *With the team's closest rivals out of the
championship, the title was theirs for the taking.*

tale

live to tell the tale → **live**
an old wives' tale → **old**
spin (sb) a yarn/tale → **spin**
a tall tale → **tall**
tell its own tale/story → **tell**
tell the same, a different, another, etc. tale/story (of sth)
→ **tell**

tales

tell tales (about sb/sth) → **tell**
tell tales out of school → **tell**

talk

be all 'talk (and no action) (*disapproving*)
be a person who talks a lot about what they are

going to do or have done without actually doing
much: *Don't listen to her promises—she's all talk
and no action.*

be the talk of sth (*informal*)
be sth that everyone is interested in and talking
about: *His collection is the talk of the Milan fashion
shows.* ◇ *Overnight, she became* ***the talk of the
town*** (= famous).

**'you can/can't talk; look who's 'talking;
you're a 'fine one to talk** (*spoken*)
you should not criticize sb because you are also
guilty of the same fault: *'He's always late for
appointments.' 'You can talk! You're hardly ever on
time yourself.'* ◇ *'George is so careless with money.'
'Look who's talking!'*

'talk about … (*spoken*)
used to emphasize sth: *Did you watch the programme
on the Labour Party last night? Talk about biased!*

talk 'big (*disapproving*)
tell people how good you are or promise many things:
The President talks big but he doesn't do anything.

talk 'dirty (*informal*)
talk to sb about sex in order to make them sexually
excited: *I love it when you talk dirty.*

talk your 'head off (*informal*)
talk a lot: *He talked his head off all evening.*

talk the hind leg(s) off a 'donkey (*informal,
humorous*)
(usually used with *can* or *could*) talk for a long
time: *He would make a good politician—he could
talk the hind legs off a donkey!*

talk 'shop
talk about your work or business in a social situation with sb who works with you: *Are you two
talking shop again? Why don't you forget business
for a while and come and meet my friends?*

talk through the back of your 'head (*informal*)
talk nonsense: *If he says that he's going to win the
prize, he's talking through the back of his head.*

talk through your 'hat (*old-fashioned, informal*)
(usually used in progressive tenses) say silly
things while you are talking about a subject you do
not understand: *Don't take any notice of him. He's
talking through his hat, as usual.*

talk to a brick 'wall (*informal*)
used when sb refuses to listen to your advice,
ideas, explanations, etc: *Talking to him is like talking to a brick wall. He just won't listen.*

talk 'tough (on sth) (*informal, especially AmE*)
tell people very strongly what you want: *Before the
elections, the party talked tough on crime, but little
has been done since they've been in power.*

talk 'turkey (*informal, especially AmE*)
discuss the practical details of sth seriously and
honestly: *Look, Mark, it's time we talked turkey.
How much money can you invest in the company?*

talk your way out of sth/doing sth
make excuses and give reasons for not doing sth;

manage to get yourself out of a difficult situation: *He tried to talk his way out of it by saying someone else was responsible.* ◇ *I'd like to see her talk her way out of this one* (= the present trouble).

be/talk at cross purposes → **cross**
fighting talk → **fighting**
knock/talk some sense into sb → **sense**
a pep talk → **pep**
pillow talk → **pillow**
(make) small talk → **small**
speak/talk of the devil → **devil**
speak/talk the same/a different language → **language**

talker

a fast talker → **fast**

talking

'now you're talking (*spoken*)

used for showing interest and enthusiasm about sth just said, for example a good suggestion: *'Why don't we go to Paris for the weekend?' 'Now you're talking!'*

,talking of 'sb/'sth (*spoken, especially BrE*)

used for saying that you intend to say more about sb/sth just mentioned: *'I was out last night with Dave, Mark and Angela ... ' 'Talking of Mark, did he tell you about his latest business idea?'*

know what you're talking about → **know**
look who's talking = you can/can't talk → **talk**

talks

money talks → **money**

tall

a ,tall 'order

a very difficult task or request: *Finishing this work by the end of the week is a tall order, but I'll try.*

a ,tall 'story (*especially BrE*) (*AmE usually* a ,tall 'tale)

a story which is very difficult to believe: *What she says about her grandfather being a foreign prince sounds like a tall story to me.* ◇ *There were many tall tales told later about the events of that day.*

great/tall oaks from little acorns grow → **oaks**
stand tall → **stand**
walk tall → **walk**

tandem

in tandem (with sb/sth)

together (with sb/sth); at the same time (as sb/sth): *These two computers are designed to work in tandem.* ◇ *She runs the business in tandem with her husband.*

tangent

go/fly off at a 'tangent (*BrE*) (*AmE* go off on a 'tangent)

change suddenly from talking or thinking about one thing to talking or thinking about another:

One moment the professor is working hard on a problem in physics, the next he's gone off at a tangent and he's talking about bees.

❷ NOTE
A *tangent* is a straight line that touches the outside of a curve but does not cross it.

tango

it takes two to tango → **two**

tantrum

throw a tantrum → **throw**

tap

(be) on 'tap

(be) ready and available for immediate use: *I've got plenty of people on tap to help us if we need them.*

tape

red tape → **red**

taped

have (got) sb/sth 'taped (*BrE, informal*)

understand sb/sth completely and have learned how to deal with them/it successfully: *He can't fool me—I've got him taped.*

tar

tar sb/sth with the same 'brush

judge a whole group of people or things unfairly because of your bad experience with one or a few of them: *Because his older brother had been a troublemaker at the school, Paul was automatically tarred with the same brush. It wasn't fair!*

spoil the ship for a ha'porth/ha'penny-worth of tar → **spoil**

target

a sitting duck/target → **sitting**

task

take sb to 'task (about/for/over sth)

criticize sb forcefully (for doing sth wrong): *I was taken to task for arriving late.* ◇ *She took the Government to task over its economic record.*

an uphill struggle/battle/task → **uphill**

taste

be in bad, the worst possible, etc. 'taste

be offensive and not at all appropriate: *Most of his jokes were in very poor taste.*

be in good, the best possible, etc. 'taste

be appropriate and not at all offensive: *They made a few jokes about the management, but it was all done in good taste.*

to 'taste

in the quantity that is needed to make sth taste the way you prefer: *Add salt and pepper to taste.*

an acquired taste → **acquired**

be a taste of things to come = be the shape of things to come → **shape**

give sb a taste/dose of their own medicine → **medicine**

leave a bad/nasty taste in the/your mouth → **leave**

there's no accounting for taste(s) → **accounting**

tat

tit for tat → **tit**

tatters

be in 'tatters

1 (of clothes) be torn in many places: *He got into a fight and came home with his clothes in tatters.*
2 (of a plan, an idea, a person's feelings, etc.) be ruined or badly damaged: *She's failed her exams, and now all her hopes of becoming a doctor are in tatters.* ◇ *His career and his reputation are both in tatters after the scandal.*

tea

wouldn't do sth for all the tea in 'China
(*informal*)

never; not for any reason at all: *'If you marry him you'll be a rich woman.' 'I wouldn't marry him for all the tea in China.'*

not be sb's cup of tea → **cup**

teach

teach your grandmother to suck 'eggs (*BrE, informal*)

tell or show sb how to do sth that they can already do well, and probably better than you can: *I don't know why he's telling Rob how to use the computer. It seems to me like teaching your grandmother to suck eggs.*

teach sb a 'lesson (also 'teach sb (to do sth))

learn from a punishment or because of an unpleasant experience, that you have done sth wrong or made a mistake: *He needs to be taught a lesson* (= he should be punished). ◇ *Losing all his money in a card game has taught him a lesson he'll never forget.* ◇ *That'll teach you! Perhaps you'll be more careful in future!*

(you can't) teach an old dog new 'tricks (*saying*)

(you can't) make old people change their ideas or ways of working, etc: *My grandmother doesn't want a computer. She says you can't teach an old dog new tricks.*

can/could teach/tell sb a thing or two (about sb/sth) → **thing**

teacup

a storm in a teacup → **storm**

teapot

a tempest in a teapot = a storm in a teacup → **storm**

tear

tear your 'hair (out) (*informal*)

be very worried or angry: *Why are you so late home? Your mother and I have been tearing our hair out wondering where you were!*

Sid was tearing his hair out trying to get the report finished on time.

tear sb ˌlimb from 'limb (*often humorous*)

attack sb very violently: *Julian looked so angry that I thought he was going to tear his brother limb from limb.*

tear (yourself/sth) 'loose (from sb/sth)

escape from sb/sth by using great force: *He put his arms round my neck but I tore myself loose and ran for help.*

tear sb 'off a strip; tear a 'strip off sb (*BrE, informal*)

criticize sb because you are angry about sth they have said or done: *The boss tore all the staff off a strip for using the Internet for personal matters during office hours.*

tear sb/sth to 'pieces/'shreds

criticize sb/sth; completely destroy sth: *The press tore the Government's economic plans to shreds.* ◇ *The Prime Minister tore his opponents' arguments to pieces.*

break/cut/tear (sth) loose from sb/sth → **loose**

rip/tear the heart out of sth → **heart**

wear and tear → **wear**

tearing

(be in) a tearing 'hurry/'rush (*especially BrE*)

(be) in a very great hurry: *I was late for a meeting and in a tearing hurry.*

tears

blood, sweat and tears → **blood**

bore sb to tears → **bore**

crocodile tears → **crocodile**

end in tears → **end**

tee

to a T/tee **→ T**

teeter

teeter on the 'brink/'edge of sth

be very close to a very unpleasant or dangerous situation: *The country is teetering on the brink of civil war.*

> ❷ **NOTE**
> If something *teeters*, it stands or moves in an unsteady way as if it is going to fall.

teeth

get your 'teeth into sth (*informal*)

put effort and enthusiasm into sth that is difficult enough to keep you interested: *This job is too easy. Why can't they give me something I can really get my teeth into?*

have 'teeth (*BrE, informal*)

(of an organization, a law, etc.) be powerful and effective: *It appears that the new legislation doesn't have any teeth, since there has been no improvement in working conditions.*

(do sth) in the teeth of danger, opposition, etc.

(do sth) when or even though it is dangerous or people oppose it, etc: *The new law was passed in the teeth of strong opposition.* ◇ *They crossed the Atlantic in the teeth of a force 10 wind.*

armed to the teeth (with sth) **→ armed**
bare your teeth **→ bare**
cut your teeth on sth **→ cut**
do sth by the skin of your teeth **→ skin**
fed up to the back teeth with sb/sth **→ fed**
get/take the bit between your teeth **→ bit**
gnash your teeth **→ gnash**
grit your teeth **→ grit**
Hell's teeth **→ hell**
kick sb in the teeth **→ kick**
lie through your teeth **→ lie**
(as) rare/scarce as hen's teeth **→ hen**
set sb's teeth on edge **→ set**
show your teeth **→ show**
sick to the back teeth of sb/sth = fed up to the back teeth with sb/sth **→ fed**
would give your eye teeth for sth/to do sth **→ eye**

teething

have, etc. 'teething problems/troubles

experience small problems or difficulties in the development of a product, business, etc., or when sth new first becomes available to the public: *If your new car is having teething troubles, take it back to the garage where you bought it.*

> ❷ **NOTE**
> When a baby is *teething*, its first teeth are starting to grow, which is painful for the baby.

telegraph

bush telegraph **→ bush**

telephone

be on the 'telephone/'phone

1 be using the telephone: *Mr Perkins is on the telephone but he'll be with you in a moment.* ◇ *You're wanted* (= sb wants to speak to you) *on the telephone.*
2 (*BrE*) have a telephone in your home or place of work: *They live on a small island and are not on the phone.*

tell

don't 'tell me (*spoken, informal*)

used to say that you know or can guess what sb is going to say, especially because it is typical of them: *Don't tell me, you were late again!*

I tell a 'lie (*spoken*)

used to say that sth you have just said is not true or correct: *We first met in 1982, no, I tell a lie, it was 1983.*

I (can/can't) 'tell you; I'm 'telling you (*spoken*)

used to emphasize what you are saying, especially when it is surprising or difficult to believe: *I can't tell you how happy I felt* (= it is difficult to describe my happiness, because it was so great). ◇ *It's not as easy as it looks, I'm telling you.*

I/I'll ,tell you 'what; I ,know 'what (*spoken*)

said before making a suggestion: *I tell you what - let's ask Fred to lend us his car.* ◇ *I know what! Why don't you buy her a CD?*

tell it how/like it 'is (*informal*)

tell sb sth honestly and directly: *All right, I'll tell it like it is. I don't love you Rachel, and I never have.*

(go) tell it/that to the ma'rines (*saying, informal*)

used to say that you do not believe what sb is saying, promising, etc: *'I'll never smoke again!' 'Yeah? Go tell that to the marines.'*

> ❶ **ORIGIN**
> This comes from the saying 'that will do for the marines but the sailors won't believe it'.

tell its 'own tale/story

explain or show sth, without the need of any more explanations or comment: *The burned buildings and broken glass in the streets tell their own story.*

'tell me (*spoken*)

used to introduce a question: *Tell me, have you had lunch yet?*

'tell me about it (*spoken*)

used to say that you understand what sb is talking about and have had the same experience: *'I get so annoyed with Steve!' 'Tell me about it. He drives me crazy.'*

tell me a'nother (*spoken*)

used for saying that you do not believe sb because they are joking or exaggerating: *'I caught a fish that weighed 5 kilos on holiday.' 'Tell me another, will you? I bet it didn't even weigh one kilo.'*

tell 'porkies (*BrE, informal, humorous*)
(usually used in progressive tenses) say sth that is not true: *Can this be true, or is somebody telling porkies?*

ℹ ORIGIN
This phrase comes from rhyming slang, in which *pork pies* stands for 'lies'.

tell the same, a different, another, etc. tale/ story (of sth)
show the same, a different, another, etc. thing: *These two photographs of the city tell a very different story.* ◇ *The faces of these children tell the same tale of hunger and misery.*

tell 'tales (about sb/sth) (*BrE*)
tell sb, especially sb in authority, that another person has done something wrong: *How did the boss know that I was late for work this morning? I think somebody's been telling tales about me.*

tell ,tales out of 'school
talk about the private affairs of a group or organization to people who do not belong to it: *I shouldn't tell tales out of school, but my company is in serious trouble.*

tell the 'time (*BrE*) (*AmE* **tell 'time**)
read the time from a clock, etc: *She's only five—she hasn't learnt to tell the time yet.*

tell sb ,where to get 'off; tell sb ,where they get 'off (*BrE, informal*)
tell sb angrily that you do not like the way they are behaving and you no longer accept it: *He gets drunk every time we go to a party, so I've told him where to get off.*

tell sb ,where to 'put/'stick sth; tell sb what they can 'do with sth (*informal*)
make it clear to sb that you are angry and are rejecting what they are offering you: *I was so furious I nearly told him where to stick his rotten job!*

tell the (whole) 'world
tell sth to everyone; tell sth publicly: *Keep your voice down! We don't want to tell the whole world about it!*

to tell (you) the 'truth
used when admitting sth: *To tell the truth, I fell asleep in the middle of her talk.*

what did I 'tell you? (also **I 'told you so**)
used for telling sb who did not listen to your warnings or take your advice that they were wrong and you were right: *'I've got terrible stomach-ache.' 'What did I tell you? You should never have drunk the tap water.'* ◇ *'She didn't like the present.' 'I told you so. I knew she didn't like perfume.'*

you ,never can 'tell; you can ,never 'tell (*saying*)
you can never be sure; you can never know exactly what will happen: *'Is he happy?' 'I don't know. You can never tell with him.'* ◇ *'Who's going to win?' 'In weather conditions like these you never can tell.'*

can/could teach/tell sb a thing or two (about sb/sth) → **thing**

hear tell (of sth) → **hear**
kiss and tell → **kiss**
live to tell the tale → **live**
not know/not be able to tell one end of sth from the other → **end**
only time will tell → **time**
time (alone) will tell → **time**

telling

you're telling 'me! (*spoken, informal*)
used for saying that you already know and completely agree with what sb has just said: *'Cooking for ten people is hard work.' 'You're telling me!'*

I'm telling you = I (can/can't) tell you → **tell**
there's no knowing/saying/telling … → **knowing**

temper

keep/lose your 'temper (with sb)
remain calm although you are annoyed/become very angry: *You must learn to keep your temper.* ◇ *He loses his temper very quickly if you argue with him.*

have (got) a quick temper → **quick**

temperature

have/run a 'temperature
have a higher body temperature than normal: *She's got a terrible headache and she's running a temperature.*

raise/lower the 'temperature (*informal*)
increase/decrease the amount of excitement, emotion, etc. in a situation: *His angry refusal raised the temperature of the meeting.* ◇ *The government tried to lower the political temperature by agreeing to some of the demands.*

take sb's 'temperature
measure the heat of sb's body, using a thermometer: *The nurse took my temperature; it was 38°.*

tempest

a tempest in a teapot = a storm in a teacup → **storm**

tempt

tempt 'fate/'providence
take a risk or do something dangerous: *'I don't think I'll insure my boat.' 'Don't tempt fate. It's best to insure it.'*

ten

,ten out of 'ten (for sth) (*BrE, often ironic*)
used to say that sb has guessed sth correctly or done sth very well: *Not brilliant, Robyn, but I'll give you ten out of ten for effort.*

,ten to 'one …
it is very likely that … ; very probably: *Ten to one they'll never find out who did it anyway.*

nine times out of ten → **nine**
two/ten a penny → **penny**

tender

(be) at a ˌtender 'age; (be) at the tender ˌage of '8, '12, etc.
(be) young: *We were sent to boarding school at a tender age.* ◇ *At the tender age of seventeen I left home.*

ten-foot

not touch sb/sth with a ten-foot pole → **touch**

tenterhooks

(be) on 'tenterhooks (*AmE* also **be on ˌpins and 'needles**)
(be) very tense, excited or anxious about what might happen: *We were kept on tenterhooks for hours while the judges chose the winner.*

❶ ORIGIN
In the past, a *tenterhook* was used to keep material stretched on a drying frame during manufacture.

tenths

possession is nine points/tenths/parts of the law → **possession**

term

(do sth) in the 'long/'medium/'short term
(do sth) looking or planning for a long/medium/short time into the future: *In the short term, we can send the refugees food and clothing, but in the long term we must do something about the underlying problems.* ▶ **ˌlong-'term, ˌshort-'term** *adjs.*: *a long-term approach* ◇ *short-term problems*

terms

be on good, bad, friendly, etc. 'terms (with sb)
have a good, bad, friendly, etc. relationship with sb: *He's not on very good terms with his wife's family.* ◇ *I'm on first-name terms with my boss now* (= we call each other by our first names).

come to 'terms with sth
learn to accept sth that is difficult or unpleasant: *He finally came to terms with his father's death.*

do sth on sb's/your (own) 'terms
do sth in a way that sb chooses/you choose because they/you are in a position of power: *They agreed to stop fighting, but on their own terms: all prisoners to be released, and talks to be held immediately.*

in terms of 'sth; in 'sth terms
used to show how sth is explained, described or judged: *In terms of money, it's a great job.* ◇ *In energy terms, this new power station can produce ten times as much as the old type.*

be on nodding terms with sb → **nodding**
be on speaking terms (with sb) → **speaking**
a contradiction in terms → **contradiction**
in glowing terms/colours → **glowing**

on the same terms (as sb/sth) = on equal terms (with sb/sth) → **equal**
say, tell sb, etc. (sth) in no uncertain terms → **uncertain**

territory

ˌcome/ˌgo with the 'territory
be a normal and accepted part of a particular job, situation, etc: *As a doctor, he has to work long hours and some weekends, but that goes with the territory, I suppose.*

on neutral ground/territory → **neutral**

test

put sb/sth to the 'test
test sb/sth; find out whether sb/sth is good, bad, true, real, etc: *The second part of the contest will put your general knowledge to the test.*

test the 'water/'waters
try to find out whether sth is likely to succeed, by asking people for their opinions before you do sth: *Your idea might not be popular with people, so before you start marketing it you should test the waters.*

the acid test (of sth) → **acid**
stand the test of time → **stand**

tested

tried and tested/trusted → **tried**

tête-à-tête

a ˌtête-à-'tête (*from French*)
a private conversation between two people: *When I last saw her, she was having a tête-à-tête with Maria.* ◇ *I hate to interrupt your tête-à-tête, but could somebody answer the phone?*

❷ NOTE
The meaning of the French phrase is 'head-to-head'.

tether

be at the end of your tether → **end**

Thames

not/never set the Thames on fire → **set**

thank

have (got) sb to thank (for sth)
used when you are saying who is responsible for sth: *I have my parents to thank for my success.*

I'll thank you (not) to do sth; I'll thank you for sth/doing sth (*formal, spoken*)
used when you are angry or annoyed, to ask sb in a formal way (not) to do sth: *I'll thank you not to interfere in my personal affairs.*

thank 'God!; thank 'goodness/'heaven(s)!
used as an expression of relief: *Thank God you've arrived. I was so worried.*
(Some people find the phrase **thank God** offensive.)

hank your lucky 'stars (that ...)
be very grateful (that ...): *You should thank your lucky stars that you're young and healthy.*

he, she, etc. won't 'thank you for sth
used to say that sb will not be pleased or will be annoyed about sth: *John won't thank you for interfering.*

thankful
be grateful/thankful for small mercies → **small**

thanks

(be) ,no thanks to 'sb/'sth
(be) in spite of sb/sth: *It's no thanks to you that we arrived on time—you kept wanting to stop!*

thanks to 'sb/'sth (*sometimes ironic*)
because of sb/sth: *We won the game thanks to a lot of hard work from everyone in the team.* ◇ *We lost the match, thanks to a few silly mistakes.*

a vote of thanks → **vote**

that

and (all) 'that (*BrE, informal*)
and that sort of thing; and all the other things: *My brother's got a farm, with chickens, cows, pigs and all that.* ◇ *Her paintings are well done and all that, but I find them rather boring.*

at 'that
1 when that happened: *He said she was a fool. At that, she walked out of the room.*
2 (*informal*) as well; either: *She suggested that we should write to our Member of Parliament, and it's not such a bad idea at that.*

is that 'so? (*informal*)
1 used for telling sb that you are not frightened by their actions or threats: *'If you don't shut your mouth I'll kick you out of the house.' 'Is that so? You just try it!'*
2 used to express surprise or interest at what sb has said: *'He owns twenty cars.' 'Is that so?'*

'not that
used to state that you are not suggesting sth: *She hasn't written—not that she said she would.*

that is (to say)
1 in other words: *I'm between jobs at the moment; that's to say unemployed.* ◇ *It cost him a week's wages, that is, £300.*
2 used to give more information or to correct what has already been said: *She's a housewife—when she's not teaching English, that is.* ◇ *Let him explain it—if he can, that is.* ◇ *Nobody wants to do it. Nobody except me, that is.*

'that's a good one (*informal*)
1 said in reply to a joke or clever remark
2 (*ironic*) said in reply to a stupid remark or action: *'Can you make dinner? I'm tired.' 'Tired? That's a good one. You've done nothing all day!'*

that's (about) 'it (*informal*)
1 used for saying that an activity, job, etc. is finished: *That's it for today. We can go home now.* ◇ *That's about it. I've said all I wanted to say.*
2 used to agree with what sb has just said: *'You mean you won't get more than £500.' 'That's about it.'*

(and/so) ,that's 'that
used to show that sth is finished or decided, and there should be no more discussion or argument: *So that's that. At last we're all agreed.* ◇ *You're going to bed now, and that's that! I don't want any argument!*

them

,them and 'us
used to describe a situation in which two groups are opposed to each other, often with one group more powerful than the other: *We should try to get away from a 'them and us' attitude between employers and workers.*

theme
variations on the theme of sth → **variations**

then

and 'then some (*spoken*)
and even more (than has already been mentioned): *It rained for two hours and then some.*

theory

in 'theory
used to say that a particular statement is supposed to be true but may in fact be wrong: *In theory, these machines should last for ten years or more.* ◇ *That sounds fine in theory, but have you really thought it through?*

there

be not all/quite 'there (*informal*)
think slowly because of low intelligence, illness, drugs, etc: *Are you sure he's all there?*

be 'there for sb
be available if sb wants to talk to you or if they need help: *You know I'll always be there for you.*

,so 'there! (*informal*)
(often said by children) used for emphasizing your satisfaction with sth or for emphasizing a refusal, etc: *I got a better mark than you. So there!* ◇ *Well, you can't have it, so there!*

(do sth) ,there and 'then; (do sth) ,then and 'there
(do sth) at that time and place; immediately: *I took one look at the car and offered to buy it then and there.*

there you 'go (a'gain)
used to criticize sb because they are behaving badly again or saying the same things again and again: *There you go again—as soon as we disagree*

you start shouting at me! ◇ *There he goes again—always complaining about something.*

there ,is 'that
said when agreeing with sth: *'Flying is quick, but it's very expensive.' 'Yes, there is that.'*

(and/but/so) there it 'is; (and/but/so) there you 'go; (and/but/so) there we/you 'are
that is the situation; those are the facts: *I don't like my job, but I need the money, so there it is.* ◇ *Soup and bread isn't the best of meals, but there you go.*

,there, 'there! (*old-fashioned*)
used to comfort a small child: *There, there! Never mind, you'll soon feel better.*

,there you 'are (also **,there you 'go**) (*spoken*)
1 used when you give sth to sb: *I've got your newspaper. There you are.* ◇ *There you go. That's £5.29 change.*
2 used when explaining or showing sth to sb: *You cook it on both sides for three minutes and there you are. The perfect steak.*
3 used when sth happens which shows that you were right: *There you are. I told you we'd miss the train.*

,there's 'sth for you (*spoken*)
used to say that sth is a very good example of sth: *She visited him every day he was in the hospital. There's devotion for you.* ◇ (*ironic*) *He didn't even say thank you. There's gratitude for you!*

'there's a good boy, girl, dog, etc. (*informal*)
used to praise or encourage small children or animals: *Finish your dinner, there's a good lad.* ◇ *Sit! There's a good dog.*

therein

therein lies … (*formal*)
used to emphasize the result of a particular situation: *He works extremely hard and therein lies the key to his success.*

thick

give sb/get a thick 'ear (*BrE, informal*)
hit sb/be hit on the side of the head, as a punishment: *If you don't behave yourself you'll get a thick ear.*

in the 'thick of sth/doing sth
1 in the busiest or most active part of sth/doing sth: *He was in the thick of preparing the food for the party, so I didn't interrupt.*
2 in the most crowded part of sth: *If there's trouble, you usually find him in the thick of it.*

,thick and 'fast
quickly and in great numbers or quantities: *Replies to our advertisement are coming in thick and fast.* ◇ *By midnight, the snow was falling thick and fast.*

(as) thick as 'thieves (with sb) (*informal*)
(of two or more people) very friendly with each other, especially in a way that makes other prople

suspicious: *Those two are as thick as thieves—the go everywhere together.*

(as) thick as two short 'planks (*informal*) (als **(as) thick as 'shit** ⚠, *slang*) (*BrE*)
(of a person) very stupid: *Because she's a mode people assume she's as thick as two short planks but she isn't.*

a thick 'head (*informal*)
a physical condition in which your head is painful or you cannot think clearly as a result of an illnes or of drinking too much alcohol: *I've got a reall thick head this morning.*

(be) thick with sth/sb
(be) full of sth/sb: *The air was thick with the scen of roses.* ◇ *The street was thick with reporters an photographers.*

through ,thick and 'thin
in spite of all the difficulties and problems; in good and bad times: *He's been a good friend to her through thick and thin.*

a bit thick/strong → **bit**
thick/thin on the ground → **ground**
(have) a thick/thin skin → **skin**

thickens
the plot thickens → **plot**

thicker
blood is thicker than water → **blood**

thief

like a ,thief in the 'night
secretly or unexpectedly: *In the end I left like a thief in the night, without telling anybody or saying goodbye.*

thieves
(there is) honour among thieves → **honour**
(as) thick as thieves (with sb) → **thick**

thin

appear, etc. out of thin 'air
appear, etc. suddenly from nowhere or nothing: *The car seemed to appear out of thin air. I didn't have time to brake.* ◇ *She seems to conjure wonderful costumes out of thin air.*

be skating/walking on ,thin 'ice
be in a risky or dangerous situation: *They were skating on very thin ice, publishing the election result before it had been confirmed.*

be/get thin on 'top (*informal*)
without much hair on the head; be/go bald: *Max is only 30 but he's already getting a bit thin on top.*

disappear, etc. into thin 'air
disappear, etc. suddenly and in a mysterious way: *The money vanished into thin air. Nobody knows what happened to it.*

have a thin 'time (of it) (*BrE, informal*)
be in an unsuccessful period in your business: *Small businesses are having a thin time of it at the moment, and many are closing down.*

(as) thin as a 'rake
(of a person) very thin: *You're as thin as a rake. You certainly don't need to diet.*

the thin ,end of the 'wedge (*especially BrE*)
used for saying that you fear that one small request, order, action, etc. is only the beginning of sth larger and more serious or harmful: *The government says it only wants to privatize one or two railway lines, but I think it's the thin end of the wedge. They'll all be privatized soon.*

spread yourself too thin ➜ **spread**
thick/thin on the ground ➜ **ground**
(have) a thick/thin skin ➜ **skin**
through thick and thin ➜ **thick**
tread/walk a fine/thin line ➜ **line**
wear thin ➜ **wear**

thing

a ,mount/ ,come to the same 'thing
it does not matter how something happens or is done, the result in the end is the same: *Whether it was your fault or his fault, it still amounts to the same thing. My car's wrecked.*

be just the 'thing (also **be the very 'thing**, *less frequent*)
be exactly what you need or want: *Hot lemon juice and honey is just the thing for a cold.* ◊ *A holiday by the sea, with plenty of swimming and walking, would be the very thing.*

be no bad 'thing (that) ...
used to say that although sth seems to be bad, it could have good results: *We didn't want the press to get hold of the story, but it might be no bad thing.*

be onto a good 'thing
be in a position or situation which brings you a lot of benefits: *They've offered her a company car and a huge salary. She's onto a good thing there.*

can/could teach/tell sb a thing or two (about sb/sth) (*informal*)
be able to help sb, or teach sb how to do sth, because you have more experience: *He thinks he knows a lot about farming, but old Bert could teach him a thing or two.*

a close/near 'thing; a close-run 'thing (*informal*)
1 a competition, election, race, etc. which you only just succeed in winning: *I know we won, but believe me, it was a near thing. They could easily have beaten us.*
2 a punishment, accident, etc. which you only just avoided: *The police searched the house but they didn't find him. It was a close-run thing.*

do your own 'thing (*informal*)
live, act or behave as you want, not as others tell you to do; be independent: *Mark's father wanted him to be a doctor, but Mark wanted to do his own thing and run an art gallery.*

for 'one thing, ...(, and for a'nother, ...)
one reason is ... , and another reason is ...: *You ought to stop smoking, you know. For one thing, you're damaging your health, and for another, you can't afford it!* ◊ *'Why don't you get a car?' 'Well, for one thing, I can't drive!'*

have (got) a 'thing about sb/sth (*informal*)
have very strong feelings, either positive or negative, about sb/sth: *I think she's got a thing about David. She keeps looking at him.* ◊ *I've got a thing about smoking, and I don't allow anybody to smoke in my house.*

it isn't my, his, etc. 'thing
it is not sth that you really enjoy or are interested in: *I'm afraid pubs and clubs aren't really my thing. I'd prefer to go to a restaurant with a few friends.*

it's ,one thing to do 'A, it's (quite) a ,nother (thing) to do 'B; A is 'one thing, B is (quite) a'nother
used for saying that you find the first thing acceptable or possible but the second thing definitely unacceptable or impossible: *It's one thing to write a short article; it's quite another to write a whole book on the subject.* ◊ *Romance is one thing, marriage is quite another.*

it's a ... thing (*informal*)
it is sth that only a particular group understands: *You wouldn't understand the attraction of fast cars—it's a man thing.*

make a (big) 'thing (out) of sth (*informal*)
make sth seem much more serious or important than it really is: *It was only a small mistake, but he made a really big thing out of it.*

,one (damned/damn) thing after a'nother (*spoken*)
used to complain that a lot of unpleasant things keep happening to you: *It's just one thing after another, isn't it? First the car wouldn't start, and then the bus was late.*

(what with) ,one thing and a'nother
(because of) several different events, tasks, duties, etc: *What with one thing and another I haven't had time to sit down all day.*

,one thing leads to a'nother (*informal*)
used to suggest that the way one event or action leads to others is so obvious that it does not need to be stated: *He offered me a ride home one night, and, well, one thing led to another and now we're engaged!*

there's no such ,thing as a free 'lunch (*spoken*)
used to say that it is not possible to get sth for nothing: *I think you should be very careful about accept-*

ing his help. Remember, there's no such thing as a free lunch.

❶ ORIGIN
In the past, taverns offered their customers a 'free' lunch, but they had to buy drinks first.

there's only ,one thing 'for it
there is only one possible course of action: *Well, there's only one thing for it, I'm afraid. You're going to have to tell him what you've done and hope he forgives you.*

the (whole) ... thing (*informal*)
a situation or an activity of the type mentioned: *She really didn't want to be involved in the whole family thing.*

the (only) thing 'is ... (*spoken*)
used before mentioning a worry or problem you have with sth: *I'd love to come—the only thing is I might be late.*

the ,thing (about/with sth) 'is (*spoken*)
used to introduce an important fact, reason or explanation: *I know you want to expand the business. The thing is, we haven't got the money to do that.* ◇ *I'm sorry I didn't call you. The thing is, I've been really busy lately.*

a thing of the 'past
sth that no longer happens or exists: *Everybody sends emails these days. Letter-writing has become a thing of the past.*

the best thing since sliced bread **→ best**
chance would be a fine thing **→ chance**
the done thing **→ done**
first thing (tomorrow, in the morning, etc.) **→ first**
(it's) a good job/thing (that) ... **→ job**
(and) a good job/thing too **→ job**
know a thing or two (about sb/sth) **→ know**
last thing (at night) **→ last**
the next best thing **→ next**
the next thing (I knew) **→ next**
not know the first thing about sb/sth **→ know**
not quite the thing **→ quite**
the real thing **→ real**
sure thing **→ sure**

things

all things con'sidered
considering all the facts, especially the problems or difficulties, of a situation: *She's had a lot of problems since her husband died but she seems quite cheerful, all things considered.*

and things (like 'that) (*spoken, informal*)
used when you do not want to complete a list: *She likes nice clothes and things like that.* ◇ *I've been busy shopping and things.*

as things 'stand
the present situation is that: *As things stand, we won't finish the job on time, but we might if we get some extra help.*

be all ,things to all 'men/'people (*saying*)
change the way you behave or what you say to t to please the people you are with: *The President attempts to be all things to all men had disastro consequences.*

'do things to sb (*informal*)
have a powerful emotional effect on sb: *That sor just does things to me.*

in all things (*formal*)
in every situation; always: *I believe in honesty i all things.* ◇ *Moderation in all things is my motto.*

(just) ,one of those 'things
used to say that unfortunate things do happe sometimes and we must accept this fact: *He doesn love me any more and there's absolutely nothing can do about it. It's just one of those things.*

other/all things being 'equal
if nothing else changes; if other condition remain the same: *Other things being equal, price will rise if people's incomes rise.*

,put things 'right
do sth to improve a difficult situation or correct mistake: *The company is inefficient. A good directo could put things right very quickly.*

'see/'hear things (*informal*)
see/hear things that are not really there: *So it wa you that was playing the piano! I thought I wa hearing things.* ◇ (*humorous*) *Tom's washing th dishes—I must be seeing things!*

these ,things are sent to 'try us (*saying*)
used to say that you should accept an unpleasan situation or event because you cannot change it *'My car broke down again.' 'Oh well, these thing are sent to try us.'*

,these things 'happen
used to tell sb not to worry about sth they have done: *'Sorry—I've spilt some wine.' 'Never mina these things happen.'*

,things that go ,bump in the 'night (*informa humorous*)
strange or frightening noises, or things that can not be explained by science: *I don't believe i ghosts or spirits, or things that go bump in th night.*

as it/things turned out **→ turned**
be/feel out of it/things **→ feel**
be a taste of things to come = be the shape of things t come **→ shape**
by/from the look(s) of it/things **→ look**
cut it/things fine **→ cut**
first things first **→ first**
have it/things/everything (all) your (own) way **→ way**
have (got) your mind on other things **→ mind**
in the nature of things **→ nature**
make the best of sth/things/a bad job **→ best**
your mind is on other things **→ mind**
of all people/places/things **→ people**
overdo it/things **→ overdo**

...sh it/things → **push**

...e/sb's scheme of things → **scheme**

...ke it/things easy → **easy**

...ke it/things one day at a time → **day**

...ork it/things (so that ...) → **work**

think

anyone would think (that) ... (also **you would have 'thought (that) ...**)

(of sb's strange or surprising behaviour) if you did not know the truth, it would seem that ...: *Don't be so nervous! Anyone would think you'd never been to a party before!*

come to 'think of it (also **'thinking about it**) (*informal*)

said when you suddenly remember or realize sth: *I first met her in 1997. No, come to think of it, it was 1996.*

give sb something to 'think about (*informal*)

do or say sth to sb which shows how angry or determined you are: *This letter will give him something to think about.*

have (got) another think 'coming (*informal*)

used for saying that sb's opinion about a future event is wrong because sth quite different will happen: *If she thinks that married life is going to be easy, she's got another think coming.*

I should think 'so/'not (also **I should think 'she, etc. 'is/'does/'did, etc.**)

used for emphasis when agreeing that sth is right or correct: *'He didn't give the waiter a tip.' 'I should think not, after such bad service.'* ◇ *'He finally apologized for what he said.' 'I should think so.'* ◇ *'I'm very angry with my son.' 'I should think you are. He's behaved very badly indeed.'*

I shudder/dread to 'think (how, what, etc. ...) (*informal, often humorous*)

I am afraid to think or ask myself about sth, because the answer might be terrible or unpleasant: *I shudder to think when he last had a bath.* ◇ *How much more work is there?' 'I dread to think!'*

if/when you 'think about it

used to draw attention to a fact that is not obvious or has not previously been mentioned: *They do have a big house, when you think about it.*

just 'think

used when you feel interest, shock or excitement at sth: *Just think of the money we spend renting this place.* ◇ *I'll be on television in front of millions of viewers! Just think!*

not 'think of sth/doing sth

(used with *wouldn't, couldn't, won't* or *can't*) definitely not do sth; never do sth: *I wouldn't think of buying one of those ugly modern houses.* ◇ *A famous man like him can't think of answering all his letters personally.*

that's what 'sb thinks (*informal*)

what sb thinks will happen will not happen, especially because the speaker is going to do sth to prevent it: *'Your team doesn't have a chance of winning.' 'That's what you think!'*

think a'gain

consider a decision again and perhaps change your idea or intention: *I'd advise you to think again before leaving your wife.*

think a'loud; think out 'loud

speak your thoughts about sth, for example a problem, to yourself or to others, probably without organizing them as in normal speech: *'What?' 'Oh, don't worry. I was just thinking out loud.'*

think (the) 'better of sb

have a higher opinion of sb: *She has behaved appallingly—I must say I thought better of her.*

think 'better of it/of doing sth

decide not to do sth that you were intending to do: *He was about to say something, but then he thought better of it and kept quiet.*

think 'big (*informal*)

have big plans for the future; be ambitious: *If you want to be successful in life, you've got to think big.*

think 'highly of sb/sth

have a very high opinion of sb/sth: *Her teachers think highly of her.* ◇ *His paintings are highly thought of by the critics.*

think 'nothing of sth/doing sth; not think 'anything of sth/doing sth

1 consider (doing) sth as normal or easy, when other people consider it as difficult, dangerous, etc: *He thinks nothing of working 14 hours a day.*
2 think that sth is not important: *I saw a man outside the door, but I didn't think anything of it at the time. I realized later that he must have been the thief.*

think nothing 'of it (*spoken, formal*)

said as a polite reply when sb has thanked you or said sorry for sth: *'I'm terribly sorry for all the trouble I've caused you.' 'Think nothing of it.'*

think on your 'feet

think very quickly: *When he asked me why I wasn't at work, I had to think on my feet and I invented an excuse about going to see the doctor.* ◇ *Lawyers in court need to be able to think on their feet.*

think out of the 'box (also **think outside the 'box**)

think about sth, or how to do sth, in a new, different or creative way (especially in business): *The company is looking for adventurous, creative people who can think out of the box and are not afraid of experimenting.* ◇ *Thinking out of the box would improve public education.*

think you 'own the place (also **behave/act as if you 'own the place**) (*disapproving*)

behave in a very confident way that annoys other people, for example by telling them what to do: *What does she think she's doing, coming in here acting as if she owns the place!*

think 'positive
think in a confident way about what you can do: *If you don't think positive, you won't win.*

'think straight
think in a clear or logical way: *You're not thinking straight. If you leave your job, how will you support your family?*

think the sun shines out of sb's arse ⚠/ backside (*BrE*) (*AmE* think the sun shines out of sb's ass ⚠) (*slang*)
have a very high opinion of sb and think that everything they do is good: *We need more money for this job. I think you should be the one to ask the boss—he thinks the sun shines out of your backside!*

(not) think 'twice about sth/doing sth
(not) think carefully before deciding to do sth; (not) hesitate: *You should think twice about employing someone you've never met.* ◇ *If they offered me a job abroad, I wouldn't think twice about taking it!*

think the 'world of sb/sth
like, admire or respect sb/sth very much: *The children think the world of their new teacher.*

to 'think (that) …
used to show that you are surprised or shocked by sth: *I can still hardly believe it! To think that the President stayed at my hotel!* ◇ *To think that he was killed on the last day of the war. It's so sad.*

who does sb think they 'are? (*disapproving, informal*)
sb has no right to behave in a certain way: *Who do you think you are, taking my books without asking?* ◇ *She just walked into my office without knocking! Who does she think she is?*

can't hear yourself think ➔ **hear**
let me see/think ➔ **let**
see/think fit (to do sth) ➔ **fit**
speak/think ill of sb ➔ **ill**

thinking
put your 'thinking cap on (*informal*)
try to solve a problem by thinking hard about it: *Now, how are we going to find this money? Let's put our thinking caps on.*

thinking about it = come to think of it ➔ **think**
to my, your, etc. way of thinking ➔ **way**
wishful thinking ➔ **wishful**

third
(give sb) the ‚third de'gree (*informal*)
question sb for a long time and in a thorough way; use threats or violence to get information from sb: *The soldiers were given the third degree in order to make them reveal the information.* ◇ *Why are you giving me the third degree?*

❶ ORIGIN
This expression comes from Freemasonry (= a secret society). In order to reach the highest level of the organization and become a *Third Degree Mason*, members are interrogated.

third time 'lucky (*AmE* also third time is th 'charm)
used when you have failed to do sth twice and ho that you will succeed the third time: *I miss again! Oh well, third time lucky!*

a fifth/third wheel ➔ **wheel**

this
‚this and 'that (also ‚this, that and the 'othe (*informal*)
a number of different things: *We talked about th and that for a while and then had dinner.*

this is 'it (*informal*)
1 said when you are agreeing that a point made b sb is important: *'People prefer their cars to pub transport, you see.' 'Well, this is it.'*
2 said when you have come to an importan moment: *Well this is it, Mike. Good luck i Australia. Don't forget to write …*

thither
hither and thither ➔ **hither**

Thomas
a doubting Thomas ➔ **doubting**

thorn
be a thorn in your 'flesh/'side
be a person or thing that repeatedly annoys you o stops you doing sth: *This patient is a real thorn i my side. He's always complaining of feeling ill an I can never find anything wrong with him.*

thought
I 'thought as much
that is what I thought or expected: *'She's been lyin to you; she hasn't really got any money at all.' 'thought as much.'*

it's the thought that counts (*saying*)
the fact that sb remembered about sth is mor important than the size or value of a present: *Sh didn't send him a present for his birthday, only card, but it's the thought that counts.*

food for thought ➔ **food**
give (sb) pause for thought ➔ **pause**
on second thought ➔ **second**
perish the thought! ➔ **perish**
a school of thought ➔ **school**
a train of thought ➔ **train**
the wish is father to the thought ➔ **wish**
without a second thought ➔ **second**
you would have thought (that) … = anyone would thin (that) … ➔ **think**

thoughts

collect yourself/your thoughts → **collect**
have second thoughts → **second**
on second thoughts → **second**
a penny for your thoughts → **penny**
read sb's mind/thoughts → **read**

thousand

a hundred/thousand/million and one (things, etc. to do, etc.) → **hundred**
not a hundred/thousand/million miles away/from here → **miles**
the sixty-four thousand dollar question → **sixty-four**

thrall

in (sb's/sth's) 'thrall; in 'thrall to sb/sth (*literary*)
controlled or strongly influenced by sb/sth: *The country's economy is largely in thrall to the big companies.*

thread

thread your way through (sth)
move through a place by moving round and between people or things: *I threaded my way through the busy streets.*

hang by a hair/a thread → **hang**
lose the drift/thread of sth → **lose**

threads

the loose ends/threads → **loose**
pick up the threads → **pick**

three

(yes sir, no sir) three bags 'full (sir) (*old-fashioned, humorous*)
said when you agree to do sth that sb asks you but think that they are rather rude or unreasonable: *Our new manager doesn't want to hear our opinions, all he wants is, 'Yes sir, no sir, three bags full sir.'*

❶ ORIGIN
This phrase is from the nursery rhyme, 'Baa, baa, black sheep'.

(give) three 'cheers (for sb/sth)
shout 'hurray' three times to show admiration or support for sb/sth: *You all deserve three cheers for working so hard.* ◇ *Three cheers for the winner— hip, hip, hurray!*

the three 'R's (*old-fashioned*)
reading, writing and arithmetic as the basic school subjects

❷ NOTE
When you say these three subjects, they all have the sound /r/ at or near the beginning of the word.

(be) three sheets to the 'wind (*old-fashioned*)
(be) drunk: *By 11 o'clock he was three sheets to the wind and we had to take him home in a cab.*

❶ ORIGIN
This idiom comes from sailing: if three *sheets* (= the ropes attached to the sails) are loose, the wind blows the sails about and the boat moves in a very unsteady way.

threshold

be on the 'threshold of sth (*formal*)
be at an important moment when sth begins, changes or develops: *The country seemed to be on the threshold of war.* ◇ *Now, on the threshold of a new career, he seems confident and happy.*

thrills

(the) thrills and 'spills (of sth) (*informal*)
the exciting mixture of sudden successes and difficulties: *He loves the thrills and spills of Grand Prix motor racing.*

throat

ram, force, thrust, etc. sth down sb's 'throat (*informal*)
try to make sb accept or believe an idea or belief by talking about it all the time: *I'm tired of having her opinions rammed down my throat all the time!* ◇ *He was always forcing Marxist theories down our throats.*

clear your throat → **clear**
cut your own throat → **cut**
have (got) a frog in your throat → **frog**
have, etc. a lump in your throat → **lump**
jump down sb's throat → **jump**
stick in your throat/craw/gullet → **stick**

throats

(be) at each other's 'throats; (be) at one another's 'throats
(be) angrily fighting or arguing with each other: *Within six months of their marriage, Sue and Rodney were at each other's throats.*

throes

in the throes of sth/doing sth
doing a difficult task; experiencing a difficult period or event: *The film's about a country in the throes of change.* ◇ *He's in the throes of divorce at the moment.*

throne

be the (real) power behind the throne → **power**

throttle

(at) full throttle → **full**

through

,through and 'through
completely (typical of sb/sth): *He's a gentleman through and through.* ◇ *This letter is my bank manager through and through.*

throw

$100, £50, etc. a 'throw (*informal*)
used to say how much items cost each: *The tickets for the dinner were £50 a throw.*

throw the ,baby out with the 'bathwater (*informal*)
lose sth that you want at the same time as you are trying to get rid of sth that you do not want: *It's stupid to say that the old system of management was all bad; there were some good things about it. The baby was thrown out with the bathwater.*

throw the 'book at sb (*informal*)
punish or criticize sb for as many things as possible: *The police stopped me for speeding and threw the book at me for everything—faulty lights, dangerous tyres, no insurance …*

throw caution to the 'wind(s) (*often humorous*)
stop caring about how dangerous sth might be; start taking risks: *I decided to throw caution to the winds and buy myself a really expensive pair of shoes.* ◇ *He threw caution to the wind and dived in after the child.*

throw down the 'gauntlet
invite sb to compete with you; challenge sb: *They have thrown down the gauntlet to the Prime Minister by demanding a referendum.*

❶ ORIGIN
A *gauntlet* is a kind of glove. In medieval times a knight threw his gauntlet at the feet of another knight as a challenge to fight. If he accepted the challenge, the other knight would pick up the glove.

throw ,good money after 'bad (*disapproving*)
spend more money in an attempt to get back the money which has been lost, although this is unlikely to be successful: *The Government was throwing good money after bad by investing money in industries that would never make a profit.*

throw your 'hand in (*informal*)
stop doing sth or taking part in sth, especially because you are not successful: *If I fail again this time, I shall throw my hand in.*

❷ NOTE
When you have no chance of winning in a game of cards, you throw your *hand* (= cards) into the middle of the table.

throw your 'hat into the ring
announce officially that you are going to compete in an election, a competition, etc: *Another candidate has now thrown his hat into the ring for the elections later this year.*

throw in your 'lot with sb
decide to join a person or an organization, so that you share their luck, both good and bad: *He left his job in the National Theatre to throw in his lot with a small travelling theatre company.*

throw in the 'towel/'sponge (*informal*)
stop doing sth because you know that you cannot succeed; admit defeat: *It's a bit early to throw in the towel—you've only just started the job.*

❶ ORIGIN
This idiom comes from boxing: throwing in the towel or sponge is a sign that a fighter accepts defeat.

throw your 'money about/around (*informal*)
spend money in a careless and obvious way: *He's always throwing his money around to try to impress people.*

throw 'money at sth (*disapproving*)
spend a lot of money trying to do sth which will probably not succeed: *They threw money at the business, but it failed in its first year.* ◇ *The government throws money at social problems but it doesn't do much good.*

throw sth 'overboard
reject or get rid of sth: *All ideas of reform were thrown overboard when the new government came to power.*

throw a 'tantrum (*BrE also* throw a 'wobbly) (*informal*)
suddenly become very angry and behave in an unreasonable way: *Your mother would throw a wobbly if she knew what we'd been doing.* ◇ *When you were a child, you were always throwing tantrums.*

throw sb to the 'wolves/'lions
allow sb to be attacked or remain in a difficult situation, perhaps because they are no longer useful or important to you: *When he became politically unpopular the rest of his party just threw him to the wolves.*

throw up your arms/hands in de'spair, 'horror, etc. (*often humorous*)
show that you disagree strongly with sth, or are very worried about sth: *When she said she wanted to get a motorbike, her parents threw up their hands in horror.*

throw your 'weight about/around (*informal*)
use your position of authority or power in an aggressive way in order to get what you want: *He started throwing his weight around, shouting at everyone and telling them what to do.*

throw yourself at sb's 'feet
ask for sb to help, protect or forgive you: *He threw himself at her feet and asked her forgiveness.*

throw yourself on sb's 'mercy (*formal*)
put yourself in a situation where you must rely on sb to be kind to you and not harm or punish you:

Throw yourself on the mercy of the court, and they might not send you to prison.

bring/call/throw sth into question → **question**
cast/shed/throw (new) light on sth → **light**
cast/draw/throw a veil over sth → **veil**
fling/sling/throw mud (at sb) → **mud**
have/throw a fit → **fit**
if you throw enough mud, some of it will stick = mud sticks → **mud**
knock/throw sb for a loop → **loop**
people (who live) in glass houses shouldn't throw stones → **people**
pour/throw cold water on sth → **cold**
put/throw sb off the scent → **scent**
put/throw a spanner in the works → **spanner**
put/throw your weight behind sth → **weight**
rule/throw sth out of court → **court**
a stone's throw → **stone**
throw a (monkey) wrench in the works = put/throw a spanner in the works → **spanner**

thrown

jump in/be thrown in at the deep end → **deep**

thrust

the cut and thrust (of sth) → **cut**

thumb

thumb your 'nose at sb/sth
show that you have no respect for sb/sth, sometimes by making a rude sign with your thumb on the end of your nose: *A photograph shows one of the crowd thumbing his nose at the speaker.*

(be) under sb's 'thumb (*informal*)
(be) completely controlled or influenced by another person: *Now that they're married, she's completely under his thumb and never sees her old friends.*

a green thumb → **green**
a rule of thumb → **rule**
stand/stick out like a sore thumb → **sore**
thumb/hitch a lift → **lift**

thumbs

be all 'thumbs (also **be all ,fingers and 'thumbs**)
be unable to hold sth without dropping or damaging it; be clumsy: *He's all thumbs when it comes to fixing machines.*

(give sb/sth/get) the thumbs 'up/'down
used to show that sth has been accepted/rejected or that it is/is not a success: *I asked him whether I could borrow the car, and he gave me the thumbs up.* ◇ *I'm afraid it's thumbs down for your new proposal—the boss doesn't like it.* ◇ *We've got the thumbs up for the new swimming pool.*

❶ ORIGIN
In contests in ancient Rome the public put their thumbs up if they wanted a gladiator to live, and down if they wanted him to be killed.

twiddle your thumbs → **twiddle**

thunder

blood and thunder → **blood**
he, she, etc. has (got) a face like thunder → **face**
his, her, etc. face is like thunder → **face**
steal sb's thunder → **steal**

tick

get, buy, etc. sth on 'tick (*old-fashioned, BrE, informal*)
get food or other goods and pay for them later: *You can only buy things on tick in small shops where they know you well.*

,tick sth off on your 'fingers
check a list of things by saying them aloud, and touching your fingers one after another at the same time

what makes sb 'tick (*informal*)
what makes sb behave or think in the way they do: *I've never really understood what makes her tick.* ◇ *Money is what makes him tick.*

❷ NOTE
Tick is the sound a watch or clock makes as the hands move forward every second.

ticket

'that's the ticket (*old-fashioned, BrE, informal*)
used to say that sth is just what is needed or that everything is just right

just the job/ticket → **job**
a meal ticket → **meal**
split the ticket → **split**

tickle

catch/take/tickle sb's fancy → **fancy**
(a bit of) slap and tickle → **slap**

tickled

be tickled 'pink (also **be tickled to 'death**)
(*old-fashioned, informal*)
be very pleased or amused: *My grandmother will be tickled pink to get an invitation to the wedding.*

tide

the tide 'turns
things change, especially for the better: *For a long time there has been little political freedom, but slowly the tide is turning.*

go, swim, etc. with/against the stream/tide → **stream**
stem the tide (of sth) → **stem**

tie

tie sb's 'hands
(often used in the passive) stop sb doing sth, by taking away their power or freedom: *Employers now*

have the right to dismiss workers who go on strike and this has tied the unions' hands considerably. ◇ *I'm afraid my hands are tied. I can't allow anyone to bring visitors into the club. It's against the rules.*

tie the 'knot (*informal*)
get married: *When did you two decide to tie the knot?*

tie one 'on (*old-fashioned, AmE, slang*)
get very drunk

tie sb/yourself (up) in 'knots
become or make sb very confused: *The interviewer tied the Prime Minister up in knots. He looked a complete fool.* ◇ *He tied himself up in knots when he tried to explain why he had lipstick on his face.*

bind/tie sb hand and foot → **hand**
the old school tie → **old**

tied

with one hand tied behind your back → **hand**

tiger

a paper tiger → **paper**

tight

in a tight 'corner/'spot (*informal*)
in a very difficult situation: *He's in a bit of a tight spot at the moment. The bank has given him one week to find £2 000.*

keep a tight 'rein on sb/sth (also **keep sb/sth on a tight 'leash**)
control sb/sth very carefully; give sb/sth very little freedom: *The company must keep a tight rein on spending.* ◇ *She keeps her children on a tight leash to make sure they don't get into trouble.*

> ❷ NOTE
> A *leash* is used to hold and control a dog, and a *rein* is used to control a horse.

a ˌtight 'squeeze
a situation where you do not have much space to put things in: *We managed to get all the luggage in the car but it was a tight squeeze.*

run a tight ship → **run**
sit tight → **sit**
sleep tight! → **sleep**

tighten

tighten your 'belt
spend less money, eat less food, etc. because there is little available: *In wartime everyone has to tighten their belts.* ◇ *We'll have to tighten our belts if we want to save any money for our holidays this year.*

tightrope

tread/walk a 'tightrope; be on a 'tightrope
be in a situation where you must act very care-

fully: *I'm walking a tightrope at the moment; one more mistake and I might lose my job.*

> ❷ NOTE
> A *tightrope* is a rope high up in the air that an acrobat walks along at a circus.

tiles

a night (out) on the town/on the tiles = (out) on the town
→ **town**

till

have (got) your ˌfingers/ˌhand in the 'till (*BrE, informal*)
steal, especially small amounts of money from a shop, business, etc. where you work: *He lost his job after they found he'd had his hand in the till.*

tiller

at the helm/tiller → **helm**

tilt

tilt at 'windmills
waste your energy attacking imaginary enemies: *For some reason he thinks everyone is out to get him, but he's really just tilting at windmills.*

> ❷ ORIGIN
> This expression comes from Cervantes' novel *Don Quixote*, in which the hero thought that the windmills he saw were giants and tried to fight them.

(at) full pelt/speed/tilt → **full**

time

(and) about 'time ('too); (and) not before 'time (*spoken*)
said when the speaker is pleased that sth has happened but thinks that it should have happened sooner: *Here comes the bus—and about time too.* ◇ *'She finally repaired the window.' 'Not before time.'* ◇ *Julia's been promoted, and not before time, considering the amount of work she does.*

against 'time (also **against the 'clock**)
if you do sth **against time**, you do it as fast as you can because you do not have much time: *We've only got two days to find a replacement, so we're racing against time.* ◇ *They're working against the clock to try and get people out of the rubble alive.*

ahead of/behind 'time
early/late: *He arrived ahead of time, and had to wait.* ◇ *The trains are running behind time again today.*

all the 'time; the whole 'time (also **against the 'clock**)
1 during the whole of a particular period of time: *The letter was in my pocket the whole time* (= while I was looking for it).
2 very often; repeatedly: *She leaves the lights on all the time.*

'any time (*spoken*)
used after sb has thanked you for helping them,
etc: *'Thanks for the lift.' 'Any time.'*

at a 'time
separately or in groups of two, three, etc. on each
occasion: *We had to go and see the principal one at a
time.* ◇ *She ran up the stairs two at a time.*

at the 'time
at a certain moment in the past; then: *I remember
watching the first men on the moon on television; I
was only six at the time.*

at 'my, 'your, etc. time of life
at my, your, etc. age (especially used about older
people): *Learn to drive at my time of life? Don't be
silly!*

**be ahead of/before/in advance of your
'time**
have ideas or invent things before people are ready
to accept them: *He was sure that it was possible to
fly to the moon, but he was ahead of his time and
people laughed at him.* ◇ *She was a feminist before
her time.*

be before sb's 'time
be before the period that a person can remember
or was involved in: *The Beatles were a bit before my
time.* ◇ *There used to be fields behind this house,
but that was before your time* (= before you started
living here).

be (stuck) in a 'time warp
not having changed at all from a time in the past
although everything else has: *Her whole house
seems to be stuck in a time warp. It's like something
out of the 1950s.*

do/serve 'time (*informal*)
be in prison: *He had done time for robbing a bank.*
◇ *Two of the gang are serving time for murder.*

every 'time
whenever there is a choice: *I don't really like
cities—give me the countryside every time.*

for the time 'being (also **for the 'moment/
'present**)
now, and for a short time in the future: *He can stay
with us for the time being until he finds a place of
his own.* ◇ *I'm happy here for the moment, but I
might want to move soon.*

from/since ,time imme'morial
from ancient times; from a very long time ago: *The
Barton family have lived in this village since time
immemorial.*

from ,time to 'time
occasionally; sometimes: *We go to the cinema from
time to time.*

give sb a rough, hard, bad, etc. 'time (of it)
(*informal*)
make sb's life very difficult because you do not like
them: *Ever since I started work here, she's been
shouting at me and giving me a hard time.*

have (got) a lot of 'time for sb/sth (*informal,
especially BrE*)
like, admire or respect sb/sth very much: *I've got a
lot of time for the police. I think they've got a very
difficult job.*

**have (got) no 'time for sb/sth; not have much
'time for sb/sth** (*informal*)
dislike and have no respect for sb/sth: *I have no
time for lazy people like him.* ◇ *I haven't got any
time for people who tell lies.*

have a (hard, rough, bad, etc.) 'time of it
(*informal*)
experience difficulties, problems, etc: *We're having a time of it at the moment with the builders in
the house.* ◇ *Businesses are having a hard time of it
at right now.*

have the ,time of your 'life (*informal*)
enjoy yourself; be very happy or excited: *The children had the time of their lives at the circus.*

have (got) 'time on your hands (*informal*)
have more free time than you want or need: *Now
the children have left home, she's got a lot more time
on her hands.*

(all) in good 'time (*spoken*)
used to say that sth will be done or will happen at
the appropriate time and not before: *Be patient,
Emily! All in good time.*

in good 'time
well before the time sth starts or happens: *Make
sure you get there in good time to buy your ticket.*

in (less than/next to) 'no time
so soon or so quickly that it is surprising: *The kids
will be leaving home in no time.* ◇ *She started
learning Chinese last year and in less than no time
she could hold a conversation in it.* ◇ *The meal was
ready in next to no time.*

(do sth) in your own good 'time (*informal*)
(do sth) when you want to, and not when other
people tell you to: *There's no point in getting impatient. She'll finish the job in her own good time.*

(do sth) in your own 'time
(do sth) in your free time, and not at work: *Please
make private phone calls in your own time, Mr
Davies, not when you are at work.*

in 'time
1 not late: *Make sure that you get here in time for
the concert.*
2 after quite a long time; eventually: *You will feel
better in time.*
3 (play, sing, or dance to music) at the right speed:
*The violins didn't seem to be in time with the rest of
the orchestra.*

it's ,high/a,bout 'time (that) … (*spoken*)
used for saying that sth should be done or happen
immediately or very soon: *It's high time that this
room was properly cleaned!* ◇ *So you've started
work! It's about time!* (= you should have started a
long time ago).

it's only, just, etc. a matter/a question of 'time (before …)
used to say that a thing will definitely happen in the future, although it may not happen immediately: *Don't worry, you'll get a job if you keep looking. It's just a matter of time.* ◇ *It's only a question of time before the fighting spreads to the city.*

keep 'time
1 (of a clock or watch) always show the correct time: *It's an old watch, but it keeps very good time.*
2 sing, play, or dance to music at the right speed: *Keep time with the music, Fiona. You're singing too fast.*

lose/waste no time (in doing sth)
do sth quickly and without delay: *As soon as she arrived back home, she lost no time in visiting all her old friends.*

make good, etc. 'time
go as fast as, or faster than you expected or hoped: *On the first part of the trip we made good time.*

make 'time (to do sth)
make sure you have enough time to do sth: *I'm very busy, but I'll try to make time to do it.*

make up the 'time
do sth at a different time, because you cannot do it at the usual or correct time: *He had a long lunch break on Tuesday and so he made up the time by working late on Wednesday.*

'many a time; 'many's the time (that) … (old-fashioned)
many times; frequently: *Many's the time we've thought about emigrating to Australia, but then we wouldn't see our grandchildren growing up.*

(the) next, first, second, etc. time a'round/ 'round
on the next, first, second, etc. occasion that the same thing happens: *He repeated none of the errors he'd made first time round.* ◇ *This time around it was not so easy.*

(there's) no time like the 'present (saying)
the best time to do sth is now: *'When do you want me to start the decorating?' 'Well, no time like the present, is there?'*

not give sb the time of 'day
refuse to speak to sb because you do not like or respect them: *Since the success of her novel, people shake her hand who once wouldn't have given her the time of day.*

of all 'time
that has ever been made, lived, etc: *Which do you think is the best film of all time?* ▶ 'all-time *adj.*: *My all-time favourite film is 'Gone with the Wind'.*

(right) on 'time (also bang on 'time) (informal)
at the correct time, neither early nor late; punctual: *I always have to wait for you—you're never on time.* ◇ *The train came in bang on time for once.*

take your 'time (over sth/to do sth/doing sth)
1 do sth as slowly as you like; do not hurry: *There's no rush—take your time.*
2 be late; do sth too slowly: *You certainly took your time to get here. I've been waiting an hour!* ◇ *The shop assistant took her time serving me.*

there's no time to 'lose; there's no time to be 'lost (saying)
you must act quickly: *Come on, there's no time to lose! The plane leaves in half an hour!*

,time after 'time; ,time and (,time) a'gain
very often; many times, repeatedly: *He makes the same mistake time after time.* ◇ *Time and again she's tried to give up smoking, but she never succeeds.*

time 'flies (saying)
time seems to pass very quickly: *How time flies! I've got to go now.* ◇ *Time has flown since the holiday began.*

> **❶ ORIGIN**
> This phrase is a translation of the Latin 'tempus fugit'.

time hangs/lies 'heavy (on your 'hands)
time seems to pass very slowly because you are bored or have nothing to do: *In prison, time hangs heavy.*

time is getting 'on
it is getting late; there is not much time left: *We'd better hurry up and finish; time's getting on.*

time is 'money (saying)
time is valuable, and should not be wasted

time is on sb's 'side (also have (got) time on your side)
sb has enough time to do sth; the more that time passes, the more sb will be helped: *Although she failed the exam, time is on her side; she is young enough to take it again next year.* ◇ *The longer we wait to sell the house, the more it will be worth, so we've got time on our side.*

the time is 'ripe (for sb) (to do sth); the time is 'ripe for sth/doing sth (literary)
it is the right time to do sth: *I think the time's ripe for him to leave home if he wants to.* ◇ *The time is ripe for a change in this country.*

time 'was (when) … (old-fashioned)
used to say that sth used to happen in the past: *Time was when you could go for a walk in the country and not see another person for miles.*

time (alone) will 'tell; only time will 'tell (saying)
used to say that you will have to wait for some time to find out the result of a situation: *Only time will tell if the treatment has been successful.*

be/live on borrowed time → **borrowed**
beat time → **beat**
better luck next time → **better**
bide your time → **bide**
big time → **big**

buy time → **buy**

do sth in your own sweet time/way → **sweet**

for the nth time → **nth**

from that day/time forth → **forth**

gain time → **gain**

half the time → **half**

have an easy time of it → **easy**

have a high old time → **high**

have a thin time (of it) → **thin**

have a whale of a time → **whale**

in the fullness of time → **fullness**

in half the time → **half**

in the nick of time → **nick**

in sb's day/time → **day**

long time no see → **long**

make up for lost time → **lost**

mark time → **mark**

once upon a time → **once**

pass the/your time (doing sth) → **pass**

pass the time of day (with sb) → **pass**

play for time → **play**

quite some time → **quite**

a race against time/the clock → **race**

stand the test of time → **stand**

a stitch in time (saves nine) → **stitch**

take it/things one day at a time → **day**

tell (the) time → **tell**

there's a first time for everything → **first**

third time is the charm → **third**

third time lucky → **third**

times

at all 'times

always: *Our representatives are ready to help you at all times.*

at 'times

sometimes: *At times I wonder whether he'll ever get a job.*

be behind the 'times

be old-fashioned in the way you live, work, think, etc: *You're behind the times if you think a visit to the dentist has to be painful.*

keep up, move, etc. with the 'times

change in the same way as the rest of society changes: *In business it's important to keep up with the times.* ◇ *People's tastes change with the times.*

at the best of times → **best**

fall on hard times → **fall**

for old times' sake → **old**

ninety-nine times out of a hundred = nine times out of ten → **nine**

(be) a sign of the times → **sign**

tin

have (got) a tin 'ear (for sth) (*informal*)

be unable to hear the difference between musical notes or to enjoy music: *Even those of us with a tin ear can recognize a waltz.*

tiny

the patter of tiny feet → **patter**

tip

be on the tip of your 'tongue

used when you are speaking and cannot remember a word, name, etc. but feel that you will remember it very soon: *What's her name? You know, that tall Italian girl ... it's on the tip of my tongue ... Claudia, that's it!*

be the tip of the 'iceberg

what you can see of a problem or difficult situation is only one small part of a much larger (hidden) problem: *The 1 000 homeless people in London sleeping in night shelters are only the tip of the iceberg. There are many thousands of homeless people in the capital.*

ℹ ORIGIN

Only ½ or ⅛ of an iceberg can be seen above the water.

tip the 'balance/'scales (also swing the 'balance)

be the reason that finally causes sb to do sth or sth to happen in one way rather than another: *They were both very good candidates for the job but she had more experience and that tipped the balance.*

tip the scales at sth

weigh a particular amount: *He tipped the scales at just over 80 kilos.*

tip sb the 'wink; tip the 'wink to sb (*BrE, informal*)

give sb secret information that they can use to gain an advantage for themselves: *'How did you know the job was available?' 'A friend tipped me the wink and so I telephoned immediately.'*

tip your hand = show/reveal your hand → **hand**

tip your hat to sb = take your hat off to sb → **hat**

tipping

it's 'tipping (it) down (*BrE, informal*)

it is raining heavily: *There's no way I'm playing football in this weather—it's tipping it down.*

tiptoe

on 'tiptoe/'tiptoes

standing or walking on the front part of your foot, with your heels off the ground, in order to make yourself taller or to move very quietly or lightly: *She had to stand on tiptoe to reach the top shelf.* ◇ *We crept around on tiptoes so as not to disturb him.*

tire

never tire of doing sth

do sth a lot, especially in a way that annoys people: *He went to Harvard—as he never tires of reminding us.*

a spare tire → **spare**

tired

be/get tired of sth/doing sth
be/get bored or annoyed with sth/doing sth: *We got tired of the country and we moved into town.* ◊ *I'm tired of listening to his complaints.*

tissue

a ,tissue of 'lies (*literary*)
a story, an excuse, etc. that is full of lies: *Don't believe her—the whole thing is a complete tissue of lies.* ◊ *This official report on the nuclear energy industry is a tissue of lies.*

tit

,tit for 'tat
(do) sth unpleasant to sb because they have done sth unpleasant to you: *He hit me, so I hit him back— it was tit for tat.*

Titanic

rearrange the deckchairs on the Titanic ➔ **rearrange**

tizzy (also tizz)

be/get in/into a 'tizzy/'tizz (about sth) (*informal*)
be/become excited, nervous or confused, especially about sth that is not important: *He was in such a tizz about his homework.*

to

,to and 'fro
from one place to another and back, repeatedly; from side to side repeatedly: *They travel to and fro between London and Paris.* ◊ *She held the baby in her arms and rocked her to and fro.*

(all) to your'self, him'self, etc.
for only you, him, etc. to have, use, etc: *The boss was away last week so we had the office to ourselves.*

toast

be the toast of ...
be sb who is praised by a lot of people in a particular place because of sth that they have done well: *Eddie was the toast of Hollywood yesterday after winning three awards for his latest film.*

propose a toast (to sb) ➔ **propose**
(as) warm as toast ➔ **warm**

-to-be

-to-be
(in compounds) future: *his bride-to-be* ◊ *mothers-to-be* (= pregnant women)

tod

on your 'tod (*old-fashioned, BrE, informal*)
on your own; alone: *Are you going to be alright here all on your tod?*

> **ⓘ ORIGIN**
> This comes from rhyming slang: after Tod Sloan, an American jockey, whose name rhymes with 'alone'.

today

here to,day, gone to'morrow
if sth is **here today, gone tomorrow**, it only exists or stays for a short time: *The restaurant staff don't tend to stay for very long—they're here today, gone tomorrow.*

toe

toe the 'line (*AmE also* **toe the 'mark**)
obey the orders and accept the ideas, aims and principles of a particular group or person: *The Prime Minister is angry because some members of the government are not toeing the line.*

from head to foot/toe ➔ **head**
from top to toe ➔ **top**

toes

keep sb on their 'toes (*informal*)
make sure that sb is ready to deal with anything that might happen by doing things that they are not expecting: *Regular surprise visits help to keep the staff on their toes.* ◊ *This job really keeps me on my toes.*

make sb's 'toes curl
make sb feel embarrassed or uncomfortable about sth: *After yesterday's embarrassing incident, she really didn't want to go to work. Just thinking about it was enough to make her toes curl.* ▶ **'toe-curling** *adj.*: *a toe-curling performance*

on your 'toes
ready to deal with anything that might happen: *We were all on our toes, waiting for the game to begin.*

,step/,tread on sb's 'toes (*informal*)
offend or annoy sb, especially by getting involved in sth that is their responsibility: *It's almost impossible to criticize the plan without treading on somebody's toes.*

toffee

can't do sth for 'toffee (*old-fashioned, BrE, informal*)
if sb **can't do sth for toffee**, they are very bad at doing it: *He can't dance for toffee!*

together

to'gether with
1 including: *Together with the Johnsons, there were 12 of us in the villa.*
2 in addition to; as well as: *I sent them my order, together with a cheque for £40.*

togged

be ˌtogged 'out/'up (in sth) (*informal*)
be wearing clothes for a particular activity or
occasion: *They were all togged up in their skiing
gear.*

toing

ˌtoing and 'froing
1 movement or travel backwards and forwards
between two or more places: *All this toing and froing between London and Paris is making him tired.*
2 a lot of unnecessary or repeated activity or discussion: *There's been a lot of toing and froing next
door today. I wonder what's happening.* ◇ *After a
great deal of toing and froing, I decided not to
change jobs after all.*

token

by the ˌsame 'token
for the same reasons: *The penalty for failure will be
high. But, by the same token, the rewards for success will be great.*

told

all 'told
(used with numbers) with everything/everyone
included: *So far there have been fourteen arrests all
told.*

I told you so = what did I tell you? → **tell**
if (the) truth be known/told → **truth**
a little bird told me (that …) → **little**

toll

take its 'toll (on sb/sth) (also **take a (heavy)
'toll (of sth)**)
have a bad effect on sb/sth; cause a lot of damage,
deaths, suffering, etc: *Smoking continues to take its
toll; it is killing more and more people each year.* ◇
*The present economic crisis is taking a heavy toll.
Thousands of firms have gone bankrupt.* ◇ *His job
is taking its toll on him. He needs a holiday.*

Tom

every/any Tom, Dick and/or 'Harry (*usually
disapproving*)
any ordinary person; people of no special value to
you: *We don't want just any Tom, Dick or Harry
marrying our daughter.*

a Peeping Tom → **Peeping**

tomorrow

do sth as if/like there's no to'morrow (*informal*)
do sth with a lot of energy, as if this is the last time
you will be able to do it: *She's spending money like
there's no tomorrow.*

here today, gone tomorrow → **today**
jam tomorrow → **jam**

ton

be/come down on sb like a ton of 'bricks
(*informal*)
criticize sb angrily because they have done sth
wrong: *The first time I made a mistake, he came
down on me like a ton of bricks.* ◇ *If I find anyone
drunk in this factory I'll be down on them like a ton
of bricks.*

weigh (half) a ton → **weigh**

tone

lower the tone (of sth) → **lower**
set the tone (of/for sth) → **set**

tongs

be/go at sb/sth hammer and tongs → **hammer**

tongue

get your 'tongue round/around sth
manage to say a difficult word correctly: *I sometimes find it difficult to get my tongue around the
word 'sixth'.*

roll/slip/trip off the 'tongue
be easy to say or pronounce: *It's not a name that
exactly trips off the tongue, is it?*

a silver/smooth tongue
the ability to talk in a very pleasing and polite way,
to make people do what you want: *It was his silver
tongue that got him the job.* ▶ **silver-tongued/
smooth-tongued** *adj.*: *smooth-tongued salesmen*

(with) tongue in 'cheek (also **with your tongue
in your 'cheek**)
if you say sth **with your tongue in your cheek**,
you are not being serious and mean it as a joke: *I
never know if Charlie's serious or if he's speaking
with tongue in cheek.* ◇ *a tongue-in-cheek remark*

be on the tip of your tongue → **tip**
bite your tongue → **bite**
(has) cat got your, his, etc. tongue? → **cat**
find your voice/tongue → **find**
have (got) a loose tongue → **loose**
have (got) a sharp tongue → **sharp**
hold your peace/tongue → **hold**
loosen sb's tongue → **loosen**
your mother tongue → **mother**
a slip of the tongue/pen → **slip**
watch your mouth/tongue → **watch**

tongues

tongues 'wag (*informal*)
there is a lot of talk about sb's private life, etc:
*Don't tell anyone your secret—you know how
tongues wag around here.*

set tongues wagging → **set**

tools

,down 'tools (BrE)
stop work, either at the end of the day or to go on strike: *The workers have threatened to down tools as a protest against the dismissals.*

the tools of the/your 'trade
the things you need to do your job: *We are proud to make David's boots, because they are the tools of his trade as a professional footballer.* ◇ *Ambulancemen now believe that helicopters are vital tools of the trade.*

toot

blow/toot your own horn = blow your own trumpet ➔ **blow**

tooth

fight tooth and nail for sb/sth ➔ **fight**
fight (sb/sth) tooth and nail ➔ **fight**
have (got) a sweet tooth ➔ **sweet**
(be) long in the tooth ➔ **long**
red in tooth and claw ➔ **red**

top

at the top of your 'voice
very loudly: *He was shouting at the top of his voice.*

be/get on 'top of sth
be able to manage and control problems and difficulties successfully: *I've finally got on top of my new job but it took a long time.*

be/go ,over the 'top (abbr. OTT) (informal, especially BrE)
behave in a wild, excited or extreme way; (of sth) be unnecessarily extreme: *She drank a bottle of champagne and danced on the table. She went completely over the top.* ◇ *His remarks were a bit over the top.*

come out on 'top (of sth)
become, etc. more successful than others: *It was a hard match but Sampras came out on top in the end.* ◇ *Our new model has come out on top in export markets this year.*

from ,top to 'bottom
completely and thoroughly: *We searched the house from top to bottom.*

from ,top to 'toe
from the head to the feet; completely: *He was all in green from top to toe.* ◇ *We were covered in mud from top to toe.*

get on 'top of sb
(of a problem, too much work, etc.) make sb feel very worried or depressed: *She's letting things get on top of her at work.*

off the ,top of your 'head (informal)
as a guess; without having time to think carefully: *Off the top of my head I'd say it would cost £1 000 to do the repairs.* ◇ *'What's the population of Liverpool?' 'I'm afraid I couldn't tell you off the top of my head.'*

on top of sb/sth
1 in addition to sth; also: *On top of his salary, he gets about £100 in commission every week.*
2 too close to sth/sb: *These houses are all built on top of one another.* ◇ *He was right on top of* (= driving very close behind) *the car in front.*

on ,top of the 'world
very happy or proud: *I'm on top of the world; I've just had a baby son.* ◇ *You'll feel on top of the world after a good holiday.*

pay, earn, charge, etc. top 'dollar
pay, earn, charge, etc. a lot of money: *If you want the best, you have to pay top dollar.* ◇ *We can help you get top dollar when you sell your house.*

,take it from the 'top (informal)
go back to the beginning of a song, piece of music, speech, etc. and repeat it: *OK, take it from the top, and no mistakes this time!*

to ,top/,cap/,crown it 'all (spoken)
used to introduce the final piece of information that is worse than the other bad things you have already mentioned: *We went to a horrible restaurant. The food was awful, the music was far too loud, and to top it all, the waiter was rude to us.*

,top and 'tail sth (BrE)
cut the top and bottom parts off fruit and vegetables to prepare them to be cooked or eaten: *There's no need to top and tail the gooseberries, just steam or bake them with sugar.*

(the) ,top 'brass (BrE, informal)
people with power and authority: *The top brass got a huge pay rise.*

,top 'dog (informal)
a person, group or country that is better or more powerful than all the others: *He's top dog in television drama now.*

(at) the top of the 'tree/'ladder
(at) the highest position in a career: *Anyone can get to the top of the ladder if they try hard enough.*

(be) ,top 'secret
used to describe very secret government information: *These defence plans are top secret, known only to a very few people.* ◇ *The file was marked TOP SECRET.*

the ,top 'ten, 'twenty, etc.
the ten, twenty, etc. best-selling pop records each week: *The song didn't even make* (= get into) *the top twenty.*

up 'top (BrE, informal)
used to talk about sb's intelligence: *He doesn't have much up top, I'm afraid.*

at the bottom/top of the pile/heap ➔ **bottom**
be/get thin on top ➔ **thin**
blow your top ➔ **blow**
head/top the bill ➔ **bill**
in the first/top flight ➔ **flight**
sleep like a log/top ➔ **sleep**

Topsy

grow like Topsy → grow

torch

put sth to the 'torch (*literary*)

set fire to sth deliberately: *The original castle was put to the torch in the 18th century, although it was rebuilt later.*

carry a torch for sb → carry

torn

that's 'torn it (*BrE, informal*)

used to say that sth has happened to spoil your plans: *'Oops, that's torn it,' she thought, as she realized she'd ruined the surprise.*

toss

not give a 'toss (about sb/sth) (*BrE, slang*)

not care at all about sb/sth: *I don't give a toss what he thinks!*

toss a 'coin; 'toss for sth (*especially BrE*)

throw a coin in the air in order to decide sth: *Right, who's going to wash the dishes tonight? Shall we toss a coin?*

> **❷ NOTE**
> Before the coin is thrown, one person chooses either 'heads' (= the side of the coin marked with a head) or 'tails' (= the other side). If the side chosen lands upwards this person wins the toss and the other person loses the toss.

argue the toss → argue

toss-up

be a 'toss-up (between A and B) (*informal, especially BrE*)

be a situation in which either of two choices, results, etc. is equally possible: *'Have you decided on the colour yet?' 'It's a toss-up between the blue and the green.'*

> **❶ ORIGIN**
> This expression refers to tossing a coin in order to make a decision about something.

touch

be, etc. in/out of 'touch (with sth)

have/not have recent knowledge or news of sth, and so fully/not fully understand it: *I try to keep in touch with what's happening by reading the newspapers.* ◇ *Our politicians are old and out of touch* (= unaware of people's real feelings).

be, keep, etc. in touch (with sb)

communicate with sb regularly: *We are in touch with our central office every day.* ◇ *I've stayed in touch with some of my university friends.*

be out of 'touch (with sb)

no longer communicate with sb, so that you no longer know what is happening to them: *Now my husband and I are divorced, people assume we're out of touch, but we're not. We see each other quite regularly.*

get in 'touch with sb/sth

make contact with sb/sth (by phone, letter, visit, etc.): *Here's my phone number in case you need to get in touch with me.*

have, etc. a ˌtouch of 'class

have, etc. quality, in design, character, etc: *His clothes are old and unfashionable, but nevertheless he has a real touch of class.*

not touch sb/sth with a 'bargepole (*BrE*) (*AmE* **not touch sb/sth with a ten-foot 'pole**) (*informal*)

refuse to get involved with sb/sth or in a particular situation: *I don't know why she's marrying that man. I wouldn't touch him with a bargepole.* ◇ *I wouldn't touch the job with a ten-foot pole.*

put sb in 'touch with sb/sth

arrange for sb to contact, meet, etc. a person or an organization that you already know: *He put me in touch with the British Council in Paris.*

a soft/an easy 'touch (*informal*)

a kind and perhaps easily deceived person whom people ask for money, help, etc: *Ask Tony to lend you some money. He's a soft touch.*

touch 'base (with sb) (*informal*)

make contact with sb again: *Mark hasn't touched base with his cousins since they were all together at a family wedding three years ago.*

touch 'bottom

1 reach the ground at the bottom of an area of water

2 (*BrE*) reach the worst possible state or condition: *Her career really touched bottom with that movie.*

touch 'wood (*BrE*) (*AmE* **knock on 'wood**) (*saying*)

used for expressing the hope that your good luck will continue: *We haven't had a serious accident yet, touch wood.*

> **❶ ORIGIN**
> In the past, trees were believed to contain guardian spirits and people touched the tree to show respect. People still touch something that is made of wood when they use this expression.

catch/touch sb on the raw → raw
the common touch → common
the finishing touch(es) → finishing
hit/touch a (raw) nerve → nerve
a light touch → light
lose your touch → lose
lose touch/contact (with sb/sth) → lose
(have) a/the magic touch → magic
(have) the Midas touch → Midas
not harm/touch a hair of sb's head → hair
strike/touch a chord (with sb) → chord
touch/tug your forelock → forelock

touch-and-go

be ˌtouch-and-ˈgo (whether …) (*informal*)
be very uncertain whether sth will happen or not;
be risky: *It was a very dangerous operation. It was
touch-and-go several times.* ◇ *It was touch-and-go
whether the work would be finished in time.*

❶ ORIGIN
This idiom possibly refers to a ship sailing in
shallow water. The bottom of the ship might
touch the sea bed, but the damage might only be
small and the ship would be able to go on with
the voyage.

touched

be touched with sth
have a small amount of a particular quality: *His
hair was touched with grey.* ◇ *Some of her poems
are touched with real genius.*

tough

be/get ˈtough (on/with sb)
be strict with sb whose behaviour you do not like;
be ready to punish sb: *It's time to get tough with
football hooligans.* ◇ *be tough on crime*

(as) tough as ˈnails (*informal*)
1 very strong and able to deal successfully with
difficult conditions or situations: *She's almost 90
but she's still as tough as nails.*
2 not feeling or showing any emotion

(as) tough as old ˈboots (*informal*)
1 (of food) be very tough and difficult to chew:
This steak's as tough as old boots.
2 very strong and able to bear pain, criticism, etc.
without complaining or giving up: *Don't worry,
she'll soon recover. She's tough as old boots.*

a tough ˈcustomer/ˈcookie (*informal*)
a person who knows what they want and is not easily influenced by other people: *Self-confident,
ambitious and positive, Paula is a tough cookie who
is bound to do well.*

a ˈtough guy (*informal*)
a strong, independent-minded person who seems
to be afraid of nothing: *The most famous 'tough
guy' in American films was John Wayne.*

tough ˈlove
treating sb in a harsh way in order to help them
improve their situation or change the way they
behave: *She believes in 'tough love' for dealing with
disruptive youngsters.*

**when the ˌgoing gets ˈtough (the ˌtough get
ˈgoing)** (*saying*)
when conditions or progress become difficult
(strong and determined people work even harder
to succeed): *I know it's going to be hard work, but
you can always call me when the going gets tough.*

hang tough → hang
a hard/tough act to follow → act
a hard/tough nut (to crack) → nut

talk tough (on sth) → talk
tough shit = tough/bad luck → luck

tour

a tour de ˈforce (*from French*)
an extremely skilful performance or achievement:
a literary/cinematic tour de force

a whistle-stop tour → whistle-stop

tow

in ˈtow (*informal*)
following closely behind; with you: *Mrs Bridge
arrived with her four children in tow.*

towel

throw in the towel/sponge → throw

tower

an ivory tower → ivory
a pillar/tower of strength → strength

town

(out) on the ˈtown (also **a night (out) on the
ˈtown/on the ˈtiles**) (*informal*)
visiting restaurants, clubs, theatres, etc. for entertainment (especially at night): *For a birthday treat
they took him out on the town.* ◇ *The students went
for a night on the tiles after the last exam.*

go to ˈtown (on/over sth) (*informal*)
put a lot of money, energy, etc. into sth: *When they
give parties they really go to town* (= spend a lot of
money, invite a lot of people, etc.). ◇ *She decided to
go to town and redecorate all the rooms in the house.*

a/the man about town → man
a one-horse town → one-horse
paint the town red → paint

trace

sink, vanish, etc. without (a) ˈtrace
disappear completely: *The boat sank without trace.*
◇ *Many pop stars sink without a trace. After five
years no one can even remember their names.*

traces

kick over the traces → kick

track

ˌback on ˈtrack
going in the right direction again after a mistake,
failure, etc: *I tried to get my life back on track after
my divorce.*

be on the right/wrong ˈtrack
be thinking or acting in the right/wrong way to
find the answer to a problem: *We haven't found a
solution to the problem yet, but I think we're on the
right track.* ◇ *You're on the wrong track, I'm
afraid. The information you want isn't here.*

be on 'track
be doing the right thing in order to achieve a particular result: *Curtis is on track for the gold medal.*

keep/lose 'track (of sb/sth)
stay/not stay informed about sb/sth; remember/forget about the number of sth, the time, etc: *It's hard to keep track of how much money we spend every month.* ◊ *I've lost track of the number of times I've lost my keys.*

a ,track 'record
all a person's or an organization's successes or failures in the past: *In business your track record is more important than your qualifications.*

off the beaten track → **beaten**

tracks

make 'tracks (for sth) (*spoken*)
leave one place to go to another: *It's getting late; I think we'd better make tracks.*

stop/halt sb in their 'tracks; stop/halt/ freeze in your 'tracks
suddenly make sb stop by frightening or surprising them; suddenly stop because sth has frightened or surprised you: *The question stopped Alice in her tracks.* ◊ *The horse* **stopped dead** *in its tracks and refused to move.*

cover your tracks → **cover**
from/on the wrong side of the tracks → **wrong**
hot on sb's/sth's tracks/trail → **hot**

trade

a ,trade 'secret
1 a secret about a particular company's method of production: *The ingredients of Coca-Cola are a trade secret.*
2 (*humorous*) a secret about how you make or do sth: *'Can I have a recipe for this cake?' 'No, you can't. It's a trade secret.'*

do a roaring trade (in sth) → **roaring**
ply for hire/trade/business → **ply**
ply your trade → **ply**
the rag trade → **rag**
the tools of the/your trade → **tools**
the tricks of the trade → **tricks**

trades

a jack of all trades → **jack**

trail

blaze a/the trail → **blaze**
hit the trail → **hit**
hot on sb's/sth's tracks/trail → **hot**

train

bring sth in its 'train (*written*)
have sth as a result: *Unemployment brings great difficulties in its train.*

in sb's 'train (*written*)
following behind sb: *In the train of the rich and famous came the journalists.*

in 'train (*formal*)
being prepared; happening: *The plans for the Queen's birthday celebrations are all in train.* ◊ *Changes to the law have been set in train.*

a train of 'thought
the connected series of thoughts that are in your head at a particular time: *The phone ringing interrupted my train of thought.*

the gravy train → **gravy**

transports

(be) in transports of joy, delight, etc. (*literary*)
(be) feeling very great joy, etc: *They were in transports of delight at the news.*

trap

fall into/avoid the trap of doing sth
do/avoid doing sth that is a mistake but which seems at first to be a good idea: *Parents sometimes fall into the trap of trying to do everything for their children.*

keep your mouth/trap shut = shut your mouth/trap/face/ gob! → **shut**
spring a trap → **spring**

travel

travel 'light
travel with very little luggage: *We're travelling light with one small bag each.*

tread

,tread the 'boards (*humorous*)
be an actor: *He has recently been treading the boards in a new play at the National.*

tread 'carefully, 'warily, etc.
be very careful about what you do or say: *The government will have to tread very carefully in handling this issue.*

tread a difficult, solitary, etc. 'path
choose and follow a particular way of life, way of doing sth, etc: *A restaurant has to tread the tricky path between maintaining quality and keeping prices down.*

,tread on sb's 'heels
follow sb closely: *In the end she left the meeting room, with her assistant treading hard on her heels.*

,tread 'water
1 keep yourself upright in deep water by moving your arms and legs
2 make no progress while you are waiting for sth to happen: *For the past year I've been treading water, in a boring job with no hope of promotion.*

step/tread on sb's toes → **toes**
tread/walk a fine/thin line → **line**
tread/walk a tightrope → **tightrope**

treat

go down a 'treat (*BrE*, *informal*)
be very successful or enjoyable: *'Did the children like the story?' 'Yes, it went down a treat.'* ◇ *Mm! ice cream. That'll go down a treat.*

treat sb like 'dirt (*informal*)
treat sb very badly and without respect: *He treated his wife like dirt. She finally left him after ten terrible years.*

trick or treat → **trick**
work a treat → **work**

treatment

give sb/get the silent treatment → **silent**

tree

be out of your 'tree (*BrE* also **be out of your 'box**) (*informal*)
crazy or strange; behaving in a crazy or stupid way, perhaps because of drugs or alcohol: *She must be out of her tree, going swimming in this weather.*

be barking up the wrong tree → **barking**
(at) the top of the tree/ladder → **top**
up a gum tree → **gum**

trees

money doesn't grow on trees → **money**
not see the forest for the trees → **see**
not see the wood for the trees → **see**

trembling

in fear and trembling (of sb/sth) → **fear**

trial

by ˌtrial and 'error
trying different ways of doing sth until you find the right one: *I didn't know how to use the camera at first, so I had to learn by trial and error.*

a ˌtrial 'run
a first try at doing sth, to test it or for practice: *Take the car for a trial run before you buy it.*

trials

ˌtrials and tribuˈlations
difficulties and troubles: *The film is about the trials and tribulations of adolescence.*

tribulations

trials and tribulations → **trials**

tribute

pay tribute to sb/sth → **pay**

trice

in a 'trice
very quickly or suddenly: *He was gone in a trice.*

trick

ˌtrick or 'treat
said by children who visit people's houses at Halloween (= October 31) and threaten to play tricks on people who do not give them sweets/candy

try, use, etc. every trick in the 'book
try any method you know to get sth or get sb to do sth you want: *He'll use every trick in the book to try and stop you.*

do the job/trick → **job**
have (got) an ace/a trick up your sleeve → **sleeve**
he, she, etc. doesn't miss a trick → **miss**
turn a trick/tricks → **turn**

tricks

a bag/box of 'tricks (*informal*)
a set of methods or equipment that sb can use: *Hotel managers are using a whole new bag of tricks to attract their guests.*

be up to your (old) 'tricks (*informal*, *disapproving*)
be acting in your usual way, which the speaker does not like: *Tom's up to his old tricks again. He's having an affair with his secretary.*

how's 'tricks? (*old-fashioned*, *informal*)
used as a friendly greeting

the ˌtricks of the 'trade
the clever or expert ways of doing things, especially used by people in their jobs: *She's only been here a couple of months, so she's still learning the tricks of the trade.*

(you can't) teach an old dog new tricks → **teach**
turn a trick/tricks → **turn**

tried

ˌtried and 'tested/'trusted (*BrE*) (*AmE* ˌtried and 'true**)
that you have used or relied on in the past successfully: *We'll be using a tried and tested technique to solve the problem.*

trim

be, keep, etc. in 'trim (*BrE*, *informal*)
be, remain, etc. fit and healthy: *For a man of his age he keeps in good trim.*

ˌtrim your 'sails
1 arrange the sails of a boat to suit the wind so that the boat moves faster
2 reduce your costs: *Increasingly, businesses are having to trim their sails in order to survive.*

trip

a guilt trip → **guilt**
roll/slip/trip off the tongue → **tongue**
take a trip down memory lane = take sb/go down memory lane → **memory**

Trojan

work like a dog/slave/Trojan → work

trolley

off your 'trolley (*BrE, informal*)
crazy; stupid: *He's completely off his trolley!*

trooper

swear like a trooper → swear

trot

on the 'trot (*BrE, informal*)
one after the other: *The bus has been late for five days on the trot.*

trouble

get sb into 'trouble (*old-fashioned*)
make a woman who is not married pregnant

give (sb) (some, no, any, etc.) 'trouble
cause problems or difficulties: *My back's been giving me a lot of trouble lately.* ◇ *The children didn't give me any trouble at all when we were out.*

take trouble over/with sth; take trouble doing/to do sth (also **go to the trouble/a lot of trouble to do sth**)
use a lot of time, care and effort in doing sth: *She takes a lot of trouble with her writing, which is why it's so good.* ◇ *I went to a lot of trouble to find a nice birthday present, but he doesn't like it.* ◇ *I don't want you to go to too much trouble.*

there's trouble brewing (*informal*)
a difficult situation is starting to develop: *There's trouble brewing in the car industry.*

a trouble 'shared is a trouble 'halved (*saying*)
if you talk to sb about your problems and worries, instead of keeping them to yourself, they seem less serious: *You really should tell someone how you feel. After all, a trouble shared is a trouble halved.*

ask for trouble/it → ask
look for trouble → look
spare no expense/pains/trouble (to do sth/(in) doing sth) → spare
that's just the trouble = that's just it → just

troubled

pour oil on troubled waters → pour

troubles

have, etc. teething problems/troubles → teething

trousers

be all mouth and (no) trousers → mouth
catch sb with their trousers down → catch
wear the trousers → wear

truant

play truant → play

truck

have/want no 'truck with sb/sth (*BrE*)
not want to deal with or be involved with sb/sth: *He'll have no truck with anyone on the political left.*

true

come 'true
(of a hope, wish, etc.) really happen: *What the fortune teller said about your future really came true.* ◇ *Winning the medal was like a **dream come true**.*

out of 'true
if an object is **out of true**, it is not straight or in the correct position: *That picture's out of true. Can you straighten it up?*

so ,bad, ,stupid, etc. it isn't 'true (*informal*)
used to emphasize that sb/sth is very bad, stupid, etc: *His brother is so lazy it isn't true!*

too ,good to be 'true
used to say that you cannot believe that sth is as good as it seems: *'I'm afraid you were quoted the wrong price.' 'I thought it was too good to be true.'*

your, his, etc. true 'colours (*BrE*) (*AmE your, his, etc. true 'colors*) (*often disapproving*)
what a person is really like: *Once he got into power he showed his true colours.*

(happen, go, etc.) true to 'form
(happen, etc.) in the usual or typical way or as you expect: *True to form, he arrived early.* ◇ *The meeting went true to form, with a lot of boring speeches.*

true to 'life
(of a book, film/movie, etc.) seeming real rather than invented: *I don't think the characters are very true to life.*

hold good/true → hold
ring true/false/hollow → ring
too right/true → right
tried and true → tried

truly

yours 'truly
1 (*informal, often humorous*) I/me: *Steve came first, Robin second, and yours truly came last.* ◇ *And of course, all the sandwiches will be made by yours truly.*
2 (**Yours Truly**) (*AmE, formal, written*) used at the end of a formal letter before you sign your name

well and truly → well

trump

a/your 'trump card
sth that gives you an advantage over other people, especially when they do not know what it is and you are able to use it to surprise them: *Many schools use small classes as their trump card in marketing campaigns.* ◇ *He waited until the last*

minute to play his trump card and tell them about his plans to cut costs.

> ❶ NOTE
> In some card games, one of the four suits is chosen to have a higher value than the others. The cards in that suit are *trump cards*.

trumpet

blow your own trumpet → **blow**

trumps

,come/,turn up 'trumps (*informal*)
1 be very helpful or generous to sb who has a problem: *I asked a lot of people if they could lend me the money, but finally it was my sister who came up trumps.*
2 do better than expected: *On the day of the match the team turned up trumps* (= won the game).

trust

in sb's 'trust; in the trust of 'sb
being looked after by sb: *The family pet was left in the trust of a neighbour.*

not trust sb an·'inch
not trust sb at all: *He says he just wants to help you but I wouldn't trust him an inch if I were you.*

take sth on 'trust
believe what sb says even though you do not have any proof or evidence to show that it is true: *I took it on trust that the painting was genuine. I had no reason to believe he would try to deceive me.*

trust 'you, 'him, 'her, etc. (to do sth) (*spoken, informal*)
used when sb does or says sth that you think is typical of them: *Trust you to forget my birthday!* ◇ *Trust it to rain at the weekend!*

trusted

tried and tested/trusted → **tried**

truth

if (the) ,truth be 'known/'told
used to tell sb the true facts about a situation, especially when these are not known by other people: *None of the students really liked the new teacher. In fact, if the truth be told, everyone was rather afraid of him.*

in 'truth (*written*)
used to emphasize the true facts about a situation: *She laughed and chatted but was, in truth, not having much fun.*

,truth is stranger than 'fiction (*saying*)
used to say that things that actually happen are often more surprising than stories that are invented

(the) ,truth will 'out (*saying*)
the truth about sth cannot be hidden for ever

bend the truth → **bend**

economical with the truth → **economical**
the fact/truth of the matter → **matter**
a home truth → **home**
the moment of truth → **moment**
the naked truth → **naked**
to tell (you) the truth → **tell**

try

try your 'hand (at sth/doing sth)
try sth for the first time, for example a skill or a sport: *I've always wanted to try my hand at painting.*

,try it 'on (with sb) (*BrE, informal*)
do sth that you know is wrong, in order to see if sb will accept this behaviour or not: *The price he asked was far too much. I think he was just trying it on.* ◇ *Don't try it on with me, pal, or you'll be sorry.*

try your 'luck (at sth)
try to do or get sth, hoping you will succeed: *A friend told me the job was available, so I thought I'd try my luck.*

try sb's 'patience
make sb feel impatient: *Jim's constant complaining was really beginning to try her patience.*

do/try your damnedest → **damnedest**
do/try your level best (to do sth) → **level**
do/try your utmost (to do sth) → **utmost**
these things are sent to try us → **things**

trying

not for lack/want of 'trying
used to say that although sb has not succeeded in sth, they have tried very hard: *He's had no success in finding a job, though not for lack of trying.*

like looking for/trying to find a needle in a haystack → **needle**

tube

go down the 'tube/'tubes (*informal*)
(of a plan, company, situation, etc.) fail: *The education system is going down the tubes.*

tuck

nip and tuck (with sb/sth) = neck and neck (with sb/sth) → **neck**

tucker

your best bib and tucker → **best**

tug

tug at sb's 'heartstrings
make sb feel strong emotions of sadness and pity: *These photographs of starving puppies are designed to tug at your heartstrings.*

touch/tug your forelock → **forelock**

tumble

rough and tumble → **rough**

tune

be ˌin/ˌout of 'tune (with sb/sth)
1 be on/not on the right musical note: *They were both singing out of tune.*
2 be in/not in agreement with sb/sth; be/not be happy or comfortable with sb/sth: *He's out of tune with modern ideas about education.* ◊ *I don't like London—I just don't feel in tune with city life.*

to the tune of £500, etc. (*informal*)
used to emphasize how much money sth has cost: *We're paying rent to the tune of £200 a week.*

call the shots/the tune ➜ **call**
change your tune ➜ **change**
dance to sb's tune ➜ **dance**
he who pays the piper calls the tune ➜ **pays**
sing a different song/tune ➜ **sing**

tunnel

(have) ˌtunnel 'vision (*disapproving*)
(have) an interest in only one small part of sth instead of the whole of it: *He's got tunnel vision about music. He thinks only the classics are worth listening to.*

(see the) light at the end of the tunnel ➜ **light**

tuppence

not care/give 'tuppence for/about sb/sth
(*old-fashioned, BrE, informal*)
think sb/sth is not important; not care about sb/sth: *She loves him, but he doesn't care tuppence for her.* ◊ *The police don't give tuppence for our rights.*

❷ NOTE
Tuppence is an old word meaning 'two pence'.

turf

a turf 'war (*informal*)
an argument or dispute about who owns or controls an area: *Turf wars are inevitable when two departments are merged.* ◊ *Street violence has escalated as a result of a turf war between rival neighbourhood gangs.*

❷ NOTE
In informal language, your *turf* is the place where you live and/or work, especially when you think of it as your own.

turkey

cold turkey ➜ **cold**
talk turkey ➜ **talk**

turn

at every 'turn
everywhere or every time you try to do sth: *I keep meeting her at every turn.* ◊ *My plans always seem to go wrong at every turn.*

by 'turn(s)
used when talking of contrasting feelings or actions which follow each other: *He looked sur-*
prised, worried and angry by turn. ◊ *When they told me I had got the job in New York, I felt by turns excited and anxious.*

do sb a good 'turn
be helpful to sb; do sb a favour: *She's done the family a lot of good turns in the past.* ◊ *I did you a good turn, now you do me one.*

do sth out of 'turn
1 do sth when you have no right to do it because another person should have done it before you; not in the correct order: *There was an argument in the doctor's waiting room because somebody had gone in to see him out of turn.*
2 say or do sth that you should not say because you have no right to or because it's not the right time or place to say it: *It is not the first time that Julia has said something out of turn.* ◊ *I apologize if I've spoken out of turn.*

give sb a 'turn (*old-fashioned*)
frighten or shock sb: *You gave me quite a turn, creeping up on me like that!*

in 'turn
1 one after another: *The teacher spoke to all of us in turn.*
2 as a result of sth in a series of events: *Increased production will, in turn, lead to higher profits.* ◊ *She was very angry with me and I in turn was very upset.*

not turn a 'hair
not show strong emotion like fear, surprise or excitement, when others expect you to: *He didn't turn a hair when the judge gave him a 20-year prison sentence.*

on the 'turn (*especially BrE*)
going to change soon: *That's the third time they've won this season. I think their luck is on the turn.*

one good ˌturn deserves a'nother (*saying*)
if sb helps you with sth, you should help them in return

a practical, ˌscientific, etc. turn of 'mind
a practical, scientific, etc. way of thinking about things: *He's got a very practical turn of mind. He can fix anything.*

take a ˌturn for the 'better/'worse
become better/worse: *The weather is taking a turn for the worse, I'm afraid.*

turn and turn a'bout (*old-fashioned*)
(of two people) (do sth) one after the other repeatedly: *'Who drove to Germany?' 'We did the driving turn and turn about.'*

turn your 'back on sb/sth
refuse to help or support sb who needs it: *She turned her back on her family when she became famous.*

turn a blind 'eye (to sth)
pretend not to see sth or know about sth: *There's so much suffering in the world, you can't just turn a blind eye to it.* ◊ *The police here turn a blind eye to a*

lot of drug taking; they're really only interested in the big drug dealers.

turn the 'corner
pass the most dangerous point of an illness or the most difficult part of sth, and begin to improve: *Now that we're beginning to pay back the money we owe, I feel we've turned the corner.* ◇ *The doctors say she's turned the corner now. She should be out of hospital soon.*

turn a deaf 'ear (to sth)
refuse to listen (to sth); ignore sth: *She turned a deaf ear to her husband's advice and ordered another large whisky.*

turn your 'hand to sth
start doing sth or be able to do sth, especially when you do it well: *Jim can turn his hand to most jobs around the house.*

turn sb's 'head
(of success, praise, etc.) make a person feel too proud in a way that other people find annoying: *You'd better stop giving me all these compliments, or you'll turn my head!*

turn in his, her, etc. 'grave (BrE) (AmE roll in his, her, etc. 'grave)
(of a person who is dead) likely to be very shocked or angry: *Beethoven would turn in his grave if he could hear the way they're playing his music.*

turn sth ,inside 'out/,upside 'down
1 make a place very untidy when you are searching for sth: *I've turned this drawer inside out but I can't find my passport.* ◇ *The thieves turned the office upside down but they didn't find anything valuable.*
2 cause large changes: *The new manager turned the old systems inside out.*

turn King's/Queen's 'evidence (BrE) (AmE turn State's 'evidence)
give information against other criminals in order to get a less severe punishment: *One of the gang turned State's evidence and identified at least three others involved in the fraud.*

turn your 'nose up at sth (informal)
refuse or reject sth because you do not think it is good enough for you: *The cat turned up his nose at the food.*

a/the ,turn of e'vents
the way things happen, especially when this is not expected: *Because of a strange turn of events at work, she has unexpectedly been offered a very good job in the sales department.*

a ,turn of 'phrase
a particular way of saying sth or describing sth: *She has a very amusing turn of phrase.*

a ,turn of the 'screw
another problem or difficulty added to a situation which is already very bad: *In this recession a rise in interest rates is just another turn of the screw for businesses.*

a ,turn of 'speed
a sudden increase in speed: *She put on a turn of speed at the end of the race and won easily.*

the ,turn of the 'year/'century
the time when a new year/century starts: *He was born around the turn of the century.*

turn on the 'heat (informal)
put increased pressure on sb in order to make them do sth: *If he doesn't pay us we'll have to turn on the heat.*

turn on the 'waterworks (informal, disapproving)
start crying, especially in order to get sympathy or attention: *You can turn off the waterworks for a start, as that won't make me change my mind.*

turn the other 'cheek
make a deliberate decision to remain calm and not to act in an aggressive way when sb has hurt you or made you angry: *It's hard to just turn the other cheek when people are criticizing you unfairly.*

ⓘ ORIGIN
This is a phrase used by Jesus in the Bible.

turn sth over in your 'mind
think about sth, for example an offer, a plan, etc., very carefully before you make a decision: *I've been turning over the job offer in my mind all weekend. I really don't know what to do.*

turn over a new 'leaf
change your way of behaving and start a better life: *This is a new project to help ex-prisoners turn over a new leaf.*

turn round/around and do sth (informal)
say or do sth unexpected and unfair: *He just turned round and told her that he was leaving. She couldn't believe it.*

turn sb's 'stomach; make sb's 'stomach turn
make sb feel sick or disgusted: *The thought of eating a raw egg turns my stomach.*

turn swords into 'ploughshares (literary)
stop fighting and return to peaceful activities: *The government has agreed to decommission some of their nuclear weapons in an attempt to turn swords into ploughshares.*

turn the 'tables (on sb)
do sth which means that you now have an advantage over sb who previously had an advantage over you: *They beat us 3-0 last year, but we turned the tables on them this year—we won 5-0.*

ⓘ ORIGIN
This idiom possibly originates from the time when furniture had more than one use. A table might have a polished surface to impress neighbours and friends, but when meal time came the surface was turned over to reveal an unpolished surface underneath.

turn 'tail (and run, flee, etc.)
run away from a fight or a dangerous situation: *As soon as he saw the police he turned tail and fled.*

turn sth to your (own) ad'vantage

use or change a bad situation so that it helps you: *She had three empty rooms in the house after her children left home, so she decided to turn this to her advantage and rent them out to students.*

,turn a 'trick/'tricks (*AmE, slang*)

have sex with sb for money: *Things got so bad for her financially that she even considered turning tricks to pay the rent.*

turn 'turtle

(of a boat) turn upside down: *We turned turtle right in front of the yacht club. It was so embarrassing.*

turn up like a bad 'penny (*informal*)

appear when you are not welcome or not wanted, especially when this happens regularly: *He turns up like a bad penny every time there's a chance of a free meal or a drink.*

come/turn up trumps → trumps
done to a turn → done
get/turn nasty → nasty
go/turn sour → sour
not do a hand's turn → hand
not know which way/where to turn → know
put/turn the clock back → clock
put/set/turn your mind to sth → mind
put/turn/send sb out to grass → grass
put/turn sth to good account → account
serve his, its, etc. turn → serve
stand/turn sth on its head → head
turn/twist the knife (in the wound) → knife
turn/spin on your heel → heel
turn to jelly = be/feel like jelly → jelly

turned

as it/things turned 'out

as later events showed: *I didn't need my umbrella as it turned out* (= because it didn't rain later).

be well, badly, etc. turned 'out

be well, badly, etc. dressed: *Her children are always smartly turned out.*

poacher turned gamekeeper → poacher
the wheel has come/turned full circle → wheel

turns

take 'turns doing sth/to do sth (*BrE* also **take it in 'turns to do sth**)

do sth one person after another: *My wife and I take it in turns to write to our daughter in Canada.* ◇ *There weren't enough computers for everybody, so we had to take turns using them.*

the tide turns → tide
the worm turns → worm

turn-up

a ,turn-up for the 'book(s) (*BrE, informal*)

an unusual or unexpected event: *Everyone thought John would win, so when Richard won it was a real turn-up for the books.*

turtle

turn turtle → turn

twain

never the ,twain shall 'meet (*saying*)

used to say that two things are so different that they cannot exist together: *People in the area where I grew up were either landowners or farmers, and never the twain shall meet.*

> ❷ NOTE
> *Twain* is an old word meaning 'two'.

twice

be 'twice the man/woman (that sb is)

be much better, stronger, healthier, etc. than sb or than before: *How dare you criticize him? He's twice the man that you are!* ◇ *I saw him today for the first time since his operation. He's twice the man he was.*

twice 'over

not just once but twice: *There was enough of the drug in her stomach to kill her twice over.*

cheap at twice the price → cheap
lightning never strikes twice (in the same place) → lightning
once bitten, twice shy → once
once or twice → once
(not) think twice about sth/doing sth → think

twiddle

,twiddle your 'thumbs (*informal*)

do nothing while you are waiting for sth to happen: *I had to sit at home twiddling my thumbs, waiting for the phone to ring.*

twinkling

(do sth) in the ,twinkling of an 'eye

(do sth) very quickly: *Her mood can change in the twinkling of an eye.*

twist

,twist sb's 'arm (*informal, often humorous*)

force or persuade sb to do sth, but not by using physical force: *'Do you think Jane will lend us her car?' 'I think we could probably twist her arm.'* ◇ *'Have another drink, Mike.' 'OK, if you twist my arm.'*

'Oh, go on then. You've twisted my arm.'

get/have your knickers in a twist → **knickers**
(drive sb/be/go) round the bend/twist → **bend**
turn/twist the knife (in the wound) → **knife**
twist/wind/wrap sb around/round your little finger → **little**

'twixt

there's many a slip 'twixt cup and lip → **slip**

two

be in two 'minds about sth/doing sth (*BrE*)
(*AmE* **be of two 'minds about sth/doing sth**)
be unable to decide about sth: *I was in two minds
about leaving London; my friends were there, but at
the same time I really wanted to work abroad.*

a 'day, 'moment, 'pound, etc. or two
one or a few days, moments, pounds, etc: *May I borrow it for a day or two?*

for two 'pins (*old-fashioned, BrE*)
used to say that you would like to do sth, even
though you know that it would not be sensible: *I
spend so much money on this car. For two pins I'd
sell it.* ◇ *I'd punch him for two pins.*

have (got) two left 'feet (*informal*)
be very awkward in your movements, especially
when you are dancing or playing a sport: *I'm a
hopeless dancer. I've got two left feet.*

in two 'shakes; in a couple of 'shakes (also **in
two shakes of a lamb's tail**, *old-fashioned*)
(*informal*)
very soon: *I've just got to make a phone call. I'll be
with you in two shakes.*

it takes 'two (to do sth) (also **it takes two to
'tango**) (*saying*)
used to say that sth cannot be the fault or responsibility of one person alone: *You've only heard his
side of the story. It takes two to have an argument,
you know.* ◇ *The company is ready to sign the agreement now, but it takes two to tango and the negotiations may continue for several days yet.*

(there are) no two ways a'bout it (*informal*)
used for saying that there is only one possible way
to consider a particular situation or fact: *There are
no two ways about it—these sales figures are terrible!*

**not have two brain cells, pennies, etc. to
rub to'gether** (*BrE, informal*)
be very stupid, have no money, etc: *How can they
afford a holiday? They haven't got two pennies to
rub together.*

‚one or 'two
a few: *We've had one or two problems—nothing serious, though.*

put ‚two and ‚two to'gether
guess the truth from what you see, hear, etc: *Sue's
car is often outside his house, but only when his wife
is at work, so it's not difficult to put two and two
together.* ◇ *He's inclined to **put two and two
together and make five** (= make an incorrect
guess from what he sees, hears, etc.).*

put/stick two 'fingers up at sb (*BrE, informal*)
form the shape of a V with the two fingers nearest
your thumb and raise your hand in the air with the
back part of it facing sb, done to be rude to them or
to show them that you are angry: *He must have
been furious—he stuck two fingers up at them and
walked out of the room.*

that makes 'two of us (*informal*)
I agree with your opinion; I am in the same situation: *'I think he's behaving very badly.' 'That
makes two of us.'* ◇ *'I'm bored with this job.' 'That
makes two of us.'*

‚two can play at 'that game (*saying*)
used when you threaten to behave as badly, etc. as
sb has just behaved towards you: *'He told the boss
that you were going home early every day.' 'Oh did
he? Well, two can play at that game. I think I'll tell
the boss about him coming in late every morning.'*

two heads are better than 'one (*saying*)
two people who are trying to solve a problem
together achieve more than one person who works
alone

two ‚sides of the same 'coin
used to talk about two ways of looking at the same
situation: *According to some people, great opportunity and great danger are two sides of the same
coin.*

two ‚wrongs don't make a 'right (*saying*)
used for saying that it is wrong or useless to harm
sb because they have harmed you: *Don't be stupid!
You want to hurt him just because he hurt you! Two
wrongs don't make a right, you know.*

two's 'company (, three's a crowd) (*saying*)
two people, especially two lovers, are happier
alone than within a group of three: *'Do you want to
come with us?' 'I don't think so. Two's company …'*

be like a dog with two tails → **dog**
a bird in the hand is worth two in the bush → **bird**
can/could teach/tell sb a thing or two (about sb/sth)
  → **thing**
cut both/two ways → **cut**
fall between two stools → **fall**
kill two birds with one stone → **kill**
know a thing or two (about sb/sth) → **know**
the lesser of two evils → **lesser**
not care two hoots (about sb/sth) = not care/give a hoot
  (about sb/sth) → **hoot**
your/sb's number two → **number**
one step forward, two steps back → **step**
stand on your own two feet → **stand**
(as) thick as two short planks → **thick**
two/ten a penny → **penny**
two sandwiches short of a picnic = a brick short of a load
  → **brick**

two-shoes

a goody two-shoes = a goody-goody → **goody-goody**

type

(not) be sb's 'type (*informal*)
(not) be the kind of person that sb likes: *Mark isn't really her type—she prefers quiet, sensitive men.* ◇ *Gerry is more my type.*

revert to type → **revert**

tyre (*BrE*) (*AmE* **tire**)

a spare tyre → **spare**

U u

ugly

an ˌugly ˈduckling (*informal*)
a person or thing that at first does not seem attractive or likely to succeed but that later becomes successful or much admired: *He's got the looks of a film star now, but he was a real ugly duckling as a child.*

❶ ORIGIN
This comes from a children's story by Hans Christian Andersen, in which a young swan is raised with ducklings. They have to stop teasing him about his ugliness when he grows into a beautiful swan.

(as) miserable/ugly as sin → sin

um

ˌum and ˈaah (about sth) (also ˌhum/ˌhem and ˈhaw, *less frequent*) (*informal*)
speak but say nothing important because you need more time to think about a problem, matter, etc: *He ummed and aahed for about half an hour and then finally said he would lend me the money.* ◇ *After a lot of umming and aahing, he finally said yes to the plan.*

umbrage

take ˈumbrage (at sth) (*formal* or *humorous*)
be offended or angry because of sth, often without a good reason: *She took umbrage at my remarks about her hair.*

unawares

catch/take sb unaˈwares
surprise sb; do sth when sb does not expect it: *Her sudden refusal took me unawares.* ◇ *You caught us unawares by coming so early.*

uncertain

say, tell sb, etc. (sth) in ˌno unˌcertain ˈterms
say, etc. (sth) clearly and forcefully: *I told him in no uncertain terms what I thought of his behaviour.*

uncharted

(be in/get into) murky/uncharted waters → waters

Uncle

Uncle ˈSam (*informal*)
a way of referring to the United States of America or the US government: *He owed $20 000 in tax to Uncle Sam.*

uncle

(and) Bob's your uncle → Bob

uncrowned

(be) the ˌuncrowned ˈking/ˈqueen (of sth)
the person considered to be the best, most famous or successful in a particular place or area of activity: *Because of her expertise, she is regarded as the uncrowned queen of music in Pakistan.*

understand

give sb to believe/understand (that) … → believe

understanding

on the underˈstanding that … (*formal*)
used to introduce a condition that must be agreed before sth else can happen: *They agreed to the changes on the understanding that they would be introduced gradually.*

understood

ˌmake yourself underˈstood
make your meaning clear, especially in another language: *He doesn't speak much Japanese but he can make himself understood.*

undertone

in an ˈundertone; in ˈundertones
in a quiet voice: *'I must leave now,' he said in an undertone.*

undivided

get/have sb's undivided atˈtention (*often humorous*)
receive sb's full attention: *I'll just finish writing this sentence, and then you can have my undivided attention.*

unearthly

at an unearthly/ungodly hour → hour

unglued

come unˈglued (*AmE, informal*)
1 become very upset: *I don't know why, but whenever I take my child to the doctor's she comes unglued.*
2 if a plan, etc. **comes unglued**, it does not work successfully: *Personally, I'm not sorry the building plans have come unglued. It means they'll leave the public park alone.*

ungodly

at an unearthly/ungodly hour → hour

unison

in unison (with sb/sth)
1 if people do or say sth **in unison**, they all do it at

the same time: *'Good morning, Mrs Crawford,' the children shouted in unison.*
2 if people or organizations are working **in unison**, they are working together, because they agree with each other: *I am pleased to report that the various committees are now working in unison to thoroughly investigate this matter.*

unknown

an ˌunknown 'quantity
a person or thing that you do not know anything or enough about: *His ability to make decisions in a crisis is an unknown quantity.* ◇ *Our new director is still an unknown quantity.*

unknown to 'sb
without the person mentioned being aware of it: *Unknown to me, he had already signed the agreement.*

unseen

sight unseen → sight

unsound

of ˌunsound 'mind (*law*)
not responsible for your actions because of a mental illness or condition: *He escaped a prison sentence by reason of unsound mind at the time the crime was committed.*

unstuck

come un'stuck (*BrE, informal*)
be unsuccessful; fail: *His plan to escape came badly unstuck.* ◇ *She came unstuck in the last part of the exam.*

untie

cut/untie the Gordian knot → **Gordian**

unturned

leave no stone unturned → **leave**

up

be up to sb
1 be sb's right to decide: *Shall we have an Indian or a Chinese meal? It's up to you.* ◇ *The decision's not up to me.*
2 be sb's responsibility or duty: *It's up to us to help people in need.* ◇ *Repairs to the house are up to the owner, aren't they?*

be up with sb/sth (*spoken*)
be wrong with sb/sth: *I could tell something was up from the looks on their faces.* ◇ *What's up with the car? It won't start.*

on the ˌup and 'up (*informal*)
1 (*BrE*) getting better, becoming more successful, etc: *Her health is on the up and up. Soon she'll be out of hospital.* ◇ *Business is on the up and up.*
2 (*AmE*) honest: *Before we give him the job, are you sure he's on the up and up?*

up a'gainst it (*informal*)
in a difficult situation: *Two of the staff are ill and the order has to be ready for delivery by this evening, so we're really up against it.*

up and a'bout (*BrE*)
out of bed after being ill or sleeping: *She was off work for a week, but she's up and about again now.* ◇ *On a Saturday he's not up and about till about eleven o'clock.*

up and 'down
sometimes good and sometimes bad: *One moment he seems well, the next he's ill again—he's up and down all the time.* ◇ *My relationship with him was very up and down.*

up and down sth
all over sth; everywhere in a place: *People up and down the country are giving money to the earthquake appeal.*

up and leave, go, etc. (*informal*)
leave, go, etc. quickly and unexpectedly: *Without saying anything, she just upped and went.*

up for sth
1 on offer for sth: *The house is up for sale.*
2 being considered for sth, especially as a candidate: *Two candidates are up for election.*
3 willing to take part in a particular activity: *We're going clubbing tonight. Are you **up for it**?*

up to sth
1 (also **up to doing sth**) physically or mentally capable of sth: *She didn't feel up to going to work today.* ◇ *At my age, I just don't think I'm up to climbing 200 steps.* ◇ *He's just not up to the job, I'm afraid.*
2 (*spoken*) doing sth, especially sth bad: *What's she up to?* ◇ *We used to get up to all sorts of things when we were that age.*

ˌup 'yours! (⚠, *slang*)
an offensive way of being rude to sb, for example because they have said sth that makes you angry: *'Go and cook me my dinner.' 'Oh, up yours! Do it yourself!'*

uphill

an uphill 'struggle/'battle/'task
something that is difficult and takes a lot of effort over a long period of time: *After the recent scandal, he faces an uphill struggle to win back public support before the next election.*

upon

(almost) u'pon you (*formal*)
if sth in the future is **almost upon you**, it is going to arrive or happen very soon: *The busy summer season was almost upon us again.*

upper

get, have, gain, etc. the ˌupper 'hand (over sb)
get, etc. power or control over sb, especially in a fight, competition, etc: *Our team gained the upper*

hand in the second half of the match. ◇ *The police claim they have the upper hand in their fight against the drug dealers.*

the ‚upper 'crust (*informal*)
people who are in the highest social class: *He was very upper crust, and the other children made jokes about the way he talked and dressed.*

> ❶ ORIGIN
> In the past, the top or *upper crust* of a loaf of bread was the best part, which the more important members of the household ate.

(keep) a stiff upper lip ➔ **stiff**

uppers

on your 'uppers (*BrE, informal*)
having very little money: *Joe paid for lunch, which was great because we were both on our uppers, as usual.*

upright

bolt upright ➔ **bolt**

ups

‚ups and 'downs
times of success, happiness, etc. and times of failure, unhappiness, etc: *I suppose every marriage has its ups and downs.* ◇ *I've watched the ups and downs of his business with great interest.*

upset

upset the/sb's 'apple cart (*informal*)
do sth that spoils a plan or stops the progress of sth: *Another, much cheaper hairdresser has opened next door, which has upset the apple cart.*

upside

turn sth inside out/upside down ➔ **turn**

upstairs

kick sb upstairs ➔ **kick**

uptake

be ‚quick/‚slow on the 'uptake (*informal*)
understand things quickly/understand even simple things with difficulty: *He's a very good worker but he's a bit slow on the uptake sometimes. You have to explain everything twice.*

use

be in/out of 'use
be (not) being used: *We'll have to find a classroom that's not in use.* ◇ *The road's out of use while it's being repaired.*

be no 'use (to sb) (also **be of no 'use,** *formal*)
be useless: *You can throw those away—they're no use to anyone.*

be of 'use (to sb) (*formal*)
be useful: *These maps might be of use to you on your holiday.* ◇ *Can I be of any use* (= can I help)?

‚come into/‚go out of 'use
start/stop being used: *When did this word come into common use?* ◇ *The present system will go out of use next year.*

have (got) no 'use for sb/sth
strongly dislike sb/sth: *I have no use for people like John. You can never trust them.*

I, you, etc. could use a 'drink, etc. (*spoken*)
I, you, etc. need a drink, etc: *We could use some extra help just at the moment.*

it's no 'use (doing sth)
used to say that there is no point in doing sth because it will not be successful or have a good result: *The bus has already gone, so it's no use running.* ◇ *It's no use. I just can't remember the word.*

make 'use of sb/sth
use sb/sth for your own advantage: *Make full use of every chance you get to speak English.*

put sth to good 'use
benefit from using sth: *She'll be able to put her experience to good use in the new job.*

use your 'head (*BrE* also **use your 'loaf**) (*informal*)
think carefully; use your intelligence: *Use your loaf! Meena can't read English, so there's no point in writing her a letter!*

> ❶ ORIGIN
> In rhyming slang, *loaf of bread* stands for 'head'.

use a ‚sledgehammer to crack a 'nut
use more force than is necessary: *It was a small and peaceful demonstration so I don't know why there was such a big police presence. It was like using a sledgehammer to crack a nut.*

what's the 'use (of doing sth)? (also **what 'use is there (in doing sth)?**)
used for emphasizing that you think an action, etc. will not achieve anything: *What's the use of worrying about the weather? You can't do anything about it.* ◇ *'Why don't you try talking to her?' 'What's the use? She's already made up her mind.'*

be no good/use to man or beast ➔ **man**
a fat lot of good/help/use ➔ **fat**

useful

make yourself 'useful
help other people: *Come on, Hannah. Make yourself useful and peel those potatoes for me.*

come in handy/useful ➔ **handy**

uses

have (got) your, his, its, etc. 'uses (*informal, often humorous*)
be useful sometimes: *I know you don't like him, but he has his uses—he's a great cook!*

usual

as 'usual

in the same way as what happens most of the time or in most cases: *Steve, as usual, was the last to arrive.* ◇ *As usual at that hour, the place was deserted.* ◇ *Despite her problems, she carried on working as usual.*

as per usual/normal → **per**
it's business as usual → **business**

utmost

do/try your 'utmost (to do sth)

try as hard as you can (to do sth): *I tried my utmost to stop them.* ◇ *Don't blame her—she did her utmost to finish it on time.*

V v

vacuum

do sth in a 'vacuum
do sth alone or separately from other people, events, etc., especially when there should be a connection: *No novel is written in a vacuum. There are always influences from past writers.* ◇ *These decisions are not made in a vacuum.*

vain

in 'vain
without success: *They tried in vain to persuade her to go.* ◇ *All our efforts were in vain.*

take sb's name in vain → **name**

valour *(BrE) (AmE* **valor)**

discretion is the better part of valour → **discretion**

value

a 'value judgement *(especially BrE) (AmE* usually **a 'value judgment)** *(disapproving)*
a judgement about sth that is based on sb's personal opinion and not on facts: *'She's quite a good driver for a woman.' 'That's a real value judgement. Women drive just as well as men.'* ◇ *He's always making value judgements.*

take sb/sth at (his, its, etc.) face value → **face**

van

in the 'van *(BrE, formal)*
at the front or in the leading position: *The eight warships in the van opened fire on the advancing fleet.*

white-van man → **white-van**

vanish

disappear/vanish off the face of the earth → **face**

vanishing

do/perform/stage a disappearing/vanishing act → **act**

variance

at 'variance (with sb/sth) *(formal)*
disagreeing with or opposing sb/sth: *These conclusions are totally at variance with the evidence.*

variations

variations on the theme of sth
different ways of doing or saying the same thing: *Her new book of short stories offers variations on the theme of man's desire to succeed.*

variety

variety is the spice of 'life *(saying)*
a variety of different activities, interests, places or people in your life makes it more enjoyable: *We never go on holiday to the same place twice. It's good to see different things, and you know what they say—variety is the spice of life.*

veil

cast/draw/throw a 'veil over sth *(written)*
say nothing or no more about something unpleasant: *Most of us prefer to cast a veil over subjects like illness and death.* ◇ *It is kinder to draw a veil over some of his later films.*

velvet

an iron fist/hand in a velvet glove → **iron**

vengeance

do sth with a 'vengeance *(informal)*
do sth with great energy or force: *After the holiday I need to start working with a vengeance.* ◇ *The rain came down with a vengeance.*

venom

spit blood/venom → **spit**

vent

give (full) 'vent to sth *(informal)*
express a strong (negative) feeling freely and forcefully: *I tried to stop myself giving full vent to my anger.*

vent your 'spleen *(literary)*
express your anger in speech or writing: *He vented his spleen on the assembled crowd.*

ventured

nothing ,ventured, nothing 'gained *(saying)*
used to say that you have to take risks if you want to achieve things and be successful: *Business is not good but she's still going to open another shop. Nothing ventured, nothing gained, I suppose.* ◇ *Go on, apply for it. You know what they say—nothing ventured, nothing gained.*

verge

on/to the verge of sth/doing sth
at or close to the point or time when sb does sth or sth happens: *She was on the verge of tears.* ◇ *The events of last year left him on the verge of a nervous breakdown.* ◇ *We're on the verge of signing a new contract.*

verse

chapter and verse → chapter

vessel

burst a blood vessel → burst

vested

have (got) a vested 'interest (in sth)
have a personal reason for wanting sth to happen, especially because you get some advantage from it: *He has a vested interest in Mona leaving the firm* (= perhaps because he may get her job).

vexed

a vexed 'question
a difficult problem that people often talk and argue about: *They're discussing the vexed question of private health insurance.*

vice

a den of iniquity/vice → den

vicious

a vicious 'circle
a difficult situation or problem where one thing makes another thing happen, which then makes the first thing happen again: *He spends too much on drink because he's worried about his financial problems, and so the situation gets worse and worse. It's a vicious circle.*

victim

fall victim (to sth) → fall

victory

a Pyrrhic victory → Pyrrhic
romp home/to victory → romp

vie

c'est la vie = that's life → life

view

(have, etc. sth) in 'view (*formal*)
(have, etc.) sth as an idea, plan, etc. in your mind: *What the protesters have in view is a world without nuclear weapons.* ◇ *He wanted to get rich, and he went abroad with this end in view.*

in view of sth
because of sth; considering sth: *In view of all this rain, the game may have to be cancelled.*

(be) on 'view
being shown or displayed to the public: *A lot of exciting new designs are on view at the Boat Show this year.*

take a dim/poor 'view of sb/sth
disagree with or dislike sb/sth: *Farmers tend to take a dim view of the public walking over their*

land. ◇ *The judge said he took a very poor view of their behaviour.*

take the view (that) (*formal*)
be sb's opinion that …: *I take the view that medical care should be provided by the State.*

(do sth) with a view to sth/doing sth (*formal*)
(do sth) with the plan or hope of (doing) sth else: *He He's painting and decorating the house with a view to selling it for a good price.*

a bird's-eye view (of sth) → bird's-eye
have (got) a ringside seat/view → ringside
in full view (of sb/sth) → full
a point of view → point
take the long view (of sth) → long
a worm's-eye view → worm's-eye

villain

the 'villain of the piece (*especially humorous*)
a person or thing that is responsible for a certain problem, difficulty, etc: *Nicolette's the villain of the piece, since she's the person who started all this trouble.*

> **❷ NOTE**
> The *villain* is the principal evil character in a book, a play, etc.

vine

wither on the vine → wither

violet

a shrinking violet → shrinking

virtue

by/in 'virtue of sth (*formal*)
because of sth: *I was invited to a party at the embassy simply by virtue of being British.*

make a ˌvirtue of neˈcessity
act in a good or moral way, and perhaps expect praise for this, not because you chose to but because in that particular situation you had no choice

ˌvirtue is its own reˈward (*saying*)
the reward for acting in a moral or correct way is the knowledge that you have done so, and you should not expect more than this, for example praise from other people or payment

a paragon of virtue → paragon

vis-à-vis

vis-à-'vis (*from French, written*)
1 in relation to: *Britain's role vis-à-vis the United States*
2 in comparison with: *It was felt that the company had an unfair advantage vis-à-vis smaller companies elsewhere.*

vision

(have) tunnel vision → tunnel

visit

a flying visit → **flying**
pay sb/sth a visit → **pay**
pay a visit to sb/sth → **pay**

vivre

joie de vivre → **joie**

voice

be in good, poor, etc. 'voice

be singing well, badly, etc: *The soprano was in excellent voice.*

give 'voice to sth

express your feelings, worries, etc: *The speaker stopped, allowing the crowd time to give voice to their frustration and feelings.*

keep your 'voice down

used to tell sb to speak more quietly: *Keep your voices down, won't you? The children are asleep.*

make your 'voice heard

express your opinions, feelings, etc. so that other people hear or notice: *This programme gives ordinary people a rare chance to make their voices heard.*

a voice (crying) in the 'wilderness

a warning of a danger given by a person or small group which most people do not pay any attention to: *A few scientists in the early 1980s were warning of the dangers of AIDS but nobody took them seriously. They were just a voice in the wilderness.*

with ˌone 'voice

(of a group of people) in complete agreement: *It's very rare to find the unions and management speaking with one voice, but on the question of safety at work there is total agreement.*

at the top of your voice → **top**
find your voice/tongue → **find**
like, love, etc. the sound of your own voice → **sound**
raise your voice → **raise**
raise a/your voice against sb/sth → **raise**
the still small voice → **still**

void

null and void → **null**

volte-face

a volte-'face (*from French, formal*)

a complete change of opinion or plan: *This represents a volte-face in government policy.*

volumes

speak volumes (about/for sb/sth) → **speak**

vote

put sth to the 'vote

decide sth by asking people for their votes: *OK, I'll put it to the vote. Put up your hands if you think*
religion should be taught in schools. ◇ *The issue was put to the vote.*

a ˌvote of 'thanks

a short formal speech in which you thank sb for sth and ask other people to join you in thanking them: *I'd like to propose a vote of thanks to Ms Waters for her interesting talk.*

ˌvote with your 'feet

show that you dislike or disagree with sth by leaving a place or an organization: *If shoppers don't like the new market, they'll vote with their feet and go elsewhere.*

vu

déjà vu → **déjà**

Ww

wag
let the tail wag the dog = the tail (is) wagging the dog → **tail**

tongues wag → **tongues**

wagging
set tongues wagging → **set**

the tail (is) wagging the dog → **tail**

wagon
be/go on the 'wagon (*informal*)
no longer drink/decide to stop drinking alcohol, either for a short period of time or permanently, especially if you drink a lot: *My brother-in-law goes on the wagon for a month after Christmas every year.* ◇ *'Would you like a gin and tonic?' 'No thanks. I'm on the wagon.'*

> **❶ ORIGIN**
> This idiom refers to the *water wagon*, which in America sprayed roads with water to prevent clouds of dust. If somebody starts drinking alcohol again, they are said to *fall off the wagon*.

hitch your wagon to sb/sth/a star → **hitch**

waifs
‚waifs and 'strays
1 people with no home, especially children in a big city: *There are lots of waifs and strays living on the streets here.*
2 (*humorous*) lonely people with nowhere else to go: *My wife is always inviting various waifs and strays from work to our house. She seems to attract them.*

wait
I, he, etc. can't 'wait; I, he, etc. can hardly 'wait
used when you are emphasizing that sb is very excited about sth or keen to do it: *The children can't wait for Christmas to come.* ◇ *I can hardly wait to see him again.*

‚wait and 'see
be patient and wait to find out about sth later: *'Where are you taking me?' 'Wait and see.'* ◇ *There's nothing we can do at the moment. We'll just have to wait and see.*

'wait for it (*spoken, especially BrE*)
1 wait until you receive the order or signal to do sth: *Are you all ready? Wait for it! Now!*
2 used for telling sb that you are about to say sth amusing or surprising: *'What did you have?' 'We had roast duck and—wait for it—caviar!'*

wait a 'minute/'moment/'second
1 wait for a short time: *Can you wait a second while I make a call?*

2 used when you have just noticed or remembered sth, or had a sudden idea: *Wait a minute— this isn't the right key.*

wait on sb ‚hand and 'foot (*disapproving*)
do almost everything for sb, for example cook meals, bring everything they ask for, etc: *My father expects my mother to wait on him hand and foot.*

'wait till/until … (*spoken*)
used to show that you are very excited about telling or showing sth to sb: *Wait till you see what I've found!*

(just) you 'wait
used to emphasize a threat, warning or promise: *All right, so you won—but just you wait till next time!* ◇ *Just you wait till your father gets home!* ◇ *I'll be famous one day, just you wait!*

lie in wait → **lie**

wait for the dust to settle = let the dust settle → **let**

waiting
an ‚accident/a di‚saster waiting to 'happen
a thing or person that is very likely to cause danger or a problem in the future because of the condition it is in or the way they behave: *For many months local residents had been complaining that the building was unsafe, and that it was an accident waiting to happen.*

keep sb 'waiting
make sb wait or be delayed, especially because you arrive late: *I'm sorry to have kept you waiting.*

(play) a 'waiting game
delay making a decision or doing sth because this puts you in a stronger position: *They're playing a waiting game, delaying their own offer until they know what the others are offering.*

what are we 'waiting for? (*spoken*)
used to suggest that you should all start doing what you have been discussing: *Well, what are we waiting for? Let's get started!*

what are you 'waiting for? (*spoken*)
used to tell sb to do sth now rather than later: *If the car needs cleaning, what are you waiting for?*

wake
in the wake of sb/sth
coming after and resulting from sb/sth; behind sb/sth: *Disease began spreading in the wake of the floods.* ◇ *The tourists left all sorts of rubbish in their wake.*

> **❷ NOTE**
> As a ship moves through the water, it leaves a *wake* (= disturbed water) behind it.

wake the 'dead

(of a noise) be very loud: *He must have heard it—that doorbell's loud enough to wake the dead.*

wake up and smell the 'coffee *(AmE, informal)*

used to tell sb that they are wrong about a particular situation or have not been aware of sth and it is time that they realized and accepted the truth: *It's time to wake up and smell the coffee: you're not going to pass this course unless you start working harder.*

wake-up

a 'wake-up call

an event that makes people realize that they must take action in a dangerous situation: *The recent storms and floods have been a wake-up call for many people about the reality of climate change.*

walk

take a 'walk *(informal, especially AmE)*

used to tell sb to go away when you are angry with them: *She told him to take a walk.*

walk all 'over sb *(informal)*

1 treat sb badly, without considering them or their needs: *Tell him what you think of him—don't let him walk all over you like that.*

2 defeat sb easily: *The only time I played chess with my wife, she walked all over me.* ▶ **'walkover** noun an easy victory: *We beat them 12-0: it was a walkover.*

walk 'free

be allowed to leave a court of law, etc., without receiving any punishment: *Family and friends of the victim were stunned as the man who they believed was guilty walked free.*

'walk it *(spoken)*

win easily in a competition: *If you play like that on the day of the match, you'll walk it.*

a walk of 'life

a person's job or position in society: *The people at the meeting came from all walks of life—students, writers, business people, and so on.* ◇ *Gardening appeals to people from every walk of life, from bus drivers to company directors.*

walk off the 'job *(AmE)*

stop working in order to go on strike: *Engineers and other employees walked off the job Tuesday to demand higher pay and shorter hours.*

walk sb off their 'feet *(informal)*

make sb walk so far or so fast that they are very tired: *She may be over seventy, but I'm sure she could walk some of you younger ones off your feet.*

walk on 'eggshells

be very careful not to upset sb: *I always felt as if I had to walk on eggshells around him so that I wouldn't hurt his feelings.*

walk the 'plank

1 (in the past) walk along a board placed over the side of a ship and fall into the sea, as a punishment

2 *(informal)* be forced to leave your job or position: *The food and the service is terrible in this restaurant. If you ask me, whoever is in charge should be made to walk the plank!*

walk the 'streets

walk around the streets of a town or city: *Is it safe to walk the streets alone at night?*

walk 'tall

feel proud and confident: *When I finally got a job after years of unemployment, I felt I could walk tall again.*

float/walk on air → **air**
go/walk down the aisle → **aisle**
(try to) run before you can walk → **run**
tread/walk a fine/thin line → **line**
tread/walk a tightrope → **tightrope**

walking

give sb their 'walking papers; get your 'walking papers *(AmE, informal)*

dismiss sb from their job; be dismissed: *The coach has been given his walking papers after the team lost again on Saturday.*

a walking 'dictionary, encyclo'pedia, etc. *(informal)*

used to describe a human or living example of the thing mentioned: *Geoff is a walking encyclopedia. He knows about everything.* ◇ *She's a walking dictionary* (= she knows a lot of words).

be skating/walking on thin ice → **thin**

wall

drive/send sb up the 'wall *(informal)*

make sb very annoyed; drive sb crazy: *That noise is driving me up the wall.*

go to the 'wall *(informal)*

fail because of lack of money: *Smaller companies are always the first to go to the wall in an economic recession.*

have (got) your 'back to the wall

be in a difficult situation with no easy solution: *Inflation and unemployment have risen this year and the Government has lost a lot of support. The Prime Minister really has his back to the wall now.*

off the 'wall *(informal)*

unusual and amusing; slightly crazy: *Some of his ideas are really off the wall.* ◇ *They've both got a rather off-the-wall sense of humour.*

be banging, etc. your head against a brick wall → **head**
be/come up against a brick wall → **brick**
a fly on the wall → **fly**
the handwriting (is) on the wall = the writing (is) on the wall → **writing**
hit a brick wall = be/come up against a brick wall → **brick**
nail sb to the wall → **nail**
talk to a brick wall → **talk**
the writing (is) on the wall → **writing**

walls

,walls have 'ears (*saying*)
somebody may be listening, so be careful what you say: *You'd better keep your voice down. Walls have ears, you know.*

be climbing the walls → climbing
these four walls → four

wand

wave a (magic) wand (and do sth) → wave

wane

be on the 'wane (*written*)
be becoming smaller or less strong: *Her interest in the project is on the wane.* ◇ *Their political power is on the wane.*

> ❷ NOTE
> When the moon is *on the wane* it appears smaller in the sky.

wax and wane → wax

want

for (the) want of sth
because of a lack of sth; because sth is not available: *For the want of a better name, I'm calling this book 'My Early Years'.* ◇ *We went to the cinema for want of anything better to do.*

in want of sth (*formal*)
needing sth: *The present system is in want of a total review.*

not want to 'know (about sth) (*informal*)
not care about sth; not want to become involved with sth: *She was in desperate need of help but nobody seemed to want to know.* ◇ *If she wants money, I don't want to know about it.*

want for 'nothing
have everything you need or want: *They both earn good salaries so their children want for nothing.*

want 'rid of sb/sth (*BrE, spoken, informal*)
want to be free of sb/sth that has been annoying you or that you do not want: *Are you trying to say you want rid of me?*

what do you 'want?
used to ask sb in a rude or angry way why they are there or what they want you to do

have/play/take/want no part in/of sth → part
have/want no truck with sb/sth → truck
have/want none of it/that → none
need/want sth like (you need/want) a hole in the head
→ hole
not for lack/want of trying → trying
want the moon = cry/ask for the moon → moon
waste not, want not → waste

war

a ,war of 'nerves
an attempt to defeat your opponents by putting pressure on them so that they lose courage or con-fidence: *A big American company is trying to take over our company; it's a real war of nerves.*

a ,war of 'words
a fierce argument or disagreement over a period of time between two or more people or groups: *the political war of words over tax*

all's fair in love and war → fair
a turf war → turf

warm

keep sb's 'seat, etc. warm (for them) (*informal*)
remain in a job, official position, etc. until sb is ready to take it, especially so that a third person cannot do so: *She's not the regular gardener—she's just keeping his place warm for him until he gets back.*

(as) warm as 'toast
pleasantly warm compared to the cold air outside etc: *I'll light the fire and we'll soon be as warm as toast in here.*

warm the 'cockles (of sb's 'heart) (*BrE*)
make sb feel happy or sympathetic: *Ah! It warms the cockles of my heart to see the children so happy.*

warmed

like death warmed over/up → death

warp

be (stuck) in a time warp → time

warpath

be/go on the 'warpath (*informal*)
be angry and ready for an argument or a fight about sth: *Look out—the boss is on the warpath again!*

warrant

sign your own death warrant → sign

wars

in the 'wars (*spoken*)
slightly injured because you have been in a fight or have hurt yourself in an accident: *My nephew Ben is always in the wars. Whenever I see him, he's covered in plasters.*

warts

,warts and 'all (*informal*)
including all the faults as well as the good points: *She still loves him, warts and all.* ◇ *This new book on Churchill describes him warts and all. It gives a very complete picture.*

> ❶ ORIGIN
> A *wart* is a small hard lump that grows on the skin and that is caused by a virus. Oliver Cromwell asked the painter Sir Peter Lely to portray him 'warts and all'.

wash

(all) come out in the 'wash (*spoken*)
1 (of mistakes, problems, difficulties, etc.) be corrected after a while, without any great harm being done: '*Some of the documents still haven't arrived!*' '*Don't worry, there's probably been a slight mix-up—it'll all come out in the wash.*'
2 (of a secret) be revealed: *You can't hide what you've done for ever. It'll come out in the wash, you know.*

it, that, etc. won't/doesn't 'wash (with sb)
used to say that sb's explanation, excuse, etc. is not valid or that you/sb else will not accept it: *That excuse simply won't wash with me.*

wash your dirty linen in 'public (*BrE, disapproving*)
talk or write about unpleasant or embarrassing private difficulties in public: *Nobody must mention these problems at the meeting. I don't want our dirty linen washed in public.*

wash your 'hands of sb/sth
refuse to deal with or be responsible for sb/sth any longer: *After the way she's behaved, I'm never going to help her again! I wash my hands of her! ◇ I can't just wash my hands of the whole business. I've got responsibilities.*

❶ ORIGIN
This idiom refers to Pontius Pilate in the Bible, who refused to take a decision about what should happen to Jesus.

waste

go/run to 'waste
not be used and therefore wasted: *What a pity to see all that food go to waste!*

waste your 'breath (on sb/sth)
speak (to sb or about sb/sth) but not have any effect: *Don't waste your breath on her. She doesn't take advice from anybody. ◇ I feel like I'm just wasting my breath trying to explain things to him.*

‚waste not, 'want not (*saying*)
if you never waste anything, for example food or money, you will have it when you need it: *Come on, finish your food, children. Waste not, want not!*

a waste of 'space (*spoken*)
a person who is useless or no good at anything: *What did you have to ask him along for? He's a complete waste of space!*

lay sth waste ➔ **lay**
lay waste to sth ➔ **lay**
lose/waste no time (in doing sth) ➔ **time**

watch

be on the 'watch (for sb/sth)
be looking carefully for sb/sth that you expect to see, especially in order to avoid possible danger: *The police warned holidaymakers to be on the watch for car thieves.*

keep 'watch (for sb/sth)
stay awake or watch sb/sth carefully in case of possible danger or problems: *I'll keep watch while you sleep. ◇ The doctors are keeping watch for any change in her condition.*

watch the 'clock (*disapproving*)
often check what time it is, because you are impatient for sth to finish or to happen: *She sits at home each evening watching the clock until her husband comes in. ◇ Someone who spends all their time watching the clock is usually not a good worker.*
▶ **'clock-watching** *noun*: *Don't spend the afternoon clock-watching.*

'watch it (*informal*)
1 used to warn sb to be careful: *Watch it! There's a car coming.*
2 used to tell sb that they are behaving badly and will be punished if they continue: *If you do that again, there'll be trouble, so watch it.*

watch sb/sth like a 'hawk
watch sb/sth very carefully: *Unless you watch him like a hawk, he'll go off without finishing the work.*

watch your 'mouth/'tongue
be careful what you say in order not to offend sb or make them angry: *Now, you just watch your mouth around your grandparents, Billy!*

watch this 'space (*informal*)
used in orders, to tell sb to wait for more news about sth to be announced: *I can't tell you any more right now, but watch this space.*

watch the 'world go by
watch what is happening around you, but do little yourself: *It was one of those cafes with a terrace where you can sit and watch the world go by.*

keep a close eye/watch on sb/sth ➔ **close**
mind/watch your language ➔ **language**
mind/watch your step ➔ **step**

watched

a watched pot never 'boils (*saying*)
used to say that when you are impatient for sth to happen, it seems to take longer: *Looking out of the window won't make him arrive any quicker! Don't you know that a watched pot never boils?*

water

be (like) water off a ‚duck's 'back (*informal*)
used to say that sth, especially criticism, has no effect on sb: *His book got bad reviews, but it was all water off a duck's back—he doesn't care at all what they say.*

be (all) water under the 'bridge (*spoken*)
be an event, mistake, etc. that has already happened and is now forgotten or no longer important: *We had a terrible quarrel five years ago but that's all water under the bridge.*

like 'water (*informal*)
in large amounts; in great quantity: *They're still*

spending money like water. ◇ *Champagne was flowing like water at the party.*

blood is thicker than water → **blood**

blow sb/sth out of the water → **blow**

dead in the water → **dead**

(in) deep water → **deep**

a fish out of water → **fish**

(come) hell or high water → **hell**

hold water → **hold**

in hot water → **hot**

keep your head above water → **head**

(take to sth) like a duck to water → **duck**

make sb's mouth water → **mouth**

pass water → **pass**

pour/throw cold water on sth → **cold**

pour oil on troubled water(s) → **pour**

test the water/waters → **test**

tread water → **tread**

you can take/lead a horse to water, but you can't make it drink → **horse**

Waterloo

meet your Waterloo → **meet**

waters

(be in/get into) murky/uncharted 'waters
(be in/get into) a difficult or dangerous situation that you do not know anything about: *As I opened up the computer to try and fix the problem, I realized that I was getting into completely uncharted waters and considered whether to leave it to the experts.*

muddy the waters → **muddy**

still waters run deep → **still**

test the water/waters → **test**

waterworks

turn on the waterworks → **turn**

wave

wave a (magic) 'wand (and do sth)
find a quick and easy way of doing sth that is very difficult or impossible; do sth as if by magic: *I'm sorry, but I can't just wave a magic wand and solve your problems.* ◇ *If you could wave a wand, what sort of house would you like?*

(on) the crest of a wave → **crest**

fly/show/wave the flag → **flag**

ride a/the wave of sth → **ride**

wavelength

be on the same 'wavelength/on different 'wavelengths (*informal*)
have the same/different opinion or feelings about sth: *I find him difficult to talk to—we're on completely different wavelengths.* ◇ *On the subject of marriage, Judith and I are on the same wavelength.*

waves

make 'waves (*informal*)
be active in a way that makes people notice you, and that may sometimes cause problems: *It's taken us a long time to find an answer to this problem, so please don't make waves now.*

wax

wax and 'wane (*literary*)
increase then decrease in strength, importance, etc. over a period of time: *The government's popularity has waxed and waned over the past year.*

> ❷ **NOTE**
> These two verbs describe the changing shape of the moon in the sky. When the moon *waxes*, more of it is visible, and when it *wanes* we see less of it.

wax 'lyrical (about sth) (*written*)
talk or write about sth with enthusiasm: *He began to wax lyrical about the new car he would buy with his earnings.*

way

across the 'way (*BrE* also **over the 'way**)
on the other side of the street, etc: *Music blared from the open window of the house across the way.*

all the 'way
1 (also **the ,whole 'way**) during the whole journey/period of time: *She didn't speak a word to me all the way back home.*
2 completely; as much as it takes to achieve what you want: *I'm fighting him all the way.* ◇ *You can count on my support—I'm with you all the way.*

(that's/it's) always the 'way (*spoken*)
used to say that things often happen in a particular way, especially when it is not convenient: *'I was already late, and then I got stuck in a traffic jam.' 'Yes, that's always the way, isn't it?'*

any way you 'slice it (*AmE, informal*)
however you choose to look at a situation: *Any way you slice it, consumers pay more for certain products in some countries than others.*

'be/be 'born/be 'made that way
(of a person) behave or do things in a particular manner because it is part of your character: *It's not his fault he's so shy—he was born that way.*

be in a bad 'way
be very ill or in serious trouble: *He was attacked in the street last night and he's in quite a bad way, I understand.* ◇ *'I hear the company's in a bad way.' 'Yes, it's lost a lot of money.'*

be on the way 'out/'in
be going out of/coming into fashion: *Short skirts are on the way out.*

be (well) on the/your way to/towards sth
be about to achieve sth in the near future (usually sth good): *We're on the way towards an election*

victory. ◇ *He's well on the way to establishing himself among the top ten players in the world.*

be under 'way
have started and be now progressing or taking place: *A major search is under way to find the escaped prisoners.* ◇ *Negotiations are under way to resolve the dispute.*

by the 'way (also **by the 'by/'bye**, *less frequent*) (*spoken*)
1 used for introducing sth you have just thought of, which may or may not be connected to what has just been said: *I had a meeting with Graham at work today ... by the way, I've invited him and his wife to lunch on Sunday.*
2 used for saying that sth is not important in the present situation or discussion: *Her academic qualifications are by the by. What we need is someone dynamic and creative.*

by way of sth
1 (of a journey) passing through a place: *They're going to Poland by way of France and Germany.*
2 as a kind of sth; as sth: *What are you thinking of doing by way of a holiday this year?* ◇ *The flowers are by way of a 'thank-you' for all her help.*

come your 'way
happen to you or come into your possession, temporarily or permanently: *Some good luck came his way.* ◇ *When my grandmother dies, quite a lot of money will be coming my way.*

do sth in a big/small 'way
do sth to a great/small extent; do sth on a large/small scale: *He's got himself into debt in a big way.* ◇ *She collects antiques in a small way.*

do sth on/along the way
1 do sth as you go somewhere: *Buy a burger and eat it on the way.*
2 do sth while you do sth else; do sth during the process of doing sth else: *I've succeeded in this business, and met a lot of nice people along the way.*

either way; one way or the other
used to say that it does not matter which one of two possibilities happens, is chosen or is true: *Was it his fault or not? Either way, an explanation is due.* ◇ *We could meet today or tomorrow—I don't mind one way or the other.*

every 'which way (*informal*)
in all directions: *Her hair tumbled every which way.*

get in the way (of sth)
prevent sb from doing sth; prevent sth from happening: *He wouldn't allow emotions to get in the way of him doing his job.*

get into/out of the way of (doing) sth
become used to doing sth/lose the habit of doing sth: *The women had got into the way of going out for a walk every evening.*

get sth out of the 'way
deal with a task or difficulty so that it is no longer

a problem or worry: *I'm glad I've got that visit to the dentist out of the way.*

get/have your (own) 'way (also **have it/ things/everything (all) your (own) 'way**)
get, believe or do what you want, usually in spite of the wishes or feelings of others: *She always gets her own way in the end.* ◇ *All right, have it your own way—I'm tired of arguing.*

give 'way
break or fall down: *The bridge gave way under the weight of the lorry.* ◇ *Her legs suddenly gave way and she fell to the floor.*

give 'way (to sb/sth)
1 allow sb/sth to go first: *Give way to traffic coming from the right.*
2 feel and express a strong emotion, without trying to hide it or stop it: *She refused to give way to despair.* ◇ *As soon as she was alone, she gave way to tears.*
3 allow sb to have what they want: *In arguments, I'm always the first to give way.* ◇ *We must not give way to their demands.*
4 be replaced by sth: *The storm gave way to bright sunshine.*

go all the 'way (with sb) (*informal*)
have full sexual intercourse with sb: *Did you go all the way?*

go a long/some way towards doing sth
help very much/a little in achieving sth: *The new law goes a long way towards solving the problem.*

go out of your 'way (to do sth)
make a special effort to do sth, usually to help or please sb: *She went out of her way to cook a really nice meal.* ◇ *I went out of my way to be nice to him.*

go your own 'way
do what you want, especially against the advice of others: *Teenagers always go their own way, and it's no use trying to stop them.*

go sb's 'way
1 travel in the same direction as sb: *I'm going your way. Do you want a lift?*
2 (of events) be favourable to sb: *Did you hear Alan got the job? It seems that things are going his way at last.*

go the way of all 'flesh (*saying*)
die

have (got) a way of doing sth
used to say that sb often does sth, or that sth often happens in a particular way, espeially when it is out of your control: *He has a way of arriving when you're least expecting him.* ◇ *Long-distance relationships have a way of not working out.*

have (got) a way with sb/sth
have a special ability to deal with sb/sth: *She's a very good teacher. She has a way with children.* ◇ *He's always had a way with horses.* ◇ *She's got a way with words* (= she is very good at expressing herself).

have your (wicked) 'way with sb (*old-fashioned, humorous*)
persuade sb to have sex with you

in a 'way; in 'one way (also **in 'some ways**)
to a certain extent (but not completely): *In a way, living in the town is better than the country, because there's much more to do.* ◇ *In one way, I'm sorry we didn't stay longer.* ◇ *I agree with you in some ways.*

in his, her, its, etc. (own) 'way
in a manner that is appropriate to or typical of a person or thing but that may seem unusual to other people: *I think she does love you in her own way.*

in the/sb's 'way
stopping sb from moving or doing sth: *You'll have to ¡move—you're in my way.* ◇ *I left them alone, as I felt I was in the way.*

a lot, not much, etc. in the way of sth
a lot, etc. of sth: *We don't do a lot in the way of exercise.* ◇ *She doesn't have much in the way of clothes.* ◇ *Is there much in the way of nightlife around here?*

keep/stay out of sb's 'way
avoid sb: *He's got a lot of work to do at the moment, so if I were you I'd stay out of his way until he's got it finished.*

make 'way (for sb/sth)
make enough space for sb/sth; allow sb/sth to pass: *Could you move your books to make way for the food?* ◇ *People made way for my wheelchair.*

make your 'way (to/towards sth)
go (to/towards sth): *Would passengers please make their way to gate 15 for the flight to Paris.* ◇ *Don't worry, we can **make our own way** to the airport* (= get there without help, a ride, etc.).

make your 'way in sth
succeed in sth, especially a job: *She's trying to make her way in the fashion business.* ◇ *The time had come to leave home and start to make his way in the world.*

¡no 'way (*informal*)
definitely not; never: *'Are you going to stay at school after you're 16?' 'No way. I want to get a job.'* ◇ *No way am I going to speak to him again!*

on your/the/its 'way
1 coming; going: *If she phones again, tell her I'm on my way* (= coming to see her). ◇ *I'd better be on my way soon* (= leave soon).
2 during the journey: *I bought some bread on the way home.*
3 (of a baby) not yet born: *She's got two children and another one on its way.*

(in) ¡one way and/or a'nother/the 'other
in various different ways now considered together: *One way and another we had a very good time when we were students.*

the ¡other way a'round/'round
1 in the opposite position, direction or order: *I think it should go on the other way round.*
2 the opposite situation: *I didn't leave you. It was the other way around* (= you left me).

out of the 'way
1 no longer stopping sb from moving or doing sth: *I moved my legs out of the way so that she could get past.* ◇ *I didn't say anything until Dad was out of the way.*
2 finished; dealt with: *Our region is poised for growth once the election is out of the way.*
3 far from a town or city: *It's a lovely place, but it's a bit out of the way.* ◇ *a little out-of-the-way place on the coast*
4 used in negative sentences to mean 'unusual': *She had obviously noticed nothing out of the way.*

¡out of your 'way
not on the route that you planned to take: *I'd love a ride home—if it's not out of your way.*

¡that's the 'way (*informal*)
used for showing pleasure or approval of what sb is doing or has done: *That's the way. Just keep playing like that and you'll win.*

that's the way the cookie 'crumbles (also **that's the way it 'goes**) (*informal*)
that is the situation and we cannot change it, so we must accept it: *She met somebody else and left me. That's the way the cookie crumbles, I suppose.*

there's more than 'one way to skin a 'cat (*saying, humorous*)
there are many different ways to achieve sth: *Have you thought about a different approach? There's more than one way to skin a cat.*

to 'my, 'your, etc. way of thinking
in my, etc. opinion: *To his way of thinking, mobile phones should be banned on public transport.*

'way back (*informal*)
a long time ago: *We've known each other since way back.* ◇ *I first met her way back in the fifties.*

a/the/sb's way of 'life
the typical pattern of behaviour of a person or group: *the British/rural/traditional way of life*

the ¡way of the 'world
what often happens; what is common: *Marriages don't always last for ever. That's the way of the world, I'm afraid.*

way to 'go! (*AmE, informal, spoken*)
used to tell sb that you are pleased about sth they have done: *Good work, guys! Way to go!*

the way to sb's 'heart
the way to make sb like or love you: *The way to a man's heart is through his stomach* (= by giving him good food).

work, etc. your way through sth
read or do sth from the beginning to the end of sth: *He worked his way through the dictionary learning ten new words every day.* ◇ *He's eating his way*

through all the restaurants that are recommended in the Good Food Guide.

be roses, roses all the way → **roses**

be (a long) way off the mark = be/fall wide of the mark → **wide**

clear the way (for sth/for sth to happen) → **clear**

do/learn sth the hard way → **hard**

do sth in your own sweet time/way → **sweet**

downhill all the way → **downhill**

feel your way → **feel**

find, etc. a/the middle way → **middle**

find your/its way (to/into …) → **find**

go back a long way → **long**

have come a long way → **long**

have (got) a long way to go → **long**

he, she, etc. couldn't punch his, her, etc. way out of a paper bag → **punch**

in the family way → **family**

in the ordinary way → **ordinary**

know your way about/around (sth) → **know**

laugh all the way to the bank → **laugh**

lead the way → **lead**

lie your way into/out of sth → **lie**

look the other way → **look**

lose your way → **lose**

not know which way/where to look → **know**

not know which way/where to turn → **know**

not stand in sb's way → **stand**

open the way for sb/sth (to do sth) → **open**

out of harm's way → **harm**

pave the way (for sb/sth) → **pave**

pay your/its (own) way → **pay**

pick your way (across, along, among, over, through sth) → **pick**

point the way (to/towards sth) → **point**

rub sb up the wrong way → **rub**

see your way (clear) to doing sth → **see**

see which way the wind blows → **see**

show the way → **show**

smooth the path/way → **smooth**

take the easy way out → **easy**

take sth the wrong way → **wrong**

talk your way out of sth/doing sth → **talk**

thread your way through (sth) → **thread**

where there's a will there's a way → **will**

wing your/its way (to …) → **wing**

work your way through college, etc. → **work**

work your way up → **work**

ways

you, etc. can't have it 'both ways

you must choose between two things even though you would like both of them: *You want an interesting job that pays well, and yet one where you don't have many responsibilities. Well, you can't have it both ways.*

in ,more ways than 'one

used to show that sth that has been said has more than one meaning: *She's a big woman, in more ways than one* (= she is big in size, and also important or powerful).

,ways and 'means

the methods and materials available for doing sth: *'How will you get the money?' 'Don't worry, there are ways and means.'*

be set in your ways → **set**

change your ways → **change**

cut both/two ways → **cut**

the error of your ways → **error**

go your separate ways → **separate**

in some ways = in a way → **way**

mend your ways → **mend**

(there are) no two ways about it → **two**

a/the parting of the ways → **parting**

swing both ways → **swing**

wayside

fall by the wayside → **fall**

weak

be/go ,weak at the 'knees (*informal*)

be/become weak because of illness, strong emotion, etc: *He felt dizzy and a bit weak at the knees.* ◇ *Her smile made me go weak at the knees* (= with nervousness, love, etc.). ▶ ,weak-'kneed *adj.* not brave or determined

the weak 'link (in the 'chain)

the point at which a system or an organization is most likely to fail: *She went straight for the one weak link in the chain of his argument.*

a weak 'moment; a moment of 'weakness

a time when you do or agree to sth you would not normally do: *In a weak moment I agreed to let them stay at our house, but later I wished I hadn't.* ◇ *I was on a very strict diet but in a moment of weakness I ate a cream cake.*

the spirit is willing but the flesh (it) is weak → **spirit**

weakness

a moment of weakness = a weak moment → **weak**

weapon

be a double-edged sword/weapon → **double-edged**

wear

,wear and 'tear

damage or loss of quality because of normal use: *After having the car for five years you expect some wear and tear.* ◇ *The guarantee does not cover normal wear and tear.*

wear your ,heart on your 'sleeve

show other people your emotions, especially love: *He wears his heart on his sleeve and often gets hurt.*

ℹ ORIGIN
This phrase is from Shakespeare's play *Othello*.

wear 'thin

begin to become less; become less interesting or amusing: *My patience is beginning to wear very thin.* ◇ *Don't you think that joke's wearing a bit thin?* (= because we have heard it many times before)

wear the 'trousers *(BrE)* *(AmE* **wear the 'pants)** *(often disapproving)*
(especially of a woman) be the partner in a marriage who makes the decisions and tells the other person what to do: *It's not difficult to see who wears the trousers in their house!*

(be) the worse for wear ➜ worse

wearing
in/wearing your birthday suit ➜ birthday

weather
keep a 'weather eye on sth/open for sth
watch sth very carefully for signs of change so that you will be prepared for a problem, difficulty, etc: *It's an ambassador's job to keep a weather eye open for any important political changes.*

under the 'weather *(informal)*
slightly ill, sick or depressed; not as well/cheerful as usual: *She was off work for two weeks and she still seems a bit under the weather.* ◇ *What's the matter with Tom? He looks a bit under the weather.*

brass monkey weather ➜ brass
make heavy weather of (doing) sth ➜ heavy
ride out/weather the storm (of sth) ➜ storm

weathers
in 'all weathers *(BrE)*
in all kinds of weather, good and bad: *She goes out jogging in all weathers.*

weave
weave your 'magic; weave a 'spell (over sb) *(especially BrE)*
perform or behave in a way that attracts and interests sb very much or makes them react in a particular way: *Will Owen be able to weave his magic against Scotland on Wednesday?*

wedding
a shotgun wedding ➜ shotgun

wedge
drive a wedge between A and B ➜ drive
the thin end of the wedge ➜ thin

wee
the wee (small) hours = the small/early hours ➜ hours

week
,week after 'week *(informal)*
continuously for many weeks: *Week after week the drought continued.*

,week by 'week
as the weeks pass: *Week by week he grew a little stronger.*

week ,in, week 'out
happening every week: *I'm tired of the same old routine week in, week out.*

a ,week to'morrow, on 'Monday, etc. *(BrE)* (also **a ,week from to'morrow, 'Monday, etc.** *AmE, BrE*)
seven days after the day that you mention: *It's my birthday a week on Tuesday.*

a week 'yesterday, last 'Monday, etc. *(especially BrE)*
seven days before the day that you mention: *It was a week yesterday that we heard the news.*

weekend
a dirty weekend ➜ dirty

weigh
weigh 'anchor
(of a ship and its passengers) leave a place: *We weighed anchor in the afternoon and started for the Philippines.*

weigh on your 'mind
(of a problem or difficulty) make you feel worried and anxious: *The safety of the missing children was weighing on their minds.*

weigh (half) a 'ton *(informal)*
be very heavy: *These suitcases weigh a ton! What have you got in them?*

weigh your 'words
carefully choose the words you use when you speak or write: *He spoke very slowly, weighing his words.*

weight
be a ,weight off your 'shoulders
used to say that you are glad that you do not have to worry about sth any longer: *Finally paying off my debts was a great weight off my shoulders.*

put/throw your weight behind sth
use all your influence and power to support sth: *Several of the country's leading politicians have thrown their weight behind the campaign.*

take the 'weight off your feet *(informal)*
used to tell sb who is tired to sit down: *Here, take the weight off your feet and I'll bring you a cup of tea and a biscuit.*

(do sth by) weight of 'numbers
(do sth by) having more people in one group than in another; (do sth by) the strength of many people: *They got what they wanted by sheer weight of numbers.*

be worth your/its weight in gold ➜ worth
carry weight ➜ carry
groan under the weight of sth ➜ groan
(take) a load/weight off sb's mind ➜ mind
pull your weight ➜ pull
throw your weight about/around ➜ throw

weird

weird and wonderful
clever (and attractive) but unusual or strange: *People were wearing all sorts of weird and wonderful clothes.*

welcome

lay, put, roll, etc. out the 'welcome mat (for sb) (*especially AmE*)
make sb feel welcome; try to attract visitors, etc: *The country has put out the welcome mat for international investors.*

outstay/overstay your 'welcome
(of a guest) stay too long so that you are no longer welcome: *We visited some friends in France, but we didn't want to overstay our welcome and left after a couple of days.*

you're 'welcome (*especially AmE*)
used as a polite reply when a person thanks you: *'Thanks for your help.' 'You're welcome.'*

well

,all being 'well
if everything happens as you expect and hope: *We'll see you in July then, all being well.*

,all very 'well/'fine (for sb) (to do sth) but ... (*informal*)
used to criticize or reject a remark that sb has made, especially when they were trying to make you feel happier about sth: *'Why don't you try to relax more?' 'Look, it is all very well to say that, but how can I possibly relax with four small children in the house?'* ◇ *It's all very well for you to suggest a skiing holiday but where are we going to find the money?*

,all well and 'good (*informal*)
good but not completely satisfactory: *That's all well and good, but why didn't he call her to say so?*

all's well that 'ends well (*saying*)
if the final result is good, earlier difficulties and problems are not important

❶ ORIGIN
This is the title of a play by Shakespeare.

as well (as sb/sth)
in addition to sb/sth; too: *Are they coming as well?* ◇ *They sell books as well as newspapers.* ◇ *She's a talented musician as well as being a photographer.*

be (just) as 'well (to do sth)
be sensible or wise (to do sth): *It's just as well to lock the door, even if you only go out of the house for a few minutes.*

be doing 'well
be getting healthier after an illness; be in good health after a birth: *Mother and baby are both doing well.*

be ,well a'ware of sth; be ,well a'ware that ...
know very well about sth: *I'm well aware of the dangers involved.* ◇ *She's well aware that not everyone agrees.*

be 'well away (*BrE, informal*)
1 be making good progress; be succeeding: *If I had another £10 000 to invest in this business, I'd be well away.*
2 be drunk: *He's well away; he's been drinking all evening.*

be ,well 'in (with sb) (*informal*)
be good friends with sb, especially sb important: *She seems to be well in with all the right people.*

be ,well 'off
1 be rich enough to have a high standard of living: *Her parents are both doctors so they're quite well off.*
2 be in a fortunate situation: *Some people don't know when they're well off. If they realized how millions of people in this world live, they wouldn't complain so much.*

be well ,off for 'sth
have as much of sth as you need or want: *We're very well off for computers in this school.*

be ,well 'out of sth (*BrE, informal*)
be lucky that you are not/no longer doing sth or involved in sth: *'I've left my job in advertising.' 'You're well out of it, John. The firm is in terrible financial trouble.'*

be ,well 'up on sth
know a lot about sth: *Are you well up on the latest developments?* ◇ *She's very well up on modern Chinese literature.*

can't/couldn't very well do sth (*informal*)
used to say that sth is not the right thing to do: *You can't very well change the arrangements now. It's too late to inform people.*

do 'well by sb
treat sb generously: *He did well by me when I needed money, and I shall always be grateful to him.*

do 'well for yourself
become successful or rich: *He's done very well for himself in the last few years—you should see his new house!*

do 'well out of sb/sth
make a profit or get money from sb/sth: *He's not doing very well out of the business at the moment, but he hopes that next year things will improve.*

do 'well to do sth
be sensible or wise to do sth: *You'd do well to remember that I'm paying the bill.* ◇ *They did well to sell when the price was high.*

it's (just) as 'well (that ...)
it is a good thing (that ...); it is lucky (that ...): *It's as well that we brought an umbrella.* ◇ *'She was wearing a crash helmet, fortunately.' 'Just as well.'*

leave/let well a'lone (*BrE*) (*AmE* let well enough a'lone)
not try to change sth or get involved in sth: *Arguments between other couples should be let well alone.*

may/might as well (do sth)
used for saying that you will do sth because it seems best in the situation that you are in, although you may not really want to do it: *Since nobody else wants the job, I might as well give it to him.* ◇ *'Are you coming to the pub?' 'Might as well.'*

(you, etc.) may/might as well be hanged/ hung for a ˌsheep as (for) a 'lamb (*saying*)
if you are going to be punished for doing sth wrong, whether it is a big or small thing, you may as well do the big thing: *I'm already late but I'll stay and have another drink. May as well be hanged for a sheep as for a lamb.*

> **❶ ORIGIN**
> In the past, the punishment for stealing any livestock (= farm animals) was death by hanging.

only too 'well
used for emphasizing that you already know about sb/sth or have already experienced sth unpleasant, etc: *'Do you know Alex Humber?' 'Only too well. He's not one of my favourite people, I'm afraid.'*

very 'well (*BrE, formal*)
used to accept sth or agree to sth, especially when you do not really want to: *'Please could I go home an hour early today, Mrs Smith?' 'Very well Emma, if you really must.'*

ˌwell and 'truly (*informal*)
completely: *We were in the middle of the forest, and well and truly lost.*

ˌwell I 'never ('did)! (*old-fashioned, informal*)
used to express surprise: *Well I never! Fancy meeting you here!*

well 'said! (*spoken*)
I agree completely: *'We must stand up for ourselves.' 'Well said, John.'*

bode well/ill (for sb/sth) → **bode**
could/might just as well … → **just**
jolly well → **jolly**
know sth full/perfectly/very well → **know**
mean well → **mean**
pretty much/well → **pretty**
he, it, etc. promises well → **promises**
sit comfortably/easily/well (with sth) → **sit**
wish sb/sth well/ill → **wish**
you know as well as I do → **know**

wet

wet the baby's 'head (*informal*)
have a drink to celebrate the birth of a baby: *Jack phoned me from the hospital and then we met in a bar to wet the baby's head.*

wet the/your 'bed
accidentally urinate (= get rid of water from your body) in your bed: *It is quite common for small children to wet their beds.*

(still) ˌwet behind the 'ears (*informal, disapproving*)
be young and with very little experience: *He's a young teacher, still wet behind the ears.*

a ˌwet 'blanket (*informal, disapproving*)
a person who is not enthusiastic about anything and who stops other people from enjoying themselves: *She was such a wet blanket at the party that they never invited her again.*

wet your 'whistle (*old-fashioned, informal*)
have an alcoholic drink

'wet yourself; wet your 'pants/'knickers
accidentally urinate (= get rid of water from your body) in your underwear: *I was laughing so much I almost wet myself!*

whack

out of 'whack (*informal, especially AmE*)
1 not appropriate or correct, especially in relation to sth else: *The Olympics have made flights and accommodation here incredibly expensive. Prices are way out of whack with normal.* ◇ *If you ask me, his priorities are all out of whack. He should find a job first, then decide where to live.*
2 (especially of a system or machine) not working as it should: *Don't bother trying to call me on my mobile. It's out of whack again.* ◇ *After years of dieting, Carol's metabolism was completely out of whack.*

whale

have a 'whale of a time (*informal*)
enjoy yourself very much; have a very good time: *The children had a whale of a time at the beach and didn't want to go home.*

Everybody had a whale of a time at the party.

whammy

a double whammy → **double**

what

and what not (*spoken*)
and other (similar) things: *The shop sells nails, screws, hammers and what not.*

give sb/get what 'for (*BrE, spoken*)
punish sb/be punished, usually severely: *I'll give her what for if she does that again.* ◇ *If you steal any more of my apples, you'll get what for.*

or 'what (*spoken*)
1 used to emphasize your opinion: *Is he stupid or what?*
2 used when you are not sure about sth: *I don't know if he's a student or what.* ◇ *Come on! Are we going or what?*

so 'what? (*spoken*)
used to show that you do not care about sth or that you think sth is not important: *'Your sister did much better than you in the exam.' 'So what?'* ◇ *So what if nobody else agrees with me?*

what? (*spoken, informal*)
1 used when you have not heard or have not understood sth: *What? I can't hear you.*
2 used to show that you have heard sb and to ask what they want: *'Mummy!' 'What?' 'I'm thirsty.'*
3 used to express surprise or anger: *'It will cost $500.' 'What?'* ◇ *'And then I asked her to marry me.' 'You what?'*

what are you 'on? (*informal*)
used when you are very surprised at sb's behaviour and are suggesting that they are acting in a similar way to sb using drugs

'what-d'you-call-him/-her/-it/-them; 'what's-his/-her/-its/-their-name
used instead of a name that you cannot remember: *She's just gone out with old what-d'you-call-him.* ◇ *Have you heard from what's-her-name from the library recently?*

what for?
for what purpose or reason?: *What is this tool for?* ◇ *What did you do that for?* (= why did you do that) ◇ *'I need to see a doctor.' 'What for?'*

what's got into sb? (*spoken*)
used to say that sb has suddenly started to behave in a strange or different way: *What's got into Alex? He never used to worry like that.*

what if ... ?
1 what would happen if ... ?: *What if the car breaks down?*
2 why should I care if ... ? what does it matter if ... ?: *'You'll fail the exam if you don't work harder, Carol.' 'What if I do? It's not the end of the world.'* ◇ *What if people are starving? It doesn't affect me.*

what 'of it? (*spoken*)
used when admitting that sth is true, to ask why it should be considered important: *Yes, I wrote the article. What of it?*

what with sth (*informal*)
because of sth or a series of things: *What with the weather and my bad leg, I haven't been out for weeks.* ◇ *I haven't had time to sit down, what with one thing and another.*

what's all 'this/'that (...)?
why is this/that happening?: *What's all this I hear about you wanting to leave?*

what's it to 'you, 'him, 'her, etc.? (*informal*)
1 (said when you are annoyed) you, etc. have no right to know sth; what does it matter to you, etc: *What's it to her how I spend my money?* ◇ *What's it to them if public transport is getting worse? They never have to use it.*

(and) what's 'more; what is 'more
(and) more importantly; (and) in addition: *I don't like pubs. They're noisy, smelly, and what's more, expensive.*

what's 'up? (*informal*)
1 what's the matter?: *What's up with him? He looks furious.*
2 (*especially AmE*) what's new?; what's happening?: *Hey Jo, what's up?*

what's 'what (*spoken*)
what things are useful, important, etc: *She certainly knows what's what.*

what's with sb? (*AmE, spoken*)
used to ask why sb is behaving in a strange way: *What's with you? You haven't said a single word all morning.*

what's with sth? (*AmE, spoken*)
used to ask the reason for sth: *What's with all this walking? Can't we take a cab?*

what's 'yours? (*informal*)
(said in a pub or bar) what would you like to drink?

whatever

or what'ever (*spoken*)
or something of a similar type: *It's the same in any situation: in a prison, hospital or whatever.*

what'ever you do
used to warn sb not to do sth under any circumstances: *Don't tell Paul, whatever you do!*

wheat

sort out/separate the ˌwheat from the 'chaff
separate people or things of a better quality from those of a lower quality: *When all the applications came in, our first task was to separate the wheat from the chaff.*

wheel

(be) at/behind the 'wheel (of sth)
driving a car: *Who was at the wheel when the car crashed?*

a fifth/third 'wheel (*AmE*)
an unwanted, extra or unnecessary person: *No, I*

don't think I'll join you. Whenever I go out with you guys I just feel like a fifth wheel.

take the 'wheel
start to drive a car, replacing sb else: When we got halfway, Sarah took the wheel and I had a rest.

‚wheel and 'deal (disapproving)
do a lot of complicated deals in business or politics, often in a dishonest way: He's spent the last three years wheeling and dealing in the City. ◇ I don't want to go into politics—there's too much wheeling and dealing. ▸ **‚wheeler-'dealer** noun

the ‚wheel has come/turned full 'circle (saying)
sth that changed greatly has now returned to its original state or position: How long does it take for the wheel of fashion to come full circle?

a big cheese/wheel → **big**
a cog in the machine/wheel → **cog**
put your shoulder to the wheel → **shoulder**
put a spoke in sb's wheel → **spoke**
reinvent the wheel → **reinvent**

wheels

(there are) ‚wheels within 'wheels
used to describe a situation which is difficult to understand because it involves complicated or secret processes and decisions: In making political agreements there are always wheels within wheels. ◇ There are wheels within wheels in this organization—you never really know what's going on.

grease the wheels = oil the wheels → **oil**
set the wheels in motion = put/set sth in motion → **motion**

where

where it's 'at (informal)
where the most exciting things are happening (in music, art, etc.): For dance music, New York's where it's at right now.

wherefores

the whys and (the) wherefores (of sth) → **whys**

whet

‚whet sb's 'appetite
make sb feel hungry; make sb interested in sth: Don't eat too much of this dish. It's only to whet your appetite for the main course. ◇ One of my teachers lent me a book about climbing, and it really whetted my appetite.

which

‚which is 'which
used to talk about distinguishing one person or thing from another: The twins are so alike I can't tell which is which.

while

while away the time, etc. (doing sth)
pass the time (doing sth), usually because you are waiting for sth or have nothing better to do: I had

ten hours to wait in Rome, so I whiled away the time wandering around the museums.

(well) worth your while (to do sth) → **worth**

whip

get, have, hold, etc. the 'whip hand (over sb)
have power or control (over sb): The government knows that the army have the whip hand. ◇ Our opponents had the whip hand over us right from the beginning.

crack the whip → **crack**
a fair crack of the whip → **fair**

whipping

a 'whipping boy
a person who is blamed or punished for the mistakes of another person: The directors are clearly responsible for what happened, but they're sure to find a whipping boy lower down the company. ◇ It was your fault, and I am not going to be your whipping boy.

> **ⓘ ORIGIN**
> In the past when a royal prince made a mistake in his lessons, another boy was whipped (= punished) for his mistakes.

whirl

give sth a 'whirl (informal)
try sth, to see if it is enjoyable, interesting, etc: I've never had Indonesian food but I'll give it a whirl.

(be) in a 'whirl
(feel) confused and excited: My mind was in a whirl as I realized that this decision would change our lives.

whisker

be, come, etc. within a whisker of sth/doing sth (BrE)
almost do sth: They came within a whisker of being killed.

do sth by a 'whisker (informal)
do sth, but nearly fail; do sth, but only just: He missed the first prize by a whisker. ◇ You escaped serious injury by a whisker, so consider yourselves very lucky.

whiskers

the cat's whiskers/pyjamas → **cat**

whistle

you, etc. can 'whistle for it (BrE, spoken)
used to say that you are not going to give sb sth that they have asked for: 'The boss wants that sales report this afternoon.' 'Well, he can whistle for it.'

whistle in the 'dark
try not to show that you are afraid, are in danger, etc: He seems confident, but he's whistling in the dark. He knows he's going to lose the game.

blow the whistle (on sb/sth) → blow
(as) clean as a whistle → clean
wet your whistle → wet

whistles

bells and whistles → bells

whistle-stop

a ˌwhistle-stop ˈtour
short visits to different places made by a politician, etc. during an election campaign, etc: *The Prime Minister left on a whistle-stop tour of the north of England today.* ◇ *The new manager's gone on a whistle-stop tour of all the offices.*

whit

not a/one ˈwhit (*old-fashioned*)
not at all; not the smallest amount: *Thank you for coming, James. Unfortunately, I don't think your presence will make a whit of difference to the outcome of this meeting, as I'm fairly sure our demands won't be met.*

white

(as) ˌwhite as a ˈsheet/ˈghost (*informal*)
very pale in the face, because of illness, fear or shock: *She went as white as a sheet when she heard the news.*

a white ˈChristmas
a Christmas when it snows: *The weathermen are predicting a white Christmas this year.*

a white ˈelephant
a thing that is useless and no longer needed, although it may have cost a lot of money: *That theatre is a real white elephant. It cost millions to build and nobody ever goes there.*

> **❶ ORIGIN**
> This comes from the story that in Siam (now Thailand), the king would give a white elephant as a present to somebody that he did not like. That person would have to spend all their money on looking after the rare animal.

a white ˈlie
a small or harmless lie that you tell to avoid hurting sb: *When she asked me if I liked her new dress I had to tell a white lie. I thought it looked awful, but I couldn't say so!*

(in) black and white → black
bleed sb dry/white → bleed
in black and white → black
whiter than white → whiter

whiter

ˌwhiter than ˈwhite
(of a person) completely honest and morally good: *The government must be seen to be whiter than white.*

white-van

ˌwhite-ˈvan man (*BrE, informal*)
used to refer to a man driving a white van in an aggressive way. Many companies use white delivery vans and their drivers are often considered stupid and rude: *The government must act before this 'white van man' explosion becomes a major hazard on UK roads.* ◇ *Who enjoys driving to work with the constant traffic jams, roadworks and the impatient hooting of white-van man?*

whizz-kid

a ˈwhizz-kid (also ˈwhiz-kid) (*informal*)
a person who is very good and successful at sth, especially at a young age: *'Who's the new manager?' 'A financial whizz-kid from Harvard Business School.'*

who

who am ˈI, are ˈyou, is ˈshe, etc. to do sth?
used when you think a person has/you have no right or authority to do sth: *Who are you to tell me I can't leave my bicycle here? It's not your house.* ◇ *I don't agree, but then who am I to say what she should do?*

who's ˈwho
people's names, jobs, status, etc: *You'll soon find out who's who in the office.*

whole

Most idioms containing **whole** are at the entries for the nouns and verbs in the idioms, for example **go the whole hog** is at **hog**.

as a ˈwhole
considered as one general group: *The population as a whole were not very interested in the issue.*

on the ˈwhole
considering everything; in general: *On the whole her school work is improving, though her spelling is still poor.*

a ˈwhole lot (*informal*)
very much; a lot: *I'm feeling a whole lot better.*

a ˈwhole lot (of sth) (*informal*)
a large number or amount: *There were a whole lot of people I didn't know.* ◇ *I lost a whole lot of money at the casino.*

the ˌwhole ˈlot
everything; all of sth: *I've sold the whole lot.*

whoop

ˌwhoop it ˈup (*informal*)
1 enjoy yourself very much with a noisy group of people: *Of course I'm in a bad mood! I've been stuck here working while you've been whooping it up in the bar with your friends!*
2 (*AmE*) make people excited or enthusiastic about sth: *The emcee came on stage and really whooped it up for the next act.*

whoopee

make 'whoopee (*old-fashioned*, *informal*)
celebrate in a noisy way: *Here's a photo of us making whoopee at Dave's wedding.*

why

why 'ever ... ?
used in questions to mean 'why?', expressing surprise: *Why ever didn't you tell us?*

,why 'not? (*informal*)
used to make a suggestion, or agree to a suggestion: *'Why not go and see a film?' 'OK.'* ◇ *'Let's go and see a film.' 'OK, why not?'*

whys

the ,whys and (the) 'wherefores (of sth)
the reasons (for sth): *I don't really want to know all the whys and the wherefores. Just tell me what happened.*

wick

get on sb's 'wick (*BrE*, *informal*)
annoy sb: *She's always talking about herself—she gets on my wick.*

wicked

there's no peace/rest for the 'wicked (*usually humorous*)
used when sb is complaining that they have a lot of work to do: *Well, it's been nice talking to you, but I really must go. No rest for the wicked!*

wicket

(be on) a sticky wicket → **sticky**

wide

be/fall wide of the 'mark (also **be (a long) way off the 'mark**)
be not at all correct or accurate: *No one knew where Bangalore was, and their guesses were all wide of the mark.*

be wide 'open
(of a competition, election, etc.) with no obvious winner: *The presidential election is wide open.*

give sb/sth a wide 'berth
avoid meeting sb; avoid going near or using sth: *He's so boring I always try to give him a wide berth at parties.* ◇ *The roads are very dangerous there— I'd give them a wide berth and go by train.*

a 'wide boy (*BrE*, *informal*, *disapproving*)
a person who is dishonest in business: *If he offers you a business deal, say no. He's a bit of a wide boy.*

(lay/leave yourself) wide 'open (to sth)
(put yourself) in a situation where you can easily be criticized, blamed, attacked, etc: *By not saying anything in your defence, you're leaving yourself wide open to their accusations.* ◇ *The soldiers were wide open to attack.*

cast/spread your net wide → **net**
far and wide → **far**

wife

(all) the world and his wife → **world**

wild

a ,wild 'goose chase
a (long) search for sth that you cannot find because you have been given the wrong information: *He gave us the wrong directions to the station and that led us off on a wild goose chase.* ◇ *Peter's story sent the police on a wild goose chase. They soon realized he'd been lying.*

wild 'horses couldn't/wouldn't drag sb there, prevent sb doing sth, etc. (*informal*, *humorous*)
nothing would make or persuade sb to go somewhere, do sth, etc: *Wild horses wouldn't keep me at home on a Saturday night.*

run wild → **run**
sow your wild oats → **sow**

wilderness

(be) in the 'wilderness
(of politicians) no longer having power, influence or importance because they no longer hold high office: *After a few years in the wilderness she was allowed to return to a job in the government.*

a voice (crying) in the wilderness → **voice**

wildest

beyond your wildest 'dreams
much greater or better than you ever expected, imagined, etc: *The success of our first album was beyond our wildest dreams.*

wildfire

spread like wildfire → **spread**

will

(do sth) against your 'will
(do sth) without wanting to: *I was forced to sign the document against my will.*

do sth at 'will
do sth when, where, how, etc. you want to: *The animals are allowed to wander at will in the park.* ◇ *The younger soldiers started shooting at will* (= they fired their guns without waiting for the order).

where there's a ,will there's a 'way (*saying*)
a person who really wants something very much and is determined to get it will find a way of getting it or doing it: *'Have you had any luck in contacting Sue?' 'Not yet, but where there's a will there's a way!'*

(do sth) with a 'will (*written*)
(do sth) with energy and enthusiasm: *She started*

digging the garden with a will. ◇ *With a will they set to work.*

of your own free will ➔ **free**

with the best will in the world ➔ **best**

willies

give sb the 'willies/heebie-'jeebies/'creeps (*informal*)
make sb feel nervous or afraid: *Being alone in this old house gives me the willies.* ◇ *She said that spiders gave her the heebie-jeebies.* ◇ *He gives me the creeps. He's got such strange eyes.*

willing

God willing ➔ **God**

show willing ➔ **show**

the spirit is willing but the flesh (it) is weak ➔ **spirit**

wills

a battle of wills ➔ **battle**

willy-nilly

do sth ,willy-'nilly (*informal*)
1 do sth whether you want to or not: *She was forced willy-nilly to accept the company's proposals.*
2 do sth in a careless way without planning: *Don't just use your credit card willy-nilly.*

❶ NOTE
This expression is a shortened form of 'willing or not willing'.

win

I, you, etc. ,can't 'win (*spoken*)
whatever you do, you cannot succeed completely or please everyone: *If I spend time with Phil, she's unhappy. If I spend time with her, he's jealous. I just can't win.* ◇ *We try to eat a healthy diet, but there are so many chemicals in food nowadays that you just can't win.* ▶ ,no-'win *adj.* (of a situation, policy, etc.) that will end badly whatever you decide to do: *They're in a no-win situation at the moment. Whatever they do, someone criticizes them.*

win sb's 'heart
make sb love you: *The children have won the old man's heart.* ◇ *The actress who played Natasha won the hearts of the audience.*

,win or 'lose
whether you succeed or fail: *Win or lose, we'll know we've done our best.*

you can't win them 'all; you 'win some, you 'lose some (*spoken*)
used to express sympathy for sb who has been disappointed about sth: *'I made a terrible speech this evening.' 'Well, you can't win them all. Don't worry about it.'*

'you win (*spoken*)
used to agree to what sb wants after you have failed to persuade them to do or let you do sth else: *OK, you win, I'll admit I was wrong.*

ask for/win sb's hand ➔ **hand**

carry/win the day ➔ **day**

win (sth)/beat sb hands down ➔ **hands**

win/earn your spurs ➔ **spurs**

wind

get 'wind of sth (*informal*)
hear about sth secret or private: *A journalist got wind of a story about the nuclear research centre.*

get/have the 'wind up (about sth) (*BrE, informal*)
become/be frightened about sth: *I heard that he's selling his business and moving away. I think he's got the wind up about something or other.*

go, run, etc. like the 'wind
go, run, etc. very fast: *We had to drive like the wind to get there in time.* ◇ *She ran like the wind.*

in the 'wind
about to happen soon, although you do not know exactly when: *I can see some changes in the wind.* ◇ *The soldiers sensed that something was in the wind.*

put the 'wind up sb (*BrE, informal*)
make sb frightened about sth: *He really put the wind up her with his stories of rats in the kitchen.*

take the 'wind out of sb's sails (*informal*)
make sb suddenly less confident or angry, especially when you do or say sth that they do not expect: *Getting beaten in the first race took the wind out of her sails.*

break wind ➔ **break**

get your second wind ➔ **second**

it's an ill wind (that blows nobody any good) ➔ **ill**

sail close to the wind ➔ **sail**

see which way the wind blows ➔ **see**

a straw in the wind ➔ **straw**

(be) three sheets to the wind ➔ **three**

throw caution to the wind(s) ➔ **throw**

twist/wind/wrap sb around/round your little finger ➔ **little**

a wind/the winds of change ➔ **change**

windmills

tilt at windmills ➔ **tilt**

window

be, go, etc. out (of) the 'window (*informal*)
(of a chance, an opportunity, a job, etc.) disappear; be lost: *All my hopes of finding a good job in television have gone out of the window.* ◇ *Don't throw this opportunity out of the window.*

a ,window of oppor'tunity
a limited period of time when you can do something that you want to do or need to do: *The government's difficulties provided the opposition with a window of opportunity to present an alternative policy to the voters.*

a ,window on the 'world
a way of learning about other people and other countries: *News programmes try to provide a window on the world.*

winds

a wind/the winds of change ➔ change

wine

,wine and 'dine (sb)

entertain sb at a good restaurant: *Our hosts wined and dined us very well.* ◇ *Too much wining and dining is making him fat.*

wing

on the 'wing (*literary*)

(of a bird) flying: *It was a lovely photograph of a bird on the wing.*

on a ,wing and a 'prayer

with only a very slight chance of success: *He started the business in his own home, on a wing and a prayer, but it looks like he's really going to make a success of it.*

> **❶ ORIGIN**
> This expression was first used in the military to describe how pilots flying very badly-damaged planes succeeded in returning to base.

take/have sb under your 'wing

give sb help and protection: *When new children arrive at the school, she takes them under her wing.*

take 'wing (*literary*)

(of a bird or aircraft) start flying away: *With a roar of engines, the plane took wing.*

'wing it (*informal*)

do sth without planning or preparing it first; improvise: *I didn't know I'd have to make a speech—I just had to wing it.*

wing your/its way (to ...)

go or be sent somewhere very quickly: *An invitation to the wedding will be winging its way to you very soon.*

wings

(wait, stand, etc.) in the 'wings

(wait, etc.) ready to do sth, especially to take the place of another person: *If the party leader should resign, there are plenty of other politicians waiting in the wings.* ◇ *There are many younger tennis players in the wings, waiting for the chance to show their abilities.*

clip sb's wings ➔ clip
spread your wings ➔ spread

wink

a nod is as good as a wink (to a blind man) ➔ nod
not get a wink of sleep = not sleep a wink ➔ sleep
a nudge and a wink ➔ nudge
nudge nudge, wink wink ➔ nudge
tip sb the wink ➔ tip

winks

forty winks ➔ forty

winner

be onto a 'winner (*informal*)

be doing sth, especially selling sth, that is likely to be successful: *He is the sole importer of this product, and he certainly thinks he's onto a winner.*

pick a winner ➔ pick

wipe

wipe the 'floor with sb (*informal*)

defeat sb completely and easily in an argument, competition, etc: *They started arguing about the education reforms, and she wiped the floor with him.* ◇ *Italy wiped the floor with Austria, beating them 5-0.*

wipe sth off the ,face of the 'earth (also wipe sth off the 'map)

completely destroy sth: *In the event of nuclear war, whole cities would be wiped off the face of the earth.* ◇ *The fall in prices wiped a lot of small businesses off the map.*

wipe the slate 'clean

agree to forget about past mistakes or arguments and start again with a relationship: *We're both to blame. Let's wipe the slate clean and start again.*

wipe the/that 'smile, 'grin, etc. off your/sb's face (*informal*)

1 used to tell sb to stop smiling, etc. because it is annoying or not appropriate: *Wipe that smile off your face or I'll send you out of the classroom.*
2 make sb feel less happy or satisfied with sth: *The news from the stock market soon wiped the smile off his face.* ◇ *I'm going to wipe that grin off his face one day.*

wire

go, come, etc. (right) down to the 'wire (*informal*)

if you say that a situation goes **down to the wire**, you mean that the result will not be decided or known until the very end: *Most people are predicting a very close match, quite possibly going right down to the wire.*

> **❷ NOTE**
> In this idiom, the *wire* refers to the finishing line in races.

a live wire ➔ live

wires

get your lines/wires crossed ➔ crossed
pull wires ➔ pull

wisdom

conventional/received 'wisdom

the view or belief that most people have: *Conventional wisdom has it that riots only ever happen in big cities.*

in your, his, etc. (infinite) 'wisdom

used when you are saying that you do not understand why sb has done sth: *The government in its wisdom has decided to support the ban.*

pearls of wisdom ➔ **pearls**

wise

be ˌwise after the e'vent (*often disapproving*)
know what should have been done in a particular situation, but only after it has happened: *'If we'd been more careful, the fire would never have happened.' 'It's no good being wise after the event—we can't do anything now.'*

be/get 'wise to sb/sth (*informal*)
be/become aware of sth or aware of sb's (usually bad) behaviour: *When did you first get wise to what was happening?* ◇ *He thought he could fool me but I'm wise to him.*

a 'wise guy (*informal, disapproving, especially AmE*)
a man who speaks or behaves as if he knows much more than other people: *OK, wise guy, what do you think we should do then?*

a word to the wise ➔ **word**

wiser

be none the 'wiser/'no wiser; not be any the 'wiser
1 not understand sth, even after it has been explained to you: *I've read the instructions, but I'm still none the wiser.*
2 not know or find out about sth bad that sb has done: *If you put the money back, no one will be any the wiser.*

wish

(just) as you 'wish (*formal, especially BrE*)
I will do what you want; I will agree with your decision: *We can meet at my house or yours, as you wish.*

I 'wish! (*spoken*)
used to say that sth is impossible or very unlikely, although you wish it were possible; if only: *'You'll have finished by tomorrow.' 'I wish!'*

the wish is father to the 'thought (*saying*)
we believe a thing because we want it to be true

❶ ORIGIN
This phrase was used in Shakespeare's play *Henry IV*.

wish sb/sth 'well/'ill (*formal*)
hope that sb/sth succeeds or has good luck/hope that sb fails or has bad luck: *I wish you well in your new job.* ◇ *She said she wished nobody ill.*

wouldn't wish sth on my, etc. worst 'enemy (*informal*)
used for saying that sth is so unpleasant, painful, etc. that you would not like anyone to experience it: *It's a terrible job—it's dirty, noisy and boring. I wouldn't wish a job like that on my worst enemy.*

your wish is my com'mand (*humorous*)
I am ready to do anything you ask me to do: *'Put the kettle on, will you?' 'Your wish is my command.'*

❶ ORIGIN
These are the words of the genie (= a spirit with magical powers) in the story about Aladdin in *The Thousand and One Nights*.

wishes

if wishes were horses, beggars would/ might ride (*saying*)
wishing for sth does not make it happen

wishful

ˌwishful 'thinking
the belief that sth you want to happen is happening or will happen, although this is actually not true or is very unlikely: *Prices seem to have stopped rising in the shops, or is that just wishful thinking on my part?*

wit

to 'wit (*old-fashioned, formal*)
used when you are about to be more exact about sth you have just referred to: *I told him I only spoke one foreign language, to wit French.*

with

be 'with sb (*informal*)
1 understand what sb is saying or explaining: *I'm sorry, but I'm not with you. What exactly did you mean by 'cut and paste'?* ◇ *'Are you with me?' 'No, you've lost me. Can you explain it again?'*
2 be in support of or agreement with sb: *'What do you think, Jonathan?' 'I'm with Sarah on this.'*
3 used to ask a customer, etc. to wait for a short time: *I'm just serving this lady. I'll be with you in a minute.*

get 'with it (*informal*)
become aware of the most recent ideas, developments, events, etc: *You never seem to know what's happening around you. Get with it, Paul. Start reading, start talking to people.*

'with it (*informal*)
1 (*old-fashioned*) (of sb/sth) fashionable and up to date: *Her clothes are very with it, aren't they?* ◇ *He was wearing very with-it sunglasses.*
2 thinking quickly and clearly: *I'm a bit tired this morning. I'm not really with it.*

with 'that (*written*)
straight after that; then: *He muttered a few words of apology and with that he left.*

wither

ˌwither on the 'vine (*formal*)
gradually come to an end or stop being effective: *He used to be so ambitious, but his ambition seems to have withered on the vine.*

witless

be scared/bored 'witless (*informal*)
be extremely frightened or bored: *Despite his reputation as a tough guy, he admits that he was 'scared witless' when he first arrived in New York.*

witness

be (a) 'witness to sth
1 (*formal*) see sth take place: *He has been witness to a terrible murder.*
2 (*written*) show that sth is true; provide evidence for sth: *His good health is a witness to the success of the treatment.*

bear/give 'witness (to sth)
provide evidence of the truth of sth: *The huge crowd bore witness to the popularity of this man.*

wits

be at your wits' 'end
be so confused or worried that you do not know what you should do: *I can't pay the bills, the bank won't lend me any money, and I don't know what to do—I'm at my wits' end.*

collect/gather your 'wits
try to become calm and think clearly: *After such a shock I found it difficult to gather my wits.*

frighten/scare sb out of their 'wits
frighten sb very much: *I was scared out of my wits when I looked out of the window and saw the aircraft's engine on fire.*

have/keep your 'wits about you
be/remain quick to think and act in a demanding, difficult or dangerous situation: *Mountaineering is dangerous, so you need to keep your wits about you.*

a battle of wits → **battle**
drive sb out of their mind/wits → **drive**
live by/on your wits → **live**
pit your wits (against sb/sth) → **pit**

wives

an old wives' tale → **old**

wobbly

throw a wobbly → **throw**

woe

,woe be'tide sb (*formal* or *humorous*)
there will be trouble for sb: *Woe betide anyone who arrives late!*

,woe is 'me! (*old use* or *humorous*)
a phrase that is used to say that you are very unhappy

wolf

keep the 'wolf from the door (*informal*)
make sure that you have enough money to pay for the basic things like food, rent, heating, etc: *Their wages are just enough to keep the wolf from the door.*

a wolf in sheep's 'clothing
a person who appears friendly and nice but is really dangerous: *He certainly seems harmless enough, but is he a wolf in sheep's clothing?*

cry wolf → **cry**
a lone wolf → **lone**

wolves

throw sb to the wolves/lions → **throw**

woman

be a man/woman of his/her word → **word**
be sb's man/woman → **man**
be your own man/woman → **man**
be twice the man/woman (that sb is) → **twice**
the inner man/woman → **inner**
like a man/woman possessed → **possessed**
make an honest woman of sb → **honest**
the man/woman in your life → **life**
a man/woman of few words → **few**
a man/woman of (many) parts → **parts**
a man/woman of the world → **world**
old woman → **old**

wonder

I ,shouldn't 'wonder (if …) (*informal*)
I would not be surprised to find out (that …): *It's paid for with stolen money, I shouldn't wonder.*

it's a 'wonder (that) … (*especially spoken*)
it is surprising or strange (that) …: *Did you see the car after the crash? It's a wonder that they survived!*

(it's) no/small/little 'wonder (that) …
it's not surprising: *If you walked all the way, it's little wonder you're late.* ◇ *'The heating's gone off.' 'I thought it was cold. No wonder!'*

a nine days' wonder → **nine**

wonderful

weird and wonderful → **weird**

wonders

,wonders (will) ,never 'cease (*spoken, usually ironic*)
used to express surprise and pleasure at sth: *'The train was on time today.' 'Wonders will never cease* (= I am surprised, because usually it is late).*'*

work/do wonders/miracles (for/on/with sb/sth) → **work**

wood

not be out of the wood(s) 'yet (*informal*)
not be free from dangers or difficulties yet: *Our sales figures look much better this month, but we're not out of the woods yet.*

dead wood → **dead**
knock on wood = touch wood → **touch**
not see the wood for the trees → **see**
touch wood → **touch**

wooden

get, win, take, etc. the ˌwooden ˈspoon (*BrE, informal*)
come last in a race or competition: *England must win this match if they are to avoid taking the wooden spoon.*

woods

a babe in the woods → **babe**
in your, this, etc. neck of the woods → **neck**

woodwork

blend/fade into the ˈwoodwork
behave in a way that does not attract any attention; disappear or hide: *I decided the best thing to do would be to try and fade into the woodwork and hope that no one noticed me.*

come/crawl out of the ˈwoodwork (*informal, disapproving*)
if you say that sb **comes/crawls out of the woodwork**, you mean that they have suddenly appeared in order to express an opinion or to take advantage of a situation: *When he won the lottery, all sorts of distant relatives came out of the woodwork.*

wool

pull the wool over sb's eyes → **pull**
wrap sb up in cotton wool → **wrap**

word

be as ˌgood as your ˈword
do what you have promised to do: *You'll find that she's as good as her word—she always comes if she says she will.*

be a man/woman of his/her ˈword
be a person who always does what he/she has promised to do: *If he said he'd help you, he will—he's a man of his word.*

by ˌword of ˈmouth
in spoken, not written, words: *The news spread by word of mouth.*

❶ NOTE
A humorous way to refer to communication through modern methods, such as email or chat rooms, is 'by word of mouse' (= a computer mouse).

(right) from the word ˈgo (*informal*)
from the very beginning: *I knew from the word go that it would be difficult.*

(not) get a word in ˈedgeways (*BrE*) (*AmE* **(not) get a word in ˈedgewise**) (*informal*)
(usually used with *can* or *could*) (not) be able to say sth, because sb else is talking too much: *I tried to tell him what I thought, but I couldn't get a word in edgeways.*

give sb your ˈword (that …); have (got) sb's ˈword (that …)
promise sb/be promised (that …): *I give you my word that I'll pay you tomorrow.* ◇ *I've got his word that he'll fix the car by the weekend.*

go ˌback on your ˈword
not do what you have promised; break a promise: *He said he wouldn't charge more than £100, but he went back on his word and gave me a bill for £120.*

have a (short) ˈword (with sb) (about sth)
have a short conversation about sth, especially in private: *Can I have a word, Marie? It's about Jane.*

have a word in sb's ˈear (*BrE*)
speak to sb in private about sth: *Can I have a word in your ear, John?* ◇ *I must have a word in her ear before the others arrive.*

in a ˈword (*spoken*)
used for giving a very short, usually negative, answer or comment: *In a word, 'stupid' is how I'd describe him.*

keep/break your ˈword
do/fail to do what you have promised: *Do you think she'll break her word and tell everyone?*

your/the last/final ˈword (on/about sth)
your, etc. final decision or statement about sth: *'Will you take £900?' 'No, £1 000 and that's my last word.'* ◇ *Is that your final word on the matter?*

(upon) my ˈword! (*old-fashioned*)
used to express surprise: *My word! That was quick!*

not be the ˈword for it
used to say that a word or expression does not describe sth fully or strongly enough: *Unkind isn't the word for it! I've never seen anyone treat an animal so cruelly!*

not/never have a good word to ˈsay for/about sb/sth (*informal*)
not/never have anything positive to say about sb/sth: *She rarely has a good word to say about her neighbours.* ◇ *Nobody has a good word to say for the new computer system.*

not a ˈword (to sb) (about sth)
do not say anything to sb/anybody about sth: *Not a word to Jean about the party—it's a surprise!* ◇ *Remember, not a word about how much it cost.*

put in a (good) ˈword (for sb)
say sth good about sb to sb else in order to help them: *If you put in a good word for me, I might get the job.*

the spoken/written ˈword
the language, in speaking/writing: *The spoken word is often very different from the written word.*

take sb at their ˈword
believe exactly what sb says or promises: *She said I could go and stay in her flat in Paris whenever I wanted, so I took her at her word.*

take sb's 'word for it (that ...)
believe sth that sb has said, (which is that ...): *You know more about cars than I do, so if you think it needs a new gearbox, I'll take your word for it.* ◇ *Can I take your word for it that the text has all been checked?*

,word for 'word
in exactly the same words; translated directly from another language: *I repeated what you said, word for word.* ◇ *It probably won't sound very natural if you translate it word for word.* ◇ *a word-for-word account, translation, etc.*

your, his, etc. ,word is 'law
used to say that sb has complete power and control: *Their father is very old-fashioned. His word is law in their house.*

your, his, etc. ,word is (as ,good as) your, his, etc. 'bond
used to say that sb always does what they promise to do: *Don't worry, you can trust my brother. His word's as good as his bond.*

your, his, etc. ,word of 'honour (BrE) (AmE your, his, etc. ,word of 'honor)
used to refer to sb's sincere promise: *He gave me his word of honour that he'd never drink again.*

a ,word to the 'wise
used to introduce some advice, especially when only a few words are necessary: *The band are now touring the UK. A word to the wise though—make sure you book tickets early.*

(not) breathe a word (about/of sth) (to sb) → **breathe**
a dirty word → **dirty**
a four-letter word → **four-letter**
hang on sb's words/every word → **hang**
have the last word → **last**
a household name/word → **household**
the last word (in sth) → **last**
leave word (with sb) → **leave**
mum's the word! → **mum**
not know the meaning of the word → **know**
the operative word → **operative**
the printed word/page → **printed**
(just) say the word → **say**
spread the word → **spread**

words

have/exchange 'words (with sb) (about sth) (especially BrE)
argue or quarrel with sb because you do not like the way they have behaved: *I had to have words with him about his behaviour.* ◇ *They both got angry and had words.*

in 'other words
expressed in a different way; that is to say: *'I don't think this is the right job for you, Pete.' 'In other words, you want me to leave. Is that it?'*

(not) in so/as many 'words
(not) in exactly the same words that sb says were used: *'Have you told John that you're leaving him?'* *'Not in so many words, no. I just said I thought it might be better if we lived apart.'* ◇ *Did he actually say in so many words that there was no hope of a cure?*

in words of one 'syllable
using very simple language so that sb will understand: *They didn't seem to understand my explanation, so I explained it all again in words of one syllable.*

put 'words in(to) sb's mouth
say or suggest that sb has said sth, when they have not: *You're putting words in my mouth. I didn't say the whole house was dirty, I just said the living room needed a clean.*

take the words (right) out of sb's 'mouth
say exactly what another person was going to say: *'The speed limit on motorways should be raised.' 'I agree completely! You've taken the words right out of my mouth!'*

too funny, sad, etc. for 'words
extremely funny, sad, etc: *The man in the post office was too stupid for words.*

words 'fail me
I cannot express how I feel (because I am too surprised, angry, etc.): *Words fail me! How could you have been so stupid?*

actions speak louder than words → **actions**
at a loss for words → **loss**
be lost for words → **lost**
eat your words → **eat**
famous last words → **famous**
hang on sb's words/every word → **hang**
a man/woman of few words → **few**
mark my words → **mark**
not mince your words → **mince**
a play on words → **play**
a war of words → **war**
weigh your words → **weigh**

work

all ,work and no 'play (makes ,Jack a dull 'boy) (saying)
it is not healthy to spend all your time working, you need to relax too

be at 'work
be having an influence or effect: *Why did they lose the election? Several factors were at work ...* ◇ *Evil forces are at work in this organization.*

go/set about your 'work
start to do your work: *She went cheerfully about her work.*

go/set to 'work (on sth) (also get (down) to 'work (on sth))
start working on a particular task: *I set to work on the car, giving it a good clean.* ◇ *I ought to get to work on that essay.*

have (got) your 'work cut out (to do sth/ doing sth) (informal)
be likely to have difficulty doing sth: *You'll have*

your work cut out to get there before nine. It's 8.30 already. ◇ *I won't be able to come with you today. I've got my work cut out for me at the moment.*

in/out of 'work
having/not having a paid job: *I've been out of work for a year.* ◇ *Is your husband in work at the moment?* ◇ *an out-of-work actor*

put/set sb to 'work (on sth)
make sb start work (doing sth): *On his first day in the office they put him to work on some typing.*

work all the ,hours God 'sends (*informal*)
work all the time: *'You look tired, Jane.' 'I'm working all the hours God sends at the moment trying to finish my thesis.'*

work your 'arse off (*BrE*) (*AmE* work your 'ass off) (△, *slang*)
work very hard

work your ,fingers to the 'bone (*informal*)
work very hard: *It's not fair—I work my fingers to the bone all day and then I have to cook and clean in the evenings.*

'work it/things (so that …) (*informal*)
plan sth carefully to get the result you want; organize or arrange sth: *Can you work it so that we get free tickets?* ◇ *I worked things so that I could take all my holidays in July and August.*

,work like a 'charm (*informal*)
quickly have the effect you want; work like magic: *I don't know what she said to him, but it worked like a charm—he's much more cooperative now.*

,work like a 'dog/'slave/'Trojan (*informal*)
work very hard: *She worked like a slave to pass her exams.*

work a 'treat (*BrE, informal*)
be very effective or successful: *His idea worked a treat.*

,work your way through 'college, etc.
have a paid job while you are a student: *She had to work her way through law school.*

,work your way 'up
start with a badly-paid, unimportant job and work hard until you get a well-paid, important job: *He's worked his way up from an office junior to managing director.*

work/do 'wonders/'miracles (for/on/with sb/sth) (*informal*)
have a very good effect (on sb/sth); quickly succeed: *Getting the job did wonders for her self-confidence.* ◇ *This washing powder will work miracles on those difficult stains.* ▶ 'miracle-worker *noun*: *I just don't have enough time to finish it. I'm sorry, but I'm not a miracle-worker.*

,work yourself/sb to 'death (*informal*)
(make sb) work very hard: *That company is working him to death.* ◇ *She works herself to death and nobody ever thanks her for anything.*

all in a day's work → **day**
the devil makes work for idle hands → **devil**

(do sb's) dirty work → **dirty**
the donkey work → **donkey**
drive/run/work yourself into the ground → **ground**
a job of work → **job**
make hard work of sth → **hard**
make light work of sth → **light**
make short work of sth/sb → **short**
many hands make light work → **hands**
a nasty piece of work → **nasty**
nice work! → **nice**
nice work if you can get it → **nice**
slog/sweat/work your guts out → **guts**
too much like hard work → **hard**
work/go like a dream → **dream**
work yourself into a lather → **lather**

worker
a fast worker → **fast**

working

be working 'overtime (*informal*)
be very active or too active: *There was nothing to worry about. It was just her imagination working overtime.*

have (got) a ,working 'knowledge of sth
know sth well enough to be able to use it: *I speak good French and I have a working knowledge of Italian and Spanish.* ◇ *I've used this software a bit so I do have a working knowledge of it.*

in (full/good) working 'order (also in running 'order)
(of a machine) in good condition; working well: *For Sale: Fridge in good working order, £50.*

firing/working on all cylinders → **cylinders**

works

,good 'works
kind acts to help others: *He was a generous man, spending thousands of pounds on various good works for the village, including the construction of a proper road.*

in the 'works
something that is **in the works** is being discussed, planned or prepared and will happen or exist soon: *The rumour is that there is a sequel to the movie in the works, although this has not been confirmed.*

the (whole) 'works (*informal*)
everything that you could want, need or expect: *We went to the chip shop and had the works: fish, chips, gherkins and mushy peas.*

gum up the works → **gum**
throw a (monkey) wrench in the works = put/throw a spanner in the works → **spanner**

world

be, live, etc. in a world of your 'own
seem not to be aware of things happening around you; be a person who has ideas that other people

think are strange: *I'm not surprised he didn't know about it—he lives in a world of his own, that boy.*

be/mean (͵all) the ˈworld to sb
be very important to sb; be loved very much by sb: *Her job means the world to her.* ◊ *They've only got one child and he's all the world to them.*

come/go ˈdown/ˈup in the world
become less/more successful; become poorer/richer: *He's come up in the world since I last saw him. That was a Mercedes he was driving, wasn't it?* ◊ *Since she left Cambridge she's gone down in the world.*

come into the ˈworld (*literary*)
be born: *Our lives changed completely when little Oliver came into the world.*

for all the ˈworld as if/though ...; for all the ˈworld like sb/sth (*written*)
exactly as if ... ; exactly like sb/sth: *She stood up and shouted at him, then sat down and went on with her work for all the world as if nothing had happened.*

have (got) the ͵world at your ˈfeet
have many advantages, and so have many opportunities to choose from; be very successful and admired: *When you're young you've got the world at your feet.* ◊ *She's got money; she's well-educated; the world is at her feet.*

in an ͵ideal/a ͵perfect ˈworld
used to say that sth is what you would like to happen or what should happen, but you know it cannot: *In an ideal world we would be recycling and reusing everything.*

in the ˈworld
used to emphasize what you are saying: *There's nothing in the world I'd like more than to visit New York.* ◊ *Don't rush—we've got all the time in the world.*

a man/woman of the ˈworld
a person with a lot of experience of life, who is not easily surprised or shocked: *She's a woman of the world. She won't mind if you talk openly about sex.*

not (do sth) for (all) the ˈworld
used to say that you would never do sth: *I wouldn't sell that picture for all the world.*

the ... of this world (*informal*)
used to refer to people of a particular type: *We all envy the Bill Gateses of this world* (= the people who are as rich and successful as Bill Gates).

out of this ˈworld (*informal*)
unusually good: *She cooked a meal which was out of this world.*

what is the world ˈcoming to? (also **I don't know ͵what the world's ˈcoming to**) (*saying*)
used as an expression of anger, shock, complaint, etc., at changes in people's behaviour, the political situation, etc: *When I read the news these days I sometimes wonder what the world's coming to.* ◊ *Instant tea? What is the world coming to?*

(all) the ͵world and his ˈwife (*informal*)
everyone; a large number of people: *Don't put our address in the newspaper. I don't want all the world and his wife knocking on the door.* ◊ *The world and his wife was in Brighton that day.*

the ͵world is your ˈoyster
you have the freedom to do what you want, go where you want, etc. in the future because you are young, successful, rich, etc: *What do you mean, you don't know what to do with your life? The world is your oyster!*

a/the ˈworld of difference (between A and B) (*informal*)
a lot of difference (between A and B): *There's a world of difference between records and CDs.*

the (whole) world ˈover
everywhere in the world: *People are the same the whole world over.* ◊ *Writers the world over joined in protest against her imprisonment.*

(think) the world ͵owes you a ˈliving (*disapproving*)
(think that) society is responsible for doing everything for you and you should not have to make any effort yourself: *Why don't you go out and get a job? The world doesn't owe you a living, you know.* ◊ *He seems to think the world owes him a living.*

be lost to the world → **lost**
be worlds/a world away (from sth) → **worlds**
the bottom drops/falls out of sb's world → **bottom**
a brave new world → **brave**
dead to the world → **dead**
do sb/sth a power/world of good → **power**
how, what, why, etc. on earth/in the world ... → **earth**
it's a small world → **small**
the next world → **next**
not be the end of the world → **end**
not have a care in the world → **care**
not long for this world → **long**
not/never set the world on fire → **set**
on top of the world → **top**
the outside world → **outside**
promise (sb) the moon/earth/world → **promise**
see the world → **see**
tell the (whole) world → **tell**
think the world of sb/sth → **think**
watch the world go by → **watch**
the way of the world → **way**
a window on the world → **window**
with the best will in the world → **best**
without a care in the world → **care**
the world outside = the outside world → **outside**

worlds

be ˈworlds/a world away (from sth)
be very different (from sth): *Life in the country today is worlds away from how it was a hundred years ago.*

be poles/worlds apart → **apart**
the best of both/all (possible) worlds → **best**
the worst of both/all (possible) worlds → **worst**

worm

the ,worm 'turns (*informal*)
even a patient, calm person will get angry if they
are repeatedly badly treated: *He's often rude to his
secretary and she doesn't say anything—but one
day the worm will turn.*

the early bird catches the worm ➔ **early**

worms

a can of worms ➔ **can**

worm's-eye

a worm's-eye 'view
the opinion of sb who is closely involved in sth: *I'm
afraid I can't give you a general overview of the
situation. I can only offer you a worm's-eye view
that is based on my own experience.*

worried

be worried 'sick; be 'sick with worry
be extremely worried: *Where have you been? I've
been worried sick about you.*

you had me 'worried (*spoken*)
used to tell sb that you were worried because you
did not understand what they said correctly: *You
had me worried for a moment—I thought you were
going to resign!*

worry

,not to 'worry (*informal, especially BrE*)
it is not important; it does not matter: *'Oh, damn!
We've missed the train!' 'Not to worry. There'll be
another one in five minutes.'*

'you should worry! (*informal*)
used for telling sb that they have no need to worry:
*You think you're going to fail the exam! You should
worry! You're the best in the class.*

be sick with worry = be worried sick ➔ **worried**

worse

be ,worse 'off
be poorer, unhappier, etc. than before or than sb
else: *The increase in taxes means that we'll be £30 a
month worse off than before.*

come off 'worse
lose a fight, competition, etc. or suffer more compared with others: *Don't worry about him. People
who try to hurt him usually find they come off a lot
worse than he does.*

**we, you, he, etc. can/could/might do 'worse
(than do sth)**
it is a good idea to do sth; sth is a good decision: *If
you're looking for a good career, you could do worse
than a job in banking.*

go from ,bad to 'worse
(of an already bad situation) become even worse:
*Under the new management things have gone from
bad to worse.*

none the 'worse for sth
1 not less valuable, attractive, enjoyable, useful,
etc. because of sth: *It's rather old-fashioned but
none the worse for that.* ◇ *She's a very strict teacher,
but none the worse for that.*
2 not injured or damaged by sth: *One of the
drivers had been in a crash but, luckily, was none
the worse for the experience.*

(be) the ,worse for 'drink
(be) drunk: *He was the worse for drink when the
time came for his speech.*

(be) the ,worse for 'wear (*informal*)
1 (be) in a poor condition because of being used a
lot: *Your dictionary is looking a bit the worse for
wear. Isn't it time you bought a new one?*
2 (be) drunk: *Ellen came back from the pub rather
the worse for wear.*

'worse ,luck (*BrE, spoken*)
used to show that you are disappointed about sth:
*I'm working tonight, so I can't come to the party,
worse luck.*

a fate worse than death ➔ **fate**
for better or (for) worse ➔ **better**
his, her, etc. bark is worse than his, her, etc. bite ➔ **bark**
so much the better/worse (for sb/sth) ➔ **better**
take a turn for the better/worse ➔ **turn**

worst

be your ,own worst 'enemy
be a person who often creates problems or difficulties for himself/herself: *He spends all his money on
drink, and then finds that he's got nothing left to
live on—if you ask me, he's his own worst enemy.*

bring out the 'worst in sb
make sb show their worst qualities: *Pressure can
bring out the worst in people.*

do your 'worst
be as harmful, unpleasant, violent, etc. as you can:
I refuse to pay this bill. Let them do their worst. ◇
*The electricity company did their worst and cut off
the supply.*

get the 'worst of it; come off 'worst
be defeated in a fight, etc.; be affected more seriously than other people, etc: *The dog had been
fighting and had obviously got the worst of it.* ◇
*Small businesses have come off worst in the eco-
nomic crisis.*

if the ,worst comes to the 'worst (*AmE also if
,worst comes to 'worst*)
if the most unpleasant or unfortunate thing happens: *If the worst comes to the worst, we'll just have
to sell the house.*

the worst of 'both/'all (possible) worlds
all the disadvantages of every situation: *Rail passengers feel that they are getting the worst of both
worlds—expensive fares and an unreliable service.*

at best/worst ➔ **best**
wouldn't wish sth on my, etc. worst enemy ➔ **wish**

worth

be 'worth it
be worth the time, money, effort, risk, etc. you have spent/taken doing sth: *A dishwasher costs a lot of money, but it's worth it.* ◇ *Don't drink and drive. It's not worth it.*

be ˌworth your/its ˌweight in 'gold
be very useful or valuable: *My assistant is worth her weight in gold.* ◇ *A reliable car is worth its weight in gold.*

do sth for ˌall you are 'worth
do sth with as much energy and effort as possible: *I shouted for all I was worth but no one heard me.*

for ˌwhat it's 'worth (*spoken*)
used to emphasize that what you are saying is only your opinion or suggestion and may not be very helpful: *That's my opinion, for what it's worth.* ◇ *This is the first drawing I made, for what it's worth.*

make sth ˌworth sb's 'while (*informal*)
pay sb well for doing sth for you: *If you can work on Saturdays and Sundays, we'll make it worth your while.*

not worth the paper it's 'printed/'written on
(of a written agreement, document, report, etc.) not having any value, especially legally, or because the person involved does not intend to do what they say they will: *The promises in this letter aren't worth the paper they're written on.*

ˌworth your/its 'salt
deserving respect, especially because you do your job well: *Any teacher worth his salt knows that students who enjoy a lesson learn the most.*

> **❶ ORIGIN**
> In Roman times, soldiers were given an allowance of salt as part of their pay.

(well) worth your 'while (to do sth)
interesting or useful to do: *It would be well worth your while to come to the meeting.*

a bird in the hand is worth two in the bush → **bird**
the game is not worth the candle → **game**
get/have your money's worth → **money**
more than your job's worth (to do sth) → **job**
worth the name = worthy of the name → **worthy**

worthy

worthy of the 'name (also **worth the 'name**)
(*formal*)
deserving to be called good: *Any doctor worthy of the name would help an injured man in the street.*

wound

rub salt into the wound/into sb's wounds → **rub**

wounds

lick your wounds → **lick**
reopen old wounds → **reopen**

wrack

wrack your brains = rack your brains → **rack**

wrap

wrap sb up in cotton 'wool (*informal*)
protect sb too much from dangers or risks: *If you keep your children wrapped up in cotton wool, they'll never learn to be independent.*

twist/wind/wrap sb around/round your little finger → **little**

wrapped

be ˌwrapped 'up in sb/sth
be so involved with sb/sth that you do not pay enough attention to other people or things: *She's so wrapped up in her own problems that she hasn't got time to listen to anyone else at the moment.*

wraps

keep sth, stay, etc. under 'wraps (*informal*)
keep sth, stay, etc. secret or hidden: *These letters have lain under wraps since the 1940s.* ◇ *Next year's event is still being kept under wraps.*

wreak

play/wreak havoc with sth → **havoc**

wrench

throw a (monkey) wrench in the works = put/throw a spanner in the works → **spanner**

wring

ˌwring your 'hands
twist and rub your hands together because you are very worried, upset or anxious: *He stood there, wringing his hands in despair.* ◇ *It's no use just wringing our hands—we must do something.*

ˌwring sb's 'neck (*spoken, informal*)
used as an expression of anger or as a threat: *If I find the person who did this, I'll wring his neck!*

wringer

put sb/go through the 'wringer (*informal*)
(make sb) have a difficult or unpleasant experience, or a series of them: *He's been through the wringer lately, what with his divorce, and then losing his job.* ◇ *Those interviewers really put me through the wringer!*

> **❓ NOTE**
> In the past, a *wringer* was a device that squeezed the water out of clothes that had been washed.

wrist

a slap on the wrist → **slap**

writ

ˌwrit 'large (*literary*)
1 easy to see or understand: *Mistrust was writ large on her face.*

2 (used after a noun) being a larger or more obvious example of the thing mentioned: *The party's new philosophies are little more than their old beliefs writ large.*

write

be nothing, not much, etc. to write 'home about (also **be nothing, not much, etc. to 'shout about**) (*informal*)
not be very good or special; be ordinary: *The play was OK, but it wasn't anything to write home about.* ◇ *The food was nothing much to shout about.*

writing

in 'writing
in the form of a letter, document, etc. (that gives proof of sth): *All telephone reservations must be confirmed in writing.* ◇ *You should get his promises in writing.*

the ˌwriting (is) on the 'wall (*AmE* the ˌhandwriting (is) on the 'wall) (*saying*)
used when you are describing a situation in which there are signs that sb/sth is going to have problems or is going to fail: *The writing is on the wall for the club unless they can find £20 000.* ◇ *The President refuses to see the handwriting on the wall* (= that he will soon be defeated).

ⓘ ORIGIN
This phrase comes from the Bible story in which strange writing appeared on a wall during a feast given by King Belshazzar, predicting his death and the end of his kingdom.

written

be written all over sb's 'face
(of an emotion) be clearly seen on sb's face: *You could see he was guilty; it was written all over his face.*

have (got) sb/sth written all 'over it (*informal*)
show clearly the influence or characteristics of sb/sth: *It's been badly organized, as usual—it's got the council written all over it.*

not worth the paper it's printed/written on → **worth**
the spoken/written word → **word**

wrong

ˌback the wrong 'horse (*BrE*)
support the person, group etc. that later loses a contest or fails to do what was expected: *I certainly backed the wrong horse when I said United would win the Cup Final.* ◇ *Many people who had voted for the party in the election were now feeling that they had backed the wrong horse.*

from/on the ˌwrong side of the 'tracks (*informal*)
from or living in a poor area or part of town: *She married a man from the wrong side of the tracks.*

get sb 'wrong (*spoken*)
not understand correctly what sb means: *Please don't get me wrong, I'm not criticizing you.*

get (hold of) the ˌwrong end of the 'stick (*BrE, informal*)
understand sth in the wrong way: *You've got the wrong end of the stick. He doesn't owe me money, I owe him!*

go 'wrong
1 make a mistake with sth: *It doesn't work. We must have gone wrong somewhere. Pass me the instruction manual.* ◇ *Where did we go wrong* (= what mistakes did we make for things to be so bad)*?*
2 (of a machine) stop working correctly: *This television keeps going wrong. I'm fed up with it.*
3 not progress or develop as well as you expected or intended: *Their marriage started to go wrong when he lost his job.* ◇ *What else can go wrong* (= what other problems are we going to have)*?*

in the 'wrong
responsible for a mistake, an accident, a quarrel, etc: *She is clearly in the wrong. She had no right to take the book.* ◇ *The accident wasn't my fault. The other driver was totally in the wrong.*

on the ˌwrong side of the 'law
in trouble with the police: *The TV presenter found himself on the wrong side of the law after hitting a cyclist while driving.*

take sth the wrong 'way
be offended by a remark that was not intended to be offensive: *Don't take this the wrong way, but don't you think you should get your hair cut?*

you can't go 'wrong (with sth) (*spoken*)
used to say that sth will always be acceptable in a particular situation: *For a quick meal you can't go wrong with pasta.*

be barking up the wrong tree → **barking**
be on the right/wrong side of 40, 50, etc. → **side**
be on the right/wrong track → **track**
get/keep on the right/wrong side of sb → **side**
get/start off on the right/wrong foot (with sb) → **foot**
get up on the wrong side of the bed = get out of bed on the wrong side → **bed**
hit/strike the right/wrong note → **note**
not far off/out/wrong → **far**
not/never put/set a foot wrong → **foot**
right a wrong → **right**
rub sb up the wrong way → **rub**

wrongs

two wrongs don't make a right → **two**

Y y

yank

yank sb's 'chain (*AmE, informal*)
tell sb sth which is not true, as a joke: *Did you mean what you said, or were you just yanking my chain?*

yards

the whole nine yards → **nine**

yarn

pitch a line/story/yarn (to sb) → **pitch**
spin (sb) a yarn/tale → **spin**

yeah

,oh 'yeah? (*spoken*)
used when you are commenting on what sb has just said: *'We're off to France soon.' 'Oh yeah? When's that?'* ◇ (*ironic*) *'I'm going to be rich one day.' 'Oh yeah?'* (= I don't believe you.)

year

,all (the) year 'round
all year; all the time: *The garden is open to visitors all year round.*

from, since, etc. the year 'dot (*AmE from, since, etc. the year 'one*) (*informal*)
from, etc. a very long time ago: *The case contained old papers going back to the year dot.*

,year after 'year
every year for many years: *They go to the same place on holiday year after year.*

,year by 'year
as the years pass; each year: *Year by year their affection for each other grew stronger.*

year ,in, year 'out
(all year and) every year: *He had travelled on the 7.40 train to London year in, year out for thirty years.*

,year on 'year
(used especially when talking about figures, prices, etc.) each year, compared with the last year: *Spending has increased year on year.* ◇ *a year-on-year increase in unemployment*

the seven year itch → **seven**
the turn of the year/century → **turn**

years

not/never in a hundred, etc. 'years (*spoken*)
used to emphasize that you will/would never do sth: *I'd never have thought of that in a million years.*

put 'years on sb
make sb feel or look much older: *The shock of losing his job put years on him.*

take 'years off sb
make sb feel or look much younger: *The new hairstyle takes years off her.*

donkey's years → **donkey**

yellow

a 'yellow streak (*disapproving*)
the quality of being easily frightened; cowardice: *He won't fight? I always thought he had a yellow streak in him.*

yes

,yes and 'no
said when you cannot answer either 'yes' or 'no' because the situation is not simple: *'Have you got a car?' 'Well, yes and no. We have, but it's not working at the moment.'*

yesterday

I wasn't born yesterday → **born**

yet

as 'yet
until now or until a particular time in the past: *an as yet unpublished report* ◇ *As yet little was known about the disease.*

yore

of 'yore (*old use* or *literary*)
long ago: *in days of yore*

young

be, stay, etc. young at 'heart
(of an old person) still feel and behave like a young person: *He says that the secret of living to 100 is to remain young at heart.*

with 'young (*formal*)
(of an animal) pregnant: *The lioness was with young.*

you're only young 'once (*saying*)
young people should enjoy themselves as much as possible, because they will have to work and worry later in their lives: *'Don't you think Tony should work over the summer holidays?' 'Well, you're only young once—there's plenty of time for that later.'*

fresh/new/young blood → **blood**
(have) an old head on young shoulders → **old**

younger

be getting 'younger (*spoken*)
used to say that people seem to be doing sth at a younger age than they used to, or that they seem younger because you are now older: *The band's*

fans are getting younger. ◇ *Why do police officers seem to be getting younger?*

not be getting any 'younger (*spoken*)
be getting older: *I can't possibly walk all the way to the beach—I'm not getting any younger, you know.*

yours

,you and 'yours (*informal*)
you and your family: *You must provide a safe future for you and yours.*

Zz

z

catch/get some 'Z's (*informal, especially AmE*)
sleep: *I headed home to catch some Z's before our night out.*

> **❷ NOTE**
> In this expression, *Z's* is pronounced /ziːz/ (or sometimes /zedz/ in British English), and is used in cartoons to represent the sound people sometimes make when they sleep.

from A to Z → A

Time to catch some Z's!

S2–3 That is to Say...

B
1 if you ask me
2 believe me
3 on the other hand
4 for one thing
5 on top of that
6 I say
7 funnily enough
8 there is that
9 can we leave it at that
10 at the end of the day

C
1 for my money; to my mind
2 I'm telling you; goodness knows
3 mind you; the other side of the coin (is that…)
4 to begin with; for a start
5 what's more; into the bargain
6 guess what; by the way
7 believe it or not; as it happens
8 you've got a point there; to be su
9 (and/so) that's that; end of stor
10 all in all; when all is said and done

E
1 Any phrase from group 1
2 Any phrase from group 5
3 Any phrase from group 2
4 Any phrase from group 3
5 Any phrase from group 6
6 Any phrase from group 4

S4 It's as Easy as ABC

A
1 keen
2 like
3 easy
4 stubborn
5 fit
6 cool
7 busy
8 flat

B
1 a beet
2 a bat
3 a brush
4 a picture
5 a flash
6 toast

C
The expressions that are NOT used are:
▶ as mad as monkeys
▶ as plain as potatoes
▶ as light as a bubble

D
1 a bird
2 hot cakes
3 a light
4 wildfire
5 a headless chicken
6 a rhinoceros
7 a leaf
8 a Cheshire cat

S5 As the Saying Goes...

A
1 Better late than never.
2 It's the thought that counts.
3 Absence makes the heart grow fonder.
4 It's no good/use crying over spilt milk.
5 Talk/Speak of the devil!
6 That's easier said than done.
7 More haste, less speed.
8 Every cloud has a silver lining.

B

A	B	Definition
1	c	vi
2	e	iii
3	f	iv
4	g	vii
5	d	i
6	b	ii
7	a	viii
8	h	v

S6 Look Here!

A

Well/Happy
She looks the picture of health.
He was all smiles.

Unwell/Ill
You look rather off colour.
He doesn't look so hot.

Well-dressed
We were all in our Sunday best.
He cut quite a dash in his suit.

Angry/Unhappy
She had a face like thunder.
He gave her a dirty look.

Old
She's starting to look her age.
He looks a bit past it.

Unattractive
He's no oil painting.
She's not much to look at.

B
1 She looked like the cat that got the cream.
2 She looked like a drowned rat.
3 He's a chip off the old block.
4 She's the spitting image of her sister/of Joan.
5 She was dressed to kill.
6 It's written all over your face.
7 She's (a bit) down in the mouth.
8 It's difficult to keep a straight face.
9 She's a sight for sore eyes.
10 She's mutton dressed (up) as lamb.

S7 It Takes all Sorts...

A

1 a man/woman of the world
2 a wolf in sheep's clothing
3 a paper tiger
4 a nosy parker
5 a wet blanket
6 a law unto himself/herself
7 a dark horse
8 a fair-weather friend
9 a rough diamond
10 a live wire
11 a shrinking violet
12 a smart alec

B

Across		Down	
1	temper	2	place
4	gab	3	shoulders
6	action	5	boo
8	donkey	7	space
9	fly	8	doom
10	clouds	11	donna
12	fogey		
13	snow		
14	fish		
15	Samaritan		

S8 We're in Business

A

1 slog your guts out
2 get the sack
3 make ends meet
4 throw in the towel
5 live beyond your means
6 make money hand over fist
7 cook the books
8 go pear-shaped
9 go like a dream
10 throw money around
11 work your way up
12 the rat race
13 a fat cat

B

a & j   b & g   c & h   d & e   f & i

C

1 … got off to a flying start **or**
   … hit the ground running
2 … sold like hot cakes **or**
   … the retailers did a roaring trade
3 … make or break **or**
   … sink or swim
4 … he came a cropper **or**
   … he fell flat on his face

S9 Just What the Doctor Ordered

A

Good Health ☺

you are in the pink
you feel like a million dollars
you are on form
you are in shape
you are as right as rain

Bad Health ☹

you are green about the gills
you have the dreaded lurgy
you have been in the wars
you feel the worse for wear
you are off your food

B

1 sick as a dog
2 clean bill of health
3 under the weather
4 turn for the worse
5 pull through
6 in great shape
7 off colour
8 on the mend
9 recharge my batteries
10 a hundred per cent
11 fighting fit
12 the picture of health

13 in a bad way
14 on his last legs
15 pins and needles
16 dropping like flies
17 fighting for his life
18 still going strong
19 be sick
20 put to sleep
21 went downhill
22 in good nick
23 flat on his back.
24 off the danger list.

S10 It's Hardly Rocket Science!

A

1 a
2 a b c
3 b
4 a b
5 a c
6 a
7 a
9 c

3 think on your feet
4 (be) slow on the uptake
5 a whizz-kid
6 you don't have to be a rocket scientist
7 not suffer fools gladly
8 not just a pretty face
9 as clever as they come
10 rack your brains
11 (be) not all there
12 get your head round sth
13 a bright spark

B

1 keep your head
2 have a good head for figures

C 👃

He really uses his loaf.
There are no flies on him.
He's nobody's fool.
He's one smart cookie.

👎

He's not the sharpest knife in the drawer.
He's as thick as two short planks.
He's two sandwiches short of a picnic.
The lights are on but nobody's home.

S11 It's the Bee's Knees!

A

1 snail   2 donkey   3 duck   4 lion   5 grasshopper

B

1 I felt like a fish out of **water** when I started in this company.
2 I decided to take the bull by the **horns** and tell the boss what I thought.
3 The tourist office sent us on a wild goose **chase** to a hotel which had closed down.
4 I always get butterflies in my **stomach** before I have to give a speech.
5 I made a real pig's **ear** of the letter so I had to do it again.
6 The boss has always got a bee in his **bonnet** about something or other.
7 I nearly let the cat out of the **bag** and told Jim about his surprise party.
8 I could talk about football till the cows **come home**, but I don't want to bore you.
9 He told us some cock and bull **story** about how he'd been in a famous band.
10 My house is quite near as the crow **flies**, but there's no direct road.

C

Hold your horses.
She had kittens.
They're crocodile tears.

Hair of the dog.
He's a dark horse.
It's gone to the dogs.

He's no spring chicken.
Don't count your chickens.
He's a lone wolf.

D

1 She had kittens.
2 Hold your horses.
3 They're crocodile tears.

4 He's a dark horse.
5 Hair of the dog.
6 Don't count your chickens.

7 He's a lone wolf.
8 It's gone to the dogs.
9 He's no spring chicken.

S12 Be a Good Sport

A

football: move the goalposts
swimming: out of your depth; be thrown in at the deep end
golf: below par; par for the course
horse-racing: win/lose by a short head
cricket: hit/knock sb for six; be on a sticky wicket
baseball: be way out in left field
boxing: pull no punches; on the ropes; out for the count

B

1 thrown in at the deep end
2 a whole new ball game
3 pulled no punches
4 on the ball
5 out of his depth
6 set the ball rolling
7 ballpark figure
8 way off the mark
9 throw in the towel
10 moving the goalposts
11 par for the course
12 knows the score
13 back to square one
14 a one-horse race

S13 All Hands on Deck!

A

1	swimming	8	anchor
2	ocean	9	wave
3	deck	10	sailing
4	sailor	11	tide
5	oyster	12	captain
6	keel	13	sink
7	bridge		

B

a the world was my oyster
b plain sailing
c run a tight ship
d an odd fish
e rock the boat
f all hands on deck
g took the wind out of my sails
h jump ship
i a drop in the ocean
j plenty more fish in the sea
k back on an even keel
l water under the bridge
m push the boat out

S14 Body and Soul

A

1	mouth
2	ear
3	nose
4	eye
5	head
6	neck
7	chest
8	shoulder
9	arm
10	stomach
11	foot
12	heel
13	leg
14	toe
15	knee

B

1 made my mouth water
2 all ears
3 no skin off my nose
4 more to it than meets the eye
5 put our heads together
6 in this neck of the woods
7 get it off your chest
8 the cold shoulder
9 my right arm
10 your eyes were bigger than your stomach
11 stand on his own two feet
12 hot on his heels
13 pulling your leg
14 to keep the class on their toes
15 weak at the knees

C

1 I nearly jumped out of my skin
2 she'll be just skin and bones
3 I had to bite my tongue
4 does he have any skeletons in the closet/cupboard?
5 by the skin of his teeth
6 she's still young at heart
7 keep your hair on
8 blood out of a stone

S15 Eat, Drink and Be Merry

B

1 She's got a lot on her plate
2 sounds to me like a recipe for disaster
3 she went bananas
4 The dinner party went pear-shaped
5 I can't cook for toffee
6 Let's talk turkey.
7 life is no picnic
8 My parents saved my bacon

C

1 tea 2 cake 3 pie 4 cookie 5 eggs 6 cherry 7 potatoes 8 bread

S16 True Colours

A

1 black 2 red 3 grey 4 white

B

1 g 2 e 3 i 4 a 5 b 6 c 7 h 8 f 9 j 10 d

C

PC Green	Can I help you, sir?
Mr Blue	I'm here to report an accident.
PC Green	Yes, I see you're hurt. Where exactly did this occur?
Mr Blue	Down by the roundabout on Main Street.
PC Green	Mm, that is a bit of a **black** spot.
Mr Blue	Anyway, this car suddenly came out in front of me. It was a real bolt from the **blue** and I couldn't stop in time.
PC Green	How serious was the accident, sir? Is the other driver OK?

Mr Blue	Oh, she was healthy enough to scream **blue** murder and attract a crowd. There wasn't even any damage and neither of us was hurt.
PC Green	How did you get that **black** eye then?
Mr Blue	We were exchanging details when she hit me. She said I was giving her a **black** look. Talk about the pot calling the kettle **black**! Anyway, I came down here to see you boys in **blue** because I want to report her.
PC Green	We'd better get this all down in **black** and **white**. Here's a pen…

S17 Naming Names

A

1 Coventry 2 China 3 Greek 4 Newcastle 5 Irish 6 Dutch 7 Rome 8 French

B

Across

1 Murphy 5 Bob 7 Job 8 Parkinson 9 Sam 12 Midas 14 Jack 15 Larry 16 Bill 17 Achilles

Down

2 Hobson 3 Dick 4 Shanks 6 Adam 7 Joe 8 Pandora 10 Charming 11 Jekyll 12 McCoy 13 Riley 14 Jane

S18 All Eyes

A

1 a 2 c 3 c 4 b 5 a 6 a 7 b 8 c

B

1 couldn't take her eyes off
2 beauty is in the eye of the beholder
3 had a roving eye
4 love is blind
5 turn a blind eye
6 looked daggers at her
7 wouldn't see me for dust
8 crying her eyes out
9 saw the light
10 swears blind

S19 All Ears

A

1 ear 2 music 3 ear 4 noise 5 ear 6 noise 7 sound 8 ear 9 ring 10 music

B

1 It has a familiar ring to it.
2 He loves the sound of his own voice.
3 It's/That's like music to my ears.
4 I'll play it by ear.
5 I'll have to face the music.
6 She has an ear for languages.
7 It goes in one ear and out the other.
8 He's a big noise.

C

Jo	I just can't **believe** my ears, it seems so incredible! So, what happened next? I'm **all** ears.
Jen	Well, later that evening, we went to Pete's. You should have heard what he was saying about Cathy! I told him to calm down but it just fell on **deaf** ears.
Jo	And?
Jen	In walked Cathy. The front door was open, only Tom didn't notice.
Jo	What happened?
Jen	Tom eventually realized, and of course we were all really embarrassed. You could've heard a **pin** drop. Nobody said a word.
Jo	What about Cathy?
Jen	Finally, she turned to Tom and said, "My ears were **burning**. I thought I'd come round here and find out exactly what you thought of me."

o Oh dear.

Jen She stormed out, packed a suitcase and left. Tom can't believe it but for **crying** out loud, what does he expect? He said some terrible things.

Jo What's the situation now?

Jen Your guess is as good as mine. Keep your ear to the **ground** and let me know if you hear anything.

S20–21 Flavour of the Month

A

Taste: mouth; sweet; bitter; flavour; sour; tongue; lips   **Smell:** odour; nose; stink; scent; sniff

B

1 tongue   **2** nose   **3** mouth   **4** sweet   **5** lips   **6** sour

C

1 – 16 – 3 – 11 – 9 – 5 – 19 – 12 – 4 – 13 – 7 – 10 – 14 – 18 – 8 – 2 – 15 – 6 – 17 – 20

D

1 never look a gift horse in the mouth
2 it was no skin off my nose
3 has the cat got your tongue?

4 butter wouldn't melt in his mouth
5 give her a taste of her own medicine

E

1 b   2 a   3 a   4 c   5 a

S22 Hands Up!

A

The words in the grid are: clutching   finger   fist   glove   grasp   hand   knuckles   palm   thumb   touch

B

1 touch   2 finger   3 hand   4 glove   5 thumb   6 knuckles   7 clutching   8 fist

C

3 – 5 – 10 – 2 – 8 – 9 – 1 – 12 – 4 – 7 – 6 – 11

S23–24 Put Yourself to the Test

1 c	11 a	21 a	31 a
2 c	12 b	22 c	32 b
3 a	13 a	23 c	33 c
4 b	14 b	24 b	34 a
5 c	15 b	25 b	35 c
6 b	16 b	26 c	36 c
7 c	17 c	27 a	37 a
8 c	18 b	28 a	38 b
9 b	19 c	29 b	39 c
10 c	20 a	30 b	40 c